Children and Books

Fifth
Edition

Children and Books

Fifth
Edition

Zena Sutherland
The University of Chicago

May Hill Arbuthnot

With Special Contributions by

Dianne L. Monson
University of Washington

Rosemary Weber
Drexel University

Dorothy M. Broderick
Dalhousie University

Scott, Foresman and Company
Glenview, Illinois
Dallas, Tex. Oakland, N.J.
Palo Alto, Cal. Tucker, Ga. Abingdon, England

Library of Congress Cataloging in Publication Data

Sutherland, Zena.
Children and books.

In 4th ed. (1972) Arbuthnot's name appeared first on the title page.

Includes bibliographies and index.
1. Children's literature—History and criticism.
I. Arbuthnot, May Hill, 1884–1969, joint author. II. Title.
PN1009.A1A7 1977 028.5 76-26136
ISBN 0-673-15037-2

2 3 4 5 6-WAK-82 81 80 79 78 77

Preface to the Fifth Edition

Children and Books is meant for all adults who are interested in bringing children and books together, but it is designed particularly for classes in children's literature in English and education departments and in library schools, in colleges and universities.

Since the first edition of *Children and Books* thirty years ago, children's books have achieved a recognition and children's literature is being accorded a respect long overdue. The body of children's literature has grown enormously, courses in the subject have multiplied, and some of the best writers today are devoting all or part of their time to writing children's books. Realization that children's literature both reflects the values of our society and instills those values in children has made increasing numbers of adults aware that children's literature is a part of the mainstream of all literature and that, like adult literature, it is worthy of our respect both for what it is and for what it does.

The title suggests the dual nature of the book's approach. The emphases are on understanding children and their needs, on perspectives and background, on criteria and types of literature, and on artists and authors. In a sense, *Children and Books* has a *major-author* approach. It is impossible to describe all of the good books that have been written for children, but it is possible to introduce readers to the works of most of the major authors and artists of the past and present. The major-author emphasis should spare the reader, particularly the new student, from floundering in a sea of titles.

Children and Books is primarily about books; since the field is so broad, to include other media would mean giving them superficial treatment that would not do them justice. There are, however, some discussions of other media in Parts Four and Five; and the bibliographies for those parts, as well as the Adult References in the appendixes, refer the reader to articles and books on related media.

Organization and Revision

With each edition of *Children and Books,* the authors and the editors have been conscious of the need to reflect changes in our society by new emphases in the text, and to reorganize the text to reflect more accurately the changes in the ways in which children's literature is taught.

In this fifth edition, newly designed, Part

One is an overview of children's needs and interests, the range of books for children, types of and criteria for evaluation of children's literature, and history and trends. Part Two discusses artists and their illustrations and includes a new chapter, "Books for Early Childhood," an addition that reflects a growing area of emphasis in children's literature and education. In Part Three, the types of literature are explored: folk tales, including tall tales; fables, myths, and epics; modern fantasy; poetry, a chapter condensed since the last edition; modern fiction and historical fiction; and biography and informational books. Material from the former chapter on animal stories has been reassigned to more specific areas, so that fanciful animal tales are discussed with other fantasy and realistic animal tales with other modern realistic fiction.

Many of the thirteen chapters in Parts One through Three have been substantially reorganized, some have been condensed and rewritten, one is new, and in all chapters the text and the bibliographies have been brought up to date, with criteria for each genre discussed at the beginning of the relevant chapter.

Part Four, Bringing Children and Books Together, is a newly written section on methodology, discussing the role of the adult and the techniques to be used in introducing children to literature and in evaluating and encouraging their responses to literature.

Part Five, which considers areas and issues relating to children and their books, has been substantially reorganized, with existing articles updated and new articles on censorship, television, sexism, and children's access to library materials. This section includes suggestions for research and bibliographies.

The Appendixes are Book Selection Aids, Adult References, Publishers and Their Addresses, Children's Book Awards, and Pronunciation Guide. There is a Subject Index in addition to the Author, Illustrator, Title Index.

Special Features

Throughout the discussions of books, authors, and artists in Chapters 1–15, and set off from the text, are "Viewpoints," brief statements from books and articles, not necessarily representing the authors' viewpoint in *Children and Books,* but suggesting some issues to explore.

The bibliographies are extensive, with books pertinent to chapter discussions listed by author and title under Adult References at the end of each chapter, and books for children, separately listed and often divided into sub-categories, in all the chapters on types of children's literature. Books mentioned in the text are not annotated; additional entries are. Some out-of-print books are included since they are still available in collections. Each reader undoubtedly will miss one or more favorite books; unfortunately, space limitations necessitate some omissions, even of books the authors would have liked to include. The age levels are suggestions only, as children of the same age often differ markedly in reading skills, interests, and social maturity. Since the text stresses the importance of books about minority groups, symbols are used in many of the bibliographies to denote books that emphasize blacks, Chicanos and Puerto Ricans, Native Americans, and religious minorities, so that such books may be more accessible to readers.

To facilitate the finding of information sources, all adult references and book selection aids are listed, together with annotations and full bibliographic information, in Appendixes A and B at the end of the book. To facilitate the finding of material about authors and artists, all references to major author or artist discussions are singled out in the index by the use of boldface type.

Acknowledgments

For various kinds of assistance in the preparation of this fifth edition, grateful acknowledgments are due to the following people:

for suggestions for revision of the fourth edition, James Haskins, Bette Peltola, and Rosemary Weber;

for her contribution of Part Four (new Chapters 14–16) on encouraging children's response to literature, Dianne L. Monson, University of Washington;

for her contribution to the revision of Chapters 6, 7, 8, 10, and 11, Rosemary Weber, Drexel University;

for her contribution to the revision of Chapter 12 and for her editing of Part Five, Areas and Issues—Children and Books, Dorothy M. Broderick, Dalhousie University;

for the articles in Part Five, Deirdre Breslin, Dorothy M. Broderick, Ken Donelson, Diane Gersoni, Theodore C. Hines, Larry N. Landrum, W. Bernard Lukenbill, Eileen Marino, Michael T. Marsden, and Anne Pellowski;

for his consulting and commentary for the special color insert, Rainey Bennett;

for their valuable suggestions as manuscript readers, Dorothy M. Broderick, Dalhousie University; Dwight L. Burton, The Florida State University; James Haskins; Bette Peltola, The University of Wisconsin–Milwaukee; Wilma J. Pyle, State University of New York, Fredonia; and Jon Stott, The University of Alberta;

for her aid in bibliographic research, Wendy Towner;

for their unflagging patience and wisdom, JoAnn Johnson and Joanne Trestrail, the editors;

for his sage counsel, moral support, and sustaining sense of humor, Alec Sutherland, my husband.

Zena Sutherland
The University of Chicago

Contents

Part 3 Exploring the Types of Literature

Chapter 11 Historical Fiction 368

Chapter 12 Biography 400

Part 5
Areas and Issues—Children and Books

Appendixes

Indexes

Children and Books

Fifth Edition

Part 1
Knowing Children and Books

Children and Their Books

Chapter 1

Books are no substitute for living, but they can add immeasurably to its richness. When life is absorbing, books can enhance our sense of its significance. When life is difficult, they can give a momentary relief from trouble, afford a new insight into our problems or those of others, or provide the rest and refreshment we need. Books have always been a source of information, comfort, and pleasure for people who know how to use them. This is as true for children as for adults.

Since that paragraph was first written—some thirty years ago—the world has undergone unprecedented change. The mood of the writers, editors, teachers, and librarians working in the field of children's literature over a quarter of a century ago was quite different from the mood of most people today. Then there was a greater sense of security about the direction of the future. Today, change has become the predominant fact of life, accelerating at such a pace that traditional values have become confused and confusing. Still, many values of the past endure, and the assumptions in past editions of *Children and Books* about the nature and the needs of children, the value of good books, and the importance of bringing children and books together continue to have validity.

Along with television, films, filmstrips, videotapes, and the like, there is today an amazing variety of material in print: picture books, some without text; easy-to-read books, invaluable for the beginning and the poor reader; poetry for and by children; folk literature that includes tales, myths, fables, epics, and legends; modern fantasy ranging from imitations of folk tales to science fiction; historical fiction and biographies; animal stories, family stories (including "problem stories"), realistic fiction about people of almost every racial and ethnic group, career stories and sports stories; informational books and how-to-do-it books. They are in every public and school library, in bookstores and drugstores, on supermarket racks and corner newsstands. There are reading kits, book-and-record sets, comic books, and children's magazines—and a great deal of print meant for adults but read also by children.

Today there is also an increased sensitivity to the variety of children in our country, children who have always been with us but who have not found their counterparts in books as they do today. We have an infinite variety of children. They are bright, average, and dull; rural, urban, small-town, migrant, suburban. They come from happy homes and homes torn by tension, from solid houses and slum tenements. Black, white, Native American, Appalachian, Chicano, Nisei; unloved and neglected, loved and cherished; bookworms and nonreaders—boys and girls whose needs to identify, to develop, to feel pride in race and acceptance in the community are being studied and served. They are infinitely different and profoundly similar.

Children's literature in recent years has taken new directions, explored new themes, and opened up possibilities for developing new attitudes. In the following chapters these changes will be discussed. Writers, artists, and editors have joined forces to make many of today's children's books so varied in content and so beautiful to look at that adults as well as children enjoy them. These books, like those for adults, range from the unreliable and trashy to the scrupulously accurate and permanently significant. The treasures must be sought for, but they are there, a wealth of fine books old and new.

If we are to find these treasures, the best books for children, we need standards for judging them.[1] But two facts we need to keep constantly before us: *a book is a good book for children only when they enjoy it; a book is a poor book for children, even when adults rate it a classic, if children are unable to read it or are bored by its content.* To bring children and books together, we must know hundreds of books in many fields and their virtues and limitations, and we must also know the children for whom they are intended—their interests and their needs.

Children's Needs

Despite social change, certain basic needs seem to be common to most peoples and most times. A child's needs are at first intensely and narrowly personal, but, as he or she matures, they should broaden and become more widely socialized. The direction they will take depends a great deal on the experiences the child encounters in the crucial early years before school. How tragically different, for example, are the experiences of the battered child living with violent, unloving, sometimes psychotic adults and the experiences of the beloved child nurtured by a warm, supportive family. Struggling to satisfy their needs, children are forever seeking to maintain the precarious balance between personal happiness and social approval, and that is no easy task. Directly or indirectly, books may help, particularly if they are books written by sensitive, thoughtful adults who are percipient observers of children and who remember their own childhoods vividly. Such books not only may help children better understand themselves and others but also should help adults better understand and empathize with their own children and with the children in their classrooms and library centers.

[1]See Chapter 2 for a discussion of criteria for judging stories for children.

The Need for Physical Well-being

A child's sense of physical security ordinarily begins in a mother's or father's arms, includes the routines of eating and sleeping, and comes gradually to encompass everything that gives a sense of comfort and well-being. For both children and adults, material satisfactions may become the chief symbols of security. The old fairy tales were told by people who seldom had enough food to eat or clothing to keep them warm. So their tales are full of brightly burning fires, sumptuous feasts, rich clothes, glittering jewels, and splendid palaces. These are humanity's age-old symbols of physical comfort and security. Undoubtedly some of the appeal of the old *Elsie Dinsmore* stories and of Frances Hodgson Burnett's *Sara Crewe* and *The Secret Garden* lay in this same incredible affluence which the characters enjoyed.

Viewpoints

. . . I became deeply dissatisfied with much of the literature intended to develop the child's mind and personality, because it fails to stimulate and nurture those resources he needs most in order to cope with his difficult inner problems. The pre-primers and primers from which he is taught to read in school are designed to teach the necessary skills, irrespective of meaning. The overwhelming bulk of the rest of so-called "children's literature" attempts to entertain or to inform, or both. But most of these books are so shallow in substance that little of significance can be gained from them. The acquisition of skills, including the ability to read, becomes devalued when what one has learned to read adds nothing of importance to one's life.—From *The Uses of Enchantment: Meaning and Importance of Fairy Tales* by Bruno Bettelheim. Copyright © 1976 by Bruno Bettelheim. Reprinted by permission of Alfred A. Knopf, Inc.

Illustration by Julia Iltis from the book Behind the Magic Line *by Betty K. Erwin. Copyright © 1969 by Betty K. Erwin. Reproduced by permission of Little, Brown and Co.*

Today, as in earlier times, material security is uncertain, and it continues to be one of people's most pressing needs. So in books as in life, the lack of security and the hunger for it often supply the motive for the action and the theme of the story. In Betty Erwin's *Behind the Magic Line,* a black family leaves their crowded, two-room city apartment to find security and a better life in a home of their own. In Betsy Byars's *After the Goat Man,* a boy lives alone with a taciturn grandfather who, until the last moment, defends their home, slated for demolition because it lies in the path of a planned superhighway. In *M. C. Higgins, the Great* by Virginia Hamilton, thirteen-year-old M. C. fears that a sliding spoil heap will destroy his mountain home; he plans ways to get the family to a safer place.[2] In Vera and Bill Cleaver's *Where the Lilies Bloom,* the doughty young heroine struggles fiercely to keep her family together, lying about her father's death to prevent the authorities from separating the children, and outmaneuvering the landlord to keep the house in which they live.

In book after book, the search for security will spellbind young readers of the old fairy tales or of the modern realistic books or of the biographies of heroes and heroines, all the way from "Dick Whittington" to *Tom Sawyer* and Berniece Rabe's *Naomi.*

The Need to Love and to Be Loved

Every human being wants to love and to be loved. This need is so pressing that when it is frustrated in one direction it will provide its own substitutes, centering upon almost anything from lap dogs to antiques. Children, too, set up their own substitutes. A child who feels out of favor or rejected may lavish an abnormal amount of affection upon a stray cat, perhaps identifying with the unwanted animal. In John Donovan's *I'll Get There. It Better Be Worth the Trip,* Davy's whole devotion is giv-

[2]*M. C. Higgins, the Great,* as well as most of the other books mentioned in this chapter, is discussed elsewhere in the text. See the Index for relevant page references.

en, after his grandmother's death, to his dog, Fred. A lonely, small boy is so anxious for a pet that he mishandles a bird in Dick Gackenbach's *Do You Love Me?* An older sister gently tells him he must treat pets with respect and then, to his joy, gives him a puppy. The small, mentally retarded boy in Louise Dickinson Rich's *Three of a Kind* is spurred to responsiveness by the love of a kitten.

It is in the family that children learn their first lessons in the laws of affectionate relationships. Books, too, exemplify these relationships. In Ellen Parsons's *Rainy Day Together*, the whole theme is love between parents and children. Not only does children's sense of security develop from these family patterns, but also their whole approach to other people and later their search for and treatment of a mate. In *Queenie Peavy* by Robert Burch, a child's personality is colored by the fact that her father, to whom she feels unswerving loyalty, is in jail. The status of the mother and the father in the family circle provides children with their first concepts of the woman's role and the man's role in life and may contribute to their consequent willingness or unwillingness to accept their own sex. In recent years, in response to a growing demand, there have been books like Betty Miles's *The Real Me* in which girls can enjoy any lively activity they like without the implication that they are behaving in an unfeminine and socially unacceptable manner, and now such girls are not always converts to ruffles in the last chapter.

Family loyalties also provide a basis for loyal friendships as children's social life widens. When family relationships are normal and happy, children start life with healthy attitudes. If they feel loved and know their love is accepted, they in turn are predisposed toward friendly relationships with people outside the family. When the reverse is true, their approach to other people is often suspicious or belligerent. Gilly, the lonely, orphaned protagonist of Julia Cunningham's *Dorp Dead*, hides his intelligence because he mistrusts adults; and Ivan, in Paula Fox's *Portrait of Ivan*, is cautious in accepting friendly overtures from adults because his mother is dead and his father shows him no affection.

Sometimes stories about family life may

Illustration by Jim Spanfeller for Where the Lilies Bloom *by Vera and Bill Cleaver. Copyright © 1969. Reproduced by permission of J. B. Lippincott Company, Publishers.*

From Do You Love Me? *by Dick Gackenbach. Copyright 1975. Reproduced by permission of The Seabury Press. (Original with color)*

interpret to fortunate children the significance of their own experiences which they might otherwise take for granted. A child may find traces of his own father in the father of Andy in Joseph Krumgold's *Onion John* or share the longing of the fatherless boy in Charlotte Zolotow's *A Father Like That*, or recognize her own mother in Mrs. March of *Little Women* or a beloved grandmother in Tomie de Paola's *Nana Upstairs and Nana Downstairs*. Children may share the brother and sister fun of Madeleine L'Engle's *Meet the Austins*, or the tender, protective relationship of a girl for a mentally retarded brother in Betsy Byars's *Summer of the Swans*, or the adventures of the cousins in Elizabeth Enright's *Gone-Away Lake*, or feel the warmth of the love between Siebren and his grandfather in Meindert DeJong's *Journey from Peppermint Street*. Through reading books such as these, they may find that their own family will mean more to them. On the other hand, children who have missed these happy experiences may find in family stories vicarious substitutes which will give them some satisfaction and supply them with new insight into what families can be.

Illustration by Emily Arnold McCully from Journey from Peppermint Street *by Meindert DeJong. Copyright © 1968. Reproduced by permission of Harper & Row, Publishers, Inc., and Lutterworth Press.*

Viewpoints

Children defend themselves, I tell you. They manifest at first a degree of inertia that resists the liveliest attacks; finally they take the offensive and expel their false friends from a domain in which they wish to remain the rulers. Nothing is done to create a common opinion among them and yet that opinion exists. They would be wholly incapable of defining the faults that displease them; but they cannot be made to believe that a book which displeases them *should* please them. Whatever their differences may be as to age, sex, or social position, they detest with common accord disguised sermons, hypocritical lessons, irreproachable little boys and girls who behave with more docility than their dolls. It is as though . . . they brought into the world with them a spontaneous hatred of the insincere and the false. The adults insist, the children pretend to yield, and do not yield. We overpower them; they rise up again. Thus does the struggle continue, in which the weaker will triumph.—Paul Hazard. *Books, Children and Men* translated by Marguerite Mitchell, The Horn Book, Inc., 1944, p. 49.

Another aspect of this need to love and to serve the beloved is the recognition of this same need in other creatures. Stories about wild animals defending their mates or their young or the herd are tremendously appealing. So, too, are stories of pets, steadfast not only in their affection for their own kind but for their human owners as well. Such stories as Sheila Burnford's *The Incredible Journey* have played upon this appeal. *A Heart to the Hawks* by Don Moser is a moving example of a boy's love for a wild creature. Fine animal stories of all kinds will undoubtedly contribute to breaking down the young child's unwitting cruelties toward animals and to building sensitivity to their needs.

Finally, the need to love and to be loved, which includes family affection, warm friendships, and devotion to pets, leads the child to look toward romance. In children's literature, romance begins early but remains impersonal. The fairy tales, with their long-delayed prince or their princess on a glass hill, are little more than abstract symbols of what is to come.

A flood of novels of romance for teenagers has been produced. While many of them are incredibly stereotyped and predictable, there are growing numbers of competent authors who write well and respect their young readers. They supply realistic pictures of family life, with boys and girls looking away from their families to a serious interest in someone of the opposite sex. And many of these books deal frankly with some of the heartbreaking problems of young people. Zoa Sherburne, for example, in *Too Bad About the Haines Girl*, handles with dignity the problem of the unwed mother. The establishment of a desirable romantic attachment is one of the most important tasks of growing up. A well-written story that shows all the complications of romance, its pitfalls and disappointments as well as its happiness, can provide young people with needed guidance in an approach to one of life's most vital problems.

Out of family affection and trust grows a kind of spiritual strength that enables human beings to surmount dangers, failures, and even stark tragedies. Such books as Louisa May Alcott's *Little Women* and the *Little House* books by Laura Ingalls Wilder leave children with the conviction that decent, kindly people can maintain an inner serenity even as they struggle with and master the problems that threaten them.

Particular religious groups and practices appear in children's books and reflect something of the diversities of belief in our modern world. *Thee, Hannah!* by Marguerite de Angeli gives a charming picture of Quaker customs. *The Bad Bell of San Salvador* by Patricia Beatty is the story of a young Comanche, captured by Mexicans, who resists Roman Catholic teaching but learns tolerance from a Swiss priest. In Mildred Jordan's *Proud to Be Amish*, the Amish people are described with sympathy. *Young Fu of the Upper Yangtze* by Elizabeth Lewis gives a rich cross section of Confucian guides to conduct. Yuri Suhl's *The Merrymaker* is a captivating picture of Jewish

Viewpoints

The evidence in young lives of the search for something and somebody to be true to is seen in a variety of pursuits more or less sanctioned by society. It is often hidden in a bewildering combination of shifting devotion and sudden perversity, sometimes more devotedly perverse, sometimes more perversely devoted. Yet, in all youth's seeming shiftiness, a seeking after some durability in change can be detected, whether in the accuracy of scientific and technical method or in the sincerity of conviction; in the veracity of historical and fictional accounts or the fairness of the rules of the game; in the authenticity of artistic production (and the high fidelity of reproduction) or in the genuineness of personalities and the reliability of commitments.—Erik H. Erikson, "Youth: Fidelity and Diversity," in *Youth: Change and Challenge*, edited by Erik H. Erikson, Basic Books, Inc., New York and London, 1963, p. 3.

Illustration by Ben F. Stahl from The Bad Bell of San Salvador *by Patricia Beatty. Reproduced by permission of William Morrow & Co., Inc.*

family life and religious observances and Sulamith Ish-Kishor's *Our Eddie* a sober one. In Judy Blume's *Are You There God? It's Me, Margaret,* the protagonist cannot decide what church to attend (her father is Jewish, her mother is not), but this indecision does not shake her deep faith. Joan Lingard's *A Proper Place* depicts the tension between present-day Irish Protestants and Roman Catholics. *Waterless Mountain* by Laura Armer and *Raven's Cry* by Christie Harris present the religion of the Navaho and Haida Indians with fidelity and beauty. Joseph Krumgold's *. . . and now Miguel* has a discussion of prayer between two teenage boys that is unique in children's literature. In Louise Fitzhugh's *The Long Secret,* Harriet gets quite different notions of God and prayer and religion from her mother, her father, and the Preacher.

Reading such books, children can find an honest picture of religious diversity as it exists today—knowledge which should help them develop respect for different groups. However firm a family may be in its adherence to a particular religious sect or in its objections to all organized religion, it will find in these books a fair picture of the world as it is today. And when children read the biographies of heroes and heroines of such divergent religious beliefs as Roger Williams, John Wesley, Anne Hutchinson, Father Damien, Florence Nightingale, Martin Buber, Mohandas Gandhi, and Martin Luther King, Jr., they may begin to understand the power religious faith can have in the lives of many people.

Viewpoints

If one dares to probe beneath the surface of the various forms of the present Negro protest to find the common compelling force, one will probably find that it is a rather simple and universal human desire. It is the desire to be respected for one's self—the desire to be seen and to be reacted to as an individual human being; the desire to be free of the shackles of being lumped, categorized, and stigmatized as an inchoate mass. The Negro has no more or less virtues or frailties than those found in other human beings. He is an individual who varies as much in courage and cowardice or ambivalence as do other human beings. He reacts to injustices and cruelties with the same patterns of accommodation, intimidation, rebellion, or philosophy as do others. He is here. Like others, throughout his life, he is in a relentless struggle against the void, the inner chaos. He is an individual. If life is to be tolerable for him he must be respected as an individual.—Kenneth B. Clark, *The Negro Protest,* Beacon Press, Boston, 1963, pp. 50–51.

The Need to Belong

Growing out of the need for security is the need of every human being to belong, to be an accepted member of a group. "My mama," or "My big brother," the young child says with pride. At first these experiences are merely egocentric extensions of children's self-love, but at least they are beginning to line themselves up with their family, and this acknowledgment of others marks their growing sense of belonging to a group. In time, these same children will identify with friends, school, and later with city and country, and perhaps with a world group.

So children's literature should reflect this expanding sense of the group. It should begin with stories about the family, the school, and the neighborhood in warm books such as Martha Alexander, Ezra Jack Keats, and Charlotte Zolotow write for the preschool child, Carolyn Haywood for the primary age, and Beverly Cleary for the middle grades. These represent happy group experiences. But there are also stories about children who must struggle anxiously to be liked by the people whose acceptance they long for. Linda in Judy Blume's *Blubber,* Paul in Constance Greene's *The Unmaking of Rabbit,* and the Guatemalan Indian boy in Ann Nolan Clark's *Santiago* are good examples. The story of the child who wins a respected place in groups that once rejected him or her is a satisfying theme from "Cinderella" to *Good-Bye to the Jungle* by John Rowe Townsend.

With the growing consciousness of a world in which all people are brought closer by the developments in communications and transportation, with children's increased awareness of such problems as war, pollution, and racial and social unrest, there is an urgent need for books in which minority peoples gain not tolerance but respect, books that attack the injustice and discrimination and apathy still prevalent in our society. The young today are aware of social ills. Exposed to the mass media and to the changing mores of the community, they need books that reflect the world in which they live but offer realistic and optimistic solutions. John Tunis, in his sports stories for the preadolescent and teenager, makes his young readers face fully the extra difficulties that beset youngsters of minority groups in winning a place on the team or in the community. This is the general theme also of Eleanor Estes's *The Hundred Dresses.* In Emily Neville's *Berries Goodman* and Hila Colman's *Mixed-Marriage Daughter,* anti-Semitism is candidly portrayed; in Kristin Hunter's *The Soul Brothers and Sister Lou,* a group of black adolescents face prejudice toward and within themselves. Sometimes the problem is not one of winning acceptance but of accepting. For example, in Ann Nolan Clark's *Little Navajo Bluebird,* an Indian child passionately rejects white society and its ways and wants to belong only to her own tribal group. Books like these parallel the need of each individual not only to belong with pride to his or her own group, but to identify warmly and sympathetically with ever widening circles of people. When a child from suburbia is stirred by *Listen for the Fig Tree* by Sharon Bell Mathis or wishes she could know Jean George's Julie in *Julie of the Wolves,* her sense of belonging is widening. A good and honest book can strengthen the pride of the minority member and enrich all who read it.

The Need to Achieve

The need for competence—the "organism's capacity to interact effectively with its environment"[3]—is a strong motivating force in human behavior. The struggle to achieve competence begins with the infant's visual exploration, with crawling, grasping, and other primitive activities, and grows into the complex physical or intellectual performances of the expert athlete, mathematician, musician, or scientist. Competence is as satisfying as inhibitions and frustrations are disruptive. To be happy or well adjusted, the child or the adult must have a satisfying sense of competence in one area or another.

In Bernard Wolf's *Don't Feel Sorry for Paul,* there is no appeal for sympathy but a sense of purpose and a determination to overcome his handicaps on the part of a seven-year-old who requires three prosthetic devices. In this true story, Paul and his family have such common sense and courage that he attends school, takes riding lessons, and achieves competence with vigor and joy.

In Mary J. Collier and Eugene L. Gaier's study "The Hero in the Preferred Childhood Stories of College Men,"[4] the important factor the book heroes had in common was that they performed their unique feats on their own. Whether it was Hansel from the old fairy tale or the realistic Tom Sawyer, the hero's competence was achieved without help from adults, and his independence was the quality that made him memorable and admired. Achieving competence may become the compensation for rejection and a step toward acceptance. This is a frequent theme in stories for children—the lonely child or the shy teenager who develops competence in some field and so wins the admiration and acceptance of the group. Taro Yashima's *Crow Boy,* Eleanor Estes's *The Hundred Dresses,* Armstrong Sperry's *Call It Courage,* Nat Hentoff's *Jazz Country,* and Judy Blume's *Blubber* are all built upon this theme.

The young child's first book heroes and heroines are doers, from Edward Ardizzone's Tim, who survived shipwreck and found his lost parents, to David of the Old Testament, who slew the giant Goliath. In later childhood and adolescence young readers enjoy the competence of heroes and heroines in adventure, mystery, and career stories and the achievements of famous men and women in biographies. *Carry On, Mr. Bowditch* by Jean Latham is a splendid, true record of competence independently achieved. More and more books are appearing that describe the

[3]Robert H. White, "Motivation Reconsidered: The Concept of Competence," *Psychological Review,* Vol. 66, No. 5, 1959, p. 297.

[4]*American Imago,* Vol. 16, No. 2, 1959.

accomplishments of blacks: biographies of Matthew Henson, Benjamin Banneker, Sojourner Truth, Elizabeth Freeman, Harriet Tubman, Shirley Chisholm, Paul Robeson, Martin Luther King, Jr., and many other Americans.

There is a stern negative aspect to this hunger for achievement. The struggle for competence may involve failures and complete frustration. Physical handicaps or mental limitations must be faced and accepted. In Jean Little's *Mine for Keeps*, a child with cerebral palsy comes home after five years in a residential school feeling fear and self-pity, but she adjusts to her own problems when she becomes involved in helping another child. Jamie, in Joe Lasker's *He's My Brother*, is a slow child whose classmates tease him, although the older brother who tells the story makes it clear that Jamie has his respect and love. In Esther Forbes's *Johnny Tremain*, Johnny's maimed hand prevents him from becoming the master silversmith he had expected to be. Emma Sterne's *Blood Brothers* tells the story of Charles Drew, a black ghetto child, who despite discrimination persists in his pursuit of a medical career and eventually becomes a distinguished pioneer in blood research. Stories of such persons who refuse to accept defeat help children in the task of growing up.

Illustration by Lewis Parker from the book Mine for Keeps *by Jean Little. Copyright © 1962 by Jean Little. Reproduced by permission of Little, Brown and Co.*

The Need for Change

Often, in our reading, after grave and factual books or books about everyday affairs, we like something light or imaginative. If we are beset with personal anxieties, we may look for a book of adventure or mystery or romance, lose ourselves completely, and come back to our own problems refreshed.

Children, too, need such liberation. Although some of them are learning in open classrooms and free schools, many children suffer more than many adults realize from the pressure of routines, adult coercion and tensions, and the necessity of conforming to a code of manners and morals whose reasonableness they do not always understand. This is especially true today, when so many aspects of our present society are being challenged by the young. Some children suffer from school failures, feelings of social or physical inferiority, difficulty in communicating with their parents, and bewilderment or resentment about the strictures of cultural patterns.

Books of many kinds may be used to meet the child's need for healthy change. The old fairy tales have about them a dreamlike quality that is a welcome change from the everyday world of here and now. Modern fantasies provide laughter and imaginative adventures that are sometimes ribtickling nonsense and sometimes humor with overtones of beauty. These range from the fun of Dr. Seuss's rambunctious *Horton Hatches the Egg* to the beauty and tragedy of Mary Norton's *The Borrowers* and the compassionate self-sacrifice of *Charlotte's Web*.

There is bland burlesque of city problems in Jean Merrill's *The Pushcart War* and of the rebellious adolescent in Hope Campbell's *Why Not Join the Giraffes?* in which a conser-

Illustration by Antony Maitland from the book The Ghost of Thomas Kempe *by Penelope Lively. Copyright © 1973 William Heinemann Ltd., London. Published by E. P. Dutton & Co., Inc. and used with their permission.*

vative teenager resists the influence of her liberated parents; there is nonsense humor in John Ciardi's *The Man Who Sang the Sillies* and in Sid Fleischman's tall-tale series of *McBroom* stories. Humor and suspense are combined in *Encyclopedia Brown Saves the Day*, Donald Sobol's story of a boy detective, and in Penelope Lively's witty fantasy, *The Ghost of Thomas Kempe*. There are adventures of the world of the future in John Christopher's *The Guardians* and suspense in Stephen Chance's *Septimus and the Danedyke Mystery*. All such stories afford children fun, pleasure, and respite. Fine poetry, too, that arrests the attention and stirs the emotions, light verse and nonsense jingles now and then—these may supply children with the inspiration or laughter for which they hunger.

The Need to Know

Parents often complain about the bothersome curiosity of children. But this need to investigate, to know for sure, is a sign of intelligence. In fact, the keener the child is mentally, the wider and more persistent his or her curiosities will be. The need to know surely and accurately is a basic hunger and one which books help satisfy.

Books about Africa, desert Indians, birds, plants, stones, stars, rockets and jets, DNA, care of pets, do-it-yourself books, and, of course, dictionaries and encyclopedias properly gauged to a child's needs are all available today. Adults need only discover children's particular interests to find books that will answer their questions reliably, stimulate new curiosities, and set them to exploring further to satisfy their need to know and give them, momentarily at least, a certain intellectual security.

Some books not only provide fascinating information but dramatically exemplify the human need to find out, to know for sure. For example, Thor Heyerdahl's *Kon-Tiki* tells the true story of five young men who set out on the flimsy raft Kon-Tiki to prove their theory of the origin and migrations of the Polynesian people. Hans Baumann's *Lion Gate and Labyrinth* tells the story of Heinrich Schliemann, who also needed to know and whose persistent curiosity and zealous investigations led to the discovery of ancient Trojan ruins. And Louis Haber's *Black Pioneers of Science and Invention* tells the stories of various people whose lives were a clear demonstration of the consuming need to know.

The Need for Beauty and Order

There is still another human need that seems curiously at odds with humanity's more utilitarian search for competence and security of various kinds. It is the need for beauty and order.

A wealth of books is available today to satisfy a child's aesthetic needs—authentic poetry, fanciful tales whose content and style are perfectly suited, books that are beautiful in themselves, books that provide various kinds of aesthetically satisfying experiences, and books that help children grow in their appreciation of beauty and order. Shirley Glubok's series about art in various cultures (*The Art of China, The Art of the New American Nation, The Art of the North American Indian, The Art of Ancient Mexico*) are simply written and related to the way people lived. *Looking at Art* by Alice Elizabeth Chase discusses the ways in which individual artists interpret landscapes, or people, or spatial relations. David Macaulay's *Cathedral, City,* and *Pyramid* are remarkable for their beautifully accurate architectural drawing. Lamont Moore's *The Sculptured Image* describes the ways by which sculptors achieve their effects. *Ballet: A Pictorial History* by Walter Terry and *The Wonderful World of Music* by Benjamin Britten and Imogen Holst are fine examples of books about the performing arts written for children by experts in their fields.

Viewpoints

Someday civilization must be simplified and made more just and decent and honest for everyone. Air and water must be cleaned up. Cities that would appall Dante must be made habitable. We must discover how to live together in moderate amity. It will take a good deal of imagination to bring so many opposites into harmony, to create an inwardly desired cohesive order out of so many contradictory compulsions, to design a civilization permitting all decent variables to live together in at least a semblance of understanding.

Perhaps only because they are fresh to experience, children are insatiably curious, wanting to understand everything. Our adult curiosity seldom ranges beyond the small worlds in which we earn our living and relax from our labors. We are not notably addicted to a passionate desire for tolerance. If only we might add a child's fresh eagerness to be friendly to our trove of all recorded knowledge, then our social, economic, and political disorder might begin to assume reasonable clarity.—Harry Behn, *Chrysalis,* Harcourt Brace Jovanovich, 1968, p. 27.

From City *by David Macaulay. Copyright 1974. Reproduced by permission of Houghton Mifflin Company.*

Whether in music, dancing, drama, story, painting, or sculpture, the artist seizes upon some aspect of life and re-creates it for us in a new form. We see it whole and understandable; people, events, and places assume a new dimension beyond the mere chronicling of facts. The artist can give us a long, clear view so that we see details in relation to the complete design. It is as if a kaleidoscope were held immovable. The colors and lines fall into logical relationship and the design stands out in bold relief, not necessarily beautiful but complete and therefore satisfying.

People are continually seeking aesthetic satisfaction in one form or another and at varying levels of taste. One may find it in the songs of a rock group. Someone else finds it in a symphony which exalts the sorrows of life to cosmic proportions. Aesthetic satisfaction comes to the small child as well as to the adult, and the development of one's taste depends not only upon one's initial capacities but also upon the material one encounters and upon how it is presented. A child who has chuckled over Miss Muffet and the spider is getting ready to enjoy the poems of A. A. Milne, and to progress to Walter de la Mare's and David McCord's poetry. A child who has been charmed with Beatrix Potter's *The Tale of Peter Rabbit* might be ready to appreciate the humor and beauty of Kenneth Grahame's *The Wind in the Willows* and the pathos of *The Hundred Penny Box* by Sharon Bell Mathis.

Children Need Good Books

Today's children, like today's adults, read for many reasons: to dream, to learn, to laugh, to enjoy the familiar and explore the unknown. They read for sheer pleasure and they absorb, in their reading, those facets of books that reflect the developmental values that are appropriate to the individual readers at each of the stages of their growth. The child is influenced by factors that have always affected children's reading: his or her sex, age, health and physical development, mental ability, emotional maturation, and home environment. But many of today's children have intellectual and social sophistication that further affects their reading habits and needs and tends to make them mature earlier than children matured in the past.

The pace of life is swifter and the media more pervasive; the problems of our society at times seem insuperable. Books may help children build a concept of the society in which they live and of their roles in that society; books may help shape and sharpen their concepts about other people and relationships; and books can contribute to an understanding of themselves.

To nurture young minds there must be books of many types. And they should be strong books, written with liveliness and honesty both in content and style, rather than little juvenile tracts designed to teach this lesson or that. There have been so many of these moralistic books that they threaten the general quality of children's books. For instance, there is the story of little Dickie or Bobbie or Jimmy who goes to kindergarten, stamps around, yells, and knocks down other people's blocks or seizes their toys. He is isolated like the bubonic plague until one day he learns to share and is, forthwith, a beloved and accepted member of the group. A juvenile "how to make friends and influence people"! Or there is the story of an obnoxious boy who says he wishes he didn't have a kid sister. But when she saves him in a social emergency his attitude changes for the better. The worst of such tracts is that children accept them and immediately assume a self-righteous attitude toward the unfortunate blunderer. "Isn't he awful?" they say virtuously. Such books may underscore a lesson, but they also encourage prigs. There are similar juvenile tracts, bogged down with preaching, in the field of race relationships. Such books, humorless and tame, offer nothing to lighten their dull didacticism.

These juvenile tracts seem thin indeed when compared with such robust tales as Wanda Gág's *Millions of Cats*, "The Three Little Pigs," Beverly Cleary's *Ramona* stories, or Scott O'Dell's *Island of the Blue Dolphins*. Such books are timeless because they are built around universal themes or needs—the desire for competence or love or accurate knowledge.

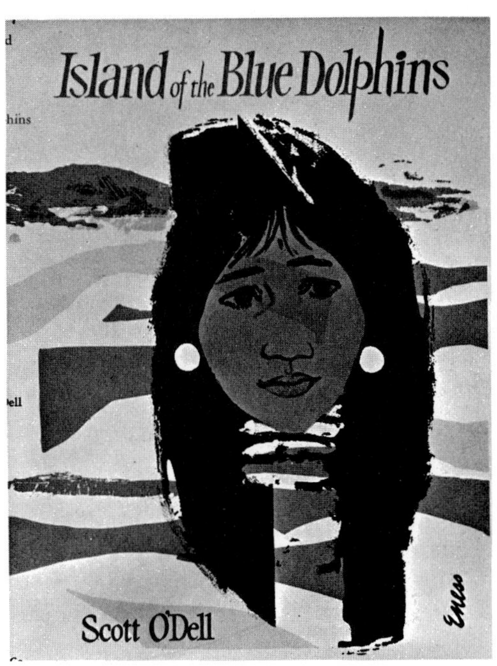

Illustration by E. Ness. From Island of the Blue Dolphins *by Scott O'Dell. Copyright © 1960 by Scott O'Dell. Reprinted by permission of the publisher Houghton Mifflin Co., Boston. (Original in color)*

It may be unwise to give children a story which deals with their particular behavior problem. In the process of growing older, a child may be confronted with pressures and problems too difficult to sustain or solve. To give such children, already harassed, a story about a person who conquers a similar fault may simply make them more self-conscious or so resentful of the virtuous example in the book that they turn with increased fervor to the uninhibited excitement of television or the comics. Children going through one of these temporary periods of rebellion or withdrawal may be helped by discovering books so absorbing, so alight with adventure or satisfying accomplishment that they are heartened in their own struggle to achieve and encouraged to believe that life is worthwhile in spite of its limitations. This is one form of indirect guidance.

Talking About Books with Children

Another method of guidance is through informal discussions of the problems these books involve, rather than of the child's own personal difficulties.[5] For example, a teacher who was reading Beverly Cleary's *Henry Huggins* to her class stopped before she read them the solution of the ethical problem Henry faces when the original owner of his dog Ribsy turns up. "What would you do if you were in Henry's place?" she asked the children, and they played out the solution then and there, with different children taking Henry's part. Their varying interpretations told the teacher much about the children's standards and attitudes, and the activity provided a good deal of fun in the process.

A classroom group discussed Kate's outrageous behavior in the first chapter of *The Good Master*. Of course they thoroughly enjoyed her antics, but they came to the conclusion that she behaved that way because she was "mad" at her father for sending her away, and so she took it out on her uncle's family. It was further agreed that most of us are likely to behave foolishly when we think we have been unjustly treated.

A problem not unlike Kate's is to be found in that splendid family story for eleven- and twelve-year-olds, *Meet the Austins* by Madeleine L'Engle. What triggered the quarrel between the older brother and sister that almost ended in tragedy for them both? The girl was the aggressor and completely unreasonable. But why? What set her off? Can the children see how the death of their beloved uncle and the arrival in the family of a spoiled brat of a girl had all the children emotionally upset and on edge? Such accumulative disturbances sometimes result indirectly in the worst explosions, as they did in this case. But the warmth and stability of family life are restored eventually in this heartwarming story.

Righteous anger over an injustice is one of the hardest emotions to handle for both children and adults. It is important that children learn early that almost everyone suffers at one time or another from this difficulty.

A Dog on Barkham Street by Mary Stolz turns on such a problem and so affords an impersonal situation for discussion. Edward is small and slight, perpetually bullied by the boy next door; Martin is big, burly, and insolent. Edward suspects that if he answered meekly he would not be tormented, but his indignation at an unprovoked insult goads him, at each encounter, into sarcasm. So the pattern repeats: Martin taunts, Edward retorts, Martin pounces and thumps until Edward says "Uncle."

A group of nine-year-olds to whom the book had been read aloud were in vehement agreement that Martin should bear the blame, save for one tall, domineering girl who felt that if Edward had ignored Martin there would have been no fight. The group then read *The Bully of Barkham Street*, an interesting companion volume that gives the same events, but from Martin's point of view. With parents who work, Martin is jealous of Edward, whose mother is always home. He eats for comfort yet hates being plump. When he does try to improve his behavior, Martin is irate that people still think of him as a bully.

Talking about the situation again, the children felt now that there was justification and guilt on both sides. One child commented that

[5]Chapter 15 discusses questioning techniques and book discussion.

this was probably true about every relationship. All of the group were now much more aware of the contributing factors (friends, school life, parental conflict) and of, as one child put it, ". . . how it balances if you aren't happy." Another discussion of the ethical issues involved was held by two sixth-grade classes, each of which had read one of the two books. Interestingly enough, these older children were able to see the implications of provocation—that is, readers of the first book did not assume that Martin was wholly to blame. They commented on the roles of Martin's parents, their lack of understanding and their need for being understood themselves. This is the sort of book that lends itself very nicely to dramatization, either as an adjunct to discussion or as a purely theatrical venture that can sharpen for each viewer the issues with which the book confronts each reader.

Sometimes the best guidance is no guidance at all, a hands-off policy until the storm passes or the tensions are eased. Tales of laughter—for example, the books by Dr. Seuss or Keith Robertson's hilarious *Henry Reed, Inc.*—are invaluable. Invaluable too are grave books like Lucy Boston's *A Stranger at Green Knowe* or Esther Hautzig's *The Endless Steppe*, so absorbing that a young reader is carried out of himself or herself and comes back re-created. Know your child and know books because for every child there is the right book at the right time.

Adult References[6]

ALMY, MILLIE. *Ways of Studying Children.*

ALMY, MILLIE, E. CHITTENDEN, and PAULA MILLER. *Young Children's Thinking; Studies of Some Aspects of Piaget's Theory.*

AMERICAN COUNCIL ON EDUCATION, COMMISSION ON TEACHER EDUCATION. *Helping Teachers Understand Children.*

ARBUTHNOT, MAY HILL. *Children's Reading in the Home.*

BRUNER, JEROME S. *Toward a Theory of Instruction.*

CHAMBERS, AIDAN. *The Reluctant Reader.*

CHILD STUDY ASSOCIATION OF AMERICA. *Insights: A Selection of Creative Literature About Childhood.*

COHEN, MONROE, ed. *Literature with Children.*

COLES, ROBERT. *Children of Crisis.*

COLES, ROBERT, and MARIA PIERS. *Wages of Neglect.*

CROSBY, MURIEL. *An Adventure in Human Relations.*

DUFF, ANNIS. *"Bequest of Wings"; A Family's Pleasures with Books.*

_____. *"Longer Flight"; A Family Grows Up with Books.*

EGOFF, SHEILA, G. T. STUBBS, and L. F. ASHLEY, eds. *Only Connect: Readings on Children's Literature.* Article by Anthony Storr, "The Child and the Book."

ERIKSON, ERIK H. *Childhood and Society.*

FADER, DANIEL N., and ELTON B. McNEIL. *Hooked on Books: Program and Proof.*

FEATHERSTONE, JOSEPH. *Schools Where Children Learn.*

FRANK, JOSETTE. *Your Child's Reading Today.*

GESELL, ARNOLD, and FRANCES ILG. *Child Development; An Introduction to the Study of Human Growth.*

HASKINS, JAMES. *Diary of a Harlem Schoolteacher.*

HAVILAND, VIRGINIA, ed. *Children's Literature; Views and Reviews.* Chapter 3, "Children: Their Reading Interests and Needs."

HENTOFF, NAT. *Our Children Are Dying;* and JOHN McPHEE. *The Headmaster.*

HERNDON, JAMES. *The Way It Spozed to Be; A Report on the Crisis in Our Schools.*

HOLT, JOHN. *How Children Fail.*

_____. *How Children Learn.*

_____. *What Do I Do Monday?*

HYMES, JAMES LEE. *Understanding Your Child.*

ILG, FRANCES L., and LOUISE BATES AMES. *Child Behavior.*

ISAACS, NATHAN. *A Brief Introduction to Piaget.*

JENKINS, GLADYS GARDNER. *Helping Children Reach Their Potential.*

JENKINS, GLADYS G., and HELEN S. SHACTER. *These Are Your Children.*

KOZOL, JONATHAN. *Death at an Early Age; The Destruction of the Hearts and Minds of Negro Children in the Boston Public Schools.*

KUJOTH, JEAN SPEALMAN. *Reading Interests of Children and Young Adults.*

LARRICK, NANCY. *A Parent's Guide to Children's Reading.*

MAIER, HENRY. *Three Theories of Child Development: The Contributions of Erik H. Erikson, Jean Piaget, and Robert R. Sears, and Their Applications.*

MATHEWS, MITFORD M. *Teaching to Read; Historically Considered.*

MAYERSON, CHARLOTTE LEON, ed. *Two Blocks Apart; Juan Gonzales and Peter Quinn.*

PIAGET, JEAN, and BARBEL INHELDER. *The Psychology of the Child.*

REID, VIRGINIA M., ed. *Reading Ladders for Human Relations.*

RICHARDSON, ELWYN. *In the Early World.*

ROBINSON, EVELYN ROSE. *Readings About Children's Literature.* Part 1, "The Child and His Reading."

SILBERMAN, CHARLES. *Crisis in the Classroom.*

SMITH, LILLIAN. *The Unreluctant Years.*

WHITE, DOROTHY MARY NEAL. *About Books for Children.*

[6]Complete bibliographic data are provided in the combined Adult References in the Appendixes.

Guiding Children's Book Selection

Chapter 2

Books are written for children, but adults buy them. Editors decide on manuscripts, reviewers make judgments, teachers and librarians exhibit books, recommend them, and otherwise guide children's reading. Parents, grandparents, uncles, and aunts select a choice volume for a favorite child. But how can adults know what book a child is going to enjoy?

Actually, they can't know with any degree of certainty. Moreover, they must face the fact that youngsters are skilled at rejecting what is not for them. A book may be judged a juvenile classic by experts in children's literature, but if it is beyond children's understanding or too subtle or sophisticated for their level of appreciation, they can turn it down with a stony indifference which leaves adults baffled and grieved. They need not mourn. Two years later a child may accept that very book with enthusiasm. It is the same with music. A simple melody may appeal to children, while a symphony may confuse them. But if their musical experiences increase as they mature, they hear parts of the symphony, its different movements, over and over, until they understand and enjoy them. Finally, when they hear the whole symphony, they can follow it with pleasure, and its great melodies sing in their memories. So some poems must be heard repeatedly, and some stories must be talked over or listened to while someone who knows and loves them reads aloud.

Through this gradual induction into better and better literature, children catch the theme and savor the beauty or the subtle humor or the meaning that eluded them at first. Sometimes an adult has the privilege of seeing this discovery take place. The children's faces come suddenly alive; their eyes shine. They may be anticipating an amusing conclusion or a heroic triumph. There is a sudden chuckle, or breath is exhaled like a sigh. The book has moved them, perhaps even to laughter or tears, but in any case there is a deep inner satisfaction, and they will turn to books again with anticipation.

This chapter will discuss criteria for book selection, the elements of literature (such as setting, viewpoint, characterization, plot, theme, and style), the role of the critic, and the range of books for children.

Knowing Children

How are adults to select these books for children? And how are adults to guide children in choosing their own books? It is evident from the discussion of children's needs in Chapter 1 that the first consideration in selecting books for a special child or a group of children must be the children themselves. The needs of children are determined by their backgrounds and attitudes, abilities and reading skills, and, of course, interests. Most small children like stories about animals and machines or vehicles, about playmates and family relationships, and about situations that reflect their own environments. They enjoy rhyme and rhythm and they are pleased by stories that demonstrate the satisfaction of having a wish fulfilled, a problem solved, a new skill learned, or a new situation taken in stride.

The beginning independent reader wants action and variety, appreciates simple or visual humor, and is beginning to be curious about the world. Some younger children enjoy word play. As their world expands, children in the primary grades become interested in children of other lands.

In the middle grades, when children have acquired a better understanding of time and a sense of history, biography begins to appeal. For a time boys tend to scorn stories in which girls are the main characters and girls tend to accept more easily protagonists of both sexes, a situation that may well change as female characters in books are given more active, interesting roles. There is often enthusiastic reaction to fantasy and nonsense humor, an interest in words, and a continuing enjoyment of action, partly seen in a devotion to series fiction, which usually leans heavily on plot. For years adults have deplored and children have relished the stereotyped *Nancy Drew* and *Hardy Boys* books; today the lively adventures of *Ramona the Pest* and *The Great Brain* have devoted followers who eagerly await each new volume.

Illustration from The Great Brain Reforms *by John D. Fitzgerald. Illustration by Mercer Mayer. Illustration copyright © 1973 by THE DIAL PRESS. Used with permission of the publisher.*

Many readers of nine, ten, and eleven become addicted to a topic or a genre; subject interests make informational books of growing importance, and children's desire for a clearer understanding of themselves and their relation to others is evident in their interest in fiction about interpersonal relationships, children of other lands and times, sex roles, and family patterns.

Young teenagers today are often concerned about their roles in society and about social problems; they talk about drugs and delinquency, student unrest, the generation gap, the role of women, the manipulations of the stock market, and the struggle for black equality. Many of them read adult books, while some may vary their reading patterns with an occasional book intended for younger children.

In selecting books for groups of children or individual children, adults should know as much as possible about children in general and about the particular children they are working with, and they can learn a great deal, as Chapter 1 suggests, by discussing books with children. Always the adult should keep in mind the goal: to make reading a pleasurable experience for children, so that it will always be one of their leisure-time activities.

Knowing Books

Adults must know a great deal about books in choosing them for children and in guiding children to them. The chapters in this book will introduce many of the fine authors of the past and present, and will also suggest criteria for judging books in each genre. These chapters are, of course, guides only. In the end, you should choose books for children on the basis of your own first-hand knowledge of the child or groups of children you are working with and of the books themselves.

The best way to know books is to read them. Book selection guides can help and lists of award books are useful, but there is no substitute for reading. Using the lists of book selection aids and prize-winning books included later in this volume is only a first step. Many of the best books are published in paperback, and children can be encouraged to start their own paperback libraries, especially if you can discuss books with knowledgeable enthusiasm. It really isn't enough to feel, "I like it," or "I don't like it." To make wise selections and to stimulate children's interest, one must know why. It is useful to keep records of such data as title, author, publisher, series, illustrator, availability in paperback, and of your opinion of plot, theme, style, characters, etc. You may also want to note passages that would be particularly enticing as baits to reading. Publishers usually suggest the reading level, but this you will want to judge for yourself. (Would a fifth-grade class enjoy this book? Could a slow reader handle it? Will the subject interest a particular child who can read but seldom does?) While you will be careful to avoid the role of censor, you should know the book well enough to judge whether it should be given to special children or recommended to a class as a whole. If you have kept records of the books you have read, you may have the great satisfaction of being able to recommend another book when a child asks, "Is there any other book just like this one?"

In some classrooms, a teacher will have enthusiastic response to *The Wind in the Willows;* in others, no response at all. In some library story hours *Mary Poppins* may produce hilarity, in others boredom—in the same library. Think how differently you would select, say, for a fourth grade of bright, enthusiastic booklovers and a fourth grade of slow, apathetic readers. Or, in working with individual children, how differently you would choose a book for a lively child with a sense of humor and a child who is quiet and thoughtful.

You can turn to review sources for opinions of books, but in the end you must rely on your

Floating away over the roofs of the houses

Illustration by Mary Shepard. Reproduced from Mary Poppins, *copyright, 1934, © 1962, by P. L. Travers, by permission of Harcourt Brace Jovanovich, Inc.*

Viewpoints

Literary criticism can be no more than a reasoned account of the feeling produced upon the critic by the book he is criticising. Criticism can never be a science: it is, in the first place, much too personal, and in the second, it is concerned with values that science ignores. The touchstone is emotion, not reason. We judge a work of art by its effect on our sincere and vital emotion, and nothing else.

. . . A critic must be able to *feel* the impact of a work of art in all its complexity and its force. To do so, he must be a man of force and complexity himself. . . . —D. H. Lawrence, *Selected Literary Criticism,* edited by Anthony Beal, Mercury Books, London, 1956, p. 118.

own judgment.[1] You should not feel restricted by children's immediate interests in choosing books because these are often narrower than they need to be and because they can change quite quickly. Children's reactions are often immediate and personal, and they often adhere conservatively to a known literary experience such as horse stories or science fiction. Teachers, parents, and librarians should keep children exploring both the best of the old books and the most promising of the new. Since new titles alone number over two thousand a year, you need some criteria to help you select wisely. To develop judgments that are reliable and useful, you need to look closely at a book, not only to appraise its total effect on you but to examine the elements that produce that effect. The traditional literary elements we will be discussing are:

1. setting
2. point of view
3. characters
4. plot
5. theme
6. style

In discussion of these elements, three books will be analyzed as examples, all realistic fiction for better comparison: Rebecca Caudill's *Did You Carry the Flag Today, Charley?* for the youngest children; Laura Ingalls Wilder's *Little House in the Big Woods* for the middle group; and John Rowe Townsend's *The Intruder* for older children.[2]

Viewpoints

Education must begin, as Dewey concluded his first article of belief, "with a psychological insight into the child's capacities, interests, habits," but a point of departure is not an itinerary. It is just as mistaken to sacrifice the adult to the child as to sacrifice the child to the adult. It is sentimentalism to assume that the teaching of life can be fitted always to the child's interests just as it is empty formalism to force the child to parrot the formulas of adult society. Interests can be created and stimulated. In this sphere it is not far from the truth to say that supply creates demand, that the provocation of what is available creates response. One seeks to equip the child with deeper, more gripping, and subtler ways of knowing the world and himself.—Jerome S. Bruner, *On Knowing,* Belknap Press of Harvard University Press, 1962, pp. 117–118.

Looking Closely at Books

Setting

Where and when did the story take place? The setting is the time and the place of the action. Its elements are the geographical location, which may be as broad as a country or city or as narrow as an isolated farm or a single classroom; and the time, which can be a historical period of several decades or more, a season, or a day. Other aspects of setting may be an occupational pattern or a general milieu or atmosphere, social or emotional. For some readers, or for some books, the setting of a story may be of paramount interest. For others, the action is all-absorbing, and the setting is of minor importance.

The setting of the story should be clear, believable, and, in the case of biography or historical fiction, authentic. A book like Irene Hunt's *Across Five Aprils* has strength in part because the author's research enabled her to reveal convincingly the tempo, the ideologies, and the language of the Civil War years—particularly in the conflict that existed in border-state families. Too often, in a mediocre book, the author substitutes for a subtly interwoven, authoritative treatment of a time or a place some laboriously detailed information awkwardly placed and often isolated from the characters and events. On the other hand, an author like Rosemary Sutcliff, who has a vast knowledge of British history, lets her characters give readers necessary details about costumes, for example, or information about military leaders, in dialogue appropriate for the

[1]Obviously there are various ways to approach a book. Frederick C. Grews in *The Pooh Perplex* (Dutton, 1963) has produced a devastating satire of various literary approaches to criticism. As Orville Prescott remarked in the *New York Times*, "In twelve glittering, brightly malicious essays he has poleaxed and then neatly eviscerated twelve varieties of currently fashionable literary criticism."

[2]Rebecca Caudill, *Did You Carry the Flag Today, Charley?* (hardback, 1966; paperback, 1971—Holt, Rinehart & Winston, Inc.). Laura Ingalls Wilder, *Little House in the Big Woods* (hardback, 1932, 1953; paperback, 1971—Harper & Row, Publishers). John Rowe Townsend, *The Intruder* (hardback, 1970—J. B. Lippincott Company).

From Did You Carry the Flag Today, Charley? *by Rebecca Caudill. Illustrated by Nancy Grossman. Copyright © 1966 by Rebecca Caudill. Copyright © 1966 by Nancy Grossman. Reproduced by permission of Holt, Rinehart and Winston, Publishers.*

period in which the book is set. A less qualified writer might introduce into the dialogue an unnatural exchange of information that has the synthetic character of a travel brochure. A mediocre story with a hospital setting might have this ridiculous remark by one nurse to another: "Oh, did you know that one must go through decompression to enter a hyperbaric oxygen chamber?" Of course, the other nurse knows it, and the reader knows she knows it. The author simply hasn't been sufficiently skilled to bring in needed scientific details in a casual, natural way.

"To get to Charley Cornett's house, you turn left off the highway at Main Street, drive to the edge of town, and cross a bridge." So begins *Did You Carry the Flag Today, Charley?* and it goes on to place Charley's home in mountain country: a small house in which Charley lives with his parents, four brothers, and five sisters. Since this is a book for reading aloud to young children, it is quite fitting that there be no specific time, but the "highway" and "drive" make it clear that it is now. No confusion here. It is in the countryside, not the city; Charley is one of a large family. All of these interpretations are within the grasp of small children.

Little House in the Big Woods begins: "Once upon a time, sixty years ago, a little girl lived in the Big Woods of Wisconsin, in a little gray house made of logs." Thus, deftly and simply, Wilder has made it clear not only that (at the time of writing) the story is set sixty years in the past, but that the little girl that was Laura Ingalls lived in pioneer fashion, in a log house. And how much more we learn about the setting because of the capitalization of "Big Woods." It immediately gives an impression of the isolation of the little gray house, and both the pinpointing of a past time and the expectation that readers will understand the locale are appropriate for the level of the readers.

In *The Intruder,* Townsend begins with "Sea, sand, stone, slate, sky." Both the staccato introduction and the paragraphs that follow, giving geographical details and historical background, lend emphasis to the importance of the place. The two-page chapter ends, "Sea, sand, stone, slate, sky. That is the landscape," a further emphasis by setting the description apart. Facing the opening lines is a map, another clue to the fact that the setting is important. Townsend assumes that his reading audience will appreciate this, and he creates, in the two pages, an atmosphere that invites an expectation of suspense that depends on the kind of reading experiences older children have had.

Point of View

Who tells the story?

The author may write as an omniscient narrator, who simply describes the characters and gives their thoughts by direct exposition, perhaps at several points in the story. Or the narrator may make no comment and simply let the characters' actions speak for them. If the story is told in first person, the voice may be that of an impartial bystander or of the principal character. In Emily Neville's *It's Like This, Cat,* in which the adolescent protagonist tells the story, we see his parents only through his eyes and must remember that the view of them is therefore limited, so that the author must use other ways of telling the reader what Dave's father is like—through the father's dialogue and actions and through another boy's reaction to him. In Hila Colman's *Claudia, Where Are You?* alternate chapters give the viewpoint of Claudia's mother (in third person) and of the runaway Claudia herself (in first person). If the author uses a diary form or a monologue, as Maia Wojciechowska does in *"Don't Play Dead Before You Have To,"* the point of view is restricted and the only change comes with changing attitudes of the speaker.

Rebecca Caudill's Charley is seen quite objectively, but the author identifies with him by making him the only character whose thoughts are given ("he remembered," "he figured out"), so that the listening or reading audience tends to empathize with him.

In *Little House*, Wilder does the same thing; the story is told in third person (although it is based on her childhood) and the emphasis is put on Laura as the main character both by introducing her first and by making the first comment on Laura from her viewpoint: "So far as the little girl could see. . . ."

In *The Intruder*, even more emphasis is given to Arnold as the protagonist, the second chapter beginning, "Arnold saw the boy and girl a few minutes before he saw the stranger," and all of the subsequent actions of the stranger (who claims that *he* is the real Arnold Haithwaite) are seen from Arnold's viewpoint as those of a mysterious intruder.

Characters

Who are the characters? How are they revealed? Do they grow and change?

It is clear from the discussion above that a major character is often distinguished by being the first person in the book to be introduced. In *The Peterkin Papers*, however, Lucretia Hale sets the lady from Philadelphia apart by introducing her only when the Peterkin family has become so befuddled that she alone can set them straight. In *Charlotte's Web*, E. B. White presents the pig, Wilbur, through a family's discussion of him. Joseph Krumgold, in . . . *and now Miguel*, opens his story with "I am Miguel."

We learn something more in his very next words: "For most people it does not make so much difference that I am Miguel. But for me, often, it is a very great trouble." The character may thus be revealed by what is said or done, or—as in the case of Wilbur—by what is said about him.

Characterization can be effected by physical description: if we read that a judge in colonial Salem has pursed lips and a frowning brow, that he is dressed in somber black and walks with stiff dignity, we anticipate his stern behavior. What characters say, what they do, how they react to others, how others talk about them are all clues to their personalities. If a major character, he or she must play a dynamic role; if the character changes, the change should be logical for the sort of person the author has drawn. There should be depth of characterization, since to emphasize only one or two traits produces a one-dimensional portrait that is often more caricature than characterization.

Characters must be both believable and consistent. Children soon learn how superficial is the patterned mystery story in which no adult contributes to the solution, while an omniscient, persistent, superintelligent child adroitly sees all clues, pursues them, and solves the mystery single-handed.

The characters should develop naturally and behave and talk in ways that are consistent with their age, sex, background, ethnic group, and education.

Whether the story is realistic or fantastic, the characters must be convincing. Although Mary Poppins is in a fanciful story, she is a very convincing character, a severe and crusty individual that no child ever forgets. When Michael asks anxiously, "Mary Poppins, you'll never leave us, will you?" the answer from his new nurse is a stern "One more word from that direction and I'll call the Policeman." Wilbur, the "radiant pig" in *Charlotte's Web*, and Toad of Toad Hall in *The Wind in the Willows* are just as convincing to children as is Harriet the spy. Long after details of plot have been forgotten, children and adults will recall with a chuckle or a warm glow of affection such characters as Jo in *Little Women*, Long John Silver, Henry Huggins, Janey the middle Moffat, Arrietty in *The Borrowers*, and

Illustration by E. H. Shepard. From The Wind in the Willows *by Kenneth Grahame. Published by Charles Scribner's Sons, 1954. Reproduced with permission of the publisher.*

dozens of other salty book characters. And it is through such well-drawn individuals that children gain new insight into their own personal problems and into their ever widening relationships with other people.

As is appropriate for small children whose chief interest is the action in a story, Caudill's Charley is revealed more by what he does than by what he says. Cheerfully obstreperous, Charley, who is five and having his first school experiences, *has* to climb an apple tree to see how apples are attached, and when the class is playing at "hoppity" like Christopher Robin, he hops right out the door. It is further revealing that when the teacher tells him to stay out in the rain, he happily pretends he is a rock and enjoys the rain. In all of his brothers' and sisters' daily inquiries about whether or not he has had the honor of being the flag-carrier, it is clear that they know their little brother and hardly expect it—yet they ask "anxiously," making it clear also that Charley is lovable and loved.

The theme of family love is strong in the *Little House* books, and the first thing we learn about Laura, as she lies in a trundle bed listening to a wolf howl, is the security she feels with Pa there to protect her. We also see in Laura's actions that she is a curious child, far less compliant than her sister Mary—and Wilder often uses Mary's behavior as a contrast to define Laura's livelier personality.

Arnold Haithwaite is revealed as an uncommunicative young man by the first passage of dialogue in *The Intruder*, yet when he confronts the intruder he makes no bones about his incredulity that they have the same name. Stalwart, inflexible, and unafraid, Arnold shows his personality in the tenacious way he insists on his identity even when the intruder has usurped his place by convincing others that he is the real Arnold Haithwaite.

Plot

What happens in the story?

Fiction for children usually focuses on what happens, what the action is. In some stream-of-consciousness novels or quiet character studies for adults, very little happens. While there are some children's books of which this is true, most of them are filled with action. Children want characters who have obstacles to overcome, conflicts to settle, difficult goals to win. It is the vigorous action in pursuit of these goals that keeps young readers racing along from page to page to find out how the central character achieves his or her ends. But achieve he or she must, in some way or other.

A plot is basically a series of actions that move in related sequence to a logical outcome; if there is no sequence or interaction, the book may have a series of episodes (in some books, particularly books of reminiscence, this can be very effective) rather than a plot or story line. Simple as it sounds, a story

Viewpoints

. . . One of the prime achievements in every good fiction has nothing to do with truth or philosophy or a *Weltanschauung* at all. It is the triumphant adjustment of two different kinds of order. On the one hand, the events (the mere plot) have their chronological and causal order, that which they would have in real life. On the other, all the scenes or other divisions of the work must be related to each other according to principles of design, like the masses in a picture or the passages in a symphony. . . . Contrasts (but also premonitions and echoes) between the darker and the lighter, the swifter and the slower, the simpler and the more sophisticated, must have something like a balance, but never a too perfect symmetry, so that the shape of the whole work will be felt as inevitable and satisfying.—C. S. Lewis, *An Experiment in Criticism,* Cambridge University Press, 1961, pp. 81–82.

needs a beginning, a middle, and an end. First the author must set the stage. Then, to have development and momentum, a plot needs conflict, opposition, or a problem. Last, there should be a definitive ending: a climax of action, or even a strong indication of future resolution. A dramatic example of a powerful ending is that of *Helter-Skelter* by Patricia Moyes, in which a young girl hunting a criminal finds that the pleasant young man in whom she has confided is himself the culprit. Alan Garner's *The Owl Service* has an equally powerful conclusion. Here a contemporary setting is the background for a frightening reenactment of a Celtic myth. In the last scene the legend is laid to rest and young Gwyn finally discovers who his father is.

Linked to the development of the plot are the characters, who affect what happens by the sort of people they are and who are, in turn, affected by what happens to them. In stories for the very young, the plot is usually simple, with no subplot, whereas older readers can both understand and enjoy the complexity of a story with many threads.

In *Charley*, the story begins with the fact that a small boy going to school for the first time is told by his brothers and sisters that one child is honored each day by being allowed to carry the flag; as the story develops it becomes evident that Charley is an unlikely candidate. Then an understanding teacher acts—and Charley proudly carries the flag.

Little House is an episodic story; although the book and its sequels show the children growing, the separate incidents of the story might often be interchanged without affecting the outcome.

The plot of *The Intruder* has high dramatic quality. (It was, in fact, filmed for television.) Arnold Haithwaite learns almost immediately that the stranger who establishes himself in Arnold's home is a threat to him—since Arnold is not quite sure of who he really is. He calls the old man with whom he lives "Dad," not having been told that he is the old man's illegitimate grandson. In the struggle for dominance between the boy and the stranger, the plot is given momentum by the fact that the stranger wants not only to take command of the household but also to commercialize the town. The fact that Arnold does not at first know his real identity gives the author an opportunity to unravel threads of past events as well as the immediate action. The conclusion fulfills the promise of the story's opening: a desperate chase on the sands, with the drowning of the criminal in the swift tide and Arnold reaching the safety of an old church, long deserted because it has been for many years cut off from the mainland at high tide.

Theme

What is the main idea of the story?

The theme of the story is its central core, its meaning. For example, the theme of *. . . and now Miguel* is the struggle to attain competence in one's chosen work and so be accepted as a responsible, mature person. The same theme appears in Bianca Bradbury's *The Loner*. In Elizabeth Coatsworth's *Bess and the Sphinx* the theme is overcoming shyness. Often in children's books the theme reflects those developmental values that are inherent in the process of growing up. The theme may be concerned with overcoming jealousy or fear, adjusting to a physical handicap, or accepting a stepparent. Books that have these or other developmental values can help not only the child who shares similar problems but also the child who does not and who needs to learn sympathy and understanding.

Viewpoints

. . . Participation in the continuity of narrative leads to the discovery or recognition of the theme, which *is* the narrative seen as total design. This theme is what, as we say, the story has been all about, the point of telling it. What we reach at the end of participation becomes the center of our critical attention. The elements in the narrative thereupon regroup themselves in a new way. Certain unusually vivid bits of characterization or scenes of exceptional intensity move up near the center of our memory. This reconstructing and regrouping of elements in our critical response to a narrative goes on more or less unconsciously. . . .
—Northrop Frye, "The Road of Excess," in *Myth and Symbol; Critical Approaches and Applications,* Northrop Frye, L. C. Knights, and others, edited by Bernice Slote, University of Nebraska Press, Lincoln, 1963, p. 9.

Not all books have such themes; some are adventure stories, some written just for fun, and some historical fiction is intended only to highlight a person, a movement, or a period. Indeed, there can be no hard and fast rule about any of the elements of fiction, since there are good books in which almost any aspect may be omitted. The elements discussed here are those which exist in most books.

The theme in *Charley* is that of achieving status and acceptance: Charley has been told that carrying the flag is the signal honor of the school day, and although he is really more excited, by the end of the story, by the fact that he owns his first book, he is well aware that the sign of approval has been carrying the flag. Although the *Little House* books are imbued with family love and pioneer courage, there really is no underlying theme. In *The Intruder*, for all the drama of the action, the theme is the boy's quest for identity.

From Thistle and Thyme *by Sorche Nic Leodhas. Illustrated by Evaline Ness. Copyright © 1962 by Leclaire G. Alger. Reproduced by permission of Holt, Rinehart and Winston, Inc.*

Style

How is the story written? How are the ideas expressed?

Style is very difficult to define. Whole books have been devoted to explaining and exemplifying it. There are many brief definitions—Jonathan Swift's "Proper words in proper places make the true definition of style"; Lord Chesterton's "Style is the dress of thoughts"; Comte de Buffon's "The style is the man." Style involves the author's choice of words, the sentence patterns (simple or involved structure, long or short sentences, arrangement of the words within the sentences), the imagery used, the rhythm of the sentences. There are many styles—as many styles as authors. As Thrall, Hibbard, and Holman say in *A Handbook to Literature*, "The best style, for any given purpose, is that which most nearly approximates a perfect adaptation of one's language to one's ideas."[3] Perhaps the best way to talk about style is simply to look at some passages. Read these excerpts from "The Three Little Pigs" and *Millions of Cats* aloud:

"Little pig, little pig, let me come in."
"No, not by the hair on my chinny-chin-chin."
"Then I'll huff and I'll puff and I'll blow your house in."

"Hundreds of cats, thousands of cats, millions and billions and trillions of cats."

Sorche Nic Leodhas has the true Scottish cadence. The first tale in her *Thistle and Thyme* begins:

An old laird had a young daughter once and she was the pawkiest piece in all the world. Her father petted her and her mother cosseted her till the wonder of it was that she wasn't so spoiled that she couldn't be borne.

How much more convincing that is than a peppering of *hoot-mon*'s and *dinna ken*'s.

Bernard Evslin, in his retelling of the Finn McCool legend, *The Green Hero*, writes of high adventure in prose that has an epic sweep, but when he is describing small events, uses unexpectedly homely and amusing language. In listing the charms of the infant girl with whom the newly born Finn is

[3]William Thrall, Addison Hibbard, and C. Hugh Holman, *A Handbook to Literature* (Odyssey, 1960), p. 474.

smitten, he concludes (after rhapsodizing about her eyes and hair), "And teeth—a full set of them—so that she was able to bite Finn quite early."

Sid Fleischman's tall tales appeal to children because they are nonsensical, but it is his crisp, casual style that gives such tales as *McBroom's Ear* humor and flavor:

I guess you've heard how amazing rich our farm was. Anything would grow in it quick. Seeds would burst in the ground and crops would shoot up right before your eyes. Why, just yesterday our oldest boy dropped a five-cent piece and before he could find it that nickel had grown to a quarter.

In *Little Calf*, a story of the first year in the life of a whale, Victor Scheffer uses words and word patterns that have a quiet, lyric quality that is admirably suited to the scene he is describing:

On a morning in early October the sea is glass, without a ripple or sound. A feather falls from the breast of an albatross winging its lonely way northwestward to the Leeward Islands and home. The plume drifts lightly to the sea and comes to rest on a mirror image. It is a day when time itself is still.

Illustration by Barbara Bascove. Reprinted by permission of Four Winds Press from The Green Hero, *© 1975 by Bernard Evslin.*

In style, as in the theme of a book, there should be appropriateness and integrity, the hallmarks of good writing. When they are absent, we often find pedestrian writing: flagrant repetitiveness, stiff dialogue, a gross exaggeration of humor or fantasy, conflict between realism and fantasy, didacticism, superciliousness ("Can YOU see the little duck in the tree?") or a use of language that is poorly chosen for the genre of the book or for the characters in it.

Rebecca Caudill's style in *Did You Carry the Flag Today, Charley?* is brisk and forthright, just as is Charley himself. Small children may not recognize the Appalachian setting, but they can hear the authenticity of the speech patterns and the fact that Charley's comments sound the way a five-year-old's should.

Once inside Miss Amburgey's schoolroom, Charley looked around. Little chairs stood in a circle, with one big chair among them. Behind the big chair was a blackboard, and in a trough underneath lay pieces of chalk. Low tables stood at one side of the room. And there—there, fastened to the wall, was the white washbowl!

Notice how much like an inquisitive child's reaction this is—and how the exclamation point prepares the way for an episode in which Charley squirts water all over himself and several others. In contrast, note the quiet simplicity and the establishment of mood in Wilder's *Little House in the Big Woods:*

She looked at Ma, gently rocking and knitting. She thought to herself, "This is now." She was glad that the cozy house, and Pa and Ma and the firelight and the music, were now. They could not be forgotten, she thought, because now is now. It can never be a long time ago.

And from *The Intruder*, an example of John Rowe Townsend's writing that shows both his gift for brief characterization and the terse dialogue that is typical of Arnold:

Illustration by Garth Williams. From Little House in the Big Woods *by Laura Ingalls Wilder. Pictures copyright 1953 by Garth Williams. Reproduced by permission of Harper & Row, Publishers, Inc., and Methuen Children's Books, Ltd., London.*

Ernest Haithwaite was a small man whose clothes now seemed a size too big for him. His features, always craggy, were sharpening with age. His hair, once plentiful, was thinning and grizzled. He shaved every Sunday, and sometimes during the week as well.

The old man was putting his cup down when a tap came on the door that led to the main house. He struggled to get up. Arnold waved him down, handed him his false teeth from the mantelpiece.

"There's a feller staying the night," the old man said.

"I know," said Arnold.

An Analysis of *Blowfish Live in the Sea*

As an example of analysis of the elements of a book (setting, point of view, characterization, plot, theme, and style) and the criteria used in assessing them, let's look at *Blowfish Live in the Sea* by Paula Fox.

It begins: "My brother, Ben, says that blowfish live in the sea. He says it in many ways. I've found it written on matchbook covers, on brown paper bags from the supermarket, in dust on the windows. That makes Mama mad because you can't get window cleaners to come anymore."[4] On the next page, we learn that this "makes my father mad," and that Ben and his sister do not have the same father. Ben's father is somewhere out west "the last I heard," and the only answer Ben gives, if asked, is "I don't know, Carrie." Carrie goes on to say that she is twelve and Ben nineteen and that his uncut hair irritates his mother and stepfather.

What a lot to learn in two pages! Carrie has first of all told us that Ben is the most important character in the story, certainly the most important to her. He prefers not to talk about his father, and Carrie's laconic "the last I heard" makes it clear that he doesn't often hear from him. The viewpoint is Carrie's, but in her comments about her parents' attitude toward one thing—Ben's hair—we suspect conflict. Then we learn Ben has dropped out of school, that after an argument with his stepfather he had stopped bringing his friends home. So the stage is set (and the setting here consists of a comfortable, conventional home and a nonconformist son).

The problem is posed when Ben gets a letter from his father, who is going to be in Boston for the weekend and wants Ben to meet him. "Can't wait," the letter ends, and the reader has been given another clue to the father who

Viewpoints

What I have been trying to say expresses my belief that the judgment of children's literature—and all the adult efforts that proceed from that judgment—must be conducted without condescension, without turning one's adult collar in an effort to define and enforce values that are somehow uniquely juvenile. On the contrary, it seems to me that the proper satisfactions of reading, even in the newly literate child—even, indeed, in the non-literate, story-listening child—provide a robust affirmation of our common humanity, our capacity, whether we are young or old, to understand and to be moved by and to gather to ourselves the products of the creative imagination.—Edward W. Rosenheim, Jr., "Children's Reading and Adults' Values." From *A Critical Approach to Children's Literature* edited by Sara Innis Fenwick. © 1967 by The University of Chicago. Reprinted by permission.

[4]From *Blowfish Live in the Sea* by Paula Fox. Copyright © 1970 by Paula Fox. Reprinted by permission of Bradbury Press, Inc.

has not been heard from for so long. Ben wants Carrie to go with him, which tells us both that he is nervous about meeting his father and that the bond between brother and sister is a strong one. All of the elements of the story have now been established and will be elaborated on, but not until the close of the book is the title explained.

In Boston, Carrie and Ben learn that Ben's father is a raffish but engaging man, a liar, a drifter who has neglected his son save for an occasional boastful letter. In fact, they get to his hotel to find a letter saying that an emergency at the ranch he runs in Arizona has forced him to leave town. "Really, so disappointed for both of us! But soon. Very soon." Ben says bluntly, "He didn't want to see me," and he goes back to the hotel and finds his suspicion verified. Mr. Felix has not left town at all.

He is in his room, not quite sober, and at first puts up a bluff about his lie. Then he admits that he, like Ben, was nervous, and having confessed this, he begins to tell the truth. He owns a motel outside of Boston, not a very profitable venture, and he talks about what a wonderful life he has had. To Carrie it is a record of failure, to Ben the freedom of his father's wanderings sounds enticing. Ben decides to stay with his father and Carrie goes home alone.

Ben's decision is the climax of the plot, and it is made credible by the friction that he has felt at home; the reader has been prepared for it both by the characterization and by the tension and apprehension of Carrie as she reacts to Mr. Felix. And for Carrie, too, the outcome is credible: she misses Ben when she is back home, but she has other interests and is not desolate.

The setting, contemporary and urban, is not a major element of the story except for its underlining of the situation: the contrast between the ordered home in New York and the seedy hotel in Boston, where the young people's expectation of what Felix will be like is shaped by that atmosphere.

The theme is love and the acceptance of frailty that love implies, exemplified both by Carrie, who adores her brother despite his moodiness and rebelliousness, and by Ben, who is old enough to understand his father's ineptitude and irresponsibility and to forgive him for them. Paula Fox is a particularly adept writer in presenting the theme of a story; she lets the characters tell the reader what their concerns are. When Carrie reminisces about an incident earlier in her childhood, she reveals both Ben's sensitivity and her own appreciation of it. And Ben, facing his father with the fact that he has been lied to for years, smiles. We know that Ben is compassionate rather than vengeful. And we know, not because the author *says* people must sometimes make difficult choices but because she *shows* us, that these things happen and that people must adjust to them.

One of the criteria for the evaluation of a book is the interaction between characters and between characters and events. Are the characters firmly enough drawn so that the reader finds their reactions to events believable? And do they, in turn, behave consistently in determining what happens? In *Blowfish Live in the Sea*, Carrie very quickly establishes her own still childlike character by her

Viewpoints

The . . . argument, 'all taste is relative', must as a matter of simple logic lead also to the conclusion that no one book is inherently better than another. If we accept this, then one of two things is true: either all books are worthless, since if preference is impossible all books are equal and therefore without *value* (for currency depends on varying stages of value); alternatively, if preference is only possible in relative judgements, then discussion is pointless, for everybody is as right as everybody else.

. . . Either some books *can* be dismissed out of hand for reasons which can be precisely given, and which depend on moral and literary principles, or all judgement is purely personal, and there are no grounds for saying that Shakespeare is better than Noël Coward. All our experience and our most valuable traditions uphold the first view: certain books are good, others are bad, and a very large number have something of both. The books are good because they comment on experience with profundity and intelligence, and occasionally with genius; and these qualities lead us to some glimpse of the truth about human experience.—Fred Inglis, *An Essential Discipline,* Methuen Educational Ltd., London, 1968, pp. 3–5.

comments on Ben and her tangential remarks about her friend Abby (an early bloomer), by her reaction to her mother's worries about Ben, and by her conversation with her father. Ben is clearly drawn through Carrie's expressed thoughts as well as by his own dialogue and his stepfather's irritation.

Some of the components of style are comparatively easy to assess: the writing flows smoothly, the dialogue really sounds like people talking, the story has suspense and momentum. Paula Fox's ability to maintain the child's point of view while writing with adult compassion and literary grace is exemplified by Carrie's memory of a family outing years before.

Once when I was standing just behind him, and he was kneeling, I'd suddenly seen how much older he was than I, how much bigger. At that same picnic, a bird had flown right into our windshield just as we parked under some trees. Ben had leaped out of the back seat and run to where the bird had fallen. Then I'd walked over and found him with the bird in his hand, a little mound of smoky feathers.

"It's dead," he said quietly.

Ben had known everything then. I thought about that bird long after winter came, and Ben standing there with it in his hand.

In this tender story of love, Paula Fox never strikes a false note, never inserts a word for effect, never uses a polysyllabic word or a quip when they are out of place. She never comes between the child and the book; it is as though she were a channel between the reader and the characters. Only when Ben is gone does Carrie learn why he wrote "Blowfish live in the sea" everywhere. His father had once sent him a dried blowfish that he had found, he wrote, in the Amazon. It was after Ben learned that blowfish live only in salt water that he inscribed his testimony of resentment against his father's betrayal. How astute of the author not to tell us this at the first, but to let us see how Ben reacts and how his leaving home to join his father indicates the softened judgment and tolerance of maturity.

Viewpoints

To judge literature in terms of the racial attitudes presented in them is actually to judge whether the writer has gone beyond and behind stereotypes, myths, and ideas about blacks to develop characters whose ethnic, social, cultural, and personal experiences mesh in all the complex ways they do in real life. The literature that will truly give black children a sense of identity will not be literature-as-morality nor literature-as-propaganda, but literature as human experience. To black children, blackness is an intrinsic and desirable component of that human experience.—Judith Thompson and Gloria Woodard, "Black Perspective in Books for Children," *Wilson Library Bulletin*, December 1969, p. 422.

The Role of the Critic

In the evaluation of children's books there should be neither a casual, uncritical approach nor a rigid adherence to the standards for adult literature. The best in children's literature, as well as the best in adult literature, will meet those standards, but it is incumbent on critics (and this includes parents) to balance each book's strengths and weaknesses and to remember that each kind of book for children has its own requirements. As Lillian Smith points out in *The Unreluctant Years:*

A child's range of choice in his reading will always depend upon what is at hand, and this will largely depend upon his elders. Mistaken ideas among adults about what books a child likes, or should like, must prevent the very object they intend: a love for books and reading. If such misunderstanding is given widespread credence it will eventually affect what books are made generally available to children. (p. 13)[5]

Adults must be wary of pedestrian books, often oversize and profusely illustrated, the kind that bookstore clerks refer to as "grandmother books": slick, busy with detail, often coy, cute, or sentimental. They must try to distinguish between what appeals to some nostalgic adults and what appeals to children. They should guard against bias, preconception, or unevaluated loyalty to a favorite childhood book.

[5]Lillian H. Smith, *The Unreluctant Years* (American Library Association, 1953).

Children's literature often reflects the values that adults think are important to encourage, and those who select books for children should be aware of the author's values and assumptions as well as of their own. If an author's attitude toward parent-child relationships, sex mores, civil rights, or any other issue is in agreement with our own, we may tend to approve of the book as a whole, but if the values and assumptions are at variance with our own, we may tend to dismiss it, regardless of its other qualities. For these reasons, it is particularly important for us to analyze books as carefully and objectively as we can. Each book must be judged on its own merits, but it is often illuminating to compare a book with the author's other books and with other authors' books on the same topic or in the same literary genre. The professional—teacher, librarian, reviewer, or editor—should know both the books themselves and the critical literature, since criticism entails making judgments that ought to be both informed and objective.

Criteria for Specific Types of Books

The special criteria for the various types of children's literature—poetry, folk tales, fables, myths, epics, modern fantasy, realistic stories, historical fiction, biography, and informational books—are discussed in succeeding chapters, and there are also evaluations of individual books, authors, and illustrators. Many different kinds of books can be judged by the criteria we have been discussing for theme, plot, setting, characters, point of view, and style. Biography, for instance, may be so evaluated, but it should also be judged by other equally important criteria (see Chapter 12). One of the essential criteria for judging informational books (see Chapter 13) is accuracy, but style, too, is important. Information can, and should, be presented in an interesting, lively fashion.

The Range of Books for Children

Because childhood should be a time of exploring many kinds of books, adults who work with children should know the different types, both to prevent children from falling into reading ruts and to encourage them to try books of many varieties.

The books discussed in the following chapters are grouped variously—some according to age level (books for early childhood), some according to approach (realistic stories), some according to genre (biography), and so on. This kind of classification, though obviously mixed and inexact, is nonetheless useful, partly because it is based to some extent on the ways that children themselves describe their books.

One means of helping a child out of a reading rut—say, all animal stories or all fairy tales—is first to discover some common elements in the books he or she enjoys and then to use these as a stimulus to change. For example, if a child who reads only animal stories has enjoyed Mehlli Gobhai's *Lakshmi, the Water Buffalo Who Wouldn't*, he or she might be led toward reading other kinds of books with some of the same elements—humor, an Indian setting, or pleasant family relationships.

Picture Stories

For prereaders and beginning readers, picture stories are enchanting. Significantly, the older stories which have lasted over the years are, for the most part, built around one or two general themes: love or reassurance, and achievement. *Peter Rabbit*, which is over seventy years old, has both. Peter has a daring adventure but returns safely to his home where his mother tucks him into bed with a justifiably punishing dose of camomile tea. Love and reassurance make Else Minarik's *Little Bear* books, and many other stories for the youngest, completely satisfying. And then, because the young child is always in an inferior position in relation to older children and adults, he or she yearns for independent achievement or competence. Hence the long life of *Mike Mulligan and His Steam Shovel*, the popularity of the *Madeline* books, and the success of the *Little Tim* stories, in which Tim triumphs gloriously over his many mishaps, such as shipwrecks and mislaying his parents—all books with themes of satisfying achievement.

In evaluating the various editions of the *Mother Goose* books or the many variations on alphabet books, the areas of decision are different. No need to wonder about the appeal of the former, since their rhyme, rhythm, and gay humor are established beyond controversy as appealing to the very young. The areas of decision lie primarily in the format of the book, the choice of rhymes included, and the illustrations. The latter are of paramount importance, too, in ABC books and are, of course, all-important in wordless picture books.

Folk Tales

Challenge and achievement are the heart of the folk-tale themes. The heroes or heroines must perform stern tasks if they are to survive, but the fact that they deal competently with glass hills, giants, witches, wicked machinations, and come through modestly triumphant is both reassuring and encouraging. Stories such as "Cinderella," "The Three Little Pigs," "The Three Billy-Goats Gruff," and "Molly Whuppie" dramatize the stormy conflict of good and evil. And they reiterate the old verities that kindness and goodness will triumph over evil if they are backed by wisdom, wit, and courage. These basic truths are the folk tales' great contribution to the child's social consciousness.

Fables, Myths, and Epics

Older children are the primary audience for the pithy—if sometimes didactic—wisdom of the fables, although many fables have been skillfully used as single versions in picture-story format. All of these forms of literature (fables, myths, and epics) have a quality of universality, and are part of the literary heritage with which all children should become familiar. They may not fully understand the complexity or symbolism of myths and legends, but they can appreciate the drama and beauty of the stories, and the great epics can satisfy a child's reverence for courage and high deeds.

Fantasy

No genre so satisfies the child's boundless imagination as does fantasy, from the adventures of Max in Maurice Sendak's *Where the Wild Things Are* to the intricate depths of Madeleine L'Engle's *A Wrinkle in Time*. It encompasses gay little picture books about friendly ghosts and little-girl witches, low-keyed modern fairy stories like Betty Brock's *No Flying in the House*, blandly told tales like Diana Jones's *The Ogre Downstairs*, the romantic adventure stories by Lloyd Alexander, the picaresque books by Joan Aiken, and the polished science fiction of Peter Dickinson. All of them can extend the reader's horizons, all of them have the action that appeals to children, many of them provide humor that ranges from daft nonsense to subtle wit, and

Viewpoints

. . . A good critic will indeed be aware of theme, plot, style, characterization, and many other considerations, some of them not previously spelled out but arising directly from the work; he will be sensitive; he will have a sense of balance and rightness; he will respond. Being only human he cannot possibly know all that it would be desirable for him to know; but he will have a wide knowledge of literature in general as well as of children and their literature, and probably a respectable acquaintance with cinema, theatre, television, and current affairs. That is asking a lot of him, but not too much. The critic (this is the heart of the matter) counts more than the criteria.

. . . If the book is for children, he should not let his mind be dominated by the fact, but neither, I believe, should he attempt to ignore it. Just as I feel the author must write for himself yet with awareness of an audience of children, so I feel the critic must write for himself with an awareness that the books he discusses are children's books.

. . . A book is a communication; if it doesn't communicate, does it not fail? True, it may speak to posterity, if it gets the chance; it may be ahead of its time. But if a children's book is not popular with children here and now, its lack of appeal may tell us something. It is at least a limitation, and it *may* be a sign of some vital deficiency which is very much the critic's concern.—Quoted by permission of the American Library Association from "Standards of Criticism for Children's Literature," John Rowe Townsend, *Top of the News,* June 1971, pp. 385–387.

almost all of them have an ingredient of durable attraction, magic.

Poetry

Poetry, too, extends children's imaginations, although in a different way. Where fantasy opens doors to things beyond belief, poetry gives new inward vision and understanding. The facile appeals of rhyme, rhythm, and repetition in simple verse and the quick humor of nonsense poetry can lead to an appreciation of the beauty of language and the crystallization in poetry of a mood, an emotion, a relationship, or the loveliness of a scene. The storytelling appeal of narrative poetry makes it a good choice for reading aloud as an introduction to the genre, and children may be led from this to lyric poetry and free verse. The increased interest of children and young people in the writing of poetry as well as in reading it is evident in the many collections and anthologies that have appeared and in the numbers of poetry magazines and workshops that have produced new young poets.

Realistic Stories

The themes of love, reassurance, and achievement are prominent in many stories of family life. For the middle years, eight to ten, the pleasant and amusing adventure stories of *Little Eddie* and *Henry Huggins* take place against a permissive family background of suburbia. So does that great family story for somewhat older readers, *Meet the Austins.* The children in these stories have their problems and difficulties, some funny, some grave; sometimes with the reassurance of family understanding and love and sometimes missing and needing them. This is also true of books about underprivileged migrant workers such as *The Maldonado Miracle* and *Roosevelt Grady.* These books broaden children's social understandings and deepen their sympathies. It is significant that the realistic stories for today's children have gone beyond such books as *The Bobbsey Twins* and *Nancy Drew* stories and present real people confronted with real problems—from earning money for a bike to rebuilding a fairly normal life in a European city in wartime *(Fly Away Home).*

Reprinted by permission of the Wm. Collins & World Publishing Co., Inc., from Roosevelt Grady by Louisa R. Shotwell, illustrations by Peter Burchard. Copyright © 1963.

This realistic fiction also acquaints children with a wider world than the city, suburbs, or regional groups of the United States. Books begin to introduce them to family life in other countries. Even in the picture-story stage, French *Madeline* and *Jeanne-Marie* are as familiar to American children as are the boys and girls of the United States in American children's books. The tens will enjoy that strange French home-in-the-making described in *Family Under the Bridge,* and the twelves will find out what happens during wartime in T. Degens's *Transport 7-41-R.* Gone are fiesta stereotypes of foreign lands and gone are the stories about a country told by an author who has never seen it or who equates contemporary life with that of a hundred years ago. *Hans Brinker* has been supplemented by Hilda van Stockum's *The Borrowed House.* Today's India is re-created by Shirley Arora in *What Then, Raman?*

There is delightful humorous realism, too, as in Keith Robertson's *Henry Reed, Inc.* From the ingenuous absurdities of Charlotte Zolotow's *When I Have a Son* and the matter-of-fact hilarity of Beverly Cleary's *Ramona the Pest* to the sophisticated humor of James Lincoln Collier's *Rich and Famous,* the young of all ages can find amusing echoes of everyday life. Wherever laughter can be found, it is important that we search for it and relish it.

Historical Fiction

Children may know Paul Revere in story or verse, but do they also know children of Revere's time—eight-year-old Sarah in *The Courage of Sarah Noble* and the twelve- or fourteen-year-old Johnny in *Johnny Tremain?* Historical fiction today is both historically authentic and well written. Indeed, in such books we find some of the best contemporary writing for children and youth. The 1961, 1962, and 1974 Newbery Medals were awarded to books of historical fiction—*Island of the Blue Dolphins, The Bronze Bow,* and *The Slave Dancer,* three books good readers of twelve and over should not miss. In each of the books mentioned in this brief sampling, the theme—from "Keep up your courage, Sarah Noble" to the message that it is only love, not hatred, that can bend a bow of bronze—speaks strongly to children of today.

Biography

Historical fiction and biography may and should be used to reinforce each other. *Johnny Tremain* makes a biography of Paul Revere infinitely more real; Cora Cheney's *The Incredible Deborah* is a stirring example of the valor of a colonial girl; and the homespun frontier boys in William Steele's stories give vivid life to the scene and times of Daniel Boone. Both historical fiction and biography impress children with a sense of the reality of other days. Begin early to introduce children to these "real stories" we call biographies. Even the youngest readers can start with Ferdinand Monjo's simply written biographies and can then move on to many excellent biographies suitable for children of each age level. Books about Paracelsus, Galileo, Joan of Arc, Columbus, Washington, Banneker, Sequoyah, Lincoln, Tubman, Bethune, Robeson, Gandhi, and many others are authentic and as fascinating as fiction.

Informational Books

The category of informational books is so broad and so diverse that almost any need a child has for facts about a subject can be satisfied. There is, however, a need for vigilance on the part of the adult to be familiar with the contents of such books, since many informational books give scant coverage or unbalanced treatment. This is an area in which the author's qualifications are important. The adult working with children should know those authors—and there are many—whose books are accurate, up-to-date, and written at the right level of complexity for their intended audience. Publishers are quick to respond to expressed needs, and the past years have seen an outpouring of books about pollution and ecology, oceanology and space science, and most of the reform and protest movements that stir our society, as well as books on the arts and sciences, humanity's past record, and our present environment. Handbooks and experiment books, reference books, do-it-yourself books, handsome art books—books by the hundreds—exist to fulfill the child's need to know. The adult can help children choose the best of these books by being aware of the accuracy of the contents, the thoroughness of the indexing (not all informational books need an index), the placement of maps and diagrams, and the organization of the material in a logical sequence.

Children need books to widen their horizons, deepen their understandings, and give them broader social insights. They also need books that minister to their merriment and increase their appreciation of beauty. They need heroism, fantasy, and down-to-earth realism. They need information about themselves and their fast-changing world, and they need books to relieve the tensions of that world. Adults may think in terms of what the child will learn, how the book may improve an attitude, correct a misconception, or ease a fear. If books do this, fine, but the child reads primarily for pleasure. For many children, the right time for a book is fleeting, and gentle guidance may be needed to expand the interests of a child who is in a reading rut so that he or she may not miss a reading experience for which there may never be another time so right.[6]

[6]For additional help in choosing books for children, see Book Selection Aids in the Appendixes.

The analyses in this chapter are meant as guidelines, not as rigid specifications. There are fine books that do not measure up to every standard of good literature but that may have particular values for a particular child, or whose strengths outweigh their weaknesses. Each book should be judged on its own merits. Wide reading at all levels and careful observation of children's reactions to books and of their individual and special interests will also help adults make wise choices in guiding young readers.

Adult References[7]

BECHTEL, LOUISE SEAMAN. *Books in Search of Children.*

CAMERON, ELEANOR. *The Green and Burning Tree.* Chapter, "Of Style and the Stylist."

CARLSEN, G. ROBERT. *Books and the Teen-Age Reader; A Guide for Teachers, Librarians, and Parents.*

CHAMBERS, AIDAN. *Introducing Books to Children.*

Chosen for Children; An Account of the Books Which Have Been Awarded the Library Association Carnegie Medal, 1936–1965.

COLBY, JEAN POINDEXTER. *Writing, Illustrating and Editing Children's Books.*

COMMIRE, ANNE. *Something About the Author; Facts and Pictures About Contemporary Authors and Illustrators of Books for Young People.*

DE ANGELI, MARGUERITE. *Butter at the Old Price.*

DE MONTREVILLE, DORIS, and DONNA HILL, eds. *Third Book of Junior Authors.*

DUNNING, STEPHEN, and ALAN B. HOWES. *Literature for Adolescents; Teaching Poems, Stories, Novels, and Plays.*

EDWARDS, MARGARET A. *The Fair Garden and the Swarm of Beasts; The Library and the Young Adult.*

EGOFF, SHEILA. *The Republic of Childhood; A Critical Guide to Canadian Children's Literature in English.*

EGOFF, SHEILA, G. T. STUBBS, and L. F. ASHLEY, eds. *Only Connect; Readings on Children's Literature.*

FENNER, PHYLLIS. *The Proof of the Pudding.*

______, ed. *Something Shared; Children and Books.*

FENWICK, SARA INNIS, ed. *A Critical Approach to Children's Literature.* Papers by Rosenheim and Nesbitt.

FIELD, CAROLYN W., ed., with VIRGINIA HAVILAND and ELIZABETH NESBITT, consultants. *Subject Collections in Children's Literature.*

FIELD, ELINOR WHITNEY, comp. *Horn Book Reflections; On Children's Books and Reading.*

FISHER, MARGERY. *Intent Upon Reading.*

______. *Who's Who in Children's Books.*

FRYATT, NORMA R., ed. *A Horn Book Sampler.*

FULLER, MURIEL, ed. *More Junior Authors.*

GILLESPIE, JOHN, and DIANA LEMBO. *Introducing Books; A Guide for the Middle Grades.*

______. *Juniorplots; A Book Talk Manual for Teachers and Librarians.*

HAVILAND, VIRGINIA. *Children's Literature; A Guide to Reference Sources.*

______, ed. *Children and Literature; Views and Reviews.* Chapter 11, "Criticism and Reviewing."

HAZARD, PAUL. *Books, Children and Men.*

HILDICK, WALLACE. *Children and Fiction.* Chapter, "Adult Responsibility: Authors' and Critics'."

HOFFMAN, MIRIAM, and EVA SAMUELS, eds. *Authors and Illustrators of Children's Books.*

HUCK, CHARLOTTE S. *Children's Literature in the Elementary School.*

KAMM, ANTONY, and BOSWELL TAYLOR. *Books and the Teacher.*

KARL, JEAN. *From Childhood to Childhood; Children's Books and Their Creators.*

KUNITZ, STANLEY J., and HOWARD HAYCRAFT, eds. *The Junior Book of Authors.*

LANES, SELMA G. *Down the Rabbit Hole; Adventures and Misadventures in the Realm of Children's Literature.*

LENSKI, LOIS. *Adventure in Understanding; Talks to Parents, Teachers and Librarians by Lois Lenski, 1944–1966.*

LEPMAN, JELLA. *A Bridge of Children's Books.*

LINES, KATHLEEN, ed. *Walck Monographs.* A series of biographies of authors.

LUKENS, REBECCA J. *A Critical Handbook of Children's Literature.*

MAHONY, BERTHA E., and ELINOR WHITNEY FIELD, eds. *Newbery Medal Books, 1922–1955.*

MEEKER, ALICE M. *Enjoying Literature with Children.*

PILGRIM, GENEVA HANNA, and MARIANNA McALLISTER. *Books, Young People, and Reading Guidance.*

QUIMBY, HARRIET, CLARA JACKSON, and ROSEMARY WEBER. *Building a Children's Literature Collection.*

ROBINSON, EVELYN ROSE. *Readings About Children's Literature.*

ROSENBLATT, LOUISE E. *Literature as Exploration.*

SAYERS, FRANCES CLARKE. *Summoned by Books; Essays and Speeches by Frances Clarke Sayers.*

SCHOOL LIBRARY JOURNAL/LIBRARY JOURNAL. *Issues in Children's Book Selection.*

SMITH, JAMES STEEL. *A Critical Approach to Children's Literature.*

SMITH, LILLIAN. *The Unreluctant Years.*

THOMISON, DENNIS. *Readings About Adolescent Literature.*

TOWNSEND, JOHN ROWE. *A Sense of Story.*

TREASE, GEOFFREY. *Tales Out of School; A Survey of Children's Fiction.* Chapter 1, "How Much Does It Matter?"

VIGUERS, RUTH HILL. *Margin for Surprise; About Books, Children, and Librarians.*

WALSH, FRANCES, ed. *That Eager Zest; First Discoveries in the Magic World of Books.*

WILSON, BARBARA KER. *Writing for Children; An English Editor and Author's Point of View.*

WYNDHAM, LEE. *Writing for Children and Teen-Agers.*

Yale French Studies: The Child's Part.

[7]Complete bibliographic data are provided in the combined Adult References in the Appendixes.

Children's Literature: History and Trends

Chapter 3

The flood of publications in children's books is so overpowering that it is important to remind ourselves that there are old books in children's literature as fresh and serviceable today as they were a hundred years ago. There are also old books for children which have been discarded, and properly so. Age is no guarantee of a book's excellence, nor recency of its significance. Some of the discards we shall glance at briefly, only to know their kind and to be wary of their reappearance in modern dress—because that is what happens. Pedantic or moral stories still appear, although they are neither as frequently published nor as highly praised as they were in the past. The successors to the penny thrillers of decades ago are churned out today in patterned style in series books, such as the *Nancy Drew* stories, and as comic books, where they outdo the penny thrillers in superficiality of characterization and plethora of action. We have not arrived at our wealth of fine modern books for children without considerable trial and error, and the errors are difficult to eradicate. We need perspective in judging children's books. We need to look at the past with modern eyes and view the present with the accumulated wisdom of the past. Where and how did children's literature begin? What has it grown out of and where is it going?

Before children can read, their acquaintance with literature begins, as it began for the race, through listening to the songs and stories of their people. All peoples had their explanations of the beginnings of the world, the coming of their own family or tribe, and the natural phenomena that delighted or terrified them. Mothers of yesterday chanted or sang to their babies. In simpler days, old women told homely tales of the beasts and kept alive legends of strange events. Grandmothers have always been the custodians of traditional tales, both of families and of the larger group, the tribe or the village. The men told stories to the adults of daring exploits and great adventures, and we may be sure the children listened. The professional storytellers, the bards or minstrels, took these tales, embroidered and polished them, and made them into the ballads or the hero tales or the epics of the people. So unwritten folk literature grew and was passed on by word of mouth for centuries before the collectors gathered it together for printing. Much of it was bloody and terrible; some of it was romantic, some coarse and humorous, told by adults to adults. Undoubtedly the children listened and loved many of these tales never intended for their ears and begged for them again and again. We say this with confidence because that is the way they have acquired much of their literature in every generation. Today, children watch adult television programs, take over adult songs, and read the same comics that adults read. They appropriate from adult material those things they understand and enjoy.

The Earliest Books

In the several centuries before the invention of movable type, all books for children were instructional, written by monastic teachers and chiefly intended for the children of wealthy families. These lesson books, often in Latin, began the tradition of didacticism that was to dominate children's books for hundreds of years and to persist as an influence into contemporary times.

Aldhelm (640?–709), abbot of Malmesbury, set the pattern used until the end of the sixteenth century of a text that was either rhymed or in question-and-answer form. In the eleventh century Anselm (1033–1109), archbishop of Canterbury, wrote an encyclopedia that treated such topics as manners and customs, natural science, children's duties, morals, and religious precepts. Such books were meant to instruct and to instill in children edifying principles of belief and conduct; they were not meant to give delight to the young.

It has been argued that the first printed book intended to be read specifically by children, apart from elementary Latin grammars, was a French courtesy book on table manners that was published a few decades after the invention of printing. In about 1487 there appeared *Les Contenances de la Table*, possibly by Jean Du Pré, which contained rhyming quatrains and was apparently very popular, since several fifteenth-century editions survive.

For Grownups: Fables, Romances, Adventures

William Caxton (1422–1491) was England's first printer. He issued a series of books which are still appearing in various versions on our publishers' book lists for children. Caxton's books included, among other titles, Sir Thomas Malory's *Morte d'Arthur, The Recuyell of the Historyes of Troye, The Boke of Histories of Jason, The Historye of Reynart the Foxe,* and *Aesop's Fables.* Tales of King Arthur still give the older child a fine introduction to romance, the story of Odysseus remains a popular adventure story, and the fables are enjoyed by young children even if they do skip the morals. Although Caxton intended his books for adults, children took many of them for themselves, and versions of these same collections continue to delight each generation.

Illustration for the William Caxton edition of Aesop's Fables.

For Children: Hornbooks and Battledores

While textbooks will not be discussed in detail, no account of children's books is complete without a word about the hornbooks and the battledores. The hornbooks, which first appeared in the 1440s, were not books at all but little wooden paddles on which were pasted lesson sheets of vellum or parchment. These sheets were covered with transparent horn and bound along the edges by strips of brass. Most of the hornbooks were two and three-fourths by five inches. The lesson sheets began with a cross followed by the alphabet (sometimes in both large and small letters) and by syllables: *ab, eb, ib,* and other vowel and consonant combinations. There would probably be "In the Name of the Father, the Son, and the Holy Ghost" and the Lord's Prayer. The hornbooks differed in content, but in general they were designed to teach the child letters and their combinations and to continue religious instruction. There is still in existence a little hornbook supposedly used by Queen Elizabeth I. We know that these first hornbooks made their way to the New World for the instruction of Puritan children.

The battledore, which was conceived by

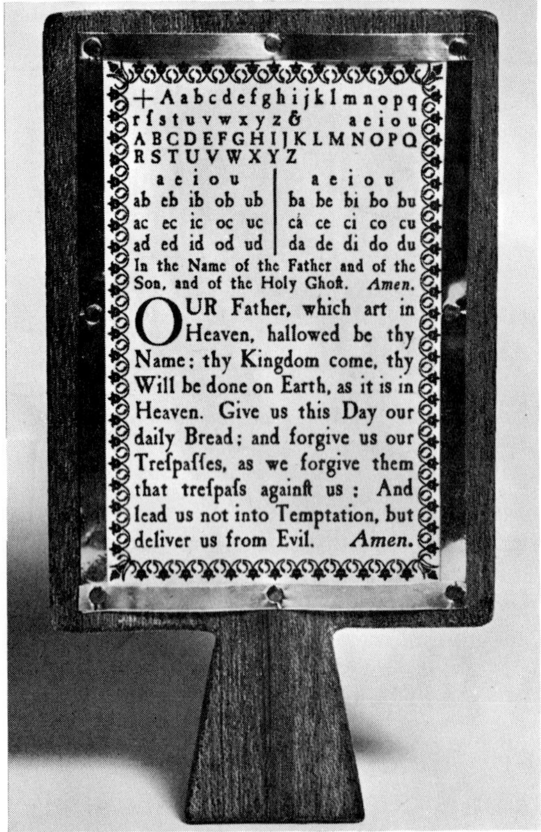

From a photograph in A Little History of the Horn-Book *by Beulah Folmsbee, The Horn Book, Inc., 1942.*

one of Newbery's helpers, was in use from about 1746 to 1770. It had three folding cardboard leaves. Unlike the hornbook, it had no religious material but contained alphabets, easy reading, numerals, and woodcut illustrations. Neither the hornbook nor the battledore ever carried anything that was remotely entertaining, so children still sampled what they could from adult books.

And a Picture Book

In 1657 a Moravian bishop and educator, John Amos Comenius (1592–1671) put into practice his belief in better education for the young by preparing what is described today as the first picture book—*Orbis Pictus* (The World Illustrated).[1] Comenius's preface indicates the author's sensitivity to children's need for interesting material: "See then here a new help for Schooles, a Picture and Nomenclature of all the chief things in the World, and of mens Actions in their way of Living!" It would serve, he hoped, "To entice Witty Children to it . . . to stir up the Attention . . . by sport, and a merry pastime." (See illustration, p. 116.)

Pedlar's Treasury: A Tu'penny Treat

Then came the chapmen, the pedlars of the seventeenth and eighteenth centuries, with newssheets, ballads, broadsides, and chapbooks tucked in among their trinkets. Chapbooks were cheap little books that could be bought for as little as a penny. They had from sixteen to thirty-two or sixty-four pages and were often not stitched but merely folded. F. J. H. Darton, in *Children's Books in England*, tells us that surviving copies have been found all carefully sewed with bits of silk or ribbon, perhaps by some child owner. The editors or compilers of these little books took the legends of antiquity, the old tales of the Middle Ages, elements of the fairy tales—any stories they could lay their hands on—and retold them in drastically condensed versions. All literary charm was lost; the grammar was often faulty, but what remained was a heightened sense of action with an adventure on almost every page. The educated upper classes of England may have frowned upon the chapbooks, but the common people of England loved them and bought them continually. Of course the children discovered them and became ardent patrons of the pedlar's treasures, too.

The stories were the kind that children have always liked—adventure stories with heroes who do things. The account of their doughty deeds fills a book: *Chapbooks of the Eighteenth Century* by John Ashton. "The History of Valentine and Orson" is the story of twin brothers who were separated in infancy, Orson to be raised by a bear and Valentine to be reared by a king of France. Later, Valentine captured the wild Orson and they performed great deeds together, each winning the hand of a lovely princess. Incidentally, the bear

[1]An edition of *Orbis Pictus*, published in 1887 by C. W. Bardeen, has been reissued by the Singing Tree Press. See Chapter 5 for further discussion of *Orbis Pictus*.

child, Orson, is a forerunner of Mowgli in Kipling's *Jungle Books*.

One favorite, "Tom Hickathrift," is a kind of early English Paul Bunyan. "At ten years old he was six feet high and three in thickness, his hand was like a shoulder of mutton, and every other part proportionable." He pulled up trees, slew giants, and felled four highwaymen at a blow.

Tom Thumb.

How *Tom Thumb* fell into the Pudding-Bowl, and of his escape out of the Tinkers Budget.

He sat upon the pudding-bowl, the Candle for to hold,

A 4 Of

From the chapbook Tom Thumb His Life and Death. *Reproduced from an edition (circa 1665) in the John G. White Collection, Cleveland Public Library.*

In contrast to the colossal Tom Hickathrift, there is Tom Thumb, whose story is told in a chapbook rhymed version of "Tom Thumb His Life and Death." The woodcuts from 1630 show this tiny hero early in his career falling into a bowl of pudding but later riding valiantly into battle atop an enormous war horse.

The attitude of serious-minded adults of the day toward these crude, often vulgar little books was generally scornful. The clergy viewed them with alarm, but at least one man of letters spoke a good word for them. Richard Steele, in *The Tatler* (No. 95), tells how his young godson was "much turned in his studies" to these histories and adds:

He would tell you the mismanagements of John Hickerthrift, find fault with the passionate temper of Bevis of Southampton and loved St. George for being the champion of England: and by this means had his thoughts insensibly moulded into the notions of discretion, virtue, and honour.

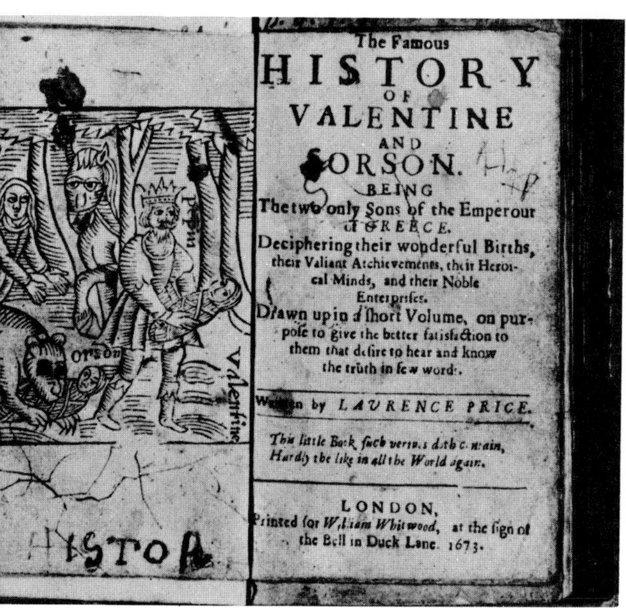

The Famous
HISTORY
OF
VALENTINE
AND
ORSON.
BEING
The two only Sons of the Emperour of GREECE.
Deciphering their wonderful Births, their Valiant Atchievements, their Heroical Minds, and their Noble Enterprises.
Drawn up in a short Volume, on purpose to give the better satisfaction to them that desire to hear and know the truth in few words.
Written by LAURENCE PRICE.
This little Book such vertues doth contain,
Hardly the like in all the World again.
LONDON,
Printed for William Whitwood, at the sign of the Bell in Duck Lane. 1673.

From Laurence Price's History of Valentine and Orson. *Reproduced from the d'Alte Welch Collection, The University Library, Department of Special Collections, University of California, Los Angeles.*

This may be a charitable interpretation of the effects of chapbook reading, but Florence Barry, in *A Century of Children's Books*, adds a cheerful note also. She says:

John Bunyan was the first to reconcile the claims of religion and romance, and he could never have written The Pilgrim's Progress *if he had not been a good customer of the pedlar in his youth.* (pp. 6–7)

Badly written, crudely illustrated, unhonored though they were, the chapbooks preserved and popularized some of the precious elements of literature that children love. But their coarseness probably paved the way for the reaction against tales, stories, and jests, the reaction which produced children's books full of somber warnings and doleful examples.

The Puritans and Perdition

Even while the chapmen were peddling their lurid, lighthearted "Histories," the religious movement was under way that was to affect life on both sides of the Atlantic. Beginning in the late 1500s, about the middle of Queen Elizabeth's reign, the English had become "the people of a book, and that book was the Bible." In London people went daily, in great crowds, to St. Paul's to hear the Bible read aloud, and small Bibles were found in homes everywhere.

A group of deeply religious people whom we know as the Puritans read their Bibles with fervor. They venerated the victims of religious persecution and studied Foxe's *Book of Martyrs* (1563), with its details of death at the stake, and gave the book to their children.

As if this legacy of terror was not enough for small Puritans to endure, a clergyman, James Janeway, wrote in 1671 or 1672 a famous book that was long popular with the heaven-bent adults who ruled over Puritan nurseries. Its full title was:

A Token For Children: *being an Exact Account of the Conversion, Holy and Exemplary Lives, and Joyful Deaths of several young Children. To which is now added, Prayers and Graces, fitted for the use of little Children.*

There were thirteen good little children in this gloomy book, and, considering their lives, it is small wonder that they died young. They spent their time trying to reform, convert, and generally improve everyone they encountered. They brooded on sin and eternal torment and the state of their souls. Morbid and unnatural as this book was with its continual dwelling on death, it grew from the earnest desire of the Puritans to make children happy—not in our modern sense of the word, but in theirs. To be happy meant to be secure in the avoidance of Hell and in the assurance of Heaven. Unfortunately their method of instilling religious ideas was chiefly through the use of fear—the fear of Hell.

Out of the Puritan world there emerged one great book for children—Bunyan's *Pilgrim's Progress* (Part I, 1678; Part II, 1684). This book was intended for adults and probably reached the children piecemeal as they listened to the adults read it aloud, or discuss it, or tell the more dramatic portions. Reviewing the story, we can easily understand why children enjoyed the book. It is told in the best tradition of the old fairy tales John Bunyan had enjoyed in chapbook form when he was a boy. Bunyan had published, also in 1678, *A Book for Boys and Girls or Country Rhymes for Children.*

John Bunyan (1628–1688), a humble tinker, confessed that one of the sins of his youth was his delight in the "History of the Life and Death of that Noble Knight Sir Bevis of Southampton." As he grew more and more religious, he put away all such light reading and turned to the Bible and to fear-inspiring books such as John Foxe's *Book of Martyrs.* He began to preach such fiery and fearsome sermons that he was locked up for nonconformity to the established Church of England. In jail

Viewpoints

. . . the evolution of juvenile literature in England has in a very real sense been an account of the gradual and often reluctant realisation that children were meant to enjoy life in their own right, and, to a great extent, on their own terms. The subject, indeed, has a wider reference than its own intrinsic importance, in reflecting a changed and broadening viewpoint towards the upbringing of children.

. . . Harking back to the Puritans and the obstinate vitality of their mental and spiritual approach to the upbringing of children, it is seen to be fundamental to their viewpoint that the only concession permissible of any important difference between children and adults implies not a smaller susceptibility to the temptations of the flesh, but a feebler capacity to withstand them.

For more than one hundred years after the time of the good, godly writers of the Commonwealth period breaks in the cloud of their sombre influence are infrequent and feeble.

. . . The significant fact is that until the eighteen-fifties and even later a carefree attitude unencumbered by moral or instructional preoccupation was strikingly exceptional in writing for children.—Percy Muir, *English Children's Books, 1600–1900,* Batsford, London, 1954, pp. 226–227.

for years with his Bible and his *Martyrs*, he began to write the story of a Christian soul on its troublesome pilgrimage through this world to everlasting life. Sir Bevis was not forgotten but was reborn as Christian; the giant Ascapart became the Giant Despair; and so, in good fairy-tale style, Christian fought monsters and enemies with properly symbolic names. But no chapbook tale was ever so somber and so dramatic as this progress of a Christian pilgrim. It begins as a dream:

As I went through the wild waste of this world, I came to a place where there was a den, and I lay down in it to sleep. While I slept, I had a dream, and lo! I saw a man whose clothes were in rags, and he stood with his face from his own house, with a book in his hand, and a great load on his back.

In its original form, with long interludes of theological moralizing, children would have difficulty reading this book, but when the dramatic story is cleared of these obstructions, it is a moving tale. In 1939 an edition abridged and illustrated by Robert Lawson was published.

The *Mayflower* reached our shores in 1620, but the great exodus of Puritans from England to the New World did not take place until around 1630. We can well imagine that those early years of colonization were too difficult for any excursions into book-producing for either children or adults, but the Puritans' passion for education could not long be submerged. The history of their activities in New England is alive with a deep and growing concern for schools and the tools of education, books. As early as 1632, there are references to hornbooks, brought from England with the crosses blotted out—crosses being for the time a religious symbol to which the Puritans objected.

The first book for children to be published in the New World appeared in 1646. It was written by John Cotton and its full title was:

Milk for Babes, Drawn out of the Breasts of Both Testaments, Chiefly for the Spirituall Nourishment of Boston Babes in either England, but may be of like Use for any Children.

Beneath this title it adds *A Catechism in Verse*, and begins:

Who is the Maker of all things?
The Almighty God who reigns on high.
He form'd the earth, He spread the sky.

It continues with all the intricate details of Puritan theology.

Editions of the *New England Primer* published as early as 1691 have been found, although it is known to have been in print before that. Its famous rhyming alphabet begins:

In Adam's fall
We sinned all.

Thy life to mend
God's Book attend.

In addition, the book contains prayers, poems, the shorter catechism, the Ten Commandments, Bible verses, and pictures. One of these is a quaint woodcut of a Dame's school; another is the picture of a mournful figure contemplating a tombstone; and the prize is a graphic illustration of the burning of Mr. John Rogers, with his wife and ten children looking on, while a jaunty man-at-arms holds them at bay. With tombs and torture, it is difficult to justify the subtitle, "An Easy and Pleasant Guide to the Art of Reading."

As late as 1832, Boston had its own descendant of Janeway's *Token*. It was written by Perkins and Marvin and the title page reads as follows:

Mary Lothrop
Who Died In
Boston
1831

The authors add in their preface that their Memoir was prepared "for the purpose of adding another to the bright pictures set before children to allure them into the paths of piety." This was a fairly large book for those days, about three by seven inches, and fully three fourths of it is devoted to the pious Mary's interminable death. The charming little frontispiece shows Mary and her little brother kneeling beside a chair, praying. The boy has struck his sister, and Mary is praying

24 NEW ENGLAND PRIMER.

Thou shalt not see thy brother s ass or his . s fall down by the way, and hide thyself from them: thou shalt surely help him to lift them up again.

THE BURNING OF MR. JOHN ROGERS.

MR. JOHN ROGERS, minister of the gospel in London, was the first martyr in Queen Mary's reign; and was burnt at Smithfield, February the fourteenth, 1554. His wife, with nine small children, and one at her breast, followed him to the stake, with which sorrowful sight he was not in the least daunted, but with wonderful patience died courageously for the gospel of JESUS CHRIST.

From The New England Primer; or An Easy and Pleasant Guide to the Art of Reading. *Massachusetts Sabbath School Society.*

him into a state of repentance. Shortly after that, Mary becomes ill and begins her preparations for death. Gloom descends for the remaining pages. It is to be hoped that Boston children who were given this "bright picture" had recourse to the lusty nonsense of *Mother Goose*. For, despite the Puritans, a pirated edition of this cheerful volume was printed in the New World in 1785.

Fairy Tales and Fables in France

Paul Hazard in his delightful *Books, Children and Men* calls attention to the early portraits of children clad in long velvet skirts, heavily plumed hats, corsets, swords, and ornaments and he remarks, "If, for centuries, grownups did not even think of giving children appropriate clothes, how would it ever have occurred to them to provide children with suitable books?"

Yet around 1697 this miracle occ[illegible] France with the publication of *Hist[illegible] contes du temps passé avec des m[illegible]* (Histories or Tales of Long Ago with [illegible] or, more familiarly, *Contes de ma M[illegible]* (Tales of Mother Goose). There is som[illegible] tion today as to whether the tales were written for adults or for children. But whatever the author's intention, they were loved by children. The stories were "La belle au bois dormant" (The Sleeping Beauty); "La petite chaperon rouge" (Little Red Riding Hood); "La Barbe Bleue" (Blue Beard); "Le Maître chat, ou le chat botté" (The Master Cat, or Puss in Boots); "Les fées" (Diamonds and Toads); "Cendrillon, ou la petite pantoufle de verre" (Cinderella, or the Little Glass Slipper); "Riquet à la houpe" (Riquet with the Tuft); and "Le petit poucet" (Little Thumb).

Did Charles Perrault (1628–1703), member of the French Academy and author of many serious but forgotten works, collect these traditional tales, or was it his eldest son, Pierre Perrault d'Armancour? "Today informed opinion in France . . . favours the son and we may very well leave it at that."[2] Perrault's Fairy Tales, we call them, and their immortality is due as much to the spontaneity and charm of the style as to the traditional content.[3]

Using Aesop and *The Fables of Bidpai* as sources, Jean de la Fontaine (1621–1695) wrote fables to amuse court circles, but they are savored by children today just as they were when they appeared as a series of twelve books in the years 1668–1694. Mme. d'Aulnoy (1650?–1705) turned the old folktale themes into ornate novels for the court. "The Yellow Dwarf" and "Graciosa and Percinet" are sometimes adapted for modern collections but are rarely seen in their original form. Mme. de Beaumont (1711–1780), busy with the education of children, also took time to write some fairy tales for them. Of these, her "Beauty and the Beast" has survived deservedly. Still others took a hand at the fairy tales, but none with the freshness of Perrault.

[2]Percy Muir, *English Children's Books, 1600–1900*, Praeger, 1969, p. 49.

[3]For a fascinating account of the "lost manuscript" of 1695, see May Hill Arbuthnot, "Puss, the Perraults and a Lost Manuscript," *Elementary English*, October 1969, pp. 715–721.

John Newbery's Books

Meanwhile, in England, it was a happy day for children, steering a perilous course between the pedlar and the Puritan, when in 1729 R. Samber translated Perrault's *Tales of Mother Goose.* No chapbook was ever so thrilling as these eight tales, no "good Godly book" was ever so beloved. At the time, they must have attracted the attention of an English publisher by the name of John Newbery, because not only did his firm later use the title *Mother Goose*, but he may also have discovered through the popularity of the tales the importance of the child as a potential consumer of books.

John Newbery was what we would call today "a character." He dabbled in many things. He wrote; he published; he befriended indigent authors; he did a flourishing business manufacturing and dispensing medicines and a "Medicinal Dictionary." In 1744, along with Dr. James's Fever Powders, Newbery offered for sale his publication:

A LITTLE PRETTY
POCKET-BOOK
Intended for the
Instruction and Amusement
of
Little Master Tommy,
and
Pretty Miss Polly.
With Two Letters from
Jack the Giant-Killer;
As also
A Ball and a Pincushion;
The Use of which will infallibly make
Tommy
a good Boy and Polly a good Girl.
To which is added,
A Little Song-Book,
Being
A New Attempt to teach Children
the Use of the English Alphabet,
by way of Diversion.[4]

For the *"amusement"* of Tommy and Polly, "by way of *diversion*"—here is a new approach to books for children and a momentous one. It marks the beginning of English books for their delight! Of course, Jack the Giant-Killer wrote two exceedingly moral letters to the readers of the *Pretty Pocket-Book.* He had evidently reformed and settled down since the chapbook days, for his lectures are as mild as milk, with no threats anywhere. The letters are followed by a series of games with rhymed directions and morals: marbles, shuttle-cock, blindman's buff, thread the needle, leap frog, and many other old favorites. There are fables, proverbs, and rules of behavior, with a rhyming alphabet and a few poems thrown in for good measure. The morals to the fables are made more romantic and palatable by the signature of Jack the Giant-Killer. The success of the *Pocket-Book* evidently encouraged the publisher because other books for children followed rapidly.

In 1765 *The Renowned History of Little Goody Two Shoes, Otherwise Called Mrs. Margery Two Shoes*, appeared. This is a short juvenile novel, the first of its kind to be written expressly for children. Oliver Goldsmith is supposed to have written *Goody Two Shoes*, which tells the story of a virtuous and clever child, Margery *Meanwell.* At the opening of the book, Margery's father suffers "the wicked persecutions of Sir Timothy *Gripe* and Farmer *Graspall*," who manage to ruin him and turn the whole family out of house and lands. The parents quickly die (evidently no Dr. James's Fever Powders available), leaving Margery and her brother Tommy destitute. Tommy goes to sea and Margery is rescued by charitable Clergyman Smith and his wife. When they buy her two shoes, the child is so overcome with pleasure that she keeps crying out, "Two shoes, Madam, see my two shoes"—hence her name.

This happiness is short-lived, for Gripe forces Smith to turn her out of the house. Back to the hedgerows once more, Margery teaches herself to read with remarkable ease by studying the schoolbooks of more fortunate children. Soon she knows more than any of them and decides to advance their learning. She makes up an alphabet of wooden blocks or "rattle traps" with both small and large letters, puts them into a basket, and goes from house to house helping children to read. Her

[4]No copies of the first English edition (1744) have survived. But in 1944, the two-hundredth anniversary of its first appearance, F. G. Melcher issued a reproduction of the first American edition, which was a reprint by Isaiah Thomas published in 1787 in Worcester, Mass. You can now examine the *Pocket-Book* gaily bedecked with a flowery gilt paper cover after Newbery's custom.

From The Original Mother Goose's Melody. *Reproduced in facsimile by W. H. Whitmore (Joel Munsell's Sons, 1899) from the edition reprinted by Isaiah Thomas of Worcester, Mass., about 1785.*

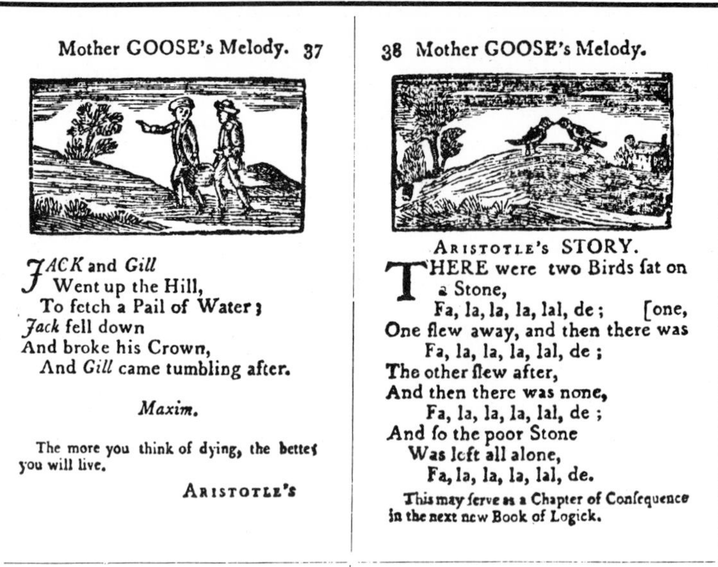

Mother GOOSE's Melody. 37

JACK and *Gill*
Went up the Hill,
To fetch a Pail of Water;
Jack fell down
And broke his Crown,
And *Gill* came tumbling after.

Maxim.

The more you think of dying, the better you will live.

ARISTOTLE's

38 Mother GOOSE's Melody.

ARISTOTLE's STORY.

THERE were two Birds ſat on a Stone,
Fa, la, la, la, lal, de; [one,
One flew away, and then there was
Fa, la, la, la, lal, de;
The other flew after,
And then there was none,
Fa, la, la, la, lal, de;
And ſo the poor Stone
Was left all alone,
Fa, la, la, la, lal, de.

This may ſerve as a Chapter of Conſequence in the next new Book of Logick.

methods apparently work like a charm, for all her young pupils respond immediately with never a "retarded reader" in the whole countryside.[5]

Goody Two Shoes is full of sociological lessons; its characters are types rather than individuals. Nevertheless, it was entertaining and it was a child's book. Many adults, notably Charles Lamb, recalled the pleasure it gave them when they read it as children.

Between 1760 and 1766, John Newbery, according to many scholars, also published the first edition of *Mother Goose*,[6] but no trace of such a book remains and no contemporary reference to or advertisement of the book has ever been uncovered.[7] On the basis of their research, Jacques Barchilon and Henry Pettit[8] now assert that there was no such publication during those years. They assume that John Newbery may have planned such a book, but not until 1781 was there an advertisement announcing the first publication by his stepson, T. Carnan, of *Mother Goose's Melody*. John Newbery's firm remained in the family for many years and continued to publish books for children.

The first American edition of *Mother Goose* appeared about 1785 and was probably a pirated reprint of an early Newbery edition. It was published by Isaiah Thomas (1749–1831), of Worcester, Massachusetts, who cheerfully and not quite legally printed his own editions of Newbery's books, possibly for mercenary motives but certainly to the benefit of young Americans. W. H. Whitmore vouched for the fact that two copies of this Isaiah Thomas edition existed in his day, and in 1889 he reproduced the book in full, calling it *The Original Mother Goose's Melody*.[9] The little book is two and one-half by three and three-fourths inches. Preface, fifty-two jingles with maxims, sixteen songs of Shakespeare, and small woodcuts are precisely the same as in the English edition. The maxims are surprising and often amusing, especially the one that follows "Margery Daw," which will surely be applauded by all bewildered readers of footnotes: "It is a mean and scandalous Practice in Authors to put Notes to Things that deserve no Notice."

It is fitting that John Newbery, this first English publisher of books for children, is hon-

[5]*The Renowned History of Little Goody Two Shoes, Otherwise Called Mrs. Margery Two Shoes.* Attributed to Oliver Goldsmith. Edited by Charles Welsh.

[6]Even the scholarly Opies give 1765–1766 in their *Oxford Dictionary of Nursery Rhymes* (Oxford, 1951), p. 33.

[7]See Chapter 4 for a discussion of *Mother Goose*. Other children's classics mentioned in this chapter are discussed more fully in later chapters. See the Index for relevant page references.

[8]*The Authentic Mother Goose Fairy Tales and Nursery Rhymes* (Alan Swallow, Denver, 1960), p. 11.

[9]W. H. Whitmore, ed. *The Original Mother Goose's Melody* (Joel Munsell's Sons, 1889). It is reproduced in facsimile from the Isaiah Thomas edition (Worcester, Massachusetts, 1785). Whitmore's introduction gives many interesting facts about the early collections of *Mother Goose*.

ored annually when the Newbery Medal is presented for the year's most distinguished literature for children written by an American citizen or resident and published in the United States.[10]

Robinson Crusoe

One book emerged from the Puritan world to mark not only the increase of cheerfulness but the beginning of contemporary adventure tales. It was Daniel Defoe's *Robinson Crusoe,* one of the most popular books in all English literature.

Defoe (1659–1731), with a wisdom far in advance of his times, wrote on banks, insurance companies, schools for women, asylums for the insane, and all sorts of social problems. He turned out bitter political and religious satires which landed him in the pillory. He rose to wealth and fame and sank to penury and prison more than once. Writing was his passion, and few men have written more continuously. His most famous book, *The Life and Strange Surprising Adventures of Robinson Crusoe,* appeared in 1719, when Defoe was sixty and nearing the end of his turbulent career. We are told four editions of it were printed in four months, and for once the old fighter enjoyed fame with no unhappy repercussions of any kind.

Why has this book commended itself to children of each succeeding generation? It was addressed to adults and originally contained masses of moral ruminations that the children must have skipped with their usual agility in the avoidance of boredom. Most children's editions today omit these tiresome reflections and get on with the story.

There was a real-life Alexander Selkirk, marooned for over four years on the island of Juan Fernandez, who not only told his story to Defoe but also gave him his papers. However, it is due to Defoe's skill that Selkirk, as Robinson Crusoe, emerges a favorite world hero. The theme itself is irresistible: man pitted against nature, one man with a whole world to create and control. He must obtain food, provide himself with clothes and shelter, fight off wild animals, reckon time, keep himself civilized and sane.

Here is a book that satisfies children's hunger to achieve competence. Identifying with Robinson Crusoe, they win an ordered, controlled place in the world by their own efforts and foresight. With the coming of Friday, they have the love of a friend whom they in turn nurture and protect. No wonder children read and reread and dramatize this book. All the details are there; every question is answered. It is reasonable and clear—a design for living, complete and satisfying.

The theme of the shipwrecked survivor was used in many books following publication of *Robinson Crusoe,* among them *The Swiss Family Robinson,* written by Johann David Wyss (1743–1818) and published in 1812. Despite its pedantic overtones, this story of a pious, energetic family on a desert island delighted worldwide audiences with its dramatic events.

Gulliver's Travels

Another remarkable book emerged from this period, a political satire not intended for children but read by them and known today as *Gulliver's Travels.* The author, Jonathan Swift (1667–1745), was born in Dublin and died there, Dean of the Cathedral. But between his birth and death, he spent considerable time in London and took an active part in the political life of the times. Recognized today as one of the greatest satirists in English literature, in his own day he was known as a pamphleteer and misanthrope.

Swift wrote his book in Ireland to lampoon the follies of the English court, its parties, its politics, and its statesmen. Worried about the reception of the book, he published it anonymously in 1726 as *Travels into Several Remote Nations of the World,* in four parts, by Lemuel Gulliver. To Swift's surprise and relief, London society, the very society he was making fun of, was highly diverted. In writing these tall tales, Swift seems to have been caught up with the richness of his own invention, and the humor sometimes overshadows the satire.

[10]For the list of books which have been awarded the Newbery Medal see "Book Awards" in the Appendix.

Children have always loved things in miniature, and they soon discovered the land of the Lilliputians. No one ever forgets Gulliver's waking to find six-inch people walking over him and Lilliputian ropes binding him. All the fascinating details are worked out to scale with logic and precision. Children are untroubled by any double meanings and like the fantasy for itself. The second journey, to the land of giants, Brobdingnag, is the next most popular, but Gulliver in an inferior position, treated like a toy, is not so appealing as the omnipotent Gulliver in Lilliput. The remaining books most children never read. As far as they are concerned, the first adventure makes the book, and it is Lilliput forever!

If Gulliver's travels had not fascinated artists, the book might not have survived in children's reading as long as it has. An early edition illustrated by Charles E. Brock (1894) and later editions illustrated by Arthur Rackham and by Fritz Eichenberg would lure anyone into reading the story.

Illustration by Louis Rhead. From Gulliver's Travels *by Jonathan Swift. Copyright 1913 by Harper & Brothers, copyright 1941 by Bertrand Rhead. Reproduced by permission of Harper & Row, Publishers.*

Poets and Children

About the time *Robinson Crusoe* and *Gulliver's Travels* were published, a gentle nonconformist preacher wrote a book of poetry for children. Isaac Watts (1674–1748) moralized in verse about busy bees and quarrelsome dogs, but he also wrote tender and beautiful hymns, many of which are found today in most hymnals. His *Divine and Moral Songs for Children* (1715) dwelt not on the fearful judgments of God, but on God "our refuge," and many a child must have been comforted by his tender "Cradle Hymn."

Toward the end of the century a major poet, William Blake (1757–1827), published a book of poems for and about children, *Songs of Innocence* (1789), each poem illustrated with Blake's own decorative designs. It is now considered an epoch-making book, but it caused no stir at the time of its publication. A companion volume, *Songs of Experience* (1794), followed. Although most of Blake's unique lyrics are for adults, some of his poetry appeals to children also.

Ann (1782–1866) and Jane (1783–1824) Taylor's *Original Poems for Infant Minds: By Several Young Persons* (1804) teaches lessons in the manner of Watts's *Moral Songs*, but with a difference. The vigorous, fun-loving Taylors usually tell good stories in their verse and reveal something of the simple, pleasant life of rural England. The book enjoyed immediate popularity and was translated into various languages, but it is best known today for the familiar "Twinkle, twinkle, little star."

The Butterfly's Ball, published in book form in 1807, was written by William Roscoe (1753–1831), a lawyer and member of Parliament, for the amusement of his little son. There is no story, but there are such fascinating details as a mushroom table with a water dock leaf tablecloth, and there are William Mulready's charming pictures of the insect guests at the ball. However, the verse is tame, and the long popularity of the poem must have been due in part to lack of better verse for children.

Didacticism in France, England, and the United States

In 1762 Jean Jacques Rousseau (1712–1778) proclaimed his theory of a new day for children through his book *Émile*. He believed in the joyous unfolding of a child's powers through a free, happy life. The child Émile was the companion of his tutor; he was free of all books except *Robinson Crusoe;* and he lived vigorously out of doors, learning from experiences and activities. Schools today reflect Rousseau's emphasis on experiences and activities.

In its day *Émile* effected a revolutionary change in people's attitudes toward both children and education. To some people, Rousseau seemed like a breeze blowing away the clouds of Puritan morbidity, and one would naturally expect the ardent Rousseau converts, if they wrote books for children, to write only the gayest ones. Instead, in France, in England, and even in the United States, they began to write painfully didactic stories, sometimes to teach religion, sometimes to inform and educate. The only thing these writers seemed to have carried over from Rousseau was the idea of following and developing the child's natural interests. In practice, they went at the business hammer and tongs. If the poor children picked strawberries, the experience was turned into an arithmetic lesson. If they rolled a snowball, they learned about levers and proceeded from those to wedges. If they took a walk, they had to observe every bird, beast, stone, and human occupation. Day and night these ardent authors stalked their children, allowing them never a moment for play or fancy but instructing and improving on every page. No longer did they threaten children with the fear of Hell, but the pressure of Information hung almost as heavily over their hapless heads.

Here was a revival of didacticism with a vengeance—not the terrifying theological didacticism of the Puritans but the intellectual and moralistic variety. Students who wish to read more about this period should study the works of the French Mme. de Genlis (1746–1830) and Armand Berquin (1749–1791) and those of such English writers as Laetitia Barbauld (1743–1825), Sarah Trimmer (1741–1810), and Hannah More (1745–1833). For most readers, a few examples of this writing will probably suffice.

One of the classic examples of the new didacticism is *The History of Sandford and Merton* (1783–1789) in four volumes by Thomas Day (1748–1789). Tommy Merton was the spoiled, helpless, ignorant son of a rich gentleman, whereas Harry Sandford was the sturdy, industrious, competent child of an honest farmer. Harry was reared out of doors and trained to work and study; there was nothing he did not know and nothing he could not do. Father Merton, handicapped by wealth though he was, saw at once the advantage of having his young darling unspoiled and trained in the ways of the honest Harry. So poor Tommy, little knowing what was in store for him, was put in the charge of the same clerical tutor who had wrought such wonders with Harry. Mr. Barlow trained both boys, but Harry was always used as the perfect example to show up the ignorance, incompetence, and general orneriness of poor Tommy. All day that worthy pair, the omniscient Barlow and the admirable Harry, instructed, disciplined, and uplifted poor Tommy. Through

Viewpoints

Not everyone will agree with me, but we are living in a time when literature aspires more and more to be didactic and utilitarian. It doesn't seem to matter what lesson it teaches—a sociological, psychological or humanistic one—as long as it teaches. There have never been more interpretations of texts or guides for readers who must be led by the hand by the critics. We are no longer allowed to enjoy a sunset without footnotes. . . . Thank God for the children. . . . The child is still selfish enough to demand an interesting story. He wants surprises and tensions. Our children, God bless them, don't read to discover their identity, as so many wiser adults pretend to do. Young as they are, fresh from the egg, they know exactly who they are, and where they belong. Neither do they read to free themselves from guilt or to quench the thirst for rebellion.—Isaac Bashevis Singer, "I See the Child as a Last Refuge," *The New York Times Book Review,* November 9, 1969, p. 66.

each of the volumes, he was plagued and polished into Rousseau-like simplicity and competence. At the end of four volumes, there he was at last—Tommy Merton remodeled, divested of all his fine apparel, his curls gone, and his life to be given over to study and philosophy forever more. Could any reform go further?

Another and perhaps the most gifted exponent of didacticism in children's books was Maria Edgeworth (1767–1849), who told her moral tales with such dramatic realism that they are still remembered. She had an excellent laboratory for developing her stories as she was the second of twenty-two children. She not only helped her father with the education of the younger ones but wrote her stories in their midst, tried them out with the children, and modified them according to their suggestions. Thomas Day himself had a hand in Maria's early education, but her own father seems to have been a greater influence in her writings than anyone else.

Maria Edgeworth wrote many short stories, some deadly dull and unnatural. But at her best, she was a born storyteller. She developed real plots—the first in children's stories since the fairy tales—with well-sustained suspense and surprise endings that took some of the sting out of the inevitable morals. While she told an interesting story, her tales carry such a heavy and obvious burden of moral lessons that her characterizations and excellent plots are sacrificed to didacticism.

One writer of the period, however, not only deplored the pedantic stories written for children but tried to provide them with more entertaining fare. Charles Lamb (1775–1835) and his sister Mary's (1764–1847) best-known contribution to children's literature is their *Tales from Shakespeare* (1806), in which they retold the plays from Shakespeare and made them more easily comprehensible and presumably more enjoyable for the young.

It was inevitable that the United States should develop its own brand of didacticism. Samuel G. Goodrich (1793–1860), who wrote under the name of Peter Parley and produced five or six volumes a year, wrote laudatory biographies of famous men and poured out a continuous stream of information in the fields of science, history, and geography. Jacob Abbott (1803–1879) launched a series in which a youth by the name of Rollo was dragged from one city and country to another, bearing up nobly under a steady barrage of travel talks and moralizing. Both men wrote well but pedantically. We shall detect some of their literary descendants in the books of today—information attractively sugared but oppressively informative nevertheless.

Our chief moralist was Martha Farquharson, pseudonym for Martha Finley (1828–1909), whose *Elsie Dinsmore* series began in 1868 and ran to twenty-six volumes. This pious heroine had a way of bursting into tears or fainting with such effect that adult sinners were converted and even Elsie's worldly father was brought to a state of repentance. Most parents developed considerable resistance to Elsie but were baffled by her powers to charm their offspring. Elsie was a spellbinder, for her author had a sense of the dramatic. To this day sensible people remember weeping over Elsie's Sabbath sit-down strike at the piano, when she refused to play the secular music for her erring father. She was made to sit on the piano stool until one of her best faints put an end to her martyrdom and Father repented. Elsie was a prig with glamour, and there is no telling how many more of her kind might have developed if certain pioneers had not appeared to clear away the artificiality and to bring laughter, fantasy, and realism to children's books.

Modern Books Begin

Even while Peter Parley was dispensing information, and Maria Edgeworth was teaching her heroines valuable lessons, and Martha Finley's heroine, Elsie Dinsmore, was piously swooning, epoch-making books in both England and the United States were appearing that were to modify the whole approach to children's literature. These children's classics, some as popular today as when they were first published, not only brought laughter, fantasy, and realism into stories for young people, but they began the trend toward better illustrations in children's books. Each of these books will be discussed in greater detail in later chapters; they are reviewed here because they are milestones in the development of children's literature.

Folk and Fairy Tales

Grimms' Popular Stories by Jacob (1785–1863) and Wilhelm (1786–1859) Grimm was translated into English by Edgar Taylor in 1823. Grimms' Fairy Tales, as they were called by the children, became as much a part of the literature of English-speaking children as the *Mother Goose* rhymes. These stories, some of them gathered by the Grimm brothers from the lips of the old storytellers, were occasionally droll but often somber and harrowing.

The *Fairy Tales* of Hans Christian Andersen (1805–1875) appeared in England in 1846, translated by Mary Howitt. Many of these stories were Andersen's own adaptations of folk tales which he, too, had heard from the storytellers. But to these he added his own fanciful inventions and immeasurably enriched the child's world of the imagination. Andersen's stories have unusual literary and spiritual values, and they are, for the most part, in a minor key, melancholy and even tragic.

Joseph Jacobs (1854–1916) was the great compiler of English folk tales; and the folklorist Andrew Lang (1844–1912) began, in 1889, with the publication of *The Blue Fairy Book*, a series that is still deservedly popular.

Illustration by George Cruikshank for Grimms' Popular Stories.

Humor

One of the first notes of gaiety was a long story poem by an American professor, Clement Moore, called "A Visit from St. Nicholas" (1822), but known to children as "The Night Before Christmas." This fast-moving, humorous ballad, full of fun, fancy, and excitement, with never a threat or a dire warning to spoil the children's delight, is as beloved now as it was in Moore's day.

Under Queen Victoria, England's industrial age flourished and grew prosperous and pompous. Then suddenly two eminent men produced books that sent the children off into gales of laughter. One, Edward Lear (1812–1888), was an artist who earned his living by making scientific paintings of birds and reptiles. When he grew too bored with the drawing room, he took refuge with the children. For them he would write absurd limericks which he illustrated on the spot. His *Book of Nonsense* (1846) not only was an unprecedented collection of amusing verses and pictures but perhaps paved the way for another excursion into absurdity.

In 1865 a book appeared that is generally considered the first English masterpiece written for children. It was *Alice's Adventures in Wonderland*. The author was Charles Lutwidge Dodgson (1832–1898), an Oxford don, a lecturer in logic and mathematics, who used the pen name Lewis Carroll. *Alice* still remains a unique combination of fantasy and nonsense that is as logical as an equation. It was first told, and later written, solely for the entertainment of children, and neither it nor its sequel, *Through the Looking Glass*, has the faintest trace of a moral or a scrap of useful information or one improving lesson—only cheerful lunacy, daft and delightful. *Alice* launched the literature of nonsense and fantasy which is told so logically and reasonably that it seems as natural as sleeping and eating.

Two more books brought laughter to children. Written in Germany in 1844 and published the next year, *Struwwelpeter* (Slovenly Peter) by Heinrich Hoffmann (1809–1894) was a collection of merry, prankish rhyming stories intended only to entertain, although the verses are regarded by some people as brutal. It is still in print, having gone into dozens

From R. Caldecott's Picture Book *by R. Caldecott. Reproduced by permission of Frederick Warne & Co., Inc., Publishers.*

of editions in English. In America, children were captivated by the antics of the Peterkin family. Lucretia Hale (1820–1900) published a series of stories about the Peterkins in magazines, collected them in a book in 1880, and gave the young an unforgettable character: the Lady from Philadelphia.

Illustrations

Both Lear's and Carroll's laughter-provoking books have delightful illustrations—Lear's own outrageous caricatures for his *Book of Nonsense* and Sir John Tenniel's inimitable drawings for Carroll's *Alice.* Deservedly famous, too, are Walter Crane, Randolph Caldecott, and Kate Greenaway,[11] whose charming watercolors brightened the pages of children's books with decorative designs, appealing landscapes, and figures which hold their own with the best in modern books.

Frederic G. Melcher in 1938 suggested a second award to the American Library Association—this time for the most distinguished picture book for children published each year in the United States. He suggested naming it the Caldecott Medal after Randolph Caldecott, a fitting memorial to the man who drew a picture of himself surrounded by children, and who left those children a legacy of gay storytelling pictures.[12]

[11]See Chapter 5 for a fuller account of illustrators of children's books.

[12]For a list of the books which have been awarded the Caldecott Medal see "Book Awards" in the Appendix.

Myths: Hawthorne and Kingsley

In the United States Greek myths were introduced to children by a gifted novelist, Nathaniel Hawthorne (1804–1864). Around 1852 *A Wonder-Book for Girls and Boys* was published, followed in 1853 by *Tanglewood Tales for Girls and Boys.* These books contain stories of the Greek gods and heroes, supposedly told to a group of lively New England children by a young college student, Eustace Bright. Eustace talks down to the children; his gods lose much of their grandeur, and his heroes are often child-sized, but the stories have a delightful style.

In England, Charles Kingsley (1819–1875), country parson, Victorian scholar, and poet, also retold the myths for children. His adaptations not only are closer to the original myths than Hawthorne's romantic versions, but convey the inner significance and grandeur of the myths in a style closer to the classic original. Here are dreams of greatness, presented with the sensitive perception of a poet. Interestingly, in Kingsley's own day these stories were less popular than his original fantasy, *The Water-Babies* (1863), which is marred for us today by its moralizing.

Fantasy

Lewis Carroll's *Alice* was the great masterpiece of fantasy and nonsense, but the nineteenth century saw the publication of several other classics in fantasy for children. In 1841,

John Ruskin (1819–1900) wrote *The King of the Golden River*, a long, serious fairy tale, and published it a decade later. In 1867, George Macdonald (1824–1905), Scottish poet and novelist, published a delightfully playful tale, *The Light Princess*, and four years later, his most important children's fairy tale, the imaginative *At the Back of the North Wind*.

Some of the other great British writers of the period tried their hands at fantasy for children. William Makepeace Thackeray (1811–1863) contributed in 1855 *The Rose and the Ring*, a long fairy tale distinguished by its blithe humor; and in 1868, Charles Dickens (1812–1870) wrote, in the best fairy-tale tradition, *The Magic Fishbone*. Dickens's earlier story, *A Christmas Carol* (1843), is firmly ensconced in the list of hardy perennials of both Christmas literature and Victoriana. Rudyard Kipling (1865–1936), storyteller and poet, Nobel Prize winner and advocate of empire, wrote *The Jungle Books* (1894) and *Just So Stories* (1902) with a warmth and affection that make his animal characters part of the permanent heritage of children's lore, along with Beatrix Potter's *The Tale of Peter Rabbit* (1901) and Kenneth Grahame's *The Wind in the Willows* (1908).

Illustration by Arthur Hughes for At the Back of the North Wind *by George Macdonald.*

From France came the stories of Jules Verne (1828–1905), who wrote for adults but whose books have fascinated children since the first, *From the Earth to the Moon*, was published in 1865. *Twenty Thousand Leagues Under the Sea* (1869) and *Around the World in Eighty Days* (1872) are still popular with adults as well as children. In Verne's work, one sees the beginning of a new genre, the science fiction story.

From Italy came *Pinocchio* by C. Collodi (pseudonym for Carlo Lorenzini, 1826–1890). Published originally in a magazine, as so many books of this period were, the story was translated in 1892 to become one of the enduring classics of the world literature for children.

Edith Nesbit (1858–1924) was one of the first and most skilled writers in combining realism and fantasy. Her first story, *The Story of the Treasure Seekers*, was published in 1899.

Realistic Stories

During the Victorian period there was an increasing awareness of, and response to, children's needs. In England the awareness was most evident in the work of Charlotte Yonge (1823–1901), who wrote family stories based on her own happy childhood, and some school stories, sentimental in tone, moral in intent, and realistic in approach. Her prolific output (well over a hundred books) was read avidly by children of the period.

In the United States our epoch-making book was a modest story of family life, *Little Women*, like Charlotte Yonge's books, based on the author's own family experiences. The author, Louisa M. Alcott (1832–1888), submitted the manuscript hesitatingly, and her publisher had to tell her as gently as possible how unacceptable it was. Fortunately, he felt some qualms about his judgment and allowed the children of his family to read the manuscript. They convinced him that he was wrong. Those astute little girls loved the book, and it has remained popular with children since its publication in 1868. The story is as genuine a bit of realism as we have ever had. Family life is there—from the kitchen to the sanctuary of the attic, from reading to giving amateur dramatics in which the homemade scenery collapses. But right as all the details are, the reason adults remember the book is the masterly characterizations of the four girls. No longer are people typed to represent Ignorance or Virtue, but here are flesh-and-blood girls, as different from each other as they could well be, full of human folly and human courage, never self-righteous, sometimes irritable but never failing in warm affection for each other. This ability to make her characters vividly alive was Louisa M. Alcott's gift to modern realism for children.

L. M. Montgomery's *Anne of Green Gables* (1904), a Canadian story of a lively, independent orphan, was as popular in the United States as it was in Canada.

In his adventure stories for boys, England's George Henty (1832–1902) used his own experiences as a correspondent to furnish the backgrounds; in the same field in the United States, William Taylor Adams (1822–1897) wrote under the fetching pen name of Oliver Optic. That best of all purveyors of rags-to-riches books, Horatio Alger (1834–1899), captivated the young with *Ragged Dick* (1867) and all the succeeding stories that flowed out in the same pattern.

So far, on both sides of the Atlantic, realistic stories for children were primarily about eminently respectable characters. When Samuel Clemens (1835–1910), or Mark Twain as he signed himself, wrote *The Adventures of Tom Sawyer* in 1876, he carried realism across the tracks. In this book Huck Finn and his disreputable father were probably the child's first literary encounters with real people who were not considered respectable but who were likable anyway. Moreover, they were not typed to show the folly of being disreputable. Huckleberry won all hearts and so nearly stole the book from Tom that he had to appear in a book of his own—*The Adventures of Huckleberry Finn* (1884). Mark Twain in these two unsurpassed books not only gave us realism with humor—in itself a new development in literature for children—but also showed warm tolerance in his presentation of people then thought socially unacceptable.

Children's Literature Comes of Age

The Victorian period saw the stream of cheerfulness in children's literature rise steadily. Many of the books written then are still popular and will be considered in detail later. This list is a reminder of these and others that are milestones in the development of children's literature from 1484 to 1908.

1484 *Aesop's Fables*, translated and printed by William Caxton.
1646 *Spiritual Milk for Boston Babes*, John Cotton.
1657 or 1658 *Orbis Pictus*, Comenius (original in Latin).
1678 *Pilgrim's Progress*, John Bunyan.
1691 *The New England Primer.*
1697 *Contes de ma Mère l'Oye*, Perrault.
1715 *Divine and Moral Songs for Children*, Isaac Watts.
1719 *Robinson Crusoe*, Daniel Defoe.
1726 *Gulliver's Travels*, Jonathan Swift.
1729 *Tales of Mother Goose*, Perrault (first English translation).
1744 *A Little Pretty Pocket-Book.*
1765 *The Renowned History of Little Goody Two Shoes.*
1781 *Mother Goose's Melody.*
1785 *Mother Goose's Melodies* (Isaiah Thomas edition).
1789 *Songs of Innocence*, William Blake.
1804 *Original Poems for Infant Minds*, Ann and Jane Taylor.
1807 *The Butterfly's Ball*, William Roscoe.
1822 *A Visit from St. Nicholas*, Clement C. Moore.
1823 *Grimms' Popular Stories* (translated into English by Edgar Taylor).
1843 *A Christmas Carol*, Charles Dickens.
1846 *Book of Nonsense*, Edward Lear.
1846 *Fairy Tales*, Hans Christian Andersen (first English translation).
1848 *Struwwelpeter*, Heinrich Hoffmann (first English translation).
1852 *A Wonder-Book for Girls and Boys*, Nathaniel Hawthorne.
1865 *Alice's Adventures in Wonderland*, Lewis Carroll (Charles Lutwidge Dodgson).

1865 *Hans Brinker, or the Silver Skates*, Mary Mapes Dodge.
1867–1876 *Sing a Song of Sixpence*, and other toy books, illustrated by Walter Crane.
1868–1869 *Little Women*, Louisa M. Alcott.
1871 *At the Back of the North Wind*, George Macdonald.
1872 *Sing-Song*, Christina Rossetti.
1876 *The Adventures of Tom Sawyer*, Mark Twain (Samuel Clemens).
1878 *Under the Window*, Kate Greenaway.
1878 *The House That Jack Built* and *The Diverting History of John Gilpin*, illustrated by Randolph Caldecott.
1880 *The Peterkin Papers*, Lucretia Hale.
1883 *Treasure Island*, Robert Louis Stevenson.
1883 *Nights with Uncle Remus*, Joel Chandler Harris.
1883 *The Merry Adventures of Robin Hood*, Howard Pyle.
1884 *Heidi*, Johanna Spyri (first English translation).
1884 *The Adventures of Huckleberry Finn*, Mark Twain (Samuel Clemens).
1885 *A Child's Garden of Verses*, Robert Louis Stevenson.
1889 *The Blue Fairy Book*, Andrew Lang.
1891 *Pinocchio*, C. Collodi (Carlo Lorenzini). First English translation.
1894 *The Jungle Books*, Rudyard Kipling.
1889 *The Story of the Treasure Seekers*, E. Nesbit.
1901 *The Tale of Peter Rabbit*, Beatrix Potter.
1903 *Johnny Crow's Garden*, L. Leslie Brooke.
1908 *The Wind in the Willows*, Kenneth Grahame.

These are individual books that were turning points in children's literature. They not only carry us into the twentieth century with distinction, but their influence is discernible in the writing of today. Laura Richards continued the deft nonsense verses of Lear and Carroll in her *Tirra Lirra* (1932). A. A. Milne's skillful light verse, *When We Were Very Young* (1924), did as much to popularize poetry for young children in schools and homes as Robert Louis Stevenson had done earlier. The small, sweet lyrics of Christina Rossetti were followed by the exquisite poetry of Walter de la Mare and by poetry with the delicacy of Aileen Fisher, the humor of David McCord, the evocative directness of Langston Hughes.

In the field of fairy tales and fantasy, *East o' the Sun and West o' the Moon* continued the interest in folklore that began with the Grimms. American children could share in the literary heritage of other lands with books like *Tales from a Finnish Tupa* (1936), Indian fables in the several versions of the Jataka stories, and Japanese folk tales in *The Dancing Teakettle* (1949). From the Uncle Remus collections there came a new consciousness of the United States as a repository of regional and racial folklore. *The Jack Tales* (1943), southern variants of European folk tales, stemmed from this interest. If the Italian fairy tale *Pinocchio* (1891) was the gay descendant of Andersen's somber toy stories, so too was the young and equally lighthearted *Winnie-the-Pooh* (1926). Gulliver's Lilliput was not more fascinating than the miniature world of *The Borrowers* (1952). *Rabbit Hill* (1944) continued the great tradition of animal fantasy begun in *The Wind in the Willows*, to be followed by *Charlotte's Web* (1952), *The Cricket in Times Square* (1960), *Animal Family* (1965), and *Watership Down* (1974). And the daft world of *Alice's Adventures in Wonderland* grew perceptibly zanier in the fantastic dreams of Dr. Seuss.

True Americana began with *Little Women* and *Tom Sawyer* and continued to flourish in

Illustration by Attilio Mussino. Reprinted with permission of Macmillan Publishing Co., Inc. from Pinocchio *by Carlo Collodi. First published in 1925. Reissued in 1969. (Original in color)*

such descendants as *Little House in the Big Woods* (1932), *Caddie Woodlawn* (1935), the three books about *The Moffats* (1941–1943), and *Across Five Aprils* (1964). It is there, too, in the fine animal story *Smoky* (1926), written in the vernacular of a cowboy, and in an excellent story of the South in the depression era, *The Rock and the Willow* (1963). And it is certainly alive in such regional stories as *Strawberry Girl* (1945), *. . . and now Miguel* (1953), and *Where the Lilies Bloom* (1969).

The picture story so charmingly begun by Beatrix Potter continues in the varied books of Wanda Gág, Maurice Sendak, Russell Hoban, and many others. And if stories of other lands began auspiciously with *Hans Brinker* and *Heidi*, they have grown and strengthened in *The Good Master* (1935), *The Wheel on the School* (1954), *The Happy Orpheline* (1957), *The Silver Sword* (1959), *Wildcat Under Glass* (1968), and *Fly Away Home* (1975). So the types of books that were turning points in children's literature at an earlier period are perpetuated today, although the kinship between the old and the new may sometimes seem remote.

Of the many good books that have been published in the twentieth century, some stand out. Probably no two people would agree on every one that merits inclusion in a list of landmark books; the older classics have proved themselves, the new ones have yet to do so. Still, some seem milestones either because they are distinguished of their kind or because they have broken new ground, or—as in the past—they are adult books that have been taken by children as their own.

1921 *The Story of Mankind*, Hendrik Willem van Loon.
1926 *Smoky, the Cow Horse*, Will James.
1926 *Winnie-the-Pooh*, A. A. Milne.
1928 *Millions of Cats*, Wanda Gág.
1928 *Abe Lincoln Grows Up*, Carl Sandburg.
1932 *Little House in the Big Woods*, Laura Ingalls Wilder.
1934 *Mary Poppins*, Pamela Travers.
1937 *The Hobbit*, J. R. R. Tolkien.
1941 *George Washington's World*, Genevieve Foster.
1941 *Paddle-to-the-Sea*, Holling C. Holling.
1943 *Homer Price*, Robert McCloskey.
1943 *Johnny Tremain*, Esther Forbes.
1944 *Rabbit Hill*, Robert Lawson.
1947 *The Twenty-One Balloons*, William Pène du Bois.
1952 *Charlotte's Web*, E. B. White.
1959 *America Is Born, a History for Peter*, Gerald W. Johnson.
1961 *The Incredible Journey*, Sheila Burnford.
1962 *The Snowy Day*, Ezra Jack Keats.
1963 *Where the Wild Things Are*, Maurice Sendak.
1964 *Harriet the Spy*, Louise Fitzhugh.
1964 *The Pushcart War*, Jean Merrill.
1964 *The Book of Three*, Lloyd Alexander.
1969 *Where the Lilies Bloom*, Vera and Bill Cleaver.
1974 *M. C. Higgins, the Great*, Virginia Hamilton.
1974 *Watership Down*, Richard Adams.

Trends in Children's Books Today

What, we may ask, are the trends in writing for children today? A glance at the past makes it clear that little today is completely new, but certainly some types of books are better written today than ever before and are enjoying such tremendous popularity that they seem to mark a trend.

An interesting phenomenon has been the growth of the picture book. Not since that famous triumvirate, Caldecott, Crane, and Greenaway, have so many artists lavished so much effort and talent on books for young children as in the last fifty years. Lynd Ward, himself an artist, wrote ". . . the book work of the thirties that is most significant in itself, and in terms of what it contributes to the world at large, was done in picture-book form."[13] Ward's own *The Biggest Bear* is an excellent example. Sharing such a book with children, adults often find themselves as charmed with the pictures as are the children. One way to teach art appreciation would be through children's picture books which run the whole gamut of styles and techniques.

[13]"The Book Artist: Yesterday and Tomorrow," in *Illustrators of Children's Books, 1744–1945*, comp. by Bertha E. Mahony, Louise P. Latimer, and Beulah Folmsbee, 1947, p. 254.

Ezra Jack Keats uses collage with great effect; Marcia Brown combines quiet colors and bold designs in handsome woodcuts. Harold Jones's pictures for *Lavender's Blue (Mother Goose)* are in strong, dark colors and in an older style of realism with impressive composition. Gerald McDermott's stylized compositions and brilliant colors are adapted from film versions of folk tales. Reflecting the emergence of pop art and grotesquerie, and possibly in ineffectual imitation of Maurice Sendak's illustrations, there have been increasing numbers of picture books, as well as illustrations in books for older children, with grim or bizarre illustrations. But despite some unfortunate and unsuccessful experiments, today's picture book is exciting art with endless possibilities.

Other trends for younger children's books include numerous wordless picture books in which the illustrations alone tell the story, concept books that clarify abstract ideas, single editions of folk tales or *Mother Goose* rhymes in growing numbers, and publication in increasing numbers of books that deal with such topics as death or senility of grandparents.

There is also an increased interest in poetry both in and out of our schools. New books of poems appear often and, what is more, they sell. Before his death, Robert Frost gave children and youth *You Come Too*, a fine selection from his poems. Harry Behn has composed some choice lyrics, and David McCord and John Ciardi enliven the scene with extraordinarily clever nonsense verse. Poetry anthologies like *Black Out Loud*, edited by Arnold Adoff, have introduced many new black American poets, and Virginia Olsen Baron's compilation of poems by young people from minority groups, *Here I Am!* reflects the interest young people have in writing poetry, as does Nancy Larrick's similar collection, *I Heard a Scream in the Streets*. An outstanding anthology of poetry by children in English-speaking countries around the world is Richard Lewis's *Miracles*. Moreover, in the schools children are speaking poetry informally or in verse choirs with unfeigned enjoyment. Such delightful books as Aileen Fisher's *Going Barefoot* or Paul Galdone's beautifully illustrated edition of *Paul Revere's Ride* might have gone unsold twenty-five years ago. Today their popularity is assured.

Illustration by Lynd Ward for The Biggest Bear. *Copyright © 1952. Reproduced by permission of Houghton Mifflin Company.*

Viewpoints

One thing that emerges clearly is that most . . . trends are pragmatic phenomena—they derive from market and/or need. So it goes back to the consumer, and you, dear reader, set the trends. Please make them good ones, I beg of you. The thing to keep in mind is that all trends start somewhere—with a prototype that is frequently the brainchild of an author who is lucky enough to have an editor who refuses to think in terms of trends. In my case, the refusal to believe in trends in what I publish comes from my staunch belief in the minority—if *I* really love a book, there's got to be a kid like me somewhere—and even if it develops that the audience and therefore the market for the book is a very select minority indeed, it was still worth publishing.—Ann Durell, "Goodies and Baddies," *The Wilson Library Bulletin*, December 1969, p. 457.

In 1921, Hendrik Willem van Loon's *Story of Mankind* launched a fresh interest in biographies and informational books, and this interest developed into two major trends. Authentic, well-written biographies are popular with adults today and equally popular with children and youth. Elizabeth Janet Gray's *Penn*, Jean Latham's *Carry On, Mr. Bowditch*, Susan Brownmiller's *Shirley Chisholm*, Dorothy Sterling's *Captain of the*

Planter: The Story of Robert Smalls, Iris Noble's *Emmeline and Her Daughters; The Pankhurst Suffragettes*—these and many others mark biography as one of the most distinguished types of juvenile literature.

As adolescents have become more sophisticated and aware and have voiced their concern with current social problems, publishers and authors have responded with books on war, the stock market, ecology, pollution, student protest, conservation, the political scene, international relations, and the role of women.

In the sciences, books have reflected the increasing complexity of school curricula and general knowledge. Each advance in space exploration produces a throng of new books, and there is a noticeable trend toward publication of such books for younger and still younger readers. Particularly evident is the growing interest in biological frontiers and in science books with sociological implications for younger children.

Numerically, informational books threaten to outdistance all other types put together. From people and places to weather and worms, from stones to stars, from dinosaurs to missiles, from insects to astronauts, science and social studies books for children pour off the presses. The books are attractive and their content is designed for particular reading levels and understanding. Their numbers and variety are so staggering that they are more than a trend; they are practically an inundation.

A frequently used technique in informational books in the social studies is the combining of photographs with a first-person text to picture a child's life in one part of another country, thus giving a detailed report rather than the usual broad, general account that covers many aspects of another land. The photodocumentary technique also has become popular in books about urban life.

Certainly the increasing number of books by, for, and about blacks constitutes one of the most significant of major trends. There were comparatively few such books earlier in the twentieth century, but the 1960s and 1970s produced a spate of them, long overdue—books that have faced the problems of black people; fiction with exciting plots, interesting settings, and well-drawn, appealing black heroes and heroines for characters; picture books in which only the illustrations indicated that the characters were black (see, for example, Ezra Jack Keats's stories about Peter in *The Snowy Day* and its sequels); biographies of long-neglected black people of note (Harriet Tubman, Frederick Douglass, Mary McLeod Bethune, Benjamin Banneker, Paul Dunbar, W. E. B. DuBois, Paul Robeson); and poetry about and by black people. Such books as Virginia Hamilton's *M. C. Higgins, the Great* or *The Hundred Penny Box* by Sharon Bell Mathis or Bette Greene's *Philip Hall Likes Me. I Reckon Maybe* are indicative of the growing maturity of the literature for and about black children, for their characters are less concerned with winning white approval than they are with facing all the problems of growing up.

Books about other minority groups have also been published in increasing numbers, although demand still exceeds supply. Virginia Driving Hawk Sneve's *High Elk's Treasure* is a contemporary novel that stresses the proud heritage of the past treasured by a young Sioux, and Winifred Madison's *Maria Luisa,* a sympathetic portrayal of a shy Chicana's encounter with prejudice in San Francisco. These and other books about members of minority groups other than black are un-

Viewpoints

Our children are black and white, as we ourselves are. We believe that they deserve to have the best books possible, not just mediocre ones, or "will do" or token integration books. We want them to have books that reflect genuine experiences and offer honest explanations. We want them to have books in which they see people like themselves and people whose facial colors and facial profiles are different from theirs. We want them to have books that show the beauty of Blacks and the beauty of Whites, the beauty of Indians and the beauty of Orientals, the beauty of Chicanos and the beauty of Puerto Ricans. The beauty of all. The beauty of people.—From *Starting Out Right* edited by Bettye I. Latimer and funded by the Office of Equal Educational Opportunity, Bulletin No. 2314, 1972, p. viii. Reprinted by permission of the Wisconsin Department of Public Instruction.

doubtedly in part a product of the trend in writing and publishing black books that raised the consciousness—and perhaps the conscience—of the children's book world. Undoubtedly this movement was also fed by the growing group consciousness of all racial and ethnic segments of the society. Illustrations show more ethnic variety, and in both fiction and nonfiction there have been many books about Chicanos, Native Americans, Puerto Ricans, and Asian-Americans.

This same group consciousness and search for identity can be seen in Canada, where an increased number of children's book awards have been established, as have several journals devoted to children's literature, where publishers have made a significant effort to increase their output in the field of children's literature, and where that output has included books that reflect both the Canadian multiethnic heritage and contemporary life.

In response to the feminist movement, there have been more biographies of women, more books in which female protagonists or minor characters play active roles or work at jobs that realistically parallel today's society. There are books like *The Real Me* by Betty Miles, in which a girl's family supports her challenge of stereotypical sex roles, *The Dollhouse Caper* by Jean O'Connell, which is a story about boys, and stories with homosexual relationships, like Sandra Scoppettone's *Trying Hard to Hear You*. Third world presses and feminist publishing houses have contributed to this still small, but growing, trend of publication.

As adult literature has become more sophisticated and frank in its use of language, and permissive in its treatment of hitherto-taboo subjects, so books for young people have to a certain degree followed suit with such books as Judy Blume's *Then Again, Maybe I Won't*, with its candid treatment of a boy's first sexual stirrings, or the frank handling of sadism in Robert Cormier's *The Chocolate War*. While many of these topical books seem concocted, there are a growing number in which controversial themes are handled with dignity and honesty—books in which sexual and psychological problems are faced, in which siblings and parents may be hostile, in which teenagers use the language that readers are well aware is used in real life. No longer are parents sacrosanct, all-wise, and benevolent; no longer do books for young people ignore drug addiction, serious maladjustment, adultery, or racial violence. Like adult books, the worst are cheap shockers; and the best—fiction and nonfiction—are thoughtful avenues to clarification or solution of attitudes and problems.

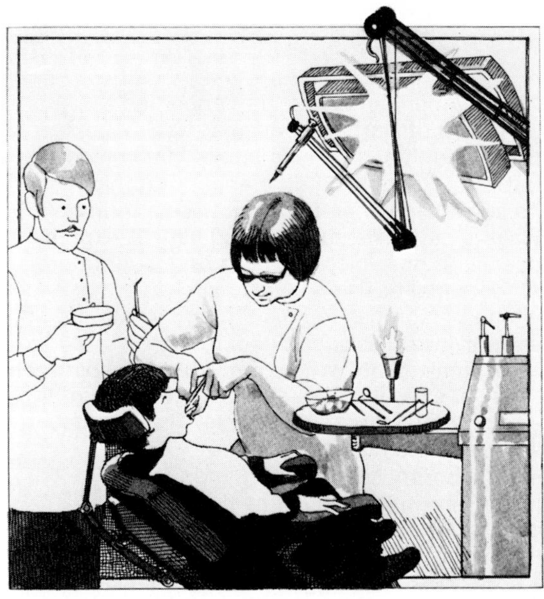

From Mothers Can Do Anything *by Joe Lasker. Copyright © 1972 by Joe Lasker. Reproduced by permission of Albert Whitman & Company, Publishers.*

While current topics often enjoy a brief popularity, there are some subjects that have interested children and young people to an extent that they have long appeared in books of fiction and nonfiction for all ages. One such topic is death, which was a familiar component of Victorian fiction and to which there was subsequently a reaction that precluded it in children's books for many years. Now death is discussed with an acceptance of its being a part of life rather than with the sanctimonious or morbid attitude of the past. From picture books like Jennifer Bartoli's *Nonna* and Charlotte Zolotow's *My Grandson Lew* to Isabelle Holland's mature *Of Love and Death and Other Journeys*, there is a range of good fiction about the death of loved ones and the

Viewpoints

Where American books are concerned the condition of North American society is being translated into children's books quite clearly, but with one notable difference from the past. As society in general does not seem to know what to say to its children and cannot express itself with one voice, we have both a literature of 'personal decision,' which suggests that each young person has to come to terms with life on an individual basis, and a literature of conformity. Many writers move uneasily between the two, exhibiting their own cloudy view of life and of contemporary problems. The form most writers use is realistic fiction or contemporary-scene fiction and they try to 'tell it like it is' in areas such as the 'personal' problems of young people, race relationships, alcoholism, drug addiction, violence, and war. . . . —Sheila Egoff, "Precepts and Pleasures: Changing Emphases in the Writing and Criticism of Children's Literature," in *Only Connect; Readings on Children's Literature,* edited by Sheila Egoff, G. T. Stubbs, and L. F. Ashley, Oxford University Press, Toronto, New York, 1969, p. 433.

adjustment to it. Books such as *Life and Death* by Herbert Zim and Sonia Bleeker or *Death Is a Noun; A View of the End of Life* by John Langone, the first for ages nine to twelve, the second for older readers, calmly discuss our fears and beliefs about dying, physiological changes, and funeral practices. Related to the subject are the problems of senility and old age; many of the stories on these topics reflect a concern about the grandparent-child relationship.

A similarly sustained interest is evident in the problems of ecology and pollution. Again, this is apparent in both factual and fictional books. For young children, Alvin Tresselt's *The Dead Tree* and Jean George's *All Upon a Stone* describe the interdependence of ecological systems, and Bill Peet's *Fly Homer Fly* concerns pollution. In Jean George's *Who Really Killed Cock Robin?* and Don Moser's *A Heart to the Hawks*, the protest against pollution and the plea for conservation are as strong as they are in such nonfiction as John Navarra's *The World You Inherit* or *The Shrinking Outdoors* by Gary Jennings.

Another trend is the publication in the United States, either in separate editions or translations, of books from other countries. Concurrently, many English-language books are translated into other languages and are therefore familiar to the children of many nations. That this trend will continue is almost assured by the increasing intercommunication among authors, illustrators, editors, librarians, and teachers who exchange journals, participate in international meetings, serve together on boards and committees, and share their concerns about children and books the world over.

The publishing world felt, in the early 1970s, repercussions of a disturbed economy, and many juvenile departments dropped books from their backlists and curtailed the number of new books they published. With higher costs for supplies and printing, the prices of children's books rose and the size of print-runs often fell. Some editors prophesied fewer colored illustrations in the years ahead. Yet sales of paperback books continued to climb and there was a fairly clear indication that two factors might have a beneficial effect on the book market: the increasing use of trade books as supplementary curricular material and the increasing awareness of and response to the need for books for young children.

What is a trend? Observe a pattern long enough and you are looking backward; to label a current change a trend is to make a judgment about the importance of a development that may prove to be ephemeral. It is within the context of the historic pattern that you must decide. It is against the background of the past—the changed concept of childhood, the establishment of universal education, the growing numbers of libraries for children, the evaluation of literary quality in the elementary school classroom—that publishers have established a broad program of special publishing for children. It is impressive by its sheer weight; it has responded with sensitivity to curricular needs and current interests; it has made reading material more accessible by mass distribution of inexpensively produced books and by a rapidly expanding production of paperback editions of established books—one of the most significant trends in bookmaking. Furthermore, many publishers are broadening their programs to include book-oriented films, film strips, cassettes, and other audiovisual media; and some have established flourishing book clubs. Without any doubt, these are exciting and productive times in the field of children's literature.

Adult References[14]

ASHTON, JOHN. *Chap-Books of the Eighteenth Century.*

BARCHILON, JACQUES, and HENRY PETTIT. *The Authentic Mother Goose Fairy Tales and Nursery Rhymes.*

BARRY, FLORENCE V. *A Century of Children's Books.*

BETT, HENRY. *The Games of Children; Their Origin and History.*

CHAMBERS, ROBERT. *Popular Rhymes of Scotland.*

COMENIUS, JOHANN AMOS. *The Orbis Pictus of John Amos Comenius.*

CROUCH, MARCUS. *Treasure Seekers and Borrowers: Children's Books in Britain, 1900–1960.*

DARLING, RICHARD L. *The Rise of Children's Book Reviewing in America, 1865–1881.*

DARTON, F. J. H. *Children's Books in England: Five Centuries of Social Life.*

DAVIS, MARY GOULD. *Randolph Caldecott 1846–1886: An Appreciation.*

DE VRIES, LEONARD. *Little Wide-Awake: An Anthology from Victorian Children's Books and Periodicals in the Collection of Anne and Fernand G. Renier.*

DOYLE, BRIAN, comp. and ed. *The Who's Who of Children's Literature.*

EDEN, HORATIA K. F. *Juliana Horatia Ewing and Her Books.*

ELLIS, ALEC. *A History of Children's Reading and Literature.*

ERNEST, EDWARD, comp., assisted by PATRICIA TRACY LOWE. *The Kate Greenaway Treasury.*

FIELD, ELINOR WHITNEY, comp. *Horn Book Reflections: On Children's Books and Reading.*

FIELD, LOUISE F. *The Child and His Book: Some Account of the History and Progress of Children's Literature in England.*

FOLMSBEE, BEULAH. *A Little History of the Horn-Book.*

FORD, PAUL LEICESTER, ed. *The New England Primer.*

FRYE, BURTON C., ed. *A St. Nicholas Anthology; The Early Years.*

GILLESPIE, MARGARET C. *Literature for Children: History and Trends.*

GOTTLIEB, GERALD. *Early Children's Books and Their Illustration.*

GREEN, ROGER LANCELYN. *Tellers of Tales.*

HALES, JOHN W., and FREDERICK J. FURNIVALL, assisted by FRANCIS J. CHILD. *Bishop Percy's Folio Manuscript.*

HALSEY, ROSALIE V. *Forgotten Books of the American Nursery; A History of the Development of the American Story-Book.*

HAVILAND, VIRGINIA, ed. *Children and Literature: Views and Reviews,* Chapter 1, "Before the Twentieth Century."

HAVILAND, VIRGINIA, and MARGARET COUGHLAN, comps. *Yankee Doodle's Literary Sampler of Prose, Poetry, & Pictures.*

HAZARD, PAUL. *Books, Children and Men.*

HEWINS, CAROLINE M. *A Mid-Century Child and Her Books.*

HÜRLIMANN, BETTINA. *Three Centuries of Children's Books in Europe.*

JORDAN, ALICE M., *From Rollo to Tom Sawyer.*

KIEFER, MONICA. *American Children Through Their Books, 1700–1835.*

LANG, ANDREW, ed. *Perrault's Popular Tales.*

MacLEOD, ANNE SCOTT. *A Moral Tale; Children's Fiction and American Culture 1820–1860.*

McGUFFEY, WILLIAM HOLMES. *Old Favorites from the McGuffey Readers.*

MAHONEY, BERTHA E., LOUISE P. LATIMER, and BEULAH FOLMSBEE, comps. *Illustrators of Children's Books, 1744–1945.*

MEIGS, CORNELIA, ANNE EATON, ELIZABETH NESBITT, and RUTH HILL VIGUERS. *A Critical History of Children's Literature.*

MOORE, ANNE CARROLL. *My Roads to Childhood.*

MUIR, PERCY. *English Children's Books, 1600 to 1900.*

OPIE, IONA and PETER. *Children's Games in Street and Playground.*

______. *The Lore and Language of Schoolchildren.*

______, eds. *The Oxford Dictionary of Nursery Rhymes.*

The Original Mother Goose's Melody, As First Issued by John Newbery, of London, about A.D. 1760.

PELLOWSKI, ANNE. *The World of Children's Literature.*

QUAYLE, ERIC. *The Collector's Book of Children's Books.*

ROSELLE, DANIEL. *Samuel Griswold Goodrich, Creator of Peter Parley; A Study of His Life and Work.*

ROSENBACH, ABRAHAM S. W. *Early American Children's Books with Bibliographical Descriptions of the Books in His Private Collection.*

ST. JOHN, JUDITH. *The Osborne Collection of Early Children's Books 1566–1910; A Catalogue,* Vols. 1 and 2.

SALWAY, LANCE. *A Peculiar Gift.*

SMITH, DORA V. *Fifty Years of Children's Books.*

SMITH, IRENE. *A History of the Newbery and Caldecott Medals.*

STEWART, CHRISTINA. *The Taylors of Ongar: An Analytical Bio-Bibliography.*

TARG, WILLIAM, ed. *Bibliophile in the Nursery.*

THWAITE, MARY F. *From Primer to Pleasure in Reading.*

TOWNSEND, JOHN ROWE. *Written for Children: An Outline of English Children's Literature.*

TUER, ANDREW W. *Pages and Pictures from Forgotten Children's Books; Brought Together and Introduced to the Reader.*

______, *Stories from Old-Fashioned Children's Books.*

VIGUERS, RUTH HILL, MARCIA DALPHIN, and BERTHA MAHONY MILLER, comps. *Illustrators of Children's Books, 1946–1956.*

WANDSWORTH PUBLIC LIBRARIES. *The Wandsworth Collection of Early Children's Books.*

WEISS, HARRY B. *A Book About Chapbooks; The People's Literature of Bygone Times.*

WELSH, CHARLES. *A Bookseller of the Last Century. Being some Account of the Life of John Newbery and of the Books he published with a Notice of the later Newberys.*

______, ed. *The Renowned History of Little Goody Two Shoes, Otherwise Called Mrs. Margery Two Shoes.*

[14]Complete bibliographic data are provided in the combined Adult References in the Appendixes.

Part 2

Discovering Books with Children

Books for Early Childhood

Chapter 4

Interest in very young children and their intellectual development has increased remarkably in recent years. Scientific research has demonstrated that fifty percent of a child's general intelligence is achieved between birth and age four, and an additional thirty percent by age eight. Children's speech and vocabulary development follows a similar pattern, with about thirty-three percent of these skills achieved by the time they are six.

Small wonder, then, that there has been a corresponding flourishing of organizations concerned solely with young children and their education, of books, journals, and articles on myriad aspects of the subject, of special schools for early education, and of books written for this group. This chapter will examine the many kinds of books there are: *Mother Goose* and other books of nursery rhymes, alphabet books and counting books, concept books and picture books without text, picture story books to be read aloud and simply written stories for beginning independent readers.

Since so often many children's first experiences with books and reading occur before they go to school, parents and other adults who are responsible for preschool children bear a large responsibility for creating an environment in which children can best develop language skills, formulate attitudes toward reading, and experience pleasure with books.

Studies of home environments of children in nursery schools show clearly how much more advanced in language skills those children are who have been sung to, read to, and talked with. In fact, there is evidence that their greatest response is to language. Infants may enjoy a mother's voice or a father's lap before they appreciate what's being read to them, but the association of books with pleasure can begin in infancy.

Children can make great discoveries about reading before learning to read for themselves. For one thing, seeing adults enjoy their own books can spur a positive attitude toward reading. Moreover, following the story as an adult reads and points out objects on the page, a child learns that the symbols in the book always go from left to right and, just as dependably, from the top to the bottom of the page. That's a big step. And then comes the marvelous realization that an "a" in one word is an "a" in another, that "c-a-t" in one book is exactly the same as "c-a-t" in another book; those are two more big steps, and they are learned most easily in a one-to-one situation when a small child and an adult, or an older child, share a book together.

Books for young children are usually referred to en masse as "picture books." The true picture book is one in which the illustrations are the dominant feature with little or no text. Brian Wildsmith's *ABC* is an excellent example, with large-scale pictures of familiar objects a child can point to and gleefully recognize. An adult may get bored the tenth time a child points and says "dog," but to the child each repetition brings the delight of corroborating a new experience. The picture book affords opportunities for self-discovery experiences, while there is a greater component of sharing in listening to a picture story book being read aloud.

A picture story book has a structured, if minimal, plot; it really tells a story, while a picture book may not. In a picture story the illustrations are so integral a part of the content that the story can be "read" by the child from the pictures (Robert McCloskey's *Make Way for Ducklings*, for example).

Look at picture books, read picture story books aloud, take children to a public library and help them choose their books. Observe their reactions. If a television program is based on a book, follow it up by getting the book if you can; the average preschooler in the United States watches television for fifty-five hours a week,[1] and any opportunity for capitalizing on that familiar medium should be seized. Talk about books you have read; tell stories if you possibly can (young children are not very demanding about technique). All of these are pleasurable shared activities, but they also prepare the child (as do street signs, magazines, and box tops) for reading independently. Chapter 1 discusses children's needs and the ways in which books can meet those needs, and Chapter 2 describes some of the criteria by which books can be evaluated. In considering books for young children, we should keep in mind those needs and those criteria as well as the limitations of experience and language of the very young. While this chapter focuses specifically on books for young children, many other books written for this age, and many of the authors and artists who excel in their creation, are discussed in the following chapter, "Artists and Children's Books," and in the later chapters on modern fantasy, realistic fiction, and informational books. You will probably find it useful to look at the following chapter on illustrators along with this chapter, since illustration is an essential element in books for the very young. The emphasis in this chapter is on the content of those books; the emphasis in the following chapter is on the artwork.

[1]A statement made by Nancy Larrick at the 1975 Conference of the N.C.T.E.

Mother Goose

Small children acquire a love for poetry as naturally as did people of early times, through hearing poems spoken or sung and through learning them, almost unconsciously, along with the speaker or singer. Long, long ago, mothers, grannies, and nurses diverted crying babies by playing with their toes—"This little pig went to market," or making a game—"Pat-a-cake, pat-a-cake," or chanting a nonsense rhyme with a catchy tune—"Hickory, dickory, dock." These old nursery ditties were easily remembered and passed on by word of mouth for generations before they achieved the permanency of print and became known as *Mother Goose*. These folk rhymes are still important not only because children and youth continue to enjoy them, but because many are skillfully composed, exuberant or dramatic, and lead naturally into modern nonsense verse and narrative poems.

Where did these verses come from? Who was Mother Goose? These are questions that occur to us as we turn over the pages of some beguiling modern editions. Although it is sometimes difficult to distinguish legend from fact, these nursery songs are linked with our historical and literary past.

The name *Mother Goose*, as Chapter 3 explains, was first associated with the eight folk tales recorded by Perrault. Andrew Lang, in *Perrault's Popular Tales*, tells us that the frontispiece of *Histoires ou contes du temps passé, avec des moralités* (Histories or Tales of Long Ago, with Morals) showed an old woman spinning and telling stories, and that a placard on the same page bore the words "Contes de ma Mère l'Oye" (Tales of Mother Goose). But the name *Mother Goose* has now become so completely associated with the popular verses that most English translations of the Perrault tales omit it from the title of the collection.

Lina Eckenstein, in *Comparative Studies* in *Nursery Rhymes* (1906), says that the name *Mother Goose* was first used in England in connection with Robert Powell's puppet shows, exhibited in London between 1709 and 1711. Powell's plays included, among others, *Robin Hood and Little John, The Children in the Wood, Whittington and His Cat*, and one called *Mother Goose*. What play did

From Oxford Nursery Rhyme Book *by Iona and Peter Opie. Reproduced by permission of The Clarendon Press, Oxford.*

Powell present under the title of *Mother Goose?* It may have been one of Perrault's stories heard from a traveler. At any rate, Perrault's *Contes de ma Mère l'Oye* was translated into English in 1729, and the popularity of the eight tales undoubtedly helped establish still more firmly that delightful nonsense name, *Mother Goose.*

Early Editions of *Mother Goose*

The next mention of the name in England is in connection with John Newbery, who is discussed in Chapter 3. At one time, Newbery was thought to have published an edition of *Mother Goose's Melody or Sonnets for the Cradle* between 1760 and 1765, but more recent research[2] suggests that he may have planned but did not publish such a book. In 1781 Newbery's stepson, T. Carnan, who continued the Newbery publishing business, advertised in the *London Chronicle* for January 2, "The first publication of *Mother Goose's Melody.*"

The first American edition of *Mother Goose* was probably a pirated reprint of an early Newbery edition, published in about 1785 by Isaiah Thomas.[3] Two more notable American editions followed the Thomas edition. Between 1824 and 1827, the Boston firm of Munroe and Francis published the *Mother Goose's Quarto, or Melodies Complete,* which contained many rhymes drawn from the Thomas reprint of Newbery's *Melody* but also many apparently old ones printed for the first time. In 1833 this firm made a reprint of the *Quarto* with the title *The Only True Mother Goose Melodies.* Both the *Quarto* and the 1833 edition are important sources for many of the later collections. These editions include, as many of our modern editions do, some poems that are not traditional, such as Walter Scott's "Pibroch of Donnel Dhu" and Shakespeare's "Jog on, jog on, the foot-path way," which are obviously out of place in a collection of folk rhymes.

Origins of the *Mother Goose* Verses

The *Mother Goose* verses underwent many changes during the years when they were passed on by word of mouth, and later when they traveled from one printed edition to another. As with the ballads, variants of the

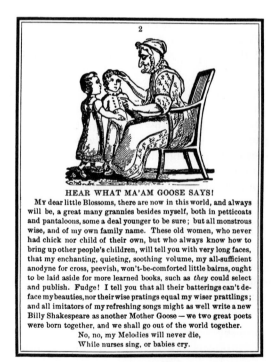

2

HEAR WHAT MA'AM GOOSE SAYS!

My dear little Blossoms, there are now in this world, and always will be, a great many grannies besides myself, both in petticoats and pantaloons, some a deal younger to be sure; but all monstrous wise, and of my own family name. These old women, who never had chick nor child of their own, but who always know how to bring up other people's children, will tell you with very long faces, that my enchanting, quieting, soothing volume, my all-sufficient anodyne for cross, peevish, won't-be-comforted little bairns, ought to be laid aside for more learned books, such as *they* could select and publish. Fudge! I tell you that all their batterings can't deface my beauties, nor their wise pratings equal my wiser prattlings; and all imitators of my refreshing songs might as well write a new Billy Shakespeare as another Mother Goose — we two great poets were born together, and we shall go out of the world together.

No, no, my Melodies will never die,
While nurses sing, or babies cry.

From The Only True Mother Goose Melodies, *an exact and full-size reproduction of the original edition published and copyrighted in Boston in the year 1833 by Munroe and Francis (Lothrop, Lee and Shepard, 1905).*

[2]Jacques Barchilon and Henry Pettit, eds. *The Authentic Mother Goose Fairy Tales and Nursery Rhymes* (Swallow, 1960).

[3]See Chapter 3 discussion.

same verses were recited or sung in different places, and which ones were the originals no one can say. Certainly they have led to considerable speculation and to some careful research. Undoubtedly many of the rhymes are mere nonsense jingles, but many others reveal interesting bits of history, old customs, manners, and beliefs. Attempts to find historical characters to fit the people of *Mother Goose* have shown more imagination than documented research. Iona and Peter Opie, scholars of distinction in the field of nursery rhymes, comment in *The Oxford Dictionary of Nursery Rhymes:*

Much ingenuity has been exercised to show that certain nursery rhymes have had greater significance than is now apparent. They have been vested with mystic symbolism, linked with social and political events, and numerous attempts have been made to identify the nursery characters with real persons. It should be stated straightway that the bulk of these speculations are worthless. Fortunately the theories are so numerous they tend to cancel each other out. The story of "Sing a song of sixpence," for instance, has been described as alluding to the choirs of Tudor monasteries, the printing of the English Bible, the malpractices of the Romish clergy, and the infinite workings of the solar system. The baby rocked on a tree top has been recognized as the Egyptian child Horus, the Old Pretender, and a New England Red Indian. Even when, by chance, the same conclusions are reached by two writers the reasons given are, as likely as not, antithetical. This game of "interpreting" the nursery rhymes has not been confined to the twentieth century, though it is curious that it has never been so overplayed as in the age which claims to believe in realism. (p. 27)

Qualities That Appeal to Children

Children enjoy the variety of subject matter and mood that continually surprises them in *Mother Goose*. It ranges from the sheer nonsense of:

Hey! diddle, diddle,
The cat and the fiddle,
The cow jumped over the moon.

to the sad and tender ballad of "The babes in the wood":

Viewpoints

. . . although each new generation of parents, grandfathers, and grandmothers sings and recites to children both the good and the inferior, only that which bests serves the children's needs and tastes remains in their memories. And when he reaches old age, everyone who heard in his childhood these folk chants passes on to his grandchildren, in his turn, the very best, the most vivid and vital. And everything that is out of tune and incongruous with the psychology of the young child is gradually forgotten and becomes extinct; . . . In this way an exemplary children's folklore has come into existence—exemplary in its language and rhythm, as well as ideally suited to the intellectual needs of the young child. . . .

The great book that is called by the English *Mother Goose* came into being exactly the same way. The rhymes comprised in *Mother Goose,* called nursery rhymes, had been subjected to the same process of collective selection, unconsciously achieved by a long sequence of generations of children. These verses had been sifted through a thousand sieves before this book came into existence.—Kornei Chukovsky, *From Two to Five,* University of California Press, Berkeley and Los Angeles, 1963, p. 94.

My dear, do you know
How a long time ago
Two poor little children,
Whose names I don't know . . .

The following list of examples, to which you can add dozens of others, suggests the variety in these verses:

People (a rich gallery of characters)
Children—Little Miss Muffet
Grownups—Old King Cole
Imaginary—Old Mother Goose when she wanted to wander
Grotesque—There was a crooked man
Children's pranks—Georgie, Porgie, pudding and pie
Animals—I had a little pony
Birds and fowl—Jenny Wren; Higgledy, piggledy, my black hen
Finger play—Pat-a-cake
Games—Ring a ring o' roses
Riddles—Little Nancy Etticoat

Counting rhymes—One, two, buckle my shoe
Counting out—Intery, mintery, cutery-corn
Alphabets—A, is an apple pie
Proverbs—Early to bed, early to rise
Superstitions—See a pin and pick it up
Time verses—Thirty days hath September
Days of the week—Solomon Grundy, born on Monday
Verse stories—The Queen of Hearts, she made some tarts
Dialogue—Who killed Cock Robin?
Songs—A frog he would a-wooing go
Street cries—Hot-cross Buns!
Weather—Rain, rain, go away
Tongue twisters—Peter Piper picked a peck of pickled peppers
Cumulative stories—This is the house that Jack built
Nonsense—Three wise men of Gotham

On the whole, descriptive nature poems, in the modern sense, are conspicuously lacking, as are fairy poems.

Lured on by the variety of these rollicking jingles, children are also captivated by their musical quality. "Sing it again," they insist, when you finish reading or singing one of their favorites. They nod their heads or rock their bodies, marking time to the rhythm. They may suit the words to their own actions.

Saying these verses, children get a happy introduction to rhyme—perfect and imperfect—to alliteration, onomatopoeia, and other sound patterns. Happily they get these without the burden of their labels and so enjoy them lightheartedly. They like the exact, neat rhyming of:

Georgie, Porgie, pudding and pie,
Kissed the girls and made them cry.
When the boys came out to play
Georgie, Porgie ran away.

But they are not disturbed by the far from perfect rhyme of:

Goosey, goosey, gander
Whither shall I wander?
Up stairs, down stairs,
And in my lady's chamber.

Alliteration, as in "Sing a song of sixpence," tickles their sound sense to a degree that astonishes us. They are also fascinated by the staccato in "Higgledy, piggledy, my black hen" and by the explosive *tle* in "She lays eggs for gen*tle*men." Indeed, the brisk tune of this ditty turns upon its lively use of consonants, the *n* sounds making it ring delightfully. One of the many values of these melodious jingles is that they accustom the ear and the tongue to the musical aspects of the English language.

There are also in *Mother Goose* small lyrics of genuine poetic charm with a more subtle music than the examples already given: "I saw a ship a-sailing," "Bobby Shaftoe," "Hush-a-bye, baby," "Johnny shall have a new bonnet," "Lavender's blue," "The north wind doth blow," and the charming:

I had a little nut tree, nothing would it bear
But a silver apple and a golden pear;
The King of Spain's daughter came to see me,
And all for the sake of my little nut tree.
I skipped over water, I danced over sea,
And all the birds in the air couldn't catch me.

All in all, the verses offer many opportunities for the development of a fine sense of the musical quality of language.

Still another characteristic of these verses that endears them to young children is their action. Jack and Jill fall down, Miss Muffet runs away, Mother Goose rides on her gander, the cow jumps over the moon, Polly puts the kettle on. Here are no meditations, no brooding introspections, no subtle descriptions. In these verses things happen as rapidly and riotously as youngsters would like to see them happening every day.

Some verses contain simple stories. "The Queen of Hearts," for example, is a slight but complete account of the innocent and industrious queen, her tarts stolen, the villain caught, punishment administered, and the villain left in a properly penitent frame of mind. Old Mother Hubbard and her bare cupboard involve considerable suspense before the tale is told out. The bewildered old woman who wakes to find her skirts cut short and so is not sure of her identity makes a story that is funny to the last line. "The babes in the wood" is a tragic tale but endurable because it is brief and is gently and sweetly told. The brevity of these verse stories makes them acceptable to children as young as two years old and they prepare children to enjoy longer and more involved prose and verse stories.

The sheer fun of *Mother Goose* keeps the verses alive in the hearts of every generation of children. What do children laugh at? It is hard to say; we can only watch and listen. Sometimes they laugh at the sound; often they laugh at the grotesque or the incongruous. Surprise and absurd antics amuse them, and broad horseplay delights them. There are plenty of examples of all these in *Mother Goose*. A man jumps into the bramble bush to scratch his eyes "*in* again"; a pig flies up in the air; Simple Simon goes fishing in his mother's pail; Humpty Dumpty has a fall (falls always bring a laugh).

Finally, children love the pictures that illustrate their favorite book. Whether the edition is so small it can be tucked into a pocket, or so enormous it must be spread out on the floor, the numerous pictures enchant them. Here they share their delight in *Mother Goose* with some of the finest illustrators of each generation, for artists also love the fun and action of these old rhymes and have lavished on them some of their best work. Just as there is endless variety in the stories, the moods, and the characters of these jingles, so there is a like variety in the size, the shape, the color, and the style of pictures that illustrate them. One adult prefers one edition, while a second adult greatly prefers another, but the children simply ask for *Mother Goose*—with colored pictures or black-and-white, simple or elaborate, commonplace or subtle.

Popular Editions

It is impractical to list all the fine editions of *Mother Goose*, but the following choices are popular with parents, teachers, librarians, and children for a variety of reasons.

Mother Goose; or, The Old Nursery Rhymes (1882), illustrated by Kate Greenaway, is a tiny book to fit small hands and pockets and to fill small hearts with delight. It contains forty-four of the brief rhymes, each with its own picture in the quaint Kate Greenaway style. The print is exceedingly small, but for nonreaders this does not matter. The illustrations are gently gay, the colors are soft, and the people exquisitely decorative.

Mother Goose; The Old Nursery Rhymes (1913), illustrated by Arthur Rackham, one of England's great artists, is a splendid edition, brought back into print in 1975. The illustrations are of three types: pen-and-ink sketches, silhouettes, and full-page color. The silhouettes are amazingly effective, for example, the dripping bedraggled cat of "Ding, dong, bell." The color plates are Rackham at his best and in many moods. These are pictures by an artist with imagination and a knowledge of folklore. (See 3, p. 68.)

A good introduction to *Mother Goose* and her world is the tried and true *The Real Mother Goose* (1965 ed.), illustrated by Blanche Fisher Wright. There are colored pictures on every page; often one picture fills a whole page, or sometimes there are two or three small ones. The characters are dressed in period costumes and can be seen distinctly by a large group of children. The colors are clear washes, sometimes soft and pale but more often bright and lively. It is a big book with a wide selection of traditional verses which the illustrations really illustrate. This is more important than some artists have realized, because small children use pictures as clues to the meaning of the text. (See 1, p. 68.)

In *Ring o' Roses* (1922), Leslie Brooke provides an imaginative and broadly humorous pictorial interpretation of the traditional verses. The characters are in English period costumes and are utterly satisfying interpretations. Simple Simon *is* Simple Simon, daft and delightful. But above all you will remember Leslie Brooke's pigs—after chuckling over them you will never again see pigs as plain pigs. This is, after all, the test of great illustrations: they do more than illustrate—they interpret the text so vividly that they become the embodiment of the words. (See 2, p. 68.)

The Tall Book of Mother Goose (1942), illustrated by Feodor Rojankovsky, is an elongated book, approximately five by twelve inches, which can be easily held. There are delightful picture spreads like the panoramic landscape of "One misty, moisty morning."

1.

2.

1. *From* The Real Mother Goose, *illustrated by Blanche Fisher Wright. Copyright 1916, renewal copyright 1944 by Rand McNally & Co. (Original in color)*

2. *Illustration by Leonard Leslie Brooke. From* Ring o' Roses. *Reproduced with permission of Frederick Warne & Co., Inc. (Original in color)*

3. *Illustration by Arthur Rackham. From* Mother Goose. *Copyright, 1931, by Arthur Rackham, 1941, by Adyth Rackham. Reproduced by permission of D. Appleton-Century Company, Inc. (Original in color)*

3.

4. *Illustration by Tasha Tudor. From* Mother Goose. *Copyright 1944 by Henry Z. Walck, Inc., Publishers. Reprinted by permission. (Original in color)*

5. *"Little Miss Muffet" from* The Tall Book of Mother Goose *illustrated by Feodor Rojankovsky, copyright 1942, copyright renewed 1970 by Western Publishing Company, Inc., reprinted by permission. (Original in color)*

6. *From* London Bridge Is Falling Down! *copyright © 1967 by Peter Spier. Reproduced by permission of Doubleday and Company, Inc. and The World's Work, Ltd., Great Britain. (Original in color)*

4.

5.

6.

7.

Jack Sprat could eat no fat,
His wife could eat no lean,
And so betwixt the two of them,
They licked the platter clean.

9.

8.

7. *From* Mother Goose *by Brian Wildsmith. Copyright © 1964. Reproduced by permission of Franklin Watts, Inc. and Oxford University Press, London. (Original in color)*

8. *Taken from* Every Child's Book of Nursery Songs *by Donald Mitchell and Carey Blyton. Copyright © 1968 by Donald Mitchell and Carey Blyton. Used by permission of Crown Publishers, Inc.*

9. *Copyright © 1963 by Philip Reed. From* Mother Goose and Nursery Rhymes. *Used by permission of Atheneum Publishers. (Original in color)*

10.

11.

12.

10. *Reprinted by permission of Coward, McCann & Geoghegan, Inc. from* The Mother Goose Treasury *by Raymond Briggs. Copyright © 1966 by Raymond Briggs.*

11. *From* Cakes and Custard *by Brian Alderson, illustrated by Helen Oxenbury. Reprinted with permission of William Morrow & Company and William Heinemann, Ltd. (Original in color)*

12. *Illustration from* Three Jovial Huntsmen *by Susan Jeffers. Reproduced by permission of Bradbury Press, Inc. (Original in color)*

An equally effective arrangement is the sequence of small pictures like those for "The three little kittens." Rojankovsky was a master of color and realistic texture. His furry kittens, feathery chicks, and woolly mufflers have a depth that almost creates a tactual sensation. His children are husky, everyday youngsters, never beautiful and often very funny. This book, with its 150 rhymes and twice as many pictures, remains popular. (See 5, p. 69.)

Tasha Tudor's illustrations have always been notable for her delicate imagination and for her use of quaint costumes. Her *Mother Goose* (1944) is six and one-half by seven and one-half inches, an agreeable size for small hands to hold. Of the seventy-seven verses, a number are unfamiliar. The action is interpreted both realistically and imaginatively. For instance, the illustration for "the cow jumped over the moon" pictures the cow running downhill with the distant moon showing through the cow's four legs. The cozy domesticity of many of the pictures is very appealing. (See 4, p. 69.)

Marguerite de Angeli's *Book of Nursery and Mother Goose Rhymes* (1954) contains 376 jingles, 260 enchanting pictures, and innumerable decorations. It is a big book, and it must have been a labor of love for the artist. Children and animals dance and prance across the pages. The book is too big for small children to handle alone, but it is fine for children and adults to look at together. The verses are not arranged in any particular order, so a nursery jingle is often followed by a ballad of sufficient substance to suit older children. However, the rich offering of verses and illustrations makes this an edition to cherish and to pass on to the next generation.

Lavender's Blue (1954), compiled by Kathleen Lines, is distinguished by Harold Jones's illustrations. Both in color and in black and white, they suggest old engravings. The pages are neatly bordered; the figures are stiffish, not stylized yet not realistic either. Although the colors are muted and there is little humor, the composition of the pictures holds your attention. "I love little pussy" is an example. Puss sits tall, solemn, and mysterious against an interior from which a door opens onto alluring streets. She is framed like a period portrait of a great lady. (See color section, Ch. 5.)

From the rich store of their scholarly study Iona and Peter Opie have compiled *The Oxford Nursery Rhyme Book* (1955), with eight hundred of the verses that have delighted children for generations. The vast collection is skillfully organized. It begins with the simplest ditties and progresses to more mature riddles, songs, and ballads. Almost every verse has a picture—small and black only, but amazingly effective. Many of the illustrations are taken from the old chapbooks and toy books. The work of Thomas and John Bewick is well represented, and the distinguished drawings of contemporary artist Joan Hassall are in keeping with their style. Students of early children's books will find this an invaluable edition, and parents will also enjoy the book. Designed as a companion volume to *The Oxford Nursery Rhyme Book* is the Opies' *A Family Book of Nursery Rhymes* (first published as *The Puffin Book of Nursery Rhymes*). Of its 358 rhymes, 200 are not included in the first book. Precise, delicate drawings by Pauline Baynes grace almost every page, and the notes at the back of the book are as entertaining as they are informative.

Brian Wildsmith's work is distinguished for its magnificent use of rich color, often in a patchwork of vibrant geometric figures. In his *Brian Wildsmith's Mother Goose* (1964) the people are gay in period clothing, and the almost theatrical quality of the pictures gives a sense of milieu as well as of the characters. (See 7, p. 70.)

Another delightful collection is *A Book of Scottish Nursery Rhymes*, edited by Norah and William Montgomerie. Most of the selections are pure Scots, but anyone can recognize and enjoy such favorites as:

"Pussy, pussy baudrons
Where have you been?"
"I've been to London,
To see the Queen!"

"Pussy, pussy baudrons,
What got you there?"
"I got a good fat mousikie,
Running up a stair!"

One of the impressive collections of the 1960s is *The Mother Goose Treasury* (1966), illustrated by Raymond Briggs. It contains over four hundred verses, most of them from the Opie collection, and each has at least one illustration. The verses and pictures, many of them small, are scattered over the pages with open-handed abandon. Occasionally there is a full-page or a double-page spread in color. The pictures are greatly varied in mood and treatment: some are bold, some delicate, some restrained, some grotesque, some humorous, but all have charm. (See 10, p. 71.)

Mother Goose and Nursery Rhymes (1963) is delightfully illustrated by Philip Reed with woodcut engravings in quiet colors, which are enhanced by being set off by ample space. The characters have an ebullient and rakish humor that captures the joyful spirit of the verses. (See 9, p. 70.)

In *Mother Goose Lost* (1971) Trevor Stubley's gay and colorful pictures illustrate a collection of unfamiliar rhymes found by Nicholas Tucker, a British psychologist, while doing research for an article. Another distinguished Englishman in the field of children's literature, Brian Alderson, includes some of his childhood favorites in addition to *Mother Goose* rhymes in *Cakes and Custard* (1975). The best collection since the one by Briggs, this handsomely designed book is illustrated by Helen Oxenbury with pictures that have wit, vigor, and superb draftsmanship. (See 12, p. 71.)

A collection of songs, many from *Mother Goose*, has been selected by Donald Mitchell and very simply arranged for piano accompaniment by Carey Blyton in *Every Child's Book of Nursery Songs* (1969). Suggestions for the use of percussion instruments or for vocal participation by children (in rounds or with spoken parts) are included. The black-and-white artwork is amusing. (See 8, p. 70.)

In recent years several very attractive editions of single verses from *Mother Goose* have been published. Both Peter Spier and Ed Emberley illustrated *London Bridge Is Falling Down*—Emberley's fanciful version has an ornate bridge but little period detail; Spier's version has minutely and humorously detailed illustrations and notes on the history of the bridge. (See 6, p. 69.) Paul Galdone and Barbara Cooney, too, have illustrated single-verse editions. Barbara Cooney has also illustrated with delightful delicacy *Mother Goose in French*, ably translated by Hugh Latham. Maurice Sendak in *Hector Protector* and *As I Went Over the Water* adds a raffish charm to two less familiar verses. For the imaginative and delicately detailed illustrations for *Three Jovial Huntsmen* (1973), Susan Jeffers won the Golden Apple at the Bienniale of Illustrations in Bratislava, an international exhibit. (See 11, p. 71.)

It is clear that no single artistic interpretation is more appropriate than any other. Whether an edition is large in size or small, whether it contains a single verse or many, the illustrations should reflect the mood of the verses, should truly illustrate them rather than being merely decorative, and should be placed on the pages so that they relate to the verses, enabling children to relate words and pictures. The latter is especially important in *Mother Goose* books in which there are several verses and illustrations on a page; the layout of the page should leave no doubt as to which illustration fits each picture. Since such layout is difficult to achieve on a crowded page, adequate spacing is an important criterion in evaluating editions. Whether illustrations are delicate or robust, they should be realistic enough for young children to see the correlation between the picture and the verse.

Viewpoints

For after all, despite the trappings, life on a block in the ghetto may not be so much unlike Tom Jones' England. Vita Sackville-West helps us remember that the eighteenth-century gentry "banged their children about physically and mentally, teaching them well in advance what to expect of life." Sometimes we forget the health and dignity that exist in the very young ghetto child. We neglect his aristocracy. The ghetto child knows by experience that he can confront and survive, which is often more than his anxious suburban counterpart knows about himself. He is a hero who needs a literature worthy of his zest and toughness, a Homer to celebrate the terror and beauty of mere existence.

I submit *Mother Goose.*—Joan Bodger, "Mother Goose: Is the Old Girl Relevant?" *Wilson Library Bulletin,* December 1969, p. 408.

Variants of *Mother Goose*

In addition to the many editions of *Mother Goose* there are several collections of nursery rhymes which are fairly close in style and content to the old English jingles.

The American Mother Goose was compiled by Ray Wood and illustrated by Ed Hargis. Children studying frontier life are interested in and amused by this collection. The verses are both rougher and funnier than the English nursery rhymes and are as indigenous to America as a "possum up a gum stump." Here is such familiar doggerel as "I asked my mother for fifteen cents," "How much wood would a woodchuck chuck," and a final section of riddles, games, and finger play. The pen-and-ink sketches are full of hilarious touches that delight adults as much as they do the children. This book is not for the youngest, but it is fun for older children.

Maud and Miska Petersham's *The Rooster Crows; A Book of American Rhymes and Jingles* was awarded the Caldecott Medal in 1946. In spite of the inclusion of such American folk rhymes as "A bear went over the mountain" and "Mother, may I go out to swim," the subtitle is difficult to justify because the collection also contains such old-world rhymes as "Sally Waters" and "Oats, peas, beans and barley grows."

A Rocket in My Pocket, compiled by Carl Withers, carries the subtitle *The Rhymes and Chants of Young Americans.* Some four hundred ditties, tongue twisters, derisive chants, and bits of pure nonsense, together with Susanne Suba's line drawings, make this an unusually beguiling book.

Did You Feed My Cow? compiled by Margaret Burroughs, an authority on Afro-American culture, is a book of street games, chants, and rhymes in which traditional folk materials have been adapted by children.

Another collection of rhymes, street chants, games, and songs, *Sally Go Round the Sun*, is based on research by the compiler, Edith Fowke, an expert on Canadian folklore. A collection of Danish nursery rhymes, *It's Raining Said John Twaining*, has been translated and illustrated by N. M. Bodecker with perky, rhythmic verses that have a humorous quality that is echoed in the illustrations. *The Prancing Pony*, translated by Charlotte De Forest, is a compilation of fifty-three favorite nursery song lyrics; the verses reflect Japanese culture but also have a universal appeal. Robert Wyndham's selections of Mandarin verses for *Chinese Mother Goose Rhymes* are beautifully illustrated by Ed Young on pages printed sideways and bordered by columns of Chinese calligraphy.

Lillian Morrison has made a delightful contribution to Americana with her small collections of riddles, auguries, school and playground chants, and amusing autograph album inscriptions. The three books in the last category—*Yours Till Niagara Falls, Remember Me When This You See*, and *Best Wishes, Amen*—are never on library shelves at commencement time.

Tongue Tanglers, compiled by Charles Francis Potter, is popular with both children and speech teachers. There are only forty-four tongue tanglers, but they are gems, and the illustrations in full color add to the hilarity. Potter's selection, chosen from thousands of tongue twisters, includes:

I saw Esau kissing Kate.
Fact is we all three saw.
I saw Esau, he saw me,
And she saw I saw Esau.

and ends with that perfect conclusion:

Tongue twisters twist tongues twisted
Trying to untangle twisted tangles
My tangs tungled now.[4]

Alvin Schwartz, in *A Twister of Twists, A Tangle of Tongues*, adds some tongue twisters on modern inventions like pre-shrunk shirts to a collection that includes old favorites.

ABC Books

While most alphabet books do help young children learn their ABC's, they also make a

[4]From *Tongue Tanglers* by Charles Francis Potter. Copyright 1962 by Charles Francis Potter. Published by The World Publishing Co.

contribution to visual literacy, helping the child organize graphic experiences. ABC books are not the only kinds of books that help children in identifying objects, but they do serve as identification books, usually comprising key words that label familiar objects or animals, less often identifying people.

Although early alphabet books like the *New England Primer* served not only to teach children letters but also to give moral instruction, the pictorial ABC books that followed *Mother Goose*'s "A Apple Pie" are all variants on that theme. Edward Lear wrote one of the funniest, all in nonsense phonetics, and it now appears in a delightful illustrated edition. Also working in the nineteenth century, Walter Crane made a charming *Baby's Own Alphabet*, and Kate Greenaway turned *A Apple Pie* into a thing of beauty.

Modern artists have also been intrigued by the austerity of a single letter and the possibilities of making it dramatic. Wanda Gág's *ABC Bunny* has a rhyming text with continuity unusual in such miscellanies. The dark woodcuts are relieved by large scarlet capital letters which suggest the small child's ABC blocks. The pictures (1, p. 76) and story make it a favorite.

Garth Williams's *Big Golden Animal ABC*, which is also available in a small edition, makes use of amusing contrast: for each letter Williams has provided a large realistic animal in full color and, on the same page, its unrealistic comic foil. The letter *A*, for instance, has a menacing Alligator with jaws agape and, near the bottom of the page, a wee rabbit on a bicycle, scuttling madly away.

Fritz Eichenberg's *Ape in a Cape*, "an alphabet of odd animals," is both funny and phonetic. The "Goat in a boat" looks properly wild-eyed (2, p. 76) like the "Fox in a box." Young children like this book, and it inspires older children to make rhymes of their own.

Roger Duvoisin's *A for the Ark*, shows Noah calling the animals alphabetically. The ducks dawdle because they like the rain. Some bears come with the *B*'s, others with *U* for ursus. On they come, comical or impressive, but all decorative in the artist's most colorful style.

Phyllis McGinley's *All Around the Town* is for older children, an alphabet of city sights and sounds in lively verse, with Helen Stone's pictures as attractive as the text. The witty lyrics combine letter sounds with the maximum rhythm and meaning. For example, one verse begins "V is for the Vendor/ A very vocal man."

In contrast to *All Around the Town*, *Bruno Munari's ABC* depends for its charm on his masterful use of color and design to build interesting associations around each letter—"A Fly/ a Flower/ a Feather/ and a Fish" with "more Flies" at the top of the page to go buzzing on through the book (3, p. 76). So arresting are his colors and use of space that the visual impact of each page is powerful.

Brian Wildsmith's ABC is a heady experience with color, an ABC book with the simplest of texts and the most glorious rainbow of subtle tints and hues. "cat CAT" says a fuchsia page with letters in three colors, and opposite, against a muted blue, is a green-eyed black cat. One of the great pleasures of this book is to flip the pages slowly and enjoy the changing colors.

Viewpoints

Until children are well into the school years, their attention is caught by objects or scenes that are strong and simple—big bold strokes, bright clear colors, sharp contrasts, and similar overstatements. They need more clues to what they're seeing, hearing, tasting, or touching than adults do. That is, much more of a building must be visible if they are going to recognize it—understandably, for they haven't seen many buildings and therefore aren't as able as adults to infer a church from a steeple or a service station from a revolving sign seen through some trees. . . . When children do become aware of details, they tend not to perceive them as parts-of-a-whole but as separate entities—smaller "wholes." This behavior was documented by William A. Miller, who tested the perception of third-graders by asking them to describe the pictures in their own school books. In each picture there were twenty to twenty-six constituent items whose perception was important to an understanding of the pictured scene. The children identified (on the average) fewer than a third of the items.—Muriel Beadle, *A Child's Mind; How Children Learn During the Critical Years from Birth to Age Five* (Garden City, New York: Doubleday & Company, Inc.), 1970, pp. 151–152.

1.

2.

3.

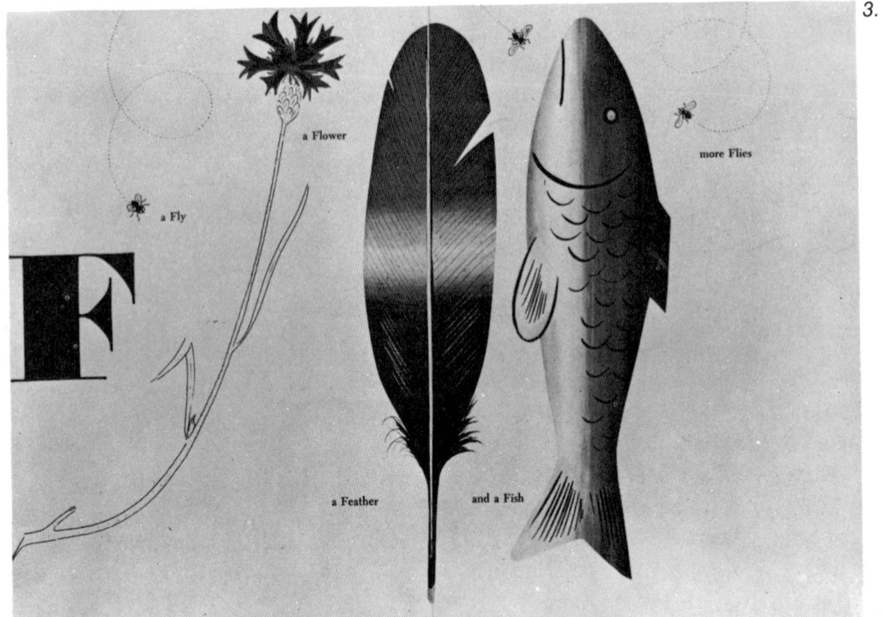

1. *Reprinted by permission of Coward-McCann, Inc. from* The ABC Bunny *by Wanda Gág. Copyright 1933 by Wanda Gág. Copyright renewed 1961 by Robert Janssen.*

2. *From* Ape in a Cape. *Copyright 1952 by Fritz Eichenberg. Reproduced by permission of Harcourt Brace Jovanovich, Inc. (Original in color)*

3. *From* Bruno Munari's ABC. *Copyright 1960 by Bruno Munari. Reproduced by permission of the publishers, The World Publishing Company. (Original in color)*

4.

Z
When zebra wears
His stripes at night
The only ones
You see are white

5.

4. *Copyright © 1965 by Artemis Verlag, Zurich, Switzerland. First U.S.A. edition 1966 by Atheneum. From* Celestino Piatti's Animal ABC. *Used by permission of Atheneum Publishers. (Original in color)*

5. *From* John Burningham's ABC, *copyright © 1964, by John Burningham, reproduced by permission of the Bobbs-Merrill Company, Inc., and Jonathan Cape Ltd., London. (Original in color)*

6.

7.

8.

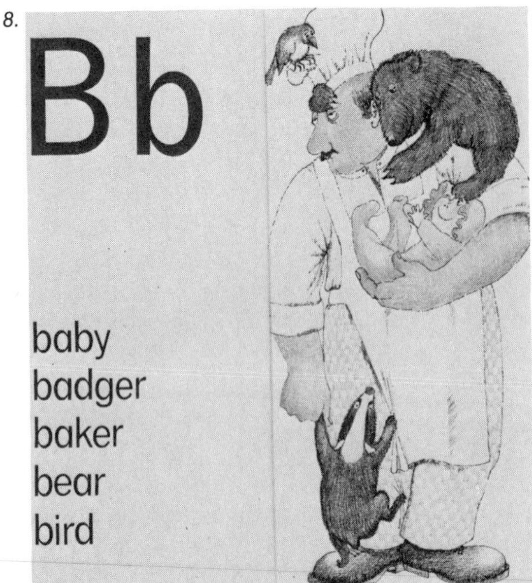

6. *From* Still Another Alphabet Book *by Seymour Chwast and Martin Stephen Moskof. Copyright © 1969. Used with permission of McGraw-Hill Book Company. (Original in color)*

7. *From* The Alphabeast Book: An Abcedarium *by Dorothy Schmiderer. Copyright © 1971 by Dorothy Schmiderer. Reproduced by permission of Holt, Rinehart and Winston, Inc. (Original in color)*

8. *Illustrations from* Helen Oxenbury's ABC of Things. *Copyright © 1972 by Helen Oxenbury. Reprinted by permission of Franklin Watts, Inc., and William Heinemann Ltd., Publishers. (Original in color)*

John Burningham's ABC has upper- and lower-case letters and illustrative words on the left-hand pages, facing stunning pictures in bold compositions (5, p. 77). The delicate details of Peter Parnall's drawings in *Apricot ABC* by Miska Miles illustrate a rhyming text that tells a story; unfortunately, on some pages the letters are partially concealed by pictorial details. *Celestino Piatti's Animal ABC* is also in rhyme, the illustrations vigorous, richly colored, and poster simple (4, p. 77). Thomas Matthiesen's *ABC* concentrates on familiar objects. Unusually good, simple color photographs face pages that have, in addition to the upper- and lower-case letters and the illustrative words, a few lines of text about the objects—"Shoes keep your feet safe when you walk. They have strings called laces, which often become untied."

Two books are especially useful for environmental awareness. Francine Grossbart's *A Big City* has words which all start with oversize capital letters: Antennas, Buildings, Cars, Doors, Elephant in a zoo, etc., on colored pages with ample blank space. Michael Deasy's *City ABC's* has photographs of urban scenes; there's variety in ethnic representation, but key words are familiar rather than urban-oriented: "gate" and "umbrella" as well as "escalator" and "manhole." In Marguerite Walters's *City-Country ABC*, half the book has a city setting; turned upside down, the other half has a country setting. The emphasis is alliterative: ". . . and W was everywhere—in the woods, in the whistling wind. There was even a woodpecker."

Among the newer books, one of the most outstanding graphically is Dorothy Schmiderer's *The Alphabeast Book*, in which each letter, framed, is reshaped in two other frames to end, in a fourth frame, as an object (7, p. 78). This is useful for visual conceptualizing as well as for learning the alphabet. *Still Another Alphabet Book* by Seymour Chwast and Martin Stephen Moskof is an unusual book, too, the pictures varied and inventive, and the entire alphabet used as a frieze on each page. Within the frieze, the letters used in the word for the pictured object are printed in a different color; for example, on the *Q* page a queenly figure is pictured and within the frieze of the alphabet the letters in "queen" are a different color from the other letters in the alphabet, a technique that intrigues children as a game and fosters reading readiness. (See 6, p. 78.)

In *Helen Oxenbury's ABC of Things* the pictures are imaginative and humorous, with letters in bold type and identifying captions on one page for the vigorous drawings on the facing page (8, p. 78). There are two letters combined on each double-page spread of *All Butterflies; An ABC* ("All Butterflies," "Cat Dance," etc.) which Marcia Brown has illustrated with woodcuts in subdued colors.

Some of the more sophisticated among the recent ABC books are Leonard Baskin's *Hosie's Alphabet*, which uses difficult words ("Omnivorous swarming locust") and stunning illustrations executed in a variety of techniques; Mitsumasa Anno's *Anno's Alphabet*, with letters shown as pieces of roughly grained wood and with intriguing objects surrounded by a delicate frame that differs on every page; and Muriel Feelings's *Jambo Means Hello*, a Swahili alphabet book illustrated by Tom Feelings with pictures in soft black and white, which gives a vivid impression of East African life as well as words and word definitions for each letter in the Swahili alphabet.

There are many other ABC books and undoubtedly more to come, but these major examples illustrate some of the various types. Since alphabet books provide graphic experience, are used for identifying objects, and often include information and concepts as well as the letters *A–Z*, a primary requisite in choosing them is clarity. Objects should be easily identifiable, and illustrations, whether drawings or photographs, should be consistent with the theme of the book if a specific theme *(A Big City)* is presented. The typeface should be clean rather than ornamented to the point of making the letter of the alphabet difficult to identify. The use of an uncommon word as the key word is inadvisable in alphabet books intended for young children; it may pique the curiosity of some but is liable to frustrate many children who cannot name the object. The illustration should match the key word, and the word itself should use the starting letter in its most commonly pronounced way: it would be unwise, for example, to use the word "children" to illustrate the letter *C*. Words, concepts, and facts are important, but children do need to know the letters of the alphabet.

Counting Books

Like alphabet books, counting books range from those that present numbers, usually numerals from one to ten, in the simplest way, to books that have continuity, tell a story, or are used by an artist as a base for elaborately imaginative shapes or situations. The same sort of clarity needed in ABC books is important in counting books: clear depiction of numerals, close relation of text to pictures, and easily identifiable objects if the objects are intended to be counted. A page crowded with vaguely drawn insects, among which are some intended to represent flies but not easily distinguishable from gnats, will only confuse the child if the text says "7—seven flies." It must be clear *what* is being counted. For very young children just beginning to familiarize themselves with the shapes of numerals and their relation to counting—often learned first by fingers—the best books are those that have plenty of open space to set off numerals and objects, those in which the numerals are large and clear.

One of the best of such books is Robert Allen's *Numbers; A First Counting Book*, which uses color photographs of familiar objects and also introduces subtly the idea that size and location do not affect components of a numerical unit. After presenting numbers one through ten with facing pictures, the text goes on to show pictures in which there are two groups: apples in a circle, and the same number in a straight line, or pictures of two groups of tomatoes of variant sizes. Young children often confuse mass and numbers, or size and position, so this serves also as a concept book.

Other books that show only groups of objects are George Mendoza's *The Marcel Marceau Counting Book*, in which the eminent mime uses hats: "1 is a farmer, 2 is a cowboy," and so on, with Marceau wearing a different hat in each picture and the assorted hats accumulating, one by one; Helen Oxenbury's *Numbers of Things*, a tall, narrow book in which the appeal lies chiefly in the deft, humorous illustrations; and Dick Rowan's *Everybody In!* which shows children of various ethnic backgrounds in a series of photographs, each with one more child joining the others in a swimming pool.

Some counting books use rhymes to add interest. Brenda Seymour's *First Counting* has rather sugary pictures, but "1 red engine for my train, 2 new boots for snow and rain," is nicely descriptive and the digits progress from one to twenty. Better illustrated, Fritz Eichenberg's *Dancing in the Moon* also goes from one to twenty, using a brief rhyming text. Both John Langstaff and Ezra Jack Keats have used the familiar counting song, *Over in the Meadow*, as the text for books that can help children learn to count while teaching them something about the animals of a meadow community. Keats's pictures of animals and Feodor Rojankovsky's, in the Langstaff book, are equally appealing in full color. Also in verse, but with more story line, is Emilie McLeod's *One Snail and Me; A Book of Numbers and Animals and a Bathtub*; the gathering of assorted creatures in a huge old tub is an entertaining concept to the young child.

Something similar is *1 One Dancing Drum* by Gail Kredenser, with Stanley Mack's pictures showing a frenetic bandmaster amassing players and instruments in a small, circular bandstand. One dancing drum, two tinkling triangles—they all pile in, but each group is a different color, so it is easy to pick out the nine tootling trombonists, some of whom are perched on top of other musicians. There is a clutter of objects in Russell Hoban's *Ten What?* but as drawn by Sylvie Selig, it's an inspired clutter. The book is also a mystery story, and the baffled detective is surrounded on page 7, where "seven houses were searched," by seven police cars, seven oversize butterflies, seven chairs out on the sidewalk, et cetera.

Donald Smith uses a farm as the setting for *Farm Numbers*, with poster-simple figures in a repeated pattern; the word and numeral for six are shown with six sheep on the page, while on the facing page the same six sheep browse near a farmhouse. In *Jeanne-Marie Counts Her Sheep*, Françoise introduces numbers through the sheep that a small French girl

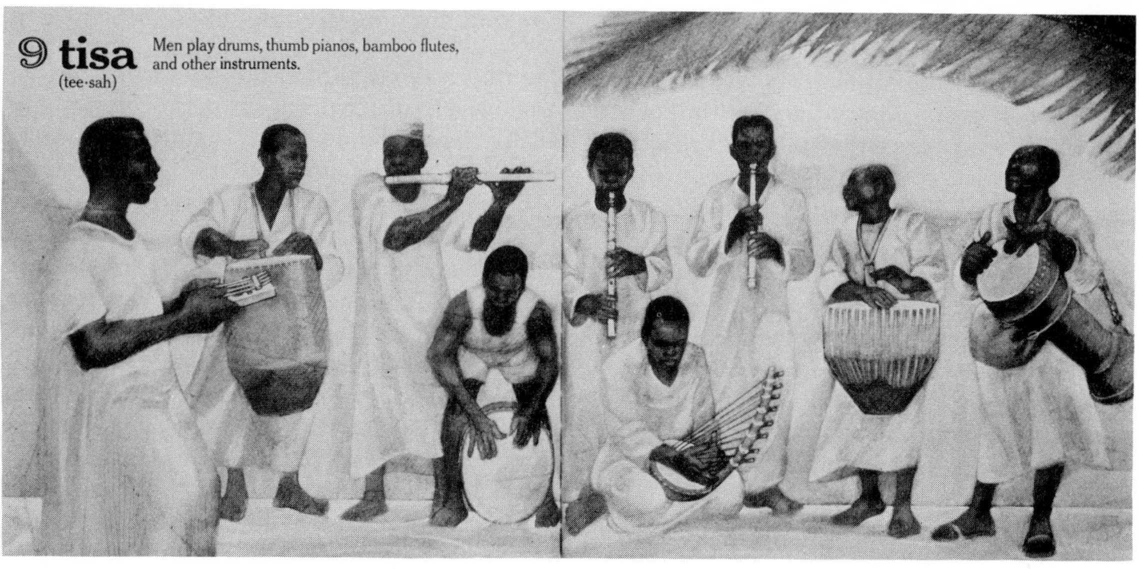

Illustration from Moja Means One: Swahili Counting Book *by Muriel Feelings with illustrations by Tom Feelings. Illustration Copyright © 1971 by Tom Feelings. Used with the permission of THE DIAL PRESS. (Original with color)*

counts in her dreams, and Dahlov Ipcar uses farms as background in both *Brown Cow Farm* and the rather more complicated *Ten Big Farms.*

Muriel Feelings's *Moja Means One* gives numerals from one to ten, the Swahili word for each numeral, phonetic pronunciation, and a sentence in which the names of objects that are to be counted are printed in red. While the geographic references may mean little to young children, the strong, soft pictures by Tom Feelings reinforce the concept of another culture.

Seymour Chwast and Martin Moskof, in *Still Another Number Book*, do not use cumulation except for a reprise at the close, but use one page for 1, two for 2. Two children are pictured: 1+ 1= 2. Five dogs? 1 + 1 + 1 + 1+ 1 = 5. The pictures are silly and gay in contemporary, almost pop, style. Another interesting variant is *The One to Fifty Book* by Anne and Alex Wyse, with pictures by Canadian children. It uses a double-page spread for each number, with a numeral, word, and the name of an object on one page, and the appropriate number of drawings of the object on the facing page. The pictures are often awkward but they have vitality and variety, only occasionally becoming confusing as when the left-hand page states "fourteen crayons" and the right-hand page shows fourteen boxes, each labeled "27 crayons." In Harris Petie's *Billions of Bugs*, the text moves from "1 Praying mantis eating a grub," to "10 Walking sticks hide in a shrub," then by tens to 100 and by hundreds to 1,000. It is not a first counting book, but an interesting expansion to use with the child who has become comfortable with numbers.

Both Ann Kirn's *Nine in a Line* and Benjamin Elkin's *Six Foolish Fishermen* are adapted from folk tales in which counting—or miscounting—is used as a humorous device; the latter especially can afford children the pleasure of seeing characters who are making an obvious mistake. Adults who are evaluating picture counting books should be wary of such pitfalls as the illustration that is out of pattern. In *The Sesame Street Book of Numbers*, for example, four objects follow the numeral 4, five follow 5, and so on—but the picture for 8 shows not eight objects, but an octopus with eight tentacles. This requires a visual sophistication that most young children have not yet achieved, although watchers of the television program on which the book is based may have no problem with it. In the same book, some of the numerals are so over-illustrated as to be difficult to read. Eve Merriam's *Project 1-2-3* is set in a large housing project, an interesting background but one that overshadows the counting function of the book, since the author gives a surfeit of information. For 7, for example, there are many signs on a basement wall: "Check faucets in building 7," "Check 7 incinerator hoppers," and others, and the text reads, "The maintenance men are busy fixing leaks and locks and lots of what gets broken. How many leaking faucets? Drip, drip, drip, drip, drip, drip, drip."

Two final counting books are delightful because of the beauty of the illustrations. Brian Wildsmith's *1, 2, 3's* has imperfections; when an arrow points to a geometric figure and the text asks "How many?" it isn't clear whether the question means green shapes or triangles. But the composition is handsome abstract art, and the colors are vividly beautiful. John Reiss, in *Numbers*, also uses rich, bright colors but the objects pictured are more familiar ones, the numerals are almost four inches high, colored backgrounds add variety to the pages, and the numbers—after moving from the traditional one to ten—go on, by tens, to 100. The final page shows a shower of a thousand raindrops falling on an umbrella held by a beaming child.

Viewpoints

The earliest years of life are most critical in terms of educational development. Though the debate concerning the source of intelligence, whether it is hereditary or environmental, goes on, there is a great deal of evidence indicating that environmental mediation or the structuring of the environment of young children in stimulating ways substantially increases their intelligence quotients. Much evidence points out that half of a child's intelligence is developed by age four and approximately two-thirds by age six. Consequently, the experiences a child has before entering kindergarten determine at least half of his or her chances for success in school. This means that parents are the child's first teachers and, along with preschool teachers, the most vital.—Arnold and Wanda Willems, "Please, Read Me a Book!" from *Language Arts*, September 1975, p. 831.

Concept Books

In the early years of childhood, when the development of language skills is of paramount importance and when the young child's curiosity creates an interest in all the relationships and categories of a complex world, one of the more difficult areas to master is that of the abstract concept. How big is "big"? How far is "far"? Time, distance, size, mass, color, shape, and the difference between "between" and "through" need to be clarified and amplified in books as well as in conversation. Some concepts have to do with physical matter and can easily be depicted visually; some concepts—time, for example—can be described in words but cannot be shown by illustrations. Concepts like the nature of love or death are abstractions and are more difficult for young children to grasp; they cannot be drawn and they are not easy to explain. Through repeated experiences, explanations, and questions young children can be helped to grasp elusive concepts of their environment.

Small children are often fascinated by their own size and growth. In *The Growing Story* Ruth Krauss explores a child's interest in his own growth, comparing that slow process with the more observable growth of plants and animals. When fall comes and the winter clothes that had been put away for him prove to be too small, the boy triumphantly discovers that he, too, is growing, though he sees no change when he looks in the mirror. Concept books explore differences and similarities in people. Ann McGovern's *Black Is Beautiful* praises the night-black sky, the rich earth, a black butterfly, and black faces; in C. Howard's *Mom and Me* a child can learn that each creature follows the pattern of its kind; in Barbara Brenner's *Faces* the photographs show not only how features vary but how they are alike in the ways they are used, incidentally presenting concepts about the senses. Several concepts are combined in Helen Borten's *Do You Know What I Know?* It explores the senses, presents environmental concepts, and also touches on colors, size differences, and personal preferences, all illustrated with a dazzling variety of styles and techniques.

Many concept books have no story line but

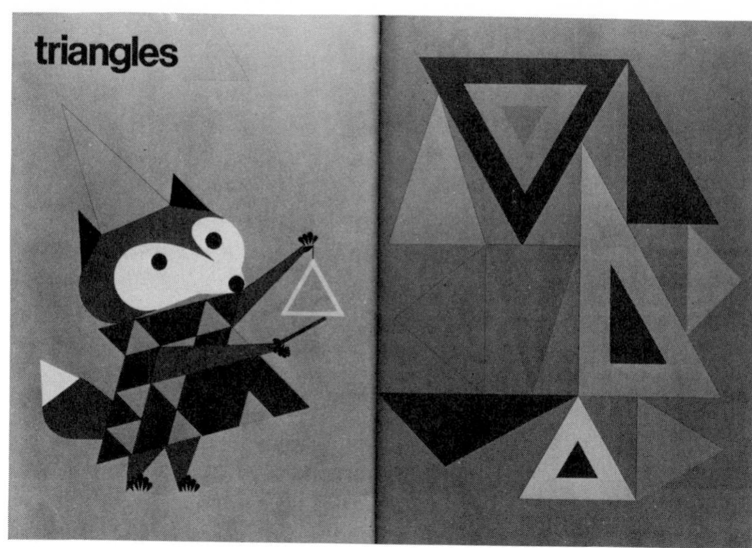

Illustration from Shapes *by John Reiss. Reproduced by permission of Bradbury Press, Inc. (Original in color)*

depend upon accurate description, repetition, and comparison to convey ideas. Books about shapes usually deal with several shapes, as do Miriam Schlein's *Shapes* and John Reiss's *Shapes*. The latter, illustrated in brilliant and effective color, goes past the familiar circle, square, and triangle to include solid forms (showing how squares form a cube) and to more complex ones like oval and rectangle. Examples of each shape are given; for oval, they are musical notes, plums, eggs, and spoons. *The Sesame Street Book of Shapes* combines drawings and photographs, so that some pages have clear presentation while in others children must find shapes within photographs, like the window panes and the patterns made by bars of a jungle gym. Tana Hoban uses photographs also in *Shapes and Things* but these are much simpler—silhouettes in white against a black page. The objects are grouped so that children can also perceive the concept of sets: kitchen utensils, tools, objects used at a desk, objects used in sewing. This book has the appeal of a simple game of identification and can be used with very young children. So can Eric Carle's *My Very First Book of Shapes*, with its heavy pages cut in two; the child matches shapes like a half-watermelon, a rectangular kite, an eye, or a worm with the solid black shapes on the second set of pages. Spiral binding makes it easy to flip back and forth.

Reiss also has created one of the best of the books on color, with a repetition of examples and—something lacking in some books on the subject—various shades of a color. A frog is in several shades of green, a pale green snake coils through the darker grass, and leaf shapes in a variety of forms are in several shades. While there is no focus on the concept of size, the book also makes it clear that all red strawberries are not the same size, that there are big and small robins with orange breasts. An unusual book on color is *The Adventures of the Three Colors* by Annette Tison and Talus Taylor, which uses transparent overlays to introduce the concept that colors can be mixed to produce another color. A large yellow butterfly on the transparent page, when put over the page with a hot-pink pig produces not just orange but, because of the placement of illustrative detail, an orange snail. The narrative framework about a boy experimenting with color mixture wavers occasionally into irrelevancy, but the book is nonetheless unique in what it achieves.

There are, of course, many books that are not written for the purpose of defining concepts that nevertheless do so, and there are also many books that could be placed as well in one group as another. Some of Tana Hoban's books, for example, that illustrate concepts by making comparisons could be placed with wordless picture books; like *Shapes and Things*, her *Look Again!* has no text but uses pages in which a cut-out square challenges the viewer to identify the portion of the picture shown and then, on a third page, shows the picture in context. Somewhat similar is *What Is It?* by Joan Loss, in which the magnified details in a full-page picture are followed by a small photograph of the whole object, relating the known object to its unfamiliar aspect.

The most effective use of comparisons is probably in those books that deal with elusive concepts: Hoban's *Push-Pull, Empty-Full,* and *Over, Under, & Through* or Peter Spier's *Fast-Slow, High-Low.* Hoban uses one set of pictures for each set of opposite terms, sharp and well-chosen photographs making the comparison very clear. Spier's book has many small drawings on each double-spread and has to be examined more carefully for differences: a couple in tennis shorts and in evening dress, two elephants touching their long trunks to the snouts of two pigs, a long and a short garden hose, the long and short hands on a clock dial, et cetera.

A lesser number of concept books are written with a narrative framework. Location and direction are emphasized in Betsy Maestro's *Where Is My Friend?* in which an elephant searches by going *through* a gate, peering *under* a rock, or looking *behind* her for the mouse which appears, beaming, *in front* of her nose. In *I Wonder What's Under* by Doris Lund, a boy stalls at bedtime by wondering if a monster is under his bed—then wondering what's under the rug that's under the bed, eventually working his way down to the earth beneath the cellar.

The concept of grouping is used in Rodney Peppe's *Odd One OuT*, the title giving a clue to the fact that there's one unit in each set that doesn't belong. A boy goes to school, window-shops, and visits a farm, a park, and a fair, in each case seeing one thing that doesn't belong: a boat on the farm, a cash register in the park, a monkey in the classroom. This does not have a strong story line, but it entertains while encouraging observation and the concept of appropriate placement.

Although there is little action in Walter Myer's *Where Does the Day Go?* it has other strong values in addition to its exploration of the mystery of night and day. The discussion among a group of children shows some of the misconceptions that can arise. The book explains natural phenomena accurately, and it presents an exemplary father who takes an evening walk with his children and their friends, commenting on the fact that people are as different as night and day, and how wonderful that is.

It is, as all parents know, important for young children to learn that parental departure is not synonymous with parental desertion. There are two books that deal nicely, but each in a different way, with the idea that

"In-Out" and illustrations from Fast-Slow, High-Low, A Book of Opposites *by Peter Spier. Reproduced by permission of Doubleday & Company, Inc. (Original in color)*

Illustration by Lois Axeman from You Go Away *by Dorothy Corey. Reproduced by permission of Albert Whitman & Company, Publishers. (Original in color)*

separation need not be traumatic. Dorothy Corey's *You Go Away* shows a baby playing peekaboo, a father tossing his child and catching him, children playing hide-and-seek, and so on. It ends with parents going off with luggage, and with the comforting "You are going far away. . . . you will come back!" In Robert Welber's *Goodbye, Hello,* a series of small creatures leave their mothers happily: "A puppy goes sniffing down the road. Goodbye, Mother . . . (page turn) Hello, toad," and "A child is watching each little creature. Goodbye, Mother . . . (page turn) Hello, teacher."

While concept books cannot be judged by exactly the same criteria as books that have a story line, it is easy to determine the effectiveness of some. Books about shapes or colors can be evaluated for their pictorial success or failure, while books that deal with emotions must be assessed for the effectiveness of the text, and that involves making a subjective judgment. Concept books can help young children see relationships between objects, or see more than one aspect of an idea, or visualize changes, or become aware of similarities or differences.

Books Without Words

While there has been debate over whether wordless books are effective in preparing children for reading, there is little question that prereaders and readers enjoy them. Such books can predispose a young child to the attitude that books are a source of pleasure, can accustom them to the left-to-right pattern of reading, and can introduce them to the concept of sequential action as pages are turned. It must be kept in mind, when evaluating these books, that they are designed to encourage not reading, but reading readiness.

Some of these books are humorous, many are inventive, and a few—like Mitsumasa Anno's *Topsy-Turvies*—are beautifully illustrated. The best wordless books have pictures so clearly drawn that the child can easily follow the plot of the story, if there is a story line. In *Topsy-Turvies,* there is a series of pictures that play with perspective or position, presenting improbabilities to challenge the young imagination. Some wordless books give information, as does Iela and Enzo Mari's *The Apple and the Moth.* The illustrations in this book follow a moth through its egg, caterpillar, cocoon, and adult stages, beginning with the moth's egg in an apple and ending with the next generation's egg in an apple blossom. The child can supply the words, but the science lesson is clear.

Books with no text that are informational are in the minority, but there are several good ones. One is Erich Fuchs's *Journey to the Moon,* which does have two pages of text about the Apollo 11 mission at the beginning of the book but which really tells the story in dramatic and sophisticated pictures. Edward Koren's *Behind the Wheel* shows what you

Viewpoints

Language can be used as a means of feeding the child with facts which he is expected to memorise, or it can be used as a means of helping the child to clarify and express ideas he had formulated himself. By comparison with original thinking, memorising is an impoverished quality of the mind. In any sphere, learning which requires the child to think for himself is far superior to the type of mini-learning which depends basically on memorising. When the child has sufficient personal experience to which the experience of others can be attached, reading and writing become a major means of imparting and articulating knowledge. In the early stages it is highly important for learning to be a thinking, rather than a mere memorising, process, for the use a person makes of knowledge is the reason for acquiring it. How he uses knowledge depends on the quality of thought he brings to the acquisition of it.—Alice Yardley, *Young Children Thinking* (London: Evans Brothers Limited), 1973, pp. 47–48.

see from the driver's seat in a series of vehicles and machines. Insets show labeled details of the controls, but there's no other text; it's an excellent book for the question and answer approach. *Family* by Ellie Simmons shows a small girl and a very pregnant mother at home; the father arrives, a smiling older woman takes over when the mother leaves for the hospital, and the child happily passes time until her mother comes home with the new baby. The illustrations are a bit sweet, but the story is perfectly clear and the attitude positive.

There are several wordless books that tell a realistic story. In Edward Ardizzone's *The Wrong Side of the Bed* a scowling child has breakfast postponed while he is scrubbed, teases a little sister and is scolded, goes outdoors and can't find anything to do; however, he comes home to a kiss and a cuddle on his mother's lap. *Hide-and-Seek* by Renate Meyer has only the slight story line of a game played by two children; intricate paintings show just glimpses of the boy's blue clothing and the girl's red outfit. In Nonny Hogrogian's *Apples*, people and animals consume the fruit offered by a pushcart vendor who goes off to replenish his supply from a stand of heavily laden apple trees.

Most of the animal stories are fanciful, but three of the better realistic stories of animals are John Hamberger's *The Lazy Dog*, in which a dog energetically chases a ball and then is so exhausted that a child has to rouse him, and *Pssst! Doggie—* and *Kitten for a Day*, both by Ezra Jack Keats. In the first of these, a cat offers, "Pssst! Doggie— Wanna dance?" and a series of pas de deux follows, with the animals imagining themselves in costumes. The closing, "That was some dance!" is followed by a refreshing nap à deux. In the second book, a friendly puppy joins a group of kittens and tries to do whatever they do (he's not very good at meowing), deciding at the end that next time they can all be puppies. There is some text, primarily "Lick, lick, lick," and "Slurp," so this isn't a true wordless book, but it is in the pattern. In *Bobo's Dream* by Martha Alexander, a boy rescues his dog's bone from a larger dog. Napping, the grateful pet dreams of protecting his boy; in the dream he is a large, fierce dog and when he wakes, he is still

From The Wrong Side of the Bed *by Edward Ardizzone. Copyright © 1970 by Edward Ardizzone. Reproduced by permission of Doubleday & Company, Inc. and The Bodley Head, London.*

so confident that he actually does frighten away a large dog. Alexander's pictures differentiate quite clearly between dream and reality.

Of the animal stories in which the creatures behave like animals but within an exaggerated or fanciful framework, the books about a boy and his frog by Mercer Mayer are among the most successful. *Frog Goes to Dinner*, for example, has bubbling humor and plenty of the action children enjoy, as the little stowaway hops out of his boy's pocket at an elegant restaurant and creates havoc. Back home, the boy is scolded and sent to his room; he obeys dejectedly, but once behind a closed door he and the frog laugh uproariously. Mayer also creates a vivid picture of children playing in *The Great Cat Chase*, with the story line crystal clear. Dressed in doll clothes, a cat jumps out of a doll carriage and is pursued by his owner, by her police-costumed friend, and by a tricycle rider. After a series of mishaps, all go home for light refreshments. In Jack Kent's *The Egg Book*, big, bright pictures tell, painlessly, that each kind of creature reproduces animals like itself, as a hen tries hopefully to hatch eggs belonging to other animals. Jose Aruego, in *Look What I Can Do*, gently and indirectly teases children's showoff instincts by having two animals compete in a follow-the-leader orgy; at the end, they are panting with fatigue but rouse themselves to sit on a third animal who says, "Look what I can do."

John Goodall's books use the device of half-pages inserted between each set of full pages, so that the turn of the half-page changes part of each illustration. In *The Ballooning Adventures of Paddy Pork* an adventurous pig rescues a piglet in distress, braves storm and sea monster in his balloon, and returns from his voyage to the plaudits of a porcine crowd. In *Naughty Nancy* the heroine is a mouse, but she is really any mischievous little girl whose pranks disrupt the very formal wedding of an older sister.

An unusual book dealing with fantasy is Lynd Ward's *The Silver Pony*. This is much longer than most wordless books and blends realism and fantasy in a story about a child who enjoys a series of flights on a magical winged horse, is injured and falls, waking to find he is ill. When he recovers, there's something better than his imaginary horse: a new pony.

In Fernando Krahn's *The Self-Made Snowman*, the plot is not wholly believable but the idea of a gigantic snowman and the Christmas setting appeal to young children. Snow falling from a mountain rolls into a ball and the wind pushes the ball along; in its slide it elongates and picks up branches that become a nose and arms; it slides right into the town square and ends up with a wreath on its head and birds perched on its nose. One of the most ingenious wordless books is *Changes, Changes* by Pat Hutchins. Like *Topsy-Turvies*, it plays with transforming shapes, but it also tells a story as two stiff little wooden dolls shift and adapt the varied shapes of building blocks to make a house, transform it into a fire engine and then into other structures, ending with another house. This has the full-circle action children find satisfying, aesthetic appeal, and the clarity of story line that marks the successful wordless book.

Since the interpretation of books without words depends entirely on the pictures, it is of paramount importance that both the immediate action of each picture and the sequence of action in all the pictures be unequivocally clear. The story line should be distinct if there is a narrative, as in the Goodall books, and the development of any informational sequence should be clear, as in Mari's *The Apple and the Moth*. These books encourage children to interpret and embellish a story; they are a good catalyst for discussion of the author's (perhaps one should say illustrator's) intent and for the child's creativity, encouraging the language skills that are so integral a part of reading readiness.

Books for Beginning Readers

Whatever method children have learned to read by, they have specific needs in the first books they read independently. The words must be simple enough for them to understand and the sentences brief enough so that the text does not appear formidable. The print should be large and clear, with adequate space between words and between lines, and with not so much text on a page that the print seems discouragingly heavy to the child.

Many children have learned to read through basal readers which include word repetition as well as the precepts mentioned above. Many of those books lack a sense of narrative, and this is one of the great assets of many of the fiction books published for first- and second-grade children today, or for those who learn to read before entering school. Since action and humor have strong appeal for young children, some of the contemporary books with these qualities are proving to be as popular as they are effective as reading materials for young children, and many of them have enough narrative flow to read aloud well also.

There have been books in the past that were suitable for the beginning reader, such as Du Bose Heyward's *The Country Bunny and the Little Gold Shoes* or even parts of Kate Greenaway's *Under the Window*, but both of these have more text on the page than would be used today, and the print of Greenaway's book is lamentably small. Two excellent books which appeared in the 1950s are Elizabeth Guilfoile's *Nobody Listens to Andrew* and *The Cat in the Hat* by Dr. Seuss. Nobody believes Andrew has anything important to say until he finally announces loudly and firmly that there is a bear in his bed; pandemonium ensues and is followed by a captured bear and a triumphantly vindicated boy. The story has mild humor in the writing style, plenty of action, and a situation most children will find familiar: being ignored. It also fulfills all the physical requisites for a beginning reader's book. Seuss, a genre unto himself, uses rhyme, repetition, and nonsense humor in *The Cat in the Hat*. This fast-moving story uses a series of incidents rather than a smooth story line as the irrepressible cat turns a household into a shambles, zooms about on a machine with mechanical arms, and goes off leaving the scene looking as placid as it was before his entry.

Most of these short books have a continuous text, but some authors have divided their texts into short, separate episodes children can handle easily, giving them also the satisfaction of having "chapters" just as older children do. Notable among this group are the books by Else Minarik and by Arnold Lobel. Minarik's *Little Bear* has four stories about an

Illustration by Maurice Sendak from Little Bear *by Else Holmelund Minarik. Copyright 1957. Reproduced by permission of Harper & Row, Publishers, Inc. and The World's Work, Ltd. (Original with color)*

ingenuous cub who makes himself some birthday soup, takes an imaginary trip to the moon, has a bedtime chat about the world's most fascinating topic (himself), and makes an interesting discovery about clothes. The warmth, tenderness, and humor of the story are echoed in Maurice Sendak's pictures. The illustrations for Lobel's books are his own, deft and direct and carefully placed on the pages so that they present no visual barrier to the print. *Mouse Tales* is a series of bedtime stories told by a father mouse to his young; it is simply written and engaging, but it was with *Frog and Toad Are Friends* that Lobel established himself as master of this form. This book was one of the finalists for the National Book Award, and its sequel a Newbery Honor Book; this despite the fact that awards for distinguished literary contributions seldom come to books for beginning readers. What Lobel achieves in these books, and in *Owl at Home*, is a pervasive feeling of amused affection blended with a wry appreciation of the foibles of the creatures in the stories. The pictures are appealing, but the smoothness of the writing and the establishment of personalities in so limited a space are the strongest aspects of these animal stories.

Humor is a component of a wide variety of stories. There is the tender ruefulness of Lillian Hoban's *Arthur's Honey Bear*, in which a small chimpanzee (who, like many animals in stories for the very young, functions as a child) decides to sell all his toys but finds that one battered bear is hard to part with. And there is the single-incident contretemps of Crosby Bonsall's *Mine's the Best*, which develops the situation of two small, hostile boys who have identical balloons. An earlier Bonsall book, *The Case of the Cat's Meow*, is a mystery story in which a cat disappears and in which readers can appreciate both the humor of the situation (Snitch is convinced his cat is so precious that somebody stole her) and the satisfying outcome (the cat has gone off to have kittens, and each child gets one as soon as the kittens are old enough). Bonsall's stories have more suspense than most, and usually they concern group activity.

An unusual fusion of fantasy and realism is found in Leonard Kessler's *Kick, Pass, and Run*, which also gives a few facts about a football game, which the animals imitate. There are perhaps too many elements in the book for a smooth blend, but there are all too few sports stories for young children. Kessler's book, like many of Bonsall's, shows black and white children in the illustrations. In Joan Lexau's *The Homework Caper* an interracial friendship is also evident in the pictures as two boys hunt frantically for a lost homework paper, eventually discovering that the little sister of one of them had substituted her "homework" for her brother's. The dialogue is direct and brisk, the solution amicable, and the story given warmth by an understanding teacher and by the boys' realization that they had thought, too, at little Susan's age, that their scribbles were valid communications.

Informational books for beginning readers present a challenge to authors, for they entail the arts of writing succinctly and sequentially and of knowing how to abridge material without omitting something of importance. Peggy Parish's *Dinosaur Time* satisfies young children's curiosity on this perennially popular subject by giving the name, its pronunciation, and a few salient facts about eleven kinds of dinosaurs. Except for the dinosaur names, the words are simple; the print is large and the information accurate. *Alligator* by Evelyn Shaw describes a life cycle in narrative form with no anthropomorphism. *Look at Your Eyes* by Paul Showers is a model of lucid simplicity in the description of some basic facts about the human eye. Anne and Harlow Rockwell use a single painting and a line or two of very large print on each page of *The Toolbox*, with a minimal explanation of the purpose of each of the items commonly found in toolboxes. Harlow Rockwell offers a variety of easy projects in *I Did It*, a "how-to" book that incorporates adeptly repeated words. Photographs illustrate Millicent Selsam's *How Puppies Grow*, which follows newly born puppies through stages of development until they are old enough to be played with and become children's pets.

One of the foremost science writers for any age level, Selsam uses a fictional framework in *Tony's Birds*, in which facts about birds are dispersed through a story of a father helping his son learn to become a bird watcher. Other natural science books in narrative form are Nathaniel Benchley's *The Several Tricks of Edgar Dolphin* and Edward Ricciuti's *Donald and the Fish That Walked*. The former injects a playful note by having the dolphin talk to people who don't understand him, and the latter capitalizes on a true event—an invasion in Florida of walking catfish that had escaped from a fish farm.

While some trade books for beginning independent readers use needed repetition in the unimaginative style of the basal readers, most trade books published today have a limited rather than a rigidly controlled vocabulary. Several publishers (Harper & Row, Crowell, Greenwillow, and Random House, for example) have excellent series designed either for early readers or for readers in the primary grades. Harper & Row has a distinguished series of history books, and Crowell an equally impressive series of science books for beginning readers.

Although standards in series are usually maintained and we may expect a certain level of quality from the better series, still each book should be judged on its own merits and evaluated by the criteria that have been discussed in this section.

Picture Story Books

The range of picture story books is enormous, but the criteria by which they can be judged are very much the same for all kinds. Whether the story is as simple as Charlotte Zolotow's *May I Visit?* or as profound psychologically as Maurice Sendak's *Where the Wild Things Are,* a story for young children should be brief, it should contain few concepts and none that are beyond comprehension if they are unfamiliar concepts, it should be written in a direct and simple style, and it should have illustrations that complement and extend the text and are never in conflict with it. These same criteria define the admirable and lasting qualities of *Peter Rabbit,* published over seventy years ago, and of *Millions of Cats,* which appeared nearly fifty years ago, as well as such treasures of the 1970s as *Frog and Toad Are Friends* or Aardema's *Why Mosquitoes Buzz in People's Ears.*

While there were illustrated books for young children early in the history of children's books, the picture book really came into its own only when printing techniques made it possible to publish books illustrated in color at a reasonable price. Illustrators like Crane, Greenaway, and Caldecott became well known, and artists who followed them in the early and mid-twentieth century produced varied and intricately developed illustrations. Many artists from other countries came to the United States, and a flourishing exchange was established in translated editions and in co-publication programs. The work of many major contributors in the first half of this century, as well as the work of today's illustrators, is discussed in Chapter 5, "Artists and Children's Books."

Most of the discussion here focuses on texts rather than on illustrations. It should be clear, however, that almost every artistic technique and medium have been used successfully in picture story books for young children. In some books the pictures serve as elements of mood, as in Uri Shulevitz's *Dawn,* while in stories like Graham Oakley's adventure tales of the church mice and their friend the church cat, or in the urban vignettes by Eleanor Schick, the illustrations are explicit representations of the setting and the action.

The world, for young children, begins at home; they are concerned with small events which to them are of great importance, with the people in their immediate circle, and with what is happening here and now. As they grow older their horizons extend to include neighbors, relatives who are not part of the immediate family, classmates in nursery

Illustration by Eleanor Schick reprinted with permission of Macmillan Publishing Co., Inc. from City in the Summer *by Eleanor Schick. Copyright © 1969 by Eleanor Schick. (Original in color)*

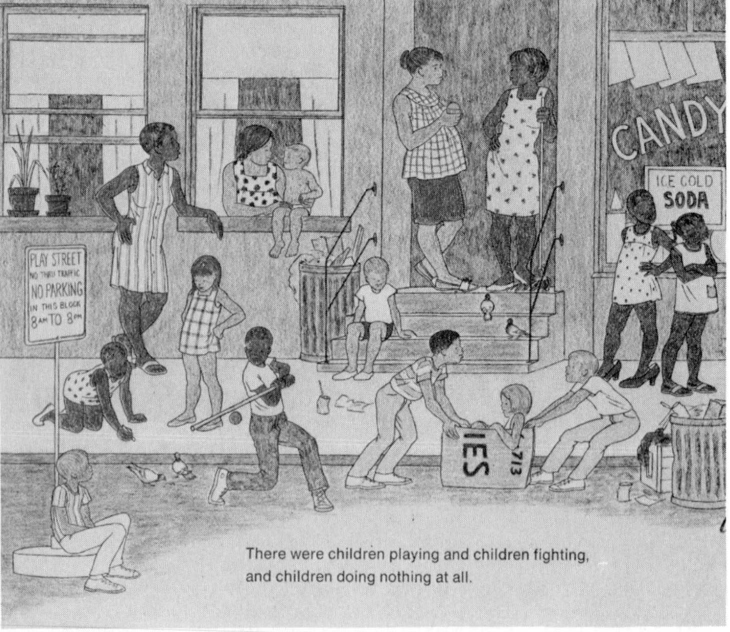

school or kindergarten, and friends. Their understanding of time, space, distance, and of relative sizes grows as they grow. Their books should take such conceptual limitations into account.

There is seldom enough time in a brief picture story book for full character development, although some may be shown by the illustrations. Many books with memorable characters like Curious George or Ferdinand the Bull or the bouncy Nora in Rosemary Wells's *Noisy Nora* achieve firm characterization by emphasis on one trait or behavior pattern. George is curious, Ferdinand likes to sit quietly and smell flowers, Nora is noisy and rambunctious. Some stories focus on a one-to-one relationship, as do Barbara Borack's *Grandpa* and Charlotte Zolotow's *Do You Know What I'll Do?* in which a child expresses her love for a baby brother. Characterization or individual relationships should be depicted without sentimentality; they should be believable and consistent.

The plot may be as simple as learning to tie a shoe, spending a first day at school or a first night away from home, or making the adjustment to the death of a pet, but it should have a structure: problem and solution, achievement of a new skill or a new experience, or the presentation of an event or an attitude that effects a change in a character or characters. There are always some books in which structure is lacking but is compensated for by the strength of some other aspect. An example is the Provensens' *Our Animal Friends at Maple Hill Farm,* in which the range of appealing creatures, lively illustrations, and witty captions carry the text along at a good pace.

Whether a picture story is realistic or fanciful, it will appeal to young children if it has humor or action. Again, some books lack these qualities but introduce a provocative concept or establish a mood so well that they appeal to children nevertheless. Although it is the text we are considering here, it should be kept in mind that in many picture story books, as in picture books, the illustrations may be so striking or so humorous as to outweigh the text and make the whole book appealing to children.

Sometimes the appealing element is the information given by the text, by the pictures, or by both. Children are always and actively curious; they are intrigued when they find that another child's family has a pattern that differs from their own or when they learn from a book what it was like in their parents' time, which to them is in a misty past. They are at the same time reassured by similarities in pattern, and they need to identify with others as their circle enlarges, just as they need that first sense of identification with the family group. Children who live in the country find the urban setting of Eleanor Schick's *Neighborhood Knight* fascinating, just as city children are interested in the details of farm life; each group receives a different kind of pleasure from books that have settings familiar to them. Black children need to see themselves in books, as do members of other ethnic groups, and each group needs to see the others as a part of our society. They must feel both accepted and accepting. Erik Erikson points out that as the child's ego develops, a major fact of psychosocial growth is the child's persistent need to identify with others, eventually achieving a sense of personal identity built on a firm base of trust and understanding.[5]

This curiosity about people can be satisfied in part by books, as can children's curiosity about themselves, animals, weather, and other aspects of their lives. How does a mother know what to do when the toaster won't work? What is a cousin? What does "dead" mean? Why won't squirrels come to be petted as puppies do? How does a dump truck work? Why doesn't the boy next door go to the same church or temple? What is that funny thing hanging around the doctor's neck? Children's questions are endless, their need to know insatiable. They have so much to learn in the early years, and they learn so quickly, that we cannot give them too many books.

Family Life

Young children take pleasure in seeing the familiar relationships of home reflected in their books, whether the characters are human or animals. Children may recognize them-

[5]Erik Erikson, *Childhood and Society* (Norton, rev. ed. 1964).

Illustration from Noisy Nora *by Rosemary Wells. Copyright © 1973 by Rosemary Wells. Used with the permission of THE DIAL PRESS. (Original with color)*

selves and their families whether a story is as quiet and realistic as Ellen Parsons's *Rainy Day Together*, which is imbued with the cozy feeling of a day spent with loving parents, or as bouncy as *Noisy Nora* by Rosemary Wells, in which a mouse child feels ignored (she's a middle child) and gets attention by making a nuisance of herself.

Very young children are most concerned with parents and their roles in respect to that center of the universe, the child. Books like Charlotte Zolotow's *When I Have a Little Girl* and *When I Have a Son* project quite naturally a child's desire to have a world in which all wishes are granted by obliging parents. A new baby in the family disturbs this world, and picture stories about sibling jealousy may help alleviate a child's feelings of guilt. In Ann Scott's *On Mother's Lap*, it is an Eskimo child who learns to share parental love, but Michael's experience is universal; in Eloise Greenfield's *She Come Bringing Me That Little Baby Girl*, Kevin is black, but his feelings of resentment at the attention paid to the new baby are common to all children. John Steptoe explores similar feelings in *Stevie*, a boldly illustrated book in which a young boy is jealous of a child his mother cares for. The tables are turned in Martha Alexander's *I'll Be the Horse If You'll Play with Me*, as Oliver (who had tried to give away baby Bonnie in *Nobody Asked Me If I Wanted a Baby Sister*) imposes on Bonnie, who learns that she, in turn, can now impose on the younger brother of whom she had been jealous.

One of the trends in books for children of all ages has been an increasing interest in grandparents. Tomie de Paola's *Nana Upstairs and Nana Downstairs* shows a small child's love for his great-grandmother and his adjustment to her death, which makes it easier to accept his grandmother's death years later. In Charlotte Zolotow's *My Grandson Lew*, the emphasis is not on the grandfather who has died as much as it is on the loving memories a mother and child share and on the comfort such sharing brings. The range of books about grandparents fortunately includes some that are warm or humorous. Barbara Borack's *Grandpa* shows the special affection between child and grandparent, and *Albert's Toothache* by Barbara Williams does the same thing in an animal story, when Grandmother Turtle is the only one who can understand how toothless Albert can possibly have a toothache. Children need both the books that will help them adjust to the senility or the death of an older person and those books that depict them as a vital part of the extended family.

Everyday Life Experiences

Closely allied to stories of home and family are books that picture children's experiences as they begin to extend their range of activities: sharing tasks and responsibilities in the home, making small forays into the outside world, becoming acquainted with neighbors. The family is still involved, but the child is growing toward independence and establishing identity, gaining self-confidence through achievement, and satisfying curiosity.

These books about everyday experiences generally deal with the fulfillment of children's needs or their acquisition of new skills or attitudes and the treatment of these subjects ranges from light to serious. There is as much to be gained from a realistic story like Robert Welber's *The Train*, in which Elizabeth's family helps her overcome her fear of crossing a meadow alone, as there is from Lillian Hoban's *Arthur's Honey Bear*. When Arthur sells his old toys, he has to adjust to the fact that he really still wants the toy bear his little sister buys; this story not only shows a child's logic and a growing ability to compromise, but suggests the way in which even young children can look back and see their own growth.

Small tasks loom large to young children, who take great pride in having their contributions recognized and who often look with envy on older brothers and sisters who go on errands. In Genevieve Gray's *Send Wendell*, the older children evade chores but Wendell—who is six—trots along with good humor when he is sent instead. He earns special recognition, thereby gaining the reward of being considered responsible. The small boy in Lorenz Graham's *Song of the Boat* who finds just the right tree for his father to use in making a canoe takes pride in his father's pleasure and in the fact that he was able to keep up with his father on the long hunt for the perfect tree. The treatment of a child's first night away from home is humorous in Bernard Waber's *Ira Sleeps Over*, but it touches on the child's very real need to have familiar objects about him, as well as on the importance of so sophisticated an event.

Stories about play are important, for children learn by playing. For them it is an important task. In *Morris's Disappearing Bag* by Rosemary Wells, there is a fanciful element, but it doesn't lessen the impact of what Morris and his brothers and sisters learn about sharing gifts. There are rhyme and rhythm in the text of William Cole's *What's Good for a Three-Year-Old?* in which a group of romping children at a birthday party discovers that each of them has a slightly different idea of what is most enjoyable. One of life's harsh lessons is learned in Russell Hoban's *A Bargain for Frances*, as the small badger strikes a disappointing bargain with her friend Thelma. There is no lesson in Petronella Breinburg's *Doctor Shawn*, only a modest, realistic picture of a group of children in imaginative play, as they take roles in the game of "playing hospital." No sex stereotypes here: Shawn and his sister take turns being nurse and doctor. Traditional sex roles are challenged in Charlotte Zolotow's *William's Doll*, in which a small boy is teased because he wants a doll; only his grandmother understands that a boy may want a doll so that he can play at being a father in just the same way that girls pretend to be mothers, that both are preparing for a future task.

Illustration by Lillian Hoban from Best Friends for Frances *by Russell Hoban. Copyright 1969. Reproduced by permission of Harper & Row, Publishers, Inc. and Faber & Faber, Ltd., London. (Original in color)*

School Stories

As more and more children participate in programs at kindergartens, nursery schools, day-care centers, or less formal group programs, the need for books that will prepare them for such experiences becomes clear. One of the simplest presentations is Harlow Rockwell's *My Nursery School*, which has little plot but shows a child taken to school by her father, having a happy morning, and being called for by her mother. The book describes playground and classroom equipment and also gently insinuates the ideas of sharing toys and working together on projects. *Did You Carry the Flag Today, Charley?* which is discussed at length in Chapter 2, gives a memorable picture of a free spirit adjusting to the strictures of the classroom. For preschool children whose older brothers and sisters seek attention by decrying school, Miriam Cohen's *Will I Have a Friend?* is a pleasant antidote. Escorted to the first day of kindergarten, a child feels bereft and lonely until the period of leg-waving antics called "rest time" when he meets a kindred spirit.

Carol Barkin and Elizabeth James, in *Sometimes I Hate School*, have faced the problem of the child who's unhappy; this is one of a series of books designed to help the young child bridge the gap between home and school environments. In this case it is a substitute for a favorite teacher who causes the hostility, but when Mr. Coleman teaches the class to make cranberry sauce, he is accepted and the child who tells the story decides he doesn't hate school after all. In a first-day-of-school story set in England, Petronella Breinburg's *Shawn Goes to School*, the combination of a smiling teacher, a real donkey to ride, and mother and big sister pointing out the charms of swings and toys, changes Shawn's sobs to a "teeny weeny smile."

Friends

Almost every aspect of friendship is explored in the many picture story books about the ups and downs of relationships: learning to share, planning projects, being jealous, having a quarrel, exchanging confidences, and, above all, having fun. One such book, Arnold Lobel's *Frog and Toad Are Friends*, has become a minor classic, with the sequel, *Frog and Toad Together*, not far behind. The stories are short and simple enough for a beginning reader but flow smoothly for reading aloud, and they have a humorous, ingenuous style.

Charlotte Zolotow's writing is notable for the combination of a loving and perceptive eye and a direct, quiet style. In *The Unfriendly Book* she describes the problem of coping with a friend who carps and criticizes other people; the William Pène du Bois illustrations show each friend first as Bertha (the carper) sees them and then as Judy sees them, a valuable lesson in differing viewpoints. *The Hating Book* explores a breakdown in friendship; when there is a confrontation, there proves to have been a mistake in communications and rapport is reestablished. Zolotow

Illustration by Arnold Lobel from Frog and Toad Are Friends *by Arnold Lobel. Copyright 1970. Reproduced by permission of Harper & Row, Publishers, Inc. and The World's Work, Ltd. (Original in color)*

isn't preaching, but two gentle lessons come through: it's better to talk it over than to sulk, and it's wise not to believe the gossip you hear.

The anguish of quarreling is handled with a light touch in Marjorie Sharmat's *I'm Not Oscar's Friend Anymore,* in which a small, brooding boy imagines Oscar moping and desolate. It is in fact the boy himself who is downcast, and when he relents and telephones Oscar, he finds that his friend doesn't even remember the fight they had. There's no cautionary note, but the message is the more effective for its ruefully comic air. The same sort of aura imbues Sharmat's *Gladys Told Me to Meet Her Here,* one of the few books about a boy-girl friendship, which describes the mixed feelings of retribution and loyalty Irving goes through as he waits for Gladys to show up at the zoo. Rosemary Wells, in *Benjamin and Tulip,* also writes of a boy and a girl, although they are animals; Benjamin's aunt tells him to go on an errand without bothering sweet little Tulip, quite unaware that sweet little Tulip beats Benjamin up every time she can. No lesson here, but it is a change to have an aggressive female, and the story and pictures are hilarious.

Viewpoints

Lillian Smith, in her book* about children's literature, designates the years of childhood as "the unreluctant years," and nowhere is this trait, this quick responsiveness, more noticeable than in the picture-book audience. The young child freely gives to writers and artists the benefit of his unprejudiced mind. Yet specific qualities in the book determine whether his reaction will be strong or weak, positive or negative. Notwithstanding initial "unreluctance," an inept or insipid book creates boredom in a child as surely as it does in anyone else and may instill suspicion about the value of books in general. On the other hand, a marked devotion occurs when strong literary or graphic elements are present, when there are illustrations, incidents, characters, or modes of expression which prove intriguing. Then the child quickly involves himself in the drama of the action, identifies with the hero, immerses himself in the setting, mimics comic characters, chants rhythmic words and phrases, and examines illustrations with an amazing awareness of mood and detail.—Donnarae MacCann and Olga Richard, *The Child's First Books; A Critical Study of Pictures and Texts,* The H. W. Wilson Company, New York, 1973, p. 8.

*Lillian Smith. *The Unreluctant Years.* (Chicago: American Library Association), 1953.

Humor

While many stories about friendship or families or school are humorous, there are some books in which humor is the most important element. Many of these are fantasies, but some realistic picture stories use exaggeration or nonsense for primary appeal. One such is Winifred Rosen's *Ralph Proves the Pudding.* Approached by a man who says he has just the right face for a television commercial, Ralph is engaged to sample and savor chocolate pudding. He doesn't like it, but enjoys the ice cream the producer provides later. Dismayed by the fact that the finished commercial shows Ralph saying "Wow!" to the pudding, when he'd really been responding to the ice cream, Ralph (and the reader) learns something about the honesty of advertising.

In Norma Farber's *Where's Gomer?* the humorous appeal is in the florid exaggeration of the rhyming text, as the crew of Noah's Ark bewails the boy who is missing at departure time. "O tempest and flood! O watery ways," his mother wails as she weeps into the stew she's cooking. In *Hamilton Duck's Springtime Story* by Arthur Getz, the humor lies in the obtuseness of the duck who thinks he's in a spring snowstorm, while the pictures show clearly that the "snow" is apple blossoms; it's a good springtime story as well as a funny one.

Tall-tale humor is the appeal in the cheerful story of *The Lady Who Saw the Good Side of Everything* by Pat Tapio. Her house washes away in a rainstorm? She needed a new house anyway. She drifts to sea on a log? She'd always wanted to see the ocean. The cartoon-strip format of *Father Christmas* by Raymond Briggs has details of the kind young children like to point out, as a grumbling Santa fills his pack, loads the sleigh, and catches cold while on his rounds. It is the combination of a realistic situation and one fanciful element that makes Margaret Mahy's *The Boy*

From Farmer Palmer's Wagon Ride, *by William Steig. Copyright © 1974 by William Steig. (Original in color)*

Who Was Followed Home diverting, although the illustrative details are often high comedy as well. Robert is pleased when a hippopotamus follows him home but his problems—and hippopotamuses—multiply until only a witch can solve the problem. In *The Backward Day* by Ruth Krauss, there's a robust, nonsensical humor in the child who puts on his clothes in reverse and comes to breakfast in the morning walking backward and wishing his parents a good night.

Bernard Waber's *I Was All Thumbs* has the double appeal of a situation in which the protagonist makes a series of errors and in which the dialogue plays with words. Children enjoy inventing disasters, and they find it more amusing than adults do if an octopus squirts ink in the wrong direction, as does Legs, the octopus-hero of this story. The title is an indication of the word-play humor, and Legs is given to remarks like, "Why complain, I thought. Why make waves," or ". . . a very fast crowd," when he tries to keep up with a school of fish. There's more slapstick in *Farmer Palmer's Wagon Ride* than is found in most of William Steig's books, but that's anything but a deterrent to children's enjoyment of this story, in which a series of minor calamities (always good for a laugh) befalls Farmer Palmer, a pig, as he makes his star-crossed way home from market.

Animals

Almost all children are interested in animal stories, whether they are creatures that behave like human beings, animals that behave like animals but can talk, or animals that behave like animals whether there are people in the story or not. Most picture stories featuring animals fall in the first category and some of them (Hoban's Frances, Lobel's Frog and Toad) have already been discussed in this chapter.

Because such stories parody the lives of human beings, it is in their perceptiveness about human foibles and emotions that their importance and appeal lie. It is not that Owl, in Arnold Lobel's *Owl at Home*, acts silly for an owl but that he acts like a silly human being as he tries frantically to be in two places at once, that children laugh at him. Nor is it because Jenny, in Esther Averill's *Jenny and the Cat Club*, is such a charming feline that she's endearing, but because she and the other cats engage in all of the often pompous procedures of formal meetings in human style. Hans Rey's Curious George and Rosemary Wells's Tulip behave as young children see themselves behave.

Arthur, in Graham Oakley's *The Church Mouse*, behaves like a mouse some of the time, like a human other times, and the story is that much funnier by contrast when Arthur practices his crawl stroke in the baptismal font. In sequels like *The Church Mice and the Moon* there is more sophistication as the author pokes fun at people; here he lampoons the scientists who are grooming two mice for a space flight. Marjorie Sharmat takes a few digs at ambitious people in *Walter the Wolf*, in which an almost-perfect little wolf who writes poetry, practices violin without being reminded, and never bites, decides that he really doesn't have to be perfect. Robert Kraus does likewise in *Owliver*, in which it is the parents of an owlet who dream of a great career for their son—Mother gives Owliver lessons in acting and tap-dancing, Father gives him doctor kits. Owliver tries everything but ends up making an independent decision. The *Little Bear* stories by Else Minarik are for independent readers, but they should also be read aloud to younger children, for they reflect all the familial relations, friendships, and imaginative play of childhood.

Stories in which animals behave as animals except that they talk are usually rather placid, since they offer less opportunity for diversity of behavior or for humor, but they are eminently suitable for the very youngest children. In Mirra Ginsburg's *The Chick and the Duckling*, for example, a newly hatched chick valiantly tries to do everything done by a duckling who was hatched a moment before him. It's a slight tale, but the two baby creatures are on the go every minute, and the painless lesson about species behavior is cheerfully presented. The idea that one is never too old to learn is clear in Leo Lionni's *In the Rabbitgarden*, where two little rabbits disobey an injunction not to eat apples *or else* (or else the fox will get them). Children may take more satisfaction than adult readers-aloud in the inference that adults aren't invariably right. *Swim, Little Duck* by Miska Miles describes an open-minded duckling's acceptance of her friends' offers to show her the best place in the world, and so learns that the pigpen and the meadow are not as nice as the pond, not for ducklings. And in Munro Leaf's *The Story of Ferdinand*, a little bull behaves almost entirely like a real bull except for the fact that he prefers to sit under a cork tree and smell flowers, not to fight. Bee-stung, he rampages about, is thought fierce, and is taken to the bull ring. Part of the humor is in the illustrations, which show the matador weeping with frustration, and part in the writing, which uses understatement and refrain ("But not Ferdinand") to achieve its effect of placidity.

Stories in which animals are seen always behaving strictly like themselves almost always have some human characters too, as a foil for the animals or as a viewpoint from which the animals are seen. *Our Animal Friends at Maple Hill Farm* by Alice and Martin Provensen has little story line but has too much text to be called a picture book, since the long and very funny captions do tell stories about the highly distinctive creatures of house and barn: the greedy, grouchy geese; a coquettish hen; or a languid Siamese who, in contrast to the other cats, is beautiful but not interesting. An old favorite is Lynd Ward's *The Biggest Bear*, in which a boy's pet cub grows older and bigger until the havoc he creates necessitates his being sent to a zoo.

Marjorie Sharmat's *Morris Brookside, a Dog* is one of the few realistic animal stories in

From The Story of Ferdinand the Bull *by Munro Leaf and Robert Lawson. Copyright 1936 by Robert Lawson (illustrations), renewed © 1964 by John W. Boyd. Reprinted by permission of The Viking Press, Inc.*

Lucky lets children walk
around her and under her.
She lets them
sit on her.
Lucky stands very quietly
when children are near.
Hold your hand flat
when you feed a pony,
or the pony may
pinch your fingers
by mistake.

From Our Animal Friends at Maple Hill Farm, *by Alice & Martin Provensen. Copyright © 1974 by Alice & Martin Provensen. Reprinted by permission of Random House, Inc. (Original in color)*

which there are no children. It is successful because of the bland style and the implicit humor of the situation which is obvious enough for the young child to see—an elderly couple dotes on the stray they've acquired to the point where they keep the dog's picture on the piano along with those of their grandchildren. In Dick Gackenbach's *Do You Love Me?* a small boy who has no playmates (he lives on a farm) accidentally kills the small bird he's found because he fondles it with such eagerness. The story can teach a child to be careful with wild creatures and to handle small ones carefully, and it has a most satisfying ending as the boy discovers that his new puppy enjoys cuddling and play as much as he does.

Adaptations of Folk Tales

In addition to the many contemporary stories that are told with the cadence and in the pattern of folk literature, stories like Wanda Gág's *Millions of Cats,* there are many picture-book versions of authentic folk tales, stories that exemplify the mores or morals of their cultures, that teach a lesson, that explain the natural phenomena of our world. Some are humorous, like Dorothy Van Woerkom's version of a German folk tale, *The Queen Who Couldn't Bake Gingerbread.* The monarch who hunts for a perfect mate is a frequent theme, but here the tables are turned twice; first, Princess Calliope demands a husband who can play a slide trombone, and second, when dreadful burning smells and squawks pervade the castle, it proves to be the king cooking and the new queen practicing the trombone. There's another kind of humor in Janina Domanska's variant of the story of the turtle who falls when he opens his mouth to speak, forgetting that the stick in his beak is carried by birds, in *Look, There Is a Turtle Flying;* here the joke is both a lesson and that familiar favorite of the young child, a disaster.

Why Mosquitoes Buzz in People's Ears, adapted by Verna Aardema from a West African folk tale, is a "why" story, but it also carries a message of justice meted out, and the brilliant illustrations add humor. The abstract and symbolic pictures by Gerald McDermott have been translated from film in *Anansi the Spider,* a creation story from the Ashanti which incorporates a folk-tale device used in other kinds of stories—the pooling of talents by a group of people, each of whom is expert in some way. *Arrow to the Sun* is an adaptation of a Pueblo Indian legend about a boy who brings the spirit of the Lord of the Sun, his father, back to the pueblo after he has been transformed into an arrow.

A favorite tale for storytellers is simply adapted by Cynthia Jameson in *The Clay Pot Boy,* the story of a pot that comes to life and voraciously devours everything in its path. Children enjoy the frenzy of the chase in this story and in Paul Galdone's version of *The*

Gingerbread Boy. Tomie de Paola's retelling of an Italian folk tale, *Strega Nona*, is imbued with robust peasant humor and stresses the poetic justice of the punishment meted out to a witch's greedy apprentice. Having heard the magic formula by which she produces pasta, he uses it in her absence, but he doesn't know how to stop the magic pot, and a river of pasta flows through the streets. The punishment? He must eat it all. A picture book version of a tale by the brothers Grimm is illustrated by Maurice Sendak so that the disdainful princess of *King Grisly-Beard*, being taught humility by her husband, takes on the vitriolic mien of Shakespeare's Katherine in *The Taming of the Shrew*. It *is* a story that espouses a traditional view of woman's role, but that is true of much in folk literature.

Informational Books

Both in fiction and nonfiction, there have been numbers of books published that satisfy young children's need to know. The best of such books deal with subjects that are within the child's experience, books like Harlow Rockwell's *My Doctor* and *My Dentist*, which describe and picture instruments and procedures, or Harriet Sobol's *Jeff's Hospital Book*, a photodocumentary about a child's hospital stay for corrective surgery. The latter, particularly, is reassuring, with a patient staff explaining everything that is going on and a beaming Jeff, after the operation, riding his tricycle and clowning self-consciously before the camera. Alvin Tresselt's *The Dead Tree* gives information about the plants and animals that live in and on a fallen tree until it becomes part of the humus that nurtures the forest. The simple, poetic text is easily comprehended, yet it teaches a valuable lesson in ecology and the life cycle of all living things.

Although written in narrative form, such books as Tomie de Paola's *"Charlie Needs a Cloak"* describe actual procedures of manufacture or craft. The little shepherd in this story shears his sheep, cards and dyes the wool, and spins the cloth for a new red cloak. A book like this is an excellent start for a discussion of where things that we use come from, a subject most children find intriguing.

There are many books about weather, seasons, and other aspects of the environment. The phenomena that are familiar to adults and to older children can amaze, delight, or baffle the very young. The art in writing such books

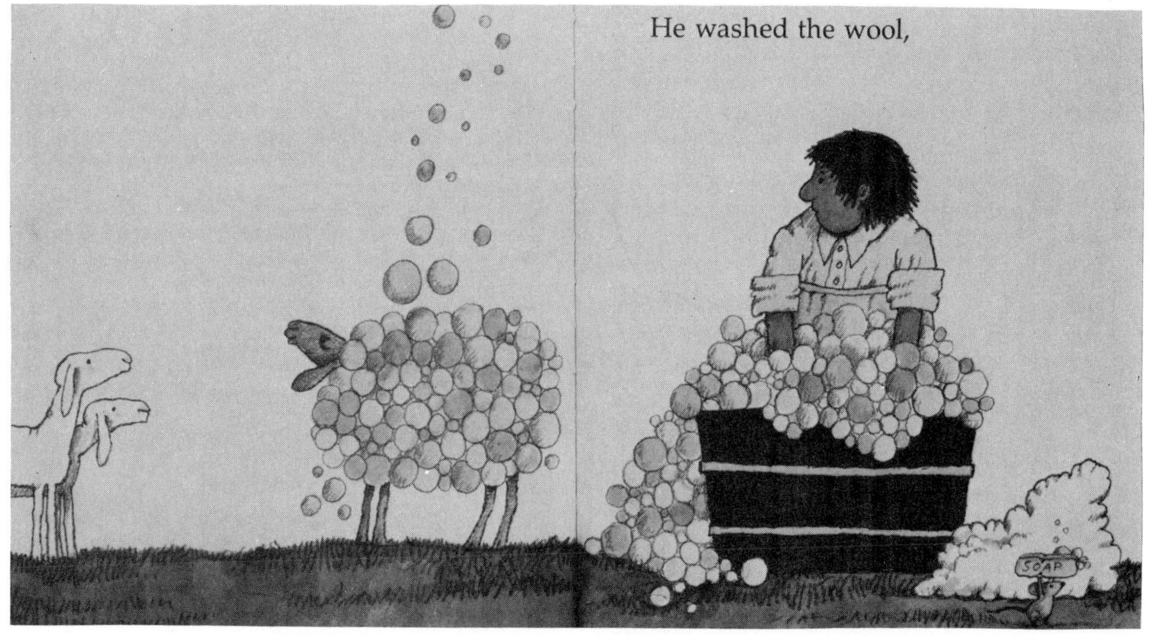

From the book "Charlie Needs A Cloak" *by Tomie de Paola. © 1973 by Tomie de Paola. Published by Prentice-Hall, Inc., Englewood Cliffs, New Jersey. (Original in color)*

involves being accurate, simple, vivid, and knowing what to omit to gain simplicity without sacrificing accuracy. One of the best of the books that present some facet of the natural environment is *Dawn* by Uri Shulevitz. Here the quiet and beautiful pictures, the hushed tone of the text, and the slow, gradual pace of the writing build to a last burst of color as full sunlight fills the scene. *The Snowy Day* by Ezra Jack Keats captures the joy a small child feels when playing in a fresh, full fall of snow. Robert McCloskey's *Time of Wonder* not only portrays vividly the ominous feeling of an approaching hurricane but also the way a family draws together to gain security when danger threatens. In Crescent Dragonwagon's *When Light Turns into Night*, a child goes off to a field at twilight to be alone with the darkening sky and the windblown grass; when she goes home to dinner it is clear that the love and security of the family circle make it possible for her to enjoy the darkening sky, another time of wonder. This is a fine book to read when a child is in a subdued, reflective mood.

These are some of the books for young children. There are many more in the succeeding chapters of this book, stories that are notable as fantasy or realism, poems and folk tales, books of fiction and books of fact that stretch across boundaries of age and sometimes of genre. This chapter is a review of the kinds of books that are appropriate for young children rather than a summary of all that exist. Because many of the picture books in Chapter 5 are also appropriate for this age group, they are listed in the bibliography that follows and are identified by the "5" that precedes them.

Like books for older children, books for the youngest reflect the changes in our society. There are still too few working mothers, although books like Joe Lasker's *Mothers Can Do Anything* and Eve Merriam's *Mommies at Work* show a wide range of working women; still too few active and independent girls; too few protagonists who are members of minority groups; but some change is evident and more will come. It is of the utmost importance that it does come, for the early years are the years in which children learn the most about their world.

Adult References[6]

ALMY, MILLIE, E. CHITTENDEN, and PAULA MILLER. *Young Children's Thinking; Studies of Some Aspects of Piaget's Theory.*

ANDERSON, ROBERT H., and HAROLD G. SHANE, eds. *As the Twig Is Bent; Readings in Early Childhood Education.*

ANDERSON, VERNA. *Reading and Young Children.*

BARCHILON, JACQUES, and HENRY PETTIT. *The Authentic Mother Goose Fairy Tales and Nursery Rhymes.*

BARING-GOULD, WILLIAM, and CEIL BARING-GOULD. *The Annotated Mother Goose.*

BEADLE, MURIEL. *A Child's Mind; How Children Learn During the Critical Years from Birth to Age Five.*

BETT, HENRY. *The Games of Children; Their Origin and History.*

CHUKOVSKY, KORNEI. *From Two to Five.*

CIANCIOLO, PATRICIA, ed. *Picture Books for Children.*

COODY, BETTY. *Using Literature with Young Children.*

DURKIN, DOLORES. *Teaching Young Children to Read.*

ECKENSTEIN, LINA. *Comparative Studies in Nursery Rhymes.*

FORD, ROBERT. *Children's Rhymes, Children's Games, Children's Songs, Children's Stories; A Book for Bairns and Big Folk.*

GESELL, ARNOLD, and others. *The First Five Years of Life; A Guide to the Study of the Preschool Child.*

GREEN, PERCY B. *A History of Nursery Rhymes.*

HALLIWELL-PHILLIPPS, JAMES O. *Popular Rhymes and Nursery Tales; A Sequel to The Nursery Rhymes of England.*

HÜRLIMANN, BETTINA. *Picture-Book World.*

HUTT, S. J., and CORINNE HUTT, eds. *Early Human Development.*

JACOBS, LELAND, ed. *Using Literature with Young Children.*

LATIMER, BETTYE I., ed. *Starting Out Right; Choosing Books about Black People for Young Children.*

MacCANN, DONNARAE, and OLGA RICHARD. *The Child's First Books; A Critical Study of Pictures and Texts.*

MILLAR, SUSANNE. *The Psychology of Play.* Chapter entitled "Phantasy, Feeling, and Make-Believe Play."

MOORE, VARDINE. *Pre-School Story Hour.*

OPIE, IONA and PETER. *Children's Games in Street and Playground.*

______. *The Lore and Language of Schoolchildren.*

______, eds. *The Oxford Dictionary of Nursery Rhymes.*

The Original Mother Goose's Melody, As First Issued by John Newbery, of London, about A.D. 1760.

PINES, MAYA. *Revolution in Learning; The Years from Birth to Six.* Particularly Chapter 11, "Early Reading."

RICHARD, OLGA. "The Visual Language of the Picture Book."

THOMAS, KATHERINE ELWES. *The Real Personages of Mother Goose.*

WHITE, DOROTHY NEAL. *Books Before Five.*

YARDLEY, ALICE. *Young Children Thinking.*

Books discussed in Chapter 5 which may also be considered books for early childhood are identified in this bibliography with a "5."

[6]Complete bibliographic data are provided in the combined Adult References in the Appendixes.

For help in locating books with special purposes or about minorities, see the section "Book Selection Aids" in the Adult References in the Appendixes. In the following bibliography these symbols have been used to identify books about a particular religious or ethnic group:

§ Black
★ Chicano or Puerto Rican
☆ Native American
● Religious minority

Mother Goose Editions

ADDAMS, Charles, ill. *The Chas. Addams Mother Goose.* Harper, 1967.

ALDERSON, BRIAN, comp. *Cakes and Custard; Children's Rhymes Chosen by Brian Alderson,* ill. by Helen Oxenbury. Morrow, 1975.

ALIKI, ill. *Hush Little Baby.* Prentice, 1968. Softly colored pictures and simple format in a charming version of an old folk lullaby.

BROOKE, L. LESLIE, ill. *Ring o' Roses; A Nursery Rhyme Picture Book.* Warne, 1922.

5 BRIGGS, RAYMOND, ill. *The Mother Goose Treasury.* Coward, 1966. Greenaway Medal.

5 CALDECOTT, RANDOLPH, ill. *Hey Diddle Diddle Picture Book.* Warne, n.d. Some of Caldecott's finest pictures accompany favorite rhymes of the nursery.

CHWAST, SEYMOUR, ill. *The House That Jack Built.* Random, 1973. A clever variation is achieved by having each stiff board page larger than the last.

5 DE ANGELI, MARGUERITE, ill. *Marguerite de Angeli's Book of Nursery and Mother Goose Rhymes.* Doubleday, 1954.

EMBERLEY, ED, ill. *London Bridge Is Falling Down; The Song and Game.* Little, 1967.

5 FRASCONI, ANTONIO, ill. *The House That Jack Built.* Harcourt, 1958.

GALDONE, PAUL, ill. *The House That Jack Built.* Whittlesey, 1961. Colorful illustrations and picture-book format give new life to an old favorite.

GREENAWAY, KATE, ill. *Mother Goose; or, The Old Nursery Rhymes.* Warne, 1882.

GROVER, EULALIE OSGOOD, ed. *Mother Goose; The Volland Edition,* ill. by Frederick Richardson. Hubbard Pr., 1971. A revised version of the 1915 publication with original illustrations.

JEFFERS, SUSAN, ill. *Three Jovial Huntsmen.* Bradbury, 1973.

LINES, KATHLEEN, ed. *Lavender's Blue,* ill. by Harold Jones. Watts, 1954.

MONTGOMERIE, NORAH and WILLIAM, comps. *A Book of Scottish Nursery Rhymes,* ill. by T. Ritchie and Norah Montgomerie. Oxford, 1965.

Mother Goose in Hieroglyphics. Houghton, 1962. An exact reproduction of an old edition of *Mother Goose* using words and rebus pictures, with an explanatory key for pictures that puzzle the reader! Originally published in Boston over a century ago.

NESS, EVALINE, ill. *Old Mother Hubbard and Her Dog.* Holt, 1972. A humorous note is added by the dog's clowning.

OPIE, IONA, ed. *Ditties for the Nursery,* ill. by Monica Walker. Walck, 1954.

OPIE, IONA and PETER, comps. *A Family Book of Nursery Rhymes,* ill. by Pauline Baynes. Oxford, 1964.

———, comps. *The Oxford Nursery Rhyme Book,* ill. from old chapbooks, with additional pictures by Joan Hassall. Walck, 1955.

RACKHAM, ARTHUR, ill. *Mother Goose; The Old Nursery Rhymes.* Watts, 1969.

REED, PHILIP, ill. *Mother Goose and Nursery Rhymes.* Atheneum, 1963.

ROJANKOVSKY, FEODOR, ill. *The Tall Book of Mother Goose.* Harper, 1942.

SENDAK, MAURICE, ill. *Hector Protector* and *As I Went Over the Water.* Harper, 1965.

SPIER, PETER, ill. *London Bridge Is Falling Down!* Doubleday, 1967.

TUCKER, NICHOLAS, comp. *Mother Goose Lost,* ill. by Trevor Stubley. T. Crowell, 1971.

TUDOR, TASHA, ill. *Mother Goose.* Walck, 1944.

WILDSMITH, BRIAN, ill. *Brian Wildsmith's Mother Goose.* Watts, 1965.

WRIGHT, BLANCHE FISHER, ill. *The Real Mother Goose.* Rand, 1916.

A Few Variants of *Mother Goose*

BODECKER, N. M., comp. *It's Raining Said John Twaining,* tr. and ill. by compiler. Atheneum, 1973.

BURROUGHS, MARGARET TAYLOR, comp. *Did You Feed My Cow? Street Games, Chants, and Rhymes,* rev. ed., ill. by Joe E. DeValasco. Follett, 1969.

DE FOREST, CHARLOTTE B. *The Prancing Pony; Nursery Rhymes from Japan adapted into English verse for children,* with "Kusa-e" ill. by Keiko Hida. Walker, 1968.

DE KAY, ORMONDE, JR. *Rimes de La Mère Ole; Mother Goose Rhymes rendered into French.* Little, 1971. More colloquial than Hugh Latham's translation. Illustrations are by Barry Zaid (pedestrian), Seymour Chwast (good), and Milton Glaser (very good).

EMRICH, DUNCAN, comp. *The Nonsense Book of Riddles, Rhymes, Tongue Twisters, Puzzles and Jokes from American Folklore,* ill. by Ib Ohlsson. Four Winds, 1970. A fine collection of Americana by an eminent folklorist. A section of notes and a bibliography are appended.

FOWKE, EDITH, comp. *Sally Go Round the Sun; Three Hundred Children's Songs, Rhymes and Games,* ill. by Carlos Marchiori. Doubleday, 1970.

How Many Strawberries Grow in the Sea? A Songbook of Mother Goose Rhymes, music by Earl Bichel, ill. by George Suyeoka. Follett, 1969.

5 KAPP, PAUL, ed. and music arr. *A Cat Came Fiddling and Other Rhymes of Childhood,* ill. by Irene Haas. Harcourt, 1956. The pictures are droll and perfect, and Burl Ives says of the music, "It sounds as though it had never been written but only sung."

LANGSTAFF, JOHN. *Ol' Dan Tucker,* ill. by Joe Krush. Harcourt, 1963. Lively picture-book retelling of Ol' Dan Tucker's endless mishaps. Music included.

LATHAM, HUGH, tr. *Mother Goose in French,* ill. by Barbara Cooney. T. Crowell, 1964.

LEACH, MARIA. *Riddle Me, Riddle Me, Ree,* ill. by William Wiesner. Viking, 1970. A collection of over two hundred riddles from folk materials the world over. Sources are given.

LOW, JOSEPH and RUTH. *Mother Goose Riddle Rhymes,* ill. by Joseph Low. Harcourt, 1953. Low has made a modern rebus from nursery rhymes that is beautiful in design and clever in conception—a brain teaser for young and old.

MITCHELL, DONALD, comp. *Every Child's Book of Nursery Songs,* arr. by Carey Blyton, ill. by Alan Howard. Crown, 1968.

MORRISON, LILLIAN, comp. *Black Within and Red Without,* ill. by Jo Spier. T. Crowell, 1953. A scholarly collection of rhymed riddles, wise, witty and often as charming as poetry. Here are traditional puzzlers from ancient Egypt, Greece, the British Isles, the Orient, and the American Ozarks.

______, comp. *A Diller a Dollar,* ill. by Marjorie Bauernschmidt. T. Crowell, 1955. Over three hundred school riddles, sayings, derisive taunts, jokes, and proverbs will be sure to enliven classroom routines.

______, comp. *Touch Blue,* ill. by Doris Lee. T. Crowell, 1958. "Signs and Spells, Love Charms and Chants, Auguries and Old Beliefs in Rhyme."

5 PETERSHAM, MAUD and MISKA. *The Rooster Crows; A Book of American Rhymes and Jingles.* Macmillan, 1945. Caldecott Medal.

POTTER, CHARLES FRANCIS, comp. *Tongue Tanglers,* ill. by William Wiesner. World, 1962.

REID, ALASTAIR, and ANTHONY KERRIGAN, tr. *Mother Goose in Spanish,* ill. by Barbara Cooney. T. Crowell, 1968.

SCHWARTZ, ALVIN. *A Twister of Twists, A Tangle of Tongues,* ill. by Glen Rounds. Lippincott, 1972.

WINN, MARIE, comp. and ed. *What Shall We Do and Allee Galloo!* ill. by Karla Kuskin. Harper, 1970. A collection of game and activity songs, each with directions for children's participation. A preface suggests ways to introduce them and appropriate times to use them.

WITHERS, CARL, comp. *A Rocket in My Pocket,* ill. by Susanne Suba. Holt, 1948.

WOOD, RAY. *The American Mother Goose,* ill. by Ed Hargis. Lippincott, 1940.

WYNDHAM, ROBERT, comp. *Chinese Mother Goose Rhymes,* ill. by Ed Young. World, 1968.

5 ZEMACH, HARVE. *Mommy, Buy Me a China Doll,* ill. by Margot Zemach. Follett, 1966.

5 ______, ed. *The Speckled Hen; A Russian Nursery Rhyme,* ill. by Margot Zemach. Holt, 1966.

ABC Books

ANNO, MITSUMASA, ill. *Anno's Alphabet; An Adventure in Imagination.* T. Crowell, 1975.

BASKIN, LEONARD, ill. *Hosie's Alphabet,* words by Hosea, Tobias and Lisa Baskin. Viking, 1972.

5 BROWN, MARCIA, ill. *All Butterflies; An ABC.* Scribner's, 1974.

5 BURNINGHAM, JOHN, ill. *John Burningham's ABC.* Bobbs, 1967.

CARLE, ERIC, ill. *All about Arthur (an absolutely absurd ape).* Watts, 1974. Arthur left Atlanta because he felt all alone, and his alliterative antics are documented by a combination of photographic and woodcut techniques. Appealingly absurd.

CHWAST, SEYMOUR, and MARTIN STEPHEN MOSKOF, ill. *Still Another Alphabet Book.* McGraw, 1969.

CRANE, WALTER, ill. *Baby's Own Alphabet.* Dodd, n.d.

DEASY, MICHAEL. *City ABC's,* photos by Robert Perron. Walker, 1974.

DUVOISIN, ROGER, ill. *A for the Ark.* Lothrop, 1952.

EICHENBERG, FRITZ, ill. *Ape in a Cape.* Harcourt, 1952.

FARBER, NORMA. *As I Was Crossing Boston Common,* ill. by Arnold Lobel. Dutton, 1975. Too complex for learning the alphabet, but the parade of exotic creatures, from angwantibo to zibet, will fascinate some children.

______. *This Is the Ambulance Leaving the Zoo,* ill. by Tomie de Paola. Dutton, 1975. A lively alphabet book also tells about an Ambulance, Bus, Cars, Drivers in a busy story that has the cumulation young children enjoy.

§5 FEELINGS, MURIEL. *Jambo Means Hello; Swahili Alphabet Book,* ill. by Tom Feelings. Dial, 1974.

FUJIKAWA, GYO, ill. *A to Z Picture Book.* Grosset, 1974. Oversize pages are filled with soft, bright pictures, first a double-page spread with the letter and many labelled words (black and white), then a double-page spread in color.

5 GÁG, WANDA, ill. *The ABC Bunny.* Coward, 1933.

GREENAWAY, KATE, ill. *A Apple Pie.* Warne, n.d.

GROSSBART, FRANCINE, ill. *A Big City.* Harper, 1966.

LEAR, EDWARD. *ABC,* penned and ill. by author. McGraw, 1965. Facsimile of a manuscript, this edition has the nonsense verses set in type at the back of the book.

McGINLEY, PHYLLIS. *All Around the Town,* ill. by Helen Stone. Lippincott, 1948.

MATTHIESEN, THOMAS. *ABC; An Alphabet Book,* photos by author. Platt, 1966.

MILES, MISKA. *Apricot ABC,* ill. by Peter Parnall. Little, 1969.

MUNARI, BRUNO, ill. *Bruno Munari's ABC.* World, 1960.

NICHOLSON, WILLIAM, ill. *An Alphabet.* Heinemann/Alan Wofsy, 1975. A handsome reprint of an 1896 Art Nouveau book, with earth-tone woodblocks illustrating "A was an Artist, B for Beggar, C is for Countess . . ."

OXENBURY, HELEN, ill. *Helen Oxenbury's ABC of Things.* Watts, 1972.

PIATTI, CELESTINO, ill. *Celestino Piatti's Animal ABC.* English text by Jon Reid. Atheneum, 1966.

ROJANKOVSKY, FEODOR, ill. *Animals in the Zoo.* Knopf, 1962. A handsome zoo alphabet book in color with an animal for every letter.

SCHMIDERER, DOROTHY, ill. *The Alphabeast Book; An Abecedarium.* Holt, 1971.

SENDAK, MAURICE, ill. *Alligators All Around,* in *Nutshell Library.* Harper, 1962.

TUDOR, TASHA, ill. *A Is for Annabelle.* Walck, 1954.

WALTERS, MARGUERITE. *The City-Country ABC; My Alphabet Ride in the City, and My Alphabet Ride in the Country,* ill. by Ib Ohlsson, Doubleday, 1966.

5 WILDSMITH, BRIAN, ill. *Brian Wildsmith's ABC.* Watts, 1963.

WILLIAMS, GARTH, ill. *Big Golden Animal ABC.* Golden Pr., 1954.

Counting Books

ALLEN, ROBERT. *Numbers; A First Counting Book,* photos by Mottke Weissman. Platt and Munk, 1968.

CARLE, ERIC, ill. *My Very First Book of Numbers.* T. Crowell, 1974. Board pages, spiral-bound, are cut horizontally so that the child can match top and bottom halves; one has a set of fruits (1 pineapple, 2 bananas) and the other has 1-10 black squares.

CHWAST, SEYMOUR, and MARTIN MOSKOF, ill. *Still Another Number Book.* McGraw, 1971.

EICHENBERG, FRITZ, ill. *Dancing in the Moon; Counting Rhymes.* Harcourt, 1955.

ELKIN, BENJAMIN. *Six Foolish Fishermen,* ill. by Katherine Evans. Childrens Pr., 1957.

§ FEELINGS, MURIEL. *Moja Means One; Swahili Counting Book,* ill. by Tom Feelings. Dial, 1971.

FRANÇOISE (Françoise Seignobosc), ill. *Jeanne-Marie Counts Her Sheep.* Scribner's, 1951.

HOBAN, RUSSELL. *Ten What? A Mystery Counting Book,* ill. by Sylvie Selig. Scribner's, 1975.

HOBAN, TANA. *Count and See,* photos by author. Macmillan, 1972. Clear, sharp photos for a text that goes from 1-15, by tens to 50, and ends with 100 peas in their pods.

IPCAR, DAHLOV, ill. *Brown Cow Farm.* Doubleday, 1959.

______, ill. *Ten Big Farms.* Knopf, 1958.

KEATS, EZRA JACK, ill. *Over in the Meadow.* Four Winds, 1972.

KIRN, ANN, ill. *Nine in a Line.* Norton, 1966.

KREDENSER, GAIL. *1 One Dancing Drum,* ill. by Stanley Mack. Phillips, 1971.

5 LANGSTAFF, JOHN. *Over in the Meadow,* ill. by Feodor Rojankovsky. Harcourt, 1957.

LEYDENFROST, ROBERT, ill. *Ten Little Elephants.* Doubleday, 1975. In the "ten little Indians" pattern.

LIVERMORE, ELAINE, ill. *One to Ten. Count Again.* Houghton, 1973. Pictures with hidden animals add a game element; part two reverses the numbering as animals leave, one by one.

McLEOD, EMILIE. *One Snail and Me; A Book of Numbers and Animals and a Bathtub,* ill. by Walter Lorraine. Little, 1961.

MAESTRO, GIULIO, ill. *One More and One Less.* Crown, 1974. One by one, ten cheerful animals arrive; one by one, they depart.

MENDOZA, GEORGE. *The Marcel Marceau Counting Book,* photos by Milton H. Greene. Doubleday, 1971.

§ MERRIAM, EVE. *Project 1–2–3,* ill. by Harriet Sherman. McGraw, 1971.

OXENBURY, HELEN, ill. *Numbers of Things.* Watts, 1968.

PETIE, HARRIS, ill. *Billions of Bugs.* Prentice, 1975.

REISS, JOHN, ill. *Numbers.* Bradbury, 1971.

§ ROWAN, DICK. *Everybody In! A Counting Book,* ill. with photos. Bradbury, 1969.

SENDAK, MAURICE, ill. *One Was Johnny; A Counting Book,* in *Nutshell Library.* Harper, 1962. A rhyming text about a small boy's problem of too many visitors who appear one by one.

§ *The Sesame Street Book of Numbers,* by Children's Television Workshop and Preschool Press. Time-Life/Little, Brown, 1970.

SEYMOUR, BRENDA, ill. *First Counting.* Walck, 1969.

SMITH, DONALD, ill. *Farm Numbers; A Counting Book.* Abelard, 1970.

WILDSMITH, BRIAN, ill. *1, 2, 3's.* Watts, 1965.

WYSE, ANNE and ALEX, ill. *The One to Fifty Book.* Univ. of Toronto Pr., 1973.

§ ZINER, FEENIE, ill. *Counting Carnival.* Coward, 1962. One by one, children form a group, with a rhyming text describing twelve costumed participants.

Concept Books

BORTEN, HELEN. *Do You Go Where I Go?* ill. by author. Abelard, 1972. Objects that can be seen at the park, the barbershop, etc., are grouped so that children may think in terms of clues and sets.

______. *Do You Know What I Know?* ill. by author. Abelard, 1970.

§ BRENNER, BARBARA. *Faces,* photos by George Ancona. Dutton, 1970.

CARLE, ERIC. *My Very First Book of Colors,* ill. by author. T. Crowell, 1974. Spiral-bound, board pages cut in half horizontally so that upper and lower can be matched. Here, each top half has a solid block of color, each bottom has a picture of a familiar object.

______. *My Very First Book of Shapes,* ill. by author. T. Crowell, 1974.

______. *My Very First Book of Words,* ill. by author. T. Crowell, 1974. In the same format as above, this appeals to a child's detective instinct and curiosity. This is for slightly older children, requiring ability to identify letter symbols before matching them to pictures of cat, boy, girl, and so on.

☆§ COREY, DOROTHY. *You Go Away,* ill. by Lois Axeman. Whitman, 1976.

§ FUJIKAWA, GYO. *Let's Play!* ill. by author. Grosset, 1975. Pictures on board pages show everyday life experiences, with some stress on directional concepts.

§ HOBAN, TANA. *Circles, Triangles and Squares.* Macmillan, 1974. Excellent photographs in which the three most familiar geometric forms occur. While a picture that has several different shapes is less explicit as a teaching tool than a page of triangles, there is an alternate value in letting the child discover forms that are not prominent.

______. *Look Again!* Macmillan, 1971.

§ ______. *Over, Under & Through.* Macmillan, 1973.

______. *Push-Pull, Empty-Full.* Macmillan, 1972.

______. *Shapes and Things.* Macmillan, 1970.

HOWARD, C. *Mom and Me,* ill. by Stu Graves. Grosset, 1975.

KRAUSS, RUTH. *The Backward Day,* ill. by Marc Simont. Harper, 1950.

______. *The Growing Story,* ill. by Phyllis Rowand. Harper, 1947.

LOSS, JOAN. *What Is It? A Book of Photographic Puzzles.* Doubleday, 1974.

LUND, DORIS HEROLD. *I Wonder What's Under,* ill. by Janet McCaffery. Parents' Magazine, 1970.

§ McGOVERN, ANN. *Black Is Beautiful,* photos by Hope Wurmfeld. Four Winds, 1969.

MAESTRO, BETSY and GIULIO, *Where Is My Friend?* Crown, 1976.

§ MYERS, WALTER. *Where Does the Day Go?* ill. by Leo Carty. Parents' Magazine, 1969.

PEPPÉ, RODNEY. *Odd One OuT,* ill. by author. Viking, 1974.

REISS, JOHN J. *Colors,* ill. by author. Bradbury, 1969.

______. *Shapes,* ill. by author. Bradbury, 1974.

SCHLEIN, MIRIAM. *Shapes.* W. R. Scott, 1952.

The Sesame Street Book of Shapes, Time-Life/Little, Brown, 1970.

SPIER, PETER. *Fast-Slow, High-Low,* ill. by author. Doubleday, 1972.

______. *Gobble, Growl, Grunt,* ill. by author. Doubleday, 1971. Engaging, realistic drawings of animals whose names and sounds are the only text enable children to acquire the concept that each creature makes a distinctive noise.

TISON, ANNETTE, and TALUS TAYLOR. *The Adventures of the Three Colors.* World, 1971.

TRESSELT, ALVIN. *It's Time Now!* ill. by Roger Duvoisin. Lothrop, 1969. Reinforces concepts of seasons by describing seasonal activities. The tone is light, the illustrations bright and vigorous.

5 ______. *White Snow, Bright Snow,* ill. by Roger Duvoi-

sin. Lothrop, 1947.

UDRY, JANICE MAY. *A Tree Is Nice,* ill. by Marc Simont. Harper, 1956. Designed to give young children awareness of the varied uses and attractions of trees.

WELBER, ROBERT. *Goodbye, Hello,* ill. by Cyndy Szekeres. Pantheon, 1974.

Wordless Books

§ ALEXANDER, MARTHA. *Bobo's Dream.* Dial, 1970.

______. *Out! Out! Out!* Dial, 1968.

ANNO, MITSUMASA. *Topsy-Turvies; Pictures to Stretch the Imagination.* Walker/Weatherhill, 1970.

ARDIZZONE, EDWARD. *The Wrong Side of the Bed.* Doubleday, 1970.

ARUEGO, JOSE. *Look What I Can Do.* Scribner's, 1971.

CARLE, ERIC. *Do You Want to Be My Friend?* T. Crowell, 1971.

CARROLL, RUTH. *Rolling Downhill.* Walck, 1973. A puppy and a kitten, entangled in yarn, roll downhill and into a series of adventures. Ending: kitten hopefully eying the basket of yarn, eager for more fun.

CARROLL, RUTH and LATROBE. *The Christmas Kitten.* Walck, 1970. Mother doesn't want the kitten that's been left by a friend, but—to her children's delight—the persistent cat reappears so many times that Mother relents.

FUCHS, ERICH. *Journey to the Moon.* Delacorte, 1969.

GOODALL, JOHN S. *The Ballooning Adventures of Paddy Pork.* Harcourt, 1969.

______. *Jacko.* Harcourt, 1972. Alternating full and half pages change the scenes in all of Goodall's books; here the pictures tell the nautical escapades of a monkey and show an eighteenth-century English setting.

______. *The Midnight Adventures of Kelly, Dot, and Esmeralda.* Atheneum, 1972. Three nursery toys come alive at night and step into a painting for a bit of fun.

5 ______. *Naughty Nancy.* Atheneum, 1975.

______. *Paddy's Evening Out.* Atheneum, 1973. Paddy Pork's visit to a theater turns into a disruption enjoyed more by the audience than the cast.

______. *Shrewbettina's Birthday.* Harcourt, 1971. A Victorian setting adds color to the story of a successful birthday party that recovers from a bad start.

HAMBERGER, JOHN. *The Lazy Dog.* Four Winds, 1971.

HOBAN, TANA. *Big Ones, Little Ones.* Greenwillow, 1976. Pictures of adult animals with their young. See titles also in bibliography for concept books.

HOGROGIAN, NONNY. *Apples.* Macmillan, 1972.

HUTCHINS, PAT. *Changes, Changes.* Macmillan, 1971.

KEATS, EZRA JACK. *Kitten for a Day.* Watts, 1974.

______. *Pssst! Doggie—.* Watts, 1973.

KENT, JACK. *The Egg Book.* Macmillan, 1975.

KOREN, EDWARD. *Behind the Wheel.* Holt, 1972.

KRAHN, FERNANDO. *April Fools.* Dutton, 1974. Two young pranksters make a monster, get lost in the woods, and use their creation, atop a long pole, to signal rescuers.

______. *The Self-Made Snowman.* Lippincott, 1974.

MARI, IELA. *The Magic Balloon.* Phillips, 1969.

MARI, IELA and ENZO. *The Apple and the Moth.* Pantheon, 1970.

MAYER, MERCER. *Ah-Choo.* Dial, 1976. An allergic elephant's sneezes cause such destruction that he lands in jail and blows his way right out.

______. *Bubble Bubble.* Parents' Magazine, 1973. A small boy sees a series of imaginary monsters in the bubbles he blows.

______. *Frog Goes to Dinner.* Dial, 1974.

______. *Frog, Where Are You?* Dial, 1969. Raffish pictures show the troubles of a boy and his dog as they hunt for a pet frog.

______. *The Great Cat Chase.* Four Winds, 1974.

MAYER, MERCER and MARIANNA. *A Boy, a Dog, a Frog and a Friend,* ill. by Mercer Mayer. Dial, 1971. Playing in a pond, the boy and his pets find a turtle and happily add it to their inner circle.

______. *One Frog Too Many.* Dial, 1975. When a baby frog is added, the older frog is jealous, but he adjusts.

MEYER, RENATE. *Hide-and-Seek.* Bradbury, 1969.

SIMMONS, ELLIE. *Family.* McKay, 1970.

UENO, NORIKO. *Elephant Buttons.* Harper, 1973. The elephant's buttons pop open to show a lion, whose buttons pop open to reveal a horse, and so on, down to a mouse. Surprise ending: an elephant balloons out when the mouse's buttons open.

5 WARD, LYND. *The Silver Pony.* Houghton, 1973.

Books for Beginning Readers

5 BENCHLEY, NATHANIEL. *Sam the Minute Man,* ill. by Arnold Lobel. Harper, 1969.

______. *The Several Tricks of Edgar Dolphin,* ill. by Mamoru Funai. Harper, 1970.

BONSALL, CROSBY. *And I Mean It, Stanley,* ill. by author. Harper, 1974. Stanley's identity is kept secret until the end of a running monologue by a small girl who is creating a sort of preschool Watts Tower.

§ ______. *The Case of the Cat's Meow,* ill. by author. Harper, 1965.

§ ______. *The Case of the Scaredy Cats,* ill. by author. Harper, 1971. The staunch crew that coped with the cat's meow finds that girls can hold their own.

______. *Mine's the Best,* ill. by author. Harper, 1973.

______. *Piggle,* ill. by author. Harper, 1973. His sisters won't play with him, so little Homer turns to his animal friends and discovers the joy of word-play. An amusing story stresses imagination and the satisfaction of the youngest when Homer's older sisters are routed by a chain of events.

BRENNER, BARBARA. *Baltimore Orioles,* ill. by J. Winslow Higginbottom. Harper, 1974. Not accurate in color, but reliable in the text that describes one oriole family through a year's life cycle.

DELTON, JUDY. *Two Good Friends,* ill. by Giulio Maestro. Crown, 1974. Duck and Bear learn that good friends must learn to tolerate each other's mildly annoying habits.

EASTMAN, PHILIP D. *Go, Dog, Go!* Random, 1961. Not the best in this type of book, but the plotless text is brisk and has a nonsense humor in a series of canine dialogues.

GREENAWAY, KATE. *Under the Window.* Warne, n.d.

GUILFOILE, ELIZABETH. *Nobody Listens to Andrew,* ill. by Mary Stevens. Follett, 1957.

HEYWARD, DU BOSE. *The Country Bunny and the Little Gold Shoes,* ill. by Marjorie Flack. Houghton, 1939.

HOBAN, LILLIAN. *Arthur's Christmas Cookies,* ill. by author. Harper, 1972. An enterprising monkey bakes cookies for Christmas giving and uses them as tree ornaments when they prove to be rock-hard. Good structure and good humor give a simple story substance.

______. *Arthur's Honey Bear,* ill. by author. Harper, 1974.

HOFF, SYD. *The Horse in Harry's Room,* ill. by author. Harper, 1970. Pictures in cartoon style illustrate a story in which a sympathetic teacher handles nicely Harry's belief in his imaginary horse.

______. *Oliver,* ill. by author. Harper, 1960. An unwanted circus elephant is so friendly and so talented as a dancer that he wins a job as a performer, much to the joy of the children who love him.

HURD, EDITH THACHER. *Johnny Lion's Rubber Boots,* ill. by Clement Hurd. Harper, 1972. One of a series of books about a lion cub who is really just like a small boy, this describes Johnny's indoor play on a rainy day and an equally satisfying puddle-romp. Lots of action, quite a bit of repetition of words.

§ KESSLER, LEONARD. *Kick, Pass, and Run,* ill. by author. Harper, 1966.

§ LEXAU, JOAN M. *The Homework Caper,* ill. by Syd Hoff. Harper, 1966.

§ ______. *The Rooftop Mystery,* ill. by Syd Hoff. Harper, 1968. Two boys cope with the traditional male embarrassment about dolls when they carry one to help on moving day. Despite the stereotypical sex role, an amusing story with problem-solution, humor, and an interracial friendship.

5 LOBEL, ARNOLD. *Frog and Toad Are Friends,* ill. by author. Harper, 1970.

5 ______. *Frog and Toad Together,* ill. by author. Harper, 1972. Short, short stories that are funnier than those of the first book and only a little less touching.

5 ______. *Owl at Home,* ill. by author. Harper, 1975.

______. *Small Pig,* ill. by author. Harper, 1969. Does a pig want his pen vacuumed? Not this piglet, who trots off for a wallow in the city and learns that what looks like delicious mud can be fast-setting cement.

MINARIK, ELSE HOLMELUND. *Father Bear Comes Home,* ill. by Maurice Sendak. Harper, 1959. The illustrations capture to perfection the ingenuous Little Bear and his loving parents in a story that has, for all its brevity, chapter divisions that look impressive to the beginning reader.

______. *A Kiss for Little Bear,* ill. by Maurice Sendak. Harper, 1968. Grandmothers do often send kisses, but seldom by as amusing a chain of helpers; Skunk breaks the chain when he finds another skunk so attractive he concentrates on kissing her rather than passing the kiss along.

5 ______. *Little Bear,* ill. by Maurice Sendak. Harper, 1957.

5 ______. *Little Bear's Friend,* ill. by Maurice Sendak. Harper, 1960. When a little girl he's become fond of leaves at the end of the summer, Little Bear's parents teach him to write so that he and Emily can communicate.

PARISH, PEGGY. *Dinosaur Time,* ill. by Arnold Lobel. Harper, 1974.

RICCIUTI, EDWARD R. *Donald and the Fish That Walked,* ill. by Syd Hoff. Harper, 1974.

ROCKWELL, ANNE. *The Toolbox,* ill. by Harlow Rockwell. Macmillan, 1971.

§ ROCKWELL, HARLOW. *I Did It,* ill. by author. Macmillan, 1974.

5 SELSAM, MILLICENT. *Benny's Animals and How He Put Them in Order,* ill. by Arnold Lobel. Harper, 1966.

______. *Greg's Microscope,* ill. by Arnold Lobel. Harper, 1963. Having coaxed his father into buying him a second-hand microscope, Greg learns how to make slides and also learns that he'll have to share the instrument with his fascinated parents.

______. *How Puppies Grow,* photos by Esther Bubley. Four Winds, 1972.

§ ______. *Tony's Birds,* ill. by Kurt Werth. Harper, 1961.

SEUSS, DR. *The Cat in the Hat,* ill. by author. Random, 1957.

______. *The Cat in the Hat Comes Back,* ill. by author. Random, 1958. A sequel to the first book has 26 cats, A-Z, who help the Cat in the Hat in a series of the silly dilemmas he creates.

SHAW, EVELYN. *Alligator,* ill. by Frances Zweifel. Harper, 1972.

______. *Octopus,* ill. by Ralph Carpentier. Harper, 1971. Succinct and accurate, an unfictionalized text about the octopus, written by a scientist, gives facts about feeding, breeding, avoiding predators, and other facets of behavior.

§ SHOWERS, Paul. *Look at Your Eyes,* ill. by Paul Galdone. T. Crowell, 1962.

Picture Story Books

5 AARDEMA, VERNA. *Why Mosquitoes Buzz in People's Ears,* ill. by Leo and Diane Dillon. Dial, 1975. Caldecott Medal.

ALEXANDER, MARTHA. *I'll Be the Horse If You'll Play with Me,* ill. by author. Dial, 1975.

______. *Nobody Asked Me If I Wanted a Baby Sister,* ill. by author. Dial, 1971.

5 ______. *Out! Out! Out!* ill. by author. Dial, 1968.

ALIKI. *June 7,* ill. by author. Macmillan, 1972.

5 AMBRUS, VICTOR. *A Country Wedding,* ill. by author. Addison, 1975.

5 ______. *The Little Cockerel,* ill. by author. Harcourt, 1968.

5 ______. *The Seven Skinny Goats,* ill. by author. Harcourt, 1970.

5 ______. *The Three Poor Tailors,* ill. by author. Harcourt, 1966.

5 ANDERSEN, HANS CHRISTIAN. *The Steadfast Tin Soldier,* ill. by Marcia Brown. Scribner's, 1953.

5 ANDERSON, LONZO. *Two Hundred Rabbits,* ill. by Adrienne Adams. Viking, 1968.

5 ARDIZZONE, EDWARD. *Little Tim and the Brave Sea Captain,* ill. by author. Walck, 1955.

5 ______. *Tim All Alone,* ill. by author. Oxford, 1957.

5 ______. *The Wrong Side of the Bed,* ill. by author. Doubleday, 1970.

AVERILL, ESTHER HOLDEN. *Jenny and the Cat Club,* ill. by author. Harper, 1973.

☆§ BARKIN, CAROL, and ELIZABETH JAMES. *Sometimes I Hate School,* photos by Heinz Kluetmeier. Raintree, 1975.

BARTOLI, JENNIFER. *Nonna,* ill. by Joan Drescher. Harvey, 1975.

BATE, LUCY. *Little Rabbit's Loose Tooth,* ill. by Diane De Groat. Crown, 1975.

☆5 BAYLOR, BYRD. *The Desert Is Theirs,* ill. by Peter Parnall. Scribner's, 1975.

5 ______. *Everybody Needs a Rock,* ill. by Peter Parnall. Scribner's, 1974.

5 BEMELMANS, LUDWIG. *Madeline,* ill. by author. Viking, 1939.

5 BISHOP, CLAIRE (HUCHET). *The Truffle Pig,* ill. by Kurt Wiese. Coward, 1971.

BORACK, BARBARA. *Grandpa,* ill. by Ben Schecter. Harper, 1967.

§ BREINBURG, PETRONELLA. *Doctor Shawn,* ill. by Errol Lloyd. T. Crowell, 1975.

§ ______. *Shawn Goes to School,* ill. by Errol Lloyd. T. Crowell, 1974.

5 BRIGGS, RAYMOND. *Father Christmas,* ill. by author. Coward, 1973.

5 ______. *Father Christmas Goes on Holiday,* ill. by author. Coward, 1975.

5 ______. *Jim and the Beanstalk,* ill. by author. Coward, 1970.

5 BROWN, MARCIA. *Dick Whittington and His Cat,* ill. by author. Scribner's, 1950.

5 ______. *Once a Mouse,* ill. by author. Scribner's, 1961. Caldecott Medal.

______. *Stone Soup,* ill. by author. Scribner's, 1947.

5 BROWN, MARGARET WISE. *The Little Island,* ill. by Leonard Weisgard. Doubleday, 1946. Published under pseudonym of Golden MacDonald. Caldecott Medal.

______. *The Runaway Bunny,* ill. by Clement Hurd, rev. ed. Harper, 1962.

BROWN, MYRA BERRY. *First Night Away from Home,* ill. by Dorothy Marino. Watts, 1960.

5 BURNINGHAM, JOHN. *The Baby; The Rabbit; The School; The Snow,* ill. by author. T. Crowell, 1975.

5 ______. *Borka; The Adventures of a Goose with No Feathers,* ill. by author. Random, 1964.

5 ______. *Mr. Gumpy's Motor Car,* ill. by author. Crowell, 1976.

5 ______. *Mr. Gumpy's Outing,* ill. by author. Holt, 1971.

5 BURTON, VIRGINIA. *The Little House,* ill. by author. Houghton, 1942. Caldecott Medal.

5 ______. *Mike Mulligan and His Steam Shovel,* ill. by author. Houghton, 1939.

CALDECOTT, RANDOLPH. *Frog He Would A-Wooing Go,* ill. by author. Warne, n.d.

5 CARIGIET, ALOIS. *Anton and Anne,* tr. by Refna Wilkin, ill. by author. Walck, 1969.

CARLSON, NATALIE SAVAGE. *Marie Louise's Heyday,* ill. by Jose Aruego and Ariane Dewey. Scribner's, 1975.

CAUDILL, REBECCA. *Did You Carry the Flag Today, Charley?* ill. by Nancy Grossman. Holt, 1966.

5 ______. *A Pocketful of Cricket,* ill. by Evaline Ness. Holt, 1964.

§5 CLIFTON, LUCILLE. *The Boy Who Didn't Believe in Spring,* ill. by Brinton Turkle. Dutton, 1973.

§5 ______. *Some of the Days of Everett Anderson,* ill. by Evaline Ness. Holt, 1970.

§ COHEN, MIRIAM. *Will I Have a Friend?* ill. by Lillian Hoban. Macmillan, 1967.

COLE, WILLIAM. *What's Good for a Three-Year-Old?* ill. by Lillian Hoban. Holt, 1974.

5 COLMONT, MARIE. *Christmas Bear,* tr. by Constance Hirsch, ill. by Feodor Rojankovsky. Golden Pr., 1966.

5 CRAFT, RUTH. *The Winter Bear,* ill. by Erik Blegvad. Atheneum, 1975.

5 DANA, DORIS. *The Elephant and His Secret,* ill. by Antonio Frasconi. Atheneum, 1974.

5 DAUGHERTY, JAMES. *Andy and the Lion,* ill. by author. Viking, 1938.

DE BRUNHOFF, JEAN. *The Story of Babar, the Little Elephant,* ill. by author. Random, 1937.

DELTON, JUDY. *Two Good Friends,* ill. by Giulio Maestro. Crown, 1974.

DE PAOLA, TOMIE. *"Charlie Needs a Cloak,"* ill. by author. Prentice, 1974.

______. *Nana Upstairs and Nana Downstairs,* ill. by author. Putnam, 1973.

5 ______, ad. *Strega Nona,* ill. by adapter. Prentice, 1975.

5 DE REGNIERS, BEATRICE SCHENK. *A Little House of Your Own,* ill. by Irene Haas. Harcourt, 1955.

5 ______. *May I Bring a Friend?* ill. by Beni Montresor. Atheneum, 1964. Caldecott Medal.

5 ______. *What Can You Do with a Shoe?* ill. by Maurice Sendak. Harper, 1955.

5 DOMANSKA, JANINA. *Din Dan Don It's Christmas,* ill. by author. Greenwillow, 1975.

5 ______. *If All the Seas Were One Sea,* ill. by author. Macmillan, 1971.

______. *Look, There Is a Turtle Flying,* ill. by author. Macmillan, 1968.

DRAGONWAGON, CRESCENT. *When Light Turns into Night,* ill. by Robert Andrew Parker. Harper, 1975.

5 ELKIN, BENJAMIN. *How the Tsar Drinks Tea,* ill. by Anita Lobel. Parents' Magazine, 1971.

5 EMBERLEY, BARBARA, ad. *Drummer Hoff,* ill. by Ed Emberley. Prentice, 1967. Caldecott Medal.

★5 ETS, MARIE HALL. *Gilberto and the Wind,* ill. by author. Viking, 1963.

5 ______. *Talking Without Words,* ill. by author. Viking, 1968.

★5 ETS, MARIE HALL, and AURORA LABASTIDA. *Nine Days to Christmas,* ill. by Marie Hall Ets. Viking, 1959. Caldecott Medal.

FARBER, NORMA. *Where's Gomer?* ill. by William Pène du Bois. Dutton, 1974.

5 FATIO, LOUISE. *The Happy Lion,* ill. by Roger Duvoisin. Whittlesey, 1954.

5 ______. *The Happy Lion's Rabbits,* ill. by Roger Duvoisin. McGraw, 1974.

5 ______. *The Happy Lion's Vacation,* ill. by Roger Duvoisin. McGraw, 1967.

5 FISHER, AILEEN. *Going Barefoot,* ill. by Adrienne Adams. T. Crowell, 1960.

5 ______. *Where Does Everyone Go?* ill. by Adrienne Adams. T. Crowell, 1961.

5 FLACK, MARJORIE. *The Story About Ping,* ill. by Kurt Wiese. Viking, 1933.

FREEMAN, DON. *Will's Quill,* ill. by author. Viking, 1975.

GACKENBACH, DICK. *Do You Love Me?* ill. by author. Seabury, 1975.

5 GÁG, WANDA. *Funny Thing,* ill. by author. Coward, 1929.

5 ______. *Millions of Cats,* ill. by author. Coward, 1928.

5 ______. *Nothing at All,* ill. by author. Coward, 1941.

5 ______. *Snippy and Snappy,* ill. by author. Coward, 1931.

GALDONE, PAUL. *The Gingerbread Boy,* ill. by author. Seabury, 1975.

______. *The Little Red Hen,* ill. by author. Seabury, 1973.

GETZ, ARTHUR. *Hamilton Duck,* ill. by author. Golden Pr., 1972.

______. *Hamilton Duck's Springtime Story,* ill. by author. Golden Pr., 1974.

GINSBURG, MIRRA, tr. *The Chick and the Duckling,* tr. from the Russian of V. Suteyev, ill. by Jose and Ariane Aruego. Macmillan, 1972.

5 GOUDEY, ALICE E. *The Day We Saw the Sun Come Up,* ill. by Adrienne Adams. Scribner's, 1961.

5 ______. *Houses from the Sea,* ill. by Adrienne Adams. Scribner's, 1959.

§ GRAHAM, LORENZ. *Hongry Catch the Foolish Boy,* ill. by James Brown, Jr. T. Crowell, 1973.

§5 ______. *Song of the Boat,* ill. by Leo and Diane Dillon. T. Crowell, 1975.

§ GRAY, GENEVIEVE. *Send Wendell,* ill. by Symeon Shimin. McGraw, 1974.

§ GREENFIELD, ELOISE. *She Come Bringing Me That Little Baby Girl*, ill. by John Steptoe. Lippincott, 1974.
5 GRIMM, JACOB and WILHELM. *King Grisly-Beard*, tr. by Edgar Taylor, ill. by Maurice Sendak. Farrar, 1973.
5 ______. *The Shoemaker and the Elves*, ill. by Adrienne Adams. Scribner's, 1960.
5 HAAS, IRENE. *The Maggie B.*, ill. by author. Atheneum, 1975.
5 HADER, BERTA and ELMER. *The Big Snow*, ill. by authors. Macmillan, 1948. Caldecott Medal.
§5 HALEY, GAIL E., ad. *A Story—A Story; An African Tale*, ill. by adapter. Atheneum, 1970. Caldecott Medal.
5 HANDFORTH, THOMAS. *Mei Li*, ill. by author. Doubleday, 1938.
HOBAN, LILLIAN. *Arthur's Honey Bear*, ill. by author. Harper, 1974.
HOBAN, RUSSELL C. *A Bargain for Frances*, ill. by Lillian Hoban. Harper, 1970.
5 ______. *Bedtime for Frances*, ill. by Garth Williams. Harper, 1960.
______. *Dinner at Alberta's*, ill. by James Marshall. T. Crowell, 1975.
5 HOFFMANN, FELIX, ad. *The Story of Christmas*, ill. by adapter. Atheneum, 1975.
5 HOGROGIAN, NONNY. *One Fine Day*, ill. by author. Macmillan, 1971. Caldecott Medal.
HOLL, ADELAIDE. *The Parade*, ill. by Kjell Ringi. Watts, 1975.
HURWITZ, JOHANNA. *Busybody Nora*, ill. by Susan Jeschke. Morrow, 1976.
HUTCHINS, PAT. *Rosie's Walk*, ill. by author. Macmillan, 1968.
5 JAMESON, CYNTHIA, ad. *The Clay Pot Boy*, ill. by Arnold Lobel. Coward, 1973.
KAHL, VIRGINIA. *The Duchess Bakes a Cake*, ill. by author. Scribner's, 1955.
★ KEATS, EZRA JACK. *Dreams*, ill. by author. Macmillan, 1974.
§5 ______. *Goggles!* ill. by author. Macmillan, 1969.
§5 ______. *Hi Cat!* ill. by author. Macmillan, 1970.
★§ ______. *Louie*, ill. by author. Greenwillow, 1975.
§5 ______. *Peter's Chair*, ill. by author. Harper, 1967.
§5 ______. *The Snowy Day*, ill. by author. Viking, 1962. Caldecott Medal.
§5 ______. *Whistle for Willie*, ill. by author. Viking, 1964.
5 KEEPING, CHARLES. *Charley, Charlotte and the Golden Canary*, ill. by author. Watts, 1967.
5 ______. *Joseph's Yard*, ill. by author. Watts, 1970.
KESSELMAN, WENDY ANN. *Time for Jody*, ill. by Gerald Dumas. Harper, 1975.
5 KINGMAN, LEE. *Peter's Long Walk*, ill. by Barbara Cooney. Doubleday, 1953.
5 KIPLING, RUDYARD. *How the Rhinoceros Got His Skin*, ill. by Leonard Weisgard. Walker, 1974.
KRAUS, ROBERT. *Milton the Early Riser*, ill. by Jose and Ariane Aruego. Windmill/Dutton, 1972.
5 ______. *Owliver*, ill. by Jose Aruego and Ariane Dewey. Windmill/Dutton, 1974.
KRAUSS, RUTH. *The Backward Day*, ill. by Marc Simont. Harper, 1950.
5 ______. *A Hole Is to Dig*, ill. by Maurice Sendak. Harper, 1952.
5 KUMIN, MAXINE, and ANNE SEXTON. *Joey and the Birthday Present*, ill. by Evaline Ness. McGraw, 1971.
5 LANGSTAFF, JOHN. *Frog Went a-Courtin'*, ill. by Feodor Rojankovsky. Harcourt, 1955. Caldecott Medal.
LAPSLEY, SUSAN. *I Am Adopted*, ill. by Michael Charlton. Bradbury, 1975. A small boy speaks of his adoption casually, he's so secure in the love of his family.
§ LASKER, JOE. *Mothers Can Do Anything*, ill. by author. Whitman, 1972.
LEAF, MUNRO. *The Story of Ferdinand*, ill. by Robert Lawson. Viking, 1936.
5 LENT, BLAIR. *John Tabor's Ride*, ill. by author. Atlantic/Little, 1966.
5 ______. *Pistachio*, ill. by author. Atlantic/Little, 1964.
LIONNI, LEO. *In the Rabbitgarden*, ill. by author. Pantheon, 1975.
5 ______. *Inch by Inch*, ill. by author. Obolensky, 1960.
5 LIPKIND, WILL. *Chaga*, ill. by Nicolas Mordvinoff. Harcourt, 1955.
5 ______. *Finders Keepers*, ill. by Nicolas Mordvinoff. Harcourt, 1951. Caldecott Medal.
5 LOBEL, ANITA. *King Rooster, Queen Hen*, ill. by author. Greenwillow, 1975.
5 LOBEL, ARNOLD. *A Zoo for Mr. Muster*, ill. by author. Harper, 1962.
5 McCLOSKEY, ROBERT. *Blueberries for Sal*, ill. by author. Viking, 1948.
5 ______. *Burt Dow, Deep Water Man*, ill. by author. Viking, 1963.
5 ______. *Make Way for Ducklings*, ill. by author. Viking, 1941. Caldecott Medal.
5 ______. *Time of Wonder*, ill. by author. Viking, 1957. Caldecott Medal.
§5 McDERMOTT, GERALD. *Anansi the Spider*, ill. by author. Holt, 1972.
☆5 ______. *Arrow to the Sun*, ill. by author. Viking, 1974. Caldecott Medal.
§5 ______. *The Magic Tree*, ill. by author. Holt, 1973.
5 ______, ad. *The Stonecutter*, ill. by adapter. Viking, 1975.
MAHY, MARGARET. *The Boy Who Was Followed Home*, ill. by Steven Kellogg. Watts, 1975.
MANUSHKIN, FRAN. *Bubblebath!* ill. by Ronald Himler. Harper, 1974.
MARSHALL, JAMES. *George and Martha*, ill. by author. Houghton, 1972.
5 MERRIAM, EVE. *Mommies at Work*, ill. by Beni Montresor. Knopf, 1961.
MILES, MISKA. *Swim, Little Duck*, ill. by Jim Arnosky. Little, 1976.
5 MILNE, A. A. *When We Were Very Young*, ill. by Ernest H. Shepard. Dutton, 1924.
5 MIZAMURA, KAZUE. *If I Built a Village . . .*, ill. by author. T. Crowell, 1971.
5 MONTRESOR, BENI. *House of Flowers, House of Stars*, ill. by author. Knopf, 1962.
5 ______. *The Witches of Venice*, ill. by author. Knopf, 1963.
5 MOSEL, ARLENE, ad. *The Funny Little Woman*, ill. by Blair Lent. Dutton, 1972. Caldecott Medal.
5 ______, ad. *Tikki Tikki Tembo*, ill. by Blair Lent. Holt, 1968.
5 NESS, EVALINE. *The Girl and the Goatherd*, ill. by author. Dutton, 1970.
§5 ______. *Josefina February*, ill. by author. Scribner's, 1963.
5 ______. *Sam, Bangs & Moonshine*, ill. by author. Holt, 1966. Caldecott Medal.
5 ______. *Tom Tit Tot*, ill. by author. Scribner's, 1965.
5 NIC LEODHAS, SORCHE. *All in the Morning Early*, ill. by Evaline Ness. Holt, 1963.
5 ______. *Always Room for One More*, ill. by Nonny Hogrogian. Holt, 1965. Caldecott Medal.
OAKLEY, GRAHAM. *The Church Cat Abroad*, ill. by author. Atheneum, 1973.
______. *The Church Mice and the Moon*, ill. by author.

Atheneum, 1974.
5 ———. *The Church Mice Spread Their Wings,* ill. by author. Atheneum, 1976.
———. *The Church Mouse,* ill. by author. Atheneum, 1972.
5 OLSEN, IB SPANG. *Smoke,* ill. by author. Coward, 1972.
5 PARNALL, PETER. *The Mountain,* ill. by author. Doubleday, 1971.
PARSONS, ELLEN. *Rainy Day Together,* ill. by Lillian Hoban, Harper, 1971.
PEARSON, SUSAN. *Izzie,* ill. by Robert Andrew Parker. Dial, 1975.
5 PETERSHAM, MAUD and MISKA. *The Box with Red Wheels,* ill. by authors. Macmillan, 1949.
5 ———. *The Christmas Child,* ill. by authors. Doubleday, 1931.
5 PETERSON, HANS. *The Big Snowstorm,* ill. by Harald Wiberg. Coward, 1976.
★5 POLITI, LEO. *Juanita,* ill. by author. Scribner's, 1948.
§5 ———. *Little Leo,* ill. by author. Scribner's, 1951.
5 ———. *Moy Moy,* ill. by author. Scribner's, 1960.
§5 ———. *The Nicest Gift,* ill. by author. Scribner's, 1973.
5 POTTER, BEATRIX. *The Tale of Peter Rabbit,* ill. by author. Warne, 1901.
PROVENSEN, ALICE and MARTIN. *My Little Hen,* ill. by authors. Random, 1973.
———. *Our Animal Friends at Maple Hill Farm,* ill. by authors. Random, 1974.
5 RANSOME, ARTHUR. *The Fool of the World and the Flying Ship,* ill. by Uri Shulevitz. Farrar, 1968. Caldecott Medal.
REY, HANS. *Curious George,* ill. by author. Houghton, 1941. And its sequels.
ROCKWELL, ANNE. *The Toolbox,* ill. by Harlow Rockwell. Macmillan, 1971.
ROCKWELL, HARLOW. *My Dentist,* ill. by author. Greenwillow, 1975.
———. *My Doctor,* ill. by author. Macmillan, 1973.
§ ———. *My Nursery School,* ill. by author. Greenwillow, 1976.
ROSEN, WINIFRED. *Ralph Proves the Pudding,* ill. by Lionel Kalish. Doubleday, 1972.
RUSS, LAVINIA. *Alec's Sand Castle,* ill. by James Stevenson. Harper, 1972.
5 RYAN, CHELI DURAN. *Hildilid's Night,* ill. by Arnold Lobel. Macmillan, 1971.
SCHICK, ELEANOR. *City in the Summer,* ill. by author. Macmillan, 1969.
5 ———. *Neighborhood Knight,* ill. by author. Greenwillow, 1976.
SCOTT, ANN. *On Mother's Lap,* ill. by Glo Coalson. McGraw, 1972.
5 SENDAK, MAURICE. *In the Night Kitchen,* ill. by author. Harper, 1970.
5 ———. *The Nutshell Library,* ill. by author. Harper, 1962.
5 ———. *Where the Wild Things Are,* ill. by author. Harper, 1963. Caldecott Medal.
SHARMAT, MARJORIE WEINMAN. *Gladys Told Me to Meet Her Here,* ill. by Edward Frascino. Harper, 1970.
———. *I'm Not Oscar's Friend Anymore,* ill. by Tony DeLuna. Dutton, 1975.
———. *Morris Brookside, a Dog,* ill. by Ronald Himler. Holiday, 1973.
———. *Morris Brookside Is Missing,* ill. by Ronald Himler. Holiday, 1974. Rebuffed when he tries to climb on Mr. Brookside's aching legs, Morris runs off. To the basement.
———. *Walter the Wolf,* ill. by Kelly Oechsli. Holiday, 1975.
5 SHULEVITZ, URI. *Dawn,* ill. by author. Farrar, 1974.
5 ———. *One Monday Morning,* ill. by author. Scribner's, 1967.
5 ———. *Rain Rain Rivers,* ill. by author. Scribner's, 1967.
SIVULICH, SANDRA STRONER. *I'm Going on a Bear Hunt,* ill. by Glen Rounds. Dutton, 1973.
SKORPEN, LIESEL MOAK. *Mandy's Grandmother,* ill. by Martha Alexander. Dial, 1975.
5 SLEATOR, WILLIAM, ad. *The Angry Moon,* ill. by Blair Lent. Little, 1970.
SOBOL, HARRIET LANGSAM. *Jeff's Hospital Book,* photos by Patricia Agre. Walck, 1975.
★ SONNEBORN, RUTH. *Friday Night Is Papa Night,* ill. by Emily McNully. Viking, 1970. A story that reflects the love and warmth in a Puerto Rican family.
STEIG, WILLIAM. *Farmer Palmer's Wagon Ride,* ill. by author. Farrar, 1974.
———. *Sylvester and the Magic Pebble,* ill. by author. Windmill/Simon, 1969. Caldecott Medal.
§5 STEPTOE, JOHN. *Stevie,* ill. by author. Harper, 1969.
5 SWIFT, HILDEGARDE. *The Little Red Lighthouse and the Great Gray Bridge,* ill. by Lynd Ward. Harcourt, 1942.
TAPIO, PAT DECKER. *The Lady Who Saw the Good Side of Everything,* ill. by Paul Galdone. Seabury, 1975.
TITUS, EVE. *Anatole in Italy,* ill. by Paul Galdone. McGraw, 1973.
TRESSELT, ALVIN. *The Dead Tree,* ill. by Charles Robinson. Parents' Magazine, 1972.
UCHIDA, YOSHIKO. *The Birthday Visitor,* ill. by Charles Robinson. Scribner's, 1975.
5 UDRY, JANICE MAY. *The Moon Jumpers,* ill. by Maurice Sendak. Harper, 1959.
§ ———. *What Mary Jo Shared,* ill. by Eleanor Mill. Whitman, 1966.
UNGERER, TOMI. *Émile,* ill. by author. Harper, 1960.
VAN WOERKOM, DOROTHY. *The Queen Who Couldn't Bake Gingerbread,* ill. by Paul Galdone. Knopf, 1975.
5 VIPONT, ELFRIDA. *The Elephant and the Bad Baby,* ill. by Raymond Briggs. Coward, 1970.
WABER, BERNARD. *I Was All Thumbs,* ill. by author. Houghton, 1975.
———. *Ira Sleeps Over,* ill. by author. Houghton, 1972.
———. *Lyle Finds His Mother.* Houghton, 1974.
5 WAHL, JAN. *Mulberry Tree,* ill. by Feodor Rojankovsky. Grosset, 1970.
WARD, LYND. *The Biggest Bear,* ill. by author. Houghton, 1952. Caldecott Medal.
§ WELBER, ROBERT. *The Train,* ill. by Deborah Ray. Pantheon, 1972.
WELLS, ROSEMARY. *Abdul,* ill. by author. Dial, 1975.
———. *Benjamin and Tulip,* ill. by author. Dial, 1973.
———. *Morris's Disappearing Bag,* ill. by author. Dial, 1975.
———. *Noisy Nora,* ill. by author. Dial, 1973.
5 WILDSMITH, BRIAN. *Brian Wildsmith's Circus,* ill. by author. Watts, 1970.
5 ———. *Brian Wildsmith's Fishes,* ill. by author. Watts, 1968.
5 ———. *Brian Wildsmith's Puzzles,* ill. by author. Watts, 1971.
5 ———. *The Little Wood Duck,* ill. by author. Watts, 1973.
WILLIAMS, BARBARA. *Albert's Toothache,* ill. by Kay Chorao. Dutton, 1974.
5 YASHIMA, TARO. *Umbrella,* ill. by author. Viking, 1958.
5 ZEMACH, HARVE. *Duffy and the Devil,* ill. by Margot Zemach. Farrar, 1973. Caldecott Medal.
5 ———. *The Judge; An Untrue Tale,* ill. by Margot Zemach. Farrar, 1969.

5 ———. *Small Boy Is Listening,* ill. by Margot Zemach. Houghton, 1959.

ZOLOTOW, CHARLOTTE. *Do You Know What I'll Do?* ill. by Garth Williams. Harper, 1958.

———. *The Hating Book,* ill. by Ben Shecter. Harper, 1969.

5 ———. *May I Visit?* ill. by Erik Blegvad. Harper, 1976.

5 ———. *Mr. Rabbit and the Lovely Present,* ill. by Maurice Sendak. Harper, 1962.

5 ———. *My Grandson Lew,* ill. by William Pène du Bois. Harper, 1974.

———. *The Unfriendly Book,* ill. by William Pène du Bois. Harper, 1975.

———. *When I Have a Little Girl,* ill. by Hilary Knight. Harper, 1965.

———. *When I Have a Son,* ill. by Hilary Knight. Harper, 1967.

———. *William's Doll,* ill. by William Pène du Bois. Harper, 1972.

Artists and Children's Books

Chapter 5

To study or discuss children's literature and not to include an examination of children's book illustration would be to ignore a significant element in the value and the appeal of these books. Just as a body of writing for children developed slowly, with youngsters at first simply appropriating those adult books that had some interest for them, so has the illustration of children's books developed slowly, bursting finally into the wealth and variety of art we have in twentieth-century books for children.

What is the explanation for today's marvelous richness in children's book illustration? The answer derives in part from the fact that the first books published for children included illustrations either to instruct, as did the courtesy books and alphabet books, or to support and extend the author's text. From the beginning, then, illustrations have served these functions. Certainly the prevalence of illustration in books for children in the past and in the present reflects an adult decision that pictures will attract and hold children's interest or will help them to learn about a subject.

Then and now, artwork in children's books served several functions: to clarify the text or to add information that is not in the text, in the case of nonfiction particularly; to enlarge or interpret the author's meaning, to evoke an appropriate mood, to establish setting or portray character in fiction; or simply to be decorative.

Art is communication, whether it is in a museum or in a book, and to judge the success of artwork in children's books we must evaluate it in terms of whether it speaks to the child. It must also be judged by how well it fits the story (or the informational text) and adapts to the confinements of page space and layout and color reproduction. And certainly we must evaluate the quality of the artwork itself, the artist's use of media and techniques.

Questions we can ask in judging the appropriateness of illustrations to text are:

—Do the pictures reflect the mood of the story, as Uri Shulevitz's do in *Dawn*? Or do they conflict with it?

—Do the pictures have any details that conflict with a textual statement? If the story describes five children, or a boy carrying a book, or a flower that is blue, the illustrations should have the right number of children, the right object under the boy's arm, the right color in the flower.

—Do the illustrations extend the text without distracting from it? If a page that shows musculature of the human body is so crowded with details that the printed information is obscured, the illustration is artistically inappropriate for the purpose of the text.

The question of whether the artwork speaks to the child is discussed under the heading "Children's Preferences" later in this chapter, but it should be kept in mind that children, especially young children, are not likely to have visual prejudices and preconceptions, and that they are a more eager audience for the artist's creative message than most adults. Certainly one way in which today's artists speak to children is to include in their illustrations youngsters of all ethnic backgrounds, drawn with no stereotypical details, and children and adults in unstereotyped sex roles. While there are no age barriers in the appreciation of art as art, illustrations must be considered in respect to the complexity of the concepts they contain and the relationship of those concepts to children's ability to understand at different ages. Most small children, for example, would find it difficult to understand the intricate details of David Macaulay's architectural drawings in *Pyramid,* drawings that speak eloquently to older children.

Finally, book illustration can be judged as art. Although individual reaction to an artist's work is subjective, all illustrations can be evaluated by artistic standards. Some of the questions we can ask in evaluating the elements in the illustration and its overall effect are:

—How does the artist use color? If the colors are bold and brilliant, do they suit the text they accompany? Or have they simply been splashed about, as colors often are in mass market books, on the premise that the brighter the page, the more it will attract children? Is color an essential element in the layout of the page? Does the color obscure or complement the lines of the drawings? Is the color reproduction of good quality?

—Does the artist use line effectively? A delicate line is appropriate for some stories, a bold one for others. Edward Ardizzone is a master of the economical line; Peter Parnall's line is spare and elegant; the light, broken line used by Robin Jacques is eminently suitable for the fairy tales he so often illustrates. Does the line express movement or is it static? Does the line give strength to the depiction of a person or object by being heavy or crosshatched? Is the line varied?

—Is the artist successful in handling shape? Whether the shape is distinct or vaguely suggested, simple or ornamented, free-flowing or rigid, the shape must suit the mood and intent of the story. How do shapes relate to each other on the page? If the drawing is realistic, is the perspective correct? Do the shapes fill the page or do they clutter it? If they represent characters, do they suggest qualities with which the author has invested them?

—Does the artist give texture to the illustrations? Arnold Lobel, in Cynthia Jameson's *The Clay Pot Boy,* gives the clay pot an unmistakable roundness and solidity; Feodor Rojankovsky's animals have an almost tactile furriness. Many artists use collage, alone or in combination with another medium, to obtain a textural difference. Barbara Cooney achieves the texture of diaphanous fabric with a thin wash of color, a representational treatment, while other artists use stylized patterns and ornamentation. A vaporous look may suggest fog, while blobs of white out of which objects emerge may fail to do so.

—How are the elements of each page or of facing pages arranged? Even when all other as-

Viewpoints

Evidence pointing to the aesthetic sensitivity of children can be gathered on all sides. They instinctively respond to balance, order, rhythm, originality—the artist's endless arrangements of color, line, shape, texture, and the writer's ingenious inventions and euphonies. But there are many exposures which can dwarf the natural growth of these responses. When the child is faced with a preponderance of inferior visual and literary impressions, a negative effect upon the development of taste and aesthetic enjoyment can be expected, as surely as a good effect can be predicted (all else remaining equal) when the child is surrounded by an artistic environment. He is not, after all, living in a vacuum.

Creating a beneficial environment for children is one of the most common objectives in education. Teachers and parents scrutinize the child and his surroundings with great care, trying to identify the activities which rouse curiosity and interest, which have strong and lasting effects and to which the child repeatedly returns. Yet they often overlook the arts or give them little emphasis, even when it is clear that few areas of experience involve children so completely and at such an instinctively high level. —Donnarae MacCann and Olga Richard, *The Child's First Books; A Critical Study of Pictures and Texts,* The H. W. Wilson Company, New York, 1973, p. 7.

From the book Strega Nona *by Tomie de Paola. © 1975 by Tomie de Paola. Published by Prentice-Hall, Inc., Englewood Cliffs, New Jersey. (Original in color)*

pects of the illustration are effective, it may fail in its intent if the composition is awkward or if there is not enough space to set off the various parts of the picture or if the illustration does not balance well in relation to the type area. The parts should have balance and direction so that the illustration has both unity and focus. Peter Parnall uses white space to give his pictures a clean, bare look and to focus the eye on elements he wishes to stress. Composition can be used to accentuate a mood or setting; Tomie de Paola, in *Strega Nona,* fills each drawing with sturdy figures in harmony with the robust and humorous folk tale and frames the drawings to suggest an onstage performance.

In evaluating the visual impact of a book, the primary concern is the illustration, but one must also consider the effect and effectiveness of the book jacket, the endpapers, the typeface used, and the way print is used on the page, particularly when it is placed in such a way that print and illustration together make a pattern. Heavy block letters do not suit a delicate fairy tale while they may be both effective and appropriate for a book of modern poetry. A clear, clean type can be lost if it is printed on a dark background or is obscured by illustrative details.

Beautiful pictures can help sell a trivial book, and sometimes poor illustrations can cause a first-rate story to be overlooked. With today's offset printing and remarkable color reproduction, the eye appeal of books is of tremendous importance, and the artist therefore plays a significant role in books for children, whether they are picture books for younger children which have little or no text, picture story books in which the illustrations are an integral part of the whole, or illustrated books in which the pictures are few and play a comparatively minor role.

From what they see in comics and slick magazines as well as in books from supermarket shelves, children know many kinds of pictures. They "read" many parts of their environment, and often have great visual sophistication and experience before they become aware of printed matter, whether in books or on box tops. Due in large part to television, children today probably have a higher degree of visual experience than children of earlier generations. Building on such experience, we can begin to lead them into an awareness of finer examples of graphic art, old and new. For, as Bertha Mahony says in *Illustrators of Children's Books,* ". . . art in children's books is a part of all art, not an isolated special field. In every period the greatest artists have shared in it."[1] But in the evaluation of illustrations as in the evaluation of stories, the children themselves must be the starting point if we are to meet their needs and extend the range of art they appreciate.

Children's Preferences

Children begin as stern literalists, demanding a truthful interpretation of the text. If a character is described as redheaded, no child is going to accept brown hair without protest. When Ludwig Bemelmans says that there are twelve little girls who go walking from Madeline's school, the child counts to see that the artist has put them all in.

Even young children observe and enjoy all the cozy details of Randolph Caldecott's *Frog He Would A-Wooing Go* or of Eleanor Schick's *Neighborhood Knight* as readily as they follow the everyday drama of weather in Uri Shulevitz's *Rain Rain Rivers*. If the illustrations interpret the story, the child will accept such varied techniques as the splashy colors of Nicolas Mordvinoff's *Finders Keepers*, Robert Lawson's finely detailed pen-and-ink sketches of landscapes and small animals, and Leo and Diane Dillon's bold patterns for *Why Mosquitoes Buzz in People's Ears*.

Being literal, the young child also wants a picture synchronized precisely with the text. When *Make Way for Ducklings* has the mother duck leading her offspring across a busy Boston thoroughfare, the child is glad that Robert McCloskey placed his unforgettable picture with the description and not a page or two later. Older children as well are irked by illustrations that appear before or after the episode they are supposed to represent.

Children are as fond of action in pictures as in stories. They love Ernest Shepard's gay action drawings of the skipping Christopher Robin, the tumult of Martha Alexander's *Out! Out! Out!* and the droll, carefree abandon of Maurice Sendak's capering children.

We know that young children also like bright colors, but not to the exclusion of black and white or the gentle colors in Adrienne Adams's illustrations for Alice Goudey's *Houses from the Sea* and the muted hues in Arnold Lobel's *Frog and Toad Together*. G. LaVerne Freeman and Ruth Sunderlin Freeman, in their evaluation of children's preferences in picture-book illustration,[2] found that children preferred bright, strong colors but that they also seemed to accept black-and-white pictures. The Freemans suggest that this acceptance may be due to familiarity with black-and-white television programs.

On the whole, there is evidence that children do prefer color to black and white in book illustrations. Yet young children delight also in Lynd Ward's powerful monochromes for *The Biggest Bear*, and older children are pleased with the fine, clear minutiae of William Pène du Bois's drawings for his *Twenty-One Balloons* or those of Edwin Tunis in *Shaw's Fortune*.

[1]The Horn Book, Inc., 1947.

[2]*The Child and His Picture Book* (Century House, rev. ed. 1967).

Illustration by Eleanor Schick is reproduced by permission of Greenwillow Books from Neighborhood Knight *by Eleanor Schick. Copyright © 1976 by Eleanor Schick.*

Adults often assume that small children do not see details in a picture, but they do. Children look for the small figures of the mice in Graham Oakley's *The Church Mice Spread Their Wings*. But the same youngster who will gloat over small details in a picture may also enjoy the bold strength of a single object by Leonard Baskin, or the sharp, clear outlines of Artzybasheff's illustrations for *The Fairy Shoemaker and Other Fairy Poems*.

Children, then, respond to a wide variety of book illustrations—even crude or saccharine drawings if they help tell the story. Their visual sensitivity can open their lives to positive early experience with books as well as enlarge their experience with art. The more they are exposed to authentic art of many styles, the greater the possibility that their tastes will diversify.

Reproducing the Work of the Artist

It's a long way from the drawing board to the finished book. We enjoy today a wealth of varied and beautiful books in part because of the technological advances in printing, in part because of the growing awareness of the importance of early childhood education, and in part because good artists, designers, and editors are dedicated to giving children the best. As Jean Karl, a children's book editor, has said:

> *It is the publisher's responsibility to choose the illustrator for a picture book, but most try to take the author's preferences into consideration, and all try to find the illustrator who will make the manuscript into a unified book. For this, the author's vision of the finished book is important, because it is part of the author's concept of what he has done.*[3]

There are many picture books in which the artist's conception of an author's characters and mood are enchanting in their perfection (for example, Garth Williams's illustrations for Natalie Carlson's *The Happy Orpheline* and Maurice Sendak's for Else Holmelund Minarik's *Little Bear* series). Some of the best picture books, however, are those written and illustrated by the same person. Rosemary Wells, Arnold Lobel, Martha Alexander, Edward Ardizzone, Maurice Sendak, Uri Shulevitz, Evaline Ness, and Marcia Brown are among the contemporary author-artists in whose books the text and illustrations perfectly complement each other. This is true also of books done for older children by such author-illustrators as Leonard Everett Fisher and Edwin Tunis.

The editor and the book designer must, in collaboration with the illustrator, consider all the visual aspects that contribute both to the beauty of a book and to its appropriateness for its intended audience—the size and clarity of the type, the leading (space between lines), the layout of the page, the amount of print on each page, as well as the illustrations. Of course such picture books as John Goodall's *Naughty Nancy* and Iela and Enzo Mari's *The Apple and the Moth* (the first, a story; the second, the record of a moth's life cycle) have no words at all, but the pictures have been so carefully planned that what happens is crystal clear. In books for older children, too, the arrangement of all visual material (Anthony Ravielli's precise drawings for *Wonders of the Human Body* are fine examples) illuminates and expands the text.

As Edward Ardizzone insists, "drawing is of paramount importance."[4] The artist must be able to draw, to interpret the story, or, in informational books, interpret accurately the given facts, and to understand the printing processes by which original artwork is converted into illustrations for a book.

There are three basic methods of reproduction—relief, intaglio, and surface or planographic printing. Each of these may be direct (done largely by hand) or indirect (done by mechanical procedures).

In *relief* the surface to be printed is raised. The most familiar examples of direct or manual techniques are probably the wood blocks or linoleum blocks on which a picture is drawn, the surrounding areas cut away, and the remaining portion inked to be impressed upon paper. The indirect or mechanical counterpart is the linecut (also called a line en-

[3]Jean Karl, *From Childhood to Childhood* (John Day, 1970).

[4]Edward Ardizzone, "Creation of a Picture Book," *Top of the News*, December 1959.

graving or line block). In this process the illustration is photographed, being mechanically reduced to correct size, on a glass plate. When the film is hardened, it is transferred to a sensitized metal plate and is developed and washed. The lines of the drawing are brought into relief by bathing the plate in acid, which eats away the part that has no lines. The plate, nailed to a wooden block so that the drawing is type-high, will print the raised design on paper.

When a drawing has shadings, a halftone engraving is made. To obtain the shadings, tones between black and white, the drawing is photographed through a halftone screen, which is crosshatched at right angles with fine lines. This breaks the pictorial copy into tiny dots: the darker the gray, the more dots to the inch. The acid etching for the halftone requires much more care than that for the simple linecut and must be done in stages so that the deeper parts can be re-etched. If colors are used, only one color can be printed at a time. A four-color picture with varying strengths requires four halftone blocks (black, yellow, magenta, and cyan blue can reproduce almost any color or shade of color) to reproduce the shading and intensity of the original.

The second method of reproduction is *intaglio*. In this process the part to be printed is below the surface rather than above the surface as in relief. Mezzotint, steel engraving, and etching are some of the direct or hand intaglio techniques. Photogravure is the indirect or mechanical technique. In this process the surface is broken into dots as for the halftone, but here each dot forms a pit—the variation is in depth rather than in size as in the halftone. The surface ink is scraped off with a knife and the remaining ink is picked out from the pits when paper is pressed on the cylinder. To print color photogravure, a separate plate must be made for each color.

The third method of reproduction is *surface* or *planographic* printing. Stencils and silk screens are examples of direct or hand techniques. Indirect or mechanical techniques include collotype (very expensive and seldom used) and lithography. Lithography is based on the principle that water and grease do not mix. The process was discovered accidentally in 1796, when Aloys Senefelder used a crayon to write a list on a slab of limestone, and then wet and inked the stone. The water repelled ink except for the writing, which didn't hold water because of the crayon grease. In today's printing, the stone is replaced by a sheet of emulsion-coated zinc on which the images are printed photographically, much in the way that halftones are produced, except that the dots are on the emulsion and will accept ink. The bare metal around the dots repels ink, and the dots are impressed in the printing process. Most lithographic work today is produced by offset process, using an extra roller to transfer the impression. The use of offset lithography for color work is one of today's most significant advances in the reproduction of illustrations.

Colors in illustrations may be mechanically separated as already mentioned, or the artist may pre-separate them; that is, make a separate drawing for each color, with transparent sheets perfectly aligned one over the other. If only two colors that do not touch each other are used, the artist can use red and black and instruct the printer to use them as keys for any other two colors.

Evidence of the importance of children's book illustration includes the establishment of the Caldecott Medal in the United States, the Greenaway Medal in England, the Howard-Gibbon Medal in Canada, and the international Hans Christian Andersen Medal for il-

Viewpoints

There is no point, for [the picture book illustrator], in trying to be purely representational. The meaning in his picture comes from the way he arranges colors, lines, shapes, and textures into a special synthesis—one that will please the senses and achieve an aesthetic experience for the reader. Object recognition is a criterion based on the commonplace. It is concerned with simple imitation. The arts are the very antithesis of commonplace standards of imitation, recognition, and the sense of familiarity derived from such considerations.—Olga Richard, "The Visual Language of the Picture Book," *The Wilson Library Bulletin,* December 1969, p. 435.

lustrators as well as authors. The American Institute of Graphic Arts now includes the names of children's book illustrators and designers in their annual "Fifty Books of the Year" and holds a biennial Children's Book Show which exhibits some one hundred books chosen for artistic and typographic merit. The Children's Book Council's annual Children's Book Showcase, and widely circulated posters by children's book illustrators call attention to Children's Book Week and also to the importance of the illustrations in books for young people.

Many of the artists who have contributed to children's books will be discussed here in chronological order, according to their birth dates. Author-artists like Maurice Sendak are discussed also in genre chapters and many creators of picture books are discussed in Chapter 4; in these other chapters, the focus is on their writing.

Woodcuts and Engravings Before 1800

In 1484 William Caxton issued the first English edition of *Aesop's Fables,* illustrated with woodcuts by some unknown artist or artists. This was an adult book, but if children saw the pictures and heard the stories, they undoubtedly took the book as their own. Since Caxton's publication of the fables these little moralities have been continuously reprinted, usually illustrated by outstanding artists who were doubtless attracted by the dramatic situations the stories embody.

Between the Caxton edition of the fables and the epoch-making *Orbis Pictus,* there were hornbooks and battledores for children but with few or no pictures. There were also the popular chapbooks, enlivened with crude woodcuts, which were beloved by the story-hungry children of the sixteenth and seventeenth centuries.

The *Orbis Pictus* of Comenius is assumed to be the first picture book prepared for children. Today, we would say that it more nearly resembles a primer. It was written in Latin in 1657 or 1658 by a Moravian bishop and translated into most European languages, including English in 1658. The pictures and text are stilted but not without charm. The word *Flores* appears above a small woodcut showing flowers in a vase and also in a field; the picture is followed by a pleasant commentary on spring flowers. Whatever the subject, there was a conscious effort to associate words and pictures and to use the latter to lead directly into the text. The *Orbis Pictus* seems tame and wooden today, but for English-speaking children it marked the beginning of picture books planned especially for them.

Even the Newbery publications, important as they are in the history of children's books, did little to advance the art of illustration. It is generally agreed that only for *Little Goody Two Shoes* (1765) did the artist (possibly Thomas Bewick) execute his woodcuts with

Flowers. XV. Flores.

Amongst the Flowers the most noted,	Inter flores notissimi,
In the beginning of the Spring are the	Primo vere,
Violet, 1. the *Crow-toes,* 2. the *Daffodil,* 3.	*Viola,* 1. *Hyacinthus,* 2. *Narcissus,* 3.
Then the *Lillies,* 4. white and yellow and blew, 5. and the *Rose,* 6. and the *Clove gilliflowers,* 7. &c.	Tum *Lilia,* 4. alba & lutea, & cœrulea, 5. tandem *Rosa,* 6. & *Caryophillum,* 7. &c.
Of these *Garlands,* 8. and *Nosegays,* 9. are tyed round with twigs.	Ex his *Serta,* 8. & *Serviæ,* 9. vientur.
There are added also *sweet herbs,* 10. as *Marjoram, Flower gentle, Rue, Lavender, Rosemary.*	Adquntur etiam *Herbæ odoratæ,* 10. ut *Amaracus, Amaranthus, Ruta, Lavendula, Rosmarinus,* (Libanotis).

From Comenius's Orbis Pictus.

From Aesop's Fables, *Thomas Bewick edition. Faithfully reprinted from rare Newcastle edition. Published by T. Saint in 1784 with the original engravings by Thomas Bewick. From the John G. White Collection, Cleveland Public Library.*

unusual grace and synchronize them with the text so that they are illustrations in the true sense of the word – interpreting or illuminating the story.

For the most part these earliest producers of crude woodcuts were minor artists, usually unknown. It was not until the advent of Thomas Bewick that children's books were adorned by a major artist.

Thomas Bewick's first book designed for children was *A Pretty Book of Pictures for Little Masters and Misses* or *Tommy Trip's History of Beasts and Birds* (1779). This book, exceedingly rare today, is an example of the artist's skill in the use of the woodcut. He developed better tools for this work, made effective use of the white line, and carried the woodcut to a new level of beauty. Most of Bewick's finest drawings seem to have been for books originally planned for adults as, for instance his various editions of Aesop's fables, particularly those of 1784 and 1818. The former was reprinted in 1878 by his publisher, T. Saint, from the original blocks. It is called *Bewick's Select Fables of Aesop and Others.* These pictures show the artist's knowledge and love of the whole outdoor world – plants, trees, birds, and beasts. Certainly Thomas Bewick, and to a somewhat lesser extent his brother John, raised the woodcut to a high level of artistic achievement.

An interesting by-product of the Bewicks' contribution is that artists of established reputations began to sign their pictures for children's books.

The Nineteenth Century

William Blake had brought delicate colors into his book for children, *Songs of Innocence* (1789), not by color printing but by hand. Color printing, however, was widely used from about 1803 to 1835, though at the beginning of the nineteenth century the most notable illustrators were still working in black and white.

Examine, in the color section, the two early colored illustrations by unknown artists, the first for *The History of the House That Jack Built* and the second for *A Continuation of the Comic Adventures of Old Mother Hubbard and Her Dog.* They are interesting proof that publishers were beginning to recognize the lure of color in books for young children.

William Mulready

The century began propitiously, then, with some color printing for children's books, but it is the work of William Mulready that first brought distinction to those early years of the century.

This illustrator is remembered for his gay, fanciful drawings for *The Butterfly's Ball* (1807) by William Roscoe. This rhymed de-

Illustration by William Mulready. From The Butterfly's Ball *by William Roscoe. Published by J. Harris, 1807.*

scription of a fairy picnic enjoyed enormous popularity for over fifty years, aided no doubt by Mulready's amusing pictures in black and white. Some of his bees, snails, butterflies, and other guests of the party have human bodies with true-to-the-species creatures atop their heads or else they are well-drawn insects or animals piloted by elfish figures perched on their backs. The mole, for instance, has a fat, blind gnome for a rider. Unfortunately, the children's books this gifted artist adorned do not stand the test of time as his drawings do. This is a fate that threatens the lasting fame of illustrators in each generation.

George Cruikshank

George Cruikshank, a great artist of this period, was a satirist and a cartoonist for England's famous *Punch*. In contrast to Mulready, Cruikshank had the good fortune to illustrate an English translation of the Grimms' *Collection of German Popular Stories* (1824 and 1826), a classic that is ageless in its appeal. In black and white, his humorous, lively, cleverly drawn pictures are the embodiment of the tales.

Sir John Tenniel

Inseparable from Lewis Carroll's *Alice's Adventures in Wonderland* (1865) and *Through the Looking Glass* (1871) are the illustrations by Sir John Tenniel, cartoonist for *Punch*. Other artists hopefully make pictures for this classic fantasy, but their illustrations usually seem inadequate when compared with Tenniel's beloved figures. Unforgettable are serious, pinafored, long-haired Alice, the smartly dressed, bustling White Rabbit, and all the other mad, topsy-turvy characters of the Wonderland and the Looking Glass worlds. Strong in line and composition, drawn with beautiful clarity and poker-faced drollery, these illustrations enhance the fantasy and give it convincing reality.

Arthur Hughes

The illustrations of Arthur Hughes are as strongly associated with George Macdonald's *At the Back of the North Wind* (1871) and *The Princess and the Goblin* (1872) as are Tenniel's illustrations with *Alice's Adventures in Wonderland*. Hughes worked in black and white and was an interpreter of fantasy, but his pictures are as different from Cruikshank's or Tenniel's as the Macdonald books are different from the Grimms' fairy tales or Carroll's *Alice*. For Macdonald's two fairy tales the never-never land of the pictures is all mystery, gentleness, and lovely innocence. These qualities carry over to Hughes's more realistic pictures for Christina Rossetti's *Sing-Song* (1872), little masterpieces of tenderness and beauty.

Walter Crane

In *English Children's Books*, Percy Muir points out in the chapter "The Importance of Pictures" that it was ". . . in the sixties that publishers began first to attempt to sell books to children mainly for the interest of the illustrations." What a line of successors that movement launched! Muir then goes on to show how much modern color printing owes to Edmund Evans, a publisher and an artist in his own right. A pioneer in color printing, Evans had long inveighed against the cheap, gaudy illustrations used in books for children. He firmly believed that even an inexpensive paperback book planned for the nursery child could be beautiful in design and color. In Walter Crane, Evans found an artist to carry out his theories.

Trained as a wood engraver, Walter Crane was greatly influenced by the work of the Pre-Raphaelites and also by his study of Japanese prints. Both of these influences are evident in his pictures—in the idealized figures of women and children and in the sparse, decorative landscapes. Between 1867 and 1876 Crane produced over thirty so-called "toy books,"[5] published chiefly by Routledge and generally undated. Crane took these books so seriously that he worked over every page, including the typography, so that it came out a well-composed whole. His *Baby's Opera* and *Baby's Bouquet* were a series of English nursery

[5]The term "toy book" is used today to mean books with pop-ups or cut-outs that make them more toys than books. The Crane "toy books" were simply books intended for the nursery prereading child.

songs with words, music, and pictures. Later he decorated, also in color, Hawthorne's *Wonder Book* (1892). (See color section.)

Kate Greenaway

Edmund Evans was greatly taken with the delicate colors and decorative borders of Kate Greenaway's pictures for her own rhymes. He printed her book *Under the Window* (1878) by a costly process that reproduced the pictures with remarkable fidelity. To her surprise, the artist found herself famous almost overnight, and she outsold all the other artists of her day, the initial sales of *Under the Window* running to some 70,000 copies. It still sells, and Evans's firm is still printing her books.

Her style was unique—graceful but static figures in quaint old-fashioned clothes, at play, at tea, or otherwise decorously engaged. The pages are gay with garlands of fruits or flowers, mostly in delicate pastel colors. Her pictures often have a gentle humor, and their grace and charm still delight the eye. (See color section.)

Illustration by Arthur Frost. From Uncle Remus and His Friends *by Joel Chandler Harris. Published 1892 by Houghton Mifflin.*

Randolph Caldecott

Randolph Caldecott, for whom the Caldecott Medal is named, was the third of Edmund Evans's famous triumvirate and, like the others, owes much to that printer's bold experiments with color printing. Caldecott succeeded and far surpassed Walter Crane in the production of illustrated toy books.

Caldecott grew up in the Shropshire country, familiar with country fairs, the hunt, dogs, horses, and the lovely English landscape, all of which are evident in his pictures. Around 1878 he began to work on the nursery toy books with which we associate his name and fame. Probably his most famous illustrations (1878) are those for William Cowper's *The Diverting History of John Gilpin* (1785). Caldecott made Cowper's poem into a picture story, funny both to children and adults and a masterpiece of droll action. No one ever drew such humorous horses or such recklessly inept riders. His illustrated *Mother Goose* rhymes in papercovered book form are among his loveliest and most original creations. Caldecott did a number of these toy books, selling at one shilling, and they have seldom been surpassed by our best and most expensive modern picture books. (See color section.)

Arthur Frost

For that classic collection *Nights with Uncle Remus*, Arthur Frost made pen-and-ink pictures as comic and irresistible as that gay rogue, Brer Rabbit himself. Whether he is "sashaying" down the road in his patched and droopy old pants or talking turkey to Tar Baby, he is a picture of rural shrewdness. Frost's whole gallery of animal folk provides as marvelous characterizations as any Caldecott ever made.

Howard Pyle

Howard Pyle was another American artist who worked in black and white. His heroic and romantic pictures for such books as *Robin Hood* (1883), *Otto of the Silver Hand* (1888), and *Men of Iron* (1890) are meticulous in their fidelity to the historical costumes and weapons of the period. Yet his elaborations of robes, courtly trappings, and tournament details are always subordinated to the interpretation of character or mood. The poignancy of young Otto's tragedy moves anyone who looks at those pictures, and, in contrast, the high good humor of Robin Hood is equally evident. Here was an author-artist with a gift for telling stories in words and pictures.

Leslie Brooke

Although some of the work of the English Leslie Brooke was published as late as 1935, he is so much in the Caldecott tradition that he seems to belong to the nineteenth century. In delicate pastel colors he provides glimpses of the English countryside, pictures as charming as any Caldecott produced. His *Mother Goose* characters in *Ring o' Roses* (1922) are delightful, and his pigs are triumphs of whimsical characterization. The *Johnny Crow* books (1903, 1907, and 1935) are his own invention. Johnny Crow is the perfect host for two parties of birds and beasts so adroitly characterized both in verse and pictures that his books are classic examples of what picture books can be in the hands of a creative artist-writer. (See color section.)

The Twentieth Century

Beatrix Potter

Beatrix Potter's *The Tale of Peter Rabbit* (1901), a milestone in children's literature, marks the beginning of the modern picture story—the book in which pictures are so integral a part of the story that the nonreading child can soon "read" the story from the pictures. In Beatrix Potter's books, her clear watercolors show small animals dressed up like human country folk pursuing their activities through fascinating English lanes and meadows or within cozy interiors. The pictures are as beautifully composed as the texts, and in her little books there is a perfect union of the two arts. (See color section.)

Arthur Rackham

Arthur Rackham, whose distinctive work is easily recognized, illustrated well over fifty books but seemed most at home in the field of folklore. His pictures for *The Fairy Tales of Grimm* (1900) made an immediate impression, and Rackham enthusiasts and collectors began with that publication. There are no fluttering fairies to be found on his pages; instead, there are earthy old gnomes, ogres, and witches, eerie, mysterious, and sometimes menacing. In black and white or full color his pictures are alive with details that the casual observer may miss—small, furry faces or elfin figures peering out from leaves or half hidden in grasses. We are told that Rackham drew his pictures before painting them, a technique that seems to strengthen them, because whether the colors are dark and somber or clear and light they have body and vitality. For *The Wind in the Willows* (1940), his characterizations of Mole, Ratty, Toad, and all the others are inimitable, and the details of picnics and cozy rooms enhance the warmth of that story. Here is an artist with unique gifts which he devoted almost entirely to the illustration of books for children. (See color section.)

Ernest H. Shepard

The deft pen of Ernest Shepard was drawing for *Punch* as early as 1907, but not until the publication of A. A. Milne's *When We Were Very Young* (1924) with the Shepard illustrations were his pen-and-ink sketches widely and affectionately known. Milne's *Winnie-the-Pooh* followed in 1926, *Now We Are Six* in 1927, and *The House at Pooh Corner* in 1928, all illustrated by Shepard. These pen-and-ink sketches of Christopher Robin, Pooh, and their companions show mood, character, and situation. Shepard's interpretative ability is shown again in illustrations for Kenneth Grahame's *The Reluctant Dragon* (1938) and *The Wind in the Willows* (1931). Even Rackham's illustrations for this latter book cannot surpass some of Shepard's sketches. Mole "jumping off all four legs at once, in the joy of living," or Toad picnicking grandly or waddling off disguised as a washerwoman—these pictures and many others are sheer perfection. In 1957 Shepard made eight color plates for *The World of Pooh* and followed, when he was eighty, with eight more for the Golden

Illustration by E. H. Shepard. From The House at Pooh Corner *by A. A. Milne. Copyright 1956, by A. A. Milne. Reproduced by permission of the publishers, E. P. Dutton & Co., Inc.*

Anniversary Edition of *The Wind in the Willows* (1959). His color plates are beautiful but add nothing to the virtuosity of his pen-and-ink sketches.

Kurt Wiese

Sent to China on business, taken prisoner by the Japanese, back to Germany by way of Australia and Africa—somewhere along the line, German-born Kurt Wiese determined to be an artist. This background of travel and of knowledge of many peoples gave color and authenticity to his illustrations for such books as Elizabeth Lewis's *Young Fu of the Upper Yangtze* (1932), Kipling's *Jungle Books* (1932), and that classic little story by Marjorie Flack, *The Story About Ping* (1933).

Perhaps the most outstanding characteristic of Kurt Wiese's work is his amazing versatility. He illustrated over a hundred books, and whether it is Ping, a Chinese duck waddling up the gangplank of his particular junk, or Felix Salten's wild and beautiful *Bambi* (1929), or his own amusing stories *Rabbits' Revenge* (1940) and the Chinese *Fish in the Air* (1948), or Claire Huchet Bishop's *The Truffle Pig* (1971), and whether he is working in black and white or full color, character and situations are illustrated with humor, fidelity to the story, and fine draftsmanship. (See color section.)

To this group of artists, born in the nineteenth century but producing in the early or middle years of the twentieth century, more names could be added. E. Boyd Smith's *The Story of Pocahontas and Captain John Smith* (1906) is a moving narrative with pictures remarkable for their composition and their interpretative quality. Jessie Willcox Smith used soft, dark colors in her illustrations for Stevenson's *A Child's Garden of Verses* (1905). She was a pupil of Howard Pyle, as was N. C. Wyeth, whose illustrations for *Robin Hood* (1917) and *Robinson Crusoe* (1920) are powerful in composition and rich in color. Thomas Handforth won the Caldecott Medal for his major contribution to children's books, *Mei Li* (1938). His black-and-white illustrations are vigorous and full of action, and they make the little Chinese heroine seem real and understandable. Another Caldecott winner is the picture book *The Big Snow* (1948) by Berta and Elmer Hader. It is typical of the Haders' work—a slight story, soft colors, and a warm feeling for birds, animals, and kindly people. Marie Hall Ets did her amusing *Mister Penny* (1935) in black and white, but her sensitive and perceptive watercolors for *Play with Me* (1955), about a little girl learning to be quiet with shy woodland creatures, are quite the

Reprinted with permission of Macmillan Publishing Co., Inc. From The Big Snow *by Berta and Elmer Hader. Copyright 1948 by Berta and Elmer Hader, renewed 1976 by Berta Hader. (Original in color)*

loveliest she has ever produced. *Nine Days to Christmas* (1959) won the Caldecott Medal but is, in spite of full, bright colors, less interesting than her earlier books. *Gilberto and the Wind* (1963) and *Talking Without Words* (1970) are among her most effective books.

No book of this size can hope to name and appraise half the talented people who are doing fine and original illustrations for children's books today. Of the sampling of these artists that follows, some were born in the nineteenth century, but most of these began their work in the thirties and some have continued producing in the years following. The exception is Wanda Gág, whose epoch-making book *Millions of Cats* appeared before the thirties.

Wanda Gág

In 1928, Wanda Gág's picture story *Millions of Cats* ushered in what came to be known as "The Golden Thirties" of picture books. It still outshines in strong story interest many of its successors. It is indeed about as close to perfection as a picture story can be. It is told with all the rhythm and cadence of the old European storytellers and is illustrated with striking black-and-white lithographs that repeat the flowing rhythm of the text. Wanda Gág was steeped in the European folk tales she heard told as a child, and so it is not surprising that her own completely fresh and original four stories have a folk flavor. They are, in addition to *Millions of Cats, Funny Thing* (1929), *Snippy and Snappy* (1931), and *Nothing at All* (1941). Her illustrations for *ABC Bunny* (1933) and for four small books of *Grimms' Fairy Tales* have the same flowing lines, dramatic black-and-white areas, and homely warmth that are characteristic of everything she did.

Marguerite de Angeli

Whether De Angeli gives us a rebellious young Quaker girl of long ago, kicking her bonnet down the stairs in *Thee Hannah!* (1940), or a too lively young pioneer schoolboy in *Skippack School* (1939), or whether she gives us some two-hundred sixty illustrations for her *Mother Goose* (1954), the people are always lovely to look at, the colors warm and soft, and the details of outdoor scenes or interiors authentic and beautifully composed. Minority groups and historical subjects have held special interest for this artist. The Pennsylvania Dutch in *Henner's Lydia* (1936), the Amish in *Yonie Wondernose* (1944), the Polish children in *Up the Hill* (1942), and the hero of her splendid historical story *Door in the Wall* (1949 Newbery Medal) are most appealing.

James Daugherty

Thomas Handforth's *Mei Li* was awarded the Caldecott Medal in 1938, but another picture story was also worthy of the award that year—*Andy and the Lion* by James Daugherty. Later, this author-artist received the Newbery Medal for his *Daniel Boone* (1939). Both books are as distinguished for their illustrations as for the text. Warm earthiness and a tender appreciation of people mark his pictures. *Andy and the Lion* is entertaining, but the pictures are unforgettable. The rear view of young Andy reaching for a book on high library shelves, or

Illustration by James Daugherty from Andy and the Lion *by James Daugherty. Copyright 1938, copyright © renewed 1966 by James Daugherty. Reprinted by permission of The Viking Press, Inc. (Original with color)*

Andy suddenly confronted with a lion in full roar, or Andy toppling over backward as he extracts the thorn—these have a great gusto. Daugherty's heroic illustrations for *Daniel Boone* (1939) have vigor, and those for *Poor Richard* (1941) reveal his wonderful gift for characterization. James Daugherty's portraits are as distinctive as the heroes they record.

Maud and Miska Petersham

Maud and Miska Petersham won the Caldecott Medal for their American Mother Goose, *The Rooster Crows* (1945) despite a black stereotype which many people found offensive and which was changed in a later edition. They celebrated the advent of a grandchild with the charming *The Box with Red Wheels* (1949), a book with bold, bright colors, strong composition, and a slight story with a surprise ending which appeals to children four to seven. However, it is their beautiful picture story of the Nativity, *The Christ Child* (1931), that has especially endeared them to many children and adults. Their pictures, historically authentic in scene, costumes, and other details, have successfully caught and interpreted for young children the tender majesty of that narrative.

Feodor Rojankovsky

Russian-born Feodor Rojankovsky has done unforgettable illustrations with earthy colors and homely, lovable, old peasant faces for Hans Christian Andersen's *The Old Man Is Always Right* (1940). There is this same earthy quality about all of Rojankovsky's people—the sturdy, unprettified children and the stocky, dumpy grownups with their warm, woolly scarves or mittens. As for his animals, there were never furrier kittens or fluffier feathered fowls. Texture, rich colors, and good draftsmanship are hallmarks of this artist. It was Rojankovsky's gay, amusing illustrations for *Frog Went a-Courtin'* (1955) by John Langstaff that won him a long deserved Caldecott Medal. He also illustrated *Over in the Meadow* (1966) with John Langstaff and Jan Wahl's *Mulberry Tree* (1970). He was one of the notable colorists among modern artists. (See color section.)

Robert Lawson

If pen-and-ink sketches can be described as witty, Robert Lawson's pictures certainly deserve the description. Who can ever forget the first glimpse of that mild young bull in *The Story of Ferdinand* (1936), peacefully inhaling the fragrance of flowers instead of snorting around the bull ring, or Mr. Popper blandly coping with his penguins in *Mr. Popper's Penguins* (1938), or the scene of the electric shock in *Ben and Me* (1939). In contrasting mood are Lawson's gravely beautiful drawings for *Pilgrim's Progress* (1939) and for *Adam of the Road* (1942), set in thirteenth-century England. Robert Lawson was a master draftsman, and every detail of scenes, costumes, and characterizations is meticulously executed. But not until he wrote as well as illustrated *Ben and Me* did his admirers realize the full scope of his talents and versatility. Text and pictures are equally amusing and full of the wry wisdom that appears again in his own *Mr. Revere and I* (1953), *Rabbit Hill* (1944 Newbery Medal), and its sequel, *The Tough Winter* (1954).

Edwin Tunis

Each book by Edwin Tunis is a product of intensive research and a model of clean draftsmanship and scrupulous accuracy. For his first six books, the line drawings were in pen and ink; to relieve strain on his arm muscles he adopted, on the advice of his physician, crayon-plus-wash both for his work in black and white and for the color drawings for *Chipmunks on the Doorstep* (1971). His books are handsome and vastly informative, *Indians* (1959) being used as a text in American Indian schools and *Weapons* (1954) as a text for the United States Air Force. *Frontier Living* (1961) was a Newbery Medal Honor Book; *The Young United States* (1969), *Colonial Living* (1957), and *Shaw's Fortune* (1966) are, like his other books, evidence that Edwin Tunis was a historian with a drawing board.

Edward Ardizzone

Only a first-rate artist like Edward Ardizzone could bless Tim with such splendid seascapes

Illustration by Roger Duvoisin. From The Happy Lion *by Louise Fatio. Copyright, 1954, by Louise Fatio Duvoisin and Roger Duvoisin. Reprinted by permission of Whittlesey House (McGraw-Hill). (Original in color)*

and glimpses of port towns. Whether the books come in the handsome, outsize edition of the first *Little Tim and the Brave Sea Captain* (1936) or in the small-size edition of *Tim All Alone* (1957), the pictures are watercolors, beautifully reproduced, full of the power of the sea and the jaunty courage of seafaring folk. Master of the economical line, Ardizzone has a droll quality that makes his figures memorable; his illustrations for Cecil Lewis's *The Otterbury Incident* (1969) and for Eleanor Estes's *Miranda the Great* (1967) are as beguiling as those for his own *The Wrong Side of the Bed* (1970). (See color section.)

Roger Duvoisin

Roger Duvoisin uses a variety of techniques and has an unfailing sense of strong composition and design. For Alvin Tresselt's books on weather and seasons, such as *White Snow, Bright Snow* (1947 Caldecott Medal), his colors are flat washes and the pictures simplified to a posterlike effect. For Louise Fatio's series of stories—*The Happy Lion* (1954), *The Happy Lion's Vacation* (1967), *The Happy Lion's Rabbits* (1974)—his pictures are in soft colors with lively details. Gian-Carlo Menotti's *Amahl and the Night Visitors* (1952) is illustrated in dark, rich colors with a somber, dramatic quality that is at one with this story from the familiar opera. Duvoisin's own books about the hippopotamus Veronica and the series of tales about the goose Petunia have rare humor. Here is a major artist giving his best to children's books. (See color section.)

Ingri and Edgar Parin d'Aulaire

Ingri and Edgar Parin d'Aulaire are the artists who brought the picture biography into its own. It is interesting that Norwegian-born Ingri and Swiss-born and French-educated Edgar should have turned to the heroes of America, their adopted land, for their subjects. After the d'Aulaires make their first sketches, they work directly on the lithograph stone, which gives their pictures unusual strength and depth. These qualities were not so effective in their *George Washington*

(1936), in which the pictures have always seemed wooden. But by the time they wrote the text and made the pictures for *Abraham Lincoln* (1939), they were using this difficult medium superbly. The colors in this book are deep and rich, and the pictures are full of authentic factual details. The lines and composition have a sort of primitive simplicity that suggests folk art. *Benjamin Franklin* (1950) is particularly rich in storytelling details, *Leif the Lucky* (1951) and *Columbus* (1955) are the most colorful, *Pocahontas* (1946) and *Buffalo Bill* (1952), the most picturesque. Their large, handsome *The Book of Greek Myths* (1962), *Norse Gods and Giants* (1967), and *Trolls* (1972) are other examples of their versatility. (See color section.)

Lynd Ward

The Biggest Bear (1952) won the Caldecott Medal for Lynd Ward, who was already a well-known illustrator, and that book seems to have overshadowed the lovely pictures he made for Hildegarde Swift's *The Little Red Lighthouse and the Great Gray Bridge* (1942). In spite of its long, awkward title, this is a significant picture story that is made doubly moving by Ward's illustrations. In both books—*The Biggest Bear*, in monochrome, and *The Little Red Lighthouse*, in dark blues and grays with touches of red—it is the artist's sure sense of dramatic contrast that tells the stories and grips and holds children's attention. In *The Silver Pony* (1973), the pictures tell the story without a text. Ward has illustrated many books written by his wife, May McNeer, among them *America's Mark Twain* (1962) and *Stranger in the Pines* (1971); he also illustrated Esther Forbes's Newbery Medal book, *Johnny Tremain* (1943).

Viewpoints

But it is not safe to identify illustration with the representational and decoration with the abstract elements of art; although this is as true as most generalizations. Both elements may be mingled in one design, and in fact must be if it is to be good. And if it were possible to divide something that is indivisible, we might say that illustration has reference to the meaning of the text and decoration to the appearance of the page. . . .

Midway between the two we have the imaginative type of illustration which rests upon the text but is itself a sort of extension of the text because it says things visually that are not possible to words.

. . .The good illustration must be a good design irrespective of the text it accompanies, and the way it fits the page is of course part of that design.—David Bland, *The Illustration of Books*, Pantheon, New York, 1952, pp. 12, 13.

Leo Politi

Leo Politi is an artist whose pictures are deceptively simple, almost primitive. Both his figures and his landscapes are stylized, but the total composition makes a beautiful design. His illustrations are colorful and appealing whether it is *Little Leo* (1951), capering gaily with his friends through Italian streets, the lovely procession of children and pets in *Juanita* (1948), the delightful little Chinese *Moy Moy* (1960), or the appealing dog in *The Nicest Gift* (1973). (See color section.)

Adrienne Adams

Houses from the Sea (1959) by Alice Goudey includes some of the loveliest watercolor illustrations Adrienne Adams has made. Since then, her pictures for the Grimms' *Shoemaker and the Elves* (1960) and Andersen's *Thumbelina* (1961) have been exceedingly popular. Her colors are warm and delicate, her pictures full of fascinating details. A most happy collaboration is evident in her delightful pictures for Aileen Fisher's *Going Barefoot* (1960) and *Where Does Everyone Go?* (1961), seasonal poems to which the pictures add lively charm. One of her most engaging conceptions has been the serried ranks of marching rabbits in her husband Lonzo Anderson's story *Two Hundred Rabbits* (1965). In Carl Withers's *Painting the Moon* (1970), the Grimm brothers' *Hansel and Gretel* (1975), and Alice Goudey's *The Day We Saw the Sun Come Up* (1961), the illustrations are particularly striking for their meticulous detail and dramatic use of color. (See color section.)

Evaline Ness

Evaline Ness uses a variety of techniques ranging from hand-worked tapestry to woodcuts printed on tissue-thin paper, with separate blocks used for each color. Her constant experimentation brings freshness to her handsomely composed illustrations. She used collage with line-and-wash for *Sam, Bangs & Moonshine,* for which she received the Caldecott Medal in 1967. For the three preceding years, the books she illustrated were Honor Books—in 1964 with illustrations for Sorche Nic Leodhas's *All in the Morning Early;* in 1965 for Rebecca Caudill's *A Pocketful of Cricket;* and in 1966 for her version of *Tom Tit Tot. Josefina February* (1963) is the first book of her own that she illustrated followed by her own *The Girl and the Goatherd* (1970); *Some of the Days of Everett Anderson* (1970) by Lucille Clifton; *The Truthful Harp* (1967) by Lloyd Alexander; and her own selection of poems about girls, *Amelia Mixed the Mustard* (1975).

From the book The Girl and the Goatherd. *Text and illustrations by Evaline Ness. Copyright © 1970 by Evaline Ness. Published by E. P. Dutton & Co., Inc., and used with their permission. (Original in color)*

Garth Williams

Garth Williams has won a formidable number of awards and prizes, including the Prix de Rome for sculpture. His first venture into children's book illustration was for E. B. White's *Stuart Little* (1945). He followed this with White's famous *Charlotte's Web* (1952)—a book that might well have received both the Newbery and the Caldecott medals. For a new edition of Laura Ingalls Wilder's *Little House* books (1953), Garth Williams spent ten years making the pictures, and as a result the pictures and stories are one. Equally successful are his illustrations for Natalie Carlson's books about the French Orphelines, Russell Hoban's *Bedtime for Frances* (1960), Margery Sharp's *Miss Bianca* (1962), and George Selden's *Harry Cat's Pet Puppy* (1974). The artist works both in black and white and full color, and his pictures are always characterized by authenticity of detail. The colors are fresh and soft, the composition vigorous. But whether the story he illustrates is realistic or pure fantasy, historical fiction or modern city life, his superb gift for characterization stands out. No pig could look more foolishly smug than Wilbur, no orphan could flee more desperately from the encircling bicyclists than Josine, no pioneers could look more cozy than the Little House dwellers.

Robert McCloskey

The first artist to be twice winner of the Caldecott Medal is Robert McCloskey, whose big, handsome picture stories are almost as popular with adults as with children. *Make Way for Ducklings* (1941 Caldecott Medal) vies with *Blueberries for Sal* (1948) in popularity. He has also illustrated Keith Robertson's *Henry Reed* stories with great humor. Only in *Time of Wonder* (1958 Caldecott Medal) and *Burt Dow, Deep Water Man* (1963) has this artist used color, but in his powerful black and whites you do not miss the color, so alive they are with realistic details and storytelling power. (See color section.)

Illustration by William Pène du Bois. From Otto and the Magic Potatoes *by William Pène du Bois. Copyright © 1970 by William Pène du Bois. Reprinted by permission of The Viking Press, Inc. (Original in color)*

William Pène du Bois

Few indeed are the children's book illustrators who can claim both a place in the New York Museum of Modern Art and a Newbery Medal. William Pène du Bois was awarded the Newbery Medal in 1948 for his *Twenty-One Balloons*, and he has written many distinguished books before and after that year, all with an illogical logic, all illustrated with paintings that are notable for their clean lines and clear colors, as evident, for example, in *Otto and the Magic Potatoes* (1970) and *Call Me Bandicoot* (1970). His boyhood love for the circus is evident in several of his books: *The Great Geppy* (1940) and *The Alligator Case* (1965). Although he has illustrated the books of other writers—George Macdonald's *The Light Princess* (1962), Rebecca Caudill's *A Certain Small Shepherd* (1965), Charlotte Zolotow's *My Grandson Lew* (1974)—the books for which he is both author and illustrator have a felicitous harmony between text and pictures seldom achieved in children's books.

Ezra Jack Keats

In a tough section of Brooklyn, eight-year-old Ezra Jack Keats discovered the beneficial side effects of painting. Some neighborhood boys snatched a painting from him, but when they learned he was the artist, they treated him with respect. The first book he wrote and illustrated, *The Snowy Day* (1963), earned him the Caldecott Medal and later was adapted into a prize-winning film at the Venice Film Festival. Keats works as a choreographer does, hanging his illustrations in rows on the walls "to pace the text." Using oils and collage, he achieves a sunny simplicity. His books include *Whistle for Willie* (1963), *Peter's Chair* (1967), *Goggles!* (a 1970 Caldecott Honor Book), *Dreams* (1974), and *Louie* (1975).

Anthony Ravielli

A painter of murals and a designer of visual training aids during World War II, Anthony Ravielli moved from there into medical illustration. After developing techniques in oil, tempera, and watercolor, he arrived at the scratchboard technique which he used for the first of his five books in the area of science, *Wonders of the Human Body* (1954). For most books he prefers to render full-color illustrations, but for *Wonders of the Human Body* he used colored inks on scratchboard. *An Adventure in Geometry* (1957) and *The World Is Round* (1963) are good examples of his technique—he designs as well as illustrates his own books. He also illustrated the 1959 edition of Charles Darwin's *The Voyage of the Beagle*, Keith Gordon Irwin's *The Romance of Chemistry* (1959), and S. Carl Hirsch's *This Is Automation* (1964), as well as his own *From Fins to Hands* (1968) and *What Is Bowling?* (1975).

Illustration by Leonard Weisgard from Wake Up and Good Night *by Charlotte Zolotow. Illustrations © 1971 by Leonard Weisgard. Reproduced by permission of Harper and Row, Publishers, Inc. and World's Work Ltd. (Original in color)*

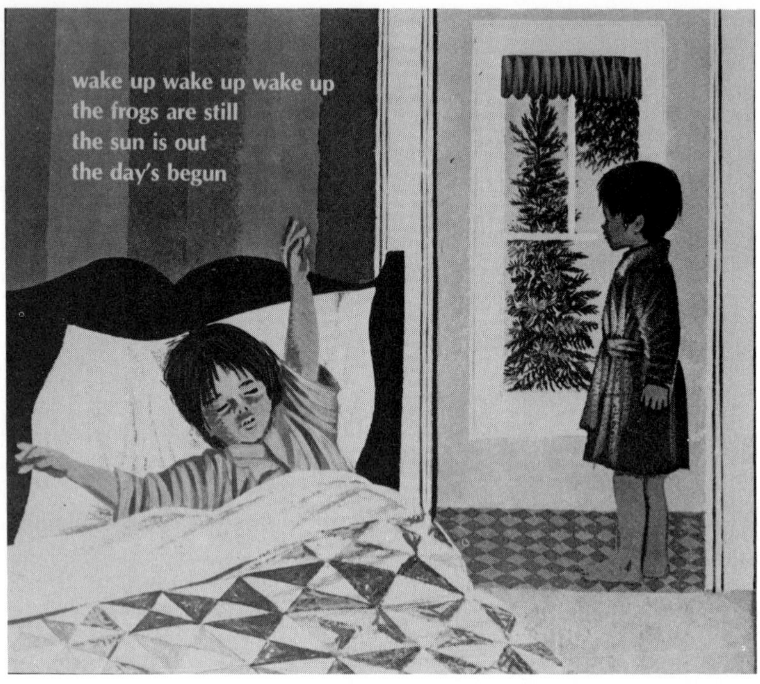

wake up wake up wake up
the frogs are still
the sun is out
the day's begun

Leonard Weisgard

Leonard Weisgard is a major illustrator whose pictures have sold many a second-rate text. He is a great colorist and his paintings are full of exquisite details of small flowers and frolicking animals and decorative birds. His illustrations for Margaret Wise Brown's *Little Island* (1946), painted on pressed wood in tempera and egg white, won him the Caldecott Medal. The seascapes are in deep blues and greens, with the island sometimes lost in mist. The landscapes are in lush yellow-greens and flashing blues. Some of the other books illustrated by this prolific artist are Sesyle Joslin's charming stories about Baby Elephant; Phyllis McGinley's *A Wreath of Christmas Legends* (1967); Charlotte Zolotow's *Wake Up and Good Night* (1971); Rudyard Kipling's *How the Rhinoceros Got His Skin* (1974); and his own *The Beginnings of Cities* (1968).

Barbara Cooney

Children were delighted by Barbara Cooney's black-and-white pictures for those two fine animal stories—Rutherford Montgomery's *Kildee House* (1949) and Barbara Reynolds's *Pepper* (1952). But in color she did not come into her own until she made the pictures for Lee Kingman's *Peter's Long Walk* (1953). They are in muted colors and interpret tenderly a child's sad homecoming which turns out cheerfully. She went on to win the Caldecott Medal for her scratchboard illustrations for *Chanticleer and the Fox* (1958), adapted from Chaucer's "The Nun's Priest's Tale" in *The Canterbury Tales*. Every detail is historically accurate, but what the children love are those pages in bright clear reds, greens, and blues, alive with action. She prefers working in full color, using acrylic paints, but has also used pen and ink for *Cock Robin* (1965), wash for the delicate pictures in Sarah Orne Jewett's *A White Heron* (1963), and charcoal for her pictures in the Grimms' *Snow White and Rose Red* (1966). Her illustrations for *Demeter and Persephone* (1972) by Penelope Proddow and *When the Sky Is Like Lace* (1975) by Elinor Horwitz exemplify both her artistic diversity and the research that results in authentic detail. (See color section.)

Marcia Brown

No generalizations about the work of Marcia Brown are possible, for she varies her style to suit the content of the story she is illustrating.

Viewpoints

Many illustrators have tried to write—with varying success—and occasionally authors have tried to draw—with less. One feels that the desire to do a book may be commendable; but without something to say to children and the means to say it, or even the desire to develop the means, one wonders at the arrogance that expects a child to be interested in halfbaked creations, texts or pictures. There is still among laymen a lack of comprehension of the discipline needed to pare a text to a basic line that looks simple. A picture book is as concise as poetry. Text and pictures combine to form an essence that expands in the child's mind.
—Marcia Brown, "One Wonders . . . ," in *Illustrators of Children's Books: 1957–1966,* compiled by Lee Kingman, Joanna Foster, and Ruth Giles Lontoft, The Horn Book, Inc., Boston, 1968, p. 24.

Her illustrations for *Stone Soup* (1947) are colorful, gay, and earthy, like the rogues who taught the villagers a more generous way of life. *Puss in Boots* (1952) is a gorgeous, flamboyant feline, well adapted to the court life into which he catapults his master. Both *The Steadfast Tin Soldier* (1953) and *Cinderella* (1955 Caldecott Medal) are in misty pinks and blues grayed down to the gentle mood of the tales. The sturdy woodcuts in brown and black for *Dick Whittington and His Cat* (1950) are as substantial as the hero, and in the alphabet book *All Butterflies* (1974) the woodcuts are in muted colors. The book that won her second Caldecott Medal, *Once a Mouse* (1961), is completely different from her earlier work. This fable of pride laid low is in jungle colors, and the stylized woodcut pictures have subtle details of expression or posture that tell the story and repay study. Marcia Brown has written and illustrated some charming stories of her own, but her major contributions to date are her brilliant interpretations of single folk tales. (See color section.)

Antonio Frasconi

Antonio Frasconi is one of the great woodcut artists of our time. His technique has softened the basic, crudely broad areas of the usual woodcut by high artistry in the use of color. He avoids the uncompromising pressure printing of the entire block by printing his woodcuts by hand and, to achieve variations of tone, rubbing a spoon over a paper laid on an inked block. Strong and vivid, his work melds the "dynamics of design and typography" with an imaginative power that pulls the young reader back to his illustrations again and again. A Uruguayan who came to the United States on a scholarship, Frasconi published his first children's book in 1955, the multilingual *See and Say*. Other Frasconi books are *The House That Jack Built* (1958), *See Again, Say Again* (1964) in four languages, *Overhead the Sun* (1969), based on lines by Walt Whitman, *The Elephant and His Secret* (1974) by Doris Dana, with bold, splashy pictures, and *One Little Room, an Everywhere* (1975), a collection of love poems edited by Myra Cohn Livingston and illustrated with small, finely detailed decorations.

Erik Blegvad

The appeal of Erik Blegvad's illustrations is in the precise detail of his tidy, humorous drawings, the delicate tints of color, and the fideli-

Illustration by Antonio Frasconi from The House That Jack Built, *copyright © 1958 by Antonio Frasconi. Reproduced by permission of Harcourt Brace Jovanovich, Inc. (Original in color)*

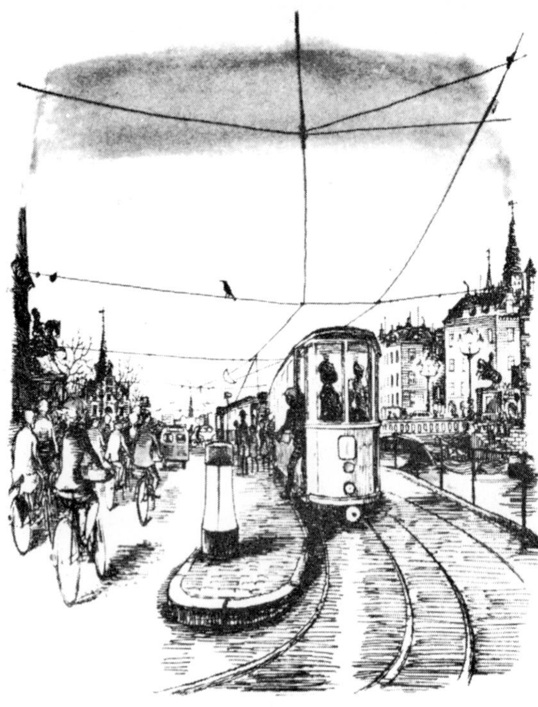

Illustration © 1965 by Erik Blegvad. From Mr. Jensen & Cat *by Lenore Blegvad. Reproduced by permission of Harcourt Brace Jovanovich, Inc. (Original in color)*

ty to the author's text. For Monica Stirling's *The Cat from Nowhere* (1969), the black-and-white drawings were done in pen and india ink. When he works in full color, he uses a transparent watercolor wash, or a mixture of watercolor and poster colors. His tender feelings for animals are apparent in Lenore Blegvad's *The Great Hamster Hunt* (1969) and in *Mr. Jensen & Cat* (1965), which has enchanting illustrations of Copenhagen. In Ruth Craft's *The Winter Bear* (1975), the full-color pictures capture the beauty of a snow scene, and in Charlotte Zolotow's *May I Visit?* (1976) they reflect both the warmth and humor of the story.

Charles Keeping

Born in Lambeth, England, Charles Keeping won the Kate Greenaway Medal in 1967 for *Charley, Charlotte and the Golden Canary*. Keeping is noted for his bold approach, his use of vivid colors, and his highly individual style. For *Joseph's Yard* (1969) he used several layers of colored acetate, with drawings in colored ink, which were then shot together as one drawing. His remarkable range shows in the bold black-and-white india-ink drawings for Rosemary Sutcliff's *Heroes and History* (1966), the unexpected perspectives in her *Knight's Fee* (1960), and in the stunning use of line and texture in *The Golden Shadow* (1973) by Leon Garfield and Edward Blishen. Only in their swirling lines is there a resemblance between his black-and-white illustrations and the vibrant color illustrations he uses in his own picture books.

Maurice Sendak

Some of Maurice Sendak's first illustrations were for humorous books like Ruth Krauss's *A Hole Is to Dig* (1952), Marcel Ayme's fantasy *The Wonderful Farm* (1951), and Beatrice de Regniers's *What Can You Do with a Shoe?* (1955). They show the tender appeal of children even when they are most absurd—round-faced children grinning fiendishly or preternaturally solemn, dressed up in adult clothes or kicking up their heels and cavorting like young colts. This artist with his flair for comic exaggeration is tremendously popular, but in his illustrations for Meindert DeJong's books, *Wheel on the School* (1954), for example, and for his own book *Kenny's Window* (1956), he shows a sensitive perception of the lonely, imaginative, struggling side of childhood, too. One book in full color is a superb example of his versatility. His pictures for Janice Udry's *Moon Jumpers* (1959) are in the green-blues of a moonlit summer's night that suggest the poetry of childhood. The same could be said of his glorious color pictures for Charlotte Zolotow's *Mr. Rabbit and the Lovely Present* (1962). Sendak's four original stories for his tiny *Nutshell Library* (1962) are exceedingly funny both in texts and illustrations.

Sendak moved into further prominence with *Where the Wild Things Are* (1963), which won the Caldecott Medal. Children rejoice over the ferocious, adoring creatures and over the small hero who, sated with adulation, goes home to reality to find his dinner waiting, still hot. Sendak's sensitivity to text and mood are evident in the contrast between his raffish humorous illustrations in the

Grimms' story *King Grisly-Beard* (1973) and his gravely beautiful and sophisticated pictures for a collection of Grimm tales, *The Juniper Tree* (1973). The delicacy of the wash drawings for Else Minarik's *Little Bear* (1957), the tenderness of the pictures in Randall Jarrell's *Animal Family* (1965), and the boldness of those in Sendak's own *In the Night Kitchen* (1970) show how completely Maurice Sendak adapts his illustrations to the story and make clear why he received the Hans Christian Andersen Medal in 1970, the first time an American artist was so honored. *Really Rosie* (1975), a paperback based on a television production, incorporates material from several Sendak books. (See color section.)

Irene Haas

Irene Haas's pictures for Paul Kapp's *A Cat Came Fiddling* (1956) show not merely children but some indescribably funny and well-characterized animals and adults. For Beatrice de Regniers's subtle little book about a child's need for privacy, *A Little House of Your Own* (1954), she has suggested the mood of quiet withdrawal in every picture. There are also sly touches of humor—for instance, in the picture of the child and cat covered up in bed, with only the cat's tail sticking out. Her illustrations for Emma Smith's *Emily's Voyage* (1966) have the same humor, but her soft, romantic pictures for Elizabeth Enright's *Tatsinda* (1963) have an appropriate fairy-tale quality. The richly ornamented, full-color pictures in *The Maggie B.* (1975) are humorous in detail but romantic in concept.

Illustration and accompanying text from In the Night Kitchen *by Maurice Sendak. Copyright © 1970. Reproduced by permission of Harper & Row, Publishers, Inc. and The Bodley Head, Ltd., London. (Original in color)*

Blair Lent

Most of Blair Lent's illustrations have been done with cardboard cuts and overlays. The 1965 Caldecott Medal Honor Book recognition was given to his illustrations for Margaret Hodges's *The Wave*, which also received a silver medal at the São Paulo Biennial in Brazil, and in 1973 Lent's pictures of impish, grotesque Japanese spirits in Arlene Mosel's *The Funny Little Woman* were awarded the Caldecott Medal. His inventive full-color paintings, which heightened the dramatic quality of William Sleator's Tlingit Indian legend, *The Angry Moon* (1970), earned him another Caldecott Honor Book recognition. *John Tabor's Ride* (1966) and *Pistachio* (1964) are examples of Lent's work as author-illustrator. He has also illustrated Franklyn M. Branley's *The Christmas Sky* (1966), Arlene Mosel's *Tikki Tikki Tembo* (1968), and Virginia Haviland's *Favorite Fairy Tales Told in India* (1973).

Brian Wildsmith

Although he says he has "abstract tendencies," Brian Wildsmith's illustrations are brilliant and strongly representational. He sees the pictorial form as being at one with the text, yet each a thing unto itself—complementary—and each able to exist without the other. All of his work is in full color; a Wildsmith trademark is the use of bright contrasting colors in a harlequin pattern. In his technique, gouache is used, moving from impasto down to almost translucent water color effects. The subjects he treats lend themselves to strong visual impact: *Brian Wildsmith's Fishes* (1968), *Brian Wildsmith's Circus* (1970), *Brian Wildsmith's Puzzles* (1971), *The Little Wood Duck* (1973), and *Brian Wildsmith's ABC*, which won the Kate Greenaway Medal for 1962 and was published in the United States in 1963. One of the major British illustrators, Wildsmith has, in addition to his own books, created illustrations for several Jean de la Fontaine fables and for *The Oxford Book of Poetry for Children* (1964), edited by Edward Blishen. (See color section.)

Margot Zemach

Margot Zemach works in ink line and wash, using color to strengthen the drawing rather than obscure it. She uses line in many ways, often boldly in central figures and sketchily in the background, or with careful detail to depict a piece of furniture and with abandon to create frilly ruffles or a curly mop of hair. Most of her books were written by her late husband. Their first was *A Small Boy Is Listening* (1959), and together they adapted and illustrated a Russian folk tale, *Salt* (1965), an Ozark folk song, *Mommy, Buy Me a China Doll* (1966), and a Russian nursery rhyme, *The Speckled Hen* (1966). In her black-and-white pictures for Isaac Bashevis Singer's *When Shlemiel Went to Warsaw* (1968), Margot Zemach demonstrates the essence of her economical use of line and adroitly echoes the peasant humor of the text. *The Judge; An Untrue Tale* (1969), a Caldecott Honor Book, has the same robust and earthy quality; this is the tale of a crusty judge who accuses defendants of telling lies and is done in by his own methods, and the pictures for the rhyming text have an inspired daftness to match. In their *Duffy and the Devil*, the Zemachs adapted a Cornish variant of the Rumpelstiltskin story. It's told with verve, and the illustrations, soft in hues but bold in composition, are humorous and vigorous. In 1974 it was awarded the Caldecott Medal.

Reprinted with the permission of Farrar, Straus & Giroux, Inc. from The Judge: An Untrue Tale *by Harve and Margot Zemach. Text copyright © 1969 by Harve Zemach, pictures copyright © 1969 by Margot Zemach. (Original in color)*

Nonny Hogrogian

For the first children's books she illustrated, Nicolete Meredith's *King of the Kerry Fair* (1960), Nonny Hogrogian used woodblocks, as she did for Robert Burns's *Hand in Hand We'll Go* (1965). The illustrations for the 1966 Caldecott Medal book, *Always Room for One More* by Sorche Nic Leodhas, were done in pen and ink, with gray wash and pastels to achieve the quality of mist and heather. Her approach to illustration is that the manuscript comes first, and the pictures grow from it, the mood of the text dictating the technique as much as possible. She used pastels to illustrate the story of the gentle, lovely *Vasilisa the Beautiful* (1970), translated by Thomas Whitney; etchings for an edition of Grimms' tales; and oil paintings for her own *One Fine Day* (1971), which was awarded the Caldecott Medal and in which the illustrations have the full and vigorous quality of the story of a sharp-nosed fox who tries to retrieve his tail. Some of the other books she has illustrated are Barbara Schiller's *The Kitchen Knight* (1965); Isaac Bashevis Singer's *The Fearsome Inn* (1967); and her own *Handmade Secret Hiding Places* (1975) in which she used pencil halftone and line. (See color section.)

Nancy Ekholm Burkert

As might be expected from an artist who sees "absolute perfection" in the compositions of

1.

1. Freely brushed color softens the engraved line, and the rhythmic pattern of the trees lends animation to an otherwise static composition that has the formal quality of a stage design. From The History of the House That Jack Built. *Reproduced from the D'Alte Welch Collection, American Antiquarian Society.*

2. The long horizontal and vertical lines of the barn are an effective foil for the animated, comic figures in a clean, simple drawing with evenly washed tints. Illustration by Leonard Leslie Brooke. From Ring o' Roses. *Reproduced with permission of Frederick Warne & Co., Inc.*

3. The sharp contrast of the slightly crude color makes the comic figures seem pasted on the flat background in this engraving. From A Continuation of the Comic Adventures of Old Mother Hubbard and Her Dog. *Reproduced from the D'Alte Welch Collection, The University Library, Department of Special Collections, University of California, Los Angeles.*

2.

3.

YES, that's the girl that struts about,
She's very proud,—so very proud!
Her *bow-wow's* quite as proud as she:
They both are very wrong to be
So proud—so very proud.

See, Jane and Willy laugh at her,
They say she's very proud!
Says Jane, "My stars!—they're very silly;"
"Indeed they are," cries little Willy,
"To walk so stiff and proud."

4. 5.

6.

4. There is subtle characterization in the figures of this skillful drawing, and clever use of background details: the window frames the proud one's head and the vine creates a fancy border. From Kate Greenaway's Under the Window. *Reproduced with permission of Frederick Warne & Co., Inc.*

5. The subtle use of color distinguishes this drawing, the gray-green of the sky blending into the only slightly lighter ground. The flat, subdued color within lines is reminiscent of Japanese prints. From Walter Crane's Baby's Bouquet. *Reproduced with permission of Frederick Warne & Co., Inc.*

6. Composed frontally in simple shapes of contrasting light and dark, the melancholy mood is deepened by the leaden colors of the foreground. Illustration by Newell Wyeth. From Treasure Island *by Robert Louis Stevenson. Copyright 1911 by Charles Scribner's Sons. Copyright 1939 by N. C. Wyeth. Reproduced with permission of Charles Scribner's Sons.*

7. This is a controlled composition, the vigorous treatment of thorny trees balancing a motionless foreground, the rosy tones of ground and sky contrasting with the gray dress, the sober face of the girl contrasting with the impish faces in the water. Mysterious and romantic, a Rackham specialty. Reprinted with permission of Macmillan Publishing Co., Inc. and Macmillan, London and Basingstoke, from English Fairy Tales *by Flora Annie Steel, illustrated by Arthur Rackham. Copyright 1918 by Macmillan Publishing Co., Inc. renewed 1946 by Mabel H. Webster.* 7.

8.

9.

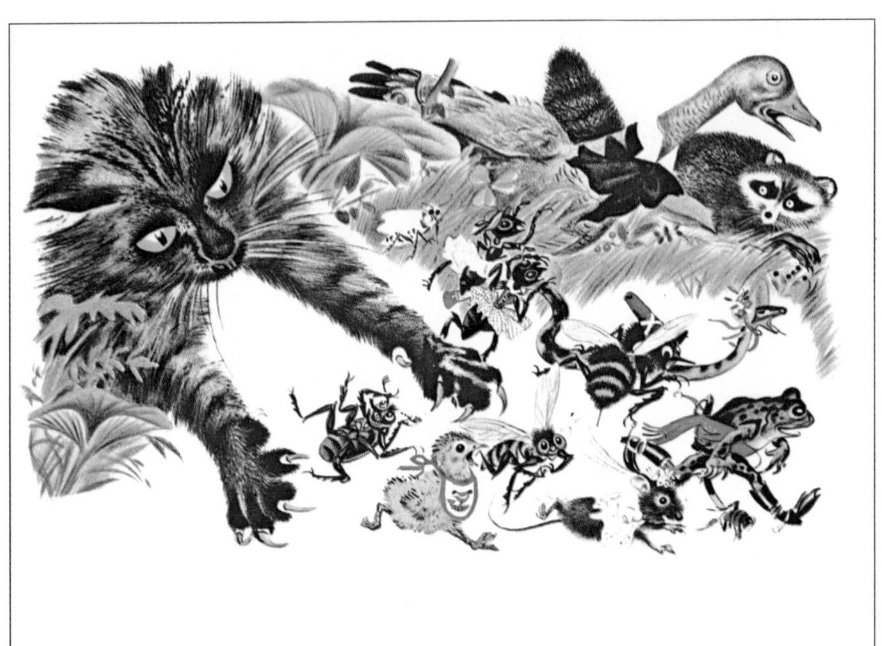

10.

8. Keenly observant, Potter gave animals human characteristics without distortion. The subdued background colors do not distract us from Peter's expression of smug contentment. From Beatrix Potter's The Tale of Peter Rabbit. *Reproduced with permission of Frederick Warne & Co., Inc.*

9. Even the perspective, running from left to right, is comic in a picture that exemplifies Caldecott's vigorous and humorous touch. Color is simple but expressive; we can enjoy all details individually and in combination. From Randolph Caldecott's Hey Diddle and Baby Bunting. *Reproduced from the D'Alte Welch Collection, Cleveland.*

10. The artist achieves lively action in a restricted space by staging smaller creatures against clear white, while larger creatures are grouped above and behind. Illustration by Feodor Rojankovsky. From Frog Went a-Courtin'. *Copyright 1955 by John M. Langstaff and Feodor Rojankovsky. Reproduced by permission of Harcourt Brace Jovanovich, Inc.*

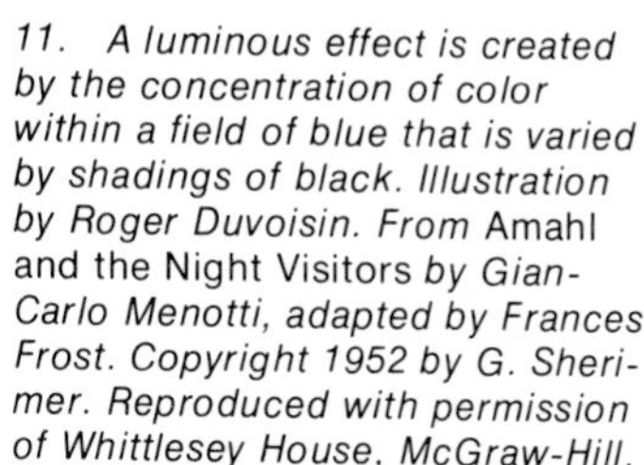

11. A luminous effect is created by the concentration of color within a field of blue that is varied by shadings of black. Illustration by Roger Duvoisin. From Amahl and the Night Visitors *by Gian-Carlo Menotti, adapted by Frances Frost. Copyright 1952 by G. Sherimer. Reproduced with permission of Whittlesey House, McGraw-Hill.*

12. An angular composition conveys a feeling of suspended motion through the lines of ripples and oars as opposed to the boat. The watercolor wash, carefully controlled, defines shapes with no use of hard lines. From Time of Wonder *by Robert McCloskey. Copyright © 1957 by Robert McCloskey. Reprinted by permission of The Viking Press, Inc.*

11.

12.

He had taken
such good care of her
that she could still dig
as much in a day
as a hundred men
could dig in a week;
at least he thought she could
but he wasn't quite sure.
Everywhere they went
the new gas shovels
and the new electric shovels
and the new Diesel motor shovels
had all the jobs. No one wanted
Mike Mulligan and Mary Anne any more.
Then one day Mike read in a newspaper that the town
of Popperville was going to build a new town hall.
'We are going to dig the cellar of that town hall,'
said Mike to Mary Anne, and off they started.

13.

14.

13. The curving block of type suggests a shovel and movement, and the loose, free drawing brings the steam shovel to life. Illustration from Mike Mulligan and His Steam Shovel *by Virginia Lee Burton. Copyright, 1939, and 1967 by Virginia Lee Demetrios. Reprinted by permission of the publisher, Houghton Mifflin Company, Boston.*

14. The solidity of the solitary figure is balanced by the delicacy of the streaks of rain in this deceptively simple illustration which is bold in composition but not heavy. The child's face glows in contrast to the cool blues and purples. From Umbrella *by Taro Yashima. Copyright © 1958 by Taro Yashima. Reprinted by permission of The Viking Press, Inc.*

15. Strong in design and simple in colors, the details of this woodcut focus the eye on the ferocious face of the tiger, with the blades of grass echoing the animal's stripes. From Once a Mouse *by Márcia Brown. Copyright 1961 by Marcia Brown. Reproduced with permission of Charles Scribner's Sons.*

16. With great economy of line, action is provided in this watercolor by the angled sails, floating objects, and variations in color within sea and sky. From Little Tim and the Brave Sea Captain *by Edward Ardizzone. Reprinted by the permission of Henry Z. Walck, Inc.*

The tiger felt offended and humiliated. He forgot all the good he had received from the old man.

"No one shall tell me that I was once a mouse. I will kill him!"

15.

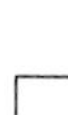

16.

17.

17. Authentically detailed, a Viking ship is the dominating object in a color lithograph that resembles an ancient map with its personified wind. The feathered edge of a huge wave evokes an image of a sea serpent, and added motion is obtained from the plunging whales and tilted ship. From Leif the Lucky *by Ingri and Edgar Parin d'Aulaire. Copyright 1951 by Doubleday, Doran & Company, Inc. Reproduced with permission of Doubleday and Co.*

18.

18. Only the two figures are in warm tones, setting them apart from the cool stillness of the summer night. Illustration by Maurice Sendak from Mr. Rabbit and the Lovely Present *by Charlotte Zolotow. Pictures copyright © 1962 by Maurice Sendak. Reproduced by permission of Harper & Row, Publishers, Inc.*

19. A complex design with multiple elements is stabilized by the vertical that runs through the butterfly and the child's figure. Watercolor and opaque are combined to give variety to this decorative illustration. From Leo Politi's Moy Moy. *Copyright 1960 by Leo Politi. Reproduced with permission of Charles Scribner's Sons.*

20. There is a surrealist quality to the huge cat, the twisting bird, and the empty, timeless street scene. Illustration by Harold Jones. From Lavender's Blue, *Mother Goose rhymes compiled by Kathleen Lines. Copyright 1954. Reproduced with permission of Franklin Watts, Inc. and Oxford University Press, London.*

19.

20.

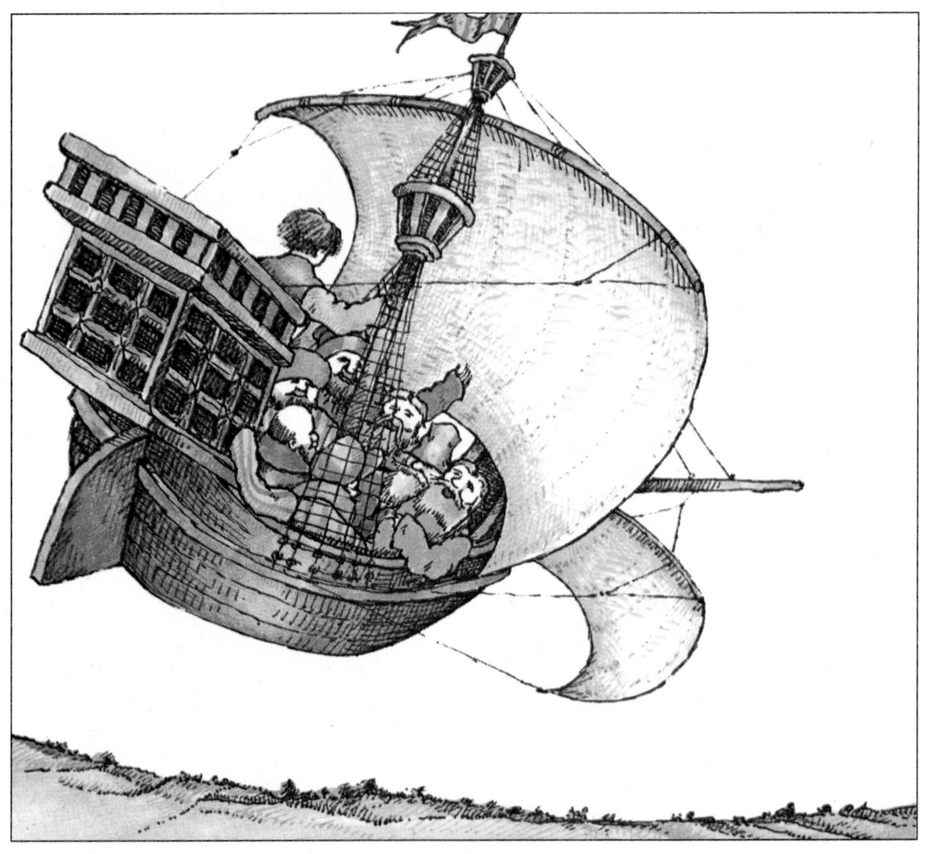

21. In this brush-and-ink painting, the large bird and branch are checked by their quiet colors, while the vivid group on the right is restrained by numbers, so that the central figure stands out. Separate figures are treated in the Chinese tradition, with each color in flat painting or simple gradations. Illustration by Nancy Ekholm Burkert from The Nightingale, *translated by Eva La Gallienne. Copyright © 1965. Reproduced by permission of Harper & Row, Publishers, Inc.*

22. The size of the figures in relation to the ship adds a comic note in a picture that resembles fifteenth-century Flemish work. Reproduced with the permission of Farrar, Straus & Giroux, Inc. From The Fool of the World and the Flying Ship, *a Russian tale retold by Arthur Ransome, illustrated by Uri Shulevitz, pictures copyright © 1968 by Uri Shulevitz.*

23. Thick, soft edges in black and deep browns frame luminous colors given a grainy texture by loosely applied pastel. Illustration from Stevie *by John Steptoe. Copyright © 1969 by John Steptoe. Reprinted by permission of Harper & Row, Publishers, Inc. and Penguin Books Ltd.*

24. Beyond the bright, jewel-toned colors, opaque and clear, this controlled abstraction has interplay between light and dark areas of the hen's body. Illustration by Brian Wildsmith for Puzzles. *Copyright © 1971. Reproduced by permission of Franklin Watts, Inc. and Oxford University Press, London.*

23.

24.

25. This oil painting is dominated by the figure in the foreground, bent and angular, her implausible grip on the pot handle adding a note of humor. Reprinted with permission of Macmillan Publishing Co., Inc. and Hamish Hamilton Children's Books Ltd., London, from One Fine Day *by Nonny Hogrogian. Copyright © 1971 by Nonny Hogrogian.*

26. A formal composition in the folk-art tradition is relieved and enriched by subtle variations of the blue sky and by the random distribution of stars. The scratch technique that allows the black base of the forms to show up as lines not only modulates but gives texture to the scene. Illustration by Janina Domanska from Din Dan Don It's Christmas. *Reprinted by permission of Greenwillow Books, a division of William Morrow & Company, Inc.*

25.

The nightingale sings his song.

26.

27.

27. The elongated forms and the angled posture of the figure are reminiscent of ancient Greek paintings in this delicate and balanced picture. The solid cluster of narcissus is in contrast to the random blossoms on the right, and the rhythm of hair and folds of the translucent garment creates an interplay between foreground and background. Illustration from Demeter and Persephone, *translated and adapted by Penelope Proddow, illustrated by Barbara Cooney. Illustrations copyright © 1972 by Barbara Cooney Porter. Reproduced by permission of Doubleday and Company, Inc.*

28.

29.

28. In the flatly designed style of Pueblo art, the illustrator achieves a dramatic effect through brilliant strips of color in sharply opposed angles around the head and the circular design on the figure. From Arrow to the Sun *by Gerald McDermott. Copyright © 1974 by Gerald McDermott. Reprinted by permission of The Viking Press.*

29. Color and exaggeration are used to heighten the comic effect in a picture that has variety in media and techniques. Illustration from Mr. Gumpy's Motor Car *by John Burningham. Copyright © 1973 by John Burningham. Reproduced by permission of Thomas Y. Crowell Company, Inc. and Jonathan Cape Ltd.*

30. All concentration of the composition is on the small, bright figures. The towering trees, with pattern gently imprinted on the paint, are both frame and contrast; and the arching branches repeat the protective curve of the boy's arms. Illustration by Adrienne Adams from Hansel and Gretel *by the Brothers Grimm, reprinted by permission of Charles Scribner's Sons. Copyright © 1975 Adrienne Adams.*

31.

31. In a simple and stylized painting, watercolor and pastel are subtly blended, with areas of color separated by a white line of varying depth that also describes detail and becomes an integral part of the design. The cast of the eye adds humor, and the curling pattern of the hat adds elegance while solidifying the composition. Illustration from Why Mosquitoes Buzz in People's Ears. *Illustrated by Leo and Diane Dillon. Illustrations Copyright © 1975 by Leo and Diane Dillon. Used with the permission of THE DIAL PRESS.*

Arthur Rackham, Nancy Burkert's work is full of exquisite detail. In her imaginative treatment of Edward Lear's *The Scroobious Pip* (1968), she is thoroughly at home with the infinite variety of nature, and both the line drawings and the full-color paintings have a firm delicacy. For Natalie Carlson's *Jean-Claude's Island* (1963) she used conté pencil and crayon, and for Eva Le Gallienne's translation of Hans Christian Andersen's *The Nightingale,* she used brush and colored ink to achieve the wonderfully rich color; the authentic detail of her illustrations for this book she provided through her study of ancient Chinese scrolls. Among the other books she has illustrated are John Updike's *A Child's Calendar* (1965), Roald Dahl's *James and the Giant Peach* (1961), and Andersen's *The Fir Tree* (1970), to which she gave pictures that are gravely sweet. (See color section.)

Diane and Leo Dillon

Leo and Diane Dillon met while attending the Parsons School of Design and have been working together as one artist since 1957. Although they have separate styles when working individually, they blend these when working on a book together and their work shows great variety of media and techniques. Their illustrations for *Why Mosquitoes Buzz in People's Ears* (1975), a West African tale retold by Verna Aardema, which was awarded the Caldecott Medal, were done with watercolor and pastels in strong, soft colors and in bold, stylized compositions inspired by the designs of African fabrics. The pictures shift so that the chain of events in an animal "why" story is seen from the animals' viewpoints. The Dillons adapt the mood and medium of their work to the text it illustrates: in the pictures for Erik Haugaard's *Hakon of Rogen's Saga* (1963), a bleak Viking tale, they use strong black-and-white woodcuts; for Natalia Belting's *Whirlwind Is a Ghost Dancing* (1974), acrylics and pastels are used for stylized, dignified pictures that reflect the grave beauty of Native American poetry and incorporate tribal motifs. The tender story of a small child's love for a very old woman in *The Hundred Penny Box* (1975) by Sharon Bell Mathis has pictures that are framed and slightly blurred in brown and white, giving the effect of an old photograph album. In Lorenz Graham's *Song of the Boat* (1975), an African tale told with the poetic language and cadence of the oral tradition, the Dillons use woodcut style, but the pictures are quite unlike the starkly dramatic illustrations of the Viking tale; the solid masses are lightened by fine lines, patterns, and designs that give variety and movement to the figures. (See color section.)

Arnold Lobel

Arnold Lobel believes that a good illustrator should have a wide repertory of styles at command, and his work shows this whether he uses wash, pencil, or pen and ink, which is his favorite medium. His first book was *A Zoo for Mr. Muster* (1962), but most of his work in the 1960s was illustrating books by other authors. For Millicent Selsam's *Benny's Animals and How He Put Them in Order* (1966), he used a raffish, sketchy line appropriate for the lightness of the story; in Nathaniel Benchley's *Sam the Minuteman* (1969), solid figures in framed drawings. In *Hildilid's Night* (1971) by Cheli Duran Ryan, a noodlehead tale, black-and-white pictures contain finely drawn parallel lines that give a soft solidity to the night scenes. This was a Caldecott Honor Book, as was *Frog and Toad Are Friends* (1971), which is discussed in Chapter 4 and which was also a National Book Award finalist. An unusual book for Lobel is his *On the Day Peter Stuyvesant Sailed into Town* (1971), historical fiction told in rhyme, in which the blue and yellow pictures are based on Dutch tiles. *Owl at Home* (1975) uses the same format as the *Frog* books, brief tales about a protagonist, but here Lobel uses soft brown tones for the humorous pictures of a silly owl rather than the greens and browns of the amphibian friends.

Raymond Briggs

Raymond Briggs is best known for illustrations of *The Mother Goose Treasury,* which won him the Kate Greenaway Medal in 1967. To complete that collection of four hundred rhymes, which he selected and illustrated, he worked for two years. Sketching with pencil and working over with pen and ink for the black-and-white pictures and with gouache for those in color, he captured the exuberance and the humor of the rhymes. A prolific worker, Briggs illustrated seven of the Coward-McCann "Champion" series in 1968 and 1969, wrote and illustrated *Jim and the Beanstalk* in 1970, and in the same year illustrated *The Elephant and the Bad Baby* by Elfrida Vipont, *The Christmas Book* compiled by James Reeves, and *The Book of Magical Beasts* edited by Ruth Manning-Sanders. His pictures are deft in composition and are gay with color and movement. For *Father Christmas* (1973) and *Father Christmas Goes on Holiday* (1975), Briggs used a cartoon format.

Victor G. Ambrus

Born in Budapest, Victor Ambrus, designer, author, and illustrator, won the Kate Greenaway Medal in 1966 for *The Three Poor Tailors*. He uses a mixture of techniques: ink, watercolor, and oil pastel. His black-and-white work, as in *Flambards in Summer* (1970) by K. M. Peyton, has the bold quality of etching. Ambrus, a collector of European military relics, provides a strong sense of action in his pictures. They are vigorous and decorative, as in *The Brave Soldier Janosh* (1966), with soldiers that are authentically swashbuckling, peasants that are stolid with a skeptical humor, and horses that seem to be cynically amused at the tall tale they are participating in. Ambrus illustrated E. M. Almedingen's *Katia* (1967) and *Fanny* (1970), Hester Burton's *Time of Trial* (1964), Barbara Picard's *The Young Pretenders* (1966), and his own *The Seven Skinny Goats* (1970) and *A Country Wedding* (1975).

Uri Shulevitz

Uri Shulevitz, who was born in Poland and spent some of his childhood years in Israel and in France, shares, he says, the belief of the prophet Isaiah—"And a little child shall lead them." He works chiefly in ink, sometimes using it in combination with wash. For the illustrations in *Maximilian's World* (1966), by Mary Stolz, he used a Japanese reed pen. In Dorothy Nathan's *The Month Brothers* (1967) and in Isaac Bashevis Singer's *The Fools of Chelm* (1973), his line drawings have a grave yet comic quality that befits the folk-tale style. In illustrating Arthur Ransome's *The Fool of the World and the Flying Ship*, for which he won the 1969 Caldecott Medal, his pictures in brilliant color are faithful to the art style of the Russian background of the book. He has illustrated with sensitivity the stories of many

Reprinted by permission of Coward-McCann, Inc. from The Elephant and the Bad Baby *by Elfrida Vipont. Illustrated by Raymond Briggs. Illustrations © 1970 by Raymond Briggs. (Original in color)*

Reprinted by permission of Charles Scribner's Sons from The Desert Is Theirs *by Byrd Baylor, illustrated by Peter Parnall. Copyright (text) © 1975 Byrd Baylor. Illustration copyright © 1975 Peter Parnall. (Original in color)*

writers, but has never surpassed the evocative mood and the harmony of pictures and text in his own *One Monday Morning* (1967), *Rain Rain Rivers* (1969), and *Dawn* (1974), which was a Hans Christian Andersen Honor Book. (See color section.)

John Burningham

An English artist, John Burningham made a spectacular entrance into the world of children's books by winning the Kate Greenaway Medal in 1963 with his first book, *Borka, the Adventures of a Goose with No Feathers*. Like most of his work, it was done largely in full color. He uses a wide range of materials: pastels, ink, crayons, montage, charcoal, gouache, and photostats, giving textural variety to his pictures. He varies the style of his work to suit the subject of the book; in *John Burningham's ABC* the composition on pages facing the letters is in bold poster style. Humor is a component of most of Burningham's work, even in the bland and dreamy pictures for *Mr. Gumpy's Outing* (1971) for which he also received the Greenaway Medal, the first time an artist had won it twice. A simply written book about a man who takes a crew of animals and children for a glorious boat ride and a high tea, it has flowery pastel pictures with a sunny, bucolic humor quite different from the bold vigor of the alphabet book illustrations. The sequel, *Mr. Gumpy's Motor Car* (1976), is less original but equally amusing; this time the children and animals have to get out and push when an old car stalls in the rain. Four small books that have bright little crayon pictures—*The Baby, The Rabbit, The School,* and *The Snow* (1975)—are nicely done for very young children. (See color section.)

Peter Parnall

Peter Parnall's drawings have a distinctive use of line and space. His work is always uncluttered, his line firm but delicate, often sinuous with movement achieved by parallels that break and flow into each other, and his drawings of flora and fauna are impeccably accurate; many examples have appeared in *Audubon Magazine* and *Scientific American*. He has illustrated books by other authors: Mary Shura's *A Tale of Middle Length* (1966), Miska Miles's *Apricot ABC* (1969), *The Fireside Song Book of Birds and Beasts* (1972) edited by Jane Yolen, and others. Parnall has the ability to draw animals in a comic spirit, as he often does in the song book, but in a book like Alice Schick's *The Peregrine Falcons* (1975) his drawings of birds are meticulously realistic. In the picture books for which Parnall is both author and illustrator, he uses space beautifully, with print and picture placed on the page to the advantage of both. *The Mountain* (1971) is a plea for the preservation of ecological balance, showing the invasion and destruction of a mountain area; color is used with restraint, on many pages only in grass and flowers, while massive tree trunks with intricate veining are drawn in black and white. Parnall's illustrations for Byrd Baylor's *Everybody Needs a Rock* (1974) contributed to its being chosen as a Notable Book by the American Library Association. In 1976 Baylor's *The Desert Is Theirs*, a story of Papago Indians illustrated with reverence and dignity by Parnall, was selected as a Caldecott Honor Book.

Gerald McDermott

Gerald McDermott is primarily a filmmaker, and his first book, *Anansi the Spider* (1972), is based on an animated film version which won the 1970 Blue Ribbon at the American Film Festival. A Caldecott Honor Book, it incorporates the graphics of the Ashanti people in its design montage. Highly stylized forms and brilliant, strident colors are used to illustrate a traditional tale of the spider-hero, Anansi, and his six sons. While the adaptation from film gives McDermott's books a static quality, the illustrations are rich and striking. All of his books are based on folk literature: *The Magic Tree* (1973) on a tale from the Congo; *Arrow to the Sun* (1974), which won the Caldecott Medal, on a Pueblo Indian tale; and *The Stonecutter* (1975) on a Japanese folk tale. (See color section.)

David Macaulay

Born in England but now living in the United States, David Macaulay has made a distinctive contribution to children's literature despite the fact that he has published only a few books. The first, *Cathedral; The Story of Its Construction* (1973) was a Caldecott Honor Book and the winner of the Deutscher Jugendbuchpreis for the best nonfiction picture book of 1975, when it was published in the German edition. A student of architecture, Macaulay has, in this and in *City; A Story of Roman Planning and Construction* (1974) and in *Pyramid* (1975), related significant architectural advances to the cultures from which they came. His meticulously detailed drawings show, step by step, the construction procedures for the edifices. Whether the scene is a sweeping panorama of a city, a cutaway drawing that shows the architectural plan, or a small picture of one facet of ornamentation, the illustrations are impressive for the masterful handling of perspective and the consistency with which the artist combines informative drawing with visual beauty.

Other Notable Artists

There are so many creative twentieth-century illustrators of children's books that it is impossible to discuss them all even briefly. Obviously this list of artists should include Henry Pitz, a prolific illustrator and author of several books on illustration; Conrad Buff, whose pictures of flora and fauna in his wife Mary's *Big Tree* (1946) are distinctive for their handling of light; Dorothy Lathrop, who won the first Caldecott Medal for the pen-and-ink sketches in *Animals of the Bible* (1937); Helen Sewell, whose work is notable for its variation of styles; Theodore Geisel, who, as "Dr. Seuss," uses cartoon art with great flair; and Ludwig Bemelmans, whose first story, *Madeline* (1939), led to other books about her adventures, all sketchily drawn but filled with humor, color, and intriguing scenes of Paris.

Virginia Burton's *Mike Mulligan and His Steam Shovel* (1939) and *The Little House* (1943 Caldecott Medal) have a swirling line and clear, bright colors (see color section); her black-and-white pictures for *Song of Robin Hood* (1947) are strikingly detailed. Nicolas Mordvinoff won the Caldecott Medal for *Finders Keepers* (1951), in which he broke away from prettified art for children and produced vigorous, humorous drawings with strong line and composition that capture the boldness of William Lipkind's text.

Other notable artists are Nicolas Sidjakov, whose stylized work for *Baboushka and the Three Kings* by Ruth Robbins was awarded the 1960 Caldecott Medal; Beni Montresor, who received the Caldecott Medal in 1965 for Beatrice Schenk de Regniers's *May I Bring a Friend?* in which elaborately decorated pictures give evidence of Montresor's career as a stage designer; and Leonard Everett Fisher, whose stark scratchboard pictures are dramatic in black and white. Leo Lionni uses collage as effectively as any artist today, and his rice-paper collage in *Inch by Inch* (1960) made the book a Caldecott Honor Book, as is *Alexander and the Wind-Up Mouse*. Lionni's *Frederick* (1967) and *In the Rabbitgarden* (1975) are animal fables that use collage and paint in handsome compositions. Tasha Tudor works in delicate pastel colors, John Steptoe in harsh, brilliant tones and a style reminiscent of Georges Rouault. (See color section.) Janina Domanska has done striking color etchings, stylized in detail, for *Under the Green Willow* (1971) and *If All the Seas Were One Sea* (1971); her *Din Dan Don It's Christmas* (1975) has the same high sense of design but uses richer colors and the motifs of Polish folk art. (See color section.)

Milton Glaser has not illustrated many books for children, but his pictures for Conrad Aiken's *Cats and Bats and Things with Wings* (1965) show amazing virtuosity, each picture in a different mood and technique. Edward Gorey's pen-and-ink illustrations are elegant and distinctive; Emily McCully's produce a free, staccato feeling. Brinton Turkle's realistic, simple pictures are as effective in creating an urban setting for Lucille Clifton's *The Boy Who Didn't Believe in Spring* (1973) as for the nineteenth-century town in *Obadiah the Bold* (1965). Ed Emberley won the Caldecott Medal for his illustrations, with a leaded-glass effect from bright colors over woodcut lines, in *Drummer Hoff* (1967), a folk verse adapted by Barbara Emberley. The Caldecott Medal for a 1970 book went to Gail Haley for *A Story, A Story*, the retelling of an African folk tale with woodcut illustrations that are occasionally crowded but have good design and vitality. Anita Lobel, an adaptable artist, is at her best in Benjamin Elkin's *How the Tsar Drinks Tea* (1971), in which the pictures, appropriately bordered, have a quality of Russian decorative art, or in *King Rooster, Queen Hen* (1975), where she fills the pages with rich textures and patterns. The soft, almost photographic drawings of Symeon Shimin, the distinctive portraiture of Ati Forberg, and the subtle shading of Tom Feelings's pictures in Muriel Feelings's *Jambo Means Hello* (1974) or in his own *Black Pilgrimage* (1972), all have a gentleness that is also strength. A bold freedom is evident in the work of Jose Aruego and Ariane Dewey, whose illustrations for *Owliver* (1974) by Robert Kraus have strength and vigor; and in the work of Tomi Ungerer, whose pictures are the visual equivalent of a comic tall tale.

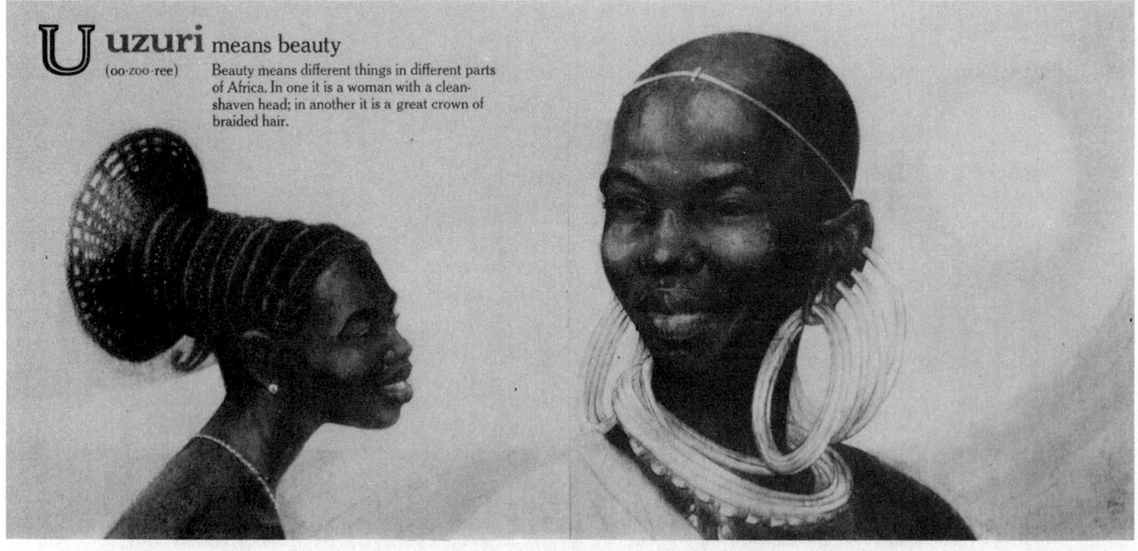

Illustration from Jambo Means Hello: Swahili Alphabet Book *by Muriel Feelings with illustrations by Tom Feelings. Illustrations Copyright © 1974 by Tom Feelings. Used with the permission of THE DIAL PRESS. (Original with color)*

Ed Young and Bernarda Bryson are outstanding for their sense of design and their use of color. John Schoenherr, Irene Brady, Olive Earle, and Hilda Simon are all notable for their scrupulously realistic pictures of animals.

The work of several illustrators is indelibly identified with the characters they have helped bring to life: Beth and Joe Krush for the stories of the Borrowers; Louis Slobodkin for the Moffats; and Paul Galdone for those mice-extraordinary, Anatole and Basil—all of these artists of course have illustrated many other books.

Jean de Brunhoff delighted children with the adventures of that suave French elephant Babar, and Françoise (Seignobosc) has given us a number of books in bright, decorative colors. The Italian artist Bruno Munari provides children with so magnificent a use of color against white space that he could train the color blind to see and rejoice. The illustrations of Swiss Felix Hoffmann for *Sleeping Beauty* (1960) and *The Story of Christmas* (1975) are in the grand style, romantic and grave. The first Hans Christian Andersen Award for illustrations went to Swiss Alois Carigiet, whose *Anton and Anne* (1969) is a good example of the vibrant delicacy of his work. In contrast, another Swiss artist, Celestino Piatti, paints in bold and brilliant modern style. The Danish artist Ib Spang Olsen, who received the Andersen Award in 1972, uses scribbly line and fresh, bright color in contrast to the gloomy smoke of a story about pollution in *Smoke* (1972). Harald Wiberg, in *The Big Snowstorm* (1976) by Hans Peterson, draws beautiful winter scenes of his native Sweden.

Two English illustrators, Margery Gill and Shirley Hughes, do work in color but are better known for their realistic, natural line drawings. C. Walter Hodges won the Kate Greenaway Medal for *Shakespeare's Theatre* (1964), and his fidelity of detail is also seen in sea scenes and the historically based tale of a rescue operation, *The Overland Launch* (1970). Paul and Dorothy Goble, although British, have made a signal contribution to our knowledge of Native Americans with magnificently detailed and historically accurate pictures in books like *Lone Bull's Horse Raid* (1973). From Japanese-born Taro Yashima have come the sensitive illustrations of

From Lone Bull's Horse Raid *by Paul and Dorothy Goble. Reproduced by permission of Bradbury Press, Inc. and Macmillan London, Ltd. (Original in color)*

children in Japan in *Crow Boy* (1955), and of a Japanese child in America in *Umbrella* (1958), and other works. (See color section.) Kazue Mizumura, who also came to the United States from Japan, has created lively pictures for the stories, set in Japan, of Yoshiko Uchida, as well as for her own *If I Built a Village . . .* (1971).

This is indeed the day of the artist in children's books, and their pictures should afford some protection from the flood of meretricious art that is so readily available. Better one good book with distinguished illustrations than a dozen stereotypes with flashy, poorly executed pictures. For children must have a chance to see truly and subtly. They must have a chance to look and look again at the illustrations in their books. Pictures can help them see the comic absurdities of life or its heroic struggles and tragedies. Pictures can give children a sudden breathtaking feeling for the beauty or the wonder of life. Such pictures deepen their perceptiveness and help them to grow.

Many of the children's books mentioned in this chapter appear in the Chapter 4 ("Books for Early Childhood") bibliography, where they are preceded by a "5" to indicate they are discussed here in Chapter 5.

Adult References[6]

ALDERSON, BRIAN. *Looking at Picture Books 1973.*
The Art of Beatrix Potter.
BADER, BARBARA. *American Picturebooks from Noah's Ark to the Beast Within.*
The Bewick Collector.
BLACKBURN, HENRY. *Randolph Caldecott; A Personal Memoir of His Early Art Career.*
CIANCIOLO, PATRICIA. *Illustrations in Children's Books.*
COLBY, JEAN POINDEXTER. *Writing, Illustrating and Editing Children's Books.* Part II, "Illustrations and Production."
COMMIRE, ANNE. *Something About the Author; Facts and Pictures About Contemporary Authors and Illustrators of Books for Young People.*
DAVIS, MARY GOULD. *Randolph Caldecott 1846–1886; An Appreciation.*
DOYLE, BRIAN, comp. and ed. *The Who's Who of Children's Literature.*
EGOFF, SHEILA. *The Republic of Childhood; A Critical Guide to Canadian Children's Literature in English.* Chapter 7, "Illustration and Design."
EGOFF, SHEILA, G. T. STUBBS, and L. F. ASHLEY, eds. *Only Connect; Readings on Children's Literature.* Part 5, "Illustration."
ENGEN, RODNEY. *Kate Greenaway.*
ERNEST, EDWARD, comp., assisted by PATRICIA TRACY LOWE. *The Kate Greenaway Treasury.*
FREEMAN, G. LAVERNE, and RUTH SUNDERLIN FREEMAN. *The Child and His Picture Book.*
FULLER, MURIEL, ed. *More Junior Authors.*
GOTTLIEB, GERALD R., and others. *Early Children's Books and Their Illustration.*
HOPKINS, LEE BENNETT. *Books Are by People.*
HUDSON, DEREK. *Arthur Rackham; His Life and Work.*
HÜRLIMANN, BETTINA. *Picture-Book World.*
KINGMAN, LEE, ed. *Newbery and Caldecott Medal Books; 1966–1975.*
KINGMAN, LEE, JOANNA FOSTER, and RUTH GILES LONTOFT, comps. *Illustrators of Children's Books, 1957–1966.*
KLEMIN, DIANA. *The Art of Art for Children's Books.*
______. *The Illustrated Book; Its Art and Craft.*
KUNITZ, STANLEY J., and HOWARD HAYCRAFT, eds. *The Junior Book of Authors.*
LANE, MARGARET. *The Tale of Beatrix Potter; A Biography.*
LEAR, EDWARD. *Lear in the Original; 110 Drawings for Limericks and Other Nonsense.*
LINDER, ENID, and LESLIE L. LINDER. *The Art of Beatrix Potter.*
MacCANN, DONNARAE, and OLGA RICHARD. *The Child's First Books; A Critical Study of Pictures and Text.*
MAHONY, BERTHA E., LOUISE P. LATIMER, and BEULAH FOLMSBEE, comps. *Illustrators of Children's Books, 1744–1945.*
MILLER, BERTHA MAHONY, and ELINOR WHITNEY FIELD, eds. *Caldecott Medal Books: 1938–1957.*
MOORE, ANNE CARROLL. *A Century of Kate Greenaway.*
MUIR, PERCY. *English Children's Books, 1600 to 1900.*
PITZ, HENRY C. *Howard Pyle; Writer, Illustrator, Founder of the Brandywine School.*
______. *Illustrating Children's Books; History, Technique, Production.*
______. *The Practice of American Book Illustration.*
______, ed. *A Treasury of American Book Illustration.*
QUINNAN, BARBARA, comp. *Fables from Incunabula to Modern Picture Books.*
RICHARD, OLGA. "The Visual Language of the Picture Book."
ROBINSON, EVELYN ROSE. *Readings About Children's Literature.* Part 5, "Illustrations and Children's Books."
VIGUERS, RUTH HILL, MARCIA DALPHIN, and BERTHA MAHONY MILLER, comps. *Illustrators of Children's Books, 1946–1956.*
WARD, MARTHA E., and DOROTHY A. MARQUARDT. *Illustrators of Books for Young People.*
WHALLEY, JOYCE IRENE. *Cobwebs to Catch Flies; Illustrated Books for the Nursery and Schoolroom, 1700–1900.*
WHITE, DOROTHY MARY NEAL. *About Books for Children.* Chapter 2, "Picture Books."
______. *Books Before Five.*

[6]Complete bibliographic data are provided in the combined Adult References in the Appendixes.

Part 3
Exploring the Types of Literature

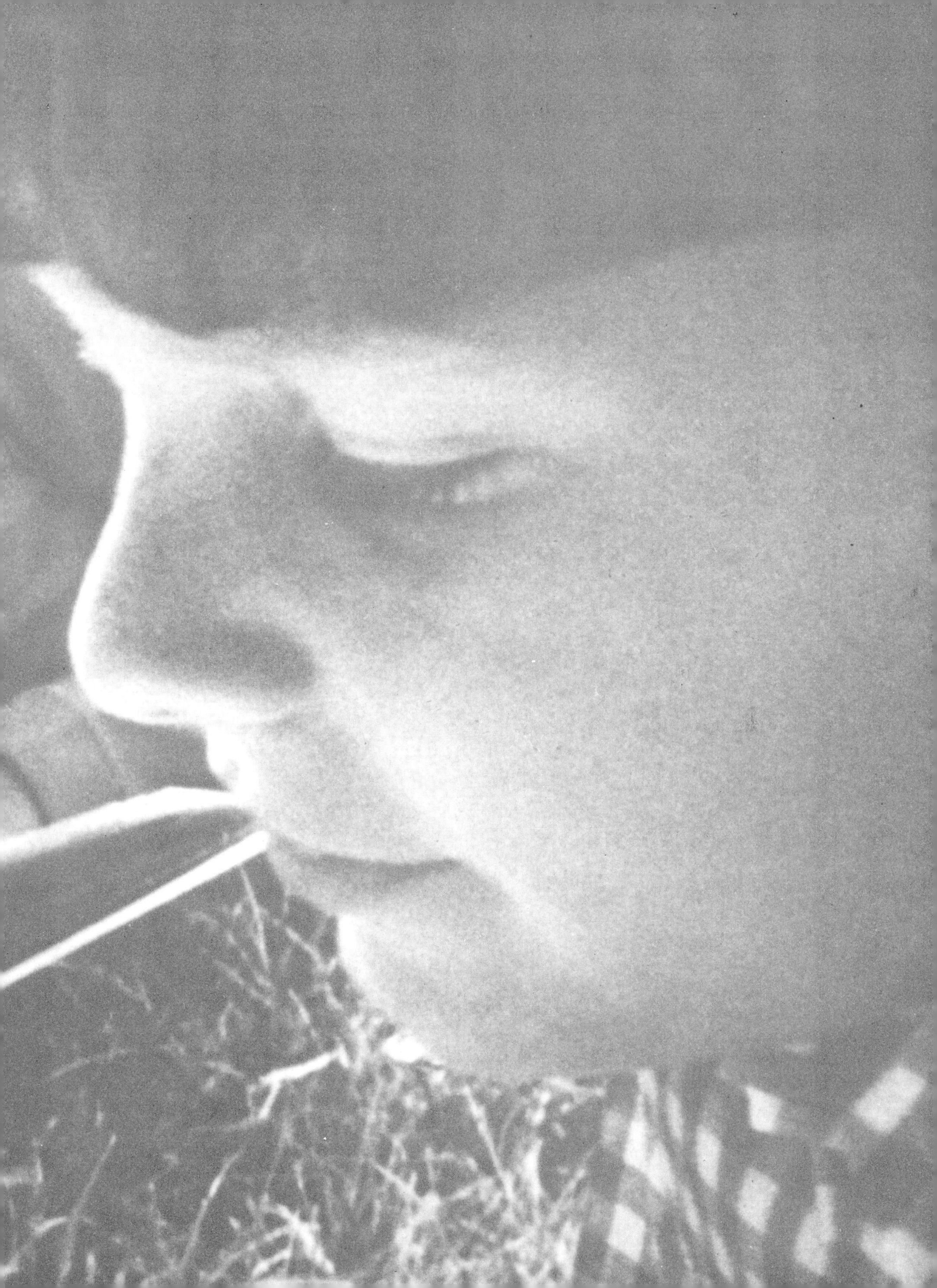

Folk Tales

Chapter 6

Folk tales, like nursery rhymes and ballads, are a part of that great stream of anonymous creation known as "folklore"—the accumulated wisdom and art of simple everyday folk. In the broadest sense of the word, folklore includes superstitions, medicinal practices, games, songs, festivals, dance rituals, old tales, verses, fables, myths, legends, and epics. Folklore is sometimes called the "mirror of a people." It reveals their characteristic efforts to explain and deal with the strange phenomena of nature; to understand and interpret the ways of human beings with each other; and to give expression to deep, universal emotions—joy, grief, fear, jealousy, wonder, triumph.

Of the many varieties of folklore, the folk tale is the most familiar and perhaps the most appealing. Interest in folk tales developed in the eighteenth century along with interest in old ballads, but in the nineteenth century a romantic interest in the old tales grew so strong that many thousands were collected all over the globe. Striking similarities were noticed among the folk tales found in different parts of the world, and many theories were advanced to explain these similarities.

Theories of Folk-Tale Origin

Monogenesis

One of the earliest explanations for the similarities among folk tales of different peoples was the Aryan myth theory. The theory asserted that all folk tales came from the Teutonic myths of a single ancestral group. This is sometimes referred to as the theory of *monogenesis* or "single origin." Although the Aryan myth theory has been refuted, it is interesting today because it has been the springboard for some other theories of folk-tale origin.

Polygenesis

One group of scholars believed in the theory of *polygenesis*, or "many origins." They asserted that human beings everywhere in the world are moved by much the same emotions—love and pity, fear and anguish, jealousy and hatred; that all people can observe the results of greed, selfish ambition, or quiet courage and kindliness; that all have seen the ways of cruel stepmothers (Were there no loving ones in the old days, one wonders?); and that all have seen neglected children come into their own. So Andrew Lang and other believers in polygenesis insisted that similar plots could develop in different parts of the world from similar situations common to all humanity. Lang used the widely disseminated story of Jason to prove his point. This theory would seem to account for the literally hundreds of variants of "Cinderella" found in Egypt, India, all parts of Europe, and among the North American Indians.

However, modern social anthropologists point out that people are *not* the same the world over. In some cultures, for instance, stepmothers may not be feared at all. The Andaman Islanders apparently are indifferent to whether the children they bring up are their own or other people's—no stepmother problem there! Another objection made to polygenesis is that the same story in all its peculiar details and chains of events could scarcely have grown up quite independently among entirely different groups isolated from each other. But whether there is any validity to the theory of polygenesis, one thing is certain: almost all peoples have produced stories and there are striking similarities among the tales of different peoples.

Remnants of Myth and Ritual

Some students, convinced that the folk tales preserve the *remnants of nature myths,* continually interpret any traditional story as a nature allegory—whether it is about sleep or forgetfulness, about a hero battling with a dragon, or about a girl being carried off by a polar bear. "Little Red Riding Hood," for instance, has been interpreted as an allegory of sunset and sunrise. The wolf is supposed to symbolize night, and in many versions he succeeds in devouring the little girl, who in her red cape represents the setting sun. This symbolic interpretation is extended in the Grimm version of the story, in which the hunters cut open the wolf and release "Little Red-Cap," the sun, from her imprisonment in the wolf, or night. The Norse "East o' the Sun" with its polar bear and its disappearing Prince was, like the Balder myth (see Chapter 7, p. 185), supposed to explain the disappearance of the sun.

Other folklorists, while not interpreting all the old stories as nature allegories, believed that many of these tales preserved *remnants of other kinds of religious myth and ritual.* For instance, Sir George Webbe Dasent thought that the Norse folk tales contained many of the elements of the Norse myths. He explained that after Christianity came to the Scandinavian countries, the old Norse gods lost their prestige and were gradually changed into the fabulous creatures of the folk tales. Odin became the Wild Huntsman riding through the sky with his grisly crew. And perhaps the nursery tale of "The Three Billy-Goats Gruff" preserves the memory of Thor's battle with the Frost Giants, for the billy goat was the ancient symbol of Thor, and the huge, stupid trolls could easily be the inglorious descendants of the Frost Giants.

Some scholars believe that cumulative tales like "The House That Jack Built" and "The Old Woman and Her Pig" have ritualistic origins. Other stories too, they think, preserve fragments of spells or incantations. In the Grimms' dramatic "The Goose-Girl," the heroine puts a spell on Conrad's hat:

Blow, blow, thou gentle wind, I say,
Blow Conrad's little hat away. . . .

Ancient superstitions and customs surrounding christenings and marriage ceremonies may also be found in the folk tales. So may propitiations of spirits, witches, the devil, or certain powerful animals (like the bear in the Norse tales).

Origins in Dreams and Unconscious Emotions

Psychoanalytic writers have studied those objects and ideas which appear frequently in fairy tales from all over the world and have asserted that they are *symbols of emotional fantasy* which all people experience. Among such supposedly universal feelings are unconscious sexual love for the parent, hatred of paternal or maternal authority, love or jealousy among brothers and sisters. The ideas and objects representing these feelings are supposed to be the same in folk tales the world over and to explain the similarities among these stories. But social anthropologists object to this theory, too. They maintain that unconscious emotions vary among different peoples and so do the symbols which represent them. The unconscious emotions described, they say, may be the characteristic product of modern urban life rather than expressions universal among all peoples, places, and times.

Some authorities think that the stories originated in the *wonderful dreams or nightmares* of the storytellers. Stories about a poor girl

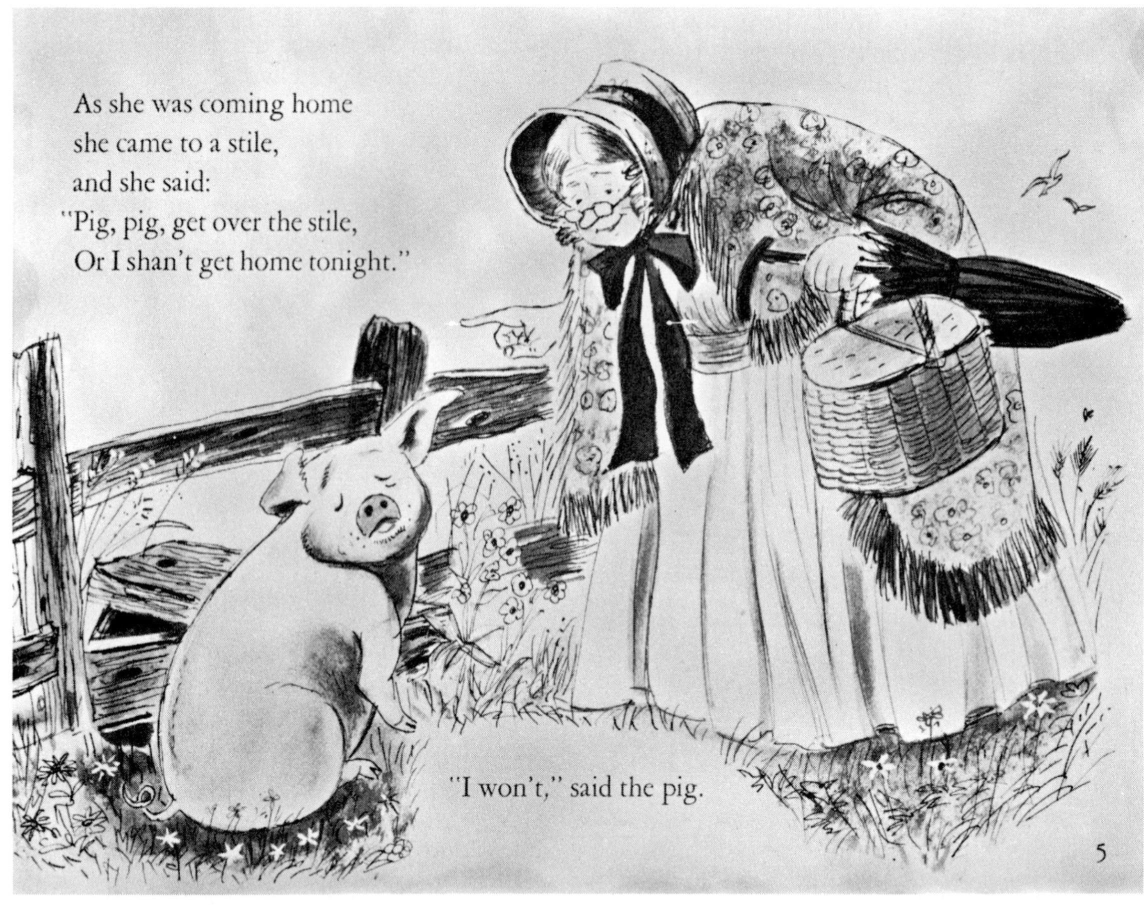
As she was coming home
she came to a stile,
and she said:
"Pig, pig, get over the stile,
Or I shan't get home tonight."
"I won't," said the pig.
5

From The Old Woman and Her Pig *by Paul Galdone. Copyright © 1960. Used with permission of McGraw-Hill Book Company.*

sent out to find strawberries in the middle of winter (some versions clothe her in a paper dress) might well grow from the bad dreams we have when the night turns cold and we find ourselves with too few blankets. Did the story of "Snow White" emerge from such a dream? Or consider the story of the poor girl in "East o' the Sun," who kissed the prince and then found herself out on a lonely road—the prince gone, the castle vanished, the little bell that fulfilled her every wish lost forever, and she in rags once more. Is she the embodiment of our anxieties and our reluctance to return from our dreams to a workaday world? So the fatal questions, impossible tasks, and endless discomforts in the folk tales may suggest some of the anxieties that haunt us in our sleep now and then. Perhaps the primitive quality of some of our dreams may also explain the shocking elements in some of the tales. These always seem less horrible in the stories than they actually should seem because they are seldom attended by any realistic details but are indeed vague, dreamlike, and evanescent.

Another phase of the psychological interpretation of folk-tale origin is the idea that the people who created the tales found in fancy the *satisfaction of unconscious frustrations or drives*. These imaginative tales provide *wish fulfillment*. That is, the oppressed peasants who produced some of the tales were "motivated by naive dreams of the success of the despised," and so they told stories about cinder lads going from wretched hovels to fabulous castles, or about a goose girl marrying the prince. It is certain that fairy tales do satisfy deep human needs, particularly the needs for security and competence. In the folk tales, banquets, servants, glittering jewels, and rich clothes are concrete symbols of success. Granting that these tales are primarily for entertainment, there seems to be little doubt that they contain a deeper meaning and an inner significance which the child or adult feels without being conscious of the cause. In discussing Perrault's fairy tales Jacques Barchilon and Henry Pettit say, "Just as the dream expresses innermost wishes in disguised form, the fairy tale masks our real wishes with the appearance of a free fantasy." And again they emphasize the symbolic character of the tales saying, ". . . the veiled symbolism of the fairy tale and its violence fulfill a need in the child's life. The fairy tale is his apprenticeship to life."[1]

Psychoanalysts also hold that "the child, through the comparison between the fantastic and the real, gradually learns to test reality. When children realize that the fairy tale is fictitious, they learn to enjoy it as fiction. This is one giant step not only in the process of rational maturation but in aesthetic development as well."[2]

[1]Jacques Barchilon and Henry Pettit, *The Authentic Mother Goose Fairy Tales and Nursery Rhymes* (Swallow, 1960), p. 27.

Viewpoints

We observe that children commonly listen to fairy tales with an air of fascinated horror, or even with gusto, and demand the reading to be repeated. Yet the gruesome figures of these tales, e.g., cannibalistic giants, enter into the frightful nightmares which so many children have to endure. It would therefore seem plain sense to avoid such horror-raising stimulation. But the matter turns out to be not so simple. We find that young children *spontaneously* create in their imagination, both consciously and still more unconsciously, the same images of horror and terror, and that they suffer from nightmares without ever having listened to a fairy story. Indeed it often happens that when their own phantasies are brought into the open by a smiling mother relating a tale of horror they thereby achieve a measure of reassurance by gradually learning that the imagery they conjure up does not correspond to any outer reality.
—Ernest Jones, "Preface," for *I Could a Tale Unfold* by P. M. Pickard, Tavistock Publications, London, and Humanities Press, New York, 1961, p. ix.

Cement of Society

In recent times the science of folklore has merged more and more into the science of social anthropology. To understand the why and wherefore of folk tales, anthropologists have lived intimately with many peoples, visiting their homes, markets, religious ceremonies, and festal celebrations. Of course they cannot visit early peoples who produced the folk tales, but their studies of modern folk societies can cast light on the origin of the old folk tales. Their conclusion may be summed up in one sentence: folk tales have been the *cement of society*. They not only expressed but codified and reinforced the way people thought, felt, believed, and behaved.

Folk tales taught children and reminded their elders of what was proper and moral. They put the stamp of approval upon certain values held by the group, and thus cemented it together with a common code of behavior. They taught kindness, modesty, truthfulness, courage in adversity—and they made virtue seem worthwhile because it was invariably rewarded and evil just as invariably punished. This idea of folk tales as carriers of the moral code helps explain the ethical significance and emotional satisfaction they still hold for us today.

Some of the explanations for the origins of folk tales are dubious, but many of them are reinforced by enough reasonable evidence to make them seem both plausible and probable. Folklorists now agree that the folk tale is created by most peoples at an early level of civilization. Historically, the tales may contain elements from past religions, rituals, superstitions, or past events. Psychologically, they may serve to satisfy in symbolic form some of humanity's basic emotional needs. Ethically, they may be "the cement of society"—reinforcing our faith in morality and the ultimate triumph of good over evil.

[2]Ibid., p. 26.

Wide Diffusion of the Folk Tales

Students have found recognizable variants of such tales as "Jason and the Golden Fleece" and "Cinderella" in the manuscripts of ancient India, Egypt, and Greece and on the lips of storytellers in Zulu huts, American Indian hogans, and Samoan villages—from the Russian steppes to African jungles and the mountains of South America. The three tasks, the flight, the pursuit, the lost slipper or sandal, and the undoing of a spell are found in innumerable societies. How were they carried?

First, of course, they were carried orally by the migrations of whole peoples. Later they traveled from one country to another with sailors and soldiers, women stolen from their tribes, slaves and captives of war, traders, minstrels and bards, monks and scholars, and young gentlemen on the grand tour. Some storytellers no doubt polished and improved the tales, while others debased them. If the folk tales traveled by land, they were passed on by many peoples and greatly changed in the process; but if they traveled by sea, they stayed closer to the originals. Sometimes one story theme would combine with others, producing either a variant of the original tale or a relatively new one. So ancient storytellers preserved old stories, produced variants of others, and occasionally dreamed up new ones to pass on. This process is one that continues even today.

The literary (or written) sources of the popular tales did not begin to circulate in Europe until around the twelfth century. Then came the Indian and Irish manuscript collections, vivid and lively importations which were no doubt partly responsible for the flowering of folk art in the thirteenth century. Ballads and stories began to bubble up everywhere, often with the same plots or themes.

During the sixteenth century, popular literature in England made a dignified beginning in print with Caxton's fine English translations of Aesop's fables, the King Arthur stories, the Homeric epics. In England, too, the chapbooks picked up fragments of tales from everywhere and kept them alive in garbled but recognizable versions, dearly beloved by the people.

Predominant Kinds of Folk Tales

No adult can read folk tales without being conscious of the varied groups into which they fall: cumulative tales, talking-beast tales, drolls or humorous tales, realistic tales, religious tales, romances, and, of course, tales of magic. Many classifications have been made, but this one seems to bring in most of the kinds and to emphasize their characteristics.

Cumulative Tales

Very young children enjoy the simplest of all stories, the cumulative or repetitional tale. Its charm lies in its minimum plot and maximum rhythm. Its episodes follow each other neatly and logically in a pattern of cadenced repetition. Sometimes, as in "The Old Woman and

Viewpoints

Children are capable, of course, of *literary belief,* when the story-maker's art is good enough to produce it.

. . . He makes a Secondary World which your mind can enter. Inside it, what he relates is "true": it accords with the laws of that world. You therefore believe it, while you are, as it were, inside. The moment disbelief arises, the spell is broken; the magic, or rather art, has failed.

. . . at no time can I remember that the enjoyment of a story was dependent on belief that such things could happen, or had happened, in "real life." Fairy stories were plainly not primarily concerned with possibility, but with desirability. If they awakened *desire,* satisfying it while often whetting it unbearably, they succeeded.

. . . The dragon had the trademark *Of Faërie* written plain upon him. . . . Of course, I in my timid body did not wish to have them in the neighbourhood. . . . This is, naturally, often enough what children mean when they ask: "Is it true?" They mean: "I like this, but is it contemporary? Am I safe in my bed?" The answer: "There is certainly no dragon in England today," is all that they want to hear. —J. R. R. Tolkien, *Tree and Leaf,* Houghton Mifflin, Boston, 1965, pp. 36–37, 40, 41.

Her Pig," the action moves upward in a spiral and then retraces the spiral downward to the conclusion. Sometimes, as in the American-English "Johnny-Cake," the Norse "Pancake," and the American "Gingerbread Boy," the action takes the form of a race, and the story comes to an end with the capture of the runaway. Fortunately, the runaway in such stories has forfeited our sympathy by stupidity ("Henny Penny"), or by impudence ("The Pancake"), so that the capture becomes merely the downfall of the foolish or the proud.

"The Pancake" is one of the most delightful of these tales. The pancake—having jumped out of the frying pan and escaped from the mother, the father, and the seven hungry children—meets a series of creatures and becomes more insolent with each encounter. The following excerpt is typical of the racing-chasing style of these little tales:

> *"Good day, pancake," said the gander.*
>
> *"The same to you, Gander Pander," said the pancake.*
>
> *"Pancake, dear, don't roll so fast; bide a bit and let me eat you up."*
>
> *"When I have given the slip to Goody Poody, and the goodman, and seven squalling children, and Manny Panny, and Henny Penny, and Cocky Locky, and Ducky Lucky, and Goosey Poosey, I may well slip through your feet, Gander Pander," said the pancake, which rolled off as fast as ever.*
>
> *So when it had rolled a long, long time, it met a pig.*
>
> *"Good day, pancake," said the pig.*
>
> *"The same to you, Piggy Wiggy," said the pancake, which, without a word more, began to roll and roll like mad.* (Tales from the Fjeld.)

Here, in the last four lines, the storyteller by an ominous tone of voice warns the children that the jig is up for the pancake. Piggy Wiggy is Fate itself.

Some cumulative stories, like "The House That Jack Built," are mere chants; others, like "The Three Little Pigs" and "The Bremen Town-Musicians," are repetitional and sequential, but have well-rounded plots. Modern examples of the successful use of this pattern are Marjorie Flack's *Ask Mr. Bear*, Wanda Gág's *Millions of Cats*, and Maurice Sendak's *One Was Johnny*.

Illustration by Hans Fischer. Reproduced from Grimm's Traveling Musicians, *by permission of Harcourt Brace Jovanovich, Inc. (Original in color)*

Talking-Beast Tales

Perhaps young children love best of all folk tales the ones in which animals talk. Sometimes the animals talk with human beings as in "Puss in Boots" but more often with other animals as in "The Cat and the Mouse in Partnership." These creatures talk every bit as wisely as humans, or as foolishly. Possibly their charm lies in the opportunity they give the reader to identify with the cleverest of the three pigs or the most powerful and efficient of "The Three Billy-Goats Gruff." Perhaps the credulity of "Henny Penny" or of the two foolish pigs ministers to the listener's sense of superiority. Certainly children are amused by these old tales for the same reasons that modern children laugh at Snoopy in Charles

Schulz's *Peanuts* cartoons. The animals in both the old and the modern creations are exaggerated characterizations of human beings, and in that exaggeration lie their humor and fascination.

These beast tales generally teach a lesson—the folly of credulity and the rewards of courage, ingenuity, and independence—though their didacticism does not stand out so much as in the fables. The stories are so lively and diverting that they are primarily good entertainment. Perhaps the most successful of the modern descendants of the ancient beast tales are Beatrix Potter's *The Tale of Peter Rabbit*, *The Tale of Benjamin Bunny*, and all her other *Tales*. These have joined the ranks of the immortals, along with "The Three Little Pigs."

The Drolls or Humorous Tales

A small body of the folk tales are obviously meant as fun and nonsense. These are the stories about sillies or numskulls, such as the Grimms' "Clever Elsie."

As you may remember, Elsie had a wooer who demanded a really clever bride. On one of his visits, Elsie's family sent her down to the cellar to draw some beer, and there, just over her head, she saw a pick-axe that had been left thrust into the masonry. Immediately she began to weep, thinking to herself,

> *"If I get Hans, and we have a child, and he grows big, and we send him into the cellar here to draw beer, then the pick-axe will fall on his head and kill him."*

She cried so hard and so long that first one member of the household and then another came down to the cellar, listened to her tale, and began to weep, too. Finally, Hans came and, hearing how things were, decided that Elsie was indeed a thoughtful, clever girl and married her. After the marriage Hans, who had evidently taken his bride's measure at last, gave Elsie a task to do in the field and left her there alone. But Elsie, unable to decide whether to work first or sleep first, finally fell asleep in the field and slept until night. Returning home in a great fright, she asked,

> *"Hans, is Elsie within?" "Yes," answered Hans, "she is within." Hereupon she was terrified, and said: "Ah, heavens! Then it is not I."*

And so she ran out of the village and was never seen again.

Like the cumulative tales, the drolls vary in the amount of plot they develop. Some have well-rounded plots; for instance, in "The Husband Who Was to Mind the House" (he does so with disastrous results) and in "Mr. Vinegar" (who trades off his cow as the start of a series of barters which brings him less and less until he has nothing left but a good cudgeling from his wife). The Norse story "Taper Tom" has not only all the droll antics to make the princess laugh but real adventure as well. Finally, the Norse "Squire's Bride" is not only a droll story but also a fine bit of adult satire on elderly wooers of young girls.

Realistic Tales

For the most part, the peoples who created these old tales seem to have had no great taste for using as story material their own "here and now," the stuff of everyday living. Even when they omit all elements of magic, they still tell a fabulous tale: the monster in "Blue Beard," for example, seems to have had some historic basis, but to young readers he is a kind of cross between an ogre and a giant. His English variant, "Mr. Fox," is even less realistic, though strictly speaking there is nothing in either story that could not have happened. Perhaps the prettiest of all realistic stories in our folk-tale collections is the Norse "Gudbrand on the Hill-side." This is "Mr. Vinegar," with a loving wife instead of a shrew. Gudbrand's old wife thinks her man can do no wrong; so, sure of his wife's love and understanding, Gudbrand makes a wager with a neighbor that his wife will not blame him no matter what he does. Just as Gudbrand expects, his wife's tender responses to his series of disastrous trades reaches a climax with her heartfelt exclamation:

> *"Heaven be thanked that I have got you safe back again; you do everything so well that I want neither cock nor goose; neither pigs nor kine."*
>
> *Then Gudbrand opened the door and said,*

"And thanks to you for that!" said the wife.

Illustration by Theodor Kittelsen for Norwegian Folk Tales *collected by Peter Christian Asbjörnsen and Jörgen Moe.*

"Well, what do you say now? Have I won the hundred dollars?" and his neighbour was forced to allow that he had.

Religious Tales

Folk tales using elements of religious beliefs are rarely found in children's collections but are fairly frequent in the complete editions of almost any group. Coming down from the morality plays of the Middle Ages, the devil and St. Peter appear usually in comic roles. The story of the devil who begged to be taken back to hell in order to escape from a shrew of a wife is a popular plot throughout Europe.

The Virgin Mary is usually introduced respectfully and even tenderly. St. Joseph is also introduced as a figure of compassion and as the administrator of poetic justice. The religious folk tales are generally either broadly comic or didactic and are, on the whole, not well adapted to children.

Romances

Romance in the folk tales is usually remote and impersonal, and the characters are often stereotypes. Aucassin and Nicolette are less interesting than their adventures. Enchantments and impossible tasks separate folktale lovers, and magic brings them together, whether they be Beauty and the Beast, the Goose Girl and the King, or the girl who traveled east o' the sun and west o' the moon to find her love.

Tales of Magic

Tales of magic are at the heart of folk tales. These are the stories which justify the children's name for the whole group—"fairy tales." Fairy godmothers, giants, water nixies, a noble prince turned into a polar bear, the North Wind giving a poor boy magic gifts to make good the loss of his precious meal, three impossible tasks to be performed, a lad searching for the Water of Life—these are

Viewpoints

. . . nothing in the entire range of "children's literature"—with rare exceptions—can be as enriching and satisfying to child and adult alike as the folk fairy tale. True, fairy tales teach little overtly about the specific conditions of life in modern mass society; these tales were created long before modern society came into being. But from them a child can learn more about the inner problems of man, and about solutions to his own (and our) predicaments in any society, than he can from any other type of story within his comprehension. Since the child is exposed at every moment to the society in which he lives, he will learn to cope with its conditions—provided, that is, that his inner resources permit him to do so. The child must therefore be helped to bring order into the turmoil of his feelings. He needs—and the point hardly requires emphasis at this moment in our history—a moral education that subtly, by implication only, conveys to him the advantages of moral behavior, not through abstract ethical concepts but through that which seems tangibly right and therefore has meaning for him. The child can find meaning through fairy tales.
—Bruno Bettelheim, "The Uses of Enchantment," *The New Yorker,* December 8, 1975, p. 50.

some of the motifs and some of the magical people that give folk tales a quality so unearthly and so beautiful that they come close to poetry. A large proportion of folk tales are based upon magic of many kinds—so it is worthwhile to study these motifs and the fairy folk who flit so mysteriously through the tales.

Fairies and Other Magic Makers

The Little People

The belief in fairies was once astonishingly widespread and persistent among Celtic peoples (particularly in Ireland and Scotland). Even when belief is gone, certain superstitions remain. From these countries comes the idea of trooping fairies, ruled over by a fairy queen, dwelling underground in halls of great richness and beauty. These fairy raths (or forts) are the old subterranean earthworks remaining today in Ireland and Scotland, with the gold and glitter of jewels added by the Celtic imagination. From these hiding places, according to tradition, the fairies emerge at night to carry off men, maidens, or children who have caught their fancy. They may put spells on the cattle or on the work of humans they dislike, or they may come to the assistance of those who win their gratitude. To eat fairy food or to fall asleep in a fairy ring (a ring of especially green grass) or under a thorn tree on May Eve or Halloween is to put yourself in the power of the fairies for a year and a day.

The name by which you refer to these blithe spirits is also a matter of importance in Celtic lore. If you want to play safe, you will never use the word f-a-i-r-y, which reminds them of the unhappy fact that they have no souls. On the Day of Judgment when humans have a chance (however slight) of going up in glory, the wee folk know full well, poor soulless creatures that they are, that they will simply blow away like a puff of down in a strong wind. So address them tactfully as "the good people," "the little people," or "the wee folk," if you would be well treated in return.

Other countries have these little creatures, too. In Cornwall, they are called pixies or piskeys, and they, like their Irish relatives, ride tiny steeds over the moors. In the Arabian tales you meet the jinns, who also live in deserted ruins, often underground, and are respectfully addressed as "the blessed ones." The German dwarfs are usually subterranean in their work and sometimes in their dwelling, too. Although they seem not to insist upon any special form of address, to treat them disrespectfully is to incur sure punishment.

The Norse hill folk live underground also, as do some of the small fairy folk of England and Scotland. There are other resemblances among these three groups. The Norse countries have house spirits, the Tomten, much like the English Lar or Lob-Lie-by-the-Fire and the Scotch Aiken-drum. All these household spirits take up their abode in a house where they are well treated and make themselves useful in many ways. They may be propitiated by bowls of milk or offerings of parsley, chives, and garlic. But woe to the misguided soul who gives them clothes! Such a gift usually offends them and always drives them away, never to return. Oddly enough, the elves in the Grimms' "Shoemaker and the Elves" were delighted by the tiny garments, but they did depart, forever.

Wise Women, Witches, and Wizards

A few of the fairy folk are consistently evil, but most of them fluctuate in their attitude toward human beings and may be either helpful or ruthless. The wise women, who come to christenings or serve as fairy godmothers, are, on the whole, a grave and serious group. They are not unlike our idea of the Fates, or Norns, who mark off the life span and foretell coming events. One of these wise women aided Cinderella, while a peevish one sent Beauty off to sleep for a hundred years.

Witches and wizards are usually wicked. They lure children into their huts to eat them, or they cast spells on noble youths and turn them into beasts. Russia has a unique witch, Baba Yaga, who lives in a house that walks around on chicken legs. When she wishes to fly, she soars off in a pestle and sweeps her way along with a besom (two objects which may have to be explained to children in advance, by the way). She has some other

Illustration by Blair Lent for Baba Yaga *by Ernest Small. Copyright © 1966 by Houghton Mifflin Company; Copyright © 1966 by Blair Lent, Jr. Reproduced by permission of Houghton Mifflin Company. (Original in color)*

unique powers that make her quite as fascinating as she is gruesome.

The magicians and sorcerers cast spells but may sometimes be prevailed upon to do a kind deed and help out a worthy youth bent on the impossible. The Celtic "Merlin" is the most romantic of all the sorcerers, but he is seldom mentioned in the folk tales. The English "Childe Rowland," however, enlists Merlin's aid in rescuing Burd Ellen from Elfland.

Occasional imps, like the German "Rumpelstiltskin" and the English "Tom Tit Tot," are hard to classify. They seem to be a kind of hybrid elf and fiend, hoping to get hold of a gay, laughing child to cheer their old age.

Giants and Ogres

Ogres and ogresses are always bloodthirsty and cruel. Giants, however, are of two kinds: the children call them "bad" and "good." The "bad giants" are a powerful clan using brute force against opponents. They swallow their antagonists whole, as tremendous power seems always to do in any age. They are ruthless and unscrupulous and must be dealt with on their own terms—deceit and trickery. But fortunately they are often thickheaded and rely too much on force, so that clever boys like Jack or the girl giant-tamer "Molly Whuppie" can outwit them and leave them completely befuddled.

The other tribe of giants we meet is the helpful one. They aid the lad who shares his last crust of bread with them, and of course their aid is magnificent. They can drink up the sea and hold it comfortably until it is convenient to release it again. They feel cold in the midst of fire and suffer from heat in solid ice. They can step lightly from mountain to mountain, break trees like twigs, and shatter rocks with a glance. The lad who lines up these giants on his side is guaranteed to win the princess and half the kingdom into the bargain. But no sluggard, no pompous pretender, no mean soul ever secures this aid. It is freely given only to honest folk about whom shines the grace of goodness.

Fairy Animals

In the world of fairy, domestic animals are as kindly disposed toward human beings as they are in the world of reality. For example, there is that handsome cat of cats, "Puss in Boots"—surely a child given a magic choice of one handy assistant from all the gallery of fairy helpers would choose the witty and formidable Puss. The Norse "Dapplegrim" is a horse of parts and does fully as well for his master as the Russian Horse of Power in "The Firebird."

Occasionally wild animals take a hand in the magic events of the folk tales. In the Norse story, a gray wolf carries the king's son to the castle of "The Giant Who Had No Heart in His Body," and in the Czech story, old Lishka the fox gives "Budulinek" a ride on her tail, to his sorrow. Wild animals may be for or against human beings. Sometimes they serve merely as transportation, but often they are the real brains of an enterprise.

Magic Objects

In "Herding the King's Hares," Espen Cinderlad receives a remarkable whistle for his kindness to an old hag. With it he can bring order to every runaway bunny in the king's herd, and finally to the royal family as well:

> *Then the king and queen thought it best to give him the princess and half the kingdom; it just couldn't be helped.*
>
> *"That certainly was some whistle," said Espen Cinderlad.*

"Molly Whuppie," when pursued by the double-faced giant, runs lightly across the Bridge of One Hair, on which the giant dares take not so much as a single step. That is the kind of power every one of us needs to develop—the power to find a bridge, however slight, on which we can run lightly away from the ogres pursuing us. The folk tales are full of these "Fools of the World," who learn how to use magic tools as the pompous and pretentious never learn to do. Espen Cinderlad, with three impossible tasks to perform, hunts around until he finds the self-propelled axe, the spade, and the trickling water that could be stopped or let loose by him alone. Each of these magic objects told him it had been waiting a long, long time, just for him. The message would seem to be that magic is always waiting for those who know how to use it.

Enchanted People

Being put under a spell is just one of the many complications that beset the heroes and heroines of the fairy tales. Childe Rowland's sister unknowingly courted disaster by running around the church "widdershins"—counterclockwise—and so put herself under the power of the fairies. "Rapunzel," of the long, long hair, was locked up in a tower by a cruel enchantress who was so clever that only a super-prince could worst her. And there are many variants of the folk tale about the royal brothers who are changed into birds, and who can be released from their enchantment only after their little sister has gone speechless for seven long years and spun each of them a shirt of thistledown. The Grimms' touching "The Frog-King" is one of many tales in which either the husband or the wife is a fairy creature or is in the power of some witch or sorcerer. Of these, the Grimms' "The Water-Nixie" is perhaps the most exciting and the Norse "East o' the Sun and West o' the Moon," the most beautiful. In all such stories only love, loyalty, and self-sacrifice can break the enchantment and restore the beloved.

On the whole, the good and evil supernatural forces in the folk tales act according to certain laws. If magic makes wishes come true and points the way to happiness, it does so only with struggles and hardships on the part of the hero or heroine. The true princess suffers pitifully before magic opens the king's eyes and he sees her for what she is—the rightful bride for his son and a gentle, loving girl. These stories are not didactic, but one after another shows that courage and simple

Viewpoints

When the fairy tales are narrated pleasantly in their original version, they will not only be entertaining, but they will also exert a doubly beneficial effect upon the development of the child. In the first place, the fairy tale awakens in the child the feeling of participation with other human beings, with people not only of his immediate environment, but of all nations. He begins to sense that he is not alone with his, at times horrid and violent, fantasies, and that the latter are meaningful and valuable sources of strength for useful sublimations, as long as they never become confused with the outward reality. He also feels understood in his most tender longings, in his highest wishes. In the second place, the fairy tale communicates to the child a dim, intuitive understanding of his own nature and of his future positive potentialities. And he starts to sense that he became a human being primarily because in this world of ours he is meant to meet challenging and wondrous adventures. And so the fairy tale nourishes the child's courage to widen his horizons and to tackle all the challenges successfully. Then only, like some of the fairy tale heroes, he can hope to become a "king" within whose maturity spiritual wisdom will harmonize with his power over earthly things.—Julius E. Heuscher, M.D., F.A.P.A., *A Psychiatric Study of Fairy Tales,* Charles C Thomas, Publisher, Springfield, Illinois, 1963, pp. 185–186.

goodness work their own magic in this world, that evil must be conquered even if it carries us to the gates of death, and that grace and strength are bestowed upon those who strive mightily and keep honest, kindly hearts.

Viewpoints

The student of fairy tales . . . is aware, of course, if he is experienced, that however ancient the stories may be he must not think of them as if they were archaeological remains, as if they were the actual objects that existed in the past; nor must he regard them (as folklorists used to do) as antiques that have been so scarred by time they have become almost unrecognizable, for this presupposes that they were once whole and perfect, and have ever since been in a state of decay. He knows instead that since they are living things, not fossils, they are subject to mutation. They are as likely to have grown as they became older, as to have shrunk. They are as likely to have acquired significance, or to have acquired fresh significance, as they have passed through sophisticated communities, as to have lost it.
—Iona and Peter Opie, *The Classic Fairy Tales*, Oxford University Press, London, 1974, p. 17.

Distinctive Elements of Folk Tales

For generation after generation, folk tales have continued to be popular with children. Modern youngsters, surrounded by the mechanical gadgets and scientific wonders of our age, are still spellbound by their magic. A brief examination of their form, style, and character portrayal may help explain the charm of the old tales for children. First of all, the form or pattern of the folk tales is curiously satisfying both to children and adults.

The Introduction

The introduction to a folk tale does exactly what its name implies. It *introduces* the reader to the leading characters, the time and place of the story, and the problem to be solved, or the conflict which is the essence of the story.

The stories often involve the element of *contrast*. Sometimes there is the uneven conflict, which always makes a story more exciting: "Hansel and Gretel" and the wicked witch—two little children pitted against an evil power; Snow White and the cruel Queen. Sometimes the contrast lies within a like group; for example, in "The Three Little Pigs," there are not only pigs and wolf but also a wise pig and foolish pigs. So in "Boots and His Brothers" the humble Boots shows the wisdom his older brothers lack. "One-Eye, Two-Eyes, and Three-Eyes" has a most unusual contrast in the three sisters. Obviously, contrast heightens the conflict and rouses the reader's sympathy for the weaker or less fortunate or more kindly member of the group.

Folk tales are *objective* and *understandable*, never abstract. They have to do with winning security, earning a living or a place in the world, accomplishing impossible tasks, escaping from powerful enemies, outwitting wicked schemes and schemers, and succeeding with nonchalance. These plots are as vital today as ever and account for the vigor of these old tales.

Time is effectively accounted for by a conventional phrase such as "Once upon a time," "Long ago and far away," "In olden times when wishing still helped one," "A thousand years ago tomorrow," or "Once on a time, and a very good time too." Such folk-tale conventions do more than convey an idea of long age; they carry the reader at once to a dream world where anything is possible.

The *scene* is even more briefly sketched. It is a road, a bridge, a palace, a forest, or a poor man's hut—a place where something is going to happen and soon. No wonder these introductions catch the child's attention. They launch the conflict with no distracting details.

Sometimes the folk tales, like the ballads, get off to such a brisk start that the introduction is almost imperceptible. This one for "The Three Billy-Goats Gruff" is a masterpiece of brevity:

Once on a time there were three Billy-goats, who were to go up to the hill-side to make themselves fat, and the name of all three was "Gruff."

On the way up was a bridge over a burn they had to cross; and under the bridge lived a great ugly

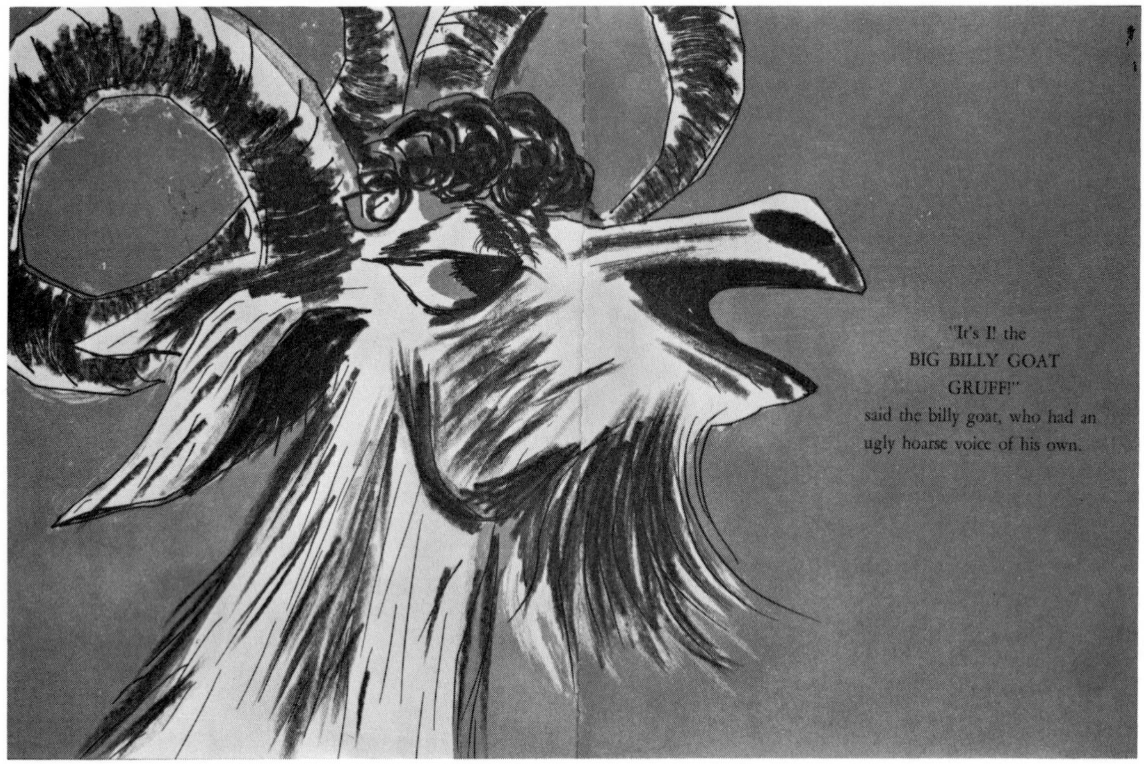

"It's I! the
BIG BILLY GOAT
GRUFF!"
said the billy goat, who had an
ugly hoarse voice of his own.

From The Three Billy Goats Gruff *by Asbjörnsen and Moe, illustrated and copyright 1957 by Marcia Brown. Reproduced by permission of Harcourt Brace Jovanovich, Inc. (Original in color)*

Troll, with eyes as big as saucers, and a nose as long as a poker.

There you are! The scene is a bridge with a pleasant stretch of grassy hillside just beyond. The characters are three earnest billy goats of the Gruff family who are desirous of getting fat on the hillside. Obstacle, Conflict, Problem live under the bridge in the person of an ugly Troll. In the fewest possible words, you have all the makings of a good plot. "The Sleeping Beauty," still a fairly uncomplicated story, must introduce the king, queen, courtiers, the grand christening for the baby princess in the palace, the good fairies for whom plates of gold have been prepared, and the evil fairy who is uninvited and minus a gold plate and therefore thoroughly angry. What will happen? This is the mark of a good introduction: it whets the appetite for more; you "go on" eagerly. For children, brevity of introduction is an important part of the charm of these folk tales. The excitement gets under way with minimum description.

The Development

The development carries forward the note of trouble sounded in the introduction. The quest begins, the tasks are initiated and performed, the flight gets under way, and obstacles of every kind appear, with the hero or heroine reduced to despair or helplessness or plunged into more and more perilous action. This is the heart of the story—action that mounts steadily until it reaches a climax, when the problem or conflict will be resolved one way or the other.

The vigorous plots of the folk tales, full of suspense and action, appeal strongly to young readers. The heroes and heroines *do* things—they ride up glass hills, slay giants who have no hearts in their bodies, outwit wolves, get their rights from the North Wind, or pitch an old witch into an oven she intended for them. Here are no brooding introspectionists but doers of the vigorous sort.

If these tales are to carry conviction, development must be both logical (in terms of the story) and plausible. When in "The Three Little Pigs" one pig is so foolish as to build a house of straw and another to build a house of sticks, you know they are doomed. But when a pig has sufficient acumen to build his house stoutly of bricks, you know perfectly well he will also be smart enough to outwit his adversaries, for such a pig will survive in any society. Another example of a logical, plausible plot development is "Clever Manka," the witty Czech story that is a favorite with older children. Manka by her cleverness wins a fine husband, a judge and burgomaster; but he warns her that she will be banished from his house if she ever uses her cleverness to interfere with his business. Knowing Manka and realizing that one cannot help using what wit the Lord gave one, you feel the conflict approaching. Of course Manka learns of a case where her husband has rendered a flagrantly unfair judgment, and in the interest of justice she interferes. She is found out and banished, but in the face of this ultimate catastrophe, she uses her wit and saves both herself and her husband from permanent unhappiness. Here is a realistic folk tale of clever mind against duller mind, with the clever one saving them both. The ending is surprising but completely logical.

Many of the tales we know preserve unity of interest. Every episode in "The Lad Who Went to the North Wind" concerns the boy's struggles to get his rights for the meal that the North Wind blew away. To achieve unity, a story must preserve a certain economy of incidents. Too many episodes, too long-drawn-out suspense, or too much magic destroys the unity of the tale. The development often contains three tasks or three riddles or three trials. Perhaps there is no particular significance in the "three" except that the old storyteller, always properly audience-conscious as a good storyteller should be, could see that suspense can be endured just so long before people get impatient. After the hero rides three times up a glass hill, the listeners demand results. Molly can use her bridge of one hair three times and after that she had better finish things off and get home. For it is on suspense that the successful development of folk-tale action depends. Suspense is built up and maintained until it reaches a peak in the climax, after which it declines and the action ends with a flourish.

The Conclusion

The conclusion usually comes swiftly and is as brief as the introduction. In "The Three Billy-Goats Gruff," the ringing challenge of the biggest billy goat announces the climax. The fight ensues, the biggest billy goat is the winner and the Gruff family is now free to eat grass and get fat for the rest of its days. In "The Sleeping Beauty," the kiss breaks the spell for the princess and the whole court, the royal wedding quickly takes place, and in most modern versions that is all, except for the conventional blessing "and they lived happily ever after."

The conclusion ends everything that was started in the introduction. Not only do the heroes and heroines achieve a happy solution for their troubles and a triumphant end to their struggles, but the villains are accounted for and satisfyingly punished. Such conclusions satisfy children's eye-for-an-eye code of ethics and apparently leave their imaginations untroubled—probably because they usually have no harrowing details and are so preposterous that they move cheerfully out of reality.

The folk tale has some conventional endings that are as picturesque as the openings. "The Three Billy-Goats Gruff" concludes

Snip, snap, snout
This tale's told out.

Other endings are: "If they haven't left off their merry-making yet, why, they're still at it"; "A mouse did run, the story's done"; "And no one need ask if they were happy"; "Whosoever does not believe this must pay a taler" (or as we should say, a dollar); "And the mouth of the person who last told this is still warm"; "And now the joy began in earnest. I wish you had been there too." For little children, the chance to vary the name in the last line of the following conclusion makes it one of their favorites.

My tale is done,
Away it has run
To little Augusta's house.

Style

One of the charms of the folk tale is the language and manner of telling the story. For these tales were never read silently; they were told until their form and language patterns were fixed. Consider "Go I know not whither, bring back I know not what," or

"Little pig, little pig, let me come in."
"No, no, by the hair of my chinny chin chin."
"Then I'll huff and I'll puff and I'll blow your house in."

Or read that matchless ending, "As for the Prince and Princess, they . . . flitted away as far as they could from the castle that lay East o' the Sun and West o' the Moon." These are brief examples of folk-tale style—frequently cadenced, sometimes humorous, sometimes romantic—with the words suited to the mood and tempo of the tale.

The beginnings and endings of the stories, of course, are particularly good examples of the storyteller's skill in establishing the predominant mood of the story, or breaking off and sending the listeners back to their workaday world. But dialogue in these old stories is also a part of their style—it runs along so naturally that real people seem to be talking. Read aloud the conversation between the old man and his wife in "Gudbrand on the Hill-side." Never once does the swift interchange of news and comments falter for a descriptive phrase such as "said he *uneasily*," or "said she *reassuringly*." Here is just a rapid, natural give-and-take between two people:

"Nay, but I haven't got the goat either," said Gudbrand, "for a little farther on I swopped it away, and got a fine sheep instead."

"You don't say so!" cried his wife; "why, you do everything to please me, just as if I had been with you. What do we want with a goat! . . . Run out child, and put up the sheep."

"But I haven't got the sheep any more than the rest," said Gudbrand; "for when I had gone a bit farther I swopped it away for a goose."

"Thank you! thank you! with all my heart," cried his wife. . . .

So they proceed from disaster to disaster without a single literary interpolation. Notice, too, that the words suffice to establish unmistakably the attitude of each speaker. Words so perfectly chosen make long descriptions unnecessary.

Another characteristic of folk-tale style is the use of rhymes. Indeed, the stories are sometimes part prose and part verse in the old sing-and-say pattern of "Aucassin and Nicolette." Cante-fables, such stories are called—that is, singing stories or verse stories. The frequency of rhymes in some of the old folk tales has caused some speculation about whether the folk tales came from the ballads or the ballads from the tales, since both often have the same subjects. This is a matter for the specialists to settle, but certainly the little rhymes add greatly to the interest of the tales.

"The Well of the World's End" ("The Frog-King") alternates prose and verse, with the frog singing over and over the same words

Viewpoints

. . . Among many peoples, at least, taletelling is a consciously acquired and practiced art, and it is obviously foolish to study this technique in the hands of bunglers. Only the best efforts of raconteurs most successful with their own audiences can form a basis for a study of style which will tell us anything of value.

That the narrative details of an oral story in any particular community are relatively fixed is clear to any student of the distribution of tales. Is the form of the narrative similarly stable, and is there an attempt to hand it on exactly as learned? How much liberty does the taleteller feel justified in taking with his stylistic effects? The answer would seem to be that the skillful raconteur usually handles his material very freely, but within traditional limits. There are certain commonplaces of events or background or of word order so traditional that they are an indispensable part of the manner of the storyteller. If he is gifted, he has a command of all these old, well-tried devices and he adds thereto his individual genius and often the genius of the man or men from whom he learned his art.
—Stith Thompson, *The Folktale,* The Dryden Press, New York, 1951, p. 450.

except for the request in the first two lines in which he raises his demands each time:

"Give me some supper, my hinny, my heart,
Give me some supper, my darling;
Remember the words you and I spake,
In the meadow, by the Well of the World's End."

Some of the prettiest verses in the folk tales are in the Grimms' "The Goose-Girl" and in the English "The Black Bull of Norroway." The former breaks into rhyme when the faithful horse, Falada, speaks to his mistress. And after he has been killed and his head nailed to the dark gateway, the Goose-Girl, who is really the princess, weeps beneath the gateway saying:

"Alas, Falada, hanging there!"

Then the head answered:

"Alas, young Queen, how ill you fare!
If this your mother knew,
Her heart would break in two."

Reprinted with permission of Macmillan Publishing Co., Inc. From Grimm's Household Stories *translated by Lucy Crane and illustrated by Johannes Troyer. Copyright 1954 by Macmillan Publishing Co., Inc.*

This piteous dialogue is followed by the song of the Goose-Girl, putting a spell on young Conrad, because he takes too much delight in her golden hair:

"Blow, blow, thou gentle wind, I say,
Blow Conrad's little hat away,
And make him chase it here and there,
Until I have braided all my hair,
And bound it up again."

The Grimms' "Cinderella," "Hansel and Gretel," "The Fisherman and His Wife," "The Juniper Tree," "Little Snow-White," and many others have memorable rhymes which some adults can still recite. The English tales are especially full of them. But many other folk tales are marked by the subtle art of the storyteller who has perfected a fine oral pattern in which rhymes frequently appear.

Character Portrayal

The interest of the modern short story frequently depends far more upon characters than upon plot or action. This is not true of folk tales. Plot is of first importance, and the characters are more or less typed. The good people in these stories are altogether good, and the wicked are so completely wicked that we waste no sympathy on them when, in the end, they are liquidated. So, too, the animals in the folk tales stand for simple traits like loyalty, cleverness, slyness, cruelty.

But look for brief flashes of characterization here and there. Cinderella is a teenage girl with her mind on balls and fine clothes. Red Riding Hood is good-hearted but irresponsible. The Lad who went to the North Wind to get his rights for the wasted meal is one of those dogged, stick-to-itive boys who, with right on his side, is going to get his way in the world or know the reason why.

Sometimes the characters are passive, like the Sleeping Beauty, but still sufficiently individual so that each one arouses different reactions. Beauty's doom, hanging over her youth and loveliness like a black cloud, inspires only pity. But the silly, feckless girl in "Tom Tit Tot," with her big appetite and meager wit, is so absurd that you don't particularly mind the hard bargain "that" drives with her.

Viewpoints

Beauty is the essence of the fairy-tale. Real ugliness has no place there—the grotesqueness of gnomes and gnarled but kindly woodcutters, and of crazy cottages which even the most backward rural authority would condemn, enters the fairy-tale only for the sake of contrast, so that the beauty of goose-girl and palace may be enhanced.

Many fairy-tales have made good ballets. Conversely, in judging a fairy-tale . . . something like the symmetry of the ballet should be sought. Observe the repetitive pattern which is so characteristic a feature of the folk-tale, and observe how the small child, hearing such a story read aloud, appreciates the repetitions and delights in the expected climax. . . . Variations, imposed upon a basic pattern, combining the expected and the unexpected in just the right proportions, give the child aesthetic satisfaction comparable with that which adults derive from good choreography or symphonic composition.—Geoffrey Trease, *Tales Out of School,* Heinemann Educational Books, London, 1964, pp. 48–49.

So while folk-tale people are strongly typed as "good" or "bad" with no subtle distinctions between, they may also be individualized. Sympathy or antagonism is aroused in different degrees by the brief characterizations. A whole portrait gallery of lads and lassies, goose-girls and princes, kings and queens remains in your memory, distinct and convincingly true to human nature.

Why Use Folk Tales with Children Today?

When the poet W. H. Auden reviewed the Pantheon edition of *Grimms' Fairy Tales* for *The New York Times* (November 12, 1944), he made this rather startling statement:

For, among the few indispensable, common-property books upon which Western Culture can be founded—that is, excluding the national genius of specific peoples as exemplified by Shakespeare and Dante—it is hardly too much to say that these tales rank next to the Bible in importance.

Later in the review he added:

It will be a mistake, therefore, if this volume is merely bought as a Christmas present for a child; it should be, first and foremost, an educational "must" for adults, married or single, for the reader who has once come to know and love these tales will never be able again to endure the insipid rubbish of contemporary entertainment.

Ethical Truth

Some people raise a great hue and cry about the ethics of the fairy tales. Of course, the folk-tale ethics are not always acceptable to the modern moral code. These stories were told by adults to adults in an age when using wits against brute force was often the only means of survival, and therefore admirable.

But folk tales are predominantly constructive, not destructive, in their moral lessons. "The humble and good shall be exalted," say the stories of "Little Snow-White," "Cinderella," "The Bremen Town-Musicians," and dozens of others. "Love suffereth long and is kind" is the lesson of "East o' the Sun" and "One-Eye, Two-Eyes, and Three-Eyes." In "The Frog-King," the royal father of the princess enforces a noble code upon his thoughtless daughter. "That which you have promised must you perform," he says sternly, and again, "He who helped you when you were in trouble ought not afterwards to be despised by you." Indeed, so roundly and soundly do these old tales stand for morality that they leave an indelible impression of virtue invariably rewarded and evil unfailingly punished.

Satisfaction of Needs

Most adults rereading these stories begin to understand Auden's feeling that they are timeless in their appeal. Plumbing, kitchen gadgets, and modes of transportation may change, but human desires and human emotions continue strong and unchanging. These old fairy tales contain in their "picture language" the symbols of some of the deepest human feelings and satisfy in fantasy human desires for security, competence, and love.

Everyone longs for security, the simple physical security of a snug house, warmth, and good food. In the fairy tales, the little hut in the forest is cozy and warm, safe from ravening wolves, and full of the peace of the fireside, with a loaf of bread baking on the hearth and a flavorsome kettle of soup on the hob. And of course there are castles, too; they may be a bit cold and drafty, but Jack or Tattercoats or Espen Cinderlad always seems to settle down very comfortably in the new grandeur. Children identify themselves with either the elegance of the castle or the snug security of the house in the woods. Both are satisfying: the castle speaks of achievement, the little hut of peace and safety.

Human beings are always in search of love. There will never be a time when people do not need loving reinforcement against the hostile world and the thought of death. The old tales are full of loving compensations for fears and hardships. Hansel reassures his little sister and protects her as long as he is able, and Gretel comes to his rescue when he is helpless and in peril. Commoners and royalty alike pursue their lost loves and endure every kind of suffering to free them from enchantments. There is cruelty in these old tales and danger, too, but the real world, like the fairy world, can be cruel and perilous. In reassuring contrast are the symbols of love, lending strength to the weak, offering sanctuary to those in peril, and in the end rewarding their faithfulness or their struggles.

People long not only for love and security but for competence. They are eager to overcome difficulties, to right wrongs, and to stand fast in the face of danger—abilities essential for heroes of any generation. The fairy tales supply unforgettable stories of wicked powers defeated and of gallant souls who in their extremity are granted supernatural strength. Whether or not children are conscious of it, these stories may become sources of moral strength—a strength which is part faith, part courage, and wholly unshakable.

Viewpoints

The fairy tale is a basic form of literature, and of art in general. The ease and calm assurance with which it stylizes, sublimates, and abstracts makes it the quintessence of the poetic process, and art in the twentieth century has again been receptive to it. We no longer view it as mere entertainment for children and those of childlike disposition. The psychologist, the pedagogue, knows that the fairy tale is a fundamental building block and an outstanding aid in development for the child; the art theorist perceives in the fairy tale—in which reality and unreality, freedom and necessity, unite—an archetypal form of literature which helps lay the groundwork for all literature, for all art. We have attempted to show, in addition, that the fairy tale presents an image of man which follows almost automatically from its over-all style. The fairy-tale style isolates and unites: its hero is thus isolated and, for this very reason, capable of entering into universal relationships. The style of the fairy tale and its image of man are of timeless validity and at the same time, of special significance in our age.—Max Lüthi, *Once Upon a Time; On the Nature of Fairy Tales,* translated by Lee Chadeayne and Paul Gottwald with additions by the author, Frederick Ungar Publishing Co., New York, 1970, p. 146.

Variety

There is a folk tale for every mood. There are drolls and romances, tales of horror and of beauty. They cover every range of feeling.

Undoubtedly their first appeal to children is *exciting action.* Things happen in these stories with just the hair-raising rapidity that children yearn for in real life and rarely find.

Sometimes there is a strange quiet about these stories. The forest is so still you can hear one bird singing; a little lamb speaks softly to a fish in a brook; the enchanted castle is silent; and the prince falls asleep by the fountain from which gently flows the water of life. Reading some of these strange tales, you feel yourself relaxing. Here there is time for everything, even a little nap by magic waters.

Children are a natural audience for folk material as is shown in the ways they use rhymes in their play, from the two-year-old murmuring nursery-rhyme refrains to the older child engaging in intricate counting-out games. Most children show a predilection for the cadence and color that are a part of the oral tradition. Children's calm acceptance of magical events and talking beasts in folk tales is not far removed from their own invention of imaginary companions. And in the enjoyment of folk tales children can assimilate a sense of their own cultural identity and an appreciation of that of others.

Collections and Collectors

French Fairy Tales

The history of Perrault's unique *Contes de ma Mère l'Oye,* published in 1697 and translated into English in 1729, has already been discussed (p. 63).

Perrault's eight stories have rather more polish and sophistication than is usual in the folk tales. In place of dull narrative, they are lively with conversations. Every necessary detail is logically provided for, or its omission underscored as a pivotal point in the plot.

Barbara Leonie Picard's *French Legends, Tales and Fairy Stories* (1955) contains four hero tales, six courtly tales of the Middle Ages, and thirteen legends, or folk tales, with no repetition of Perrault's famous eight. There is more magic in these tales than in Perrault's; the epic tales are full of battles and various complexities, the courtly tales are highly romantic, and the folk tales, though they contain some variants of familiar themes, are more mature in style than the stories they resemble. Good readers will enjoy this collection, and the storyteller will find fresh and exciting material in such stories as "The Grey Palfrey," "The Mouse-Princess," "The Stones of Plouhinec," and "Ripopet-Barabas."

In 1968, Geneviève Massignon's annotated, scholarly collection *Folktales of France* was published by the University of Chicago Press in the Folktales of the World series, a varied and representative selection. A collection long out of print has been made available again with the republication of the Comtesse d'Aulnoy's *The White Cat and Other Old French Fairy Tales* (1967), edited and translated by Rachel Field.

German Folk Tales

The conscientious Grimm brothers (Jacob, 1785–1863; Wilhelm, 1786–1859) began collecting tales with a passionate concern for sources. They were university professors—philologists—and their interest in sagas, ballads, popular tales, and all forms of traditional literature was at first secondary to their interest in the roots and development of the German language. This interest in grammar remained paramount with Jacob, but Wilhelm gradually became more interested in the tales than in any other phase of their work. When they began their collection, it was not with children in mind. They undertook their research as a part of a vast and scholarly study of language origins.

When *Kinder- und Hausmärchen*[3] appeared in 1812 (the second volume in 1815), it caused no particular stir in literary circles. Some critics considered the stories boorish; their publisher friend Brentano thought them slovenly; and yet somehow, in spite of the reviews, the stories were received with an unprecedented enthusiasm. Edition followed edition; translations began, first into Danish, Swedish, and French, then into Dutch, English, Italian, Spanish, Czech, and Polish—in all, some seventeen different languages.

The plots of these tales appeal to all ages

[3]*Nursery and Household Tales* is the usual translation, but for the German *Märchen* we have no precise translation. *Märchen* is legend, fiction, a cock-and-bull story, romance—in short, a fairy tale.

From Grimm's Fairy Tales *by Arthur Rackham. All rights reserved. Reprinted by permission of The Viking Press.*

Reprinted with permission of Macmillan Publishing Company, Inc. From About Wise Men and Simpletons *translated by Elizabeth Shub, illustrated by Nonny Hogrogian. Copyright © 1971 by Nonny Hogrogian.*

from the seven-year-olds to adults, while the style has the peculiarly spellbinding quality of the great storytellers. The Grimms were fortunate in their sources. Besides the "story-wife," Frau Viehmann, there were Wilhelm Grimm's wife, Dortchen Wild, and her five sisters, who had been raised with these old tales and could tell them with effortless fluency. Other relatives, in-laws, and neighbors contributed to the collection.

To reread these stories is to find refreshment. Here are somber tales of children turned out to fend for themselves who find love and security after all their hardships. Here are fools, cheerful and irresponsible, and royal youths and maidens, dispossessed, reduced to misery and humiliation, but keeping their innate kindness and tenderness, and so finding love. Here youth responds to the call of great tasks and accomplishes the impossible. These stories color readers' attitudes toward life, toward human relationships, and toward moral standards. They are both fantasy and reality, and they are supremely entertaining. A two-volume edition of the Grimms' tales, *The Juniper Tree and Other Tales from Grimm,* as translated by Randall Jarrell and Lore Segal in a forthright fashion, has been superbly illustrated by Maurice Sendak. Seldom have tales and illustrations been so perfectly matched. Sendak's work is imaginative, tender but terrible, a tour de force. A number of both European and American artists have illustrated individual tales by the Grimm Brothers. Felix Hoffmann is notable for his strong delineation of characters, sturdy and realistic, as in *The Sleeping Beauty.* Nancy Ekholm Burkert has individualized each dwarf in *Snow White and the Seven Dwarfs* with tenderness and delicacy. Trina Schart Hyman has given us another detailed interpretation of the same story. Adrienne Adams's handsome illustrations for tales like

From The Juniper Tree and Other Tales from Grimm, *selected by Lore Segal and Maurice Sendak, translated by Lore Segal, illustrated by Maurice Sendak, pictures Copyright © 1973 by Maurice Sendak. Reprinted with permission of Farrar, Straus & Giroux, Inc.*

Illustration by Felix Hoffmann. From Grimm's The Sleeping Beauty, *copyright 1959, by H. R. Sauerlander & Co., Aarau. Reprinted by permission of Harcourt Brace Jovanovich, Inc., and Oxford University Press. (Original in color)*

Hansel and Gretel are deft and darkly colorful. An outstanding contemporary scholar of folklore, Kurt Ranke, has compiled a collection for the Folktales of the World series—*Folktales of Germany,* which includes stories from all German-speaking territories except Switzerland (stories of Switzerland are in a separate volume). Like the other books in the series, this has a wealth of background information about the folklore of the country and a useful section of notes and indexes.

Norwegian Folk Tales

When people talk about the Scandinavian folk tales, they usually mean a particular book, *East o' the Sun and West o' the Moon,* the collection most people have known and loved, in one edition or another, all their lives. These stories probably rank with *Grimms' Fairy Tales* in their continuous popularity, and for similar reasons. They have the ring of complete sincerity and the oral charm of the storyteller's art at its best. They were recorded by Peter Christian Asbjörnsen (1812–1885) and Jörgen E. Moe (1813–1882), and turned into matchless English by a British scholar, Sir George Webbe Dasent (1817–1896), who was influenced by Jacob Grimm.

Peter C. Asbjörnsen and Jörgen Moe were devoted friends from early boyhood. Both became interested in gathering the popular tales of their native Norway from the lips of old storytellers who were still relating them as they had received them from the lips of preceding generations. When Asbjörnsen, a zoologist, started out on a scientific expedition, he followed his folklore hobby in his spare time. Indeed the two activities could be admirably combined. Searching for specimens and studying the terrain of the countryside carried him into the isolated districts where storytelling was still the chief source of indoor entertainment. Moe spent his holidays similarly employed, traveling to remote parts of the country and gathering the legends and stories of the district from the storytellers.

While in Stockholm in a diplomatic post, Sir George Webbe Dasent had the great good fortune to meet Jacob Grimm, who urged him to begin a thorough study of the language of the North, especially Icelandic. This Dasent did, and his first publication was an English translation of the *Prose, or Younger Edda,* followed by his *Grammar of the Icelandic or Old Norse Tongue,* and eventually an *Icelandic-English Dictionary.* In the midst of a remarkably strenuous life of study, translations, journalism, and travel, he became interested in the Norse folk tales and made his masterly translations of the Asbjörnsen-Moe collections, *Popular Tales from the Norse* (1859) and *Tales from the Fjeld* (1874), the two sources for all subsequent English editions.

Folktales of Norway, edited by Reidar Christiansen, is another volume in the Folktales of the World series. In a fascinating foreword, the editor for the series, Richard Dorson, an eminent folklorist of the United States, traces the historical development of the Norwegian tale. As in the other volumes, the provision of a glossary, an index of motifs, and a bibliography make this book of inestimable value to the scholar. Other outstanding collections are *Scandinavian Legends and Folk-Tales,* by Gwyn Jones; *Norwegian Folk Tales,* translated by Pat Shaw Iversen and Carl Norman; two compilations by Mary Hatch, *Danish Tales* and *More Danish Tales;* and Sigrid Undset's adaptations from the Asbjörnsen and Moe collections, *True and Untrue, and Other Norse Tales.*

From East of the Sun and West of the Moon *by Ingri and Edgar Parin d'Aulaire. Copyright 1938, renewed 1966, © 1969 by Ingri and Edgar Parin d'Aulaire. Reprinted by permission of The Viking Press, Inc.*

While the general mood of the Norwegian tales is serious, which is true of most folk tales, there is much more humor, or buoyancy, in the Norse collection than in the German. The people make the best of things with an amusing nonchalance.

There are no fairies in the gauzy-winged tradition, but there is a great deal of magic. Trolls, hill folk, giants, hags, and witch-wives are plentiful. A delightful combination of text and illustrations by Ingri and Edgar d'Aulaire, *Trolls,* is a definitive resource for details. There are magic objects in these tales—fiddles, axes, tablecloths, rams, and sticks. Winds talk and take a hand in the affairs of humans now and then. A polar bear (another symbol of the North) and a great dun bull are both men under enchantments, and there are the colossal horse Dapplegrim, the kindly wolf Gray-legs, and talking beasts of every variety.

Rhymes are infrequent, but one of the prettiest of them is the spell "Katie Woodencloak" casts on the Prince:

Bright before and dark behind,
Clouds come rolling on the wind;
That this Prince may never see
Where my good steed goes with me.

For storytelling, "The Pancake" is probably the finest of all cumulative stories because of its humor and rollicking movement. "The Cock and Hen That Went to Dovrefell" has a witty surprise ending that is far more satisfying than its English equivalent, "Henny Penny." These tales, like the Grimms', run the whole gamut from sheer nonsense to the romantic and heroic. They are classics and matchless entertainment which all children should have a chance to hear.

British Folk Tales

When Joseph Jacobs (1854–1916) began compiling the English folk tales, his objective was different from that of the Grimms or of the men who had preceded him in the English field. He intended his collection not for the archives of the folklore society but for the immediate enjoyment of English children. So Jacobs omitted incidents that were unduly coarse or brutal, adapted the language somewhat, especially dialect, and even deleted or changed an occasional episode. He was scrupulous in recording these alterations. At the back of his books, in a section for adult readers called "Notes and References," he gives the sources for each tale and its parallels, and then notes the changes he made.

Jacobs obtained a few of his tales from oral storytellers—some from Australia and one from a gypsy are mentioned. But most of his tales he obtained from printed sources, which he acknowledged. All in all, Joseph Jacobs was a sound enough folklorist. As a matter of fact, he was editor of the British journal *Folk-Lore*. But his greatest contribution is probably in selection and adaptation. Had it not been for his collections, many of these tales might still be gathering dust in antiquarian volumes.

These English tales of Jacobs are remarkable for three things: the giant-killers, the humor, and the large number suitable for the youngest children. From these collections of Jacobs come the favorites, "The Story of the Three Bears," "The Story of the Three Little Pigs," "Henny Penny," "Johnny-Cake," "The Old Woman and Her Pig," and many others.

"Tom Tit Tot," one of the stories which Jacobs rescued from the dusty oblivion of the journal *Folk-Lore*, is undoubtedly the most hilarious of all the variants of "Rumpelstiltskin." This is indeed an admirable example of the cheerfulness in the British stories. The superiority of this version lies in the full and consistent characterization of the silly girl, the impishness of "that," and the amusing hints as to the personality of the king.

The tales of giant-killers are another striking feature of the English collections, beginning with the old national hero story "St. George and the Dragon," and continuing through "Tom Hickathrift," "Jack the Giant Killer," and their only feminine rival, the resourceful "Molly Whuppie." These stout characters who make away with monsters were multiplied and perpetuated by the chapbooks, and their adventures have remained popular with British children ever since.

Jacobs remained the chief source of English folk tales until, beginning in 1954, volumes of English, Scottish, and Welsh folk tales were issued in the Oxford Myths and Legends series. Beautifully told, handsome in format and illustrations, these three books have greatly expanded the range of British folk tales.

James Reeves's *English Fables and Fairy Stories* includes many of the old favorites as well as such delightful additions as "The Pedlar's Dream," "The Two Princesses," and "The Fish and the Ring." The style is distinguished, the stories are varied in mood, and they read or tell beautifully.

Folktales of England, edited by Katharine M. Briggs and Ruth L. Tongue (Folktales of the World series), is a collection derived almost exclusively from oral sources. Many of the tales are relics of pagan superstition, many are based on local folk history. The material is

Reproduced with the permission of Farrar, Straus & Giroux, Inc. From Duffy and the Devil, *a Cornish tale retold by Harve Zemach, illustrated by Margot Zemach, Copyright © 1973 by Farrar, Straus & Giroux, Inc. (Original in color)*

Viewpoints

. . . Fairy tales are survivors. Authorless, timeless, placeless, they are also flawless. . . .

And in their character how they vary! Some have morals, some laugh in the face of morals; some are savage, some merry; some are marvelously decked out, some plain. But they survive alike because they are all good stories.

Their plots have never been surpassed and are still in service. They have action—unflinching, unremitting, sometimes circular. They appeal to the senses, they charm the memory. Their formal structure pleases the sense of order and design; their conversation is suitable, intense, pragmatic, well-timed, and makes sense for its own story alone.

Children like fairy tales also because they are wonderfully severe and uncondescending. They like the kind of finality that really slams the door. "Then the Wolf pounced upon Red Riding Hood and ate her up." And fairy tales are not innocent; they have been to the end of experience and back.—Eudora Welty, "And They All Lived Happily Ever After," *The New York Times Book Review*, November 10, 1963, p. 3.

divided by types of tales: jocular tales, tall tales, modern legends, wonder tales, etc.

Welsh Legends and Folk Tales by Gwyn Jones includes some of the hero tales of King Arthur and his knights. There are such romances as "Pwyll and Pryderi," "How Trystan Won Esylit," and three about the fairy "Woman of Llyn-Y-Fan." The folk tales are full of magic, incantations, fairy folk, and difficult names.

In *Peter and the Piskies; Cornish Folk and Fairy Tales*, Ruth Manning-Sanders has compiled a lively selection of stories about the small supernatural creatures of Celtic lore. All of her anthologies are excellent.

Harve and Margot Zemach's *Duffy and the Devil* is a highly comic Cornish variant of "Rumpelstiltskin."

The *Scottish Folk Tales and Legends* by Barbara Ker Wilson are largely unfamiliar. There are simple nursery tales for small children, broadly comic stories for older children, a few horrific scare tales, and stories of romantic beauty. Through them all runs the Gaelic fairy lore—spells, enchantments, magic, and many sorts of fairy creatures, sometimes kind, often menacing.

The delightful books by Sorche Nic Leodhas—*Claymore and Kilt, Gaelic Ghosts, Ghosts Go Haunting, Heather and Broom, Sea-Spell and Moor Magic*, and *Thistle and Thyme*—will further enrich the Scottish lore with both humor and romance. These stories have been written in such perfect storytelling form that they may be read or told without modification, and their charm is irresistible.

African Folk Tales

Although some books tapped the wealth of African folk material before the 1960s, in that decade began an outpouring of such material.

From Heather and Broom *by Sorche Nic Leodhas. Illustrated by Consuelo Joerns. Copyright © 1960 by Leclaire G. Alger. Reproduced by permission of Holt, Rinehart and Winston, Inc.*

Reprinted by permission of Coward, McCann and Geoghegan, Inc. from More Tales from the Story Hat *by Verna Aardema, illustrated by Elton Fax. Copyright © 1966 by Coward-McCann, Inc.*

Among the earlier collectors—Harold Courlander, Wilfrid Hambly, Russell Davis, Brent Ashabranner—the most prolific has been Courlander, whose general and regional collections are a rich lode of cultural information as well as a source of pleasure for readers and storytellers. West African tales are retold delightfully by Verna Aardema in *Tales from the Story Hat* and its companion volume, as well as in *Tales for the Third Ear*. East African tales are well represented in three fine collections: Humphrey Harman's *Tales Told Near a Crocodile*, Eleanor Heady's *When the Stones Were Soft*, and W. Moses Serwadda's *Songs and Stories from Uganda*. Folk tales from South Africa are smoothly retold by Aardema in *Behind the Back of the Mountain*. In addition to the many collections of regional and tribal tales, there are distinguished single-tale editions, such as Gerald McDermott's brilliantly illustrated adaptation of a Congolese tale, *The Magic Tree*, and Aardema's *Why Mosquitoes Buzz in People's Ears* with the Dillons' bold illustrations. Some of the most notable among the steadily growing number of general collections are Joyce Cooper Arkhurst's *The Adventures of Spider*, Hugh Sturton's *Zomo the Rabbit*, Frances Carpenter's *African Wonder Tales*, and Edna Mason Kaula's *African Village Folktales*. An excellent source book is *African Folktales and Sculpture*, second edition, edited by Paul Radin and James Johnson Sweeney.

The stories reflect the fact that the oral tradition is still very strong in Africa, with the tales pertinent to contemporary life and the written language echoing the cadence of speech. Many of the tales are about animal heroes like Ananse, the clever spider; many explain natural phenomena as does the literature of any people who live close to nature; many have a wry and sophisticated humor.

Illustration by Vera Bock. From Arabian Nights, *edited by Andrew Lang. Copyright, 1898, 1946 by Longmans, Green and Co. Reproduced by permission of David McKay Company.*

The Arabian Nights

The origin of *The Arabian Nights* is confused and lost in antiquity, partly because these stories belonged to the people and were not considered polite literature. In the Moslem world they circulated only in the coffee houses and the market place. The stories are very old, some of them seeming to stem from ancient India, others from North Africa, with an early collection from Persia. A Frenchman, Antoine Galland, made his translation of them in 1704 from a manuscript sent to him from Syria but written in Egypt. The stories were fortunate in falling into the hands of a translator who was also a skillful storyteller. These tales of the Orient were given a Gallic touch, so they lack nothing of drama or color. Today, children have turned away from all but a few of these exceedingly long stories.

Illustration by Fritz Eichenberg. From Padre Porko *by Robert Davis. Copyright 1939 by Robert Davis. Reproduced by permission of Holiday House.*

Russian Folk Tales

A. N. Afanasiev (1826–1871) collected the Russian folk tales as the Grimm brothers collected the German, and there is now an English translation of the complete Afanasiev collection in the Pantheon edition, newly reissued in 1975. These stories are for adult students of folklore, not for children. They are bloody and horrible but full of excitement and color. Certain of these tales are rather generally familiar to American children—"The Snow Maiden" (sometimes called "Snegourka"), "The Firebird," and "Sadko." Every one of these lends itself to dramatization as well as to storytelling. These and other popular Russian stories are nicely told in Arthur Ransome's *Old Peter's Russian Tales*.

Miriam Morton's impressive anthology, *A Harvest of Russian Children's Literature*, has a sizable section of folk tales, and many tales have been published singly in illustrated editions. Two of Alexander Pushkin's poetic retellings of classic tales, *The Tale of the Czar Sultan* and *The Tale of the Golden Cockerel*, have been opulently illustrated by I. Bilibin.

Spanish Folk Tales

One American storyteller, Ruth Sawyer, thought the Irish stories were matched only by the Spanish, and her own collection seems to bear out her opinion. New and delightful stories for telling can be found in every one of the collections of Spanish tales listed in the bibliography for this chapter. The stories for the youngest children are full of fun, those for the older ones full of grace. *Padre Porko*, for instance, is one of the most enchanting series of talking-beast tales to be found anywhere. The Padre, the gentlemanly pig, is both astute and benignant, and his canny solutions of neighborhood difficulties are made with great elegance.

Excellent collections have come to us in translation from many parts of the world. There are Dorothy Sharp Carter's *The Enchanted Orchard*, tales from the Central American cultures, and her delightful retellings of stories from the West Indies, *Greedy Mariani*.

Virginia Haviland has selected thirty-two stories from around the world for *The Fairy Tale Treasury*, robustly illustrated by Raymond Briggs. *The Classic Fairy Tales*, selected and introduced by scholars Iona and Peter

Opie, gives us twenty-four familiar fairy tales as they first appeared in English.

Two subject-oriented collections of note are Maria Leach's *Whistle in the Graveyard*, devoted to ghost stories, and Rosemary Minard's *Womenfolk and Fairy Tales*, a bringing together of folk tales with women as the main characters.

Many individual folk tales have been published in a picture-book format. Tomie de Paola's *Strega Nona* is a delightful noodlehead tale from Italy, while Arlene Mosel's *The Funny Little Woman*, with distinctive illustrations by Blair Lent, is from Japan.

It is likely that your librarian can provide native folk tales for practically any country you can name. Some of these have been better translated and adapted than others, but there is scarcely a collection not worth examining.

Illustration copyright © 1974 by Atheneum Publishers. Illustration by Trina Schart Hyman from Greedy Mariani and Other Folk Tales of the Antilles *selected and adapted by Dorothy Sharp Carter (A Margaret K. McElderry Book). Used by permission of Atheneum Publishers.*

Folk Tales in the United States

The United States is the fortunate recipient of folklore and folk tales from all over the world. This rich heritage falls into four large categories: (1) tales from black Americans, including the collections known as the Uncle Remus stories; (2) tales from the North American Indians; (3) variants of the European stories; and (4) tall tales. In the general discussion of folk tales few references are made to these American types, for definite reasons. In the first place, the European collections came into print long before American stories developed, and so they rather set the standard or pattern of such tales. Moreover, American collected tales differ in so many respects from those of the European groups that they often prove the exception to the very principles discussed as typical. They are, besides, far from a homogeneous group—no generalizations will cover all four varieties. An Uncle Remus tale differs from an American Indian story quite as much as both of them differ from their European relatives or the tall tale differs from all three. In short, each of the four types of American folk tales needs to be considered separately.

Black Folklore

Joel Chandler Harris (1848–1908) became interested in collecting the tales he heard the plantation slaves tell. Born in Georgia and raised on such stories as a child, he knew black dialect, humor, and picturesque turns of speech. Moreover, he had a deep love for the stories and for the people who told them.

The stories, told by Uncle Remus, a plantation slave, are mostly talking-beast tales and the hero is Brer Rabbit, the weakest and most harmless of animals, but far from helpless. Through his quick wit, his pranks, and his mischief, he triumphs over the bear, the wolf, the fox, and the lesser animals. Like the French "Reynard the Fox," he is a trickster, but unlike Reynard, he is never mean or cruel, only a practical joker now and then, a clever fellow who can outwit the big brutes and turn a misfortune into a triumph. No matter what happens to him or what he does, he remains completely lovable.

Reprinted from Brer Rabbit and His Tricks, *text* © *1967, by Ennis Rees, and illustrations* © *1967, by Edward Gorey, a Young Scott Book, by permission of Addison-Wesley Publishing Company.*

These stories are, of course, reminiscent of the talking-beast tales of other countries. Some of them may have had their roots in India, but it is generally agreed that most of them originated in Africa or were created in this country. Variants of "The Tar Baby" are found in many lands, but there is a special flavor to the Uncle Remus stories. They show a homely philosophy of life, flashes of poetic imagination, a shrewd appraisal of human nature, a love of mischief, a pattern and style unsurpassed by any other beast tales.

These stories do have their limitations, and the dialect is chief of them. Children in the South may be fortunate enough to hear these tales read by adults who can do justice to the flavorsome dialect. But even when the stories are turned into standard English, they retain their witty folk flavor, just as tales translated from the Norwegian or East Indian or American Indian do. Perhaps translation is the answer here, too. Ennis Rees, in *Brer Rabbit and His Tricks* and *More of Brer Rabbit's Tricks*, has provided such translations with great success. The simplest version for children is Margaret Wise Brown's edition of *Brer Rabbit*.

Other objections to these stories are raised by modern American blacks. In the article entitled "Uncle Remus for Today's Children" (*Elementary English*, March 1953), Margaret Taylor Burroughs points out that the tales are full of offensive terms for blacks. She objects to the intrusion of old "Uncle's" personality and point of view. These sometimes add to the wit and wisdom of the stories, but she cites some deplorable examples also. These objections point up the fact that the great body of seven hundred *Uncle Remus Tales* will survive chiefly as source material for gifted storytellers.

The mighty deeds of John Henry, the black folk hero, are described in books by Harold Felton and by Ezra Jack Keats, and Keats has also provided bold, impressive illustrations. An excellent and varied collection of black Americana is Harold Courlander's *Terrapin's Pot of Sense*.

North American Indian Tales

The collecting of North American Indian tales began with the sporadic records of missionaries and explorers, but not until the 1830s was there any serious attempt to bring together the rich body of existing material. Henry Rowe Schoolcraft, a government agent for the Ojibwa Indians, zealously recorded their myths and legends, although not in pure form. Since his time, ethnologists and folklorists in the United States and Canada have collected a voluminous and varied storehouse of Native American folklore.

While there are recurring themes and vari-

Viewpoints

Beware . . . of the defensive argument now used by "folklore" writers to justify their tampering with sources: "We have the same right as the original storytellers to tell a folktale in our own way." There is no more fundamental fallacy in the presentation of folk materials than this notion. The carrier of oral folk traditions continually alters the tale, song or saying he has heard; such change is at the very heart of oral, unrehearsed narration. But the calculating money-writer, using the very different medium of print in a self-conscious effort to reach readers who already associate "folklore" with froth and fun, is the voice not of the folk but of the mass culture.—Richard M. Dorson, *American Folklore,* The University of Chicago Press, Chicago and London, 1959, p. 4.

ants of specific tales, and even variants of European folk tales, the extant material provides a body of literature that differs distinctly according to region and tribe. Because the American Indian has a reverence for natural things, an affinity for the creatures of the earth and for the earth itself, much of the lore is concerned with nature as a part of religious beliefs and practices. Myths and legends that explain the origins of natural phenomena or the attributes of wild creatures are common to all the Native American cultures, since all of them invested living things with magical powers.

The major types of tales are creation myths; trickster tales, often humorous, in which the hero is either in human or in animal form, as in the stories of Coyote or Rabbit; journeys to another world, a story type that often reflects mores and taboos of a tribe; hero tales, often including tests for maturity or courage; and marriages between human beings and animals. Each region usually had its own cycle of traditional tales, and as with folklore diffusion everywhere, there are themes and patterns that occur in different regions.

Native Variants of European Tales

The Southern "The Gingerbread Boy," printed in *St. Nicholas* in 1875, "Johnny-Cake" in Jacobs's *English Fairy Tales,* and Ruth Sawyer's story, "Journey Cake, Ho!" are all variants of the Scotch "The Wee Bannock" or the Norse "The Pancake." There are undoubtedly dozens of other European folk tales extant in this country in characteristically modified form, but so far the most amusing and significant collections are *The Jack Tales* and *Grandfather Tales* by Richard Chase, collected from American mountain people. Chase's account of these gay-hearted people makes you wish there were more of the stories. He has recorded them in the vernacular of the mountain people who have modified them to local speech and customs. The god Wotan or Woden appears, ancient, mysterious, but as helpful to Jack as he was to Sigurd or Siegfried. Jack is a country boy, unassuming but resourceful, and never nonplussed by the most fantastic adventures. The language is ungrammatical and sometimes rough, but it is humorously effective when handled by as gifted a storyteller as Richard Chase. The mood is decidedly comic, the setting rural. City children may not know "The Old Sow and the Three Little Shoats," but they'll recognize it as "The Three Little Pigs." Many of the tales have been found elsewhere in this country.

Tall Tales

The characteristic of the tall tale that distinguishes it from other humorous stories is its blatant exaggeration. Our older tall tales—with their swaggering heroes who do the impossible with nonchalance—embody delusions of power: dreams of riding a cyclone or mowing down forests, or, in short, blithely surmounting any and every obstacle. They are such flagrant lies that the lyingest yarn of all is the best one, provided it is told with a straight face and every appearance of truth. Babe, Paul Bunyan's blue ox, measures "forty-two axhandles between the eyes—and a tobacco box—you could easily fit in a Star tobacco box after the last axhandle." Pecos Bill, after riding the cyclone successfully, must figure a convenient way of getting down. In short, one characteristic of tall-tale humor is that there must be a great show of reasonableness and precise detail in the midst of the most hilarious lunacy.

There are no complete or satisfying answers to the questions about where all these tales came from or who started them. Some of the older stories are classified as folk tales, but many are probably best described as "fake lore."[4] But regardless of their origins, they are almost invariably humorous. The New England coast produced Captain Stormalong. Paul Bunyan and his blue ox came from the lumber camps. The Western plains started Pecos Bill and his horse the Widow Maker on their careers. Mike Fink was a keelboatman on the Mississippi, while Davy Crockett, Tony Beaver, and John Henry all belong to the South. One artist has covered a map of the United States with these heroes,[5] and it is the most astonishing array of rip-roaring he-men imaginable. Walter Blair has contributed to the tall tale in *Tall Tale America* as has Adrien Stoutenburg in *American Tall Tales* and *American Tall-Tale Animals*. Moritz Jagendorf has compiled several volumes of regional material: *New England Bean Pot*, a book of tales from the middle Atlantic region, and *Folk Stories of the South*. Of the several collections by Maria Leach, an outstanding one is *The Rainbow Book of American Folk Tales and Legends*, which includes tall tales.

The multiplicity of folk-tale collections does not mean necessarily that we should use more of them. Most teachers and librarians are probably using them less than they once did because other types of fiction for children have improved in quality. But we should know that there are now available many national collections of these old tales, and we should select from them a moderate number of suitable variety and use them in balanced proportion to other reading material.

Adult References[6]

AFANASIEV, ALEXANDER N., comp. *Russian Fairy Tales.*

ASBJÖRNSEN, PETER C., and JÖRGEN MOE. *Norwegian Folk Tales.*

______. *Popular Tales from the Norse.*

BARCHILON, JACQUES, and HENRY PETTIT. *The Authentic Mother Goose Fairy Tales and Nursery Rhymes.*

BAUGHMAN, ERNEST. *A Type and Motif Index of the Folktales of England and North America.*

BETTELHEIM, BRUNO. *The Uses of Enchantment; Meaning and Importance of Fairy Tales.*

BRIGGS, KATHARINE M. *A Dictionary of British Folk-Tales in the English Language.*

______. *The Personnel of Fairyland; A Short Account of the Fairy People of Great Britain for Those Who Tell Stories to Children.*

BRUNVAND, JAN H. *The Study of American Folklore, an Introduction.*

COLUM, PADRAIC, ed. *A Treasury of Irish Folklore.*

COOK, ELIZABETH. *The Ordinary and the Fabulous; An Introduction to Myths, Legends, and Fairy Tales for Teachers and Storytellers.*

DE AUGULO, JAIME. *Indian Tales.*

DORSON, RICHARD M. *American Folklore.*

______. *Buying the Wind; Regional Folklore in the United States.*

______, ed. Folktales of the World series.

______, ed. *Folktales Told Around the World.*

EASTMAN, MARY HUSE. *Index to Fairy Tales, Myths and Legends.*

Funk and Wagnalls Standard Dictionary of Folklore, Mythology and Legend.

GRIMM, JACOB and WILHELM. *The Complete Grimm's Fairy Tales.*

IRELAND, NORMA. *Index to Fairy Tales, 1949–1972; Including Folklore, Legends and Myths in Collections.*

JACOBS, JOSEPH. See listings of his collections of English, Celtic, and Indian folk tales in the following bibliography. They contain significant introductions, and the notes in each appendix are treasures of folklore information.

KRAPPE, ALEXANDER HAGGERTY. *The Science of Folk-Lore.*

PERRAULT, CHARLES. *Perrault's Complete Fairy Tales.*

RAMSEY, ELOISE, comp. *Folklore for Children and Young People; A Critical and Descriptive Bibliography for Use in the Elementary and Intermediate School.*

THOMPSON, STITH. *The Folktale.*

______, comp. *One Hundred Favorite Folktales.*

TRAVERS, PAMELA L. *About the Sleeping Beauty.*

ULLOM, JUDITH C., comp. *Folklore of the American Indians; An Annotated Bibliography.*

ZIEGLER, ELSIE. *Folklore; Annotated Bibliography and Index to Single Editions.*

[4]See particularly Richard M. Dorson, "Twentieth-Century Comic Demigods," *American Folklore* (University of Chicago Press, 1959), pp. 214–226.

[5]See Glen Rounds's end pages for Walter Blair's *Tall Tale America*, an amusing group of fabulous stories.

[6]Complete bibliographic data are provided in the combined Adult References in the Appendixes.

General Collections

BAKER, AUGUSTA, comp. *The Golden Lynx and Other Tales*, ill. by Johannes Troyer. Lippincott, 1960.

______. *The Talking Tree and Other Stories*, ill. by Johannes Troyer. Lippincott, 1955. Two fine selections by a noted storyteller. 8-11

BROOKE, L. LESLIE, ed. *The Golden Goose Book*, ill. by ed. Warne, 1906. "The Golden Goose," "Tom Thumb," "Three Little Pigs," and "Three Bears" are delightfully illustrated. 5-10

CHILD STUDY ASSOCIATION OF AMERICA. *Castles and*

Dragons; Read-to-Yourself Fairytales for Boys and Girls, ill. by William Pène du Bois. T. Crowell, 1958. 9-12

DE LA MARE, WALTER. *Tales Told Again,* ill. by Alan Howard. Knopf, 1959. Gracefully told versions of familiar tales. 9-12

HAVILAND, VIRGINIA, ed. *The Fairy Tale Treasury,* ill. by Raymond Briggs. Coward, 1972. 9-11

JACOBS, JOSEPH. *The Pied Piper and Other Tales,* ill. by James Hill. Macmillan, 1963. An attractively illustrated edition. 10-12

JOHNSON, EDNA, EVELYN SICKELS, and FRANCES CLARKE SAYERS. *Anthology of Children's Literature.* Houghton, 1969. The chapter on "Folk-Tales" contains a good selection. 10 up

LEACH, MARIA. *The Rainbow Book of American Folk Tales and Legends,* ill. by Marc Simont. World, 1958. Regional lore, proverbs, riddles, tall tales, and folk tales of North and South America. 9-12

OPIE, IONA and PETER. *The Classic Fairy Tales.* Oxford, 1974. 9 up

PROVENSEN, ALICE and MARTIN, comps. *The Provensen Book of Fairy Tales,* ill. by comps. Random, 1971. A dozen modern fairy stories illustrated with gay, colorful pictures. 9-11

RACKHAM, ARTHUR, comp. *Arthur Rackham Fairy Book,* ill. by comp. Lippincott, 1950. A choice of Rackham's favorite tales. 8-10

______, ill. *Fairy Tales from Many Lands.* Viking, 1974. A reissue of a 1916 title with beautiful, full-color plates. 10-11

ROSS, EULALIE, comp. *The Buried Treasure and Other Picture Tales,* ill. by Joseph Cellini. Lippincott, 1958. Tales from the Picture Tales series. 7-10

______. *The Lost Half-Hour,* ill. by Enrico Arno. Harcourt, 1963. Good storytelling material. 9-11

UNITED NATIONS WOMEN'S GUILD. *Ride with the Sun; Anthology of Folk Tales and Stories from the United Nations,* ed. by Harold Courlander, ill. by Roger Duvoisin. McGraw, 1955. Each story has been approved by the U.N. representative of the country from which it comes. 10-12

WIGGIN, KATE DOUGLAS, and NORA A. SMITH, eds. *The Fairy Ring,* rev. by Ethna Sheehan, ill. by Warren Chappell. Doubleday, 1967. A good new edition of an old favorite. 9-11

WITHERS, CARL. *A World of Nonsense, Strange and Humorous Tales from Many Lands,* ill. by John E. Johnson. Holt, 1968. Fifty examples of the universal appeal of nonsense and exaggeration. 9-11

Subject Collections

BELTING, NATALIA. *Calendar Moon,* ill. by Bernarda Bryson. Holt, 1964. The text, which is composed of folklore and myth from widely varied peoples, moves through the calendar year in this distinctive, strikingly illustrated book. 10-13

______. *The Earth Is on a Fish's Back; Tales of Beginnings,* ill. by Esta Nesbitt. Holt, 1965.

______. *Elves and Ellefolk; Tales of the Little People,* ill. by Gordon Laite. Holt, 1961. 8-12

GARNER, ALAN, ed. *A Cavalcade of Goblins,* ill. by Krystyna Turska. Walck, 1969. An excellent anthology of excerpts, poems, and stories from worldwide sources. A treasure for storytellers. 9-12

HARDENDORFF, JEANNE B., comp. *Tricky Peik and Other Picture Tales,* ill. by Tomie de Paola. Lippincott, 1967. A collection of trickster tales. 9-11

LEACH, MARIA, ed. *How the People Sang the Mountains Up; How and Why Stories,* ill. by Glen Rounds. Viking, 1967. Legends about natural phenomena from many lands. 10-12

______. *Whistle in the Graveyard; Folktales to Chill Your Bones,* ill. by Ken Rinciari. Viking, 1974. 9-11

MANNING-SANDERS, RUTH. *A Book of Charms and Changelings,* ill. by Robin Jacques. Dutton, 1972.

______. *A Book of Devils and Demons,* ill. by Robin Jacques. Dutton, 1970.

______. *A Book of Dragons,* ill. by Robin Jacques. Dutton, 1965.

______. *A Book of Ghosts and Goblins,* ill. by Robin Jacques. Dutton, 1969.

______. *A Book of Magic Animals,* ill. by Robin Jacques. Dutton, 1975.

______. *A Book of Mermaids,* ill. by Robin Jacques. Dutton, 1968.

______. *A Book of Witches,* ill. by Robin Jacques. Dutton, 1966.

______. *A Book of Wizards,* ill. by Robin Jacques. Dutton, 1967.

______. *The Red King and the Witch; Gypsy Folk and Fairy Tales,* ill. by Victor Ambrus. Roy, 1965. Each has a delightful style and well-chosen tales. 9-11

______. *Tortoise Tales,* ill. by Donald Chaffin. Nelson, 1974. 5-8

MINARD, ROSEMARY, ed. *Womenfolk and Fairy Tales,* ill. by Suzanna Klein. Houghton, 1975. 9-11

SAWYER, RUTH. *Joy to the World; Christmas Legends,* ill. by Trina Schart Hyman. Little, 1966.

______. *The Long Christmas,* ill. by Valenti Angelo. Viking, 1941. Tales by a great storyteller. 8-12

SPICER, DOROTHY. *13 Dragons,* ill. by Sofia. Coward, 1974. Varied and sprightly. 9-11

Collections and Single Tales

African and Ethiopian

AARDEMA, VERNA. *More Tales from the Story Hat,* ill. by Elton Fax. Coward, 1966. 7-10

______. *Tales for the Third Ear; From Equatorial Africa,* ill. by Ib Ohlsson. Dutton, 1969. Nine folk tales retold from original sources that give verbatim versions of African storytellers. Full of action and humor and an excellent source for storytelling. 8-10

______. *Tales from the Story Hat,* ill. by Elton Fax. Coward, 1960. 8-12

______, ad. *Behind the Back of the Mountain; Black Folktales from Southern Africa,* ill. by Leo and Diane Dillon. Dial, 1973. 9-11

______, ad. *Why Mosquitoes Buzz in People's Ears; A West African Folk Tale,* ill. by Leo and Diane Dillon. Dial, 1975. A "why" tale retold with verve and magnificently illustrated. Caldecott Medal. 5-8

ARKHURST, JOYCE COOPER. *The Adventures of Spider,* ill. by Jerry Pinkney, Little, 1964. 8-10

ARNOTT, KATHLEEN. *African Myths and Legends,* ill. by Joan Kiddell-Monroe. Walck, 1963. Tales from south of the Sahara tell of "animals, humans and superhumans." 11 up

BURTON, W. F. P. *The Magic Drum; Tales from Central Africa,* ill. by Ralph Thompson. Criterion, 1962. Short tales with a fablelike quality that are favorites in the Congo. Illustrated with humor and imagination. 9-12

COURLANDER, HAROLD. *The King's Drum and Other Stories,* ill. by Enrico Arno. Harcourt, 1962. Almost thirty stories from Africa identified by tribal sources. Excellent notes are appended on the origins or interpretations of these folk tales. 9-13

COURLANDER, HAROLD, and GEORGE HERZOG. *The Cow-Tail Switch, and Other West African Stories,* ill. by Madye Lee Chastain. Holt, 1947. Seventeen tales, told in lively style and revealing much about the customs of the people. 10-12

COURLANDER, HAROLD, and WOLF LESLAU. *The Fire on the Mountain and Other Ethiopian Stories,* ill. by Robert W. Kane. Holt, 1950. Outstanding in style, illustrations, and content. 10-14

COURLANDER, HAROLD, and ALBERT PREMPEH. *The Hat-Shaking Dance, and Other Tales from the Gold Coast,* ill. by Enrico Arno. Harcourt, 1957. Humorous, droll, or wise are these twenty-one tales of Anansi. 9-12

DAYRELL, ELPHINSTONE. *Why the Sun and the Moon Live in the Sky; An African Folktale,* ill. by Blair Lent. Houghton, 1968. A story about the beginnings of time from the Efik-Ibibio peoples. Beautifully stylized artwork is based on African sources. 5-7

FUJA, ABAYOMI. *Fourteen Hundred Cowries and Other African Tales,* ill. by Ademola Olugebefola. Lothrop, 1971. Unusual stories recorded many years ago by a Yoruba scholar. 9-12

GILSTRAP, ROBERT, and IRENE ESTABROOK. *The Sultan's Fool and Other North African Tales,* ill. by Robert Greco. Holt, 1958. Eleven wise and witty tales, excellent for reading aloud and storytelling. 9-12

GUIRMA, FREDERIC. *Tales of Mogo; African Stories from the Upper Volta,* ill. by author. Macmillan, 1971. Eight stories of the Mossi people, which tell of animals, magic, and folk wisdom. 9-11

HALEY, GAIL E., ad. *A Story, A Story; An African Tale,* ill. by adapter. Atheneum, 1970. The story explains the origin of that favorite African folk material, the spider tale. Caldecott Medal. 5-7

HARMAN, HUMPHREY. *Tales Told Near a Crocodile; Stories from Nyanza,* ill. by George Ford. Viking, 1967. 10-11

HEADY, ELEANOR. *When the Stones Were Soft; East African Fireside Tales,* ill. by Tom Feelings. Funk, 1968. 9-11

HOLLADAY, VIRGINIA, comp. *Bantu Tales,* ed. by Louise Crane, ill. by Rocco Negri. Viking, 1970. Nineteen short, well-told tales. 9-11

KAULA, EDNA MASON. *African Village Folktales,* ill. by author. World, 1968. 9-11

McDERMOTT, GERALD, ad. *The Magic Tree; A Tale from the Congo,* ill. by adapter. Holt, 1973. 5-7

RADIN, PAUL, and JAMES JOHNSON SWEENEY. *African Folktales and Sculpture,* 2nd ed. Pantheon, 1964. 13 up

SERWADDA, W. MOSES. *Songs and Stories from Uganda,* transcribed and ed. by Hewitt Pantaleoni, ill. by Leo and Diane Dillon. T. Crowell, 1974. 8-10

Arabian

BROWN, MARCIA. *The Flying Carpet,* ill. by author. Scribner's, 1956. This story, so much a part of our language and so difficult to find, is beautifully retold and illustrated. 6-10

COLUM, PADRAIC, ed. *The Arabian Nights; Tales of Wonder and Magnificence,* ill. by Lynd Ward. Macmillan, 1964. Republished after thirty years, in a new and attractive edition, this outstanding collection will appeal to younger readers. 10-14

LANG, ANDREW, ed. *Arabian Nights,* ill. by Vera Bock. McKay, 1946. Fine black-and-white drawings and large print make this a favorite edition for children's reading. 10-14

WIGGIN, KATE DOUGLAS, and NORA SMITH, eds. *Arabian Nights, Their Best Known Tales,* ill. by Maxfield Parrish. Scribner's, 1909. Here are the favorite stories—"Aladdin," "Ali Baba," "The Voyage of Sinbad the Sailor"—gorgeously illustrated in color and well told. 10-14

Canadian

BARBEAU, MARIUS. *The Golden Phoenix; and Other French-Canadian Fairy Tales,* retold by Michael Hornyansky, ill. by Arthur Price. Walck, 1958. Notes as to their origin give these eight tales a special interest. Told with humor and zest. 10-13

CARLSON, NATALIE SAVAGE. *The Talking Cat and Other Stories of French Canada,* ill. by Roger Duvoisin. Harper, 1952. Tales told with vitality and humor and excellent for reading aloud. 8-11

Chinese

BIRCH, CYRIL. *Chinese Myths and Fantasies,* ill. by Joan Kiddell-Monroe. Walck, 1961. Ghosts and magicians and plain folk, too, are characters in this absorbing collection of tales. 11 up

KNIGHT, MARY. *The Fox That Wanted Nine Golden Tails,* ill. by Brigitte Bryan. Macmillan, 1969. A fox learns that transformations bring no happiness. An imaginative, elegant treatment of a familiar theme. 8-9

MOSEL, ARLENE, ed. *Tikki Tikki Tembo,* ill. by Blair Lent. Holt, 1968. An amusing picture book to read aloud. The wash illustrations have an appropriately Oriental beauty. 5-7

RITCHIE, ALICE. *The Treasure of Li-Po,* ill. by T. Ritchie. Harcourt, 1949. These six original fairy tales are told with all the sincerity and dignity of the folk tales which they resemble. 10-14

WOLKSTEIN, DIANE. *8,000 Stones; A Chinese Folktale,* ill. by Ed Young. Doubleday, 1972. A small boy ingeniously contrives a solution to his ruler's problem: how to weigh an elephant. 8-9

YOLEN, JANE H. *The Emperor and the Kite,* ill. by Ed Young. World, 1967. A tale of ancient China about Djeow Seow, who was so tiny her father the Emperor never noticed her until she saved his life. 5-8

Czechoslovakian

FILLMORE, PARKER. *Shepherd's Nosegay,* ed. by Katherine Love, ill. by Enrico Arno. Harcourt, 1958. Eighteen tales of Finland and Czechoslovakia compiled from Fillmore's out-of-print collections. Excellent for telling and reading aloud. 9-12

HAVILAND, VIRGINIA, ad. *Favorite Fairy Tales Told in Czechoslovakia,* ill. by Trina S. Hyman. Little, 1966. 8-10

Danish

HATCH, MARY COTTAM. *13 Danish Tales, Retold,* ill. by Edgun (pseud.). Harcourt, 1947. These stories are excellent for reading or storytelling, and are carefully adapted from the Bay translation. 9-13

______. *More Danish Tales, Retold,* ill. by Edgun (pseud.). Harcourt, 1949. 9-13

HAVILAND, VIRGINIA, ad. *Favorite Fairy Tales Told in Denmark,* ill. by Margot Zemach. Little, 1971. Six tales are retold with directness and simplicity. Useful as a source for storytelling as well as for independent reading. 9-11

JONES, GWYN. *Scandinavian Legends and Folk Tales* (see Norwegian tales).

English, Scottish, and Welsh

BRIGGS, KATHARINE, and RUTH TONGUE, eds. *Folktales of England.* Univ. of Chicago Pr., 1965. (Folktales of the World series) 10 up

BROWN, MARCIA. *Dick Whittington and His Cat,* ill. by author. Scribner's, 1950. A lively, readable adaptation of this classic hero tale with strong linoleum cuts in two colors. 4-8

CARRICK, MALCOLM, ad. *The Wise Men of Gotham,* ill. by adapter. Viking, 1975. Blithe and bouncy noodlehead tales. 9-11

COLWELL, EILEEN. *Round About and Long Ago; Tales from the English Counties,* ill. by Anthony Colbert. Houghton, 1974. Brisk, straightforward retellings of twenty-eight tales. 9-12

GALDONE, PAUL, ill. *The Old Woman and Her Pig.* McGraw, 1960. The old nursery favorite is reintroduced as a lively picture book. Another nursery classic made into a picture book by the artist is *Old Mother Hubbard and Her Dog* (1960). 4-7

JACOBS, JOSEPH, ed. *English Fairy Tales,* ill. by John D. Batten. Putnam, n.d.

______. *More English Fairy Tales,* ill. by John D. Batten. Putnam, n.d.

These not only are reliable sources for the favorite English tales but also are appealing to children in format and illustrations. 9-12

JONES, GWYN. *Welsh Legends and Folk Tales,* ill. by Joan Kiddell-Monroe. Walck, 1955. Retellings of ancient sagas as well as folk and fairy tales are included. Illustrations in color are particularly outstanding. 11-14

MANNING-SANDERS, RUTH. *Peter and the Piskies; Cornish Folk and Fairy Tales,* ill. by Raymond Briggs. Roy, 1966. 10-12

NESS, EVALINE. *Tom Tit Tot,* ill. by author. Scribner's, 1965. A very attractive picture-book variation of the Rumpelstiltskin story, good for storytelling or for reading aloud. 5-8

NIC LEODHAS, SORCHE (pseud.). *Always Room for One More,* ill. by Nonny Hogrogian. Holt, 1965. A picture-book version of an old Scottish song. Handsome illustrations. Caldecott Medal. 5-8

______. *By Loch and by Lin,* ill. by Vera Bock. Holt, 1969. 9-12

______. *Claymore and Kilt,* ill. by Leo and Diane Dillon. Holt, 1967. 12-14

______. *Gaelic Ghosts,* ill. by Nonny Hogrogian. Holt, 1964. 10-12

______. *Ghosts Go Haunting,* ill. by Nonny Hogrogian. Holt, 1965. 10-12

______. *Heather and Broom,* ill. by Consuelo Joerns. Holt, 1960. 10-12

______. *Sea-Spell and Moor-Magic; Tales of the Western Isles,* ill. by Vera Bock. Holt, 1968. 9-11

______. *Thistle and Thyme,* ill. by Evaline Ness. Holt, 1962. 10-12

REEVES, JAMES. *English Fables and Fairy Stories,* ill. by Joan Kiddell-Monroe. Walck, 1954. An attractive collection of nineteen tales illustrated in two colors. 10-14

STEEL, FLORA ANNIE. *English Fairy Tales,* ill. by Arthur Rackham, with an afterword by Clifton Fadiman. Macmillan, 1962. This book has the imaginative pictures of Rackham and the excellent adaptations of Steel. All the favorites are here. 8-12

WILSON, BARBARA KER. *Scottish Folk Tales and Legends,* ill. by Joan Kiddell-Monroe. Walck, 1954. In addition to the folk tales, a section of stories on the legendary exploits of the Fians is included. Attractive format and illustrations. 11-14

ZEMACH, HARVE. *Duffy and the Devil; A Cornish Tale Retold,* ill. by Margot Zemach. Farrar, 1973. Caldecott Medal. 5-8

Finnish

BOWMAN, JAMES CLOYD, and MARGERY BIANCO. *Tales from a Finnish Tupa,* from a tr. by Aili Kolehmainen, ill. by Laura Bannon. Whitman, 1936. Here are the everyday folk tales of the Finnish people, not the epic stories. Beautifully told, with effective illustrations. 10-14

FILLMORE, PARKER. *Shepherd's Nosegay* (see Czechoslovakian tales).

GINSBURG, MIRRA, tr. *How Wilka Went to Sea,* ed. by the translator, ill. by Charles Mikolaycak. Crown, 1975. Finno-Ugric and Turkic tales abounding in witches, giants, and wizards. 9-11

French

D'AULNOY, MARIE C. *The White Cat and Other Old French Fairy Tales* by Mme. La Comtesse d'Aulnoy, tr. by Rachel Field, ill. by Elizabeth MacKinstry. Macmillan, 1928, 1967. 8-11

MASSIGNON, GENEVIEVE, ed. *Folktales of France,* tr. by Jacqueline Hyland. Univ. of Chicago Pr. 1968. (Folktales of the World series) 10 up

PERRAULT, CHARLES. *Cinderella; or The Little Glass Slipper,* ill. by Marcia Brown. Scribner's, 1954. Attractive pastel illustrations. Caldecott Medal. 5-9

______. *Puss in Boots,* ill. by Marcia Brown. Scribner's, 1952. Wonderful pictures enliven this story of the faithful cat who helps to make a lord of his poor young master. 6-9

______. *Puss in Boots,* ill. by Hans Fischer. Harcourt, 1959. A noted Swiss artist interjects a subtle humor of his own into the pictures and his retelling of Perrault's tale. 5-8

PICARD, BARBARA LEONIE. *French Legends, Tales and Fairy Stories,* ill. by Joan Kiddell-Monroe. Walck, 1955. A rich and varied source of folklore ranging from epic literature to medieval tales; from legends to fairy tales. 10-14

German

GRIMM, JACOB and WILHELM. *About Wise Men and Simpletons; Twelve Tales from Grimm,* tr. by Elizabeth Shub, ill. by Nonny Hogrogian. Macmillan, 1971.

Newly translated from the less familiar first edition, pithy versions of familiar tales. 9-11

______. *Grimm's Fairy Tales,* tr. by Mrs. E. V. Lucas and others, ill. by Fritz Kredel. Grosset, 1945. An edition that is thoroughly satisfactory to children. The excellent translation is supplemented by bright, appealing pictures. 9-12

______. *Grimm's Fairy Tales; Twenty Stories,* ill. by Arthur Rackham. Viking, 1973. Selections from an edition long out of print, illustrated with beauty and vigor. 9-11

______. *Hansel and Gretel,* tr. by Charles Scribner, ill. by Adrienne Adams. Scribner's, 1975. 8-10

______. *The Juniper Tree and Other Tales from Grimm,* 2 vols., selected by Lore Segal and Maurice Sendak, tr. by Lore Segal with four tales tr. by Randall Jarrell, ill. by Maurice Sendak. Farrar, 1973. 9 up

______. *Red Riding Hood,* retold by Beatrice Schenk de Regniers, ill. by Edward Gorey. Atheneum, 1972. A verse retelling, with distinctively Gorey illustrations. 7-8

______. *The Shoemaker and the Elves,* ill. by Adrienne Adams. Scribner's, 1960. Colorful illustrations add new beauty to one of the Grimms' best-loved tales for little children. 3-6

______. *The Sleeping Beauty,* ill. by Felix Hoffmann. Harcourt, 1960. Richly toned pictures. Other Grimm tales illustrated by this artist include *The Wolf and the Seven Little Kids* (1959), *The Seven Ravens* (1963), and *Hans in Luck* (1975). 5-9

______. *Snow White,* tr. by Paul Heins, ill. by Trina Schart Hyman. Little, 1974. 9-11

______. *Snow White and the Seven Dwarfs,* freely tr. and ill. by Wanda Gág. Coward, 1938.

______. *Snow-White and the Seven Dwarfs; A Tale from the Brothers Grimm,* tr. by Randall Jarrell, ill. by Nancy Ekholm Burkert. Farrar, 1972. 9-11

______. *Tales from Grimm,* freely tr. and ill. by Wanda Gág. Coward, 1936.

______. *Three Gay Tales from Grimm,* tr. and ill. by Wanda Gág. Coward, 1943. Wanda Gág's narration is lively, natural, and simple. So are the illustrations. 8-12

______. *The Traveling Musicians,* ill. by Hans Fischer. Harcourt, 1955. Distinctive illustrations in color make this an outstanding folk-tale picture book. 5-8

HAUFF, WILHELM. *Dwarf Long-Nose,* tr. by Doris Orgel, ill. by Maurice Sendak. Random, 1960. Poor Jacob displeases a witch and spends years as an ugly dwarf before regaining his true form and a handsome bride as well. An excellent translation, appealingly illustrated. 9-11

PICARD, BARBARA LEONIE. *German Hero-Sagas and Folk-Tales,* ill. by Joan Kiddell-Monroe. Walck, 1958. *Siegfried* and other sagas, as well as such folk tales as *Ratcatcher of Hamelin,* give children a broader background of German lore than the more familiar Grimm tales. 11-14

RANKE, KURT, ed. *Folktales of Germany,* tr. by Lotte Baumann. Univ. of Chicago Pr., 1966. (Folktales of the World series) 10 up

Indian and Pakistani

BROWN, MARCIA. *Once a Mouse,* ill. by author. Scribner's, 1961. The timid mouse was changed by a kindly hermit into a cat, a dog, and then a tiger who became so cruel he had to be punished. Caldecott Medal. 5-8

DE ROIN, NANCY, ed. *Jataka Tales,* ill. by Ellen Lanyon. Houghton, 1975. A sampling of the animal fables attributed to Buddha. 8-9

GRAY, JOHN E. B. *India's Tales and Legends,* ill. by Joan Kiddell-Monroe. Walck, 1961. Truly distinguished retellings of India's rich lore, which will appeal to older children. 11 up

HITCHCOCK, PATRICIA. *The King Who Rides a Tiger and Other Folk Tales from Nepal,* ill. by Lillian Sader. Parnassus, 1966. A dozen colorful, varied tales, retold in a light and graceful style. 9-11

JACOBS, JOSEPH, ed. *Indian Fairy Tales,* ill. by J. D. Batten. Putnam, 1969. Like Jacobs's other collections, these stories are selected from manuscript sources. They also throw light on fable and folk-tale origins. 9-12

Irish

COLUM, PADRAIC. *The King of Ireland's Son,* ill. by Willy Pogány. Macmillan, 1921, 1967. Seven Irish folk tales about a brave young royal lad. 10-12

DANAHER, KEVIN. *Folktales of the Irish Countryside,* ill. by Harold Berson. White, 1970. Fourteen tales heard by the author from six storytellers. Delightful to read alone or aloud, and a good source for storytellers. 10-12

HAVILAND, VIRGINIA, ad. *Favorite Fairy Tales Told in Ireland,* ill. by Arthur Marokvia. Little, 1961. "Old Hag's Long Leather Bag" and "Billy Beg and the Bull" are among the popular tales included in this attractive, large-print collection. 8-11

JACOBS, JOSEPH. *Munachar and Manachar; An Irish Story,* ill. by Anne Rockwell. T. Crowell, 1970. The cumulation and the nonsense humor are appealing. Good for storytelling or reading aloud. 5-7

______, ed. *Celtic Fairy Tales,* ill. by John D. Batten. Putnam, 1892.

______, ed. *More Celtic Fairy Tales,* ill. by John D. Batten. Putnam, n.d. Jacobs includes Welsh, Scotch, Cornish, and Irish in his two Celtic collections. His copious notes are of great value. 9-12

MacMANUS, SEUMAS. *Hibernian Nights,* ill. by Paul Kennedy. Macmillan, 1963. The "last of the great Irish storytellers" compiled this rich collection of twenty-two of his favorite tales chosen from his earlier books. 11 up

O'FAOLAIN, EILEEN. *Irish Sagas and Folk-Tales,* ill. by Joan Kiddell-Monroe. Walck, 1954. This distinguished collection contains epic tales and folk tales to delight both reader and storyteller. 10-14

Italian

CHAFETZ, HENRY. *The Legend of Befana,* ill. by Ronni Solbert. Houghton, 1958. The old Italian Christmas legend beautifully retold and illustrated. 5-9

DE PAOLA, TOMIE, ad. *Strega Nona; An Old Tale Retold,* ill. by adapter. Prentice, 1975. 7-8

HAVILAND, VIRGINIA, ad. *Favorite Fairy Tales Told in Italy,* ill. by Evaline Ness. Little, 1965. 8-10

JAGENDORF, M. A. *The Priceless Cats and Other Italian Folk Stories,* ill. by Gioia Fiamenghi. Vanguard, 1956. An attractive and gay collection for the children's own reading. 10-13

Japanese

BARUCH, DOROTHY. *Kappa's Tug-of-War with Big Brown Horse,* ill. by Sanryo Sakai. Tuttle, 1962. Retelling of an old legend of a little water-imp who steals what he wants, and is at last outwitted by Farmer Shiba. 6-8

McALPINE, HELEN and WILLIAM, comps. *Japanese Tales and Legends,* retold by the McAlpines, ill. by Joan Kiddell-Monroe. Walck, 1959. A choice selection of folklore, legends, and epic tales. 10-14

McDERMOTT, GERALD, ad. *The Stonecutter; A Japanese Folk Tale,* ill. by adapter. Viking, 1975. Brilliant, monolithic art effectively presents the tale of a stonecutter who craves power. 5-8

MOSEL, ARLENE, ad. *The Funny Little Woman,* ill. by Blair Lent. Dutton, 1972. Caldecott Medal. 5-8

STAMM, CLAUS, ed. *Three Strong Women; A Tall Tale from Japan,* ill. by Kazue Mizumura. Viking, 1962. A sturdy girl, her mother, and her grandmother train a cocky young wrestler to new heights of strength for a court performance. A humorous read-aloud, color illustrated. 8-11

______. *The Very Special Badgers; A Tale of Magic from Japan,* ill. by Kazue Mizumura. Viking, 1960. An amusing and humorous tale of how two badger clans settle a dispute. 8-10

UCHIDA, YOSHIKO. *The Dancing Kettle and Other Japanese Folk Tales,* retold, ill. by Richard C. Jones. Harcourt, 1949. Fourteen folk tales, some of them familiar, many of them new, make this a welcome addition to folklore collections.

______. *The Magic Listening Cap; More Folk Tales from Japan,* ill. by author. Harcourt, 1955. This second collection is illustrated with the distinctive simplicity characteristic of Japanese art. 9-12

Mexican and South American

CARTER, DOROTHY SHARP, ad. *The Enchanted Orchard; And Other Folktales of Central America,* ill. by W. T. Mars. Harcourt, 1973. 10-12

FINGER, CHARLES J. *Tales from Silver Lands.* Doubleday, 1924. The author gathered these outstanding folk tales from the Indians during his South American travels. Newbery Medal. 10-14

JAGENDORF, M. A., and R. S. BOGGS. *The King of the Mountains; A Treasury of Latin American Folk Stories,* ill. by Carybé. Vanguard, 1960. More than fifty tales, listed by country of origin. 10-14

Norwegian

ASBJÖRNSEN, PETER C., and JÖRGEN MOE. *East o' the Sun and West o' the Moon,* ill. by Hedvig Collin. Macmillan, 1953. An attractive edition of a title which first appeared twenty-five years earlier. Based on the Dasent translation. 10-14

______. *East o' the Sun and West o' the Moon,* ill. by Kay Nielsen. Doubleday, 1922. Fifteen favorite stories with highly imaginative illustrations. 10-14

______. *Norwegian Folk Tales* (see Adult References, this chapter). 10-13

______. *The Squire's Bride,* ill. by Marcia Sewall. Atheneum, 1975. A hilarious tale enhanced by comic black-and-white pencil drawings. 8-10

______. *The Three Billy Goats Gruff,* ill. by Marcia Brown. Harcourt, 1957. A favorite folk tale appears in brightly colored picture-book format. 4-7

CHRISTIANSEN, REIDAR T., ed. *Folktales of Norway,* tr. by Pat Shaw Iversen. Univ. of Chicago Pr., 1964. (Folktales of the World series) 10 up

D'AULAIRE, INGRI and EDGAR. *Trolls,* ill. by authors. Doubleday, 1972. 8-10

HAVILAND, VIRGINIA, ad. *Favorite Fairy Tales Told in Norway,* ill. by Leonard Weisgard. Little, 1961. Seven familiar tales, handsomely illustrated in three colors. Includes "Why the Sea Is Salt," "Taper Tom," and "Princess on the Glass Hill." 8-11

JONES, GWYN. *Scandinavian Legends and Folk Tales,* ill. by Joan Kiddell-Monroe. Walck, 1956. Another Oxford contribution to folk-tale collections, this contains several of the familiar stories. Others are hero tales and unusual examples of folklore told with humor and impressive art. 8-12

UNDSET, SIGRID, ed. *True and Untrue and Other Norse Tales,* ill. by Frederick T. Chapman. Knopf, 1945. A good collection for storytelling and for children's own reading. The author's foreword on the subject of folklore will appeal to the student. 10-13

Polish

BORSKI, LUCIA M., and KATE B. MILLER. *The Jolly Tailor, and Other Fairy Tales,* ill. by Kazimir Klephacki. McKay, 1957. Reissued after many years, this collection translated from the Polish offers fine material for reading and storytelling. 9-12

HAVILAND, VIRGINIA, ad. *Favorite Fairy Tales Told in Poland,* ill. by Felix Hoffmann. Little, 1963. Six tales are retold and illustrated here. Large-print format appeals to younger readers. 8-10

SINGER, ISAAC BASHEVIS. *When Shlemiel Went to Warsaw; And Other Stories,* tr. by author and Elizabeth Shub, ill. by Margot Zemach. Farrar, 1968. Eight stories, some based on traditional Jewish tales. The cadence of the writing is especially evident when read aloud. Good for storytelling. 10 up

______. *Zlateh and Goat,* tr. by author and Elizabeth Shub, ill. by Maurice Sendak. Harper, 1966. Seven tales based on middle-European Jewish folk material, told and illustrated with distinction. 10-12

ZAJDLER, ZOE, comp. *Polish Fairy Tales,* ill. by Hazel Cook. Follett, 1968. A more extensive collection than the Borski or Haviland collections. Good for storytelling or independent reading. 9-11

Russian

AFANASYEV, ALEXANDER. *Soldier and Tsar in the Forest; A Russian Tale,* tr. by Richard Lourie, ill. by Uri Shulevitz. Farrar, 1972. A younger, virtuous brother ousts an older one. Illustrations are brilliant and Slavic in feeling. 5-8

DANIELS, GUY, tr. *Foma the Terrible; A Russian Folktale,* ill. by Imero Gobbato. Delacorte, 1970. A funnier Russian noodlehead there never was. Adapted from the Afanasiev collection. 5-8

DOWNING, CHARLES. *Russian Tales and Legends,* ill. by Joan Kiddell-Monroe. Walck, 1957. Epic, folk, and fairy tales gathered from many areas of Russia. 11 up

DURHAM, MAE. *Tit for Tat and Other Latvian Folk Tales,* ill. by Harriet Pincus. Harcourt, 1967. Mischievous tales told in a direct, colloquial style which is echoed in the pictures. 9-11

GINSBURG, MIRRA, tr. *The Kaha Bird; Tales from the Steppes of Central Asia,* ill. by Richard Cuffari. Crown, 1971. Nineteen stories from a dozen cultures, many with a robust, sly humor. 9-11

———, tr. *The Lazies; Tales of the Peoples of Russia,* ed. by translator, ill. by Marian Parry. Macmillan, 1973. Fifteen humorous tales. 8-10

MORTON, MIRIAM, ed. *A Harvest of Russian Children's Literature.* Univ. of Calif. Pr., 1967. All ages

PROKOFIEFF, SERGE. *Peter and the Wolf,* ill. by Warren Chappell. Knopf, 1940. Delightful picture-book story about young Peter, who outwitted the wolf to rescue the duck. Excerpts from the musical score accompany the text. 7-10

PUSHKIN, ALEXANDER. *The Tale of the Czar Sultan,* tr. by Patricia Lowe, ill. by I. Bilibin. T. Crowell, 1975. 8-10

———. *The Tale of the Golden Cockerel,* tr. by Alessandra Pellizone, ill. by I. Bilibin. T. Crowell, 1975. 8-10

RANSOME, ARTHUR. *Old Peter's Russian Tales,* ill. by Dmitri Mitrokhim. Nelson, 1917, 1976. This is the teacher's most practical source for the Russian tales. They are in admirable style for telling or reading aloud or dramatizing. 8-12

———, ad. *The Fool of the World and the Flying Ship; A Russian Tale,* ill. by Uri Shulevitz. Farrar, 1968. A retelling of a Russian tale is brought to life with these vigorous and colorful illustrations. Caldecott Medal. 5-8

ROBBINS, RUTH. *Baboushka and the Three Kings,* ill. by Nicolas Sidjakov. Parnassus, 1960. The familiar Russian folk tale of the selfish old woman and the Wise Men is enhanced by striking modern illustrations. Caldecott Medal. 5-10

WHITNEY, THOMAS P., tr. *The Story of Prince Ivan, the Firebird, and the Gray Wolf,* ill. by Nonny Hogrogian. Scribner's, 1968. A classic Russian fairy tale with a melodramatic plot. 8-10

———, tr. *Vasilisa the Beautiful,* ill. by Nonny Hogrogian. Macmillan, 1970. From the Afanasiev collection, a version of the Cinderella story. Handsome illustrations. 9-11

WYNDHAM, LEE, comp. *Tales the People Tell in Russia,* ill. by Andrew Antal. Messner, 1970. Ten tales, told with gusto, for which sources are cited in an appended note. Also contains three fables and a short list of proverbs. 8-10

ZEMACH, HARVE, ad. *Salt; A Russian Tale,* from a literal translation by Benjamin Zemach of the Russian of Alexei Afansev, ill. by Margot Zemach. Follett, 1965. A picture-book version of a Russian story, with the familiar pattern of the youngest brother surmounting all difficulties and winning a princess. Attractively illustrated. 5-8

Spanish

BOGGS, RALPH STEELE, and MARY GOULD DAVIS. *The Three Golden Oranges and Other Spanish Folk Tales,* ill. by Emma Brock. McKay, 1936. Stories for older children, romantic and exciting. One remarkable ghost story. 10-12

DAVIS, ROBERT. *Padre Porko,* ill. by Fritz Eichenberg. Holiday, 1958. Padre Porko, the gentlemanly pig, has all the benignancy of the Buddha animals, and a certain mannerly elegance besides. Amusing tales, enhanced by good pen-and-ink sketches. 8-12

EELLS, ELSIE SPICER. *Tales of Enchantment from Spain,* ill. by Maud and Miska Petersham. Dodd, 1956. These are romantic tales, rich in magic. 10-14

HAVILAND, VIRGINIA, ad. *Favorite Fairy Tales Told in Spain,* ill. by Barbara Cooney. Little, 1963. Six delightful Spanish tales retold. 8-10

JIMENEZ-LANDI, ANTONIO. *The Treasure of the Muleteer and Other Spanish Tales,* tr. by Paul Blackburn, ill. by Floyd Sowell. Doubleday, 1974. Regional tales which reflect Moorish and Christian traditions. 10-13

Swiss

DUVOISIN, ROGER. *The Three Sneezes and Other Swiss Tales,* ill. by author. Knopf, 1941. Humorous tales, many of which are based on the theme of the stupid fellow who succeeds. 9-12

MÜLLER-GUGGENBÜHL, FRITZ. *Swiss-Alpine Folk-Tales,* tr. by Katharine Potts, ill. by Joan Kiddell-Monroe. Walck, 1958. These tales are a distinguished collection of national folklore in the Oxford series of Myths and Legends. 10-14

United States and Canada: Indian and Eskimo Tales

BELTING, NATALIA M. *The Long Tailed Bear and Other Indian Legends,* ill. by Louis F. Cary. Bobbs, 1961. Animal legends of twenty-two tribes make this a valuable source. The large-print format will appeal to children, and storytellers will welcome the tribal identification preceding each story. 8-10

COURLANDER, HAROLD. *People of the Short Blue Corn; Tales and Legends of the Hopi Indians,* ill. by Enrico Arno. Harcourt, 1970. Tales that reflect the cultural patterns, the beliefs, and the humor of the Hopis. 9-11

FIELD, EDWARD, comp. *Eskimo Songs and Stories,* tr. by the compiler, collected by Knud Rasmussen, ill. by Kiakshuk and Pudlo. Delacorte, 1973. Rhythmic and vigorous, this collection reflects the cultural patterns of the tribes of the Hudson Bay area. 9-12

FISHER, ANNE B. *Stories California Indians Told,* ill. by Ruth Robbins. Parnassus, 1957. A dozen Indian myths told with zest and ranging from creation myths to humorous tales. 9-12

GILLHAM, CHARLES EDWARD. *Beyond the Clapping Mountains; Eskimo Stories from Alaska,* ill. by Chanimum. Macmillan, 1943. Illustrated by an Eskimo girl, these are unusual and highly imaginative tales. 10-12

HARRIS, CHRISTIE. *Once Upon a Totem,* ill. by John Frazer Mills. Atheneum, 1963. Five superb tales of the Indians of the North Pacific. 9-12

———. *Once More Upon a Totem,* ill. by Douglas Tait. Atheneum, 1973. Three tales based on legends of the Northwest Coast Indians. 9-12

HEADY, ELEANOR B. *Tales of the Nimipoo; From the Land of the Nez Percé Indians,* ill. by Eric Carle. World, 1970. Twenty "why" tales with coyote as the hero. 8-10

HILLERMAN, TONY, ad. *The Boy Who Made Dragonfly; A Zuni Myth,* ill. by Laszlo Kubinyi. Harper, 1972. How the first Corn Priest is chosen and the dragonfly made. 10-12

HODGES, MARGARET, ad. *The Fire Bringer; A Paiute Indian Legend,* ill. by Peter Parnall. Little, 1972. Retold with a spare dignity beautifully echoed in the illustrations. 8-10

HOUSTON, JAMES. *Kiviok's Magic Journey; An Eskimo Legend,* ill. by author. Atheneum, 1973. A vigorous and dramatic retelling of one of the most popular legends of the Eskimo folk hero. 8-10

McDERMOTT, GERALD, ad. *Arrow to the Sun; A Pueblo Indian Tale,* ill. by adapter. Viking, 1974. Stylized designs and stunning color effectively complement the story of the Boy who brings the spirit of the Lord of the Sun to his pueblo. Caldecott Medal. 5-8

MACMILLAN, CYRUS. *Glooskap's Country, and Other Indian Tales,* ill. by John A. Hall. Walck, 1956. First published in 1918 as *Canadian Wonder Tales,* this is one of the finest collections of Indian stories available. They range from simple "how" stories to complex and mystical tales of magic, superbly told and illustrated. 8-12

MARTIN, FRAN. *Nine Tales of Coyote,* ill. by Dorothy McEntee. Harper, 1950. Authentic tales of Coyote, the Indian animal god. The stories are lively and have a quality of suspense. Illustrations are in color.

______. *Raven-Who-Sets-Things-Right; Indian Tales of the Northwest Coast,* ill. by Dorothy McEntee. Harper, 1975. Tales of a trickster-creator, smoothly told. 9-10

REID, DOROTHY N. *Tales of Nanabozho,* ill. by Donald Grant. Walck, 1963. Stories of the mythical Ojibwa hero to whom Longfellow gave the Iroquois name of Hiawatha. 9-12

SLEATOR, WILLIAM, ad. *The Angry Moon,* ill. by Blair Lent. Little, 1970. An adaptation of a legend of the Tlingit Indians of Alaska, the writing simple and staccato. An interesting legend useful for storytelling, with attractive illustrations. 5-7

United States: Afro-American Tales

BROWN, MARGARET WISE. *Brer Rabbit; Stories from Uncle Remus,* ill. by A. B. Frost. Harper, 1941. 8-10

CHESNUTT, CHARLES W. *Conjure Tales,* retold by Ray Anthony Shepard, ill. by John Ross and Clare Romano. Dutton, 1973. These stories by a black author, first published in 1899, are vigorous and humorous. 10-14

COURLANDER, HAROLD. *Terrapin's Pot of Sense,* ill. by Elton Fax. Holt, 1957. Americana collected in rural regions from black storytellers. 8-11

FELTON, HAROLD. *John Henry and His Hammer,* ill. by Aldren Watson. Knopf, 1950. 10-12

HARRIS, JOEL CHANDLER. *Brer Rabbit,* ill. by A. B. Frost. Harper, 1941.

______. *Complete Tales of Uncle Remus,* ed. by Richard Chase. Houghton, 1955.

______. *The Favorite Uncle Remus,* ill. by A. B. Frost; ed. by George Van Santvoord and Archibald C. Coolidge. Houghton, 1948. 10 up

KEATS, EZRA JACK. *John Henry: An American Legend,* ill. by author. Pantheon, 1965. 5-8

REES, ENNIS. *Brer Rabbit and His Tricks,* ill. by Edward Gorey. W. R. Scott, 1967. 5-8

______. *More of Brer Rabbit's Tricks,* ill. by Edward Gorey. W. R. Scott, 1968. 5-8

United States: Variants of European Tales

CHASE, RICHARD, ed. *Grandfather Tales,* ill. by Berkeley Williams, Jr. Houghton, 1948. 9-12

______. *Jack and the Three Sillies,* ill. by Joshua Tolford. Houghton, 1950. 8-10

______. *The Jack Tales,* ill. by Berkeley Williams, Jr. Houghton, 1943. 9-12
American versions of old-world tales from the Cumberlands and the Smokies.

JAGENDORF, MORITZ. *New England Bean Pot; American Folk Stories to Read and Tell,* ill. by Donald McKay. Vanguard, 1948. Folk tales of six New England states told with zest and humor. Other titles in this regional series are: *Sand in the Bag and Other Folk Stories of Ohio, Indiana and Illinois,* ill. by John Moment. Vanguard, 1952; *Upstate, Downstate; Folk Stories of the Middle Atlantic States,* ill. by Howard Simon. Vanguard, 1949; and *Folk Stories of the South,* ill. by Michael Parks. Vanguard, 1973. 10-14

SAWYER, RUTH. *Journey Cake, Ho!* ill. by Robert McCloskey. Viking, 1953. Mountain folk-tale version of *The Pancake.* Lively illustrations make this an attractive picture book. 6-10

United States: Tall Tales

BLAIR, WALTER. *Tall Tale America: A Legendary History of Our Humorous Heroes,* ill. by Glen Rounds. Coward, 1944. 10-14

BOWMAN, JAMES CLOYD. *Mike Fink,* ill. by Leonard Everett Fisher. Little, 1957. Mike Fink was one of the greatest legendary riverboatmen, and his adventures are related in tall-tale tradition. 11 up

______. *Pecos Bill,* ill. by Laura Bannon. Whitman, 1937. Pecos Bill is the gayest of our heroes and the closest to the child's sense of humor. The illustrations add to the book's appeal. 9-12

CREDLE, ELLIS. *Tall Tales from the High Hills,* ill. by author. Nelson, 1957. Lively folk tales from the North Carolina Blue Ridge country, fine for reading and telling. 9-12

FELTON, HAROLD W. *Bowleg Bill, Seagoing Cowpuncher,* ill. by William Moyers. Prentice, 1957. Tall-tale nonsense about a cowboy who solves his problems in his own cowboy way. 10 up

LENT, BLAIR. *John Tabor's Ride,* ill. by author. Atlantic, 1966. A tall tale based on a New England legend about a shipwrecked sailor. The appeal of the telling is in the exaggeration, the fantastic situations, and the abundance of salty marine terms. 5-8

McCLOSKEY, ROBERT. *Burt Dow, Deep-Water Man; A Tale of the Sea in the Classic Tradition,* ill. by author. Viking, 1963. Jonah's story pales by comparison with this exuberant tall tale. 5-8

MALCOLMSON, ANNE. *Yankee Doodle's Cousins,* ill. by Robert McCloskey. Houghton, 1941. This is one of the finest collections of real and mythical heroes of the United States. 10-14

PECK, LEIGH. *Pecos Bill and Lightning,* ill. by Kurt Wiese. Houghton, 1940. A brief edition with copious illustrations to aid the slow reader. 8-12

ROUNDS, GLEN. *Ol' Paul, the Mighty Logger,* ill. by author. Holiday, 1949. These Paul Bunyan stories are retold with an earthy, exuberant zest. 10 up

SCHWARTZ, ALVIN, comp. *Whoppers; Tale Tales and Other Lies,* ill. by Glen Rounds. Lippincott, 1975. Notes and sources are given for over a hundred whoppers, from one-liners to longer tales. 9-12

SHAPIRO, IRWIN. *Heroes in American Folklore,* ill. by Donald McKay and James Daugherty. Messner, 1962.

Five tall-tale heroes include Casey Jones, Joe Magarac, John Henry, Steamboat Bill, and Old Stormalong.

———. *Yankee Thunder, the Legendary Life of Davy Crockett,* ill. by James Daugherty. Messner, 1944. The author is torn between writing about the real Davy and the mythical Davy, but chooses the latter—"Yaller blossom of the forest, half horse, half snapping turtle, the ring-tailed roarer. . . ." The pictures are as vigorous as the hero. 10-14

SHEPHARD, ESTHER. *Paul Bunyan,* ill. by Rockwell Kent. Harcourt, 1941. The most complete edition of these tales, this book also has Rockwell Kent's superb pictures. 10-14

STOUTENBURG, ADRIEN. *American Tall Tales,* ill. by Richard M. Powers. Viking, 1966. Eight stories, each about a tall-tale hero. 9-11

United States: Tales in Picture-book Form and General Collections

EMBERLEY, BARBARA, ad. *Drummer Hoff,* ill. by Ed Emberley. Prentice, 1967. An adaptation of a folk verse, with bouncy rhythm and the twin appeals of rhyme and repetition for the very young. Delightful illustrations. Caldecott Medal. 5-7

JAGENDORF, MORITZ, ed. *The Ghost of Peg-leg Peter and Other Stories of Old New York,* ill. by Lino S. Lipinsky. Vanguard, 1966. Tales range from ghost stories of early settlers to a tale about Fiorello La Guardia. 10-13

SPIER, PETER. *The Erie Canal,* ill. by author. Doubleday, 1970. The words of the rollicking song are the text. The illustrations have fascinating details and are faithful to the time and locale. 9-11

Other Countries

BATES, DAISY, comp. *Tales Told to Kabbarli,* retold by Barbara Ker Wilson, ill. by Harold Thomas. Crown, 1972. Daisy Bates devoted many years to recording aboriginal lore in Australia. 10 up

BELPRÉ, PURA. *Once in Puerto Rico,* ill. by Christine Price. Warne, 1973.

———. *The Tiger and the Rabbit and Other Tales,* ill. by Tomie de Paola. Lippincott, 1965.

———. *Perez and Martina,* ill. by Carlos Sanchez. Warne, 1961.

Tales of Puerto Rico. 9-11

CARPENTER, FRANCES. *The Elephant's Bathtub; Wonder Tales from the Far East,* ill. by Hans Guggenheim. Doubleday, 1962. Burma, Cambodia, Malaya, Vietnam, and other lands of the Far East are represented in the twenty-four tales of humor and enchantment. 11-14

CARTER, DOROTHY SHARP, ad. *Greedy Mariani; And Other Folktales of the Antilles,* ill. by Trina Schart Hyman. Atheneum, 1974. 9-11

COURLANDER, HAROLD. *The Tiger's Whisker and Other Tales and Legends from Asia and the Pacific,* ill. by Enrico Arno. Harcourt, 1959. More humorous and philosophic tales gathered by a folklorist who has made a significant contribution to the lore of faraway lands. 9-13

CURCIJA-PRODANOVIC, NADA. *Yugoslav Folk-Tales,* ill. by Joan Kiddell-Monroe. Walck, 1957. 10-14

DEUTSCH, BABETTE, and AVRAHM YARMOLINSKY. *Tales of Faraway Folk,* ill. by Irena Lorentowicz. Harper, 1952. A unique collection of tales from Baltic, Russian, and Asiatic lands. 9-12

———. *More Tales of Faraway Folk,* ill. by Janina Domanska. Harper, 1963. Fifteen more tales, many from the U.S.S.R. 7-11

GRAHAM, GAIL B., ad. *The Beggar in the Blanket; And Other Vietnamese Tales,* ill. by Brigitte Bryan. Dial, 1970. Eight folk tales translated from French language sources in Vietnam. There is less drama here than in most folk literature and more projection of cultural patterns. 9-11

JEWETT, ELEANORE MYERS. *Which Was Witch? Tales of Ghosts and Magic from Korea,* ill. by Taro Yashima (pseud. for Jun Iwamatsu). Viking, 1953. Fourteen stories with sparkle and suspense, excellent for storytelling. 9-13

JUNNE, I. K. *Floating Clouds, Floating Dreams; Favorite Asia Folk Tales.* Doubleday, 1974. Tales of eleven Asian countries, told in a very readable style. 9-11

KEELY, H. H., and CHRISTINE PRICE, ads. *The City of the Dagger; And Other Tales from Burma,* ill. by Christine Price. Warne, 1971. Folklore and legends with historical bases are mingled in intricate and often lengthy tales of magical events, many of which concern hero-kings of the past. 10-12

KELSEY, ALICE GEER. *Once the Hodja,* ill. by Frank Dobias. McKay, 1943. Twenty-four tales from Turkey filled with humor and simple wisdom.

———. *Once the Mullah,* ill. by Kurt Werth. McKay, 1954. Stories told by Mullah give insight into Persian life and folklore. 9-12

OLENIUS, ELSA, comp. *Great Swedish Fairy Tales,* tr. by Holger Lundbergh, ill. by John Bauer. Delacorte, 1973. Illustrated by a major Swedish illustrator in a romantic, turn-of-the-century style which suits the gentle magic in the tales. 9-11

PARKER, K. LANGLOH. *Australian Legendary Tales,* selected and ed. by H. Drake-Brockman, ill. by Elizabeth Durack. Viking, 1966. A selection of Australian aboriginal tales first published at the turn of the century. Much violence and fascinating cultural detail. 11-14

SHERLOCK, PHILIP M. *Anansi, the Spider Man; Jamaican Folk Tales,* ill. by Marcia Brown. T. Crowell, 1954. These stories are told by Jamaicans with simplicity and charm. 9-12

SHERLOCK, PHILIP and HILARY. *Ears and Tails and Common Sense.* T. Crowell, 1974. Stories from the Caribbean told with verve and humor. 9-11

SHULEVITZ, URI. *The Magician,* ad. from the Yiddish of I. L. Peretz. Macmillan, 1973. A Passover story about the prophet Elijah, nicely retold and handsomely illustrated.

TASHJIAN, VIRGINIA A., ed. *Once There Was and Was Not,* based on stories by H. Toumanian, ill. by Nonny Hogrogian. Little, 1966. Seven Armenian folk tales, many with familiar elements, beautifully illustrated. A pleasure to read aloud and a good source for storytelling. 9-11

———, ed. *Three Apples Fell from Heaven; Armenian Tales Retold,* ill. by Nonny Hogrogian. Little, 1971. 9-11

VO-DINH, ad. *The Toad Is the Emperor's Uncle; Animal Folktales from Viet-Nam,* ill. by adapter. Doubleday, 1970. Stories that reflect humor as well as ethical principle. 9-11

Fables, Myths, and Epics

Chapter 7

Fables, myths, and epics, like the ballads and folk tales, are a part of the great stream of folklore. While they are not generally so popular with children as the folk tales, they have made an equally important contribution to our literary heritage. The fables have colored our attitudes toward moral and ethical problems. The myths and the epics have become a part of our everyday symbols in both writing and speech. All these three types of literature, while fundamentally different from each other, have one characteristic in common: they have a strong moral flavor.

Fables, Parables, Proverbs

Fables are brief narratives which take abstract ideas of good or bad, wise or foolish behavior and attempt to make them concrete and striking enough to be understood and remembered. The chief actor in most fables is an animal or inanimate object which behaves like a human being and has one dominant trait. Whether the characters are humans or beasts, they remain coldly impersonal and engage in a single significant act which teaches a moral lesson. These are the essential elements of the true fable.

Fables have a teasing likeness to proverbs and parables. All three embody universal truths in brief, striking form; and all three are highly intellectual exercises, as exact as an equation. Of the three, the *proverb* is the most highly condensed commentary on human folly or wisdom. It tells no story but presents a bit of wisdom succinctly:

A soft answer turneth away wrath: but grievous words stir up anger. (Proverbs 15:1)

Better is a dry morsel and quietness therewith, than a house full of feasting with strife. (Proverbs 17:1)

It is interesting to find many examples in *Japanese Proverbs* by Rokuo Okada that are amazingly like Biblical proverbs in their implications:

He who wants to shoot the general must first shoot his horse.

A cornered mouse bites the cat.[1]

Perhaps the fable grew out of the proverb, to dramatize its pithy wisdom in story form.

The *parable* is like the fable in that it tells a brief story from which a moral or spiritual truth may be inferred. But its characters, unlike the personified animals or objects of most fables, are generally human beings, like the Wise and Foolish Virgins, or the Prodigal Son, or the Good Samaritan. If the story is told in terms of animals or objects, they are never personified but remain strictly themselves. That is, the seed that falls upon rocky ground has nothing to say for itself, and the house

[1]From *Japanese Proverbs* by Rokuo Okada. Copyright by the Japan Travel Bureau. In *Japan Times Weekly*, December 1, 1962.

that was built upon sand goes down in the flood strictly a house. The parables use people or things as object lessons.

There are obvious differences among the stories discussed in the following pages under *Fable Collections*. Some are typical fables, some are parables, others resemble folk tales, and many contain maxims or proverbs. All of them, however, embody moral or spiritual wisdom.

From Aesop's Fables *by Boris Artzybasheff. Copyright 1933 by Boris Artzybasheff. All rights reserved. Reprinted by permission of the Viking Press, Inc.*

Fable Collections

If you say "fables" to an English-speaking child, he thinks at once of *Aesop's Fables*. To a French child, La Fontaine and "fables" are inseparably associated, and so in the Orient it is *The Panchatantra, The Fables of Bidpai*, or the *Jatakas*. These major collections of fables, while resembling each other, also show striking differences.

Aesop's Fables

Some modern scholars doubt whether Aesop really existed. G. K. Chesterton suggests that he may be as completely fictitious a character as that other slave, Uncle Remus, who also told beast tales. But his name and fame persist through one edition of the fables after another. Aesop is said to have lived in Greece between 620 and 560 B.C. and is thought to have been a Samian slave. Because free speech under the Tyrants was risky business, Aesop is supposed to have used the fables for political purposes, protecting himself and veiling his opinions behind the innuendos of these little stories. Legend has it that he was deformed and that he was hurled off a cliff, whether for his deformity or for his politics is not known. All we know is that the picturesque legends about Aesop have survived with his name.

Translated into Latin in the first and third centuries, the Aesop fables became the textbooks of the medieval schools. In Latin they found their way into England, France, and Germany, were translated into several languages, and were among the first books to be printed by Caxton when he started his famous press in England. Evidently there was infiltration from other sources. Joseph Jacobs said he could mention at least seven hundred fables ascribed to Aesop, although the first known collection of them, made by Demetrius of Phalerum about 320 B.C., contained only about two hundred. Since India, like Greece, had long used the beast tale for teaching purposes, undoubtedly some of the Indian fables gravitated, in the course of time, to the Aesop collection. From whatever source they came, once included in Aesop they assumed the Aesop form, which is now regarded as the pure fable type. It is a brief story with inanimate objects or animals most frequently serving as the leading characters, and with the single action of the narrative pointing to an obvious moral lesson. James Reeves in his *Fables from Aesop* points out that the virtues which Aesop praises are not the heroic ones but rather "the peasant virtues of discretion, prudence, moderation and forethought. . . . That is why Aesop . . . has always had the affection and regard of ordinary people."

The Panchatantra

The Panchatantra, meaning "five books," was composed in Kashmir about 200 B.C.,[2] and is

[2] *The Panchatantra*, translated by Arthur W. Ryder (University of Chicago Press, 1925), p. 3.

the oldest known collection of Indian fables. *The Hitopadesa*, or Book of Good Counsel, is considered only another version of *The Panchatantra*,[3] and still another is called *The Fables of Bidpai*. These collections were translated into Persian, Arabic, Latin, and many other languages. In the Latin version the tales became popular throughout medieval Europe.

After the extreme condensation of Aesop, the stories of *The Panchatantra* seem long and involved. They are a textbook on "the wise conduct of life," intricate stories-within-stories, and are interrupted with philosophical verses so numerous that the thread of the story is almost forgotten. Some of these poems are sixteen or twenty verses long, but the quatrain is the more usual type.

A friend in need is a friend indeed,
Although of different caste;
The whole world is your eager friend
So long as riches last.

Make friends, make friends, however strong
Or weak they be;
Recall the captive elephants
That mice set free.[4]

These verses are summaries of the stories which seem more like folk tales than fables. On the whole, *The Panchatantra* is for adults rather than children.

The *Jatakas*

Another collection of ancient Indian fables is the group called the *Jatakas*. The time of their origin is not definitely known. They were in existence in the fifth century A.D., but carvings illustrating Jataka stories have been found which were made as early as the second or third centuries B.C.

Jatakas is a Buddhist name for stories concerning the rebirths of Gautama Buddha, who, according to tradition, was reincarnated many times in the forms of different animals until he became at last Buddha, the Enlightened

[3]Joseph Gaer, *The Fables of India* (Little, Brown, 1955), p. 53.
[4]*The Panchatantra*, op. cit., pp. 5, 273.

From The Fables of India *by Joseph Gaer, by permission of Little, Brown and Co. Copyright 1955 by Joseph Gaer.*

One. These beast tales, then, are really about a man living briefly as an animal, consorting with other animals, and deriving from these experiences certain ethical lessons.

Joseph Gaer tells us that there are two or three thousand of these stories. Generally, the introduction and body of the tale are in prose, but the conclusions are often verses. Comparatively few of them are suitable for children and then only with considerable adaptation. Joseph Gaer's versions, in *The Fables of India*, keep close to the original form of the Jatakas. Some Jatakas resemble parables from the Bible. Still others are like short folk tales with self-evident morals.

The Fables of La Fontaine

In the twelfth century, Marie de France introduced and popularized the fable in France. Others followed her lead, but Jean de La Fontaine (1621–1695), a contemporary of Charles Perrault, made the fable so completely and gracefully his own that the French coined a word for him, *le fablier*, "the fable-teller."

La Fontaine was a skilled poet and wrote his fables in graceful verses which are delightful to read and easy to memorize. There are charming bits of description in these fables which reveal the birds and little beasts and the forests and meadows of the beautiful Champagne countryside where La Fontaine grew up. The courtier and the man of the world show themselves in the shrewd appraisals of character and the worldly philosophy that permeate the fables:

Now, as everyone knows, white paws do not grow on wolves.

My dear Mr. Crow, learn from this how every flatterer lives at the expense of anybody who will listen to him. This lesson is well worth the loss of a cheese to you.[5]

La Fontaine used for his sources the Latin versions of Aesop and *The Fables of Bidpai*, and the versions of his predecessor, Marie de France. In spite of the verse form and the characteristic bits of philosophy, these fables of La Fontaine are closer to the Aesop pattern than to the tales from India. They maintain the brevity, the predominant use of animal characters, and, above all, the single striking episode which points up the moral.

Fable Editions

The fables are both didactic and universal, with their universality making their didacticism bearable if not enjoyable. Children are made uncomfortable by a story that preaches directly, but if they see that the lessons of the fables apply to everyone, they can better appreciate their wisdom and humor.

Excellent collections available today are *Aesop's Fables*, edited and illustrated by Boris Artzybasheff; a newly illustrated edition of *The Fables of Aesop*, edited by Joseph Jacobs; James Reeves's *Fables from Aesop;* and Anne Terry White's *Aesop's Fables*. Reeves has varied the concise narrative form by introducing conversation among the animals, and Anne Terry White has retold the stories in an easy, simple style appropriate for younger children. Louis Untermeyer, in his *Aesop's Fables*, gaily illustrated by Alice and Martin Provensen, has provided an edition of stories humorous and colorful enough to read aloud to children as young as six or seven.

The trend to present the fables in a form appropriate for younger children is most obvious in the publication of single-fable editions, such as Mary Calhoun's *Old Man Whickutt's Donkey;* Jean Showalter's *The Donkey Ride;* and Brian Wildsmith's *The Miller, the Boy, and the Donkey*. Wildsmith has retold and illustrated several other La Fontaine fables in addition to this favorite. In *John J. Plenty and Fiddler Dan*, John Ciardi has told the story of the improvident grasshopper and the industrious ant in an amusing verse version. There are also some attractive adaptations of fables from India for young children. Notable among them are Marcia Brown's Caldecott Medal book, *Once a Mouse*, an animal fable illustrated by color woodcuts; and Paul Galdone's *The Monkey and the Crocodile*, an adaptation of a Jataka tale.

Another collection that has both fables and folk tales is Mirra Ginsburg's *Three Rolls and One Doughnut: Fables from Russia*, which has a vivacious style. A source of Russian fa-

[5]From *The Fables of La Fontaine*, translated by Margaret W. Brown (Harper, 1940), pp. 6, 8, and 19.

Viewpoints

In every age [*Aesop's Fables*] has had the distinction of being approved of and adapted for the young reader. In style the Aesopian fable is akin to the folk-tale, but, unlike most other traditional lore, it had the good fortune in the ancient world to be moulded into an acceptable form. Often made into a schoolbook and burdened with added moralities, it never lost those pristine characteristics which endeared it to young or unsophisticated minds. Brevity in telling, clarity of style, animal characters with human attributes, pithy lessons about human conduct; these were all features to give life to the fables in every generation. There is little of high ethical purpose in the episodes: they are more like a fascinating looking-glass reflecting the follies of mankind.—M. F. Thwaite, *From Primer to Pleasure*, The Library Association, London, 1963, p. 7.

From Chanticleer and the Fox, *adapted by Barbara Cooney from Chaucer's* Canterbury Tales, *Copyright © 1956 by Thomas Y. Crowell Co., Inc., with permission of the Publisher. (Original in color)*

bles is Ivan Krylov's *Fifteen Fables of Krylov*, in a colloquial translation by Guy Daniels. A delightful single-fable edition is Barbara Cooney's Caldecott Medal book *Chanticleer and the Fox*, which is based on Geoffrey Chaucer's "The Nun's Priest's Tale" from *The Canterbury Tales*. There are a number of fables in modern dress—a particularly good one is Jean Merrill's *The Black Sheep*, which is far longer than the usual compressed fable form but, in the true spirit of the fable, teaches a lesson about blind conformity.

Myths

The fables are simple, highly condensed lessons in morality. The myth is far more complicated. It attempts to explain—in complex symbolism—the vital outlines of existence:

> *(1) cosmic phenomena (e.g., how the earth and sky came to be separated); (2) peculiarities of natural history (e.g., why rain follows the cries or activities of certain birds); (3) the origins of human civilization (e.g., through the beneficent action of a culture-hero like Prometheus); or (4) the origin of social or religious custom or the nature and history of objects of worship.*[6]

It also attempts to make more acceptable the painful realities of existence—danger, disease, misfortune, and death—by explaining them as part of a sacred order in the universe.

The explanations may seem irrational and inconsistent to the science-minded modern. This is because they are not scientific hypotheses but were created by and appeal to the imagination. The truth of the myth was unquestioned by primitive peoples because it was so closely associated with their sacred beliefs. For them, both nature and society were areas of reverent acceptance—not of objective study, as they are in this age of scientific inquiry.

Evolution of Myths

A number of writers have called attention to the various levels of myth development, their evolution from primitive to highly complex symbolic stories. These developmental stages are important to us because they throw light upon the various types of stories (for example, the *pourquoi* tales) included in myths and help to explain their suitability, or lack of it, as story material for children.

The early part of this evolution is, of course, shrouded in the darkness of prehistoric times. Much research has been devoted to it, but the outlines are still only dimly understood. For one thing, the evolution of myth and religion differs from people to people. Suffice it to say that the Greeks, like many other peoples, passed through a primary stage in which they worshiped an impersonal force believed to pervade all aspects of the universe: sun, moon, crops, rivers. The early Greeks performed rites to propitiate these bodiless forces so that they would grant to the world fertility and life. Later these nature forces were personified in the myths.

[6]William Reginald Halliday, "Folklore," in an earlier edition of the *Encyclopaedia Britannica*.

Myths, then, did give body—both animal and human—to the mystic forces that early people felt in the universe. As these ideas developed, the tendency was to give complex human form to these impersonal forces. These bright sky-dwellers were created in humankind's own image but surpassed humanity in beauty, wisdom, and power.

Imagining these supernatural beings in their own likeness, the people interpreted a flood to mean that the river god was angry with them and intended to punish them. Drouths, earthquakes, good crops and bad crops were all dependent on how humanity stood in the graces of these nature gods. These primitive beginnings of myth were polytheistic; that is, they developed many gods.

Presently these beings developed relationships among each other, assumed certain powers, and suffered limitations of power. Thus in the Greek mythology the first gods were all brothers and sisters—Hestia, Demeter, Hera, Poseidon, Hades, and Zeus. Because Zeus saved them from destruction, he was chosen the supreme ruler, the sky god, while Poseidon ruled the waters and Hades, who dwelt below the earth, ruled the dominion of the dead. From their matings, their children, and the powers and limitations of each of these three powerful brothers arose endless squabbles that bear a melancholy resemblance to the earthly rows of humans.

Each god or goddess came to assume certain powers although every one except Zeus knew distinct limitations to power and was vulnerable to misfortunes in certain respects, even as humans are. Balder, the Norse sun god, whose mother, Frigga, made everything except the mistletoe promise not to harm him, was slain by the insignificant shrub which Frigga had thought too harmless to bother about. Balder the Beautiful died; he went out to sea in his fiery ship, burning like the autumn foliage; the earth wept for him, and cold and darkness followed—a picture of the coming of autumn and winter in the north country. So these deities developed relationships and powers but were subject to certain limitations from other powers.

The extension of a god's powers soon turned him or her into a symbolic figure, standing for certain abstract virtues. So Zeus, from being at first merely a sky god, became the symbol of power and law. Apollo began as the sun god, a beautiful young man with a fiery chariot to drive across the sky daily. Then he became also the god of health and healing, the patron god of physicians. Finally this idea of healing was expanded to include the related but less physical concept of purification, and Apollo then stood for the abstract idea of purity. In some such way as this, many of the gods evolved from mere nature personifications to become symbols of abstract moral attributes.

In some mythologies less sophisticated than the Greeks' the deities have never signified anything more than spirits of earth, sky, sun, moon, or even animals. The American Indian "Old Man Coyote" is such a deity. On the other hand, the Navaho "Turquoise Woman" is not merely a sky goddess but seems to be also a symbol of beauty in the highest sense, meaning harmony and goodness.

Finally, when the gods had come to stand for moral attributes and powers, the next and last stage of myth-making was the development of a priesthood, temples, and a ritual of worship. Then the myth was an organized religion. Apollo had a great temple at Delphi with priests, an oracle, vestal virgins, and elaborate ceremonies and rituals. The Apollo cult represents the last and most complex stage of myth-making, which the mythologies of only highly civilized people attain.

Viewpoints

The great fantasies, myths, and tales are indeed like dreams: they speak *from* the unconscious *to* the unconscious, in the *language* of the unconscious—symbol and archetype. Though they use words, they work the way music does: they short-circuit verbal reasoning, and go straight to the thoughts that lie too deep to utter. They cannot be translated fully into the language of reason, but only a Logical Positivist, who also finds Beethoven's Ninth Symphony meaningless, would claim that they are therefore meaningless. They are profoundly meaningful, and usable—practical—in terms of ethics; of insight; of growth.—Ursula K. Le Guin, "The Child and the Shadow," *Quarterly Journal of the Library of Congress,* April 1975, p. 141.

Types of Myth Stories

Among the simplest of myth stories are the why stories, or *pourquoi* tales. Why the woodpecker has a red head and how the arbutus came to be are from the North American Indians. In both Greek and Norse myths these *why* stories become more complex than in the American Indian woodpecker and arbutus examples. Take, for instance, the Greek explanation of summer and winter; the story goes that Demeter (the earth mother) has been deprived of her beautiful child Persephone (the grain), who has been carried off by Hades to his realm below the ground. Demeter seeks her child, weeping, but Persephone must remain in Hades' underworld for six months of each year, leaving earth to darkness and cold. Such a story is neither simple nor fully explanatory for children. In much the same vein, the North American Indians of the Southwest have their desert seasonal story of little Burnt-Face, the scorched earth, who sees the invisible chief, the spring rains, and is made beautiful by him and becomes his bride. To children, these are just good fairy tales, as interesting and objective as "Cinderella." However, if in the study of Greeks or Desert Indians you explain to the children the possible meaning of these stories for the people who created them, they are surprised and charmed with the secondary meaning.

From Persephone and the Springtime *by Margaret Hodges, by permission of Little, Brown and Co. Illustrations Copyright © 1973 by Arvis Stewart. (Original in color)*

Some of the myths warn against particular sins. Pride seems to be especially offensive to the gods. Arachne was turned into a spider because she boasted of her weaving. Bellerophon, after he captured the winged horse, Pegasus, became so sure of himself that he attempted to ride into Zeus's dwelling and was promptly struck blind for his presumption. Some of these myths are almost like fables, and, like the fables, they could be summarized with a maxim or proverb.

Many of the myths are, on the whole, too adult in content and significance to be appropriate story material for children. But the simpler tales among them are accepted by the children exactly as they accept any folk tale. One of their favorites is "King Midas," who wished that everything he touched would turn into gold and soon found himself starving in the midst of plenty. Well-told versions of such stories are suitable for children and may be used with or without the background of the people and their mythology.

The ways of the gods with humans are the subject of another group of stories which includes "King Midas." One of the most delightful is "Bellerophon and Pegasus." Bellerophon, a handsome youth, is sent by his host, Iobates, to kill the chimera, which is devastating Lycia. Although Iobates is sure the mission will mean the boy's death, the gods take pity upon Bellerophon and send him the winged Pegasus. That Pegasus, the winged horse of the gods, means "poetry" does not enter children's heads, but that Bellerophon could not kill the terrible chimera until he had first captured and tamed Pegasus makes a good adventure story of unusual beauty. Such stories are really hero tales with a background of myth and they comprise a particularly good group of stories for children. Some of them, like those in the *Odyssey*, later developed into national epics. Stories of the gods' amatory adventures among humans are legion and are not often adapted for children.

Finally, the ways of the gods with other gods furnish us with another body of myth stories, often complex in their significance and adult in content. Here we encounter nature myths which even the folklorists interpret differently and which leave the reader baffled and a bit weary with all the things which aren't what they seem. Frazer's *Golden Bough* is a repository for these tales. In the Greek stories we find involved accounts of creation whose interpretation is decidedly speculative. And throughout the accounts of the gods and their escapades are endless double meanings which may start simply with Gaea, a personification of the Earth, who is touched by Eros (Love) and bears Uranus (Heaven). Moving and profound is the story of Prometheus, the Titan, who dared the wrath of the gods to bring fire to humanity and suffered endless tortures as a result. Prometheus is so noble a symbol of sacrifice that poets and painters have repeatedly used his story as a subject. But these myths, with their symbolism and inner meanings, are both complex and abstract, and some people feel that they have no place in children's literature.

Viewpoints

. . . Myths are original revelations of the preconscious psyche, involuntary statements about unconscious psychic happenings, and anything but allegories of physical processes. Such allegories would be an idle amusement for an unscientific intellect. Myths, on the contrary, have a vital meaning.

. . . there is no longer any question whether a myth refers to the sun or the moon, the father or the mother, sexuality or fire or water; all it does is to circumscribe and give an approximate description of an *unconscious core of meaning.* The ultimate meaning of this nucleus was never conscious and never will be. It was, and still is, only interpreted, and every interpretation that comes anywhere near the hidden sense (or, from the point of view of scientific intellect, nonsense, which comes to the same thing) has always, right from the beginning, laid claim not only to absolute truth and validity but to instant reverence and religious devotion. Archetypes were, and still are, living psychic forces that demand to be taken seriously.—C. G. Jung, "The Psychology of the Child Archetype," *Essays on a Science of Mythology* by C. G. Jung and C. Kerényi, translated by R. F. C. Hull, Bollingen Series XXII, Princeton University Press, Second Edition, 1969, pp. 73, 75.

Sources of Mythologies

Greek Myths

Most of the Greek myths came to us by way of the poet Hesiod, who is supposed to have lived during the eighth century B.C. While he was guarding his father's flocks, so the story goes, the Muses themselves commissioned him to be their poet. So a poet he became, winning a contest and gratefully dedicating a tripod to the Muses, who had shown him the way.

His first famous poem, *Works and Days*, contains the earliest known fable in Greek, "The Hawk and the Nightingale."

Theogony, another poem attributed to Hesiod, contains the Greek myths of the creation and the history of Zeus and Cronus, including Zeus's great battle with the Titans. Hesiod's picture of the defeated Titans, confined and guarded by giants and by Day and Night, is a convincing one.

Hesiod is credited with bringing together in organized form the major portion of Greek mythology. The English translation, although in prose, is good reading.

Roman Myths

The Roman versions of the Greek myths are available to us in the more familiar *Metamorphoses* of the Latin poet Ovid. Born in 43 B.C., Ovid belonged to a wealthy and privileged family. He was educated under famous Roman teachers and became a poet against his father's wishes.

The *Metamorphoses* consists of fifteen books recounting tales of miraculous transformations, hence the title. It begins with the metamorphosis of Chaos to order, follows the Greek development of gods and humans, recounts innumerable *why* stories of flowers, rivers, rocks, and the like. It concludes, appropriately enough, with Julius Caesar turned into a star, and Ovid himself on his way to some form of immortality. These stories, even in our English prose translations, are amazingly dramatic. It is interesting to check modern versions with these stirring tales of Ovid, which are the source of most adaptations.

Norse Myths

Whether the Norse myths began in Norway, Greenland, Ireland, Iceland, or England, it was in Iceland that they were preserved orally and first written down. Iceland, remote from the rest of the world and settled largely by Norwegians, held to the old language, once the speech of all Northern peoples, and so kept the stories alive in their original form. The two collections are the *Elder* or *Poetic Edda*, and the *Younger* or *Prose Edda*.

The *Poetic* and the *Prose Eddas* follow the sing-and-say style, with the difference that the *Poetic Edda* is mostly verse with brief prose passages, and the *Prose Edda* is mostly prose with interspersed poetic passages. Both are difficult books, but there are several adaptations to use with children.

The word *Edda* was originally the name or title for a great-grandmother. In time it came to stand for the Norwegian court-meter or the art of poetry. In both senses it seems to imply something traditional. The *Elder* or *Poetic Edda* (thirty-four poems) contains the Prophecy, which tells how the world was created, how the gods came to be, and how they fell. There is a book of proverbs, and finally there is the story of Sigurd the Volsung, the Norse epic. These heroic lays were supposedly collected from oral tradition by Saemund the Learned and committed to writing about the eleventh or twelfth century. By then they must have been exposed to Christian ideas and to other cultures, but they remain, nevertheless, primitive and vigorous.

The *Younger* or *Prose Edda* was not collected until the thirteenth century. The first book, "The Beguiling of Gylfi," contains the bulk of the Norse myths. It was the work of Snorri Sturluson, an Icelander who combined a greedy and traitorous character with a real reverence for the traditional literature he recorded so faithfully.

Viewpoints

There is another door that can be opened by reading legends and fairy tales, and for some children, at the present time, there may be no other key to it. *Religio,* in one Latin sense of the word, implies a sense of the strange, the numinous, the totally Other, of what lies quite beyond human personality and cannot be found in any human relationships. This kind of "religion" is an indestructible part of the experience of many human minds, even though the temper of a secular society does not encourage it, and the whole movement of modern theology runs counter to it. In Christian "religious instruction" there is likely to be less and less *religio:* it may very well be in reading about a vision of the flashing-eyed Athene or the rosy-fingered Aphrodite that children first find a satisfying formulation of those queer prickings of delight, excitement and terror that they feel when they first walk by moonlight, or when it snows in May, or when, like the young Wordsworth, they have to touch a wall to make sure that it is really there. Magic is not the same as mysticism, but it may lead towards it; it is mystery "told to the children."—Elizabeth Cook, *The Ordinary and the Fabulous,* Cambridge University Press, London, 1969, p. 5.

Why Use the Myths with Children?

It is the rare child who is not enchanted with the stories of mythology. The sky-dwellers of the Greeks and Romans not only left a mark on our language, but they continue to spellbind each succeeding generation of children. Bellerophon taming the winged horse, Icarus plummeting through the sky into the sea, Hermes stepping cloudward on his winged sandals—these somehow catch the imagination with their dramatic beauty. It is not an accident that most of the examples of myths in the preceding pages have been from the Greek. If children can sample only one mythology, it should be the Greek or its Roman adaptation. Our language and our thinking are full of words and ideas derived from these sources.[7] For example, *titanic* comes from the powerful Titans; *erotic* from Eros, the god of love; *panic* from the god Pan; and *cereal* from Ceres, the grain goddess. Minerva with her owl gazes down on us in our libraries. Venus, rising from her sea shell, advertises bath salts or cosmetics. There is a dramatic quality about the myths which has so captured the

[7]There is a book devoted to such sources: Isaac Asimov, *Words from the Myths* (Houghton, 1961).

imaginations of poets that poetry, and English poetry in particular, is filled with classical allusions. Not to know Greek-Roman mythology is to grope more or less blindly through the arts, particularly literature.

But the Norse myths too should be part of the experience of English-speaking children. The people who composed them were a vital source of our customs, laws, and speech. Yet the myths which are their finest expression and the clearest mirror of their life are not nearly so familiar to most of us as the myths of the ancient civilizations of Greece and Rome. The Norse gods do not have the beauty and grace of the classic deities, but they are cast in heroic mold, and there is a grandeur about the tales that is hard to match. Such stories as "How Thor Found His Hammer," "The Apples of Iduna," "Thor's Visit to the Giants," and "The Death of Balder" are fascinating with or without a study of the people.

Both Greek and Norse mythologies, moreover, furnish the background for the great national epics of those countries. Children must know Greek mythology in order to understand the *Iliad* or the *Odyssey,* and they must know Norse mythology in order to understand the ideals and motives of the heroic characters in the Norse epic *Sigurd the Volsung,* or in Wagner's opera cycle *The Ring of the Nibelungs,* the Teutonic form of the Sigurd epic.

These are a few of the reasons that myths should be used with older children, but the chief reasons are, after all, the beauty and the imaginative quality of the tales themselves.

What Versions of the Myths to Use

The chief difficulty in using mythology with children is to select satisfactory versions of the stories. Nathaniel Hawthorne, artist though he was, did not scruple to turn the gods into petulant children. He told an entrancing story, but he lost almost completely the dignity of the gods, and sometimes he even lost the significance of the story.

Good versions of the myths for children have been made and new ones are still appearing. General standards should help us in selecting the best of these.

Although some adaptation may be necessary, myths should not be written down to children. When this is done, the author is usually trying to retell myths to children who are too young for them. Six- and seven-year-old children can take only the bare bones of these stories, but children from nine or ten years old to fourteen can enjoy rich versions of some of the originals. For example, Krystyna Turska's adaptation of *Pegasus* makes the myth of the winged horse and his bold rider vividly real with its beautiful illustrations. In the home, some children may read myths earlier, but in the mixed groups of the average classroom, the appeal of myths is distinctly to older children.

Finally, adaptations should be simple enough to be thoroughly comprehensible to children without sacrificing either the spirit or the richness of the originals. Too often, in order to simplify these stories, an adapter reduces the colorful details of the original to drab outlines, devoid of charm. Simplification of some of the words is permissible and even essential. But reject an adaptation that omits the rich, descriptive details of Ovid's tale. It would be a pity to miss the pictures of the palace, the chariot, and the horses of the Sun, the account of Apollo's love and anxiety for the reckless youth, the portrayal of the boy's terror of the lonely heavens, and the descriptions of the rushing speed, the earth aflame, and finally the Jovian bolt.

According to these standards, what versions of the myths are best to use with children? There has been a flood of new adaptations and some new editions of old versions. Of the latter, one of the best is *The Heroes* by Charles Kingsley, Victorian scholar and poet. His stories of Perseus, Theseus, and Jason have a nobility that should prove a wholesome antidote to the banality of much of our mass entertainment. Padraic Colum's *The Golden Fleece* and *The Children's Homer* are superb storytelling for good readers, and the d'Aulaires' big, handsome *Book of Greek Myths* represents years of preparation. The stories are brief but have continuity; the copious and colorful illustrations are uneven in quality but imaginative. This is a splendid book for classroom use. It is also interesting to see how the myths appeal to poets, beginning

Illustration by William Stobbs. Reproduced from The Gorgon's Head. © *1961 by Ian Serraillier. By permission of Henry Z. Walck, Inc.*

with Kingsley and Colum. In 1960, British poet Robert Graves brought out his version, *Greek Gods and Heroes,* a lively text that makes clear what is often confusing. And Ian Serraillier, another poet, has told the stories of Perseus, in *The Gorgon's Head,* and Theseus, in *The Way of Danger,* with dramatic beauty. Both can be read by children or may serve as sources for storytelling. The illustrations suggest figures on Greek vases. Other tales by Serraillier include *Heracles the Strong,* illustrated with woodcuts that echo the vigor of the story; *The Clashing Rocks,* the story of Jason; and *A Fall from the Sky,* the story of Daedalus.

The eleven stories from Greek mythology adapted by Katherine Miller in *Apollo* are told in competent but not impressive brief versions. Olivia Coolidge's twenty-seven myths in *Greek Myths,* on the other hand, are mature in approach and are well told. Leon Garfield and Edward Blishen's *The God Beneath the Sea,* a flowing narrative version that clarifies the complexities of Olympian relationships, won the 1970 Carnegie Medal. Their later book, *The Golden Shadow,* takes the life of Heracles as its central theme. *Strangers Dark and Gold* by Norma Johnston is a stirring synthesis of three early versions of Jason's quest for the Golden Fleece. Two very good source books are Edith Hamilton's *Mythology,* which gives excellent background, and Roger Lancelyn Green's *A Book of Myths,* which gives variants of myths from many of the ancient lands. Examine these editions and choose the one or two that best suit your needs as sources for storytelling or references for the children to read themselves.

When you want to use Norse myths and hero tales, turn again to Padraic Colum, to his *Children of Odin,* a stirring and understandable version of those complex tales. Less difficult for younger readers are Catharine Sellew's *Adventures with the Giants* and *Adventures with the Heroes* and Ingri and Edgar Parin d'Aulaire's *Norse Gods and Giants.* In this last book, the author-artists have illustrated with big, bold pictures and have retold Norse myths in a straightforward style with occasional passages in which the oral tradition is evident. Although *Legends of the North* by Olivia Coolidge has a contemporary tone and lacks the lyric quality of the Colum tales, it has a special quality of vigorous spontaneity. An early adaptation that still serves well is Abbie F. Brown's *In the Days of Giants,* while Dorothy Hosford's *Sons of the Volsungs* and *Thunder of the Gods* cover the myths and the hero cycles in superb style, either for storytelling or reading by the children themselves. These are, however, the most difficult of all stories to tell.

Epic and Hero Tales

In the source collections of myths, both Greek and Norse, there are (in addition to the stories of the gods) tales of human heroes buffeted violently by gods and humanity but daring greatly, suffering uncomplainingly, and enduring staunchly to the end. Such tales, having a human hero as the focus of the action and embodying the ideals of a culture, are called epics.

From Norse Gods and Giants *by Ingri and Edgar Parin d'Aulaire. Copyright © 1967 by Ingri and Edgar Parin d'Aulaire. Reproduced by permission of Doubleday & Company, Inc.*

Characteristics of the Epic

Epics are sometimes written in verse, as in the *Iliad* or the *Sigurd Saga*, and sometimes in prose, as in Malory's *Morte d'Arthur*. The adventures of the legendary hero Robin Hood were preserved by the ballads. The term *epic* is often used quite flexibly to include such dissimilar materials as the great philosophical poem from the Hebrew, the Book of Job, the slight and romantic *Aucassin and Nicolette* from the medieval French, and the comparatively modern *Paradise Lost* by the English poet John Milton.

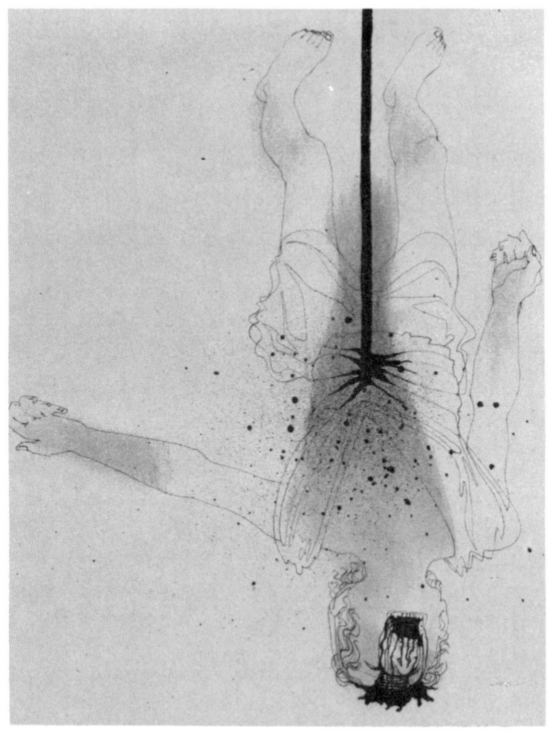

From The Golden Shadow *by Leon Garfield and Edward Blishen. Illustrated by Charles Keeping. Illustration copyright © 1973 by Charles Keeping. Reprinted by permission of Pantheon Books, a division of Random House, Inc.*

Most of us, however, think of epics as a cycle of tales, such as the *Odyssey* or the *Iliad*, gathered around one hero. These two heroic narratives have come to typify this particular field of literature. In them, legendary heroes pursue legendary adventures, aided or hindered by partisan gods who apparently leave Olympus for the express purpose of meddling in human affairs. In short, myth may still be with us in the epic, but the dramatic center of interest has shifted from the gods to a human hero. We have moved from Olympus to earth; we have transferred our sympathies from gods to humans, from divine adventures to human endeavors.

The epic is strongly national in its presentation of human character. Odysseus may have never lived, but he is the embodiment of the

Greek ideals of manly courage, sagacity, beauty, and endurance. Sigurd is the personification of Norse heroism; King Arthur is the code of chivalry in the flesh; and Robin Hood is the mouthpiece for England's passionate love of freedom and justice, as he is the ideal of hardy, jovial English manhood. Study the epic hero of a nation and you discover the moral code of that nation and era—all its heroic ideals embodied in one character.

The *Iliad* and the *Odyssey*

The *Iliad* and the *Odyssey* are attributed to Homer, a legendary Greek poet. Songs about the seige of Troy are known to have been sung shortly after the events took place, although the first written forms of the epics did not appear until some six hundred years later. What Homer composed and what he compiled cannot be established, but the great epics known by his name were studied and recited by educated Greeks and there were apparently texts or arrangements of them from around 560 to 527 B.C. Authentic texts are established by 150 B.C. The date of Homer's birth has been variously estimated as from 1159 B.C. to 685 B.C., but by the time stories of Homer's life began to appear, nothing was authentically known about him. George Gilbert Aimé Murray sums up this disputable evidence in the following fashion:

The man "Homer" cannot have lived in six different centuries nor been born in seven different cities; but Homeric poetry may well have done so. The man cannot have spoken this strange composite epic language, but the poetry could and did.[8]

The *Iliad* is certainly complex and long, but the adventures in the *Odyssey*, or *Ulysses*, are exciting and understandable to children. A combined edition, *The Iliad and the Odyssey of Homer* adapted by Alfred J. Church, has versions that are well suited to the nine- to eleven-year-old reader, as are the versions in the handsomely illustrated *The Iliad and the Odyssey* adapted by Jane Werner Watson. For a slightly older reader, Padraic Colum's *The Children's Homer* is a distinguished retelling. But for readers of twelve or older, Barbara Leonie Picard's *The Odyssey of Homer* gives more depth in its perceptive portrayal of character.

In this epic the Greek ideals of cool intelligence, patience, and resourcefulness are found in both Penelope and Odysseus. They exhibit these qualities and hold tenaciously to their goals even when humans and gods are arrayed against them. Over "the misty sea," "the wine-dark sea," Odysseus sailed for twenty years and none could stay him. This is a story of fortitude which every generation of children should know.

Sigurd the Volsung

The Norse epic *Sigurd the Volsung* is not so well known as it deserves to be. There is a rugged nobility about the saga stories which some children especially appreciate. Because these tales reflect a simpler social order, many people consider them better suited to children than the Greek epics. This is a debatable point, since anyone who has ever tried to

Viewpoints

[The heroic ideal] had risen into the consciousness of the authors of the Sagas; it was not far from definite expression in abstract terms. In this lay the danger. An ideal, defined or described in set terms, is an ideal without any responsibility and without any privilege. It may be picked up and traded on by any fool or hypocrite. Undefined and undivulged, it belongs only to those who have some original strength of imagination or will, and with them it cannot go wrong.

All is well, however, so long as this heroic ideal is kept in its right relation, as one element in a complex work, not permitted to walk about by itself as a personage. This right subordination is observed in the Sagas, whereby both the heroic characters are kept out of extravagance . . . and the less noble or the more complex characters are rightly estimated. [The Sagas] are imaginative, dealing in actions and characters; they are not ethical or sentimental treatises, or mirrors of chivalry.—W. P. Ker, *Epic and Romance,* Macmillan, London, 1931, pp. 202–203, 206.

[8]George Gilbert Aimé Murray, "Homer," in an earlier edition of the *Encyclopaedia Britannica.*

From The Iliad and the Odyssey *adapted by Jane Werner Watson. Illustrations by Alice & Martin Provensen. Copyright 1956 by Western Publishing Company, Inc. reprinted by permission. (Original in color)*

tell the saga of Sigurd knows all too well its difficulties. Obscurities in the text, difficult names much alike, and unpalatable social relationships upon which the main action of the story depends make this an epic which calls for expert handling.

Certainly the saga has some elements of violence in common with those crime stories which the modern child may be reading in the newspapers or seeing in the movies or on television. But their differences are important. In the latter, the tales of blood and murder are often sordid, ignobly motivated, and horrifying. In the Sigmund-Sigurd stories, there is the nobility of great heroism, of keeping your word even though it costs you your life, of self-sacrifice for a great cause, of death rather than dishonor, of ideals of race and family, of intrepid courage and perseverance.

Robin Hood

Of all the hero cycles, *Robin Hood* is unquestionably the children's favorite. It may not be the loftiest epic, and Robin Hood may not be the noblest hero, but his mad escapades, his lusty fights, his unfailing good humor when beaten, his sense of fair play, and, above all, his roguish tricks and gaiety practically define "hero" for children. Children should read *Robin Hood*, see it in a movie or television version, and read it again. Indeed, no other hero lends himself so readily to dramatization on screen or in classroom as does this gallant leader of the outlaws.

Children enjoy hearing some of the ballads of Robin Hood read aloud, but the prose version by Howard Pyle, with his spirited illustrations, is the text they should know. It is hard reading for most children, and if they can't read it for themselves, they should hear it. For the lucky superior readers, it remains for generation after generation of children one of the most exciting narratives in all literature. Other rewarding versions of the story are Geoffrey Trease's *Bows Against the Baron* and J. Walker McSpadden's *Robin Hood and His Merry Outlaws*, which is told in a simple but lively style and illustrated with the jaunty drawings of Louis Slobodkin.

King Arthur and the Knights of the Round Table

Opinions differ as to the appropriateness of the King Arthur stories for young children. Certainly they are more mature in content and significance than either the *Odyssey* or *Robin Hood*. The individual adventures of some of the knights are as understandable as those

THE MERRY FRIAR CARRIETH ROBIN ACROSS THE WATER

From The Merry Adventures of Robin Hood *by Howard Pyle. Copyright, 1946, by Charles Scribner's Sons. Reproduced by permission of the publishers.*

of the Sherwood Forest band, but the ideals of chivalry are far subtler than the moral code of Robin Hood and his men. Often brave deeds are performed for the love of a fair lady, and many feel the cycle is better for the adolescent period when romance is uppermost and codes of conduct are taken seriously.

On the other hand, there are unusually good juvenile editions of the Arthur tales for children which, simplified though they are, satisfy the child's love of knights and knightly adventures. Two of the older editions of the stories of King Arthur and his court remain deservedly popular: Sidney Lanier's *The Boy's King Arthur* and Howard Pyle's *The Story of King Arthur and His Knights,* which Pyle both told and romantically illustrated. Barbara Leonie Picard's *Stories of King Arthur and His Knights* uses lucid language and evokes a feeling of the period, as does Mary MacLeod's *The Book of King Arthur and His Noble Knights,* but MacLeod's book does not achieve the stylistic level of Picard's. Several books tell separate episodes from the Arthurian legend: Barbara Schiller's *The Kitchen Knight;* the collection of four Arthurian tales in T. H. White's *The Once and Future King* that begins with *The Sword in the Stone,* Ian Serraillier's poetic *The Challenge of the Green Knight,* the story of Sir Gawain's battle against the knight who had issued a challenge to the company at Camelot; and Constance Hieatt's scholarly version of the same story, *Sir Gawain and the Green Knight.* Hieatt's *The Joy of the Court* tells the romantic story of Erec and Enid, as does Barbara Schiller's *Erec and Enid.* Teachers who love the Arthur stories will have listeners who enjoy them. Certainly a saturation with any of these hero cycles is an enriching experience.

It is the gentleness and beauty of these stories and the idealistic character of King Arthur and his knights which sometimes furnish children with their first idea of strength in gentleness, of the power that comes through disciplined restraint. Not that children can put these qualities into words, but the qualities are there, embodied in the strong, gentle men who are the heroes of these tales.

The *Ramayana* and the Mahabharata

There was no English version of the *Ramayana* for children until Joseph Gaer's *The Adventures of Rama* was published. This mythepic of India tells how the god Vishnu came down to earth as Prince Rama, a mortal, to save humanity from the evil powers of Ravan. Once on earth, Rama behaves much like other epic heroes. He fights innumerable battles, marries the beautiful Sita, suffers banishment, gives way to suspicion and jealousy, and is put to shame by the gentle Sita's trial by fire. After that, all goes well, and throughout the ten thousand years of Rama's reign

Unknown were want, disease and crime,
So calm, so happy was the time.

The individual stories resemble Greek myths rather more than the usual epic does. The illustrations suggest dance, in which form the adventures of Rama are often shown in India. A splendid edition of the *Ramayana* has been adapted by Elizabeth Seeger, who has also retold one of India's great hero tales in *The Five Sons of King Pandu*, the story of the Mahabharata. Both books are beautifully illustrated in the Indian tradition, and both have the rolling prose that is so suitable to the intricacies of the stories and to their lofty themes.

Other Epics and Hero Tales

The length and complexity of the epic form may seem a deterrent to young readers, but it allows time for real characterization and for a continual iteration of the moral code. Although the great national epics and hero tales are of particular interest to students of literature and to folklorists, they can be enjoyed by the adolescent reader; and many of the single episodes, especially those of the hero tales, can be appreciated by the preadolescent.

From the book Beowulf: Dragon Slayer *by Rosemary Sutcliff. Illustration by Charles Keeping. Illustration copyright, ©, 1962 by The Bodley Head, Ltd. Published by E. P. Dutton & Co., Inc. and used with their permission.*

Reprinted from The Ramayana, *text © 1969, by Elizabeth Seeger, and illustrations © 1969 by Gordon Laite, A Young Scott Book by permission of Addison-Wesley Publishing Company. (Original in color)*

An excellent introduction to the genre is *Hero Tales from Many Lands*, edited by Alice Hazeltine. Her selection of retellings is discriminating, and the book includes sources, background notes, and a glossary. Barbara Leonie Picard's *Hero Tales of the British Isles* also has notes that give historical information.

Beowulf, the oldest epic in English, has been retold in several editions for the young reader. Two versions that can be enjoyed by ten- to twelve-year-olds are Dorothy Hosford's *By His Own Might, The Battles of Beowulf* and Robert Nye's *Beowulf, A New Telling*, a quite simple prose interpretation of the epic poem. For older children, an outstanding prose version is Rosemary Sutcliff's *Beowulf*, which has a poetic grandeur of style. Ian Serraillier's *Beowulf, the Warrior* is in sonorous and stately verse.

The Babylonian story of Gilgamesh has been retold in several editions; the most notable both in style and illustration is that of Bernarda Bryson. A version that is easier to read is edited by Anita Feagles: *He Who Saw Everything, The Epic of Gilgamesh*. The ornate, mythic style of Jennifer Westwood's *Gilgamesh, and Other Babylonian Tales*, has flavor but limits the book to older readers.

The deeds of Cuchulain, the Irish warrior-hero who was the descendant of a god, are combined in a continuous story in Rosemary Sutcliff's *The Hound of Ulster*. Another Irish hero, Finn MacCool, leader of the Fenians, is described by Sutcliff in *The High Deeds of Finn MacCool*, a vigorous account of the Fenian legends. These legends are also related in vivid style in *The Tangle-Coated Horse and Other Tales* by Ella Young and are given a sophisticated, witty retelling in *The Green Hero* by Bernard Evslin.

From continental Europe come other tales of heroes: stories of the legendary Spanish hero, the Cid; the story of Roland from France; in romantic tales from the Kiev cycle, *The Knights of the Golden Table* by E. M. Almedingen; *The Nibelungenlied* from Germany.

Tales from other parts of the world, too, are becoming available for children. Marcia Brown, in *Backbone of the King*, retells the Hawaiian epic of the courtier Pakaa and his son Ku. Dale Carlson's *Warlord of the Gengi* recounts the valorous deeds of a Japanese folk hero. Roland Bertol's *Sundiata, The Epic of the Lion King*, tells of the hero-king who founded the African empire of Mali.

Fable, myth, and epic are different from each other in many ways, yet all three are a part of the great stream of folk literature and are also embodiments of moral truths in story form.

The *fable* teaches briefly and frankly and provides children with their first excursion into the realm of abstract ideas and intellectual speculations about conduct.

The *myth* teaches through symbols which grow more and more complex. The symbolism soon ceases to have the simple, obvious moral of a fable and becomes as complicated as life, and it is then proportionately difficult for a child to understand. Fortunately, the myth stories possess a beauty that is satisfying in itself.

The *epics* have a triple value. They contribute to an appreciation of world literature, to an understanding of national ideals of behavior, and to a comprehension of the dimensions of the valor and nobility of heroism for all humanity.

Adult References[9]

ASIMOV, ISAAC. *Words from the Myths.*
AUSLANDER, JOSEPH, and FRANK ERNEST HILL. *The Winged Horse; The Story of Poets and Their Poetry.*
BULFINCH, THOMAS. *Age of Fable; or, Stories of Gods and Heroes.*
EASTMAN, MARY HUSE. *Index to Fairy Tales, Myths and Legends.*
FRAZER, SIR JAMES GEORGE. *The Golden Bough.*
Funk and Wagnalls Standard Dictionary of Folklore, Mythology and Legend.
GUERBER, HELENE A. *Myths of Greece and Rome.*
HOMER. *The Iliad.*
______. *The Odyssey.*
IRELAND, NORMA. *Index to Fairy Tales, 1949–1972: Including Folklore, Legends and Myths in Collections.*
KIRK, G. S. *Myth.*
MUNCH, PETER A. *Norse Mythology, Legends of Gods and Heroes.*
OVID. *The Metamorphoses.*
RANK, OTTO. *The Myth of the Birth of the Hero: A Psychological Interpretation of Mythology.*
SCHWAB, GUSTAV. *Gods and Heroes.*
SMITH, RUTH, ed. *The Tree of Life.*
TATLOCK, JESSIE M. *Greek and Roman Mythology.*
Volsunga Saga: The Story of the Volsungs and Niblungs, with Certain Songs from the Elder Edda.

Aesop's Fables

Aesop's Fables, tr. by V. S. Vernon Jones, ill. by Arthur Rackham. Watts, 1967. This is one of the most satisfactory editions both for children and adults. Chesterton's introduction should not be missed. The illustrations appeal to older children. 10-14

Aesop's Fables, ill. by Fritz Kredel. Grosset, 1947. An attractive, readable edition which contains over 150 fables. 10-14

Aesop's Fables, ill. by Jacob Lawrence. Windmill, 1970. Stark, sophisticated illustrations for a compilation of eighteen fables, moderately well told. 9-11

ARTZYBASHEFF, BORIS, ed. *Aesop's Fables*, ill. by ed. Viking, 1933. 12-14

EVANS, KATHERINE. *A Bundle of Sticks*, ill. by author. Whitman, 1962. An amusing modern picture-book adaptation of the Aesop fable for younger readers. Other adaptations by this author include *The Boy Who Cried Wolf* (1960) and *A Camel in the Tent* (1961). 5-8

The Hare and the Tortoise, ill. by Paul Galdone. McGraw, 1962. Action-filled color illustrations for this Aesop fable heighten suspense for the youngest. 4-7

[9]Complete bibliographic data are provided in the combined Adult References in the Appendixes.

JACOBS, JOSEPH, ed. *The Fables of Aesop*, ill. by David Levine. Macmillan, 1964. 9-11

KENT, JACK, reteller. *Fables of Aesop*, ill. by reteller. Parents' Magazine, 1972. 7-9

______, reteller. *More Fables of Aesop*, ill. by reteller. Parents' Magazine, 1974. Free adaptations from the Vernon-Jones version, with simple language and comic pictures. 5-7

REES, ENNIS, ad. *Lions and Lobsters and Foxes and Frogs*, ill. by Edward Gorey. Scott/Addison, 1971. Seventeen selections taken from *Fables from Aesop* (Oxford, 1966) by Rees are here illustrated by Gorey's amiable, wild-eyed beasts. 8-10

REEVES, JAMES, ad. *Fables from Aesop*, ill. by Maurice Wilson. Walck, 1962. In his selection of fifty fables, the narrator has introduced brief dialogue and descriptive phrases to enliven them, while keeping to the spirit of the original. Illustrations, many in color, are exceptional in quality. 9-13

SHOWALTER, JEAN B., ad. *The Donkey Ride*, ill. by Tomi Ungerer. Doubleday, 1967. 5-9

Three Aesop Fox Fables, ill. by Paul Galdone. Seabury, 1971. Large figures, with humor and movement, make this good for group showing. 4-7

UNTERMEYER, LOUIS, ed. *Aesop's Fables*, ill. by Alice and Martin Provensen. Golden Pr., 1965. 6-9

WHITE, ANNE TERRY, ed. *Aesop's Fables*, ill. by Helen Siegl. Random, 1964. 8-10

La Fontaine's Fables

CALHOUN, MARY. *Old Man Whickutt's Donkey*, ill. by Tomie de Paola. Parents' Magazine, 1975.

LA FONTAINE, JEAN DE. *The Fables of La Fontaine*, tr. by Marianne Moore. Viking, 1954. These fables retain their original verse form in this translation. A scholarly edition which includes La Fontaine's twelve books of fables and his own original preface. Chiefly an adult source.

______. *The Hare and the Tortoise*, ill. by Brian Wildsmith. Watts, 1967.

______. *The Miller, the Boy and the Donkey*, ill. by Brian Wildsmith. Watts, 1969. Big pages, big print, and jewel-tone colors make these and other single-title editions by Wildsmith attractive. 5-8

Other Fables

ANDERSEN, HANS CHRISTIAN. *The Ugly Duckling, The Emperor's New Clothes*, and others (see Bibliography, Chapter 8).

BRENNER, ANITA. *A Hero by Mistake*, ill. by Jean Charlot. W. R. Scott, 1953. Afraid of his own shadow, this little man accidentally captures some bandits, is hailed as a hero, and learns to behave like one. 6-8

BROWN, MARCIA. *Once a Mouse* (see Bibliography, Chapter 6).

CHAUCER, GEOFFREY. *Chanticleer and the Fox*, ad. and ill. by Barbara Cooney. T. Crowell, 1958. Pictures of colorful beauty and design add delight to the old fable of the crafty fox and the vain cock. Caldecott Medal. 6-9

CIARDI, JOHN. *John J. Plenty and Fiddler Dan*, ill. by Madeleine Gekiere. Lippincott, 1963. 4-9

DAUGHERTY, JAMES. *Andy and the Lion* (see Bibliography, Chapter 4).

GAER, JOSEPH. *The Fables of India*, ill. by Randy Monk. Little, 1955. Beast tales from three outstanding collections of Indian fables: the *Panchatantra*, the *Hitopadesa*, and the *Jatakas*. The stories are entertainingly presented, and there is excellent background material on the known history of fable literature for the student. 12-16

GALDONE, PAUL. *The Monkey and the Crocodile*, ill. by author. Seabury, 1969. 5-7

GINSBURG, MIRRA. *Three Rolls and One Doughnut: Fables from Russia*, ill. by Anita Lobel. Dial, 1970. 6-10

KRYLOV, IVAN. *Fifteen Fables of Krylov*, tr. by Guy Daniels, ill. by David Pascal. Macmillan, 1965. 12 up

MERRILL, JEAN. *The Black Sheep*, ill. by Ronni Solbert. Pantheon, 1969. 9-11

Greek and Roman Myths and Epics

CHURCH, ALFRED JOHN, ad. *The Aeneid*. Macmillan, 1962. A simplified and dignified version. 10-14

______, ad. *The Iliad and the Odyssey of Homer*, ill. by Eugene Karlin. Macmillan, 1964. 10-14

______, ad. *The Odyssey of Homer*, ill. by John Flaxman. Macmillan, 1951. First published in 1906, this attractively done edition is an excellent source for children to read or adults to tell. Stories are arranged in chronological order. 10-14

COLUM, PADRAIC. *The Children's Homer*, ill. by Willy Pogany. Macmillan, 1925, 1962. A distinguished version in cadenced prose, simple but in the spirit of the original. Vigorous illustrations.

______. *The Golden Fleece*, ill. by Willy Pogany. Macmillan, 1921, 1962. A companion edition to *The Children's Homer*, and equally fine. 10-14

COOLIDGE, OLIVIA E. *Greek Myths*, ill. by Edouard Sandoz. Houghton, 1949. Twenty-seven of the best known Greek myths. Here the gods are not idealized, but the stories have authenticity. 10-16

D'AULAIRE, INGRI and EDGAR PARIN. *Ingri and Edgar Parin d'Aulaire's Book of Greek Myths*, ill. by authors. Doubleday, 1962. 8-11

DE SELINCOURT, AUBREY. *Odysseus the Wanderer*, ill. by Norman Meredith. Criterion, 1956. A lusty, modern retelling of the Odyssey that should lure many young readers into an acquaintance with this epic before high-school days. 11 up

GARFIELD, LEON, and EDWARD BLISHEN. *The God Beneath the Sea*, ill. by Zevi Blum. Pantheon, 1971. 11-14

______. *The Golden Shadow*, ill. by Charles Keeping. Pantheon, 1973. 12-16

GATES, DORIS. *The Golden God: Apollo*, ill. by Ted CoConis. Viking, 1973. The Apollo myths brought together into a coherent whole. Gates has done the same thing for the myths concerning Zeus in *Lord of the Sky: Zeus* (Viking, 1972); for the Athena myths in *The Warrior Goddess: Athena* (Viking, 1973); and for the Heracles myths in *Mightiest of Mortals: Heracles* (Viking, 1975). 10-11

GRAVES, ROBERT. *Greek Gods and Heroes*, ill. by Dimitris Davis. Doubleday, 1960. 12-15

______. *The Siege and Fall of Troy*, ill. by C. Walter Hodges. Doubleday, 1963. An easy-to-follow narrative history of the Trojan War. 12-16

GREEN, ROGER LANCELYN. *Heroes of Greece and Troy; Retold from the Ancient Authors*, ill. by Heather Copley and Christopher Chamberlain. Walck, 1961. The tales of the Heroic Age have been woven into a unified whole, from the coming of the Immortals to Odysseus, the last of the heroes. Beautifully written, and with an introduction that will give insight into the great variety of classic sources used in this fine version. 12 up

______, ed. *A Book of Myths,* ill. by Joan Kiddell-Monroe. Dutton, 1965. 10-12

HAMILTON, EDITH. *Mythology,* ill. by Steele Savage. Little, 1942. 12 up

HAWTHORNE, NATHANIEL. *The Golden Touch,* ill. by Paul Galdone. McGraw, 1959. The old tale of King Midas is imaginatively illustrated with gold-toned pictures. 6-9

JOHNSTON, NORMA. *Strangers Dark and Gold.* Atheneum, 1975. 12-16

KINGSLEY, CHARLES. *The Heroes,* ill. by Vera Bock. Macmillan, 1954. Beautifully retold tales which make a fine cycle for the storyteller. 10-14

______. *The Heroes,* ill. by Joan Kiddell-Monroe. Dutton, 1963. 9-12

LANG, ANDREW. *The Adventures of Odysseus,* ill. by Joan Kiddell-Monroe. Dutton, 1962. Andrew Lang's distinguished retellings of Homer's *Iliad* and the *Odyssey* are reissued in handsome new format. Originally published in his *Tales of Greece and Troy* (1907). 12 up

MacPHERSON, JAY, *Four Ages of Man,* ill. St. Martin's, 1962. Beautifully narrated stories from the Greek myths organized around four periods: "creation and the coming of the gods; pastoral life and the ordering of the seasons; the adventures and the labors of the heroes; war, tragic tales, and decline into history." 13 up

MILLER, KATHERINE. *Apollo,* Houghton, 1970. 9-11

PICARD, BARBARA LEONIE. *The Iliad of Homer,* ill. by Joan Kiddell-Monroe. Walck, 1960. A truly distinguished retelling of the *Iliad,* with characters sympathetically portrayed. *The Odyssey of Homer* (1952) is an equally fine companion volume. 12-15

REEVES, JAMES. *The Trojan Horse,* ill. by Krystyna Turska. Watts, 1969. A Trojan boy describes the invasion of his city. 9-10

SELLEW, CATHARINE. *Adventures with the Gods,* ill. by George and Doris Hauman. Little, 1945. An introduction to the more familiar myths, simply written for younger children. 9-12

SERRAILLIER, IAN. *The Clashing Rocks: The Story of Jason,* ill. by William Stobbs. Walck, 1964. 10-13

______. *A Fall from the Sky: The Story of Daedalus,* ill. by William Stobbs. Walck, 1966. 10-13

______. *The Gorgon's Head; The Story of Perseus,* ill. by William Stobbs. Walck, 1962. 12-14

______. *Heracles the Strong,* ill. by Rocco Negri. Walck, 1970. 10-13

______. *The Way of Danger; The Story of Theseus,* ill. by William Stobbs Walck, 1963. 12-14

SEWELL, HELEN. *A Book of Myths,* sel. from Bulfinch's *Age of Fable,* ill. by Helen Sewell. Macmillan, 1942, 1964. Some people dislike, others are enthusiastic about the stylized illustrations in black and white, or sharp blue, black, and white. They are undeniably authentic in spirit and detail. 10-14

TAYLOR, N. B. *The Aeneid of Virgil,* ill. by Joan Kiddell-Monroe. Walck, 1961. The epic of Aeneas and his journeys after the burning of Troy, retold in an excellent prose version. 13-15

TOMAINO, SARAH F., ad. *Persephone; Bringer of Spring,* ill. by Ati Forberg. T. Crowell, 1971. A graceful retelling of the Greek legend with delicate and dramatic illustrations. 8-10

TURSKA, KRYSTYNA. *Pegasus,* ill. by author. Watts, 1970. 9-11

WATSON, JANE WERNER. *The Iliad and the Odyssey,* ill. by Alice and Martin Provensen. Golden Pr., 1964. 11-13

Norse Myths and Epics

BROWN, ABBIE FARWELL. *In the Days of Giants,* ill. by E. B. Smith. Houghton, 1902. This is a sterling adaptation of the Norse myths. 10-14

COLUM, PADRAIC. *Children of Odin,* ill. by Willy Pogany. Macmillan, 1920, 1962. Norse myths and hero tales retold in a continuous narrative ending with the death of Sigurd. Our best source for children. In fine modern format. 10-14

COOLIDGE, OLIVIA. *Legends of the North,* ill. by Edouard Sandoz. Houghton, 1951. A wide variety of stories includes tales of the northern gods and heroes, the Volsungs, and other sagas. 12-14

D'AULAIRE, INGRI and EDGAR PARIN. *Norse Gods and Giants,* ill. by authors. Doubleday, 1967. 8-11

HOSFORD, DOROTHY G. *Sons of the Volsungs,* ill. by Frank Dobias. Holt, 1949. A splendid version of the Sigurd tales adapted from William Morris's *The Story of Sigurd the Volsung and the Fall of the Niblungs.* 11-14

______. *Thunder of the Gods,* ill. by George and Claire Louden. Holt, 1952. Distinguished retellings of the Norse myths: stories of Odin, Thor, Balder, Loki, and other familiar tales. Excellent for storytelling or reading aloud. 11-14

SCHILLER, BARBARA, ad. *Hrafkel's Saga; An Icelandic Story,* ill. by Carol Iselin. Seabury, 1972. A family saga about one of the ancient Icelandic chieftains, told directly in heroic style. 11-13

SELLEW, CATHARINE. *Adventures with the Giants,* ill. by Steele Savage. Little, 1950. 8-11

______. *Adventures with the Heroes,* ill. by Steele Savage. Little, 1954. Retold in simple language are the stories of the Volsungs and Nibelungs. 9-12

English Epics and Hero Tales

HIEATT, CONSTANCE. *The Castle of Ladies,* ill. by Norman Laliberte. T. Crowell, 1973. One of Gawain's romantic quests, adroitly retold. 10-12

______. *The Joy of the Court,* ill. by Pauline Baynes. T. Crowell, 1970. 9-11

______. *Sir Gawain and the Green Knight,* ill. by Walter Lorraine. T. Crowell, 1967. 10-12

HOSFORD, DOROTHY G. *By His Own Might; The Battles of Beowulf,* ill. by Laszlo Matulay. Holt, 1947. 11-16

LANIER, SIDNEY. *The Boy's King Arthur,* ill. by N. C. Wyeth, ad. from Sir Thomas Malory's *History of King Arthur and His Knights of the Round Table.* Scribner's, 1942. An authoritative and popular version of this hero cycle; the best one to use for reading or telling. 10-14

MacLEOD, MARY. *Book of King Arthur and His Noble Knights,* ill. by Henry C. Pitz. Lippincott, 1949. 9-13

McSPADDEN, J. WALKER. *Robin Hood and His Merry Outlaws,* ill. by Louis Slobodkin. World, 1946. 9-12

MALORY, SIR THOMAS. *Le Morte d'Arthur,* ill. by W.

Russell Flint. London: Warner, publisher to the Medici Society [1921]. 2 vols. Children who are superior readers are fascinated with this source of the Arthur stories. 12-16

NYE, ROBERT. *Beowulf: A New Telling,* ill. by Allan E. Cober. Hill, 1968. 10-12

PICARD, BARBARA L. *Hero Tales of the British Isles,* ill. by Eric Fraser. Criterion, 1963. 10-13

______. *Stories of King Arthur and His Knights,* ill. by Roy Morgan. Walck, 1955. 10-13

PYLE, HOWARD. *The Merry Adventures of Robin Hood of Great Renown in Nottinghamshire,* ill. by author. Scribner's, 1946. This is the great prose edition of the Robin Hood tales, the best source for reading and telling. 12-14

______. *Some Merry Adventures of Robin Hood,* rev. ed., ill. by author. Scribner's, 1954. This book contains a dozen stories adapted from the longer book, and would serve as an introduction for younger readers. 10-13

______. *The Story of King Arthur and His Knights,* ill. by author. Scribner's, 1933. Any Pyle edition is written with grace and distinction. This is no exception. 12-14

ROBBINS, RUTH. *Taliesin and King Arthur,* ill. by author. Parnassus, 1970. The young poet Taliesin entertains King Arthur's court with his storytelling. The book mingles fact and fiction and the style is poetic. 9-11

SCHILLER, BARBARA. *Erec and Enid,* ill. by Ati Forberg. Dutton, 1970. 9-11

______. *The Kitchen Knight,* ill. by Nonny Hogrogian. Holt, 1965. 9-11

______, ad. *The Wandering Knight,* ill. by Herschel Levit. Dutton, 1971. A retelling of the deeds of the young Lancelot. 9-11

SERRAILLIER, IAN. *Beowulf, the Warrior,* ill. by Severin. Walck, 1961. 12 up

______. *The Challenge of the Green Knight,* ill. by Victor Ambrus. Walck, 1967. 12-14

Song of Robin Hood, ed. by Anne Malcolmson, music arr. by Grace Castagnetta, ill. by Virginia Lee Burton. Houghton, 1947. Eighteen ballads illustrated with distinguished black-and-white drawings. Traditional music for many of the ballads is included. The book is the result of careful research in art and music as well as in selection of the ballads. 10-14

SUTCLIFF, ROSEMARY. *Beowulf,* ill. by Charles Keeping. Dutton, 1962. 11 up

______. *Tristan and Iseult.* Dutton, 1971. A tender retelling of a great love story. 11-14

TREASE, GEOFFREY. *Bows Against the Barons,* ill. by C. Walter Hodges. Hawthorne, 1967. 10-12

Other National Epics

ALMEDINGEN, E. M. *The Knights of the Golden Table,* ill. by Charles Keeping. Lippincott, 1964. 12-15

______. *The Story of Gudrun;* based on the third part of the Epic of Gudrun, ill. by Enrico Arno. Norton, 1967. A German tale retold with a dignity appropriate to the romantic sweep of a medieval epic. 12-15

BERTOL, ROLAND. *Sundiata: The Epic of the Lion King,* ill. by Gregorio Prestopino. T. Crowell, 1970. 9-12

BOSLEY, KENNETH, reteller. *The Devil's Horse: Tales from the Kalevala.* Pantheon, 1971. Robust, colloquial retelling of the Finnish heroic ballads. 10 up

BROWN, MARCIA. *Backbone of the King,* ill. by author. Scribner's, 1966. 10-12

BRYSON, BERNARDA. *Gilgamesh,* ill. by author. Holt, 1967. 11-14

CARLSON, DALE. *Warlord of the Gengi,* ill. by John Gretzer. Atheneum, 1970. 11-14

DAVIS, RUSSELL, and BRENT K. ASHABRANNER. *Ten Thousand Desert Swords; The Epic Story of a Great Bedouin Tribe,* ill. by Leonard Everett Fisher. Little, 1960. The Bani Hilal were a great and ancient warrior tribe, and their legends are superbly retold for the discriminating reader. 12 up

DEUTSCH, BABETTE. *Heroes of the Kalevala,* ill. by Fritz Eichenberg. Messner, 1940. This version has not only literary distinction but continuity. Text and illustrations bring out the lusty humor of the tales. 10-14

EVSLIN, BERNARD. *The Green Hero; Early Adventures of Finn McCool,* ill. by Barbara Bascove. Four Winds. 1975. A sophisticated, witty retelling in a sequential narrative. 11-14

FEAGLES, ANITA. *He Who Saw Everything; the Epic of Gilgamesh.* Scott/Addison, 1966. 9-11

GAER, JOSEPH. *The Adventures of Rama,* ill. by Randy Monk. Little, 1954. One of the best-loved epics of India is the story of Prince Rama and of his wife Sita, stolen from him by a demon king. The careful selection of incidents makes this an absorbing and unified tale. 12-14

GOLDSTON, ROBERT. *The Legend of the Cid,* ill. by Stephane. Bobbs, 1963. A simple version of the adventures of the Spanish hero. 10-13

HAZELTINE, ALICE, ed. *Hero Tales from Many Lands,* ill. by Gordon Laite. Abingdon, 1961. 11-15

HODGES, ELIZABETH JAMISON. *A Song for Gilgamesh,* ill. by David Omar White. Atheneum, 1971. The story of a young potter of Sumer is woven around the journey of Gilgamesh to the Land of the Living. 11-13

HODGES, MARGARET. *Myths of the Celts,* ill. by Eros Keith. Farrar, 1973. Short tales, well told. 9-11

PICARD, BARBARA LEONIE. *Tales of Ancient Persia.* Walck, 1973. Based on a portion of the epic poem *Shah-Nama,* a retelling in flowing narrative style. 12-14

SEEGER, ELIZABETH. *The Five Sons of King Pandu,* ill. by Gordon Laite. Scott/Addison, 1969. 12 up

______. *The Ramayana,* ill. by Gordon Laite. Scott/Addison, 1969. 12 up

SEREDY, KATE. *The White Stag,* ill. by author. Viking, 1937. Based on the legend of the founding of Hungary, a tale of the hero Bendeguz and his son Attila. Newbery Medal. 10-14

The Song of Roland, tr. by Merriam Sherwood, ill. by Edith Emerson. McKay, 1938. This is one of the finest translations of the story of Roland for younger readers, and is illustrated with distinctive line drawings. 12-16

SUTCLIFF, ROSEMARY. *The High Deeds of Finn MacCool,* ill. by Michael Charlton. Dutton, 1967. 11-14

______. *The Hound of Ulster,* ill. by Victor Ambrus. Dutton, 1964. 11-14

UDEN, GRANT, ad. *Hero Tales from the Age of Chivalry; Retold from the Froissart Chronicles,* ill. by Doreen Roberts. World, 1969. Twelve tales by the great poet-historian of the fourteenth century. Historically interesting, romantic in approach. 11-13

WESTWOOD, JENNIFER. *Gilgamesh and Other Babylonian Tales.* Coward, 1970. 12 up

YOUNG, ELLA. *The Tangle-Coated Horse and Other Tales: Episodes from the Fionn Saga,* ill. by Vera Bock. McKay, 1968. 12-14

Modern Fantasy

Chapter 8

The younger child who has explored *Mother Goose* and the simpler folk tales and the older child who has gone beyond these to myths and epics are both ready for wider reading experiences. While folk literature is full of the truths that generations have deemed worthy of remembering and passing on to their children, and modern realistic fiction presents the facts of present-day life, fantasy is the art form that many modern writers have chosen to present another kind of truth, to lay out for children the realities of life—not in a physical or social sense, but in a psychological sense.

One of the things that a child may learn about life is that, although in the physical realm manipulated by human beings nothing is certain but change, in the world of the human mind the old verities do not change. People are still concerned about good and evil, and seek to tip the balance toward good. People still seek to live in harmony with nature, as far as possible, as evidenced by their concern for animals and in their appreciation of forests, fields, streams. People seek in the mundane, everyday world some touch of magic, and they look curiously toward the future as it may be on earth or among the stars.

The folk tale often was a realistic story of daily events, but just as often a magical element was injected by means of supernatural beings such as fairies, elves, magicians, ogres, or dragons, or supernatural objects: a pot that skipped, a ship that flew. Folk tales with these magical elements were at times characterized as fairy tales, and we have continued to use this term for tales by modern writers which echo the folk-tale pattern.

Although the distinction between the old folk tale and the modern literary fairy tale is useful to adults, it is of no importance to children. Magic is magic to them whether they find it in Grimm, Andersen, or Dr. Seuss. Children do not think of their stories in the conventional categories of literature or of libraries but describe their favorites broadly as animal stories or funny stories or true stories or fairy tales, by which they mean any tale of magic, old or modern. Eleanor Cameron, in *The Green and Burning Tree,* says,

> *If we do not quibble over fineness of categories, we then avoid the danger of becoming one of that company of scholars (some of the folklorists among them) who seem to care less about experiencing the truth and beauty of a tale than in being "correct" in putting it into this compartment or that.*[1]

The characteristics of the folk and fairy tales that make them particularly appealing to children are the same ones which make fantasy attractive. In fact, interesting story patterns, distinctive style, and memorable characterizations are essential to any good story for children. The special quality of fantasy is that it concerns things that cannot really happen or

[1]Eleanor Cameron, *The Green and Burning Tree* (Atlantic-Little, Brown, 1969). p. 12.

that it is about people or creatures who do not exist, yet within the framework of each story there is a self-contained logic, a wholeness of conception that has its own reality. If it does not, it fails. Some modern fantasies err because they are over-whimsical or unduly sophisticated or, worse still, because they talk down to children. As we select from the new fantasy being published each year, let's keep in mind (along with good story patterns, style, and characterizations) sincerity, directness, and imagination as essential characteristics.

From the single, short fairy tale modeled after the folk tale by such early writers as Perrault, writers of fantasy moved into the longer book-length tale, where they had more room to present the ambiguities and problems of humanity trying to live up to its best sense of self. J. R. R. Tolkien, Lloyd Alexander, Susan Cooper, Ursula Le Guin, and C. S. Lewis all found that more than one volume was needed to explore the implications of the basic struggle between good and evil. All but one of these, Susan Cooper, found it necessary to create different worlds for their characters.

Besides the use of other-worldly settings and supernatural beings, human or animal, writers of fantasy may manipulate time, create talking animals and toys, give life to inanimate objects, and endow children with extraordinary abilities. A writer of fantasy may combine many of these elements in a tale, as C. S. Lewis does in his Narnia series. We find that events which take many days in Narnia have taken no time in the children's usual world. Lewis also uses talking animals—the lion, Aslan; Reepicheep, the mouse—and the children's bravery and ability to reason lead to the rescue of several enchanted or imprisoned Narnians. Sometimes writers use only one element which is fantastic and tell an otherwise perfectly realistic story, as L. M. Boston does in *The Children of Green Knowe*. Here the happenings are realistic, except that Tolly sees and plays with children who lived three hundred years before him.

While any work of imagination may be serious or humorous according to the intent of the author, playfulness and humor seem to have a particular place in fantasy. The exaggeration which is often found in this type of writing can be a rich source of humor, and children can also find humor in stories with one or two fantastic elements which contrast satisfyingly with ordinary, everyday events. In her *Miss Osborne-the-Mop*, Wilson Gage presents children with the possibilities of housework done by a mop-come-alive. It's fun to see how a talking mouse might have influenced Ben Franklin, in *Ben and Me* by Robert Lawson.

Whatever the imaginative work the writer of fantasy produces, and whatever elements of magic and the supernatural enter into it, the whole must be acceptable to us as readers, must have consistency and logic, so that we say to ourselves, "I never thought of it that way. But why not?"

The development of modern fantasy has been so astonishing and varied that it merits detailed examination. Because there are so many of these tales, this chapter can consider only a few—stories which have remained favorites over the years, recent ones which have attained great popularity, and certain ones which illustrate trends.

Viewpoints

I feel that if you are going to use fantasy, that is if you are going to write in this peculiar way, then you must relate this to the known facts, that is to the material world. It goes back to my original point that mythology is not an escape, it is not an entertainment. It is an attempt to come to terms with reality. . . . it is a clarification.

. . . anybody could write a story about a moonlit hillside near Tintagel with some nice romantic ruins and have a unicorn careering across the landscape and that would be lovely. It would also be a pastiche of everything that has ever been written about unicorns since about 1400 and would not add anything to anybody's experience and therefore, to my mind, would not be worth writing.—Alan Garner, "Coming to Terms," *Children's Literature in Education*, July 1970 (#2) p. 17.

Early Writers —Lasting Influences

Many early writers of fantasy began by using their imaginations to embellish folk and fairy tales. Indeed, in the seventeenth century at the time of Louis XIV, much of the French court was engaged in this pastime. The cult continued for some fifty years and produced the memorable fairy tales of Perrault, Comtesse d'Aulnoy, and Madame Le Prince de Beaumont. Perrault produced a small volume of eight stories, including "The Sleeping Beauty," "Little Red Riding Hood," "Cinderella," and "Puss-in-Boots." These tales are adorned with fairy godmothers, fabulous footwear, and talking beasts. Both "The White Cat" by d'Aulnoy and "Beauty and the Beast" by Le Prince de Beaumont feature a human-turned-animal whose bewitchment is broken by the love and constancy of a human.

Hans Christian Andersen's first stories for children were likewise elaborations of familiar folk and fairy tales, but he soon began to allow his imagination full rein in the invention of plot, the shaping of character, and the illumination of the human condition. These later creations, solely from Andersen's fertile imagination, are called literary fairy tales, to distinguish them from the fairy tales of unknown origin, those created by common folk. Andersen's work served as inspiration for other writers.

Reprinted by permission of the Wm. Collins & World Publishing Co., Inc., from The King of the Golden River *by John Ruskin, illustrations by Fritz Kredel. (Original in color)*

John Ruskin, influential British literary critic, wrote "The King of the Golden River" (1841), in which the younger, kinder brother wins the inheritance. Howard Pyle, American illustrator par excellence of Robin Hood and King Arthur, wrote and illustrated his own fairy tales at the end of the last century. Oscar Wilde's allegories "The Happy Prince" and "The Selfish Giant" were sophisticated morality tales. Wilde's literary fairy tales, while having supernatural beings as characters, were concerned with good and evil rather than with magic for its own sake. The point of the tale was the human, not the marvelous, element.

The early writers of fantasy—Perrault, Ruskin, Pyle, Wilde, and especially Andersen—had a lasting influence on the form. They were all authors of highly regarded literature for adults; they had proven their ability to write well, and, in Pyle's case, to illustrate successfully. These men were not unknowns, seeking to carve out a career, but well-known writers, adding a new area to an already established reputation. Except for Oscar Wilde, most of what these writers produced for adults is not read so often today as their works for children. They set high standards for those who followed.

Hans Christian Andersen

Hans Christian Andersen (1805-1875) was born in Odense, Denmark, of a peasant family. His cobbler father owned a few books which his son also cherished, while his uneducated mother worked hard to support her unusual, artistic son in the years between his father's death and Andersen's move to Copenhagen at age fourteen.

Andersen had no doubt that his talents would make him famous, and had no hesitation in presenting his work to play producers, singers, and ballet masters. He became a pupil in the Royal Theatre's schools of dancing and singing and then, following the recommendation of the theater board, he went back to grammar school for five years to get the education he lacked. He was unhappy as a gram-

Illustration by Erik Blegvad. Reproduced from Hans Christian Andersen's The Swineherd, *© 1958 by Erik Blegvad, by permission of Harcourt Brace Jovanovich, Inc. (Original in color)*

mar-school student, much older than his fellows, physically ill-proportioned, forbidden by his friends to spend his time writing rather than learning, tongue-lashed by the harsh schoolmaster with whom he lived as well as worked.

Andersen's first book, a travel diary of a walking trip, appeared in 1829, published by himself. From that time on, Andersen's life pattern was set: alternately traveling and living in a few rooms or with friends in Denmark, writing continuously—a diary, letters to friends, novels, and tales. His first volume of *Fairy Tales, Told for Children* appeared in 1835, and included "The Tinderbox," "Little Claus and Big Claus," "The Princess and the Pea," and "Little Ida's Flowers." Andersen, although he longed for a home of his own, never married. He was attracted to several women, including the singer Jenny Lind, but his proposals were not accepted. His many friends tried to assuage his loneliness, but in spite of his success Andersen remained unsure of himself in social relationships. He was no supporter of organized religion, but he did have an abiding faith in God, often expressed in his tales. Andersen poured himself into his writing; it became the vehicle for expressing his emotions, flashes of humor, commentaries on life, and the follies of humankind. Some of his stories are retellings of folk tales: "Little Claus and Big Claus," "The Princess and the Pea," "The Emperor's New Clothes," "The Wild Swans," "The Swineherd," "Clod Hans," and "What Father Does Is Always Right." In these, Andersen took the traditional story and added to it his own interpretation of character, providing motivation for the action in the tale. The heroes and heroines are not stereotypes; they live and breathe and become individuals, named or not. The princess who can feel a pea under twenty mattresses can never be confused in our thinking with any other princess, sensitive though she may be. And no emperor save Andersen's would walk in a procession wearing invisible clothing. Andersen imparted such life to these characters that we feel empathy for the emperor and his courtiers, none of whom naturally wish to admit they are stupid or unfit for office.

But it is in Andersen's own creations, his literary fairy tales, that his genius for characterization is shown. As we read "The Little Mermaid," we shudder at the pain the mermaid must feel as she puts foot to ground, and yet, so persuasive is Andersen's art that, in spite of the physical agony, we still agree with her that the prince is worth dying for.

"The Ugly Duckling" is, rightly or wrongly, seen as symbolic of Andersen's own life. The animosity of the neighbors to the "different" one seems so natural that we wonder if we

Viewpoints

. . . deeper meaning is essential in fantasy. For the characters involved, there is no need for very deep thought. They can enjoy the pleasure of realizing their dearest wishes, only occasionally speculating about their origin. Sometimes (as in E. Nesbit's stories) they can be changed a little, can learn a little from their adventures, as they miraculously travel the world, change their shape, or exploit the power of a button, a lamp-post or a pencil. But the reader who vicariously enjoys these delights should expect something more. The fantasy should exercise his imagination. For the characters in the story there is little time for Why and How. Questions are blown away as they rush from one adventure to another. But the reader can and should ask How and Why. He should be left with a sense of expansion, as if he himself had been flying on a magic carpet and breathing an air more rarefied than his accustomed oxygen. . . . – Margery Fisher, *Intent Upon Reading,* Watts, 1961, pp. 149–150.

ourselves would have seen the promise implicit in the awkward creature. The conversations in the poultry-yard ring true both to human nature and the human ear. What mother would not say, "He is my own child and, when you look closely at him, he's quite handsome . . ."? Because of Andersen, every "ugly duckling" promises a swan.

Andersen's ability to draw character does not rest on extensive description. In a few carefully chosen words he establishes important qualities, leaving our imaginations so stimulated that we supply the rest of the picture. Of the hero of "The Steadfast Tin Soldier" Andersen says, ". . . he stood as firm and steadfast on his one leg as the others did on their two."[2] Later, when the soldier has been attracted to the paper ballerina, Andersen says, "She stood as steadfast on the toes of her one leg as the soldier did on his. His eyes never left her, not even for a moment did he blink or turn away." After the soldier's adventures, the hero finds himself momentarily safe back in the playroom, only to be tossed into the stove. But here again Andersen tells us: "He looked at the ballerina, and she looked at him. He could feel that he was melting; but he held on as steadfastly as ever to his gun and kept his gaze on the little ballerina in front of the castle." The only description that Andersen has given us of the soldier is that he has a red and blue uniform, and a rifle. The outward description is not important; what Andersen is emphasizing is the constancy of this character.

Along with his ability to write with the directness of colloquial speech, Andersen was a master of bringing to light the incongruity which underlies humor. In describing the feast to be set before the guests in "The Hill of the Elves," he tells of salads made of toadstool seeds, garnished with moist snouts of mice and dressed with hemlock juice, and pronounces it a "festive – though a bit conservative – menu."

Andersen's fantasies do not lack supernatural beings or things, and many of them have other-worldly settings, talking animals, and personifications of inanimate objects. But his main contribution was to make us look more sharply at daily life through the window of his imagination.

[2]Hans Christian Andersen. "The Steadfast Tin Soldier" from *The Complete Fairy Tales and Stories* translated by Erik Christian Haugaard. Copyright © 1974 by Erik Christian Haugaard. Reprinted by permission of Doubleday & Company, Inc.

Tales with Folk-Tale Elements

Writers of fantasy since the time of Andersen and the French court writers before him have used folk-tale elements in their creations. Especially in the realm of the picture book, their works are often considered so authentic as to be classified as folk tales themselves. One such is *Millions of Cats* (1928) by Wanda Gág. The old man and the woman in the tale who want a cat find themselves forced to choose among "hundreds of cats, thousands of cats, millions and billions and trillions of cats." Told with the simplest of language, the barest of characterization, but with a consummate style which has omitted all but the essential words, illustrated with Gág's own flowing, childlike black-and-white drawings, this story truly seems to be a long-forgotten folk tale, the only fantasy being the number of cats and the method of reducing them to one.

They came to a pond.
"Mew, mew! We are thirsty!" cried the
Hundreds of cats,
Thousands of cats,
Millions and billions and trillions of cats.

Illustration from Wanda Gág's Millions of Cats. *Copyright 1928 by Coward-McCann, Inc. Copyright renewed 1956 by Wanda Gág. Reproduced with permission of the publisher.*

The Five Chinese Brothers (1938), written by Claire Huchet Bishop and illustrated by Kurt Wiese, falls into the same category. The story of each identical brother coming home to say goodbye to his mother before his execution and being replaced by a brother talented enough to escape the new form of death, with the final escape of the brothers from execution, mirrors the old belief that if you're clever enough to keep from being killed, you're good enough to live. The use of wit to escape evil is a familiar plot in folk tales. Here again the economy of words and the use of only essential line in the illustrations suggest the folk tale.

James Thurber

The Great Quillow
Many Moons

The humor James Thurber showed as a cartoonist and as the author of delightfully satiric fables is evident in his fairy tales for children. *The Great Quillow* (1944) is about a toymaker who is the only person in his village clever enough to think of a way to rid the town of a voracious giant who is depleting the communal larder. Quillow's attendance at meetings of the town council enables Thurber to poke sly fun at the prim requirements of parliamentary procedure.

In *Many Moons* (1943), for which Louis Slobodkin's illustrations won the Caldecott Medal, the Little Princess Lenore lies ill, saying that only if she can have the moon will she recover. The King consults his assorted wise men, who are equally long-winded, opinionated, and useless. Only the jester has the wisdom to consult the Princess, who makes it clear that to her the moon is golden and small, since she can obscure it by holding up her thumb. She is delighted with the small golden globe the jester brings.

Thurber's light, seemingly effortless tales with their subtle wit have a surface simplicity that many children can enjoy, while those of wider experience can appreciate his perceptive delineation of human nature. Thurber's stories are certainly in Andersen's fairy-tale tradition.

J. R. R. Tolkien

The Hobbit

No other fantasy of our time has appealed to as broad an age range of readers as has *The Hobbit* (1937); children are enthralled by it, and adults probe and discuss the inner meanings of the book and of its companion tale, *The Lord of the Rings*, a complex three-volume sequel. Professor Tolkien was an eminent philologist and an authority on myth and saga, and his knowledge provided so firm a base for the mood and style of his writing that there is no need for scholarly demonstration. Middle-earth *is*. Tolkien wrote of it as easily as one writes about one's own home, and the familiarity of approach lends credence to the world he created.

The hero of *The Hobbit* is Bilbo Baggins, a little creature who is neat and quiet, who loves his material comforts, and who has no desire to do great deeds. When he is tricked into going along on a quest, however, the little hobbit rises to the occasion to show that the common person (or hobbit) is capable of heroism.

There are several qualities that contribute to the stature of *The Hobbit*. The adventures are exciting, the characters are differentiated and distinctive, and the book bubbles with humor. One of the amusing qualities is the aptness of the invented personal and place names. Bilbo's mother's unmarried name was Bella-

Illustration from The Hobbit *by J. R. R. Tolkien. Copyright © 1966 by J. R. R. Tolkien. Reprinted by permission of the publisher Houghton Mifflin Company, Boston.*

donna Took, perfectly in accord with her reputation as a hobbit who had had a few adventures before she settled down as Mrs. Baggins. And what an admirable name for a dragon—Smaug, and what an equally appropriate name for his lair—the Desolation of Smaug. Perhaps a special appeal lies in the very fact that Bilbo Baggins is a quiet little creature, and that his achievements are due to a stout heart, tenacity, and loyalty to his friends rather than to great strength or brilliance. He puts heroism within the grasp of each reader. Many folk-tale elements are present—the human-beast, elves, the enchanted artifact—all woven naturally into the tale.

C. S. Lewis

The *Narnia* Stories

Well known as a theologian, poet, and author, C. S. Lewis created for children the strange new world of Narnia, which they first enter through an old wardrobe. *The Lion, the Witch, and the Wardrobe* (1950), about the adventures of four children, is the first of a series of seven books. Narnia is no Utopia. In fact, once the children have become kings and queens of Narnia, they find themselves engaged in the endless conflict between good and evil, symbolized by the benignant Lion Aslan and the malicious Witch. After reigning for many years, the children return to their own world only to find that they have not even been missed, the time scheme in Narnia having differed so from their own.

Prince Caspian carries the children back to Narnia for further adventures. *The Magician's Nephew* goes back to the creation of Narnia by the Lion. When the Lion sings into existence the world, the stars, the land, and then the creatures, the sheer goodness of creation is too much for the Witch. She flees, but the reader knows she will return. *The Last Battle* concludes the series. As the title implies, the loyal followers of the king of Narnia are making their last stand against the forces of evil which seek to destroy the noble Lion Aslan and the world he has created.

Another theologian, Chad Walsh, considers Lewis's *The Last Battle* probably the best of the series, full of Christian symbolism, and a "deeply moving and hauntingly lovely story apart from its doctrinal content." Lewis's stories are so clearly based on Christian theology and the Bible that we sometimes do not recognize the folkloric elements in the tales—the sacrifice of a king for the good of his people, the talking animals and trees, the healing apple.

While Lewis's style verges on the avuncular at times, it is perfectly suited to these Chronicles, where the children are definitely children and not expected to display qualities more appropriate for adults. The children are, on the whole, honest, steadfast, persevering, and able to resist temptation; the larger tasks are always accomplished with the aid of an adult, or a supernatural helper. It is taken for granted that the children do not have to *prove* their inherent goodness; rather there is sorrow that at times one or another of them may fall short of the best of which a child is known to be capable.

Lloyd Alexander

The *Prydain* Books
The Marvelous Misadventures of Sebastian

Lloyd Alexander had planned, in writing about Prydain, only to adapt the Welsh legends he loved, but he became so engrossed in the project that, as he said in his Newbery Medal acceptance speech, "it grew into something much more ambitious."

The first of the Prydain five-book cycle is *The Book of Three* (1964), in which Taran, the hero, is introduced. Taran, Assistant Pig-Keeper, does not have great status, but of course few pig-keepers are responsible for such a pig as Hen Wen, who utters prophecies by using letter sticks. When Taran goes forth with the great warrior Gwydion to fight against the evil Horned King, they must first find the lost Hen Wen to learn from her of the king. The Horned King has sworn allegiance to Arawn, Lord of the Land of Death. On the quest, Taran and Gwydion are joined by the capricious Princess Eilonwy, the Caliban-like creature Gurgi, and the boastful harpist, Fflewddur Fflam.

Each of the characters is strongly drawn. Unforgettable is the crafty, toadying, whimpering but loyal Gurgi, whose rhymed speech delights readers. The histrionics of Fflewddur have a touch of Mr. Micawber as he pontificates and prevaricates, but his harp, given him by Taliesin, is a rein on his fancy, for whenever he lies, a string breaks.

In the second book, *The Black Cauldron,* Taran again goes on a quest, this time to the Land of Death, where Arawn creates his Cauldron-Born creatures who live on after death. In *The Castle of Llyr*, the Princess Eillonwy is kidnaped, and it is then that Taran first realizes his love for that saucy girl. In *Taran Wanderer* the hero goes forth to seek his true identity and learns that his worth, whatever it is, is dependent on his ability and his accomplishments rather than on his position. The final book in the Prydain cycle, *The High King* (1968), was awarded the Newbery Medal. It tells of the last conflict between Taran and the Death Lord.

Alexander's fantasy is based firmly upon legend, with a multitude of natural and supernatural characters, and some halfway between. Indeed, we learn at the end that all of the major characters except Taran himself are from the Summer Land, where they live forever. Alexander creates distinctive characters, and he is a true master of the light, sophisticated style, preferring discussion to action, although there are great goings and comings in these books. There is much humor as well, but it is the wry shrug of the adult and not the slapstick antic of the child.

Alexander uses many elements of folk literature in his tales—the magic bauble or light that Eilonwy carries, the ability of the pig to prophesy, the magic cauldron and sword, the inexhaustible knapsack of food.

Throughout the books runs the muted theme of the hero, the champion of good against the forces of evil—not just the external manifestations of it, but the evil within oneself—the hero who emerges triumphant at the end.

Another intricate tale by Alexander, *The Marvelous Misadventures of Sebastian* (1970), received the National Book Award. A young eighteenth-century musician goes off on a series of romantic adventures. The fantasy is slight here, being a matter of the exaggeration of reality rather than the creation of a new world or supernatural beings. Alexander's later books, *The Wizard in the Tree* (1975) and *The Cat Who Wished to Be a Man* (1973), have one or two magical characters, but portray human nature quite realistically.

Ursula Le Guin

A Wizard of Earthsea
The Tombs of Atuan
The Farthest Shore

Ursula Le Guin, like Tolkien, has created a world of her own, Earthsea. It is a place of wizards and mages, spells and charms. *A Wizard of Earthsea* (1968) introduces us to Ged, or Sparrowhawk, seventh son of a seventh son, and tells of his education as a wizard. At one point in his training, Ged cannot resist the temptation to show off his powers, and lets loose a nameless evil to roam the world. He struggles first to escape it, and finally realizes that he cannot avoid it and must meet it head on. *The Tombs of Atuan* (1971) introduces us to Arha, trained from early childhood to be the high priestess of the Kargad Lands, a part of Earthsea. Ged comes to the sacred precincts, searching for half of a magic amulet. He not only finds it, but frees Arha from her servitude to the dark gods. *The Farthest Shore* (1972) shows us Ged as the Archmage, setting out to discover the reason for the decline in potency of the wizards throughout Earthsea. With him goes Arren, destined to be the king of all the lands of Earthsea.

Le Guin is adept at creation of character, concentrating her efforts on her protagonists, defining minor characters in relationship to them. Ged's nature is built up gradually, through action and reaction, and because we learn to know him in this way, we accept him fully. There are marvels and mysteries aplenty—the ability to raise a favorable wind, to talk to dragons—but these are of minor importance to the tale of Ged as a person. Part of Le Guin's power as a storyteller lies in her style—serious, spare, precise. Not for her the earthy humor of Tolkien or the sophisticated wit of Alexander. The measured cadence of the language seems to be a retelling in a more modern idiom of an old, old tale.

Text copyright © 1972 by Ursula Le Guin
Illustrated by Gail Garraty
From The Farthest Shore
Used by permission of Atheneum Publishers

Susan Cooper

Over Sea, Under Stone
The Dark Is Rising
Greenwitch
The Grey King

A young British writer now resident in the United States has written a series of books about the eternal battle between good and evil. In *Over Sea, Under Stone* (1965) Simon, Jane, and Barnaby go to Cornwall on vacation with their parents and an old, white-haired professor friend of the family, Merriman Lyon. There they discover a chalice, believed to be the Grail, but lose in the sea an ancient map and key to the runes on the Grail.

In *The Dark Is Rising* (1973) we meet Will Stanton, seventh son of a seventh son, and youngest of the Old Ones, an ageless people whose destiny is to fight against evil until the end. In this tale Will learns he is one of them. His education in his heritage is undertaken in part by Merriman Lyon, another of the Old Ones.

Jane is the heroine of *Greenwitch* (1974). The Grail has been stolen, and the children go to Cornwall with Uncle Merry and Will Stanton to recover it. Because Jane has wished for the happiness of the Greenwitch, a time-honored offering fashioned by the women of the village and given to the sea, instead of wishing for herself, Greenwitch gives Jane the map and rune-key from the depths of the ocean. It has lain protected in its lead case since its loss in the first book. The Grail is also recovered.

Will Stanton is the major character in *The Grey King* (1975), a Newbery Medal book. He is sent to Wales to recover from a severe ill-

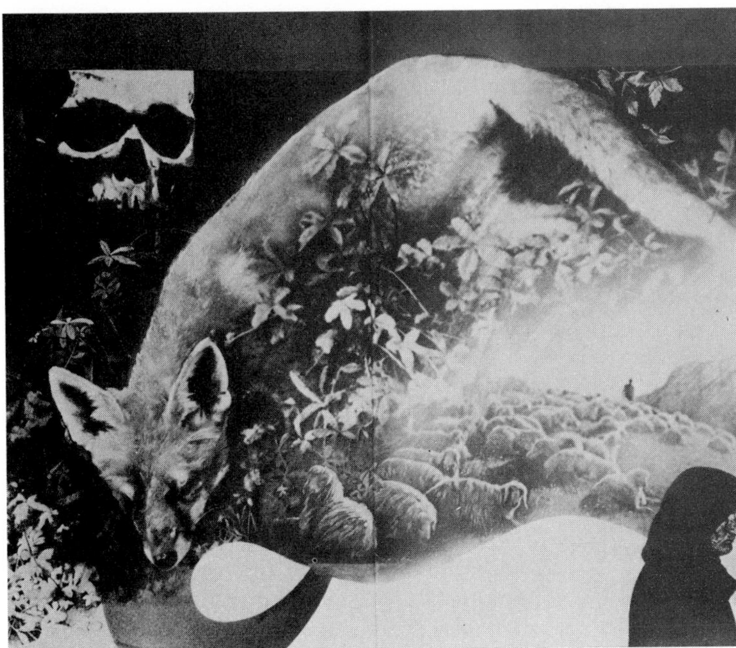

Illustration by Michael Heslop from The Grey King *(A Margaret K. McElderry Book). Copyright © 1975 by Susan Cooper. Used by permission of Atheneum Publishers and Chatto & Windus, Ltd., London.*

ness, and meets King Arthur's son, Bran, sent forward in time as a baby to protect him from the forces of evil. Bran realizes his heritage, and the sleepers, horsemen from Arthur's time, are awakened to ride against evil in the crucial battle.

Cooper has made increasing use of legend and folklore with each book in the series. Since we have accepted these elements in the stories previously, we are willing to immerse ourselves more deeply as the tale progresses. Setting is important in all of these stories, providing an atmosphere in which old tales naturally come true. Characterization is vivid, especially of the three children and Will Stanton, and there is much action, described in rich, meaning-laden language.

Other Tales with Folk-Tale Elements

Alan Garner has drawn heavily on the legends of Cheshire to tell *The Weirdstone of Brisingamen* and its sequel, *The Moon of Gomrath.* Garner's earlier stories are filled with action at the expense of character development, but in *The Owl Service,* which won a Carnegie Medal, we come to know the young people well as they mysteriously reenact a Welsh legend, their actions inhibited and dictated by the English class structure which circumscribes their lives.

William Mayne has written a few stories including folkloric elements, most notably *Earthfasts,* in which two boys are the means by which a soldier comes alive out of the past. In *A Game of Dark,* a boy escapes the pain of not loving his dying father through retreating into the medieval world. Mayne is a skilled writer, but not all of his fantasies carry conviction.

Barbara Leonie Picard's fairy tales have the true cadence and spirit of folk material. Her *The Faun and the Woodcutter's Daughter, The Goldfinch Garden, The Lady of the Linden Tree,* and *The Mermaid and the Simpleton* have many familiar folk-tale themes, but they are freshly conceived, and the stories are written with a grave simplicity that makes them particularly enjoyable when read aloud.

Scottish folklore provides background and atmosphere in Mollie Hunter's *The Kelpie's Pearls, The Walking Stones,* and *A Stranger Came Ashore.* The rhythm of her writing lends credence to these tales of supernatural beings and happenings.

Rosemary Harris, a Carnegie Medal winner for *The Moon in the Cloud,* has used the ancient story of Noah and the flood and built a sophisticated, amusing tale. *The Seal-Singing* is based on the Celtic belief in seals as supernatural beings.

Tales of Pure Imagination

While many writers of fantasy have chosen to use motifs from folklore in their work, others have created magical and unusual characters and happenings which seem unlike anything that has gone before.

Lewis Carroll, Charles Kingsley, and George Macdonald all wrote fantasies in the late nineteenth century. Kingsley's *The Water-Babies* (1863) and Macdonald's *At the Back of the North Wind* (1871) and his Princess and Curdie stories are still enjoyed by a few children, but these tales seem overly long and very moralistic to modern readers. Lewis Carroll's tales, on the other hand, are full of pure nonsense and rare humor.

Lewis Carroll

Alice's Adventures in Wonderland
Through the Looking Glass

The "Alice" books cannot be accounted for on the basis of anything that had preceded them. Charles Lutwidge Dodgson was a sober, sedate cleric who lectured in mathematics at Christ Church, Oxford. Dr. Liddell, a colleague, had three little girls of whom Alice was evidently Dodgson's favorite:

Child of the pure unclouded brow
And dreaming eyes of wonder!

So he described her, in the introductory poem to *Through the Looking Glass.* The charming photographs he has left of her bear out his description. Dodgson used to tell stories to these little girls, teasing them by breaking off in the middle with "And that's all till next time." Whereupon "the cruel Three" would cry, "But it *is* the next time!"

Then came that famous summer afternoon (the fourth of July, by the way) when Dodgson rowed his little friends up the Cherwell River to Goodstow, where they had tea on the riverbank. There the young man told them the fairy tale of "Alice's Adventures Under Ground." Alice hoped there'd be nonsense in it, and no hopes ever materialized more gloriously. The next Christmas, Dodgson wrote his story as a gift for "a dear child in memory of a Summer day."

Three years after the famous picnic, the story appeared in book form, somewhat enlarged, with the new title *Alice's Adventures in Wonderland* and with Sir John Tenniel's matchless illustrations. That was 1865, and six years later the companion volume appeared, both books under the pseudonym Lewis Carroll.

Then a strange thing happened. Charles Lutwidge Dodgson, still very much the obscure mathematician, found Lewis Carroll a famous person—sought after, praised, discussed, even advertised. Gentle, sensitive soul that he was, Dodgson was horrified. He announced firmly that "Mr. Dodgson neither claimed nor acknowledged any connection with the books not published under his name." If the name "Lewis Carroll" was supposed to provide Charles Dodgson with a shield against publicity, it was a dismal failure. Instead it practically obliterated the mathematician. Nothing else he ever wrote enjoyed anything like the success of his two popular companion volumes about Alice.

Does anyone who has read the *Adventures in Wonderland* ever forget those opening paragraphs, with the child's comment on books?

Illustration by Sir John Tenniel. From Alice's Adventures in Wonderland, *by Lewis Carroll.*

Alice was beginning to get very tired of sitting by her sister on the bank, and of having nothing to do: once or twice she had peeped into the book her sister was reading, but it had no pictures or conversations in it, "and what is the use of a book," thought Alice, "without pictures or conversations?"

Then plop! Right into the third short paragraph comes the White Rabbit, with waistcoat and watch. Down he goes into the rabbit hole, murmuring "Oh dear! Oh dear! I shall be too late!" And down the rabbit hole after him goes Alice, "never once considering how in the world she was to get out again." From then on madness takes over.

Alice encounters strange creatures. There is the smiling Cheshire Cat who can vanish leaving only his grin behind. There is the Queen of Hearts who disposes of all who disagree with her with a simple "Off with her head!" and the Red Queen who has to run for dear life in order "to keep in the same place." All these characters talk nonsense in the gravest way. The best example is "A Mad Tea-Party," where the conversation reminds you uncomfortably of some of the disjointed small talk which you have not only heard but perhaps, horrid thought, even contributed to. The characters appear and disappear, behave with a kind of wild logic, and burst into verses which sing in your head in place of the serious poetry you might prefer to recall. Carroll's characters are masterpieces; it's not so much what they do but what they are that we remember—Alice's matter-of-fact acceptance of all events, puzzling out the sense (surely there must be some!) in this world that others have organized; the Red Queen's determination to have the last (and only) word.

The puzzling question is, when do children enjoy *Alice?* Needless to say, it should never be required reading. Some children heartily dislike fantasy and to make them read *Alice* would be to turn reading into a penalty instead of a delight. When college students are asked what books they remember enjoying as children, there is often more disagreement over *Alice* than over any other book. Some disliked it heartily or were bored by it; some say *Alice* was one of their favorite books, not as children but at the high-school age. This is perhaps where it really belongs. Most of those who liked *Alice* as children, ten or under, had heard it read aloud by adults who enjoyed it. Those who had to read the book for themselves rarely found it funny until they were older.

Sir John Tenniel in his illustrations for *Alice* has fixed forever the face, figure, and dress of this beloved little girl. Long, straight hair, a grave, prim face, a neat, perky dress covered with a pinafore, and the straight, slim legs clad in horizontally striped stockings make an appealing figure which no one ever forgets. The Tenniel white rabbit is an equally unforgettable figure with his sporty tweed coat, his massive gold watch and chain, his swagger walking stick—just the kind of fellow who *would* keep the Duchess waiting. The drawings are so alive, so profoundly interpretative, so right, that it's almost impossible to think of these characters except as Tenniel pictured them.

James Barrie

Peter Pan

Of all Sir James Barrie's delightful plays, none has been so popular as *Peter Pan* (1904). Exquisitely performed by Maude Adams at the beginning of the century and by Mary Martin in a musical version in the middle of the century, it has been as popular with adults as with children. The book *Peter and Wendy* was made from the play. Barrie has, like Carroll, created memorable characters: Peter Pan, the boy who will not grow up; Tinker Bell, the guardian fairy; and the three children—Wendy, John, and Michael—who go off with Peter Pan to Never Never Land. Their adventures with pirates, Indians, and a ticking crocodile are exciting, but in the end they return to their parents to begin the serious business of growing up. When at one point Tink's life is in danger (she drinks some poison intended for Peter Pan by the evil Captain Hook), only one thing will save her, and so Peter calls through the dusk to all children, "Do you believe in fairies?" And of course, Barrie has made her real to all of us. *Peter and Wendy* is not the masterpiece that *Alice in Wonderland* is, but the names of some of the characters have become household words.

William Pène du Bois

The Twenty-One Balloons

The fantasies of William Pène du Bois are as orderly and logical as mathematics, and his illustrations have the same graceful balance. He himself credits his passion for order to his regimented school life at Lycée Hoche, for which he is as grateful as he is for glorious weekly excursions to the French circus. These and other lifelong interests are reflected in his books—his love of France, the circus, all forms of mechanized transportation, islands, Utopias, and explosions! Look at some of his most notable books: *Bear Party* is a reasonable fable of some quarrelsome bears who grow genuinely fond of each other when they have a fancy dress party. A bear Utopia results. *The Giant* is a logical story of an eight-year-old giant, already seven stories tall but wistfully amiable. He can disrupt a whole city and send the people into a panic by picking up streetcars or automobiles or people for a better look. It is all drawn to scale as precisely as an architect's plan. In *Lazy Tommy Pumpkinhead* the author takes a healthy poke at the electronic age and what can happen when machines fail.

And best of all there is his Newbery Medal book, *The Twenty-One Balloons* (1947). When its hero, Professor William Waterman Sherman, tires of teaching little boys arithmetic, he sets off in a balloon to see the world and be alone. He tells his story of landing on the island of Krakatoa (a real island, by the way) and finding its inhabitants inventors of the most amazing super-gadgets. These are described in detail and drawn meticulously. Since the island is volcanic, the people have planned a machine for escape should the volcano erupt, and of course it does. And off they go in their airy-go-round. Related with the utmost simplicity, the story piles up suspense until the explosion is a relief.

Du Bois's characters are amiable, but he is more interested in machinery than in personality. He handles the practical details with a deft agility that we can only admire.

Illustration by Beth and Joe Krush. Reproduced from The Borrowers, *copyright, 1952, 1953, by Mary Norton, by permission of Harcourt Brace Jovanovich, Inc.*

Mary Norton

The Borrowers

As British as tea for breakfast, but with action, suspense, and characters of universal appeal, *The Borrowers* (1953) by Mary Norton was immediately popular in the United States as well as in Great Britain.

Borrowers are not fairies but small creatures who live in old houses and take their names from the places they inhabit—the Overmantels, for instance, the Harpsichords, and the Clocks, who live under a huge old grandfather's clock in the hall. Homily, Pod, and their daughter Arrietty Clock are the only surviving family of Borrowers in the old house. When a Borrower is seen, there is nothing for him to do but emigrate. Only Pod, climbing curtains with the aid of his trusty hatpin, borrowing a useful spoon now and then or a bit of tea or a portrait stamp of the Queen, only Pod has escaped detection. Arrietty is the problem now. Arrietty wants to see the world and she goes exploring, happily and trustingly even after the boy sees her. They become fast friends, but even the boy cannot prevent the disastrous ending. It is so catastrophic that young readers could not accept it as final. There had to be a sequel, and so we follow the fortunes of these fascinating characters in *The Borrowers Afield, The Borrowers Afloat,* and *The Borrowers Aloft,* with which the series ends, although Homily reminisces about a past event in *Poor Stainless.*

No briefing of these stories can give any conception of their quality. Every character is unforgettably portrayed. There is poor Homily with her hair forever awry, loving but a chronic worrier, "taking on" first and then going capably to work. Pod is the sober realist, a philosopher and a brave one. Arrietty is youth and adventure, springtime and hope, too much in love with life to be afraid even of those mammoth "human beans." To read these books aloud is to taste the full richness of their humor and good writing.

Lucy M. Boston

The *Green Knowe* books

Another distinguished English fantasy, beautifully written and completely absorbing, is *The Children of Green Knowe* (1955) by Lucy M. Boston. It goes back in time from the present and a boy named Tolly to the seventeenth century and three children of his family who died in the great plague.

A lonely child, Tolly is sent to live with his great-grandmother, Mrs. Oldknow, at the family's ancient manor house, The Green Knowe. He is soon aware of the presence of other children who come and go. He hears them but cannot see them although he knows his grandmother sees them. She shows him the portrait of the three and tells him the story of each child and their great horse Feste, and presently Tolly sees them also, but he can never touch them. Playing with these children from the past involves Tolly in a terrifying situation. He is saved by St. Christopher, and the story ends serenely.

There are more books in this setting— *Treasure of Green Knowe,* in which Tolly and his great-grandmother again appear; *An Enemy at Green Knowe,* in which Tolly meets a practitioner of black magic; and *The River at Green Knowe,* in which a new set of characters appears. *A Stranger at Green Knowe,* one of the most moving boy and animal tales ever written, brings an escaped zoo gorilla to sanctuary at Green Knowe. In all of these stories real life and fantasy are successfully mingled.

Boston's stories are never commonplace. They grow naturally out of the characters of Mrs. Oldknow and Tolly, interacting with the past which is still present in the old house, a subtle juxtaposition of present and historical time.

A. Philippa Pearce

Tom's Midnight Garden

Philippa Pearce won the Carnegie Medal for *Tom's Midnight Garden* (1959), an engrossing fantasy with time as a theme. Young Tom, much bored by life in his aunt and uncle's apartment, hears an ancient clock strike thirteen. Immediately he slips into an enchanting garden where he plays with Hatty, a child from the past. Their play is imaginative but made credible because of the logic of "Time no longer," the motto on the clock. These strange midnight adventures of Tom's are la-

Illustrations by Susan Einzig for Tom's Midnight Garden *by A. Philippa Pearce. Copyright 1958 Oxford University Press. Reproduced by permission of J. B. Lippincott Company.*

ter explained somewhat by what adults might call thought-transference. However, they seem quite clear and uncomplicated to readers once they accept Tom's timeless midnight garden. Pearce's style is serene, unhurried, reflective—giving us time to absorb the experience as Tom lives it.

As in all of these tales of pure imagination, it is character that counts. We think at first that it is the action in the tale that delights us. Then we realize that any adventure would be exciting, providing that it happened to Alice, or Arrietty, or Tolly, or Tom.

Penelope Farmer

Charlotte Sometimes
The Summer Birds
A Castle of Bone

Charlotte Sometimes (1969) also has the time-shift theme that is a familiar one in fantasy, but it has seldom been used more dramatically, perhaps because Charlotte alternates between two worlds. Somehow, while in boarding school, Charlotte finds that she is back in the days of World War I and that her name is Clare. Slowly she begins to realize that Clare is her double and that whenever she is in Clare's world, her own place is taken by her doppelgänger. The mystery and suspense are maintained to the end.

In *Emma in Winter* (1966) Charlotte's sister finds that she shares the same dreams as a boy she dislikes, a boy she and Charlotte met in *The Summer Birds,* the most moving of these books. In *The Summer Birds* (1962), a strange boy teaches the sisters to fly, and then all the children in their school enjoy the soaring bliss and freedom of flight. When the summer ends, they learn the boy's identity and the magic is lost. They are again earthbound. *The Summer Birds* has an almost palpable aura of magic and an ending with all the inevitability of Greek drama.

In *A Castle of Bone* (1972) four children discover that what seems to be an ordinary cupboard reduces anything put into it to an earlier state of being. A pigskin wallet becomes a squealing piglet; a boy becomes a baby. The problem is: how does one restore the diminished object or person?

Viewpoints

In almost any fantasy of time travel, or of the mingling of different times, there inevitably arises the intriguing question of who, rightfully, is a ghost to whom, it being usually a matter of whose time the scene is being played in, though this is not invariably easy to decide—the mood or feeling being often ambiguous or even wittily paradoxical. . . .

. . . traveling back and forth in Time, or on different levels of Time, meeting one's self or others coming and going or existing in various dimensions at once, can all become enormously complicated so that the writer, not to speak of the reader, is continually required to keep his wits about him.

But happenings and devices in themselves, no matter how outré and mind-bending, are not what give lasting nourishment. They do not deeply satisfy and some of us they do not satisfy at all. For what one remembers from the great piece of writing is the voice speaking in a way that is indefinably different from any other voice, the unforgettable personalities, the sense of a profound life that can go on after the story is ended. . . .—Eleanor Cameron, *The Green and Burning Tree,* Little, Brown, Boston, Toronto, 1969, pp. 90, 76–77.

Although Farmer's style is smooth, and her characterizations perceptive, we remember the moods and settings of her stories rather than the people in them. We admire her ingenuity but we don't agonize over her characters' problems as we do over those of the Borrowers. The actual workings of the fantastic elements are a little too obvious.

Maurice Sendak

Where the Wild Things Are
Higglety Pigglety Pop!
In the Night Kitchen
Nutshell Library

Maurice Sendak's versatility and craftsmanship as an artist are discussed in Chapter 5. They are qualities that contribute both to the books he has illustrated for other authors and to those he has written himself. The integrity of his conception and the respect he has for children are nowhere more evident than in his own books of fantasy. Best known of his books is the 1964 Caldecott winner, *Where the Wild Things Are,* a picture book that was greeted with delight by many and apprehension by some. Max is a small boy whose noisy ebullience causes his mother to call him a Wild Thing. "I'll eat you up!" he retorts, and is sent to his room, where he solaces himself by imagining a kingdom of wild things, fanged and clawed, all bowing respectfully to their beloved ruler, Max, king of all the wild things. "Let the wild rumpus start," he proclaims, and a mammoth frolic takes place. When Max leaves, his creatures plead with him to stay because they love him so. But he goes back to his room, to real life, and to his supper waiting for him, "and it was still hot." The psychological implications are sound. Children see the reassurance in Max's return home from his fantasy land when he "wanted to be where someone loved him best of all."

The subtitle of *Higglety Pigglety Pop!* (1967) is *There Must Be More to Life.* Its heroine is Jenny, who has everything a dog could want and leaves home because she is not content. She wants something she does not have, and feels "there must be more to life" than having everything. Jenny was drawn from life, immortalizing a dearly loved household pet in soft and amusing black-and-white pictures that are quite different from the bold exaggeration and flamboyance of the wild things. Jenny eventually becomes the leading lady of the World Mother Goose Theater starring as The Dog (typical Sendak humor) in a production of "Higglety Pigglety Pop!" Written with bland directness that belies the nonsensical situation, the story ends with a poignant note from Jenny to her old master in which she says that she cannot tell him how to get to Castle Yonder, because she doesn't know where it is. "But if you ever come this way, look for me."

Maurice Sendak's childhood memories are the basis for much of the setting for *In the Night Kitchen* (1970). The delicious smells of baking coming from the room below, the buildings, seen against a night sky, and the "Mickey Oven" label (Sendak has an impressive collection of Mickey Mouse objects) all contribute to the story of a small boy who, in his dream, falls down into the night kitchen where three identical bakers (all Oliver Hardy) try to stir him into the batter. Sendak's draftsmanship is particularly impressive in these illustrations, and both the pictures and the story are remarkable in their identification with a child's vision.

The four irresistible books that make up Maurice Sendak's tiny *Nutshell Library* (1962) are illustrated with impish, round-faced boys. The text of the four little books is as original as the pictures. *One Was Johnny* is a counting book, which winds up and down in fine, cumulative style. *Pierre,* subtitled "a cautionary tale," describes the horrible fate of a boy who keeps saying "I don't care." But the ending is droll. *Alligators All Around* is one of the funniest alphabet books yet, and *Chicken Soup with Rice* is hilarious nonsense about the months of the year. These are funny books, original and beguiling, in miniature form.

Other Tales of Pure Imagination

The field of fantasy has attracted a number of excellent writers. In England, Penelope Lively won a Carnegie Medal for *The Ghost of Thomas Kempe,* the tale of a boy who must learn to deal with the demands of a not easily satisfied poltergeist. In *The House at Norham Gardens* the heroine dreams at night of the events of her grandfather's scientific expedition to New Guinea, while in the daytime she copes with school and life with two elderly aunts on a diminished income.

Jane Langton has taken the Concord, New Hampshire, terrain as her own, sages and all, and has constructed ingenious adventures for Eddy and Eleanor in *The Diamond in the Window, The Swing in the Summerhouse,* and *The Astonishing Stereoscope.* The window, the swing, and the stereoscope project the children into magical times and places.

Antoine de Saint-Exupéry's *The Little Prince* is a poetic, practically plotless fairy tale, whimsical and sophisticated in its concern with the inconsistencies of human behavior. The prince, who comes to earth from another planet, tells much of the story in dialogue form. The lack of action and the allusiveness of the dialogue limit the book's appeal to those readers who appreciate style

Reproduced with the permission of Farrar, Straus & Giroux, Inc. from Knee-Knock Rise by Natalie Babbitt, Copyright © 1970 by Natalie Babbitt.

and theme above all else.

The Animal Family by Randall Jarrell also has a poetic quality but is more cohesive in plot and is more smoothly written than *The Little Prince.* Alone in his home near the sea, a hunter falls in love with a mermaid, who comes to live with him. Their family is increased by a shipwrecked boy, a bear, and a lynx, and together they live in love and peace. The writing has a subtle simplicity and ingenuous humor that succeed both in making the element of fantasy believable and in avoiding any semblance of sentimentality.

Natalie Babbitt's *Knee-Knock Rise,* in which a whole village is terrified by the terrible Megrimum (that doesn't exist), and her more poetic *The Search for Delicious* are both lightened by humor. *The Devil's Storybook* contains ten original tales in which the devil generally is worsted. *Tuck Everlasting* poses the interesting question: would one want to live forever? Babbitt's ingenious plots are amusingly farfetched. She delights in word play as much as does Carl Sandburg in his *Rootabaga Stories,* with their garrulous humor.

In Elizabeth Coatsworth's *Cricket and the Emperor's Son,* Cricket, a small apprentice, tells a tale each night to the little Prince who cannot sleep, the stories coming from a magic paper that never comes to an end. Coatsworth's Newbery Medal book, *The Cat Who Went to Heaven,* which also has a Japanese setting, is about a struggling young artist who is commissioned to paint a picture for the temple. The temple priest refuses to accept the picture because it shows a cat in the procession of animals approaching Buddha. The little household cat that had been a model for the picture dies, and a miracle occurs; the painted cat now appears at the head of the procession, under the hand of Buddha, which is stretched out in blessing. Coatsworth's tales are well written, whatever the genre.

Modern Stories of Talking Beasts

The talking beasts in the folk tales were, on the whole, a cheerful lot. Silly creatures were liquidated, but the wise pig survived, and smart billy goats gained the grassy hillside in spite of the troll. There was no brooding and no melancholy until Andersen's *Fairy Tales,* whose Ugly Duckling not only was mistreated by others but suffered spiritually. In the two English talking-beast masterpieces, *The Tale of Peter Rabbit* and *The Wind in the Willows,* there are animals with limitations who make mistakes and commit follies which they shake off with blithe determination. It is the tone and pattern of these lively tales rather than "The Ugly Duckling" which are dominant in animal fantasy. In many of these stories the only fantasy is the animal as near-human, living in human-type surroundings. The humor of these tales generally has the slapstick element that children enjoy.

Beatrix Potter

The Tale of Peter Rabbit

Beatrix Potter, English novelist of the nursery and cheerful interpreter of small animals to small children, has left her own account of how she happened to write her classic, *The Tale of Peter Rabbit*. In a letter to *The Horn Book*, May 1929, she said:

. . . About 1893 I was interested in a little invalid child. . . . I used to write letters with pen and ink scribbles, and one of the letters was Peter Rabbit.

Noel has got them yet; he grew up and became a hard-working clergyman in a London poor parish. After a time there began to be a vogue for small books, and I thought "Peter" might do as well as some that were being published. But I did not find any publisher who agreed with me. The manuscript—nearly word for word the same, but with only outline illustrations—was returned with or without thanks by at least six firms. Then I drew my savings out of the post office savings bank, and got an edition of 450 copies printed. I think the engraving and printing cost me about £11. It caused a good deal of amusement amongst my relations and friends. I made about £12 or £14 by selling copies to obliging aunts. I showed this privately printed black and white book to Messers. F. Warne & Co., and the following year, 1901, they brought out the first coloured edition.

Commenting on her method of writing the author adds:

My usual way of writing is to scribble, and cut out, and write it again and again. The shorter and plainer the better. And read the Bible (unrevised version and Old Testament) if I feel my style wants chastening.[3]

Children quickly learn by heart these apparently simple little stories[4] of Beatrix Potter's, and how they relish the names of her characters: Flopsy, Mopsy, and Cottontail, Jemima Puddle-Duck, Pigling Bland, Mrs. Tiggy-Winkle, Benjamin Bunny, Peter Rabbit. The stories are plotted carefully, with plenty of suspense to bring sighs of relief when the conclusion is finally reached. Children chuckle over the funny characters, the absurd predicaments, and the narrow escapes. They pore over the clear watercolor illustrations, which are full of action, and absorb delightedly the lovely details of landscapes, old houses, fine old furniture and china.

Children can soon "read" Peter's adventures for themselves, they know them so well; but the charms of that humorous and exciting plot never grow stale—disobedient Peter in Mr. MacGregor's cabbage patch, very complacent at first, then pursued and thoroughly frightened but still keeping his wits about him; next, Peter at home, properly repentant, chastened by his mother, but snug in bed at last and secure. Here is a cheerful Prodigal Son, child-size.

Rudyard Kipling

Just So Stories

Living in India for many years and thus familiar with the Indian Jatakas and the usual pattern of a "why" story, Rudyard Kipling wrote the *Just So Stories* (1902), his own collection of explanatory tales, in amusing imitation of the old form. "How the Whale Got His Throat" and "How the Leopard Got His Spots" begin seriously and end with a logical kind of nonsense that reminds us of *Alice*.

The children's favorite is "The Elephant's Child." This story explains how the elephant's "blackish, bulgy nose, as big as a boot" grew to the long trunk we see today. It was all because of the "'satiable curtiosity" of the Elephant's Child who, after innumerable spankings, ran away to seek knowledge by the banks of "the great grey-green, greasy Limpopo River."

These are stories to be read aloud. They are cadenced, rhythmic, and full of handsome, high-sounding words which are both mouth-filling and ear-delighting. Children soon catch on to the grandiloquent style and absurd meanings. The mock-serious tone of these pseudo-folk tales adds to their humor.

In contrast to the *Just So Stories*, Kipling's *Jungle Books* (1894) stand the test of time due in part to his scrupulous avoidance of the temptation to humanize the animals. They may talk but they remain true to their natures. Children get from these stories about the boy Mowgli and the animals who raise him an insight into that wild-animal nature, into the

[3]Beatrix Potter. From a letter to *The Horn Book Magazine*, May 1929. Copyright 1929 by The Horn Book, Inc.
[4]Among the companion volumes to Peter Rabbit are *The Tale of Benjamin Bunny, The Tailor of Gloucester, The Tale of Squirrel Nutkin, The Tale of Jemima Puddle-Duck, The Tale of Mrs. Tiggy-Winkle,* and *The Tale of Tom Kitten*.

curious likeness of animals and humans, and into the still more curious lines of demarcation.

Kenneth Grahame

The Wind in the Willows

Kenneth Grahame was a lovable, literary, out-of-doorish sort of Englishman with a gift for storytelling. For his small son, nicknamed "Mouse," he used to spin continuous tales at bedtime. Once Mouse refused to go to the seaside because his trip would interrupt the adventures of Toad, to which he was listening. In order to persuade the child to go, his father promised to send him a chapter in the mail daily, and this he did. Sensing their value, the nursery governess who read the chapters to Mouse mailed them back to his mother for safekeeping. From these letters and bedtime stories grew *The Wind in the Willows* (1908).

Each chapter tells a complete adventure of the four friends—reflective Mole, kindly old Water Rat, shy Badger, and rich, conceited, troublesome Toad. The friends "mess around in boats," have picnics, dine elegantly at Toad Hall, get lost in the Wild Wood, rescue Toad from his life of folly, and even encounter once "The Piper at the Gates of Dawn." But how to explain the appeal of this book?

In the first place, the sensory experiences make the reader one with Mole or Ratty. You can feel the sunshine hot on your fur; you, too, waggle your toes from sheer happiness or stretch out on some cool dock leaves or explore the silent silver kingdom of the moonlit river. Earth and water, a green world of woods and meadows speak to you from every page.

The humor of *The Wind in the Willows*, particularly the humor of the conversations, is subtle, but Toad's antics, his bemused pursuit of his latest fad, his ridiculous conceit, the scrapes he gets into, and the efforts of his friends to reform him furnish enough broad comedy to satisfy everyone. The dialogue is so natural you might know that it grew not from written but from oral composition. It is that of the born storyteller, used to children's predilection for talk, improvising dialogue in his own fluent, individual vein. What talk it is—funniest when it is most grave, revealing more of the speaker than any explanatory paragraph.

For example, Toad, having dragged his friends Rat and Mole on an uncomfortable journey across the country in a cart, remarks fatuously:

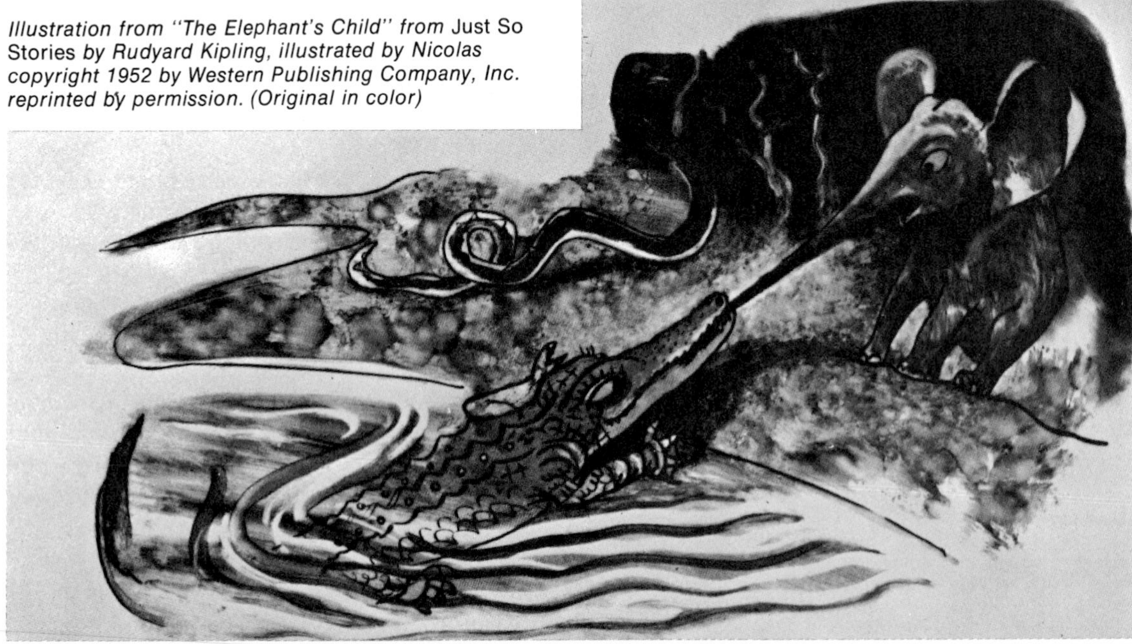

Illustration from "The Elephant's Child" from Just So Stories *by Rudyard Kipling, illustrated by Nicolas copyright 1952 by Western Publishing Company, Inc. reprinted by permission. (Original in color)*

New Folks co-ming, Oh my! New Folks co-ming, Oh my! New Folks co-ming, Oh my! Oh my! Oh my!

From Rabbit Hill *by Robert Lawson. Copyright 1944 by Robert Lawson. Reprinted by permission of The Viking Press, Inc.*

". . . This is the real life for a gentleman! Talk about your old river!"

"I don't talk about my river," replied the patient Rat. "You know I don't, Toad. But I think about it," he added pathetically, in a lower tone: "I think about it—all the time!"

The Mole reached out from under his blanket, felt for the Rat's paw in the darkness, and gave it a squeeze. "I'll do whatever you like, Ratty," he whispered. "Shall we run away to-morrow morning, quite early—very early—and go back to our dear old hole on the river?"

"No, no, we'll see it out," whispered back the Rat. "Thanks awfully, but I ought to stick by Toad till this trip is ended. It wouldn't be safe for him to be left to himself. It won't take very long. His fads never do. Good night!"[5]

No preaching about the duties of a friend, just patient, enduring friendship, loyal in service and understanding!

These conversations are as much a part of the style as the descriptions which make the book one of the masterpieces of English literature.

None of these things—sensory appeal, humor, dialogue, or descriptions—accounts for the hold this book takes upon the heart and the imagination. As in Andersen's *Fairy Tales,* it is the inner significance of the story that counts. First of all, there is the warm friendliness of the animals. Each one makes mistakes, has his limitations, but no one ever rejects a friend. The three put up with Toad's escapades as long as they can; then they join together and reform him in spite of himself. Together they endure perils and pitfalls and come safely through only because they help each other. This continual kindliness, the overlooking of other people's mistakes, and the sympathetic understanding which pervade every page warm the reader's heart. There are no hidden meanings or didacticism here, just reassurance and comfort.

[5]From *The Wind in the Willows* by Kenneth Grahame; copyright 1908, 1935 by the publishers, Charles Scribner's Sons.

Robert Lawson

Ben and Me
Rabbit Hill

Robert Lawson, with his easy storytelling style and beautiful illustrations, added much to the glory of the talking-beast tale. Children consider *Ben and Me* (1939) one of the genuinely funny books. These biographical memoirs of Benjamin Franklin are supposedly written by Amos, a cheeky mouse who modestly admits that he supplied Ben with most of his ideas. The two were almost frozen and Ben had a case of sniffles when Amos thought of the idea of a stove. Ben was a little slow at catching on but finally worked out a very satisfactory contraption. Amos admits that he thoroughly disapproved of Ben's experiments with electricity, but he stuck by his friend in spite of many a shock and some novel results caused by Amos's interference. A series of these fantastic biographies followed.

Good as his humorous biographies are, Lawson really came into his own as a creative writer with *Rabbit Hill* (1944), a Newbery Medal winner. This is the story of Father and Mother Rabbit, their high-leaping son, Little Georgie, aged Uncle Analdas, and a host of other animals. The story begins with the pleasant rumor that new folks are moving into the big house. The question is, what kind of folks will they turn out to be—mean and pinching, or planting folks with a thought for the small creatures who have always lived on the hill? The new folks begin well with a sign "Please Drive Carefully on Account of Small Animals." They plant gardens without fences, sow fields without traps, provide generous "garbidge," and permit no poison. They rescue little Willie from drowning and Little Georgie from an automobile accident. Their crowning beneficence is a beautiful pool and feeding station for their animal friends.

The Tough Winter (1954) is the sequel to *Rabbit Hill*. It tells a moving story of what happens to small beasts when snow and ice last too long and there are no kindhearted human beings to help.

These books may not have the superlative literary qualities of *The Wind in the Willows*, but they are exceedingly well written and marvelously illustrated. All of the animals, from suspicious Uncle Analdas to worrying Mother Rabbit, are delightfully individualized.

E. B. White

Charlotte's Web

E. B. White, essayist and editorial writer for *The New Yorker*, noted for his lucid, effortless prose, wrote *Stuart Little*, the story of a baby who resembled a mouse, "in fact he was a mouse." Some children liked Stuart's adventures, but many adults were disturbed by the biology of this mouse child of a human family. *The Trumpet of the Swan*, the story of a mute swan who learned to play an instrument so that he could woo his beloved, is a fascinating blend of fantasy and realistic details. But White's masterpiece is *Charlotte's Web* (1952).

Fern, a farmer's child, persuades her father to give her a runt of a pig he is about to butcher. Fern names her pet "Wilbur," and raises him with a doll's nursing bottle for a feeder. But when Wilbur gains girth, he is firmly banished to the barnyard, and here the fantasy begins. Fern spends long periods of time watching Wilbur daily and discovers that she understands what the animals are saying to each other. Wilbur has learned about the fall butchering and he doesn't want to die. Charlotte, the aloof, intelligent spider, feels sorry for the silly little pig and promises to save him. Her devices for doing this are unique and exceedingly funny. The progress of Wilbur, the "radiant pig," involves all the people on two farms and most of the barnyard creatures, including Templeton, the selfish rat. In the end, Wilbur is saved but Charlotte dies, true to her kind, leaving hundreds of eggs. Birth and death and life go on in their strange and moving cycles.

Illustration by Garth Williams from Charlotte's Web *by E. B. White. Copyright 1952 by E. B. White. Reprinted by permission of Harper & Row, Publishers, Inc. and Hamish Hamilton Children's Books Ltd.*

Charlotte's Web is a fantasy universally acclaimed by adults and universally loved by children. Wilbur is a true pig—he relishes slops and good soft muck. But he also is a child, lonesome, without a friend, turning to Charlotte for understanding, reassurance, entertainment, love, and finally a solution to his most urgent problem. Wilbur is no hero: he weeps at the thought of death. But he is obedient and tries his best to live up to all the good things Charlotte weaves about him in her web.

White's writing style is confidential and intimate; he's telling a story just for you, and readers and listeners respond openly to the humor and pathos of these adventures.

George Selden

The Cricket in Times Square
Tucker's Countryside
Harry Cat's Pet Puppy

The Garth Williams illustrations add immeasurably to the charm of Selden's books, as they do for *Charlotte's Web*. In *The Cricket in Times Square* (1960) the New York setting provides a solid base of realism—the animal characters live in the Times Square subway station. Tucker is a tough, slangy city mouse, a pure Damon Runyon character, and his friend Harry Cat is a sage creature who joins him in welcoming the cricket Chester, who has been brought into town in somebody's picnic basket. Chester is also befriended and given publicity by Mario, the boy whose parents run the station newspaper stand. The cricket makes a name for himself when it is discovered that he has perfect pitch and is a concert-grade chirper. The style is breezy, the dialogue entertaining, the whole situation fresh and imaginative.

In *Tucker's Countryside* (1969) Chester, who has gone back to Connecticut, appeals to his old friends to help save the meadow in which he and his country friends live. The stratagem that saves the day is amusingly all too possible.

In *Harry Cat's Pet Puppy* (1974), Harry adopts a dog and experiences all the problems of an anxious parent, compounded by the large size of the pup.

Like E. B. White, Selden brings his animal characters so vivdly to life that they are unforgettable personalities, and the books pay tribute to the tenderness and loyalty of friendship.

Other Examples of Talking Beasts

Humans have observed and lived with animals for a long time, frequently identifying closely with them. It is no wonder that authors have chosen to make beasts talk and that their readers accept these tales so readily. Two recent books in this category have been awarded prizes: *Mrs. Frisby and the Rats of NIMH* by Robert O'Brien and *Watership Down* by Richard Adams. O'Brien's Newbery Medal tale has some science-fiction aspects, as he tells the story of the rats who have been used as experimental subjects to see how certain injected substances affect their ability to learn, and who escape the National Institute of Mental Health and set up their own society. O'Brien's tale is rich in circumstantial detail, fact piled upon fact, yet compactly and reasonably told. The rabbits in Richard Adams's Carnegie Medal book also seek a new home and, urged forward by a foreboding vision, find it on Watership Down. Adams creates not only a series of adventures, but a folklore for his migrating rabbits. Theirs is an epic struggle, serious, believable, although carried out by what we're accustomed to think of as small, rather helpless animals.

In *The Bat-Poet*, Randall Jarrell wrote a story of grave sweetness, a quality echoed in the Maurice Sendak illustrations. This is a small homily on the writing of poetry. His creatures speak and think, and the poetry written by the bat gives marvelously vivid pictures of the owl, the mockingbird, the chipmunk, and the bat.

Copyright © 1971 by Robert C. O'Brien
Illustrations by Zena Bernstein
from Mrs. Frisby and the Rats of NIMH

Illustration by Louis Darling is reproduced by permission of William Morrow & Co., Inc. from Runaway Ralph *by Beverly Cleary.*

Most of the fantasy tales about animals are humorous, as are Margery Sharp's *Miss Bianca* stories. Miss Bianca is the most genteel of mice, but her courage is unbounded. With her faithful (but quite ordinary) admirer, Bernard, she embarks on adventures as lurid and melodramatic as those of any detective story, but she is always calm, always completely in charge of the situation.

Another popular talking animal is the enterprising young mouse, Ralph, who makes friends with a boy in Beverly Cleary's *The Mouse and the Motorcycle* and continues his adventures in *Runaway Ralph*. The husband-and-wife team of Louise Fatio and Roger Duvoisin has produced the series of *Happy Lion* books. Not only are these stories well told with good plots, sly humor, and surprise endings, but the pictures are rich in details that children pore over. A series of tales about *A Bear Called Paddington* by Michael Bond disarmingly describes life in a middle-class English family; the Browns adopt a small bear from Peru found wandering about in a railway station with a tag that pleads, "Please look after this bear." William Steig, well known as a creator of adult cartoons, has given us droll, sophisticatedly simple animal characters in *Dominic*. For the younger child, an engaging young donkey is the central character in his Caldecott Medal book, *Sylvester and the Magic Pebble*.

Talking-beast stories are perhaps the first kind of fantasy that younger children encounter, and there have been an enormous number published, especially in the last several decades. All sorts of creatures, from pandas to goldfish, are talking and adventuring. Two favorites are Margaret Wise Brown's *Goodnight Moon* and Marjorie Flack's *Ask Mr. Bear*, both of which have humor and warm, reassuring family relationships.

Over thirty years old but still appealing are the *Curious George* stories by H. A. Rey. Children easily identify with a monkey who can't help getting into trouble just because he wants to *know* about things.

Modern talking-beast tales should be chosen with discrimination. We can do no better than to reread Beatrix Potter and *The Wind in the Willows* when we are in doubt about the qualities that should distinguish the best new animal fantasies.

Sylvester Duncan lived with his mother and father at
Acorn Road in Oatsdale. One of his hobbies was collecting
pebbles of unusual shape and color.

Illustration by William Steig from Sylvester and the Magic Pebble © *by William Steig 1969. Reprinted by permission of Windmill Books/Simon and Schuster. (Original in color)*

Personified Toys and Inanimate Objects

Although the fanciful story about the secret life of toys and other inanimate objects was Andersen's invention, it took the writers of the twentieth century to use this form at the child's level, with an inventiveness and charm that already have made some of these stories children's classics. Andersen's tales of the little china shepherdess and the chimney sweep or the steadfast tin soldier are faintly sad and decidedly adult. Later writers have avoided both these pitfalls. Their dolls, trains, and airplanes are usually cheerful and lively.

Carlo Lorenzini

The Adventures of Pinocchio

The Italian classic *Pinocchio,* written in 1880 by a witty Tuscan, Carlo Lorenzini (pseudonym Collodi), was apparently first translated into English and published in the United States in 1892. From then on, it has held a place in the affections of American children and has undoubtedly influenced American writers.

The story concerns a rogue of a puppet which old Geppetto painstakingly carves out of wood. Hardly has the poor wood-carver finished when the saucy creature makes off in pursuit of his own sweet way. Pinocchio is full of good resolutions: to buy new clothes for his dear papa Geppetto, to go to school, to learn his lessons, and to be a good boy generally. Instead, he wastes his money, lies about it, plays hooky from school, and chooses bad companions. Every time he lies to his friend the Blue Fairy, his nose grows longer, until soon he can't turn around in a room without colliding with the walls. The climax is his journey to the Land of Toys, where there is never any school and where he finds presently that he has grown a fine pair of donkey ears and a body to match. Saved again and again by the good Blue Fairy, he learns that she is ill and starving. He is roused at last, earns money to feed and care for both Geppetto and the Fairy, and wakes in the morning to find himself no longer a puppet but a real boy, living with Geppetto in a well-kept home.

Viewpoints

Melancholy men, they say, are the most incisive humorists; by the same token, writers of fantasy must be, within their own frame of work, hardheaded realists. What appears gossamer is, underneath, solid as prestressed concrete. . . .

Once committed to his imaginary kingdom, the writer is not a monarch but a subject. Characters must appear plausible in their own setting, and the writer must go along with their inner logic. Happenings should have logical implications. Details should be tested for consistency. Shall animals speak? If so, do *all* animals speak? If not, then which—and how? Above all, why? Is it essential to the story, or lamely cute? Are there enchantments? How powerful? If an enchanter can perform such-and-such, can he not also do so-and-so?

. . . And, as in all literature, characters are what ultimately count. . . . Fantasy . . . goes right to the core of a character, to extract the essence, the very taste of an individual personality. This may be one of the things that makes good fantasy so convincing.—Lloyd Alexander, "The Flat-heeled Muse," *The Horn Book,* April 1965, pp. 142, 143–144, 145.

This is the children's own epic, presenting young readers with themselves in wood, full of good resolutions, given to folly, sliding through somehow, but with one difference—Pinocchio always comes out on top and never quite loses face. But he does learn his lesson, and readers never doubt it.

A. A. Milne

Winnie-the-Pooh
The House at Pooh Corner

A. A. Milne's *Winnie-the-Pooh* (1926) and *The House at Pooh Corner* (1928) are different from anything that preceded them. They seem to have grown naturally out of poems about Christopher Robin and Pooh, and they also developed, as the author says, from his small son's demands to hear a story for Pooh:

"What sort of stories does he like?"
"About himself. Because he's that sort of Bear."
"Oh, I see." . . .
So I tried.

The accommodating Milne forthwith began to spin a series of tales about Pooh, when he lived in the forest "under the name of Sanders." He calls on Rabbit and eats so much that he sticks in the door and can't get out. He flies up in a balloon to get some honey out of a tree, tries to imitate a cloud in order to distract the suspicious bees, and finally has to have the balloon shot in order to get down. There are adventures with Piglet, Eeyore the old donkey, Kanga, and Little Roo. *The House at Pooh Corner* introduces Tigger, a new and amusing character, but the tales go on in much the same vein.

Ernest Shepard's illustrations make it clear that most of the animals are really toys like Winnie-the-Pooh. The pictures are full of the fascinating details Shepard knows children and adults will enjoy. For instance, Mr. Owl's house has two signs at the door. One, under the knocker, says

PLES RING
IF AN RNSER
IS REQIRD

The other, under the bell rope, reads

PLEZ CNOKE
IF AN RNSR
IS NOT REQID

From The Little House *by Virginia Lee Burton. Copyright © renewed 1969 by George Demetrios. Reprinted by permission of the publisher Houghton Mifflin Company, Boston. (Original in color)*

The stories are unusual in that Christopher goes in and out of them on a familiar forest-dwelling level with the animals, but in the end he brings everything back to reality when he sets off up the stairs of his own house, headed for a bath, dragging Pooh by one leg. The stories are finished, Christopher is himself, and Pooh is Pooh.

Christopher is omnipotent in these tales, surely a heady experience for children subject to the whims and demands of their elders. Milne's facility with words delights both children and adults, making this an excellent choice for parent-child sharing. His tone is childlike, innocent, uncondescending, allowing children to laugh at themselves without the necessity of looking to adults for cues.

Virginia Burton

Mike Mulligan and His Steam Shovel
The Little House

Virginia Burton used her brush and words in the happiest possible combination. *Mike Mulligan and His Steam Shovel* (1939) tells the story of Mike, who owns a fine steam shovel with which he does important jobs of excavation until his machine, Mary Anne, is outmoded by new and more powerful models. Then Mike reads about a town which wishes to have a cellar dug for its town hall. Mike and Mary Anne hasten to the scene and offer to dig it in one day or no pay. The city fathers agree, seeing a chance to get their excavation done for nothing, since such a feat seems obviously impossible. The next morning Mary Anne and Mike go to work. Dirt flies in all directions, the watching crowds grow to a mob, and at last, exactly on the hour, the excavation is finished, deep and well squared-off at the corners. The only trouble is that Mike, in his excitement, has dug himself in, and there is no way of getting Mary Anne out. So Mary Anne becomes the furnace of the new town hall and Mike her attendant. Both live a warm, prosperous, and respected life ever after.

Burton's machine stories have certain marked characteristics which help to explain their popularity. The plot always involves a staggering task or action and has considerable suspense. The illustrations heighten the feeling of action by swirling, circular lines that rush across the page and stem from or center on the cause of it all. You can almost see movement in the pictures of Mary Anne tearing around the hole with dirt flying all directions and of the crowd of tiny figures with their gaze focused on the snorting steam shovel.

But *The Little House,* the winner of the Caldecott Medal for 1943, is Virginia Burton's finest and most distinguished book. A house in the country presently finds itself in the center of a village, and then in the midst of a great city where it is an insignificant obstruction between skyscrapers, with elevated trains overhead, subways beneath, and swarms of people everywhere. Rescued by the descendants of its builder, the little house is taken back to the country where it can once more watch the cycle of the four seasons revolving in ordered beauty.

There is a significance to this book that should make it permanently valuable as literature and art. The evolution of cities in all their complexity and the resultant loss of some of the sweetness of earth and sky are implied in text and picture. The pattern of every picture is the same—rhythmical curving lines which in the country are gracious and gentle but in the city become more and more violent and confused. The house has only a delicately suggested face, and the personification is subordinate to the pattern of these illustrations, something for children and adults to study with growing astonishment and delight.

Burton's personification is much more evident in art than in text, but no one doubts that Mike speaks Mary Anne's thoughts or that the story discloses the Little House's thoughts, though it doesn't speak aloud.

Rumer Godden

The Dolls' House
Impunity Jane
Miss Happiness and Miss Flower

The most common type of personification for younger children is found in doll stories. The novelist Rumer Godden has written a series of them unsurpassed in variety and charm, for her dolls have distinct personalities and in her books they talk and act in character. Only in one respect are they alike. In the hands of their owners they are often misunderstood and badly treated, and always helpless, except for the sheer force of their unique personalities. The first of the series, *The Dolls' House* (1947, 1962), is one of the most dramatic. An exquisite old Victorian doll house is inhabited by proper, genteel dolls. When a strange, haughty doll is added to the group, a doll-sized tragedy takes place, but this ending is as gentle as the spirit of the old house.

Illustration by Adrienne Adams. From Impunity Jane *by Rumer Godden. Copyright 1954 by Rumer Godden. By permission of The Viking Press, Inc. (Original with color)*

Then there is *Impunity Jane* (1954), so called because the clerk tells the buyers that this finger-sized doll can be dropped "with impunity." But her owner does not think much of Jane, so she relegates her to a stuffy old doll house where she sits for years, bored and pining for adventure. When a small boy named Gideon carries her off in his pocket, life begins for Jane. What that boy thinks up for Jane to do! She sails his boat, flies his airplanes, rides on his bicycle, dwells in igloos and wigwams, and generally enjoys life. When Gideon's conscience forces him to own up to his kidnaping, the solution is a joyous one, and he and Jane return happily to a life of exploration and adventure.

In contrast to the intrepid Jane, *Miss Happiness and Miss Flower* (1961) are two exquisite Japanese dolls, almost too gentle to enjoy any adventures. Yet they are the promoters of a long series of activities which help a homesick, timid little girl and quell a jealous one. These dolls give rise to another series of adventures in a book called *Little Plum*. In this story the interest centers less on the dolls and more on their owner Belinda's naughty curiosity and behavior in relation to a new child next door. However, the culmination of the amusing action is a most felicitous Feast of the Dolls in Japanese style. Other doll stories by Godden are *Candy Floss, The Fairy Doll, Home Is the Sailor,* and *The Story of Holly and Ivy*.

Other Stories about Inanimate Objects

Two doll stories have won the Newbery Medal, *Hitty* by Rachel Field and *Miss Hickory* by Carolyn Sherwin Bailey. Hitty is carved from mountain ash and travels around the world, while Miss Hickory is an apple tree twig with a hickory nut head who lives all her life on the same farm. Both dolls live through adversity bravely and boast definite personalities, many cuts above today's mass-produced dolls.

In *The Dollhouse Caper* Jean O'Connell has written a satisfying story about a family of dolls who come to life when no people are about and who worry about being discarded by their owners, three brothers who are growing up. This book has good characterization, sturdy plot, and smooth writing style.

One of the most touching stories about a toy is Russell Hoban's *The Mouse and His Child*. They are a single unit, a wind-up tin toy that has been discarded. Repaired by a tramp, they go on a quest for love and security. The story has humor and tenderness, and an adventurous plot with general appeal. While the sophistication of its latent meaning and social comment and the difficulty of the vocabulary put special demands on readers, it is well worth the effort.

The Return of the Twelves by Pauline Clarke is an ingenious story about some wooden soldiers that had once belonged to the children of the famous Brontë family. Years after the Brontë times, eight-year-old Max Morley finds the Twelves and learns that they "freeze" when they are observed. He wins their confidence and they talk of the past. Max and his sister decide that the soldiers belong in their old home, Haworth, and let them march off rather than offend their dignity by carrying them. Winner of the Carnegie Medal, the book has a polished style, delightful individual characterizations of the soldiers, and enough literary references to intrigue adults as well as young readers.

Quite unlike any other heroine is *Miss Osborne-the-Mop* by Wilson Gage. Jody, who has discovered that she has the magical power of making objects materialize, soon wishes she had never used her power, since Miss Osborne, a mop brought to life, is a tart character who insists on Jody's participation in a vigorous clean-up campaign.

Humorous Fantasy

While a number of the fantasies mentioned so far in this chapter, such as those by Thurber, Alexander, Carroll, Kipling, Lawson, White, Selden, and Milne, have a great deal of humor, it is the humor of word play or sly remarks on the foibles of animals or humans, a sophisticated humor which demands a certain level of maturity for fullest enjoyment.

Other fantasies have an open, slapstick-style of humor, the kind that is obvious at all levels of understanding and causes us to laugh aloud. Lucretia Hale's *The Peterkin Papers*, stories of a family who cannot solve

Viewpoints

Inventiveness, remember, is not to be judged by how *far out* the imagination of the writer may take his readers, but rather by the degree to which he can make the readers believe in the world he has created. And after they have believed, finally returning to their own world, to what measure then will their own world seem different to them?—James E. Higgins, *Beyond Words; Mystical Fancy in Children's Literature,* Teachers College Press, Columbia University, New York, 1970, p. 28.

the most obvious problems without the advice of "the lady from Philadelphia," is a nineteenth-century example.

P. L. Travers

Mary Poppins
Mary Poppins Comes Back

P. L. Travers grew up in Australia, where high, wild winds blow everyone into a dither and make almost anything possible. So an east wind blows *Mary Poppins* (1934) straight into the nursery of the Banks family, and a west wind carries her off. The children first see her coming up the walk, bag in hand, and the next thing she strikes the house with a bang. Once their mother has engaged her as a nurse, Mary slides lightly *up* the banisters as neatly as the children slide down. When she opens her bag, they see it is quite empty, but out of it she takes everything from a folding cot to a bottle of medicine from which she doses the children with incredibly delicious liquid, tasting of strawberry ice or lime-juice cordial or whatever you prefer.

The Poppins books are extremely British, with cooks, gardeners, maids, nannies, nurseries, and teas. The humor is sometimes adult and sometimes whimsical, but children who like these books like them enormously and wear them to shreds with rereadings; others dislike them with hearty scorn. The character of Mary Poppins herself has a flavor all its own. Vain, stern, crotchety, continually overtaken by magic but never admitting it, she is adored by the children she disciplines and enchants.

Theodor Seuss Geisel

And to Think That I Saw It on Mulberry Street
The 500 Hats of Bartholomew Cubbins

Theodor Seuss Geisel chose his middle name for a pen name and then added the "Dr." as a purely honorary touch. His first book for children was *And to Think That I Saw It on Mulberry Street* (1937). A small boy sees only a horse and a wagon on Mulberry Street but begins working up a bigger and bigger yarn to tell his father. Each succeeding page pictures the next addition to his tale until finally two pages across are necessary to get everything in. Then his father fixes him with a cold stare and his tale diminishes suddenly, leaving only the horse and wagon on Mulberry Street.

This rhymed narrative was only a sample of more and better nonsense to come. Of all the Seuss books *The 500 Hats of Bartholomew Cubbins* (1938) is certainly one of the best. Bartholomew Cubbins takes off his hat to the King only to find the royal coach stopping, and the King commanding him to take off his hat. Puzzled, he puts his hand to his head and finds a hat there. He jerks it off hastily only to find another in its place, and another, and another, and another. He is seized and threatened with death, but still the hats continue to crown his bewildered head. Finally the King sees upon the boy's head the most gloriously regal hat he has ever beheld. In exchange for this elegant hat, he spares Bartholomew's life, and, as the befeathered hat goes on the King's head, Bartholomew finds his own head bare at last. The outline of this story gives no idea of the humor of both pictures and text. This story has a lively sequel, *Bartholomew and the Oobleck.*

Dr. Seuss has the cartoonist's gift for expressing a great deal of humor in a single line or word, and he has maintained the ability to create in uncluttered pictures and text the kind of humor the younger child best enjoys—endless word play, incongruous situations, much action, sure punishment for the truly wicked. His heroes win out not because of brute strength but because the usual cycle of life, gamely lived through, comes round to their side once again.

Seuss has written numerous zany stories, nonsense with basic sense and, at times, basic vocabulary. Children enjoy them all.

Astrid Lindgren

Pippi Longstocking

A Swedish writer is responsible for creating a superchild, the heroine of *Pippi Longstocking* (1950). Pippi is an outrageous and delightful child who lives competently with her monkey and horse and, in this book and its sequels, takes control of any situation in which she finds herself. She curbs some bullying boys, disrupts a school session, and outwrestles two policemen when they try to take her to an orphanage. Indeed, after carrying one in each hand, she sets them down so hard that it is some time before they can get up. Then they report she is not a fit child for the orphanage!

Pippi's antics are exceedingly funny to children. She is a child in charge of her own world, with a sea-captain father conveniently away on the high seas, a chest of gold for sundries, and the warmest of hearts, except for interfering adults.

Jean Merrill

The Pushcart War

Certainly one of the most original fantasies of our time, *The Pushcart War* (1964), has all the ingredients of good fiction. The characters are unusual and distinctively drawn, the setting is colorful, the plot has a tight structure, the style is light and polished, and the theme is significant. Add humor, pace, and the element of fantasy made wholly believable, and the result is sheer delight. The place is New York City, and the problem is that there are so many huge trucks that traffic on Manhattan Island is in a constant snarl. The three big men in trucking decide that the first step in their campaign to eliminate other vehicles is to attack the pushcart owners. But the little people won't be put down; they fight with pins, and the ensuing number of flat tires puts such a strain on repair facilities that trucks are left stranded all over the island. Led by General Anna, the brave little army of pushcart owners outwits the big business sharks, to say nothing of the mayor whose attitude has been swayed by making him a stockholder. In the most ingenuous fashion, Jean Merrill attacks both corruption in political office and monopoly in business, and she does it with a bland humor that avoids any note of bitterness. The characters and the situation are given validity by an introduction that cites invented sources and by a foreword that is written by an invented historian. The concept is original and the development of the story line amusing, but it is the dialogue that gives the book flavor. In the pushcart owners' strategy session, Old Anna says, "Of course, we have got to fight." "Fight the trucks?" a colleague asks. "How can the pushcarts fight the trucks?" Anna's reply is a clincher: "Maybe you'd rather be dead?"

Reprinted from The Pushcart War, *text © MCMLXIV, by Jean Merrill and illustrations © MCMLXIV, by Ronni Solbert, a Young Scott Book, by permission of Addison-Wesley Publishing Company.*

Other Humorous Fantasy

At the outset, *Mr. Popper's Penguins* by Richard and Florence Atwater gives every indication of being a simple, realistic story about a paperhanger with a passion for the Antarctic. The narration is grave and dignified, skidding suddenly into understated nonsense with the addition of penguin Captain Cook to the family.

Oliver Butterworth's *The Enormous Egg* blandly injects the hatching of a dinosaur into the modern scene, and Scott Corbett's *Ever*

Ride a Dinosaur? tells of a brontosaurus (who can make himself invisible) sneaking in to have a look at the dinosaur exhibit at the New York Museum of Natural History. Butterworth's *The Trouble with Jenny's Ear* is the hilarious tale of a small girl whose extrasensory perception is used to advantage in television appearances. Corbett's *The Limerick Trick* and others in the series are rollicking adventure tales that have an element of magic and a large portion of breezy slapstick.

Joan Aiken's humor tends toward sophistication and language play, but her ability to exaggerate gives her work the slapstick surprise that children appreciate. Her Gothic tale, *The Wolves of Willoughby Chase*, drips with Victorian sentimentality and drama. In *Nightbirds on Nantucket* and *Black Hearts in Battersea* Aiken displays a Dickensian relish for names that indicate character, and a sense of the ludicrous that results in such situations as a pink whale obligingly towing a transatlantic cannon. *Smoke from Cromwell's Time and Other Stories* is a good collection of short stories on fanciful themes, and *The Whispering Mountain* is a broad burlesque of the fanciful adventure story. It has a rollicking plot that incorporates a spurned grandchild, a magic harp, a foreign potentate, and a breed of little men who live in a mountain; and it has a spectrum of dialects overdone to the point of absurdity.

From The Ghost in the Noonday Sun *by Sid Fleischman. Illustrated by Warren Chappell. Copyright © 1965 by Albert S. Fleischman. By permission of Little, Brown and Co. in association with the Atlantic Monthly Press.*

From Nightbirds on Nantucket *by Joan Aiken, illustrated by Robin Jacques. Copyright © 1966 by Joan Aiken. Reproduced by permission of Doubleday & Company, Inc.*

Sid Fleischman's stories are also large-canvas affairs. In *The Ghost in the Noonday Sun*, a pirate kidnaps a boy who can, he thinks, lead him to the treasure of the man he murdered. A tropic isle, plank-walking, buried treasure, and mutinous pirates are just a few of the standard ploys at which the author pokes fun. In *Chancy and the Grand Rascal* the young hero (so skinny he has to stand twice to cast a shadow) goes off to find his little sister Indiana, meets a rogue and shyster, Colonel Plugg, and then finds his uncle, whose ability to lie magnificently routs even the lying Plugg. *By the Great Horn Spoon* is a picaresque tale about the California Gold Rush, in which Young Jack and the family butler, Mr. Praiseworthy, go off to recoup their losses. In the McBroom stories, Fleischman has used the tall-tale style of humor to excellent advantage.

What's humorous in one culture is not necessarily funny in another, but Tove Jansson, whose work received the Hans Christian Andersen Award, is popular internationally. Her books about those engaging imaginary creatures the *Finn Family Moomintroll* have a daft logic all their own.

Science Fiction

Science fiction and fantasy are closely related genres, and they are sometimes difficult to distinguish clearly from one another. At one time science fiction was clearly an extrapolation from known scientific facts. That is, the events of a story were possible, given the advances promised by fact or theory, though perhaps many years in the future. Fantasy, on the other hand, was clearly unreality in the physical sense—talking animals, supernatural beings, a parallel world. Some novels of the future contain unreal elements and may be called science fantasy, but contemporary science fiction often becomes a vehicle for commentary on what social scientists and physical scientists are telling us are facts. What kinds of new governments might we evolve? What stresses will crowding bring? How will we handle the social problems brought on by an ever lengthening life span? Today's science fiction brings our judgment into play. We ask ourselves: what is right? what is wrong? and find ourselves not far from those fantasies that address the eternal battle between good and evil.

Children of today have seen the fulfillment of many prophecies of science fiction of the past. They seem readier at times than adults to welcome the future. Usually science fiction for children is less bleak than that written for adults, emphasizing the adventure of exploring the unknown, and the fascination of seeing another world and its inhabitants.

Viewpoints

The technology in science fiction is often a pretext, the ship that steers us off into the orbit of other worlds, provinces of an interstellar anthropology. But even there, in the silence of those infinite spaces, something like the spirit of technology still presides, a sense of intellectual gadgetry. These other worlds are devised rather than developed, they are theorems rather than places, and this is not the expression of an incidental failing in a lot of science fiction writers, but an essential aspect of the genre. Its thin characters and sketchy locations, the general lack of texture and density in its portrayed planets, are flaws only if we are looking for the complication of life which fiction so often provides. If we are looking, in Scholes's phrase, for "some projected dislocation of our known existence," then these flaws help to lighten our baggage for us, become the agents of a transparency which allows us to see through the text to the bones of its ingenuity. A good science fiction story always sounds good in summary, because it depends not on a seen universe or a recollected emotion but on a radical thought.—From "Coffee Break for Sisyphus" by Michael Wood in *The New York Review of Books*, (October 2, 1975), p. 3.

Robert Heinlein

Tunnel in the Sky
Podkayne of Mars

The fun and danger of *Tunnel in the Sky* (1955) and Robert Heinlein's many other books about interspace travel is that they seem completely reasonable and factual. No "airy-go-rounds" in these tales. Instead we have to pinch ourselves to remember that we are not pioneering on Mars, sending colonies to Ganymede, or commuting to Hespera. The stories are so well told they carry the reader along in a state of almost unbearable suspense. Although many science-fiction stories include girls, few of them have a girl as the central character. In *Podkayne of Mars* (1963) a sixteen-year-old girl goes on her first trip to Earth and is kidnaped on a Venus stopover. Children just beginning to read science fiction enjoy Heinlein because he is technically accurate without being difficult.

Madeleine L'Engle

A Wrinkle in Time

Madeleine L'Engle's notable book *Meet the Austins* is a fine realistic family story. The opening of *A Wrinkle in Time* (1963 Newbery Medal) suggests that it will be a similar kind of story. A storm is raging outside, but within the cozy kitchen Meg Murry and her brother, precocious five-year-old Charles Wallace Murry, are having hot cocoa with their mother. Into this family group comes a strange old woman, Mrs. Whatsit. She explains that she was "caught in a down draft and blown off course." But having finished her cocoa, she departs with one final word to the mother, ". . . there *is* such a thing as a tesseract." That is what the children's scientist father had been working on for the government when he disappeared. The next day, Meg, Charles Wallace, and Calvin O'Keefe, a friend, meet Mrs. Whatsit and two other strange old women, who warn the children that their father is in grave danger and that only they can save him and only if they are willing to tesseract. This involves the "fact" that the shortest distance between two points is not a straight line, but a fold or wrinkle. The children prove to be only too willing to try it. There follows in the complex course of the rest of the book a battle between good and evil, love and hate. In the end Meg's love triumphs and her father is saved. All of them tesseract back to earth where their lives pick up as they were except for their new-found knowledge of good and evil.

This space story is written in terms of the modern world in which children know about brainwashing and the insidious, creeping corruption of evil.

A second story about the Murrys is *A Wind in the Door* in which Charles, the youngest, seems near death. With the help of otherworldly teachers, Meg learns to extend her love even to those who do not seem to deserve it in order to save Charles.

L'Engle's books are complicated in their blend of science, philosophy, religion, satire, and allegory, but her ability to draw character and concoct adventurous situations attracts readers.

John Christopher

The White Mountains trilogy

Christopher's stories of the future are written with a breadth of conception and a fidelity of detail that lend conviction. He succeeds admirably in *The White Mountains* (1967) in establishing the believability of his twenty-first-century world. In this world, machine creatures called Tripods control the earth and perpetuate their mastery over human beings by inserting steel caps in the skulls of all children when they reach the age of fourteen, an operation that renders them forever subservient. Three boys—Will, Henry, and Beanpole—have heard that there is a haven in a land the ancients called "Switzerland," and having learned from a Vagrant that free people live in the White Mountains, they decide to escape before they are capped. They have a hazardous but successful journey to a small colony of free humans who live secluded in a mountain. In the second volume, *The City of Gold and Lead* (1967), Will takes part in an athletic contest, the winners of which are to have the privilege of serving the Masters, the Tripods. The other boys go in a spirit of sacrifice; Will goes as a spy. In *The Pool of Fire* (1968) Will describes the intricate sabotage by which the Tripods are defeated, and the new freedom of humankind to set up its own government. As has happened before, there is quarreling and competition, so Will gives up his own plans to work with a small group of people whose goals are world unity and peace. The ending is sober and realistic, a reminder that vigilance against tyranny must be constant. The whole concept of the trilogy is developed with pace and skill—the pitting of good against evil, in a world where few can see the evil, adding suspense to the well-structured action.

The Guardians is science fiction without a fantasy element. It is set in the year 2052, when England is divided into two societies: the megalopolis, huge and sprawling, sharply divided by a frontier from the rest of England, a world occupied by the landed gentry and their servants.

In his later books for children, *The Lotus Caves, Dom and Va,* and *The Prince in Wait-*

ing trilogy, Christopher has used new settings and time periods, but has not succeeded in creating characters as credible as Will. All of Christopher's books are concerned with serious human problems and humanity's environment; his gift as a science-fiction writer is his ability to treat these problems seriously without making a tract out of an absorbing adventure story.

Peter Dickinson

The Weathermonger
Heartsease
The Devil's Children

An editor of the English humor magazine *Punch* and the author of adult mystery stories, Peter Dickinson was immediately successful as a writer for children. His first book, *The Weathermonger* (1969), is a vigorous and well-written fantasy about an England of the near future, a time in which the British Isles have become mysteriously subject to a state of feudalism in which any mechanical object is taboo, and in which the weather is controlled by magic. Geoffrey, a young weathermonger, escapes to France and comes back secretly with his younger sister on a mission, the cause of the enchantment. The plot is inventive, the characterization vivid, and the thoroughly contemporary dialogue, often lightly humorous, a good contrast to the mystic elements of the story.

The second book in this trilogy about England in the time of the Changes is *Heartsease* (1969). Only a few people are unmarked by the hatred of machines, the fear of strangers, the belief in witches. Margaret and her cousin Jonathan find a "witch," buried beneath a pile of stones but still alive. He is an American, and he can hardly believe the hysteria and bigotry of the villagers who attacked him. The children plan to help him escape, and they eventually get the man on board the tugboat *Heartsease* and take off, pursued by angry villagers. The book is, as are its companion volumes, an indictment of prejudice. It is also the most dramatic of the three, with a taut suspense in the escape and chase sequences.

In *The Devil's Children* (1970) a small girl who has been left alone in London joins a group of Sikhs, who are unaffected by the prevailing thrall that grips the native population. She is used by them to prevent their making innocent blunders, and she clings to them at first for security despite the fact that they are reviled as the Devil's Children by the villagers in the area where they settled. But she comes to respect them for their intelligence and good will, as the village people eventually do also. Logical plot development, strong characterization, and a sprightly writing style add to the appeal of a cracking good tale. These are superb examples of one facet that is common to many science-fiction stories: the expressed belief in brotherhood and love as necessary ingredients in a shrunken world.

From Heartsease *by Peter Dickinson. Illustrated by Nathan Goldstein. Copyright © 1969 by Peter Dickinson. By permission of Little, Brown and Co.*

Other Examples of Science Fiction

There are several writers whose science-fiction stories for older readers are good if not distinguished and whose audience greets each new volume avidly.

Andre Norton's earlier stories were concerned with voyages to other worlds through space or time and with problems in dealing with different types of intelligent life. She has made a specialty of the possibilities of communication between humans and animals in such tales as *Moon of Three Rings* and *The Zero Stone*. Recently her stories have moved into the realm of fantasy, but she continues to create credible, interesting characters and to spin breathtaking adventures. Most of Alice M. Lightner's books have a medical theme, like that of *Doctor to the Galaxy*, in which a problem of medical research is pursued on a mythical planet. In her *The Galactic Troubadours*, however, the theme is the revival of musical performance in a society that frowns on young people who aren't satisfied with perfectly good taped music. Also realistic rather than fantastic is Sylvia Engdahl's *Journey Between Worlds*, which explores the theme of prejudice of Terrans against Martian colonists. In *Enchantress from the Stars* and *The Far Side of Evil*, she explores the possibilities of control of physical phenomena by mental means. Other dependably good writers are Alan Nourse and Suzanne Martel, whose *The City Under Ground* is on a theme that has often been used by writers of adult science fiction: the emergence of a new civilization, conscious of ethical values, from the ruins of the old.

Children enjoy stories about robots, such as Lester Del Rey's *The Runaway Robot* and Carol Ryrie Brink's *Andy Buckram's Tin Men*. *The Runaway Robot* is set in the future when robots are common, but it is an uncommon robot that becomes so close a friend of his human companion that the two run away together. Andy in *Andy Buckram's Tin Men* is a twelve-year-old who builds four robots out of tin cans, but not until they are struck by lightning during a storm do the four come alive and save Andy's life during the flood caused by the storm.

For younger children, anywhere from eight to eleven, there are numerous amusing space fantasies. Ruthven Todd's *Space Cat*, Patricia Wrightson's *Down to Earth*, Jerome Beatty's *Matthew Looney* stories, Jay Williams and Raymond Abrashkin's *Danny Dunn* books, Louis Slobodkin's *Space Ship Under the Apple Tree*, and Eleanor Cameron's *Wonderful Flight to the Mushroom Planet*, together with their sequels, make absorbing reading and good introductions to this popular type of literature.

Books That Stir Controversy

Since we must be persuaded by writers of fantasy and science fiction to suspend the rules of the everyday world that we all have known from childhood, it is no wonder that books of this type may stir controversy.

It is hardly necessary to say that a book is not likely to excite discussion if it does not have some excellent qualities. Books that are patterned in plot and pedestrian in style fall by the wayside; books that have a few minor flaws outweighed by their strengths can be enjoyed by successive waves of young readers; and books that are the best of their kind live on to become classics.

Some of the controversial books of the past can be seen, in retrospect, to have been breakers of barriers and small classics of their time. Sometimes it is the content, sometimes the treatment, sometimes only a small facet of the story that causes disagreement about a book.

Certainly one perennial bone of contention has been the Oz books of L. Frank Baum. *The Wizard of Oz* and, to a lesser degree, its sequels have remained favorites of many children despite the fact that many authorities in the field of children's literature feel that the style is flat and dull, and that the inventiveness of the first book was followed by mediocrity and repetition in subsequent volumes. Another book that has been condemned for other reasons by some adults is Helen Bannerman's *The Story of Little Black Sambo*, which is set in India. It is offensive because of the illustrations and because the names "Sambo," "Mumbo," and "Jumbo" have derogatory connotations.

Also attacked, with considerable justification it would seem, as casting aspersion on black people, are the *Dr. Dolittle* books by Hugh Lofting, one of which (*The Voyages of Dr. Dolittle*) won the Newbery Medal in 1923.

Children have enjoyed the humorous reversal of roles in the series, with animals guiding and taking care of helpless human beings, and the gravity with which preposterous events are treated. Although the stories have action and humor, they also have disturbing racial epithets, illustrations, and incidents, and some adults have suggested that the offending sections be deleted in new editions of the books.

Quite another sort of difference of opinion has been generated by the books of Julia Cunningham, some of which are fantasy (*Viollet*, in which a bird, a fox, and a man unite to save the life of a gentle old man) and others (like *Dorp Dead*) which can be taken as fantasy or as realism. Indeed, some of the controversy has been on this very point. Some adults dislike the books because they are sophisticated, complex, and heavy with symbolism and psychological import; others defend the books on the grounds that the symbolism and the author's concern with the struggle between good and evil in our society entitle the stories to be classed among the significant books of our time. Most agree that the writing style is polished and distinctive.

The characters and plots developed by Roald Dahl, primarily an adult author, have also generated sharp debate. In *Charlie and the Chocolate Factory* five children win a contest to enter a wonderfully ingenious manufacturing plant invented by Willy Wonka and operated by pygmies—a device that has been criticized as antiblack. Criticism has also been directed at Dahl's stereotyping of character as a means of discoursing on social behavior. *The Magic Finger* is simpler in structure and stronger in its message: shooting animals for sport is deplorable. An indignant eight-year-old girl points her magic finger at her neighbors who are hunters. The father and sons shrink to tiny winged creatures and the ducks grow enormous, sprout arms that can hold guns, and move into the family's house. Able to understand the animal point of view,

Illustration by William Pène du Bois for The Magic Finger *by Roald Dahl. Copyright © 1966. Reproduced by permission of Harper & Row, Publishers, Inc.*

Viewpoints

Fantasy is probably the most sophisticated form of fiction being written today. Not only must it conform to and meet all the standards of good novel writing; it must also use the fantastic, wholly or partially, directly or indirectly, to express what cannot be expressed in any other way. Fantasy carries the reader into a universe beyond everyday reality, where the restraints of time, gravity, and mortality no longer operate. But the strange world projected by fantasy is not a disorderly one. Its conditions are as practical and as consistent as our own. . . .

The purpose of fantasy is not to escape reality but to illuminate it: to transport us to a world different from the real world, yet to demonstrate certain immutable truths that persist even there—and in every possible world.—Sheila Egoff, *The Republic of Childhood,* Oxford University Press, Toronto, 1967, pp. 133, 134.

the hunters make a pact with the ducks. Less humorous than *Charlie*, this has better construction and a light, easy style. *James and the Giant Peach*, which tells of a boy's flight in a peach made gigantic by magic, shows Dahl's ingenuity in constructing a novel type of spaceship.

Ian Fleming's *Chitty-Chitty-Bang-Bang* is a burlesque of detective stories by a popular writer of adult detective fiction. The marvelous car Chitty-Chitty can rise to an occasion both literally and figuratively, since she takes to air and can (and does) take charge of events when the going gets rough in her family's encounter with a gang of French smugglers. The sophisticated style and zany story line have amused children, and the book has been used as the script for a film, but the sophistication of the parody and the style are felt by many adults to be inappropriate for the audience most interested in stories of animated machines.

Edward Eager's stories (*Magic or Not? The Well Wishers, Half Magic, Seven-Day Magic*, and others) have intriguing plots and a good style, save for those books in which segments are purportedly but unconvincingly told by the child characters. The author has been criticized by those who feel his material is derivative and his children precocious.

The writing of Norton Juster in *The Phantom Tollbooth* delights many readers, young and old, who are intrigued by words and word play (a light meal consists of lights; a bee is a Spelling Bee) and by the Bunyan-like place names (for example, the Mountain of Ignorance and the Foothills of Confusion). To others the dependence on latent meanings and on comprehension of allusions makes the book seem heavily burdened with references that will daunt many readers.

Under each category of modern fantasy many more authors and books could be listed. Most of the examples discussed in this chapter are outstanding because they pointed the way or were exceptions or became classics or seem likely to attain that distinction. Even with innumerable omissions, the list is a long one, and the numbers of these books are increasing yearly. Authors discussed here are generally outstanding in craftsmanship, inventiveness, and creation of character. They have something to say and they say it well.

Most children enjoy fantasy as a change from the here and now, as a breathing space in the serious process of growing up. It is a rare child who does not like some fantasies, and most children enjoy many of them. Adults sometimes wonder why. The probable reason is that they provide children with a flight into other worlds, incredible, exciting, satisfying. Fantasy frees children's own imaginations and helps them to face reality with more creativity and spontaneity of thought. Hans Christian Andersen, Kenneth Grahame, Beatrix Potter, Mary Norton, E. B. White, C. S. Lewis, Lucy Boston, and others have shown children that much of the joy of life depends upon your willingness to take different points of view.

Adult References[6]

ALDISS, BRIAN. *The True History of Science Fiction.*

BLOUNT, MARGARET. *Animal Land; The Creatures of Children's Fiction.*

BOVA, BEN. *Through Eyes of Wonder; Science Fiction and Science.*

BREDSDORFF, ELIAS. *Hans Christian Andersen; The Story of His Life and Work.*

CAMERON, ELEANOR. *The Green and Burning Tree; On the Writing and Enjoyment of Children's Books.* Part 1, "Fantasy."

CARROLL, LEWIS [pseud.]. *The Annotated Alice; Alice's Adventures in Wonderland & Through the Looking Glass.*

COLLINGWOOD, STUART DODGSON. *The Life and Letters of Lewis Carroll (Rev. C. L. Dodgson).*

CREWS, FREDERICK C. *The Pooh Perplex; A Freshman Casebook.*

EGOFF, SHEILA, G. T. STUBBS, and L. F. ASHLEY, eds. *Only Connect; Readings on Children's Literature.* Part 2, "Fairy Tales, Fantasy, Animals."

FIELD, ELINOR WHITNEY, comp. *Horn Book Reflections.* Part 5, "Fantasy, Yesterday and Today."

GODDEN, RUMER. *Hans Christian Andersen: A Great Life in Brief.*

GREEN, PETER. *Kenneth Grahame.*

HAZARD, PAUL. *Books, Children and Men.*

HEARN, MICHAEL. *The Animated Wizard of Oz.*

HELMS, RANDEL. *Tolkien's World.*

HIGGINS, JAMES E. *Beyond Words; Mystical Fancy in Children's Literature.*

LANE, MARGARET. *The Tale of Beatrix Potter; A Biography.*

LENNON, FLORENCE BECKER. *Victoria Through the Looking Glass.*

LEWIS, C. S. *Of Other Worlds; Essays and Stories.*

STIRLING, MONICA. *The Wild Swan; The Life and Times of Hans Christian Andersen.*

[6]Complete bibliographic data are provided in the combined Adult References in the Appendixes.

TOWNSEND, JOHN ROWE. *Written for Children.* Chapter 13, "Fantasy Between the Wars."

WILLIAMS, SIDNEY H., and FALCONER MADAN. *The Lewis Carroll Handbook.*

For additional titles for the youngest children, see the Picture Story Books bibliography, Chapter 4.

Children's Books

ADAMS, RICHARD. *Watership Down.* Macmillan, 1974. Carnegie Medal. 12 up

AIKEN, JOAN. *Black Hearts in Battersea,* ill. by Robin Jacques. Doubleday, 1964. 9-12

______. *The Kingdom and the Cave,* ill. by Victor Ambrus. Doubleday, 1974. 9-11

______. *Nightbirds on Nantucket,* ill. by Robin Jacques. Doubleday, 1966. 10-12

______. *Not What You Expected.* Doubleday, 1974. A collection of short stories. 10 up

______. *Smoke from Cromwell's Time; and Other Stories.* Doubleday, 1970. 10-12

______. *The Whispering Mountain,* ill. by Frank Bozzo. Doubleday, 1969. 10-14

______. *The Wolves of Willoughby Chase,* ill. by Pat Marriott. Doubleday, 1963. 11-13

ALEXANDER, LLOYD. *The Black Cauldron.* Holt, 1965. 11-13

______. *The Book of Three.* Holt, 1964. 11-13

______. *The Castle of Llyr.* Holt, 1966. 10-13

______. *The Cat Who Wished to be a Man.* Dutton, 1973. 10-12

______. *The Foundling and Other Tales of Prydain,* ill. by Margot Zemach. Holt, 1973. Six stories written with grace and humor. 9-11

______. *The High King.* Holt, 1968. Newbery Medal. 11-13

______. *The Marvelous Misadventures of Sebastian.* Dutton, 1970. National Book Award. 9-11

______. *Taran Wanderer.* Holt, 1967. 11-13

______. *The Wizard in the Tree,* ill. by Laszlo Kubinyi. Dutton, 1975. 9-11

ANDERSEN, HANS CHRISTIAN. *The Complete Andersen,* tr. by Jean Hersholt, ill. by Fritz Kredel. Heritage, 1952. Jean Hersholt captures both the spirit and fine literary style of Andersen in this translation of 168 tales. 12 up

______. *The Complete Fairy Tales and Stories,* tr. by Erik Christian Haugaard. Doubleday, 1974. Translated in a flowing style, in the cadence of the oral tradition. 9 up

______. *Fairy Tales,* ed. by Svend Larsen, tr. by R. P. Keigwin, ill. by Vilhelm Pedersen. Scribner's, 1951. Nineteen favorite tales in a translation very faithful to the Danish original. 12 up

______. *It's Perfectly True, and Other Stories,* tr. by Paul Leyssac, ill. by Richard Bennett. Harcourt, 1938. This translation of twenty-eight stories by a famous Danish storyteller has been a favorite collection for younger readers. 11-14

______. *Seven Tales,* tr. by Eva Le Gallienne, ill. by Maurice Sendak. Harper, 1959. Favorite stories chosen for their appeal to younger readers. 7-12

______. Some single-story editions:

The Emperor and the Nightingale, ill. by Bill Sokol. Pantheon, 1959. 9-10

The Fir Tree, ill. by Nancy Burkert. Harper, 1970. 9-11

The Little Match Girl, ill. by Blair Lent. Houghton, 1968. 9-11

The Nightingale, tr. by Eva Le Gallienne, ill. by Nancy Burkert. Harper, 1965. 9-11

The Steadfast Tin Soldier, tr. by M. R. James, ill. by Marcia Brown. Scribner's, 1953. 6-10

The Swineherd, tr. and ill. by Erik Blegvad. Harcourt, 1958. 5-9

Thumbelina, tr. by R. P. Keigwin, ill. by Adrienne Adams. Scribner's, 1961. 6-9

The Ugly Duckling, tr. by R. P. Keigwin, ill. by Johannes Larsen. Macmillan, 1967. 6-9

The Wild Swans, ill. by Marcia Brown. Scribner's, 1963. 6-10

ANNETT, CORA. *How the Witch Got Alf,* ill. by Steven Kellogg. Watts, 1975. A little donkey tries everything, even singing, to get attention. 8-9

ARTHUR, RUTH M. *Requiem for a Princess,* ill. by Margery Gill. Atheneum, 1967. Having worried herself sick over the discovery that she is adopted, fifteen-year-old Willow spends her nights in dreams in which she lives the life of a sixteenth-century Spanish girl whose portrait she has seen. 11-14

ATWATER, RICHARD and FLORENCE. *Mr. Popper's Penguins,* ill. by Robert Lawson. Little, 1938. 8-12

BABBITT, NATALIE. *The Devil's Storybook,* ill. by author. Farrar, 1974. Ten lively stories about an arrogant devil. 9-11

______ *Knee-Knock Rise,* ill. by author. Farrar, 1970. 9-11

______. *The Search for Delicious.* Farrar, 1969. 9-11

______. *The Something,* ill. by author. Farrar, 1970. A pithy and funny story about Milo, a hairy little cave dweller, who is afraid of Something in the night. It turns out to be a modern girl. When they meet in dreams, both stoutly declare they are not afraid of each other. 4-6

______. *Tuck Everlasting,* ill. by author. Farrar, 1975. 9-11

BAILEY, CAROLYN. *Miss Hickory,* ill. by Ruth Gannett. Viking, 1968. Newbery Medal. 10-13

BANNERMAN, HELEN. *The Story of Little Black Sambo,* ill. by author. Lippincott, 1923 (first pub. in 1900). Historically interesting but unacceptable. 4-7

BARRIE, SIR JAMES. *Peter Pan,* ill. by Nora Unwin. Scribner's, 1950. Peter Pan and all his delightful companions are visualized for the children by Nora Unwin's illustrations for this edition. 9-12

BAUM, L. FRANK. *The Wizard of Oz,* ill. by W. W. Denslow. Reilly, 1956 (first pub. in 1900). This edition has many of the original illustrations. 8-11

BEATTY, JEROME, JR. *Matthew Looney in the Outback,* ill. by Gahan Wilson. Scott/Addison, 1969. One of a popular series. 9-12

BELLAIRS, JOHN. *A Figure in the Shadows,* ill. by Mercer Mayer. Dial, 1975. More adventures in a sequel to the title below.

______. *The House with a Clock in Its Walls,* ill. by Edward Gorey. Dial, 1973. An orphaned boy discovers the excitement of living with an uncle who has magical powers. 10-12

BIANCO, MARGERY WILLIAMS. *The Velveteen Rabbit,* ill. by William Nicholson. Doubleday, 1926, 1958. How a very old toy rabbit becomes real and goes off into the real world. 4-7

BISHOP, CLAIRE. *The Five Chinese Brothers,* ill. by Kurt Wiese. Coward, 1938. 5-10

BOMANS, GODFRIED. *The Wily Wizard and the Wicked Witch; And Other Weird Stories,* tr. by Patricia Crampton, ill. by Robert Bartelt. Watts, 1969. A collection of original fairy tales with unusual treatment and a refreshing blend of orthodox magic and brisk touches of humor. 9-11

BOND, MICHAEL. *A Bear Called Paddington,* ill. by Peggy Fortnum. Houghton, 1960. 8-10

______. *Paddington on Top,* ill. by Peggy Fortnum. Houghton, 1975. One in a series of amusing sequels. 8-10

______. *The Tales of Olga da Polga,* ill. by Hans Helweg. Macmillan, 1973. Episodic chapters about a complacent, mendacious guinea pig. 8-10

______. *Olga Meets Her Match,* ill. by Hans Helweg. Hastings, 1975. And his name is Boris! 8-10

BONTEMPS, ARNA, and JACK CONROY. *The Fast Sooner Hound,* ill. by Virginia Lee Burton. Houghton, 1942. How this tall-tale hound could outrun any train, even the Cannon Ball, is gravely related and hilariously pictured. 8-12

BOSTON, LUCY M. *The Castle of Yew,* ill. by Margery Gill. Harcourt, 1965. An imaginative adventure which takes place in a topiary garden.

______. *The Children of Green Knowe,* ill. by Peter Boston. Harcourt, 1955.

______. *An Enemy at Green Knowe,* ill. by Peter Boston. Harcourt, 1964.

______. *The Guardians of the House,* ill. by Peter Boston. Atheneum, 1975. Objects in an old house catapult a curious boy into a series of adventures.

______. *Nothing Said,* ill. by Peter Boston. Harcourt, 1971. In this blend of realism and fantasy, a child meets a dryad.

______. *The River at Green Knowe,* ill. by Peter Boston. Harcourt, 1959.

______. *The Sea Egg,* ill. by Peter Boston. Harcourt, 1967. Two small boys find a stone that hatches into a water creature through whom they learn the magical secrets of the sea.

______. *A Stranger at Green Knowe,* ill. by Peter Boston. Harcourt, 1961. Carnegie Medal.

______. *Treasure of Green Knowe,* ill. by Peter Boston. Harcourt, 1958. 9-11

BOVA, BENJAMIN. *End of Exile.* Dutton, 1975.

______. *Exiled from Earth.* Dutton, 1971.

______. *Flight of Exiles.* Dutton, 1972. Exiled from earth because they will upset the political equilibrium, a group of scientists sets out aboard a space ship to find a new home. Suspense, drama, and a satisfying ending in this trilogy. 11-13

BRINK, CAROL RYRIE. *Andy Buckram's Tin Men,* ill. by W. T. Mars. Viking, 1966. 10-11

BROCK, BETTY. *No Flying in the House,* ill. by Wallace Tripp. Harper, 1970. Annabel discovers she is part fairy. 7-9

BROOKS, WALTER. *Freddy and the Men from Mars.* Knopf, 1954.

______. *Freddy Goes to Florida.* Knopf, 1949. Between these two books lies a long series of Freddy stories that enjoy great popularity. 9-12

BROWN, MARGARET WISE. *Goodnight Moon,* ill. by Clement Hurd. Harper, 1947. 4-6

BURTON, VIRGINIA LEE. *The Little House,* ill. by author. Houghton, 1942. Caldecott Medal. 5-8

______. *Mike Mulligan and His Steam Shovel,* ill. by author. Houghton, 1939. 6-8

BUTTERWORTH, OLIVER. *The Enormous Egg,* ill. by Louis Darling. Little, 1956. 9-13

______. *The Trouble with Jenny's Ear,* ill. by Julian de Miskey. Little, 1960. 9-11

BYFIELD, BARBARA NINDE. *The Haunted Tower,* ill. by author. Doubleday, 1976. A retired detective who lives with a crotchety ghost solves a mystery. Very tongue-in-cheek. 8-10

CAMERON, ELEANOR. *The Court of the Stone Children.* Dutton, 1973. Visiting a museum, Nina meets a ghost-girl from the Napoleonic period. National Book Award. 10-12

______. *Stowaway to the Mushroom Planet,* ill. by Robert Henneberger. Little, 1956.

______. *The Wonderful Flight to the Mushroom Planet,* ill. by Robert Henneberger. Little, 1954. 9-11

CARROLL, LEWIS [pseud. for Charles Lutwidge Dodgson]. *Alice's Adventures in Wonderland* and *Through the Looking Glass,* ill. by John Tenniel. Heritage, 1944 (first pub. in 1865 and 1871). One of the best-loved and most quoted fantasies for children.
Ill. by John Tenniel. Grosset, 1963.
Ill. by John Tenniel. Macmillan, 1963.
Ill. by John Tenniel. World, 1946.
Ill. by Arthur Rackham. Watts, 1966. 10 up

CHRISMAN, ARTHUR BOWIE. *Shen of the Sea; Chinese Stories for Children,* ill. by Else Hasselriis. Dutton, 1925; redesigned, 1968. Brisk and humorous fairy tales that were awarded the 1926 Newbery Medal. 10-12

CHRISTOPHER, JOHN. *Beyond the Burning Lands.* Macmillan, 1971. A sequel to *The Prince in Waiting.*

______. *The City of Gold and Lead.* Macmillan, 1967.

______. *Dom and Va.* Macmillan, 1973.

______. *The Guardians.* Macmillan, 1970.

______. *The Lotus Caves.* Macmillan, 1969.

______. *The Pool of Fire.* Macmillan, 1968.

______. *The Prince in Waiting.* Macmillan, 1970.

______. *The White Mountains.* Macmillan, 1967.

______. *Wild Jack.* Macmillan, 1974. A twenty-third-century Robin Hood tale. 11-14

CLARKE, ARTHUR C. *Dolphin Island.* Holt, 1963. A fine science-fiction tale of teenage Johnny Clinton, who becomes interested in dolphins when they rescue him from drowning. 12-15

CLARKE, PAULINE. *The Return of the Twelves,* ill. by Bernarda Bryson. Coward, 1964. Carnegie Medal; British title is *The Twelve and the Genii.* 10-12

CLEARY, BEVERLY. *The Mouse and the Motorcycle,* ill. by Louis Darling. Morrow, 1965. 9-11

______. *Runaway Ralph,* ill. by Louis Darling. Morrow, 1970. 8-10

COATSWORTH, ELIZABETH. *The Cat Who Went to Heaven,* ill. by Lynd Ward. Macmillan, 1930 and 1959. Newbery Medal. 10-14

______. *Cricket and the Emperor's Son,* ill. by Juliette Palmer, Norton, 1965. 10-11

______. *Marra's World,* ill. by Krystyna Turska. Greenwillow, 1975. A lonely, motherless girl finds affection, in an eerie, haunting story. 9-11

______. *Pure Magic,* ill. by Ingrid Fetz. Macmillan, 1973. The story of a boy who could change into a fox. 9-10

COBALT, MARTIN. *Pool of Swallows.* Nelson, 1974. Humor, mystery, and ghosts are combined in a sophisticated story from England. 11-15

COLLODI, CARLO [pseud. for Carlo Lorenzini]. *The Adventures of Pinocchio,* tr. by Carol Della Chiesa, ill. by Attilio Mussino. Macmillan, 1963.
Ill. by Charles Mozley, large type ed. Watts, 1967. 9-12

COOPER, SUSAN. *The Dark Is Rising,* ill. by Alan E. Cober. Atheneum, 1973.

______. *Greenwitch.* Atheneum, 1974.

______. *The Grey King,* ill. by Michael Heslop. Atheneum, 1975. Newbery Medal.

______. *Over Sea, Under Stone,* ill. by Margery Gill. Harcourt, 1965. 10-12

CORBETT, SCOTT. *Ever Ride a Dinosaur?* ill. by Mircea Vasiliu. Holt, 1969. 9-11

______. *The Hockey Trick,* ill. by Paul Galdone. Little, 1974. 8-11

______. *The Limerick Trick,* ill. by Paul Galdone. Little, 1964. 8-11

CRESSWELL, HELEN. *The Bongleweed.* Macmillan, 1973. A mysterious plant takes over a garden. 9-11

______. *The Piemakers,* ill. by W. T. Mars. Lippincott, 1968. A pie for 2000 people takes everyone's cooperation. A clever, humorous tale. 9-11

CUNNINGHAM, JULIA. *Dorp Dead,* ill. by James Spanfeller. Pantheon, 1965. 12 up

______. *Maybe, a Mole,* ill. by Cindy Szekeres. Pantheon, 1974. Adventures of a not-blind mole and his animal friends, who learn respect and trust. 8-10

______. *Viollet,* ill. by Alan E. Cober. Pantheon, 1966. 10-11

CURRY, JANE LOUISE. *Mindy's Mysterious Miniature,* ill. by Charles Robinson. Harcourt, 1970. Mindy and her neighbor, Mrs. Bright, are captured by a Mr. Putt, who has inherited a magic contraption that miniaturizes houses and the people in them. The concept is entertaining and the writing has suspense and pace. 9-11

______. *The Watchers.* Atheneum, 1975. A time travel fantasy set in the Appalachians. 11-13

DAHL, ROALD. *Charlie and the Chocolate Factory,* ill. by Joseph Schindelman. Knopf, 1964. 10-11

______. *James and the Giant Peach*, ill. by Nancy E. Burkert. Knopf, 1961. 10-11

______. *The Magic Finger*, ill. by William Pène du Bois. Harper, 1966. 10-11

DE BRUNHOFF, JEAN. *The Story of Babar, the Little Elephant*, ill. by author. Random, 1937. A series of these books follows and has been continued since the author's death by his son Laurent. 5-8

DE LA MARE, WALTER. *A Penny a Day*, ill. by Paul Kennedy. Knopf, 1960. Walter de la Mare brings poetic beauty to his prose style in six tales of fantasy which offer choice reading aloud. Followed by a companion volume, *The Magic Jacket* (1962). 10-13

______. *The Three Royal Monkeys*, ill. by Mildred Eldridge. Knopf, 1948. Originally published as *The Three Mulla-Mulgars*, this distinguished fantasy is a long story of the adventures of three young monkeys who go in search of their father, a prince from the valley of Tishner. 12-15

DEL REY, LESTER. *The Runaway Robot.* Westminster, 1965. 11-14

DICKINSON, PETER. *The Devil's Children*. Little, 1970. 10-14

______. *Emma Tupper's Diary*, ill. by David Omar White. Atlantic/Little, 1971. A hoax involving sea monsters is at the center of this lively story set in the Scottish highlands. 10-13

______. *The Gift.* Atlantic/Little, 1974. Davy's ability to read minds leads to a frightening adventure. 10-14

______. *Heartsease.* Little, 1969. 10-14

______. *The Weathermonger.* Little, 1969. 10-14

DOLBIER, MAURICE. *Torten's Christmas Secret,* ill. by Robert Henneberger. Little, 1951. A fresh, gay Christmas story involves Santa's toy factory. 4-8

DONOVAN, JOHN. *Family.* Harper, 1976. A touching story about a group of laboratory apes is told by one of their number. 11 up

DRUON, MAURICE. *Tistou of the Green Thumbs,* ill. by Jacqueline Duhème. Scribner's, 1958. A subtle allegory. 9-11

DRURY, ROGER. *The Finches' Fabulous Furnace*, ill. by Erik Blegvad. Little, 1971. The fabulous furnace, it turns out, is a small volcano in the Finches' cellar. 9-11

DU BOIS, WILLIAM PÈNE. *The Alligator Case,* ill. by author. Harper, 1965. An unusually alert boy detective starts working on the case before the crime is committed. 9-11

______. *Bear Party*, ill. by author. Viking, 1951 and 1963. 5-8

______. *Call Me Bandicoot*, ill. by author. Harper, 1970. Fourth in the author's series on the seven deadly sins, this has stinginess as the leit-motif, but the imaginative embroidery of the central character's storytelling almost eclipses the theme. Witty and sophisticated, with elegant illustrations. 10-14

______. *The Giant*, ill. by author. Viking, 1954. 9-12

______. *Great Geppy*, ill. by author. Viking, 1940. The Great Geppy, detective, is the only red-and-white striped horse in the world. When he attempts to solve the Bott Circus Case, the stripes are a great asset. 10-14

______. *The Horse in the Camel Suit,* ill. by author. Harper, 1967. The boy detective who solved the *Alligator Case* pits his skill against a troupe of entertainers who turn out to be horse thieves in disguise. 9-11

______. *Lazy Tommy Pumpkinhead,* ill. by author. Harper, 1966. 7-9

______. *Otto and the Magic Potatoes,* ill. by author. Viking, 1970. The broadly nonsensical story of Otto the giant dog and his master who are kidnaped. 9-11

______. *Peter Graves,* ill. by author. Viking, 1950. Houghton was an inventor who was always having to be rescued by the fire department. A boy, Peter Graves, went to see him with hair-raising results. 10-14

______. *The Twenty-One Balloons,* ill. by author. Viking, 1947. Newbery Medal. 10-12

EAGER, EDWARD M. *Half Magic,* ill. by N. W. Bodecker. Harcourt, 1954.

______. *Magic or Not?* ill. by N. M. Bodecker. Harcourt, 1959.

______. *Seven-Day Magic,* ill. by N. M. Bodecker. Harcourt, 1962.

______. *The Well-Wishers,* ill. by N. M. Bodecker. Harcourt, 1960. 9-11

ENGDAHL, SYLVIA. *Beyond the Tomorrow Mountains,* ill. by Richard Cuffari. Atheneum, 1973. The story of a young man's maturing in a world that is rebuilding after earth is doomed. 11-14

______. *Enchantress from the Stars,* ill. by Rodney Shackell. Atheneum, 1970. 11-14

______. *The Far Side of Evil,* ill. by Richard Cuffari. Atheneum, 1971. 11-14

______. *Journey Between Worlds*, ill. by James and Ruth McCrea. Atheneum, 1970. 11-14

ENRIGHT, ELIZABETH. *Tatsinda,* ill. by Irene Haas. Harcourt, 1963. This original fairy tale offers children penetrating social comment, coupled with the suspense of a well-told story. 9-12

______. *Zeee,* ill. by Irene Haas. Harcourt, 1965. A small, grumpy fairy is befriended by a Person. 9-11

ERWIN, BETTY. *Who Is Victoria?* ill. by Kathleen Anderson. Little, 1973. A poltergeist in the form of a girl appears in a small Wisconsin town. Unsentimental treatment of old age and death. 9-11

ESTES, ELEANOR. *The Witch Family,* ill. by Edward Ardizzone. Harcourt, 1960. Their pleasant game of drawing witches leads two small girls into incredible adventures when their witches come alive! 10-12

ETS, MARIE HALL. *Mister Penny,* ill. by author. Viking, 1935. Mister Penny's good-for-nothing animals reform and help him in an amusing book. 6-8

______. *Mister Penny's Race Horse,* ill. by author. Viking, 1956. All the animals get into mischief going to the Fair, and Limpy finds that he can be a race horse. 6-8

FAIRSTAR, MRS. [pseud. for Richard Horne]. *Memoirs of a London Doll,* ill. by Emma L. Brock. Macmillan, 1968 (first pub. in 1846). 9-12

FARMER, PENELOPE. *A Castle of Bone.* Atheneum, 1972. 10-12

______. *Charlotte Sometimes,* ill. by Chris Connor. Harcourt, 1969.

______. *Emma in Winter,* ill. by James J. Spanfeller. Harcourt, 1966. 10-12

______. *The Summer Birds,* ill. by James J. Spanfeller. Harcourt, 1962.

______. *William and Mary.* Atheneum, 1974. Two children come to grips with their separate family problems while being transported to other times and places. 10-12

FATIO, LOUISE. *The Happy Lion,* ill. by Roger Duvoisin. Whittlesey, 1954. The first in a consistently popular series. 5-7

FERMAN, EDWARD L., and ROBERT P. MILLS, eds. *Twenty Years of the Magazine of Fantasy and Science Fiction.* Putnam, 1970. Some of the best science fiction writers who published in the magazine are represented here, though not all at their best. 11 up

FIELD, RACHEL. *Hitty; Her First Hundred Years,* ill. by Dorothy P. Lathrop. Macmillan, 1929. Newbery Medal. 11-14

FLACK, MARJORIE. *Ask Mr. Bear,* ill. by author. Macmillan, 1932, 1958. 3-7

FLEISCHMAN, SID. *By the Great Horn Spoon!* ill. by Eric von Schmidt. Little, 1963. 10-12

______. *Chancy and the Grand Rascal,* ill. by Eric von Schmidt. Little, 1966. 10-12

______. *The Ghost in the Noonday Sun,* ill. by Warren Chappell. Little, 1965. 10-12

______. *McBroom's Ear,* ill. by Kurt Werth. Norton, 1969. Another blithe tall tale about the marvelous McBroom farm which produces magnificent crops of food and stories. Enjoyable for reading aloud or storytelling. *McBroom the Rainmaker* (Grosset, 1973) is another title in this enjoyable series. 8-11

FLEMING, IAN. *Chitty-Chitty-Bang-Bang; The Magical Car,* ill. by John Burningham. Random, 1964. 10-11

GÁG, WANDA. *Millions of Cats,* ill. by author. Coward, 1928. 5-8

______. *Nothing at All,* ill. by author. Coward, 1941. Through the use of a magic phrase, a lonesome little invisible puppy becomes "see-able," and finds a happy home. 5-7

GAGE, WILSON. *Miss Osborne-the-Mop,* ill. by Paul Galdone. World, 1963. 9-11

GARD, JOYCE. *Talargain.* Holt, 1965. Talargain, the hero, was a foundling in seventh-century England. He had learned to swim with the seals who saved his life when he came home to save his king. 11-14

GARFIELD, LEON. *The Restless Ghost; Three Stories,* ill. by Saul Lambert. Pantheon, 1969. Three splendid ghost stories, all set in the past and all with an authentic ring. 12-15

GARNER, ALAN. *The Moon of Gomrath.* Walck, 1967. 10-12

______. *The Owl Service.* Walck, 1968. Carnegie Medal. 10-12

______. *The Weirdstone of Brisingamen.* Walck, 1969. 10-13

GODDEN, RUMER. *Candy Floss,* ill. by Adrienne Adams. Viking, 1960. 8-10

______. *The Dolls' House,* ill. by Tasha Tudor. Viking, 1962. 8-10

______. *The Fairy Doll,* ill. by Adrienne Adams. Viking, 1956. 7-10

______. *Home Is the Sailor,* ill. by Jean Primrose. Viking, 1964. 10-11

______. *Impunity Jane,* ill. by Adrienne Adams. Viking, 1954. 8-10

______. *Little Plum,* ill. by Jean Primrose. Viking, 1963. 8-11

______. *Miss Happiness and Miss Flower,* ill. by Jean Primrose. Viking, 1961. 8-11

______. *The Mousewife,* ill. by William Pène du Bois. Viking, 1951. Expanded into a story from a note in Dorothy Wordsworth's journal, this is an exquisitely written little fable of the friendship of a mouse and a dove. 7-10

______. *The Story of Holly and Ivy,* ill. by Adrienne Adams. Viking, 1958. 7-9

GRAHAME, KENNETH. *The Reluctant Dragon,* ill. by Ernest H. Shepard. Holiday, 1953. A subtly amusing tale about a boy who makes friends with a dragon and arranges to have him meet and fight St. George. 9-11

______. *The Wind in the Willows,* ill. by Ernest H. Shepard. Scribner's, 1953 (first pub. in 1908). 10-12

GRIPE, MARIA. *The Glassblower's Children,* ill. by Harald Gripe. Delacorte, 1973. Two children are kidnaped and held in a castle in this tale in a Gothic vein. 9-11

HALE, LUCRETIA P. *Peterkin Papers,* ill. by Harold Brett. Houghton, 1960 (first pub. in 1880). 10-12

HARRIS, ROSEMARY. *The Moon in the Cloud.* Macmillan, 1970. Carnegie Medal. 10-13

______. *The Seal-Singing.* Macmillan, 1971. 11-14

______. *The Shadow on the Sun.* Macmillan, 1970. A sequel to *The Moon in the Cloud.* The vigorous characterization and dialogue make this as diverting as its predecessor. 10-13

HEINLEIN, ROBERT A. *Have Space Suit—Will Travel.* Scribner's, 1958. An improbable but convincing tale of two youngsters who journey through space and save humanity from immediate destruction. 12-16

______. *Podkayne of Mars; Her Life and Times.* Putnam, 1963. 12-15

______. *Tunnel in the Sky.* Scribner's, 1955. 11-13

HOBAN, RUSSELL C. *The Mouse and His Child,* ill. by Lillian Hoban. Harper, 1967. 9-11

______. *A Near Thing for Captain Najork,* ill. by Quentin Blake. Atheneum, 1976. A wild spoof of adventure tales, hilariously larded with Victorian niceties. 8-10

HUNTER, MOLLIE. *The Kelpie's Pearls,* ill. by Joseph Cellini. Funk, 1966. 10-13

______. *A Stranger Came Ashore.* Harper, 1975. 11-13

______. *The Walking Stones,* ill. by Trina Schart Hyman. Harper, 1970. 10-12

JANEWAY, ELIZABETH. *Ivanov Seven,* ill. by Eros Keith. Harper, 1967. An uproarious spoof about the Russian army discipline upset by an ingenuous peasant. 11-14

JANSSON, TOVE. *Finn Family Moomintroll,* ill. by author. Walck, 1965. One of a successful series. 9-12

JARRELL, RANDALL. *The Animal Family,* ill. by Maurice Sendak. Pantheon, 1965. 10-12

______. *The Bat-Poet,* ill. by Maurice Sendak. Macmillan, 1967. 10 up

JONES, DIANA WYNNE. *The Ogre Downstairs.* Dutton, 1975. Adroit blending of fantasy and realism in a story about stepbrothers who become friends through magic. 10-11

JONES, ELIZABETH ORTON. *Twig,* ill. by author. Macmillan, 1943. When Twig found the red tomato can in the yard, she thought it would make a beautiful home for a fairy. And a fairy did come to delight a city child. 8-10

JUSTER, NORTON. *The Phantom Tollbooth,* ill. by Jules Feiffer. Random, 1961. 11-13

KARL, JEAN. *The Turning Place; Stories of a Future Past.* Dutton, 1976. Short stories blend to give a picture of a changed earth. 10-15

KÄSTNER, ERICH. *The Little Man,* ill. by Rick Schreiter, tr. by James Kirkup. Knopf, 1966. The diverting adventures of little Maxie, two inches high, who becomes a circus performer. Written in lively style by a distinguished German author. 10-11

______. *The Little Man and the Big Thief,* ill. by Stan Mack. Knopf, 1970. Tiny Maxie finds a friend his own size. 9-11

KENDALL, CAROL. *The Gammage Cup,* ill. by Erik Blegvad. Harcourt, 1959. Children who enjoy Tolkien's *The Hobbit* will appreciate this tale of mild revolt among the Minnipins, or little people, and its surprising outcome. A protest against conformity. 10-13

______. *The Whisper of Glocken,* ill. by Imero Gobbato. Harcourt, 1965. A continuation of the chronicles of the Minnipins. 10-12

KINGSLEY, CHARLES. *The Water-Babies,* ill. by Harold Jones. Watts, 1961. 8-12

KIPLING, RUDYARD. *The Elephant's Child,* ill. by Leonard Weisgard. From the *Just So Stories,* 1902. Walker, 1970. 9-11

______. *Just So Stories,* ill. by author. Doubleday, 1902.
Ill. by J. M. Gleeson. Doubleday, 1912, 1946.
Ill. by Nicolas [pseud. for Nicolas Mordvinoff]. Doubleday, 1952. 8-12

______. *The Jungle Book,* ill. by Philip Hays. Doubleday, 1964. Stories of India and the jungle life of the boy Mowgli, adopted by a wolf pack. 9-13

LANGTON, JANE. *The Astonishing Stereoscope,* ill. by Erik Blegvad. Harper, 1971. 10-12

______. *The Diamond in the Window,* ill. by Erik Blegvad. Harper, 1962. 11-14

______. *The Swing in the Summerhouse,* ill. by Erik Blegvad. Harper, 1967. 10-12

LAURENCE, MARGARET. *Jason's Quest,* ill. by Steffan Torell. Knopf, 1970. A quest takes an oddly matched band of small animals to London. 9-11

LAWSON, JOHN. *The Spring Rider.* T. Crowell, 1968. A dreamlike fantasy in which a boy and his sister mingle with the soldiers who fought a Civil War battle on the area now farmed by their family. 11-13

______. *You Better Come Home with Me,* ill. by Arnold Spilka. T. Crowell, 1966. Like the preceding title, the plot is not always clear, but the style is lyric and subtle. 11-12

LAWSON, ROBERT. *Ben and Me,* ill. by author. Little, 1939. 9-12

______. *Mr. Revere and I,* ill. by author. Little, 1953. Revere's ride from his horse's point of view. 11-14

______. *Rabbit Hill,* ill. by author. Viking, 1944, 1968. Newbery Medal. 9-12

______. *The Tough Winter,* ill. by author. Viking, 1970. 9-12

LE GUIN, URSULA K. *The Farthest Shore,* ill. by Gail Garraty. Atheneum, 1972. National Book Award. 11-14

______. *The Tombs of Atuan,* ill. by Gail Garraty. Atheneum, 1971. 11-14

______. *A Wizard of Earthsea,* ill. by Ruth Robbins. Parnassus, 1968. 11-14

L'ENGLE, MADELEINE. *A Wind in the Door.* Farrar, 1973. 11-14

______. *A Wrinkle in Time.* Farrar, 1962. Newbery Medal. 11-14

LEWIS, CLIVE STAPLES. *The Lion, the Witch, and the Wardrobe,* ill. by Pauline Baynes. Macmillan, 1950. Other titles in the Narnia series, in order of appearance, are: *Prince Caspian* (1951), *The Voyage of the Dawn Treader* (1952), *The Silver Chair* (1953), *The Horse and His Boy* (1954); *The Magician's Nephew* (1955), and *The Last Battle* (1956). 8-12

LIGHTNER, ALICE. *Doctor to the Galaxy.* Norton, 1965. 11-14

______. *The Galactic Troubadours.* Norton, 1965. 12-14

LINDGREN, ASTRID. *Pippi Longstocking,* tr. by Florence Lamborn, ill. by Louis S. Glanzman. Viking, 1950. Followed by several hilarious sequels. 9-12

______. *The Tomten,* adapted from a poem by Viktor Rydberg, ill. by Harald Wiberg. Coward, 1961. Unforgettably lovely pictures of the wintry Swedish countryside illustrate the story of a kindly little troll. Equally attractive is *The Tomten and the Fox* (Coward, 1966). 5-7

LIVELY, PENELOPE. *The Ghost of Thomas Kempe,* ill. by Antony Maitland. Dutton, 1973. Carnegie Medal. 9-11

______. *The House in Norham Gardens.* Dutton, 1974. 11-14

LOFTING, HUGH. *The Story of Dr. Dolittle,* ill. by author. Lippincott, 1920. 9-12

______. *The Voyages of Dr. Dolittle,* ill. by author. Lippincott, 1922. Newbery Medal. 9-12

MACDONALD, GEORGE. *At the Back of the North Wind,* ill. by George and Doris Hauman. Macmillan, 1950.

______. *The Light Princess,* ill. by William Pène du Bois. T. Crowell, 1962.

______. *The Light Princess,* ill. by Maurice Sendak. Farrar, 1969.

______. *The Princess and Curdie,* ill. by Nora S. Unwin. Macmillan, 1954.

______. *The Princess and the Goblin,* ill. by Nora S. Unwin. Macmillan, 1964.
Attractive editions of old favorites. 9-12

McGINLEY, PHYLLIS. *The Plain Princess,* ill. by Helen Stone. Lippincott, 1945. In this parody of a fairy tale, the heroine's appearance improves as she becomes less selfish. 7-10

McHARGUE, GEORGESS. *Stoneflight,* ill. by Arvis Stewart. Viking, 1975. Janie finds that the stone griffin on her New York rooftop can come to life and give her needed security. 10-12

______, comp. *Hot and Cold Running Cities; An Anthology of Science Fiction.* Holt, 1974. A well-chosen collection of tales about the future. 12 up

McKILLIP, PATRICIA. *The Forgotten Beasts of Eld.* Atheneum, 1974. Sybel, who's called all the legendary beasts to her side, finds love is more important than power. 12-14

MARTEL, SUZANNE. *The City Under Ground,* tr. by Norah Smaridge, ill. by Don Sibley. Viking, 1964. 11-14

MAYNE, WILLIAM. *Earthfasts.* Dutton, 1967. 11-14

______. *A Game of Dark.* Dutton, 1971. 10-13

MAZER, NORMA. *Saturday, the Twelfth of October.* Delacorte, 1975. A girl goes back in time and lives with a primitive tribe. 11-13

MERRILL, JEAN. *The Pushcart War,* ill. by Ronni Solbert. Scott/Addison, 1964. 10-12

MILNE, A. A. *The House at Pooh Corner,* ill. by Ernest Shepard. Dutton, 1928.

______. *Winnie-the-Pooh,* ill. by Ernest Shepard. Dutton, 1926.

These stories were reprinted in 1961, with larger type and more attractive format.

______. *The World of Pooh,* ill. by E. H. Shepard. Dutton, 1957. Distinctive color illustrations give a festive air to this new large-print volume, containing *Winnie-the-Pooh* and *House at Pooh Corner.* 8-10

MOON, SHEILA. *Knee-Deep in Thunder,* ill. by Peter Parnall. Atheneum, 1967. A most unusual fantasy in which the characters seem to have been brought together by some mysterious force in order to travel and struggle toward an unseen goal. 12 up

MORGAN, HELEN. *Satchkin Patchkin,* ill. by Shirley Hughes. Macrae, 1970. Eight short tales that are particularly suited for reading aloud or for storytelling. Good style, satisfying action. 8-10

NORTON, ANDRE. *The Crystal Gryphon.* Atheneum, 1972. Kerovan, who has hoofs instead of feet, proves worthy of his betrothed. 12-14

______. *The Jargoon Pard.* Atheneum, 1974. Set in a medieval world. Companion volume to the preceding title. 12-14

______. *Lavender-green Magic,* ill. by Judith Gwyn Brown. T. Crowell, 1974. A time-travel adventure with a black heroine. 12-14

______. *Moon of Three Rings.* Viking, 1966. 12-14

______. *The Zero Stone.* Viking, 1968. 12-14

NORTON, MARY, *Bed-Knob and Broomstick,* ill. by Erik Blegvad. Harcourt, 1957. Prim Miss Price was studying how to be a witch when the Wilson children discovered her. The bit of magic she gave them to ensure silence leads to some enchanting adventures. 9-13

______. *The Borrowers,* ill. by Beth and Joe Krush. Harcourt, 1953. Carnegie Medal. This book was followed by *The Borrowers Afield* (1955), *The Borrowers Afloat* (1959), *The Borrowers Aloft* (1961). 9-12

______. *Poor Stainless,* ill. by Beth and Joe Krush. Harcourt, 1971. 8-10

NOURSE, ALAN E. *The Universe Between.* McKay, 1965. A tale of parallel universes, stressing the need for meaningful communication. 11-13

O'BRIEN, ROBERT C. *Mrs. Frisby and the Rats of NIMH,* ill. by Zena Bernstein. Atheneum, 1971. Newbery Medal. 9-11

______. *Z for Zachariah.* Atheneum, 1975. A taut science fiction story of the last people left in the world. 11 up

O'CONNELL, JEAN S. *The Dollhouse Caper,* ill. by Erik Blegvad. T. Crowell, 1976. 8-10

ORGEL, DORIS. *Phoebe and the Prince,* ill. by Erik Blegvad. Putnam, 1969. The hero is a flea with a distinguished past. Brisk and silly fun. 5-9

ORMONDROYD, EDWARD. *All in Good Time,* ill. by Ruth Robbins. Parnassus, 1975. In a sequel to *Time at the Top,* families from two time periods merge. 10-13

______. *Broderick,* ill. by John Larrecq. Parnassus, 1969. An industrious mouse finds fame and fortune as a surfer. A delightful story, told with a straight face in polished style. 5-7

______. *Theodore,* ill. by John M. Larrecq. Parnassus, 1966. When he is caught in a laundromat load, Theodore, an aging toy bear, must arrange a few small capers to return him to his ordinary dirty state. A good read-aloud story. 3-6

______. *Time at the Top,* ill. by Peggie Bach. Parnassus, 1963. The elevator stops at an extra floor and Susan finds an 1890 family and home. 10-13

PARKER, RICHARD. *A Time to Choose; A Story of Suspense.* Harper, 1974. A nicely plotted story of movement between two periods of time. 11-14

PEARCE, A. PHILIPPA. *Tom's Midnight Garden,* ill. by Susan Einzig. Lippincott, 1959. Carnegie Medal. 10-13

PECK, RICHARD. *The Ghost Belonged to Me.* Viking, 1975. A boy of 1913 helps a restless ghost in her efforts to be reburied with her family, in a witty and nostalgic fantasy. 11-13

PEYTON, KATHLEEN. *A Pattern of Roses,* ill. by author. T. Crowell, 1973. The lives of a boy of the present and his counterpart in the past are strangely, convincingly linked. 11-14

PICARD, BARBARA LEONIE. *The Faun and the Woodcutter's Daughter,* ill. by Charles Stewart. Criterion, 1964. 10-12

______. *The Goldfinch Garden,* ill. by Anne Linton. Criterion, 1965. 9-12

______. *The Lady of the Linden Tree,* ill. by Charles Stewart. Criterion, 1962. 10-12

______. *The Mermaid and the Simpleton,* ill. by Phillip Gough. Criterion, 1969. 9-11

POTTER, BEATRIX. *The Tale of Peter Rabbit,* ill. by author. Warne, 1903. Between 1903 and 1930, nineteen books were published in the series. 3-8

PREUSSLER, OTFRIED. *The Satanic Mill,* tr. by Anthea Bell. Macmillan, 1973. A prize-winning German book about an evil miller-magician whose apprentices are doomed to die. 11-14

PYLE, HOWARD. *Pepper and Salt,* ill. by author. Harper, 1923 (first pub. in 1885). Eight fairy tales, wittily retold and well illustrated.

______. *Wonder Clock,* ill. by author. Harper, 1943 (first pub. in 1887). Twenty-four delightful tales, a companion volume to the one above. 10-12

REY, HANS A. *Curious George,* ill. by author. Houghton, 1941. And its sequels. 4-8

RODGERS, MARY. *A Billion for Boris.* Harper, 1974. Annabel and her friend Boris find a television set that gives the news of the next day. Including stock market prices! 9-11

______. *Freaky Friday.* Harper, 1972. What would a girl do if she woke one morning and found she'd turned into her mother? Annabel tells us what. 9-11

RUSKIN, JOHN. *The King of the Golden River,* ill. by Fritz Kredel. World, 1946. 10-14

SAINT-EXUPÉRY, ANTOINE DE. *The Little Prince,* tr. by Katherine Woods, ill. by author. Harcourt, 1943. 12 up

SANDBURG, CARL. *Rootabaga Stories,* ill. by Maud and Miska Petersham. Harcourt, 1922. 8-12

SELDEN, GEORGE. *The Cricket in Times Square,* ill. by Garth Williams. Farrar, 1960. 9-12

______. *The Genie of Sutton Place.* Farrar, 1973. A genie released from a carpet accomplishes minor and major miracles in a city story. 10-11

______. *Harry Cat's Pet Puppy,* ill. by Garth Williams. Farrar, 1974. 8-11

______. *Tucker's Countryside,* ill. by Garth Williams. Farrar, 1969. 9-11

SENDAK. MAURICE. *Higglety Pigglety Pop! or There Must Be More to Life,* ill. by author. Harper, 1967. 8-10

———. *In the Night Kitchen,* ill. by author. Harper, 1970. 5-7

———. *Nutshell Library,* ill. by author. Harper, 1962. 4-7

———. *Where the Wild Things Are,* ill. by author. Harper, 1963. Caldecott Medal. 5-7

SEUSS, DR. [pseud. for Theodor Seuss Geisel]. *And to Think That I Saw It on Mulberry Street,* ill. by author. Vanguard, 1937. 5-8

———. *Bartholomew and the Oobleck,* ill. by author. Random, 1949. 5-8

———. *The Cat in the Hat,* ill. by author. Random, 1957. The Cat provides novel entertainment for two housebound children. 5-8

———. *The Cat in the Hat Comes Back!* ill. by author. Random, 1958. More fun with the Cat and his helpers. Easy-to-read stories. 5-8

———. *The 500 Hats of Bartholomew Cubbins,* ill. by author. Vanguard, 1938. 6-10

SHARP, MARGERY. *The Rescuers,* ill. by Garth Williams. Little, 1959. Witty fantasy of three brave mice who rescue a Norwegian poet from imprisonment in a deep, dark dungeon. *Miss Bianca* (1962) relates another brave rescue. 10-13

SINGER, ISAAC BASHEVIS. *The Fearsome Inn,* tr. by author and Elizabeth Shub, ill. by Nonny Hogrogian. Scribner's, 1967. A fanciful tale mingling the Polish-Jewish humor and gusto with the fairy tale genre most deftly. The illustrations have a graceful vitality and a restrained use of color. 10-12

SLEIGH, BARBARA. *Carbonel: The King of the Cats,* ill. by V. H. Drummond. Bobbs, 1957. Humorous magical tale of two children who rescue the king of cats from the spell of an old witch. 9-12

———. *The Kingdom of Carbonel,* ill. by D. M. Leonard. Bobbs, 1960. Carbonel battles for the rights of his royal kittens. 9-12

SLOBODKIN, LOUIS. *Space Ship Under the Apple Tree,* ill. by author. Macmillan, 1967. Eddie's farm vacation at Grandmother's proves anything but quiet when he is joined by Marty, the little man from Martinea, complete with his space ship. First in a series. 8-10

SMITH, AGNES, *An Edge of the Forest,* ill. by Roberta Moynihan. Viking, 1959; Westwind Press, 1974. An allegory of peaceful coexistence. 11-14

SNYDER, ZILPHA KEATLEY. *And All Between,* ill. by Alton Raible. Atheneum, 1976. The two factions in *Below the Root* confront each other in a suspenseful story. 10-12

———. *Below the Root,* ill. by Alton Raible. Atheneum, 1975. A science fantasy set in a community of tree-dwellers. 10-12

———. *Eyes in the Fishbowl,* ill. by Alton Raible. Atheneum, 1968. Dion explores a department store at night and finds that odd things happen. 11-14

STEELE, MARY Q. *Journey Outside,* ill. by Rocco Negri. Viking, 1969. The Raft People float down the dark underground river, looking for a Better Place, but the boy Dilar leaves and makes his way to the strange world of grass and sunshine where he encounters several cultures, each convincingly portrayed. 10-12

STEELE, WILLIAM O. *Andy Jackson's Water Well,* ill. by Michael Ramus. Harcourt, 1959. Andy Jackson achieves the incredible by bringing back water to drought-ridden Nashville. A hilarious tall tale that is ideal for storytelling. 9-13

STEIG, WILLIAM. *Dominic,* ill. by author. Farrar, 1972. 9-11

———. *The Real Thief,* ill. by author. Farrar, 1973. An upright goose, guard of the royal treasury, is falsely accused of theft and exonerated when the real thief is caught. 8-10

———. *Sylvester and the Magic Pebble,* ill. by author. Simon, 1969. Caldecott Medal. 5-7

STOCKTON, FRANK RICHARD. *The Bee-Man of Orn,* ill. by Maurice Sendak. Holt, 1964. The Bee-Man is completely content until he is informed that he has been transformed from some other sort of thing. A charming story, republished with Sendak's delightful illustrations. 10-12

———. *The Griffin and the Minor Canon,* ill. by Maurice Sendak. Holt, 1963. The lonesome last griffin, curious as to how he looks, flies far from his native haunts to see his statue on an old church. His reception by the people, and especially by the Minor Canon, makes this an intriguing tale. 6-10

STOLZ, MARY S. *Belling the Tiger,* ill. by Beni Montresor. Harper, 1967. A pointed message in this humorous story. 7-10

———. *Cat in the Mirror.* Harper, 1975. The heroine, Erin, escapes her present unhappiness by moving in time to a household in ancient Egypt. 11-13

STORR, CATHERINE. *The Chinese Egg.* McGraw, 1975. Two English children share precognitive visions that solve a kidnaping. 12 up

THURBER, JAMES. *The Great Quillow,* ill. by Doris Lee. Harcourt, 1944. 8-11

———. *Many Moons,* ill. by Louis Slobodkin. Harcourt, 1943. Caldecott Medal. 7-10

———. *The Thirteen Clocks,* ill. by Marc Simont. Simon, 1950. The cold Duke's hold over Princess Saralinda is broken when Prince Zorn brings him 1000 jewels and the Princess's warmth restarts the clocks. 11-12

———. *The Wonderful O,* ill. by Marc Simont. Simon, 1957. Life without "O" goes on, but love, even footnotes, are lost. 10 up

TODD, RUTHVEN. *Space Cat,* ill. by Paul Galdone. Scribner's, 1952. Flyball was a daring cat, and when he accompanied his favorite pilot on a trip to the moon, he not only saved his life but made an important scientific discovery. First of a series. 8-10

TOLKIEN, JOHN R. R. *Farmer Giles of Ham,* ill. by Pauline Diana Baynes. Nelson, 1962. Humorous tale of a simple farmer who finds himself rescuing his village from dragons! 9-12

———. *The Hobbit,* ill. by author. Houghton, 1938. 5-8

TRAVERS, P. L. *Mary Poppins,* ill. by Mary Shepard. Harcourt, 1934.

———. *Mary Poppins Comes Back,* ill. by Mary Shepard. Harcourt, 1935.

———. *Mary Poppins in the Park,* ill. by Mary Shepard. Harcourt, 1952.

———. *Mary Poppins Opens the Door,* ill. by Mary Shepard and Agnes Sims. Harcourt, 1943. 8-12

WARRICK, PATRICIA, and MARTIN H. GREENBERG, eds. *The New Awareness; Religion Through Science Fiction,* Delacorte, 1975. Most of the selections in this anthology are written with skill and insight. 13 up

WHITE, E. B. *Charlotte's Web,* ill. by Garth Williams. Harper, 1952. 10 up

———. *Stuart Little,* ill. by Garth Williams. Harper, 1945. 9-11

———. *The Trumpet of the Swan,* ill. by Edward Frascino. Harper, 1970. 9-11

WILDE, OSCAR. *The Happy Prince and Other Stories,* ill. by Peggy Fortnum. Dutton, 1968. 9-11

———. *The Selfish Giant,* ill. by Gertrude and Walter Reiner. Harvey, 1968. 9-11

WILLIAMS, JAY, and RAYMOND ABRASHKIN. *Danny Dunn and the Antigravity Paint,* ill. by Ezra Jack Keats. McGraw, 1956. One of a popular series. 10-12

WILLIAMS, URSULA MORAY. *Island Mackenzie,* ill. by Edward Ardizzone. Morrow, 1960. The two survivors from a shipwreck—Miss Pettifer and the captain's cat—find themselves on the same island. A fine mixture of humor, fantasy, and suspense. 10-12

______. *The Moonball,* ill. by Jane Paton. Meredith, 1967. A group of resourceful English children appoint themselves protectors of the moonball—a weird, silky-haired, grapefruit-size, living object—which a professor wishes to subject to scientific investigation. 7-9

______. *The Toymaker's Daughter,* ill. by Shirley Hughes Meredith, 1968. A doll wants desperately to become a real child. 9-10

WRIGHTSON, PATRICIA. *Down to Earth,* ill. by Margaret Horder. Harcourt, 1965. 10-12

______. *The Nargun and the Stars.* Atheneum, 1974. Friendly spirits help an Australian family battle the Nargun, an ancient creature of living stone. 10-12

YOLEN, JANE H. *The Girl Who Cried Flowers, and Other Tales,* ill. by David Palladini. T. Crowell, 1974. Five tales with a folklore flavor. 8-10

______. *The Magic Three of Solatia,* ill. by Julia Noonan. T. Crowell, 1974. A romantic adventure tale. 10-11

______. *The Seventh Mandarin,* ill. by Ed Young. Seabury, 1970. Beautifully illustrated tale, in legend style, of seven mandarins who guarded their king, long ago in an eastern land. Good style and good storytelling, despite a rather pallid ending. 7-9

______, comp. *Zoo 2000; Twelve Stories of Science Fiction and Fantasy Beasts.* Seabury, 1973. 11 up

Poetry

Chapter 9

Poetry can bring warmth, reassurance, even laughter; it can stir and arouse or quiet and comfort. Above all it can give significance to everyday experience. To miss poetry would be as much of a deprivation as to miss music. For these reasons it is essential that we know poetry and that we know how to introduce it to children. The experience of poetry should come with so much pure pleasure that the taste for it will grow and become a permanent part of a child's emotional, intellectual, and aesthetic resources.

For some years, there has been a ground swell of interest in poetry, both in producing it for young people and in encouraging them to write it. Not all of the qualities that distinguish poetry from prose are common to all its forms, but basic to the genre are the concentration or crystallization of mood, emotion, or experience; the use of words or sounds that are evocative; and the use of imagery, oblique or vividly clear. Most poetry provides the satisfaction and challenge of pattern and uses words in a way that is more musical or rhythmic than all but the most lyric prose. The alliteration and refrain that can be obtrusive or redundant in prose become, in a good poem, part of its appeal; in a mediocre poem, an abuse of these devices or a rigid adherence to rhyme, especially when it is forced, can result in doggerel. Rhyme and rhythm, particularly attractive to younger children, reinforce aural enjoyment, for poetry must be heard to be fully savored. The essence of poetry is revelation: by the way words are put together, by the richly imaginative use of those words, by the condensation of the poet's conviction, we see with sharpened understanding our own experiences or share with quickened empathy the experiences or dreams of others.

Definitions of poetry are, of course, valueless to children, but they are valuable to adults since they throw light on the manner in which to present poetry.

Robert Frost said that "A poem is a momentary stay against confusion. Each poem clarifies something. . . . A poem is an arrest of disorder."[1] Frost implied that our experiences come pellmell, but a poem sorts them out, gives them order and meaning—not merely the essence of an experience but its significance.

Others define poetry:

Absolute poetry is the concrete and artistic expression of the human mind in emotional and rhythmical language.—Encyclopaedia Britannica

The essence of poetry is invention; such invention as, by producing something unexpected, surprises and delights.—Samuel Johnson

If I read a book and it makes my whole body so cold no fire can ever warm me, I know that is poetry. If I feel physically as if the top of my head

[1]John Ciardi, "Robert Frost; Master Conversationalist at Work," *Saturday Review*, March 21, 1959.

were taken off, I know that is poetry. These are the only ways I know it. Is there any other way?— Emily Dickinson

If you examine these definitions and others, you will discover certain ideas recurring: poetry surprises and delights; it sings like music; it makes you feel intensely; poetry gives you an arresting thought often in rhythmic words, plus a shiver up your backbone. When poetry means these things to you, you have genuinely enjoyed it: it becomes a part of you. When it leaves you just where you were, neither aroused nor amused, neither enchanted nor solaced, then poetry has not happened to you; it has passed you by. So it is with children.

Elements of Good Poetry

But how about adults who enjoy doggerel, and children who accept anything that rhymes? Does enjoyment make poetry of these jingles they read? Perhaps for them it does temporarily, but doggerel need not remain their top level of appreciation. Good taste in any field—music, interior decoration, clothes, poetry—is largely a matter of experience. As we become familiar with the best in one field, we gain discrimination there, while in another field in which our experience is limited we may show very poor taste. Harry Behn says, "I believe that children's judgment of what books are best for them to expand into is better than *our* judgment if we make the best as easily available as television."[2] Children's taste will improve if they have repeated experiences with good poetry.

Singing Quality: Melody and Movement

One of the most important characteristics of good poetry is its singing quality, its melody and movement. In the nonsense jingles and humorous verse, for example, words and lines trip along with the lightness of children jumping rope. Clumsy doggerel—in contrast to the verses of Lear, Richards, and Milne—is heavy footed, and its words and lines have no sparkle. If, as Lillian Smith says in *The Unreluctant Years*, the verses of Milne and Lear are not true poetry, they are certainly as debonair and as skillfully written as light verse can be. If a poem is in a mysterious or meditative or wistful mood, the lines move slowly and the words fall subtly on the ear. These are clues to reading poetry aloud and emphasizing the musical pattern. On the whole, the poetry small children like is more lively and lilting than poetry for adults. The fact that children enjoy marked rhythms and crisp rhymes accounts for their ready acceptance of second-rate verse if it has these characteristics. But if their ears become attuned to the subtleties and varieties of rhythmic patterns found in poems like those by Stevenson, De la Mare, and Behn, they may detect the labored rhythms and forced rhymes which characterize most mediocre verse.

Words of Poetry

Poetry uses strong, vigorous words or evocative, rich words or delicate, precise words that

Viewpoints

In choosing poems for young children . . . we would do well to remember that wit has its beginnings in simply being funny, or in the Comic Spirit, if I may borrow an almost-classic designation. . . . I have had the experience of reading Carl Sandburg's "Arithmetic" to several groups of nine- and ten-year-olds. The laughter is a little tentative at first, then grows to a shout as they begin to recognize their own struggles and puzzlements. What astonishes them most, however, is the realization that this set of lines, with its combination of truthfulness and absurdity, its juxtaposition of arithmetic problems and fried eggs, is a poem. One can almost hear the wheels go round as the children begin to consider the question of what poetry is. Now, "Arithmetic" is not "Paradise Lost," but doesn't it achieve for the nine-year-old that crystallization of experience, that new way of looking at something we knew all along, that we call poetry? Another way of putting it is to say that poetry is partly about something you know and partly about something you don't know quite yet. Children are quick to grasp this idea. . . .—Helen Plotz, "All Who Hide Too Well Away," *The Horn Book,* April 1959, pp. 113, 114.

[2]Harry Behn, *Chrysalis* (Harcourt Brace Jovanovich, 1968), p. 16.

define with accuracy. Of course, prose may employ the same words, but poetry ordinarily uses them with greater condensation and in more melodious combinations so that their effect is more striking. Think of the amusing "sneezles and freezles" of Christopher Robin, of John Updike's "stripped and shapely Maple" grieving in November for "the ghosts of her departed leaves," or of Blake's "echoing green," which suggests the calls and shouts of children at their play. Read through these poems and notice both the exact, descriptive words and the sensory, connotative words and phrases which distinguish good poetry from the ordinary: "the still dark night," "skipping along alone," "rain in the city" falling "slant-wise where the buildings crowd," "soaked, sweet-smelling lane," "Apple trees are snowing." Words that stir the imagination, that speak to the senses, that provoke laughter, that move us deeply and strongly—such words are part of the secret of good poetry.

Illustrations on pages 246 and 247 by Trina Schart Hyman, © 1972 by Harcourt Brace Jovanovich, Inc. and reproduced with their permission from Listen, Children, Listen *by Myra Cohn Livingston.*

Content of Poetry

While poetry has strong emotional appeals, it is built around subjects or ideas, and appeals to the intellect as well as the emotions. Even a slight verse like "Little Miss Muffet" has a well-defined idea—security, fright, escape. Children's emotional response to poetry depends upon their grasp of the content. Of course poetry may have almost as varied subject matter as prose, but like any of the other arts, it must invest that content with arresting significance. A slippery baby in a bathtub is Carl Sandburg's "fish child," and Marianne Moore's jellyfish is "an amber-tinctured amethyst." John Ciardi's "thin grin-cat" stalking a bird is ominous in its suggestion of hunger and anticipated satisfaction. So poetry takes the strange or everyday facts of life and gives them fresh meaning. We see colors that seem new because poetry has revealed them.

Selecting Poetry for Children

When we choose a poem for children, we may well test it with these questions: First, *does it sing*—with good rhythm, true, unforced rhymes, and a happy compatibility of sound and subject—whether it is nonsense verse or narrative or lyric poetry? Second, *is the diction distinguished*—with words that are rich in sensory and connotative meanings, words that are unhackneyed, precise, and memorable? Third, *does the subject matter of the poem invest the strange or the everyday experiences of life with new importance and richer meaning?* When a poem does these three things, it is good poetry.[3]

People who do not like poetry usually have had unpleasant introductions to poems when they were children. Poetry should be chosen and presented to children with care if we wish to make it appealing to them. Following are some suggestions for do's and don't's:

- Don't introduce poetry by dissecting it.
- Don't read poetry aloud without practicing enough to read it well.
- Don't confuse poems that are *about* children with poems that are *for* children.
- Don't present poems that are too long, or that have long descriptive passages.
- Don't choose poems that have involved figures of speech or obsolete language.
- Don't introduce poetry by having children read it silently.
- Don't require children to memorize poetry.
- Don't use poetry as a reading exercise.
- Don't select poems that are pedantic or that are about a subject in which children probably have a minimal interest, such as reflections on growing old.
- Don't select poems with obscure meanings or language too difficult for the child's comprehension.

[3]Many of the poems cited in this chapter appear in *Time for Poetry*, Third Edition (Scott, Foresman, 1968) and *The Arbuthnot Anthology of Children's Literature*, 4th ed. (Scott, Foresman, 1976).

- Do read poetry aloud often.
- Do provide a variety of poems in records, books, and tapes.
- Do make several anthologies available to children.
- Do select contemporary poetry as well as older material.
- Do help children avoid sing-song reading aloud.
- Do choose poems with comprehensible subject matter.
- Do encourage the writing of poetry.
- Do choose poems that have action or humor.
- Do try choral readings.

These are general suggestions, and are not meant to imply that all figures of speech should be shunned, or that all subject matter in poetry should be wholly within the child's experience, but that such aspects of poetry should be given careful consideration before poems are introduced to children.

We would do well to remember how important it is that children still in the process of learning to read should hear most of their poetry before they are asked to cope with it on the printed page; children's reading abilities are behind their listening abilities in the first few years of school, and so the effort of reading poetry may, during those years, be greater than the pleasure of reading poetry. It is also important to keep in mind that today's poets are more understandable to today's children than are most of the older poets, whose work may be better understood and more easily introduced when children reach junior or senior high school.

To Make Poetry-Lovers of Children

Know What Children Like About Poetry

This brings us to the delight of using poetry with children. We must know what they like about poetry and how to expose them to it so the liking grows. Research findings indicate that children's poetry preferences have remained stable throughout the years.[4] Students in the upper elementary grades dislike sentimental poems, preferring those that are humorous; they prefer poetry with everyday language and content to poetry with figurative language or to traditional poetry, and they have a strong liking for poems written in narrative form.

Fortunately, poetry's first and strongest appeal is its *singing quality*, the *melody* and *movement* of the word patterns and the lines. Walter de la Mare calls these qualities "tune and runningness," and they make poetry an aural art like music, to be heard and spoken just as music is to be heard and played. Our business as adults is to savor this singing quality of verse and to learn how to maintain it in our reading.

Next, children like the *story* element in poetry, from "Little Miss Muffet" to "The Highwayman." This is so strong an interest that we should search for fine narrative poetry for every age level. Children will accept the feeblest doggerel if it tells a story. Often the surprising and provocative little story suggestions in the poetry of Walter de la Mare account for the children's enjoying subtler and lovelier verse than they would otherwise appreciate.

Nonsense and *humor* in poetry have great appeal to children. They delight in the daft lunacy of cows jumping over the moon and they move happily from the gaiety and nonsense of *Mother Goose* and Edward Lear to the modern hilarity of Shel Silverstein and John Ciardi. They enjoy the sound of nonsense words, alliteration, and the repetition of phrases in a refrain. But on the way, nonsense merges naturally into light verse. Children chuckle over the gay drama of "The King's Breakfast" and a few years later are grinning over the more intellectual humor of "Macavity the Mystery Cat." For humor can be subtle, and well-written humorous verse is an exercise not only in ear training but also in quick associations, double meanings, satire, or witty implications.

The *sensory content* of poetry (the words and images that evoke seeing, hearing, touching, tasting, smelling responses) constitutes one of its strongest appeals, or, in some cases, accounts for its failure with certain children. If the sensory content is familiar or understandable, then they respond to it with zest. Over half the children in the United States are from urban areas while a large proportion of our poetry is distinctly rural in its sensuous imagery. (Of course, this situation is changing as more and more of the recent poetry has an urban setting.) The city child and the country child have certain experiences in common—wind, rain, snow, sun, moon, stars, heat, cold, fog—but how differently these experiences impinge on the consciousness of each of them. Take snow, for instance, which in the crowded areas of the city is soon a blackish, soggy slush. How, then, can the city child, who knows neither down, nor lambs, nor

But OSTRICHES
never
can fly at all.
They're far too big
and their wings
too small.

Illustration by Peter Parnall for But Ostriches . . . *by Aileen Fisher. Text copyright © 1970 by Aileen Fisher, illustrations copyright © 1970 by Peter Parnall. Reprinted with permission of Thomas Y. Crowell Company, Inc., New York, Publishers.*

[4]Ann Terry, *Children's Poetry Preferences; A National Survey of Upper Elementary Grades.* National Council of Teachers of English, 1974.

even clean, soft snow (at least for very long), respond to the feeling of stepping upon "white down," of walking upon "silver fleece," as described in Elinor Wylie's "Velvet Shoes"? By the time these are laboriously explained, there is not much left of the dreamlike quality of that walk

At a tranquil pace,
Under veils of white lace.[5]

In the last several years, fortunately, more and more city poems have appeared. In a poem from *I Thought I Heard the City,* Lilian Moore captures the beauty and quiet of snow in an urban setting.

Snowy Morning[6]

Wake
gently this morning
to a different day.
Listen.
There is no bray
of buses,
no brake growls,
no siren howls and
no horns
blow.

There is only
the silence
of a city
hushed
by snow.

There are now many anthologies intended particularly for city children: for example, Robert Froman's *Street Poems,* Nancy Larrick's *On City Streets,* Arnold Adoff's *City in All Directions,* and Lee Bennett Hopkins's *City Talk.*

Poetry should be comprehensible to children, but that does not mean they must have experienced everything they read about. Few children have had an opportunity to observe an ostrich closely, yet how enticingly Aileen Fisher leads them to an easy understanding of ostriches by contrasting ostriches with birds that *are* familiar.

Most birds surely
Walk quite poorly
Most birds merely
hop around.

They're securest,
swiftest, surest
on their wings
above the ground,
but OSTRICHES . . . .[7]

In this way, with humor, suspense, rhyme, and rhythm, the child is led through enjoyment to comprehension.

Provide Children with Rich Poetry Experiences

Children's encounters with poetry should include three types of response—*enjoyment, exploration,* and *deepening understandings.* These do not occur always as separate steps but simultaneously. Certainly, children must start with enjoyment or their interest in poetry dies. But if from the beginning they find delight in the poems they hear, they are ready and eager to explore further—more books and more poems of different sorts. Even the youngest children can learn to see implications beyond the obvious. To read for veiled meanings is to identify oneself with the poet, to ask the poet's questions. This is reading for deeper understanding, taking a thoughtful look at what lies beneath the surface. Enjoyment, exploration, and deeper understanding must all be part of children's experience with poetry if we are to help them to love it.

Read Poetry to Children

Poetry began as a spoken art; people listened to it and remembered it because rhyme and meter made it easier to recall than prose. So it

[5]From "Velvet Shoes" from *Collected Poems of Elinor Wylie.* Copyright 1921, 1932 by Alfred A. Knopf, Inc. Reprinted by permission.

[6]"Snowy Morning." Text copyright © 1969 by Lilian Moore. From *I Thought I Heard the City.* Used by permission of Atheneum Publishers.

[7]From *But Ostriches . . .* by Aileen Fisher, copyright © 1970 by Aileen Fisher, used by permission of Thomas Y. Crowell Company, Inc., publishers.

Viewpoints

While in all other Arts it is agreed that a student should be trained only on the best models, wherein technique and aesthetic are both exemplary, there has been with respect to Poetry a pestilent notion that the young should be gradually led up to excellence through lower degrees of it; so that teachers have invited their pupils to learn and admire what they expected them to outgrow: and this was carried so far that writers, who else made no poetic pretence, have good-naturedly composed poems for the young, and in a technique often as inept as their sentiment.—Robert Bridges, *The Chilswell Book of English Poetry,* compiled by Robert Bridges, Longmans and Green and Co., London, 1924, p. ix.

should begin for children. Poetry should be heard because of its inherent lyric qualities. Adults should read or speak it aloud and encourage children to join in until, without even realizing it, they have memorized effortlessly dozens of poems which they can speak naturally and gaily. (See Part 4 for a discussion of reading poetry aloud.) Speaking or reading poetry to children should continue all through their childhood.

By the time of early adolescence most children have mastered the mechanics of reading and if their childhood experiences with poetry have been happy, they will go on reading it on their own.

Poetry should never be used as a reading exercise. When children have to struggle with a poem as a reading lesson, they are baffled and discouraged. John Erskine, writing for older students, says in *The Kinds of Poetry:* "The office of the teacher of poetry is easily defined; it is to afford a mediation between great poets and their audience." With children, effective oral reading is the surest mediation.

Mother Goose is a natural starting point with children from two to six or seven years old. Her pages are alive with "tune and runningness" and children respond with vigor. They soon discover that "Ride a cock horse" is a gallop and "To market, to market" is an everyday walk, quite unlike the military tread of "The grand Old Duke of York." Body movement of young children is a natural response to these nursery rhymes. They don't know that it is meter and rhyme, line and word patterns that produce these contagious rhythms, but they feel the "goingness" of the verses. This easy, natural introduction can provide a firm foundation for later interest. *Mother Goose* is discussed more fully in Chapter 4, "Books for Early Childhood."

The introduction to poetry for older children should begin as painlessly as it begins for the prereaders. That is, they should hear many poems vigorously read aloud for sheer pleasure, with no analysis during this exploratory stage. Some poetry should be slipped in and introduced with a comment like: "A new poem is like new music. Sometimes you have to hear it several times before you know whether or not you like it." Older children may not always respond with body movements, but they may well identify the gallop of Stevenson's "Windy Nights" or the rattling rhythm of McCord's "The Pickety Fence" even though they cannot analyze the mood in words.

Explore Poetry Books with Children

In the process of enjoying poetry, children will encounter many books and different types of verse. Their explorations will include books by a single author and anthologies of poetry by many poets.

Anthologies are invaluable, and there is no reading experience more satisfying, either in a classroom, a library, or at home, than to settle down with your children to explore a new anthology. Needless to say, you will have explored it first to know its range and contents and to have chosen in advance a group of poems that you feel sure the children will understand and enjoy. Modern anthologies usually provide a high quality of poetry selections and convenient subject matter arrangements, and they rescue from oblivion such out-of-print treasures as "The Pirate Don Durk of Dowdee," "Overheard on a Saltmarsh," and the best of Winifred Welles and Mary Austin. Classrooms and homes should own several anthologies. Here are a few criteria for selecting an anthology from among the many excellent ones available:

1. Examine the author index to discover the range and quality of writers represented. Does it lean heavily on poets of the past, Eugene Field, Riley, Stevenson, Longfellow, or are the best of these balanced by many good modern poets?

2. How many poems does the book contain? Oddly enough, one anthology will contain over five hundred poems while another at approximately the same price will include two to three hundred. If the quality of the two books is equally good, the first is obviously a better choice.

3. Look for indexes and classifications. The indexes should include authors, titles, and, preferably, first lines. Teachers will find classifications by subjects equally important—such groupings as people, animals, nonsense, magic, our country, seasons, and the like. Organization by subjects is far more important than organization by grades. Indeed, grade levels for poems are impossible and undesirable, no matter how teachers yearn for them, because children's tastes and capacities vary as much as the poems themselves and depend on their varied experiences.

4. Format is important. A heavy volume may be useful in the school library as a reference book, but it will not be good for a child to use or an adult to handle with the child. Good paper, clear type, well-spaced pages, all add to the attractiveness of a book.

Some anthologies not only meet these basic criteria, but provide extra dividends in the form of attractive illustrations, brief introductions to or explanations of poems, and suggestions for reading aloud and choral speaking.

Teach children how to explore and use an anthology. A forthcoming festival, for example, means a search for the best Halloween or Christmas poems. Undoubtedly the greatest value of a fine anthology is the feeling it gives children for the range and variety of poetry. They will look, browse further, and make discoveries.

In the same way, children should become acquainted with the books of single poets, not merely Stevenson's *A Child's Garden of Verses*, but David McCord's *For Me to Say*, Harry Behn's *Little Hill*, June Jordan's *Who Look at Me*, and others. This exploration of the works of individual poets guarantees that the child will encounter a range of poetry from the imaginative and subtle lyrics of Walter de la Mare to the robust nonsense of John Ciardi. Such exploration will also help children to grow emotionally, aesthetically, and intellectually with poetry.

Deepen Children's Understanding of Poems

A third phase of poetry experience involves a more intellectual response than either enjoyment or exploration. It is what John Ciardi has called "reading in depth" or reading for a more complete understanding of the poet's meaning. With the youngest children this begins with talking about word meanings and background experiences and with older children it progresses to a fuller consciousness of implications, double meanings, possible symbols, and even to some analysis of form.

To help younger children understand the

From For Me to Say *by David McCord. Illustrated by Henry B. Kane. Copyright © 1970 by David McCord. By permission of Little, Brown and Co.*

meaning of a poem, we often need to evoke or supplement their background of experience. For instance, suppose a child has never seen a subway. Explain how it is built and operated. Then the "underground caves" of Bobbi Katz's "Things to Do If You Were a Subway" become clear. Or suppose a child has never seen a snail. Show a picture of a snail or bring one to school. Then Hilda Conkling's "Little Snail" with "his house on his back" will be visually clear. Walter de la Mare never says in his poem "The Huntsmen" that it is about three boys riding their hobbyhorses upstairs, and so unless children understand this, the "clitter clatter" of those wooden sticks on the stair and the whole meaning of the poem will be obscure.

Sometimes the musical pattern of a poem affects its meaning in ways even very young children can sense. For instance, five-year-olds know that the words in Stevenson's "The Swing" really swing and that the words of Milne's "Hoppity" do hop with Christopher Robin to the very last line which hops to a standstill. Hearing poetry read with an emphasis on its musical patterns, young children can be trained to the point where they are aware, consciously or unconsciously, of what the patterns are making them feel or understand.

Or take Elizabeth Coatsworth's beautiful study in contrasts—"Swift things are beautiful," p. 280. Help the children to hear how the words and lines of the first stanza hurry along, with no long, sonorous vowels or words to delay the crisp, brisk movement. But in the second verse, the long vowels in such mouth-filling phrases as "The pause of the wave/That curves downward to spray" and the heavy last lines, "And the ox that moves on/In the quiet of power," compel a slow, deliberate reading. You simply cannot dash off those last lines briskly.

These brief, simple examples of the way poets use the words and patterns of their verse to suggest action, mood, or meaning are obvious enough for children and are the beginnings of a deeper look at the poetry they enjoy. This deeper look will carry them into the below-the-surface meaning or implications or symbols the poet uses.

Undoubtedly, some teacher has already helped students discover the remarkable likeness of themes in Gerald Johnson's *America Is Born* and Robert Frost's poem "The Gift Outright." In his book Johnson says:

> *At the start nobody intended to become an American, but everybody did if he stayed in this country. They were changed simply by living (here). . . . George Washington still thought of himself as a trueborn Englishman, although it was impossible for him to be anything of the sort.*
>
> *What made us Americans was not long and careful thinking about it, but simply seeing what had to be done and doing it. What had to be done here was not exactly what had to be done in England; and in doing it we became something different from Englishmen.* (p. 140)

Read the children this and then read "The Gift Outright" several times until they see the connection. Because of the concepts involved, this is not a poem for use with younger children.

The Gift Outright[8]

The land was ours before we were the land's.
She was our land more than a hundred years
Before we were her people. She was ours
In Massachusetts, in Virginia,
But we were England's, still colonials,
Possessing what we still were unpossessed by,
Possessed by what we now no more possessed.
Something we were withholding made us weak
Until we found out that it was ourselves
We were withholding from our land of living,
And forthwith found salvation in surrender.
Such as we were we gave ourselves outright
(The deed of gift was many deeds of war)
To the land vaguely realizing westward,
But still unstoried, artless, unenhanced,
Such as she was, such as she would become.

The relation between this poem and the Johnson passage lies, of course, in the lines, "She was our land more than a hundred years/Before we were her people." Why? Be-

[8]"The Gift Outright." From *The Poetry of Robert Frost* edited by Edward Connery Lathem. Copyright 1916, 1923, 1928, 1934, © 1969 by Holt, Rinehart and Winston, Inc. Copyright 1936, 1942, 1944, 1951, © 1956, 1962 by Robert Frost. Copyright © 1964, 1970 by Lesley Frost Ballantine. Reprinted by permission of Holt, Rinehart and Winston, Inc. and Jonathan Cape Ltd. for the Estate of Robert Frost.

cause we were "Possessed by what we now no more possessed"—in other words, England. Which is just another way of saying what Gerald Johnson said. Older children can readily fill in the wars involved in "(The deed of gift was many deeds of war)," but it is more important to challenge the children with those enigmatic last lines—"Such as she was, such as she would become." What would they like our country to become, our United States? This is important because the answer may well lie with them, the children of today, the adults of tomorrow. What would they have our country become that it is not today? The children's answers may not be profound—neither would the answers of most adults—but at least the poem will have made them look beneath the surface of evolving life in their own country and sense the fact that they, too, are going to play a part in its future. This poem is a perfect example of Frost's own pronouncement that "Each poem clarifies something."

The children who are reading and writing poetry today are searching and probing issues and problems of our time. They want, in addition to poetry that is beautiful in its grace and melody, poetry that is beautiful in strength and candor. They need to explore the new forms, to hear the angry voices, for they are, many of them, angry about what is happening in their world. They should read Coatsworth, De la Mare, and Frost, but they should also read Nikki Giovanni, Vanessa Howard, Leonard Cohen, Mari Evans, Karl Shapiro, and the many other poets who are most immediately concerned, as the children are, with the way things are now.

The Range of Poetry for Children

Although some children cling to one genre or subject in their reading, most like variety, and their preferences change with mood and age. Fortunately, there is such variety in poetry as to satisfy any taste: narrative, dramatic, or lyric; bound verse or free; poems about animals, people, nature, fairies, emotions, causes; poems that are thoughtful or stirring, tender or hilarious. Here we shall cross the lines of form and content in discussing both the wide variety of poetry for children and the poetry children are writing today. We shall consider poetry ranging from nonsense verse and the more serious poems about children's everyday experiences to the quiet probings of Langston Hughes's poetry and the patterned intricacies of poems by May Swenson and Myra Cohn Livingston.

A poem may be written in free verse, which has no requirements of rhyme and meter, or in bound verse, which does. It can be narrative, dramatic, or lyric. Dramatic poetry, a form seldom used in children's poems, reveals the personality of a character primarily through his or her speech or through the speech of other characters. Narrative poetry tells a story and is enjoyed by children for that reason, whether the poems are long and serious or brief and humorous. Lyric poems, which are usually short, express an emotion of some kind, often highly personal, and may range in content from the expression of a child's delight in "wiggly mud" to a sad farewell to departing summer.

Nonsense Verse

A good way to introduce children to poetry is with nonsense verse. For young children the gay tradition of nonsense verse was given a rousing start by *Mother Goose*'s rhymes (see Chapter 4). Children enjoy these amusing jingles, and most adults find a lifelong source of fun in humorous limericks and verse.

Not all people and not all ages are amused by the same jokes. Two-year-olds may chuckle over the hissing s's of "sing a song of sixpence." The hilarity of older children is roused by other forms of nonsense. Just listen to seven-year-olds enjoying Laura Richards's "Eletelephony" (see p. 270).

Nonsense verse, if it is skillfully composed, introduces the child to rhyme, rhythm, and meter and to various types of verse patterns. The neatly turned limerick and the patter of humorous couplets or quatrains in exact meter train the ear to enjoy the sound of words and rhythms, a training that should carry over to catching similar sound patterns in poetry of a higher order.

From Nonsense to Humor

Although no hard and fast line divides humor from sheer nonsense, there is, nevertheless, a difference. Nonsense is more daft, more impossible, while humorous verse deals with the amusing things that befall real people, or might conceivably befall them. Edward Lear and Laura E. Richards sometimes wrote humorous verse, but for the most part their verse is hilarious nonsense. In contrast, A. A. Milne wrote occasional nonsense, but on the whole his poems involve people and situations that are amusingly possible, however improbable they may be.

Usually "The King's Breakfast" is the favorite with most Milne addicts. This starts reasonably with the king asking for a little butter on the "Royal slice of bread," and it moves along smoothly until the sleepy Alderney upsets all royal regularity by suggesting "a little marmalade instead." From then on the dialogue becomes entirely daft, reaching a joyous climax when the king bounces out of bed and slides down the banisters. This is, of course, the essence of the fun—the incongruity of a king who is so deeply concerned with marmalade that he whimpers, sulks, bounces, and slides down banisters. The verse pattern of each episode reinforces the mood.

Other writers of humorous verse before the 1950s include the once popular James Whitcomb Riley and Eugene Field. Riley's verses have a mild humor, but they rarely bubble or sparkle. Field's "The Duel" is still enjoyed by children of five or six. This mock tragedy about the gingham dog and the calico cat who "ate each other up" has a pleasant swing and a delightful refrain. Another tragicomic verse is Vachel Lindsay's "The Potatoes' Dance," which tells of the blighted romance of a "tiny Irish lady" and a hapless sweet potato.

Humorous Verse Since the Fifties. One of the most outstanding and prolific writers of humorous verse for children since the 1950s is David McCord, who wrote for adults before he began writing for children. McCord's poems are not all humorous, but the best of them have a captivating playfulness and ebullience which infectiously communicate an enjoyment of words and word play.

William Cole's *Oh, What Nonsense!* and *Oh, How Silly!* are anthologies of humorous poems, the first containing many counting rhymes and jump-rope chants, the second song lyrics and folk rhymes. In both books, the illustrator, Tomi Ungerer, wittily echoes the gay and deft silliness.

In each of her collections of poetry, Eve Merriam provides some amusing gems. Like David McCord, she sometimes uses poetic forms to explain the forms themselves, giving six examples of the couplet in "Couplet Countdown" and demonstrating in "Leaning on a Limerick" both the form and the playful use of words at which she excels.

For older readers, Myra Cohn Livingston's *Speak Roughly to Your Little Boy* is both diverting and instructive. It is a collection of parodies and burlesques, each paired with the original material on which it was based. Some of the selections will also be enjoyed by younger children who can recognize little nuggets of burlesque like J. B. Morton's "Now We Are Sick."

Since anthologists have not found all the humorous verse that has been written, it is a rewarding activity for teachers to make a collection of favorites, or to encourage children to make such a collection. Clever, well-written verses which provoke a chuckle are worth having not only because they bring laughter into a world in need of laughter, but because their rollicking jingles cultivate the

From Oh, What Nonsense! *by William Cole and Tomi Ungerer. Illustrations copyright © 1966 by Tomi Ungerer. Reprinted by permission of The Viking Press, Inc.*

ear and lead naturally and painlessly to the enjoyment of lyric poetry.

Poetry of the Child's Everyday World

The world of fantastic nonsense and the child's everyday world of people, pets, and the outdoors may seem far apart. Yet many poets move easily from one to the other and, like the child, are at home in both worlds.

Actually, in the years before Edward Lear introduced his madcap world of nonsense, children had been given to understand that life was not only real but decidedly earnest. Poems were written and read to children for the purpose of improving their manners and uplifting their morals. Yet didactic as some of these early efforts seem today, they marked a dawning recognition of the child's everyday world of people and play, both real and imaginative. Slowly the idea took form and grew, the idea of a child not as a small adult but as an intensely active person, functioning in a world of his or her own.

The poems of Kate Greenaway marked the transition from verse written for children's instruction to verse written for their entertainment, verse which records the play world from the child's point of view. Even though her verses are often wooden and occasionally unchildlike, they reflect a new consciousness of real children and their everyday play.

Other poets caught this new point of view and began to write a new kind of verse for and about children. Their poems reflect both the child's everyday world of active play and the inner world of imaginative play.

Robert Louis Stevenson wrote only one book of poetry for children, *A Child's Garden of Verses*, but with that one book he became one of the great children's poets. His poems are truly childlike in their approach to play and in the manner in which they mirror the small adventures of a child's day. They are rhythmic and musical, and they see both the imagined and the real with a child's clear eye.

Eleanor Farjeon wrote skillful nonsense verse. Her lyrics are tender and beautiful, and her poetry reflects a sure knowledge of the child's world and wonderment. Her first book, for which she wrote her own music, was *Nursery Rhymes of London Town*. Her writing has zest and playfulness, enjoyment of words, and a variety of subjects and patterns with a seeming spontaneity and an unquestionable charm.

Elizabeth Madox Roberts had the ability to see, feel, and think in a childlike manner that strikes the adult as unerringly right and true. Her single book of poetry for children, *Under the Tree*, uses words and phrases that sound like a child speaking, but only an artist could have chosen words so brilliantly descriptive. Her narrative is as direct as prose, with no pretentiousness, no fanciness, no ethereal theme, but the imagery, the sensitivity, and the identification with the concerns of children bring her poems directly into the child's world of poetry.

John Updike, distinguished as a writer for adults and as the 1964 winner of the National Book Award for Fiction, has, in *A Child's Calendar*, written with fresh imagery about the familiar phenomena of the child's changing year.

June[9]

The sun is rich,
And gladly pays
In golden hours,
Silver days,

And long green weeks
That never end
School's out. The time
Is ours to spend.

The playground calls,
The ice-cream man,
And, after supper,
Kick-the Can.

The live-long light
Is like a dream,
And freckles come
Like flies to cream.

Here is just a sampling of the many poets who have brought their lyric gifts to interpret the everyday world the child sees and won-

[9]"June" from *A Child's Calendar*, by John Updike and Nancy Burkert. Copyright © 1965 by authors. Reprinted by permission of Alfred A. Knopf, Inc.

Illustration by Nancy Burkert from A Child's Calendar *by John Updike. Copyright © 1965 by John Updike and Nancy Burkert. Reprinted by permission of Alfred A. Knopf, Inc. (Original in color)*

ders about. Of all the poems available for children, however, those that tell a story have a special appeal for poetry lovers as well as for self-proclaimed detesters of poems.

Traditional Ballads

The ancient ballads are often, because of their dialect and archaic language, difficult for children to read or sing. Yet children are universally fond of poems that tell a story, and a more rousing collection of stories would be hard to find. Both the folk ballads and modern story poems have a common appeal; they tell a story in concentrated form, with a maximum of excitement and a minimum of words. Children may make little distinction between the types, for what they enjoy is the swift movement of verse or melody enhancing the dramatic appeal of a good story. The search for these story poems carries us back into folk rhymes and forward to present-day narrative poems, ranging from hilarious nonsense to romance and noble tragedy.

Traditional ballads were passed on by word of mouth long before they were printed, and they were so popular and so rapidly carried about by sailors and travelers that it is difficult today to determine whether a ballad is Danish, Scottish, English, or German in origin. The English and Scottish ballads flourished from the thirteenth to the middle of the sixteenth century. However, it was not until 1765, when Bishop Percy collected and published many of them in his famous *Reliques*, that they became widely known and appreciated; the ballads that this collection contained had been found by chance in an ancient manuscript. They inspired Sir Walter Scott and others after him to search for and preserve other original ballad materials.

Characteristics of the Traditional Ballads. The old ballad was a song story and its singing quality is still evident in the lilting verses and refrains and in the lively tunes that accompany the words. "Bonny Barbara Allan," for example, tells a tragic tale swiftly and movingly, but the opening verse suggests at once that here is a song:

In Scarlet Town, where I was bound
There was a fair maid dwelling.
Whom I had chosen to be my own,
And her name it was Barbara Allan.

The tune of "The Gypsy Laddie," or its more familiar folk-song variant, "The Raggle, Taggle Gypsies," is a compelling one, but the ballad is also dramatic for reading. Even the most tragic ballads, like "Edward" or "Lord Randal," have wistful, tender airs that somehow soften the tragedy.

In many ballads this songlike quality is enhanced by refrains which seem made for dancing. It is a good idea to help children respond to the musical character of the ballads by having them sing some or try to suit rhythmic movements to the words of others or even try lively dance steps to the lustier refrains.

Perhaps the most striking characteristic of the ballads is their dramatic and rapidly unfolding plots. In "Edward," for example, you sense immediately that something is wrong; then you learn that Edward has killed his own father, but not till the last stanza do you know that the mother herself planned the crime and persuaded her son to commit it.

There are of course some comic plots, too, but they are distinctly in the minority. "The Crafty Farmer" outwitting the thief is one of the children's favorites, and they like even better the broad slapstick farce of the stubborn old couple in "Get Up and Bar the Door." The folk-tale plot of trial by riddle with a bright person substituting for a stupid one is amusingly used in "King John and the Abbot of Canterbury" ("King John and the Bishop").

Illustration by Virginia Burton. From Song of Robin Hood *edited by Anne Malcomson. Reproduced with permission of Houghton Mifflin Company.*

Viewpoints

. . . Ballads are widely considered to be plotted narratives, rising from relatively trained minds, taken over and fostered by the folk until they become the verses and masterpieces that our collectors uncover.

The word "plotted" is of particular significance. . . . Plotting is honored by the tradition in which the Anglo-American ballad is born, but there is little evidence to support a contention that the folk, in whose oral heritage the ballad lives, care very much at all for unified action. Their myths and their tales lack unified action, except as a vestige. Generally, the folk tend to discard plotting in favor of something one might call "impact" or "emotional core.". . .

A ballad survives among our folk because it embodies a basic human reaction to a dramatic situation. This reaction is reinterpreted by each person who renders the ballad. As an emotional core it dominates the artistic act, and melody, setting, character, and plot are used only as means by which to get it across. This core is more important to the singer and the listeners than the details of the action themselves. —Tristram P. Coffin, "Mary Hamilton and the Anglo-American Ballad as an Art Form," in *The Critics and the Ballad,* readings selected and edited by MacEdward Leach and Tristram P. Coffin, Southern Illinois University Press, Carbondale, 1961, pp. 245, 246, 247.

On the whole, ballad plots are more likely to be tragic than humorous. They celebrate bloody and terrible battles, ghosts that return to haunt their true or their false loves, fairy husbands of human maids, infanticide, murder, faithless love punished, faithful love not always rewarded—sad, sad romance and tragedies in every possible combination.

Incremental repetition is an aid to storytelling. This is a ballad convention in which each verse repeats the form of the preceding verse but with a new turn that advances the story. Reading ballads that use incremental repetition, you will find it easy to imagine a leader starting the pattern by asking the question, a crowd of people singing the refrain, and the same leader, or perhaps the next person in the circle, answering the question.

The author always remains anonymous. Reference to the storyteller is comparatively rare, perhaps only in an opening line. The storyteller merely records the facts of the adventure as objectively as possible and remains completely anonymous.

The ballads, as we have observed, run the whole gamut of subjects and emotions. Here are some categories with a few examples:

Farce—The Crafty Farmer; Get Up and Bar the Door

Comedy—King John and the Abbot of Canterbury (King John and the Bishop); A Gest of

Robyn Hode (with the exception of the account of Robin Hood's death)
Crime—Edward; The Bonny Earl of Murray; Lord Randal; The Twa Sisters
Noble tragedy—Sir Patrick Spens; The Hunting of the Cheviot; The Battle of Harlaw; The Battle of Otterburn (the ballads of the great battles are generally too involved for the elementary school)
Romance—Lizie Lindsay; Bonny Barbara Allan; The Raggle, Taggle Gypsies (The Gypsy Laddie)
Fairylore—The Wee Wee Man; Tam Lin; Hind Etin
Ghost story—The Wife of Usher's Well
Melodrama—The Daemon Lover (James Harris); Lord Randal; Bonny Barbara Allan

Folk Ballads in the United States. Early settlers brought the old Scottish and English ballads to this country, and children in states as remote from each other as Pennsylvania and Texas, or Wisconsin and the Carolinas, heard their parents and their grandparents singing the same ballads that *their* grandparents had sung in the mother country. "Bonny Barbara Allan," for example, was carried by the colonists and pioneer families from one end of the United States to the other.

The collection compiled by Francis Child (1825–1896) of Harvard stimulated such an interest in these old story songs that collectors began to search for and record their American variants. They found, as you might expect, a large number of ballads being sung or recited throughout the country, but especially in the Southern mountains. There the mountaineers, cut off from the mainstream of immigration and changing customs, had preserved the songs their ancestors brought with them. Sometimes "Barbara Allan" was "Barbery Allen" or "Barbara Ellen," but in every version she was the same heartless girl whose cruelty caused her lover's death. "Lord Randal" might be hailed democratically as "Johnny Randall," or even "Jimmy Randolph," but he was still begging his mother to make his bed soon for he was "sick at the heart and fain wad lie down." Sometimes the verses had been so altered and patched together that they were incoherent. Most of the ballads had, however, come through with less change than you might naturally expect from several hundred years of oral transmission.

Cecil J. Sharp (1859–1924), an English musician, made early and outstanding collections of these descendants of Scottish-English ballads in the Southern mountains of the United States. His books are valuable contributions to the ballad literature of America, and other collectors have followed his lead. Older children will enjoy the ballads in Sharp's first two volumes, while children as young as three and four are charmed with the *Nursery Songs*.[10]

Once the collectors set to work gathering American variants of the old-world ballads, they began to encounter new ballads and folk songs that are as native to the United States as buckwheat cakes and hominy grits. Here was a rich treasure of ballad-making still in the process of creation. These songs achieve a wistful melancholy or a happy-go-lucky philosophy or a sheer braggadocio distinguishing certain groups of hardy settlers or certain workers such as the Western cowboys.

The native ballads of the United States tell, on the whole, fewer coherent and dramatic stories than do the Scottish-English ballads; but they sing with or without the music. The Negro spirituals reach heights of religious fervor never attained in any old-world ballad, but for their full beauty they need their music. The cowboys' ballads have sometimes a philosophic or a wistful air that is more in the mood of a song than of a story. The language is easier for us, even the dialect or vernacular, but some of it is rather rough.

With the increasing popularity of folk singing in the middle period of the twentieth century, there has been a renaissance of the ballad form. The outstanding performer-composers are the heroes of the young, the guitar the indispensable instrument, the ballad their own song. And, for the younger children, there is an echoing trend in the publication of single songs in illustrated editions.

Once children realize that ballads are still remembered and treasured, they may turn

[10]C. J. Sharp, compiler, *English Folk Songs from the Southern Appalachians* (Oxford, 1953); *American-English Folk Songs* (Schirmer, 1918); *Nursery Songs from the Appalachian Mountains* (Novello, 1921–1923).

collectors and discover some ballads in their own families or communities. Once they realize that ballads are still being made not merely by professional poets imitating old forms but by isolated peoples celebrating tragic, comic, or dramatic events, the children, too, may wish to try group composition of a ballad. It is fun and less difficult than it sounds. Radio, newspapers, and television make constant use of such events for sketches and dramas. Why not try casting them into ballad form?

Narrative Poems

The story poems and the old ballad form have proved as attractive to poets as they have to readers. The rapid action, the refrains and repetition, and the rhythm all contribute to the interest and impetus of story poems.

For the youngest children, from five to eight or nine, there are two masterpieces—"A Visit from St. Nicholas" by Clement Clarke Moore and "The Pied Piper of Hamelin" by Robert Browning.

It is interesting to recall that Robert Browning wrote his "The Pied Piper of Hamelin" for the amusement of a sick child, with the special intention of supplying him with subject matter he could illustrate. Perhaps this accounts, in part, for the visual quality of the poem, which has endeared it to illustrators. The story of "The Pied Piper" is too familiar to need reviewing, but particular qualities of the poem are worth noting. In the first place, the story moves rapidly. Words hurry and trip along, episodes follow each other swiftly, and lines have the racing tempo first of the scurrying rats and later of the skipping children. The dramatic conflict between greed and honor is sufficiently objective for children to understand, and they approve of the Piper's retributive revenge.

For broad comedy Eugene Field's "The Duel" (the tale of "the gingham dog and the calico cat") and Laura Richards's "The Monkeys and the Crocodile" are perennial favorites. William Allingham's "The Fairy Shoemaker" and Laura Richards's "Little John Bottlejohn" are unusual fairy and mermaid poems, the latter simple enough for the five-year-olds. Willis Barnstone's *A Day in the Country* is a narrative in free and fluid verse, a sunny story of a child's happy summer day. An amusing venture into history is Arnold Lobel's *On the Day Peter Stuyvesant Sailed into Town*. In Natalie Babbitt's *Dick Foote and the Shark*, the poetic hero saves his own life and that of his terrified father by so doggedly spouting poetry from the bow that the befuddled shark swims away.

The story of Noah's Ark, more than slightly adapted, has two verse versions: *The Cruise of the Aardvark*, in which Ogden Nash's pompous hero discovers belatedly that he is not on an ordinary pleasure cruise; and Countee Cullen's *The Lost Zoo*, which is a good choice for reading aloud to younger children. A lasting favorite is "Custard the Dragon" by Ogden Nash. Search your anthologies and books by single poets for more story poems, because even the fives and sevens enjoy the swiftness and suspense which the rhythmic flow of verse gives to a story.

Children in the middle grades may like Longfellow's moving "The Wreck of the Hesperus." Also tragic, and of high poetic beauty, is Edna St. Vincent Millay's "The Ballad of the Harp-Weaver." This the twelves and fourteens should not miss. It is a fantasy, eerie and wistful, built around a mother's love and sacrifice for her child. A poem as full of pity and tenderness as this lovely ballad will help to balance the stark and often brutal tragedies to which children are exposed through newspapers and television.

Scott's "Young Lochinvar," a gay, swashbuckling romance with a galloping tempo, is particularly enjoyed by older children; "The Highwayman" by Alfred Noyes is a favorite romance. William Cowper's "John Gilpin" is only one of many humorous ballads they enjoy. May Sarton has written with sensitivity and grace "The Ballad of Ruby," based on an episode described in Robert Coles's *Children of Crisis*. It tells of a small black child's experience of discrimination when she goes to school. And let's not forget that gem of Americana, Ernest L. Thayer's "Casey at the Bat."

For eleven- to fourteen-year-olds there are many story poems about great events in history. Certainly they should hear "The Landing of the Pilgrim Fathers" by Felicia Dorothea Hemans, with its unforgettable picture of that desolate arrival and its significance in our history. Children may also thrill to the galloping hoofbeats of Longfellow's "Paul Revere's Ride" before they meet the more complex and workaday Revere of the biographies. Arthur Guiterman has written a number of fine historical ballads, but especially recommended are his "Daniel Boone" and "The Oregon Trail." These are significant both as poems and as history. In *Independent Voices,* Eve Merriam has written poems that tell, in a variety of rhyming verse patterns and with a vivid sense of the dramatic, the stories of many great American men and women. In Rosemary and Stephen Benét's *A Book of Americans,* there are many poems you will wish to use with history, but the pair, "Nancy Hanks" and "Abraham Lincoln," are the great favorites.

These poems are typical of the fine narrative verse about people and events in United States history. Such poems can be introduced casually as the history chronology unfolds, or the children may become interested in the theme of heroism and start searching for hero poems of their own.

Lyric Poetry

Ask any teacher or parent who reads aloud to children what kind of poems they like best and the answer will be, "Funny ones."

The rhythm and melody of verse are primary sources of satisfaction to children just as are the rhythm and melody of music. But it is a long way from the tumpity-tump skips and gallops of early childhood to Bach and Beethoven and it is just as far from *Mother Goose* and Edward Lear to Walter de la Mare and Robert Frost. If we are to help children grow up successfully in poetry, we should start where the children are.

For instance, children begin as young as two years old to play with words and respond to their sounds. "Pickle-lillie, pickle-lillie," chants one child, savoring the ear-tickling *l*'s with evident enjoyment. "Upsey-daisy," sings another with broad smiles. Other children are caught by the charm of other words and phrases, and without knowing why, they respond to the mood evoked by the words. In some such accidental way, children's taste for lyric poetry may begin. It is the responsibility of parents, librarians, and teachers to provide poetry experiences for children that will help them grow up happily with poetry.

Viewpoints

The lyric has to be condensed and intense and its technical achievement must be sophisticated and impeccable. As a result the level of workmanship is very high. This is a fine ideal, yet the final test of lyric poetry is that it should get off the ground, and should not be so cumbered with craft that it can't use its wings. We miss the rhythms of pure song in most contemporary verse. Yeats and Walter de la Mare were perhaps the last in that tradition. . . . —Elizabeth Drew, *Poetry,* W. W. Norton, and Co., New York, 1959, pp. 48–49.

It is not that lyric poetry is characteristically obscure or that its sound is more important than its meaning. But authentic poetry not only conveys meaning but generally evokes an emotional response. Children who have the good fortune to hear a poem that gives them a shiver up their backbones or a swift upsurging flood of elation or a sense of quiet and peace are discovering some of the joys of poetry.

From the great body of English lyric verse, children will appropriate certain poems that suit them, and when they have spoken them repeatedly until they know them, the verses become truly their own. They will ask about them, too, and through discussions meaning will be enriched. If most children still prefer the lightest of light verse, just remember that most adults do, too.

William Shakespeare is one of those poets who, although writing for adults, has songs that children enjoy. Children hearing the songs of Shakespeare without being forced to analyze or memorize them soon know the poems by heart, and the words sing in their heads like a popular tune. "Jog on, jog on," from *The Winter's Tale,* is a good march for any excursion of children, and Ariel's song, "Where the bee sucks," from *The Tempest,* is a pleasant fairy poem. "Who is Sylvia?" from *The Two Gentlemen of Verona;* "When icicles hang by the wall," *Love's Labour's Lost;* and "Hark, hark! the lark," *Cymbeline*—these poems have a singing quality and a simplicity of content that bring them within the enjoyment range of older children, especially if they hear the poems before they read them.

William Blake's *Songs of Innocence* is a landmark in English literature as well as in children's literature. The average child may not particularly enjoy some of the more difficult poems, but will enjoy many of them if they are read aloud by someone who likes their melodies. For Blake's poems are songs, full of cadences and lovely sounds.

Christina Rossetti provides the young child with an ideal introduction to lyric poetry in the verses of *Sing Song*, published in 1872. Many of the verses have homely, familiar subjects, but they are written with lyric grace and with a subtle simplicity in the choice of words. What gentleness there is in "The Caterpillar":

Brown and furry
Caterpillar in a hurry
Take your walk
To the shady leaf or stalk
Or what not,
Which may be the chosen spot.
No toad spy you,
Hovering birds of prey pass by you;
Spin and die,
To live again a butterfly.

Many poets of the twentieth century have written outstanding lyric poetry, including Walter de la Mare and Eleanor Farjeon, Sara

Illustration by Arthur Hughes for Sing Song *by Christina Rossetti (1872 edition).*

Teasdale and Elizabeth Coatsworth. Eve Merriam, in *It Doesn't Always Have to Rhyme*, and Harry Behn, in *The Golden Hive*, or Langston Hughes, in "Snail" or "Dream Variations," have written lines as musical as any lyric poets of the past.

Poetry of Nature

Most of the poets discussed in this category are dissimilar in most respects, but they have one characteristic in common: they observe nature with sensitive interpretation and an imaginative turn that kindles a responsive spark in the reader.

The poems of Sara Teasdale are largely descriptive and often too subtle for the child under ten, but their lyric beauty and poignance captivate some children. Elizabeth Coatsworth's poems are less musical but rich with imagery, less complex but lucid and gay with a quick appeal.

Aileen Fisher, many of whose longer poems (*Once We Went on a Picnic* and *Listen, Rabbit*) have been published singly in picture-book form, has been a prolific writer of verses for children. Her writing is pleasant and patterned, and all of her nature poetry reflects both her awareness of the child's interests and her own deep love of the outdoors and of small, wild creatures.

The Danish explorer Knud Rasmussen brought back from his fifth expedition to the Arctic a large collection of Eskimo poems. A selection from these has been made into a beautiful book for children, *Beyond the High Hills*, illustrated with breathtaking color photographs by a missionary priest, Father Guy Mary-Rousselière. The result is sheer beauty pictorially and verbally, with a dramatic re-creation of Eskimo thoughts, feelings, and way of life. These verses are in free form and have great strength and maturity. The bitter contrast between the two seasons is evident in this—

There is joy in
Feeling the warmth
Come to the great world
And seeing the sun
Follow its old footprints
In the summer night.

There is fear in
Feeling the cold
Come to the great world
And seeing the moon
—Now new moon, now full moon—
Follow its old footprints
In the winter night.[11]

To read these poems with the loneliness and beauty of the photographs is a moving experience. They will give children more of Eskimo life and thought than many factual books. *The Wind Has Wings,* a varied and handsomely illustrated collection of Canadian poetry compiled by Mary Downie and Barbara Robertson, includes Eskimo and French songs.

Mary Austin's *The Children Sing in the Far West,* published in 1928, is an older collection of children's poems about America's Southwest. Teachers should slip in some of her best and most characteristic poems now and then—"Charms," "Prayers," and "A Song of Greatness," for example—and at least a few of the children will respond.

A Song of Greatness[12]

When I hear the old men
Telling of heroes,
Telling of great deeds
Of ancient days,
When I hear that telling
Then I think within me
I too am one of these.

When I hear the people
Praising great ones,
Then I know that I too
Shall be esteemed,
I too when my time comes
Shall do mightily.

These poems give young readers a new understanding of and respect for Native Americans. At her best, Mary Austin transcends local color and writes with universal significance.

The Trees Stand Shining, a selection of poetry of the North American Indians, has been compiled by Hettie Jones. The poems are, in fact, untitled songs, fragmentary and brief, often with the terse quality of haiku, that show the affinity the Indian feels for the beauty and strength of nature. Humanity's close relationship to nature is also depicted in John Bierhorst's anthology *In the Trail of the Wind: American Indian Poems and Ritual Orations.* This volume includes poems of the Maya, the Aztec, and the Eskimo as well as those of North American Indian tribes. William Brandon's collection, *The Magic World: American Indian Songs and Poems,* is unusual for its inclusion of a large number of Nahuatl ceremonial songs.

In *A Few Flies and I,* some of the poems of the great Japanese poet Issa have been brought together by Jean Merrill and Ronni Solbert. Richard Lewis, in *Of This World,* also chose some of the Issa poems that show an infinite tenderness toward the small creatures of the world.

Of all the books that share this affection for animals, Carmen Bernos de Gasztold's *Prayers from the Ark* and *The Creatures' Choir,* translated from the French by Rumer Godden, are the most beguiling, each poem a percipient picture of the animal that speaks.

The Hedgehog[13]

Yes, Lord, I prick!
Life is not easy—
but You know that—
and I have too much on my shoulders!
I speak of my prickles
but thank You for them.
You at least
have understood me,
that is why You made me
such a pinball.
How else can I defend myself?
When people see me,
my anxious nose
searching for the fat slugs

[11]"There is joy." Reprinted by permission of The World Publishing Company from *Beyond the High Hills: A Book of Eskimo Poems* edited by Knud Rasmussen. Copyright © 1961 by The World Publishing Company.

[12]"A Song of Greatness" from *The Children Sing in the Far West.* Copyright renewed 1956 by Kenneth M. Chapman and Mary C. Wheelwright. Reprinted by permission of the publisher, Houghton Mifflin Company.

[13]From *The Creatures' Choir* (British Title: *The Beasts' Choir*), by Carmen Bernos de Gasztold, translated by Rumer Godden. Copyright © 1965 by Rumer Godden. Reprinted by permission of The Viking Press, Inc., and Macmillan London and Basingstoke.

that devastate the garden,
why can't they leave me alone?
Ah! But when I think proper,
I can roll myself up
into my hermit life.

Amen

Two other books about wild creatures are *Cats and Bats and Things with Wings* by Conrad Aiken and *Brownjohn's Beasts* by the British poet Alan Brownjohn, whose animals, like those of Carmen Bernos de Gasztold, speak for themselves—and with great wit.

Poetry from Around the World

There Are Two Lives, edited by Richard Lewis, is one of the many other books that are bringing poetry of other lands to English-speaking children. Producing such books is a phenomenon not wholly new but noticeably burgeoning. Lewis chose Japanese and Chinese poetry for *Moment of Wonder* and selected haiku for younger readers in *In a Spring Garden*. He selected poems of the haiku poet Issa in *Of This World* and edited the work of another great haiku poet in *The Way of Silence: The Prose and Poetry of Basho*. Japanese poems are also found in Virginia Baron's *The Seasons of Time*, a selection of ancient tanka poetry, and Harry Behn's two collections of haiku, *Cricket Songs* and *More Cricket Songs*. Nursery rhymes of other lands are discussed in Chapter 4.

Illustration by Jean Primrose. From The Creatures' Choir *by Carmen Bernos de Gasztold, translated by Rumer Godden, decorations by Jean Primrose. Copyright © 1965 by Rumer Godden. Illustrations reprinted by permission of The Viking Press, Inc.*

In William Jay Smith's *Poems from France* and Kenneth Canfield's *Selections from French Poetry*, each poem in French has the English translation on the facing page. Undoubtedly the French poetry best known to English-speaking children is that of de Gasztold, whose two books were just mentioned.

In Jean Longland's *Selections from Contemporary Portuguese Poetry*, Seymour Resnick's *Spanish-American Poetry* and *Selections from Spanish Poetry*, and Richard Lewis's *Still Waters of the Air: Poems by Three Modern Spanish Poets*, again the English translation is printed on the page facing the original. These are all intended for older readers.

Also bilingual are the poems in Mario Benedetti's *Unstill Life*, an introduction to the Spanish-American poetry of Latin America; and the poems in Michael de Luca and William Giulianos's *Selections from Italian Poetry*.

Vladimir Rus's *Selections from German Poetry* and Helen Plotz's *Poems from the German*, both of which provide the poems in the original and in English translation, are for older children. For younger readers there are several editions of Heinrich Hoffmann's *Slovenly Peter*, now a children's classic, one version of which was translated by Mark Twain.

The first section of Miriam Morton's anthology *A Harvest of Russian Children's Literature* has verses for young children, and there are a few other poems in the book, notably a long narrative poem, "The Little Humpbacked Horse," a fairy tale in verse that is also popular in Russia in dramatized form. Ivan Krylov's *The Fifteen Fables of Krylov* has a dry wit.

From India there is the poetry in Gwendolyn Reed's *The Talkative Beasts: Myths, Fables and Poems of India*, and in Rabindranath

Tagore's slim volume *Moon, For What Do You Wait?* In *We, the Vietnamese: Voices from Vietnam,* edited by François Sully, there is a representative section of poetry from a portion of "Kim Van Kieu," Vietnam's best-known epic poem, to folk songs of protest and the poetry of today's underground.

The indefatigable Richard Lewis has selected some of the poetry of ancient Greece for *Muse of the Round Sky* and has chosen poems and songs of primitive peoples of the world for *Out of the Earth I Sing,* most of the selections being from African and North American Indian tribes. *A Crocodile Has Me by the Leg,* compiled by Leonard Doob, has African poems that clearly stem from the oral tradition and have folk wisdom and humor.

For *The Singing and the Gold,* an excellent anthology of world literature compiled by Elinor Parker, many poets contributed to the translations of poetry from thirty-four different languages. It is probable that this trend toward international diffusion of an art that is, of all types of literature, the one most elemental, perceptive, and universal will increase as our children grow toward a world less partitioned by boundaries than the world of the past.

Poetry by Children

There have always been children who wrote poetry, and there have been some—like Hilda Conkling and Aliki Barnstone—whose writing has been published and extolled. Never before today, however, has there been such a poetic ferment, so much encouragement by adults working with children in small groups and in classrooms, so many young people forming their own groups to read, write, and discuss poetry.

One of the most sympathetic and informed explorations of this activity is in *Somebody Turned on a Tap in These Kids,* edited by Nancy Larrick and containing articles by such poets as June Jordan, Myra Cohn Livingston, and Eve Merriam, and by others who work with children. In *Poetry Is,* Ted Hughes, a British poet, addresses his remarks about technique, acuity of observation and expression, and imagery, to young people. In *Let Them Be Themselves,* author Lee Bennett Hopkins discusses poetry as one of the ways in which the language arts program may be enriched for disadvantaged children.

Not every child is capable of writing poetry, and it is true that some of the work being done with children is directed as much toward therapeutic as esthetic goals, but the amount of fine poetry that has been published is a testament to the emotional and imaginative capacity of the young. The work of one outstanding young black writer, Vanessa Howard, has been included in several anthologies of poetry by children. The two following poems are examples of the inward vision and of the poetry of protest.

Truly My Own[14]

I think if I searched a thousand lands
and twice the number in rainbows,
I'd never find one human being
who chose the things I chose
a person who wanted the things I wanted
or sought what I sought to be

I'd never find one human being
like or comparison to me
and if I traveled seven seas
I would still be alone
for there is no one who thinks like me
for my dreams are truly my own.

And, untitled:

I am frightened that
the flame of hate
will burn me
will scorch my pride
scar my heart
it will burn and i
cannot put it out,
i cannot call the fire department
and they cannot put out the flame
within my soul
i am frightened that the flame
of hate will burn me
if it does
I will die[14]

[14]"Truly My Own" and "I am frightened that" by Vanessa Howard from *The Voice of the Children* collected by June Jordan and Terri Bush. Copyright © 1968 by The Voice of the Children, Inc. Reprinted by permission of Holt, Rinehart and Winston, Inc. and Julian Bach Literary Agency, Inc.

Illustration by Emily Arnold McCully from the book Here I Am! *edited by Virginia Olsen Baron. Illustrations copyright © 1969 by Emily Arnold McCully. Published by E. P. Dutton & Co., Inc. and used with their permission.*

The Voice of the Children, compiled by June Jordan and Terri Bush, comprises some of the best of the poetry written in a creative writing workshop; Virginia Baron's anthology *Here I Am!* contains poems written by young people from diverse minority groups. "Inevitable poets," Arnold Adoff calls the young people whose poems poured in from all parts of the country to be selected for *it is the poem singing into your eyes.* Kenneth Koch's *Wishes, Lies, and Dreams* contains both the author's description of his work with children in a New York City school and their poetry.

I Heard a Scream in the Streets, edited by Nancy Larrick, is a collection of poems written by young people in the city. Her other anthology of children's poetry, *Green Is Like a Meadow of Grass,* shows the results of children's observation of nature, encouraged by teachers motivated in a poetry workshop.

Miriam Morton has gathered Russian children's poems in *The Moon Is Like a Silver Sickle,* and Richard Lewis has gathered children's poetry in several fine anthologies: *Miracles,* a collection of poetry by children of the English-speaking world; *The Wind and the Rain,* nature poems; and *There Are Two Lives,* poems by Japanese children, a collection in which restraint in the use of language is the most marked difference between these poems and those of American children. One of the most touching collections of children's poetry is *I Never Saw Another Butterfly,* poems written by Jewish children in a concentration camp. Many of the poems are remarkable for their courage, vision, and compassion.

Poetry for Now

In the explosive increase of children's interest in reading and writing poetry, there are several striking trends. One is the subject matter with which the young are concerned: they are writing poems about anything and everything they see around them, and although they are still aware of natural beauty and intrigued by the intricacies and mystery of themselves and other people, some of their poetry seethes with anger, sees beauty as well as despair in the urban scene, and faces with candor the afflictions of the world they inherit. In form, too, there is a new freedom: most of the poetry they write and much of the poetry they read is free verse, some of it in shaped patterns, like that of May Swenson's "Redundant Journey," in which the print forms a sinuous pattern on the page, or it is the concrete poetry that moves from the oral tradition to appeal to the eye. Free verse, of course, is not new, but it has never been so enthusiastically employed.

Young people are reading avidly the contemporary multi-ethnic voices of protest. There is a marked increase in the numbers of black poets being heard and being represented in anthologies of modern poetry chosen especially for young readers. And—no surprise in a world in which communication has brought peoples closer to each other—there is a growing amount of poetry from other cultures now available in English.

Viewpoints

The search for what is real has led many a poet and his readers to topics once thought of as unpoetic: traffic lights, for example, and escalators, subways and littered sidewalks. On crowded streets and in cluttered hallways man's inhumanity to man shows up dramatically. Adults who have equated poetry with "a host of golden daffodils" may find it difficult to accept this harsh reality for children. Yet this is the children's world, too. . . .

It should not surprise us, then, to find that today's children seek the realistic poetry of bolder voices, speaking in a blunt conversational style. They like poems which debunk the phony and unveil hypocrisy. I think this is one of the reasons why they are held by Eve Merriam's *The Inner City Mother Goose,* which is a biting commentary on the injustices of the American ghetto.

"This is real," explained one fourteen-year-old. "The trouble with poetry at school is it's all covered over with the beautiful."—Nancy Larrick, "Poetry That's Real," *Somebody Turned on a Tap in These Kids,* edited by Nancy Larrick, Delacorte Press, New York, 1971, pp. 4–5.

There is no age limit for poetry that is distinguishably, and often distinctively, contemporary. Some of the urban poetry written for very young children is concerned with subjects and problems that were never mentioned in children's literature before, an acknowledgment of the sophistication of the young. "The City Question" in Robert Froman's *Street Poems* poses the problem of the man lying on the sidewalk. Wino? Junkie? Or ill? Is he dangerous, or should one try to help? Another poem is called "Hail, Polluters." Froman plays with shapes in this intriguing book that manipulates print to accentuate the message of the words; the names of objects in a garbage heap are, for example, actually piled helter-skelter; and in a poem about a dandelion, the print forms a stem and a flower head. Ian Hamilton Finlay's *Poems to Hear and See* are experiments in form by a poet who is a participant in the Concrete Poetry movement, which intends the word to stand for itself as does an ideogram.

In *Mazes* by Muriel Rukeyser, a picture-book format and color photographs are the setting for a poem about a child who explores his surroundings, a lovely lyric but complex enough to make demands on the reader. In Nikki Giovanni's *Ego-Tripping and Other Poems for Young People,* some of the poems are tender, some angry; all are a celebration of being black. May Swenson's poetry has enormous vitality and impact, and is filled with striking images, with patterns in print that she calls Shape Poems, and with the Riddle Poems that require the reader to make personal contribution toward interpretation. June Jordan's *Who Look at Me* is a long poem that moves, as in a gallery, from one portrait to another of black people. The paintings are by distinguished artists, the poem a passionate statement of the dignity, the pain, the anger, and the pride of the black people.

Who see the block we face
the thousand miles of alabaster space
inscribed keep off keep out don't touch
and Wait Some More for Half as Much?[15]

Robert Hayden, himself a poet, has compiled the work of American black poets in *Kaleidoscope,* an anthology that begins with the poetry of the "Sable Muse" of colonial times, Phillis Wheatley, and proceeds chronologically, with biographical notes, to contemporary writers. Arnold Adoff, in *I Am the Darker Brother* and *Black Out Loud* confines his selections to the work of modern black poets; such established writers as Langston Hughes, LeRoi Jones, Mari Evans, and Arna Bontemps are included, but there are many poems by writers less well known.

There are a dozen or so very good anthologies of modern poetry for young people, and many of them include poems by older poets who have struck a note consonant with today's themes, or poems that are the lyrics of contemporary ballads and protest songs. David Morse's selections in *Grandfather Rock* have been made to show the kinship between such lyrics and poems from Homer's time on; indeed, Morse, in his preface, refers to such poetry as "the rock and roll of the past."

[15]From *Who Look at Me* by June Jordan. Copyright © 1969 by June Jordan. Used by permission of Thomas Y. Crowell Company, Inc., publisher, and Joan Daves.

Among the best of the anthologies of modern poetry are *Lean Out of the Window* by Sara Hannum and Gwendolyn Reed; *Sounds and Silences: Poetry for Now* by Richard Peck; and *Reflections on a Gift of Watermelon Pickle* by Stephen Dunning, Edward Lueders, and Hugh L. Smith. Additional anthologies including other collections by these same compilers will be found in the bibliography.

Young poetry lovers do read the poetry of the past, but for most of them the modern poets have a greater appeal, speaking as they do to the issues, and in the language of the present. There has been no lessening of admiration for the poems of Emily Dickinson, Robert Frost, Edna St. Vincent Millay, and W. H. Auden, but there are other poets whose names (in addition to those already mentioned in this chapter) crop up in almost every anthology index: Babette Deutsch, James Dickey, Galway Kinnell, Denise Levertov, Richard Wilbur, Rod McKuen, Howard Nemerov, Pauli Murray. Indeed, almost every contemporary poet is represented and has his or her faction of admirers.

One fact that emerges from a survey of poetry for children is that poets can no more be pigeonholed than light can be captured and boxed. Another fact is that a poem, more than any other kind of literature, has no boundaries and that a suggestion for a reading level is only that—an indication that for many children the poem will probably be most appreciated at a certain age. For children often have a far greater comprehension in listening to a poem than in reading it for themselves, and the poem that awakens a response will produce more attention and understanding on the part of the reader or listener than the poem that can be accepted placidly.

Not every poem is for every child, and some poetry needs intellectual as well as emotional participation. As Agnes Repplier says, in her introduction to a poetry anthology:

> *In the matter of poetry, a child's imagination outstrips his understanding; his emotions carry him far beyond the narrow reach of his intelligence. He has but one lesson to learn,—the lesson of enjoyment.*[16]

[16]From *An Anthology of Modern Verse*, ed. by A. Methuen (Methuen, 1921), p. xiii.

The Range of Poets for Children

In contemplating the poetry that children enjoy, it is clear that the range is as varied as the children themselves. Some of the poets who are favorites did not write for children at all; some—like Theodore Roethke and Randall Jarrell—wrote occasionally for them; and others wrote only for them. Those contemporary poets who write in protest or who experiment with form are read as avidly as are the more conventional poets, old and new.

Early Writers—Lasting Influences

Many of the earliest writers of poetry for children wrote a few poems that are still read and loved, but they are revered more for the impetus they gave to writing for children than for the writing itself. Isaac Watts, a preacher who decided that "What is learnt in verse, is longer retained in the memory, and sooner recollected," put his homilies in *Divine and Moral Songs for Children* in 1715. The visionary artist and author William Blake in *Songs of Innocence* (1789) created mood and conveyed ideas through rhythmic verse that speaks to the emotions and to the imagination.

Two sisters, Ann and Jane Taylor, wrote poems as moralistic and didactic as those of Watts, but they wrote wholly for children, and among the *Original Poems for Infant Minds* (1804) there were some that had suspense. They are best remembered for "Twinkle, twinkle, little star." Christina Rossetti's masterpiece is undoubtedly "Goblin Market," which appeared in 1862, a narrative poem that has suspense, vivid imagery, and colorful descriptions. Her *Sing Song* (1872) is a lighthearted nursery classic but it has more complexity than does *Mother Goose*, and it makes subtle and repeated use of vowel and consonant sounds to suggest the feeling or idea described by the words. Emily Dickinson's work has become increasingly beloved by the young. Her poems were revolutionary in their time: short, usually in four-line stanzas, sharply perceptive, often somber but at times playful or witty. There are several editions of her poems that have been chosen for children: *Letter to the World* (1969), edited by Rumer

Godden; *Poems* (1964), edited by Helen Plotz; and *Poems for Youth* (1934), edited by Alfred Hampson.

Lewis Carroll's poetry is much funnier in context, in *Alice's Adventures in Wonderland* (1865) and *Through the Looking-Glass* (1871), than it is when read separately, but his nonsense verses can be enjoyed alone. Ebullient, daft, and rhythmic, poems like "Jabberwocky" have enchanted word-lovers for a century. Carroll's writing is discussed more fully in Chapter 8. Kate Greenaway's verses were undistinguished, but they are simple, childlike, and mildly humorous; without the illustrations upon which her reputation rests, the poems in such books as *Under the Window* (1879) probably would not have survived.

In briefly examining the work of some of the major contributors to children's poetry, who will be discussed in chronological order by their dates of birth, it is possible to see both the diversity and the pattern not only of what children read but of what their society's changing ideas of a child's capabilities and preferences have been.

Illustration by Kate Greenaway for "Susan Blue." From Marigold Garden, *published by Frederick Warne & Company. (Original in color)*

There was an Old Man on
whose nose
Most birds of the
air could repose;
But they all flew away at the closing of day,
Which relieved that Old Man and his nose.

From Edward Lear's The Complete Nonsense Book.

Edward Lear

The Book of Nonsense
Nonsense Songs and Stories
Whizz!

In England, about 1820, several small books of limericks appeared, the first of which, *Anecdotes and Adventures of Fifteen Gentlemen,* Edward Lear probably read. The limerick form set Lear to writing some of the most famous nonsense in the English language and illustrating it with sketches so amusing that a Lear limerick without the Lear drawing is only half as funny as the two together.

It was while Lear was at work as an illustrator of flora and fauna that the Earl of Derby discovered him and invited the young artist to come down to his country estate and make drawings of his collection of birds and animals. During his stay with this family (he was eventually employed by four Earls of Derby), he began the nonsense verses, and Lear the artist became also Lear the humorist.

It was to the Earl's grandchildren that Lear must have shown his limericks as he produced them—limericks and sketches that were published in 1846 as the first *Book of Nonsense.* For Lear himself, writing them must have been great fun. They were a rest from those painstakingly detailed scientific

Illustration by Leslie Brooke. From Nonsense Songs *by Edward Lear. Published and copyrighted by Frederick Warne & Co., Inc. Reproduced with the permission of the publishers.*

drawings, they were a safe release for his high spirits, and above all they must have been a blessed escape from the illness which pursued but never conquered him.

The second book, *Nonsense Songs and Stories*, published in 1871, includes a variety of humorous verses, among them the pseudo-serious narrative poems that seem all the funnier because they are gravely told.

Lear's made-up words are one of the most obvious sources of amusement in these jingles. You find the Pobble who has no toes, the Quangle Wangle with the beaver hat, and the amorous Yonghy-Bonghy Bò. The words in Lear's five different sets of alphabet rhymes are mostly of this tongue-twister variety. Of these five alphabet rhymes, none is better than the one that begins

A was once an apple-pie,
Pidy,
Widy,
Tidy,
Pidy,
Nice insidy,
Apple-Pie!

Lear was an excellent craftsman. His meters are exact, his rhymes neat and musical, and his verse has a pleasant sound even at its wildest. Much of it is decidedly melodious. Children linger over the refrains; they also like the ridiculous and eccentric characters in these verses and are especially entertained by the mad troop that populates the limericks, six of which are used as a continuous text illustrated by Janina Domanska in *Whizz!*

Laura E. Richards

Tirra Lirra; Rhymes Old and New

Laura E. Richards's father was Samuel Gridley Howe, who devoted himself to such diverse

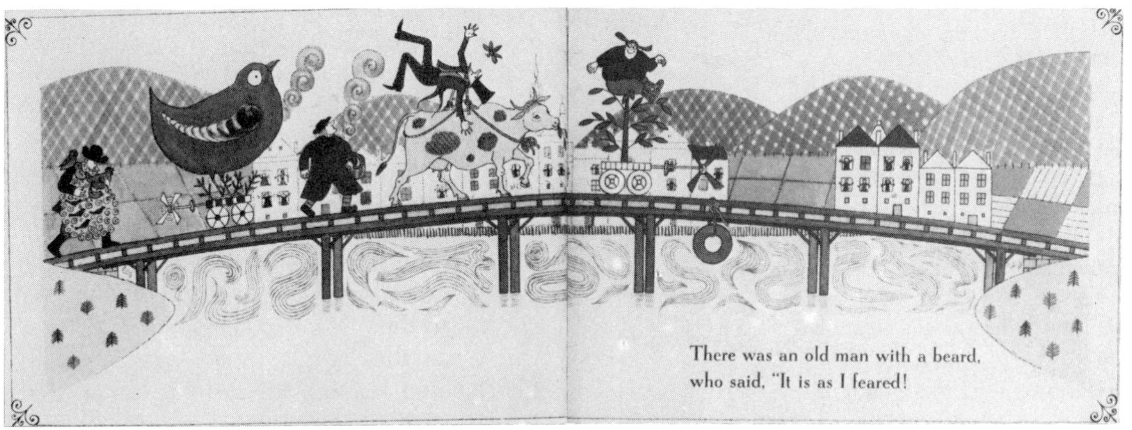

There was an old man with a beard,
who said, "It is as I feared!

Reprinted with permission of Macmillan Publishing Co., Inc. and Hamish Hamilton Children's Books Ltd. from Whizz! *by Edward Lear, illustrated by Janina Domanska. Illustration Copyright © 1973 by Janina Domanska. (Original in color)*

social causes as the Greek War for Independence, the education of the blind, and the founding of the first school for feebleminded children. Her mother, Julia Ward Howe, was the author of "The Battle Hymn of the Republic." It is not surprising that the children in this family in turn scribbled stories and poetry.

The poems of Laura Richards have a spontaneity and a freshness that are equaled only by their lyric quality. It was her husband who suggested that she send some of her verses to the new magazine for children, *St. Nicholas*, and this she did. From then on, stories and poems came from her pen at an amazing rate. Between stories and biographies, the verses continued to "bubble up" with undiminished charm. But it wasn't until 1932 that a book of her verses called *Tirra Lirra; Rhymes Old and New* was published—a book which she dedicated to her youngest grandchild and to her eldest great-grandchild.

Laura Richards's verses abound in humorous, made-up words. Lear gave us "meloobious" and "torrible," and Carroll presented us with "galumphing," "beamish," and "whiffling," but Richards matches them with "Muffin Bird," "Rummyjums," "bogothybogs," "Lolloping Lizard," and "a Glimmering Glog." Moreover, no one can play with words with more joyous confusion than she. Children from five to any age have always found much to chuckle over in

Eletelephony[17]

Once there was an elephant,
Who tried to use the telephant—
No! no! I mean an elephone
Who tried to use the telephone—
(Dear me! I am not certain quite
That even now I've got it right.)

Howe'er it was, he got his trunk
Entangled in the telephunk;
The more he tried to get it free,
The louder buzzed the telephee—
(I fear I'd better drop the song
Of elephop and telephong!)

[17]"Eletelephony" and "The Umbrella Brigade." From *Tirra Lirra* by Laura E. Richards. Copyright 1935 by Laura E. Richards; Copyright © 1960 by Hamilton Richards. Reprinted by permission of Little, Brown and Co.

Like "Eletelephony," "Some Fishy Nonsense," "Doggerel," "Sir Ringleby Rose," and many other jingles depend for their fun upon this juggling with words.

But Richards carries her fun beyond mere play with words. She has, in addition to the verse-maker's skill, the dramatic art of a first-rate storyteller. The gentle tale of "Little John Bottlejohn," lured away by a cajoling mermaid; the gory record of "The Seven Little Tigers and the Aged Cook," the exciting "The Monkeys and the Crocodile"—these and a dozen others depend for their interest upon the skillful storytelling of the author as well as upon her irrepressible sense of the absurd.

Her characters and situations are also a source of amusement for the children. And even four- and five-year-olds feel superior when they giggle understandingly over the blunders of the two dogs "Jippy and Jimmy."

Laura Richards has caught in her verses some of the singing quality of words that chil-

From Tirra Lirra: Rhymes Old and New *by Laura E. Richards. Illustrated by Marguerite Davis. Copyright 1930, 1932, 1934 by Laura E. Richards. Copyright 1955 by Little, Brown and Company. By permission of Little, Brown and Co.*

dren enjoy. To test this quality, read aloud the chorus of "The Umbrella Brigade":

But let it rain,
Tree-toads and frogs,
Muskets and pitchforks,
Kittens and dogs!
Dash away! plash away!
Who is afraid?
Here we go,
The Umbrella Brigade![17]

This lyric quality not only gives distinction to her most extravagant nonsense but makes children more sensitive to the musical qualities of words.

Robert Louis Stevenson

A Child's Garden of Verses

The title "poet laureate of childhood" has often been bestowed upon Robert Louis Stevenson, who first captivated adult readers with his essays and fiction, then caught and held the affectionate regard of children with *A Child's Garden of Verses.* This collection appeared in 1885 as *Penny Whistles,* with sixty-three poems and this fond dedication to Stevenson's childhood nurse: "To Alison Cunningham (From Her Boy)." Not all these poems are for children; a few of them are merely about children or are adult reminiscences of childhood. Such poems creep into almost every collection of juvenile poetry but are nevertheless to be avoided; for example, Stevenson's "Whole Duty of Children," or the rarely included "To Any Reader" and "To Willie and Henrietta."

With these exceptions, no careful reading of the poems can fail to leave you impressed with the author's genuine understanding of children. The opening poem, "Bed in Summer," is every child's complaint:

And does it not seem hard to you,
When all the sky is clear and blue,
And I should like so much to play,
To have to go to bed by day?

His children get up shivering with cold on winter mornings; they yearn to travel; they discover the sea miraculously filling up their holes on the beach; they struggle with table manners; they have a deep respect for "System," an orderly world; they enjoy good days and bad ones, mostly good; they watch for the lamplighter; they wonder why they can't see the wind; and they enjoy a world of play and a world of the imagination as well. Children's interest in tiny things is found not only in "The Little Land" but over and over again in other verses. Here are real children, many-sided and with many interests.

Especially true to child life are the poems involving dramatic play. Imagination transforms a clothes basket into a boat. Climbing up in the cherry tree, the child glimpses not merely the next-door garden but foreign lands and even fairyland. In "A Good Play," the children explain:

We built a ship upon the stairs
All made of the back-bedroom chairs.

The poems bristle with the properties and imaginative transformations of that arch magician, the child of about four to seven years old.

People have complained that this child of the *Verses* is a solitary child, and they have read into the poems some of the pathos of Stevenson's frailty as a child. But if you study these verses, you will find several children playing pirates in the "Pirate Story"; building ships together in "A Good Play"; or being mountaineers in "The Hayloft," to mention only a few. These give us a fair proportion of other children and of social play. They emphasize also the normal play activities of healthy children. Nothing of the invalid here!

Perhaps the largest group of poems under a single general classification is made up of those concerned with night. What an imaginative group it is, and sometimes scary, too. There are two poems in this night group which are also notable for their rhythm. "Shadow March" is in perfect marching time, but it is an eerie, frightening march of bogies and shadows, not to be used before the children are seven or eight years old and strong enough to stand it. Less scary and still finer is that pounding gallop called

Windy Nights

Whenever the moon and stars are set,
Whenever the wind is high,
All night long in the dark and wet,
A man goes riding by.
Late in the night when the fires are out,
Why does he gallop and gallop about?

Whenever the trees are crying aloud,
And ships are tossed at sea,
By, on the highway, low and loud,
By at the gallop goes he,
By at the gallop he goes, and then
By he comes back at the gallop again.

From Peacock Pie, *by Walter de la Mare, illustrated by Barbara Cooney. Illustration copyright © 1961 by Barbara Cooney. Reprinted by permission of Alfred A. Knopf, Inc.*

This example of rhythm illustrates another of the outstanding qualities in Stevenson's *Child's Garden of Verses*: the poems are markedly lyrical. Of course, numbers of them have been set to music, but they sing anyway, without benefit of notes. Take the concluding line of "A Good Boy": "And hear the thrushes singing in the lilacs round the lawn." Or listen to the refrain in "The Wind":

O wind, a-blowing all day long,
O wind, that sings so loud a song!

Go through page after page of these poems and you'll find their melody singing in your memory.

Although teachers and parents who were raised on *A Child's Garden of Verses* may feel that the verses are overfamiliar, they must not forget that these poems are new to each generation of children. "The Cow," "My Shadow," "The Swing," "Winter-time," and "Time to Rise," in addition to the verses already quoted, are enduring favorites, and children should not miss them. New poets of childhood may make their contributions, but Robert Louis Stevenson has left to young children a legacy of small lyrics.

Walter de la Mare

Rhymes and Verses: Collected Poems for Children
Peacock Pie

Adults and children of the English-speaking world lost a great lyric poet when Walter de la Mare died in 1956. For eighteen years he wrote stories and poems and published them under the pseudonym of Walter Ramal. The treasured *Songs of Childhood* was published in 1902 when he was working as a statistician.

All of his poems for young people are now collected in *Rhymes and Verses*. (There is also *Come Hither*, De la Mare's own selection of poems for children.) *Peacock Pie* has been reissued and is a choice book for the special child to own. Many of his poems are difficult; nevertheless his work contains some poetry that should not be missed. Choose your favorite poems; try them with children; then try certain others that are beautiful but that are not so sure to be enjoyed at first hearing. Who knows what words will catch the imagination of children? When you are using the poetry of a great lyric poet, be adventurous and try a wide selection for the sake of that occasional child who may suddenly be carried away by the magic of poetry.

One characteristic of Walter de la Mare's poems is the use of the unanswered question which leaves the reader wondering. Many of his poems have this enigmatic quality. Of course, too much ambiguity may be discouraging to those children who are literal creatures and like things straight and plain. A little, however, stimulates children's imagination and provokes not only a healthy speculation but the ability to transcend the factual and go over into the world of dreams.

De la Mare could be direct and clear when he wished to, and his children are real flesh-and-blood children. The account of "Poor Henry" swallowing physic is as homely a bit of family life as you can find anywhere. Small children enjoy the matter-of-fact subject matter and the straightforward treatment of such poems as "Chicken," "The Barber's," and the Elizabeth Ann parts of "A Child's Day." Even these poems for the youngest children, however, are illumined with little touches that invariably lift them above the world of the commonplace.

There are many nature poems in *Rhymes and Verses*. Throughout the poems you find intimate glimpses of flowers, birds, beasts, the sea, and the countryside—all caught and colored with the poet's own peculiar insight. No poetry is more intensely visual than De la Mare's. A "sun-washed drift of seabirds," "rain-sweet lilac on the spray," and, for another sensory experience, those "chuffling" pigs making their "grizzling, gruzzling and greedy" sounds.

Forrest Reid characterizes Walter de la Mare's poetry by saying that it is chiefly "poetry of imagination and *vision* with its hints of loveliness belonging to a world perhaps remembered, perhaps only dreamed, but which at least is not *this* world."[18] The fairy poems, with a great range of mood and style, begin at nonsense level with such delightful absurdities as "Tillie," the old woman who swallowed some magic fern seeds when she yawned and has ever since been floating around on the wind.

Illustration by Boris Artzybasheff for Walter de la Mare's "Sleepyhead" from The Fairy Shoemaker and Other Fairy Poems.

That De la Mare's work for children has the same beauty found in his books for adults is not surprising when he himself said in his introduction to *Bells and Grass*, "I know well that only the rarest kind of best in anything can be good enough for the young." If anyone has given children "the rarest kind of best" in poetry, it is Walter de la Mare.

Robert Frost

You Come Too

Robert Frost was four times the recipient of the Pulitzer Prize for poetry. In 1950 the United States Senate adopted a "resolution of felicitation" on his seventy-fifth birthday, and in 1961, President-elect John F. Kennedy invited Frost to read one of his poems at the

[18]*Walter de la Mare: A Critical Study*. Faber and Faber Ltd., 1929.

Illustration by Thomas W. Nason from You Come Too *by Robert Frost. Copyright © 1959, by Holt, Rinehart and Winston, Inc. Reproduced by permission of Holt, Rinehart and Winston, Inc.*

inaugural ceremony, the first time a poet had been so honored.

In 1962, the poet's eighty-eighth year, a new book of his poems was published, *In the Clearing*, an arresting title for a last book. Frost died early in 1963. John Ciardi wrote of him, "If he is half radiance he is also half brimstone, and praise be. His best poems will endure precisely because they are terrible—and holy."[19]

Which of Robert Frost's poems are simple enough for young children? The poet answered this question with the title of his own selections—*You Come Too, Favorite Poems for Young Readers*. In this book young children will enjoy the riddle about the grasshopper, "One Guess," and the amusing "Fireflies in the Garden." Children can understand "Blue-Butterfly Day" with that wonderful line, "But these are flowers that fly and all but sing."

For the nines and tens and older, almost any poem in this collection will carry meaning, more meaning perhaps for the rural than for the urban child. The latter probably has never "out-walked the furthest city light," nor watched "A Hillside Thaw," nor tried "Mending Wall." But fortunately we can all learn by vicarious experiences, and in every poem, the pictures or episodes or ideas are sharply and clearly told with words that have a tonal beauty as captivating as music.

Robert Frost once said, "Every poem is a new metaphor inside or it is nothing"[20]—which implies that the surface meaning of a poem is only the beginning. Frost's poems grow in richness with thoughtful rereading. We may not wish to discuss the various levels of meaning in every poem, but it would be a pity to leave children with nothing more than the obvious scenes the verses report. "A Drumlin Woodchuck" is, for instance, the amusing soliloquy of a canny old denizen of a hilltop (drumlin) telling how he has managed to evade the hunters. Here is the last verse—

It will be because, though small
As measured against the All,
I have been so instinctively thorough
About my crevice and burrow.[21]

Here is obviously more than meets the eye. The poet himself referred to it as "my most Vermonty poem." And it is obviously rich, good-humored satire. It might be the poet speaking for himself or anyone who is trying to maintain a little privacy, to protect the right to be oneself, to live one's own life, to keep one's own secrets. Older boys and girls fighting for a place of their own can appreciate this. "The Road Not Taken" has a different meaning for every human being. Even twelve-year-olds can sense the choices that lie ahead. "Two Tramps in Mud Time" is more difficult—must we *not* work at work we love, if someone else needs such work? That is a difficult social problem. What should the poet have done?

Poems such as these from this one small collection of Frost's poetry will help the children move gradually from the purely objective to deeper meanings. Slipped in among the lighter fare, these poems should be read

[19]"Robert Frost: American Bard," *Saturday Review*, March 24, 1962, p. 15.

[20]Charles R. Anderson, "Robert Frost," *Saturday Review*, February 23, 1963, p. 20.

[21]"A Drumlin Woodchuck." From *The Poetry of Robert Frost* edited by Edward Connery Lathem. Copyright 1916, 1923, 1928, 1934, © 1969 by Holt, Rinehart and Winston, Inc. Copyright 1936, 1942, 1944, 1951, © 1956, 1962 by Robert Frost. Copyright © 1964, 1970 by Lesley Frost Ballantine. Reprinted by permission of Holt, Rinehart and Winston, Inc. and Jonathan Cape Ltd. for the Estate of Robert Frost.

and discussed, paralleled with personal experiences or the experiences of people we know or of people from history, and then they should be read still again for pure enjoyment and enriched meaning. Children should encounter some of Robert Frost's poems so that they can live with the poetry over the years. The poems will grow in significance as the children grow in years and experience.

Carl Sandburg

Early Moon
Wind Song

Carl Sandburg was almost forty years old before he began to be recognized as a writer. He became the author of what is certainly one of the greatest biographies of Abraham Lincoln, *The Prairie Years* and *The War Years*, and he occupies a secure position in American letters.

The publication of his *Chicago Poems* in 1915 created a sensation and brought down upon his head both praise and hostility. Critics seemed to feel either that poetry was going rapidly downhill or that here was another Walt Whitman, a prophet of a new day. His two books of poetry for children are *Early Moon* (1930) and *Wind Song* (1960), both included in *The Sandburg Treasury* along with *Rootabaga Stories, Prairie-Town Boy,* and *Abe Lincoln Grows Up*.

Sandburg's verse is free, the language sturdy and direct, the subjects often indicating his interest in all things American and his sympathy for its little people. Here is an example of his robust simplicity:

Bubbles[22]

Two bubbles found they had rainbows on their curves.
They flickered out saying:
"It was worth being a bubble just to have held that rainbow thirty seconds."

Older children can also appreciate the ironical "Southern Pacific." Its biting brevity is exceedingly effective. Easier for them to understand are "Summer Grass" (waiting for rain), "Again?" (about a skyscraper), the poignant "Buffalo Dusk" (good for Western units), "People Who Must" (about a steeplejack), "Manual System" (about a switchboard operator), and the fine "To Beachey, 1912" (which might be about any aviator of any year).

Sandburg has given some good advice in "Primer Lesson." If you read this to children, let them talk it over.

Primer Lesson[23]

Look out how you use proud words.
When you let proud words go, it is not easy to call them back.
They wear long boots, hard boots; they walk off proud; they can't hear you calling—
Look out how you use proud words.

Eleanor Farjeon

Eleanor Farjeon's Poems for Children
The Children's Bells
Kings and Queens

When Eleanor Farjeon began to write, she always took her manuscripts to her father's study, pushed them under the door, and then ran away. "I had a stomach-ache till he came and told me if he liked it," she wrote. "He never kept me waiting. Even if he was writing his own stories, he stopped at once to look at my last poem, and came straight to the Nursery to talk it over with me."

Her first book was the amusing *Nursery Rhymes of London Town,* for which she wrote her own music. This was followed by the lively historical nonsense, *Kings and Queens*, and from then on she wrote prolifically, both prose and poetry.

Kings and Queens, written with her brother Herbert, was republished in 1953 and will delight children wrestling with the solemnity of English history. For instance, "Henry VIII"[24] opens with:

[22]"Bubbles" © 1960 by Carl Sandburg. Reprinted from his volume, *Wind Song*, by permission of Harcourt Brace Jovanovich, Inc.

[23]From *Slabs of the Sunburnt West* by Carl Sandburg, copyright, 1922 by Harcourt Brace Jovanovich, Inc.; renewed, 1950, by Carl Sandburg. Reprinted by permission of the publishers.

[24]"Henry VIII" by Herbert and Eleanor Farjeon from *Kings and Queens*. Reprinted by permission of Harold Ober Associates Incorporated. Copyright 1933, 1961 by Eleanor Farjeon.

Bluff King Hal was full of beans;
He married half a dozen queens;
For three called Kate they cried the banns,
And one called Jane, and a couple of Annes.

And it continues with blithe irreverence to account for the six ladies and their much-marrying spouse.

At their best, Eleanor Farjeon's poems for children, whether nonsense or serious lyrics, are skillfully written. Her rhythms are often as lively as a dance; her meters and rhyme schemes are varied and interesting; and her subject matter has exceptional range.

Unfortunately, the quality of her poems is uneven. She is not, for instance, so adroit at describing the modern child's everyday activities as A. A. Milne, but the moment she turns imaginative, something wonderful happens. Take, for example, that curious and lovely night poem, whose very title arrests attention:

The Night Will Never Stay[25]

The night will never stay,
The night will still go by,
Though with a million stars
You pin it to the sky.
Though you bind it with the blowing wind
And buckle it with the moon,
The night will slip away
Like sorrow or a tune.

This poem might well give children their first sense of time, rushing irresistibly along in a pattern of starry nights that will not stand still. Not that children can so translate the poem, but they will say it and say it again, because both the ideas and the words are as haunting as a melody. In *The Children's Bells*, her "What Is Time?" supplements this poem in a gayer mood. Children like the sound of her companion poems, "Boys' Names" and "Girls' Names," and the surprise endings amuse them.

Of her fairy poems, "City Under Water" is perhaps the loveliest and the most usable for children. There are not many of these, but they are invariably good fairy lore and are well written.

One of Eleanor Farjeon's most valuable contributions is her Christmas poetry, which is unique in its variety and spirit. Sometimes the poems have the hushed reverential mood of a Christmas hymn; sometimes they are gay and rollicking. There are no poems more true to the Christmas spirit, thoughtful, tender, imaginative. Her "Prayer for Little Things" is often used at Christmas but is actually timeless in its appeal.

Eleanor Farjeon was the first writer for children to receive the Hans Christian Andersen Award when it was established in 1956, and each year in her memory the Children's Book Circle in England presents the Eleanor Farjeon Award for "distinguished services to children's books."

A. A. Milne

When We Were Very Young
Now We Are Six

While still a young man, A. A. Milne established himself as a successful writer for adults and as a member of the London literary world. After the First World War, a son was born to the Milnes—Christopher Robin. As soon as he could talk he gave himself the name of "Billy Moon," and "Moon" he was called by everyone. For this reason, Milne explains, the name "Christopher Robin" always seemed to belong entirely to the public's little boy, not to his own.

At the time Milne was writing plays and other adult literature, he gave his wife a verse about Christopher Robin—"Vespers"—which she sent off to a magazine and which was accepted for publication. Then Rose Fyleman, who was publishing a magazine for children, asked Milne to contribute some children's verses. At first he refused but then changed his mind and sent the poems. When both the editor and the illustrator advised him to write a whole book of verses, he felt it was a foolish thing to do, but again he complied. The result was *When We Were Very Young*, a major sensation in children's books both in England

[25]"The Night Will Never Stay." From the section "Meeting Mary" in *Poems for Children* by Eleanor Farjeon. Copyright, 1951, by Eleanor Farjeon. Reprinted by permission of J. B. Lippincott Company and David Higham Associates, Ltd. for Michael Joseph Ltd.

and America. It shares with the second book, *Now We Are Six*, an undiminishing popularity year after year. Milne's plays are amusing, but it is probable that his reputation as a writer will rest more securely upon his two books of verse for children and his two books of stories about Pooh than upon any of his adult stories and dramas.

Milne had a remarkable ability of presenting small children as they are. He gives us their bemused absorption in their private inner world of make-believe, their blithe egotism, their liking for small animals, their toys and games, and the peculiar angle from which they view the odd behavior of those adults who move vaguely on the fringe of their private world.

Christopher Robin speaks for the imaginations of children around four to six years old. His make-believe world is not peopled with the fairies of the eight-year-old but is just the everyday sort of play of the nursery-age child.

The egocentricity of the young child's thought and language has never been recorded more accurately than it was by A. A. Milne. Christopher Robin goes to the market looking for a rabbit and is naively astonished that the market men should be selling mackerel and fresh lavender when *he*, Christopher Robin, wants rabbits. He catalogues his articles of clothing, fascinating because they are his. You can hear the smug emphasis on the personal pronoun. Changing the guard at Buckingham may be very impressive, but the child's only concern is, "Do you think the King knows all about Me?" This is a typical four-year-old, thinking and speaking of everything in terms of himself.

Illustration by E. H. Shepard. From the book When We Were Very Young *by A. A. Milne. Copyright, 1924, by E. P. Dutton & Co., Inc. Renewal, 1952, by A. A. Milne. Reproduced by permission of the publishers.*

Viewpoints

. . . I know that a great many children did, and do, like *When We Were Very Young.* I think that such merit as attaches to the verses for this (as distinct from the illustrations to which the book is so obviously indebted) was won by taking pains: more pains, perhaps, than is usual. Whatever else they lack, the verses are technically good. The practice of no form of writing demands such a height of technical perfection as the writing of light verse in the Calverley and *Punch* tradition. *When We Were Very Young* is not the work of a poet becoming playful, nor of a lover of children expressing his love, nor of a prose-writer knocking together a few jingles for the little ones; it is the work of a light-verse writer taking his job seriously even though he is taking it into the nursery. It seems that the nursery, more than any other room in the house, likes to be approached seriously. —A. A. Milne, *Autobiography,* E. P. Dutton and Co., New York, 1939, p. 282.

Knowing children's interests, Milne reflects them in his writing. There we find the child's love of small animals and toys. The verses are full of the small child's activities, also. He stalks down the sidewalk missing all the lines. He sits on the stairs and meditates, or he goes hoppity, hoppity, hop. On the whole, he is a busy, active child, immersed in his own affairs and oblivious of any world beyond his own horizon. We can analyze Milne's tripping trochees, his iambs and dactyls, but these academic labels do not seem to convey any idea of the fluid and flashing use he made of words, rhyme, and rhythm to convey character, mood, and action. When Christopher Robin hops through the jingle called "Hoppity," the lines go in exactly the pattern of a child's hop, ending with a big one and a rest, just as hopping always does. But best of all is that juvenile meditation "Halfway Down." Ernest Shepard's sketch, too, has caught the mood of suspended action that is always overtaking small children on stairs. (See the discussion of Shepard's work in Chapter 5.) Why they like to clutter up stairs with their belongings and their persons Milne knew, and he has told us with arresting monosyllables that block the way as effectually as Christopher Robin's small person blocks the stairs. In this first stanza from "Halfway Down"[26] notice "It" and "Stop," which sit as firmly in the middle of the verse as Christopher on the stair.

Halfway down the stairs
Is a stair
Where I sit.
There isn't any
Other stair
Quite like
It.
I'm not at the bottom,
I'm not at the top;
So this is the stair
Where
I always
Stop.

Over and over again, Milne makes a monosyllable or a single word equal three or four words in a preceding line by sheer intensity. It is a device that compels correct reading of the lines, regardless of scansion.

With all of these virtues, it is not surprising that some moderns have come to feel that Milne is the greatest poet for children, certainly their favorite poet. However, delightful as Milne's verses are, they do not cover the full range either of children's interests or of their capacity for enjoying poetry. Many poets achieve greater lyric beauty, more delicate imagery, and deeper feeling for the child's inner world, but certainly we shall never encounter a writer who understood more completely the curious composite of gravity and gaiety, of supreme egotism and occasional whimsy that is the young child.

[26]"Halfway Down." From the book *When We Were Very Young* by A. A. Milne. Decorations by E. H. Shepard. Copyright 1924 by E. P. Dutton & Co., Inc. Renewal, 1952, by A. A. Milne. Published by E. P. Dutton & Co., Inc. Reprinted by permission of The Canadian Publishers. McClelland and Stewart Limited, Toronto, E. P. Dutton & Co., Inc., and Methuen & Co. Ltd.

Elizabeth Madox Roberts

Under the Tree

Elizabeth Madox Roberts won several poetry prizes during the period when she was writing the novels for which she is known. The poems that brought a prize while she was in college were later published as *Under the Tree* (1922). A year before her death, a second volume of poems, *Song in the Meadow,* appeared.

Her one book of poems for children is unlike any other juvenile poetry. It has an air of deceptive simplicity that gives the unwary reader no immediate clues to the artistry which makes these poems emotionally satisfying and full of everyday enchantment. Some lines from "The Worm" will serve as an example:

Dickie found a broken spade
And said he'd dig himself a well;
And then Charles took a piece of tin,
And I was digging with a shell.

Then Will said he would dig one too.
We shaped them out and made them wide,
And I dug up a piece of clod
That had a little worm inside.

We watched him pucker up himself
And stretch himself to walk away.
He tried to go inside the dirt,
But Dickie made him wait and stay.

His shining skin was soft and wet.
I poked him once to see him squirm.
And then Will said, "I wonder if
He knows that he's a worm."[27]

[27]"The Worm" and "Mr. Wells." From *Under the Tree* by Elizabeth Madox Roberts. Copyright 1922 by B. W. Huebsch, Inc., renewed 1950 by Ivor S. Roberts. Reprinted by permission of The Viking Press, Inc.

The children are digging, but notice that they are digging with a broken spade, a piece of tin, and a shell—tools accepted as a matter of course by the child. Then the worm distracts them from their original plan of digging a well, and they experiment with it for a while until a strange idea makes them forget their experiments.

The Roberts child ruminates about things, wonders, and has several scares, but is never fairy-conscious or full of delicate whimsies, having instead a wholesome earthiness and a healthy identification with and delight in nature.

The poems are full of pleasant people and reflect the child's interest not only in other children, but in the grownups at home and abroad. Father fills the little girl's mug at milking time and sings or tells stories to all the children. Mother sends them on picnics and corrects their manners. The townspeople vary from pretty "Miss Kate-Marie," the Sunday school teacher, to Mr. Pennybaker, who makes faces when he sings bass, and the notable Mr. Wells:

Mr. Wells[27]

On Sunday morning, then he comes
To church, and everybody smells
The blacking and the toilet soap
And camphor balls from Mr. Wells.

He wears his whiskers in a bunch,
And wears his glasses on his head.
I mustn't call him Old Man Wells—
No matter—that's what Father said.

And when the little blacking smells
And camphor balls and soap begin,
I do not have to look to know
That Mr. Wells is coming in.

The intense curious interest that children feel toward the strange antics of grownups is reflected in poem after poem and is summarized in the amusing "People Going By."

Reading these poems, you realize their integrity. No word, no line is dressed up or prettified to sound cute. Cuteness afflicts some modern verse for children and is indeed the curse of juvenile poetry. Here in these poems by Elizabeth Madox Roberts is complete fidelity to child nature. They are grave, simple, and full of the unconscious beauty of children's narratives when they are moved to tell you earnestly of something they enjoy. You can live with these poems, use them year after year, and never exhaust their richness. No adult can read them without knowing much more about children when finished, and no child can hear them without feeling a kinship with that child who likes to play with wiggle-tails, smell the aromatic herbs of fennel, and eat cherry pie, but who occasionally suffers from every child's all-too-familiar fears.

Viewpoints

We have a cliché we use too often when we discuss the reading of poems. We talk about "levels." We say, at this level it means this; at a second level something quite different; at a third . . . at a fourth. . . . It is a word which saves time perhaps and may even mean something as a shorthand sign but as a metaphor it is deceptive. It implies that a poem is like an apartment house: you climb from one story to the next and each floor is separate and distinct: the rooms—the arrangement of the rooms—are identical but everything else is different . . . the furniture . . . the view. One does not read a poem in this way. . . .

. . . And one does not read one's self *up* or *down*. One stands there and reads *through:* through the sounds, but never leaving the sounds, into their references, through the references to the images they make, through the images to their relation to each other, through their relation to each other to the feel of meaning. It is perspective one reads for in a poem, and perspective includes the near things as well as the far and includes them all at the same time and in the same scene.—Archibald MacLeish, *Poetry and Experience,* Houghton Mifflin, Boston, 1961, pp. 85–86.

Elizabeth Coatsworth

Summer Green
Poems
The Sparrow Bush
Down Half the World

Elizabeth Coatsworth's *The Cat Who Went to Heaven* won the Newbery Medal for 1930 but is not as popular with children as her historical tales such as *Away Goes Sally, Five Bushel Farm*, and *The Fair American*. Within the pages of these books are some of her best poems, and her poetry is collected in *Summer Green, Poems, The Sparrow Bush*, and *Down Half the World*.

A certain style in her poetry is well illustrated by the frequently quoted "Swift things are beautiful," from *Away Goes Sally:*

Swift things are beautiful:
Swallows and deer,
And lightning that falls
Bright-veined and clear,
River and meteors,
Wind in the wheat,
The strong-withered horse,
The runner's sure feet.

And slow things are beautiful:
The closing of day,
The pause of the wave
That curves downward to spray,
The ember that crumbles,
The opening flower
And the ox that moves on
In the quiet of power.[28]

Here are the comparisons that the author uses not incidentally but as the theme of the entire poem. You can find other examples of contrasts in all three books. Building a poem around a series of comparisons seems to be a favorite pattern for Elizabeth Coatsworth. It is an exceedingly provocative one for children to study and to try for themselves in their own writing.

Another aspect of her style is the smooth, flowing lines that fall so gently on the ear. Poem after poem has this quietness. The lyric text of *Under the Green Willow*, a picture book, has a subdued, rhythmic quality. Although the lines can frolic now and then, slow-moving calmness predominates. For this reason, reading many of the poems at a time is monotonous.

On the whole these poems are not markedly musical, but they are rich in sensory words; for instance: fallen apples that "smell cidery on the air," sleigh bells that ring "icily sweet," and little buds "no larger than a mouse's ear." You can find examples of her use of words which make you see, smell, taste, touch, and hear.

Her nature poems seem to fall into two classes. Some are straight nature descriptions, and others are brief, lovely descriptions which lead toward, or climax in, a human mood or situation. One of the finest examples of the second type, "How gray the rain," from *Five Bushel Farm*, ends with

Serene and bright
The rainbow stands
That was not anywhere before,
And so may joy
Fill empty hands
When someone enters through a door.[29]

These poems linking together nature and human concerns are notable but they may prove a bit subtle for children and may require discussion before the literal-minded children catch their implications. But the nature descriptions are understandable to all children.

The verses lack the epigrammatic and sparkling quality of similar poems by Christina Rossetti but have instead a straightforward simplicity. In *The Fair American* there is the philosophic

To have nothing at all
Is to have much still.[30]

The poetry of Elizabeth Coatsworth is more ideational than most juvenile verse. It belongs chiefly to older children and will stretch their minds and imaginations.

[28] "Swift things are beautiful." Reprinted with permission of The Macmillan Company and Blackie & Son Limited from *Away Goes Sally* by Elizabeth Coatsworth. Copyright 1934 by The Macmillan Company, renewed 1962 by Elizabeth Coatsworth Beston.

[29] "How gray the rain." Reprinted with permission of The Macmillan Company and Blackie & Son Limited from *Five Bushel Farm* by Elizabeth Coatsworth. Copyright 1939 by The Macmillan Company, renewed 1967 by Elizabeth Coatsworth Beston.

[30] "To have nothing at all." Reprinted with permission of The Macmillan Company and Blackie & Son Limited from *The Fair American* by Elizabeth Coatsworth. Copyright 1940 by The Macmillan Company, renewed 1968 by Elizabeth Coatsworth Beston.

Rachel Field

Taxis and Toadstools
Poems

Rachel Field must have been a delightful human being, judging from the amusing account of her early years she wrote for *The Junior Book of Authors*, which gives the impression of a warm, vivid personality, full of exuberance, loving people and the outdoor world.

After college, she settled in New York to begin the serious business of writing. Her *Six Plays* was published in 1924, and that same year her poems for children, *The Pointed People*, appeared. These attracted favorable attention even though they appeared at the same time that A. A. Milne's *When We Were Very Young* was creating a sensation. Two years later her second book of poems, *Taxis and Toadstools*, was published.

From 1924 to 1942, in a period of only eighteen years, she published some thirty-six books, many of which she herself illustrated. Among her best-known books for children are *Calico Bush*, a historical novel; and the 1930 Newbery Medal book, *Hitty*, the story of a hundred-year-old doll.

An inland child once said with awe that she was going to spend the summer on an island. "A real island with the sea all around; just think, with the sea on every side of us!" she breathed, bringing to mind Field's lines:

If once you have slept on an island
You'll never be quite the same.

Over and over, Rachel Field catches the curious wonderment of children. She shows a child turning back to look at the china dog with the "sad unblinking eye" and wishing for magic words to bring him to life; or wondering if skyscrapers ever want to lie down and never get up! These are authentic child-thoughts, and children respond to their integrity with spontaneous pleasure.

Out of doors, the children of her poems voice that curious kinship with birds, beasts, and growing things that is part of the magic of childhood. Children go to the woods for wild strawberries and forget that there is anything else in the world to do but "fill my hands and eat." They understand the wild creatures, and when they see "The Dancing Bear," they know at once something is wrong, for his eyes look bewildered "like a child's lost in the woods at night."

Field's unique contribution to children's verse is perhaps the three groups of city poems in her *Taxis and Toadstools* called "People," "Taxis and Thoroughfares," and "Stores and Storekeepers."

In the collection of her verses called *Poems*, children like "Good Green Bus," "At the Theater," "The Florist Shop," "The Animal Store," and the favorite "Skyscrapers."

One of the most pleasant poems in this group is "City Rain." The first verse is so clear a picture that children often want to illustrate it. The cozy feeling in the second verse is heightened by the rainy sound of that next-to-the-last line, with its humming *n*'s and *ing*'s:

City Rain[31]

Rain in the city!
I love to see it fall
Slantwise where the buildings crowd
Red brick and all.
Streets of shiny wetness
Where the taxis go,
With people and umbrellas all
Bobbing to and fro.

Rain in the city!
I love to hear it drip
When I am cosy in my room
Snug as any ship,
With toys spread on the table,
With a picture book or two,
And the rain like a rumbling tune that sings
Through everything I do.

Rachel Field's poetry never attains the power and sureness of her best prose, but the complete absence of artificiality or juvenile cuteness in these poems commends them to both children and adults.

[31]"City Rain" copyright 1926 by Doubleday & Company, Inc. from the book *Taxis and Toadstools* by Rachel Field. Reprinted by permission of Doubleday & Company, Inc. and World's Work Ltd.

David McCord

Far and Few
Take Sky
Every Time I Climb a Tree
For Me to Say
Away and Ago

Speaking at a conference on children's literature, David McCord gave as one of his rules for writing for children:

> *First, just be a child before you grow up and let nothing interfere with the process. Write it all* out *of yourself and* for *yourself. . . . Next, never take the phrase "writing verse for children" seriously. If you write for them you are lost. Ask your brain's computer what you know about a child's mind. The answer is zero.*[32]

McCord first began writing verse at fifteen, encouraged, he believes, by two solitary years on an Oregon ranch. *Far and Few,* his first book for children, with his fifteenth book of verse, a choice collection of poems. They range from pure nonsense to quiet little meditations that reflect, perhaps, those solitary years out of doors.

Far and Few opens with a poem about "Joe," the greedy squirrel who keeps the birds waiting. It closes with "Fred," an intrepid flying squirrel, the original glider. Children and adults who feed birds will recognize both these characters. Here is

Joe[33]

We feed the birds in winter,
And outside in the snow
We have a tray of many seeds
For many birds of many breeds
And one gray squirrel named Joe.
  But Joe comes early,
  Joe comes late,
  And all the birds
  Must stand and wait.
And waiting there for Joe to go
Is pretty cold work in the snow.

[32]From David McCord's "Poetry for Children," in *A Critical Approach to Children's Literature,* ed. by Sara Innis Fenwick. University of Chicago Press, 1967, p. 53.

[33]"Joe" by David McCord from *Far and Few.* Copyright 1952 by David McCord. Reprinted by permission of Little, Brown and Co. and Curtis Brown, Ltd.

From Take Sky *by David McCord. Illustrated by Henry B. Kane. Copyright © 1961, 1962 by David McCord. By permission of Little, Brown ahd Co.*

Other small beasts are presented—bats, grasshoppers, a snail, starfish, and an especially convincing crowd of crows "spilling from a tree." For sheer nonsense, "Five Chants," "Who Wants a Birthday?" and "Isabel Jones & Curabel Lee" are fun. Children under six like to roll the onomatopoetic refrains of "Song of the Train" and "The Pickety Fence" on their tongues. But it takes a perceptive older child to appreciate "The White Ships," "The Shell," "The Starfish," and "The Star in the Pail."

Take Sky, McCord's second book of verse for children, is on the whole more completely humorous than *Far and Few.* His "Write Me a Verse" should appeal to youngsters wrestling with verse forms. In these poems couplets, quatrains, limericks, and triolets are amusingly defined and illustrated. However, there is also much entertainment in this book for the youngest children. In "Sing Song," "Three Signs of Spring," "Sally Lun Lundy," and many other verses, McCord has a wonderful time playing with the sounds of words. He also makes many clever uses of dialogue. The poems in *Away and Ago* are also light and sunny; in this collection he writes about parties, balloons, baseball, and holidays, and in "Like You As It" he plays with words. The poet savors language, but he holds it—like the master craftsman he is—firmly in check.

Harry Behn

The Golden Hive
The Little Hill
Windy Morning
The Wizard in the Well

Harry Behn has written both prose and poetry for children, and has translated Japanese haiku with precise and delicate sensitivity in *Cricket Songs* and *More Cricket Songs*, both of which are illustrated by reproductions of paintings by Japanese artists.

In his book on poetry, *Chrysalis*, Behn points out that children see a world in every least little thing, and his poems explore with an ever-fresh awareness children's delight in little things about them. *The Golden Hive* is for older readers and includes some fine lyric poems, of which "The Painted Desert" and "Summer" are particularly evocative. His other small books of verse, decorated by the author, speak to young children, five to nine, with lyric charm and unusual variety. There are a few nonsense jingles like "Mr. Pyme," "Dr. Windikin," "Shopping Spree," and the lively "Tea Party."

There are many verses about the child's play world, both real and imaginative. "The New Little Boy" is refreshingly antisocial. "Picnic by the Sea" is a child's view of the queer grownups who sit sunning themselves when there are so many wonders to be explored. "Hallowe'en" is a particularly shivery celebration of that favorite festival and is delightful for verse choirs to speak for their own pleasure or for an appreciative audience.

Behn's unique contribution is found in those poems where he is helping the child to look at everyday experiences with the eyes of the spirit. Notice the philosophy in

Others[34]

Even though it's raining
I don't wish it wouldn't.
That would be like saying
I think it shouldn't.
I'd rather be out playing
Than sitting hours and hours
Watching rain falling
In drips and drops and showers,
But what about the robins?
What about the flowers?

Read aloud "Early Awake," "Trees," "Spring," "Spring Rain," "The Little Hill," "Lesson," and you will feel the reassurance, the acceptance, and the happy peace that emanate from these and many other poems.

Stephen Vincent Benét
Rosemary Carr Benét

A Book of Americans

Stephen Vincent Benét, a member of a famous family of writers, published his first book of verse while he was a student at Yale University. Twice winner of the Pulitzer Prize for poetry, Benét is probably best known for his epic poem about the Civil War, *John Brown's Body*. With his wife, Rosemary, he wrote *A Book of Americans*, in which popular figures in American history are described in moods ranging from the nonsensical to the deeply serious.

"Pilgrims and Puritans" is a humorous presentation of the two sides of these colonists. It reads in part:

Pilgrims and Puritans[35]

The Pilgrims and the Puritans
Were English to the bone
But didn't like the English Church
And wished to have their own
And so, at last, they sailed away
To settle Massachusetts Bay.

[34]"Others." From *The Wizard in the Well*, © copyright 1956 by Harry Behn. Reprinted by permission of Harcourt Brace Jovanovich, Inc.
[35]From *A Book of Americans*. Copyright 1933 by Rosemary and Stephen Vincent Benét. Copyright renewed © 1961 by Rosemary Carr Benét. Used by permission.

The stony fields, the cruel sea
They met with resolution
And so developed, finally,
An iron constitution
And, as a punishment for sinners,
Invented boiled New England dinners.

Children like "Captain Kidd," "Peregrine White and Virginia Dare," and the larruping "Theodore Roosevelt." These are genuinely funny. The poem about the Wright brothers is particularly appreciated today by nine- and ten-year-olds for its humorous account of a momentous event in human history.

This is not great poetry, but it gives the reader a series of vivid portraits of some great Americans, written with vigor and simplicity. It can be a delightful addition to the study of the lives of these Americans or of periods in American history.

Langston Hughes

Don't You Turn Back

Langston Hughes began writing verse while he was in high school and later joined the New York group of black writers of the Harlem Renaissance movement. Much of his poetry is in a spirit of racial pride and protest. The poem "I, Too" is in many anthologies, including Lee Bennett Hopkins's selection of Hughes's poems for children, *Don't You Turn Back:*

I, Too, Sing America[36]

I am the darker brother.
They send me to eat in the kitchen
When company comes,
But I laugh,
And eat well,
And grow strong.

Tomorrow,
I'll be at the table
When company comes.
Nobody'll dare
Say to me,
"Eat in the kitchen,"
Then.

Besides,
They'll see how beautiful I am
And be ashamed—

I, too, am America.

Although many of his poems speak for and about black people, Hughes also wrote poetry that speaks for all humankind.

Silence[37]

I catch the pattern
Of your silence
Before you speak.

I do not need
To hear a word.

Illustration copyright © 1969 by Ann Grifalconi. Reprinted from Don't You Turn Back *by Langston Hughes, by permission of Alfred A. Knopf, Inc.*

[36]"I, Too" Copyright 1926 and renewed 1954 by Langston Hughes. Reprinted from *Selected Poems of Langston Hughes,* by permission of Alfred A. Knopf, Inc.

In your silence
Every tone I seek
Is heard.

These are both serious poems, but there is an ironic humor in much of Hughes's writing, both poetry and prose. Although he wrote several books for children (on jazz, on Africa, on black heroes), his poetry was not created for them. They have, however, overruled him and claimed his poetry for their own. Children enjoy its candor, its humor, and the melodic style that is often reminiscent of ballads and the blues. His last book, published after his death, is *Black Misery,* a series of pithy sentences that are a bitter comment on what a black child faces in our society.

David Littlejohn says of Langston Hughes:

> *By moulding his verse always on the sounds of Negro talk, the rhythms of Negro music, by retaining his own keen honesty and directness, his poetic sense and ironic intelligence, he has maintained through four decades a readable newness distinctly his own.*[38]

Aileen Fisher

Going Barefoot
But Ostriches . . .
Feathered Ones and Furry
Do Bears Have Mothers, Too?

Aileen Fisher sold her first verses to *Child Life Magazine* while working in Chicago. Yearning to return to the outdoors, she decided to buy a one-way ticket to Colorado, and there she has stayed, writing poetry about the wild creatures she loves. She has also written some excellent biographies and several collections of plays, and has published many books of poetry in addition to the titles listed above. Her topics cover the seasons, children's pets, nature as the child encounters it.

With *Going Barefoot* Fisher attained a new freedom of verse patterns, a lighter, gayer touch, and a melodic line that makes this book a delight to read aloud either at one sitting or in parts day by day. It begins with the boy's question—

How soon
how soon
is a morning in June,
a sunny morning or afternoon
in the wonderful month
of the Barefoot Moon?[39]

Then the young philosopher observes that rabbits go barefoot all year round, so do raccoons, bees, cats, deer, and other creatures, while he must suffer the handicap of socks, shoes, and even galoshes. At last comes the day when he and his mother consult the calendar and the narrative reaches a triumphant conclusion—

June![39]

The day is warm
and a breeze is blowing,
the sky is blue
and its eye is glowing,
and everything's new
and green and growing . . .

My shoes are off
and my socks are showing . . .

My socks are off . . .

Do you know how I'm going?
BAREFOOT!

This is free and melodic and as full of movement as the restless child waiting for the big day of emancipation from shoes. The poetry about the rabbits, the kangaroos, and other creatures may be read and enjoyed separately or enjoyed as part of the whole. Adrienne Adams's illustrations in full color, with authentic paw prints adorning the end pages, add enchantment to this delightful book. The

[37]"Silence," from *Fields of Wonder* by Langston Hughes. Copyright 1947 by Langston Hughes. Reprinted by permission of Alfred A. Knopf, Inc.

[38]David Littlejohn, *Black on White; A Critical Survey of Writing by American Negroes.* Viking, 1969 (originally published in 1966 by Grossman).

[39]"How soon" and "June." From *Going Barefoot* by Aileen Fisher, copyright © 1969 by Aileen Fisher, used by permission of Thomas Y. Crowell Company, Inc., publisher.

Viewpoints

Poetry is essentially a game, with artificial rules, and it takes two—a writer and a reader—to play it. If the reader is reluctant, the game will not work.

. . . Poetry, . . . is a kind of musical word game which we value because of its expressive qualities. Not all poems are equally musical, or equally playful, or equally expressive. Nor are they necessarily musical, playful, or expressive in the same way. But we can consider these three qualities as the basic constituents of poetry. . . . If a piece of writing is neither especially rhythmical nor especially ironic or metaphorical in its language, it is not poetry, regardless of its dramatic situations or the ideas it presents.—Robert Scholes, *Elements of Poetry,* Oxford University Press, New York, Toronto, London, 1969, pp. 1, 7, 60.

autumnal *Where Does Everyone Go?* is not quite so exhilarating but exceedingly pleasant to hear and look at. *Up, Up the Mountain* and *In the Middle of the Night* are lyric comments on the beauties of nature; *Feathered Ones and Furry* and *But Ostriches . . .* communicate with humor an affection for animals and an appreciation of the beauty of nature. The poems in *Do Bears Have Mothers, Too?* are addressed to young animals by their mothers; fresh and breezy, they are permeated with fond maternal pride.

Theodore Roethke

I Am! Says the Lamb
Dirty Dinky and Other Creatures

Theodore Roethke received many awards and honors for his poetry, including Guggenheim and Ford Foundation Fellowships, the Pulitzer Prize in 1954, and the National Book Award posthumously in 1965.

Some of his poems are included in anthologies for young people, but *I Am! Says the Lamb* and *Dirty Dinky* are the only collections that can be enjoyed as a whole by children. The rhythm and the sharp imagery appeal to children, who enjoy the poet's wit and his occasional pithy bluntness. Roethke wrote with an ebullience and humor that are especially appealing in such nonsense poems as "The Kitty-Cat Bird." That some of his other poems can be enjoyed by children is obvious on reading

The Bat[40]

By day the bat is cousin to the mouse.
He likes the attic of an aging house.

His fingers make a hat about his head.
His pulse beat is so slow we think him dead.

He loops in crazy figures half the night
Among the trees that face the corner light.

But when he brushes up against a screen
We are afraid of what our eyes have seen:

For something is amiss or out of place
When mice with wings can wear a human face.

It is interesting to compare this poem with "Man and Bat" by D. H. Lawrence and with the poem that begins, "A bat is born . . ." in Randall Jarrell's *The Bat-Poet.*

[40]"The Bat," copyright 1938 by Theodore Roethke, from the book *Collected Poems of Theodore Roethke.* Reprinted by permission of Doubleday & Company, Inc. and Faber and Faber Limited.

Pictures copyright © 1975 by Diane Dawson
From See My Lovely Poison Ivy *by Lilian Moore*
Used by permission of Atheneum Publishers

Lilian Moore

I Feel the Same Way
I Thought I Heard the City
Sam's Place; Poems from the Country
See My Lovely Poison Ivy

Lilian Moore decided, in her capacity as an editor, that writers often use too many words. This knowledge and her years of experience as a specialist in reading problems have influenced her poetry, which is simple and direct, yet fluent and witty in a way that younger children can comprehend and appreciate. In "Winter Cardinal" she creates a vivid image with elegance and restraint:

Winter Cardinal[41]

Fat
and elegantly
crested,
clinging to the branch
of the stripped tree
like
one bright leaf that
bested
every wind and lived to
show
its red
against
the astonished snow.

Moore has written several stories for children and compiled some poetry anthologies, but it is her own poetry that makes a unique contribution. Children respond to the humor and incongruity of the lighthearted poems in *See My Lovely Poison Ivy*, especially those in which there is a surprising turn, as there is in

Bedtime Stories[42]

"Tell me a story,"
Says Witch's Child.

"About the Beast
So fierce and wild.

About a Ghost
That shrieks and groans.

A Skeleton
That rattles bones.

About a Monster
Crawly-creepy.

Something nice
To make me sleepy."

[41]"Winter Cardinal" from *Sam's Place* by Lilian Moore. Text copyright © 1973 by Lilian Moore. Used by permission of Atheneum Publishers.
[42]"Bedtime Stories" from *See My Lovely Poison Ivy* by Lilian Moore. Text copyright © 1975 by Lilian Moore. Used by permission of Atheneum Publishers.

Hilda Conkling

Poems by a Little Girl
Shoes of the Wind

That a little girl living much in the company of her poet-mother should begin "talking" her own poems is not surprising, but the quality of Hilda Conkling's poems *is*. They are beautiful both in ideas and in expression.

When Hilda was ten years old, *Poems by a Little Girl* was published with a laudatory introduction by the poet Amy Lowell. Hilda's mother said the poems often came when they were walking or just conversing. Hilda never hesitated for a word, and the mother made notes as best she could. Later she read her copy to Hilda, who would correct any word that had been inadvertently changed. The poems stand exactly as the child spoke them. When Hilda was twelve, her second book, *Shoes of the Wind*, was published (selections from the two books have been published under the title *Silverhorn*). After her second book, there were no more poems from Hilda so far as we can discover. Speculations as to why she ceased writing are beside the point. Our concern is with these poems that have important qualities for children.

First of all, their lack of rhyme is sometimes an asset. The time always comes when children are obsessed with rhyming everything and calling it poetry; then it is a good thing to read them some of young Hilda's verses and say, "Here is poetry written by a little girl. It has no rhyme. Why do you suppose it is called poetry?" That question puzzles some children, but eventually they arrive at certain unmistakably poetic qualities in these unrhymed stanzas. "She *sees* things good," one child said after hearing "Moon Song." Another child, hearing "Chickadee" and "Red Rooster," thought the poet remembered how things *sounded*. Eventually, they discover that it is the fresh or different way in which she tells something with just a few words that makes these little verses different from prose. For instance:

Tree-toad is a leaf-gray shadow
That sings.
Tree-toad is never seen
Unless a star squeezes through the leaves,
Or a moth looks sharply at a gray branch.[43]

Hilda Conkling's free style is, then, a salutary antidote for the rhyming passion when it produces only doggerel and seems to handicap the development of original observation and expression. Her limitation for children is that she is predominantly descriptive. She is chiefly concerned with finding the precise words that tell how something looked or felt or appealed to her imagination. While many of her verses contain remarkably fine and discriminating observations, too much of this kind of detailed description overwhelms children.

John Ciardi

I Met a Man
The Man Who Sang the Sillies
You Read to Me, I'll Read to You

John Ciardi has for a number of years been active as a teacher, lecturer, critic, and writer. Much of his poetry for both adults and children has a brisk candor. In his poetry for children, though, the humor and nonsense soften a forthrightness that is sometimes tart. Many of his poems are satirical comments on the reprehensible behavior of children, a vein most appreciated by the sophisticated reader. However, the topics he develops are usually fresh and original, as, for example, "How to Tell the Top of a Hill," "The River Is a Piece of the Sky," "The Reason for the Pelican." And when he chooses a familiar subject like "Halloween," he treats it freshly, so that it is unlike any other Halloween poem ever written—dramatic and weird, and a brain-tickler for the oldest and best readers.

The omission of words in "Summer Song" makes a good language game.

Summer Song[44]

By the sand between my toes,
By the waves behind my ears,
By the sunburn on my nose,
By the little salty tears
That make rainbows in the sun
When I squeeze my eyes and run,
By the way the seagulls screech,
Guess where I am? At the. . . . . !
By the way the children shout
Guess what happened? School is . . . !
By the way I sing this song
Guess if summer lasts too long?
You must answer Right or . . . . . !

One of Ciardi's interesting experiments in verse for children is *I Met a Man*, written with a controlled vocabulary of some four hundred words. It was planned as a first book for his own child to read and it moves from easy to more difficult in both words and content. "Poetry," the author says, "is especially well designed to lead the child to such recognition [of new words] for rhyme and pattern are always important clues."

Ciardi continued his experiment with a limited vocabulary in *You Read to Me, I'll Read to You*, in which he alternates a poem the child is supposed to read with one for the adult to read, unrestricted by word lists. These, too, are clever verses. In *The King Who Saved Himself from Being Saved*, Ciardi tells an amusing and pointed story that spoofs the stereotypical hero who insists on improving a situation with which everyone else concerned is perfectly content. This narrative poem is illustrated by Edward Gorey, whose elegant grotesquerie is admirably suited to Ciardi's wit.

[43]From "Tree-Toad" from *Summer-Day Song* by Hilda Conkling. Copyright 1920, renewed 1948 by Hilda Conkling. Reprinted by permission of Random House, Inc.

[44]"Summer Song." From the book *The Man Who Sang the Sillies* by John Ciardi. Copyright, ©, 1961, by John Ciardi. Reprinted by permission of J. B. Lippincott Company.

Kaye Starbird

Speaking of Cows
A Snail's a Failure Socially
Don't Ever Cross a Crocodile
The Pheasant on Route Seven

Kaye Starbird wrote verses as a child and she had poems published in magazines while she was still in college. She has written both satirical verse and serious poetry for adults. In her writing for children she uses a conversational tone and sees everyday experiences from the child's point of view.

Her poems present a child voicing his or her honest opinions or questions about the bugs, beasts, people, and ideas he or she encounters. There is the lizard O'Toole, "living his life in a quiet way," but still unloved. There is "My Cousin Kitty," who, no matter what wonders you show her, continues to cry "I want a balloon." The poems about the kitten in the mailbox, the toad that needed a baby-sitter, the naughty imaginary sprite who takes over the body of a child who is misbehaving—these and many others are inventive and skillfully composed.

With each book, Kaye Starbird has grown as a poet. Her verse patterns are more deft, her moods more varied. Compare, for example, the humor of the first of the following poems with the nostalgic thoughtfulness with which the second, "One Leaf," begins.

A Snail's a Failure Socially[45]

A snail's a failure socially,
Which means you very seldom see
A crowd of happy, laughing snails
Collected all at once.
The reason's this: when asked to dine
A snail could answer "Yes" or "Fine,"
But if he lived a field away
The trip would take him months.

In short, the most excited snail,
Though pleased to hit the party trail,
Could promptly tidy up and take
A shortcut through the clover;
But asked to Easter luncheon—say—
And getting there Columbus Day,
There'd be at least an even chance
He'd find the party over.

One Leaf[46]

At least a month away from the autumn season
I saw a leaf from the maple break and fall,
Fluttering down for no apparent reason
One windless day when nothing else moved at all.

Eve Merriam

Finding a Poem
It Doesn't Always Have to Rhyme
There Is No Rhyme for Silver
Out Loud

Eve Merriam is a teacher of creative writing as well as a writer of prose and poetry for adults and for children. Her first book of poetry for adults, *Family Circle*, won the Yale Series of Younger Poets prize.

Merriam's verse is varied in form, inventive, and often humorous. It usually speaks directly to the child's experience and is especially appealing to the reader who enjoys word-play. Her essay on "Writing a Poem," in *Finding a Poem*, describes the poet's search for the exact word or phrase to express and illuminate her meaning. Both this essay and the chapter entitled " 'I,' Says the Poem" in Nancy Larrick's *Somebody Turned on a Tap in These Kids* are good reading for anyone working with children.

Some notion of the range of her poetry can be seen in two contrasting poems:

Landscape[47]

What will you find at the edge of the world?
A footprint,
a feather,
desert sand swirled?
A tree of ice,
a rain of stars,
or a junkyard of cars?

[45]"A Snail's a Failure Socially." From the book *A Snail's a Failure Socially* by Kaye Starbird. Copyright © 1966 by Kaye Starbird. Reprinted by permission of Paul R. Reynolds, Inc., 599 Fifth Avenue, New York, N.Y. 10017.

[46]"One Leaf." From the book *The Pheasant on Route Seven* by Kaye Starbird. Copyright, ©, 1968, by Kaye Starbird. Reprinted by permission of J. B. Lippincott Company.

What will there be at the rim of the world?
A mollusc,
a mammal,
a new creature's birth?
Eternal sunrise,
immortal sleep,
or cars piled up in a rusty heap?

Ping-Pong[47]

Chitchat
wigwag
rickrack
zigzag

knickknack
gewgaw
riffraff
seesaw

crisscross
flip-flop
ding-dong
tiptop

singsong
mishmash
King Kong
bong.

"Landscape" has the provocative imagery and the concern with today's problems that are typical of Eve Merriam's poetry and are qualities that she encourages in the writing of her students. The intensity of her protest against social ills is most clearly seen in *The Inner City Mother Goose*, a collection of angry poems written for adults but relished by many young people.

"Ping-Pong" is a good example of the way she uses words for aural effect; bouncy and rhythmic, the poem evokes the patterned clicking of the game's sound. In *There Is No Rhyme for Silver* and *It Doesn't Always Have to Rhyme*, Merriam—like David McCord—uses poems to illustrate such terms as cliché, homonym, limerick, onomatopoeia, simile, and metaphor.

[47]"Landscape" and "Ping-Pong" by Eve Merriam from *Finding a Poem*. Copyright © 1970 by Eve Merriam. Reprinted by permission of Atheneum Publishers, and Eve Merriam c/o International Famous Agency.

Gwendolyn Brooks

Bronzeville Boys and Girls

Gwendolyn Brooks's first poem was published when she was thirteen; in 1949 she won the annual prize given by *Poetry* magazine, and in 1950 she received the Pulitzer Prize for Poetry, never before awarded to a black writer.

In all her poetry there is a concern for racial and personal identity. Dan Jaffer says,

The label "Black poetry" ignores Gwen Brooks' ability to speak as a hunchbacked girl, a male preacher, a white spokesman, in varying voices all clearly her own . . . it forgets that though Gwen Brooks learns from Langston Hughes, she also learns from T. S. Eliot; and that she must be more than a replica of either or both.[48]

Her poems for and about children, *Bronzeville Boys and Girls*, speak for any child of any race. Each of the poems is named for a boy or girl. They show a rare sensitivity to the child's inner life—the wonderments, hurts, and gay sense of make-believe and play. Here are two in contrasting mood.

[48]"Gwendolyn Brooks: An Appreciation from the White Suburbs," by Dan Jaffe. From *The Black American Writer*, v. 2, ed. by Christopher Bigsby (Everett/Edwards, 1969).

Viewpoints

Gwendolyn Brooks has always been committed and lyrical and relevant. Before it was fashionable, she was tone deep in blackness. In the fifties, she was writing poems about Emmett Till and Little Rock and the black boys and girls who came North looking for the Promised Land and found concrete deserts. In fact, she has always written about the sounds and sights and flavors of the black community. Her poems are distinguished by a bittersweet lyricism and an overwhelming concreteness. . . . Her poems celebrate the truth of her life. They celebrate the truth of blackness, which is also the truth of man.—From *To Gwen With Love* edited by Patricia L. Brown, Don L. Lee, and Francis Ward. Johnson Publishing Co., Chicago, 1971, pp. 3, 1.

Illustration by Roni Solbert from Bronzeville Boys and Girls *by Gwendolyn Brooks. Copyright © 1956 by Gwendolyn Brooks Blakely. Reproduced by permission of Harper & Row, Publishers, Inc.*

Cynthia in the Snow[49]

It SUSHES.
It hushes
The loudness in the road.
It flitter-twitters,
And laughs away from me.
It laughs a lovely whiteness,
And whitely whirs away,
To be
Some otherwhere,
Still white as milk or shirts.
So beautiful it hurts.

Vern[49]

When walking in a tiny rain
Across the vacant lot,
A pup's a good companion—
If a pup you've got.

And when you've had a scold,
And no one loves you very,
And you cannot be merry,
A pup will let you look at him,
And even let you hold
His little wiggly warmness—

And let you snuggle down beside.
Nor mock the tears you have to hide.

William Jay Smith

Laughing Time
Boy Blue's Book of Beasts
Mr. Smith and Other Nonsense

William Jay Smith won, among other honors, the Young Poets' Prize of *Poetry* magazine in 1945. He has served as Consultant in Poetry to the Library of Congress, and has written poetry for children as well as poetry and criticism for adults.

"I like this book," said the King of Hearts.
"It makes me laugh the way it starts!"

"I like it also," said his Mother.
So they sat down and read it to each other.[50]

The verses in *Laughing Time* are not too subtle for very young children and not too simple for the sevens and for the adults who must, perforce, read them aloud.

Children enjoy the idea behind "The Toaster."

A silver-scaled Dragon with jaws flaming red
Sits at my elbow and toasts my bread.
I hand him fat slices, and then, one by one,
He hands them back when he sees they are
done.[50]

Boy Blue's Book of Beasts is equally good nonsense about animals wild and tame—considerably wilder in verse form! There is "a tough Kangaroo named Hopalong Brown/Boxed all the badmen out of town" and "Trim my whiskers! Bless my soul!/Here comes a big brown one-eyed Mole." "A long-haired Yak" in a barber's chair presents a problem and so does a little Raccoon who

[49]"Cynthia in the Snow" and "Vern" from *Bronzeville Boys and Girls* by Gwendolyn Brooks. Copyright © 1956 by Gwendolyn Brooks Blakely. Reprinted by permission of Harper & Row, Publishers.

[50]"The King of Hearts" and "The Toaster" from *Laughing Time* by William Jay Smith. Copyright © 1955 by William Jay Smith. Reprinted by permission of William Jay Smith and Little, Brown and Co. in association with the Atlantic Monthly Press.

wants to be something else. All the verses are cleverly written. Smith's *Typewriter Town* is less successful, but it is good to discover a writer of poetry for adults who starts his own children with the musical inventions of nonsense verse.

William Jay Smith is also co-editor with Louise Bogan of an excellent anthology, *Golden Journey: Poems for Young People;* and with Virginia Haviland of an annotated bibliography, *Children and Poetry,* which includes a good listing of poetry anthologies.

May Swenson

Poems to Solve
More Poems to Solve

May Swenson writes with sharp imagery, her free and flowing verse filled with an awareness of sensory stimuli and imaginative vision.

Her poems are studded with evocative phrases that spring to life; in "At Truro," for example

The sea is unfolding scrolls
and rolling them up again.
It is an ancient diary

the waves are murmuring.
The words are white curls,
great capitals are seen.[51]

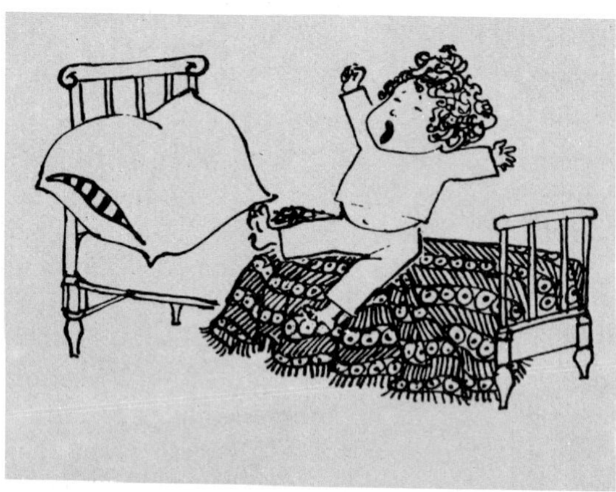

Illustration by Jacqueline Chwast. Reproduced from Wide Awake and Other Poems, *© 1959, by Myra Cohn Livingstone, by permission of Harcourt Brace Jovanovich, Inc.*

In the preface to *More Poems to Solve,* she discusses the patterns of words in her poems, and explains that "Riddles, Shapes, Riddle-Shapes, Word-Things, Shape-Word-Things (not to mention the poems whose modes, by contrast, are more conventional) all present some unexpected facet or internal feature to be discovered *as part* of the recognition to be reached for in each." Her poems to solve, then, at least invite and at most demand the participation of the reader.

Myra Cohn Livingston

Whispers and Other Poems
Wide Awake and Other Poems
A Crazy Flight and Other Poems
The Way Things Are and Other Poems

Myra Cohn Livingston was interested in writing and music throughout all her school years, finally abandoning her music study to become a writer and teacher. As a teacher of creative writing, she feels very strongly about the paramount importance of free expression. As she has said in "What the Heart Knows Today":[52]

Happily, we are no longer concerned with those who copy patterns or fill in blanks; the beginning acceptance of blank verse, free verse, haiku has helped somewhat to break the rhyme barrier, but we have a long way to go before we can succeed in recognizing that the tools of poetry are not poetry.

Nevertheless, her own mastery of rhyme and meter makes it clear that she herself is in command of the tools of poetry. Most of her books of verse (some of which are listed above) deal with the sensory experiences, activities, and imaginings of young children.

Whispers[53]

Whispers
  tickle through your ear
  telling things you like to hear.
Whispers
  are as soft as skin
  letting little words curl in.
Whispers
  come so they can blow
  secrets others never know.

Wide Awake[54]

I have to jump up
out of bed
and stretch my hands
and rub my head
and curl my toes
and yawn
and shake
myself
all wideawake!

Although *A Crazy Flight and Other Poems* is for children eight to eleven, there are no age barriers to the enjoyment of poetry, and many of Livingston's selections may please both the read-aloud audience and adults. A recognition of changing speech patterns can be observed in "The Sun Is Stuck":[55]

The sun is stuck.
I mean, it won't move.
I mean it's hot, man, and we need a red-hot
poker to pry it loose,
Give it a good shove and roll it across the sky
And make it go down
So we can be cool,
Man.

Livingston has also edited an anthology for children, *Listen, Children, Listen,* and an excellent anthology for adolescent poetry lovers—*A Tune Beyond Us*—which includes many poems from other languages. As she says in "Editor's Note": "This collection has been chosen, largely, from the lesser known works of great poets or from the work of little-known poets: A German who tells of a railroad man in Ohio, an Irishman who sees the Devil, a Latin poet of the ninth century writing of Easter Sunday . . . an American speaking of flying saucers. . . . In an age of science and definition, it sometimes seems important to reflect that art escapes definition by its appeal to man's senses, sensitivities, and emotions."

Here, then, are some of the poets who have written joyously and seriously for children. There are of course many other poets whose work is cherished by children, such as Dennis Lee or Karla Kuskin, whose gay, simple verses appeal to younger children, or Mary O'Neill, whose *Hailstones and Halibut Bones* is a happy experiment with words and colors, associating colors with objects, moods, and feelings. Most anthologies include one or more of the poems of James Tippett, E. V. Rieu, James Reeves, William Allingham, Frances Frost, Vachel Lindsay, Sara Teasdale, and Rose Fyleman. With the flourishing of new black poets, older boys and girls read with interest some of the earlier writers like Paul Laurence Dunbar and Countee Cullen. The bibliography at the end of this chapter reflects children's interest in modern poetry. It cannot possibly cite all of the anthologies that have now been published for children and young people, but it includes some excellent general anthologies and a selection of subject anthologies.

Not all of the poets discussed in this chapter and listed in the bibliography have been gifted with lyric genius, but each one has made a contribution which serves to underscore the fact that *children like poetry*. If the lesser of our poets are at first more popular with children than our major poets, it is probably because they are direct and clear; they choose subjects children can understand easily, and they treat the subject briefly and cheerfully. These are standards we must respect in our choice of verse for children. We must remember, too, that they may turn away from obscurity in a poem just as many adults do; that they will endure length usually only in narrative verse that is swift-moving and exciting; and that in general they shun long descriptions. So lyric poets who catch their favor generally do so with poetry that is brief and gay, or markedly melodious. And of course many young people prefer the poetry

[51]"At Truro." Reprinted by permission of Charles Scribner's Sons from *More Poems to Solve* by May Swenson. Copyright © 1971 May Swenson.
[52]"What the Heart Knows Today" by Myra Cohn Livingston. From *Somebody Turned on a Tap in These Kids*, ed. by Nancy Larrick. Delacorte, 1971, p. 11.
[53]"Whispers" from *Whispers and Other Poems*. Copyright © 1958 by Myra Cohn Livingston. Reprinted by permission of McIntosh and Otis, Inc.
[54]"Wide Awake" from *Wide Awake and Other Poems*, © 1959 by Myra Cohn Livingston. Reprinted by permission of Harcourt Brace Jovanovich, Inc.
[55]"The Sun Is Stuck" from *A Crazy Flight and Other Poems* by Myra Cohn Livingston. Copyright © 1969 by Myra Cohn Livingston. Reprinted by permission of McIntosh and Otis, Inc.

that speaks to the problems and issues of today.

The poetry in Randall Jarrell's fantasy *The Bat-Poet* is graceful and perceptive, but no more so than the creative musing of the little brown bat who, disappointed at the criticism of his poetry, says, "The trouble isn't making poems, the trouble's finding somebody that will listen to them."[56] Children are listening. They are listening to older poets and younger ones, to poetry of all peoples the world over, to poems that make them laugh and cry and question and see or feel things they have never seen or felt before.

Adult References[57]

ARNSTEIN, FLORA. *Children Write Poetry: A Creative Approach.*

AUSLANDER, JOSEPH, and FRANK ERNEST HILL. *The Winged Horse; The Story of Poets and Their Poetry.*

BEHN, HARRY. *Chrysalis; Concerning Children and Poetry.*

BREWTON, JOHN E. and SARA W., comps. *Index to Children's Poetry.*

CIARDI, JOHN, and MILLER WILLIAMS. *How Does a Poem Mean?*

DEUTSCH, BABETTE. *Poetry in Our Time.*

DREW, ELIZABETH, and GEORGE CONNOR. *Discovering Modern Poetry.*

DUNNING, STEPHEN. *Teaching Literature to Adolescents: Poetry.*

EASTMAN, MAX. *The Enjoyment of Poetry.*

ESBENSEN, BARBARA JUSTER. *A Celebration of Bees; Helping Children Write Poetry.*

FRANKENBERG, LLOYD. *Pleasure Dome: On Reading Modern Poetry.*

HAVILAND, VIRGINIA, and WILLIAM JAY SMITH, comps. *Children and Poetry; A Selective Annotated Bibliography.*

HILLYER, ROBERT. *In Pursuit of Poetry.*

HOPKINS, LEE BENNETT. *Let Them Be Themselves.*

HUBER, MIRIAM BLANTON. *Story and Verse for Children.*

HUGHES, TED. *Poetry Is.*

ISAACS, J. *The Background of Modern Poetry.*

KOCH, KENNETH. *Rose, Where Did You Get That Red?*

———. *Wishes, Lies, and Dreams; Teaching Children to Write Poetry.*

LARRICK, NANCY, ed. *Somebody Turned on a Tap in These Kids.*

LIVINGSTON, MYRA COHN. *When You Are Alone/It Keeps You Capone; An Approach to Creative Writing with Children.*

RIBNER, IRVING, and HARRY MORRIS. *Poetry: A Critical and Historical Introduction.*

SANDBURG, CARL, ed. *The American Songbag.*

SANDERS, THOMAS E. *The Discovery of Poetry.*

SHAW, JOHN MACKAY. *Childhood in Poetry: A Catalogue.*

TERRY, ANN. *Children's Poetry Preferences: A National Survey of Upper Elementary Grades.*

WITUCKE, VIRGINIA. *Poetry in the Elementary School.*

[56]Randall Jarrell, *The Bat-Poet*, Macmillan, 1967, p. 15.

[57]Complete bibliographic data are provided in the combined Adult References in the Appendixes.

In the following bibliography these symbols have been used to identify books about a religious or a particular ethnic group:

§ Black
★ Chicano or Puerto Rican
☆ Native American
● Religious minority

Children's Books: Anthologies

There are so many good anthologies of poetry for children that it is not possible to list them all here. The following are especially useful for reasons the text or the notes make clear.

§ ABDUL, RAOUL, ed. *The Magic of Black Poetry,* ill. by Dane Burr. Dodd, 1972. Includes poems from many countries. 11 up

ADAMS, ADRIENNE, comp. *Poetry of Earth,* ill. by author. Scribner's, 1972. Discriminating, and good for reading aloud to younger children. 8-10

§ ADOFF, ARNOLD, ed. *Black Out Loud,* ill. by Alvin Hollingsworth. Macmillan, 1970. 11-14

———. *City in All Directions,* ill. by Donald Carrick. Macmillan, 1969. 12 up

§ ———. *I Am the Darker Brother,* ill. by Benny Andrews. Macmillan, 1968. 11 up

———. *it is the poem singing into your eyes; anthology of new young poets.* Harper, 1971. 10 up

§ ———, ed. *My Black Me; A Beginning Book on Black Poetry.* Dutton, 1974. 8-11

§ ———, ed. *The Poetry of Black America; An Anthology of the 20th Century.* Harper, 1973. 12 up

ADSHEAD, GLADYS L., and ANNIS DUFF, eds. *An Inheritance of Poetry,* ill. by Nora S. Unwin. Houghton, 1948. A large collection of unusual poems, chiefly for adolescents, but with some exquisite bits for children. 10-16

ALDAN, DAISY, comp. *Poems from India,* ill. by Joseph Low. T. Crowell, 1969. A collection of poems ranging from ancient times to the present, conservative and idealistic, on the whole. 14 up

§ ALLEN, SAMUEL, ed. *Poems from Africa,* ill. by Romare Bearden. T. Crowell, 1973. Broad in geographical and chronological scope. 12 up

ARBUTHNOT, MAY HILL, and SHELTON L. ROOT, JR., eds. *Time for Poetry,* 3rd gen. ed., ill. by Arthur Paul. Scott, Foresman, 1968. There are more than seven hundred poems in this newest edition of a favorite collection, ranging from *Mother Goose* to T. S. Eliot. The discussion of reading poetry to children and using poetry in verse choirs and the notes throughout the text are invaluable for adults. 4-14

Association for Childhood Education, Literature Committee. *Sung Under the Silver Umbrella,* ill. by Dorothy Lathrop. Macmillan, 1935, 1962. A small collection of choice poetry, including selections from the Bible, modern poems, nonsense verse, and Japanese haiku. 4-9

★●§ BARON, VIRGINIA, ed. *Here I Am! An Anthology of Poems Written by Young People in Some of America's Minority Groups,* ill. by Emily Arnold McCully. Dutton, 1969. 8-11

———. ed. *The Seasons of Time; Tanka Poetry of An-*

cient Japan, ill. by Yasuhide Kobashi. Dial, 1968. Dial, 1968. 11 up

★●§ ______. *Here I Am! An Anthology of Poems Written by Young People in Some of America's Minority Groups,* ill. by Emily Arnold McCully. Dutton, 1969. 8-11

BEHN, HARRY, tr. *Cricket Songs; Japanese Haiku,* with pictures selected from Sesshu and other Japanese masters. Harcourt, 1964. 10 up

______, tr. *More Cricket Songs,* ill. with pictures by Japanese masters. Harcourt, 1971. 10 up

☆ BELTING, NATALIA MAREE, comp. *Our Fathers Had Powerful Songs,* ill. by Laszlo Kubinyi. Dutton, 1974. Nine poems from American and Canadian Indian tribes. 9-12

☆ ______, comp. *Whirlwind Is a Ghost Dancing,* ill. by Leo and Diane Dillon. Dutton, 1974. Chiefly poems of creation or natural phenomena from North American Indian tribes. 9 up

BENEDETTI, MARIO, ed. *Unstill Life,* tr. by Darwin Flakoll and Claribel Alegria, ill. by Antonio Frasconi. Harcourt, 1969. 11 up

☆ BIERHORST, JOHN, ed. *In the Trail of the Wind,* ill. Farrar, 1971. 12 up

BLISHEN, EDWARD, comp. *Oxford Book of Poetry for Children,* ill. by Brian Wildsmith. Watts, 1963. An excellent anthology covering a wide variety of subjects and styles with superb illustrations. 9-12

BOGAN, LOUISE, and WILLIAM JAY SMITH, eds. *The Golden Journey; Poems for Young People,* ill. by Fritz Kredel. Reilly, 1965. 10-14

☆ BRANDON, WILLIAM, ed. *The Magic World: American Indian Songs and Poems.* Morrow, 1971. 11 up

BREWTON, SARA and JOHN, comps. *Birthday Candles Burning Bright; A Treasury of Birthday Poetry,* ill. by Vera Bock. Macmillan, 1960. A delightful anthology of poems arranged by age groups, illustrating the general fun of birthdays and including a choice selection of Christmas poems. 5 up

______, comps. *Laughable Limericks,* ill. by Ingrid Fetz. T. Crowell, 1965. 9 up

______, comps. *Sing a Song of Seasons,* ill. by Vera Bock. Macmillan, 1955. Poems of school days and vacation time. 6-12

CANFIELD, KENNETH, ed. *Selections from French Poetry,* ill. by Tomi Ungerer. Harvey, 1965. 12 up

☆ CLYMER, THEODORE, ed. *Four Corners of the Sky; Poems, Chants, and Oratory,* ill. by Marc Brown. Little, 1975. Poems of Native American cultures. 10 up

COLE, WILLIAM, ed. *Beastly Boys and Ghastly Girls,* ill. by Tomi Ungerer. World, 1964. Varied and humorous. 10-12

______, ed. *The Birds and the Beasts Were There,* ill. by Helen Siegl. World, 1963. A choice and lovely collection of verses about animals, birds, and insects, both real and fantastic. 6 up

______, comp. *A Book of Animal Poems,* ill. by Robert Parker. Viking, 1973. 9 up

______, ed. *A Book of Nature Poems,* ill. by Robert Andrew Parker. Viking, 1969. 10-14

______, ed. *Humorous Poetry for Children,* ill. by Ervine Metzl. World, 1955. 8 up

______, ed. *Oh, How Silly!* ill. by Tomi Ungerer. Viking, 1970. 8-10

______, ed. *Oh, What Nonsense!* ill. by Tomi Ungerer. Viking, 1966. 9-11

______, comp. *Pick Me Up; A Book of Short Short Poems.* Macmillan, 1972. Two hundred brief poems. 9 up

______, ed. *Poems for Seasons and Celebrations,* ill. by Johannes Troyer. World, 1961. From the year's beginning to its end, poems follow the cycle of seasons and holidays in a refreshing collection of modern and traditional verses. 8-15

______, comp. *Poems from Ireland,* ill. by William Stobbs. T. Crowell, 1972. Old and new material. 12 up

______, comp. *Poems from Italy.* T. Crowell, 1972. A bilingual anthology. 12 up

______, ed. *Poems of Magic and Spells,* ill. by Peggy Bacon. World, 1960. Goblins and ghosts, witches and other magical creatures are highlighted in a novel and attractive anthology. 9-13

______, ed. *The Poet's Tales: A New Book of Story Poems,* ill. by Charles Keeping. World, 1971. From folk ballads to sophisticated modern poems. 10-14

COLUM, PADRAIC, ed. *Roofs of Gold; Poems to Read Aloud.* Macmillan, 1964. The editor's favorites from Shakespeare to Dylan Thomas. 11-15

DE FOREST, CHARLOTTE B., ad. *The Prancing Pony; Nursery Rhymes from Japan,* adapted into English verse for children, ill. by Keiko Hida. Walker, 1968. 3-7

DE LA MARE, WALTER, ed. *Come Hither,* 3rd ed., ill. by Warren Chappell. Knopf, 1957. 12 up

______, ed. *Tom Tiddler's Ground,* ill. by Margery Gill. Knopf, 1962. First American edition of a choice compilation of verses for younger children. As in *Come Hither,* De la Mare's perceptive notes distinguish his anthologies. 9 up

DE LUCA, MICHAEL, and WILLIAM GIULIANOS, eds. *Selections from Italian Poetry.* Harvey, 1966. 13 up

§ DOOB, LEONARD, ed. *A Crocodile Has Me by the Leg; African Poems,* ill. by Solomon Irein Wangboje. Walker, 1967. 9-14

DOWNIE, MARY, and BARBARA ROBERTSON, comps. *The Wind Has Wings; Poems from Canada,* ill. by Elizabeth Cleaver. Walck, 1968. 9-12

DUNNING, STEPHEN, EDWARD LUEDERS, and HUGH SMITH, comps. *Reflections on a Gift of Watermelon Pickle.* Scott, Foresman, 1967. 11 up

______, comps. *Some Haystacks Don't Even Have Any Needle,* ill. Scott, Foresman, 1969. A splendid collection of poems complemented by reproductions of modern art in full color. 11 up

EATON, ANNE THAXTER, comp. *Welcome Christmas!* ill. by Valenti Angelo. Viking, 1955. A garland of some fifty Christmas poems, chosen with exquisite taste and given decorations of fitting beauty. all ages

FERRIS, HELEN, comp. *Favorite Poems Old and New,* ill. by Leonard Weisgard. Doubleday, 1957. A splendidly varied collection of over 700 poems. 5 up

FLEMING, ALICE, comp. *Hosannah the Home Run! Poems About Sports.* Little, 1972. 10 up

FUJIKAWA, GUY, comp. *A Child's Book of Poems,* ill. by comp. Grosset, 1969. A profusely and attractively illustrated collection of poems, standard fare. Selections are not grouped or arranged. 3-7

FYLEMAN, ROSE, ed. *Picture Rhymes from Foreign Lands.* Lippincott, 1935. 5-8

GREGORY, HORACE, and MARYA ZATURENSKA, eds. *The Crystal Cabinet,* ill. by Diana Bloomfield. Holt, 1962. A refreshingly original anthology of lyric poetry, wide in range, from Chinese translations to poems by Edith Sitwell. 12 up

HANNUM, SARA, and JOHN TERRY CHASE, comps. *The Wind Is Round,* ill. by Ron Bowen. Atheneum, 1970. 10 up

HANNUM, SARA, and GWENDOLYN REED, comps. *Lean Out of the Window; An Anthology of Modern*

Poetry, ill. by Ragna Tischler. Atheneum, 1965. 10-14

§ HAYDEN, ROBERT, ed. *Kaleidoscope; Poems by American Negro Poets.* Harcourt, 1967. 13 up

HILL, HELEN, and AGNES PERKINS, comps. *New Coasts and Strange Harbors; Discovering Poems,* ill. by Clare Romano and John Ross. T. Crowell, 1974. Chiefly mid-twentieth-century poets. 12 up

HOPKINS, LEE BENNETT, comp. *City Talk,* ill. with photos by Roy Aranella. Knopf, 1970. 7-9

______, comp. *Good Morning to You, Valentine,* ill. by Tomie de Paola. Harcourt, 1976. A useful collection of lighthearted poems. 7-10

______, comp. *I Think I Saw a Snail; Young Poems for City Seasons,* ill. by Harold James. Crown, 1969. A selection of poems (four or five for each season) by accepted authors. A few are not particularly city poems. 5-8

☆ HOUSTON, JAMES, ed. *Songs of the Dream People,* ill. by author. Atheneum, 1972. Chants and poems from North American Eskimo and Indian songs. 9 up

HOWARD, CORALIE, comp. *Lyric Poems,* ill. by Mel Fowler. Watts, 1968. 11-14

● *I Never Saw Another Butterfly.* McGraw, 1964. 7-12

☆ JONES, HETTIE, ed. *The Trees Stand Shining; Poetry of the North American Indians,* ill. by Robert Andrew Parker. Dial, 1971. 8-11

★§ JORDAN, JUNE, and TERRI BUSH, comps. *The Voice of the Children.* Holt, 1970. 10 up

LARRICK, NANCY, ed. *Green Is Like a Meadow of Grass,* ill. by Kelly Oechsli. Garrard, 1968. 5-9

§ ______, ed. *I Heard a Scream in the Streets; Poems by Young People in the City,* ill. with photos by students. Evans, 1970. 10 up

§ ______, ed. *On City Streets,* ill. with photos by David Sagarin. Evans, 1968. 10-14

______, comp. *Room for Me and a Mountain Lion; Poetry of Open Space.* Evans, 1974. 10 up

LEWIS, RICHARD, ed. *I Breathe a New Song: Poems of the Eskimo,* ill. by Oonark. Simon, 1971. Poems that reflect the Eskimo's life and closeness to nature. 9 up

______, ed. *In a Spring Garden,* ill. by Ezra Jack Keats. Dial, 1965. 5-9

______, ed. *Miracles.* Simon, 1966. all ages

______, ed. *The Moment of Wonder; A Collection of Chinese and Japanese Poetry,* ill. with paintings by Chinese and Japanese masters. Dial, 1964. all ages

______, ed. *Muse of the Round Sky; Lyric Poetry of Ancient Greece,* tr. by Willis Barnstone and others. Simon, 1969. 8 up

☆ ______, ed. *Out of the Earth I Sing; Poetry and Songs of Primitive Peoples of the World.* Norton, 1968. 8 up

______, ed. *Still Waters of the Air; Poems by Three Modern Spanish Poets,* ill. by Arvis Stewart. Dial, 1970. 11 up

______, ed. *There Are Two Lives; Poems by Children of Japan,* tr. by Haruna Kimura. Simon, 1970. 8-10

______, ed. *The Wind and the Rain,* ill. with photos by Helen Buttfield. Simon, 1968. 8-10

LIVINGSTON, MYRA COHN, ed. *Listen, Children, Listen,* ill. by Trina Schart Hyman. Atheneum, 1972. 5-8

______, ed. *One Little Room, an Everywhere,* ill. by Antonio Frasconi. Atheneum, 1975. Love poems from a dozen countries, from Biblical times to today. 11 up

______, ed. *Speak Roughly to Your Little Boy; A Collection of Parodies and Burlesques, Together with the Original Poems, Chosen and Annotated for Young People,* ill. by Joseph Low. Harcourt, 1971. 11 up

______, ed. *A Tune Beyond Us,* ill. by James J. Spanfeller. Harcourt, 1968. 12 up

______. *What a Wonderful Bird the Frog Are; An Assortment of Humorous Poetry and Verse.* Harcourt, 1973. 9 up

LONGLAND, JEAN, ed. *Selections from Contemporary Portuguese Poetry.* Harvey, 1966. 11 up

LOWER, THELMA, and FREDERICK COGSWELL, comps. *The Enchanted Land; Canadian Poetry for Young Readers.* Gage, 1967. A well-rounded selection. 9-12

McDONALD, GERALD D., comp. *A Way of Knowing; A Collection of Poems for Boys,* ill. by Clare and John Ross. T. Crowell, 1959. A varied and popular collection, representative of modern and traditional poets. Appeals to girls as well as to boys. 10 up

MacKAY, DAVID, comp. *A Flock of Words,* ill. by Margery Gill. Harcourt, 1970. 11 up

METCALF, JOHN, comp. *The Speaking Earth; Canadian Poetry.* Van Nostrand, 1973. 10 up

MOORE, LILIAN, and JUDITH THURMAN, comps. *To See the World Afresh.* Atheneum, 1974. An outstanding anthology. 10 up

MORRISON, LILLIAN, comp. *Best Wishes, Amen; A New Collection of Autograph Verses,* ill. by Loretta Lustig. T. Crowell, 1974. 9-13

______, comp. *Touch Blue; Signs and Spells, Love Charms and Chants, Auguries and Old Beliefs, in Rhyme,* ill. by Doris Lee. T. Crowell, 1958. 6-13

______, comp. *Yours till Niagara Falls,* ill. by Marjorie Bauernschmidt. T. Crowell, 1950. 9-13

MORSE, DAVID, ed. *Grandfather Rock.* Delacorte, 1972. 11 up

MORTON, MIRIAM, ed. *A Harvest of Russian Children's Literature.* Univ. of Calif. Pr., 1967. all ages

______, comp. *The Moon Is Like a Silver Sickle; A Celebration of Poetry by Russian Children,* ill. by Eros Keith. Simon, 1972. 9-13

NASH, OGDEN, comp. *I Couldn't Help Laughing.* Lippincott, 1957. 12-14

______, comp. *The Moon Is Shining Bright as Day,* ill. by Rose Shirvanian. Lippincott, 1953. 12-14

NESS, EVALINE, comp. *Amelia Mixed the Mustard and Other Poems,* ill. by comp. Scribner's, 1975. Twenty poems about girls. 8-10

OPIE, IONA and PETER, eds. *The Oxford Book of Children's Verse.* Oxford, 1973. A broad selection, chronologically arranged, also has adult reference use because of the Opies' notes. 5-13

Pandora's Box. Canadian Council of Teachers of English, 1973. Poems written by children for a poetry contest. 8-12

PARKER, ELINOR, comp. *The Singing and the Gold,* ill. by Clare Leighton. T. Crowell, 1962. 12 up

PECK, RICHARD, ed. *Sounds and Silences: Poetry for Now.* Delacorte, 1970. 12 up

PLOTZ, HELEN, comp. *The Earth Is the Lord's; Poems of the Spirit.* T. Crowell, 1965. Emphasizes work of contemporary poets. 11 up

______, comp. *Imagination's Other Place; Poems of Science and Mathematics,* ill. by Clare Leighton. T. Crowell, 1955. 12 up

______, comp. *The Marvelous Light; Poets and Poetry.* T. Crowell, 1970. The poets and their work reflect a variety in style and mood. 11 up

______, comp. *Poems from the German,* ill. by Ismar David. T. Crowell, 1967. 11 up

______, comp. *Untune the Sky: Poems of Music and the Dance.* T. Crowell, 1957. Ranges from reverence to gaiety. 10 up

READ, HERBERT. *This Way, Delight,* ill. by Juliet Kepes.

Pantheon, 1956. Includes an excellent essay, "What Is Poetry?" 8-12

REED, GWENDOLYN, comp. *Out of the Ark; An Anthology of Animal Verse,* ill. by Gabriele Margules. Atheneum, 1968. Old favorites and some lesser-known poems representing many centuries. Useful for independent reading or for reading aloud. 10-14

______, comp. *The Talkative Beasts: Myths, Fables and Poems of India,* ill. by Stella Snead. Lothrop, 1969. 8-12

RESNICK, SEYMOUR, ed. *Selections from Spanish Poetry,* ill. by Anne Marie Jauss. Harvey, 1962. 11 up

______, ed. *Spanish-American Poetry; A Bilingual Selection,* ill. by Anne Marie Jauss. Harvey, 1964. 11 up

RUS, VLADIMIR, ed. *Selections from German Poetry,* ill. by Elizabeth Korolkoff. Harvey, 1966. 13 up

SCHAEFER, CHARLES, and KATHLEEN MELLOR, comps. *Young Voices; The Poems of Children.* Bruce, 1971. 9-11

SECHRIST, ELIZABETH, comp. *One Thousand Poems for Children,* based on the selections of Roger Ingpen, ill. by Henry C. Pitz. Macrae, 1946. A tremendous collection, excellent for a reference source in school or home. all ages

SEEGER, RUTH CRAWFORD, ed. *Let's Build a Railroad,* ill. by Tom Funk. Dutton, 1954. 4-9

SMITH, WILLIAM JAY, ed. *Poems from France,* ill. by Roger Duvoisin. T. Crowell, 1967. 9 up

SULLY, FRANÇOIS, ed. *We, the Vietnamese: Voices from Vietnam.* Praeger, 1971. Includes poetry. 13 up

SUMMERFIELD, GEOFFREY, ed. *First Voices; The Fourth Book.* Knopf, 1973. In unfortunately small print, this and the three preceding volumes in the series offer a broad range of poems. 10-13

TOWNSEND, JOHN ROWE, comp. *Modern Poetry,* ill. with photos by Barbara Pfeffer. Lippincott, 1974. Poems that reflect the concerns of three decades, 1940s–1960s. 11 up

TRIPP, WALLACE, comp. *A Great Big Ugly Man Came Up and Tied His Horse to Me; A Book of Nonsense Verse,* ill. by comp. Little, 1973. 7-9

UNTERMEYER, LOUIS, ed. *Rainbow in the Sky,* ill. by Reginald Birch. Harcourt, 1935. Untermeyer was one of the first and most indefatigable anthologists for children. This is only one of his many books. They lean heavily on old and familiar poems. 7-12

☆ WOOD, NANCY, comp. *Prose and Poetry of the Pueblos,* ill. by Frank Howell, Doubleday, 1974. Thoughts of older members of the Taos. 10 up

Children's Books: By Individual Poets

AIKEN, CONRAD. *Cats and Bats and Things with Wings,* ill. by Milton Glaser. Atheneum, 1965. 5-8

ALDIS, DOROTHY. *All Together; A Child's Treasury of Verse,* ill. by Helen D. Jameson. Putnam, 1952. Poems about everyday happenings. 5-9

______. *Quick as a Wink,* ill. by Peggy Westphal. Putnam, 1960. Insect poems. 4-7

ALLINGHAM, WILLIAM. *The Fairy Shoemaker and Other Fairy Poems,* ill. by Boris Artzybasheff. Macmillan, 1928. Poems by Allingham, Walter de la Mare, and Matthew Arnold. 9-12

______. *Robin Redbreast and Other Verses,* ill. by Kate Greenaway, Helen Allingham, Caroline Paterson, and Harry Furness. Macmillan, Little Library, 1930. Contains his best-known poem, "The Fairies." 7-12

ARMOUR, RICHARD. *All Sizes and Shapes of Monkeys and Apes,* ill. by Paul Galdone. McGraw, 1970. 5-8

______. *A Dozen Dinosaurs,* ill. by Paul Galdone. McGraw, 1967. 6-9

______. *Odd Old Mammals; Animals After the Dinosaurs,* ill. by Paul Galdone. McGraw, 1968. 9-11
In all his books, Armour's blithe verses give accurate information about animals.

AUSTIN, MARY. *The Children Sing in the Far West,* ill. by Gerald Cassidy. Houghton, 1928. 8-12

BABBITT, NATALIE. *Dick Foote and the Shark,* ill. by author. Farrar, 1967. 9-11

______. *Phoebe's Revolt,* ill. by author. Farrar, 1968. 8-9

BARNSTONE, WILLIS. *A Day in the Country,* ill. by Howard Knotts. Harper, 1971. 5-8

BEHN, HARRY. *The Golden Hive,* ill. by author. Harcourt, 1966. 9-12

______. *The Little Hill,* ill. by author. Harcourt, 1949.

______. *Windy Morning,* ill. by author. Harcourt, 1953.

______. *The Wizard in the Well,* ill. by author. Harcourt, 1956. 5-9

BELLOC, HILAIRE. *The Bad Child's Book of Beasts,* ill. by B. T. B. Knopf, 1965. Horrendous nonsense. 6-9

______ *Cautionary Verses,* ill. by B. T. B. and Nicolas Bentley. Knopf, 1959. 9-12

______. *Matilda, Who Told Lies and Was Burned to Death,* ill. by Steven Kellogg. Dial, 1970. A spoof of a Victorian morality tale. 9-12

BENÉT, ROSEMARY, and STEPHEN VINCENT. *A Book of Americans,* rev. ed., ill. by Charles Child. Holt, 1952. 8-14

BLAKE, WILLIAM. *Songs of Innocence,* ill. by Harold Jones. Barnes, 1961. A welcome edition which contains nineteen of Blake's more childlike poems. 6 up

BODECKER, N. M. *Let's Marry Said the Cherry and Other Nonsense Poems,* ill. by author. Atheneum, 1974. Deft, amusing verses. 9-11

BROOKE, L. LESLIE. *Johnny Crow's Garden.* Warne, 1903.

______. *Johnny Crow's New Garden.* Warne, 1935.

______ *Johnny Crow's Party.* Warne, 1907. 3-7

______ *Leslie Brooke's Children's Books,* 4 vols. Warne, n.d. 5-12

______. *Ring o' Roses* (see Bibliography, Chapter 4).

§ BROOKS, GWENDOLYN. *Bronzeville Boys and Girls,* ill. by Ronni Solbert. Harper, 1956. 7-11

BROWNJOHN, ALAN. *Brownjohn's Beasts,* ill. by Carol Lawson. Scribner's, 1970. 9-11

CARMER, CARL. *The Boy Drummer of Vincennes,* ill. by Seymour Fleishman. Harvey, 1972. A narrative poem about the Illinois frontier in 1779. 8-10

CARROLL, LEWIS. *Alice's Adventures in Wonderland* (see Bibliography, Chapter 8).

______. *The Annotated Snark,* with an introduction and notes by Martin Gardner. Simon, 1962. The full text of Lewis Carroll's great nonsense epic *The Hunting of the Snark* and the original illustrations by Henry Holiday.

______. *Poems of Lewis Carroll,* comp. by Myra Cohn Livingston, ill. by John Tenniel and others. T. Crowell, 1973. 5 up

CAUDILL, REBECCA. *Come Along!* ill. by Ellen Raskin. Holt, 1969. Haiku poems about the year's cycle. 7-9

CAUSLEY, CHARLES. *Figgie Hobbin,* ill. by Trina Schart Hyman. Walker, 1974. Ranges from nonsense verse to poignant or narrative poems. 8-10

CHAUCER, GEOFFREY. *A Taste of Chaucer,* selections from *The Canterbury Tales,* chosen and ed. by Anne

Malcolmson, ill. by Enrico Arno. Harcourt, 1964. A careful and discriminating adaptation of—and introduction to—Chaucer for young people. The introduction describes Chaucer and the period in which he lived. 12 up

CIARDI, JOHN. *Fast and Slow,* ill. by Becky Gaver. Houghton, 1974. A selection of light, humorous poems, with much word-play. 9-11

———. *The Reason for the Pelican,* ill. by Madeleine Gekiere. Lippincott, 1959. 5-9
Nonsense verses and imaginative poems in this collection launched John Ciardi's books for children. Others are:

———. *I Met a Man,* ill. by Robert Osborn. Houghton, 1961. 4-8

———. *The King Who Saved Himself from Being Saved,* ill. by Edward Gorey. Lippincott, 1965. 9-11

———. *The Man Who Sang the Sillies,* ill. by Edward Gorey. Lippincott, 1961. 4-8

———. *Scrappy the Pup,* ill. by Jane Miller. Lippincott, 1960. 4-8

———. *Someone Could Win a Polar Bear,* ill. by Edward Gorey. Lippincott, 1970. 5-8

———. *You Read to Me, I'll Read to You,* ill. by Edward Gorey. Lippincott, 1962. 5-8

§ CLIFTON, LUCILLE. *Some of the Days of Everett Anderson,* ill. by Evaline Ness. Holt, 1970. 5-7

COATSWORTH, ELIZABETH. *Away Goes Sally* (see Bibliography, Chapter 11).

———. *Down Half the World,* ill. by Zena Bernstein. Macmillan, 1968. 12 up

———. *The Fair American* (see Bibliography, Chapter 11).

———. *Five Bushel Farm* (see Bibliography, Chapter 11).

———. *The Sparrow Bush,* ill. by Stefan Martin. Norton, 1966. 9-12

———. *Summer Green,* ill. by Nora S. Unwin. Macmillan, 1948. 7 up

———. *Under the Green Willow,* ill. by Janina Domanska. Macmillan, 1971. 5-7

COLE, WILLIAM. *What's Good for a Four-Year-Old?* ill. by Tomi Ungerer. Holt, 1967. One of a series. 3-4

CONKLING, HILDA. *Poems by a Little Girl.* Lippincott, 1920. 6-10

———. *Shoes of the Wind.* Lippincott, 1922. 6-10

———. *Silverhorn; The Hilda Conkling Book for Other Children,* ill. by Dorothy P. Lathrop. Stokes, 1924.

CULLEN, COUNTEE. *The Lost Zoo,* ill. by Joseph Low. Follett, 1969. 10 up

DE GASZTOLD, CARMEN BERNOS. *The Creatures' Choir,* tr. by Rumer Godden, ill. by Jean Primrose. Viking, 1965. 11 up

———. *Prayers from the Ark,* tr. by Rumer Godden. Viking, 1962. 12 up

DE LA MARE, WALTER. *Peacock Pie,* ill. by Barbara Cooney. Knopf, 1961. 6 up

———. *Rhymes and Verses: Collected Poems for Children,* ill. by Elinore Blaisdell. Holt, 1947. 5 up

DE REGNIERS, BEATRICE SCHENK. *May I Bring a Friend?* ill. by Beni Montresor. Atheneum, 1964. A young child brings his (animal) friends with him when invited to visit the king and queen. Caldecott Medal. 5-7

———. *Something Special,* ill. by Irene Haas. Harcourt, 1958. 3-6

DICKINSON, EMILY. *Letter to the World,* ed. by Rumer Godden, ill. by Prudence Seward. Macmillan, 1969.

———. *Poems,* ed. by Helen Plotz, ill. by Robert Kipness. T. Crowell, 1964.

———. *Poems for Youth,* ed. by Alfred Hampson. Little, 1934. 11 up

FARJEON, ELEANOR. *The Children's Bells,* ill. by Peggy Fortnum. Walck, 1960.

———. *Eleanor Farjeon's Poems for Children.* Lippincott, 1951. 5-12

———. *Then There Were Three,* ill. by Isobel and John Morton-Sale. Lippincott, 1965. 4-7

FIELD, EUGENE. *Poems of Childhood,* ill. by Maxfield Parrish. Scribner's, 1904. First published in 1896. 8-12

FIELD, RACHEL. *Poems,* ill. by author. Macmillan, 1957. Favorite selections from this versatile author's earlier books with a few new poems. 6-12

———. *Taxis and Toadstools,* ill. by author. Doubleday, 1926. 7-12

FINLAY, IAN HAMILTON. *Poems to Hear and See.* Macmillan, 1971. 8-10

FISHER, AILEEN. *But Ostriches . . . ,* ill. by Peter Parnall. T. Crowell, 1970. 8-10

———. *Feathered Ones and Furry,* ill. by Eric Carle. T. Crowell, 1971. 5-8

———. *Going Barefoot,* ill. by Adrienne Adams. T. Crowell, 1960. 4-8

———. *In the Middle of the Night,* ill. by Adrienne Adams. T. Crowell, 1965. 5-7

———. *Listen, Rabbit,* ill. by Symeon Shimin. T. Crowell, 1964.

———. *Once We Went on a Picnic,* ill. by Tony Chen. T. Crowell, 1975. 4-7

———. *Runny Days, Sunny Days; Merry Verses,* ill. by author. Abelard, 1958. 6-8

———. *Up, Up the Mountain,* ill. by Gilbert Riswold. T. Crowell, 1968. 8-10

———. *Where Does Everyone Go?* ill. by Adrienne Adams. T. Crowell, 1961. 4-8

FROMAN, ROBERT. *Street Poems.* McCall, 1971. 8-10

FROST, FRANCES. *The Little Naturalist,* ill. by Kurt Werth. Whittlesey, 1959. Poems of nature. 8-12

———. *The Little Whistler,* ill. by Roger Duvoisin. Whittlesey, 1949. Poems of the seasons. 8-12

FROST, ROBERT. *Complete Poems of Robert Frost.* Holt, 1949.

———. *In the Clearing.* Holt, 1962.

———. *You Come Too,* ill. by Thomas W. Nason. Holt, 1959. 11 up

FYLEMAN, ROSE. *Fairies and Chimneys.* Doubleday, 1944. Deftly combines fantasy and reality. 8-10

§ GIOVANNI, NIKKI. *Ego-Tripping and Other Poems for Young People,* ill. by George Ford. Lawrence Hill, 1974. Poems selected by the poet from her published works. 11 up

GREENAWAY, KATE. *Marigold Garden,* ill. by author. Warne, 1910.

———. *Under the Window,* ill. by author. Warne, 1910. 4-7

HOBERMAN, MARY ANN. *Hello and Good-By,* ill. by Norman Hoberman. Little, 1959. 4-9

HOFFMANN, HEINRICH. *Slovenly Peter, or Pretty Stories and Funny Pictures for Little Children.* Tuttle, 1969. 5-8

HOLMAN, FELICE. *At the Top of My Voice; and Other Poems,* ill. by Edward Gorey. Norton, 1970. Wry, humorous poems. 8-10

———. *I Hear You Smiling and Other Poems,* ill. by Laszlo Kubinyi. Scribner's, 1973. Free and metric verse; thoughtful and ebullient poems. 8-10

§ HOWARD, VANESSA. *A Screaming Whisper,* photos by

J. Pinderhughes. Holt, 1972. One of the most promising young poets writes with depth and insight. 11 up

§ HUGHES, LANGSTON. *Black Misery,* ill. by Arouni. Eriksson, 1969. 10-14

§ ______. *Don't You Turn Back,* selected by Lee Bennett Hopkins, ill. by Ann Grifalconi. Knopf, 1969. 10 up

§ ______. *Fields of Wonder.* Knopf, 1947. 11 up

§ ______. *Selected Poems of Langston Hughes.* Knopf, 1959. 11 up

HUGHES, TED. *Season Songs,* ill. by Leonard Baskin. Viking, 1975. Poems and pictures about the seasons are equally beautiful. A stunning book. 11 up

ISSA. *A Few Flies and I; Haiku by Issa,* ed. by Jean Merrill and Ronni Solbert, from tr. by R. H. Blyth and Nobuyaki Yuasa, ill. by Ronni Solbert. Pantheon, 1969. 8-11

JARRELL, RANDALL. *The Bat-Poet.* Macmillan, 1967. 9-11

§ JOHNSON, JAMES WELDON. *God's Trombones,* ill. by Aaron Douglas. Viking, 1927. Seven verse sermons. Introduction discusses dialect and vernacular. 11 up

§ JORDAN, JUNE. *Who Look at Me.* T. Crowell, 1969. 10 up

KRYLOV, IVAN. *The Fifteen Fables of Krylov,* tr. by Guy Daniels, ill. by David Pascal. Macmillan, 1965. 10-12

KUMIN, MAXINE. *No One Writes a Letter to the Snail,* ill. by Bean Allen. Putnam, 1962. Fresh, bouncy verses. 8-10

KUSKIN, KARLA. *The Bear Who Saw the Spring,* ill. by author. Harper, 1961. A most amiable bear inducts a small dog into the beauties of each of the four seasons. Rhyming text makes this a delightful read-aloud picture book. 5-6

______. *Near the Window Tree,* ill. by author. Harper, 1975. Each poem has a prefatory note, explaining how it came to be written. 7-9

LEAR, EDWARD. *The Complete Nonsense Book,* ed. by Lady Strachey. Dodd, 1942. This volume includes both books referred to in the text: *The Book of Nonsense* and *Nonsense Songs and Stories.* These are available in the original attractive separate volumes from Warne. 8-14

______. *Le Hibou et la Poussiquette,* tr. by Francis Steegmuller, ill. by Barbara Cooney. Little, 1961.

______. *Incidents in the Life of My Uncle Arly,* ill. by Dale Maxey. Follett, 1969.

______. *The Jumblies,* ill. by Edward Gorey. W. R. Scott, 1968.

______. *The Owl and the Pussy Cat,* ill. by William Pène du Bois. Doubleday, 1962.

______. *The Owl and the Pussy-Cat,* ill. by Dale Maxey. Follett, 1970. 5-8

______. *The Quangle-Wangle's Hat,* ill. by Helen Oxenbury. Watts, 1969. 4-8

______. *The Scroobious Pip,* completed by Ogden Nash, ill. by Nancy Ekholm Burkert. Harper, 1968. Stunning, imaginative pictures. 9 up

______. *Whizz!* ill. by Janina Domanska. Macmillan, 1973. 4-6

LEE, DENNIS. *Alligator Pie,* ill. by Frank Newfeld. Houghton, 1975. Bouncy, sunny verse by an eminent Canadian poet. 5-8

LENSKI, LOIS. *City Poems,* ill. by author. Walck, 1971. Most of the poems are new and their chief attraction is, for the urban child, the familiarity of the sights and activities they describe. 5-7

LEWIS, RICHARD, comp. *Of This World; A Poet's Life in Poetry,* ill. with photos by Helen Buttfield. Dial, 1968. 10 up

______. *The Way of Silence; The Prose and Poetry of Basho.* Dial, 1970. 10 up

LINDSAY, VACHEL. *Johnny Appleseed, and Other Poems,* ill. by George Richards. Macmillan, 1928. 10 up

______. *Springfield Town Is Butterfly Town,* ed. by Pierre Dussert, ill. by Vachel Lindsay. Kent State Univ. Pr., 1969. 7-11

LIVINGSTON, MYRA COHN. *A Crazy Flight; And Other Poems,* ill. by James Spanfeller. Harcourt, 1969. 8-11

______. *Happy Birthday!* ill. by Erik Blegvad. Harcourt, 1964. 5-7

______. *The Malibu and Other Poems,* ill. by James Spanfeller. Atheneum, 1972. Varied, spontaneous writing. 10-12

______. *The Moon and a Star and Other Poems,* ill. by Judith Shahn. Harcourt, 1965. Poems about familiar phenomena or activities. 5-8

______. *The Way Things Are and Other Poems,* ill. by Jenni Oliver. Atheneum, 1974. Brief poems written from the child's viewpoint. 9-11

______. *Whispers and Other Poems,* ill. by Jacqueline Chwast. Harcourt, 1958. 5-8

______. *Wide Awake and Other Poems,* ill. by Jacqueline Chwast, Harcourt, 1959. 5-8

LOBEL, ARNOLD. *On the Day Peter Stuyvesant Sailed into Town,* ill. by author. Harper, 1971. 5-8

McCORD, DAVID. *All Day Long; Fifty Rhymes of the Never Was and Always Is,* ill. by Henry B. Kane. Little, 1966. 9-11

______. *Away and Ago,* ill. by Leslie Morrill. Little, 1975. Clever word-play and a sense of fun prevail. 8-11

______. *Every Time I Climb a Tree,* ill. by Marc Simont. Little, 1967. 7-9

______. *Far and Few: Rhymes of the Never Was and Always Is,* ill. by Henry B. Kane. Little, 1952. 5-10

______. *For Me to Say: Rhymes of the Never Was and Always Is,* ill. by Henry B. Kane. Little, 1970. 9-11

______. *Take Sky: More Rhymes of the Never Was and Always Is,* ill. by Henry B. Kane. Little, 1962. 8 up

McGINLEY, PHYLLIS. *All Around the Town* (see Bibliography, Chapter 4).

______. *Mince Pie and Mistletoe,* ill. by Harold Berson. Lippincott, 1961. 6-12

______. *A Wreath of Christmas Legends,* ill. by Leonard Weisgard. Macmillan, 1967. 10-13

MERRIAM, EVE. *Catch a Little Rhyme,* ill. by Imero Gobbato. Atheneum, 1966. 5-9

______. *Finding a Poem,* ill. by Seymour Chwast. Atheneum, 1970. 11 up

______. *Independent Voices,* ill. by Arvis Stewart. Atheneum, 1968. 10-12

______. *It Doesn't Always Have to Rhyme,* ill. by Malcolm Spooner. Atheneum, 1964. 10-14

______. *Out Loud.* Atheneum, 1973. Fresh, perceptive, vivid writing. 10-13

______. *There Is No Rhyme for Silver,* ill. by Joseph Schindelman. Atheneum, 1962. Jaunty little verses full of rhythm, nonsense, and child appeal, for the youngest. 5-7

MILNE, A. A. *Now We Are Six,* ill. by Ernest Shepard. Dutton, 1927.

______. *When We Were Very Young,* ill. by Ernest Shepard. Dutton, 1924. These verses were reprinted in 1961, in larger type and more attractive format.

______. *The World of Christopher Robin,* ill. by Ernest Shepard. Dutton, 1958. The complete verses from *Now We Are Six* and *When We Were Very Young* appear in attractive single-volume format with eight new color illustrations. 5-10

MIZUMURA, KAZUE. *I See the Winds,* ill. T. Crowell, 1966. A small book with a brief poem on each page, and on the facing page an illustration. The illustrations vary from attractive to lovely; the poetry ranges from adequate to good. 8-10

MOORE, LILIAN. *I Feel the Same Way,* ill. by Robert Quackenbush. Atheneum, 1967. 6-9

______. *I Thought I Heard the City,* ill. by Mary J. Dunton. Atheneum, 1969. 8-10

______. *Sam's Place; Poems from the Country,* ill. by Talivaldis Stubis. Atheneum, 1973.

______. *See My Lovely Poison Ivy; And Other Verses about Witches, Ghosts and Things,* ill. by Diane Dawson. Atheneum, 1975. 8-10

NASH, OGDEN. *The Cruise of the Aardvark,* ill. by Wendy Watson. Evans, 1967. 7-9

______. *Good Intentions.* Little, 1942. 10 up

O'NEILL, MARY. *Hailstones and Halibut Bones,* ill. by Leonard Weisgard. Doubleday, 1961. 6 up

ORGEL, DORIS. *The Good-Byes of Magnus Marmalade,* ill. by Erik Blegvad. Putnam, 1966. Amusing, not-so-fond farewell remarks by a small boy. 8-9

PRELUTSKY, JACK. *A Gopher in the Garden; And Other Animal Poems,* ill. by Robert Leydenfrost. Macmillan, 1967. 9-10

______. *Toucans Two,* ill. by José Aruego. Macmillan, 1970. Entertaining light verse. 5-8

RASMUSSEN, KNUD, comp. *Beyond the High Hills: A Book of Eskimo Poems,* ill. by Guy Mary-Rousselière. World, 1961. 7 up

RICHARDS, LAURA E. *Tirra Lirra; Rhymes Old and New,* ill. by Marguerite Davis, foreword by May Hill Arbuthnot. Little, 1955. 5-12

RIEU, E. V. *The Flattered Flying Fish,* ill. by E. H. Shepard. Dutton, 1962. Lovely light verses that savor of Milne and Lewis Carroll and yet have a special quality of their own. There is a tenderness when touching on a child's woes and a happy imaginativeness in the nonsense rhymes. 7-12

RILEY, JAMES WHITCOMB. *The Gobble-uns'll Git You Ef You Don't Watch Out!* ad. from "Little Orphant Annie," ill. by Joel Schick. Lippincott, 1975. The illustrations give new humor to a once-popular poem. 8-9

ROBERTS, ELIZABETH MADOX. *Under the Tree,* ill. by F. D. Bedford. Viking, 1922. 6-10

ROETHKE, THEODORE. *Collected Poems.* Doubleday, 1966. 12 up

______. *Dirty Dinky and Other Creatures; Poems for Children,* selected by Beatrice Roethke and Stephen Lushington. Doubleday, 1973. Chiefly animal poems, most of them humorous. 8-11

______. *I Am! Says the Lamb,* ill. by Robert Leydenfrost. Doubleday, 1961. 10 up

ROSSETTI, CHRISTINA. *Goblin Market,* ill. by Arthur Rackham. Watts, 1970. 9 up

______. *Goblin Market,* ill. by Ellen Raskin. Dutton, 1970. 9 up

______. *Sing Song,* ill. by Marguerite Davis. Macmillan, 1952. 4-10

RUKEYSER, MURIEL. *Mazes,* ill. with photos by Milton Charles. Simon, 1970. 8-10

SANDBURG, CARL. *Early Moon,* ill. by James Daugherty. Harcourt, 1930. 10-14

______. *The Sandburg Treasury; Prose and Poetry for Young People,* ill. by Paul Bacon. Harcourt, 1970. 10-14

______. *Wind Song,* ill. by William A. Smith. Harcourt, 1960. Poems chosen for child appeal cover a wide range of subjects from prayers and people to nature and nonsense. 11-14

SILVERSTEIN, SHEL. *Where the Sidewalk Ends; The Poems and Drawings of Shel Silverstein.* Harper, 1974. Fresh, breezy poetry; much of it has a pointed message for today. 8-11

SMITH, WILLIAM JAY. *Boy Blue's Book of Beasts,* ill. by Juliet Kepes. Little, 1957. 5-9

______. *Laughing Time,* ill. by Juliet Kepes. Little, 1955. 4 up

______. *Mr. Smith and Other Nonsense,* ill. by Don Bolognese. Delacorte, 1968. 8-12

______. *Typewriter Town.* Dutton, 1960.

STARBIRD, KAYE. *Don't Ever Cross a Crocodile,* ill. by Kit Dalton. Lippincott, 1963. 5-10

______. *The Pheasant on Route Seven,* ill. by Victoria de Larrea. Lippincott, 1968. 10-13

______. *A Snail's a Failure Socially; And Other Poems, Mostly About People,* ill. by Kit Dalton. Lippincott, 1966. 9-11

______. *Speaking of Cows,* ill. by Rita Fava. Lippincott, 1960. 5-10

STEVENSON, ROBERT LOUIS. *A Child's Garden of Verses.* There are many editions of this classic. These are representative:
Ill. by Jessie Willcox Smith. Scribner's, 1905, 1969. A large book with appealing pictures in soft colors.
Ill. by Tasha Tudor. Walck, 1947. A full edition with pictures in soft pastels using the young Robert Louis himself as the child.
Ill. by Brian Wildsmith. Watts, 1966. The loved and familiar poems are illustrated with the usual Wildsmith riot of color. 5-9

SWENSON, MAY. *More Poems to Solve.* Scribner's, 1971. 10 up

______. *Poems to Solve.* Scribner's, 1969. 12 up

TAGORE, RABINDRANATH. *Moon, For What Do You Wait?* ed. by Richard Lewis, ill. by Ashley Bryan. Atheneum, 1967. 9 up

TEASDALE, SARA. *Stars To-night,* ill. by Dorothy Lathrop. Macmillan, 1930. 8-12

TIPPETT, JAMES S. *I Live in a City.* Harper, 1924. 5-7

UPDIKE, JOHN. *A Child's Calendar,* ill. by Nancy Ekholm Burkert. Knopf, 1965. 8-10

WATSON, CLYDE. *Father Fox's Pennyrhymes,* ill. by Wendy Watson. T. Crowell, 1971. 3-6

WELLES, WINIFRED. *Skipping Along Alone.* Macmillan, 1931. Imaginative poems with a lyric quality. 7-9

WILBUR, RICHARD. *Opposites,* ill. by author. Harcourt, 1973. A series of verses deftly explains opposite terms. 10-12

Adult References: The Ballads

ABRAHAMS, ROGER, and GEORGE FOSS. *Anglo-American Folksong Style.*

BRAND, OSCAR. *The Ballad Mongers; Rise of the Modern Folk Song.*

CHILD, FRANCIS JAMES, ed. *English and Scottish Popular Ballads.*

COFFIN, TRISTRAM P. *The British Traditional Ballad in North America.*

FRIEDMAN, ALBERT B. *The Viking Book of Folk Ballads of the English Speaking World.*

HALES, JOHN W., and FREDERICK J. FURNIVALL, assisted by FRANCIS J. CHILD. *Bishop Percy's Folio Manuscript.*

HODGART, M. J. C. *The Ballads.*

KITTREDGE, GEORGE LYMAN, ed. *English and Scottish Popular Ballads; Student's Cambridge Edition.*
KRAPPE, ALEXANDER HAGGERTY. *The Science of Folk-Lore.*
LEACH, MAC EDWARD. *Folk Ballads and Songs of the Lower Labrador Coast.*
______, ed. *The Ballad Book.*
LOMAX, JOHN A., ed. *Songs of the Cattle Trail and Cow Camp.*
LOMAX, JOHN A., and ALAN LOMAX, comps. *American Ballads and Folk Songs.*
______, eds. *Cowboy Songs and Other Frontier Ballads.*
MYRUS, DONALD. *Ballads, Blues and the Big Beat.* Chapter, "Poems, Protests, and Put Downs."
POUND, LOUISE. *Poetic Origins and the Ballad.*
______, ed. *American Ballads and Songs.*
SCOTT, JOHN ANTHONY. *The Ballad of America; The History of the United States in Song and Story.*
SHARP, CECIL J. *Nursery Songs from the Appalachian Mountains.*
______, comp. *English Folk-Songs from the Southern Appalachians.*
Some British Ballads.

Ballad Sources

BAKER, LAURA NELSON. *The Friendly Beasts,* ill. by Nicolas Sidjakov. Parnassus, 1957. Reverent and beautiful illustrations enhance this version of an old English carol of the first Christmas eve, when animals talked in the stable at Bethlehem. 4 up

BENÉT, STEPHEN VINCENT. *The Ballad of William Sycamore,* ill. by Brinton Turkle. Little, 1972. A pioneer describes the joys of his simple, rugged life. Nice to read aloud to younger children, too. 9-11

BONI, MARGARET BRADFORD, ed. *Fireside Book of Folk Songs,* arr. for piano by Norman Lloyd, ill. by Alice and Martin Provensen. Simon, 1966. A beautiful collection of many types of folk songs to be enjoyed by the whole family. 8 up

BROWNING, ROBERT. *The Pied Piper of Hamelin,* ill. by Kate Greenaway. Warne, n.d. Kate Greenaway made some of her loveliest pictures for this poem.

______. *The Pied Piper of Hamelin,* ill. by Harold Jones. Watts, 1962. An attractive, color-illustrated, new edition. 6-12

COLE, WILLIAM, ed. *Story Poems New and Old,* ill. by Walter Buehr. World, 1957. Over 90 story poems include traditional ballads, old favorites, and choice modern verses. 9 up

DE REGNIERS, BEATRICE SCHENK. *Catch a Little Fox,* ill. by Brinton Turkle. Seabury, 1970. Variations on a folk rhyme have sprightly illustrations. 4-7

FELTON, HAROLD W., ed. *Cowboy Jamboree: Western Songs and Lore,* music arr. by Edward S. Breck, ill. by Aldren A. Watson, foreword by Carl Carmer. Knopf, 1951. This small collection of only twenty songs is especially valuable because of the little introductions to each song. 6 up

FERRIS, HELEN, comp. *Love's Enchantment,* ill. by Vera Bock. Doubleday, 1944. A collection of romantic ballads. 12 up

LANGSTAFF, JOHN. *Frog Went a-Courtin',* ill. by Feodor Rojankovsky. Harcourt, 1955. Caldecott Medal. 4-6

______. *The Golden Vanity,* ill. by David Gentleman. Harcourt, 1972. Romantic illustrations echo the mood of a story about a clever cabin boy. 9-12

______, comp. *Hi! Ho! The Rattlin' Bog; And Other Folk Songs for Group Singing,* with piano settings by John Edmunds, et al., with guitar chords suggested by Happy Traum, ill. by Robin Jacques. Harcourt, 1969. 12 up

LANGSTAFF, NANCY and JOHN, eds. *Jim Along, Josie; A Collection of Folk Songs and Singing Games for Young Children,* ill. by Jan Pienkowski. Harcourt, 1970. A good collection of folk songs, action songs, and singing games with a discussion of their use with children. 5-8

LONGFELLOW, HENRY WADSWORTH. *Paul Revere's Ride,* ill. by Paul Galdone. T. Crowell, 1963. Illustrations in rich color capture the somber beauty of the night and the colonial countryside. 8 up

MALCOLMSON, ANNE, ed. *Song of Robin Hood,* music arr. by Grace Castagnetta, ill. by Virginia Burton. Houghton, 1947. A collector's item, this beautiful book is invaluable as a source both for ballad text and music. 12 up

MANNING-SANDERS, RUTH, ed. *A Bundle of Ballads,* ill. by William Stobbs. Lippincott, 1961. More than sixty traditional ballads, varied in mood and theme, introduce children to an absorbing poetic form. 12 up

MOORE, CLEMENT CLARK. *The Night Before Christmas,* ill. by Arthur Rackham. Lippincott, 1954. A fine edition with Rackham's lovely pictures. 4-7

______. *The Night Before Christmas,* ill. by Leonard Weisgard. Grosset, 1949. Bold, bright colors and design characterize this big modern edition. 4-7

NIC LEODHAS, SORCHE. *By Loch and By Lin.* Holt, 1969. Flavorful retellings of tales from Scottish ballads. 9-12

PARKER, ELINOR, comp. *100 Story Poems,* ill. by Henry C. Pitz. T. Crowell, 1951. All the favorite old story poems are here. 8-14

______, comp. *100 More Story Poems,* ill. by Peter Spier. T. Crowell, 1960. 8-14

POUND, LOUISE, ed. *American Ballads and Songs.* Scribner's, 1922, 1972. Selections are divided by type; no music is included. 11 up

RITCHIE, JEAN. *The Swapping Song Book,* ill. with photos by George Pickow. Walck, 1964. all ages

ROUNDS, GLEN, ed. *The Strawberry Roan,* ill. by ed. Golden Gate, 1970. Humorous pictures in a format for younger readers. 6-9

SCHREITER, RICK, ill. *The Derby Ram.* Doubleday, 1970. Intricate, almost Hogarthian illustrations enliven a robust nursery ballad. 7-9

SEEGER, RUTH CRAWFORD. *American Folk Songs for Christmas,* ill. by Barbara Cooney. Doubleday, 1953.

______. *Animal Folk Songs for Children: Traditional American Songs,* ill. by Barbara Cooney. Doubleday, 1950. An interesting introduction discussing this native animal folklore. Songs and illustrations are excellent. 4 up

SERRAILLIER, IAN. *Robin and His Merry Men; Ballads of Robin Hood,* ill. by Victor G. Ambrus. Walck, 1970. In both dialogue and exposition, this retelling keeps to the style and the cadence of the ballad form. 12-14

SPIER, PETER, ill. *The Fox Went Out on a Chilly Night.* Doubleday, 1961. The old folk song enjoys a handsome picture-book setting of New England at harvest time. Illustrations in color and music appended. 5 up

TAYLOR, MARK. *Old Blue: You Good Dog You,* ill. by Gene Holtan. Golden Gate, 1970. The illustrations complement the humor of a folk-based tall tale retold with zest. 8 up

Modern Fiction

Chapter 10

While there are signs that moralistic and sentimental didacticism is not dead, present-day realistic fiction is predominantly honest. Most authors assume, as did Samuel Clemens in *The Adventures of Tom Sawyer* (1876), that children are sensible, normal human beings, interested in how other children and adults get along in the world. Modern realistic fiction for children includes, along with a great number of mediocre stories, some of the finest children's books ever written.

Realistic stories may be just as exciting or humorous or romantic or imaginative as fantasy, but they are always plausible or possible. In a realistic story everything that happens *could* happen. Sometimes the adventures of the hero or heroine may seem rather improbable but still merit the classification of realistic because they are possible. A realistic story is a tale that is convincingly true to life.

Realistic fiction for children includes historical novels (Chapter 11), stories about peoples of other lands, and stories about contemporary life in the United States, the last two categories the major concern of this chapter. Such books help children better understand the problems and issues of their own lives, empathize with other people, and see the complexities of human relationships.

The books discussed in this chapter have been divided into three major groups: books for the youngest children, many of which are also discussed in Chapter 4, books for the middle group, and books for older children. These divisions are not hard and fast, since many children read above their usual reading level when they are interested or may go back to a childhood favorite of their past reading experience. And many adults have found that they can read aloud books intended for children older than those in their audience. The reading levels suggested in the bibliography of this chapter are equally flexible. Besides the three major categories, there are three minor categories: animal stories, sports stories, and mysteries—three of the favorite subject-matter interests of children.

The stories in this chapter are not divided by ethnic or regional groups or by countries. The chapter bibliography, however, is marked so that those who are interested, say, in finding books about black children can do so; and the Subject Matter Index, too, will help readers find such stories.

In the past ten years or so, realistic fiction has shown more change than any other kind of books for children. Chapter 1 touches briefly on those changes and Chapter 3, pages 54–58, discusses some of the present-day trends: the increased number of books by and about blacks; the growing publication in the United States, either in separate editions or translations, of books from other countries; and, particularly notable, the greater frankness in language and the treatment of hitherto taboo subjects.

Criteria for Realistic Stories

How can we evaluate this wealth of realistic fiction for children, when it ranges from picture stories for the youngest to mystery stories and romance for young people? First of all, it may be helpful to review the section in Chapter 2 entitled "Looking Closely at Books," pp. 21–27, and to consider in these books just how effectively setting, point of view, characters, plot, theme, and style are handled. The primary consideration is the power of the story to captivate readers and keep them racing along from page to page, while having sufficient literary distinction to develop children's taste.

Most of this fiction, in addition to telling good stories, satisfies some of children's basic needs. From *One Morning in Maine* to *Where the Lilies Bloom* there is continual emphasis on winning or holding security. The satisfaction of belonging is very important in *Plain Girl, Little Navajo Bluebird,* and *Are You There God? It's Me, Margaret.* Loving and being loved is a powerful motive in *Wild in the World* and *Zeely.* Children's love of change and fun is a motivating force in *Henry Huggins* and *Little Eddie.* The need to know is important in *Tom Sawyer, Portrait of Ivan, . . . and now Miguel, Roosevelt Grady,* and in the mystery tales. The need for competence is a strong motivating force in *Yonie Wondernose* and *My Side of the Mountain,* and in many other realistic stories of the past and present.

If these books center on children's basic needs; if they give them increased insight into their own personal problems and social relationships; if they show that people are more alike than different, more akin to each other than alien; if they convince young readers that they can do something about their lives – have fun and adventures and get things done without any magic other than their own earnest efforts – then they are worthwhile books for children to read.

Stories About Minority Groups

No other country in the world has the variety of peoples to be found in the United States. There are such regional groups as the Southern mountain people, the Cajuns, and the migrant groups that follow the crops – picking cotton or beans or strawberries or oranges. Then there are the close-knit communities of immigrants and their descendants making a little Italy or Hungary or Sweden within a larger community. There are groups representing all the major and innumerable minor religious sects, and Americans of every racial background. Since all of these diverse peoples have contributed richly to the life of the nation, it is important that children should meet them vicariously in books in order that they may meet them in person sympathetically and with respect. Children see in books their own images, and if these are distorted or if there is stigma by omission, such self-images are damaged. And it is especially important that the minority group is pictured not as "them" but as "one of us," that the books about children of minority groups show the diversity within the group rather than a stereotype. When there is a need and a response, as there has been for books about black children, there are always the twin specters of the bandwagon book, tailored to fit the need, and of the

Viewpoints

The only obligation to which in advance we may hold a novel, without incurring the accusation of being arbitrary, is that it be interesting. . . . The ways in which it is at liberty to accomplish this result (of interesting us) strike me as innumerable, and such as can only suffer from being marked out or fenced in by prescription. They are as various as the temperament of man, and they are successful in proportion as they reveal a particular mind, different from others. A novel is in its broadest definition a personal, a direct impression of life: that, to begin with, constitutes its value, which is greater or less according to the intensity of the impression. But there will be no intensity at all, and therefore no value, unless there is freedom to feel and say. The tracing of a line to be followed, of a tone to be taken, of a form to be filled out, is a limitation of that freedom and a suppression of the very thing that we are most curious about. – Henry James, "The Art of Fiction," in *Makers of Literary Criticism* (vol. II), compiled and edited by A. G. George, Asia Publishing House, London, 1967, p. 352.

Illustration by Elsa Beskow from Pelle's New Suit. *Harper & Row, Publishers, 1929. Reprinted by permission of Stig Beskow, Stockholm. (Original in color)*

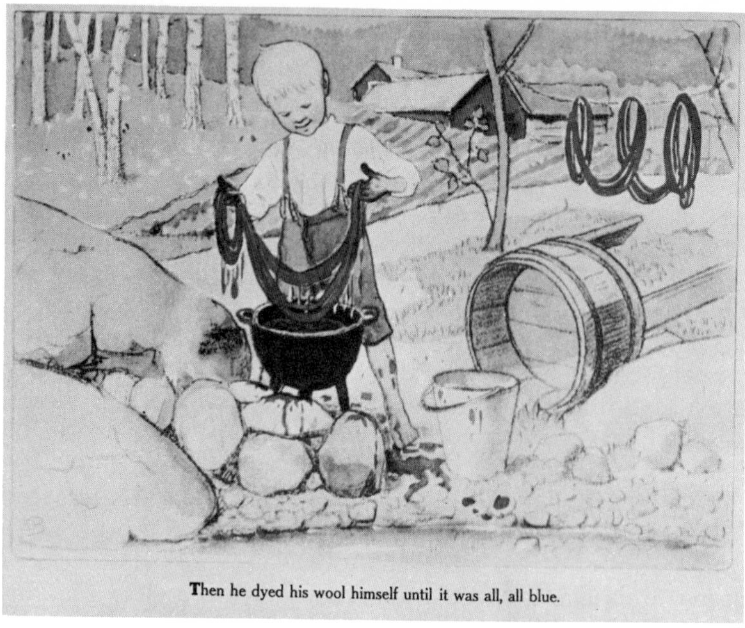

Then he dyed his wool himself until it was all, all blue.

tract, written with good intent but too burdened by its message to be a good story. Some of these books may be useful temporarily despite their mediocrity, but it is to be hoped that the day will come when there are so many good books for and about every kind of child that we can dismiss those that do not meet all the standards of good literature.

Stories About Children from Other Lands

In early stories about other lands there was a tendency to present the picturesque at the expense of the usual. Readers were given the China of bound feet, the Holland of wooden shoes and lace caps, South America by way of a primitive type of Indian tribe. Some of these faults are still to be found in recently published books (both those written in the United States and those selected for importation from other countries), but such misconceptions are becoming far less common. We must check the information given in such stories against what we know to be true of the present everyday life of people. And we must question any implication that a way of life of people we don't know is queer or quaint rather than simply different. In many of these books the themes are universal, and the stories point up the fact that differences between children of one country and those of another are superficial, based on cultural factors to be valued and preserved rather than on inherent factors.

Books for Younger Children

Our youngest children, anywhere from two years old to seven, seem to have a special need for stories that are as factual and personal as their fingers and toes and the yards and neighborhoods they are beginning to explore.

Forerunners

In the 1920s Lucy Sprague Mitchell called attention to the lack of realistic stories for children under five, and supplied stories centering on the child's own activities, using the child's own language. In 1929 an example of realism for the youngest came from the Swedish. It was a translation of *Pelle's New Suit* (1929), told and illustrated by Elsa Beskow. Text and pictures in color tell how the little boy Pelle needs a new suit. He raises his own lamb and then, for each person who helps him with his suit, he performs some useful service. He follows the tailoring even as he assists the tailor. Finally, for his Sunday best he triumphantly wears his beautiful blue suit.

The most notable of the early followers of Lucy Sprague Mitchell was Margaret Wise Brown, who wrote also under the name of Golden MacDonald. Her *The City Noisy Book* (1939), intended to stimulate the sensory perceptions of young children, was a pioneer and was followed by several more *Noisy* books. Then there was a series contrasting bigness and littleness. The hero of *The Little Fisherman* caught little fish and the big fisherman caught big fish, and so on. Brown's contribution lay chiefly in her sensitive perception of the child's sensory responses to the big, booming confusion of the world.

The books by Margaret Wise Brown launched a torrent of awareness compositions for the young. There were books about night sounds, day smells, wetness, coldness, and colors. By the 1950s it began to look as if we were in for a kind of pernicious anemia of theme and plot, with language experiences in place of stories and pitter-patter in place of events. These books give children back themselves with little more—no rich entertainment, no additional insight, and no laughter.

Marjorie Flack's *Wait for William* (1935) is a "here and now" story whose whole plot turns on a small boy's struggle to get his shoelaces tied. Any four-year-old can understand and sympathize with William's predicament, and so can adults.

These early examples of realism for the youngest have been followed by a continuing spate of books impressive in their variety, written and illustrated by authors and artists of distinction, and reflecting not only the needs and interests of young children but also the diversity and the changes within our society.

Alvin Tresselt

Hide and Seek Fog
White Snow, Bright Snow

Midway between the awareness and the theme-plot schools of writing for young children lie the picture stories of Alvin Tresselt and Leo Politi. Tresselt constructs his stories about weather and nature in simple, rhythmic prose, and with Roger Duvoisin's pictures, they develop a real sense of drama. *Hide and Seek Fog* (1965), for example, describes how the fog affects sea and seaside activities. These little everyday miracles of the weather are made exciting, something to be watched and enjoyed, never feared. Texts and pictures are full of reassurance and beauty. *White Snow, Bright Snow* won the 1948 Caldecott Medal for Duvoisin.

Leo Politi

Pedro and other stories

Leo Politi's picture stories are simple in theme and plot and are frequently centered on the activities of small children living in a homogeneous racial group in the midst of one of our big cities. *Pedro, the Angel of Olvera Street* (1946) and *Juanita* (1948) are both about the Mexican-Americans of Los Angeles—*Pedro* tells of Olvera Street at Christmas time and *Juanita* of the Olvera pre-Easter ceremony, the Blessing of the Animals. *Song of the Swallows*, the 1950 Caldecott Medal book, tells of the coming of spring to the old mission of Capistrano. *Moy Moy* (1960) is about a little Chinese-American girl observing the Chinese New Year. *Little Leo* (1951) journeys to Italy and converts a whole village of children to the charms of playing Indian. In *Three Stalks of Corn* (1976) a small girl learns Mexican legends from her grandmother. An affectionate understanding of children is reflected in every book and every picture Politi has made.

Edward Ardizzone

The *Little Tim* stories

Even young children need a touch of wildness now and then, which is precisely what the English writer Ardizzone gives them in *Little Tim and the Brave Sea Captain* (1936), his spirited account of Tim's adventures at sea. It all starts with Tim, who plays in and out of boats on the beach. How he becomes a stowaway, learns to be an efficient if reluctant deckhand, and experiences shipwreck makes a thrilling story for the five- to eight-year-olds. Ardizzone's watercolors are as vigorous as his tale. Here is realism for the youngest at its most adventurous level. Tim is a do-it-yourself hero if ever there was one, and his competence and achievements through a series of stories rouse the admiration of his young devotees. Ardizzone's books introduce other heroes, but Tim is still the favorite young hero.

Robert McCloskey

Make Way for Ducklings
Time of Wonder

Robert McCloskey was the first artist to win the Caldecott Medal twice, 1942 and 1958. If you look over his picture stories—*Make Way for Ducklings* (1941), *One Morning in Maine* (1952), and *Time of Wonder* (1957)—you discover that they are all built on a theme of reassurance. Children know the ducklings will come safely through their first perilous trip in city traffic because their mother has them in charge. And in that superb book in full color, *Time of Wonder*, the safe, secure world of woods and beach is threatened by the oncoming darkness of a hurricane. How the family prepares for and survives this menace is so convincingly told and pictured that children feel they too can meet and endure danger. The pictures in the first two books have humor and strength, and some of the paintings in *Time of Wonder* have a breathtaking beauty. (See color section.) McCloskey's books for older children, *Homer Price* (1943) and *Centerburg Tales* (1951), are both written with a humor that has given them enduring popularity.

Carolyn Haywood

"B" Is for Betsy
Little Eddie

With the *Betsy* and the *Little Eddie* books of Carolyn Haywood, children progress from the picture story to the illustrated story, with the pictures of secondary importance to the tale.

He planted himself in the center of the road, raised one
hand to stop the traffic, and then beckoned with the other,
the way policemen do, for Mrs. Mallard to cross over.

Illustration by Robert McCloskey from Make Way for Ducklings *by Robert McCloskey. Copyright, 1941, by Robert McCloskey; copyright © renewed 1969 by Robert McCloskey. By permission of the Viking Press, Inc.*

Another mark of increasing maturity is that against a familiar background of family life, the young heroes and heroines move into an ever widening circle of neighborhood and school adventures, camps, and even travel.

"B" Is for Betsy (1939) launched the series of books about the everyday activities of a little girl in suburbia. As she grew with each succeeding book, her experiences widened. While the characters in these books remained very close to stereotypes, it was the interpretation of their activities or the problems connected with school or camp or typical mistakes and accidents that held the attention of young readers. These gave the child greater self-knowledge, more understanding of other people and experiences, and a greater confidence in approaching their years of growing up.

With *Little Eddie* (1947) Carolyn Haywood developed a real boy, and laughter began. Eddie is as earnest as Betsy, but much more alive. He is an avid collector of "valuables," which his long-suffering family calls "junk." Still the family endures patiently even an old but full-sized fire engine. In *Eddie's Pay Dirt* (1953), our hero is confronted with a grave ethical problem. His father helps him see it, but wisely leaves the decision to Eddie. *Eddie's Happenings* (1971) and the more recent *Eddie's Valuable Property* (1975) show many signs of Eddie's maturity.

These simply written stories have a warmth and a directness that win and hold young readers.

Taro Yashima

Crow Boy

Taro Yashima's striking picture stories are set in his native Japan. *Plenty to Watch* (1954) by Taro and Mitsu Yashima tells of the shops and workers that Japanese children stop to watch as they walk home from school. The stores and the workers may differ from their American counterparts, but the story of children's insatiable curiosity is universal.

Crow Boy (1955), Taro Yashima's third book, was a Caldecott Honor Book and also won the Child Study Award. It has unusual social values as well as pictorial beauty. Crow

Illustration by Taro Yashima from Crow Boy *by Taro Yashima. Copyright 1955 by Mitsu and Taro Yashima. By permission of the Viking Press, Inc. (Original in color)*

Boy is a small, silent child who walks to school alone, sits alone, and does not talk. The children call him derisively "Chibi"—tiny boy. But a new schoolmaster discovers that the small outcast walks in from a great distance. He knows where wild potatoes and wild grapes grow, and he knows every call the crows make and can imitate them perfectly. When he does this for the children they call him "Crow Boy" with respect, and he is one of them at last. Not since Eleanor Estes's *The Hundred Dresses* has this theme of the outsider been so sensitively handled.

Joan Lexau

Olaf Reads
Benjie

Joan Lexau's stories have diversity of style, mood, and subject, but all of them have an understanding of the child's viewpoint, whether they are written for older readers or for kindergarten children. Her books for the youngest children are permeated with love and humor.

Illustration from Benjie on his Own *by Joan Lexau. Illustrated by Don Bolognese. Illustrations Copyright © 1970 by Don Bolognese. Reprinted with the permission of the DIAL PRESS. (Original in color)*

Olaf Reads (1961) is an amusing tale of a child so enthralled by his new prowess that he takes literally a sign that says "Pull," and finds the whole school responding with a fire drill. In *Benjie* (1964), a very shy black child discovers, when he hunts for his grandmother's lost earring, that it isn't really so hard to talk to people; in *Benjie on His Own* (1970) he learns that he can call on his neighbors for help when his grandmother is ill. *Finders Keepers, Losers Weepers* (1967) is for beginning readers, a story of a small boy's trials in taking care of his still smaller sister. *Striped Ice Cream* (1968) tells of a child in a working-class family who, tired of hand-me-down dresses from her sisters, is thrilled by a new dress *and* striped ice cream for her birthday. *Me Day* (1971) describes a small boy's joy in seeing his father, who has left home, on his birthday. *Come Here, Cat* (1973) is almost wordless, the tale of a small girl's pursuit of a reluctant cat.

Ezra Jack Keats

The Snowy Day
Goggles!

The Snowy Day (1962), Ezra Jack Keats's Caldecott Medal book, started a trend of showing black children in illustrations with no reference to racial identity in the text. Keats has continued to write stories about Peter's adventures in the city and other urban stories as well. The settings of these tales are crowded with buildings, junky vacant lots, and, most of all, with people. The smaller children play around and between the older ones, keeping their own favorite playthings through wit, as Peter does in *Goggles!* (1969), when some older boys covet the motorcycle goggles he has found.

In *Whistle for Willie* (1964) Peter learns to whistle at last, spurred on by the need to call his dog. Roberto has difficulty sleeping in *Dreams* (1974), and an inadvertent action helps to save a cat trapped by a dog. *Louie* (1975) doesn't talk until the day he sees Gussie, a puppet, and finds something to love. The slight plots are bolstered by the vibrant illustrations, filled with children of different ethnic groups.

Charlotte Zolotow

Big Sister and Little Sister
The Hating Book
William's Doll

Few writers for small children so empathize with them as does Charlotte Zolotow, whose books—with some exceptions—are really explorations of relationships cast in story form and given vitality by perfected simplicity of style and by the humor and tenderness of the stories. *Big Sister and Little Sister* (1966) is typical of Zolotow's later books, exploring the balances in a one-to-one relationship. *The Hating Book* (1969) describes the ups and downs of friendship. The mother of a fatherless child listens, in *A Father Like That* (1971), to her son's catalog of virtues in his dream-father, who would *never* show off at parent-teacher meetings. *Janey* (1973) is a story of a best friend's moving away. In *William's Doll* (1972), Zolotow shows that little boys as well as little girls may want a doll to play with. Zolotow's understanding of children's emotional needs and problems, and her ability to express them with candor have made her one of the major contemporary writers of realistic books for small children.

Martha Alexander

Out! Out! Out!
The Story Grandmother Told
Sabrina

Tidy, charming little drawings in soft colors add to the appeal of Martha Alexander's realistic stories. In *Out! Out! Out!* (1968) she tells a story without words, the pictures showing the delightful commotion that ensues when a bird flies into the house. In *The Story Grandmother Told* (1969) a bright-faced black child prompts Gramma to tell a favorite tale by telling it herself. *Sabrina* (1971) finds, when she starts nursery school, that other girls like her unusual name. Bonnie, often taken advantage of by her older brother, finds herself on top in *I'll Be the Horse If You'll Play with Me* (1975). Each story touches on some familiar situation, and the behavior of the children is convincingly natural.

Other Books for Younger Children

The profusion of picture-story books and books for the beginning reader makes it impossible to include every one of the many worthy books that have been published. Lois Lenski, whose regional stories are discussed later in this chapter, pioneered in realism in books for the youngest children. The series that began with *The Little Auto* (1934) and the later series about Debby and Davy are direct and simple, with no wasted words. The engagingly homely children and deft humor of Harriet Pincus's illustrations add immeasurably to the bland text of Lore Segal's *Tell Me a Mitzi*, which has three stories of family life—as it really is. One tale is totally and amusingly improbable, but Mitzi and her little brother Jacob remain sturdily childlike.

Grandparents are a part of life for younger children. *Kevin's Grandma* (1975) by Barbara Williams shows both a sedate and an adventurous model. *Grandpa's Maria* (1974) by Hans-Eric Hellberg tells of Maria's dependence on Grandpa for stability when her mother goes to a rest home. The locale is Sweden, but the need for security is universal. Max Lundgren, in *Matt's Grandfather* (1972),

Illustration by Harriet Pincus. Reprinted with permission of Farrar, Straus & Giroux, Inc. from Tell Me a Mitzi, *text copyright © 1970 by Lore Segal, pictures copyright 1970 by Harriet Pincus. (Original in color)*

another story set in Sweden, draws a realistic picture of a small child's acceptance of a senile grandparent.

Death is also a part of life, and an increasing number of books even for younger children show this. In *Nonna* (1975) by Jennifer Bartoli, a grandmother is remembered by her grandson. Tomie de Paola's *Nana Upstairs and Nana Downstairs* (1973) shows Tommy's adjustment to one death and, much later, to another. The difficulty of adjusting to the death of a sibling, and particularly of a twin, is honestly portrayed in *My Twin Sister Erika* (1976), a story by Ilse-Margret Vogel, set in Germany.

Another part of life often passed by earlier was the handicapped or mentally retarded child. In *He's My Brother* (1974) by Joe Lasker, a child who is simply slow is the center of interest. *Howie Helps Himself* (1974) by Joan Fassler describes Howie's final triumph of being able to manipulate his wheelchair by himself.

Of the trends observable in contemporary publishing, the increased number of books about black children is a major one. Some of the books are simply affirmations of pride, like Jean Bond's *Brown Is a Beautiful Color* (1969) or Ann McGovern's *Black Is Beautiful* (1969), and some are stories of black children showing competence, as in Janice Udry's *Mary Jo's Grandmother* (1970); overcoming jealousy and learning to love, as Robert does in John Steptoe's beautifully illustrated *Stevie* (1969); or as Johnetta does in Lucille Clifton's *My Brother Fine with Me* (1975). Some books show adjustments to crowded living arrangements, as in June Jordan's *New Life: New Room* (1975) or a child seeking quiet in a crowded home, as in Elizabeth Hill's *Evan's Corner* (1967). In some, the theme is one of problems raised by racial prejudice, such as Billy meets in *A New Home for Billy* (1966) by May Justus. In this story, a black family, anxious to move from a tenement to a house in the country, encounters barriers before they find a community that welcomes them.

Illustration by Emily A. McCully from Friday Night Is Papa Night *by Ruth A. Sonneborn and Emily A. McCully. Illustrations copyright © 1970 by Emily A. McCully. Reprinted by permission of The Viking Press, Inc. (Original with color)*

Ruth Sonneborn's stories are about Puerto Rican children in the United States; they are stories of universal problems and joys, like the happiness of having the family all together in *Friday Night Is Papa Night* (1970), rather than of difficulties faced because the children are Puerto Rican. *Magdalena* (1971) by Louisa Shotwell is the story of a lively Puerto Rican child and her beloved grandmother. There is still a paucity of books about other minority groups for the youngest readers, but this will surely change.

Almost every trend in realistic fiction for older children seems to be followed by a similar trend in books for younger children. Topics that have been hitherto abjured are emerging, as does divorce in Beth Goff's *Where Is Daddy?* (1969).

Although children in the United States are enjoying more books from other countries than ever before, there are fewer picture stories being written about children of other lands. However, the sprightly stories of Françoise, and Ludwig Bemelmans's *Madeline* (1939) are still read and loved. Marie Hall Ets is one of the few authors who writes about Mexican children; her *Bad Boy, Good Boy* (1967) describes the problems of learning a new language and the effect of marital conflict on a child, while *Gilberto and the Wind* (1963) is a simpler story of a child's play.

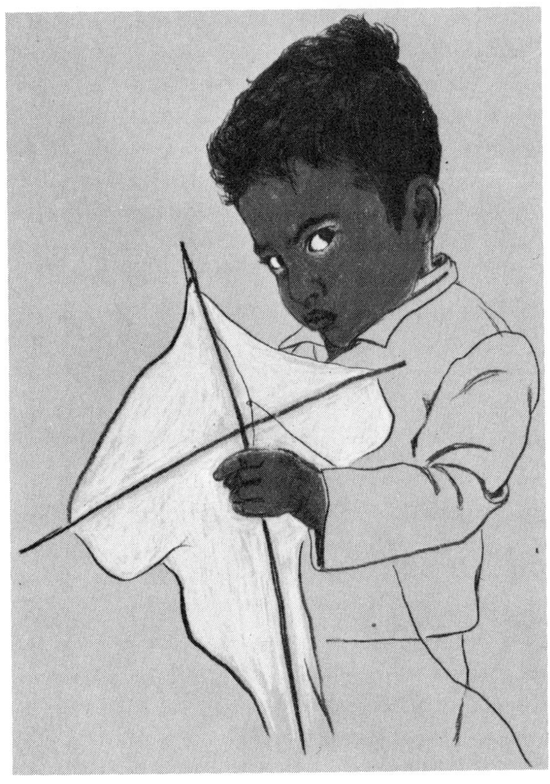

Illustration by Marie Hall Ets from Gilberto and the Wind *by Marie Hall Ets. Copyright © 1963 by Marie Hall Ets. Reprinted by permission of The Viking Press, Inc. (Original with color)*

Books for the Middle Group

Before examining present-day realistic stories for the middle and older children, it may be helpful to review some of the classic realistic stories that have been landmarks in the history of children's literature and that are popular still: *The Adventures of Tom Sawyer* (1876), *Little Women* (1868), *Hans Brinker, or the Silver Skates* (1865), *Heidi* (1884), and *The Secret Garden* (1909).

Forerunners

A century ago, Samuel Clemens (Mark Twain) introduced children to the seamy side of village life in *Tom Sawyer*. At that time, automobiles, superhighways, airplanes, and television had not tied the small towns so intimately to the large cities that there was little difference between the two. There in *Tom Sawyer* was the isolated country town Samuel Clemens himself had grown up in, with respectable churchgoers on one side and the village ne'er-do-wells on the other. Tom was the link between the two groups. By way of his friendship with Huck, the son of the town drunkard, he knew all the shady characters as well as his Aunt Polly's churchgoing friends. He saw a grave robbery and a murder and had other hair-raising adventures. This book gives children chills up and down their spines, but it is not lurid or sensational. Along with the excitement and the humor, there is a steady emergence of Tom's code: he keeps his word to a friend; he may be scared to death, but he sees things through; in real peril, he protects a weaker person; he uses his head, keeps cool, and keeps trying. This is as good a code today as it ever was.

Louisa May Alcott's *Little Women* deals with a family of four girls of teen age, but it is to preadolescents that this book makes the greatest appeal, because of their interest in what lies just ahead, their first sense of romance, their dream of being grown up. Many young readers still enjoy *Little Women* as their great-great-grandparents did. Here is the first great juvenile novel of family life—a warm, loving family group, struggling with poverty and with individual problems but sustained by an abiding affection for each other and an innocent kind of gaiety that could make its own fun. Not until the Laura Ingalls Wilder series do we again encounter such a picture of a family, and in no one of the Wilder series is each member of the group more distinctly drawn than are the unforgettable Beth, Jo, Meg, and Amy. Here is characterization that makes each girl a real human being—exasperating, lovable, heroic, absurd, delightful.

Little Women also provides a wholesome introduction to romance and to the inevitability of death even among loved ones, who, because they are loved, seem somehow invulnerable. There is a continuity in social relationships, with the home as the necessary core of all happy living.

Hans Brinker, or the Silver Skates by Mary Mapes Dodge and *Heidi*, written in German by Johanna Spyri, a Swiss, and translated into English in 1884, introduced children in the United States and Canada to daily life in other lands through a strong and engaging story, a tradition that has continued. *Hans Brinker, or the Silver Skates* was immediately successful. It was translated into many languages, and the Dutch people accepted it as the best picture of childhood in Holland that had ever been written up until that time.[1] Dodge had become deeply interested in the history of the Dutch republic and had saturated herself with the best references she could find on the subject. When she began to write her book she had a twofold purpose: to tell a story about the children of Holland and to weave into that story as much of the history and customs of the people as she could.

Heidi uses the most popular of all themes—a variation of Cinderella, the unwanted, neglected child who comes into her own—but there is a convincing quality about *Heidi* which many modern Cinderellas lack. The child is full of the joy of living. She skips and leaps and she falls in love with an apparently grouchy old grandfather, the goats, and the mountains, all with equal vehemence and loyalty. No child who has read and loved *Heidi* will ever enter Switzerland without a feeling of coming home. This is what books about other lands should do for children—leave them feeling forever a part of that country, forever well disposed toward the people. Such stories of other people create no sense of oddity, no feeling of irreconcilable differences, but a desire to know these people so like themselves.

For a long period after *Tom Sawyer, Little Women, Hans Brinker,* and *Heidi* appeared, there was as little substantial realism for older children as there was for the youngest. Frances Hodgson Burnett's *The Secret Garden* did in some measure span the gap between these older books and those realistic stories which are comparatively recent. It has maintained a following of devoted readers to this very day, telling a fairy tale of unimaginable riches, of children misunderstood and suffering but conquering all. Burnett enjoys describing great wealth and then showing how it often brings neither a normal nor a happy life—very consoling to those without such wealth. The heroine of *The Secret Garden*, Mary, is plain and bad tempered as well as orphaned and neglected. In the huge estate where she is sent to live, Mary discovers a secret garden, a master with a crooked back, and his ailing son, Colin. Martha, the hearty Yorkshire maid, provides a healthy contrast, and Martha's little brother, Dickon, is the very spirit of the earth as is his wise, kind mother, who has love enough for her own brood of twelve and for the poor little rich children besides. Among them, they get the wretched Colin into the secret garden with Mary. Under Dickon's guidance, the children make the garden grow and bloom once more, without realizing that in the process they, too, will grow and bloom.

Armstrong Sperry

Call It Courage

Call It Courage (1940), a Newbery Medal book, is an exciting story about Mafatu, the son of a

Reprinted with permission of Macmillan Publishing Co., from Call It Courage *by Armstrong Sperry. Copyright 1940 by Macmillan Publishing Co., Inc. renewed 1968 by Armstrong Sperry.*

[1]Bertha Mahony and Elinor Whitney, comps., *Realms of Gold in Children's Books*. Garden, 1929, p. 611.

Polynesian chief, rejected by his people for his cowardice and marooned on a desert island. This island proves to be the sinister shrine of cannibals. Mafatu maintains life, develops all the necessary arts and skills, makes his own weapons and his own canoe, finally escapes the cannibals, and returns home a hero. This book about the conquest of fear can give young readers the courage to face their own fears with a sense of ultimate triumph.

Eleanor Estes

The *Moffat* stories

Within the United States one of the most captivating book families is unquestionably the Moffats, created by Eleanor Estes. There are three of these books—*The Moffats* (1941), *The Middle Moffat* (1942), and *Rufus M.* (1943).

The stories are set in the 1910s, but the characters and their problems are so real and so universal they seem timeless. There is no general theme, no long suspense, and no exciting climax to these books. Each chapter is a complete episode in the life of one of the Moffats.

The ultimate humor in these situations is provided by the artist, Louis Slobodkin. The Moffat tales and Slobodkin's illustrations represent the perfect union of story and pictures—Rufus M. leaping for a deadly catch in a baseball game; Janey viewing the world amiably from an upside-down angle, looking between her own stout legs, head almost on the ground.

Also illustrated by Slobodkin, Estes's *The Hundred Dresses* (1944) is one of the most effective indictments of prejudice in children's literature, and a poignant story told in an easy, natural style. Wanda Petronski is an outsider, poor and ill-clad, who wears the same dress every day. Taunted, she says she has a hundred dresses at home. She does, and she's drawn them all. Her pictures, exhibited at school, win a medal, but Wanda isn't there. A note from her father says they have moved to a place where "No more holler Polack. No more ask why funny name. . . ." Eleanor Estes was awarded the Newbery Medal for *Ginger Pye* (1951), a story about a family that loses its dog and finds him through the kind

Illustration by Louis Slobodkin. Reproduced from The Middle Moffat *copyright, 1942, 1970, by Eleanor Estes, by permission of Harcourt Brace Jovanovich, Inc.*

offices of three-year-old Uncle Benny. The plot in *The Alley* (1964) revolves around burglary, but the book's appeal is in its picture of a small faculty community. In *The Coat-Hanger Christmas Tree* (1973), a child adjusts to her mother's refusal to have a real tree.

Estes creates real children wrapped up in their own concerns, playing, interacting, paying scant attention to mere adult problems.

Elizabeth Enright

The Saturdays
Gone-Away Lake

Elizabeth Enright had a gift for realism. *The Saturdays* (1941) introduces the four Melendys, ranging in age from six to thirteen, and deals with their $1.60 Saturdays. These are achieved by pooling all their allowances and by permitting one child to use the whole amount for a Saturday, each in turn. The results are often startling and always amusing. *The Four Story Mistake* (1942) and *Then There Were Five* (1944) continue the family activities in the country and lead to the adoption of a country boy.

The Melendy family has been almost superseded by the popular cousins in *Gone-Away Lake* (1957) and its sequel. In the first book, Portia and her cousin Julian discover an abandoned colony of summer cottages near a swamp that was once a lovely, sparkling lake. In the second book, *Return to Gone-Away* (1961), the family makes the joyous decision to restore one of the old houses and live there the year round. Enright's style is so forthright and lively that this unusual setting becomes completely real and the reader shares the family's joy in that final decision.

The Newbery Medal was given to Enright's *Thimble Summer* (1938), a family story set on a Midwestern farm in the midst of a burning drouth. Just as the drouth is broken by a drenching rain, Garnet finds a silver thimble, which she is convinced will bring her a lucky summer.

Enright's children are, like those created by Estes, very real, although somewhat more venturesome.

Marguerite de Angeli

Bright April
Yonie Wondernose
Thee, Hannah!

Bright April (1946) was one of the earliest books to focus on a black child's problems. The youngest in a prosperous, middle-class family, April finds a happy solution to her difficulties with a prejudiced member of her Brownie troop. There are many books for and about black children now, and books that show urban ghetto life, not just comfortable middle-class surroundings, but this was a rarity when it was published. Marguerite de Angeli was also a pioneer in relating stories about the minority groups around her home in Philadelphia. Her stories are slight, but the warm pictures she paints, both with colors and words, of Amish, Quaker, and Pennsylvania Dutch children are important. *Henner's Lydia* (1936), *Skippack School* (1939), *Yonie Wondernose* (1944), and *Thee, Hannah!* (1940) are all pleasant stories about interesting people.

Yonie Wondernose with his wondering is a favorite, especially when, like the hero of the folk tale, his wondering pays off and he proves his courage as well. Particularly appealing, too, is the little Quaker girl in *Thee, Hannah!* who despises her Quaker garb until she finds herself chosen, because of it, to serve a great cause at the time of the Civil War. The young girl in *Henner's Lydia* can still be seen on countless Amish farms, learning to be like Mother.

From Cotton In My Sack *by Lois Lenski*
Copyright 1949 by Lois Lenski
Reproduced by permission of J. B. Lippincott Company

Of first importance are de Angeli's illustrations. These are beautiful in color with springtime freshness and innocence. To be sure, her children—whatever their sex, nationality, or disposition—have always the same little heartshaped faces and wistful beauty, but they have also a skipping gaiety which is natural to childhood.

Virginia Sorensen

Plain Girl
Miracles on Maple Hill

Plain Girl (1955) is another delightful story about the Amish in Pennsylvania. Ten-year-old Esther is both worried and pleased when she knows she must attend a public school. But she makes friends and is surprised to find that her very best friend, she of the glorious pink dress, actually admires Esther's plain clothes. In *Miracles on Maple Hill*, awarded the 1957 Newbery Medal, ten-year-old Marly and her family move to the country in hopes that her father will regain his health after being a prisoner of war. The "miracle" happens, and the family decides to stay at Maple Hill. *Lotte's Locket* (1964) is the brisk and appealing story of a Danish child's adjustment to the fact that she is going to move to the United States. The story has good background material about Copenhagen and Danish holiday customs. In *Around the Corner* (1971) a black family welcomes white newcomers to their neighborhood. Sorensen's stories are quiet and understated, but persuasive in their serenity.

Lois Lenski

Strawberry Girl
Cotton in My Sack
Boom Town Boy

In 1946, when the Newbery Medal was given to Lois Lenski's *Strawberry Girl*, attention was called to a unique series of books about regional groups from all over the United States.

Lois Lenski began her series with *Bayou Suzette* (1943), a story about the French-speaking people in the bayou section of Louisiana. After *Strawberry Girl* of Florida came *Blue Ridge Billy* (1946), about the North Carolina mountain group, and *Judy's Journey* (1947), which followed the crop-pickers from California to Florida and back to New Jersey. There are many more, including *Project Boy* (1954), which is set in a veterans' housing project and *High-Rise Secret* (1966), in a high-rise housing project.

Strawberry Girl (1945) is typical of these books at their best. It is the story of Birdie Boyer's family, newly moved to Florida's backwoods for the purpose of raising small crops of "sweet 'taters," strawberries, oranges, and the like.

In *Cotton in My Sack* (1949), everyone in the family, except the baby, toils endlessly picking cotton, only to indulge in a once-a-week orgy of aimless spending. In *Boom Town Boy* (1948), Orvie's family strikes oil and goes on a spending spree that is silly and purposeless.

The values of this series are to be found in its objective realism and compassion. Young members of disadvantaged families meet families like their own in these regional stories of Lois Lenski's. And they take heart, because always the ups and downs of these hard-pressed, courageous people yield a ray of hope. Things are, or give promise of becoming, better. And to the children of more affluent families, these books give a picture of a kind of family love and loyalty that may be new to them.

Beverly Cleary

Henry Huggins
Ramona the Pest
Mitch and Amy

Beverly Cleary's *Henry Huggins* books are pure Americana, from supermarkets to backyard barbecues, delightfully humorous.

The Huggins family is an average group. The parents are sympathetic to Henry's enterprises but not overly indulgent. All the children in the stories are pursuing their own goals with the frustrations usual to children. The first book begins with Henry's determination to keep and support a stray dog he has acquired and named Ribsy. After Ribsy has been accepted, the next problem concerns the speedy multiplication of a pair of guppies Henry buys at a sale. By midsummer the neighborhood is glutted with guppies and they are occupying his mother's entire supply of mason jars. This is a dilemma in the canning season! Then when the original owner of Ribsy turns up and claims his dog, Henry is in a still more serious spot. He earnestly wants to do the right thing, but he also wants Ribsy. The solution is a masterly piece of diplomacy.

There are several other books about Henry and even one about *Ribsy* (1964). Each book is built around a real struggle on Henry's part and involves some very funny situations before a hard-won success.

There are two delightful books about Henry's nemesis. Ramona is probably the first kindergarten dropout on record in *Ramona the Pest* (1968), having become convinced that the teacher, whom she adores, doesn't love her any more. We follow *Ramona the Brave* (1975) to first grade, where she finds the basics boring, but life still worth living. A serious problem for many children is presented in a realistic and encouraging way in *Mitch and Amy* (1967). Mitch and Amy are fourth-grade twins, he a slow reader and she a proficient one. They are, except when under attack, very competitive, yet it is Amy that finds the book that starts Mitch on the path to self-motivated reading.

Cleary's characters are real boys and girls, convincingly alive, and the style of the books is correspondingly plain and everyday, but filled with the type of humor that appeals to her young audience.

Meindert DeJong

The Wheel on the School
Journey from Peppermint Street

The Wheel on the School (1954), a tenderly told story which won the Newbery Medal, gives a remarkably detailed picture of life in a Dutch fishing village and also has unusual social values. The story begins in the tiny village school, when Lina, the only girl, asks, "Do you know about storks?" This leads to more questions, "Why are there no storks in Shora?" and "How can we bring them back?" These two questions launch a series of activities that begins with the six children and the schoolmaster but presently draws into the circle every person in the village. Everything is ready for the storks when a terrible storm kills or drives off course hundreds of the birds. But at last the storks do settle in Shora again.

Although the book is long for its story, it reads aloud wonderfully and can promote many discussions about the people, the lonely land of sea and sky that is Holland, and the wonder of those great birds that fly home all the way from Africa.

Journey from Peppermint Street (1968), which won the National Book Award for Children's Literature, is set in Holland in the early 1900s. Beautifully written, it is the story of a small boy who goes with his grandfather on a long night walk to visit an "inland aunt." The relationship between the old man and the child, the satisfaction at conquering his nervousness in a strange place, and the confidence gained by little Siebren as he meets new people, have a universality that transcends the setting.

Another story set in Holland is *Far Out the Long Canal* (1964). Because the ice has been bad for several years, and he has had a long illness, nine-year-old Moonta is the only child in town who cannot skate. Any reader can sympathize with his embarrassment, his secret struggles, and the alternate teasing and comfort he gets from friends and family. *The House of Sixty Fathers* (1956) is a vividly realistic story, set in China, of a boy who searches for his lost family.

Although DeJong's style is often repetitious and occasionally ponderous, he has the gift of wonder and delight. Whatever the outward action of his tales, it is the inner grace of his children and animals that moves readers, young or old. It is not surprising that in 1962 he won the Hans Christian Andersen International Award for his contribution to the world of children's literature.

Illustration by Maurice Sendak from The Wheel on the School *by Meindert DeJong. Copyright, 1954, by Meindert DeJong. Reprinted by permission of Harper & Row, Publishers, Inc.*

Natalie Savage Carlson

The Family Under the Bridge
The Happy Orpheline
The Empty Schoolhouse

Some of the gayest stories about Paris are Natalie Carlson's *The Family Under the Bridge* (1958) and her series about the Orphelines. *The Family Under the Bridge* has to do with the post–World War II period in Paris when housing was difficult to find. The hero is an elderly, jaunty hobo named Armand, completely averse to work, family life, and especially "starlings," as he calls children. Armand has found himself a snug corner under an old bridge. So imagine his horror to return

Illustration by Garth Williams from The Family Under the Bridge *by Natalie Savage Carlson. Pictures copyright © 1958 by Garth Williams. Reprinted by permission of Harper & Row, Publishers, Inc.*

there one night and find it occupied by three children. This is the beginning of the end for carefree, soft-hearted Armand. His series of adventures with the starlings are sometimes very funny and sometimes sad, but in the end he finds himself the adopted grandfather of a family. No pathos here, just a determined struggle for a stable, decent way of life.

The books about the Orphelines reverse the usual pattern of sad, sad orphans hoping to be adopted. These French orphans love their home to the point where their one fear is adoption. When in *The Happy Orpheline* (1957) poor Brigitte is about to be adopted, she knows she must perform a very wicked deed of some kind to prove she isn't fit for adoption. What she does is hilarious and makes a fitting if confused climax to the adventures of the twenty Orphelines who are still twenty strong at the end. *A Brother for the Orphelines* (1959) and *A Pet for the Orphelines* (1962) are fun, too, and follow the pattern of the others. Each chapter is a complete adventure in the course of which young readers see French life from a child's view.

Emma, who tells the story of *The Empty Schoolhouse* (1965), has dropped out of school but is proud of her bright little sister Lullah. Lullah is black, her friend Oralee white, and they are delighted that there is going to be an integrated school in their Louisiana parish. There is trouble, though, and parents keep their children away. When Lullah is hurt in a racial incident, the rift between her and Oralee grows—but it is healed, and the episode shocks some parents into a reversal of their decision. The first-person narrative gives consistency and immediacy to an honest and thoughtful story.

Ann Aurelia and Dorothy (1968) is another book about an interracial friendship, and *Marchers for the Dream* (1969) tells about an eleven-year-old girl who goes with her grandmother to Washington to join the Poor People's March. *The Half Sisters* (1970) and its sequel, *Luvvy and the Girls* (1970), are amusing stories about Luvvy, one of six sisters, who longs to be old enough to go away to a Catholic boarding school but finds when she does that there are adjustments to be made. Set early in the century, the stories have good period details and lively characters.

Whatever their settings, Carlson's stories have realistic characters who often display a gentle humor.

Keith Robertson

The *Henry Reed* stories

Children need books also which demonstrate that life is not always earnest, that it can in fact be highly entertaining. *Henry Reed, Inc.* (1958) is such a book. It is Henry's private journal. On a visit to his uncle and aunt who live in the country near Princeton, Henry hears all about the research at that university; so he decides to go into research. He takes over an old barn and paints an enormous sign: HENRY REED, RESEARCH. To the sign, a girl who finds her way into this intellectual domain adds: PURE AND APPLIED. She wants her name added too, but Henry is adamant—she must prove her worth first. Their research activities make this book hilarious reading.

Other Henry Reed stories are direct narrative, equally amusing and often mirroring some new social trend. In *Henry Reed's Big Show* (1970), for example, Henry and Midge put on a rock music festival. These books are highly exaggerated in the pace of their plots, but in every separate episode the activities of the ploymasters Henry and Midge are within the realm of possibility.

Robertson, a versatile author, writes another type of story in *In Search of a Sandhill Crane* (1973). Fifteen-year-old Link spends the summer with an elderly aunt in the Michigan woods, and becomes passionately interested in sandhill cranes. The story is well structured, with a wealth of natural lore, and sympathetic, convincing characters.

Mary Stolz

By the Highway Home
The Noonday Friends
A Wonderful, Terrible Time

Mary Stolz is a prolific author and one of the few authors who write with admirable perception for all ages. *A Dog on Barkham Street* (1960) and *The Bully of Barkham Steet* (1963) were considered in Chapter 1 as companion volumes that narrate the same events from different viewpoints.

In *By the Highway Home* (1971), the death of an older brother, the loss of the father's job, and a subsequent move to a new home create problems of adjustment for a girl of thirteen. A lost job also adds to the tensions in *The Noonday Friends* (1965), in which Franny can see her friend only at lunchtime because Franny must take care of her little brother after school. The story is perceptive in reflecting the way emotions are affected by circumstances and in drawing the relationship between Franny and the small brother who depends on her.

The two friends in *A Wonderful, Terrible Time* (1967) are black girls who go to an interracial summer camp. Sue Ellen is apprehensive; Mady is thrilled and enjoys every moment. Sue Ellen never wants to talk about serious things; Mady—whose father had been killed in a voter registration drive—does. Integration is not the issue of the book but is one of several problems considered to show the differences in the reactions of the two girls.

Illustration by Louis S. Glanzman for A Wonderful, Terrible Time *by Mary Stolz. Pictures copyright © 1967 by Louis S. Glanzman. Reproduced by permission of Harper & Row, Publishers, Inc.*

The problems a close-knit family faces when one of them—in this case the mother—dies, are honestly and perceptively described in *The Edge of Next Year* (1974). *Lands End* (1973) contrasts life for the only child of staid parents with that of a child from the large, noisy family next door.

Stolz brings a special sense of reality to her characters; they are well developed, sympathetically presented, and worth knowing.

Jean Little

Mine for Keeps
Home from Far
Look Through My Window

Born blind, Canadian Jean Little understands the child who is different, and has the ability to spin a good story which makes such differences natural and comprehensible. In *Mine for Keeps* (1962), Sally, who has cerebral palsy, comes home after five years at a school for handicapped children, her apprehension about getting along mixed with self-pity. Through the help of her family and through her own interest in others, Sally gradually overcomes her fears and becomes more independent. The story treats the difficulties of a handicapped child matter-of-factly and emphasizes the point that the family has to adjust to the situation and that each of them makes mistakes. In the sequel, *Spring Begins in March* (1966), Sally smooths the way of her little sister.

In *Home from Far* (1965) Jenny's twin brother Michael is killed, and soon after the accident, Jenny's parents bring two foster children into the home, one named Mike and the same age as Jenny. This is a sensitive study of the attitudes and emotions of children, particularly of Jenny, who at first bitterly resents Mike, and of Mike, who misses his real father.

Viewpoints

Fiction at its best, then, is the fruit of perfect self-identification of the writer with his materials—with beings, with situations, with objects, with time and place. It is the application of life of a heightened perception which experiences people and all things as if the writer *were* those people, those things. For the fiction writer "There, but for the grace of God, go I" is heightened to "There go I," is heightened to "While there is a poorer class, I belong to it, while there is a criminal class, I am of it, while there is a soul in jail, I am not free." It is the literal self-identification "with every fault, frailty and futility," and also with every magnification and enhancement of the human being. It is to see within, it is to see through, it is to see all material, as it were, as intimate and as *warm* as one's self. These walls, this separation of being which we set up and imagine, are specious. The appearance—and this is what the realist deals with—is separative; but the consciousness, which the creative writer deals with, is one.—Zona Gale, "Writing as Design," in *The Writer and His Craft,* edited by Roy W. Cowden, The University of Michigan Press, Ann Arbor, 1954, p. 35.

In *Look Through My Window* (1970) Emily's family takes in four little cousins whose mother is hospitalized. From resentment, Emily moves to love and acceptance, and her horizons are further broadened by a new friend who has one Jewish parent. The discussions between Emily and Kate are candid, those between Emily and her mother tender and sensible, and those between Kate and her father perceptive and honest, as they talk about what it is to be Jewish. In the sequel, *Kate* (1971), the girl moves further to explore her ambivalence and to discover why her father had severed connections with his family. Jean Little has a rare ability to see problems and their ramifications from the viewpoint of the child.

Marilyn Sachs

The *Amy and Laura* stories
The *Peter and Veronica* stories
Marv

In *Amy Moves In* (1964), Amy's family moves in the 1930s to another section of the Bronx; the pleasant family story about the Sterns ends with mother going into a hospital. In *Laura's Luck* (1956) Laura and Amy go off to camp, Laura jealous of her younger sister because she adjusts so much more easily. Laura gains confidence and decides she likes camp in a story that is, like the first book, lightly humorous and realistic in dealing with small problems. Not until the third book, *Amy and Laura* (1966), is there a real problem in interpersonal relationships. Laura finds it difficult to accept her invalid mother, away so long, and is relieved at the close of the story when Mama rebels and declares she is going to run her home and be a mother, not a liability.

In *Veronica Ganz* (1968) and *Peter and Veronica* (1969), Marilyn Sachs introduces a perennial bully who becomes friends with the smallest boy in class. Peter, in the second book, is first angry with his mother because she doesn't want his non-Jewish friend to come to his bar mitzvah, then—after he has persuaded his mother—angry at Veronica because she doesn't show up. Both in the candor with which Peter and Veronica discuss their mothers' prejudices and in the new maturity with which they mend their quarrel the story is honest and percipient. In later years, Veronica's daughter is named after a dead aunt who perished in a fire while warning others of the danger. But Mary Rose Ramirez finally learns *The Truth About Mary Rose* (1973): she was not a paragon.

Marv (1970) tells of a boy who admires his sister Frances more than anyone else in the world, and repeatedly tries to impress her with his accomplishments, always seeking her approval. There are poignant moments and funny ones, but the book's import is the resilience with which youth strives for competence and approval.

A broken home and a mother unable to face reality create a burden impossible for Fletcher and Fran Ellen to shoulder in *The Bears' House* (1971). Fantasies about the dollhouse in her classroom serve as a release for Fran Ellen's emotions. Finally, adults intervene in the situation. In *Dorrie's Book* (1975), the heroine copes with her feelings as five new members join a hitherto quiet family—triplet babies and two older abandoned children.

Sachs has a sympathetic understanding of children's concerns and problems, and handles conflicts between generations honestly and realistically. Her dialogue is fresh, breezy, and often very funny.

Illustration by Louise Fitzhugh from Harriet the Spy *by Louise Fitzhugh. Copyright © 1964 by Louise Fitzhugh. Reproduced by permission of Harper & Row, Publishers, Inc. and McIntosh and Otis, Inc.*

Louise Fitzhugh

Harriet the Spy
The Long Secret

The very funny and very touching story of *Harriet the Spy* (1964) aroused vigorous controversy for the portraits it drew of prying, quarrelsome Harriet and of her parents, too busy with their social life to pay much attention to their child until she was in real trouble. Eleven-year-old Harriet aspires to be a writer, and, encouraged by her nurse Ole Golly, keeps notes about everything that happens to her and her friends and to the people she studies on her after-school spy route. She keeps notes on her thoughts and observations, too, as when, on the way to see Ole Golly's "family," she writes:

> *This is incredible. Could Ole Golly have a family? I never thought about it. How could Ole Golly have a mother and father? She's too old for one thing and she's never said one word about them and I've known her since I was born. Also she doesn't get any letters. Think about this. This might be important.*

The sequel, *The Long Secret* (1965), is less intense, more sophisticated, and equally funny at times. Harriet, curious as ever but now on very close terms with her parents, is at the beach for the summer. So is the shy Beth of *Harriet the Spy*, now terrified because her mother, a jet set butterfly, has come to disrupt the quiet life Beth and her grandmother lead. The inclusion of an evangelist family, several jaded characters of the jet set, and a wise old man make the book more cluttered and not as effective as *Harriet*, but it has two episodes that are particularly perceptive. In one, Harriet and her mother have a serious discussion of faith and religion, and in the other Harriet and her friends talk about menstruation, a long-standing taboo subject in children's books.

While Harriet has problems many children don't want, she also has a brash courage many children envy. Her honesty makes her an irresistible character.

Robert Burch

Queenie Peavy
Simon and the Game of Chance

Queenie Peavy (1966) is a story of the Depression era, set in Georgia, where Queenie, thirteen, has a deserved reputation as a troublemaker and a hoyden. Fiercely loyal to her father, who is in jail, she faces a painful readjustment when he comes home, shows neither affection nor responsibility, breaks his parole, and is returned to jail. Queenie, a staunch little character, realizes that any change in her status must now come from her own changed attitude and behavior. Candid in treatment of the father, this is one of the books that lucidly exemplifies the end of the perfect-parent image in children's literature.

The father in *Simon and the Game of Chance* (1970) is also the harsh character of the story, stern and tyrannical, a man whose rigidity affects the whole life of the family. Simon's immediate problem is his fear that he is in some way responsible for the death of his sister's fiancé, since he had resented the planned marriage. Like Queenie, Simon adjusts in a way consistent with his character and his need to be loved and accepted.

Joey's Cat (1969), a pleasant story for younger children, is about a small black boy who is delighted when his mother changes her mind and lets him bring his cat and her kittens into the house.

Paula Fox

Maurice's Room
A Likely Place
The Stone-Faced Boy
Portrait of Ivan

With the publication of *Maurice's Room* (1966) it became immediately clear that Paula Fox was one of the best new writers in the field of children's literature. Her style is quiet, her vision penetrating, her understanding of children deep and sympathetic. Maurice is an only child whose room is a haven for anything and everything he finds. His parents attempt subtle distractions, but there is no stopping a born collector: when the family moves to the country, Maurice is bored until he sees the barn, full of Old Things.

A Likely Place (1967) is a testament to the joy of competence. Lewis, tired of the adults who want to help or to improve him, takes great delight in his friendship with an elderly gentleman who treats him as an equal.

In *The Stone-Faced Boy* (1968) a child who is shy and withdrawn in the midst of a boisterous family takes refuge in looking impassive. Only one elderly great-aunt sees what lies behind the stoic facade. This empathetic relationship between a child and someone outside his immediate family is used again in *Portrait of Ivan* (1969), in which lonely Ivan's friendship with the artist who is painting his portrait helps Ivan gain confidence to approach his busy, remote father. The writing is skilled, and the characters are superbly drawn. *Blowfish Live in the Sea* (1970) is discussed at some length in Chapter 2. *How Many Miles to Babylon?* (1967) is the story of a black child persecuted by a gang of older boys. With the historical novel, *The Slave Dancer* (1973), Fox won the Newbery Medal.

Eleanor Clymer

My Brother Stevie
The Spider, the Cave and the Pottery Bowl
The House on the Mountain

"She was always going away, even before Pa died, and leaving us with Grandma," twelve-

Drawings copyright © 1971 by Ingrid Fetz
From The Spider, the Cave, and the Pottery Bowl
by Eleanor Clymer
Used by permission of Atheneum Publishers

year-old Annie says of her mother in *My Brother Stevie* (1967). This is a sober and convincing story about what can happen to children who feel rejected. Annie worries about the gang her younger brother is in, but her concern is not as effective as the affection of a wise, warm teacher. Another book with an urban setting, *The Big Pile of Dirt* (1968), tells a story of children with no play space who enjoy the pile of dirt left by demolition. It is all the more poignant for being told in matter-of-fact style.

In *The Spider, the Cave and the Pottery Bowl* (1971) young Kate goes back to her mother's home on the mesa, the Indian village where grandmother teaches her to make pottery. The story is a simple one, but it is imbued with the dignity of tradition and has a positive approach: Kate is irked when a white tourist is patronizing but she is no less proud of her heritage.

The House on the Mountain (1971) has a slight plot, but in the story of a group of black children, enthralled by a little house they see on a country outing, there is a touching yearning for space and beauty, and a moving pride in their dignified withdrawal when the angry owners find them inside the house.

The story of Julius, who was placed with his younger half-brother in a children's shelter, is told in *Luke Was There* (1973). Luke, a black social worker, becomes the one stable person in Julius's life. When Luke leaves to do alternate service as a conscientious objector, Julius runs away. The resolution of the story shows Julius growing in understanding as sympathetic adults help him.

Clymer's writing skill is evident in her use of contemporary themes and the freshness she brings to each story.

Zilpha Keatley Snyder

The Egypt Game
The Changeling

One of the notable books of 1967 and a Newbery Honor Book, *The Egypt Game* is an absorbing story of sustained, imaginative group play and of interracial friendship. Surprisingly for a child's book, the characters include a murderer who almost captures one of the girls. The children are vividly real, their Egypt Game absorbing, their conversation and personalities distinctive.

In *The Changeling* (1970) a quiet child from a conservative family becomes friends with an unusual girl and only years later realizes how much the disreputable and wildly imaginative Ivy contributed to her own growth and flexibility.

The interest of the young in astrology and the supernatural is reflected in *The Headless Cupid* (1971), in which an unhappy adolescent persuades her newly acquired stepbrothers and stepsisters to become her disciples in the occult. Only when there seems to be evidence of a poltergeist does Amanda lose her pose of superiority. *The Velvet Room* (1965) is the story of Robin, one of the children in a family of migrant workers, who finds a haven in the Velvet Room, the library of a deserted house. While there are elements of mystery, the book is less a mystery than a story of the need for security and belonging.

In *The Witches of Worm* (1972) Snyder explores the problems of a girl angry at her whole world, who says that Worm, her cat, makes her do witchlike things.

These stories are realistic but often involve some supernatural elements which give them an eeriness seldom found in children's books at this level.

Virginia Hamilton

Zeely
The Time-Ago Tales of Jahdu
M. C. Higgins, the Great

A gifted black writer, Virginia Hamilton has shown versatility with each of her books. In *Zeely* (1967) a child visiting in the country is smitten by the beauty of a neighbor who looks like a Watusi queen. The book is impressive both as a picture of a girl's crush on an adult and as a record of a child's growing understanding of racial identity.

The danger posed by the Cumberland Mountain slag heap under whose shadow his family lives makes M.C., thirteen, long to have his family move. But M.C.'s experiences with a folklorist and a girl from "outside," as well as his father's attachment to his ancestral home, make his dreams seem impossible. *M. C. Higgins, the Great* (1974), written in an intricate yet graceful style, won both the Newbery Award and the National Book Award in 1975.

In *The Time-Ago Tales of Jahdu* (1969) and *Time-Ago Lost; More Tales of Jahdu* (1973), Lee Edward stays each day with Mama Luka until his mother is home from work, and each day he hears another story of the legendary Jahdu, crafty and powerful. The tales are beautifully told in the folk tradition, and the small boy learns the joy of being black and proud.

The House of Dies Drear (1968) is a dramatic story set in an old house that had been a station on the Underground Railroad; and *The Planet of Junior Brown* (1971), a memorable book for older readers, is an imaginative and touching story of a friendship between two boys who are loners, each in a different way.

Hamilton is a skilled writer, presenting the black experience with singular distinction of style and viewpoint, and with nuances of meaning for the more mature or culturally aware reader.

Illustration from Zeely by Virginia Hamilton. Illustrations by Symeon Shimin. Illustration © Macmillan, 1967.

Vera and Bill Cleaver

Ellen Grae
Where the Lilies Bloom
I Would Rather Be a Turnip

Although there had been other books about children of divorce before *Ellen Grae* (1967) was published, none had so firmly stated by implication the fact that a parent's love and responsibility are not changed by divorce. Ellen Grae tells her own story, and it becomes instantly apparent that she is an accomplished and artistic teller of tall tales and that she is a child with great sensitivity and loyalty. Despite the seriousness of the problem that faces Ellen Grae and despite its less than satisfactory resolution, the story is permeated with humor. Its sequel, *Lady Ellen Grae,* has less impact but is written with vivacity and sharp characterization. The hero of *Grover* (1970) is

Ellen Grae's friend, and his adjustment to his mother's suicide (she has cancer) and to his father's grief is described in a story that shows the sensitivity of the young.

The heroine of *Where the Lilies Bloom* (1969) is one of the strongest characters in children's fiction. Fourteen-year-old Mary Call Luther buries her father herself, and valiantly tries to hold together the family—which includes a mentally retarded older sister—so that the four children will not be sent to a county charity home. This is an excellent example of the need for security as well as of the need to achieve. Another strong character, Fern Drawn in *Dust of the Earth* (1975), works at the difficult job of sheepherding to help her family survive, and has the joy of seeing a disparate group of children and parents become a united family.

In *I Would Rather Be a Turnip* (1971) twelve-year-old Annie Jelks faces a problem that is seldom presented in children's books, the acceptance of an illegitimate child. Annie is aware that everyone in her small town knows that her sister's child was born out of wedlock, and when eight-year-old Calvin comes to live with Annie and her father, she is jealous of her father's love for the boy and apprehensive about the feelings of her friends. The Cleavers deal perceptively with the intricacies of serious problems yet lighten the stories with humor. These books are prime examples of the changes that have occurred in what has been considered appropriate in children's books.

Elaine Konigsburg

From the Mixed-Up Files of Mrs. Basil E. Frankweiler
Jennifer, Hecate, Macbeth, William McKinley, and Me, Elizabeth
(George)
About the B'nai Bagels

In 1968 Elaine Konigsburg made history in children's books when her *From the Mixed-Up Files of Mrs. Basil E. Frankweiler* was awarded the Newbery Medal and her *Jennifer, Hecate, Macbeth, William McKinley, and Me, Elizabeth* was voted a Newbery Honor Book. They were her first two books. *From the*

Copyright © 1967 by E. L. Konigsburg
From From the Mixed-Up Files of Mrs. Basil E. Frankweiler
Used by permission of Atheneum Publishers

Mixed-Up Files is an engaging story of two children who leave home and take up residence in the Metropolitan Museum of Art, the details of the expedition capably planned by the older child, Claudia. The unlikely setting is made believable by the bland perfection of details.

Jennifer, Hecate is a story of interracial friendship and sustained imaginative play in which Jennifer, a self-declared witch, permits Elizabeth (who tells the story) to become her apprentice. Both in the relationship between the two protagonists and in their relationships to others there is delightful warmth and humor.

(George) (1970) deals with a serious problem, the schizoid personality, yet the book has high humor, tenderness, and a lively plot. The distinctive achievement of *(George)* is that it enables the reader to see that the child with

psychological problems is not beyond the pale: Ben is human, intelligent, loving.

About the B'nai Bagels (1969) is a cheerful story, less dramatic than the other Konigsburg books, but enjoyable for the felicity with which Mark describes the awfulness of having his mother manage his Little League team, the nervous pleasure of his first look at a girly magazine, and the indignation aroused by his first encounter with anti-Semitism. *Altogether, One at a Time* (1971) is a collection of four deftly written short stories, different in plot and mood, alike in their theme of compromise with circumstance. *The Dragon in the Ghetto Caper* (1974) tells of the friendship between lonely, eleven-year-old Andy and Edie, a lonely housewife, as they unwittingly become involved in the numbers racket.

Whatever her theme, Konigsburg's stories are amusingly told, with solid substance underneath.

Constance Greene

A Girl Called Al
I Know You, Al

There is poignant sympathy for the girl in Constance Greene's *A Girl Called Al* (1969). Plump and caustic, Al is a nonconformist who is won over by the understanding friendship of the building superintendent and who is catapulted into maturity by his death. *I Know You, Al* (1975) tells us more about Al as she faces the problems in her life: being the only girl in the class who hasn't yet begun to menstruate, being too plump, not liking her mother's suitor, and meeting the father she hasn't seen for eight years. Both these stories are entertaining, warm, and perceptive.

Greene turns to boys and their problems in *The Unmaking of Rabbit* (1972). Paul is shorter than the other boys in his class and has large ears that stick out. He lives with Gran; his mother, even when she remarries, has no place for him. Paul gathers his courage, reads a paper in class about refusing to join a group for break-ins, and is invited to join another group for sleep-outs. He firmly renounces the name Rabbit. *The Ears of Louis* (1974) are also large, but Louis learns to overlook the teasing. Both stories are realistic and written with ease and humor, with sympathetic characters who have believable problems.

Maria Gripe

Hugo and Josephine
The Night Daddy

In her stories about Swedish children, Maria Gripe has shown us that children have similar problems, no matter what their country of origin. *Josephine* (1970), *Hugo* (1970), and *Hugo and Josephine* (1969) describe the problems of the preacher's youngest daughter, who's not sure she's wanted, in and out of school, and her relationship with Hugo, a true individualist. Hugo comes to school when he can spare the time from more important forest pursuits, but he is so gravely sensible and logical that even the teacher accepts his behavior. Josephine learns from Hugo to question other people's conclusions and interpretations, and not to be jealous when Hugo has other friends.

The Night Daddy (1971) and *Julia's House* (1975) tell of the relationship between Julia and Peter, who stays with her when her nurse mother is on night duty. The affection that grows between the two is sympathetically depicted. In the second book we see an older Julia, dividing her loyalties now between Peter and her school friends and teacher. In the meantime, Peter's attention has been caught by a small boy who appears as the main character in *Elvis and His Secret* (1976) and *Elvis and His Friends* (1976). Peter's supportive affection helps Elvis to find his own identity.

Winner of the Hans Christian Andersen Award in 1974, Gripe is distinguished for the depth of her characterizations and the sensitivity with which she portrays relationships. She has the rare ability to be childlike without being childish; she understands the children and so do we. We enter willingly into their joys and sorrows, defeats and triumphs.

Judy Blume

Are You There God? It's Me, Margaret
Then Again, Maybe I Won't

Judy Blume has written a number of frank stories that discuss problems formerly referred to only in veiled terms in books for children. In *Are You There God? It's Me, Margaret* (1970), Margaret and her friends are concerned with physical maturity: when will they begin to menstruate? and when will their breasts develop? Margaret is also confused about religion; will she be Jewish like her father or Christian like her mother? She doesn't solve all her problems but does decide that her faith is strong, that she can worship in her own way, whatever her formal affiliation.

In *Then Again, Maybe I Won't* (1971), Blume writes with sympathetic insight about an adolescent boy disturbed by his family's changed attitude when they become well-to-do, and by his first sexual stirrings. Karen adjusts to divorce in *It's Not the End of the World* (1972), and in both *Deenie* (1973) and *Blubber* (1974), the protagonists are troubled by adjustment to physical handicaps, concerned not only with their health but also with the effects that their appearance may have on their peer groups.

Blume is astute in her choices of contemporary themes; her dialogue is natural, her characters believable, and her style direct and unaffected. Her stories have a pervasive sense of humor as well as an affectionate understanding of children and young people.

Viewpoints

In the name of realism, book reviewers applaud books crammed with relentless, so-called documentation of pathology flowering from a pivotal, perverted faith in a pathogenic, miserable and hopeless condition of being which is, allegedly, our realistic condition. In the name of realism, the writer finds himself or herself encouraged or forcibly spurred to invent problems, to build conflicts, to design characters of incredible fallibility and self-centered inconsequence.

In the name of realism, the equally creative work of inventing solutions or of inhibiting the development of conflicts by designing characters or their environment so that conflict would seem actually contrived, or of research obdurately directed toward uncovering of little known genuine heroes, heroines, and verifiable happy and peaceful ways of living—this equally creative work, more often than not, is unmistakably discouraged and ridiculed, even at the proposed stage when the publisher and the other media get hold of a creative writer and thinker.—June Jordan. From "Young People: Victims of Realism in Books and in Life," *Wilson Library Bulletin*, October 1973, p. 143. Copyright © 1973 by The H. W. Wilson Company. Reprinted by permission.

Other Books for the Middle Group

In books for children, realism in the 1970s tends to mirror the contemporary scene, but there have been fine realistic stories written in the past and so vividly true to life that they, too, are enjoyed by today's children. One of these is Ruth Sawyer's Newbery Medal book, *Roller Skates* (1936), in which ten-year-old Lucinda makes friends as she skates about New York. Another example is Ursula Nordstrom's *The Secret Language* (1960), in which a homesick child adjusts to the pattern of life at boarding school. Louisa Shotwell's *Roosevelt Grady* (1963) concerns a migrant family's desire for a settled life and educational opportunities.

One of the notable developments in the books of the 1970s has been the increasing number of stories about lively, independent girls. Meg is an eleven-year-old who starts a consciousness-raising group in *The Manifesto and Me—Meg* (1974) by Bobbi Katz. Maggie, of Dorothy Crayder's *She, the Adventuress* (1973), proves self-reliant when she travels alone on a ship bound for Italy. With brotherly and parental support, Barbara takes over her brother's newspaper route, overturning company rules in *The Real Me* (1974) by Betty Miles.

As is true of books for other age groups, books for the middle group show an increased awareness of children's concern with such situations as death, particularly the death of a family member; adjustment to living with grandparents; and the relationship between children and mentally retarded siblings. Betsy Byars won the Newbery Medal in 1971 for *Summer of the Swans*, the story of a sister's care and responsibility for a mentally retarded brother. Both her *After the Goat Man* (1974) and *The House of Wings* (1972) deal perceptively with boys and their relationships with grandfathers who have lived solitary lives. In Kathryn Ewing's *A Private Matter*

(1975), a child who lives alone with her mother, and who has accepted an elderly neighbor as substitute father, must adjust to his moving away. Another kind of acceptance is needed in Rose Blue's *Grandma Didn't Wave Back* (1972), wherein a child reluctantly accepts the fact that only a nursing home will provide the constant care Grandma needs. *A Taste of Blackberries* (1973) by Doris Buchanan Smith candidly explores the grief and guilt felt by a boy when his best friend dies of a bee sting.

Maturity and perspective gained through the solution of problems in personal relationships are particularly well handled in Eleanor Cameron's *A Room Made of Windows* (1971) in which a self-centered adolescent learns to respond to the needs of others. *To the Green Mountains* (1975), also by Cameron, is a skillful evocation of life in a small town for Kath, whose mother manages a hotel and supports a ne'er-do-well husband. The intricacies of relationships are delicately explored, as Kath matures enough to understand others' difficulties and how they affect her own problems.

Illustration from Me and Arch and the Pest *by John Durham, Illustrations by Ingrid Fetz. Copyright © 1970 by Ingrid Fetz. Reprinted by permission of Four Winds Press, a division of Scholastic Magazines, Inc.*

Among the many books now available about black children in the United States, some have an interracial theme while others are about only black children. Two good examples of the former are John Durham's *Me and Arch and the Pest* (1970), the story of two boys who acquire a large dog, especially appealing because of the warm relationships, the natural dialogue, and the candid, casual way in which Arch and Bit discuss their parents' unreasonable attitudes toward large dogs, the difference in their color (Bit is white, Arch black) and the difference between natural speech and schoolroom language, and Barbara Cohen's *Thank You, Jackie Robinson* (1974), the story of a fatherless white boy whose mother runs an inn and who finds a man-to-man relationship with Davey, the black chef, who likes baseball as much as Sam does. Some of the excellent stories in the latter group are *Sister* (1974) by Eloise Greenfield, Bette Greene's *Philip Hall Likes Me. I Reckon Maybe* (1974), Betty Erwin's *Behind the Magic Line* (1969), and Michele Murray's *Nellie Cameron* (1971). In *Sister,* a girl of thirteen is torn between finding her own path to maturity and following that of an older sister whom she's always adored but who now seems to be heading for trouble. In Greene's story about a loving family of rural Arkansas, the protagonist is an eleven-year-old who is torn between admiration for her first love and a stifled conviction that she's as bright as he is—maybe brighter. *Behind the Magic Line* is also a good family story, but more serious in its presentation of the problems of ghetto living. Nellie Cameron has a troubling personal problem, her feelings of rejection complicated by academic failure; attendance at a reading clinic gives her new confidence based on success.

Children's problems are much alike everywhere in the world despite the fascinating differences of setting and idiomatic language. This is true of Rumer Godden's *The Kitchen Madonna* (1967), a tender story about an aloof child who reaches out to help the homesick Ukrainian maid in his London home, and equally true of E. W. Hildick's *Louie's Snowstorm* (1974), a funny, fast-paced Christmas story in which an American girl plays a lively role. One is an urban story of a single child, told in graceful, polished prose, and the other a rollicking tale of a group of children, but both reflect basic needs. In *What the Neighbors Did and Other Stories* (1973), A. Philippa Pearce tells eight warm, realistic tales about children in a Cambridgeshire village. All British books, each is unique.

The Australian stories of Reginald Ottley and Joan Phipson, too, demonstrate that children are much the same wherever they happen to live, but the most moving story from an Australian author is probably Patricia Wrightson's *A Racecourse for Andy* (1968), its main character a gentle, mentally retarded child whose mistaken belief that he owns a race track is treated with great sympathy and understanding by all his friends.

The universality of childhood experience is clear in Hilda Van Stockum's Irish stories about the O'Sullivan family, in Shirley Arora's tale of a boy in India, *"What Then, Raman?"* (1960), in books from all parts of the world. The mother who works while father studies is a familiar phenomenon in our country, but nobody has been more perceptive about the implications of this life-style for children than Anne-Cath. Vestly in her story of a Norwegian family, *Hello, Aurora* (1974). Mary-Joan Gerson, in *Omoteji's Baby Brother* (1974), explores the effect of a baby's advent for a small Nigerian boy. Uganda in the 1940s is the setting for a quiet, serious story of the effects of education for *Mukasa* (1973) by John Nagenda. Through these books children may learn to feel more at home in their expanded world.

Books for Older Children

Although there have been many changes in realistic fiction for younger children and for children in the middle group, the most striking changes have been in realistic fiction for older children. In the most recent books, subjects which were once taboo or elided, such as premarital pregnancy or illegitimate children, are fairly common, and the image of the perfect parent appears in fewer and fewer stories. Problems that confront today's youth are treated with understanding: the generation gap, the drug scene, the dissatisfaction with a materialistic society. And the language used reflects the speech of today, both in the admission of words that were once considered shocking and in the use of black English. Some of the stories are didactic, but the best fiction can win young people because it shows their world and its relationships as they know them to be.

Evelyn Sibley Lampman

Treasure Mountain
Navaho Sister
Half-Breed

Evelyn Lampman has concentrated on writing stories about Native American children who are faced with conflicting ways of life. In *Treasure Mountain* (1949) an American Indian brother and sister from a government school spend a summer with their great-aunt who is a full-blooded "blanket Indian." Accustomed to white ways, the children at first are shocked by their aunt's customs and beliefs, but as the summer passes their respect and love for her grow. The title comes from the children's hunt for treasure to raise the money for taxes, but the primary interest in this story lies in their deepened appreciation of values in the old ways of life as well as in the new.

In *Navaho Sister* (1956) orphaned Sad Girl goes to a government school where she feels isolated and is thoroughly unhappy. The episodes in the book bring out the difficult adjustment a Native American child must make to a modern school. Sad Girl's need to be more outgoing and tolerant is a problem in social adjustment most children can understand.

The story of a twelve-year-old *Half-Breed* (1967) is set in Oregon Territory, where Hardy has come to find his white father and finds instead an aunt who had not known Hardy existed. Hardy is homesick and his father is too much of a wanderer to make a home for his son, but the boy becomes so fond of Aunt Rhody that he is content. The plot is thin, but the style, the setting, and the boy's need to belong and to establish his identity are strong.

In *The Year of Small Shadow* (1971) an eleven-year-old American Indian boy comes to stay with a white lawyer for a year while his father is in jail. While visiting his aunt in Montana, Jamie becomes friendly with a Cheyenne boy, and helps him replace a medicine bag in its rightful burial site in *Rattlesnake Cave* (1974), a story which has good style and good pace.

Lampman always treats Native American culture and beliefs with respect, and her stories show children coping with change while keeping what's good from the past.

Ann Nolan Clark

Secret of the Andes
Santiago
Medicine Man's Daughter

In My Mother's House (1941) and *Secret of the Andes* (1952) represent something of Clark's range of experience with primitive peoples. Furthermore, she is able to interpret their ways of life so that modern children respect them, and her writing reflects her love for them. *Secret of the Andes*, a Newbery Medal winner, is the story of a dedicated Peruvian Indian boy, the last of a royal line, who has been brought up in the mountains and grows to understand his heritage and his responsibilities. *Santiago* (1955) is about a Guatemalan youth, raised in a Spanish home but determined to find his place in the world as an Indian. Both of these perceptive stories are beautifully written. *Medicine Man's Daughter* (1963) is the story of a girl who, at fifteen, has been chosen by her father as his successor. Stunned when a white man heals a child she cannot help, Tall-Girl rides off to a mission school and in time learns to appreciate the values of both cultures. The story moves slowly, but the information about Navaho life is interesting and the book sustains the mood of Tall-Girl's dedication.

For younger children Clark has written books that give authentic pictures of the life and ideals of the desert Indians. For older and younger children, she writes with a sense of the inner life and ideals of a people. Her cadenced prose is beautiful and unique.

Joseph Krumgold

. . . and now Miguel
Onion John

Joseph Krumgold has given the preadolescent two fine stories of growing up, both winners of the Newbery Medal.

The members of young Miguel's family in *. . . and now Miguel* (1953) have been sheepherders for generations, first in Spain, now in the Southwest country around Santa Fe, New Mexico. Twelve-year-old Miguel is struggling to prove to his father that he is as mature and competent a sheep man as his adored brother Gabriel, who is eighteen. This is a universal problem, differing only in its symbols for the city boy, the coastal boy, or Miguel, the sheepherder. His attempts to prove his maturity and responsibility supply the action of the story. After many disheartening blunders, success comes, but it is tempered with regret. This book, written in the first person, may have to be introduced to children, but it is well worth the time and effort. Here are strong family love and loyalty with a profound respect for the family tradition of work, and here is pride in the expert performance of that work. Here too is the hero worship of a younger for an older brother. There is a feeling for the cycle of the seasons, each one bringing its special work and special satisfactions. And finally there is a closeness to God that makes prayer a natural part of life.

Onion John (1959) was not so universally approved as *Miguel* but it too is concerned with problems in family relationships that are part of growing up. Andy is temporarily fascinated by a picturesque old hobo who lives in a shanty at the edge of town. This hero worship causes the first rift between Andy and his father. The story of the whole town trying to uplift and "do good" to the old tramp is an exceedingly funny and characteristic bit of Americana. But not until Onion John has fled from his do-gooders does Andy realize that he would rather be exactly like his father—the respected owner of the town hardware store—than anyone else.

In *Henry 3* (1967) a boy and his family are in a setting of suburban affluence that seems to encourage conformist behavior. The boy is disturbed by the values of adults and the superficial standards by which many people live.

Florence Crannell Means

Knock at the Door, Emmy
Us Maltbys
Our Cup Is Broken

Knock at the Door, Emmy (1956) is the story of the child of a migrant family who is bent on receiving an education, using public libraries avidly, going to school whenever she can. Emmy's single-minded tenacity finally brings her a college scholarship and a chance to reach her goal of doing social work with migrant people.

Us Maltbys (1966) is an excellent book about the acceptance of foster children. The two Maltby girls are stunned when their parents announce that they are going to take in five teenage girls with problems, and both the Maltby girls and their foster-sisters have a slow and often painful period of adjustment. Mrs. Maltby then decides to test the town rule that no black may stay overnight and brings home a baby boy after the family has discussed her proposal and agreed to it. Hoping that little Jamie will charm people into accepting him, the Maltbys give a party—and their hopes are realized. This is an interesting contrast to John Neufeld's *Edgar Allan* (see bibliography), in which the outcome is quite different.

Our Cup Is Broken (1969) is heavy with tragedy, but it is, like other books by Means, a searching exploration of a social problem. Sarah had lived with a white family since she was twelve, and went back to her Hopi village in deep despair because the parents of the white boy who was in love with her had ruthlessly broken up the attachment. She found herself no more at home in the Hopi community than she had been in the white, and the bitter story of intercultural conflict ends with marriage and a move to a new community only after Sarah has been raped and borne a blind child.

Shuttered Windows (1938), which was one of the earliest books to portray blacks realistically, describes the problems faced by a young girl from the north who comes to a South Carolina island.

Jean George

My Side of the Mountain
Julie of the Wolves

My Side of the Mountain (1959) is the record of a New York City boy who breaks away from his family to prove that he can maintain life completely on his own in a mountain wilder-

Illustration by John Schoenherr from Julie of the Wolves *by Jean Craighead George. Illustrations copyright © 1972 by John Schoenherr. Reproduced by permission of Harper & Row, Publishers, Inc.*

ness for a year. This competent young nonconformist writes, "I am on my mountain in a tree home that people have passed without ever knowing I am here. The house is a hemlock tree six feet in diameter, and must be as old as the mountain itself." How fourteen-year-old Sam perfects his house and how he makes a lamp from deer fat in a turtle's shell, clothes from deerskins, flour from acorns, and a balanced diet from roots, wild onions, leaves, and livers of animals make absorbing reading. Only the concluding reunion with his family seems mildly contrived.

In *Julie of the Wolves* (1972), George not only tells the story of a girl caught between two cultures—Eskimo and white—but offers fascinating facts about the ways of the wolves. Julie learns to communicate with a small pack of wolves and thus gets food when she is starving on the Arctic tundra. The book won the Newbery Medal and is a good example of George at her best; she is more a naturalist than a narrator, and excels in descriptions of wilderness flora and fauna.

Dorothy Sterling

Mary Jane

Dorothy Sterling's *Mary Jane* (1959) faces fully the violence that met the first black children to try out school integration in a segregated community. Mary Jane's grandfather is a scientist and former college professor, living in quiet retirement on his farm. When Mary Jane tells him that in the autumn she is going to enter the white high school in order to get certain subjects not taught in their segregated school, her grandfather tries gently to prepare her for trouble. When she returns home, her lawyer father tries to do so also, but Mary Jane is adamant. Nothing, not even her father and the police escort, has prepared her for the jeering, howling mob shouting, "Go back to Africa," or the white mothers' faces distorted with hate, yelling, "Pull her black curls out," or the boys inside the school chanting, "We don't want her. . . . She's too black for me." Mary Jane is frightened right down to the pit of her stomach, but, along with one black boy, she keeps her chin up and stays in school.

The indignities they suffer in and out of school are many, but Mary Jane wins the friendship of one white girl. With Sally's encouragement and the understanding kindness and backing of two teachers, Mary Jane hangs on. By the year's end, things are better and the future a shade more hopeful. Is this too easy and too quick a conclusion? Who can say? Another middle-class story, *Mary Jane* was a strong statement at the time it appeared. Both black and white children must have courage and hope. Books can help to build both.

Madeleine L'Engle

Meet the Austins

Meet the Austins (1960), another family-centered book, is one of the first since *Little Women* to handle the death of a loved one so well.

The story begins in a modern kitchen where mother is preparing a gala dinner for a visiting relative. The small children are underfoot with dog and toys, the twelve-year-old daughter is doing her homework, and the record player is midway through Brahms's Second Piano Concerto when the telephone rings. It announces the death of a beloved uncle in an airplane crash. The next night, realizing that the two oldest children are not sleeping, the mother gets them up and dressed and they drive up the mountain to talk. The children demand bitterly why God had to take a good man like Uncle Hal, and the mother replies, "Sometimes it's very hard to see the hand of God instead of the blind finger of Chance. That's why I wanted to come out where we could see the stars." They talk it out quietly in between long, healing silences, and then they go home. The children's ups and downs, a serious brother-sister conflict, some funny and some grave situations—all develop against a background of family love. This is a fine family story, as unusual and provocative a book as is the first chapter.

The Moon by Night (1963) is a sequel in which the family goes on a camping trip and Vicky, now fourteen, is concerned with some of the problems of a maturing adolescent: boys, faith, prejudice, and society's values.

Aimée Sommerfelt

The Road to Agra
Miriam
My Name Is Pablo

Aimée Sommerfelt is a distinguished Norwegian writer whose familiarity with India gives *The Road to Agra* (1961) a convincing background. It won the Norwegian State Prize for Children's Literature, as did its sequel, *The White Bungalow* (1964). In the first book, a boy of thirteen takes his small sister on the long trek to Agra, where he hopes her rapidly deteriorating eyesight can be saved. Turned away from the hospital, the children are picked up and cared for by a UNICEF unit. Impressed by this, Lalu decides, in the second book, to become a doctor—but he is needed at home, and is himself surprised that he is content to stay there. The books give a vivid picture of Indian village life, but their power lies in the universality of the theme of the choice that many young people must make.

Miriam (1963) is the story of a Jewish family in occupied Norway during World War II, a candid picture of the range of attitudes toward Jews among the Norwegians, and, again, a book with far wider implications than the immediate setting.

My Name Is Pablo (1966) is set in Mexico City, where young Pablo has been sent to a reformatory for shining shoes without a license. Released, he fears reprisal from two tough boys who have tried to get him to help them sell marijuana. Colorful and candid, the book gives a stirring picture of the pressures that operate on the poor in an urban environment.

Emily Neville

It's Like This, Cat
Berries Goodman
Garden of Broken Glass

There is no startling drama in *It's Like This, Cat* (1963), a Newbery Medal book, but it is impressive both for its lightly humorous, easy style and the fidelity with which it portrays a fourteen-year-old boy, Dave, who tells the story. Dave has found the first girl with whom he really feels comfortable (her mother is delightfully sketched as an urban intellectual), and he learns, by seeing the relationship between his father and his friend, that his father really is a pretty good guy. The experience of seeing one's parents through a friend's eyes is a common one, usually revelatory and seldom touched on in books for young people.

Berries Goodman (1965) looks back on the two years in which his family lived in a suburb, years in which he had a friend who was Jewish and learned the subtle signs of adult prejudice: the nuances of tone and the light dismissal of subjects with painful implications. He also learns that Sidney's mother is just as biased. The book is an invitation to better understanding, and its serious import is not lessened by a light humor.

A convincing tale of urban life, set in a lower-class St. Louis neighborhood, *Garden of Broken Glass* (1975) is the story of four eighth-graders and their intertwined lives. Brian, white, is in a depressed state most of the time because of his alcoholic mother. Dwayne, Melvita, and Martha, black, deal with their problems practically and help Brian grow in understanding.

Neville understands adolescents and their need to work out relationships and roles. Her style is matter-of-fact but quietly compelling.

Ivan Southall

Hills End
Ash Road
Let the Balloon Go

One of Australia's most notable writers of children's books, Ivan Southall is particularly adept at placing his child characters in a situation of stress or danger, and showing in realistic and exciting fashion how the common sense and courage of the young can prevail over obstacles. In *Hills End* (1963) a group of children who have been exploring a cave with their teacher come back to find their hometown flooded and deserted, and so they organize for survival and rehabilitation. In *Ash Road* (1966), which won the Australian Children's Book of the Year Award, three boys

Reprinted with permission of Macmillan Publishing Co., Inc. from Benson Boy by Ivan Southall, illustrations by Ingrid Fetz. Illustration Copyright © 1973 by Macmillan Publishing Co., Inc.

who have been careless while camping start a bush fire. The suspense is built by Southall's use of fragmented incidents fitted together in jigsaw pattern.

Many of Southall's books concern a group, but in *Let the Balloon Go* (1968) the supreme effort of a spastic child, the great achievement of climbing a tree, is as tense and exciting as the flood or the fire of the earlier books. The theme of the story is that all young people want a chance to make their own decisions and take their own risks. Perry of *Benson Boy* (1973) must get his mother, who's having a baby, to the hospital on a wild, stormy night after his father has been knocked unconscious by a fall. This calls not only for physical strength and courage, but for the fortitude to ask help from an estranged neighbor. All of Southall's books combine a faith in the abilities of the young and a dramatic setting in which they demonstrate their capability. *To the Wild Sky* (1967) also won the Book of the Year Award in Australia.

Hila Colman

Classmates by Request
The Girl from Puerto Rico
Claudia, Where Are You?

Carla is one of a group of white high-school students who have asked to transfer to an all-black school in *Classmates by Request* (1964). Her overtures of friendship are rejected by Ellen, who has remained aloof from her family's participation in the campaign for civil rights and who is angry because neither her father nor any other black man was asked to serve on a commission appointed by Carla's father. It is Ellen's father who emerges as the pacifier, stating bluntly that he is not qualified and should not have been asked, and that his friendship with Carla's father is not impaired. The two girls end by marching together in a demonstration. The ending is a bit pat, but the subjects of school integration and race relations are made an integral part of the story rather than a springboard, and the changing attitudes of Ellen and Carla develop naturally out of events.

The Girl from Puerto Rico (1961) has a slight plot but a warm understanding of the situation of the newly arrived Puerto Rican who comes to the United States in happy anticipation and is unprepared for cultural differences, dismayed by housing conditions, and shocked by the discrimination against her people.

A story about the generation gap, *Claudia, Where Are You?* (1969), is Colman's most effectively written book. The chapters tell the story, alternately, from Claudia's point of view and from her mother's. A successful woman who deludes herself into thinking always that everything around her is just what she wants it to be, Claudia's mother cannot understand her daughter's rebellion against her own values. Claudia runs away to the East Village, calling on her parents only when she needs money. Her distraught mother cannot understand Claudia's need for freedom; Claudia cannot live in suburban affluence. The characterization is excellent, the theme universal, the unsweetened ending faithful to the theme.

The difficulties of early marriage are candidly explored in *After the Wedding* (1975). Colman writes easily and prolifically on current themes.

Maia Wojciechowska

Shadow of a Bull
Tuned Out
"Don't Play Dead Before You Have To"

Shadow of a Bull (1964) richly deserved its Newbery Award, for in the conflict of a Spanish boy torn between his inclination and obligation, there are the themes of youth's similar conflict in any time and place, and of the courage of a boy who dares to admit he is afraid. Manolo, whose father had been the greatest bullfighter in Spain, is being trained in his footsteps by the hopeful elders of his Andalusian village. He knows himself a coward, yet he practices and prays—and when he is eleven and has had his first experience in the ring, he decides he is through.

In *Tuned Out* (1968) an adolescent boy's journal describes, in a stark and honest story, the painful experiences of a loved and respected older brother who has become a drug addict. The sober message is particularly effective because it is seen through the younger boy's eyes.

"Don't Play Dead Before You Have To" (1970) explores the sense of commitment and the values of young people in a time of protest. The literary form is unusual, the book being a long monologue by teenager Byron, babysitting a five-year-old genius who immediately accepts all Byron's shallow values. But Byron changes through the course of the book, and—although the form becomes monotonous—there is great impact in his growing concern for others and in his intense yearning for a better world. It is this belief that our only hope is in young people which particularly distinguishes Maia Wojciechowska's writing.

Frank Bonham

Durango Street
The Nitty Gritty
The Vagabundos

Although *Durango Street* (1965) has a black youth as its protagonist, it is less about black delinquents than it is about the slum neighborhood that breeds delinquency. Rufus is a paroled adolescent more suspicious of the social worker assigned to his case than he would be if Alex Robbins were white. While the patient, firm Robbins does have a realistically small effect on Rufus and his gang, the book is more interesting as a fictional study of gang behavior and protocol than as a story.

In *The Nitty Gritty* (1968), another black adolescent is torn between the indolent life of his favorite uncle and the benefits of continuing his education. Again, the story lacks impetus but is perceptive in interpretation of character and motivation, its candor lightened by moments of humor.

In *The Vagabundos* (1969) a white adolescent follows the trail of his father, who has disappeared from home. By the time he catches up with his father, Eric understands why the simple life of the local fishermen, the vagabundos, holds more satisfaction than do the indolence and boredom of retirement. The book has vivid characterization of the Americans and Mexicans Eric meets, the suspense of the chase, and a perceptive delineation of the relationship between father and son.

Susan Hinton

The Outsiders
That Was Then, This Is Now

The Outsiders (1967) are the members of a tough, lower-class gang who have a running feud with a middle-class gang. Ponyboy is the outsider who tells the story, stark and vivid, of running off to a hideout with a pal who has committed murder. The two give themselves up, and Ponyboy's pal dies in the hospital. Ponyboy faces the fact that the advantage is with those on the inside of society's line, yet knows that if he cannot have help, he must and will help himself and end the vicious circle of hostility and reprisal. Honest and forthright, the story shows the desperation of the need to belong; it has also a bittersweet quality, especially in young Ponyboy's relationship with his older brothers.

The young author's candor and insight that made the book so popular are evident also in her *That Was Then, This Is Now* (1971), which is basically a story of friendship and the choice that teenaged Byron must make when he finds that his best friend is pushing dope. Especially bitter because he has seen drugs ruin a younger boy of whom he is fond, Byron turns Mark in—and hates himself. The characters are vividly real, and no didactic tract on drug abuse could be more convincing than is the story seen from the viewpoint of an adolescent who has himself been a fringe delinquent. *Rumble Fish* (1975) is the tragic story of two brothers—Motorcycle Boy, who has lost his will to live and is killed after committing a senseless robbery, and Rusty-James, the younger, who idolizes his brother and is almost destroyed by his death.

Nat Hentoff

Jazz Country
I'm Really Dragged But Nothing Gets Me Down

In *Jazz Country* (1965) Tom Curtis is a trumpet player who describes the people whose influence has helped him decide to go to college rather than join a band. Most of the jazzmen he meets are black, and Tom is white; he finds that his new friends will accept no phonies and that he has to prove himself before he is accepted by them. A fine book about jazz and about New York City, this is distinguished for its candor about racial attitudes and relationships.

In *I'm Really Dragged But Nothing Gets Me Down* (1968) not a great deal happens, but a great deal is there: it is the scope of understanding and the depth of perception that give vitality and impact to a story of the unsure adolescent and the generation gap. Jeremy and his father don't understand each other, but then Jeremy hardly understands himself. He is in conflict about the draft, unsure of his goals, worried about his responsibilities. The same theme is explored in Barbara Wersba's *Run Softly, Go Fast* (1970), also a perceptive study of a father and son who are at odds, but it lacks the sense of dramatic conflict of the Hentoff book, largely because *I'm Really Dragged* makes both viewpoints understandable. *In the Country of Ourselves* (1971) is a tough, honest account of the protest and rebellion in a high school, an upheaval in which faculty, students, and community forces are split and struggling for power. *This School Is Driving Me Crazy* (1975) is not only a vehicle for Hentoff's criticisms of schools, but also an interesting story of relationships between students and teachers, father and son.

Kristin Hunter

The Soul Brothers and Sister Lou
Guests in the Promised Land

Which side was she on? Lou, at fourteen, wasn't militant, but she didn't trust white policemen, and she warned the gang with whom she sang that a policeman was near and was acting provocative. She knew the gang carried weapons, but she also saw an unarmed boy shot by the police, and found it hard to believe that any white people had good motives. Yet the more she learned of her black heritage, the more proud and confident Lou became, until she made her decision: moderation, not militancy. *The Soul Brothers and Sister Lou* (1968) has too many episodes and a weak ending (sudden success as a vocal group), yet the book is valuable because it gives a vivid and honest picture of one segment of black society and of the dilemma of its young people. In *Guests in the Promised Land* (1973) Hunter's eleven short stories, varied and vigorous, examine facets of the problems of the black child in a white world.

John Rowe Townsend

Trouble in the Jungle
Good Night, Prof, Dear
Noah's Castle

John Rowe Townsend is one of the major writers of realistic fiction for young people in England. His *Trouble in the Jungle* (1969) tells of some slum children who show their mettle when they are temporarily abandoned by adults. To avoid being forced into an institution, the two older children take the younger ones to a refuge in a deserted warehouse and have a dangerous skirmish with criminals who also seek a hideout. The story, which has good characterization and pace, ends on a realistic note: the shiftless father and his mistress return, and the children go back to their home. Although published earlier in the United States (1967), *Good-Bye to the Jungle* is a sequel in which the family moves to a better home and a better life.

Hell's Edge (1969) was a runner-up for the Carnegie Medal when it was first published in England. It is the story of a grimy Yorkshire town, Hallersage, in which several young people are interested in an urban renewal project. There is an element of mystery, but this is not a mystery story.

In *Good Night, Prof, Dear* (1971) a shy and overprotected sixteen-year-old falls in love with a waitress he meets when his parents are away on a trip. Although the girl verges on a fallen-woman-with-heart-of-gold type, it is the contrast between her knowledgeable resilience and Graham's diffidence and insecurity that gives the story its real drama. *The Intruder*, another story about a sixteen-year-old, is discussed in Chapter 2.

Noah's Castle (1976) is a compelling, all-too-possible family story. Foreseeing food shortages, Father buys and barricades a huge house, stocks it, and prepares to survive. What his family thinks of all this precipitates more problems.

Townsend has an ear for dialogue, as well as an understanding of adolescent psychology. His books are written with economy of structure and vitality of motive, the style utterly appropriate to the tale.

Illustrations copyright 1969 by W. T. Mars for Trouble in the Jungle *by John Rowe Townsend. Copyright 1961. Reproduced by permission of J. B. Lippincott Company.*

Theodore Taylor

The Cay

Although the fact that German submarines are attacking islands along the Venezuelan coast during World War II serves as a catalyst for Phillip's departure, this is in no sense a historical novel, since all of the action takes place on a small Caribbean island, *The Cay* (1969), with only two characters. The ship Phillip and his mother are on is torpedoed and the boy finds himself, some hours later, alone on a raft with Timothy, an old man. Infected by his mother's prejudice, Phillip feels only aversion for his black companion at first, but he becomes totally dependent on Timothy when he goes blind as a delayed result of the shipwreck injury. Slowly, patiently, stubbornly, Timothy teaches the boy to fend for himself, refusing to coddle him—and when old Timothy dies, Phillip knows how much he has come to love and respect the wise and charitable man. The bleakness of the setting is a dramatic foil for the action, and there is taut suspense within the economical framework of the plot.

John Donovan

I'll Get There. It Better Be Worth the Trip
Wild in the World

In a compassionate story of childhood's end, John Donovan draws a picture of thirteen-year-old Davy, caught and shaped by his environment in *I'll Get There. It Better Be Worth the Trip* (1969). His beloved grandmother has just died, and Davy comes to New York to live with his mother, a divorced, bitter alcoholic. All he clings to is his beloved dog, and the dog irritates his mother. Sent to a boy's school, Davy meets another pupil adjusting to bereavement, and the two have a brief homosexual relationship. It is handled with great dignity and compassion, not the core of the book but one of the scarring episodes that make Davy know his strength must be in himself.

Wild in the World (1971) is a quite different and an even stronger book, memorable for its stark setting and the dramatic impact of a solitary boy's deep need for love and companionship. John lives alone on a remote mountainside farm until a stray dog—or it may be a wolf, John is not sure—learns to trust him. For the first time, John plays and laughs with the creature he has named "Son." When John dies, still alone, and neighbors find him, his "Son" is chased off but steals back later to sleep and keep his vigil in John's house.

Richard Peck

Don't Look and It Won't Hurt
Representing Super Doll

The second of three daughters, Carol had to take care of her younger sister after their parents' divorce in *Don't Look and It Won't Hurt* (1972). Mom, already bitter, didn't want Carol to have boyfriends and refused to have anything to do with her oldest daughter, Ellen, when she became pregnant. It was Carol who went to Chicago to see Ellen and beg her to come home. A gentle, loving girl, Carol had learned to look away from pain that cannot be alleviated; she has had heavy burdens, but they have made her understanding and mature rather than bitter like her mother.

In *Representing Super Doll* (1974) a beautiful but not very astute girl, Darlene, goes to New York for one round of a teenage beauty contest. Her ambitious mother convinces Verna, Darlene's classmate, to go along as companion. Verna, level-headed and intelligent, scorns the whole proceeding and goes home—and Darlene does the same. To her mother's fury, she has quit just before the final round. The message is firmly feminist, but Peck does not let the message obscure the story; the plot is solid, the characters strong, and the treatment of adolescent concerns balanced.

Dreamland Lake (1973) has a wry humor in the classroom scenes to offset the somberness of a story in which two boys, finding a vagrant's corpse in an amusement park, become so engrossed in making a mystery of a natural death that they carelessly bring about another death. Another story of suspense is *Through a Brief Darkness* (1973), in which a sixteen-year-old girl discovers that her father is a prominent underworld figure. While this has some conventional mystery story elements, it also has good pace and dialogue that is natural. Dialogue is one of the strong aspects in all Peck's stories, and his books are notable for their fresh viewpoints and their vitality.

Norma Klein

Mom, the Wolf Man, and Me
Confessions of an Only Child

While Norma Klein has written for several age levels, her greatest impact is in stories for younger adolescents. The "me" in *Mom, the Wolf Man, and Me* (1972) is Brett, an illegitimate child, who loves living alone with her mother and hopes that life will never change. Then the "wolf man," the owner of an Irish wolfhound, comes along, and the possibility of a change looms. Brett's mother is candid and open, and the suitor as concerned with Brett's feelings as with her mother's.

Many of Klein's stories are about single-parent homes, divorce, remarriage, and the adaptability required of children, as in *It's Not What You Expect* (1973) and *Taking Sides* (1974). But *Confessions of an Only Child* (1974) tells of eight-year-old Tonia's feelings before the birth and death of a premature baby brother, and her acceptance of the brother born a year later.

Klein is a thoughtful connoisseur of real people and sets down her observations skillfully for us. Her children are not divorced from adult problems and relationships, but live closely, in their urban existences, with real and surrogate parents, who are inevitably frank and open about their emotions. Only occasional older people—grandmothers, babysitters—ever suggest that different values might be held by other adults.

From Confessions of an Only Child, *by Norma Klein, illustrated by Richard Cuffari. Copyright © 1974 by Pantheon Books, a Division of Random House, Inc. Reprinted by permission of Pantheon Books, a Division of Random House, Inc.*

M. E. Kerr

Dinky Hocker Shoots Smack
Is That You, Miss Blue?

With *Dinky Hocker Shoots Smack* (1972), a fresh, perceptive advocate for adolescents appeared in the person of M. E. Kerr. Dinky Hocker spends all her money for food and has no dates. Because he wants to take Dinky's visiting cousin to a dance, Tucker finds P. John, a plump square, for Dinky, and instant rapport follows, with Weight Watchers for two. Dinky's parents, who help everyone but their own child, find P. John too reactionary and break up the romance. Dinky's revenge is to inscribe "Dinky Hocker shoots smack" on all the buildings and sidewalks in the neighborhood. Hilariously funny but touching at the same time, this has an excellent style and convincing characterizations.

The problems that come with a parent who is a celebrity are those of Adam in *The Son of Someone Famous* (1974). Alternating chapters by Adam and by Brenda Belle Blossom, his girlfriend, allow Kerr to tell the story from two points of view and yet to keep it intimate and personal.

Flanders is sent to a private girls' boarding school in *Is That You, Miss Blue?* (1975). Angry with her mother for leaving home and with her father for apparently deserting her, Flan learns through her school experiences that everyone needs understanding love, even parents and teachers.

Fifteen-year-old Suzy, the narrator of *Love Is a Missing Person* (1975), tells of the problems of her sister, Chicago, and her search for love with someone else's boyfriend. Kerr never offers easy answers to the situations and experiences her characters are involved in, but presents them sympathetically, honestly, and compassionately.

Sharon Bell Mathis

Listen for the Fig Tree
The Hundred Penny Box

An eloquent spokesperson for black culture has created a realistic and moving story of relationships between generations in *Listen for the Fig Tree* (1974). Muffin, who is sixteen and blind, finds that coping with her grief-stricken Momma is a hard task, for Momma, mourning her husband's death, has taken to drink. Muffin's solace lies in her plans to attend her first celebration of the African Kwanza, and she makes a dress for the occasion, a dress in which she looks beautiful—too beautiful. A neighbor attempts rape; other neighbors rescue her, and one makes her a new dress. Muffin has a glorious time at Kwanza, and—although she comes home to find Momma still drinking, still insistent that Daddy's coming home—she faces her problems with new courage, courage gained from the feelings of solidarity and strength she had gained at Kwanza.

A story that is primarily for children in the middle grades, *The Hundred Penny Box* (1975) is so tender and delicate that it appeals to many older readers as well. A small boy becomes his great-great-aunt's confidant and protector when his mother wants to get rid of Aunt Dew's big box of pennies. But Michael knows that without her pennies, one for each year of her life, something vital will leave Aunt Dew's life.

Mathis is very successful in delineating characters and establishing setting. Her writing is effectively restrained, her stories convincing and candid.

From The Hundred Penny Box *by Sharon Bell Mathis*
Text Copyright © 1975 by Sharon Bell Mathis
Illustrations Copyright © 1975 by Leo and Diane Dillon
Reprinted by permission of The Viking Press
(Original with color)

Other Books for Older Children

In Mildred Lee's *The Skating Rink* (1969) a shy fifteen-year-old boy's life is changed by the skating rink, because the owner teaches Tuck to skate so expertly that he is able to partner an exhibition skater on opening night. Tuck works doggedly to achieve competence and realizes he has won respect, not for his performance but for his application. Lee's *The Rock and the Willow* (1963) was chosen a Notable Book, and deservedly. It is a powerful and incisive story set in rural Alabama during the Depression years, bleak in its honest portrayal of a hard life, with young Enie bearing the brunt of caring for the family after her mother's death and grudgingly accepting a stepmother. The characters are cameo-clear, and Enie's dream of getting away from home and going to college is realistically achieved.

An unusual setting for another Depression era story is the Montana ranch on which Adrienne Richard's *Pistol* (1969) works as a wrangler, grows from boy to man, and goes home to see with a new perspective that his father is a weakling and that he must leave home permanently to find freedom. The story has a serious theme but is lightened by delightful scenes of cowboy humor.

William Armstrong's *Sounder* (1969), a Newbery Medal book, is the grim and moving story of a black sharecropper's family whose father is jailed for stealing food for his wife and children.

Spanish Harlem is the setting for *Nilda* (1973) by Nicholasa Mohr, a sharp and candid picture of the life of a barrio child. A new arrival in Harlem, Phyl learns that although Edith is slovenly, her kindness is a bulwark in Rosa Guy's *The Friends* (1973). Alice Childress tells a dramatic, moving story in *a HERO ain't nothin' but a Sandwich* (1973). Thirteen-year-old Benjie insists that he can do without dope any time he wants, but his friends and relatives are more realistic.

The consistent and distinctive first-person style of Scott O'Dell's *Child of Fire* (1974) brings vividly to life an adolescent Chicano boy, seen through the eyes of a parole officer.

Our Eddie (1969) by Sulamith Ish-Kishor is the trenchant story of a tyrannical father so dedicated to helping others that he neglects his own family. The Raphels are English Jews who have moved to New York, where Papa refuses to see that Eddie is truly ill, and only after the boy's death softens his behavior somewhat to his other children.

A naturalist in the making, Mike fights futilely against the development of the rural areas near his home, while at the same time remaining a typical young adolescent. Don Moser's *A Heart to the Hawks* (1975) is a convincing character study.

The establishment wins also in *The Chocolate War* (1974) by Robert Cormier. In an all-boy Catholic high school, Jerry's hazing by the Vigils includes an order to refuse to sell chocolates in the school's annual fund-raising event. Jerry obeys, but when the order is rescinded, he stands pat. Retribution inevitably follows in this sobering, dramatic story.

There are school problems also in *Marly the Kid* (1975) when Marly runs away from a nagging mother to her father and stepmother. Her new life becomes easier as she gains insight and perspective about herself in this perceptive character study by Susan Beth Pfeffer.

Paula Danziger's *The Cat Ate My Gymsuit* (1974) shows how much an innovative teacher means to bored, self-hating Marcy. When the teacher is fired, Marcy and her friends lead a protest, which her formerly timid mother joins.

The Pigman (1968) was what John and Lorraine called Mr. Pignati, whom they had met when pretending to collect for a charity. The lonely, elderly man is delighted to have the young people as friends, but when he comes back from a hospital stay to find them having a wild party, Mr. Pignati is stunned. Remorseful, they try to make amends, but the old man has had too much excitement and dies of a stroke. Only then do John and Lorraine know that each person's cage is of his own making: "there was no one else to blame any more . . . And there was no place to hide." Told alternately by John and Lorraine, this story by Paul Zindel shows more clearly than a reporter could the restless, pliant amorality that so often marks adolescent behavior, and the deep sensitivity beneath it.

A dignified, perceptive story of a homosexual relationship, *Trying Hard to Hear You* (1974) by Sandra Scoppettone tells of a crucial summer in the lives of a group of adolescents.

Other popular books about young people today include Lee Kingman's *The Peter Pan Bag* (1970), in which a girl participates in communal living in Boston and finds her new acquaintances serious about establishing their independence but often pathetic or irritatingly irresponsible; and Barbara Rinkoff's *Member of the Gang* (1968), in which a probation officer convinces one boy that delinquent behavior has only one outcome—trouble (a particularly effective story because it shows the potency of the need to belong and because the probation officer realistically has only moderate success with the gang).

The girl in Barbara Corcoran's *Sam* (1967) has been taught by her father, who keeps her on their island home until she is in high school because he so mistrusts people, but Sam discovers for herself that there are all kinds of people, and that even those like Uncle Everett, a weakling and a gambler, have some good things about them. In *A Dance to Still Music* (1974), Margaret, deaf after an illness, rebels by running away when her mother plans to put her in a special school. In Corcoran's and Bradford Angier's *A Star to the North* (1970) a brother and sister learn to accept each other's inadequacies on a trek through the Canadian wilderness.

K. M. Peyton's *Pennington's Heir* (1974), which follows *Pennington's Last Term* (1971) and *The Beethoven Medal* (1972), about a brilliant young pianist with a rebellious temper, is also a story of an early, forced marriage. Peyton's ability to create vigorous, believable characters and situations is enhanced by her polished writing style.

A good story which may help readers to understand to some extent the bitterness rampant in Northern Ireland today is Joan Lingard's *The Twelfth Day of July* (1972), the first of several stories about Protestant Sadie and Catholic Kevin.

It is interesting that two prize books from Holland are about children in other countries. Siny van Iterson's *Pulga* (1971) is the story of a Colombian waif who gets a job as a trucker's helper and gains self-confidence from his experience; and Jaap Ter Haar's *Boris* (1970) is a story of brotherhood set in Russia. One of the best of the translations from Russia is Vadim Frolov's *What It's All About* (1968), in which a teenage boy copes with the bitter fact that his mother has left his father to be with another man. Sasha's self-doubt, his budding love affair, and his relationships with classmates give the story balance and depth.

Hesba Fay Brinsmead's *Pastures of the Blue Crane* (1966) is set in Australia, its theme the intrinsic worth of all men. A girl of sixteen who has been living in boarding schools inherits property and finds, in her new home, that her most trustworthy friend is Perry, a quartercaste. Indignant at the slurs cast on him, Amaryllis is not dismayed when she discovers that she herself is not, as she had always assumed, all white.

Miners in Australia's opal fields work in a harsh, uncompromising setting, which imposes unusual pressures on families. Both Colin Thiele's *Fire in the Stone* (1974) and Mavis Thorpe Clark's *Spark of Opal* (1973) tell of the effects of this life on children, white and aborigine, as they wait for that lucky strike.

One of the best of the stories of conflict and resolution between the old ways and the new is *Sunrise Tomorrow* (1973) by Naomi Mitchison, a story of Botswana. Convincingly drawn characters show the different roles in which young people can contribute to a developing nation.

Of William Mayne's books for older children, *A Swarm in May* (1957) is the most distinctive. Set in a choir school in England, it has a colorful atmosphere, delightful characterization and dialogue, a polished and witty style, and a considerable amount of information about church music. The story line is solid, and the ingenious ploys of the boys make this one of the most entertaining of all school stories.

Although the story takes place during the blitz of London, *Fireweed* (1970) by Jill Paton Walsh is not historical fiction, but a tender story of two adolescents who find each other and set up housekeeping in an abandoned building, their relationship innocent and touching. When Julie is hurt in a bombing, Bill realizes that he loves her, but when he visits her in the hospital and meets her family, he is snubbed by them and thinks she too is rejecting him. A convincing and dramatic story is given poignancy by the wholly unsentimental writing.

Animal Stories

Almost all children are interested in animals. Rhymes about "The Three Little Kittens" or the mouse that ran up the clock are early favorites, and *Mother Goose* is supplemented by the more realistic animal picture books. With these, children learn to name all the beasts under the sun from hippopotamuses to anteaters. The folk tales with animal heroes come next and seem never to wear out their welcome. "The Three Little Pigs," "The Little Red Hen," and all the other favorites are heard over and over with endless satisfaction. Children progress from these to the more complex, realistic stories about animals, and for many people the interest lasts a lifetime.

Animal stories can be divided into three groups: those in which animals behave like human beings, those in which they behave like animals save for the fact that they can talk, and those in which they behave like animals. Many of the books in the first two categories can be found in Chapter 4, Books for Early Childhood, and in Chapter 8, Modern Fantasy; there are, of course, many animal stories in folk literature as well. The realistic tales range from lighthearted picture books like Nathan Zimelman's *The Lives of My Cat Alfred* (1976) to humorous stories like Phil Stong's *Honk: the Moose* (1935) or the substantial books by Walt Morey.

A primary criterion for realistic fiction about animals is that the animals be objectively portrayed. The author should not interpret behavior or motives through giving the animal powers of speech or thought. Any conjecture about motives of animal protagonists should agree with the interpretation of animal behavior as reliable observers have recorded it. Since tragedy often occurs in the lives of animals, stories about them often are dramatic or melancholy. In evaluating such books, we need to be more than ordinarily alert to what is a true and consistent story, and to what is

From The Incredible Journey *by Sheila Burnford. Copyright © 1960, 1961 by Sheila Burnford. Reprinted by permission of Little, Brown and Co.—Atlantic Monthly Press and Hodder and Stoughton Limited.*

pure sentimentality or animal melodrama. A little melodrama or a few mediocre books are not going to hurt children, but they should not miss the great animal tales in a welter of second-rate ones.

Among the great stories is Sheila Burnford's *The Incredible Journey* (1961), a detailed account of three heroic animals who travel through 250 miles of Canadian wilderness to the place and people that mean home and love to them. Attacked by wild creatures, delayed by well-meaning people, crossing hazardous terrain, a cat and two dogs struggle on to find their family. The animals are never humanized or sentimentalized, and they are described with dignity and restraint in a moving and beautifully written story.

Many of the best books about animals are written by authors who specialize in this area. Marguerite Henry, for example, who is probably the most successful writer of horse stories we have ever had, bases each book on thorough research; the stories are well told, the animal heroes are true to their species, and the people are often as memorable as the animals. For *King of the Wind* (1948), which won the Newbery Medal, the author investigated the history of the great Godolphin Arabian, which sired a line of thoroughbreds and changed the physical conformation of racehorses. It is one of the most exciting horse stories ever written. Almost as popular is *Misty of Chincoteague* (1947), a history of the little wild horses on a Virginia island. In *Gaudenzia* (1960) and *White Stallion of Lipizza* (1964), Henry bases her stories on the annual horse race held in Siena and on the Lipizzaners, the precision drilled performing horses of the Spanish Riding School of Vienna.

Other authors who have written prolifically in the field of realistic animal fiction are Walt Morey, Jim Kjelgaard, C. W. Anderson, Jean Doty, and Jean George. All of Morey's books are set in the far North or Northwest, and are imbued with his love for that region and his affection for animals. In *Gentle Ben* (1965) and in *Gloomy Gus* (1970), the protagonists are bears, animal personalities that are as vivid as the perceptively characterized human beings among whom they live. *Kävik the Wolf Dog* (1968) is the dramatic story of a mistreated animal that is being sent to Seattle, escapes, and makes his way back to Alaska and the only person who had been kind to him. In *Year of the Black Pony* (1976) a boy on an Oregon farm tames and trains a spirited pony, a plot that is deftly meshed with a tender family story. Kjelgaard specializes in dog stories, of which the best known is *Big Red* (1956), which was followed by several books about progeny of the lovable and courageous Irish setter. Anderson and Doty specialize in horse stories, Anderson with the "Blaze" series for younger children, splendidly illustrated by the author, and with stories of racehorses for older children, and Doty with simply written stories for the middle grades as well as her more intricate mystery story, *The Crumb* (1976). Jean George wrote many stories on a life-cycle pattern with John George: *Vulpes, the Red Fox* (1948) and *Bubo, the Great Horned Owl* (1954), for example, both make it clear that George is not only an animal lover, but a skilled naturalist. Some of her finest books are *Gull Number 737* (1964), the story of a boy who becomes so interested in his father's research on herring gulls that he develops his own project; *Coyote in Manhattan* (1968), in which a wild animal, loose in Central Park, is eventually captured; and *Julie of the Wolves* (1972), discussed earlier in this chapter.

One of the most touching and trenchant animal stories is *The Yearling* (1938) by Marjorie Kinnan Rawlings. Although written for adults, it has been discovered by children even as they discover certain adult books and make them their own in every generation. A lonely boy and his pet deer grow up together in the Florida wilderness, but when the growing animal begins to eat the family's scanty crops, the boy's father issues an order: the deer must be shot. Added to the boy's anguish over losing his pet are his own guilt feelings and his anger at his father. This is more tragic than most of the stories in which children give up wild pets, but there are many in which a child feels anguish because a wild creature grows from a baby to a size where it must be returned to live with its own kind.

From the book Rascal *by Sterling North. Illustration by John Schoenherr. Illustration copyright © 1963 by E. P. Dutton & Co., Inc., publishers, and used with their permission.*

Some animal stories are factual, based on an author's experience with wildlife. Perhaps the best known of these is Sterling North's *Rascal* (1963), which was so popular that the author wrote a simplified version, *Little Rascal*, two years later—a better adaptation than most books rewritten for children. A description of the engaging ways of a pet raccoon, the first-person account is always objective in observations of animal behavior. Also based on observation is Emil Liers' *An Otter's Story* (1953), a delightful book about one family of playful, affectionate freshwater otters in which the author makes clear their usefulness in the balance of nature both for farmers and for fishermen.

The English naturalist Joyce Stranger has, in *Lakeland Vet* (1972), so skillfully woven incidents about animals into the fictional account of a veterinarian's hard life that his love and compassion for all living things are more impressive than the story line. The same sense of compassion is strong in Meindert DeJong's *Along Came a Dog* (1958), illustrated by Maurice Sendak. Gentle but never sentimental, DeJong's stories about animals have a quiet, poignant appeal; here the animals have strong personalities, as a stray dog establishes himself as the protector of a crippled, doughty little hen.

Realistic animal stories for young children are on the whole a cheerful group, often containing excellent illustrations. Although many of Marjorie Flack's books were about dogs, the abiding favorite has been *The Story About Ping* (1933), with Kurt Wiese's pictures catching the spirit of a brisk, homey tale about a rebellious little duck that lives on a boat in the Yangtze River. Lynd Ward's *The Biggest Bear* (1952) is a delectable comedy about a pet bear that grows from a cute baby into a large animal that causes so many problems that the only solution is sending it to a zoo. Liesel Skorpen's *Bird* (1976) is a diverting story about a boy who is convinced the nestling he's rescued needs his help to fly. Alma Whitney's *Leave Herbert Alone* (1972) is amusing in a wry way, as a small girl is so anxious to show her love for a cat that she frightens him and has to learn a gentler approach.

Marjorie Sharmat's two stories about a dog taken in by an elderly couple, *Morris Brookside, a Dog* (1973) and *Morris Brookside Is Missing* (1974) are distinctive in their bland, quiet style; the humor lies in the situation, for Mr. and Mrs. Brookside so dote on Morris that his puppies' pictures are right up there on the piano with those of their grandchildren. In Beverly Cleary's *Socks* (1973) the advent of a baby is told from a cat's viewpoint. Socks had been a pampered pet until the intruder came along, and he's resentfully jealous until the baby gets big enough to turn into a playmate. Socks always behaves and thinks like a cat, never a person, yet Cleary invests him with a definite personality in this delightful tale.

The animal stories by Miska Miles have in common a quiet tone, an absence of anthropomorphism, and, in most of them, a consistency in the way they reflect an animal's life from its own viewpoint. In *Nobody's Cat* (1969) a tough, self-sufficient alley cat awakens sympathy by being just what he is: lean, homely, and lonely. There is no sentimentality, no happy ending to his adventures. Other stories are *Mississippi Possum* (1965), *Eddie's Bear* (1970), *Wharf Rat* (1972), and *Otter in the Cove* (1974).

It matters little where an animal story is set, since the interest and affection children feel for creatures, wild or tame, is universal. In *Just a Dog* by Helen Griffiths (1975) the story of a mongrel pup is set in Madrid, but the incidents could be duplicated in any city. Anne de Roo's *Cinnamon and Nutmeg* (1974) takes place in New Zealand, where a farm child, knowing her father won't let her keep the calf and kid she's found, hides them in an abandoned house and gives them loving care. A Scottish farm is the setting for Alec Lea's *Temba Dawn* (1975); when the farm is sold, young Rob succeeds in convincing his father to take a pet calf, Temba Dawn, with them, in an honest and moving story. Most of Lucy Boston's writing is fantasy, but she uses the same setting, an English country house, for *A Stranger at Green Knowe* (1961), a powerful and original story about the understanding and affection between a gorilla that has escaped from a zoo and a young refugee.

There is rarely any need to urge children to read stories about animals. Pet stories bring out children's desire to nurture and protect, and, as they mature, they learn about the piteous vulnerability of animals at the hands of cruel owners or hunters and trappers. Such stories encourage a compassionate sense of kinship with animals. Many of these books teach sex casually in the course of an absorbing story. For children who have little or no knowledge of breeding and the raising of young, these stories are especially valuable. From the stories that center on the proper training of dogs and horses, young readers gain a background for the training of their own pets. There is, of course, a great deal of overlap between such stories and informational books. Much of the fiction gives accurate information, and many informational books about animals have a narrative framework; indeed, it is at times difficult to decide in which class a book belongs.

Best of all, these four-footed characters display some of the very qualities that children admire in human beings—courage in the face of danger, fortitude in suffering, loyalty to cubs, mate, or owner, and finally, a gay, frolicsome zest for life that is much like the child's own frisky, coltish enjoyment of each day. These are all good reasons why the child enjoys fine books about animals.

Since the mere nature of the wild animal's life means chiefly pursuit or being pursued, escape or death; and since the drama of a pet's

Viewpoints

It is obvious that the naturalist would not indulge in anthropomorphism—the endowment of animals with human traits. It is not so clear that the writers of even the best animal stories should not or do not do so. Some transfer of human intelligence and emotion to the animal character can, in good hands, heighten the emotional impact of a story and strengthen the rapport between writer and reader. . . . But it takes a sure sense of the limits of credibility to keep the realistic animal story from being maudlin or, worse, so confused as to be neither animal story nor outright fantasy.—Sheila Egoff, *The Republic of Childhood*, Oxford University Press, Toronto, 1967, p. 107.

life turns upon the upsetting of its happy security with a tragic or triumphant outcome, there is bound to be a certain similarity in these tales. Too many of them in a row are monotonous or overly harrowing. Such stories should be read along with other books. But any child is the richer for having had his or her sympathies expanded and tenderness stirred by such great animal books as *Along Came a Dog, Gentle Ben,* and *The Yearling.* Any child is the poorer for having missed the drama of *King of the Wind, The Incredible Journey,* and *A Stranger at Green Knowe.*

Sports Stories

If there is one fault common to most sports stories, it is the formula plot: the beginner, from school playground to professional team, who can't get along with another member of the team or the whole team or the coach because he or she is cocky or wants things his or her own way, eventually rises to heights of glory and acceptance by all by saving the final game in the final minute of play. Another fault common to such stories is the thin plot wrapped around long and often tedious game sequences. Perhaps more than any other kind of realistic fiction, the sports story needs good characterization and good style to give it depth, especially since there is usually little variation in setting and often little opportunity for a meaningful theme.

There are few realistic sports stories for the beginning reader, but Leonard Kessler's *Here Comes the Strikeout* (1965) has simplicity, humor, and an emphasis on perseverance and achievement. Bobby (white) cannot get a hit until he has been coached by his friend Willie (black) and has worked hard to correct his faults. Leonard Shortall, in a good story for seven- to nine-year-olds, describes a boy's first attempts at skiing in *Ben on the Ski Trail* (1965). Beman Lord has written several books for this age group, one of which, *Shrimp's Soccer Goal* (1970), reflects the increasing interest in that sport and is unusual in presenting a woman teacher as the founder and coach of the team. Another good soccer story from Sweden is Kerstin Thorvall's *Gunnar Scores a Goal* (1968).

The popularity of each individual sport is echoed proportionately in children's books, with baseball and football stories far outnumbering all others. One of the most dependable writers for the nine-to-eleven group is Matt Christopher, whose productivity is impressive. *Johnny Long Legs* (1970) and *Tough to Tackle* (1971) are examples of his style: simple, undistinguished plots; good game descriptions; and an emphasis on sportsmanship and team effort. *The Baseball Bargain* (1970) by Scott Corbett has more depth, since the protagonist is tempted to steal a mitt and strikes a bargain with the storekeeper whereby he earns it by working in the store—*if* he can first do three good deeds in a day. Corbett's light, easy style and humor make this a pleasant tale with serious overtones—and good baseball. Alfred Slote's *Stranger on the Ball Club* (1970) also is concerned with ethical values and has good sports writing and deeper characterization than is found in most books at this level; his *Matt Gargan's Boy* (1950) has good game sequences in a story about Danny, son of a major league baseball player, who resents having a girl on his team, especially a girl whose father is courting Danny's divorced mother. William Pène du Bois, in *Porko von Popbutton* (1969), writes a merry tale of ice hockey at a boys' school.

Margaret Potter's *The Touch-and-Go Year* (1969) is flawed by several uses of coincidence in the plot, but is otherwise a fine story about a boy who works to become a professional tennis player—a sport that receives rather scant attention.

The response by publishers to the demand for more books about blacks and other minority groups has included sports fiction, but many of these stories seem obtrusive in their inclusion of such minorities. Indeed, one of the formulas has seemed to be the team in which each player represents a different ethnic background. Stories that approach the particular problems of the black player in sports with honesty and concern are rare, and therefore John Tunis's *All-American* (1942) was all the more exciting when it appeared. It tells the story of a boy who plays high-school football and learns to appreciate each player for his own worth and to fight discrimination. In Jesse Jackson's *Anchor Man* (1947) an influx of black students into a small-town school leads to misunderstanding on both sides, and the author gives a good study of a range of attitudes. Two of the more recent books that deal incisively with the special problems of the black player are Robert Lipsyte's *The Contender* (1967), in which a Harlem youth decides, after a successful start in a boxing career, to get an education instead; and Donald Honig's *Johnny Lee* (1971), a story of a black baseball rookie who finds discrimination as well as friendship on the team and in the Virginia town where he plays in a minor league.

In Honig's *Way to Go, Teddy* (1973), a young baseball player is in conflict with the father who wants him to become a lawyer. The details of a rookie's life are lively and authentic; the author was a professional ball player. Another story with rare depth and characterization is *Stubborn Sam* by William Gault. Sam Bogosian goes to college as his father asks—but he still wants to play baseball, and does. In Robert Weaver's *Nice Guy, Go Home* (1968), an Amish boy is drawn into a civil rights conflict in the town where his pro team plays; although he respects the Amish ideals, Johnny cannot remain neutral when he sees injustice.

As in other kinds of fiction, sports stories follow trends and issues. In the past, books about girls' sports have been undistinguished, but more are beginning to appear. *Not Bad for a Girl* by Isabella Taves (1972) is based on a real case of a girl who is put on a Little League team by a sympathetic coach. Sharon plays well, but there is such abuse and persecution by local residents that the coach and Sharon are expelled. The realistic ending gives more impact to the exposure of sexism than any formula happy ending could. Another baseball story, *Something Queer at the Ball Park* by Elizabeth Levy (1975), is a less serious tale with a slightly slapstick mystery element, but it does feature a girl who plays on a team on which the issue of sex roles doesn't even arise. In *Rod-and-Reel Trouble* by Bobbi Katz (1974), a girl who has always wanted to enter an annual fishing contest gets a chance when it is, for the first time, open to girls as well as boys; the story has a protagonist who is courageous, sensible, and persistent. In Scott Corbett's *The Hockey Girls* (1976), a group of high-school girls are horrified when they discover that an athletic program has been set up for girls, since not any of them are interested in sports. But the field hockey coach, an elderly English teacher, is competent and enthusiastic, and the girls find, once they have attained proficiency, that they enjoy the game.

The interest in the problem of drugs is reflected in William Heumann's *Fastbreak Rebel* (1971), in which the white protagonist on a pro basketball team encourages his coach to sign on a black player who has given up drugs and is especially anxious to show the young people of his deprived neighborhood that there is a better way than the marijuana-to-heroin path.

Although few American readers understand the fine points of cricket, nobody can miss the high-spirited humor of P. G. Wodehouse's *Mike and Psmith* (1969), first published in 1909, but a timeless piece of school humor. Shinty is enough like hockey to be comprehensible to fans, and Margaret MacPherson's *The Shinty Boys* (1963) has a cohesive plot, plenty of action, lively characters, and the flavorful dialogue and atmosphere of the Isle of Skye. Last, for really mature readers, *Today's Game* (1965), by Martin Quigley, is valuable both because of the author's expert knowledge of baseball behind the scene and because of the brisk, professional approach to the problems

Viewpoints

Literature has been instrumental in aggravating the racism of America. It is not duly recognized as such. Nevertheless, it is powerful in its racist hypnosis. We have attempted to show some of the ways in which this hypnotic process begins in books for the very young. Perhaps the most serious offense committed by the literary world has been the virtual exclusion of Black people from children's books. On the one hand, the omission itself strengthens the omnipotence of white supremacy. On the other, it is part of the myth complex appropriate to the racism of American culture—it is a way of acting out that Black people do not exist or count.—From "Moving Beyond Token Integration" in *Starting Out Right* edited by Bette I. Latimer and funded by the Office of Equal Educational Opportunity, Bulletin No. 2314, p. 24. Reprinted by permission of the Wisconsin Department of Public Instruction.

of a manager, his moves and counter-moves in a crucial game. This is a side of baseball seldom described, and it paves the way for some of the adult baseball classics such as *Bang the Drum Slowly* by Mark Harris and *The Long Season* by Jim Brosnan.

Mystery and Adventure

A classification of children's books which cuts across all groups of realistic fiction in all countries and times is the mystery story. The mystery tale is certainly a striking example of the way in which children's books parallel predominant trends in adult reading interests. With mothers, fathers, and even grandparents all devoted to the "whodunit" school of writing, it is not surprising to find a seven-year-old marching into the children's room of a library and demanding a good mystery story.

Not only do adventure and mystery stories cut across realistic fiction, but also infringe with impunity on historical fiction, as do many of Mollie Hunter's books: are they historically based tales of adventure or are they historical tales filled with dramatic incidents? Townsend's *The Intruder* and Virginia Hamilton's *The House of Dies Drear*, both mentioned earlier in this chapter, seem primarily realistic stories, yet they may well be considered mystery tales.

The extreme popularity of the mystery tale at present may be a fad as far as children are concerned, artificially stimulated by adult emphasis. An element of mystery has always been a source of interest in a story and always will be. But when innumerable books are written merely for the sake of the mystery, the pattern and mood of such tales are liable to become tiresomely repetitious and the stories are likely to be trash. At their worst, such books are marked by preposterous plots, details left unaccounted for, too many episodes, violence piled upon violence, typed characters, and, finally, poor style.

The virtues of good mystery tales for children are numerous, but first among these is the atmosphere of excitement and suspense which serves as the most tempting of all baits for nonreaders. Comic-strip-addicted and television-fed children demand a highly spiced book fare if they are going to read at all, and these mystery tales are usually adventure stories with plenty of breathtaking action to keep young thrill-seekers absorbed. Another useful feature of such stories is that they help establish a much needed reading skill—rapid silent reading. Children unconsciously speed up their usual reading rate under the stimulus of an agreeable suspense. They will cover pages of a mystery tale at breakneck speed in their desire to find the answers and solve the mystery. This rapid rate of silent reading, together with a little skipping or skimming on the way, is a useful habit for fiction readers to establish—the younger the better.

Finally, if children can be supplied with adventure and mystery stories which are also well written and not too difficult for them to read, unbookish children can be persuaded to read a better type of literature than they might otherwise attempt.

The appeal of suspense often leads children to read above their usual level. Older children will plunge happily into adult mystery stories, and children in the middle grades may have favorite authors whose books are intended for older children. Even the youngest now have mystery tales: short, easy to read, and wisely laced with humor. Some of these are Joan Lexau's *The Rooftop Mystery* (1968) and *The Homework Caper* (1966); Ben Shecter's *Inspector Rose* (1969), which has a circus setting, Elizabeth Levy's *Something Queer Is Going On* (1973), and Crosby Bonsall's stories—*The Case of the Cat's Meow* (1965) and others with a lively interracial cast.

Popular with the eight-to-ten age group are the tales by Donald Sobol about a boy detective; in *Encyclopedia Brown Saves the Day* (1970) the astute ten-year-old solves a series of short mysteries, with answers at the back of the book. Catherine Storr's *Lucy* (1968) is determined to be a detective, and, much to her surprise, she effects the capture of a gang of thieves.

For the nine- to eleven-year-olds, there's an enticing locked room in Elizabeth Ladd's *A Mystery for Meg* (1962). Erich Kästner's *Emil and the Detectives* was published in 1930, but the charm of this German author's style is such that the book is still enjoyed. This is true as well for William Mayne's *The Battlefield*

(1967), in which the Yorkshire setting adds to the appeal of a mystery about some odd, carved, apparently very old stones.

It is for the ten- to twelve-year-olds that mystery stories begin to appear in large numbers, although any true fan will read any good mystery—and even some not so good. In Eleanor Cameron's *A Spell Is Cast* (1964), there are logical explanations for all the things that puzzle Cory, and the book has fine characterization. Although the plot of Frank Bonham's *Mystery in Little Tokyo* (1966) is somewhat contrived, Bonham draws a fine picture of the Japanese section of Los Angeles as a solid neighborhood community with rich tradition. A good story with a country setting is Wilson Gage's *The Ghost of Five Owl Farm* (1966), with a haunted house and Something in the barn.

Two books for this age group that are notable both for their distinctive style and their well-paced plots are William Mayne's *The Changeling* (1963) and Philippa Pearce's *The Minnow Leads to Treasure* (1958). In Mayne's book, three children zealously unravel the mystery of events in the life of an elderly woman who cannot remember anything that happened before she was twenty. In *The Minnow*, two boys recover a family treasure that had been lost since the time of the Armada. To the lure of the subject and the suspense of the story are added superbly natural characters, humor, and an evocative atmosphere of long, golden summer days. In Florence Hightower's *The Fayerweather Forecast* (1967), the style is lively and there are some highly entertaining episodes, such as the one in which mother is working for a new school and little Bitsy obligingly quavers out a pitiful tale about the horrors of the decrepit old school. A kidnaping is solved by a doughty girl in Dorothy Crayder's *She and the Dubious Three* (1974), and the heroine is herself kidnaped in Margaret Storey's *Ask Me No Questions* (1975). Two writers whose tales of adventure and suspense are dependably exciting are Karin Anckarsvärd of Sweden and Nina Bawden of England.

Catch as Catch Can (1970) by Josephine Poole is an English mystery story in which two children witness an incident on a train and are pursued by criminals, a basic plot often used in adult tales and here executed with finesse. In Keith Robertson's *The Money Machine* (1969), two boys pursue the trail of a counterfeiter, and in Eva-Lis Wuorio's *Save Alice!* (1968) three children have a romping journey through Spain, trying to discover why Alice (a bird) had been shoved into their car and what the dastardly villains who did it are up to. In addition to the fun, the story has delightful dialogue between the British and American contingents of the party.

When we come to the mystery and adventure tales for children of eleven and up, we face an avalanche. One of the great classic tales of adventure is Robert Louis Stevenson's *Treasure Island* (1883), which has been published in many fine editions. The story of Long John Silver and his pirate crew has suspense, masterly characterization, a rousing plot, and an adroit contrast in moral codes. *Crystal Mountain* (1955) by Belle Dorman Rugh was a Newbery Honor book. Set in Lebanon, the story has good intercultural relations as well as an interesting setting and the satisfying solution to a minor mystery. Among Keith Robertson's mysteries for this age group are *Three Stuffed Owls* (1954) and *Ice to India* (1955), a sea story with a wonderfully villainous villain.

One of the master storytellers of our time in the realm of high adventure is Leon Garfield. His stories are set in the eighteenth century, abound in picturesque language, period details, complicated plots, exaggerated characters (usually of very high or very low estate), and are written so deftly that the wildly implausible is made wholly convincing. In *Black Jack* (1968), for example, a hanged man revives, captures an orphaned boy and holds up a coach from which an insane girl escapes. The boy and girl join a caravan, she regains her sanity, her father is murdered, she goes to an asylum, the repentant highwayman rescues her, and the boy and girl sail off as stowaways in his uncle's ship, presumably to a much quieter life.

In Henry Winterfeld's *Mystery of the Roman Ransom* (1971) the exuberant boys of ancient Rome who solved a puzzler in *Detectives in Togas* (1956), again become involved in a dramatic detective venture when a slave from Gaul tells them he bears a secret message that a senator is doomed to die. The boys are all sons of senators, and they immediately spring into action, lots of it. The story has the pace and suspense that a good mystery story should have, and although it has no historical significance, it gives a modicum of information about ancient Rome; it also has a minor anti-slavery message, vigorous style, and good characterization.

From France come the mystery stories of Paul Berna, whose *A Truckload of Rice* (1970) is a good example of the solid plots, lively chase sequences, and Parisian settings characteristic of most of his books.

The books of Philip Turner are more boys-and-ploys than they are mysteries, though in *Colonel Sheperton's Clock* (1966) the boys, busily investigating an old mystery, find themselves involved with criminals. The first sequel, *The Grange at High Force* (1967), was awarded the Carnegie Medal, and all of the books are distinguished by a vivid picture of an English town and by the sparkling dialogue, which is tossed back and forth from boy to boy like a ping-pong ball.

Roderic Jeffries, who writes adult mysteries as Jeffrey Ashford, excels at logical plot construction and authoritative details in police procedure in *Patrol Car* (1967) and *River Patrol* (1969).

Felicity Bell tells her own story in Patricia Moyes's *Helter-Skelter* (1968), an artfully plotted tale of a security leak at a British naval research base, during which the heroine confides in the culprit himself and endangers her life thereby.

In Madeleine L'Engle's rather involved adventure story, *The Arm of the Starfish* (1965), a precocious girl of twelve is kidnaped. Her father is a marine biologist working on regeneration of parts, and there are spies and agents prying about the Portuguese island that is the setting. Despite the complications of plot, the story is strong in appeal because of its theme of the triumph of good over evil, or at least of the humane over the inhumane. This is true also of the sequel, *Dragons in the Waters* (1976).

Two authors who have written many suspense stories are Phyllis Whitney and Eilis Dillon. Whitney's *Secret of the Spotted Shell* (1967) is set in the Virgin Islands, and is casual in its acceptance of the mixed racial background of many residents. Eilis Dillon's stories are set in her native Ireland, and each has distinctive characterization and dialogue flavored, rather than burdened, with the musical cadence of Irish speech. In a skillfully constructed, well-paced story, *A Herd of Deer* (1970), Peter Regan is hired as a spy by a man who suspects his hostile neighbors of depleting his herd.

A fledgling spy almost muffs his first assignment in Christopher Nicole's *Operation Destruct* (1969), a story that has the mad pace of the adult spy stories it mocks, light humor, and refreshing variation in detail, such as the pretty girl reporter who is far more adept than the hero and who falls for a pop singer. William Mayne's *Ravensgill* (1970) unfolds and clarifies an old family feud in a tale taut with suspense and delightfully imbued, as are so many Mayne stories, with Yorkshire atmosphere. In his *Pool of Swallows*, written under the pseudonym of Martin Cobalt, (1974), a brilliant blend of ghostly happenings, humor,

Viewpoints

The short story, like any form of literature that pretends to the status of art, must become an organic whole. While it is composed of various identifiable elements, each must be seen as having its existence only in relation to the others and each must contribute a proper share toward the achieving of a final, integrated form. Incident must not exist for its own sake, as it does in anecdote and sometimes does in certain forms of popular fiction. Action must grow out of the conflicting motives of its characters. Similarly, atmosphere should not display a merely sentimental grouping of oddities, as it sometimes did in what we call "local color" stories. Creation of atmosphere must become one of the techniques whereby the total scene achieves its appropriate tone as the result of an underlying consistency of attitude towards the subject. Theme, or "meaning," represents not the mere drawing of a moral or the delivering of a message. The idea must be embodied in the total form, must become as much an integrated segment of the total work as are the characters and the place where they act.—Ray B. West, Jr., *The Art of Writing Fiction,* Thomas Y. Crowell Co., New York, 1968, p. 121.

and suspense, the mysterious pools that suddenly swirl and flood prove to have a logical explanation.

Frank Bonham's *Mystery of the Fat Cat* (1968) is set in a poor neighborhood, Dogtown, where the fate of the Boys' Club is contingent upon a cat. The boys suspect that the cat's caretaker has substituted another animal so that he will not lose his job (he is paid out of an estate which goes to the Boys' Club after the cat's death). The efforts of the boys to prove a fraud has been perpetrated are exciting and believable, and the inclusion of a mentally retarded child as a sympathetic character who contributes to the solution is a bonus.

Of the many mystery anthologies, one that approaches the quality of the best compilations for adults is Joan Kahn's *Some Things Fierce and Fatal* (1971). Other anthologies and single mysteries are given in the bibliography for this chapter.

The books discussed here should suffice to show how mystery cuts across most forms of fiction. Unlike adult "whodunits," the juvenile stories seldom involve murder. Rather, the element of mystery is introduced to heighten interest and suspense. Few of these books have literary distinction, though many are competently written, and mystery tales for children are particularly valuable when, in the course of exciting action, they also emphasize desirable attitudes and social relationships.

The books mentioned in this chapter do not by any means exhaust the list of good realistic fiction for children and young people. To give only the best to children, the adult should be aware of the pedestrian books that are written as "bandwagon" books to satisfy a demand, and should evaluate new books with a critical appraisal of how well they meet the standards discussed in Chapter 2 and fulfill the needs discussed in Chapter 1. The best in this genre will always be those books that depict life honestly and accurately. They are the ones that are interesting in themselves, that present characters who evoke understanding or even self-identification, and that give children new insights into experiences both familiar and unknown.

Adult References[2]

CLARK, ANN NOLAN. *Journey to the People.*

DUNNING, STEPHEN, and ALAN B. HOWES. *Literature for Adolescents; Teaching Poems, Stories, Novels, and Plays.*

EGOFF, SHEILA. *The Republic of Childhood; A Critical Guide to Canadian Children's Literature in English.* Part 4, "The Realistic Animal Story."

EGOFF, SHEILA, G. T. STUBBS, and L. F. ASHLEY, eds. *Only Connect; Readings on Children's Literature.* Part 6, "The Modern Scene."

ELLIS, ANNE W. *The Family Story in the 1960's.*

FENWICK, SARA INNIS, ed. *A Critical Approach to Children's Literature.* "Literature for Children Without" by Marion Edman.

HILDICK, WALLACE. *Children and Fiction.*

HOPKINS, LEE BENNETT. *Books Are by People.*

LEPMAN, JELLA. *A Bridge of Children's Books.*

REID, VIRGINIA M. ed., *Reading Ladders for Human Relations.*

WHITE, DOROTHY, and MARY NEAL. *Books Before Five.*

For additional titles for the youngest children, see the Picture Story Books bibliography, Chapter 4.

For help in locating books with special purposes or about minorities, see the section "Book Selection Aids" in the Adult References in the Appendixes. In the following bibliography these symbols have been used to identify books about a particular religious or ethnic group:

§ Black
★ Chicano or Puerto Rican
☆ Native American
● Religious minority

Some Forerunners of Realistic Fiction

ALCOTT, LOUISA M. *Little Women,* ill. by Barbara Cooney. T. Crowell, 1955 (first pub. in 1868–69).

______. *Little Women,* ill. by Jessie W. Smith. Little, 1968. 10-13

BURNETT, FRANCES HODGSON. *The Secret Garden,* ill. by Tasha Tudor. Lippincott, 1962 (first pub. in 1909). 9-11

DODGE, MARY MAPES. *Hans Brinker, or the Silver Skates,* ill. by Hilda Van Stockum. World, 1948 (first pub. in 1865). 10-12

SPYRI, JOHANNA. *Heidi,* ill. by Greta Elgaard. Macmillan, 1962 (first pub. in 1884). 9-11

TWAIN, MARK (pseud. for Samuel Clemens). *The Adventures of Huckleberry Finn,* ill. by John Falter. Macmillan, 1962 (first pub. in 1885). 10 up

______. *The Adventures of Tom Sawyer,* ill. by John Falter. Macmillan, 1962 (first pub. in 1876). 10-14

______. *The Adventures of Tom Sawyer* and *The Adventures of Huckleberry Finn,* ill. by Norman Rockwell, 2 vols. in 1. Heritage, 1952. 10-14

[2]Complete bibliographic data are provided in the combined Adult References in the Appendixes.

Realistic Fiction: The United States

§ ADOFF, ARNOLD, ed. *Brothers and Sisters; Modern Stories by Black Americans.* Macmillan, 1970. A discriminating selection of twenty short stories about black youth, varied in period, setting, style, and mood, chosen from a 40-year span. 12 up

§ AGLE, NAN HAYDEN. *Maple Street,* ill. by Leonora E. Prince. Seabury, 1970. A black Baltimore neighborhood is kind to a hostile white family in time of trouble. 8-10

ALCOCK, GUDRUN. *Run, Westy, Run,* ill. by W. T. Mars. Lothrop, 1966. A runaway finds there is no magic ending. 10-11

ALEXANDER, MARTHA G. *I'll Be the Horse If You'll Play with Me,* ill. by author. Dial, 1975. 5-7

______. *Out! Out! Out!* ill. by author. Dial, 1968. 3-5

§ ______. *Sabrina,* ill. by author. Dial, 1971. 3-5

§ ______. *The Story Grandmother Told,* ill. by author. Dial, 1969. 3-6

ANGELO, VALENTI. *The Bells of Bleecker Street,* ill. by author. Viking, 1949. An Italian neighborhood comes vividly to life in this amusing story of twelve-year-old Joey's struggles to return the toe from a statue of St. John. 10-13

§ ARMSTRONG, WILLIAM. *Sounder,* ill. by James Barkley. Harper, 1969. Newbery Medal. 12-15

★●☆ ASSOCIATION FOR CHILDHOOD EDUCATION. *Told Under the Stars and Stripes,* ill. by Nedda Walker. Macmillan, 1945. An interracial collection. 8-12

☆ BAKER, BETTY. *Little Runner of the Longhouse,* ill. by Arnold Lobel. Harper, 1962. Little Runner finally gains his reward of maple sugar in the Iroquois New Year rites. An amusing repetitive Indian tale for beginning readers. 6-7

☆ ______. *The Shaman's Last Raid,* ill. by Leonard Shortall. Harper, 1963. Two Apache children of today learn something of their tribal culture when great-grandfather visits them. 9-11

★ BARTH, EDNA. *The Day Luis Was Lost,* ill. by Lilian Obligado. Little, 1971. Newly arrived in the city, a Puerto Rican child has trouble finding his way to school. 8-10

BARTOLI, JENNIFER. *Nonna,* ill. by Joan Drescher. Harvey, 1975. 7-9

§ BARTUSIS, CONSTANCE. *Shades of Difference.* St. Martin's, 1968. A perceptive, candid story of the problems of being completely unprejudiced as a white boy becomes friendly with black members of a recreation center. 13-15

§ BEIM, LORRAINE and JERROLD. *Two Is a Team,* ill. by Ernest Crichlow. Harcourt, 1945. A black and a white youngster learn to cooperate. 5-8

★ BELPRE, PURA. *Santiago,* ill. by Symeon Shimin. Warne, 1969. Missing his pet, left behind in Puerto Rico, a child finds that his picture of her brings him a new friend. 8-9

§ BERENDS, POLLY BERRIEN. *The Case of the Elevator Duck,* ill. by James K. Washburn. Random, 1973. Gilbert, bright, black, bespectacled, finds a duck in the housing project elevator, where no pets are allowed, and finally finds a home for it. A natural, funny story. 8-10

BLUE, ROSE. *Grandma Didn't Wave Back,* ill. by Ted Lewin. Watts, 1972. 8-10

● BLUME, JUDY. *Are You There God? It's Me, Margaret.* Bradbury, 1970. 10-12

______. *Blubber.* Bradbury, 1974. 9-11

______. *Deenie.* Bradbury, 1973. 10-13

______. *It's Not the End of the World.* Bradbury, 1972. 9-11

______. *Then Again, Maybe I Won't.* Bradbury, 1971. 10-12

§ BOND, JEAN. *Brown Is a Beautiful Color,* ill. by Barbara Zuber. Watts, 1969. 5-7

§ BONHAM, FRANK. *Durango Street.* Dutton, 1965. 4 up

§ ______. *The Nitty Gritty,* ill. by Alvin Smith. Dutton, 1968. 11-14

★ ______. *Viva Chicano.* Dutton, 1970. A Chicano youth on parole fights to escape from the burdens that have trapped him into delinquency. 13-16

BORACK, BARBARA. *Someone Small,* ill. by Anita Lobel. Harper, 1969. A tender, realistic, low-keyed story about a little girl who gets a pet bird. The bird eventually dies, is buried, and life goes on. 5-7

BRADBURY, BIANCA. *Andy's Mountain,* ill. by Robert MacLean. Houghton, 1969. A warm and lively picture of a cantankerous and determined old man who refuses to give up his farm to the state for a highway and of the love and loyalty between him and his grandson. 10-12

______. *The Loner,* ill. by John Gretzer. Houghton, 1970. Twelve-year-old Jay's resentment of his older brother Mal works itself out in the course of a summer job. Easy writing style, realistic incidents, and spare structure give the book vitality and verisimilitude. 10-12

BROOKS, JEROME. *Uncle Mike's Boy.* Harper, 1973. A boy adjusting to his parents' divorce and the death of a small sister finds his uncle a source of support and understanding. A warm, sensitive, at times touching, story. 10-12

BROWN, MARGARET WISE. *The Dead Bird,* ill. by Remy Charlip. W. R. Scott, 1958. A simple story of some children's burial of a bird. 5-7

______. *The Little Fisherman,* ill. by Dahlov Ipcar. W. R. Scott, 1945. 4-6

______. (Golden MacDonald, pseud.). *The Little Island,* ill. by Leonard Weisgard. Doubleday, 1946. Gentle descriptive prose. Caldecott Medal. 4-8

______. *The City Noisy Book,* ill. by Leonard Weisgard. Harper, 1939. 4-6

BROWN, MYRA BERRY. *First Night Away from Home,* ill. by Dorothy Marino. Watts, 1960. The mingled qualms and joys of that experience. 4-6

☆ BUFF, MARY. *Dancing Cloud,* rev. ed., ill. by Conrad Buff. Viking, 1957. The Navaho Indians depicted in beautiful prose and pictures. 8-10

☆ BUFF, MARY and CONRAD. *Hah-Nee of the Cliff Dwellers,* ill. by Conrad Buff. Houghton, 1956. A story of the great pueblo cities of the Southwest. 10-12

● ______. *Peter's Pinto,* ill. by Conrad Buff. Viking, 1949. A Utah ranch summer is highlighted for Peter when he acquires a wild pinto pony of his own. Mormon background. 9-11

☆ BULLA, CLYDE. *Eagle Feather,* ill. by Tom Two Arrows. T. Crowell, 1953. Eagle Feather, a young Navaho, loved the outdoor life of a shepherd and had no wish to go to school until changed circumstances made school a longed-for goal. 7-10

☆ ______. *Indian Hill,* ill. by James Spanfeller. T. Crowell, 1963. Adjustment of a Navaho Indian family moved from a reservation to a city apartment. 8-10

______. *Shoeshine Girl,* ill. by Leigh Grant. T. Crowell, 1975. Sarah Ida takes a job shining shoes for spending money, and changes for the better as a result of her relationship with her boss. Quiet but satisfying. 8-10

§ BURCH, ROBERT. *Joey's Cat,* ill. by Don Freeman. Viking, 1969.

§ ______. *Queenie Peavy,* ill. by Jerry Lazare. Viking, 1966. 11-14

______. *Simon and the Game of Chance,* ill. by Fermin Rocker. Viking, 1970. 10-12

BUTLER, BEVERLY. *Light a Single Candle.* Dodd, 1962. The stirring story of Cathy Wheeler, blinded at fourteen, and her courageous struggle to regain her place in the school crowd. 12-15

BYARS, BETSY C. *After the Goat Man,* ill. by Ronald Himler. Viking, 1974. 10-12

______. *Go and Hush the Baby,* ill. by Emily A. McCully. Viking, 1971. An appealing story about Will, who is asked by his mother to pacify the baby just as he is about to leave the house, bat in hand. 2-5

______. *The House of Wings,* ill. by Daniel Schwartz. Viking, 1972. 9-12

______. *The Summer of the Swans,* ill. by Ted CoConis. Viking, 1970. Newbery Medal. 10-12

§ CAINES, JEANNETTE FRANKLIN. *Abby,* ill. by Steven Kellogg. Harper, 1973. A small black girl learns about her adoption. 3-6

CAMERON, ELEANOR. *A Room Made of Windows,* ill. by Trina Schart Hyman. Little, 1971. 10-13

§ ______. *To the Green Mountains.* Dutton, 1975. 10-13

CAMPBELL, HOPE. *Why Not Join the Giraffes?* Norton, 1968. Suzie's stuffy boyfriend almost makes her regret her nonconformist parents. 11-14

§ CARLSON, NATALIE SAVAGE. *Ann Aurelia and Dorothy,* ill. by Dale Payson. Harper, 1968. 8-10

§ ______. *The Empty Schoolhouse,* ill. by John Kaufmann. Harper, 1965. 9-11

______. *The Half Sisters,* ill. by Thomas di Grazia. Harper, 1970. 9-11

______. *Luvvy and the Girls,* ill. by Thomas di Grazia. Harper, 1971. 8-11

§ ______. *Marchers for the Dream,* ill. by Alvin Smith. Harper, 1969. 9-11

§ CAUDILL, REBECCA. *A Certain Small Shepherd,* ill. by William Pène du Bois. Holt, 1965. An Appalachian Christmas story, movingly told. 9-11

______. *Did You Carry the Flag Today, Charley?* ill. by Nancy Grossman. Holt, 1966. 5-7

______. *A Pocketful of Cricket,* ill. by Evaline Ness. Holt, 1964. On his first day of school Jay takes a pet cricket with him in his pocket. A charming picture book that captures a universal quality of childhood. 5-7

★§ CHILD STUDY ASSOCIATION OF AMERICA. *Families Are Like That!* ill. by Richard Cuffari. T. Crowell, 1975. Ten stories of family life and relationships. 7-9

§ CHILDRESS, ALICE. *a HERO ain't nothin' but a Sandwich.* Coward, 1973. 11-14

☆ CLARK, ANN NOLAN. *Along Sandy Trails,* photos by Alfred A. Cohn. Viking, 1969. Not really a story, this book with its beautiful color photos follows an Indian child in the Arizona desert and gives a feeling of the peaceful life and of the color and beauty of the dry land's flowering. 8-10

☆ ______. *In My Mother's House,* ill. by Velino Herrera. Viking, 1941. 8-12

☆ ______. *Little Navajo Bluebird,* ill. by Paul Lantz. Viking, 1943. 8-12

☆ ______. *Medicine Man's Daughter,* ill. by Donald Bolognese. Farrar, 1963. 11-13

CLARK, MARGERY (pseud. for Mary E. Clark and Margery C. Quigley). *The Poppy Seed Cakes,* ill. by Maud and Miska Petersham. Doubleday, 1924. Amusing tales of lively Andrewshek. 7-9

CLEARY, BEVERLY. *Ellen Tebbits,* ill. by Louis Darling. Morrow, 1951. The trials and tribulations of being in third grade. 8-12

______. *Fifteen,* ill. by Beth and Joe Krush. Morrow, 1956. Jane at fifteen wants above all a handsome boyfriend. Her progress, along with the essential family life of fifteen-year-olds, is told with a light and satisfying reality. 12-15

______. *Henry Huggins,* ill. by Louis Darling. Morrow, 1950. And other books in the series. 8-10

______. *Jean and Johnny,* ill. by Beth and Joe Krush. Morrow, 1959. The author creates a sympathetic family life around fifteen-year-old bespectacled Jean and the cocky senior who temporarily captures her heart. 12-15

______. *Mitch and Amy,* ill. by George Porter. Morrow, 1967. 9-11

______. *Ramona the Brave,* ill. by Alan Tiegreen. Morrow, 1975. 8-10

______. *Ramona the Pest,* ill. by Louis Darling. Morrow, 1968. 8-10

______. *Ribsy,* ill. by Louis Darling. Morrow, 1964. 9-11

CLEAVER, VERA and BILL. *Dust of the Earth.* Lippincott, 1975. 11-14

______. *Ellen Grae,* ill. by Ellen Raskin. Lippincott, 1967. 9-11

______. *Grover,* ill. by Frederic Marvin. Lippincott, 1970. 9-11

______. *I Would Rather Be a Turnip.* Lippincott, 1971. 10-12

______. *Lady Ellen Grae,* ill. by Ellen Raskin. Lippincott, 1968. 9-11

______. *Where the Lilies Bloom,* ill. by Jim Spanfeller. Lippincott, 1969. 11-14

§ CLIFTON, LUCILLE. *Don't You Remember?* ill. by Evaline Ness. Dutton, 1973. A charming black family story, with a four-year-old who remembers everything. 3-5

§ ______. *My Brother Fine with Me,* ill. by Moneta Barnett. Holt, 1975. 7-9

§ ______. *The Times They Used to Be,* ill. by Susan Jeschke. Holt, 1974. 10-11

CLYMER, ELEANOR. *The Big Pile of Dirt,* ill. by Robert Shore. Holt, 1968. 8-10

§ ______. *The House on the Mountain,* ill. by Leo Carty. Dutton, 1971. 8-9

§ ______. *Luke Was There,* ill. by Diane de Groat. Holt, 1973. 9-12

______. *My Brother Stevie.* Holt, 1971. 9-11

☆ ______. *The Spider, the Cave and the Pottery Bowl,* ill. by Ingrid Fetz. Atheneum, 1971. 8-10

______. *We Lived in the Almont,* ill. by David K. Stone. Dutton, 1970. The first-person account of Linda and her family who move into the once elegant Almont apartments. A perceptive picture of the concerns of a young adolescent and a small group of varied tenants. 9-11

●§ COHEN, BARBARA. *Thank You, Jackie Robinson,* ill. by Richard Cuffari. Lothrop, 1974. 9-11

COLLIER, JAMES LINCOLN. *Rich and Famous; The Further Adventures of George Stable.* Four Winds, 1975. 11-14

______. *The Teddy Bear Habit, or How I Became a Winner,* ill. by Lee Lorenz. Norton, 1967. Fast pace and fast humor in the TV and recording industry as 13-year-old George's agent tries to make him a star. 10-12

COLMAN, HILA. *After the Wedding.* Morrow, 1975. 12-16

§ ______. *Classmates by Request.* Morrow, 1964. 12-15

______. *Claudia, Where Are You?* Morrow, 1969. 12-15

★ ______. *The Girl from Puerto Rico.* Morrow, 1961. 12-15

§ CONE, MOLLY. *The Other Side of the Fence,* ill. by John Gretzer. Houghton, 1967. It's hard to side with the minority when a black family moves into the neighborhood. 8-10

CONFORD, ELLEN. *Felicia the Critic,* ill. by Arvis Stewart. Little, 1973. Why did people get so irritated when Felicia just used common sense and told the truth? Funny, completely natural dialogue. 10-12

______. *The Luck of Pokey Bloom,* ill. by Bernice Loewenstein. Little, 1975. Pokey's tries at winning various contests lend themselves to humor. Good parent-child relationships in a warm family story. 9-11

______. *Me and the Terrible Two,* ill. by Charles Carroll. Little, 1974. Dorrie can hardly believe it when the new next-door neighbors turn out to be boys—and twins, at that. 9-11

CORCORAN, BARBARA. *A Dance to Still Music,* ill. by Charles Robinson. Atheneum, 1974. 11-13

______. *The Long Journey,* ill. by Charles Robinson. Atheneum, 1970. Laurie, thirteen, is sent on horseback by her grandfather across the state of Montana to find her uncle. The story has pace and suspense, memorable characters, an appealing heroine, and a satisfying ending. 10-12

______. *Sam,* ill. by Barbara McGee. Atheneum, 1967. 11-14

● CORMIER, ROBERT. *The Chocolate War.* Pantheon, 1974. 12-16

CRAIG, MARGARET MAZE. *Now That I'm Sixteen.* T. Crowell, 1959. A teen-age story of real substance, in which Chip, a boy classmate, steers timid, insecure Beth on the road to genuine popularity and success. 12-15

CRAYDER, DOROTHY. *She, the Adventuress,* ill. by Velma Ilsley. Atheneum, 1973. 9-11

CRETAN, GLADYS YESSAYAN. *All Except Sammy,* ill. by Symeon Shimin. Little, 1966. The misfit in a musical Armenian-American family, Sammy finds status and satisfaction in art. 8-10

DANZIGER, PAULA. *The Cat Ate My Gymsuit.* Delacorte, 1974. 11-13

§ DE ANGELI, MARGUERITE. *Bright April,* ill. by author. Doubleday, 1946. 8-11

● ______. *Henner's Lydia,* ill. by author. Doubleday, 1936. 8-10

______. *The Lion in the Box,* ill. by author. Doubleday, 1975. An old-fashioned Christmas story. 9-11

● ______. *Skippack School,* ill. by author. Doubleday, 1939 and 1961. 9-11

● ______. *Thee, Hannah!* ill. by author. Doubleday, 1940. 9-11

● ______. *Yonie Wondernose,* ill. by author. Doubleday, 1944. 6-9

DE PAOLA, TOMIE. *Nana Upstairs and Nana Downstairs,* ill. by author. Putnam, 1973. 5-8

DE REGNIERS, BEATRICE. *A Little House of Your Own,* ill. by Irene Haas. Harcourt, 1955. A house of your own is important to even the youngest child. 5-7

______. *The Snow Party,* ill. by Reiner Zimnik. Pantheon, 1959. On a lonely Dakota farm, a blinding snowstorm brings a houseful of company to a little old woman who pined for a party. 5-9

☆ DISTAD, ANDREE. *Dakota Sons,* ill. by Tony Chen. Harper, 1972. When Tad made friends with an Indian boy, he found out just how pervasive prejudice could be. 9-11

DIXON, PAIGE. *May I Cross Your Golden River?* Atheneum, 1975. Eighteen-year-old Jordan and his family must adjust to the knowledge of his certain death. Handled with conviction and dignity. 12-15

DODD, WAYNE. *A Time of Hunting.* Seabury, 1975. Jess loved hunting, but gradually he learned to value life for all, and put hunting behind him. Taut, smooth, believable. 11-14

DONOVAN, JOHN. *I'll Get There. It Better Be Worth the Trip.* Harper, 1969. 11-14

______. *Wild in the World.* Harper, 1971. 11-14

§ DURHAM, JOHN. *Me and Arch and the Pest,* ill. by Ingrid Fetz. Four Winds, 1970. 8-10

☆ EMBRY, MARGARET. *Shadi.* Holiday, 1971. A story of cultural conflict for an adolescent Navajo girl. 11-14

ENRIGHT, ELIZABETH. *The Four-Story Mistake,* ill. by author. Holt, 1942. 9-11

______. *Gone-Away Lake,* ill. by Beth and Joe Krush. Harcourt, 1957. 8-10

______. *Return to Gone-Away,* ill. by Beth and Joe Krush. Harcourt, 1961. 8-10

______. *The Saturdays,* ill. by author. Holt, 1941. 9-12

______. *Then There Were Five,* ill. by author. Holt, 1944. 10-13

______. *Thimble Summer,* ill. by author. Holt, 1938. Newbery Medal. 10-12

§ ERWIN, BETTY. *Behind the Magic Line,* ill. by Julia Iltis. Little, 1969. 9-11

ESTES, ELEANOR. *The Alley,* ill. by Edward Ardizzone. Harcourt, 1964. 9-11

______. *The Coat-Hanger Christmas Tree,* ill. by Suzanne Suba. Atheneum, 1973. 9-11

______. *Ginger Pye,* ill. by author. Harcourt, 1951. Newbery Medal. 9-11

______. *The Hundred Dresses,* ill. by Louis Slobodkin. Harcourt, 1944. 9-11

______. *The Middle Moffat,* ill. by Louis Slobodkin. Harcourt, 1942. 9-11

______. *The Moffats,* ill. by Louis Slobodkin. Harcourt, 1941 and 1968. 9-11

______. *Rufus M.,* ill. by Louis Slobodkin. Harcourt, 1943. 9-11

★ ETS, MARIE HALL. *Bad Boy, Good Boy,* ill. by author. T. Crowell, 1967. 5-8

★ ______. *Gilberto and the Wind,* ill. by author. Viking, 1963. No indication is given as to whether the Mexican child is in Mexico or the U.S. 3-5

______. *Just Me,* ill. by author. Viking, 1965. A very small boy describes his imaginative imitating of farmyard animals as he plays alone. 3-6

______. *Play with Me,* ill. by author. Viking, 1955. An exquisite picture story showing how a little girl makes many animal friends when she learns to be still in the woods. 3-6

EWING, KATHRYN. *A Private Matter,* ill. by Jean Sandin. Harcourt, 1975. 9-10

FARLEY, CAROL. *The Garden Is Doing Fine,* ill. by Lynn Sweat. Atheneum, 1975. Corrie refuses to face the fact that her father is dying until she sees herself as his garden. 10-14

FASSLER, JOAN. *Howie Helps Himself,* ill. by Joe Lasker. Whitman, 1974. 6-8

§ FAULKNER, GEORGENE, and JOHN BECKER. *Melindy's Medal,* ill. by Elton C. Fax. Messner, 1945. A humorous and tender story of a black girl, Melindy, who is boundlessly happy when the family moves to a new housing project. When a fire breaks out at her school, Melindy proves her bravery. 8-10

● FEAGLES, ANITA. *Me, Cassie.* Dial, 1968. Her mother's liberal causes almost crowd Cassie out of her home. An amusing, sophisticated tale. 12-15

● FENTON, EDWARD. *Duffy's Rocks.* Dutton, 1974. Timothy, raised by his grandmother, can't rest until he sees his father for himself. An outstanding story of a Roman Catholic family in the Depression years. 11-13

● FITZGERALD, JOHN DENNIS. *The Great Brain Does It Again,* ill. by Mercer Mayer. Dial, 1975. One of a series about a Roman Catholic family living in a Mormon town. J.D. tells anecdotes about his older brother, who can talk his way out of anything. Lively and funny. 10-12

FITZHUGH, LOUISE. *Harriet the Spy,* ill. by author. Harper, 1964. 10-12

______. *The Long Secret,* ill. by author. Harper, 1965. 11-13

§ ______. *Nobody's Family Is Going to Change.* Farrar, 1974. A black father scoffs at the daughter who wants to be a lawyer like him, but Emma won't change her mind. 10-11

FLACK, MARJORIE. *Wait for William,* ill. by author and R. A. Holberg. Houghton, 1935. 4-8

FOX, PAULA. *Blowfish Live in the Sea.* Bradbury, 1970. 11-14

§ ______. *How Many Miles to Babylon?* ill. by Paul Giovanopoulos. White, 1967. 9-10

______. *A Likely Place,* ill. by Edward Ardizzone. Macmillan, 1967. 9-11

______. *Maurice's Room,* ill. by Ingrid Fetz. Macmillan, 1966. 8-10

______. *Portrait of Ivan,* ill. by Saul Lambert. Bradbury, 1969. 10-12

______. *The Stone-Faced Boy,* ill. by Donald A. MacKay. Bradbury, 1968. 9-11

☆ FREDERICKSEN, HAZEL. *He-Who-Runs-Far,* ill. by John Houser. W. R. Scott, 1970. The book is chiefly devoted to years spent by Pablo, a Papago Indian, in the government school where he learns English and the white man's ways. He becomes convinced he must bring understanding and change to his people but realizes as the book closes that they are not yet ready to accept his ideas. 10-13

GAGE, WILSON. *Big Blue Island,* ill. by Glen Rounds. World, 1964. When Darrell is sent to live with a great-uncle on an island in Tennessee, he is bored and resentful. The depiction of the boy is powerful: a child who has no parents, no education, and no future begins to feel that he has a place and a role. 10-12

______. *Dan and the Miranda,* ill. by Glen Rounds. World, 1962. Dan chose spiders for his school science project, and the family, especially his sister, regarded the choice with mixed feelings! A delightful family tale developed around a nature theme. 9-10

★ GALBRAITH, CLARE K. *Victor,* ill. by Bill Comerford. Knopf, 1971. Victor has a hard time with a new language, and is delighted when Mamacita shows up at school on Parents' Night and airs her secretly learned English. 8-9

GATES, DORIS. *Blue Willow,* ill. by Paul Lantz. Viking, 1940. A story of migratory farm workers and ten-year-old Janey's longing for a permanent home. 10-12

GEORGE, JEAN. *My Side of the Mountain,* ill. by author. Dutton, 1959. 11-14

GOFF, BETH. *Where Is Daddy? The Story of a Divorce,* ill. by Susan Perl. Beacon, 1969. 3-5

GOFFSTEIN, M. B. *Two Piano Tuners,* ill. by author. Farrar, 1970. Orphaned Debbie lives with her grandfather, an expert piano tuner. He wants Debbie to be a concert pianist; she wants to be a piano tuner as good as Grandpa. The story has humor, affection, and charm. 8-9

GONZALES, GLORIA. *The Glad Man.* Knopf, 1975. Melissa organizes community support for an old man living in a bus near a dump, and finds she's done more harm than good. 9-11

§ GRAHAM, LORENZ. *North Town.* T. Crowell, 1965.

§ ______. *South Town.* Follett, 1958.

§ ______. *Whose Town?* T. Crowell, 1969.

In these books the Williams family leaves the South because of discrimination, but finds much discrimination in the North as well. David, a teenager, wavers between militancy and moderation. 11-14

§ GREENE, BETTE. *Philip Hall Likes Me. I Reckon Maybe,* ill. by Charles Lilly. Dial, 1974. 9-11

● ______. *Summer of My German Soldier.* Dial, 1973. A mistreated Jewish girl living in a small Arkansas town in the 1940s befriends an escaped German prisoner. 11-14

GREENE, CONSTANCE C. *The Ears of Louis,* ill. by Nola Langner. Viking, 1974. 8-10

______. *A Girl Called Al,* ill. by Byron Barton. Viking, 1969. 9-11

______. *I Know You, Al,* ill. by Byron Barton. Viking, 1975. 8-11

______. *Leo the Lioness.* Viking, 1970. The theme of the adolescent who grows into a more mature person is handled unusually well here. The writing is convincingly that of a teenager, the dialogue is excellent, and the relationships are drawn sympathetically. 10-12

______. *The Unmaking of Rabbit.* Viking, 1972. 9-11

§ GREENFIELD, ELOISE. *Sister,* ill. by Moneta Barnett. T. Crowell, 1974. 10-12

§ GUY, ROSA. *The Friends.* Holt, 1973. 12-15

HAMILTON, GAIL. *Titania's Lodestone.* Atheneum, 1975. Priscilla is pleasantly surprised when her Gypsy-like parents are accepted in a small Massachusetts town, and she herself grows in understanding and perspective. 10-13

§ HAMILTON, VIRGINIA. *The House of Dies Drear,* ill. by Eros Keith. Macmillan, 1968. 11-14

§ ______. *M. C. Higgins, the Great.* Macmillan, 1974. Newbery Medal, National Book Award. 11-13

§ ______. *The Planet of Junior Brown.* Macmillan, 1971. 12-14

§ ______. *Time-Ago Lost; More Tales of Jahdu,* ill. by Ray Prather. Macmillan, 1973. 8-10

§ ______. *The Time-Ago Tales of Jahdu,* ill. by Nonny Hogrogian. Macmillan, 1969. 8-10

§ ______. *Zeely,* ill. by Symeon Shimin. Macmillan, 1967. 9-11

HAYWOOD, CAROLYN. *"B" Is for Betsy,* ill. by author. Harcourt, 1939, 1968. And other books in the series. 6-8

______. *Eddie's Happenings,* ill. by author. Morrow, 1971. 8-10

______. *Eddie's Pay Dirt,* ill. by author. Morrow, 1953. 8-10

______. *Eddie's Valuable Property,* ill. by author. Morrow, 1975. 7-9

______. *Little Eddie,* ill. by author. Morrow, 1947. And other books in the series. 7-9

HEILBRONER, JOAN. *The Happy Birthday Present,* ill. by Mary Chalmers. Harper, 1962. Peter and Davy, with little money and endless time, shop thoroughly for mother's birthday gift. One of the most delightful of the books for beginning readers. 6-7

●§ HENTOFF, NAT. *I'm Really Dragged But Nothing Gets Me Down.* Simon, 1968. 14-17

●§ ______. *In the Country of Ourselves.* Simon, 1971. 12-17

§ ______. *Jazz Country.* Harper, 1965. 13 up

______. *This School Is Driving Me Crazy.* Delacorte, 1975. 10-13

§ HILL, ELIZABETH. *Evan's Corner,* ill. by Nancy Grossman. Holt, 1967. 5-7

HINTON, S. E. *The Outsiders.* Viking, 1967. 13-15

______. *Rumble Fish.* Delacorte, 1975. 12-16

______. *That Was Then, This Is Now.* Viking, 1971. 13-15

HOBAN, RUSSELL C. *Herman the Loser,* ill. by Lillian Hoban. Harper, 1961. A most refreshing picture story of a little boy with a talent for losing who one day becomes a victorious finder. 5-6

______. *The Sorely Trying Day,* ill. by Lillian Hoban. Harper, 1964. A family finds that hostile or friendly behavior can have a chain effect. 5-7

HOLLAND, ISABELLE. *Amanda's Choice.* Lippincott, 1970. Twelve-year-old Amanda is an *enfant terrible.* When Manuel, a nineteen-year-old musical prodigy from a New York slum, comes to occupy the guest cottage at her family's summer home, Amanda feels he is the first person who understands her. Memorable characterization and good style. 12-14

______. *The Man Without a Face.* Lippincott, 1972. A boy from an all-female household finds help in an older man's affection. A dignified treatment of a homosexual incident. 12-15

______. *Of Love and Death and Other Journeys.* Lippincott, 1975. When her mother dies, Meg leaves Europe for a new home in New York with a father she's never known. A sophisticated story with superbly drawn characters. 12-15

HOLMAN, FELICE. *Slake's Limbo.* Scribner's, 1974. Slake lives in a hideaway in the New York subway for four months, existing like a Crusoe, through resourcefulness. A smooth, novel tale. 10-12

HUNT, IRENE. *Up a Road Slowly.* Follett, 1967. Julie Trelling, left motherless at age seven, is sent to live with an aunt and uncle who provide her with insight into the qualities necessary to become a mature, happy individual. Newbery Medal. 11-14

§ HUNTER, KRISTIN. *Guests in the Promised Land.* Scribner's, 1973. 12-15

§ ______. *The Soul Brothers and Sister Lou.* Scribner's, 1968. 12-15

● ISH-KISHOR, SULAMITH. *Our Eddie.* Pantheon, 1969. 11-14

JACKSON, JACQUELINE. *The Paleface Redskins,* ill. by author. Little, 1958. A family summer is enlivened by imaginative play. 9-11

§ JACKSON, JESSE. *Call Me Charley,* ill. by Doris Spiegel. Harper, 1945. 10-13

§ ______. *Charley Starts from Scratch.* Harper, 1958. 12 up Two sensitive stories of a black boy who lives in a white neighborhood. After high school, Charley finds many doors closed to him until he comes in first in Olympic trials.

§ ______. *Tessie,* ill. by Harold James. Harper, 1968. A black girl wins a scholarship to an all-white private school, and firmly insists on making the best of both worlds. 11-14

JOHNSON, ANNABEL and EDGAR. *The Grizzly,* ill. by Gilbert Riswold. Harper, 1964. David accompanies his father to the woods for a weekend of fishing. The dangers they encounter, the relationship between father and son who hardly know each other since the parents have been separated for some years—all this is perceptively and convincingly described. 11-14

§ JORDAN, JUNE. *New Life: New Room,* ill. by Ray Cruz. T. Crowell, 1975. 5-8

● JORDAN, MILDRED. *Proud to Be Amish,* ill. by W. T. Mars. Crown, 1968. Katie has a hard time with guilt feelings when she envies the dress of a child who's not plain. 10-11

§ JUSTUS, MAY. *New Boy in School,* ill. by Joan Balfour Payne. Hastings, 1963. Lennie must adjust to being the only black boy in his class. 7-8

§ ______. *A New Home for Billy,* ill. by Joan Balfour Payne. Hastings, 1966. 5-8

KATZ, BOBBI. *The Manifesto and Me—Meg.* Watts, 1974. 9-12

§ KEATS, EZRA JACK. *Dreams,* ill. by author. Macmillan, 1974. 3-6

§ ______. *Goggles!* ill. by author. Macmillan, 1969. 5-7

§ ______. *Louie,* ill. by author. Greenwillow, 1975. 5-8

§ ______. *The Snowy Day,* ill. by author. Viking, 1962. Caldecott Medal. 5-7

§ ______. *Whistle for Willie,* ill. by author. Viking, 1964. 3-6

KERR, M. E. *Dinky Hocker Shoots Smack.* Harper, 1972. 11-14

______. *Is That You, Miss Blue?* Harper, 1975. 12-16

______. *Love Is a Missing Person.* Harper, 1975. 12-15

______. *The Son of Someone Famous.* Harper, 1974. 12-15

KINGMAN, LEE. *The Peter Pan Bag.* Houghton, 1970. 13-16

______. *The Year of the Raccoon.* Houghton, 1966. Joey is an ordinary middle child who is helped to overcome feelings of inferiority and inadequacy through his attachment to a pet raccoon. 11-14

KLEIN, NORMA. *Confessions of an Only Child,* ill. by Richard Cuffari. Pantheon, 1974. 9-11

______. *It's Not What You Expect.* Pantheon, 1973. 11-14

______. *Mom, the Wolf Man, and Me.* Pantheon, 1972. 10-13

______. *Taking Sides.* Pantheon, 1974. 11-13

§ KONIGSBURG, E. L. *Altogether, One at a Time,* ill. by Gail E. Haley and others. Atheneum, 1971. 9-11

______. *The Dragon in the Ghetto Caper,* ill. by author. Atheneum, 1974. 10-12

______. *From the Mixed-Up Files of Mrs. Basil E. Frankweiler,* ill. by author. Atheneum, 1967. Newbery Medal. 10-12

______. *(George),* ill. by author. Atheneum, 1970. 11-14

§ ______. *Jennifer, Hecate, Macbeth, William McKinley, and Me, Elizabeth,* ill. by author. Atheneum, 1967. 9-11

KRAUSS, RUTH. *A Hole Is to Dig,* ill. by Maurice Sendak. Harper, 1952. Definitions you won't find in any dictionary! 5-7

______. *A Very Special House,* ill. by Maurice Sendak. Harper, 1953. An imaginative spree by a small child who, for once in his life, does everything he shouldn't. 4-7

§ KREMENTZ, JILL. *Sweet Pea; A Black Girl Growing Up in the Rural South,* ill. with photos by author. Harcourt, 1969. Ten-year-old Sweet Pea tells her own story: living with a working mother and four little brothers in a rented house in rural Alabama, a hard but not intolerable life with family love and religion looming large. Good photos. 8-10

★ KRUMGOLD, JOSEPH. *. . . and now Miguel,* ill. by Jean Charlot. T. Crowell, 1953. Newbery Medal. 13-17

______. *Henry 3,* ill. by Alvin Smith. Atheneum, 1967. 11-14

______. *Onion John,* ill. by Symeon Shimin. T. Crowell, 1959. Newbery Medal. 11-14

☆ LAMPMAN, EVELYN SIBLEY. *Half-Breed,* ill. by Ann Grifalconi. Doubleday, 1967. 15-17

☆ ______. *Navaho Sister,* ill. by Paul Lantz. Doubleday, 1956. 10-13

☆ ______. *Rattlesnake Cave,* ill. by Pamela Johnson. Atheneum, 1974. 9-11

☆ ______. *Treasure Mountain,* ill. by Richard Bennett. Doubleday, 1949. 12-14

☆ ______. *The Year of Small Shadow.* Harcourt, 1971. 10-12

LASKER, JOE. *He's My Brother,* ill. by author. Whitman, 1974. 7-9

☆ LAURITZEN, JONREED. *The Ordeal of the Young Hunter,* ill. by Hoke Denetsosie. Little, 1954. A distinguished story of a twelve-year-old Navaho boy who grows to appreciate what is good in the cultures of the white man and the Indian. Background of the story is Flagstaff, Arizona.. 11-14

LEE, MILDRED. *The Rock and the Willow.* Lothrop, 1963. 14-16

______. *The Skating Rink.* Seabury, 1969. 11-13

L'ENGLE, MADELEINE. *Meet the Austins.* Vanguard, 1960. 10-13

______. *The Moon by Night.* Ariel, 1963. 11-14

LENSKI, LOIS. *Bayou Suzette,* ill. by author. Stokes, 1943. 8-10

______. *Blue Ridge Billy,* ill. by author. Lippincott, 1946. 8-10

______. *Boom Town Boy,* ill. by author. Lippincott, 1948. 8-12

______. *Cotton in My Sack,* ill. by author. Lippincott, 1949. 8-12

______. *High-Rise Secret,* ill. by author. Lippincott, 1966. 8-9

______. *Judy's Journey,* ill. by author. Lippincott, 1947. 8-10

______. *The Little Auto,* ill. by author. Walck, 1934. The first in a popular series about Mr. Small. 5-7

______. *Project Boy,* ill. by author. Lippincott, 1954. 7-9

______. *Strawberry Girl,* ill. by author. Lippincott, 1945. Newbery Medal. 9-12

★ LEWITON, MINA. *Candita's Choice,* ill. by Howard Simon. Harper, 1959. A warm and understanding story of an eleven-year-old who adjusts slowly to the move from Puerto Rico to New York. When she has a chance to return, Candita decides to stay in New York where she no longer feels an alien. 9-11

§ LEXAU, JOAN. *Benjie,* ill. by Don Bolognese. Dial, 1964. 5-7

§ ______. *Benjie on His Own,* ill. by Don Bolognese. Dial, 1970. 5-8

______. *Come Here, Cat,* ill. by Steven Kellogg. Harper, 1973. 5-7

______. *Finders Keepers, Losers Weepers,* ill. by Tomi de Paola. Lippincott, 1967. 6-8

§ ______. *Me Day,* ill. by Robert Weaver. Dial, 1971. 5-8

______. *Olaf Reads,* ill. by Harvey Weiss. Dial, 1961. 6-7

§ ______. *Striped Ice Cream,* ill. by John Wilson. Lippincott, 1968. 7-9

LINDQUIST, JENNIE. *The Golden Name Day,* ill. by Garth Williams. Harper, 1955. A warm story of a Swedish-American family. 8-10

McCLOSKEY, ROBERT. *Blueberries for Sal,* ill. by author. Viking, 1948. Sal gets home safely after following a bear in the blueberry patch. 4-7

______. *Centerburg Tales,* ill. by author. Viking, 1951. Humorous stories. 10-12

______. *Homer Price,* ill. by author. Viking, 1943. Lively, funny stories about an irrepressible boy; one of the first books to spoof comic books. 9-12

______. *Lentil,* ill. by author. Viking, 1940. A boy saves the day in a small town's welcome to a returning citizen by playing the harmonica. 7-9

______. *Make Way for Ducklings,* ill. by author. Viking, 1941. Caldecott Medal. 6-8

______. *One Morning in Maine,* ill. by author. Viking, 1952. 5-7

______. *Time of Wonder,* ill. by author. Viking, 1957. Caldecott Medal. 8-10

§ McGOVERN, ANN. *Black Is Beautiful,* ill. by Hope Wurmfeld. Four Winds, 1969. 5-8

McKAY, ROBERT. *Dave's Song.* Meredith, 1969. Well written, this book is both realistic and romantic. Kate (who considers Dave a loner, an oddball) and Dave (who considers Kate, but secretly) are drawn together in their reaction to the unjust treatment of a rehabilitated ex-convict. 12-15

§ MATHIS, SHARON BELL. *The Hundred Penny Box,* ill. by Leo and Diane Dillon. Viking, 1975. 8-11

§ ______. *Listen for the Fig Tree.* Viking, 1974. 12-16

MAZER, HARRY. *The Dollar Man.* Delacorte, 1974. Marcus longs to know his father, but finds the reality disappointing. Believable and touching. 11-14

MAZER, NORMA FOX. *A Figure of Speech.* Delacorte, 1973. A moving, realistic story of a child's love for her grandfather. 11-14

MEANS, FLORENCE CRANNELL. *Knock at the Door, Emmy,* ill. by Paul Lantz. Houghton, 1956. 12-14

☆ ______. *Our Cup Is Broken.* Houghton, 1969. 12-15

§ ______. *Shuttered Windows,* ill. by Armstrong Sperry. Houghton, 1938. 11-14

★§ ______. *Us Maltbys.* Houghton, 1966. 11-14

MILES, BETTY. *The Real Me.* Knopf, 1974. 9-11

MITCHELL, LUCY SPRAGUE. *Here and Now Story Book,* rev. and enl. ed., ill. by H. Willem Van Loon and Christine Price. Dutton, 1948 (first pub. in 1921). Stories with little plot, but centered on the child's own activities, told in the child's words. 2-7

★ MOHR, NICHOLASA. *Nilda,* ill. by author. Harper, 1973. 11-14

★ ______. *El Bronx Remembered; A Novella and Stories.* Harper, 1975. A varied group of stories, atmospheric and told with simplicity of style. 12-14

MOSER, DON. *A Heart to the Hawks.* Atheneum, 1975. 12-15

§ MURRAY, MICHELE. *Nellie Cameron,* ill. by Leonora E. Prince. Seabury, 1971. 9-11

NESS, EVALINE. *Sam, Bangs & Moonshine,* ill. by author. Holt, 1966. Sam is a small, mendacious girl and Bangs is her cat and moonshine is the word for all the lies she tells. Attractive illustrations. Caldecott Medal. 5-7

§ NEUFELD, JOHN. *Edgar Allan.* Phillips, 1968. A poignant story of a white family's adoption of a black child, and the pressure that forces them to give him up. 11-14

§ NEUMEYER, PETER. *The Faithful Fish,* ill. by Arvis L. Stewart. W. R. Scott, 1971. The children of a white family are followed by those of a black family in a vacation cottage where fishing is the great attraction. 5-8

● NEVILLE, EMILY. *Berries Goodman.* Harper, 1965. 11-14

______. *Fogarty.* Harper, 1969. A fine, thoughtful book about a young college dropout whose plans to be a playwright come to naught but who realizes there is another place in the world for him. 13-15

§ ______. *Garden of Broken Glass.* Delacorte, 1975. 12-14

______. *It's Like This, Cat,* ill. by Emil Weiss. Harper, 1963. Newbery Medal. 11-14

§ NEWELL, HOPE. *A Cap for Mary Ellis.* Harper, 1953. Two young nursing students enter as the first black trainees in a New York State hospital. There they make a happy adjustment to the new life, their fellow workers, and the patients. The story is told with warmth and humor. Followed by *Mary Ellis, Student Nurse* (1958). 12-16

NORDSTROM, URSULA. *The Secret Language,* ill. by Mary Chalmers. Harper, 1960. 7-9

★ O'DELL, SCOTT. *Child of Fire.* Houghton, 1974. 12-15

§ PANETTA, GEORGE. *The Shoeshine Boys,* ill. by Joe Servello. Grosset, 1971. Tony, an Italian-American, becomes a shoeshine boy to help out with the finances when his father loses his job. He joins forces with MacDougal Thompson, a black boy, and the Black and White Shoeshine Company is a great success. 8-10

PECK, RICHARD. *Don't Look and It Won't Hurt.* Holt, 1972. 11-14

______. *Dreamland Lake.* Holt, 1973. 11-13

______. *Representing Super Doll.* Viking, 1974. 11-15

______. *Through a Brief Darkness.* Viking, 1973. 11-14

● PECK, ROBERT NEWTON. *A Day No Pigs Would Die.* Knopf, 1972. Anecdotal story of a Shaker boy on a Vermont farm, where families have strong ties. 12-16

PEVSNER, STELLA. *A Smart Kid Like You.* Seabury, 1975. 10-12

PFEFFER, SUSAN BETH. *The Beauty Queen.* Doubleday, 1974. Kit's mother badgers her into entering a beauty contest when she wants to join a little theater group. 11-14

______. *Marly the Kid.* Doubleday, 1975. 11-14

★ POLITI, LEO. *Juanita,* ill. by author. Scribner's, 1948. 5-7

______. *Little Leo,* ill. by author. Scribner's, 1951. 5-8

______. *Moy Moy,* ill. by author. Scribner's, 1960. 5-7

★ ______. *Pedro, the Angel of Olvera Street,* ill. by author. Scribner's, 1946. 6-9

★ ______. *Song of the Swallows,* ill. by author. Scribner's, 1949. Caldecott Medal. 5-7

★ ______. *Three Stalks of Corn,* ill. by author. Scribner's, 1976. 5-8

RABE, BERNIECE. *Naomi.* Nelson, 1975. Life on a Missouri farm during the Depression years, with superstition and religion strong influences on daily life. 11-14

RASKIN, ELLEN. *Spectacles,* ill. by author. Atheneum, 1968. An amusing picture book about the trials and errors of a small girl who myopically sees strange creatures and finally is won over to wearing glasses. 5-7

RICH, LOUISE DICKINSON. *Three of a Kind,* ill. by William M. Hutchinson. Watts, 1970. A foster child forgets her own problems in helping the four-year-old autistic grandson of the couple she lives with. Realistic characters and a warmly portrayed Maine setting. 9-11

RICHARD, ADRIENNE. *Pistol.* Little, 1969. 12-15

§ RINKOFF, BARBARA. *Member of the Gang,* ill. by Harold James. Crown, 1968. 10-12

ROBERTSON, KEITH. *Henry Reed, Inc.,* ill. by Robert McCloskey. Viking, 1958. 11-13

______. *Henry Reed's Big Show,* ill. by Robert McCloskey, Viking, 1970. 10-12

______. *In Search of a Sandhill Crane,* ill. by Richard Cuffari. Viking, 1973. 10-13

§ RODMAN, BELLA. *Lions in the Way.* Follett, 1966. A story of school integration in a Tennessee town. 11-14

§ ROSE, KAREN. *A Single Trail.* Follett, 1969. Ricky is white and entering a new sixth grade after nine moves. Earl is black and antagonistic in school. Their friendship comes very slowly with help from an understanding teacher. The story has a sturdy honesty. 10-11

● ______. *There Is a Season.* Follett, 1967. Katie Levin dates a new neighbor, a Roman Catholic boy, but finds that religious pressures interfere. 11-14

● SACHS, MARILYN. *Amy and Laura,* ill. by Tracy Sugarman. Doubleday, 1966. 9-11

● ______. *Amy Moves In,* ill. by Judith G. Brown. Doubleday, 1964. 9-11

______. *The Bears' House,* ill. by Louis Glanzman. Doubleday, 1971. 9-12

______. *Dorrie's Book,* ill. by Anne Sachs. Doubleday, 1975. 10-12

● ______. *Laura's Luck,* ill. by Ib Ohlsson. Doubleday, 1965. 9-11

● ______. *Marv,* ill. by Louis Glanzman. Doubleday, 1970. 9-12

● ______. *Peter and Veronica,* ill. by Louis Glanzman. Doubleday, 1969. 9-12

★ ______. *The Truth About Mary Rose,* ill. by Louis Glanzman. Doubleday, 1973. 9-12

● ______. *Veronica Ganz,* ill. by Louis Glanzman. Doubleday, 1968. 10-12

SAWYER, RUTH. *Roller Skates,* ill. by Valenti Angelo. Viking, 1936. Newbery Medal. 12-13

SCHULMAN, L. M., ed. *A Woman's Place; An Anthology of Short Stories.* Macmillan, 1974. Chosen with taste, these stories reflect the theme of woman's role in a world in which she is not treated as man's equal. 12-16

SCOPPETTONE, SANDRA. *Trying Hard to Hear You.* Harper, 1974. 13-18

§ SCOTT, ANN HERBERT. *Sam,* ill. by Symeon Shimin. McGraw, 1967. Although the story is more an expanded situation than a plot, it is a pleasant and realistic picture of Sam and his black, middle-class family. 3-6

SEGAL, LORE. *Tell Me a Mitzi,* ill. by Harriet Pincus. Farrar, 1970. 5-7

SHARMAT, MARJORIE WEINMAN. *Gladys Told Me to Meet Her Here,* ill. by Edward Frascino. Harper, 1970. When Gladys is late meeting Irving at the zoo, he indulges himself alternately in daydreams of his best friend suffering and memories of her staunch loyalty. As enjoyable for the adult reader-aloud as for the young listener. 5-7

______. *Goodnight Andrew Goodnight Craig,* ill. by Mary Chalmers. Harper, 1969. Two small boys, who have gone to bed, get noisier and noisier until their father comes in with an ultimatum. The illustrations echo the engaging tone of the story, which is all in dialogue. 4-6

______. *Maggie Marmelstein for President,* ill. by Ben Shecter. Harper, 1975. 9-11

§ SHEARER, JOHN. *I Wish I Had an Afro,* ill. with photos by author. Cowles, 1970. The candor and pathos of the text are uncommon and the quality of the photos is exceptional. 9-11

SHERBURNE, ZOA. *Leslie.* Morrow, 1972. A girl's reluctant first try with marijuana leads to serious consequences. 12-16

______. *Stranger in the House.* Morrow, 1963. Adjustment to the return home of a mother from a mental hospital. 13-15

______. *Too Bad About the Haines Girl.* Morrow, 1967. Melinda, a teenager, finds that a premarital pregnancy affects others as well as herself. 13-17

§★ SHOTWELL, LOUISA R. *Adam Bookout,* ill. by W. T. Mars. Viking, 1967. An interracial story set in Brooklyn. Adam finds he can't avoid problems by moving from one relative's house to another. 9-11

★ ______. *Magdalena,* ill. by Lilian Obligado. Viking, 1971. 10-12

§ ______. *Roosevelt Grady,* ill. by Peter Burchard. World, 1963. 9-11

SHULEVITZ, URI. *One Monday Morning,* ill. by author. Scribner's, 1967. A fine read-aloud book about the imaginative play of a small, solitary child. The setting is urban, inner city, lower class. 5-7

SKORPEN, LIESEL MOAK. *Elizabeth,* ill. by Martha Alexander. Harper, 1970. Kate was disappointed when she got a rag doll for Christmas instead of the one she wanted. How she came to love the rag doll is told without sentimentality. 5-7

SMITH, DORIS BUCHANAN. *Kelly's Creek,* ill. by Alan Tiegreen. T. Crowell, 1975. An appealing story of a boy with a learning disability. 9-11

______. *Kick a Stone Home.* T. Crowell, 1974. A fifteen-year-old learns to accept herself, as well as her father's new wife. 11-14

______. *A Taste of Blackberries,* ill. by Charles Robinson, T. Crowell, 1973. 9-11

☆ SMUCKER, BARBARA. *Wigwam in the City,* ill. by Gil Miret. Dutton, 1966. One of the few stories about discrimination against Indians in an urban setting. A Chippewa family in Chicago turns to the American Indian Center for help. 10-12

☆ SNEVE, VIRGINIA DRIVING HAWK. *High Elk's Treasure,* ill. by Oren Lyons. Holiday, 1972. A story of a Sioux Indian family that makes clear the attitudes of contemporary Indians of different generations. 9-12

SNYDER, ZILPHA KEATLEY. *The Changeling,* ill. by Alton Raible. Atheneum, 1970. 10-12

§ ______. *The Egypt Game,* ill. by Alton Raible. Atheneum, 1967. 9-12

______. *The Headless Cupid,* ill. by Alton Raible. Atheneum, 1971. 9-11

______. *The Velvet Room,* ill. by Alton Raible. Atheneum, 1965. 10-12

______. *The Witches of Worm,* ill. by Alton Raible. Atheneum, 1972. 11-13

★ SONNEBORN, RUTH. *Friday Night Is Papa Night,* ill. by Emily A. McCully. Viking, 1970. 6-7

§ SORENSON, VIRGINIA. *Around the Corner,* ill. by Robert Weaver. Harcourt, 1971. 10-12

______. *Miracles on Maple Hill,* ill. by Beth and Joe Krush. Harcourt, 1956. Newbery Medal. 10-12

● ______. *Plain Girl,* ill. by Charles Geer. Harcourt, 1955. 9-11

§ SPRAGUE, GRETCHEN. *A Question of Harmony.* Dodd, 1965. Values are clarified when three young people are refused service in a snack bar because one of them is black. 12-15

§ STEPTOE, JOHN. *Stevie,* ill. by author. Harper, 1969. 5-7

§ STERLING, DOROTHY. *Mary Jane,* ill. by Ernest Crichlow. Doubleday, 1959. 10-13

STOLZ, MARY. *The Bully of Barkham Street,* ill. by Leonard Shortall. Harper, 1963. 10-12

______. *By the Highway Home.* Harper, 1971. 11-13

______. *A Dog on Barkham Street,* ill. by Leonard Shortall. Harper, 1960. 10-12

______. *The Edge of Next Year.* Harper, 1974. 10-13

______. *Lands End,* ill. by Dennis Hermanson. Harper, 1973. 10-12

★ ______. *The Noonday Friends,* ill. by Louis S. Glanzman. Harper, 1965. 9-11

______. *Who Wants Music on Monday?* Harper, 1963. A sharply perceptive story of a sensitive adolescent who sees clearly the shallowness of her popular older sister, the amiable stupidity of her mother. Also candid are the discussions between her brother and his black college roommate. 13-15

§ ______. *A Wonderful, Terrible Time,* ill. by Louis S. Glanzman. Harper, 1967. 9-11

TALBOT, CHARLENE JOY. *A Home with Aunt Florry.* Atheneum, 1974. Orphaned Wendy and Jason are sent to New York City to live with an aunt who lives in a condemned building and is an inveterate scrounger. Adjustment is not easy. 10-13

★ ______. *Tomas Takes Charge,* ill. by Reisie Lonette. Lothrop, 1966. Two motherless Puerto Rican children, fearing the dreaded Welfare, hide in an abandoned New York building when their father fails to come home. The boy's tender protection of his older, timid sister is beautifully drawn. 9-12

§ TANNER, LOUISE. *Reggie and Nilma.* Farrar, 1971. Nilma, a black woman, and her son, Reggie, enjoy a close relationship with the white family she works for. When Reggie is wrongly suspected of robbing the white family's apartment, the breach is irreparable. Despite the serious problems, the story is not somber. 11-15

● TAYLOR, SYDNEY. *All-of-a-Kind Family,* ill. by Helen John. Follett, 1951.

● ______. *All-of-a-Kind Family Downtown,* ill. by Beth and Joe Krush. Follett, 1972.
Stories about a New York Jewish family of the 1900s, which seems to run only to girls. 9-11

§ TAYLOR, THEODORE. *The Cay.* Doubleday, 1969. 12-15

★ THOMAS, DAWN C. *Mira! Mira!* ill. by Harold L. James. Lippincott, 1970. A Puerto Rican child adjusts to a move to New York not through the usual pattern of recognition in some situation but rather when he sees his first snowfall which he feels "fell from the sky to say 'Welcome.'" 5-7

TRESSELT, ALVIN. *Hide and Seek Fog,* ill. by Roger Duvoisin. Lothrop, 1965. 5-8

______. *White Snow, Bright Snow,* ill. by Roger Duvoisin. Lothrop, 1947. Caldecott Medal. 5-7

TURKLE, BRINTON. *The Sky Dog,* ill. by author. Viking, 1969. A satisfying story for the read-aloud audience about a boy who finds and keeps a stray dog. Simply and touchingly told and engagingly illustrated. 4-6

UCHIDA, YOSHIKO. *The Birthday Visitor,* ill. by Charles Robinson. Scribner's, 1975. A young Japanese-American girl finds that a visiting minister from Japan doesn't spoil her birthday. 7-9

______. *The Promised Year,* ill. by William M. Hutchinson. Harcourt, 1959. A Japanese girl visits the United States. 9-11

UDRY, JANICE MAY. *The Moon Jumpers,* ill. by Maurice Sendak. Harper, 1959. Beautiful color illustrations enhance this mood picture book which describes children frolicking in the moonlight until bedtime interrupts their imaginative play. 5-8

§ ______. *Mary Jo's Grandmother,* ill. by Eleanor Mill. Whitman, 1970. 5-7

§ WALDRON, ANN. *The Integration of Mary-Larkin Thornhill.* Dutton, 1975. A white minister's daughter is assigned to a black junior high school in the South. 10-13

WALLACE, BARBARA BROOKS. *Victoria.* Follett, 1972. A boarding-school story with a self-centered, complex, and touching heroine. 9-12

§ WEIK, MARY HAYS. *The Jazz Man,* ill. by Ann Grifalconi. Atheneum, 1966. A story that combines harsh realism and brooding lyricism gives a poignant picture of a crippled child in Harlem. This has had high praise for its tender treatment of the child and harsh criticism for the depiction of parental neglect. 9-11

WERSBA, BARBARA. *The Dream Watcher.* Atheneum, 1968. Albert is an adolescent loner until he meets an old woman who tells him about her glamorous career on the stage and becomes his friend. When she dies, he is shocked to find she had lied to him about almost everything, but he realizes keenly that she gave him something precious and durable. Excellent characterization. 11-14

● ______. *Run Softly, Go Fast.* Atheneum, 1970. 13-15

WIER, ESTER. *The Loner,* ill. by Christine Price. McKay, 1963. A boy with no name, no home, no family, is taken in by a woman sheepherder, and he learns what it means to give oneself completely to a job. Vivid characterization, a notable theme. 11-14

§ WILKINSON, BRENDA. *Ludell.* Harper, 1975. Three years in the life of a black girl in a small Georgia town in the 1950s. 11-13

WILL and NICOLAS. *Russet and the Two Reds,* ill. Harcourt, 1962.

______. *The Two Reds,* ill. Harcourt, 1950.

Slight but lively stories with the realism of city streets. 5-8

WILLIAMS, BARBARA. *Kevin's Grandma,* ill. by Kay Chorao. Dutton, 1975. 4-6

WOJCIECHOWSKA, MAIA. *Don't Play Dead Before You Have To.* Harper, 1970. 13-15

______. *Tuned Out.* Harper, 1968. 14-16

YASHIMA, TARO. *Umbrella,* ill. by author. Viking, 1958. To small Momo it seemed that rain would never come so that she might use her new blue umbrella and bright red boots. New York background. 4-6

YORK, CAROL BEACH. *Nothing Ever Happens Here.* Hawthorn, 1970. Young Elizabeth lives a quiet life in a dull town, but the author has written a truly touching book about the ordinary lives around her. Perceptive characterization. 11-14

ZINDEL, PAUL. *The Pigman.* Harper, 1968. 12-14

ZOLOTOW, CHARLOTTE. *Big Sister and Little Sister,* ill. by Martha Alexander. Harper, 1966. 5-7

______. *A Father Like That,* ill. by Ben Shecter. Harper, 1971. 5-7

______. *The Hating Book,* ill. by Ben Shecter. Harper, 1969. 5-7

______. *Janey,* ill. by Ronald Himler. Harper, 1973. 7-8

______. *William's Doll,* ill. by William Pène du Bois. Harper, 1972. 5-8

______, comp. *An Overpraised Season; 10 Stories of Youth.* Harper, 1973. A varied collection of short stories about the bittersweet problems of adolescents, especially their relationships with adults. 11-16

Realistic Fiction: Other Lands

Africa

§ BØDKER, CECIL. *The Leopard,* tr. by Gunnar Poulsen. Atheneum, 1975. When a leopard steals a calf, Tibeso sets out to see a wise man and becomes involved with a thief. Set in Ethiopia. 10-12

§ BRADLEY, DUANE. *Meeting with a Stranger,* ill. by E. Harper Johnson. Lippincott, 1964. An American comes to an Ethiopian village to teach sheep-raising and is tested by the boys. 10-12

§ CLIFFORD, MARY LOUISE. *Salah of Sierra Leone,* ill. by Elzia Moon. T. Crowell, 1975. A boy is uncertain which side is right in the political maneuvering surrounding the 1967 elections. 11-13

§ DINNEEN, BETTY. *Lion Yellow.* Walck/McKay, 1975. A Kenyan game park is threatened with closing. 10-12

§ ______. *A Lurk of Leopards,* ill. by Charles Robinson. Walck, 1972. Karen lives in a suburb of Nairobi and happens upon a female leopard. Knowing she should report the presence of a dangerous animal, Karen equivocates. 10-13

§ FEELINGS, MURIEL. *Zamani Goes to Market,* ill. by Tom Feelings. Seabury, 1970. Adventures of a small boy in Ghana. 5-8

§ GERSON, MARY-JOAN. *Omoteji's Baby Brother,* ill. by Elzia Moon. Walck, 1974. 8-9

§ GRAHAM, LORENZ B. *I, Momolu,* ill. by John Biggers. T. Crowell, 1966. Taken to Liberia's Cape Roberts after he has hurt a soldier who playfully dressed his son in a uniform, Flumbo realizes that not all soldiers are evil. 12-15

§ ______. *Song of the Boat,* ill. by Leo and Diane Dillon. T. Crowell, 1975. 8-9

§ MIRSKY, REBA. *Seven Grandmothers,* ill. by W. T. Mars. Follett, 1955. A sequel to the title below.

______. *Thirty-one Brothers and Sisters,* ill. by W. T. Mars. Follett, 1952. Life in a Zulu village. 9-11

§ MITCHISON, NAOMI. *Sunrise Tomorrow; A Story of Botswana.* Farrar, 1973. 12-15

§ NAGENDA, JOHN. *Mukasa,* ill. by Charles Lilly. Macmillan, 1973. 9-11

§ STEVENSON, WILLIAM. *The Bushbabies,* ill. by Victor Ambrus. Houghton, 1965. A most unusual story, both in the setting and in the beautifully built-up relationship between two people different in age, sex, race, and station. The story moves from one dangerous episode to another across wild African country. 11-14

§ WELLMAN, ALICE. *Tatu and the Honey Bird,* ill. by Dale Payson. Putnam, 1972. A small boy helps his sister get an education too. Set in Angola. 8-10

Australia and New Zealand

§ BRINSMEAD, HESBA FAY. *Pastures of the Blue Crane.* Coward, 1966. 13-15

CLARK, MAVIS THORPE. *Spark of Opal.* Macmillan, 1973. 11-14

OTTLEY, REGINALD. *The Bates Family.* Harcourt, 1969. The Bates family, ten strong, has no home but a wagon as they work as drovers in the outback. 10-13

______. *Boy Alone,* ill. by Clyde Pearson. Harcourt, 1966. The story of a young adolescent in the Australian outback. The atmosphere is wonderfully created; the writing is perceptive. Followed by *Roan Colt* (1967) and *Rain Comes to Yamboorah* (1968). 10-12

PHIPSON, JOAN. *Birkin,* ill. by Margaret Horder. Harcourt, 1966. An engaging story about several children in a small Australian town who care for a calf. Plenty of action and humor. 10-12

______. *The Boundary Riders,* ill. by Margaret Horder. Harcourt, 1963. The suspense-filled journey to safety of three Australian children and their dog. 10-13

______. *The Family Conspiracy,* ill. by Margaret Horder. Harcourt, 1964. The large Barker family lives on an isolated Australian sheep station. A warm and convincing family story with good characterization and an unsentimental ending. 10-11

______. *Polly's Tiger,* ill. by Erik Blegvad. Dutton, 1974. Polly has problems making friends in a new home. 8-9

SOUTHALL, IVAN. *Ash Road,* ill. by Clem Seale. St. Martin's, 1966. 11-14

______. *Benson Boy,* ill. by Ingrid Fetz. Macmillan, 1973. 10-12

______. *Hills End.* Macmillan, 1963, 1974. 11-14

______. *Let the Balloon Go,* ill. by Ian Ribbons. St. Martins, 1968. 11-13

______. *To the Wild Sky,* ill. by Jennifer Tuckwell. St. Martin's, 1967. 12-14

SPENCE, ELEANOR, *Jamberoo Road,* ill. by Doreen Roberts. Roy, 1969. Two orphans, Cassie and Luke, go to the prosperous Marlow homestead as governess and stable boy. The book has a bit of everything: drama and love interest, excellent characterization, good plot, and an interesting Australian setting. 11-14

______. *The Nothing Place,* ill. by Geraldine Spence. Harper, 1973. Glen has many problems adjusting to deafness, and the sympathy of his new friends seems a hindrance rather than a help. 10-12

SUTHERLAND, MARGARET. *Hello, I'm Karen,* ill. by Jane Paton. Coward, 1976. Karen's life in New Zealand. 7-8

THIELE, COLIN. *Blue Fin.* Harper, 1974. Snook's skipper father is firmly convinced that his son can't do anything right on a tuna boat, but Snook gets an opportunity to prove his worth in this exciting tale. 11-14

______. *Fire in the Stone.* Harper, 1974. 11-14

WRIGHTSON, PATRICIA. *A Racecourse for Andy,* ill. by Margaret Horder. Harcourt, 1968. 10-12

Canada

CORCORAN, BARBARA, and BRADFORD ANGIER. *A Star to the North.* Nelson, 1970. 11-14

LITTLE, JEAN. *Home from Far,* ill. by Jerry Lazare. Little, 1965. 10-13

● ______. *Kate.* Harper, 1971. 10-13

● ______. *Look Through My Window,* ill. by Joan Sandin. Harper, 1970. 9-11

______. *Mine for Keeps,* ill. by Lewis Parker. Little, 1962. 10-12

______. *Spring Begins in March,* ill. by Lewis Parker. Little, 1966. 10-12

______. *Stand in the Wind,* ill. by Emily Arnold McCully. Harper, 1975. Martha and Ellen entertain two American sisters, who at first seem hardly worth knowing. 9-11

Central and South America

BEHN, HARRY. *The Two Uncles of Pablo,* ill. by Mel Silverman. Harcourt, 1959. Small Pablo copes with two antagonistic uncles as well as his own problem of trying to gain an education. An appealing story of Mexico written by a poet very popular with children. 9-11

BONHAM, FRANK. *The Vagabundos.* Dutton, 1969. 12-15

BUFF, MARY and CONRAD. *Magic Maize,* ill. by authors. Houghton, 1953. Guatemalan Indians and their problems. 9-12

BULLA, CLYDE. *Benito,* ill. by Valenti Angelo. T. Crowell, 1961. The encouragement of a successful artist helps orphaned Benito assert his need for time from the endless farm drudgery at Uncle Pedro's to develop his talent. 8-10

CLARK, ANN NOLAN. *Santiago,* ill. by Lynd Ward. Viking, 1955. 12-14

______. *Secret of the Andes,* ill. by Jean Charlot. Viking, 1952. Newbery Medal. 12-14

ETS, MARIE HALL, and AURORA LABASTIDA. *Nine Days to Christmas,* ill. by Marie Hall Ets. Viking, 1959. Ceci, a little girl of Mexico, discovers the fun of Christmas with her first piñata. Caldecott Medal. 5-8

GARRETT, HELEN. *Angelo the Naughty One,* ill. by Leo Politi. Viking, 1944. The amusing reform of a small Mexican boy who did not like to take baths. 6-9

NESS, EVALINE. *Josefina February,* ill. by author. Scribner's, 1963. A warm, quiet read-aloud story set in Haiti. 5-7

O'DELL, SCOTT. *The Black Pearl,* ill. by Milton Johnson. Houghton, 1967. The stark simplicity of the story and the deeper significance it holds in the triumph of good over evil add importance to the book, but even without that it would be enjoyable as a rousing adventure tale with beautifully maintained tempo and suspense as Ramon searches for a giant black pearl in the waters of Baja California. 12-17

RHOADS, DOROTHY M. *The Corn Grows Ripe,* ill. by Jean Charlot. Viking, 1956. Twelve-year-old Tigre, spoiled and lazy, grows up suddenly when his father is injured. Background of the story is Yucatan, among the Mayan Indians. 9-12

ROY, CAL. *The Legend and the Storm,* ill. by author. Farrar, 1975. The extensive and bitter student uprising in Mexico in 1968 seen from the viewpoint of fifteen-year-old Rafa. 13-16

SOMMERFELT, AIMÉE. *My Name Is Pablo,* tr. by Patricia Crampton, ill. by Hans Norman Dah. Criterion, 1966. 11-14

STOLZ, MARY. *The Dragons of the Queen,* ill. by Edward Frascino. Harper, 1969. A simply written tale which contrasts new ways of life with the old in Mexico. 10-12

______. *Juan,* ill. by Louis S. Glanzman. Harper, 1970. A story of an orphaned boy, this has fine characterization. 9-11

SURANY, ANICO. *Ride the Cold Wind,* ill. by Leonard Everett Fisher. Putnam, 1964. The story of a small Peruvian boy who wishes to go fishing with his father on Lake Titicaca. He and his sister go boating alone, and when a storm comes up, must be rescued. An appealing theme and setting. 8-10

VAN ITERSON, S. R. *Pulga,* tr. from the Dutch by Alexander and Alison Gode. Morrow, 1971. 11-14

China and Japan

BRO, MARGUERITE. *Su-Mei's Golden Year,* ill. by Kurt Wiese. Doubleday, 1950. It is Su-Mei and her friends of the younger generation who save their Chinese village from famine when the wheat crop is endangered. 11-14

BUCK, PEARL. *The Big Wave,* ill. by Hiroshige and Hokusai. Day, 1948. Jiya leaves the coast after a tidal wave destroys his home and the entire fishing village. When he is grown, he courageously returns to his traditional occupation. There is a heroic quality in the telling which makes this Japanese story a memorable one. 9-13

DeJONG, MEINDERT. *The House of Sixty Fathers,* ill. by Maurice Sendak. Harper, 1956. 11-13

HANDFORTH, THOMAS. *Mei Li,* ill. by author. Doubleday, 1938. The pleasant adventures of a little Chinese girl at the Fair. Caldecott Medal. 5-8

MATSUNO, MASAKO. *A Pair of Red Clogs,* ill. by Kazue Mizumura. World, 1960. A little Japanese girl damages her new red clogs by playing a game with them. Beautifully illustrated in color, with a universal theme. 5-8

UCHIDA, YOSHIKO. *Hisako's Mysteries,* ill. by Susan Bennett. Scribner's, 1969. Although there is some awkwardness in the appearance of Hisako's father, who was presumed dead, the book is otherwise well written and interesting both for the picture of life in Japan today and of a typical thirteen-year-old. 10-12

———. *Sumi and the Goat and the Tokyo Express,* ill. by Kazue Mizumura. Scribner's, 1969. Sumi has a brief but delicious moment in the limelight when she is the only one who can get old Mr. Oda's goat to move from the path of the new Tokyo express. A charming book. 7-9

VINING, ELIZABETH GRAY. *The Cheerful Heart,* ill. by Kazue Mizumura. Viking, 1959. Tomi and her family return to Tokyo after World War II and start life anew. 9-11

YASHIMA, MITSU and TARO. *Plenty to Watch,* ill. by Taro Yashima. Viking, 1954. 8-10

YASHIMA, TARO. *Crow Boy,* ill. by author. Viking, 1955. 8-10

England, Ireland, Scotland, Wales

ARDIZZONE, EDWARD. *Little Tim and the Brave Sea Captain,* ill. by author. Walck, 1955 (first pub. in 1936). First of several books about Tim's adventures at sea. 4-6

———. *Nicholas and the Fast Moving Diesel,* ill. by author. Walck, 1959. Two small boys avert a train wreck when fireman and engineer become ill. High adventure for the youngest. 5-7

ARUNDEL, HONOR. *The Blanket Word.* Nelson, 1973. Jan realizes that love, the blanket word, can mean something besides entanglement. Typical of Arundel's candid, sympathetic teenage novels. 12-15

CRESSWELL, HELEN. *The Night Watchmen,* ill. by Gareth Floyd. Macmillan, 1970. Josh and Caleb, the most distinctive pair of tramps in contemporary fiction, fascinate young Henry with their enthralling talk and their do-as-you-please life. Not deep characterization, but marvelously vivid characters. 9-11

DIVINE, DAVID. *The Stolen Seasons.* T. Crowell, 1970. Two British children and their American friend organize an expedition to get over Hadrian's Wall without being spotted. The first part of the book is entertaining, the second tense with suspense when they flee some men, who have stolen a valuable artifact and know the children have seen them. 11-14

GARNETT, EVE. *The Family from One End Street,* ill. by author. Vanguard, 1960. The story of the big, cheerful Ruggles family who live in a poor neighborhood. Carnegie Medal. 11-13

GODDEN, RUMER. *The Kitchen Madonna,* ill. by Carol Barker. Viking, 1967. Dour Mr. McFadden turns neighborly when ten-year-old Selina becomes his friend. 8 up

———. *Mr. McFadden's Hallowe'en.* Viking, 1975. 8-12

HILDICK, E. W. *Louie's Snowstorm,* ill. by Iris Schweitzer. Doubleday, 1974. 10-12

● LINGARD, JOAN. *Across the Barricades.* Nelson, 1973. Catholic Kevin and Protestant Sadie fall in love in the beleaguered Belfast of today. 11-15

● ———. *Into Exile.* Nelson, 1973. Kevin and Sadie, now married, find their religious differences cannot be ignored, especially after Kevin's father is killed by a bomb. 12-15

● ———. *A Proper Place.* Nelson, 1975. Kevin and Sadie struggle to make ends meet in Liverpool. 12-15

● ———. *The Twelfth Day of July; A Novel of Modern Ireland.* Nelson, 1972. 11-13

MACKELLAR, WILLIAM. *Wee Joseph,* ill. by Ezra Jack Keats. McGraw, 1957. Young Davie prayed hard, and a small miracle and a great scientific event combine to save Wee Joseph, his runt puppy, from being drowned. A heartwarming story of Scotland. 8-10

McLEAN, ALLAN CAMPBELL. *Storm over Skye,* ill. by Shirley Hughes. Harcourt, 1957. A story rich in Scottish atmosphere tells of two brothers' efforts to solve the sheep stealing that has thrown their community into an uproar. A bit of romance, too. 13-16

McNEILL, JANET. *The Battle of St. George Without,* ill. by Mary Russon. Little, 1968. Urban children in a fight for turf. 10-12

———. *Goodbye, Dove Square,* ill. by Mary Russon. Little, 1969. In this sequel to the above title, all the Dove Square residents have left the area, cleared for renewal. A realistic picture of urban life. 10-13

———. *The Other People.* Little, 1970. Kate visits her aunt's guest house, which she had envisioned as a glamorous resort, and finds it shabby and filled with unexciting people. Her initiative and sympathy are the fulcrum for events that change, to some extent, the lives of most of the others and her own as well. Well-drawn characters. 11-13

———. *We Three Kings.* Little, 1974. Estranged cousins are brought together as they salvage a Nativity play almost ruined by a delinquent gang. 9-11

MAYNE, WILLIAM. *A Grass Rope,* ill. by Lynton Lamb. Dutton, 1962. Four children investigate an old legend about a unicorn. Carnegie Medal. 10-12

———. *A Swarm in May,* ill. by C. Walter Hodges. Bobbs, 1957. 11-13

MORGAN, ALISON. *A Boy Called Fish,* ill. by Joan Sandin. Harper, 1973. The story of a boy and his dog, set in rural Wales. 9-11

———. *Pete.* Harper, 1973. Pete, thought by his mother to be on a school trip, runs off from Wales to Scotland to join his father, on a job there, finding both enemies and friends on the way. 10-12

———. *Ruth Crane.* Harper, 1974. Ruth has problems dealing with a younger brother after the death of her father and the hospitalization of her mother and sister after an automobile accident. Set in Wales. 11-14

NESBIT, EDITH. *The Conscience Pudding,* ill. by Erik Blegvad. Coward, 1970. A Christmas story taken from *The New Treasure Seekers,* one of the books about the Bastable children that have become classics. When money is short, the children plan and produce an elaborate Christmas pudding. The period details are charmingly picked up in the illustrations. 9-11

PEARCE, PHILIPPA. *A Dog So Small,* ill. by Antony Maitland. Lippincott, 1963. An unusual story of a gentle, withdrawn young boy's obsessive desire to own a dog. 10-12

———. *What the Neighbors Did and Other Stories,* ill. by Faith Jaques. T. Crowell, 1973. 9-12

PEYTON, K. M. *The Beethoven Medal,* ill. by author. T. Crowell, 1972. 12-15

———. *Pennington's Heir.* T. Crowell, 1974. 12-15

———. *Pennington's Last Term,* ill. by author. T. Crowell, 1971. 12-15

RANSOME, ARTHUR. *Swallows and Amazons,* ill. by Helene Carter. Lippincott, 1931. First of a series of stories about four children who live in the Lake District in England. 12-13

ROBINSON, JOAN G. *Charley,* ill. by Prudence Seward. Coward, 1970. The story of Charley who, through a misunderstanding, believes she is unwanted by the aunt to whom she is sent and runs away. Good characters, plenty of action, and the perennial appeal of making-it-on-your-own. 9-11

ROBINSON, VERONICA. *David in Silence,* ill. by Victor Ambrus. Lippincott, 1966. The story, set in a small English town, concerns a new boy, David, who has always been deaf. A poignant and interesting story about the isolation and hostility that often are the lot of the deaf. 10-12

STREATFEILD, NOEL. *Ballet Shoes,* ill. by Richard Floethe. Random, 1950. The hard work and unwavering determination that it takes to become a ballet dancer. 11-13

______. *The Children on the Top Floor,* ill. by Jillian Willett. Random, 1965. Life with a television celebrity. 10-12

______. *The Family at Caldicott Place,* ill. by Betty Maxey. Random, 1968. Life is difficult when the father of the family is recovering from a deep neurosis. 9-11

______. *Thursday's Child,* ill. by Peggy Fortnum. Random, 1971. A foundling girl finds her place in life. 9-11

TATE, JOAN. *Wild Boy,* ill. by Susan Jeschke. Harper, 1973. The friendship between two boys, both solitary people. Set in Yorkshire. 10-12

TOWNSEND, JOHN ROWE. *Good-bye to the Jungle.* Lippincott, 1967. 12-14

______. *Good Night, Prof, Dear.* Lippincott, 1970. 12-14

______. *Hell's Edge.* Lothrop, 1969. 11-14

______. *The Intruder.* Lippincott, 1970. 11-14

______. *Noah's Castle.* Lippincott, 1976. 10-14

______. *Trouble in the Jungle,* ill. by W. T. Mars. Lippincott, 1969. 10-12

TURNER, PHILIP. *War on the Darnel,* ill. by W. T. Mars. World, 1969. Three lively English boys engage in a mighty battle with another set of boys who have set up a river barricade. Good characterization and even better dialogue. 10-14

VAN STOCKUM, HILDA. *The Cottage at Bantry Bay,* ill. by author. Viking, 1938.

______. *Francie on the Run,* ill. by author. Viking, 1939.

______. *Pegeen,* ill. by author. Viking, 1941. 10-12

WALSH, JILL PATON. *Fireweed.* Farrar, 1970. 11-14

France

BEMELMANS, LUDWIG. *Madeline,* ill. by author. Viking, 1939. Other titles in the series include the Caldecott Medal book *Madeline's Rescue* (1953), *Madeline and the Bad Hat* (1957), *Madeline and the Gypsies* (1959). 5-7

BISHOP, CLAIRE HUCHET. *All Alone,* ill. by Feodor Rojankovsky. Viking, 1953. Villagers in the French Alps learn to work together when two children, herding in the mountains, are isolated by an avalanche. 9-11

______. *Pancakes-Paris,* ill. by Georges Schreiber. Viking, 1947. A half-starved postwar French child receives a miraculous package of American pancake mix. How he meets two American soldiers and gets the recipe makes a heart-warming tale. 8-12

CARLSON, NATALIE SAVAGE. *A Brother for the Orphelines,* ill. by Garth Williams. Harper, 1959.

______. *The Family Under the Bridge,* ill. by Garth Williams. Harper, 1958.

______. *The Happy Orpheline,* ill. by Garth Williams. Harper, 1957.

______. *The Orphelines in the Enchanted Castle,* ill. by Adriana Saviozzi. Harper, 1964. The fourth book about the lively French orphans who live—this time in a small castle—with Madame Flattot. A light and charming story with important (but not obtrusive) overtones about social behavior. 9-11

______. *A Pet for the Orphelines,* ill. by Fermin Rocker. Harper, 1962. 8-10

Germany

BENARY-ISBERT, MARGOT. *The Ark,* tr. by Clara and Richard Winston. Harcourt, 1953. The Lechow family, a mother and four children, are trying to reestablish a somewhat normal life in a bombed-out city. 12-14

______. *Rowan Farm,* tr. by Richard and Clara Winston. Harcourt, 1954. The family from *The Ark* welcomes home their father. Two superlative stories. 13-17

PETRIDES, HEIDRUN. *Hans and Peter,* ill. by author. Harcourt, 1963. Two boys have the satisfaction of seeing a hut raised through their own efforts. 7-9

VOGEL, ILSE-MARGRET. *My Twin Sister Erika,* ill. by author. Harper, 1976. 6-9

VON GEBHARDT, HERTHA. *The Girl from Nowhere,* tr. by James Kirkup, ill. by Helen Brun. Criterion, 1959. No one believes her father will return, but a little German girl's faith surmounts mockery and pity and is happily rewarded. 10-13

Holland

DeJONG, MEINDERT. *Far Out the Long Canal,* ill. by Nancy Grossman. Harper, 1964. 10-13

______. *Journey from Peppermint Street,* ill. by Emily Arnold McCully. Harper, 1968. National Book Award. 9-11

______. *Shadrach,* ill. by Maurice Sendak. Harper, 1953. A sensitive study of a boy and his pet rabbit. 9-12

______. *The Wheel on the School,* ill. by Maurice Sendak. Harper, 1954. Newbery Medal. 9-12

DODGE, MARY MAPES. *Hans Brinker; or the Silver Skates* (see Forerunners).

India

ARORA, SHIRLEY. *The Left-Handed Chank.* Follett, 1966. A village in India accepts modern ideas. 11-14

______. *"What Then, Raman?"* ill. by Hans Guggenheim. Follett, 1960. A shy, earnest boy, the only person in his village who has learned to read, finds that his accomplishment carries with it the responsibility to help others. 10-12

BOTHWELL, JEAN. *The Little Flute Player,* ill. by Margaret Ayer. Morrow, 1949. Minor disasters stalk Teka, the little village flute player, and grow into tragedy when famine comes. The ten-year-old boy takes his father's place and saves his family from starvation. 9-12

GOBHAI, MEHILL. *Lakshmi; The Water Buffalo Who Wouldn't,* ill. by author. Hawthorn, 1969. A simply written story about a family in India today. The tale has humor as well as an interesting setting, and the theme (mother and son amused at the come-down of father) a broad applicability. 7-9

MEHTA, RAMA. *The Life of Keshav; A Family Story from India.* McGraw, 1969. A very good story of contemporary India, the young protagonist caught between traditional patterns of living and the desire for an education that will inevitably change those patterns. 11-14

RANKIN, LOUISE. *Daughter of the Mountains,* ill. by Kurt Wiese. Viking, 1948. Tells of the journey of a little Tibetan village girl to far-off Calcutta in search of her stolen puppy. 10-13

SINGH, REGINALD LAL, and ELOISE LOWNSBERY. *Gift*

of the Forest, ill. by Anne Vaughan. McKay, 1942 and 1958. In this distinguished story of rural India, Young Bim, a Hindu boy, finds a tiger cub and cares for it until he is forced to return it to the jungle. 11-14

SOMMERFELT, AIMÉE. *The Road to Agra,* ill. by Ulf Aas. Criterion, 1961. 10-11

———. *The White Bungalow,* ill. by Ulf Aas. Hale, 1963. 10-12

Italy

BETTINA (pseud. for Bettina Ehrlich). *Pantaloni,* ill. by author. Harper, 1957. Colorfully illustrated, this is a warm story of Italian village life and of a little boy's search for his lost dog. 5-8

FLETCHER, DAVID. *Confetti for Cortorelli,* ill. by George Thompson. Pantheon, 1957. To be in the Children's Fancy Dress Parade, Angelo, an orphan of Sicily, needed a costume. How he earned it and gained a home as well makes an original and distinctive story. 6-8

REGGIANI, RENEE. *The Sun Train,* tr. from the Italian by Patrick Creagh. Coward, 1966. A mature story about a family that moves from an almost-feudal society in Sicily to find other problems just as serious in a contemporary Italian urban setting. 11-14

Russia

● CORCORAN, BARBARA. *The Clown.* Atheneum, 1975. Liza, a diplomat's daughter who speaks Russian, helps to smuggle a Russian Jewish clown out of the country. Fast-paced adventure. 10-13

FROLOV, VADIM. *What It's All About,* tr. by Joseph Barnes. Doubleday, 1968. 13-15

KASSIL, LEV. *Once in a Lifetime,* tr. by Anne Terry White. Doubleday, 1970. The first-person story of a thirteen-year-old Russian girl's experience as a movie find. The story has a Moscow setting, with good balance of school and family life and excellent characterization. 11-14

KORINETZ, YURI. *There, Far Beyond the River,* tr. by Anthea Bell, ill. by George Armstrong. O'Hara, 1973. 10-12

MAYAKOVSKY, VLADIMIR. *Timothy's Horse,* ad. by Guy Daniels, ill. by Flavio Costantini. Pantheon, 1970. A rhyming text that tells of a small boy whose wish comes true when he and his father buy a hobby horse. Marvelous illustrations. 5-7

TER HAAR, JAAP. *Boris,* tr. from the Dutch by Martha Mearns, ill. by Rien Poortvliet. Delacorte, 1970. 10-12

Scandinavia

ANCKARSVÄRD, KARIN. *Aunt Vinnie's Invasion,* tr. by Annabelle MacMillan, ill. by William M. Hutchinson. Harcourt, 1962. The six Hallsenius children live with Aunt Vinnie for a year. This is an amusing story of modern Sweden. 10-13

———. *Doctor's Boy,* tr. from the Swedish by Annabelle MacMillan, ill. by Fermin Rocker. Harcourt, 1965. A lively tale set early in the twentieth century. 10-12

BESKOW, ELSA. *Pelle's New Suit,* ill. by author. Harper, 1929. 12-15

FREUCHEN, PETER. *Whaling Boy,* ill. by Leonard Everett Fisher. Putnam, 1958. Per List, not quite twelve, finds life aboard a Danish whaling ship a rugged and adventurous experience. A powerfully written and moving story. 10-13

FRIIS-BAASTAD, BABBIS. *Don't Take Teddy,* tr. from the Norwegian by Lise Sømme McKinnon. Scribner's, 1967. A moving story about a small boy who protects his older retarded brother. 10-13

GRIPE, MARIA. *Elvis and His Friends,* tr. from the Swedish by Sheila LaFarge, ill. by Harald Gripe. Delacorte, 1976. 9-11

———. *Elvis and His Secret,* tr. from the Swedish by Sheila LaFarge, ill. by Harald Gripe. Delacorte, 1976. 9-11

———. *Hugo,* tr. from the Swedish by Paul Britten Austin, ill. by Harald Gripe. Delacorte, 1970. 9-11

———. *Hugo and Josephine,* tr. from the Swedish by Paul Britten Austin, ill. by Harald Gripe. Delacorte, 1969. 7-8

———. *Josephine,* tr. from the Swedish by Paul Britten Austin, ill. by Harald Gripe. Delacorte, 1970. 7-8

———. *Julia's House,* tr. from the Swedish by Gerry Bothmer, ill. by Harald Gripe. Delacorte, 1975. 10-11

———. *The Night Daddy,* tr. from the Swedish by Gerry Bothmer, ill. by Harald Gripe. Delacorte, 1971. 9-11

HELLBERG, HANS-ERIC. *Grandpa's Maria,* tr. from the Swedish by Patricia Crampton, ill. by Joan Sandin. Morrow, 1974. 8-9

JANSSON, TOVE. *The Summer Book,* tr. from the Swedish by Thomas Teal. Pantheon, 1975. Describes the small events of sun-filled days spent by Sophia and her grandmother on an island one summer. For the perceptive reader. 11-13

LINDE, GUNNEL. *The White Stone,* tr. by Richard and Clara Winston, ill. by Imero Gobbato. Harcourt, 1966. Set in Sweden, the story of two children whose friendship ended a rather lonely life for each of them. The writing style is light and amusing and the relationship between the two is charming. 10-11

LINDGREN, ASTRID. *The Children on Troublemaker Street,* tr. by Gerry Bothmer, ill. by Ilon Wiklund. Macmillan, 1964. Swedish children of today and their many activities. 7-9

———. *Rasmus and the Vagabond,* tr. by Gerry Bothmer, ill. by Eric Palmquist. Viking, 1960. Written in a more serious vein than the author's *Pippi Longstocking* series, this is an appealing story of a runaway orphan and the part-time tramp who befriended him. 9-12

LUNDGREN, MAX. *Matt's Grandfather,* tr. by Ann Pyk, ill. by Fibben Hald. Putnam, 1972. 5-7

● SOMMERFELT, AIMÉE. *Miriam,* tr. by Pat Shaw Iversen. Criterion, 1963. 12-15

SORENSON, VIRGINIA. *Lotte's Locket,* ill. by Fermin Rocker. Harcourt, 1964. 9-11

UNNERSTAD, EDITH. *The Saucepan Journey,* ill. by Louis Slobodkin. Macmillan, 1951. The Larsson children, all seven of them, spend a wonderful summer in the traveling caravan, helping father sell his saucepans through Sweden. 9-12

VESTLY, ANNE-CATH. *Hello, Aurora,* tr. from the Norwegian by Eileen Amos, adapted by Jane Fairfax, ill. by Leonard Kessler. T. Crowell, 1974. 8-10

Switzerland

CHÖNZ, SELINA. *A Bell for Ursli,* by Alois Carigiet. Walck, 1953. One of the most beautiful picture stories to come out of Europe, this is also the exciting story of a small Swiss boy determined to have the largest bell to ring in the spring procession. 6-9

RUTGERS VAN DER LOEFF-BASENAU, ANNA. *Avalanche!* tr. by Dora Round, ill. by Gustav Schrotter. Morrow, 1958. Holland's prize-winning children's book for 1955 tells the dramatic story of an avalanche that struck the tiny Swiss village of Urteli and how it affected three young boys. 11-13

SPYRI, JOHANNA. *Heidi* (see Forerunners).

ULLMAN, JAMES RAMSEY. *Banner in the Sky.* Lippincott, 1954. A story of the self-discipline and stern code of ethics that governs the Alpine guides. 12-14

Other countries

AYER, JACQUELINE. *Nu Dang and His Kite,* ill. by author. Harcourt, 1959. A colorful introduction to Siamese life is provided by this story of a small boy's search along the river banks for his lost kite. *The Paper Flower Tree* (1962) is the story of a little girl of Thailand who at last finds her longed-for ornamental tree. 6-8

BALET, JAN B. *Joanjo; A Portuguese Tale*, ill. by author. Delacorte, 1967. The story of Joanjo, a small Portuguese boy, and his acceptance of the independent life of the fisherman after dreams of glory. 5-7

BONZON, PAUL-JACQUES. *The Orphans of Simitra,* tr. from the French by Thelma Niklaus, ill. by Simon Jeruchim. Criterion, 1962. Orphaned by an earthquake in Greece, Porphyras and his little sister find a new home in Holland. The homesick Marina disappears and Porphyras works his way to Paris in search of her. Sensitively written and rich in background of people and places. 11-14

HOUSTON, JAMES. *Akavak; An Eskimo Journey,* ill. by author. Harcourt, 1968. Young Akavak sets out on a dangerous journey along with his grandfather. They reach their goal after seeming to be hopelessly lost, because of the acumen of the old man and the determination of the young one, and the courage of both. The stark illustrations reflect the elemental isolation of the setting. 9-11

KRUMGOLD, JOSEPH. *The Most Terrible Turk; A Story of Turkey,* ill. by Michael Hampshire. T. Crowell, 1969. Uncle Mustafa and Ali are all that are left of a once-large family. Their relationship is warm and appealing, and the setting, Turkey today, is interesting. 8-10

MERRILL, JEAN. *Shan's Lucky Knife,* ill. by Ronni Solbert. W. R. Scott, 1960. Young Shan outwits the tricky boatman who has taken all his possessions. An excellent read-aloud tale with a Burmese background and folk-tale flavor. 7-10

SEREDY, KATE. *The Good Master,* ill. by author. Viking, 1935. A family who live on a Hungarian ranch in the early 1900s teach wild Kate gentler ways. 10-12

______. *The Singing Tree,* ill. by author. Viking, 1939. Another story of Kate, set during World War I. 10-14

SHANNON, MONICA. *Dobry,* ill. by Atanas Katchamakoff. Viking, 1934. Newbery Medal. Dobry, a Bulgarian peasant boy, finds himself longing both to stay at home and to go away to become a sculptor. A rich, multifaceted picture of a culture. 10-13

SPERRY, ARMSTRONG. *Call It Courage*, ill. by author. Macmillan, 1940. Newbery Medal. Published in England as *The Boy Who Was Afraid.* 10-13

● TAYLOR, SYDNEY. *A Papa Like Everyone Else,* ill. by George Porter. Follett, 1966. 9-11

● WATSON, SALLY. *To Build a Land,* ill. by Lili Cassel. Holt, 1957. War-orphaned Leo and his small sister, rescued from the streets of Naples, find a new life in a children's camp in Israel. 11-14

WOJCIECHOWSKA, MAIA. *Shadow of a Bull,* ill. by Alvin Smith. Atheneum, 1964. Newbery Medal. 12-15

WUORIO, EVA-LIS. *The Island of Fish in the Trees,* ill. by Edward Ardizzone. World, 1962. The day-long adventure of two little sisters who trail the doctor around the island to get him to mend their broken doll. The setting is the Balearic Islands, and both story and pictures are exceptionally appealing. 7-9

Animal Stories

AGLE, NAN HAYDEN. *My Animals and Me,* ill. with photos by Emily Hayden. Seabury, 1970. Reminiscences of an animal lover in a book that combines warmth, humor, family anecdotes, and memories of beloved pets in a rural pre–World War I background. 8-10

ANDERSON, CLARENCE. *Billy and Blaze*, ill. by author. Macmillan, 1936, 1962. And its sequels. 5-8

BAUDOUY, MICHEL-AIMÉ. *Old One-Toe,* tr. by Marie Ponsot, ill. by Johannes Troyer. Harcourt, 1959. French children sympathize with a hunted fox. 11-13

BOSTON, LUCY M. *A Stranger at Green Knowe*, ill. by Peter Boston. Harcourt, 1961. Carnegie Medal. 11-14

BUFF, MARY and CONRAD. *Elf Owl,* ill. by Conrad Buff. Viking, 1958. A story of the desert, beautifully illustrated. 5-8

BURNFORD, SHEILA. *The Incredible Journey*, ill. by Carl Burger. Little, 1961. Canadian Library Association Medal. 11 up

CLARK, BILLY C. *The Mooneyed Hound,* ill. by Nedda Walker. Putnam, 1958. Jeb's handicapped dog proves his mettle as a hunter in the field trials. 9-11

CLEARY, BEVERLY. *Socks,* ill. by Beatrice Darwin. Morrow, 1973. 9-11

DeJONG, MEINDERT. *Along Came a Dog,* ill. by Maurice Sendak. Harper, 1958. 10-12

______. *The Last Little Cat,* ill. by Jim McMullan. Harper, 1961. The timid seventh kitten strays away from his friend, the old blind dog, and encounters many cat enemies before he reaches home and safety. 8-10

DE ROO, ANNE. *Cinnamon and Nutmeg.* Nelson, 1974. 9-11

DOTY, JEAN. *The Crumb.* Greenwillow, 1976. 10-12

FISHER, AILEEN. *Valley of the Smallest: The Life Story of a Shrew,* ill. by Jean Zallinger. T. Crowell, 1966. 11-14

FLACK, MARJORIE. *Angus and the Ducks,* ill. by author. Doubleday, 1930, 1939. First of a series about a frisky, curious Scottish terrier. 4-7

______. *The Story About Ping,* ill. by Kurt Wiese. Viking, 1933. 5-8

GALL, ALICE CREW, and FLEMING CREW. *Splasher,* ill. by Else Bostelmann. Walck, 1945. A flood is a great adventure for a young muskrat and his friends. 8-10

§ GATES, DORIS. *Little Vic*, ill. by Kate Seredy. Viking, 1951. When Pony River, a black boy, sees Little Vic, he believes the colt will be as great as his sire, Man o' War. The boy endures every hardship willingly in his devotion to the colt. 9-12

GEORGE, JEAN. *Coyote in Manhattan,* ill. by John Kaufman. T. Crowell, 1968. 11-13

______. *Gull Number 737.* T. Crowell, 1964. 12-15

______. *Julie of the Wolves*, ill. by John Schoenherr. Harper, 1972. Newbery Medal. 10-13

GEORGE, JOHN and JEAN. *Bubo, the Great Horned Owl,* ill. by Jean George. Dutton, 1954. 11-14

______. *Vulpes, the Red Fox,* ill. by Jean George. Dutton, 1948. 10-14

GIPSON, FRED. *Old Yeller,* ill. by Carl Burger. Harper, 1956. Travis's mongrel dog is bitten by a rabid wolf while loyally defending his family. He becomes infected and has to be destroyed. This is a moving tale of a boy and his dog, set in pioneer Texas of the 1870s. In a sequel, *Savage Sam* (1962), Travis, now fifteen, is aided by Old Yeller's equally gallant son in rescuing two small children from Apache captivity. 11-14

GRIFFITHS, HELEN. *Just a Dog,* ill. by Victor Ambrus. Holiday, 1975. 10-12

HALLARD, PETER. *Puppy Lost in Lapland,* ill. by Wallace Tripp. Watts, 1971. An injured puppy struggles for survival in the wilderness. 10-12

HENRY, MARGUERITE. *Gaudenzia; Pride of the Palio,* ill. by Lynd-Ward. Rand, 1960. 11-14

______. *Justin Morgan Had a Horse,* ill. by Wesley Dennis. Rand, 1954. A story of the development of the Morgan breed of horses. 9-14

______. *King of the Wind,* ill. by Wesley Dennis. Rand, 1948. Newbery Medal. 9-14

______. *Misty of Chincoteague,* ill. by Wesley Dennis. Rand, 1947. 9-14

______. *White Stallion of Lipizza,* ill. by Wesley Dennis. Rand, 1964. 11-13

HOLLING, HOLLING C. *Pagoo,* ill. by author and Lucille W. Holling. Houghton, 1957. A quietly paced, beautifully illustrated life story of a hermit crab. 9-12

JAMES, WILL. *Smoky, the Cowhorse,* ill. by author. Scribner's, 1926. Newbery Medal. The adventures of a range horse. 11-16

KJELGAARD, JIM. *Big Red,* ill. by Bob Kuhn. Holiday, 1956. 12-16

LATHROP, DOROTHY. *Who Goes There?* ill. by author. Macmillan, 1935, 1963. Lovely pictures of small forest creatures. 6-10

LEA, ALEC. *Temba Dawn.* Scribner's, 1975. 10-12.

LEIGHTON, MARGARET. *Comanche of the Seventh,* ill. by Elliot Means. Farrar, 1957. In the life story of Comanche, the horse that survived Custer's Last Stand, the author achieves an absorbing animal tale. 11-15

LIERS, EMIL. *An Otter's Story,* ill. by Tony Palazzo. Viking, 1953. 10-13

LINDQUIST, WILLIS. *Burma Boy,* ill. by Nicolas Mordvinoff. Whittlesey, 1953. A thrilling tale of an elephant of the teakwood forests which goes wild, and of young Haji, the elephant boy, who wins his confidence and saves the villagers from disaster. 9-11

McNEER, MAY. *My Friend Mac,* ill. by Lynd Ward. Houghton, 1960. An orphaned and fast-growing moose provides plenty of diversion for lonely little Baptiste of the Canadian woods. 7-9

MAXWELL, GAVIN. *The Otters' Tale,* ill. with photos. Dutton, 1962. A juvenile edition of the author's memorable nature tale of his otter pets, *Ring of Bright Water.* 12-15

MILES, MISKA. *Eddie's Bear,* ill. by John Schoenherr. Little, 1970. 5-8

______. *Mississippi Possum,* ill. by John Schoenherr. Little, 1965. 7-9

______. *Nobody's Cat,* ill. by John Schoenherr. Little, 1969. 8-9

______. *Otter in the Cove,* ill. by John Schoenherr. Little, 1974. 8-10

______. *Wharf Rat,* ill. by John Schoenherr, Little, 1972. 7-9

MONTGOMERY, RUTHERFORD. *Kildee House,* ill. by Barbara Cooney. Doubleday, 1949. Story of an elderly would-be hermit who, building a house in the redwood forest, soon finds it filled with small animals and visited by warring children. The tragicomic episodes make this a nature story of unusual sensitivity and beauty. 10-13

MOREY, WALT. *Gentle Ben,* ill. by John Schoenherr. Dutton, 1965. 11-14

______. *Gloomy Gus.* Dutton, 1970. 10-12

______. *Kävik the Wolf Dog,* ill. by Peter Parnall. Dutton, 1968. 11-14

______. *Year of the Black Pony.* Dutton, 1976. 10-12

MOWAT, FARLEY. *Owls in the Family,* ill. by Robert Frankenberg. Little, 1962. A funny and heartwarming story of two owls of Northern Canada, told by their youthful rescuer. 9-12

MUKERJI, DHAN GOPAL. *Gay-Neck,* ill. by Boris Artzybasheff. Dutton, 1927, 1968. Gay-Neck's training as a carrier pigeon in India made him valuable as a messenger in France during World War I. Newbery Medal, 1928. 11-14

NORTH, STERLING. *Little Rascal,* ill. by Carl Burger. Dutton, 1965. 9-11

______. *Rascal: A Memoir of a Better Era,* ill. by John Schoenherr. Dutton, 1963. 12 up

O'HARA, MARY(pseud. for Mary Sture-Vasa). *My Friend Flicka.* Lippincott, 1941. Horsebreeding on a Western ranch. 12 up

RAWLINGS, MARJORIE KINNAN. *The Yearling,* ill. by N. C. Wyeth. Scribner's, 1938, 1962. 12 up

ROUNDS, GLEN. *The Blind Colt,* ill. by author. Holiday, 1941, 1960.

______. *Stolen Pony,* ill. by author. Holiday, 1948, 1969. Two stories with a background of the Dakota Badlands. With the care and training given by a ten-year-old boy, the blind colt earns his right to live. The sequel tells how the pony was stolen by horse thieves and then abandoned, to make his way home with the aid of a faithful dog. 9-12

SANDBURG, HELGA. *Anna and the Baby Buzzard,* ill. by Brinton Turkle. Dutton, 1970. A true story. 5-7

SCHEFFER, VICTOR B. *Little Calf,* ill. by Leonard Everett Fisher. Scribner's, 1970. A narrative about a sperm whale. 12 up

SETON, ERNEST T. *Lives of the Hunted,* ill. by author. Schocken, 1967. A favorite realistic saga. 10 up

SHARMAT, MARJORIE WEINMAN. *Morris Brookside, a Dog,* ill. by Ronald Himler. Holiday, 1973. 5-8

______. *Morris Brookside Is Missing,* ill. by Ronald Himler. Holiday, 1974. 5-8

SKORPEN, LIESEL MOAK. *Bird,* ill. by Joan Sandin. Harper, 1976. 5-8

STONG, PHIL. *Honk: the Moose,* ill. by Kurt Wiese. Dodd, 1935. 9-10

STRANGER, JOYCE. *Lakeland Vet.* Viking, 1972. 11 up

WALKER, DAVID E. *Big Ben,* ill. by Victor Ambrus. Houghton, 1969. Fine writing style and characterization in this story about a St. Bernard who is unjustly suspected of being a sheep-killer. 9-11

WARD, LYND. *The Biggest Bear,* ill. by author. Houghton, 1952. Caldecott Medal. 5-8

WHITNEY, ALMA MARSHAK. *Leave Herbert Alone,* ill. by David McPhail. Addison, 1972. 3-6

ZIMELMAN, NATHAN. *The Lives of My Cat Alfred,* ill. by Evaline Ness. Dutton, 1976. 5-8

Sports Stories

BISHOP, CURTIS. *Little League Victory.* Lippincott, 1967. Ed's temper tantrums make it difficult for him to be accepted as a member of the team, but he succeeds in getting over this obstacle. 9-11

CHRISTOPHER, MATT. *Johnny Long Legs,* ill. by Harvey Kidder. Little, 1970. 9-11

______. *Tough to Tackle,* ill. by Harvey Kidder. Little, 1971. 8-10

CORBETT, SCOTT. *The Baseball Bargain,* ill. by Wallace Tripp, Little, 1970. 9-11

______. *The Hockey Girls.* Dutton, 1976. Published simultaneously in Canada by Clarke, Irwin. 9-11

DU BOIS, WILLIAM PÈNE. *Porko von Popbutton,* ill. by author. Harper, 1969. 9-11

GAULT, WILLIAM. *Stubborn Sam.* Dutton, 1969. 11-14

GLANVILLE, BRIAN. *Goalkeepers Are Different.* Crown, 1972. Game descriptions and facts about public relations and international competition are authoritative in a story about a new member of an English pro soccer team. 11-14

§ HEUMANN, WILLIAM. *Fastbreak Rebel.* Dodd, 1971. 11-14

§● HIGDON, HAL. *The Electronic Olympics.* Holt, 1971. A blithe tale of a computerized Olympics and an affable African track star. 11-14

§ HONIG, DONALD. *Johnny Lee.* McCall, 1971. 10-14

______. *Way to Go, Teddy.* Watts, 1973. 11-14

§ JACKSON, JESSE. *Anchor Man,* ill. by Doris Spiegel. Harper, 1947. 12 up

KATZ, BOBBI. *Rod-and-Reel Trouble,* ill. by Janet LaSalle. Whitman, 1974. 8-10

§ KESSLER, LEONARD. *Here Comes the Strikeout,* ill. by author. Harper, 1965. 7-8

KNUDSON, R. R. *Zanballer.* Delacorte, 1972. While the diary form isn't quite convincing, Zan does convey her determination that a girls' football team has a place in school sports. 11-14

● KONIGSBURG, E. L. *About the B'nai Bagels,* ill. by author. Atheneum, 1969. 10-12

LEVY, ELIZABETH. *Something Queer at the Ball Park,* ill. by Mordicai Gerstein. Delacorte, 1975. 7-9

§ LIPSYTE, ROBERT. *The Contender.* Harper, 1967. 12-15

LORD, BEMAN. *Shrimp's Soccer Goal,* ill. by Harold Berson. Walck, 1970.
All of Lord's stories about several sports are sound and enjoyable for readers in the middle group. 8-10

MacPHERSON, MARGARET. *The Shinty Boys,* ill. by Shirley Hughes. Harcourt, 1963. 11-13

POTTER, MARGARET. *The Touch-and-Go Year.* Meredith, 1969. 10-12

§ QUIGLEY, MARTIN. *Today's Game.* Viking, 1965. 13 up

RENICK, MARION. *Boy at Bat,* ill. by Paul Galdone. Scribner's, 1961. An amusing story of a boy who gets into one baseball game and demands that his family now call him "Lefty." 7-9

______. *Take a Long Jump,* ill. by Charles Robinson. Scribner's, 1971. A track story that also has good family relationships. 9-11

SHORTALL, LEONARD. *Ben on the Ski Trail,* ill. by author. Morrow, 1965. 7-9

SLOTE, ALFRED. *Hang Tough, Paul Mather.* Lippincott, 1973. A poignant first-person story by a leukemia victim who tries to keep up with his greatest interest, playing Little League ball. 9-12

______. *Matt Gargan's Boy.* Lippincott, 1975. 9-11

______. *Stranger on the Ball Club.* Lippincott, 1970. 9-11

§ ______. *Jake.* Lippincott, 1971. A small boy's uncle gives up his free time to coach a baseball team. 9-11

TAVES, ISABELLA. *Not Bad for a Girl.* Evans/Lippincott, 1972. 9-11

THORVALL, KERSTIN. *Gunnar Scores a Goal,* tr. from the Swedish by Anne Parker, ill. by Serge Hollerbach. Harcourt, 1968. 8-10

TOWNE, MARY. *First Serve,* ill. by Ruth Sanderson. Atheneum, 1976. Thirteen-year-old Dulcie is torn between her desire to enter competitive tennis and her fear that her older sister, who also plays, will feel hurt. 11-14

§ TUNIS, JOHN. *All-American,* ill. by Hans Walleen. Harcourt, 1942. 10-14

______. *The Duke Decides,* ill. by James MacDonald. Harcourt, 1939.

______. *The Iron Duke,* ill. by Johan Bull. Harcourt, 1938. Among the best college stories we have for the precollege boy. *The Iron Duke* is about an Iowa boy's adjustments to Harvard. *The Duke Decides* finds him a member of the Olympic track team. 12-16

● ______. *Keystone Kids.* Harcourt, 1943. A fine sports story for the teen age—the happy resolution of anti-Semitic feeling is achieved by the students. 12-16

● WEAVER, ROBERT. *Nice Guy, Go Home.* Harper, 1968. 12-15

WODEHOUSE, P. G. *Mike and Psmith.* Meredith, 1969. 11 up

Mystery and Adventure

ANCKARSVÄRD, KARIN. *The Robber Ghost,* tr. from the Swedish by Annabelle Macmillan, ill. by Paul Galdone. Harcourt, 1961. The disappearance of money from the post office housed in a wing of an old and supposedly haunted Swedish castle arouses the detective instincts of young schoolmates Michael and Cecilia. Good atmosphere and suspense for both boys and girls. 10-12

BERNA, PAUL. *A Truckload of Rice,* tr. from the French by John Buchanan Brown, ill. by Prudence Seward. Pantheon, 1970. 10-12

BONHAM, FRANK. *Mystery in Little Tokyo,* ill. by Kazue Mizumura. Dutton, 1966. 10-12

§★ ______. *Mystery of the Fat Cat,* ill. by Alvin Smith. Dutton, 1968. 10-14

§ BONSALL, CROSBY. *The Case of the Cat's Meow,* ill. by author. Harper, 1965. All of the Bonsall books are charming and useful. 7-8

BRANFIELD, JOHN. *The Poison Factory.* Harper, 1972. An English girl investigates the possibility that her father's death was caused by nerve gas. 11-14

CAMERON, ELEANOR. *A Spell Is Cast,* ill. by Beth and Joe Krush. Little, 1964. 10-12

______. *The Terrible Churnadryne,* ill. by Beth and Joe Krush. Little, 1959. Did a strange prehistoric creature really stalk San Lorenzo peak? Tom and Jennifer and the whole town of Redwood Cove are caught up in the strange controversy. A unique, well-written tale of suspense. 9-12

CHANCE, STEPHEN. *Septimus and the Danedyke Mystery.* Nelson, 1973. A former member of the CID investigates the theft of a valuable religious relic. 11 up

COBALT, MARTIN. *Pool of Swallows.* Nelson, 1974. 11-15

CRAYDER, DOROTHY. *She and the Dubious Three,* ill. by Velma Ilsley. Atheneum, 1974. 10-12

DILLON, EILIS. *A Herd of Deer,* ill. by Richard Kennedy. Funk, 1970. 12-15

______. *The Singing Cave,* ill. by Stan Campbell. Funk,

1960. Suspense and mystery abound in this outstandingly written tale of the discovery and disappearance of Viking remains from a cave on an Irish isle. 12-15

GAGE, WILSON. *The Ghost of Five Owl Farm,* ill. by Paul Galdone. World, 1966. 10-12

GARFIELD, LEON. *Black Jack,* ill. by Antony Maitland. Pantheon, 1968. 11-14

———. *The Sound of Coaches,* ill. by John Lawrence. Viking, 1974. A picaresque period tale of a foundling who searches for facts about his real parents. Robust characters, rich dialogue, vigorous style. 12-16

GIBSON, WALTER B., ed. *Rogues' Gallery; A Variety of Mystery Stories,* ill. by Paul Spina. Doubleday, 1969. A better than usual anthology of mystery and detective stories, each one prefaced with a page of information about the author or the background for the particular story. 13 up

HIGHTOWER, FLORENCE. *Dark Horse of Woodfield,* ill. by Joshua Tolford. Houghton, 1962. The Woodfield home was a shabby relic, but it housed Buggsie and Maggie Armistead, who trained a horse, solved a mystery, and even bred cocoons to restore the family fortunes. A highly humorous and substantial family story with a background of New England. 11-13

———. *The Fayerweather Forecast,* ill. by Joshua Tolford. Houghton, 1967. 10-13

———. *The Ghost of Follonsbee's Folly,* ill. by Ati Forberg. Houghton, 1958. The newly bought dilapidated house in the country soon had the young Stockpoles trying to solve the mystery of its strange sounds and another puzzle as well. 11-14

———. *Mrs. Wappinger's Secret,* ill. by Beth and Joe Krush. Houghton, 1956. Eccentric Mrs. Wappinger of a Maine resort island is quite sure she has ancestral buried treasure somewhere on her property. Young Charlie Porter, summer visitor, is more than delighted to aid her in a secret treasure-hunting alliance. 11-14

JEFFRIES, RODERIC. *Patrol Car.* Harper, 1967.

———. *River Patrol.* Harper, 1969. 11-14

KAHN, JOAN, ed. *Some Things Fierce and Fatal.* Harper, 1971. 11-14

KÄSTNER, ERICH. *Emil and the Detectives,* ill. by Walter Trier. Doubleday, 1930. 9-11

LADD, ELIZABETH. *A Mystery for Meg,* ill. by Mary Stevens. Morrow, 1962. 9-11

L'ENGLE, MADELEINE. *The Arm of the Starfish.* Farrar, 1965. 12-15

———. *Dragons in the Waters.* Farrar, 1976. 11-15

LEVY, ELIZABETH. *Something Queer Is Going On,* ill. by Mordicai Gerstein. Delacorte, 1973. 7-9

§ LEXAU, JOAN. *The Homework Caper,* ill. by Syd Hoff. Harper, 1966. 6-7

§ ———. *The Rooftop Mystery,* ill. by Syd Hoff. Harper, 1968. 6-8

LINDGREN, ASTRID. *Bill Bergson Lives Dangerously,* tr. by Herbert Antoine, ill. by Don Freeman. Viking, 1954.

———. *Bill Bergson, Master Detective,* tr. by Herbert Antoine, ill. by Louis Glanzman. Viking, 1952. These two stories from the Swedish are told with considerable humor in spite of their dramatic plots. In *Bill Bergson, Master Detective* Bill and his friends Anders and Eva Lotta track down stolen jewels and restore them to the police. In the other book they identify a murderer. 10-13

McLEAN, ALLAN CAMPBELL. *Master of Morgana.* Harcourt, 1959. Sixteen-year-old Niall solves the mystery of his older brother's injuries in this suspense-filled tale of fishermen and poachers on the Isle of Skye. 13-15

MAYNE, WILLIAM. *The Battlefield,* ill. by Mary Russon. Dutton, 1967. 9-11

———. *The Changeling,* ill. by Victor G. Ambrus. Dutton, 1963. 10-12

———. *Ravensgill.* Dutton, 1970. 12-15

MEADER, STEPHEN. *The Fish Hawk's Nest,* ill. by Edward Shenton. Harcourt, 1952. Exciting tale of smuggling on the New Jersey coast in the 1820s. Good characterizations and background. 11-14

MOYES, PATRICIA. *Helter-Skelter.* Holt, 1968. 12-15

NICOLE, CHRISTOPHER. *Operation Destruct.* Holt, 1969. 12-15

PEARCE, PHILLIPA. *The Minnow Leads to Treasure,* ill. by Edward Ardizzone. World, 1958. 10-12

POOLE, JOSEPHINE. *Catch as Catch Can,* ill. by Kiyo Komoda. Harper, 1970. 10-12

RASKIN, ELLEN. *The Tattooed Potato and Other Clues.* Dutton, 1975. A spoof of detective fiction has zany characters and plenty of action. 10-12

ROBERTS, WILLO DAVIS. *The View from the Cherry Tree.* Atheneum, 1975. Preparing for a wedding, Rob's family is too busy to listen to his story of a neighbor's fall, which he's seen from a tree. Only the murderer pays attention. 10-13

ROBERTSON, KEITH. *The Crow and the Castle,* ill. by Robert Greiner. Viking, 1957. A superior mystery tale involving two youthful amateur detectives. 11-14

———. *Ice to India,* ill. by Jack Weaver. Viking, 1955. 12-14

———. *The Money Machine,* ill. by George Porter. Viking, 1969. 10-12

———. *Three Stuffed Owls,* ill. by Jack Weaver. Viking, 1954. 12-14

RUGH, BELLE DORMAN. *Crystal Mountain,* ill. by Ernest H. Shepard. Houghton, 1955. 11-13

SHECTER, BEN. *Inspector Rose,* ill. by author. Harper, 1969. 6-8

SOBOL, DONALD. *Encyclopedia Brown Saves the Day,* ill. by Leonard Shortall. Nelson, 1970. 8-10

STEVENSON, ROBERT LOUIS. *Treasure Island,* ill. by C. B. Falls. World, 1946 (first pub. in 1883).

———. *Treasure Island,* ill. by N. C. Wyeth. Scribner's, 1945. 11-16

STOREY, MARGARET. *Ask Me No Questions.* Dutton, 1975. 10-12

STORR, CATHERINE. *Lucy,* ill. by Victoria de Larrea. Prentice, 1968. 8-10

TURNER, PHILIP. *Colonel Sheperton's Clock,* ill. by Phillip Gough. World, 1966.

———. *The Grange at High Force,* ill. by W. T. Mars. World, 1967. Carnegie Medal. 11-14

WHITNEY, PHYLLIS. *Mystery of the Green Cat.* Westminster, 1957. The discovery of a message long hidden in a ceramic cat brings peace to an old neighbor. 11-14

§ ———. *Secret of the Spotted Shell,* ill. by John Mecray. Westminster, 1967. 11-14

WINTERFELD, HENRY. *Detectives in Togas,* tr. from the German by Richard and Clara Winston, ill. by Charlotte Kleinert. Harcourt, 1956. 10-12

———. *Mystery of the Roman Ransom,* tr. from the German by Edith McCormick, ill. by Fritz Biermann. Harcourt, 1971. 10-13

WUORIO, EVA-LIS. *Save Alice!* Holt, 1968. 10-12

Historical Fiction Chapter 11

We require that modern fiction for children depict life honestly and accurately. This is also a major requisite for historical fiction. Children can check the experiences described in modern fiction against their own lives and those of their friends or can confirm them through the mass media. But children bring to historical fiction little knowledge of particular periods of history, either through study or reading, and must rely on the author's accuracy in this field.

Generally, the writer of historical fiction aims consciously to tell a story set in a past time, a time about which the majority of the book's readers will have no direct knowledge. In order to tell a story which has the flavor of a chosen time, the author becomes as familiar as possible with the period through reading contemporary accounts in books, newspapers, and magazines, through historical studies, or through the use of interviews or oral history records. The writing of the book then becomes an expression of assimilated knowledge and vicarious experience. Characters may be actual historical personages, or they may be created by the author, people like ourselves inside, although their clothing and habits may be very different. The author shows how these people are directly affected by their environment. Details of daily life—food, clothing, shelter—come naturally into the story as the characters deal with their problems. Emotions grow naturally out of the problems, and we see how these people were prepared physically and spiritually by their cultural background to meet their daily challenges.

Elizabeth George Speare's *The Witch of Blackbird Pond* is a good example of what we are discussing. Kit, raised in Barbados, comes to live with Puritan relatives in Connecticut in the 1600s and finds a serious, hard way of life, very different from the relaxed and carefree life she had known. Adaptation to her changed environment is not easy for Kit, and her involvement in a witchcraft trial is a logical development in a plot set in New England in the 1600s.

A war story almost always involves battles; still the weapons used, the style of warfare, the support systems, all differ from war to war, from period to period. The Revolutionary War described in Leonard Wibberley's *Treegate* series is very different from World War II, as seen through the eyes of German Hans in James Forman's *The Horses of Anger*. The experiences of the characters reflect the times. In all cases, the plot in a historical novel grows directly out of the period described.

One of the most difficult tasks of the writer of historical fiction is to present natural conversations. If the words and sentence patterns are so archaic as to break the reader's concentration, the author is in difficulty. If the conversations are too contemporary in tone, the mood of the story may be destroyed. For children just mastering their own tongue, language—especially dialect—may be an overwhelming problem in reading historical fiction.

A time sense is also difficult for children to gain; they see their own parents' childhoods as being long ago and World Wars I and II as immeasurably distant in time. Names of historical characters may be difficult, and events taking place outside their own countries have a quality near fantasy for many children. Interest may lag if the author spends too much time building setting; conversely, bewilderment may result if not enough background is presented for full understanding of the plot.

As in any story for children, however, an exciting plot, realistic characters, judicious use of dialogue and dialect, a universal theme, and a strong sense of place and time will help a child over the difficulties created by lack of knowledge.

The successful writer of historical fiction is aware that historical points of view change with time and that treatment of character and fact is inevitably affected by the way these things are viewed in the period in which the author is writing. Thus the treatment of women, blacks, and Native Americans in historical fiction changed drastically in the 1970s and the writer should understand this change and see it in its historical perspective.

Occasionally a story is set in a historical period but it could just as well happen today: the social conditions of the times seem to have little impact on the characters' lives and seem to be of minor concern to the author. We can make this another test of historical fiction: Does the author intend to create a vivid picture of another historical period and is that picture vital to the telling of the story? If not, we may have an interesting story, but it is not historical fiction. Tales which were contemporary when written and which are still read by succeeding generations, such as Louisa May Alcott's *Little Women*, have become historical fiction in a sense, but they were not created as historical fiction and they, and others like them, will be considered in this book as realistic fiction.

Where do we draw the line between historical fiction and modern realistic fiction? For the purposes of this chapter we will discuss only those books whose backgrounds are no later than World War II. The books are divided into those for younger readers, the middle group, and older readers, and are arranged within each group by the period or year of the setting for the title discussed, or the first title if there are several titles. All of the books, in varying degrees, comply with the major requirements of good historical fiction for young readers. The research and the authoritative historical milieu are there, but they do not overpower the story. You will note that no single book ever presents all points of view. This need not be a problem if you choose books that present a balance.

What is the value of historical fiction for the children of today? The past is not simply a listing of dates and events, as important and momentous as these may be. The past is people and how people managed to live and love and find joy in accomplishment whatever the times. The historical novel clothes the bare historical facts with trappings of a thousand tiny details, bringing emotion and insight to scholarship. Children learn facts in social

Viewpoints

"History is people." I have said this often enough to adults as well as to children, and this is the sum of all my research; this is the basis of everything I have learned about the historical novel. History is ordinary people shaped and shaken by the winds of their time, as we in our time are shaped and shaken by the wind of current events. And so, to write about the people of any time, one must know them so well that it would be possible to go back and live undetected among them.

Rather than writing from the outside looking in, then, one will write from the inside looking out. Then also, as when a raised window permits interior and exterior to merge in the air and sunlight flowing into a room, the past will merge with the present. The feelings of past and present will be shared. There will be engagement between reader and characters, irrespective of superficial differences in dress, speech, and habit; and in identifying with these characters, the reader will find his own identity.—Mollie Hunter. From *The Last Lord of Redhouse Castle.* ©1975 by Mollie Hunter. Reprinted by permission of A. M. Heath & Company Ltd.

studies and history; it is the interpretation of the facts in historical fiction that makes them feel "We were there!"

Early Writers of Historical Fiction

Not all of the early historical fiction written for the children of the United States is still worth reading. A few writers, however, produced books which are as rewarding now as they were when first published.

Howard Pyle was steeped in the traditions and customs of the Middle Ages. He not only wrote fascinating stories about them, but provided powerful illustrations for his own books from a seemingly inexhaustible storehouse of detailed information. His running narrative is always clear, direct, and vigorous. Old speech forms add to the flavor of his tales without unduly impeding the reader.

Otto of the Silver Hand (1888) is a horrifying tale of the robber barons of Germany. One of these had plundered ruthlessly. For revenge, his enemies struck off the hand of his only son, the delicate Otto. Later, because of the silver substitute, the boy was known as Otto of the Silver Hand. The story presents two phases of the life of the period: the turbulent life within the castle strongholds of the robber barons and the peaceful, scholarly pursuits of the monks within their great monasteries. The mutilation of the boy is gently handled, underscoring the infinite pathos of a child in the power of cruel men.

In Pyle's *Men of Iron* (1892), sixteen-year-old Myles Falworth is sent to be a squire to a powerful earl. There he learns that his own father is practically an outlaw, suspected of plotting to take the king's life. In the earl's great castle, Myles is trained in all the intricate feats of knighthood and in the code of chivalry and he is eventually knighted. He frees his father from suspicion and wins the earl's daughter for his wife. Myles has to battle with his own impulsiveness and his too-quick temper as well as with his enemies. This remains an outstanding book about medieval England.

Cornelia Meigs was interested not only in our historical past but also in the beginnings of ideas and their development. Her stories are always something more than historical fiction. Indeed, she manages frequently to illuminate certain problems of the present.

For example, *Clearing Weather* (1928) deals with Nicholas Drury's struggles to keep alive his uncle's shipbuilding business in the discouraging days following the American Revolution. Only through the cooperation of the whole community is the little town able to reestablish itself. The theme of community cooperation is still a good one.

Master Simon's Garden (1929) carries a still more striking theme. In the little Puritan New England settlement called Hopewell, where everything is done for utility and thrift, Master Simon develops his beautiful garden—a riot of colorful flowers and sweet herbs. It is an expression of his philosophy of tolerance and love in complete contrast to the intolerance and suspicion of some of his neighbors.

While Meigs was not a creator of memorable characters, her plots are absorbing and often exciting, stronger because of their genesis

Illustration by Howard Pyle from Otto of the Silver Hand *by Howard Pyle. Copyright, 1916, by Anne Poole Pyle. Reprinted by permission of the publisher, Charles Scribner's Sons.*

in a strong theme. It is the theme which gives unity to the action and significance to the conclusion.

One of the finest books Rachel Field ever wrote is *Calico Bush* (1931), the story of Marguerite Ledoux, a French bound-out girl of thirteen, who travels to the state of Maine with a Massachusetts family in 1743. On the long sail from Marblehead to Mount Desert, Marguerite comes to know the Sargent family and proves to them her grit and resourcefulness. She remains, nevertheless, a servant and an alien in their midst. There are brief days of joy in the new settlement, but there are tragic and frightening days, too—the Sargent baby is burned to death, and an Indian raid is diverted only by Marguerite's courage and ingenuity. At the end of the story, the Sargents gratefully offer Marguerite her freedom, but she will not leave them. The picture of the times and the people is authentic and well balanced. The hardships, the monotony, and the perils of pioneer life are there, unvarnished and frightening. The compensatory rewards may seem slight to modern readers, but there can be no doubt in their minds about the sturdy, undismayed character of these settlers.

Books for Younger Children

For young children who have little understanding of the past, historical fiction should be presented very simply, focusing on a person or just a few people, or on one problem or event. The story needs action and drama, and should avoid any references to events that demand knowledge not provided in the book. Historical fiction for young children is generally about exciting people in history to whom they have frequently been introduced by the mass media—knights, pirates, Vikings, soldiers, pioneers, American Indians—whether these characters are real or invented.

Clyde Robert Bulla

John Billington, Friend of Squanto
The Sword in the Tree

Clyde Bulla's books for children are written in a simple style which does not condescend to young readers. He has the ability to concentrate on one aspect of character, and to describe events which enhance that aspect. In *Squanto* (1954) and *John Billington, Friend of Squanto* (1956), Bulla gives a brief picture of the Pilgrims of Plymouth Colony. *The Sword in the Tree* (1956) tells of treachery punished when a young boy asks King Arthur's help. Other books by Bulla take place during the Viking explorations of America, and in the early days of the settlement of the Middle and Far West of the United States.

Alice Dalgliesh

The Courage of Sarah Noble
Adam and the Golden Cock

Alice Dalgliesh has the ability to create realistic child characters and to make their concerns important to us without losing sight of the historical elements of her tales.

The Courage of Sarah Noble (1954) is richly historical and, according to Dalgliesh, a real episode of 1707. Eight-year-old Sarah is sent into the wilderness to cook and care for her father because her mother cannot leave or move a sick baby. Before Sarah and her father set off, her mother wraps the little girl in a cloak as warm as her love and says, "Keep up your courage, Sarah Noble." When wolves threaten them in the forest, or they sleep in strange cabins with unfriendly folk, or Sarah is left alone with an Indian family, she wraps her mother's cloak and her words warmly about her and keeps up her courage.

Another tale of colonial times is *The Thanksgiving Story* (1954), a fictional account of the voyage of the *Mayflower* and the first year at Plymouth, culminating in the Thanksgiving feast with the Indians. Centered on the experiences of the Hopkins family, especially the children, it is a remarkably moving story, told with dignity and avoiding stereotyped episodes.

The Fourth of July Story (1956) must have been more difficult to write, with its large gallery of leading characters and the complex theme of independence and restoration of good relationships with England. But again Dalgliesh has selected her people and episodes so carefully that the story is dramatic

Illustration by Brinton Turkle from Obadiah the Bold *by Brinton Turkle. Copyright © 1965 by Brinton Turkle. Reprinted by permission of The Viking Press, Inc. (Original in color)*

and not too complicated for the understanding and enjoyment of children.

Adam and the Golden Cock (1959) is a Revolutionary War story in which a boy is caught in the conflict between friendship and loyalty, for Adam's friend Paul is from a Tory family. Children of today, aware of conflicting opinions about controversial issues, may see the timeless application of such conflict.

Brinton Turkle

Obadiah the Bold

Set in the early nineteenth century, *Obadiah the Bold* (1965) is an engaging tale of the dreams of glory of a small Quaker boy who wants to become a pirate. He decides he will be a sailor like Grandfather after Father very cleverly talks about how brave a man Captain Obadiah Starbuck had been. The text has minimal historical significance, but the illustrations show details of early Nantucket, and both this book and its sequel, *Thy Friend, Obadiah* (1969), give children a sense of the period, the Quaker community, and the loving kindness of family life. The soft details of the illustrations are charming in themselves and they are accurately informative in showing costume, architecture, and artifacts of the period.

Ferdinand Monjo

The Drinking Gourd

A fine story about the Underground Railroad is told in *The Drinking Gourd* (1970), in which young Tommy Fuller, sent home from church because of a prank, wanders into the barn and finds a runaway slave family. The explanation given Tommy of the Railroad clarifies it for readers as well as for Tommy, and he understands for the first time the degradation of slavery and the danger runaways face. When a search party comes along, Tommy quickly pretends that he himself is running away from home; the marshal laughs and decides not to search the hay wagon, and so Tommy helps the cause. That night Father explains that he is, he knows, breaking a law but that he must. These are *people.* The story has suspense and action, and in Tommy's participation there is both the joy of achievement and an appreciation of ethical issues.

In later books Monjo has woven stories around historical personages such as Benjamin Franklin (*Poor Richard in France*, 1973), Thomas Jefferson (*Grand Papa and Ellen Aroon*, 1974), and Abraham Lincoln (*Gettysburg*, 1976). Using a child of the family to tell the story, Monjo has effectively presented these men from a child's point of view. Whether these books are classified as historical fiction or biography, there is a sense of history and an emphasis on such qualities as courage, loyalty, and family love.

Other Books for Younger Children

Although *The Apple and the Arrow* (1951) by Mary and Conrad Buff is set in 1292, the story of Switzerland's revolt against Austria has pertinence for young readers today. The tale of the legendary William Tell's leadership is seen from the point of view of the young son from whose head, according to the story, the apple was shot.

Wilma Pitchford Hays has written a number of short, informational books with a historical setting. *May Day for Samoset* (1968) and *Christmas on the Mayflower* (1956) are typical and show the author's knowledge and interest in historical details, which are somewhat purposefully inserted in the tales.

One of the gayest books of historical fiction for young children is Arnold Lobel's *On the Day Peter Stuyvesant Sailed into Town* (1971), delightfully illustrated by the author, a story in rhythmic verse that describes the irascible governor's successful efforts to clean up New Amsterdam.

Lobel's book also is representative of the growing number of books of historical fiction written for beginning readers. Others are Nathaniel Benchley's *Sam the Minuteman* (1969), a lively story of the American Revolution, and Betty Baker's *The Pig War* (1969), based on a dispute between the United States and Great Britain in 1859 over possession of an island.

Based on a true incident, *Martin and Abraham Lincoln* by Catherine Coblentz was first published in 1947 and reissued twenty years later. The dialogue between the President and the small boy gives information about the American Civil War, and the story not only characterizes Lincoln but poignantly shows how the duress of war affects a child.

Books for the Middle Group

By the time they reach the middle grades, children have acquired some sense of the past and some perspective on its relation to the present. Their lively curiosity leads to conjecture about people of other times, and historical fiction that tells a good story about such people satisfies both their need to know and their appreciation of action. In the books for this group, most of the stories stress courage and problem-solving, and the preponderance of historical fiction is set in the comparatively familiar bounds of our own country's past.

Marguerite de Angeli

The Door in the Wall

Marguerite de Angeli's Newbery Medal book, *The Door in the Wall* (1949), is set in thirteenth-century England. Robin's noble father is off to the wars and his mother is with the queen when the plague strikes. Robin falls ill, unable to move his legs, and is deserted by the servants. Brother Luke finds the boy, takes him to the hospice, and cares for him. To the despairing Robin he says, "Always remember . . . thou hast only to follow the wall far enough and there will be a door in it." The monks teach the boy to use his hands and his head, "For reading is another door in the wall. . . ."

Robin learns to swim and to get around swiftly on his crutches, but his bent back never straightens. However, his spirit is strong, and he plays so heroic a part in saving a beleaguered city that the king honors him, and his parents are moved with joy and pride. This heartwarming story is beautifully illustrated in the author's most colorful style. The characters are less convincing than the situations, but the book is frequently of great interest to children.

Jean Fritz

The Cabin Faced West
Brady

In *The Cabin Faced West* (1958) there isn't much to console Ann. She misses her cousin in Gettysburg and there isn't another child in the pioneer country of Western Pennsylvania for her to play with until she finds a boy her own age. The high point of the story is a surprise visit from George Washington, an episode based on historical fact, but the most engaging incident is the one in which Ann's mother stops her work to play tea party with the lonely child.

Brady (1960) is a more mature story, set in the years just before the Civil War. Living in an area where people's feelings are divided, Brady is embarrassed by his father's strong anti-slavery feelings until events move him to take a position of responsibility. Both books are smoothly written and are convincing in their setting and in period details, but *Brady* also has a depth that stems from strong characterization and a vivid portrayal of the moral issues involved in the Abolitionist position.

Fritz's later novels, *Early Thunder*, set in 1775 Salem, and *I, Adam*, set in nineteenth-century New England, also have strong characters and serious discussions. We appreciate the problems of the characters, but we don't feel close to them. On the other hand, the humor of which Jean Fritz is capable shines out abundantly in her *Who's That Stepping on Plymouth Rock?* (1975), representative of the brief, factual tales for younger readers that are her recent work.

Elizabeth Coatsworth

Away Goes Sally
Five Bushel Farm
The Fair American

Elizabeth Coatsworth is an experienced, interesting writer whose works encompass poetry, fantasy, and historical fiction for a range of ages. When writing for older children, she is a strong delineator of character rather than an inventor of exciting episode. *Away Goes Sally* (1934) introduces us to an early nineteenth-century family of three sisters and two brothers who are raising an orphaned niece. The interplay of family relationships is excellent, especially when Uncle Joseph finds a way to move to Maine even when Aunt Nanny has said she will not leave her home. He simply builds her a small house on a sledge and transports everyone in comfort during the snowy winter months. *Five Bushel Farm* (1939) introduces us to Andrew, a sea captain's son who is out of touch with his father through no fault of his own, and who becomes a member of Sally's family in Maine. *The Fair American* (1940) takes the two children on a sea voyage where they help to save a French boy fleeing from the terrorists after the French Revolution.

All the small details of living are interestingly worked into the stories; the children are obedient but resourceful; family cooperation is the normal state of affairs.

Carol Ryrie Brink

Caddie Woodlawn

Like *The Perilous Road*, *Caddie Woodlawn* (1935) belongs to the Civil War period, but the war plays no part in the story. Caddie and her family live in Wisconsin when Indians are considered a menace, but life on the whole is fairly comfortable. Red-headed Caddie and her two brothers extract every possible bit of fun and adventure the frontier settlement can yield. Caddie's long friendship with the Indians and her courageous personal appeal to them helps prevent a threatened uprising.

The fun Caddie gets out of life suggests the usefulness of this book in the historical group in counteracting the overseriousness of much historical fiction.

Laura Ingalls Wilder

Little House in the Big Woods
and other stories

As has been noted, children's sense of the past is a confused one at best. Gas lights are more incredible to them than candlelight, and horse-and-buggy travel quite as odd as a trip by canal boat. Indeed, it may be easier for them to understand and enter into the colonial period of American history than into the more immediate past. The pioneering and settling of the Midwest have fewer picturesque details than has the dramatic first colonization. Frontier life has more humdrum struggle, less romantic adventure. Until Laura Ingalls Wilder undertook the writing of her family's experiences in settling the Midwest, there were no books of this period which really held children's interest.

Children love all the "Little House" books and grow up with the Ingalls girls and the Wilder boys, from *Little House in the Big Woods* (1932) to the romantic *These Happy Golden Years* (1943) when Laura Ingalls and Almanzo Wilder are married. The first book appeals to children of eight or nine; the latter is written for the almost-grown-up youngster, who by this time may feel that Laura is an old and dear friend. Few other books give children this sense of continuity and progress.

The saga begins with the Ingalls family in their log cabin in the Wisconsin forests, in *Little House in the Big Woods*. The children are all girls. The oldest is Mary (who later goes blind), then the active Laura, and baby Carrie. Grace eventually displaces Carrie as the baby. In this first book we become acquainted with Ma's skill in cooking wonderful, triumphant meals out of limited resources, and especially we know her good bread, baked every Saturday. It fills the small cabin with its delicious fragrance and nourishes the girls' growing bodies even as Pa's gay songs and fiddle music nourish their spirits. Here, too, we first see the little china woman which Ma is to carry with her through all their journeys. She puts it over the fireplace only when the dwelling is worthy, a real house and home. All these things give the children a sense of comfort and security.

Next, the family moves out to the wild Kansas country and begins the adventures described in the *Little House on the Prairie* (1935). *On the Banks of Plum Creek* (1937) finds the Ingalls family in Minnesota; *By the Shores of Silver Lake* (1939) carries them to the Dakota Territory, where they remain either on their lake or in town.

Farmer Boy (1933) begins the account of the Wilder family of boys on their prosperous New York farm. We follow Almanzo Wilder from his first day at school to the proud moment when he is given his own colt to break and train. In this book the modern child is given incidentally a sense of money values in terms of human labor. Almanzo knows fifty cents as so many hours of backbreaking toil over the family potato crop.

The Long Winter (1940) finds the Ingalls family living in town. Of the whole series, this book is one no modern child should miss. One blizzard follows another until the railroads cease to run and the little town is cut off from supplies for months. Fuel gives out, and the family has to twist straw into sticks to burn. Ma devises a button lamp to save oil. All day the sound of their little hand mill is heard as different members of the family take turns grinding wheat, their last stand against hunger. Finally the wheat begins to give out, and the whole community faces starvation. Then it is Almanzo Wilder, not Pa Ingalls, who rides out into the snow-driven prairie to buy

Viewpoints

. . . the historical novelist does not merely acquire information about the past, but absorbs it into his mind. Atmosphere comes out in his books as the overflow of a personality that has made a peculiar appropriation of history. It comes as part of the man himself.

. . . The virtue and power of the novelist's depiction of men, is not that he observes perpetually and arranges data, but that he enters into the experiences of others, he runs his life into the mould of their lives, he puts himself under the conditioning circumstances of their thinking. He can feel with people unlike himself and look at the world with their eyes and grapple with the issues of life that meet them, because he can put himself in their place, that is to say, because his experience is not entirely and merely his own. It is precisely because personality is not cut off from personality, and a man is not entirely locked up within himself, . . . that the novelist can so to speak transpose himself and catch life into a person other than himself.—H. Butterfield, *The Historical Novel,* Cambridge University Press, London, 1924, pp. 107, 111.

wheat from a farmer who has it. He succeeds, and the conclusion of the book is happy and humorous. *Little Town on the Prairie* (1941) and *These Happy Golden Years* (1943) carry Laura into teaching and then into marriage with Almanzo. *The First Four Years* (1971), a posthumously published book, tells of Laura and Almanzo's first years as struggling farmers. In *These Happy Golden Years,* a title which speaks for the whole series, Laura Ingalls Wilder wrote in her daughter's copy:

And so farewell to childhood days,
Their joys, and hopes and fears.
But Father's voice and his fiddle's song
Go echoing down the years.[1]

Other Books for the Middle Group

Jane Flory's historical stories are set in and around nineteenth-century Philadelphia. *Faraway Dream* (1968) tells of an orphan apprenticed to a milliner, while *A Tune for the Towpath* (1962) introduces us to a lockkeeper's daughter whose home lies beside a busy Pennsylvania canal.

Carolina's Courage (1964) by Elizabeth Yates is one of many tales of the wagon trains that crossed the great plains. Lonzo Anderson's *Zeb* (1966) is a taut story of a boy who survives a winter alone in the wilderness when his father and older brother are accidentally killed. In *Trouble River* (1969) by Betsy Byars, Dewey escapes the Indians by rafting himself and his querulous grandmother down river.

Two good Civil War stories for the middle group are F. N. Monjo's *The Vicksburg Veteran* (1971) and Rhoda Bacmeister's *Voices in the Night* (1965). In the Monjo story, General Grant's son participates in the Union victory that gains control of the Mississippi; in the Bacmeister story, a small girl visiting a family that operates a station for the Underground Railroad uses her wits to help one runaway escape. In Anna Gertrude Hall's *Cyrus Holt and the Civil War* (1964), a boy of nine finds the war exciting when it starts but as time goes by becomes increasingly aware of the men wounded and dead, and of the growing burden of deprivation and unwonted responsibilities.

The story of the Battle of Little Big Horn is told by fifteen-year-old Red Hawk in *Red Hawk's Account of Custer's Last Battle* (1970) by Paul and Dorothy Goble. Red Hawk, the only fictional character, says sadly, "Once all the earth was ours; now there is only a small piece left which the White Men did not want." He knows that the cause is lost despite the victory won by the Indians. The list of sources indicates the research that gives the book its authenticity of historical detail.

The Peppermint Pig (1975) by Nina Bawden shows an English family temporarily forced to live with relatives as their fortunes fail around the turn of the century, while *Carrie's War* (1973) describes the lives of World War II evacuees in the English countryside. Bawden is skilled in creating credible characters and evoking sympathy for them.

For children who have never experienced the horror of war, books that tell of the plight of children in wartime can evoke some understanding. Alki Zei's *Wildcat Under Glass* (1968, first published in 1963 in Greece) is a story of life under the oppression of dictatorship as experienced by a child, Melia, who lives on a Greek island during the time of prewar German occupation. The story, which begins in August 1936, has drama and momentum, and is particularly effective in showing the reactions of the very young to a rigid regime. In *Petros' War* (1972), Zei describes, from the point of view of a ten-year-old boy, the Italian occupation of Athens during World War II.

In Susan Cooper's *Dawn of Fear* (1970), a small group of boys, busy with their games and school, are shocked into awareness and fear when one of their number is killed in an air raid.

The effect of the Germans on the lives of European Jews is graphically portrayed in Johanna Reiss's *The Upstairs Room* (1972), where Annie lives hidden away in a farmhouse in wartime Holland. In *A Pocket Full of Seeds* (1973) by Marilyn Sachs, French Nicole arrives home for lunch one day to find her family completely gone. Judith Kerr, in *When*

[1]Irene Smith, "Laura Ingalls Wilder and the Little House Books," *The Horn Book,* September–October 1943, p. 306. Delightful account of the author, with family photographs of Ma, Pa, the four girls, and Almanzo.

From A Pocket Full of Seeds *by Marilyn Sachs, illustrated by Ben Stahl. Copyright © 1973 by Marilyn Sachs. Reproduced by permission of Doubleday & Company, Inc.*

Hitler Stole Pink Rabbit (1971), follows a family as they flee from Germany to Switzerland to France to escape extinction. They come finally to wartime England in *The Other Way Round* (1975), a sequel for older readers.

Books for Older Children

Older readers can range through many time periods, and in their historical fiction there is no need to avoid the complexities of social movements and relationships that existed in the past as they do today. Erik Haugaard's Hakon can move from one cultural pattern to another, Rosemary Sutcliff's Aquila can have a divided allegiance that young people understand. They can enjoy the rich tapestry of a story that has intricate patterns of action in an unfamiliar setting and appreciate the implications that past events have for the present.

Lucile Morrison

The Lost Queen of Egypt

Lucile Morrison's *The Lost Queen of Egypt* (1937) is a thrilling story. It begins about 1580 B.C. in the royal nurseries of Akhenaten, Pharaoh of Egypt, and Nefertiti, his queen. Their six little daughters are being arrayed for the arrival of the Great Royal Mother, who decides that three of the little girls must be betrothed at once to guarantee the succession. Ankhsenpaaten is relieved when the soldierly Tutankhaten is chosen for her; since he alone of the royal blood has shown a reckless courage and vitality equal to her own.

Later, a series of deaths calls this popular young pair to the throne; they become Tutankhamon and Ankhsenamon and seem destined to happiness and a long reign. Instead, the young king dies by poisoning and the queen is trapped in the palace to be forced either to marry the traitorous Ay or to die herself. Describing how Kenofer the artist rescues her, and how, in disguise, they turn to the river and live on their boat like hundreds of humble river people, gives the author an opportunity to compare ways of life for queen and commoner.

Illustration by Franz Geritz from The Lost Queen of Egypt *by Lucile Morrison. Copyright 1937 by Frederick A. Stokes Company. Copyright © renewed 1965 by Lucile Morrison. Reproduced by permission of J. B. Lippincott Company.*

Eloise Jarvis McGraw

Mara, Daughter of the Nile

Another novel of ancient Egypt is *Mara* (1953), a hair-raising tale of royal intrigue, spies, and true love, in the days when a female Pharaoh, Hatshepsut, has usurped the throne from the rightful king. Mara is a slave who vaguely remembers better days and is determined to escape. She is bought by a mysterious man who offers her luxury if she will serve at court as a spy for the queen. She accepts, and also sells her services as a spy for the king to a young nobleman, Lord Sheftu. Eventually, her love for Sheftu and a deep pity for the wronged king change her from a liar and a cheat to a selfless heroine who endures torture rather than betray her new loyalties. The action is terrifying. Detailed pictures emerge of the daily life of different classes—shopkeepers, rivermen, soldiers, slaves, and royalty.

A second book about ancient Egypt by this writer is *The Golden Goblet* (1961). While it is not quite so powerful a tale as *Mara*, it, too, affords a detailed picture of the times, with a vigorous plot and convincing characters.

Olivia E. Coolidge

Egyptian Adventures

Olivia E. Coolidge is a scholar, and in the course of her entertaining *Egyptian Adventures* (1954) she gives children lively pictures of the Egyptians' superstitions and magic, harvests and hunts, festivals and funerals. The characters emerge fully drawn and colorfully alive. These twelve well-written stories will do much to develop children's feeling for the people and adventures of a far-distant past.

Men of Athens (1962), *Roman People* (1959), and *People in Palestine* (1965) are in the same format, each tale complete in itself and the whole giving a remarkably vivid picture of the diversity of the culture in a historical period. *The King of Men* (1966) is a complex and absorbing novel based on the Agamemnon legend, and *Marathon Looks on the Sea* (1967) provides a sharp immediacy to the Battle of Marathon. The central character is a boy torn between allegiance to his own Greek people and to the Persian king who has become his friend. *The Maid of Artemis* (1969) tells of a year in the life of an Athenian girl and her choice for the future. In all these books, the combination of scholarly research and a fine writing style re-creates the period so convincingly that the reader has no sense of a disparate culture; each detail of rites and customs, of mores and superstitions, is an integral part of the story.

Henry Treece

Viking's Dawn

An English poet, critic, and teacher, Henry Treece was distinguished both for the sonorous quality of his prose and for his ability to create convincingly the mood and language of the distant past. *Viking's Dawn* (1956) is the first of a trilogy about Harald Sigurdson who, in the eighth century, was the only man on his crew to return from a voyage filled with disasters. In *The Road to Miklagard* (1957) Sigurdson becomes a Moorish slave and travels to Constantinople and then to Russia; and in *Viking's Sunset* (1961) the Vikings come to a new land and live with Eskimos and Indians.

Treece uses ancient Britain as a setting for lively tales like *The Centurion* (1967), a story of a Roman legionnaire. His last book, *The Dream Time* (1967), takes us back to Stone Age Britain. Like Rosemary Sutcliff, Treece was so steeped in history that his stories have a remarkable unity: details of dress and architecture, language, and references to other events have a consistency that makes his books convincing and alive.

Erik Christian Haugaard

Hakon of Rogen's Saga

Hakon of Rogen's Saga (1963) is not a traditional saga but a realistic story taking place in the last days of the Vikings. The rocky, mountainous island of Rogen, where Hakon was born, has been handed down in his family from father to son for generations. To Hakon,

Rogen Island and his powerful father seem indestructible and their home the best of all places to live, especially after Thora, his gentle stepmother, comes bringing love to both the boy and his father. But Thora was a kidnapped bride, and so when spring comes, her father sends three ships and many men to bring her back. When the bloody battles are over, Hakon is an orphan at the mercy of his treacherous uncle, who wants Rogen for his own. How Hakon suffers enslavement and brutal treatment, bides his time, finds a hideout in the mountain caves, mobilizes his few loyal men, and eventually takes Rogen again reads much like an old Norse saga. The author, a Dane familiar with Icelandic sagas, says at the beginning:

"Your dog, your horse, your friend, and you yourself: all shall die. Eternally live only your deeds and man's judgment over them," this was the credo of the Vikings.

Throughout the book their philosophy of living and dying is stated or chanted and at the end of the book when Hakon has won Rogen and rescued Helga, with whom he had been raised, he says to her:

That is everyone's birthright, his freedom, and the gods have only one message for us, that we must live.

In this book the Vikings are of heroic stature and the author clothes their story with nobility.

Its sequel, *A Slave's Tale* (1965), is told by the small slave girl Helga, to whom Hakon is like a beloved brother. Their affection ripens into love, but this is a minor facet of the story, which is primarily a tale of a voyage to Frankland in a longboat. The writing, in explication and dialogue as well as in the period details, vividly creates the historical milieu and has the sweep and cadence of a Norse epic.

The Rider and His Horse (1968) is set in ancient Israel at the final battle between the Jews and Romans at Masada, while *The Untold Tale* (1971) gives an all-too-clear picture of life for the poor in Denmark in the 1600s. Haugaard's heroes always face horror realistically and unflinchingly, and tragedy is as often the outcome as is triumph.

Rosemary Sutcliff

The Lantern Bearers
Dawn Wind

Most critics would say that at the present time the greatest writer of historical fiction for children and young people is unquestionably Rosemary Sutcliff. Her books are superior because they are authentic records of England's earliest history with its bloody raids and its continuous wars for occupation by Norsemen, Romans, Normans, and Saxons, and also because every one of her memorable books is built around a great theme. Her characters live and die for principles they value and that people today still value.

The theme of all her stories, as Margaret Meek[2] points out, is "the light and the dark. The light is what is valued, what is to be saved beyond one's own lifetime. The dark is the threatening destruction that works against it." In *The Lantern Bearers* (1959)[3] the blackness of despair is concentrated in the heart of Aquila, a Roman officer who, when a Saxon raid sweeps down on his father's farm, sees his father slain, and his sister Flavia carried off by the raiders. He himself is left tied to a tree for the wolves and later made a slave by another band. Years later, after he has escaped his thralldom, an old friend says to him:

It may be that the night will close over us in the end, but I believe that morning will come again. . . . We are the Lantern Bearers, my friend; for us to keep something burning, to carry what light we can forward into the darkness and the wind.

No briefing of these stories can give any conception of their scope and power. They may be difficult, not because of vocabulary, but because of the complexities of the plots in which many peoples are fighting for dominance.

Fortunately, *Dawn Wind* (1962), one of the finest of the books, is also the least complex. Chronologically it follows *The Lantern Bearers*, but it is complete in itself and will undoubtedly send many readers to the trilogy.

[2] *Rosemary Sutcliff*. A Walck Monograph, Walck, 1962.
[3] *The Lantern Bearers* is the third book in a trilogy which also includes *The Eagle of the Ninth* and *The Silver Branch*.

Drawing by Richard Cuffari, reprinted by permission of Henry A. Walck, from The Capricorn Bracelet *© 1973 by Rosemary Sutcliff.*

For the fourteen-year-old hero Owain, the light of the world seems to have been extinguished. He finds himself the sole survivor of a bloody battle between the Saxons and the Britains in which his people, the Britains, are completely destroyed. In the gutted remains of the city from which he had come, the only life the boy finds is a pitiable waif of a girl, lost and half-starved. At first Owain and Regina are bound together in mutual misery, but eventually they are united in respect and affection. So when Regina is gravely ill, Owain carries her to a Saxon settlement, even though he knows what will happen to him. The Saxons care for the girl but sell Owain into slavery. Like Aquila, Owain can do nothing less than serve his master with all his skill and strength. This proud, competent youth is loved and trusted by his master and his family. If sometimes despair almost overcomes Owain, his work, in which there is both conflict and triumph, absorbs him. After eleven years, he is freed and sets out at once to find his people and Regina, who has never doubted he would come for her.

So life is not snuffed out by the night. A dawn wind blows and two people start all over again with those basic qualities that have always made for survival. Whether it is her great trilogy or *The Shield Ring* (1957) or *The Outcast* (1955) or *Warrior Scarlet* (1958) or her later, less complex tales, *The Capricorn Bracelet* (1973) and *The Witch's Brat* (1970), Rosemary Sutcliff gives children and youth historical fiction that builds courage and faith that life will go on and is well worth the struggle.

Cynthia Harnett

Nicholas and the Wool-Pack
Caxton's Challenge

Cynthia Harnett's sketches add to the wealth of informative detail about fifteenth-century England in *Nicholas and the Wool-Pack*, winner of the Carnegie Medal in 1951 under its British title, *The Wool-Pack*. It is not only an exciting story with an element of mystery, but also a colorful picture of the weaving industry and of everyday life of the period. Nicholas, an apprentice to his father, a wool merchant, foils the two Lombardians who are secretly attempting to ruin his father.

Another smoothly written story of the same period is *Caxton's Challenge* (*The Load of Unicorn* [1968] in the British edition), which gives a vivid picture of London at that time, both the text and the maps indicating the careful research that lends authenticity to historical fiction. Again an apprentice is a leading character; Bendy is entranced by the printing machines of his master, William Caxton, and becomes involved in the struggles Caxton has against the resentful scriveners.

The Writing on the Hearth (1971) embroils would-be Oxford scholar Stephen in fifteenth-century English politics. Harnett's stories are solid and sedate, well researched and meticulous in detail.

Elizabeth Janet Gray Vining

Adam of the Road
I Will Adventure

Elizabeth Gray Vining is a born storyteller, although paradoxically her stories are weak in plot construction. Her books develop little excitement; the conflicts are mild, with no breath-taking suspense leading to a climax. Yet she is a careful historian, and her tales have all the authentic minutiae of everyday life long ago which make history convincing. But chiefly she is concerned with people.

In *Adam of the Road* (1943), for which the author won the Newbery Medal, the protagonist happened to have lived in the thirteenth century instead of today. Adam's two loves are his golden cocker spaniel and his minstrel father, but he loses them both for a time. How he seeks the two of them up and down the roads of old England gives children a glimpse into every variety of medieval life—that of jugglers, minstrels, plowmen, and nobles, as real as the people today.

The hero of *I Will Adventure* (1962) is Andrew Talbot, a most beguiling young imp, who takes to himself a line from Shakespeare's *Romeo and Juliet,* "I will adventure." Andrew is journeying to London to be a page to his uncle Sir John Talbot when he has the good luck to hear this play and, by way of a fight with one of the boy players, meets Master Burbage and Shakespeare himself. Andrew is all for signing up with the players, but they won't take him, though Shakespeare, grieving for his own boy Hamnet, lets Andrew ride with him for a day's journey. Through Andrew's eyes the reader comes to know intimately many facets of London life in 1596, especially the theater, the plays, and the audiences. Andrew's problems are happily solved, thanks to Shakespeare and a sympathetic uncle.

The Taken Girl (1972) moves us from England to Philadelphia during pre–Civil War days, when Veer, an orphaned servant girl, works with John Greenleaf Whittier in the Abolitionist movement.

Illustration by Corydon Bell. From I Will Adventure *by Elizabeth Janet Gray. Copyright © 1962 by Elizabeth Janet Gray. Reprinted by permission of The Viking Press, Inc.*

Marchette Chute

The Wonderful Winter
The Innocent Wayfaring

Marchette Chute, the author of *Shakespeare of London* and similar studies of Chaucer and Ben Jonson for adult readers, has also written some delightful stories for young people. *The Wonderful Winter* (1954) carries young readers straight into Shakespeare's theater with young Robin, Sir Robert Wakefield, who has escaped from an intolerable home situation. London seems to spell starvation for him until he is befriended by some actors and is taken into the home of the famous John Heminges. Through the warmth and affection of this crowded household, young Robin learns to give and accept love and gaiety. Meanwhile he works and plays small parts in the Burbage Theater, knows the great Shakespeare, and falls in love with *Romeo and Juliet.* When Robin returns to his castle and his duties, he is happy and confident as a result of his wonderful winter.

The Innocent Wayfaring (first published in 1943 and reissued in 1955) is fourteenth-century England brought vividly and authentically to life. Anne is so averse to learning the arts of housewifery that she runs away from her convent school with the prioress's pet monkey for company. The monkey is responsible for her meeting Nick, a poet and a most resourceful young man. He tries to get away from her, but Anne sticks like a burr. Their adventures provide a view of fourteenth-century life, from seamy inns to manor houses. After three days Nick takes Anne back to her family with the agreement that when she has learned housewifery and he his father's business, Nick will come for her. Meanwhile, they have the memory of three enchanting days which led them back to home and responsibility.

Both books are beautifully written by a scholar who can paint a glowing background for her charming stories.

Barbara Willard

The Lark and the Laurel

While several American writers, notably Laura Ingalls Wilder and Leonard Wibberley, have followed a family through the years, Barbara Willard has spanned more than a hundred years of English history, from the early sixteenth century to the mid–seventeenth century, through a family living in Ashdown Forest, in and around a house called Mantlemass. The first of the series, *The Lark and the Laurel* (1970), tells of a child marriage for political ends. The cycle continues with *The Sprig of Broom* (1971), which introduces Richard Plashet, or Plantagenet, unacknowledged son of Richard III, and his son, Medley, who marries into the Mantlemass Manor family. *A Cold Wind Blowing* (1972) shows how the family weathers the Reformation, while in *The Iron Lily* (1973) an unacknowledged Medley woman takes over as the iron-willed mistress of her husband's forge at his death. Mantlemass is destroyed in the last tale, *Harrow and Harvest* (1974), when civil war erupts. Willard has a strong feeling for place, and it is the locale we remember as much as the events and people.

Patricia Clapp

Constance

With the exception of one character, all of the people described by *Constance* (1968) in her journal existed, and the events are based on the real life of an ancestress of Patricia Clapp's husband. The historical details are smoothly woven into the story, and the description of the early days of the Plymouth Colony is unusually vivid. As she tells of her growing understanding of the Indians, her relationship with her stepmother, her doubts about herself, and her friendship with the young man she will marry, Constance is always a convincing character. The book, which concludes with her marriage in 1626, is particularly valuable because of the graphic depiction of the hardships of the first grim winter and the struggles of the colonists with their English backers.

Hester Burton

Beyond the Weir Bridge
Time of Trial

Beyond the Weir Bridge (1970) is a vivid piece of historical writing, consistent in language and viewpoint, informative about the period in which it is set, and a truly dramatic story. Richard and Richenda, whose fathers had been killed in 1644 in Cromwell's service, are both fond of shy, bookish Thomas although he is a Royalist. Richenda, indeed, comes to love him when they are grown and with him joins the Quakers, a denomination then reviled. It is only when Richard, who has become a doctor, sees Thomas's faith bring him to plague-ridden London to help as best he can, that he understands the true humility of the Quaker credo.

Time of Trial, winner of the 1963 Carnegie

Medal, also is concerned with the courage of the nonconformist. Seventeen-year-old Margaret Pargeter is the daughter of a London bookseller who is sent to prison for advocating social reform and for printing a book judged inflammatory. *Kate Ryder* (1975) is a compelling tale of England's Civil War, with another strong heroine. Burton's characters always reflect the mores and customs in a time of change, yet are developed as distinctive individuals, and her stories are all the more convincing because her characters' goals are realistically modest.

Mollie Hunter

The Ghosts of Glencoe
The Stronghold

Ensign Robert Stewart, the protagonist of Mollie Hunter's *The Ghosts of Glencoe* (1969), is an officer of the king's army, dedicated to keeping peace in the Highlands. Like many other Scottish officers, Ensign Stewart is torn between loyalty to his king and sympathy for his own people. Shaken by the vengefulness of those who do not share that sympathy, Stewart finally warns the rebels when an attack is planned. The dialogue rings true, and the period details are as meticulously correct as is the historical material.

This careful treatment of fact is a firm base in all of Mollie Hunter's books, although most of them are more highly fictionalized than is *The Ghosts of Glencoe. The Spanish Letters* (1967) is a cloak-and-dagger adventure story, set in Edinburgh in the late sixteenth century, in which two Spanish agents are allied with Scottish traitors planning to abduct King James. *The Lothian Run* (1970) is a tale of spies and smugglers which, like *The Spanish Letters*, is full of plot and counterplot, romantic and sinister. Less dramatic but just as suspenseful is the more somber *A Pistol in Greenyards* (1968), a tale of the Highland evictions of the tenant farmers in the 1850s.

The Thirteenth Member (1971) deals with a coven of witches and part of a plot to kill James I of Scotland. In *The Stronghold* (1975), winner of a Carnegie Medal, Hunter's ability to construct a convincing tale from historical fragments is very evident. In this book Coll discovers a way to build the multi-storied tower within which his small Scottish tribe can withstand Roman raids during the first century A.D.

Elizabeth George Speare

The Witch of Blackbird Pond
The Bronze Bow

The Witch of Blackbird Pond was the winner of the 1959 Newbery Medal. Orphaned Kit, luxuriously raised in tropical Barbados, comes to live with her Puritan relatives in Connecticut. These cousins try to be kind but they disagree with Kit about almost everything. Her silk dresses and befeathered bonnets scandalize the whole community, and Kit willfully flouts local customs in many

Viewpoints

If writing historical novels has its own special pleasures, it also has its own special difficulties—especially if one knows that one's books are going to be read primarily by children. Children are not less intelligent than grownups. The problem is that they *know* less. In particular, they know less history. The first difficulty, then, is to give the historical setting of one's story and to impart the necessary historical facts without appearing to teach or to preach and—what is more important—without slowing up the pace of the narrative. Both the child and the writer want to hurry on to the action of the story. Yet, if the historical background is not firmly painted in, both child and author come to grief. The characters in the story move in a kind of featureless limbo, and both reader and writer lose interest in them. For this reason, I find the writing of the first chapter of every novel extremely difficult. There is so much to do all at the same moment: there are the characters to describe, the geographical setting to depict, the plot to be introduced, and, on top of all, the problem of history. I know from children themselves that I have not entirely mastered this difficulty, for I sometimes receive letters which begin: "I liked your story except for the beginning which I found boaring [sic]."—Hester Burton, "The Writing of Historical Novels," *The Horn Book*, June, 1969, p. 276.

ways, most seriously by making friends with an old Quaker woman, Hannah Tupper, the suspected witch of Blackbird Pond. Kit's recklessness climaxes in her arrest, imprisonment, and trial for witchcraft. This terrifying experience brings Kit to realize that no one of us can live without family or friends. Her stern old uncle defends her even at considerable danger to himself and his family. A forlorn waif Kit had befriended stands by her, and her disapproving, seafaring beau Nat finally manages to extricate Kit. The strength of this book lies in its theme and its well-drawn characters. They are neither wholly good nor wholly bad but a very human mixture of heroism and bigotry, frailty and courage, rebellious recklessness and generous loyalty.

The 1962 Newbery Medal winner, *The Bronze Bow,* is set in Israel during the time Jesus lived. The title comes from II Samuel 22: 35—"He trains my hands for war, so that my arms can bend a bow of bronze." This verse fascinates young Daniel, who, along with many Israelites, is looking for the Deliverer to drive the cruel Romans out of their land. Daniel had seen his mother and father wantonly slain by these conquerors. Blinded by his hatred, Daniel kills his sister's hope of love, thereby driving her into mental darkness. Not until he has seen his mute but devoted follower killed and has almost lost his love, Thacia, does Daniel come face to face with the healing love of Jesus. Then at last he understands that it is not hatred and violence, but only love that is strong enough to bend the bow of bronze.

John and Patricia Beatty

At the Seven Stars
Who Comes to King's Mountain?

John and Patricia Beatty's historical novels are based on sound research, and their aim is to entertain rather than to instruct their readers. As Patricia Beatty says, "We hope that our books are more than escape fiction, but we are aware that all fiction offers escape."[4] In *At the Seven Stars* (1967) a fifteen-year-old boy from Philadelphia comes to London in 1752 and meets some of the very real people of that turbulent period. Richard becomes involved in the struggle between the Hanoverian and Stuart supporters, takes refuge in William Hogarth's home, is imprisoned, escapes, enlists the aid of the actor David Garrick, and gets back to America with the help of the Duke of Newcastle. *Who Comes to King's Mountain?* (1975) shows the difficulties a Scottish South Carolina boy has in serving with the rebels rather than the British during the last years of the Revolution. There is never a dearth of action in books by the Beattys or in the books that Patricia Beatty writes alone. In *Hail Columbia* (1970), for example, a suffragette in Oregon in 1893 stirs up the town of Astoria by her vigorous dedication to causes.

Esther Forbes

Johnny Tremain

Esther Forbes received the 1942 Pulitzer Prize for her adult biography *Paul Revere and the World He Lived In.* Her *Johnny Tremain,* which was an outgrowth of the research expended on *Paul Revere,* received the 1944 Newbery Medal. In her Newbery acceptance speech, she explained that while she was working on the adult biography she had to stifle any tendency toward fiction. But she was continually teased by the story possibilities of Boston's apprentices, who were always getting into scrapes of one kind or another. To illustrate her point, she related the hilarious doings of one of these apprentices who precipitated the Boston Massacre, and she concluded:

> *In this way an apprentice of whom we know nothing except that he was "greasy and diminutive" played his minute part in our history and disappears forever. I'd like to know more of him.*[5]

So she promised herself that as soon as possible she would write some fiction about the apprentices. The resulting book, *Johnny Tremain,* represents a high point in American his-

[4]Patricia Beatty, "The Two-headed Monster," *The Horn Book,* February 1967, p. 100.

[5]Esther Forbes, "The Newbery Medal Acceptance," *The Horn Book,* July–August 1944, p. 264.

Illustration by Lynd Ward from Johnny Tremain *by Esther Forbes. Copyright, 1943 by Esther Forbes Hoskins. Copyright © 1971 by Linwood M. Erskine, Jr. Reprinted by permission of Houghton Mifflin Company. (Original with color)*

torical fiction for children and young people.

Johnny Tremain tells the story of a silversmith's apprentice who lived in the exciting days that marked the beginning of the American Revolution. Johnny's master is second only to the famous Paul Revere as a silversmith, but Johnny knows that he himself is unrivaled among all apprentices. Competent and cocky, a humble artist but an unbearably conceited boy, Johnny is harsh and overbearing with his fellow apprentices and ambitious for himself. Just as he achieves a notable design, the apprentices decide to play a joke on him. The results are far worse than they intended. Not only is Johnny's design lost but he is left with a burned hand, maimed for life. His career as a silversmith is over even before it is well begun. Out of work and embittered, he still must stand on his own feet or go under. He stands.

This is the beginning of a story that carries Johnny and his friend Rab into the thick of Boston's pre-Revolutionary activities. In the first little skirmish of the Revolution, men and boys lined up in the square—some to die. But they knew what they were dying for, Forbes assures us, and they believed it "was worth more than their own lives."

Johnny Tremain has so many values they are difficult to summarize. Johnny's bitterness over his maimed hand is understandable. This book gives no one-sided account of pre-Revolutionary days but makes the colonists and redcoats come alive as histories never seem to. The British, especially, are amazingly human in their forbearance, while the confusion and uncertainty of the colonists are frighteningly real. All the details of the everyday life of the period are expertly woven into the story, never dragged in for themselves.

Rebecca Caudill

Tree of Freedom

Tree of Freedom (1954), a story about the Revolutionary War period, is sound historical fiction because of its vivid characterizations and homely details of everyday living, which make the past understandable and natural. Each child of a family moving to Kentucky may take one prized possession. Stephanie carries an apple seed, because that is what her grandmother brought from France. When Noel, the eldest son, wants to take his dulcimer, it starts anew the feud between father and son. But the mother intervenes, "Twon't hurt him any. An' a little music won't hurt Kentucky, either. . . . He's got his rifle, ain't he, as well as his dulcimore? He'll use it like a man. See if he don't." And he does, but the quarrel is not resolved until the end of the war.

Another fine story is Caudill's *The Far-Off Land* (1964), in which a young girl is taken by flatboat in 1780 from the Moravian settlement in Salem to French Lick. Although she becomes accustomed to the rough ways of the settlers, Ketty cannot accept their hostile behavior toward Indians, since she has been brought up to practice brotherly love. The characterization is strong, the period details convincing and smoothly incorporated into the story.

Leonard Wibberley

The *Treegate* series

Leonard Wibberley paints his stories of Peter Treegate's adventures during the Revolutionary War on a broad canvas. In the first book, *John Treegate's Musket* (1959), John Treegate is a solid, respectable Boston citizen who is loyal to his king, but his son Peter becomes increasingly convinced of the rectitude of the patriot cause and fights against the British at Bunker Hill. In *Peter Treegate's War* (1960), Peter becomes a war prisoner, escapes, crosses the Delaware with Washington, and goes to the southern mountains. *Sea Captain from Salem* (1961) tells the story of Peace of God Manly, who saved Peter's life in the first book, and who is sent on a mission by Benjamin Franklin, in an effort to win French support for the cause. The move to France gives the series variety, and the plot provides some rousing sea battles. In *Treegate's Raiders* (1962), Peter is on a recruiting trip through the mountains, trying to persuade Scottish settlers to forget their clan loyalties and feuds and unite as Americans, the same problem handled by the Beattys in *Who Comes to King's Mountain?* The story has vivid martial scenes and ends with the defeat of Cornwallis. All the books give realistic pictures not only of the Revolutionary War but of the significance of that war to the ordinary citizen of the time and to history. In *Leopard's Prey* (1971), *Red Pawns* (1973), and *The Last Battle* (1976), Wibberley moves to the events surrounding the War of 1812, his young protagonists, the two nephews of Peter Treegate.

William O. Steele

Wayah of the Real People
The Perilous Road
The Far Frontier

Few writers re-create wilderness life more vividly and movingly than William Steele. His stories are well written in the vernacular of the times, with good dialogue, plenty of suspense and action, and flesh-and-blood characters—grownups who struggle and survive in a tough pioneer world and expect their children to do the same; frontier boys, ignorant, prejudiced, or wrong-headed, but resourceful and enduring. The significant thing about William Steele's boys is that life changes and develops them, so that the reader sees them grow.

Wayah of the Real People (1964) is an unusual story about a Cherokee boy's year of schooling at Brafferton Hall in mid–eighteenth-century Williamsburg. Wayah suffers all the problems of any child placed in an environment culturally different from his own. Afraid that he has changed, Wayah finds when he has returned to the Real People, that his year away has helped him mature.

In *The Perilous Road* (1958), young Chris Brabson, who hates the Yankees, cannot understand how his parents can accept the fact that his older brother has joined the Union Army. After Union soldiers have raided the Brabson livestock, Chris tries a bit of revenge and is surprised, when he gets to know some of the soldiers, that they are people like himself. The story has action and suspense, and, like many of Steele's other books, is set in the Tennessee mountain region.

The Far Frontier (1959) shows another strong-willed boy who is outraged when he finds himself bound out to an absent-minded scientist from Philadelphia. But before their long, danger-beset journey through the Tennessee wilderness is over, Tobe has acquired a deep respect for his brave, eccentric companion. Best of all, the boy survives with a lasting hunger for learning and is well on his way with both reading and figuring. Tobe and the naturalist, Mr. Twistletree, are a memorable pair.

Evelyn Lampman

The Tilted Sombrero
Cayuse Courage

Evelyn Lampman's *The Tilted Sombrero* (1966) takes place at the start of the Mexican War of Independence in 1810, and it includes some real people prominent in that struggle, primarily Father Hidalgo y Costilla, the priest who led the first Indian revolt against Spain. In addition to historical interest, however, the story gives a vivid picture of the stratification of Mexican society. Its protagonist, Nando, is a proud Creole whose family has always been loyal to Spain, and at first he is greatly displeased to learn that his family is not pure Creole, that they have an Indian grandmother. Won over to the patriot cause, Nando changes his attitude. The book has a colorful setting and an action-filled plot, but it is the theme of rebellion against oppression that is its most memorable element. Another historical period (1847) is the setting for a fine pioneer story, *Tree Wagon* (1953), and Lampman's sympathetic identification with Native Americans is evident in both *Cayuse Courage* (1970), a story of the Whitman Massacre told from the viewpoint of a young Indian boy, and *Once Upon the Little Big Horn* (1971), a detailed account of the four-day struggle commonly known as "Custer's Last Stand," also described in *Red Hawk's Account of Custer's Last Battle* by Paul and Dorothy Goble. *White Captives* (1975) is based on the experience of several children taken from a wagon train by an Apache raiding party in 1851.

Scott O'Dell

Island of the Blue Dolphins
The King's Fifth

There seem to be more good realistic stories about the American Indian set in the past than in the present. Of these stories of the past, the most powerful is *Island of the Blue Dolphins* (1961 Newbery Medal).

In the early 1800s off the coast of California, a twelve-year-old Indian girl boards a ship that is to carry the tribe away from their island home where they are being harried and destroyed by Aleutian seal hunters. But when Karana sees that her little brother has accidentally been left behind, she jumps off the moving ship and swims back to him and their island home. A pack of wild dogs kills her brother and begins to stalk the solitary girl. This is the beautifully told story of her survival on the island for eighteen years. She has to prepare her own weapons, build a shelter with a strong fence, maintain a continual search for food, replace her worn out clothes, all with an eye on the savage pack of dogs. The need to love and nurture is strong. So when she wounds the leader dog, she nurses him back to health and he becomes her inseparable companion and defender. Shining through her struggles and hardships are her quiet resignation, her endurance, her genuine love for her island home, and the great fortitude and serenity she develops. The story of Karana is historically true. Her incredible battles with a bull sea elephant, a devilfish, and the ferocious dogs, and, above all, her years of solitude command the reader's humble admiration for human courage.

Also based on history is the story told by Esteban in *The King's Fifth* (1966), his reminiscences of the journey made as a fifteen-year-old cartographer to Coronado. Put ashore to find Coronado's camp, his small group has a dangerous journey searching for the fabled gold of Cibola, and Esteban is later imprisoned on the charge that he has withheld the king's share of the treasure. The transitions between past and present are smoothly bridged, and the historical details are used to enhance rather than obscure an adventurous tale.

Weyman Jones

The Talking Leaf
The Edge of Two Worlds

In two stories about Sequoyah, Weyman Jones brings vividly to life the half-white Cherokee who conceived the idea of giving his people a written alphabet. In *The Talking Leaf* (1965) a young Cherokee, Atsee, had hoped to become a great scout like his father but finds that times have changed, that the Cherokee nation has to change as well. Knowing that his people must become literate, Atsee seeks Sequoyah. Sympathetic, dignified, and beautifully written, the story is moving, its theme apparent in Sequoyah's comment when Atsee asks bitterly if the bolt he is making for a bridge is so that the whites can come into Cherokee country more easily. "Part of growing up," Sequoyah says, "is learning that a bridge goes two ways." In *The Edge of Two Worlds* (1968) a white boy who is the only survivor of an Indian attack on a wagon train travels for mutual protection with Sequoyah, now an old man, but when the time comes that they part, the boy has learned to respect and trust the gentle and dignified Indian. There is no stereotype, no sentimentality in these stories, but a deep understanding and reverence for the man who learned to interpret the written word so that he might help his people.

Christie Harris

Raven's Cry
West with the White Chiefs

Raven's Cry (1966) was given the Canadian Library Association's award as the best children's book of the year in English. The dramatic and impressive story describes the dreadful consequences for the Haida people when white men came in 1775 to hunt sea otter, cheating the people and destroying their way of life until only a handful remained. The story is told from the Indian viewpoint, in a vigorous narrative that is complemented by the strong illustrations of Bill Reid, a descendant of the last Haida chief, who duplicates the form of Haida art.

West with the White Chiefs (1965) is based on the journal written by two Englishmen, a story of high adventure in which a small party crosses the Rockies in 1863. The characterization of the whites and Indians, who become friends on the journey, is excellent, and there is some comedy in the pedantic, quarrelsome schoolmaster who foists himself on the party of explorers.

Betty Baker

The Dunderhead War
Walk the World's Rim

The Dunderhead War (1967) is one of the few good books for young people about the Mexican War, which serves as a background for Betty Baker's story of seventeen-year-old Quincy, who is too young to enlist, but travels with his Uncle Fritz and shares some of the adventures of the volunteers. Uncle Fritz has just come to the United States, and his complacent superiority and criticism of that "army of dunderheads" give an outsider's viewpoint and add humor to a lively story.

Many of Baker's books, from stories for beginning readers to serious fiction for adolescents, are about Native Americans. Two of the best are *Walk the World's Rim* (1965), the story of the black slave Esteban who wandered across the country with Cabeza de Vaca and became the hero of the Indian boy Chakoh; and *And One Was a Wooden Indian* (1970), a sensitive novel about a young Apache of the nineteenth century and his first encounter with white people.

Harold Keith

Rifles for Watie

Rifles for Watie, winner of the 1958 Newbery Medal, is substantial historical fiction. The hero of the book is young Jefferson Davis Bussey, who despite his name is a Kansas farm boy and a rabid Unionist. Once in the army, Jeff's name and his stubborn forthrightness get him into trouble with a brutal officer, who persecutes him endlessly. Finally, Jeff is sent as a spy behind the Rebel lines to try to discover where Confederate Stand Watie, full-blooded Cherokee Indian, is getting the new rifles issued for the Union armies. Jeff is captured by the Rebels, but his name, together with a plausible story, allays suspicions. Jeff lives, works, and fights with this Indian regi-

Illustration by Peter Burchard. Reprinted by permission of Coward, McCann & Geoghegan, Inc., from Jed *by Peter Burchard. Copyright © 1960 by Coward, McCann, Inc.*

ment for fourteen months. When he finally gets his information and escapes to the Northern side, he leaves his Confederate friends with real regret. He leaves them also with the disturbing realization that heroic, well-intentioned men are fighting and dying on both sides in this horrifying struggle.

Keith has created unforgettable characters and has given us all the hunger, dirt, and weariness of war to balance the heroism of men and boys on both sides.

Peter Burchard

Bimby
Jed

Peter Burchard's approach to the writing of historical fiction is to pinpoint his theme by using a compressed, concise account of an incident or a single day and creating thereby a dramatic impact. In *Bimby* (1968) he follows a young slave through one crucial day in which the boy sees an old friend killed and also learns that his father had died of the punishment he received when he tried to escape. Knowing that she will never see her son again, Bimby's mother gives him information that will enable him to escape, both of them aware that life without freedom is empty. The writing is subdued, so that the poignancy and tension of the story emerge from the events themselves.

In *Jed* (1960), Burchard again avoids didacticism and lets the ethical implications of a boy's conduct make their own impact on the reader. Although he is only sixteen, Jed has already fought at Shiloh, and he is disturbed by the behavior of some of the Yankee soldiers who are his companions at arms. Foraging is stealing, and war is no excuse; war, in fact, is not glamorous. When he finds a small boy who has been hurt, Jed takes the child back to his Confederate family and befriends them. *The Deserter* (1974) is a Civil War spy story.

K. M. Peyton

The *Flambards* trilogy

Before K. M. Peyton's *Flambards* trilogy, she produced a series of excellent adventure stories, many of which are set in the past but have little sense of history. With the publication of *Flambards* (1968), Peyton made the Edwardian period an integral part of the book. Flambards is the Russell estate to which Christina Parsons, a young orphan, comes to live with her uncle and his two sons, Mark and Will. World War I is looming, and quiet Will is enthralled by flying. The emphasis on the first frail, experimental planes is a major part of the story, although the plot focuses on Christina's rejection of the powerful bully Mark and her love for Will. One of the ways in which Peyton reflects the changing mores of the period is in Christina's ambivalence about servants: she resents her uncle's treatment of them, yet cannot quite feel that the groom, Dick, is a person.

The book was a runner-up for the Carnegie Medal, which was won by Peyton for the second book of the three, *The Edge of the Cloud* (published in the United States in 1970). In this book Will and Christina take refuge with an aunt in Battersea, since Mark and his father were irate because of Christina's choice. For two years they are engaged, Christina always apprehensive because of Will's dangerous vocation. The story ends with their marriage, but it is less a love story than an account of the early days of flying, with its stunt men, and the camaraderie of the still-small group of flyers.

In *Flambards in Summer* (1970) the time is 1916, and Christina is a widow. She finds that Mark has an illegitimate son and brings the boy to Flambards, the neglected estate that she now manages. Eventually she falls in love again. It is significant of the changes in Christina and of the changes in the times that Dick, the former groom, is the man she plans to wed. The characterization is strong and the heroine's development into maturity is a convincing characterization and also a microcosmic picture of the new social structure that came out of World War I.

Elizabeth Foreman Lewis

Young Fu of the Upper Yangtze
To Beat a Tiger

Elizabeth Lewis, who lived long in China, wrote *Young Fu of the Upper Yangtze*, winner of the 1933 Newbery Medal. It is the exciting story of a thirteen-year-old Chinese country boy who is brought to the rich city of Chungking in the 1930s and apprenticed to a skillful coppersmith. In time, Young Fu becomes a fine craftsman, but neither easily nor quickly. Meanwhile, he explores the great city and finds everywhere the conflict of old and new ideas. Fu is no idealized hero but exhibits the usual contradictory human traits. He is brave and honest, yet he wastes his master's time and gets into trouble. He works hard, grows skillful, and then gets unbearably cocky. He is frugal one moment and wasteful the next.

Lewis has a later book, *To Beat a Tiger* (1956), for teenagers and young adults. It is the grim story of sixteen Chinese boys living by their wits on the outskirts of Shanghai. They all know the proverb, "To beat a tiger, one needs a brother's help." Their tiger is starvation and death, and so they lie, steal, and cheat, but share their wretched scraps of food, their hut, filthy rags, and scanty heat. Death strikes one of the gang, and the chance to rise by sheer villainy claims another. Nationalists and Communists are not named, but the two factions are there and the boys are involved. It is a complex story, but once the large gallery of characters is identified, the plot gains momentum and suspense is high.

While Lewis creates many unusual happenings and adventures for her characters, it is in the presentation of the people that she excels. Even minor characters have individuality and presence, and linger in the reader's memory.

Other Books for Older Children

A story of ancient times is Madeleine Polland's *To Tell My People* (1968). A British girl, taken by Roman invaders, is sent to Rome as a slave. When she escapes and returns to her colony, she hopes to share with her people the knowledge she has gained, but they are ignorant and only sneer. She had hoped to bring them peace; they will do nothing but fight. Polland has set several books in this era, telling believable stories with strong characters.

Hans Baumann's stories are always exciting, even though sometimes slowed down by details. In *I Marched with Hannibal* (1962), an old man tells two children about his boyhood experiences, a narrative device that gives the book a sense of immediacy and scope for vivid personal accounts of the marches and battle scenes. Baumann's historical personages are never stock characters but are vividly depicted to add depth to stories with authentic background.

The Namesake (1964) and *The Marsh King* (1967) by Cyril Walter Hodges are sequential tales of King Alfred's struggle against the Danish invaders, stories full of action and fascinating historical details. Another English writer, Geoffrey Trease, moves his hero in *The Red Towers of Granada* (1967) from England in the time of Edward I to Spain. Cast out of his village as a leper, young Robin learns from a Jewish doctor that he has only a minor skin disease. When the doctor leaves England for Spain, Robin goes with him.

Fifteenth-century Poland is the setting for

Illustration by C. Walter Hodges. Reprinted by permission of Coward, McCann & Geoghegan, Inc., and G. Bell & Sons, Ltd., London, from The Marsh King *by C. Walter Hodges. Copyright © 1967 by C. Walter Hodges.*

Eric Kelly's 1929 Newbery Medal book, *The Trumpeter of Krakow,* a story based on the oath of the Krakow trumpeters to sound their defiant song every hour. The setting is colorful, the story intriguing both because it has dramatic adventure and because it gives an absorbing picture of the problems of the Polish people.

I, Juan de Pareja (1965), for which Elizabeth Borton de Trevino was awarded the Newbery Medal, is the story of the black slave of the painter Velazquez. Written in autobiographical form, it comes close to biography, but is told as a story. An aspiring artist himself, de Pareja painted secretly until his master realized that here was another artist—and freed him. In de Pareja's descriptions of court affairs and of Velazquez as a person, there is appeal for the reader interested in history and in art, and the story itself moves with pace and dignity.

Another story with a black protagonist is Ann Petry's *Tituba of Salem Village* (1964), a dramatic fictionalization of the inexorable hysteria of the Salem witch-hunt and trials. In Alice Marriott's *Indian Annie: Kiowa Captive* (1965), Annie comes to love her foster parents and marries into the tribe. The story is set in the antebellum years, and Annie is struck by the fact that a freed slave cannot identify, as she does, with another minority group.

E. M. Almedingen has written many charming historical novels set in Russia, most of them based on family records. *Katia* (1967) is an adaptation of a great-aunt's memoirs, published in Russia in 1874. *Young Mark* (1968) is the true and romantic story of Almedingen's great-great-grandfather, who became a court favorite because of his beautiful singing, grew wealthy, and established the family fortune. The writing is intricate and mature, but the style and the fidelity of the historical background are very appealing.

No group of stories within the genre of historical fiction demonstrates so clearly that literature is an international heritage as do the books about World War II. From Denmark comes Anne Holm's *North to Freedom* (1965), the story of a boy of twelve who escapes from a prison camp in eastern Europe and makes his way to his mother in Copenhagen. Josef Carl Grund's *Never to Be Free* (1970) and Hans Peter Richter's *Friedrich* (1970), both translated from the German, are alike in being told by boys who are at first loyal to Hitler but who change; in Grund's book Gustav is disillusioned by his army experience; in Richter's, the boy who tells the story is disillusioned by what happens to his Jewish friend Friedrich. Both stories are all the more effective for their portrayal of ordinary people. This is also true of a book from France, Colette Vivier's *House of the Four Winds* (1969), for the people who live in the house (an apartment building) are a cross-section of middle-class Parisians, and their valor (or cowardice) during the German occupation has a homeliness that makes the historical period come alive. Margaret Balderson's *When Jays Fly to Barbmo* (1969) moves slowly, but the style fits the bleak setting of a

Illustration by Victor Ambrus. Reprinted with the permission of Farrar, Straus & Giroux, Inc. and Oxford University Press, London. From Katia *by E. M. Almedingen, illustrated by Victor Ambrus, copyright © 1966 by E. M. Almedingen.*

Norwegian island where the German invaders burn the farmhouses.

In Hester Burton's *In Spite of All Terror* (1969), a girl who has been sent out of London for her safety comes back to do her bit on the eve of Dunkirk. One of the most powerful books in this group is Erik Haugaard's *The Little Fishes* (1967), told by a twelve-year-old waif in wartime Italy. Guido lives by stealing because he must to exist. Children compete with adults for survival, yet Guido has faith in humanity. Terrible and true, the story is a testament of hope as much as it is an indictment of war.

Printing a Danish underground paper brings death to Peter's father in *A Kind of Secret Weapon* (1969) by Elliott Arnold. Nathaniel Benchley's *Bright Candles* (1974) shows other facets of the Danish resistance to the Nazi occupation, from sabotage to nationwide support of the Jews. Suspense and vigorous action are hallmarks of books by this versatile writer.

The ravages of war are a recurrent theme in James Forman's books. *Horses of Anger* (1967), like Grund's *Never to Be Free,* concerns a Nazi soldier who begins to doubt the propaganda he has heard and to understand his own prejudice. In Forman's *The Traitors* (1968), a Bavarian pastor suffers because his congregation and his only child espouse the Nazi cause, and he joins the underground rebellion. Forman's books are mature and sophisticated, often profound and provocative, demanding the most of a young reader.

It is only now, some thirty years later, that we are beginning to see a number of books for children on the Jewish experience during, before, and after World War II, many of them written out of personal knowledge. Perhaps the time lapse was necessary to enable authors to approach the theme with some objectivity. It may also be because we are less inclined in these days of the pervasiveness of the mass media to shelter children from the misdeeds of adults. We are more willing to present life whole, the bad—although not dwelt upon at length—with the good. We are also awaking to the fact that children do not come equipped with a value system, that good citizenship and character must be taught.

The bicentennial celebration in the United States led to an increased publication of historical fact and fiction for young and old to answer demands for information only partially met through the mass media. It seems logical to expect that the coincidence of the two-hundredth year of nationhood and the problems the United States now faces in the ecological and political areas will encourage a continuing interest in the past, an interest in how our ancestors met the many problems of a new environment and a new government.

Viewpoints

The historical novelist with a proper respect for history has a very stiff task before him; . . . the atmosphere of belief, the attitudes and assumptions of society that he conveys, must be in accordance with what is known of the mental and emotional climate of the place and period. It is by the striking of a false note here that one distinguishes the writer who has "got up" his subject, however painstakingly, from the one who has really soaked himself in it.—Helen Cam, *Historical Novels,* The Historical Society, London, 1961, pp. 4, 8.

Since we are more willing to present all sides of life to children, we have also been more ready to treat historical personages with humor and humanity, to make them come alive as people. Authors are beginning to realize that children as well as adults have an interest in the sources, primary and secondary, that have been used to build a picture of the past.

As the world becomes more nearly the "global village" foreseen by Marshall McLuhan, we will undoubtedly see historical fiction set in many more countries than the United States and the United Kingdom. Increased opportunities for travel mean an upswing in interest in places and people no longer remote and unknown.

Adult References[6]

American Historical Fiction and Biography for Children and Young People.

EGOFF, SHEILA. *The Republic of Childhood; A Critical Guide to Canadian Children's Literature in English.* Part 3, "Historical Fiction."

EGOFF, SHEILA, G. T. STUBBS, and L. F. ASHLEY, eds. *Only Connect: Readings on Children's Literature.* Part 3, "Historical Fiction."

European Historical Fiction and Biography for Children and Young People.

FIELD, ELINOR WHITNEY, comp. *Horn Book Reflections.* Part III, "Recreating Other Times."

A Guide to Historical Fiction.

History in Children's Books.

World Culture.

Some historical fiction titles may be found in the bibliography for Chapter 10. In the following bibliography these symbols have been used to identify books about a religious or a particular ethnic group:

- § Black
- ★ Chicano or Puerto Rican
- ☆ Native American
- ● Religious minority

Historical Fiction: The Ancient World

ANDREWS, J. S. *The Man from the Sea.* Dutton, 1971. Their men lost in a storm, the survivors in an early fishing village are aided by a trader from the south. A taut, well-told tale. 11-14

BAUMANN, HANS. *I Marched with Hannibal,* tr. by Katherine Potts, ill. by Ulrik Schramm. Walck, 1962. 12-15

BEHN, HARRY. *The Faraway Lurs.* World, 1963. Tribes of differing cultures meet in early Denmark, with tragic consequences for two young people. 12-15

BULLA, CLYDE ROBERT. *Viking Adventure,* ill. by Douglas Gorsline. T. Crowell, 1963. A Viking's son grows into a man on the long voyage to Wineland and home again. 8-10

COOLIDGE, OLIVIA. *Egyptian Adventures,* ill. by Joseph Low. Houghton, 1954. 12-16

______. *King of Men,* ill. by Ellen Raskin. Houghton, 1966. 12 up

______. *The Maid of Artemis,* ill. by Bea Holmes. Houghton, 1969. 10-14

______. *Marathon Looks on the Sea,* ill. by Erwin Schachner. Houghton, 1967. 12-15

______. *Men of Athens.* Houghton, 1962. 12-15

● ______. *People in Palestine.* Houghton, 1965. 12 up

______. *Roman People,* ill. by Lino Lipinsky. Houghton, 1959. 12-15

FYSON, J. G. *The Three Brothers of Ur,* ill. by Victor G. Ambrus. Coward, 1966. Lively tale of a trader's household in the ancient city. 10-14

GARD, JOYCE. *The Mermaid's Daughter.* Holt, 1969. An intricate novel set in Britain at the time of the Roman occupation, based on the mermaid-goddess cult. 11-14

HAUGAARD, ERIK CHRISTIAN. *The Rider and His Horse,* ill. by Leo and Diane Dillon. Houghton, 1968. 12-17

HAYS, WILMA PITCHFORD. *The Story of Valentine,* ill. by Leonard Weisgard. Coward, 1956. A vivid story of a Christian priest who, when imprisoned, achieved a miracle of faith. 9-12

LAWRENCE, ISABELLE. *The Theft of the Golden Ring,* ill. by Charles V. John. Bobbs, 1948. A complex and exciting story. 11-14

LINEVSKI, A. *An Old Tale Carved Out of Stone,* tr. by Maria Polushkin. Crown, 1973. The trials of a young, insecure shaman as he tries to lead his tribe wisely in early Siberia. 11-15

McGRAW, ELOISE JARVIS. *The Golden Goblet.* Coward, 1961. 11-15

______. *Mara, Daughter of the Nile.* Coward, 1953. 11-15

MADDOCK, REGINALD. *The Great Bow,* ill. by Victor Ambrus. Rand, 1968. A tightly constructed and convincing story about prehistoric people. Atta is a thoughtful fourteen-year-old who fails his test of manhood because he does not want to kill. 10-12

MORRISON, LUCILE. *The Lost Queen of Egypt,* ill. by Franz Geritz and Winifred Brunton. Lippincott, 1937. 12-14

POLLAND, MADELEINE. *To Tell My People,* ill. by Richard M. Powers. Holt, 1968. 11-13

☆ SCHWEITZER, BYRD BAYLOR. *One Small Blue Bead,* ill. by Symeon Shimin. Macmillan, 1965. Beautifully illustrated, a rhyming text tells a story of primitive people in Arizona. 7-9

SPEARE, ELIZABETH G. *The Bronze Bow.* Houghton, 1961. Newbery Medal. 12 up

TREECE, HENRY. *The Centurion,* ill. by Mary Russon. Meredith, 1967. 11-15

European Historical Fiction

ALMEDINGEN, E. M. *Katia,* ill. by Victor G. Ambrus. Farrar, 1967. This has often been classified as a biography. 11-14

______. *Young Mark: The Story of a Venture,* ill. by Victor G. Ambrus. Farrar, 1968. 12-15

ARNOLD, ELLIOTT. *A Kind of Secret Weapon.* Scribner's, 1969. 10-13

[6]Complete bibliographic data are provided in the combined Adult References in the Appendixes.

AVERY, GILLIAN. *A Likely Lad,* ill. by Faith Jacques. Holt, 1971. A true Victorian tale. Willy prefers school to trade, to the amazement of his parents. 11-15

BALDERSON, MARGARET. *When Jays Fly to Barbmo,* ill. by Victor G. Ambrus. World, 1969. 11-14

BAWDEN, NINA. *Carrie's War.* Lippincott, 1973. 10-14

______. *The Peppermint Pig.* Lippincott, 1975. 10-14

BEATTY, JOHN and PATRICIA. *At the Seven Stars,* with Hogarth prints and line drawings of Douglas Gorsline. Macmillan, 1963. 12-14

______. *Master Rosalind.* Morrow, 1974. A fascinating and lively picture of Elizabethan theatrical life and the court and criminal circles of the time. 12-14

BENCHLEY, NATHANIEL. *Beyond the Mists.* Harper, 1975. An old Viking recalls his days with Leif Ericson. 12-15

● ______. *Bright Candles.* Harper, 1974. 12-15

BENTLEY, PHYLLIS. *The Adventures of Tom Leigh,* ill. by Burt Silverman. Doubleday, 1964. 10-14

______. *Forgery.* Doubleday, 1968. 10-14

______. *Oath of Silence,* ill. by Burt Silverman. Doubleday, 1967. Set in England's Yorkshire in the early nineteenth century, these three stories bring the problems of the weavers, facing mechanization, to life. 11-14

BUFF, MARY. *The Apple and the Arrow,* ill. by Conrad Buff. Houghton, 1951. 9-12

BULLA, CLYDE. *The Sword in the Tree,* ill. by Paul Galdone. T. Crowell, 1956. 8-10

● BURTON, HESTER. *Beyond the Weir Bridge,* ill. by Victor G. Ambrus. T. Crowell, 1970. 12-15

______. *Castors Away!* ill. by Victor G. Ambrus. World, 1962. A story centering on the great naval battle at Trafalgar. 12-15

______. *The Henchmans at Home,* ill. by Victor G. Ambrus. T. Crowell, 1972. Stories of two generations of a family, during the time of Nelson and the Battle of Trafalgar, and the Victorian era. 12-15

______. *In Spite of All Terror,* ill. by Victor G. Ambrus. World, 1969. 11-14

______. *Kate Ryder,* ill. by Victor G. Ambrus. T. Crowell, 1975. 12-15

______. *No Beat of Drums,* ill. by Victor G. Ambrus. World, 1967. In 1830 English farmhands try to unite to gain a living wage and are punished by transportation to Tasmania. 12-15

______. *Time of Trial,* ill. by Victor G. Ambrus. World, 1964. Carnegie Medal. 12-15

CHUTE, MARCHETTE. *The Innocent Wayfaring,* ill. by author. Dutton, 1955.

______. *The Wonderful Winter,* ill. by Grace Golden. Dutton, 1954. 11-14

COOLIDGE, OLIVIA. *Tales of the Crusades,* ill. adapted from prints by Gustave Doré. Houghton, 1970. Each of the stories that chronicle some facet of the long years of the Crusades is a splendid entity, wonderfully evocative and vividly written. The book does not give a cohesive picture of all those centuries but is impressive both as a literary and a historical work. 13 up

COOPER, GORDON. *An Hour in the Morning,* ill. by Philip Gough. Dutton, 1974. 10-11

______. *A Time in a City,* ill. by Robin Jacques. Dutton, 1975. Twelve-year-old Kate Bassett's life as she goes into service before World War I in an English rural community and then in a town. Fully detailed social history. 12-15

COOPER, SUSAN. *Dawn of Fear,* ill. by Margery Gill. Harcourt, 1970. 10-11

DARKE, MARJORIE. *A Question of Courage.* T. Crowell, 1975. A fine story about women's suffrage is set in Birmingham and London before the first world war. 12-14

DE ANGELI, MARGUERITE. *The Door in the Wall,* ill. by author. Doubleday, 1949. Newbery Medal. 8-11

DEGENS, T. *Transport 7-41-R.* Viking, 1974. A grim tale of the aftermath of war as evacuees return to Cologne in 1946. 11-14

FORMAN, JAMES. *Horses of Anger.* Farrar, 1967. 13 up

______. *Ring the Judas Bell.* Farrar, 1965. A story of Greece just after the time of the Nazi occupation when the Andarte were kidnapping children from the villages. A dramatic and sophisticated story; honest, grim, and moving. 13 up

● ______. *The Traitors.* Farrar, 1968. 13 up

GRUND, JOSEF CARL. *Never to Be Free,* tr. by Lucile Harrington. Little, 1970. 12-15

HARNETT, CYNTHIA. *Caxton's Challenge,* ill. by author. World, 1960. Carnegie Medal. 12-16

______. *Nicholas and the Wool-Pack,* ill. by author. Putnam, 1953. 11-15

______. *The Writing on the Hearth.* Viking, 1973. 12-15

HAUGAARD, ERIK CHRISTIAN. *Hakon of Rogen's Saga,* ill. by Leo and Diane Dillon. Houghton, 1963. 11-14

______. *The Little Fishes,* ill. by Milton Johnson. Houghton, 1967. 12 up

______. *A Slave's Tale,* ill. by Leo and Diane Dillon. Houghton, 1965. 11-14

______. *The Untold Tale,* ill. by Leo and Diane Dillon. Houghton, 1971. 12-15

HODGES, C. WALTER. *Columbus Sails,* ill. by author. Coward, 1950. This well-liked story of Columbus and his voyages is fiction based on facts and is tremendously moving. 11-14

______. *The Marsh King,* ill. by author. Coward, 1967. 12-15

______. *The Namesake,* ill. by author. Coward, 1964. 12-14

HOLM, ANNE. *North to Freedom,* tr. from the Danish by L. W. Kingsland. Harcourt, 1965. 11-13

HUNTER, MOLLIE. *The Ghosts of Glencoe.* Funk, 1969. 11-14

______. *The Lothian Run.* Funk, 1970. 12-15

______. *A Pistol in Greenyards.* Funk, 1968. 11-14

______. *The Spanish Letters.* Funk, 1967. 12-15

______. *The Stronghold.* Harper, 1974. Carnegie Medal. 10-14

______. *The Thirteenth Member.* Harper, 1971. 12-15

● ISH-KISHOR, SULAMITH, *A Boy of Old Prague,* ill. by Ben Shahn. Pantheon, 1963. A graphic story of life in the Jewish ghetto in 1540 Poland. 10-12

JENSEN, NIELS. *Days of Courage,* tr. by Oliver Stallybrass. Harcourt, 1973. A village's lone survivor of the great plague of medieval Europe rebuilds his life. A compelling tale. 12-15

KELLY, ERIC. *The Trumpeter of Krakow,* rev. ed. Macmillan, 1966. Newbery Medal. 12-14

● KERR, JUDITH. *The Other Way Round.* Coward, 1975. 12-15

● ______. *When Hitler Stole Pink Rabbit.* Coward, 1972. 10-12

● LEVITIN, SONIA. *Journey to America,* ill. by Charles Robinson. Atheneum, 1970. The first-person story of a young Jewish girl and her family from Germany in the late 30s. Dramatic and well written. 10-12

LEWIS, HILDA. *The Gentle Falcon.* Criterion, 1957. A poignant and moving story of little Princess Isabella of France, who was married to Richard II of England when she was seven. Romantic in vein and rich in historical detail. 12 up

LOVETT, MARGARET. *Jonathan.* Dutton, 1972. The grinding poverty of 1815 England as seen in the struggles of a boy to care for orphaned children. 11-14

MacPHERSON, MARGARET L. *The Rough Road,* ill. by Douglas Hall. Harcourt, 1966. Jim finds life difficult indeed living with unkind foster parents on the Isle of Skye during the depression of the 30s. Vivid atmosphere, characterization, and dialogue. 12-15

MONJO, FERDINAND N. *The Sea Beggar's Son,* ill. by C. Walter Hodges. Coward, 1975. A stirring tale of a Dutch hero of the seventeenth century. 9-12

NÖSTLINGER, CHRISTINE. *Fly Away Home,* tr. by Anthea Bell. Watts, 1975. A gripping survival story set in World War II Vienna. 11-14

OLIVER, JANE [pseud.]. *Faraway Princess,* ill. by Jane Paton. St. Martin's, 1962. Princess Margaret, in flight from England after the Norman Conquest, finds sanctuary in Scotland and later a throne. Excellent historical fiction. 10-13

PEYTON, K. M. *The Edge of the Cloud,* ill. by Victor G. Ambrus. World, 1970. Carnegie Medal.

______. *Flambards,* ill. by Victor G. Ambrus. World, 1968.

______. *Flambards in Summer,* ill. by Victor G. Ambrus. World, 1970. 12-15

PICARD, BARBARA LEONIE. *Lost John,* ill. by Charles Keeping. Criterion, 1962. John, who has left home to avenge his father's death, is captured by outlaws and becomes one of them. Set in the Middle Ages. 11-14

PLOWMAN, STEPHANIE. *Three Lives for the Czar.* Houghton, 1970. The fascinating first-person story of Andrei Hamilton, whose family had for many generations lived in Russia and whose childhood playmate had been the Grand Duchess Olga. Successfully combines romantic appeal and sociological value. 13 up

POLLAND, MADELEINE. *Children of the Red King,* ill. by Annette Macarthur-Onslow. Holt, 1961. Grania and Fergus, children of Ireland's embattled king, are sent as captives to their father's enemy. The events leading to reunion with their father offer a vivid story of the Norman Conquest. 11-13

POPE, ELIZABETH. *The Perilous Gard,* ill. by Richard Cuffari. Houghton, 1974. Set in Elizabethan times. A courageous girl, banished from the then-Princess Elizabeth's side to a remote castle, battles the occult. 11-14

PYLE, HOWARD. *Men of Iron,* ill. by author. Harper, 1891.

______. *Otto of the Silver Hand,* ill. by author. Scribner's, 1888. 10-14

● REISS, JOHANNA. *The Upstairs Room.* T. Crowell, 1972. 9-12

● RICHTER, HANS PETER. *Friedrich,* tr. from the German by Edite Kroll. Holt, 1970. 11-14

● SACHS, MARILYN. *A Pocket Full of Seeds,* ill. by Ben Stahl. Doubleday, 1973. 9-12

SERRAILLIER, IAN. *The Silver Sword,* ill. by C. Walter Hodges. Criterion, 1959. The unforgettable journey of four children who make their way from Warsaw to Switzerland and safety during World War II. 11-14

● SLOBODKIN, FLORENCE. *Sarah Somebody,* ill. by Louis Slobodkin. Vanguard, 1970. The warm and sympathetic story of a nine-year-old girl in a Polish village in 1893 who gets a chance to learn to read and write—and to become somebody 8-10

● SUHL, YURI. *The Merrymaker,* ill. by Thomas di Grazia. Four Winds, 1975. Turn-of-the-century Eastern Europe is the setting for a story of a poor Jewish family. 9-12

● ______. *On the Other Side of the Gate.* Watts, 1975. A young Jewish couple in World War II Poland smuggle their baby to safety in a suspenseful tale. 12-16

SUTCLIFF, ROSEMARY. *The Capricorn Bracelet,* ill. by Richard Cuffari. Walck, 1973. 11-14

______. *Dawn Wind,* ill. by Charles Keeping. Walck, 1962; Walck, 1973.

______. *The Eagle of the Ninth,* ill. by C. Walter Hodges. Walck, 1954. The story of a lost legion in Roman Britain of the second century.

______. *The Lantern Bearers,* ill. by Charles Keeping. Walck. 1959. Carnegie Medal.

______. *The Mark of the Horse Lord.* Walck, 1965. Set in Scotland during the second century, this exciting adventure novel is fast paced with no slackening of suspense up to the last stunning episode.

______. *The Outcast,* ill. by Richard Kennedy. Walck, 1955. Unwanted by either Briton tribesmen or the Romans, orphaned Beric is forced to build a new life. Service as a galley slave is an unforgettable part of the story.

______. *The Shield Ring,* ill. by C. Walter Hodges. Walck, 1957. Eleventh-century England is the background for this tale of Norsemen against Norman invaders, and of the advance of two young people in the war-torn land.

______. *The Silver Branch.* Walck, 1958. Two young Romans, involved in the bitter intrigue between the ruler of Roman Britain and his rival, play a heroic part in bringing an assassin to justice.

______. *Warrior Scarlet,* ill. by Charles Keeping. Walck, 1958. In a unique tale of Bronze Age England, Drem kills his wolf and regains his tribal status despite a crippled arm. 12-16

______. *The Witch's Brat,* ill. by Richard Lebenson. Walck, 1970. An evocative story of Norman England, based on the actual founding of St. Bartholomew's Hospital. The story has strong, taut structure and good characterization, but is most distinguished by the colorful picture of a historical period. 11-14

● TREASE, GEOFFREY. *The Red Towers of Granada,* ill. by Charles Keeping. Vanguard, 1967. 11-14

TREECE, HENRY. *The Dream Time,* ill. by Charles Keeping. Meredith, 1968. 11-14

______. *The Road to Miklagard,* ill. by Christine Price. Criterion, 1957. 11-14

______. *Viking's Dawn,* ill. by Christine Price. Criterion, 1956. First in an absorbing trilogy of eighth-century Viking life, in which youthful Harald Sigurdson accompanies his father on his first dangerous sea journey. In *The Road to Miklagard* (1957) his voyages are interrupted when he becomes a Moorish slave. In *Viking's Sunset* (1961) Harald, now a chieftain, sails his longboat to the shores of Lake Superior, and death intervenes on this last voyage. Harald's life saga conveys the vast scope of early Viking travels. 11-14

______. *Viking's Sunset.* ill. by Christine Price. Criterion, 1961. 11-14

§ TREVINO, ELIZABETH B. DE. *I, Juan de Pareja.* Farrar, 1965. Newbery Medal. 12-15

TUNIS, JOHN R. *Silence over Dunkerque.* Morrow, 1962. The evacuation of Dunkirk is the dramatic background for the story of British Sergeant Williams stranded in enemy-occupied France. A powerful story. 12-15

VAN STOCKUM, HILDA. *The Winged Watchman*, ill. by author. Farrar, 1962. The Verhagen family, in constant danger from an informer, conceals a British pilot during the occupation. 10-12

VINING, ELIZABETH GRAY. *Adam of the Road*, ill. by Robert Lawson. Viking, 1942. Newbery Medal. 12-14

______. *I Will Adventure*, ill. by Corydon Bell. Viking, 1962. 11-14

● VIVIER, COLETTE. *The House of the Four Winds*, tr. and ed. by Miriam Morton. Doubleday. 1969. 11-14

WALSH, GILLIAN PATON. *The Huffler*, ill. by Juliette Palmer. Farrar, 1975. A Victorian adventure set on an English canal boat. 10-12

WATSON, SALLY. *Mistress Malapert*. Holt, 1955. A lively tale of an ancestor of the heroine in *Jade* (1968). 11-14

WELCH, RONALD. *Tank Commander*. Nelson, 1974. A compelling story of an officer's experiences in World War I. 12-15

WILLARD, BARBARA. *A Cold Wind Blowing*. Dutton, 1973. 11-15

______. *Harrow and Harvest*. Dutton, 1975. 11-15

______. *The Iron Lily*. Dutton, 1974. 11-15

______. *The Lark and the Laurel*. Dutton, 1970. 11-15

______. *The Sprig of Broom*. Dutton, 1972. 10-14

WILLIAMS, URSULA MORAY. *The Earl's Falconer*, ill. by Charles Geer. Morrow, 1961. Training falcons was not the privilege of peasant boys, but young Dickon's rare talent earned him the Earl's favor. A colorful tale of medieval England. 11-14

ZEI, ALKI. *Petros' War*, tr. by Edward Fenton. Dutton, 1972. 10-14

______. *Wildcat Under Glass*, tr. from the Greek by Edward Fenton. Holt, 1968. 10-12

United States Historical Fiction

ANDERSON, LONZO. *Zeb*, ill. by Peter Burchard. Knopf, 1966. 10-14

☆ ARMER, LAURA ADAMS. *Waterless Mountain*, ill. by Sidney Armer and Laura Adams Armer. McKay, 1931. An early Newbery Award book, the story of Dawn Boy, a Navajo boy destined to be a medicine man. 11-15

§ BACMEISTER, RHODA. *Voices in the Night*, ill. by Ann Grifalconi. Bobbs, 1965. 9-11

§ BACON, MARTHA. *Sophia Scrooby Preserved*, ill. by David Omar White. Atlantic, 1968. A romantic tale of a cultured black girl whose lively adventures are described in the mannered style of early English novelists. 11-13

☆ BAKER, BETTY. *And One Was a Wooden Indian*. Macmillan, 1970. 11-15

______. *The Dunderhead War*. Harper, 1967. 11-14

______. *The Pig War*, ill. by Robert Lopshire. Harper, 1969. 7-8

☆§ ______. *Walk the World's Rim*. Harper, 1965. 11-14

BALL, ZACHARY [pseud.]. *North to Abilene*. Holiday, 1960. The thousand-mile cattle drive from Texas to Abilene challenges the resourcefulness of orphaned Seth in this fine tale of the early cattle industry. 12-15

BEATTY, JOHN and PATRICIA. *Who Comes to King's Mountain?* Morrow, 1975. 11-15

BEATTY, PATRICIA. *Hail Columbia*, ill. by Liz Dauber. Morrow, 1970. 10-12

______. *A Long Way to Whiskey Creek*. Morrow, 1971. Set in Texas in 1879, a story in which two boys overcome the lingering hostility between Northern and Southern supporters. 10-12

______. *O the Red Rose Tree*, ill. by Liz Dauber. Morrow, 1972. A lively tale of Oregon in the 1890s. 9-12

☆ BELL, MARGARET. *Daughter of Wolf House*. Morrow, 1957. The coming of the white trader and his sons to the Alaskan salmon country changes the lives of the Indian villagers and brings romance to Nakatla, granddaughter of the chief. 12-15

BENCHLEY, NATHANIEL. *Sam the Minuteman*, ill. by Arnold Lobel. Harper, 1969. 7-9

BOLTON, CAROLE. *Never Jam Today*. Atheneum, 1971. Young Maddy becomes involved, through her Aunt Augusta, in the cause of women's suffrage. A realistic story with a commendable conclusion: Maddy passes up two love interests for the time being in favor of college and a career. 11-14

☆ BRINK, CAROL RYRIE. *Caddie Woodlawn*, ill. by Kate Seredy. Macmillan, 1935. Newbery Medal. 9-12

BULLA, CLYDE ROBERT. *Down the Mississippi*, ill. by Peter Burchard. T. Crowell, 1954. Erik leaves his Minnesota farm to go down the river on a log raft as a cook's helper. Storms and an Indian raid add plenty of excitement. 8-10

☆ ______. *John Billington, Friend of Squanto*, ill. by Peter Burchard. T. Crowell, 1956. 7-9

______. *Riding the Pony Express*, ill. by Grace Paull. T. Crowell, 1948. An easy-to-read but never commonplace story of a boy who carried the mail in an emergency. 8-10

§ BURCHARD, PETER. *Bimby*, ill. by author. Coward, 1968. 9-11

______. *The Deserter*. Coward, 1974. 10-12

______. *Jed*, ill. by author. Coward, 1960. 10-13

______. *North by Night*, ill. by author. Coward, 1962. Swift moving escape tale of two Yankee soldiers from a South Carolina Confederate prison. 12 up

BYARS, BETSY. *Trouble River*, ill. by Rocco Negri. Viking, 1969. 9-12

CATTON, BRUCE. *Banners at Shenandoah*. Doubleday, 1955. Bruce Catton, Pulitzer Prize winner, writes absorbingly of Civil War days in this story of young Bob Hayden, flag bearer for General Sheridan. 12-16

● CAUDILL, REBECCA. *The Far-Off Land*, ill. by Brinton Turkle. Viking, 1964. 12-14

______. *Tree of Freedom*, ill. by Dorothy Bayley Morse. Viking, 1949. 12-14

☆ CLAPP, PATRICIA. *Constance; A Story of Early Plymouth*. Lothrop, 1968. 12-15

CLARK, ANN NOLAN. *Year Walk*. Viking, 1975. A sixteen-year-old Basque sheepherder comes to Idaho in the early 1900s. 8-11

CLARKE, MARY STETSON. *The Glass Phoenix*. Viking, 1969. The beginnings of a glass works in Sandwich, Mass., in 1830. 11-15

CLARKE, TOM E. *The Big Road*. Lothrop, 1965. Vic Martin runs away from home in 1933 and finds life during the Depression difficult. 12-15

COATSWORTH, ELIZABETH. *Away Goes Sally*, ill. by Helen Sewell. Macmillan, 1934.

______. *The Fair American*, ill. by Helen Sewell. Macmillan, 1940.

______. *Five Bushel Farm*, ill. by Helen Sewell. Macmillan, 1939. 10-12

COBLENTZ, CATHERINE. *Martin and Abraham Lincoln*, ill. by Trientja. Childrens Pr., 1967. 7-10

COLLIER, JAMES LINCOLN, and CHRISTOPHER COLLIER. *My Brother Sam Is Dead*. Four Winds, 1974. Tim Meeker tells of problems in Connecticut in 1775 after his father is imprisoned and his brother joins the rebels. 11-14

CONSTANT, ALBERTA WILSON. *Those Miller Girls!* ill. by Joe and Beth Krush. T. Crowell, 1965. A period story set in Kansas early in the century. The motherless Miller girls come with their father to his new job at Eastern Kansas Classical College. 10-12

DALGLIESH, ALICE. *Adam and the Golden Cock,* ill. by Leonard Weisgard. Scribner's, 1959. 8-9

☆ ______. *The Courage of Sarah Noble,* ill. by Leonard Weisgard. Scribner's, 1954.

______. *The 4th of July Story,* ill. by Marie Nonnast. Scribner's, 1956.

☆ ______. *The Thanksgiving Story,* ill. by Helen Sewell. Scribner's, 1954. 7-10

EDMONDS, WALTER D. *Bert Breen's Barn.* Little, 1975. Tom Dolan, son and grandson of ne'er-do-wells, steadily works toward his goal of owning an old but sturdy barn. A finely detailed study of country life in the early twentieth century. 12-15

☆ ______. *The Matchlock Gun,* ill. by Paul Lantz. Dodd, 1941. Newbery Medal. Describes an Indian attack on colonial settlers. A book which gives only one side of red-white relations. 10-12

§ FALL, THOMAS. *Canalboat to Freedom,* ill. by Joseph Cellini. Dial, 1966. Orphaned Benja is indentured as a canalboat worker. There he meets Lundius, a freed slave who becomes his friend and teacher. When Lundius is killed working for the Underground Railroad, Ben grieves. The emphasis in the story is on their developing friendship and on Ben's gradual realization of the horrors of slavery. 11-14

☆ FIELD, RACHEL. *Calico Bush,* ill. by Allen Lewis. Macmillan, 1931. 10-14

FINLAYSON, ANN. *Rebecca's War,* ill. by Sherry Streeter. Warne, 1972. A lively tale of the British occupation of Philadelphia. 11-14

______. *Redcoat in Boston,* ill. by Peter Landa. Warne, 1971. Harry Worrilow, a British soldier on duty in Boston at the time of the Boston Massacre, decides to become an American. *Greenhorn on the Frontier* (Warne, 1974) tells of Harry's efforts to settle near Fort Pitt. 11-14

FLEISCHMAN, SID. *Mr. Mysterious & Company,* ill. by Eric von Schmidt. Little, 1962. Traveling under their intriguing stage name, the delightful Hackett family give magic shows in small pioneer towns as they work their way west from Texas to a San Diego ranch. A very different and appealing story of the early West. 10-12

FLORY, JANE. *Faraway Dream.* Houghton, 1968. 9-11

______. *The Liberation of Clementine Tipton.* Houghton, 1974. 9-11

______. *A Tune for the Towpath.* Houghton, 1962. 9-11

FORBES, ESTHER. *Johnny Tremain,* ill. by Lynd Ward. Houghton, 1943. Newbery Medal. 12-14

☆ FORMAN, JAMES. *The Life and Death of Yellow Bird.* Farrar, 1973. The story of some of the Indians who did not come to government reservations after the battle at Little Bighorn in 1867. 12-16

§ FOX, PAULA. *The Slave Dancer,* ill. by Eros Keith. Bradbury, 1973. A white boy of 1840 is impressed into work on a slave ship. Newbery Medal. 11-14

§ FRITZ, JEAN. *Brady,* ill. by Lynd Ward. Coward, 1960. 10-13

______. *The Cabin Faced West,* ill. by Feodor Rojankovsky, Coward, 1958. 8-10

______. *Early Thunder,* ill. by Lynd Ward. Coward, 1967. Set in Salem in 1775, the story of a boy whose loyalty moves from King to Patriot cause. 11-14

______. *I, Adam,* ill. by Peter Burchard. Coward, 1963. A good period story, set in New England in the mid-19th century, about a young man who decides that his real goal is an education. 11-14

GAUCH, PATRICIA LEE. *This Time, Tempe Wick?* ill. by Margot Tomes. Coward, 1974. Tempe prevents colonial soldiers from requisitioning her horse. 8-10

☆ GOBLE, PAUL and DOROTHY. *Red Hawk's Account of Custer's Last Battle,* ill. by authors. Pantheon, 1970. 10-12

☆ HAIG-BROWN, RODERICK. *The Whale People,* ill. by Mary Weiler. Morrow, 1963. A dignified picture of the great whale hunters and the training of a young Indian chief. 10-12

HALL, ANNA GERTRUDE. *Cyrus Holt and the Civil War,* ill. by Dorothy Bayley Morse. Viking, 1964. 9-11

HAUGAARD, ERIK CHRISTIAN. *Orphans of the Wind,* ill. by Milton Johnson. Houghton, 1966. A sea story set during the Civil War. 10-12

HAYS, WILMA PITCHFORD. *Christmas on the Mayflower,* ill. by Roger Duvoisin. Coward, 1956. 7-9

☆ ______. *May Day for Samoset,* ill. by Marilyn Miller. Coward, 1968. 7-9

☆ ______. *Pilgrim Thanksgiving,* ill. by Leonard Weisgard. Coward, 1955. The story of the first Thanksgiving. 7-9

HUNT, IRENE. *Across Five Aprils.* Follett, 1964. An impressive book both as a historically authenticated Civil War novel and as a beautifully written family story. The realistic treatment of the involved emotional conflicts within a border-state family is superb. 12 up

JOHNSON, ANNABEL and EDGAR. *Torrie.* Harper, 1960. It took the grim realities of a covered-wagon journey to California to jolt rebellious fourteen-year-old Torrie from her self-centered ways. Family relationships are well depicted in this pioneer story of the 1840s. 13-15

☆ JONES, WEYMAN. *The Edge of Two Worlds,* ill. by J. C. Kocsis. Dial, 1968. 10-13

☆ ______. *The Talking Leaf,* ill. by Harper Johnson. Dial, 1965. 10-12

☆ KEITH, HAROLD. *Rifles for Watie.* T. Crowell, 1957. Newbery Medal. 12-16

☆ LAMPMAN, EVELYN. *Cayuse Courage.* Harcourt, 1970. 11-14

☆ ______. *Once Upon the Little Big Horn,* ill. by John Gretzer. T. Crowell, 1971. 10-12

☆ ______. *Tree Wagon,* ill. by Robert Frankenberg. Doubleday, 1953. 10-13

☆ ______. *White Captives.* Atheneum, 1975. 11-13

☆ LATHAM, JEAN. *This Dear-Bought Land,* ill. by Jacob Landau. Harper, 1957. An outstanding story of Captain John Smith and the settlement of Jamestown. 11-14

LENSKI, LOIS. *Puritan Adventure,* ill. by author. Lippincott, 1944. Massachusetts is the background of this vivid tale of colonial times. A lighthearted young aunt from England visits a strict Puritan family, bringing gaiety and laughter with her. 11-14

§ LEVY, MIMI COOPER. *Corrie and the Yankee,* ill. by Ernest Crichlow. Viking, 1959. Corrie, a little black girl on a South Carolina plantation, rescues a wounded Yankee soldier and helps him to safety. 10-13

LOBEL, ARNOLD. *On the Day Peter Stuyvesant Sailed into Town,* ill. by author. Harper, 1971. 5-8

LOWREY, JANETTE. *Six Silver Spoons,* ill. by Robert Quackenbush. Harper, 1971. A British soldier helps two children carry safely the silver spoons made by Paul Revere during the Revolutionary War. 6-8

☆ McGRAW, ELOISE JARVIS. *Moccasin Trail.* Coward, 1952. A white boy attacked by a grizzly is rescued and raised by the Crow Indians. When he meets his family, his conflicts are convincingly portrayed. 11-14

☆ MARRIOTT, ALICE. *Indian Annie: Kiowa Captive.* McKay, 1965. 11-14

MEIGS, CORNELIA. *Clearing Weather,* ill. by Frank Dobias. Little, 1928. 11-14

———. *Master Simon's Garden,* ill. by John Rae. Macmillan, 1929. 11-14

§ MONJO, FERDINAND. *The Drinking Gourd,* ill. by Fred Brenner. Harper, 1970. 7-8

———. *Gettysburg: Tad Lincoln's Story,* ill. by Douglas Gorsline. Windmill/Dutton, 1976. 8-11

———. *Grand Papa and Ellen Aroon,* ill. by Richard Cuffari. Holt, 1974. Thomas Jefferson as seen by his favorite grandchild. 7-9

☆ ———. *Indian Summer,* ill. by Anita Lobel. Harper, 1968. A Kentucky family defends itself against Indian attack while their father is away fighting with George Washington. 7-8

———. *Poor Richard in France,* ill. by Brinton Turkle. Holt, 1973. Franklin's grandson reports on his exploits in France. 7-9

———. *The Vicksburg Veteran,* ill. by Douglas Gorsline. Simon, 1971. 7-10

☆ O'DELL, SCOTT. *Island of the Blue Dolphins.* Houghton, 1960. Newbery Medal. 11-14

☆ ———. *The King's Fifth,* ill. by Samuel Bryant. Houghton, 1966. 12-15

☆ ———. *Sing Down the Moon.* Houghton, 1970. Bright Morning is a young Navaho girl whose tribe is forced from their homes by white people and driven to Fort Sumner. She persuades her husband to escape and they start their peaceful life anew. The simple, almost terse, style makes more vivid the tragedy and danger. 11-14

☆ ———. *Zia.* Houghton, 1976. This sequel to *Island of the Blue Dolphins* is set in California. 10-13

§ PETRY, ANN. *Tituba of Salem Village.* T. Crowell, 1964. 12-15

POPE, ELIZABETH MARIE. *The Sherwood Ring,* ill. by Evaline Ness. Houghton, 1958. Beautifully told romances of Revolutionary times and of today are skillfully interwoven in a story rich in suspense and mystery. 12-16

RICHARD, ADRIENNE. *Wings.* Little, 1974. Pip and her brother live in southern California in the 1930s, enthralled by movies and airplanes and their mother's unorthodox friends. 10-14

☆ SANDOZ, MARI. *The Story Catcher,* ill. by Elsie J. McCorkell. Westminster, 1963. The dramatic and moving story of Lance, a young Sioux brave who longs to achieve status with his people. The blending of style and subject is impressive. 11-14

SCHAEFER, JACK. *Mavericks,* ill. by Lorence Bjorklund. Houghton, 1967. This is a deeply romantic picture of the old West, written in a strong and flavorful prose, moving back and forth from old Jake Hanlon's past to the present. 12-15

☆ SHARP, EDITH LAMBERT. *Nkwala,* ill. by William Winter. Little, 1958. Stirringly written historical tale of a young Spokane Indian who at last wins his adult name. 11-13

☆ SPEARE, ELIZABETH GEORGE. *Calico Captive,* ill. by W. T. Mars. Houghton, 1957. Stirring junior novel of Miriam Willard, a young Indian captive taken to Canada during the French and Indian Wars. 11-15

● ———. *The Witch of Blackbird Pond.* Houghton, 1958. Newbery Medal. 12-16

STEELE, WILLIAM O. *The Buffalo Knife,* ill. by Paul Galdone. Harcourt, 1952. A thousand-mile flatboat trip is an exciting adventure for a boy of nine. 9-12

———. *The Far Frontier,* ill. by Paul Galdone. Harcourt, 1959. 10-14

———. *The Perilous Road,* ill. by Paul Galdone. Harcourt, 1958. 11-13

☆ ———. *Wayah of the Real People,* ill. by Isa Barnett. Holt, 1964. 11-13

———. *Wilderness Journey,* ill. by Paul Galdone. Harcourt, 1953. A sickly boy becomes a resourceful pioneer. 9-12

TAYLOR, THEODORE. *Teetoncey,* ill. by Richard Cuffari. Doubleday, 1974.

———. *Teetoncey and Ben O'Neal,* ill. by Richard Cuffari. Doubleday, 1975. Teetoncey is the one female survivor of a shipwreck off Cape Hatteras in 1898. The first book tells of her rescue, while the second recounts the struggle to recover valuable cargo aboard the sunken ship. 10-13

● TURKLE, BRINTON. *Obadiah the Bold,* ill. by author. Viking, 1965. 8-9

● ———. *Thy Friend, Obadiah,* ill. by author. Viking, 1969. 7-9

UCHIDA, YOSHIKO. *Journey to Topaz,* ill. by Donald Carrick. Scribner's, 1971. A Japanese-American family is sent to a World War II relocation center in Utah. 10-12

———. *Samurai of Gold Hill,* ill. by Ati Forberg. Scribner's, 1972. A well-paced story of a group of Japanese immigrants who come to California in 1869. 10-12

VINING, ELIZABETH GRAY. *The Taken Girl.* Viking, 1972. 11-14

WIBBERLEY, LEONARD. *John Treegate's Musket.* Farrar, 1959. First in an outstanding series. Other titles are: *Peter Treegate's War* (1960), *Sea Captain from Salem* (1961), *Treegate's Raiders* (1962). 12-15

———. *The Last Battle.* Farrar, 1976. 11-14

§ ———. *Leopard's Prey.* Farrar, 1971. 11-14

———. *Red Pawns.* Farrar, 1973. 11-14

WILDER, LAURA INGALLS. *The First Four Years,* ill. by Garth Williams. Harper, 1971. Found among the author's papers after her death, and published without revision, this is the story of her first years as a farmer's wife on a South Dakota homestead. The same charm and virtues as the Little House books. 10-14

———. *Little House in the Big Woods,* ill. by Garth Williams. Harper, 1953. Other titles in the series are: *Little House on the Prairie, On the Banks of Plum Creek, By the Shores of Silver Lake, Farmer Boy, The Long Winter, Little Town on the Prairie, These Happy Golden Years.* 9-14

☆ WILSON, HAZEL. *His Indian Brother,* ill. by Robert Henneberger. Abingdon, 1955. Based on a true incident of the 1800s is this story of Brad Porter, left alone in a Maine pioneer cabin and rescued from starvation by an Indian chief and his son. 10-14

☆§ WOJCIECHOWSKA, MAIA. *Odyssey of Courage: The Story of Álvar Núñez Cabeza de Vaca,* ill. by Alvin Smith. Atheneum, 1965. Cabeza de Vaca's journey, stressing his affection for the Indians and their regard for him. 12-14

☆§ WORMSER, RICHARD. *The Black Mustanger,* ill. by Don Bolognese. Morrow, 1971. Set in Texas in the period after the Civil War, the story of a white boy whose mentor is a cowboy, half black and half Apache. 10-14

§ WRISTON, HILDRETH. *Susan's Secret,* ill. by W. T. Mars. Farrar, 1957. Suspense-filled story of a little Vermont girl who undertook her absent family's task of guiding fugitive slaves to the next Underground station. 9-12

☆ YATES, ELIZABETH. *Carolina's Courage,* ill. by Nora S. Unwin. Dutton, 1964. 8-10

YEP, LAURENCE. *Dragonwings.* Harper, 1975. A fascinating view of life in the Chinese community of San Francisco in the first years of the twentieth century, including a description of the earthquake. 10-14

Historical Fiction: Other Countries

BARTOS-HÖPPNER, B. *Hunters of Siberia,* tr. by Anthea Bell. Walck, 1969. A novel set in the early part of the century that is both a plea for conservation of wild life and a remarkable picture of a way of life now ended. 12-15

BAUMANN, HANS. *Sons of the Steppe.* Walck, 1958. Authentic background adds to the story of two of Genghis Khan's grandsons. 12-16

CHAUNCY, NAN. *Hunted in Their Own Land,* ill. by Victor G. Ambrus. Seabury, 1973. The tragic story of the gradual annihilation of the aborigines in Tasmania by the whites. 12-15

DICKINSON, PETER. *Dancing Bear,* ill. by David Smee. Little, 1973. In Byzantium in 558, Silvester, a slave, accompanied by a bear and a holy man, searches for his mistress who was kidnapped by the Huns. 10-14

☆ HARRIS, CHRISTIE. *Raven's Cry,* ill. by Bill Reid. Atheneum, 1966. 10-15

☆ ______. *West with the White Chiefs,* ill. by Walter Ferro. Atheneum, 1965. 11-15

☆ HOUSTON, JAMES. *The White Archer; An Eskimo Legend,* ill. by author. Harcourt, 1967. Kungo is a young Eskimo who vows revenge when his parents are killed and his sister is taken captive by a band of Indians. The description of his years of cold, patient planning is in low key. 10-12

☆ LAMPMAN, EVELYN. *The Tilted Sombrero,* ill. by Ray Cruz. Doubleday, 1966. 11-14

LEWIS, ELIZABETH FOREMAN. *To Beat a Tiger; One Needs a Brother's Help,* ill. by John Heuhnergarth. Holt, 1956. 14-17

______. *Young Fu of the Upper Yangtze,* ill. by Kurt Wiese. Holt, 1932. Newbery Medal. The 1973 edition of this book contains illustrations by Ed Young. 13-15

MUHLENWEG, FRITZ. *Big Tiger and Christian,* ill. by Rafaello Busoni. Pantheon, 1952. Long but well-sustained story of the journey of two boys across China and the Gobi Desert in the 1920s. 11-13

PATERSON, KATHERINE. *The Master Puppeteer,* ill. by Haru Wells. T. Crowell, 1976. 11-15

______. *Of Nightingales That Weep,* ill. by Haru Wells. T. Crowell, 1974. 11-15

______. *The Sign of the Chrysanthemum,* ill. by Peter Landa. T. Crowell, 1973. 8-11

Three novels of feudal Japan.

RITCHIE, RITA. *The Golden Hawks of Genghis Khan,* ill. by Lorence F. Bjorklund. Dutton, 1958.

______. *Secret Beyond the Mountains.* Dutton, 1960.

______. *The Year of the Horse,* ill. by Lorence F. Bjorklund. Dutton, 1957. These are outstanding tales of the years of Mongol supremacy. 12-15

● VINEBERG, ETHEL. *Grandmother Came from Dworitz; A Jewish Story,* ill. by Rita Briansky. Tundra, 1969. The first of a series of books on the origins of Canadians (a French edition of each will be published), the story based on the life of the author or illustrator of the book. The text here is sedate but the material is fascinating, giving a vivid picture of the restrictions upon nineteenth-century Russian Jews, their communal life, and their emigration. 9-12

WALSH, JILL PATON. *The Emperor's Winding Sheet.* Farrar, 1974. The siege and fall of Constantinople through the eyes of a shipwrecked English boy. Graphic without being unduly violent. 11-14

§ WATSON, SALLY. *Jade.* Holt, 1968. A lively tale of an eighteenth-century girl who becomes a pirate. 11-14

Biography

Chapter 12

Biography may be defined as that branch of literature that deals with the history of individual men's and women's lives. Thus the three essential ingredients of good biography are history, the person, and literary artistry. Facts should be authentic and verifiable; the subject should be considered as an individual rather than as a paragon or type; and the writing should be a conscious work of art. This description—with some amplification—not only defines the genre, but suggests the standards by which it can be judged.

Biography as History

Authenticity

If a biography is the history of a person's life, it should be as accurate and authentic as research can make it. That statement is true for all biographies, but its application varies, depending on the nature of the biographee's contributions, and the life the person led. Even today, we know very little about Emily Dickinson's life, and authors wishing to write books about Dickinson are forced to do a great amount of internal analysis of her poems for insights into the kind of person who might have written them. For literary figures, internal analysis of their writings is essential regardless of how much we know about their public and private lives. When they leave detailed diaries or journals, as the writer André Gide did, the biographer is faced with a different problem: the mass of information must be checked against the recorded impressions of the people named by Gide. If these seem contradictory, the biographer must discover what the attitude of Gide's contemporary was—friendly, worshipful, or definitely antagonistic. This may involve consulting the available writings of still other contemporaries who knew both individuals and who in turn left records of their relationships.

When the subject of a biography is a famous public figure, such as George Washington, the search for authenticity takes the biographer to government archives for official papers relating to Washington's life as president. But that is only the beginning, for the same checking and cross-checking with contemporaries' opinions must be pursued. The mass of documents is overwhelming, but rarely definitive, and a good biographer alerts the reader that what is being written is based on known available evidence. A good biographer resembles a good detective, following clues, interviewing people, hearing what the subject has to say, and then—and only then—reaching a tentative conclusion that is presented to readers, who serve as the jury.

Accuracy and authenticity are easier to achieve when writing about people of the past. They are very difficult to achieve when writing of the living or the recently dead. In biography for children, much of what we know is true may be deleted because it is contrary to the image children's authors and publishers wish to convey to young readers. The problem of accuracy can be demonstrated by looking at three biographies of Martin Luther King, Jr., written for children of elementary school age. The easiest of the books, *The Picture Life of Martin Luther King, Jr.* by Margaret B. Young, covers the tumultuous year of the Montgomery, Alabama, bus boycott in one sentence: "After a year the laws were changed." Ed Clayton's *Martin Luther King; The Peaceful Warrior* and James T. deKay's *Meet Martin Luther King, Jr.* contain more detail about the violence of that year but raise questions about their own authenticity. Is Clayton right when he says that the bomb attempt on King's house found Mrs. King and their daughter in danger ("Coretta grabbed their infant daughter and ran to the rear of the house")? Or is deKay more accurate in telling us that Coretta King was talking to a friend while Yoki (the daughter) slept in a back room? This particular example of discrepancy may seem minor, but it alerts us to the fact that very few biographies for children can be considered accurate or authentic because the authors are simplifying information for young readers, and seldom engage in primary source research, relying rather on secondary accounts of the events.

Objectivity

The *Talmud* says "We see things as we are, not as they are," a statement which reminds us that all data are filtered through human minds. The best biographers are aware of their own biases and take special care to be sure they do not interfere with the search for whatever degree of truth can be found. Good biographers know they are not free to offer personal opinions as fact or to present an interpretation for which there is no evidence. They let deeds speak for themselves. If the behavior of the subject seems ambiguous, the author may speculate about the contradictory evidence, but may not take sides or tell the reader what to think. Was Sam Houston completely honest and disinterested in his dealings with the Indians and with his Cherokee foster father? Marquis James in *The Raven*, a biography of Sam Houston, never tells us how he regards Houston's actions. He presents the evidence and lets us draw our own conclusions. And readers of *The Raven* may differ in their judgment of Sam, just as Sam's contemporaries themselves differed.

It also follows that the biographer may report only those words and thoughts which were recorded, either by the subject or by those contemporary observers in a position to know. Some biographers have got around this strict limitation by saying, "Perhaps he thought . . ." or "Perhaps he meant what he said, who knows?" Lytton Strachey uses this device repeatedly in his *Queen Victoria*.

Viewpoints

As to the question about the moral obligation of the author to distinguish between fact and fiction in juvenile biography—the author should not pretend to be writing one hundred percent fact if he is introducing invented scenes and dialogue. What I imagine is always based on facts that make the scenes possible and usually even likely. I make the dialogue as plausible as I can, and I always use historical dialogue whenever history obliges me by preserving the words I happen to need.

So much for the line between fact and fiction. Even more important are the needs of the present times. We need to inspire our gifted young people to make an attempt at greatness. We need to make them want to reach out after that splendid, elusive, brass ring known as achievement and make it theirs. Our age is more tawdry than we wish it to be, and we yearn for some heroes and heroines for ourselves and for the future. I have not yet utterly abandoned the Western world. It has produced many men and women who still make my skin prickle. I have not yet abandoned the American experiment, for it has produced large numbers of people whom I wish I might have emulated. That is why I would like my books to arouse young people. To make them understand that all great human beings were once uncertain children, unaware of their powers. I want my books to incite children to dare to do something marvelous. For, if they dare, perhaps they will succeed.
—F. N. Monjo. "Great Men, Melodies, Experiments, Plots, Predictability, and Surprises," *The Horn Book Magazine*, October 1975.

From Benjamin Franklin *by Thomas Fleming. Engraving from The Granger Collection.*

When the gouty old king whom she was to succeed asked the young Victoria for her favorite tune, she replied without a moment's hesitation, "God Save the King." This, Strachey tells us, "has been praised as an early example of a tact which was afterwards famous." Then he adds cryptically, "But she was a very truthful child, and perhaps it was her genuine opinion." He closes his book with a dramatic use of this device. Describing the dying queen, old, blind, and silent, he suggests that she *may perhaps* have recalled her past. Then, as if Victoria were thinking aloud, he briefly and tenderly reviews her life, going back to the little girl in "sprigged muslin, and the trees and the grass at Kensington." Jeanette Eaton also uses it in her account of the dying Washington in *Leader by Destiny*. It is a legitimate device, but when it is overused it may become a not too subtle method of influencing the opinions of the reader.

Documentation

For many people, one of the most important tests of a good biography is the accuracy and thoroughness of its documentation. Nicolson in *The Development of English Biography* insists that a biography should be as scrupulously documented as history. Strachey's *Queen Victoria* is a model in this respect, for every incident and every description is conscientiously documented in the footnotes.

In the past, few juvenile biographies were documented by footnotes, although most authors did supply sources in a separate section, a bibliography, or an afterword. Some juvenile biographies, such as *W.E.B. DuBois* by Virginia Hamilton do contain footnotes as well as extensive bibliographies. Others, such as *Fanny Kemble's America* by John Anthony Scott, are written by people whose authority has been established by their adult writings on the subject. Whether children read the footnotes or are impressed by the author's qualifications is not important. What matters is that these changes reflect an increased concern on the part of authors and publishers to give young readers the best biographies possible within the restrictions imposed by age.

Biography as the Individual

All of us are familiar with older biographies which presented Washington the ever truthful, Lincoln the sad, and Benjamin Franklin the thrifty. Franklin seems to have been cast in the role of the thrifty merely because he wrote a number of wise saws on the desirability of this virtue. As a matter of fact, he sent home from England a continual stream of handsome and extravagant presents, such as silver-handled knives, fine china, a whole box of table glass, carpets, even a harpsichord for Sally.[1] Later, in France, his bills for his wine cellar were lavish, and he finally remarked plaintively that frugality was "a virtue I never could acquire in myself."[2] So "perhaps," as the biographers say, his adages on thrift were reminders for his unthrifty self, as well as for the rest of the world.

Franklin is indeed a good example of a figure almost spoiled for young people in the past because he had been typed as a paragon. Today in the new biographies, such as Thom-

[1] Carl Van Doren, *Benjamin Franklin*, pp. 276–277.
[2] Ibid., p. 637.

as Fleming's *Benjamin Franklin,* young people and even children may catch a glimpse of the real Franklin—witty, worldly, urbane, adored by the ladies and adoring them in turn, equally at home in the wilderness and in the court, a scientist, a man of letters, a diplomat, an amateur musician, lazy and prodigiously industrious, in short, a composite of strength and weakness on a grand scale, with a tremendous brain directing the whole. To have made Franklin, of all men, into the image of a stuffy prig was a crime. To rediscover the whole Franklin and reveal him to this generation, as Carl Van Doren has done, is a crowning achievement of modern biography.

Another achievement of current biography for both adults and children is the growing recognition that white males were not the only members of the human race to lead exciting lives and to contribute to civilization, but that women and members of racial and ethnic minorities also have a rich heritage, and have made significant contributions.

The Whole Person

James Boswell's *Life of Samuel Johnson* (1791) is considered one of the greatest biographies in the English language and it is as fully developed a portrait as we could wish for. But, despite Boswell's early demonstration of what a good biography should be, the majority of biographies for both adults and children have treated their subjects as paragons rather than as fallible human beings.

Why this idealization took place is a complex story, but basically biography was treated less as a literary genre than as a political and social tool. In the United States, following the publication of *The Life and Memorable Acts of George Washington* (1800) by the Reverend Mason Weems, the pattern was set for American biographers to depict the country's leaders as paragons. Part of this impetus came from the religious leaders of the nation; part of it came from the historians who were depicting the new nation as fulfilling its "Manifest Destiny." In England, the rise of what we now term Victorian morality dictated that the more human side of people be suppressed, and political factors here, too, influenced whom biographers saw as worthy.

In scholarly biographies, read only by university professors and lay people deeply interested in the person being written about, it has been customary throughout most of the past two centuries to depict the subject as a whole person. Popular biographies, on the other hand, written for the general adult public, have traditionally ignored the personal life if the subject had what were termed "vices." When writing for children the cleansing process was taken a step further and personal tragedies and failures were passed over. In many cases, juvenile biographies did not even depict the person's death.

As society's values have changed and new areas of research have developed, the content acceptable in juvenile biographies has also changed. Divorce is not now seen as a vice, to be suppressed, but as an event to be explained. Describing incidents of failure, rather than lessening a person's worth, shows readers that all people face setbacks at some point in their lives. And we are coming to understand that death is a part of life and cannot be ignored.

By broadening the parameters of what constitutes acceptable content in juvenile biographies, we have also broadened the range of people who can be written about. When the older, rigid standards were in effect, it was impossible for an author to think of writing a juvenile biography about Margaret Sanger, the great birth-control pioneer, or about blacks like Malcolm X who had led horrendous childhoods.

This new openness does not mean that anything and everything is acceptable in a juvenile biography. While the definition of what constitutes good taste has changed, the concept itself remains. Authors must always be sure that they are not sensationalizing any events of a person's life. They must be able to point out if a particular fact in their subject's life was very important to the individual being written about, or if it was an idiosyncrasy. Boswell tells us that Samuel Johnson would sneak out after dark to buy oysters for his cat. He did not want the servants to know what he was up to. That was an idiosyncrasy. Had he been sneaking out to visit a mistress, that information would be more important to an understanding of Johnson.

Vivid Details

One of the best methods of assuring that the whole person is presented in a biography is to steep it with rich and arresting details. An adolescent or an adult reading about how Samuel Johnson always had to go through a door on one particular foot finds that information interesting. The reader may already know that certain baseball players always touch third base on their way to the outfield. Few of us, whether children or adults, can easily identify with people who have changed history—whether through politics or breaking Babe Ruth's home-run record—and these human details help us know that great feats in life are accomplished by human beings and not by paragons.

In the past, biographies written for young people failed at precisely this point. They told children about the large affairs in which their subjects played a part but neglected to give any account of the individuals' amusing idiosyncrasies, peculiar bents, and special talents which made them unique. Children delight in Franklin's account of himself as a boy floating in a pond on his back propelled by a kite;[3] or in the story of Davy Crockett crossing an icy river in December, sometimes in and sometimes out of the water, but managing to keep dry his keg of gunpowder, a bundle, and his gun, "Betsy";[4] or of Lewis and Clark, the intrepid explorers, feeling uncomfortable when the Indians at a ceremonial feast served a stewed dog, reminding them of their own Spot;[5] or of Lincoln holding a child upside down to make tracks on the ceiling as a joke on the stepmother he dearly loved, a joke he righted with a fresh coat of whitewash.[6]

To be told that Penn dressed in sober clothes is dull enough. To learn that even after he turned Quaker he still loved good apparel and went to meet the velvet-clad Lord Baltimore in sober brown but cut by the best London tailor from the finest materials—ah, that is more human.[7] To read that Penn was tried for holding a meeting with other Quakers is dreary, but young people warm immediately to the picture of Penn on trial, shut up in a cage at the back of the courtroom, shouting out his own defense so effectively that he won the jury to his side and later won the right of the jury to have its decisions upheld in the English courts.[8] Little incidents and big ones which reveal spirited human beings who will not be downed and who travel their own unique way bring the individual to life for the reader. Revealing details are the very essence of good biography.

Biography as Literature

If biography is a branch of literature, then it, like any other work of art, should be a consciously planned composition. It has a subject, a theme, unity attained through that theme, style, a pattern of the whole, and a pattern of the parts. These may not be evident to the casual reader, but if the life is written with any skill, they are there.

Theme and Unity

Biography, like history, is based on documented facts. No liberties may be taken with these facts; no flights of fancy are permissible. The biographer begins by assembling all the documents and examining all the evidence. But good biographers feel that they should not give all their accumulated research to the reader in its endless and often trivial details. They recognize that there is a difference between the rich and arresting details discussed earlier and endless presentation of trivia. Each biographer must choose those details which will most truly reveal the subject as the author has come to know him or her. It is in this matter of selection and organization that the biography ceases to be purely history and becomes a work of art. For the author, in reading all the sources and weighing all the evidence, gradually develops a theme. The theme of a biography makes a fundamental statement about the person's life as seen by the biographer. This theme is not, and never

[3]Carl Van Doren, *Benjamin Franklin*, p. 17.
[4]Constance Rourke, *Davy Crockett*, pp. 94–97.
[5]Julia Davis, *No Other White Men*, p. 71.
[6]Ingri and Edgar d'Aulaire, *Abraham Lincoln* (unpaged).
[7]Elizabeth Janet Gray Vining, *Penn*, p. 206.
[8]Ibid., Chapter 15.

can be, the total truth about the person's life, but if it has emerged from the research, it provides readers with a unified view of the man or woman being written about. Biographers fail to write good biography if they approach the research process with a theme in mind, for then, despite all good intentions, they will make the data fit their preconceptions.

Turning to children's or young people's biographies, we often find the theme in the title—*Carry On, Mr. Bowditch* (Nathaniel Bowditch), *Invincible Louisa* (Louisa M. Alcott), and *Susette La Flesche: Voice of the Omaha Indians.*

In *Leader by Destiny,* the life of George Washington, Jeanette Eaton shows how over and over again circumstances and the times interfered with Washington's life and called him to other ways of living. He might have been a homespun frontiersman, playing a gallant part no doubt, but his brother's death gave him Mount Vernon and turned him into a country gentleman. This role was forwarded by his neighbor's wife, the lovely Sally Fairfax (destiny again), who taught him the manners and ways of gentlemen. Then the country squire was called upon for soldiery and more soldiery, and finally he was made the head of the Continental Army. Seven long years of campaigning followed, with his whole heart yearning for the gracious life of Mount Vernon. Then came peace and a chance to realize his desires, but destiny called him once more, this time to the presidency, the gravest responsibility an American had ever faced. Washington played a great part in every role he undertook, but it would seem that these roles were not of his own choosing. He would have been a leader in any situation, but destiny called him to national greatness.

Similar in theme is James Haskins's *Ralph Bunche: A Most Reluctant Hero.* Bunche's life was filled with "firsts": the first black to earn a Ph.D. in political science; the first black to have a desk in the State Department; and the first American black to win the Nobel Peace Prize. He was a man who seemed always to be in the right place at the right time and his skills were recognized and appreciated by the world's leaders. He would have been content to teach, write, and spend time with his family, but world events called him, like Washington, to greatness.

From Susette La Flesche: Voice of the Omaha Indians *by Margaret Crary. Photograph from the Nebraska State Historical Society.*

Not all biographies adhere so closely and obviously to theme and unity as those just cited, certainly not the early examples of biography. But modern biographies, including those for young people, seem to follow this pattern and are organized around a theme which gives a dramatic unity to the book.

Style and Pattern

If biography is to be judged as literature, it must also have a pleasing style. As one authority has said, style is "the auditory effect of prose." The prose must be good to read and it must be appropriate to the subject matter and to the mood of the story.

A fine example of style and pattern in biography is Carl Sandburg's *Abe Lincoln Grows Up,* adapted from the first twenty-seven chapters of his book for adults, *The Prairie Years.* Picking the book up anywhere, you discover that it reads aloud so easily and naturally you just keep reading. Of Tom Lincoln, the father, Sandburg writes:

He wasn't exactly lazy, he was sort of independent, and liked to be where he wasn't interfered with. . . . He was a wild buck at fighting, when men didn't let him alone. A man talked about a woman once in a way Tom Lincoln didn't like. And in the fight that came, Tom bit a piece of the man's nose off. . . . Though he was short spoken, he knew yarns, could crack jokes, and had a reputation as a story-teller when he got started. (pp. 12–13)

Of Nancy Hanks, Sandburg writes differently:

The Lincolns had a cabin of their own to live in. It stood among wild crab-apple trees.

And the smell of wild crab-apple blossoms . . . came keen that summer to the nostrils of Nancy Hanks.

The summer stars that year shook out pain and warning, strange laughters, for Nancy Hanks. (p. 30)

A different use of pattern is well illustrated by the opening chapter of Elizabeth Gray Vining's *Penn,* written under her unmarried name, Elizabeth Janet Gray. She describes Penn's father, young Captain Penn, already rising in the English navy, in which eventually he becomes admiral; his wife with her Irish estates; the king with his two sons, James and Charles; a shoemaker named George Fox; an eight-month-old heiress, Gulielma Springett; and the lusty baby, William Penn.

And all these scattered lives were to play their part in the life of the baby who slept and cried and ate and slept again in sight of the steep walls of the old, grim Tower, into which had gone, down the centuries, many prisoners, young and old, frightened and defiant; and from which fewer had come out. The Tower too had its part. (p. 7)

Here, we are told, are all the threads of the story, all the important elements in the life of the baby, who grew to be the man of whom it was said later, "the world has not yet caught up with William Penn." There in that first chapter are the small patterns which will make up the large pattern.

These examples show how biography, although as scrupulously documented as history, may become in the act of composition a branch of literature. Yet good adult biographies are as sound sources for facts as histories. This may also be true of biographies for children and young people but with certain differences.

Biography for Children

Historically, juvenile biographies have differed greatly from adult biographies, but the gap between the two has narrowed as children have become more knowledgeable and adults have become more respectful of children's abilities. While not all current biographies are documented, more and more of them contain footnotes and bibliographic references since the authors know they may be reviewed by people who know the subject as well as by people who are engrossed by the story.

No longer do authors systematically and automatically suppress the human weaknesses of their subjects or avoid relating personal tragedies. As was indicated earlier in the discussion of "The Whole Person," a new level of integrity has been achieved in the writing of juvenile biography.

However, differences remain. Biographies for children will probably never approach the level of documentation that is found in the scholarly adult biographies. Children who

Viewpoints

Biography *is* a craft—like all the other arts—in that it employs techniques which can be learned by anybody, which are outside personal commitment. It can be loosely called a science in that, for part of his labors, the biographer proceeds inductively: he collects facts in order to arrive at conclusions from them. It is an art, however lowly, because the biographer is himself interfused into what he has made, and, like the novelist and the painter, shapes his material in order to create effects.

. . . The novelist's pen is a delicate instrument. If the biographer holds something like that pen in one hand, he has to wield a shovel with the other. His ore is not inner experience, the quicksilver stuff of gland and nerve. It is brute matter, wrested from the earth. . . . To exist at all, it must feed upon the truth of facts, and yet to exist on its highest level, it must pursue the truth of interpretation.—Paul Murray Kendall, *The Art of Biography.* W. W. Norton and Co., New York, 1965, p. xii.

can cope with that kind of writing should be introduced to the adult biographies and allowed to find their own levels of understanding.

But if we compare juvenile biography with the popularized adult biographies, we find very few differences, and those that do exist are in favor of the juvenile authors. No biography for children exploits the person being written about to the degree that popularizations for adults do. If personal scandal is introduced into a juvenile biography, it is because it is absolutely vital for understanding the life of the woman or man being written about. In adult biographies, such scenes are often present to titillate the reader rather than to shed light on the subject.

Biographers for young readers usually feel that it is legitimate to cast known facts about an episode into actual dialogue and to interpret the thoughts of their characters; that is, they put words into their subjects' mouths and thoughts into their heads for which there is no documentary evidence. Popularized adult biographies do the same. The authors' excuse, and it is a legitimate one, is that this technique produces a more dramatic narrative.

Undocumented dialogue produces one of two hybrids of genuine biography: first, there is *fictionalized biography*, in which the facts are documented and only a few liberties are taken, such as occasional dialogue for which there is no record; and, second, there is *biographical fiction*, which takes a historical character as a basis for a story semihistorical in nature.

Fictionalized Biography

Most biographies for children are fictionalized. That is, they are based on careful research, but known facts are often presented in dramatic episodes complete with conversation. For instance, Elizabeth Vining, in relating the moving quarrel between Admiral Penn and his young son lately turned Quaker, begins the account with the old Admiral exploding wrathfully, ". . . three people you may *not* thee and thou – the King, the Duke of York, and myself." This speech is much more exciting than the plain statement, "The Admiral objected to his son's Quaker use of thee and thou." The quarrel continues the next day, climaxing in the Admiral's terrible threat:

> *"I am going to kneel down and pray to God that you may not be a Quaker, nor go ever again to any more of their meetings."*

and in William's frenzied reply:

> *"Before I will hear thee pray after any such manner," he cried, "I'll leap out of the window."*

It was a high window, too, and, according to Vining, William was saved only by the interruption of one of his father's most elegant friends come to call. Since Vining is a scrupulous research scholar, she probably had some sort of documentary evidence for this quarrel. She does, for instance, give the Admiral's actual letters to William summoning him home for this grim conference. Assuming then that there is a historical basis for the scene, we accept the dialogue, which certainly heightens the drama, the words fairly crackling with suppressed emotion.

Perhaps fictionalized biography is the best pattern of biography for young people and children. There is no doubt that dialogue based on facts, written by a scholar and an artist, brings history to life and re-creates living, breathing people, who make a deep impression on children.

Biographical Fiction

Jean Lee Latham's Newbery Medal book, *Carry On, Mr. Bowditch*, is sometimes catalogued as fiction, but the reason is not clear. In her acceptance speech the author describes her book as fictionalized biography. She probably makes no more use of imaginary dialogue than does Vining in *Penn*, which is listed as biography. *Mr. Bowditch* does include perhaps a dozen imaginary characters, such as members of ships' crews, but the author adds that "there are about four dozen historical characters . . . handled with accuracy as to time, place, and personality."[9] Certainly this book,

[9] *Horn Book*, August 1956.

based on all the historical documents available, is a magnificent record of a little-known genius. In purpose and in effect on the reader it is biography.

These distinctions among different types of historical literature are not greatly important to the children's use of the books. When young people read biographical fiction, they might be warned, "This is the way it may have happened, but history does not tell us for sure." And when they read biography or even fictionalized biography, they might be told, "Insofar as the author can find historical records, this is the way it *did* happen."

Briefly, the chief distinctions between good biographies for adults and those for children are that, in the latter, sources are less often stated, unsavory episodes are usually omitted, and recorded events are more likely to be enlivened with imaginary dialogue. On the whole, however, modern biographies for children represent scholarly research and conscientious retelling of events in a dramatic style. Such characteristics make these books some of the finest modern contributions to children's literature.

Viewpoints

Biography, like fiction, should have its characters so completely realized, its background so true, that everything that happens will seem inevitable. But the characters in the series books are all of a pattern. There is a convention that great men and women invariably started out as normal and likeable youngsters, good mixers, and good sports. There is no inkling of the fact that loneliness and oddity often bear a dark fruit of their own. . . .

In two popular biographies in the Childhood of Famous Americans Series, *Nancy Hanks, Kentucky Girl,* and *Mary Todd Lincoln,* the heroines are so conventional as to be startling to anyone who has read Carl Sandburg's *Abraham Lincoln.* Mary Todd's disastrous disposition, which was to harry the great president so sorely, is passed off as "that terrible Todd temper." She is represented as spunky and lovable, gay, generous, and impulsive, flying off the handle, shaking her curls, and stamping her little foot.

. . . What is gained by telling children that the great of the world have always been well adjusted and genteel?—Fran Martin, "Stop Watering Down Biographies." Reprinted from *Junior Libraries,* December 1959. Published by R. R. Bowker Company. (A Xerox company) Copyright © 1959 by R. R. Bowker Company.

Work Methods of Biographers

From book-jackets, authors' notes, lists of suggested readings, prefatory remarks, articles by authors on their research methods, and even from those pages in which writers express thanks to those who have helped them, it is clear that the research for biographies for children is taken very seriously indeed. Evidence of careful documentation is found in more and more books for younger and younger children.

Dorothy Sterling, for example, when working on *Captain of the Planter,* a biography of Robert Smalls, went to Beaufort and Charleston, where she talked to people who had known Smalls, and had two visits with his son. She pored over old newspapers and photographs, ransacked library collections and archives, and picked up every lead by correspondence.

Aileen Fisher and Olive Rabe, in "Writing About the Alcotts,"[10] explain how they used the source material collected and published by others and the biographies of men and women who had played a part in the Alcotts' lives, reading whatever could be found about the family and the period. Each worked on the same chapter separately; one welded the two versions and the other edited and revised the resulting chapter. The authors decided to write the story from the viewpoint of a family member so that the book would have an intimate feeling, although they knew it restricted the action to what could be observed.

There are small variations in the ways in which authors patiently dig, sift, compare, record, and revise, but one thing is paramount: a respect for the truth. Marchette Chute says it beautifully:

[10]Aileen Fisher and Olive Rabe, "Writing About the Alcotts," *Horn Book,* October 1968.

To put the whole thing into a single sentence: you will never succeed in getting at the truth if you think you know, ahead of time, what the truth ought to be.[11]

The Series

The Bobbs-Merrill Childhood books seem to have launched, in 1932, the biography fever with both children and publishers. As a result, not only is the numerical impact of these books staggering, but the duplication of biographies has reached the point where it is a major feat of memory to recall which George Washington is whose and whose Abraham Lincoln is which.

It would be convenient to be able to make a judgment of each series as a whole, but this is impossible, because within one set of books some are thin or pedestrian and others are of major importance. Although it is difficult to select from a list, it is wasteful for schools or homes or libraries to order every one of any series. It is best to watch for authoritative reviews of individual books. Many of the books discussed in this chapter are from one or another of the series. However, since each series is designed to perform a definite function in the child's reading program, several should be familiar to adults working with children.

Two outstanding series for the beginning reader are the Harper and Row "I Can Read" history books and the Young Crowell Biographies. The former includes several life stories told from the child's viewpoint; the latter emphasizes minority group members, although it does not focus on them exclusively. The Bobbs-Merrill Childhood of Famous Americans series has high-interest low-vocabulary books, rigidly patterned and often determinedly merry and gay. The Random House Step-Up Books, the Putnam See-and-Read Books, and the Watts Picture Life series are all simply written and variable in quality. The Garrard Discovery Books follow a set format, and although there are exceptions, many of the titles in this extensive series for young children are bland or stilted.

Scribner's Initial Biographies by Genevieve Foster are well written, brief, and useful—but staid in tone. Like the Foster books, the Grosset and Dunlap Signature Books, which the publishers call "life stories," are for the middle grades, but are often highly fictionalized and sometimes of dubious accuracy.

In 1950, Random House launched the Landmark Books, presenting people, movements, and moments in history that have been landmarks in our national life. Some of the contributors are notable, and some of the books are of superior literary quality, but in a series as extensive as this one, it is not surprising that high standards are not always maintained.

The Crowell biographies of women and of poets are outstanding series books for older readers, as are the Harper and Row Breakthrough Books, which emphasize, as the title indicates, a breakthrough in achievements or in human relations. Putnam publishes both a Sports Hero series and an American Hero series, which, like the Houghton Mifflin North Star series, contains lives of heroes in American history. The Horizon Caravel Books and the American Heritage Junior Library are both distinguished for their profuse and beautiful illustrations as well as for the accuracy of the material.

Collective Biographies

Because of the brevity of treatment of each subject in collective biographies, they will not be discussed singly in this chapter. However, many are included in the bibliography, since this form of the genre serves two purposes admirably. The collective biography is an excellent choice for the child whose span of attention is limited, and for the reader who is particularly interested in the career, race, sex, period, or country that is the common denominator for the collection. This is an especially popular form for sports biographies—or biographical sketches—but it is also used widely to catch the interest of those children who are infatuated, say, with ballet or medicine (*anything* about ballet or medicine) or with women who broke into new professional fields or with black scientists. This is not to suggest that collective biographies are catch-

[11]Marchette Chute, "Getting at the Truth," *Saturday Review*, September 19, 1953.

alls: such books as Isaac Asimov's *Breakthroughs in Science* (1960) or *Leaders of New Nations* (1968) by Leonard Kenworthy and Erma Ferrari are exciting books and an irreplaceable contribution to children's literature.

The following discussions of biographies are grouped under three main divisions: Biographies for the Youngest, Biographies for the Middle Group, and Biographies for Older Readers. Within each of these main groups, the discussions are arranged according to the birth date of the subjects of the biographies, so that there is a chronological progression within each section.

The main emphasis throughout is on the authors who are outstanding biographers. However, most of the author-title subsections not only highlight one biography of the author and give some indication of the range of his or her work, but also mention parallel biographies of the principal subject by other authors.

Illustration by Rocco Negri from The One Bad Thing About Father *by F. N. Monjo. Pictures copyright © 1970 by Rocco Negri. Reprinted by permission of Harper & Row, Publishers, Inc. (Original with color)*

Books for Younger Children

Young children do not have the sense of time necessary to appreciate biography as history. Nor do they have the ability to empathize that makes biography a source of heroes and heroines for older readers. But young children do enjoy a good story and those biographies designed to be read aloud serve that purpose. Young children are also exposed to much more information these days and biographies for them familiarize them with the people behind the names they hear in their everyday lives, such as Washington, Lincoln, and Columbus, who have holidays named after them; and people who have airports, schools, and highways named after them, such as Martin Luther King, Jr., John Kennedy, and others.

There have been some good biographies for young children in the past; they are still valuable, especially for reading aloud. What is flourishing now is the simply written life story or partial biography for the beginning independent reader. The best of this kind are just as accurate as books for older readers, but the person's life is often seen from a child's viewpoint—as in Ferdinand Monjo's *The One Bad Thing About Father*, which gives a son's-eye-view of Theodore Roosevelt. For the young child whose time sense cannot fully encompass the past, this is perhaps the best—but not the only—way to give a biography immediacy and reality.

Alice Dalgliesh

The Columbus Story

The text of the picture biography *The Columbus Story* (1955) is less than thirty pages long. It is vividly alive and re-creates with simple dignity, in a direct writing style, the boyhood of Columbus and the struggles he had in getting support for his first successful voyage.

The book carries Columbus through that journey, with none of the tragedy of the later years, and can be read aloud to children as young as five or six. Some second-graders and most third-graders can read it for themselves. Leo Politi's brilliantly colored illustrations complement the dignified tone of the story.

With Dalgliesh's gift for making the past come alive for children (see Chapter 11), it is logical that she should also succeed in writing enjoyable biographies for young children. In her picture biography for readers in the middle grades, *Ride on the Wind* (1956), she describes the dramatic solo flight of Charles Lindbergh across the ocean in "The Spirit of St. Louis."

Of the other biographies or partial biographies of Columbus written for young children, two gauged for the beginning reader are Gertrude Norman's *A Man Named Columbus* (1960), slight but useful because of its simplicity; and Clara Ingram Judson's *Christopher Columbus* (1960), a straightforward account in which style is sacrificed to the demands of a controlled vocabulary. An appendix in Ann McGovern's *The Story of Christopher Columbus* (1963) gives information about the way facts were obtained from source materials.

Patricia Miles Martin

Pocahontas

Patricia Miles Martin begins her story of *Pocahontas* (1964) when the Indian girl is eleven years old and sees an English ship arrive. She learns English, becomes friendly with the Jamestown colonists, marries John Rolfe when she is grown, and dies in England, homesick and ready to return to America. Written for beginning independent readers, the book is hampered stylistically by the demands of a limited vocabulary, but it is not dull and not unduly fictionalized. The story of Pocahontas has all the requisites of romantic drama, although there is some question about whether the familiar scene in which she saves the life of John Smith did occur, since Smith did not include it in the first edition of his own book.

Jan Wahl's *Pocahontas in London* (1967) focuses on the Indian girl's experiences in London. However, the writing is stiff and the book notable only for the brilliant color and striking composition of John Alcorn's illustrations. A good choice for reading aloud to young children is *Pocahontas* (1949) by Ingri and Edgar Parin d'Aulaire, with its direct approach, large and colorful pictures, and emphasis on action. (See also Bulla's *Pocahontas and the Strangers.*)

Daniel Boone (1965) is a good example of the many other biographies that Patricia Martin has written for young readers, most of them about famous persons in America's history. *Daniel Boone* tends to be somewhat oversimplified in style, with short sentences and large print, but it gives the major facts about Boone's life at a level comprehensible to the beginning reader. These books are useful but not outstanding, giving young children information rather than an understanding of the biographee's role in history.

Clyde Robert Bulla

Squanto, Friend of the Pilgrims

Children are usually enthralled by the amazing story of Squanto's life. He was taken to England in 1605 and lived there for eight years. Then he returned to this country with John Smith only to be captured and sold to Spain by slave hunters. In Spain he was rescued by the friars and returned once more to his native land. The story is beautifully told by Clyde Bulla, who has a gift for writing easy-to-read books that are never commonplace. His historical tales have a pleasant lilt and swing and substantial content. *Squanto* was published in 1954 with the subtitle *Friend of the White Men*, and in 1969 the title was changed to *Squanto, Friend of the Pilgrims*. The book has the same virtues as Bulla's historical fiction, the genre used in *John Billington, Friend of Squanto* (1956). The other biographies of Squanto for this age group are dull and stilted when compared to Bulla's story.

Bulla's *Pocahontas and the Strangers* (1971) is written for eight- to ten-year-olds, but the suspense of the story and the simplicity of style make it appropriate for reading aloud to younger children, especially if read in installments. Other good biographies by Bulla for the beginning independent reader are *Song of St. Francis* (1952), *Lincoln's Birthday* (1966), and *Washington's Birthday* (1967).

Aliki Brandenburg

A Weed Is a Flower

Aliki Brandenburg, who writes as "Aliki," illustrates her own books. In *A Weed Is a Flower* (1965), a biography of George Washington Carver, her pictures show a realistic range of skin tones. The story of the great black naturalist is told in a dry, quiet style with a simple vocabulary. The title is based on a comment attributed to Dr. Carver: "A weed is a flower growing in the wrong place." Born of slave parents, Carver worked his way through school, leaving the college where he had been a student and then a faculty member to join the staff of Tuskegee Institute at the invitation of Booker T. Washington. His distinguished career in agricultural research brought him many honors, and he is probably, along with Martin Luther King, Jr., the most popular black person of note as a subject of biographies for children. Another biography for this group is *George Washington Carver* (1960) by Samuel and Beryl Epstein, a stolid and factual account.

Aliki also has written and illustrated attractive picture biographies: *The Story of Johnny Appleseed* (1963) and *The Story of William Penn* (1964). The latter, like *A Weed Is a Flower*, invests its subject with dignity and stature.

From the book A Weed Is a Flower: The Life of George Washington Carver *by Aliki. © 1965 by Aliki Brandenburg. Published by Prentice-Hall, Inc., Englewood Cliffs, New Jersey. (Original in color)*

Ingri and Edgar Parin d'Aulaire

Abraham Lincoln

The picture-book biographies of Ingri and Edgar Parin d'Aulaire are a real contribution to the youngest. They are large books, copiously illustrated with full-page lithographs in deep, glowing colors on alternate pages, and with black-and-whites and innumerable small pictures in between. These small pictures fulfill a definite purpose in each book, sometimes adding droll touches to the interpretation of the hero's character, sometimes showing something of his work or progress. In *Benjamin Franklin* (1950), for instance, the decorative borders throughout the book carry a series of Franklin's wise sayings. These are fun for children to discover and read, and they make *Poor Richard's Almanac* more real. Throughout the series, the illustrations are somewhat stylized and occasionally stiff. But this is a minor criticism of pictures that are usually alive with action and full of humor.

Study the details of the pictures in *Abraham Lincoln* (1939). No need to talk about the doorless dwellings—in one picture a horse has stuck his head into the single room of the cabin and seems to be taking a neighborly interest in the new baby. Notice the little boys' single galluses upon which hang all the responsibility for holding up their scanty pants. No need to say that Mary Todd was something of a termagant, nor that she had a few problems to contend with in Abe. That picture of

From Abraham Lincoln *by Ingri and Edgar Parin d'Aulaire. Copyright 1939 by Doubleday & Company, Inc. Reprinted by permission of the publisher. (Original in color)*

the wildly disordered parlor, with Abe on the floor in stocking feet, and with Mary, arms akimbo, reflected in the elegant mirror, is a demonstration of their fundamental unlikeness. The book is full of just the sort of sly humor that characterized Abe.

In the early d'Aulaire books, the texts were simple and the life stories were incomplete. But with *Benjamin Franklin, Pocahontas* (1949), *Buffalo Bill* (1952), and *Columbus* (1955), the content grew richer, with more details. In the case of *Columbus,* the man's whole life is related, even those tragic last voyages.

A weakness in the d'Aulaires' writing is their propensity for using "never" and "always." They tell children in their *George Washington* (1936) that "He learned to be good and honest and never tell a lie." After recounting a delightful incident in which young Ben Franklin spent too much money for a whistle, they say "That was the only time Benjamin ever spent a penny unwisely." Hopefully children will not take too seriously these overstatements of virtue and will remember the more human aspects of the men being written about.

Of the many biographies of Abraham Lincoln, one of the best is Clyde Bulla's *Lincoln's Birthday* (1966). Wilma Hays's *Abe Lincoln's Birthday* (1961), despite the similarity of title, is fiction, based on the events of Lincoln's twelfth birthday. Clara Ingram Judson's *Abraham Lincoln* (1961) has a rather flat style, but is useful because it is easy to read, factually accurate, and balanced in coverage.

Tobi Tobias

Maria Tallchief

Tobi Tobias has had a lifetime interest in the dance and she writes of Maria Tallchief, world renowned ballerina, with clarity and admiration. She conveys to young readers the dedication and hard work that go into making a person a superstar. Tobias handles tastefully Tallchief's divorce from choreographer George Balanchine and, without belaboring the point, informs readers that family life is very difficult to combine with a ballet career.

Another dance biography by Tobias is *Arthur Mitchell* (1975), a book about the man whose determination to dance overcame the bias against black ballet dancers. In *Marian Anderson* (1972), Tobias recounts the story of the woman who made musical history with one of the great voices of the twentieth century. Tobias's interest in the arts goes beyond music and dance and is reflected in her biography *Isamu Noguchi; The Life of a Sculptor* (1974).

Other Books for Younger Children

There have been increasing numbers of very simply written biographies to satisfy the curiosity of children in the primary grades. While the majority of them are about famous men and women in American history, there are also numerous biographies of famous sports figures, people in the news, and little known people who have careers of interest to children.

Maggi Scarf's *Meet Benjamin Franklin* (1968) touches on the most familiar events and achievements in Franklin's life. In *The Story of Ben Franklin* (1965), Eve Merriam gives a brief but balanced treatment of Franklin as a family man. Ormonde De Kay's *Meet Andrew Jackson* (1967) is one of the better books in the Random House Step-Up Series.

Martin Luther King, Jr., is a favorite subject, and a favorite book with young readers is Margaret B. Young's *The Picture Life of Martin Luther King, Jr.* (1968). Other figures in the news who have been written about in an easy-to-read style include *Gordon Parks* (1971) by Midge Turk, the story of a versatile and creative black photographer and writer; Ruth Franchere's *Cesar Chavez* (1970), a good picture of the plight of the migrant worker and of the Chicano labor leader; and *Rosa Parks* (1973) by Eloise Greenfield, the story of the woman who precipitated the Montgomery bus strike by refusing to move to the back of the bus.

Marshall and Sue Burchard have developed a satisfactory style and format for their sports hero biographies and have offered young readers the opportunity to read about hockey stars *Bobby Orr* (1973) and *Phil Esposito* (1975), tennis great *Billie Jean King* (1975), and baseball's *Henry Aaron* (1974).

While young children may not be familiar with the writings of Langston Hughes and James Weldon Johnson they can, nevertheless, find much to interest them in Alice Walker's *Langston Hughes, American Poet* (1974) and Ophelia Egypt's *James Weldon Johnson* (1974), both of which reflect the consistently high quality of the Crowell Biography Series. This series is one of the most balanced, containing biographies of women, blacks, Native Americans, and other minorities, as well as biographies about such people as *Eleanor Roosevelt* (1970) by Jane Goodsell and *The Ringling Brothers* (1971) by Molly Cone, which tells of a circus-smitten family who achieved the dream so many children have.

Illustration copyright © 1974 by Moneta Barnett from James Weldon Johnson *by Ophelia Settle Egypt, reprinted by permission of Thomas Y. Crowell Company, Inc., publisher.*

Books for the Middle Group

Children in the middle grades want to know everything there is to know about their special heroes and heroines, the doers—from explorers and scouts of the Old West to today's astronauts and baseball stars. Children are not usually ready for career stories unless they are stories of action, nor are they concerned with character development. Least of all are most children able to appreciate an account of the pursuit of an abstract idea. Penn, with his deep concern for Quakerism and social ideals, is a hero for older children, as is Jefferson, who was so predominantly a man of ideas.

However, through their reading of fairy tales and realistic fiction, children arrive gradually at some broad standards of right and wrong. They may not understand altruism or self-abnegation, but they know all about fair play, kindness, bravery, and justice. These actions they respect, and they admire the heroes and heroines who embody these virtues.

The increasing awareness on the part of authors and editors that young readers like their biographies to be tales of action and achievement rather than stories of the childhood pranks of a great man or woman, straightforward and accurate rather than adulatory, has brought a decided improvement in most of the books for this age group.

Aileen Fisher

Jeanne d'Arc

Aileen Fisher's *Jeanne d'Arc* (1970) is beautifully illustrated with Ati Forberg's quiet, reverent pictures. The story begins with Jeanne at the age of eleven, listening to her father's angry plaints about the English invaders and to his expressed hope that the Dauphin somehow could ascend the throne left vacant by his father's death. When first Jeanne sees a dazzling light and hears a voice tell her that she will be guided by the saints, she is happy and trustful but not, in her piety, surprised. The faith she has in her power to defeat the English and to see the Dauphin crowned, and the tragedy of her imprisonment and death are described with grave simplicity. Aileen Fisher writes in a direct and unembellished prose appropriate to Jeanne's modesty and conviction and she successfully portrays her as a heroine by describing her acts rather than by commenting on them.

In *Joan of Arc; Her Life as Told by Winston Churchill* (1969), reprinted from Churchill's *A History of the English-Speaking Peoples*, comments by the author such as these are frequent: "Unconquerable courage, infinite compassion, the virtue of the simple, the wisdom of the just, shone forth in her." For older readers, Albert Paine's *The Girl in White Armor* (1967; abridged from an earlier version) is well written, historically accurate and detailed, and broad in scope.

Fisher, in collaboration with Olive Rabe, has also written *We Alcotts* (1968), which is for older readers. The biography is told by Mrs. Alcott—in language delightfully stately and appropriate for the period—and focuses on the family's participation in the intellectual ferment of their circle, the abolitionist movement, and new educational theories.

Illustration by William Stobbs. From Columbus, Finder of the New World *by Ronald Syme. Copyright 1952 by William Morrow and Company, Inc. Reprinted by permission of the publishers.*

Ronald Syme

Columbus, Finder of the New World

Ronald Syme's series of biographies of explorers began as easy-to-read books for the middle and upper grades—Columbus, Cortes, Champlain, Balboa, Magellan, and others—and broadened to include more detailed biographies of La Salle, John Smith, and Henry Hudson. *Columbus, Finder of the New World* (1952) is typical of the style and approach of all the books. Christopher Columbus is a difficult character to present in a full biography, since the drama of his life rises grandly to the successful conclusion of his first voyage. After that, failure and tragedy take over. It is greatly to Syme's credit that he presents the gloom as well as the glory. In this brief, well-written biography, the Admiral of the Ocean Sea goes down to his death apparently defeated, but his name and his achievements live after him.

Other biographies of Columbus that readers of nine to twelve may enjoy are Armstrong

Sperry's *Voyages of Christopher Columbus* (1950) and Clara Ingram Judson's *Admiral Christopher Columbus* (1965), not to be confused with her biography of Columbus for younger children. For another slant on the Admiral, children can read Nina Brown Baker's *Amerigo Vespucci* (1956), which, in discussing why America was named for Amerigo rather than for Columbus and in discussing the relationship between the two explorers. gives a picture of Columbus that helps explain his downfall.

In addition to his books about explorers, Syme has written several biographies of heroes of Latin American countries. For older children, *Bolivar the Liberator* (1968) is a good example of the dramatic pattern of events, set off by a restrained style, that makes Ronald Syme's books as exciting as they are informative. Bolivar became president of the Republic of Great Columbia, which included Venezuela, Colombia, Peru, Ecuador, and Bolivia. Although his fortune and his power were lost, and he died in poverty and isolation, Bolivar's reputation as the most important political figure in South American history has grown with the passing of time. "Few liberators," comments Syme, "have lived long enough to enjoy the benefits derived from their achievement of victory for others." As always, Syme is candid in appraisal and lucid in explaining the complexities of political upheaval. These are characteristics also of *Garibaldi; The Man Who Made a Nation* (1967), of *Toussaint; The Black Liberator* (1971), and of *Zapata, Mexican Rebel* (1971), the latter for readers of nine to twelve, simply written, not as smooth in style as the books for older readers but just as objective.

Harold W. Felton

Mumbet; The Story of Elizabeth Freeman

In our era of consciousness of the exclusion, for many years, of the black contributors to American history, such heroes as Benjamin Banneker and Matthew Henson and such heroines as Sojourner Truth and Mary McLeod Bethune have been described many times. Elizabeth Freeman, though, is one heroine whose true story, dramatic and courageous, is seldom heard. Harold Felton's *Mumbet* (1970) tells how Elizabeth had become "Mumbet" to the Ashleys, the Massachusetts family whose slave she was. When Elizabeth heard of the new Massachusetts constitution which stated that all men were created equal, she called on a lawyer who had visited the Ashley home. He argued her case and in 1781 the black slave won her freedom in the courts of Massachusetts. Uneducated but intelligent, firm in her resolve, Elizabeth Freeman is a fascinating heroine, her triumph given suspense by the obstacles put in her way by the Ashleys, and her later years graced by the indomitable way in which she drove Shays' raiders from the lawyer's home.

Adroitly fictionalized, *Mumbet* is written in a vigorous style, the lengthy introduction making evident the research (with many sources quoted) that provided a firm base for the biography.

Harold Felton's other books are primarily about the heroes of America's tall tales or about such black heroes of the West as *Jim Beckwourth* (1966) and *Edward Rose* (1967), all action-filled stories.

Genevieve Foster

The Initial Biographies

The Initial Biographies by Genevieve Foster are brief and add little to our knowledge of the American heroes they describe, but they are written in restrained literary style and provide children with a summary of each person's childhood, youthful struggles, and mature contributions. *George Washington* (1949) has the same accuracy that distinguishes Foster's *George Washington's World*, but is more simplified, yet not written down. Many of the legendary exploits are omitted. In *Abraham Lincoln* (1950) the legends are included and explained—especially the Ann Rutledge affair. Her *Theodore Roosevelt* (1954) makes lively reading as she captures the exuberance of the man.

In *The World of William Penn* (1973), Foster looks at what happened during Penn's lifetime in England, the Continent, the Far East, and colonial America. While not a full biography, it is engrossing reading.

Doris Faber

I Will Be Heard; The Life of William Lloyd Garrison

The subject of Doris Faber's *I Will Be Heard; The Life of William Lloyd Garrison* (1970) is no idealized figure: opinionated, irascible, with no small estimate of his own ability, he was a man whose greatest virtues were a belief in the equality of man and an unwillingness to compromise in any way in the pursuit of that belief. It was a meeting with Benjamin Lundy, whose experiences in the South had caused him to devote his life to speaking against slavery, that started Garrison on the long fight for abolition of that evil. Reviled for many years for the stridency of his views, Garrison did not catch up with the times—the times caught up with him. By the time the Civil War was over, he—who had been threatened, mobbed, and jailed—was lauded and cheered, welcomed by the President, and carried through the streets of Charleston by freed slaves. Through Garrison's biography, the whole pattern of the fight against slavery can be seen. Describing her sources in an afterword, Faber notes that much of the material about abolition is not readily available but was gathered from the files of contemporary journals and from the four-volume biography published by Garrison's sons. Older readers may prefer Jules Archer's *Angry Abolitionist; William Lloyd Garrison* (1969).

Other Faber biographies for the middle group include *Horace Greeley; The People's Editor* (1964), and *Franklin D. Roosevelt* (1974). For older children, Faber has written *Oh, Lizzie; The Life of Elizabeth Cady Stanton* (1972), the famous nineteenth-century feminist.

Clara Ingram Judson

Abraham Lincoln, Friend of the People

Clara Ingram Judson began writing biography in 1939 with a modest little book about Frances Willard called *Pioneer Girl*. That was followed by *Boat Builder; The Story of Robert Fulton* (1940) and others. In 1950, when her *Abraham Lincoln, Friend of the People* appeared, it was evident that this writer, competent in so many fields, had attained new stature as a biographer. It was also evident that Judson's research into source materials was to yield a fresh slant on the man. Her careful studies convinced her, for example, that Abe's childhood was no more "poverty stricken" than that of most of the neighbors. She also brought out the warm family love and loyalty of the Lincoln clan, and Abe himself emerges as a real person.

Many think *Abraham Lincoln, Friend of the People* is the finest book in Judson's biography series. Certainly it can take its place with the Sandburg and Daugherty Lincolns. The illustrations are unique also. In addition to the pen-and-ink drawings, there are colored photographs of the Lincoln dioramas from the Chicago Historical Society. These pictures are eye-catching and vivid.

Clearly, Judson believed the only justification for new biographies of such well-known national figures as George Washington, Thomas Jefferson, Andrew Jackson, and Theodore Roosevelt is that they throw fresh light on, and give children new facts or a new point of view about, the man. Before she wrote a biography, she read the letters, journals, or papers of her hero, searched contemporary magazines and newspapers, and studied the life of the times. As a result, she rescued Washington from the stereotypes that had nearly obliterated him. She even made Jefferson, the man of ideas, intelligible to children. Judson's writing is sometimes stilted, but somehow her deep love of family, her respect for all kinds of people, and her sense of the struggles through which these men came to greatness communicate themselves to children.

Other Books for the Middle Group

Many biographies for the middle grades seem to have been published with more thought for their usefulness as supplementary curricular material than for their literary merit, but they should be used for that purpose and for giving information only if better books are not available. Fortunately, there are now so many good biographies that a reader who enjoys the genre and is not just seeking information about a particular individual has a wide choice.

Reprinted by permission of Coward, McCann & Geoghegan, Inc. from Where Was Patrick Henry on the 29th of May? *by Jean Fritz. Illustrations copyright © 1975 by Margot Tomes.*

For Alcott fans, Helen Papashvily's *Louisa May Alcott* (1965) gives a brisk and capable summary of the writer's work and family life. *Nothing Is Impossible; The Story of Beatrix Potter* (1969) by Dorothy Aldis is simply written and uses extracts from Potter's letters and journal to give added color and establish atmosphere. Margaret Davidson's *The Story of Eleanor Roosevelt* (1969) is a good biography of that indomitable woman for this age group. Arnold Dobrin tells the story of another strong woman in *A Life for Israel; The Story of Golda Meir* (1974).

Jean Fritz brings skill and spirit to her biographies and two of the most enjoyable for this age group are *Where Was Patrick Henry on the 29th of May?* (1975) and *Why Don't You Get a Horse, Sam Adams?* (1974). Sam Adams is also the subject of Fayette Richardson's *Sam Adams; The Boy Who Became Father of the American Revolution* (1975). Ferdinand Monjo adds to Lincolniana in *Me and Willie and Pa* (1973), the story of the Lincoln years in the White House as told by Tad. An excellent biography of an explorer is Jean Latham's *Far Voyager; The Story of Captain Cook* (1970).

Arnold Adoff's *Malcolm X* (1970) is very simply written; *The Life of Malcolm X* (1971) by Richard Curtis, for the more mature reader, is candid and comprehensive; and *The Picture Life of Malcolm X* (1975) by James Haskins is simply written but straightforward.

Martin de Porres, Hero (1954) by Claire Huchet Bishop is a moving story of the Peruvian child, half-black, half-Spanish, who devoted his adult life in the sixteenth century to helping the poor and who was beatified in 1837.

Although the writing in Mary Malone's *Actor in Exile; The Life of Ira Aldridge* (1969) is not outstanding, the dramatic story of the black actor makes fascinating reading. With no chance of gaining a place in American theater, Aldridge went to England in 1824. There was prejudice enough there to make his career difficult, but in time he was acclaimed a great tragedian.

With as many biographies as are published today, it is impossible to mention them all. Additional titles are listed in the chapter bibliography, and more are available through sources cited in Appendix A, Book Selection Aids.

Books for Older Children

Children in the middle grades usually demand action, but adolescent readers are also interested in men and women of ideas and ideals. While they enjoy a biography that is dramatic and well told, they may also read biographies for their historical background, their association with causes and movements, or their association with a field in which the reader has a special interest. One reader may consume avidly any biography with a Civil War background; another, any book about a musician; others, books about people whose lives as dancers, chemists, doctors, or teachers satisfy an orientation toward the profession.

Throughout this chapter, parallel biographies have been mentioned, and they exist in profusion for older readers. Adults working with children will want to know such books so that they may help children explore various presentations. Comparing Catherine Owens Peare's *Mahatma Gandhi; Father of Nonviolence* (1969, rev. ed.) and Olivia Coolidge's *Gandhi* (1971), the reader can see that Peare's book with its fictionalized, rather informal narrative style is easier to read and more dramatic, but that Coolidge's is more detailed, dignified, and analytical. Jeanette Eaton's *Gandhi; Fighter Without a Sword* (1950) is notable for the perceptive picture it gives of Gandhi as a man and a spiritual leader. Comparing biographies gives children an opportunity to understand how emphasis, style, and author's viewpoint, the amount of fictionalization or of documentation, and the amount of historical background or period details can shape a book.

Sidney Rosen

Galileo and the Magic Numbers

From the moment Master Jacopo Borghini introduced the young Galileo to the Pythagorean magic numbers, his life as a physicist and astronomer was determined. Although money was a problem, Galileo acquired an education and, eventually, a teaching position. His annoying habit of asking "Why?" and "How do you know?" made him unpopular with his teachers and colleagues as well as with Roman Catholic authorities. In *Galileo and the Magic Numbers* (1958), Rosen shows clearly the heroism of the man who defied the theological beliefs of his time to make important contributions to human knowledge.

Wizard of the Dome (1969) is an appealing biography for the general reader, since Rosen portrays Buckminster Fuller as a lively, tenacious inventor whose patterns of success and failure as a designer-inventor have a cliffhanger appeal; to the scientifically oriented girl or boy, it has the added attraction of presenting with unusual clarity the theories for which Fuller is now famous. Out of his concepts about the tetrahedron in nature and the application of geodesic structure have come his now-famous geodesic dome construction. The book has a good balance of personal life and of information about Fuller's professional career; it is written in a dignified but informal style, and it makes clear the importance and the innovatory nature of his work. In *Doctor Paracelsus* (1959), Rosen tells the story of Theophrastus Bombastus von Hohenheim, a Swiss doctor who rebelled against superstitions of medical belief and practices of the early sixteenth century.

Elizabeth Yates

Amos Fortune, Free Man

Born an African prince, sold in Boston, well treated by a series of masters, Amos Fortune learned the tanner's trade and eventually bought his freedom. After that, this humble, mighty soul devoted everything he earned to buying freedom for other slaves. Freedom and education were the greatest things in his life. He died a respected member of the little New Hampshire town of Jaffrey, where he had lived so long. When Elizabeth Yates saw the tombstone of Amos, she tells us, she knew she must write his biography. *Amos Fortune, Free Man* (1951 Newbery Medal winner) is written with warmth and compassion. Since most books about slavery deal with the South, it is important to have this picture of slave-running and sales in the North. The details are grim, but Amos Fortune carried suffering lightly because his eyes were on the freedom of the future. It is this characteristic of Fortune's, so clearly depicted by Yates, that causes some modern critics to disparage the book. They disapprove of the quiet way Amos Fortune bore his enslavement with courage and dignity, forgetting the circumstances under which he achieved his own personal integrity and offered the chance to live free to other blacks.

In *Prudence Crandall; Woman of Courage* (1955), Yates writes of the Quaker schoolmistress who engendered bitter hostility in 1833 when she opened a school for black girls in a Connecticut town.

James Daugherty

Poor Richard

For superior readers with mature interests, Daugherty's *Poor Richard* (1941) has unusual distinction. This book covers Franklin's whole life, his manifold activities, and his amazing talent for friendship among people of all varieties and ages. The chapter called "An American in Paris" opens in this way.

One man alone captured a city. An American had taken Paris single-handed.

All the king's horses and all the king's men could not do what the friendly seventy-year-old journeyman printer was doing in spite of himself. He was surprised and pleased to find himself a hero. He was ready to act the part, knowing all that it might mean for America.

The chapter includes a visit with John Paul Jones, "a one-man navy," and a little later we are treated to the scandalized Abigail Adams's report of a dinner where Mme. Helvétius sat with one arm around Franklin's shoulder and the other on the chair of Abigail's own John. "After dinner," wrote the outraged Mrs. Adams, "she threw herself on a settee where she showed more than her feet." Here, obviously, is a somewhat mature interpretation of the times, written and illustrated with Daugherty's usual gusto and swing.

Daugherty's *Abraham Lincoln* (1943) covers Lincoln's whole life. This book avoids the usual anecdotes found in most of the other juveniles, and with remarkable clarity and power tells the story of Lincoln in relation to the stormy war years. A reviewer summarizing Daugherty's contribution in his three biographies writes:

. . . "Daniel Boone," "Poor Richard" and now "Abraham Lincoln"—are linked together in unity of spirit, an appreciation, in the true sense, of the restless, surging, visionary America which, with all its faults, has borne Titans.[12]

There is something in the spirit which animates Daugherty's pen and brush that seems particularly adapted to the interpretation of titans. His *Abraham Lincoln* illustrations show all the rowdy vigor of his earlier drawings, but predominant in the book is the brooding melancholy of the strangest and perhaps loneliest of our great Presidents. *Abraham Lincoln* is the most serious of Daugherty's three biographies, as we should expect, and is a magnificently clear if tragic picture of this great man.

Daugherty's *Daniel Boone* (1939), for which he won the Newbery Medal, is a spirited biography that has been attacked for bigotry in recent years by some critics. It is true that this book reflects the "Manifest Destiny" theory of the westward movement in American history. It is true that both Indians and blacks are treated in an offhand manner by Daugherty. But that is how Boone would have perceived them and to criticize Daugherty for not making Boone a twentieth-century liberal is overstepping the boundaries of critical analysis.

For a fuller biography of the man at a more mature level, children should read John Mason Brown's *Daniel Boone.*

[12]Ellen Lewis Buell, "The Story of Honest Abe," a review of Daugherty's *Abraham Lincoln* in *The New York Times Book Review*, December 19, 1943.

Nardi Reeder Campion

Patrick Henry, Firebrand of the Revolution

Patrick Henry was one of the leaders of the American Revolution, and yet his character and achievements have always been open to question. In her book *Patrick Henry* (1961), Campion shows why. She never glosses over the weaknesses of her hero. As a boy, growing up in a cultured home where education was highly valued, he was lazy and irresponsible and soon discovered that he could talk himself out of most scrapes. He developed a fine speaking voice and a feeling for words and the cadence of language that were to be his greatest assets as long as he lived. Amiable and talented, he married when he was still penniless, failed twice at storekeeping, but, with three children to support, decided to become a lawyer. For once he studied intensively, if briefly, and became a close friend of the scholarly Jefferson. Once admitted to the bar, he won an unpopular case against the clergy and the king that rocked the State and made him famous.

This was the beginning. Caught up in the rising tide of pre-Revolutionary activity, Patrick Henry in the Virginia House of Burgesses became the spellbinding voice of the Revolutionists. And somehow, that dream of freedom from tyranny and a union of the colonists so possessed the man that it forged him into a finer person than he had been. Yet after years of devoted friendship, Jefferson broke with him completely and denounced him venomously. Campion records his words and accusations but concludes that there were no valid stains on Henry's honor.

On July 5, 1776, he was overwhelmingly elected first governor of Virginia, an office which he administered wisely and well in five different terms. Jefferson was wrong, the author concludes, and this strange, passionate "Son of Thunder" died gently and courageously, much loved by his family and his State. This is a fascinating and carefully documented biography, well adapted to elementary school children but enjoyed at high-school level also.

Leonard Wibberley

Man of Liberty; A Life of Thomas Jefferson

In the years 1963-66, Leonard Wibberley published four volumes about the life of Thomas Jefferson. In 1968, a condensed and slightly revised volume incorporated the volumes into *Man of Liberty; A Life of Thomas Jefferson.*

In his prefatory note for *Man of Liberty,* Wibberley says that he felt his task as a biographer was to round out the picture usually given of Jefferson the statesman by including more information about his personal life. However, the comments he makes about his sources are much more specific and detailed than such notes usually are. Wibberley's choice of material clearly is based on exhaustive as well as discriminating research. He concludes, "I do not think that, however much I had read about Jefferson, I could have written this book about him without having lived in America. It is something that is in the air, and if you press me to say what that something is, I have to answer: Jefferson."[13]

This admiration is not explicit in the text itself. Wisely, Wibberley draws Thomas Jefferson (and the historical figures with whom he lived and worked) so astutely that the man's intellect, ability, and versatility speak for him. The biography is mature in approach, an excellent source of information about the period as well as a fascinating study of Jefferson.

Viewpoints

. . . we cannot thank [the biographer] sufficiently for what he does for us. For we are incapable of living wholly in the intense world of the imagination. The imagination is a faculty that soon tires and needs rest and refreshment. But for a tired imagination the proper food is not inferior poetry or minor fiction—indeed they blunt and debauch it—but sober fact, that 'authentic information' from which, as Lytton Strachey has shown us, good biography is made. When and where did the real man live; how did he look; did he wear laced boots or elastic-sided; who were his aunts, and his friends; how did he blow his nose; whom did he love, and how; and when he came to die did he die in his bed like a Christian, or . . . .—Virginia Woolf, "The New Biography," *The New York Herald Tribune,* October 30, 1927. Reprinted in *Granite and Rainbow* by Leonard Woolf, Harcourt, Brace, New York, 1958, p. 155.

Jeanette Eaton

Leader by Destiny

Washington is undoubtedly one of the most difficult figures to bring alive for children, both because he has been belittled by the trivial anecdotes told about him and because he has the subtle, intangible qualities of a highly civilized human being. Self-discipline and restraint are not easy for children to understand or to appreciate, and for this reason in particular Washington is a better character for adolescents than for children.

The best juvenile biography of Washington, Jeanette Eaton's *Leader by Destiny* (1938), is for the teen age, but it is such an extraordinary book that adults could also profit by reading it. You catch in it, for instance, Washington's lifelong regret for his inadequate education. You also find in this book Washington's single indiscretion, in his relations to his friend's wife, the beautiful Sally Fairfax. He wrote her one letter declaring his love. This letter Sally kept secret until the day of her death, and it remained secret for a hundred years after. In this book you see Washington's affectionate relations with his wife's children, and you see Martha herself as a charming and devoted wife to Washington, who came to appreciate her more and more. This book will help young

[13]Leonard Wibberley, *Man of Liberty* (Farrar, 1968), pp. v, vii.

Illustration by John O'Hara Cosgrave II. From Carry On, Mr. Bowditch *by Jean Lee Latham. Copyright, 1955, by Jean Lee Latham and John O'Hara Cosgrave II. Reproduced by permission of the Houghton Mifflin Company.*

people and adults know Washington as a very human, often bewildered man with a remarkable gift for inspiring confidence in others.

Elizabeth Ripley

Hokusai

To supplement her background of art education, Elizabeth Ripley studied numerous sources to gain information for her biographies of artists. For *Hokusai* (1968), her story of the Japanese artist (1760–1849), she spent a month in Japan to get background. One of the best in a series of good books, *Hokusai* is particularly charming because of the vivacity and humor of the artist himself. Dismissed by his master from a print design shop because of his unorthodox approach to art, Hokusai lived in poverty until he at long last became famous for the beauty of his prints. A nonconformist, a showman, a cheerful spendthrift, he died at eighty-nine after having changed his name fifty times and having squandered his money. He chose his own tombstone inscription: "Old Man Mad About Painting."

In *Michelangelo* (1953) Ripley shows the artist as almost the victim of his two gifts for painting and for sculpture. Painting with its vision of endless details seemed to enslave him, while sculpture freed his energies and let his creative spirit soar. Each of the books in Elizabeth Ripley's series follows a similar pattern, with a brief coverage of the artist's childhood and youth and, with the beginning of his productivity, a discussion of his life as it related to his major works.

Another excellent biography of Michelangelo is Robert Coughlan's *The World of Michelangelo 1475–1564* (1966) in the Time-Life Library of Art, written for the mature reader. The text gives full historical background and a discussion of the artist's work, as well as a perceptive picture of the man. The book is profusely illustrated with reproductions of Michelangelo's paintings and photographs of his sculpture.

Esther M. Douty

Forten the Sailmaker; Pioneer Champion of Negro Rights

James Forten, born ten years before the American Revolution in the Colony of Pennsylvania, was the grandson of a slave and the son of a father both free and proud. When he was eight, he began his schooling with the gentle Quaker Anthony Benezet. At fourteen he signed on a privateer as powder boy, was captured by the British, and gave up his chance to go home as an exchange prisoner to a white friend who was ill. Released later, he shipped to England and worked as a stevedore, returning to Philadelphia to become an apprentice in the sail loft, where his industry and ability so impressed the white owner that he offered to sell the business to James. Thus he became an independent man, *Forten the Sailmaker* (1968), who in time became wealthy and influential in the community.

In 1800, Forten and other free blacks of the city petitioned Congress for a revision of the Fugitive Slave Act, and throughout the rest of his life he gave generously of his time and his fortune helping others, buying the freedom of many slaves, working with the Underground Railroad. Over three thousand people, white and black, attended the funeral of this quiet and respected citizen of Philadelphia.

Carefully written, the book is based on extensive research, both the bibliography and the author's acknowledgments showing Esther Douty's meticulous probing. The book is a good example of how biography shows the valor of a lifetime dedicated to a worthy cause.

The information garnered for this book has also been used in part as background for Douty's *Charlotte Forten; Free Black Teacher* (1971), which is mentioned in the discussion of Longworth's biography of Charlotte Forten.

Jean Lee Latham

Carry On, Mr. Bowditch

Between the great leaders in the American Revolution and the sturdy frontier people of the push westward is the unique figure of Nathaniel Bowditch. Born in Salem, Massachusetts, in 1773, he never had a day's schooling after he was ten years old. Yet he became an outstanding astronomer, mathematician, and author of *The New American Practical Navigator*, published in 1802 and still a basic text of modern navigation.

When Nathaniel was twelve, his father bound him out for nine years to a ship's chandlery. The boy was near despair, when an old fellow told him, "Only a weakling gives up when he is becalmed! A strong man sails by ash breeze!" That is, he "sails" his boat with ash oars. So Nat sailed. His story is one of continuous toil in the chandlery by day and with books at night. Then came the end of his indenture, and a knowledgeable young man set off on the first of his five adventurous voyages. There is romance in Nat's story, and some tragic as well as some extremely humorous episodes. The climax came when Harvard, a university to which he had yearned to go, bestowed upon this unschooled but brilliant scientist an honorary degree. It is a thrilling story of New England fortitude and love of learning. Jean Latham has told it splendidly, and strong illustrations add to the distinction of this 1956 Newbery Medal book.

Another Latham biography of a great American navigator is *Trail Blazer of the Seas* (1956), the story of Matthew Maury, who worked to establish a naval academy. *Young Man in a Hurry; The Story of Cyrus W. Field* (1958) is a true story but is as exciting as adventure fiction.

Elisabeth Kyle

Girl with a Pen; Charlotte Brontë

Elisabeth Kyle's *Girl with a Pen* (1964) is a story of Charlotte Brontë's life from her seventeenth year to her thirty-first. Competently fictionalized, the biography evokes vividly the bleak parsonage and the beloved moorland country, the affection among the Brontë children, and the growing development of their literary interests.

Particularly engaging is the section that describes the reception at the London publishing house of Smith and Elder of a book titled *Jane Eyre* by a writer who called herself

Currer Bell. The subsequent acclaim of the book is followed by Charlotte's timid report to her father that she had had a book published and his announcement to her sisters: "Girls, do you know that Charlotte has been writing a book, and it is much better than likely?"

The portraits of Charlotte and her sisters are candid, and the impression of their restricted horizons is so strong that the reader is always conscious of the courage it must have taken the three Brontë sisters as women—and particularly as women from a modest parsonage—to submit their manuscripts.

In her afterword, Kyle refers to this book as a story rather than a biography, but it succeeds in the task of a good biography: it reveals the character of its subject and her achievements, and in stimulating interest in its subject, this captivating biography—or story, as Kyle describes it—is exceptionally successful.

Another of Kyle's lively biographies of writers is *Great Ambitions; A Story of the Early Years of Charles Dickens* (1968), covering in great detail Dickens's life between the ages of twelve and twenty-seven. Kyle has also written *Duet; The Story of Clara and Robert Schumann* (1968).

Viewpoints

Certainty of knowledge not only excludes mistake, but fortifies veracity. What we collect by conjecture, and by conjecture only can one man judge of another's motives or sentiments, is easily modified by fancy or by desire; as objects imperfectly discerned take forms from the hope or fear of the beholder. But that which is fully known cannot be falsified but with reluctance of understanding, and alarm of conscience: of understanding, the lover of truth; of conscience, the sentinel of virtue.

He that writes the life of another is either his friend or his enemy, and wishes either to exalt his praise or aggravate his infamy: many temptations to falsehood will occur in the disguise of passions, too specious to fear much resistance. Love of virtue will animate panegyric, and hatred of wickedness embitter censure. The zeal of gratitude, the ardour of patriotism, fondness for an opinion, or fidelity to a party, may easily overpower the vigilance of a mind habitually well disposed, and prevail over unassisted and unfriended veracity.—Samuel Johnson, *The Rambler,* No. 60, Sat., Oct. 13, 1750.

James Playsted Wood

Spunkwater, Spunkwater! A Life of Mark Twain

"The United States has always paid its entertainers extravagantly," says James Wood in *Spunkwater, Spunkwater!* (1968). "Whatever his other excellences, and he had many—and whatever deep, dark mystique ingenious critics have read into his life and work—Mark Twain was first and last an entertainer. It was his celebrity as an entertainer that led to his being enthroned as the American sage. He was the articulate and even voluble symbol of the kind of practical wisdom Americans most admired. He was about as tragic as anyone else, applauded and honored everywhere he went, who was having a wonderful time. . . ." Such candid comment is typical of the fresh and thoughtful approach of James Wood, whose sophisticated style pays readers the compliment of assuming that they will appreciate the nuance of humor and oblique reference.

Mark Twain's life as river pilot, newspaperman, author, lecturer, caustic world traveler, and deeply devoted husband and father is familiar material, included in most of the biographies of Twain. Wood gives an added dimension by his perceptively analytical discussion of Twain's volatile and ebullient personality and by his criticism of Twain's writing. A list of important dates and a bibliography add to the book's general usefulness, and some delightful photographs add to its appeal.

The mature wit and percipience of Wood's analysis of Twain are also evident in his other biographies of writers. In *The Lantern Bearer; A Life of Robert Louis Stevenson* (1965), he is candid in appraisal of Stevenson as a romantic, often illogical man and a superb craftsman. Wood's *The Admirable Cotton Mather* (1971) is particularly interesting because he disputes Mather's reputation as vindictive and bigoted.

Polly Longsworth

I, Charlotte Forten, Black and Free

Polly Longsworth's *I, Charlotte Forten* (1970) is based on Ray Allen Billington's edition of Charlotte's diary, and, according to the author in her acknowledgments, is "as close a re-creation of Miss Forten's life and experiences as I am capable of achieving." This explains why the biography begins with Charlotte's sixteenth year, when she came to Salem, Massachusetts, so that she might attend an unsegregated school.

As the granddaughter of the wealthy and respected James Forten, she had been brought up in a home in which good breeding and cultural interests were taken for granted, and in which the leaders of the antislavery movement were accustomed guests. Charlotte continued to meet in Salem such dignitaries as Whittier, Garrison, Douglass, and Phillips, and she decided to devote her life to helping her own people.

Having become a teacher, she volunteered to join the Port Royal Commission that was going to the South Carolina Sea Islands to teach the neglected blacks of Saint Helena. In 1864, she came North to attend her father's funeral, and there the biography ends, although a final chapter describes the Grimké family and her marriage to Francis Grimké, and speaks briefly of their joint years of dedication to helping the black cause through the hard days of antebellum disillusionment.

The book is written in first person, in a heavy and rather ornate style appropriate for a nineteenth-century woman of good family. It is nevertheless an exciting book, in part because the pages read like a roll call of all the early crusaders against slavery, in part because the events are intrinsically dramatic, and in part because the picture of a frail and gentle girl so unselfishly devoted to a cause is romantic in the best sense.

Esther Douty's *Charlotte Forten; Free Black Teacher* (1971), a biography for the middle grades, is based on the diary also, but written in third person; it, too, ends with Charlotte Forten's return to the North after her father's death. An afterword briefly describes her subsequent life. More fictionalized than the Longsworth book, this has a few childhood episodes that contribute little to the book and includes some quotations from the diary. Otherwise the books cover most of the same incidents and major events, though there is much more detail and more background in Longsworth's account.

Another outstanding biography by Longsworth is *Emily Dickinson; Her Letter to the World* (1965), written in a quiet style that is a good foil for the romantic subject, and with a balanced attention to the poet's writing and to her personal life.

Dorothy Sterling

Captain of the Planter; The Story of Robert Smalls

Robert Smalls's owner was Henry McKee. Because he could earn more money for McKee by being hired out, Smalls was sent to Charleston, where he worked in a sailing loft and watched the pilots carefully until he became adept at handling boats himself. In 1861, Smalls shipped on the *Planter* as a deckhand. The ship was in the service of the Confederate Navy, and it was the resemblance between its captain and himself that gave Smalls his great idea: an idea that would bring him freedom and put the ship into Union hands. At three A.M. on the morning of May 13, 1862, the black crew quietly maneuvered the ship out of the harbor, stopping to take on some of their wives and children; they were given freedom to pass by the sentinel at Fort Sumter, and the crew proudly hailed a Union ship and turned the *Planter* over to the Union.

Disappointed by the fact that the Union Army included no black troops, Smalls visited President Lincoln and persuaded him to change his policy. Dedicated to the causes of freedom and equality, he became a public speaker and a member of Congress.

Dorothy Sterling's story of Robert Smalls, well documented by a list of sources and an extensive bibliography, is dramatic because of its subject matter: Smalls's personal achievement and the events of the years of the Civil War and the Reconstruction. What Sterling had added to the inherent drama of the *Captain of the Planter* (1958) is a powerful picture of the tragedy of the postwar years and a personal portrait of a man whose true greatness lay not in one single courageous act but in the fact that he never compromised his principles for the sake of expediency.

Other biographies by Sterling are *Freedom Train; The Story of Harriet Tubman* (1954), and *The Making of an Afro-American; Martin Robison Delaney 1812–1885* (1971), an extensively documented account of an early exponent of black nationalism. While Dorothy Sterling has written stories, informational books on such diverse topics as caves and caterpillars, and series books, her strongest commitment is clearly to the cause of black equality. Young readers who enjoy her biographies may also want to read her study of events related to the Emancipation Proclamation in *Forever Free* (1963), her history of the American civil rights movement in *Tear Down the Walls!* (1968), and *Speak Out in Thunder Tones* (1973) and *The Trouble They Seen* (1976), both compilations of statements by black people, covering the years 1787–1877.

Shannon Garst

Crazy Horse

Toward the end of the period of westward expansion came the terrible struggles between the advancing hordes of whites and the defending Indians. Several fine biographies of Indian leaders of this period give children the story of these events from the Indians' point of view. *Crazy Horse* (1950) is one of the best of these. It begins with Crazy Horse's training as a boy, shows his bitter experiences with the bad faith and cruelties of the whites and his growing determination to stop their invasion at all costs. The end is sheer tragedy. Crazy Horse is defeated, his people scattered or herded into a reservation, and Crazy Horse, rather than submit, fights to his death. No child who reads this moving record will ever believe the cruelties were all on one side.

Shannon Garst also writes sympathetically of the Sioux way of life in *Sitting Bull, Champion of His People* (1946) and of Sitting Bull's tenacious and courageous fight in a losing battle against white encroachment. Garst's *Kit Carson, Trailblazer and Scout* (1942) is a lively book of frontier life, full of action and the romance of the Old West.

Shirley Graham

Booker T. Washington

Although Shirley Graham's late husband, William E. B. DuBois, had major philosophical differences with Booker T. Washington, Graham writes objectively and sympathetically of the man in her biography *Booker T. Washington* (1955).

Born a slave, Booker was nine when the Emancipation Proclamation brought him freedom and an opportunity to go to West Virginia, where he worked in a salt mine and a coal mine. He took the name "Washington," in fact, from the name of the salt mine and the "Taliaferro" from the name of his father. Bent

Viewpoints

For how can a book be educational which discourages children from reading? What is educational about a book which is so thin in its characterization, so stilted in its prose, and so contrived in its plotting that the young reader goes to it as to a penance, eyeing his baseball mitt for succor. Unfortunately, there are quite a number of such "educational" books published today. . . . In a large part they consist of the lives of famous men who, judging by the books, could hardly be said to have lived at all. They seem merely to have passed through the Ten Commandments, nodding dutifully to each one of them, never guilty of an error of judgment, let alone a sin, and then died honored by their countrymen, who secretly must have been very glad to get rid of them. . . . But it is a paradox of writing that books which are written for the purpose of being educational (I exclude school books from this discussion) are not. The very emphasis on being educational kills the spirit of the book. While those which are written with a love of a story or of a character or of a time or a place are educational, for something comes to life from between the pages and we stand on Tower Hill in the sixteenth century and hear the executioner cry in anguish, "God pardon me," as he brings down his ax and severs the head of Sir Thomas More from his body. . . .—Leonard Wibberley, "The Land of the Ever Young," *The California Librarian*, January, 1962, pp. 19–20.

on getting an education, young Washington worked doggedly to pay his way through Hampton Institute, his academic prowess earning him an appointment as principal of Tuskegee, the new normal school that became Tuskegee Institute.

Although Booker T. Washington became famous for his development of Tuskegee, for bringing George Washington Carver to the faculty, for dining with Presidents, and for being the first black man to get an honorary degree from Harvard University, he has always stirred some controversy because of the stand he took on race relations in the famous speech often referred to as the "Atlanta Compromise." In her biography, Shirley Graham has submerged any difference in viewpoint she might have with Washington. Her story is told with an understanding of how Washington's life and experience shaped his ideas. The biography is adroitly fictionalized, many of the incidents based on Washington's autobiography *Up from Slavery*, with anecdotes and dialogue woven smoothly into the narrative. A bibliography gives sources, and a lengthy index makes textual material accessible.

An interesting contrast to Booker T. Washington's story is found in *W. E. B. DuBois* (1972) by Virginia Hamilton, and older children should be encouraged to read this and think about those differences in philosophies between the two men. DuBois was an aristocrat in every sense of the word. He received a doctorate from Harvard, where he studied under such men as William James and George Santayana. He spent two years studying at the University of Berlin. The story of how the scholar became a political activist and one of the most important black leaders in the history of the United States is fascinating.

Shirley Graham has also written *The Story of Phillis Wheatley* (1949), which is well researched but more fictionalized; *Your Most Humble Servant* (1949), the story of Benjamin Banneker; and *His Day Is Marching On* (1971), memoirs of her husband, W. E. B. DuBois.

Mature readers will want to read Booker T. Washington's autobiography *Up from Slavery* and *The Souls of Black Folks* by W. E. B. DuBois.

Catherine Owens Peare

The Louis D. Brandeis Story

Catherine Owens Peare is never adulatory in her attitude toward the men and women whose biographies she writes, but her affection and respect for her subjects are usually clear, as they are in *The Louis D. Brandeis Story* (1970). Coming from a close-knit Austrian-Jewish family that had migrated to Louisville, Brandeis grew up in a circle in which it was taken for granted that cultural, academic, and political interests would be shared and discussed. An ardent student, Louis Brandeis made a distinguished record at Harvard Law School.

With a passion for justice and a concern for the underprivileged, Brandeis became a respected figure in the legal hierarchy of Boston, and grew wealthy enough to espouse reform measures and to takes cases without a fee to protect the public interest against the depredations of big business monoliths. In his years as an associate justice of the Supreme Court, he won distinction for his idealism, his concern for humanity, and his farseeing understanding of ethical and social implications of the issues involved in cases heard. An ample bibliography of sources is included with Peare's story of his life.

Many of Peare's biographies are concerned with public figures: *The Herbert Hoover Story* (1965) stresses Hoover's role in humanitarian projects, and *The Woodrow Wilson Story* (1963), Wilson's idealism and his influence on world events. In *Mary McLeod Bethune* (1951), she draws an exciting picture of the remarkably energetic black educator.

Iris Noble

Emmeline and Her Daughters; The Pankhurst Suffragettes

Emmeline and Her Daughters (1971), like many of Iris Noble's other biographies, describes with enthusiastic sympathy a pioneer in a reform movement, a champion of a cause. The book's bibliography includes works by Emmeline Pankhurst and by each of her three daughters, clearly the source of many of the intimate details that give the account vitality and authenticity. The tumultuous record of the Pankhursts is seen both as a personal narrative and as the opening salvo in the long battle for equality for women.

Emmeline Pankhurst had been a demure, cultured Victorian wife and mother until the day her husband, who had long fought for feminine liberation, challenged her to take an active part in the struggle. He began her education as a militant participant by taking her to hear debates in Parliament, helping her organize the Women's Franchise League, and encouraging her to run for a minor political office. She was forty when he died, and without his backing her role was even more difficult. It was her daughter Christabel who conceived the idea of a new organization, "*of* women *for* women, one that will lead all the women of Britain into militant action." So the Women's Social and Political Union was born, the group that was a vigorous spearhead for feminine equality. The actions taken against this dedicated army of women led them to mass demonstrations and acts of violence, but their courage in the face of brutal reprisals eventually won them public admiration, the support of much of the press, and, in 1928, at long last, full suffrage.

Iris Noble deals objectively with dramatic and important events and shows the long struggle as not only a dominating motive in the lives of the four Pankhurst women but the cause of a bitter rupture between Christabel and Sylvia Pankhurst.

Objectivity in reporting and sympathetic understanding of a crusader's ardor are also evident in Noble's *Susan B. Anthony* (1975), the story of the persistent crusader for women's rights. In *Empress of All Russia* (1966), Noble combines broad historical coverage with a vigorous, perceptive characterization of Catherine the Great.

The obstacles that faced women during the nineteenth century are made clear in Patricia Clapp's biography of Elizabeth Blackwell, *Dr. Elizabeth; The Story of the First Woman Doctor* (1974). Written in the first person, this biography is never guilty of over-dramatization.

That the fight begun by the Pankhursts and Anthony is not over can be seen in two very fine biographies of Shirley Chisholm, the first black woman to serve in the United States Congress. Susan Brownmiller's *Shirley Chisholm* (1970) is for slightly younger readers than James Haskins's *Fighting Shirley Chisholm* (1975). Haskins writes here, as in all his books, with a candidness still rare in children's books.

Howard Greenfeld

Gertrude Stein; A Biography

Of the several biographies of Gertrude Stein that were written for young people in honor of the hundredth year of her birth, Howard Greenfeld's *Gertrude Stein* (1973) is the most sensitive in depicting her personality and the most thorough in analyzing her writing and her role in the turbulent artistic and literary circles of Paris. Greenfeld provides evidence of painstaking research with a lengthy bibliography of sources, and he uses many quotations from Stein's writing or from current articles to corroborate his statements.

The balanced treatment of personal and artistic facets that Greenfeld uses in the Stein biography is also a strong feature of his *Pablo Picasso* (1971) and *Marc Chagall* (1967). In

From Gertrude Stein: A Biography *by Howard Greenfeld. Photograph from Yale University, the Beinecke Rare Book and Manuscript Library Collection of American Literature.*

F. Scott Fitzgerald (1974), Greenfeld describes the tragedy of Fitzgerald's life with a compassion that never lapses into sentimentality or melodrama. He achieves, in all his biographies, a polished, dignified writing style, and he succeeds in presenting knowledgeable, candid, and vivid pictures of individuals while making clear their roles in artistic or literary history.

Miriam Gurko

Restless Spirit; The Life of Edna St. Vincent Millay

Miriam Gurko's *Restless Spirit* (1962) is a mature and thoughtful biography for adolescent readers. Her sources include published and unpublished material, letters, and interviews. "Curiously, as the mass of notes grew, the more elusive the subject seemed to become," Gurko states in her foreword. And she goes on, "From this assortment of fact and characterization I have had to select those elements which appeared the most credible, and which seemed to have undergone the least alteration as a result of the passage of time or the presence of certain personal factors."

Brought up by her mother after her parents had separated, Vincent and her sisters had a childhood in which they early became self-reliant. Vincent wrote poetry at the age of five, and many of her childhood poems were published in *The St. Nicholas Magazine*. She had already published "Renascence" and become modestly famous when she entered Vassar at the age of twenty-one. After her graduation, Edna, who no longer used "Vincent" as her name, went to New York to join in the intellectual ferment of Greenwich Village life and in the activities of the newly formed Provincetown Players. After several abortive love affairs, she married Eugen Boissevin, a marriage that was ideal for a poet, since Eugen felt it his role to protect Edna and encourage her work.

The biography includes quotations from Edna St. Vincent Millay's poetry only when they are relevant to the text, and Gurko has integrated smoothly the personal material, the background of the artistic and literary circles in which Edna moved, and the discerning discussion of the poet's work and its place in modern poetry.

Toby Shafter's biography *Edna St. Vincent Millay; America's Best-Loved Poet* (1957) is lighter in style, with much more fictionalization and with approximately half the book devoted to Millay's childhood. However, it is factually reliable and a good introduction for less mature readers.

Other biographies by Miriam Gurko include *Clarence Darrow* (1965), interesting both as an account of the famous Scopes trial and as a study of the nonconformist lawyer who was a defender of unpopular causes. Much of the story also reflects the history of the labor movement. *The Lives and Times of Peter Cooper* (1959), as the title indicates, is concerned with other figures as well as with that of the protagonist, for the inventor and industrialist Cooper was constantly involved in industrial, political, and educational movements.

Leo Gurko

Ernest Hemingway and the Pursuit of Heroism

Leo Gurko, in *Ernest Hemingway* (1968), writes for the adolescent reader who is seriously interested in Hemingway as a writer rather than as a person. Only the first quarter of this biography is devoted to Hemingway's life. Colorful to the point of flamboyance, Ernest Hemingway was a nonconformist adolescent in a conventional suburban home. When he refused to go to college and was rejected by the Army during the First World War, he joined the staff of the Kansas City *Star* as a cub reporter until he discovered that he could serve with the Red Cross. Much of his experience in Italy appears in *A Farewell to Arms*. His years in Paris, his service in Spain during the Civil War, his string of marriages, and his winning of the Nobel Prize for Literature are described in a concise and objective account. The remainder of the book is devoted to an astute critical analysis of Hemingway's writing, learned but never dry, in which Gurko explores the persistence of the theme of heroism, not the heroism of great deeds but the heroism of the individual who struggles for humanity and his own salvation.

In *The Two Lives of Joseph Conrad* (1965) Gurko again relates, in polished prose style, the man and his experiences to the content of his books (in which there are often thinly disguised counterparts of the people and the incidents in the subject's own life). *Tom Paine; Freedom's Apostle* (1957) is more simply written than Gurko's other books and equally objective and perceptive.

Theodora Kroeber

Ishi; Last of His Tribe

At the end of the nineteenth century a small band of Yahi Indians lived in solitude and secrecy at the foot of Mount Lassen, their way of life threatened by the white settlers and seekers of gold. *Ishi* (1964) and his people knew that they could survive only if they remained hidden, their ancient villages having been destroyed by the ruthless invaders. As long as they could, the people clung to the sacred ways, the quiet and peaceful pattern of Yahi life. One by one, the others died, and Ishi was alone. "There is nothing to wait for in this empty land, nothing—I am free to go." And so he left, and took the trail to the west, lost his way, and met the saldu, the whites.

Viewpoints

A biography is not an encyclopedia, it is the story of a life. George Macaulay Trevelyan has said it is in narrative that modern historical writing is weakest. I think this happens when the writer tries to crowd too much information on his page at one time, or, sinning in the opposite direction, assumes the reader is familiar with names and events simply because he, the writer, knows them so well. All this information, gathered in the library, has its place, a canny page or paragraph where it will fit painlessly—which means clearly and entertainingly, so that the reader will feel he has made a discovery.—Catherine Drinker Bowen, *Biography: The Craft and the Calling*, Little, Brown and Co., 1968, pp. 50–51.

To his surprise, they did not kill him; a Stranger was brought, a museum-saldu, who spoke in the tongue of the People, and took Ishi on a train. And so Ishi came to live with the whites in peace, an adviser to the museum people on the ways and the crafts of the Yahi. One of the most striking aspects of *Ishi* is the consistency with which Theodora Kroeber maintains Ishi's viewpoint; even after he comes to live and work with the museum staff, the relationships are seen through Ishi's eyes, and the writing continues to have the beautiful cadence and dignity of Yahi. At the end,

> *Death came to him as he wished— with his friends in the museum-watgurwa. Majapa and the museum men released his spirit in the old Yahi way. And they saw to it that Ishi had with him those things that a Yahi hunter must take from the World of the Living, for the journey to the west. . . .*

The names used are always the Yahi names that Ishi had given.

Alfred Kroeber was Curator of the Museum of Anthropology and Ethnology at the University of California when Ishi was brought there, and his wife had the benefit of his professional knowledge as well as first-hand information from Ishi. Such familiarity permits a biographer to incorporate cultural details so that they are as intrinsic a part of a life story as they are in *Ishi*, and in Theodora Kroeber's anthropological study for adult readers, *Ishi in Two Worlds*.

Milton Meltzer

Langston Hughes

Perhaps because *Langston Hughes; A Biography* (1968) is about a colleague and friend, it has an immediacy and warmth that Meltzer's other biographies do not have. Perhaps it is that the poet himself sheds light and grace. "Within a few years of his first book," Meltzer says, "he was the poet laureate of his people." Hughes's life and work were a testament to his belief that it was a proud thing to be black, his poetry more bittersweet than bitter.

In Topeka, Kansas, he was the only black child in school; he spent some time on his

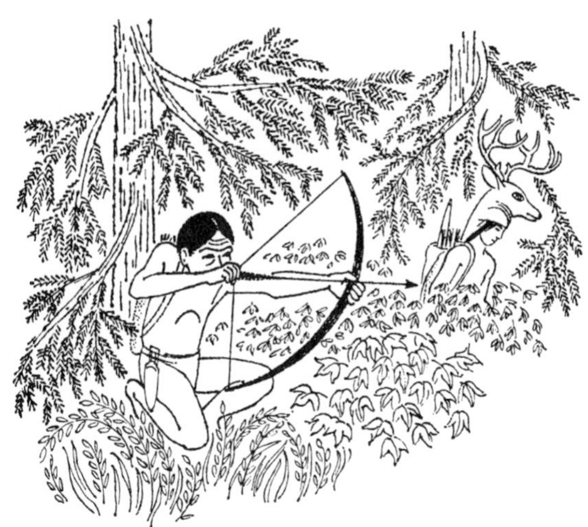

Illustration by Ruth Robbins for Ishi, Last of His Tribe *by T. Kroeber. Copyright 1965. Reproduced by permission of Parnassus Press.*

father's Mexican ranch; he washed dishes in a Paris cafe and worked on a Staten Island truck farm. While working as a waiter in a Washington hotel, he put three of his poems on Vachel Lindsay's table, and that night Lindsay read the poems aloud in public. He went to Spain as a reporter during the Civil War there, and he traveled in Asia and in Russia—in short, he had an exciting and colorful life.

But his travels, his involvement in causes, and his amazingly varied and prolific outpouring of magnificent prose and poetry are almost overshadowed by his passion for truth and justice. That is what Milton Meltzer has succeeded in conveying to the readers of *Langston Hughes*.

The reader will want to explore Hughes's poems, some of which are discussed in the poetry chapters; his short stories, the amusing stories about "Simple," with *The Best of Simple* (1961) comprising selections from earlier books; and his two autobiographical books, *I Wonder as I Wander* (1956, reprinted 1964) and *The Big Sea* (1963).

In an article on the distortions in children's history books, Milton Meltzer says,

> *Biography is another way to re-create the past. The life of a Tom Paine, a Benjamin Banneker, a Sojourner Truth . . . lets the reader see history from inside, from the mind and heart of an individual struggling to reshape his own time. In history books, Wendell Phillips and William Lloyd Garrison are only a paragraph or a line, too often dismissed as irresponsible fanatics. Or there is a glancing reference to that other "fanatic," Thaddeus Stevens, painted darkly in the sky of Washington like some vulture hovering over the capital to pick the bones of Southern heroes ennobled in defeat.*[14]

Meltzer's *Thaddeus Stevens* (1967) destroys this picture and presents a mature and thoughtful biography of the Pennsylvania lawyer whose tenure in the national Congress was marked by bitter opposition from the South, particularly because of his battle against the fugitive slave laws. Thaddeus Stevens was a champion of public education and racial equality, his efforts on behalf of black people's civil rights continuing after the Civil War and through the years of Reconstruction. Meltzer's description of those years and of Stevens's leadership in the move to impeach President Andrew Johnson is direct and vigorous, one of the most valuable aspects of a fine biography that does, indeed, see history from the viewpoint of "an individual struggling to reshape his own time."

Tongue of Flame; The Life of Lydia Maria Child (1965) and *A Light in the Dark; The Life of Samuel Gridley Howe* (1964) are, like the Stevens biography, imbued with enthusiasm for the causes to which the subjects were dedicated, yet they are not eulogistic in tone. Howe was a pioneer in work for the blind and for prison reform, in programs to aid the mentally retarded, and provided help to fugitive slaves. Lydia Child founded the first children's magazine in this country, ran a newspaper, and was a pioneer in the fight against slavery. Meltzer has let their amazing records speak for them, serving their reputations simply by recording their lives.

Other Books for Older Children

By far the greatest number of biographies are written for readers in the upper grades and high school. Many are, of course, read by

[14]Milton Meltzer, "The Fractured Image," *Library Journal*, Oct. 15, 1968, p. 3923.

younger children. It is not possible to include discussion of all the fine books that are available; fortunately reference books in the field of biography make the material easily accessible to readers seeking information about individuals' lives. Here will be added just a few more outstanding biographies to indicate further the scope of the genre.

Margaret Leighton's *Cleopatra; Sister of the Moon* (1969) gives a good picture of the complicated pattern of Mediterranean countries and depicts Cleopatra not as a siren but as an intelligent woman aware of the transitory nature of her power. In Alice Curtis Desmond's *Cleopatra's Children* (1971) the picture of shifting alliances, feuds, and intrigue is even stronger.

Cornelia Spencer writes objectively and authoritatively of one of China's most important figures in *Sun Yat-sen, Founder of the Chinese Republic* (1967). For insight into the China of today, an excellent title is Jules Archer's *Chou En-lai* (1973).

Among the notable biographies of American historical figures are Esther Forbes's *America's Paul Revere* (1946); Edwin P. Hoyt's *William McKinley* (1967), which stresses McKinley's role as an internationalist ahead of his time; and *Andrew Jackson, Soldier and Statesman* (1963) by Ralph K. Andrist, which is profusely illustrated with material from the time, as is the pattern with other American Heritage books.

Ann Petry has told a well-documented story of another famous American in *Harriet Tubman; Conductor on the Underground Railroad* (1955). The dramatic story of this courageous woman is also told in Hildegarde Swift's *Railroad to Freedom* (1932).

One slave who did not escape was Peter Still, who worked all his life to save enough money to buy his freedom. Still's story is told by Peggy Mann in *The Man Who Bought Himself; The Story of Peter Still* (1975).

Fanny Kemble, the great nineteenth-century Shakespearean actress, cared enough about freeing the slaves that it cost her her marriage to Pierce Butler, Jr., the loss of her children, and divorce at a time when divorce was thoroughly disapproved of. Her story is told with vigor by John Anthony Scott in *Fanny Kemble's America* (1973).

Invincible Louisa; The Story of the Author of Little Women (1968) by Cornelia Meigs was first published in 1933 and won the Newbery Medal. It gives a remarkably broad view of the period and of the people in Louisa May Alcott's life as well as a perceptive study of Alcott herself.

The 1969 National Book Award went to Isaac Bashevis Singer for *A Day of Pleasure; Stories of a Boy Growing Up in Warsaw*. Illustrated with photographs of the Singer family and of scenes of Warsaw, the nineteen autobiographical stories, told in delightful style, provide a lively picture of the ghetto community and of the author as a child.

Biography, like many other literary forms, reflects contemporary interests, and so there have been increasing numbers of books about minority group representatives in the United States, about leaders of other countries, and about women. One such is James Terzian and Kathryn Cramer's *Mighty Hard Road; The Story of Cesar Chavez* (1970), which is liberally fictionalized but a good study both of Chavez and of the migrant workers' struggle against exploitation. Another is James Haskins's *Adam Clayton Powell; Portrait of a Marching Black* (1974) which presents a very human picture of the flamboyant black leader.

Virginia Hamilton's *Paul Robeson; The Life and Times of a Free Black Man* (1974) is a moving biography of the great black artist whose political views caused him so much trouble.

Until recently almost all books about Native Americans focused on tribal chiefs, but in recent years authors have begun to give us the stories of lesser known figures. Among the best of these are Margaret Crary's *Susette La Flesche; Voice of the Omaha Indians* (1973), which tells the story of a courageous woman who fought against nineteenth-century injustices perpetrated against the Poncas, and Patrick Des Jarlait's autobiography *Patrick Des Jarlait; The Story of an American Indian Artist* (1975), which is enhanced by examples of Des Jarlait's brilliant watercolors.

At every level of writing for children, but most particularly for those of junior high school age and up, biographers have made great strides in presenting human portraits of the people being written about. Authors, publishers, librarians, teachers, and parents have come to understand that protecting children from knowledge of the human foibles of a person is giving them less than the truth. Children have a right to the truth, the whole truth, so that they may understand more clearly the men and women about whom they are reading.

Adult References[15]

ALTICK, RICHARD D. *Lives and Letters; A History of Literary Biography in England and America.*

BERRY, THOMAS ELLIOTT, ed. *The Biographer's Craft.*

BOWEN, CATHERINE DRINKER. *Biography; The Craft and the Calling.*

CLIFFORD, JAMES L. *From Puzzles to Portraits; Problems of a Literary Biographer.*

_____, ed. *Biography as an Art.*

CRAVEN, PAUL R. *Biography.*

FISHER, MARGERY. *Matters of Fact.* Chapter 4, "Biography."

HOTCHKISS, JEANETTE, comp. *American Historical Fiction and Biography for Children and Young People.*

_____, comp. *European Historical Fiction and Biography for Children and Young People.*

NICHOLSEN, MARGARET. *People in Books; A Selective Guide to Biographical Literature Arranged by Vocations and Other Fields of Reader Interest.*

SILVERMAN, JUDITH. *An Index to Young Readers' Collective Biographies.*

STANIUS, ELLEN, comp. *Index to Short Biographies; For Elementary and Junior High Grades.*

In the following bibliography these symbols have been used to identify books about a religious or a particular ethnic group:

§ Black
★ Chicano or Puerto Rican
☆ Native American
● Religious minority

Collective Biographies

§ ALEXANDER, RAE PACE, comp. *Young and Black in America.* Random, 1970. Well-known black men and women describe the problems they encountered in their youth. 11 up

§● ASIMOV, ISAAC. *Breakthroughs in Science,* ill. by Karoly and Szanto. Houghton, 1960. 11 up

BAKELESS, KATHERINE. *Story-Lives of American Composers,* rev. ed. Lippincott, 1962.

_____. *Story-Lives of Great Composers,* rev. ed. Lippincott, 1962.

For each collection, nineteen composers have been selected. 12-15

● BEARD, ANNIE E. S. *Our Foreign-Born Citizens,* 6th ed. T. Crowell, 1968. Short biographies of Americans of foreign birth or parentage. 10-14

BEARD, CHARLES AUSTIN. *The Presidents in American History,* rev. ed. Messner, 1974. Offers good historical background for each Presidential career. 12-16

BENÉT, LAURA. *Famous American Poets,* ill. with photos. Dodd, 1950. Over twenty poets both recent and past are introduced in brief biographies. 11-14

§ BONTEMPS, ARNA. *Famous Negro Athletes.* Dodd, 1964. Short sketches include personal and career information. 10-12

§● BUCKMASTER, HENRIETTA. *Women Who Shaped History.* Macmillan, 1966. A fine collective biography of Dorothea Dix, Prudence Crandall, Elizabeth Stanton, Harriet Tubman, and Mary Baker Eddy. 12-15

§● COHEN, TOM. *Three Who Dared.* Doubleday, 1969. Three young men who risked their safety to help bring civil rights to southern black people. 11-14

COY, HAROLD. *The First Book of Presidents,* rev. ed., ill. by Manning Lee. Watts, 1973. A useful ready reference source. 8-10

CRAWFORD, DEBORAH. *Four Women in a Violent Time.* Crown, 1970. Mary Dyer, Anne Hutchinson, Penelope Van Princes, and Deborah Moody fought for personal liberty in colonial times. 11-14

DAUGHERTY, SONIA. *Ten Brave Men,* ill. by James Daugherty. Lippincott, 1951. Good accounts of such national heroes as Roger Williams, Patrick Henry, Thomas Jefferson, and Andrew Jackson.

_____. *Ten Brave Women,* ill. by James Daugherty. Lippincott, 1953. 11-15

§ DOBLER, LAVINIA, and WILLIAM A. BROWN. *Great Rulers of the African Past,* ill. by Yvonne Johnson. Doubleday, 1965. Five brief biographies of rulers of African kingdoms during the years 1312–1617. 10-13

DUNSHEATH, PERCY. *Giants of Electricity.* T. Crowell, 1967. Useful both for its biographical and scientific information. 12 up

FANNING, LEONARD M. *Fathers of Industries.* Lippincott, 1962. Emphasis is on men who from industrial revolution days to the present have contributed significantly to inventions having social and economic significance. 12 up

FISHER, AILEEN, and OLIVE RABE. *We Alcotts,* ill. by Ellen Raskin. Atheneum, 1968. 11-14

FREEDMAN, RUSSELL. *Teen-Agers Who Made History.* Holiday, 1961. Stories of eight famous people of the past and present who became eminent in their careers before the age of twenty. 12-14

§ HASKINS, JAMES. *A Piece of the Power; Four Black Mayors.* Dial, 1972. Getting elected is not a guarantee of power or support as these black leaders discovered. 12-15

HIRSHBERG, AL. *The Greatest American Leaguers.* Putnam, 1970. Typical of many such sports biographies, this is breezy and anecdotal. 10-14

JOHNSTON JOHANNA. *Women Themselves,* ill. by Deanne Hollinger. Dodd, 1973. Brief biographical descriptions of fourteen women. 9-12

§ JONES, HETTIE. *Big Star Fallin' Mama; Five Women in Black Music.* Viking, 1974. Good view of popular music through the lives of Ma Rainey, Bessie Smith, Mahalia Jackson, Billie Holiday, and Aretha Franklin. 12 up

KENNEDY, JOHN. *Profiles in Courage,* Young Readers Memorial ed. abr. Harper, 1964. The Pulitzer Prize was awarded this compilation of stories of men who took courageous stands in some decisive moments

[15]Complete bibliographic data are provided in the combined Adult References in the Appendixes.

in our history. 10-12

§ KENWORTHY, LEONARD, and ERMA FERRARI. *Leaders of New Nations,* ill. by Michael Lowenbein. Doubleday, 1968. Revised edition of 1959 title, with four new leaders added and older material brought up to date. 12 up

LEVY, ELIZABETH. *Lawyers for the People; A New Breed of Defenders and Their Work.* Knopf, 1974. An exciting overview of the lawyers working to defend the public. 11-15

§ McNEER, MAY, and LYND WARD. *Armed with Courage,* ill. by Lynd Ward. Abingdon, 1957. Brief, entertaining biographies of seven dedicated men and women: Florence Nightingale, Father Damien, George W. Carver, Jane Addams, Wilfred Grenfell, Gandhi, and Albert Schweitzer. 9-12

§ MITCHISON, NAOMI. *African Heroes,* ill. by William Stobbs. Farrar, 1969. Eleven tales of great Africans from the sub-Sahara, told in the fluent prose of a storyteller. Much history is included, but the book's impact lies in the richness and dignity of the people and their complex traditions. 12 up

MONTGOMERY, ELIZABETH RIDER. *The Story Behind Great Stories,* ill. by Elinore Blaisdell. Dodd, 1947.

______. *The Story Behind Modern Books.* Dodd, 1949. Short sketches about authors and illustrators of children's books, both classic and recent. 11 up

ORR, FRANK. *Hockey's Greatest Stars.* Putnam, 1970. A Canadian sportswriter gives a lively and informative account of twenty-odd outstanding players. 10-13

§ RICHARDSON, BEN. *Great American Negroes,* rev. by William A. Fahey, ill. by Robert Hallock. T. Crowell, 1956. Vivid accounts of twenty black people who have overcome obstacles and who have contributed to American culture in many fields. 12-16

§ ROLLINS, CHARLEMAE HILL. *They Showed the Way; American Negro Leaders.* T. Crowell, 1964. Each life story is very brief, but the book is valuable for information about black leaders not available elsewhere. Other Rollins biographies are about black poets and black entertainers. 11-14

ROSENBLUM, MORRIS. *Heroes of Mexico.* Fleet, 1970. A survey of emperors, revolutionaries, artists, statesmen, and others who influenced the country's development. 12 up

SABIN, FRANCENE. *Women Who Win,* ill. with photos. Random, 1975. Both amateur and professional athletes are included. 11-14

§ SHOEMAKER, ROBERT H. *The Best in Baseball,* rev. ed. T. Crowell, 1974. From Ty Cobb and Babe Ruth to Cincinnati's Johnny Bench. 10 up

§ STEVENSON, JANET. *Pioneers in Freedom; Adventures in Courage.* Reilly, 1969. Life histories of men and women, slave and free, who had the courage to fight for the truths stated in the Declaration of Independence. 9-11

STODDARD, HOPE. *Famous American Women.* T. Crowell, 1970. An unusually good collective biography, distinguished by a sprightly style, a variety of fields of endeavor, and the evidence of careful research that makes the book a reference source as well as entertaining reading. 11-15

SULLIVAN, GEORGE. *Queens of the Court,* ill. with photos. Dodd, 1974. Brisk, informal portraits of modern tennis greats. 11-14

§ TERKEL, LOUIS. *Giants of Jazz,* ill. with photos. T. Crowell, 1975. A fine overview of jazz musicians and the music they make. 12-16

§ WALKER, GRETA. *Women Today; Ten Profiles.* Hawthorn, 1975. Interesting collection of modern women working in a variety of occupations. 11-14

●§ WEBB, ROBERT. *Heroes of Our Time.* Series 1. Watts, 1964. Followed by companion volumes; Series 4, for example (Watts, 1969), describes influential leaders of their countries and includes Brandt, Dayan, Gandhi, Ho Chi Minh, and others. 11-13

WEINBERG, ARTHUR and LILA. *Some Dissenting Voices; The Story of Six American Dissenters.* World, 1970. Life stories of Steffens, Debs, Darrow, Altgeld, Addams, and Ingersoll, with emphasis on their ideas. 11-15

YOUNG, BOB and JAN. *Liberators of Latin America.* Lothrop, 1970. Eleven biographical sketches are preceded by a chapter giving historical background and a concluding section on the rise of the new republics. 11-14

§ YOUNG, MARGARET B. *Black American Leaders.* Watts, 1969. 10-14

§ ______. *The First Book of American Negroes,* ill. with photos. Watts, 1966. 10-14

Individual Biographies

§ AARON, HENRY LOUIS (1934–)

Burchard, Marshall and Sue. *Henry Aaron; Sports Hero,* rev. ed., ill. with photos. Putnam, 1974. 8-11

Gutman, Bill. *Hank Aaron.* Grosset, 1973. This book about baseball's superstar is useful for slow older readers as well as young readers. 8-10

Young, B. E. *The Picture Story of Hank Aaron,* ill. with photos. Messner, 1974. Emphasis is on Aaron's breaking Babe Ruth's home-run record. 7-10

ADAMS, SAMUEL (1722–1803)

Chidsey, Donald Barr. *The World of Samuel Adams.* Nelson, 1974. An affectionate but not laudatory biography of the querulous patriot. 12-15

Fritz, Jean. *Why Don't You Get a Horse, Sam Adams?* ill. by Trina Schart Hyman. Coward, 1974. 8-10

Richardson, Fayette. *Sam Adams; The Boy Who Became Father of the American Revolution,* ill. by William Sauts Bock. Crown, 1975. 8-10

ADDAMS, JANE (1860–1935)

Meigs, Cornelia Lynde. *Jane Addams; Pioneer for Social Justice.* Little, 1970. The writing has warmth and cohesion and gives a vivid picture of an era in this excellent biography of an important social reformer. 11-15

ALCOTT, LOUISA MAY (1832–1888)

Meigs, Cornelia. *Invincible Louisa.* Little, 1968 (first pub. in 1933). Newbery Medal. 12-14

Papashvily, Helen. *Louisa May Alcott,* ill. by Bea Holmes. Houghton, 1965. 11-14

§ ALDRIDGE, IRA (1807–1867)

Malone, Mary. *Actor in Exile; The Life of Ira Aldridge,* ill. by Eros Keith. Crowell-Collier, 1969. 9-11

ALLEN, ETHAN (1738–1789)

Holbrook, Stewart. *America's Ethan Allen,* ill. by Lynd Ward. Houghton, 1949. Spirited illustrations in color add to the dramatic story of the "Green Mountain Boys" and their fighting leader. 11-15

§ ANDERSON, MARIAN (1902–)

Tobias, Tobi. *Marian Anderson,* ill. by Symeon Shimin. T. Crowell, 1972. 7-9

ANTHONY, SUSAN B. (1820–1906)

Noble, Iris. *Susan B. Anthony.* Messner, 1975. 11-14

§ ARMSTRONG, LOUIS (1900–1971)
Eaton, Jeanette. *Trumpeter's Tale; The Story of Young Louis Armstrong,* ill. by Elton Fax. Morrow, 1955. Good biographical writing, and a good history of the development of jazz. 12-14

ASOKA, EMPEROR OF INDIA (3rd century B.C.)
Lengyel, Emil. *Asoka the Great; India's Royal Missionary.* Watts, 1969. The life of the man who spread Buddhism to India, China, and Japan. This is one of a series, "Immortals of Philosophy and Religion," that includes St. Augustine, Confucius, Martin Luther, Moses Maimonides, and St. Francis. 12 up

BACH, JOHANN SEBASTIAN (1685–1750)
Wheeler, Opal, and Sybil Deucher. *Sebastian Bach; the Boy from Thuringia,* ill. by Mary Greenwalt. Dutton, 1937. An easy, popular introduction to this composer. 9-10

BALBOA, VASCO NÚÑEZ DE (1475–1517)
Syme, Ronald. *Balboa, Finder of the Pacific,* ill. by William Stobbs. Morrow, 1956. Other explorer biographies include *Champlain of the St. Lawrence* (1952), *Henry Hudson* (1955), *Magellan, First Around the World* (1953). 10-12

§ BANNEKER, BENJAMIN (1731–1806)
Graham, Shirley. *Your Most Humble Servant; Story of Benjamin Banneker.* Messner, 1949. 14 up

BARTON, CLARA (1821–1912)
Boylston, Helen Dore. *Clara Barton, Founder of the American Red Cross,* ill. by Paula Hutchison. Random, 1955. Emphasizes Barton's work as a Civil War nurse rather than as the founder of the American Red Cross. 9-12

§ BECKWOURTH, JAMES PIERSON (1798–1867)
Felton, Harold. *Jim Beckwourth; Negro Mountain Man,* ill. with photos and prints of the period and maps. Dodd, 1966. 11-14

BEETHOVEN, LUDWIG VAN (1770–1827)
Wheeler, Opal. *Ludwig Beethoven, and the Chiming Tower Bells,* ill. by Mary Greenwalt. Dutton, 1942. Not a fully candid biography, but appealing to younger children. 9-10

● BERNSTEIN, LEONARD (1918–)
Ewen, David. *Leonard Bernstein; A Biography for Young People.* Chilton, 1960. Story of the notable American composer and conductor. 13 up

§ BETHUNE, MARY McLEOD (1875–1955)
Peare, Catherine Owens. *Mary McLeod Bethune.* Vanguard, 1951. 13-15
Sterne, Emma Gelders. *Mary McLeod Bethune,* ill. by Raymond Lufkin. Knopf, 1957. A substantial biography about the child of a slave-born mother who did so much to advance the education of her people. 12-16

BLACKWELL, ELIZABETH (1821–1910)
Clapp, Patricia. *Dr. Elizabeth; The Story of the First Woman Doctor.* Lothrop, 1974. 11-15

BOLIVAR, SIMON (1783–1830)
Syme, Ronald. *Bolivar the Liberator,* ill. by William Stobbs. Morrow, 1968. 9-12

BOONE, DANIEL (1734–1820)
Brown, John Mason. *Daniel Boone; The Opening of the Wilderness,* ill. by Lee J. Ames. Random, 1952. Fine characterization adds distinction to this biography of the Kentucky pioneer. 12-15
Daugherty, James. *Daniel Boone,* ill. by author. Viking, 1939. Newbery Medal. 12-15
Martin, Patricia Miles. *Daniel Boone,* ill. by Glen Dines. Putnam, 1965. 7-9

BOWDITCH, NATHANIEL (1773–1838)
Latham, Jean Lee. *Carry On, Mr. Bowditch,* ill. by John O'Hara Cosgrave II. Houghton, 1955. Newbery Medal. 11-15

● BRANDEIS, LOUIS (1856–1941)
Peare, Catherine Owens. *The Louis Brandeis Story.* T. Crowell, 1970. 11-13

BRONTË, CHARLOTTE (1816–1855)
Kyle, Elisabeth. *Girl with a Pen; Charlotte Brontë.* Holt, 1964. 12 up
Vipont, Elfrida. *Weaver of Dreams; The Girlhood of Charlotte Brontë.* Walck, 1966. A good biography of Charlotte Brontë, giving a quite absorbing and dramatic picture of the isolated family. Some instances of fairly florid writing and imaginary conversation. 11-14

BUCK, PEARL (1892–1973)
Block, Irving. *The Lives of Pearl Buck; A Tale of China and America.* T. Crowell, 1973. Smoothly written and balanced biography of an amazing woman who was both a talented writer and a compassionate human being. 12 up

§ BUNCHE, RALPH (1904–1971)
Haskins, James. *Ralph Bunche: A Most Reluctant Hero,* ill. with photos. Hawthorn, 1974. 12-16

BUONARROTI, MICHELANGELO (1475–1564)
Coughlan, Robert. *The World of Michelangelo.* Time-Life, 1966. Like other volumes in the magnificent Time-Life Library of Art, this is profusely illustrated with reproductions of the artist's work. 12 up
Ripley, Elizabeth. *Michelangelo.* Walck, 1953. 12-15

CABOT, JOHN (1450–1498)
Hill, Kay. *And Tomorrow the Stars; The Story of John Cabot,* ill. by Laszlo Kubinyi. Dodd, 1968. An excellent biography, convincingly fictionalized and carefully researched, giving vivid pictures of the dream-driven mariner Cabot and of Venice at the zenith of her power. Canadian Library Association Award. 12 up

§ CAMPANELLA, ROY (1921–)
Schoor, Gene. *Roy Campanella; Man of Courage.* Putnam, 1959. A warm life story of the Dodger catcher who fought against crippling injuries. 9-11

CARSON, CHRISTOPHER (1809–1868)
Bell, Margaret E. *Kit Carson, Mountain Man,* ill. by Harry Daugherty. Morrow, 1952. A short dramatic biography with large print and many illustrations. 8-11
Garst, Shannon. *Kit Carson, Trail Blazer and Scout,* ill. by Harry Daugherty. Messner, 1942. 11 up

CARSON, RACHEL (1907–1964)
Sterling, Philip. *Sea and Earth; The Life of Rachel Carson.* T. Crowell, 1970. A beautifully balanced biography, written with skill and restraint. 12 up

§ CARVER, GEORGE WASHINGTON (1864?–1943)
Aliki. *A Weed Is a Flower; The Life of George Washington Carver,* ill. by author. Prentice, 1965. 5-8

CASSATT, MARY (1845–1926)
McKown, Robin. *The World of Mary Cassatt,* ill. with photos. T. Crowell, 1972. A balanced portrait of the artist and the art world in which she worked. 12-16
Wilson, Ellen. *American Painter in Paris; A Life of Mary Cassatt.* Farrar, 1971. Photographs and reproductions of paintings enliven the story of a distinguished artist. 11 up

CATHER, WILLA SIBERT (1873–1947)
Franchere, Ruth. *Willa,* ill. by Leonard Weisgard. T. Crowell, 1958. Willa Cather's pioneer childhood in Nebraska is vividly portrayed, and younger readers unfamiliar with her novels will enjoy the biography as

a good story. 11-14

CATHERINE II, EMPRESS OF RUSSIA (1729–1796)
Noble, Iris. *Empress of All Russia; Catherine the Great.* Messner, 1966. 12-15

● CHAGALL, MARC (1887–)
Greenfeld, Howard. *Marc Chagall.* Follett, 1967. 12-15

§ CHAMBERLAIN, WILT (1936–)
Rudeen, Kenneth. *Wilt Chamberlain,* ill. by Frank Mullins. T. Crowell, 1970. The basketball star is described in a simply written and balanced book. 7-9

CHAPLIN, CHARLES (1889–)
Jacobs, David. *Chaplin, the Movies, and Charlie,* ill. with photos. Harper, 1975. A total picture of the man who gave pleasure to millions as a comic/commentator on our human frailties. 12 up

CHAPMAN, JOHN (1774–1845)
Aliki. *The Story of Johnny Appleseed,* ill. by author. Prentice, 1963. 7-8
Hunt, Mabel Leigh. *Better Known as Johnny Appleseed,* ill. by James Daugherty. Lippincott, 1950. The life of John Chapman, "American pioneer, missionary, and apple lover," based on old legends and reminiscences gathered by the author. 12-16

★ CHAVEZ, CESAR (1928–)
Franchere, Ruth. *Cesar Chavez,* ill. by Earl Thollander. T. Crowell, 1970. 7-9
Terzian, James, and Kathryn Cramer. *Mighty Hard Road; The Story of Cesar Chavez.* Doubleday, 1970. 11-14

CHILD, LYDIA MARIA (1802–1880)
Meltzer, Milton. *Tongue of Flame; The Life of Lydia Maria Child.* T. Crowell, 1965. 13-15

§ CHISHOLM, SHIRLEY (1924–)
Brownmiller, Susan. *Shirley Chisholm,* ill. Doubleday, 1970. 10-14
Haskins, James. *Fighting Shirley Chisholm,* ill. with photos. Dial, 1975. 12-16

CHOU EN-LAI (1898–1976)
Archer, Jules. *Chou En-lai.* Hawthorn, 1973. 12-15

CHUKOVSKY, KORNEI (1882–1969)
Chukovsky, Kornei. *The Silver Crest; My Russian Boyhood,* tr. by Beatrice Stillman. Holt, 1976. A delightful reminiscence by a major Russian writer for children. 11 up

CHURCHILL, SIR WINSTON LEONARD SPENCER (1874–1965)
Coolidge, Olivia. *Winston Churchill and the Story of Two World Wars,* ill. with photos. Houghton, 1960. The twentieth century becomes vividly alive and significant in this story of the great British statesman. 13-16

CLEMENS, SAMUEL LANGHORNE (1835–1910)
Eaton, Jeanette. *America's Own Mark Twain,* ill. by Leonard Everett Fisher. Morrow, 1958. Mississippi riverboat days and life in the West are absorbing highlights of this well-rounded story of one of America's most colorful authors. 12-16
McNeer, May. *America's Mark Twain,* ill. by Lynd Ward. Houghton, 1962. Colorful illustrations and a lively text make this biography attractive to a wide range of readers. 10-14
Wood, James Playsted. *Spunkwater, Spunkwater! A Life of Mark Twain,* ill. with photos. Pantheon, 1968. 11-15

CLEOPATRA, QUEEN OF EGYPT (69–30 B.C.)
Desmond, Alice Curtis. *Cleopatra's Children,* ill. with maps, charts, and photos. Dodd, 1971. 11-14
Leighton, Margaret. *Cleopatra; Sister of the Moon.* Farrar, 1969. 12-15

CODY, WILLIAM (BUFFALO BILL) (1846–1917)
d'Aulaire, Ingri and Edgar Parin. *Buffalo Bill,* ill. by authors. Doubleday, 1952. 7-9

COLUMBUS, CHRISTOPHER (1451–1506)
Dalgliesh, Alice. *The Columbus Story,* ill. by Leo Politi. Scribner's, 1955. 8-10
d'Aulaire, Ingri and Edgar Parin. *Columbus,* ill. by authors. Doubleday, 1955. 7-9
Judson, Clara Ingram. *Admiral Christopher Columbus,* ill. by W. T. Mars. Follett, 1965. 10 up
McGovern, Ann. *The Story of Christopher Columbus.* Random, 1963. 7-10
Norman, Gertrude. *A Man Named Columbus,* ill. by James Caraway. Putnam, 1960. 7-8
Sperry, Armstrong. *Voyages of Christopher Columbus,* ill. by author. Random, 1950. 8-10
Syme, Ronald. *Columbus, Finder of the New World,* ill. by William Stobbs. Morrow, 1952. 10-13

CONRAD, JOSEPH (1857–1924)
Gurko, Leo. *The Two Lives of Joseph Conrad.* T. Crowell, 1965. 13 up

COOK, JAMES (1728–1779)
Latham, Jean. *Far Voyager; The Story of James Cook,* maps by Karl W. Stuecklen. Harper, 1970. 10-13
Syme, Ronald. *Captain Cook; Pacific Explorer,* ill. by William Stobbs. Morrow, 1960. The English navigator's eighteenth-century explorations of the South Pacific climax a fast-paced, fully illustrated biography. 10-13

COOPER, PETER (1791–1883)
Gurko, Miriam. *The Lives and Times of Peter Cooper,* ill. by Jerome Snyder, diagrams by Ava Morgan. T. Crowell, 1959. 12 up

CRANDALL, PRUDENCE (1803–1889)
Yates, Elizabeth. *Prudence Crandall; Woman of Courage,* ill. by Nora S. Unwin. Aladdin, 1955. 12-15

☆ CRAZY HORSE, OGLALA CHIEF (1842?–1877)
Garst, Doris Shannon. *Crazy Horse, Great Warrior of the Sioux,* ill. by William Moyers. Houghton, 1950. This biography gives good perspective on why the Indians so bitterly opposed the white men. 12-15
Meadowcroft, Enid. *The Story of Crazy Horse,* ill. by William Reusswig. Grosset, 1954. Biography of the Oglala chief who opposed Custer and who died escaping imprisonment. 9-12

DAMIEN, FATHER (1840–1889)
Roos, Ann. *Man of Molokai; The Life of Father Damien,* ill. by Raymond Lufkin. Lippincott, 1943. Moving story of a great modern saint who spent his life in the service of lepers. 11-14

DARROW, CLARENCE (1857–1938)
Faber, Doris. *Clarence Darrow; Defender of the People,* ill. by Paul Frame. Prentice, 1965. A balanced and objective book. 10-12
Gurko, Miriam. *Clarence Darrow.* T. Crowell, 1965. 13 up

● DAVID, KING OF ISRAEL
Bolliger, Max. *David,* ill. by Edith Schindler. Delacorte, 1967. The life of David up to the point of his becoming King of Israel. 9-12

DA VINCI, LEONARDO (1452–1519)
Noble, Iris. *Leonardo da Vinci; The Universal Genius,* ill. Norton, 1965. Despite a considerable amount of fictionalization, the painter comes alive as a distinctive personality. 11-14

DEBS, EUGENE VICTOR (1855–1926)
Noble, Iris. *Labor's Advocate; Eugene V. Debs.* Messner, 1966. Portrays the movements in which Debs

was a pioneer. 11-14

§ DELANY, MARTIN ROBISON (1812-1885)
Sterling, Dorothy. *The Making of an Afro-American; Martin Robison Delany 1812-1885.* Doubleday, 1971. 11 up

☆ DES JARLAIT, PATRICK (1921-1972)
Des Jarlait, Patrick. *Patrick Des Jarlait; The Story of an American Indian Artist,* as told to Neva Williams. Lerner, 1975. 11-14

DICKENS, CHARLES (1812-1870)
Kyle, Elisabeth. *Great Ambitions; A Story of the Early Years of Charles Dickens.* Holt, 1968. 12-15

DICKINSON, EMILY (1830-1886)
Fisher, Aileen, and Olive Rabe. *We Dickinsons; The Life of Emily Dickinson as Seen Through the Eyes of Her Brother Austin,* ill. by Ellen Raskin. Atheneum, 1965. 12-15
Longsworth, Polly. *Emily Dickinson; Her Letter to the World.* T. Crowell, 1965. 13 up

§ DOUGLASS, FREDERICK (1817?-1895)
Douglass, Frederick. *Life and Times of Frederick Douglass,* ad. by Barbara Ritchie. T. Crowell, 1966. First published in 1842 and last revised by the author in 1892. This is a very good adaptation with no deletion of important material. 11-15
Graham, Shirley. *There Was Once a Slave; The Heroic Story of Frederick Douglass.* Messner, 1947. 12 up

§ DREW, CHARLES RICHARD (1904-1950)
Bertol, Roland. *Charles Drew,* ill. by Jo Polseno. T. Crowell, 1970. First director of the Red Cross Blood Bank, the distinguished black doctor fought prejudice throughout his life. 7-9

§ DuBOIS, W. E. B. (1868-1963)
Hamilton, Virginia. *W. E. B. DuBois; A Biography,* ill. with photos. T. Crowell, 1972. 12-16
Lacy, Leslie Alexander. *Cheer the Lonesome Traveler; The Life of W. E. B. DuBois,* ill. by James Barkley and with photos. Dial, 1970. An excellent biography for young people of one of the most eminent black American leaders. The writing style is brisk, competent, and dispassionate. 12-15

§ DUNBAR, PAUL LAURENCE (1872-1906)
Gayle, Addison. *Oak and Ivy; A Biography of Paul Laurence Dunbar.* Doubleday, 1971. A candid account of the black writer. 11-14

EDISON, THOMAS ALVA (1847-1931)
North, Sterling. *Young Thomas Edison,* ill. by William Barss. Houghton, 1958. Outstanding biography of Edison both as a man and as an inventive genius. 11-15

ELEANOR OF AQUITAINE (1122?-1204)
Konigsburg, Elaine. *A Proud Taste for Scarlet and Miniver,* ill. by author. Atheneum, 1973. Not quite biography, something more than historical fiction, this is a delightful look at Eleanor, Henry II, and the people surrounding them. 12-16

ELIZABETH I, QUEEN OF ENGLAND (1533-1603)
Hanff, Helene. *Queen of England; The Story of Elizabeth I,* ill. by Ronald Dorgman. Doubleday, 1969. 10-13
Vance, Marguerite. *Elizabeth Tudor, Sovereign Lady,* ill. by Nedda Walker. Dutton, 1954. This story is sympathetically and dramatically told and should be a stimulus to further historical reading. 12-15

ERICSSON, JOHN (1803-1889)
Burnett, Constance Buel. *Captain John Ericsson; Father of the "Monitor."* Vanguard, 1961. Failure as well as success marked the life of the Swedish-born genius. 12-16

ERIKSSON, LEIF (b. tenth century)
Shippen, Katherine. *Leif Eriksson; First Voyager to America.* Harper, 1951. Well-written, exciting biography of the explorer of Vinland. 11-13

ESPOSITO, PHILLIP (1942-)
Burchard, Marshall and Sue. *Phil Esposito; Sports Hero.* ill with photos. Putnam, 1975. 8-11

FIELD, CYRUS (1819-1892)
Latham, Jean-Lee. *Young Man in a Hurry; The Story of Cyrus Field,* ill. by Victor Mays. Harper, 1958. An account of the laying of the Atlantic cable and of the unconquerable Cyrus Field. 12 up

FITZGERALD, F. SCOTT (1896-1940)
Greenfeld, Howard. *F. Scott Fitzgerald.* Crown, 1974. 12-15

§ FORTEN, CHARLOTTE (1838-1914)
Douty, Esther M. *Charlotte Forten; Free Black Teacher.* Garrard, 1971. 9-11
Longsworth, Polly. *I, Charlotte Forten, Black and Free.* T. Crowell, 1970 11-14

§ FORTEN, JAMES (1766-1842)
Douty, Esther M. *Forten the Sailmaker; Pioneer Champion of Negro Rights,* ill. with photos. Rand, 1968. 12-15

§ FORTUNE, AMOS (1709?-1801)
Yates, Elizabeth. *Amos Fortune, Free Man,* ill. by Nora S. Unwin. Dutton, 1950. Newbery Medal. 10-13

FRANCIS OF ASSISI, SAINT (1182-1226)
Bulla, Clyde. *Song of St. Francis,* ill. by Valenti Angelo. T. Crowell, 1952. The appealing story of St. Francis of Assisi presented in simple fashion for younger readers. 8-10

FRANKLIN, BENJAMIN (1706-1790)
Daugherty, Charles Michael. *Benjamin Franklin; Scientist-Diplomat,* ill. by John Falter. Macmillan, 1965. This very simple biography gives a quite adequate biographical outline. Barely fictionalized and not condescending. 8-10
Daugherty, James. *Poor Richard,* ill. by author. Viking, 1941. 12-15
d'Aulaire, Ingri and Edgar Parin. *Benjamin Franklin,* ill. by authors. Doubleday, 1950. 7-9
Eaton, Jeanette. *That Lively Man, Ben Franklin,* ill. by Henry C. Pitz. Morrow, 1948. Franklin's many-sided career, from printer to ambassador. 11-14
Fleming, Thomas J. *Benjamin Franklin.* Four Winds, 1973. Insightful and witty with information not found in most other juvenile biographies. 11-14
Fritz, Jean. *What's the Big Idea, Ben Franklin?* ill. by Margot Tomes. Coward, 1976. Breezy, but balanced and authoritative. 8-10
Merriam, Eve. *The Story of Ben Franklin,* ill. by Brinton Turkle. Four Winds, 1965. 7-9
Scarf, Maggi. *Meet Benjamin Franklin,* ill. by Harry Beckhoff. Random, 1968. 7-11

§ FREEMAN, ELIZABETH (1744?-1829)
Felton, Harold W. *Mumbet; The Story of Elizabeth Freeman,* ill. by Donn Albright. Dodd, 1970. 9-11

FULLER, RICHARD BUCKMINSTER (1895-)
Rosen, Sidney. *Wizard of the Dome; R. Buckminster Fuller, Designer for the Future.* Little, 1969. 12 up

FULTON, ROBERT (1765-1815)
Judson, Clara Ingram. *Boat Builder; The Story of Robert Fulton,* ill. by Armstrong Sperry. Scribner's, 1940. 9-11

GALILEI, GALILEO (1564-1642)
Bixby, William, and the editors of *Horizon* Magazine, in consultation with Georgio De Santillana. *The Universe of Galileo and Newton,* ill. American

Heritage, 1964. A most impressive dual biography, beautifully illustrated and written in a lively style. The scientific material is authoritative. 13 up

Rosen, Sidney. *Galileo and the Magic Numbers,* ill. by Harve Stein. Little, 1958. 12 up

GANDHI, MOHANDAS K. (1869–1948)

Coolidge, Olivia. *Gandhi.* Houghton, 1971. 11-14

Eaton, Jeanette. *Gandhi; Fighter Without a Sword,* ill. by Ralph Ray. Morrow, 1950. 13-15

Peare, Catherine Owens, *Mahatma Gandhi; Father of Non-violence.* Hawthorne, 1969. 12 up

GANNETT, DEBORAH (SAMPSON) (1760–1827)

McGovern, Ann. *The Secret Soldier; The Story of Deborah Sampson,* ill. by Ann Grifalconi. Four Winds, 1975. A simply written account of the woman who donned men's clothing to serve in the Continental Army. 8-10

GARIBALDI, GIUSEPPE (1807–1882)

Syme, Ronald. *Garibaldi; The Man Who Made a Nation,* ill. by William Stobbs. Morrow, 1967. 11-14

GARRISON, WILLIAM LLOYD (1805–1879)

Archer, Jules. *Angry Abolitionist; William Lloyd Garrison.* Messner, 1969. 12 up

Faber, Doris. *I Will Be Heard; The Life of William Lloyd Garrison.* Lothrop, 1970. 9-12

GAUTIER, FELISA RINCON DE (1897–)

Gruber, Ruth. *Felisa Rincon de Gautier; The Mayor of San Juan,* ill. with photos. T. Crowell, 1972. A biography that combines Puerto Rican history with the life of an amazing woman. 11-14

☆ GERONIMO, APACHE CHIEF (1829–1909)

Wyatt, Edgar. *Geronimo, the Last Apache War Chief,* ill. by Allan Houser. Whittlesey, 1952. The story of a great Indian hero. 11-14

● GERSHWIN, GEORGE (1898–1937)

Ewen, David. *The Story of George Gershwin,* ill. by Graham Bernbach. Holt, 1943. Memories of an American composer of popular music by a personal friend. 12-16

GOGH, VINCENT VAN (1853–1890)

Dobrin, Arnold. *I Am a Stranger on the Earth; The Story of Vincent Van Gogh,* ill. with reproductions. Warne, 1975. Effectively conveys the essence of Van Gogh's personality and the reproductions convey the essence of his work. 10-12

GRAHAM, MARTHA (1894–)

Terry, Walter. *Frontiers of Dance; The Life of Martha Graham,* ill. with photos. T. Crowell, 1975. A nice combination of objectivity and affection makes the great dancer real as both artist and person. 11 up

GREELEY, HORACE (1811–1872)

Faber, Doris. *Horace Greeley; The People's Editor,* ill. by Paul Frame. Prentice, 1964. 9-12

GRIEG, EDVARD (1843–1907)

Kyle, Elisabeth. *Song of the Waterfall; The Story of Edvard and Nina Grieg.* Holt, 1970. Also gives a good picture of life in nineteenth-century Norway. 10-12

GUION, CONNIE M. (1882–1971)

Campion, Nardi Reeder, with Rosamond Wilfley Stanton. *Look to This Day!* ill. with photos. Little, 1965. A long, lively biography of Dr. Connie Guion, a famous physician and delightful character. Her story gives interesting glimpses of the beginnings of higher education for women. 12-15

HAMILTON, ALICE (1869–1970)

Grant, Madeleine P. *Alice Hamilton; Pioneer Doctor in Industrial Medicine.* Abelard, 1968. The inspiring story of a woman whose career encompassed both science and social reform. 12-14

HANCOCK, JOHN (1737–1793)

Fritz, Jean. *Will You Sign Here, John Hancock?* ill. by Trina Schart Hyman. Coward, 1976. An amusing but accurate biography of a signer of the Declaration of Independence, and president of the Continental Congress. 8-10

● HAUTZIG, ESTHER

Hautzig, Esther. *The Endless Steppe; Growing Up in Siberia.* T. Crowell, 1968. The true and harrowing story of five arduous years spent by Esther and her family in forced labor in Siberia, all the more effective because it is told with direct simplicity and no bitterness. 11-15

HEMINGWAY, ERNEST (1899–1961)

Gurko, Leo. *Ernest Hemingway and the Pursuit of Heroism.* T. Crowell, 1968. 14 up

HENRY, PATRICK (1736–1799)

Campion, Nardi Reeder. *Patrick Henry; Firebrand of the Revolution,* ill. by Victor Mays. Little, 1961. 12 up

Fritz, Jean. *Where Was Patrick Henry on the 29th of May?* ill. by Margot Tomes. Coward, 1975. 8-10

HERSCHEL, SIR WILLIAM (1738–1822)

Crawford, Deborah. *The King's Astronomer; William Herschel.* Messner, 1968. Although highly fictionalized, the dialogue uses language that seems so right for the period that it is an asset to the book. A good balance of personal and scientific material. 11-14

HITLER, ADOLF (1889–1945)

Shirer, William L. *The Rise and Fall of Adolf Hitler,* ill. with photos. Random, 1961. In this biography of the Nazi dictator, emphasis is on political events, stirringly recorded for younger readers. 11-14

HOKUSAI (1760–1849)

Ripley, Elizabeth. *Hokusai.* Lippincott, 1968. 11-14

● HOOVER, HERBERT CLARK (1874–1964)

Peare, Catherine Owens. *The Herbert Hoover Story.* T. Crowell, 1965. 11-14

HOUSTON, SAM (1793–1863)

James, Bessie and Marquis. *Six Feet Six.* Bobbs, 1931. 10-12

HOWE, SAMUEL GRIDLEY (1801–1876)

Meltzer, Milton. *A Light in the Dark; The Life of Samuel Gridley Howe.* T. Crowell, 1964. 12-15

§ HUGHES, JAMES LANGSTON (1902–1967)

Meltzer, Milton. *Langston Hughes; A Biography.* T. Crowell, 1968. 12 up

Walker, Alice. *Langston Hughes, American Poet,* ill. by Don Miller. T. Crowell, 1974. 7-9

HUMBOLDT, ALEXANDER, FREIHERR VON (1769–1859)

Thomas, M Z. (pseud.). *Alexander von Humboldt,* tr. by Elizabeth Brommer, ill. by Ulrik Schramm. Pantheon, 1960. Von Humboldt's adventures in the South American jungles are vivid and unforgettable in this life story of the explorer-naturalist. 11-15

☆ ISHI (d. 1916)

Kroeber, Theodora. *Ishi; Last of His Tribe,* ill. by Ruth Robbins. Parnassus, 1964. 12 up

JACKSON, ANDREW (1767–1845)

Coit, Margaret L. *Andrew Jackson,* ill. by Milton Johnson. Houghton, 1965. A perceptive biography, not adulatory but candid about the deficiencies that made Jackson so controversial a figure. 12-15

De Kay, Ormonde. *Meet Andrew Jackson,* ill. by Isa Barnett. Random, 1967. 7-9

Remini, Robert. *The Revolutionary Age of Andrew Jackson.* Harper, 1976. A vigorous and authoritative presentation. 12 up

§ JACKSON, MAHALIA (1911–1972)
Jackson, Jesse. *Make a Joyful Noise Unto the Lord! The Life of Mahalia Jackson, Queen of Gospel Singers,* ill. with photos. T. Crowell, 1974. Excellent biography of a woman of courage, vitality, and integrity. 11-14

JEFFERSON, THOMAS (1743–1826)
Fleming, Thomas J. *Thomas Jefferson.* Grosset, 1971. 11-14
Lisitzky, Gene. *Thomas Jefferson,* ill. by Harrie Wood. Viking, 1933. A well-balanced picture of the many facets of this complex man. 12-16
Wibberley, Leonard. *Man of Liberty; A Life of Thomas Jefferson.* Farrar, 1968.

JOAN OF ARC, SAINT (1412–1431)
Churchill, Winston. *Joan of Arc; Her Life as Told by Winston Churchill,* ill. by Lauren Ford. Dodd, 1969. 8 up
Fisher, Aileen. *Jeanne d'Arc,* ill. by Ati Forberg. T. Crowell, 1970. 8-10
Paine, Albert. *The Girl in White Armor,* ill. by Joe Isom. Macmillan, 1967 (first pub. in 1927). 11-14

§ JOHNSON, JAMES WELDON (1871–1938)
Egypt, Ophelia Settle. *James Weldon Johnson,* ill. by Moneta Barnett. T. Crowell, 1974. 8-10

JONES, JOHN PAUL (1747–1792)
Sperry, Armstrong. *John Paul Jones; Fighting Sailor,* ill. by author. Random, 1953. The life of the naval hero who suffered ingratitude and injustice throughout his career. 10-13

☆ JOSEPH, NEZ PERCÉ CHIEF (1840–1904)
Davis, Russell, and Brent Ashabranner. *Chief Joseph, War Chief of the Nez Percé.* McGraw, 1962. The tragic story of a peace-loving chief forced into war as his people opposed the westward movement. 12-16

KEMBLE, FRANCES ANN (1809–1893)
Scott, John Anthony. *Fanny Kemble's America.* T. Crowell, 1973. 12-16

KING, BILLIE JEAN (1943–)
Burchard, Marshall and Sue. *Sports Hero: Billie Jean King,* rev. ed., ill. with photos. Putnam, 1975. 8-11

§ KING, MARTIN LUTHER, JR. (1929–1968)
Clayton, Ed. *Martin Luther King; The Peaceful Warrior,* ill. by David Hodges. Prentice, 1964. 9-11
De Kay, James T. *Meet Martin Luther King, Jr.,* ill. with photos and drawings by Ted Burwell. Random, 1969. 7-9
Patterson, Lillie. *Martin Luther King, Jr.; Man of Peace,* ill. by Victor Mays. Garrard, 1969. 8-9
Young, Margaret B. *The Picture Life of Martin Luther King, Jr.,* ill. with photos. Watts, 1968. 7-8

LAFAYETTE, MARIE JOSEPH PAUL YVES ROCH GILBERT DU MOTIER, MARQUIS DE (1757–1834)
Eaton, Jeanette. *Young Lafayette,* ill. by David Hendrickson. Houghton, 1932. 12-16
Gottschalk, Fruma. *The Youngest General; A Story of Lafayette,* ill. by Rafaello Busoni. Knopf, 1949. The author had access to unusual original sources in writing this life of Lafayette. 10-14

☆ LA FLESCHE, SUSETTE (1854–1903)
Crary, Margaret. *Susette La Flesche; Voice of the Omaha Indians.* Hawthorn, 1973. 11-14

LAWRENCE, THOMAS EDWARD (1888–1935)
MacLean, Alistair. *Lawrence of Arabia.* Random, 1962. The absorbingly told life story of the great military leader in the Arab-Turkish revolt. 11-14

LAWSON, ROBERT (1892–1957)
Jones, Helen L., ed. *Robert Lawson, Illustrator,* ill. Little, 1972. Lawson's illustrations and his editor's commentary should interest students of children's literature as well as young readers who have enjoyed his books. 10 up

LEE, ROBERT EDWARD (1807–1870)
Commager, Henry Steele. *America's Robert E. Lee,* ill. by Lynd Ward. Houghton, 1951. Lee is a hero all America should be proud of, and this biography shows why. 11-15

LILIUOKALANI, QUEEN OF THE HAWAIIAN ISLANDS (1838–1917)
Wilson, Hazel. *The Last Queen of Hawaii; Liliuokalani,* ill. by W. T. Mars. Knopf, 1963. Includes some Hawaiian history. 11-14

LINCOLN, ABRAHAM (1809–1865)
Bulla, Clyde. *Lincoln's Birthday,* ill. by Ernest Crichlow. T. Crowell, 1966. 8-9
Coolidge, Olivia. *The Apprenticeship of Abraham Lincoln.* Scribner's, 1974. A serious study for older readers describing the first fifty years of Lincoln's life. 13 up
Daugherty, James. *Abraham Lincoln,* ill. by author. Viking, 1943. 12-15
d'Aulaire, Ingri and Edgar Parin. *Abraham Lincoln,* ill. by authors. Doubleday, 1939. Caldecott Medal. 12-14
Fisher, Aileen. *My Cousin Abe,* ill. by Leonard Vosburgh. Nelson, 1962. Dennis Hanks tells the story of his younger relative with the warmth and tenderness inspired by the close family relationship. Although introducing a narrator, the author faithfully follows the details of Lincoln's life. 11-15
Foster, Genevieve. *Abraham Lincoln; An Initial Biography,* ill. by author. Scribner's, 1950.
Hays, Wilma P. *Abe Lincoln's Birthday,* ill. by Peter Burchard. Coward, 1961. 7-10
Judson, Clara Ingram. *Abraham Lincoln,* ill. by Polly Jackson. Follett, 1961. 7-9
______. *Abraham Lincoln, Friend of the People,* ill. by Robert Frankenberg and with photos. Follett, 1950. 11-15
Monjo, Ferdinand N. *Me and Willie and Pa,* ill. by Douglas Gorsline. Simon, 1973. 8-10
Phelan, Mary Kay. *Mr. Lincoln's Inaugural Journey,* ill. by Richard Cuffari. T. Crowell, 1972. Lincoln's leisurely trip from Springfield to Washington, D.C., is suspense laden, even if most readers know the assassination plot was not successful. 10-12
Sandburg, Carl. *Abe Lincoln Grows Up,* ill. by James Daugherty. Harcourt, 1928. 11-16

LINCOLN, MARY TODD (1818–1882)
Randall, Ruth Painter. *I Mary,* ill. with photos. Little, 1959. A sincere and honest biography of Mary Todd Lincoln which helps to dispel some of the unhappy legends associated with her life. 12-16

LINDBERGH, CHARLES (1902–1974)
Dalgliesh, Alice. *Ride on the Wind,* ill. by Georges Schreiber. Scribner's, 1956. 7-9

LONDON, JACK (1876–1916)
Franchere, Ruth. *Jack London; The Pursuit of a Dream.* T. Crowell, 1962. The author has skillfully conveyed the poverty, the rough adventurous life, and the taste of glory achieved by London in his brief forty years, without emphasizing the details more suited to an adult biography. 12 up

§ LOVE, NAT (1854?–1921?)
Felton, Harold W. *Nat Love, Negro Cowboy,* ill. by David Hodges. Dodd, 1969. Gives a lively picture of the Old West. 9-10

LUTHER, MARTIN (1483–1546)
Fosdick, Harry Emerson. *Martin Luther,* ill. by Steele Savage. Random, 1956. Written by one of the best-known Protestant ministers, this is a thoughtful biography of the great reformer. 12-16
McNeer, May. *Martin Luther,* ill. by Lynd Ward. Abingdon, 1953. The fighting spirit of Martin Luther makes his life story both difficult and thrilling. Superb illustrations add distinction to this book. 12-14

McKINLEY, WILLIAM (1843–1901)
Hoyt, Edwin P. *William McKinley.* Reilly, 1967. 13-15

§ MALCOLM X (1925–1965)
Adoff, Arnold. *Malcolm X,* ill. by John Wilson. T. Crowell, 1970. 8-10
Curtis, Richard. *The Life of Malcolm X.* Macrae, 1971. 11-15
Haskins, James. *The Picture Life of Malcolm X,* ill. Watts, 1975. 8-10

§ MARSHALL, THURGOOD (1908–)
Young, Margaret B. *The Picture Life of Thurgood Marshall.* Watts, 1971. 8-10

§ MARTIN DE PORRES, SAINT (1579–1639)
Bishop, Claire Huchet. *Martin de Porres, Hero,* ill. by Jean Charlot. Houghton, 1954. 12-14

MATHER, COTTON (1663–1728)
Wood, James Playsted. *The Admirable Cotton Mather,* Seabury, 1971. 13 up

MAURY, MATTHEW FONTAINE (1806–1873)
Latham, Jean Lee. *Trail Blazer of the Seas,* ill. by Victor Mays. Houghton, 1956. Absorbing story of the scientific U.S. Naval Lieutenant Matthew Fontaine Maury, who studied winds and currents to reduce ships' sailing time. 11-15

● MEIR, GOLDA (1898–)
Dobrin, Arnold. *A Life for Israel; The Story of Golda Meir.* Dial, 1974. 9-12

MICHELANGELO. See BUONARROTI, MICHELANGELO.

MILLAY, EDNA ST. VINCENT (1892–1950)
Gurko, Miriam. *Restless Spirit; The Life of Edna St. Vincent Millay.* T. Crowell, 1962. 13 up
Shafter, Toby. *Edna St. Vincent Millay; America's Best-Loved Poet.* Messner, 1957. 12 up

§ MITCHELL, ARTHUR (1934-)
Tobias, Tobi. *Arthur Mitchell,* ill. by Carole Byard. T. Crowell, 1975. 8-10

MOZART, JOHANN CHRYSOSTOM WOLFGANG AMADEUS (1756–1791)
Komroff, Manuel. *Mozart,* ill. by Warren Chappell and with photos. Knopf, 1956. Written to commemorate the two-hundredth anniversary of Mozart's birth, this is an outstanding biography. 11-15
Monjo, Ferdinand N. *Letters to Horseface; Being the Story of Wolfgang Amadeus Mozart's Journey to Italy 1769-1770 When He Was a Boy of Fourteen,* ill. by Don Bolognese and Elaine Raphael. Viking, 1975. 10-12
Wheeler, Opal, and Sybil Deucher. *Mozart, the Wonder Boy,* ill. by Mary Greenwalt. Dutton, 1934. A simply written account. 9-10

MUIR, JOHN (1838–1914)
Swift, Hildegarde. *From the Eagle's Wing; A Biography of John Muir,* ill. by Lynd Ward. Morrow, 1962. A fascinating biography for budding naturalists. 12 up

MUSIAL, STANLEY FRANK (1920–)
Robinson, Ray. *Stan Musial; Baseball's Durable "Man."* Putnam, 1963. Comments from Musial's colleagues attest to the popularity of "Stan the Man." 10-12

NEWTON, SIR ISAAC (1642–1727)
See Bixby entry under GALILEO.

NIGHTINGALE, FLORENCE (1820–1910)
Nolan, Jeannette Covert. *Florence Nightingale,* ill. by George Avison. Messner, 1946. Florence Nightingale's life story stresses her work rather than her personal life. 11-14

NOGUCHI, ISAMU (1904–)
Tobias, Tobi. *Isamu Noguchi; The Life of a Sculptor,* ill. T. Crowell, 1974. 8-10

§ NORTHUP, SOLOMON (1808–?)
Knight, Michael, ed. *In Chains to Louisiana.* Dutton, 1971. Adapted from Northup's autobiography in which he told of being kidnapped and sold into slavery. 11-15

ORR, ROBERT (1948–)
Burchard, Marshall and Sue. *Bobby Orr; Sports Hero,* ill. with photos. Putnam, 1973. 8-10

PAINE, THOMAS (1737–1809)
Coolidge, Olivia E. *Tom Paine, Revolutionary.* Scribner's, 1969. An infinitely detailed and vivid picture of affairs in France, England, and the colonies during Paine's career, and an objective picture of the man. Sophisticated biographical writing. 12 up
Gurko, Leo. *Tom Paine; Freedom's Apostle,* ill. by Fritz Kredel. T. Crowell, 1957. 12 up

PANDIT, VIJAYA LAKSHMI (NEHRU) (1900–)
Guthrie, Anne. *Madame Ambassador; The Life of Vijaya Lakshmi Pandit,* ill. with photos. Harcourt, 1962. Both an absorbing personal story of India's stateswoman and a unique picture of India's changing history. 13-16

PANKHURST, EMMELINE (1858–1928)
Noble, Iris. *Emmeline and Her Daughters; The Pankhurst Suffragettes.* Messner, 1971. 11-14

PARACELSUS, PHILIPPUS (1493–1541)
Rosen, Sidney. *Doctor Paracelsus,* ill. by Rafaello Busoni. Little, 1959. 12-16

§ PARKS, GORDON (1912–)
Turk, Midge. *Gordon Parks,* ill. by Herbert Danska. T. Crowell, 1971. 7-8

§ PARKS, ROSA (1913–)
Greenfield, Eloise. *Rosa Parks,* ill. by Eric Marlow. T. Crowell, 1973. 7-9
Meriwether, Louise. *Don't Ride the Bus on Monday,* ill. by David Scott Brown. Prentice, 1973. A more detailed portrait than the Greenfield title, this conveys the quiet courage and determination Rosa Parks demonstrated when she set off the Montgomery bus boycott. 8-10

● PENN, WILLIAM (1644–1718)
Aliki. *The Story of William Penn,* ill. by author. Prentice, 1964. 8-9
Foster, Genevieve. *The World of William Penn,* ill. by author. Scribner's, 1973. 9-12
Vining, Elizabeth Gray. *Penn,* ill. by George Gillett Whitney. Viking, 1938. 12-16

PETER THE GREAT (1672–1725)
Putnam, Peter Brock. *Peter, The Revolutionary Tsar,* ill. by Laszlo Kubinyi. Harper, 1973. A good place to begin understanding Russian history is with the tsar who had unlimited power except when it came to changing minds. 12 up

PETIGRU, JAMES (1789–1863)
Edwards, Sally. *The Man Who Said No.* Coward, 1970. James Petigru was an established member of South Carolina society, but he was also a Unionist and opposed to the spread of slavery. A good biogra-

phy with well-integrated historical background and with restrained fictionalization. 12-15

PICASSO, PABLO (1881–1973)
Greenfeld, Howard. *Pablo Picasso; An Introduction.* Follett, 1971. 12-15

§ PIPPIN, HORACE (1888–1946)
Rodman, Selden, and Carole Cleaver. *Horace Pippin; The Artist As a Black American.* Doubleday, 1972. Full-color paintings by an eminent black artist add to the appeal of the first biography of Pippin for children. 11-13

☆ POCAHONTAS (1595?–1617)
Bulla, Clyde. *Pocahontas and the Strangers.* T. Crowell, 1971. 8-10
d'Aulaire, Ingri and Edgar Parin. *Pocahontas,* ill. by authors. Doubleday, 1949. 7-9
Martin, Patricia Miles. *Pocahontas,* ill. by Portia Takakjian. Putnam, 1964. 7-8
Wahl, Jan. *Pocahontas in London,* ill. by John Alcorn. Delacorte, 1967. 8-9

POLK, JAMES KNOX (1795–1849)
Severn, William. *Frontier President: James K. Polk.* Washburn, 1965. A light tone makes this competent biography especially readable. 12-15

POTTER, BEATRIX (1866–1943)
Aldis, Dorothy. *Nothing Is Impossible; The Story of Beatrix Potter,* ill. by Richard Cuffari. Atheneum, 1969. 9-11
Lane, Margaret. *The Tale of Beatrix Potter; A Biography,* ill. by Beatrix Potter. Warne, 1946. Delightful story of the Victorian artist whose Peter Rabbit tales have delighted young children. 13-16

§ POWELL, ADAM CLAYTON, JR. (1908–1972)
Haskins, James. *Adam Clayton Powell; Portrait of a Marching Black,* ill. with photos. Dial, 1974. 12 up

REED, JOHN (1887–1920)
Hovey, Tamara. *John Reed; Witness to Revolution.* Crown, 1975. John Reed was a superb journalist who covered strikes, wars, and revolutions and whose radical politics endeared him to some and alienated him from many. 12-16

REVERE, PAUL (1735–1818)
Forbes, Esther. *America's Paul Revere,* ill. by Lynd Ward. Houghton, 1946. Vigorous prose and superb illustrations do much to illumine the history of the Revolutionary period. 11-15

RICHTER, HANS PETER (1925–)
Richter, Hans Peter. *I Was There,* tr. by Edite Kroll. Holt, 1972. Richter's story begins at age eight when he joined the Hitler youth movement and ends with him and his friends in the Third Reich Army. A dramatic, forceful book. 11-15

RINCON, FELISA DE GAUTIER. See GAUTIER, FELISA RINCON DE.

RINGLING BROTHERS
Cone, Molly. *The Ringling Brothers,* ill. by James and Ruth McCrea. T. Crowell, 1971. 7-9

RIZAL, JOSÉ (1861–1896)
Reines, Bernard. *A People's Hero; Rizal of the Philippines.* Praeger, 1971. A foresighted leader who fought against Spanish tyranny and was executed in 1896, Rizal was ahead of his time in the battle for equality and civil rights. 7-11

§ ROBESON, PAUL (1898–1976)
Hamilton, Virginia. *Paul Robeson; The Life and Times of a Free Man,* ill. with photos. Harper, 1974. 12 up

§ ROBINSON, JOHN (1919–1972)
Robinson, Jackie, and Alfred Duckett. *Breakthrough to the Big Leagues.* Harper, 1965. Candid about Robinson's problems as the first black player in the major leagues, and very well written. 11-14
Rudeen, Kenneth. *Jackie Robinson,* ill. by Richard Cuffari. T. Crowell, 1971. 7-9

ROOSEVELT, ELEANOR (1884–1962)
Davidson, Margaret. *The Story of Eleanor Roosevelt.* Four Winds, 1969. One of the better biographies of an indomitable woman. 9-11
Goodsell, Jane. *Eleanor Roosevelt,* ill. by Wendell Minor. T. Crowell, 1970. 8-10

ROOSEVELT, FRANKLIN DELANO (1882–1945)
Faber, Doris. *Franklin D. Roosevelt,* ill. Abelard, 1974. 8-11
Peare, Catherine Owens. *The FDR Story,* ill. T. Crowell, 1962. A remarkably perceptive biography of Roosevelt as an individual and as a political figure. 12-15

ROOSEVELT, THEODORE (1858–1919)
Foster, Genevieve. *Theodore Roosevelt,* ill. by author. Scribner's, 1954. 9-12
Monjo, Ferdinand. *The One Bad Thing About Father,* ill. by Rocco Negri. Harper, 1970. 7-8

§ ROSE, EDWARD (1811–1834)
Felton, Harold W. *Edward Rose, Negro Trail Blazer,* ill. with photos and prints of the period, and maps. Dodd, 1967. 10-14

☆ ROSS, JOHN (1790–1866)
Clark, Electa. *Cherokee Chief; The Life of John Ross,* ill. by John Wagner. Crowell-Collier, 1970. John Ross was a man whose Scottish ancestors had married into the Cherokee Nation and whose integrity earned him the respect of white statesmen as well as the leadership of his tribe. A dramatic and tragic story of the persecution of the Cherokee people. 10-14

§ RUSSWURM, JOHN BROWN (1799–1851)
Sagarin, Mary. *John Brown Russwurm; The Story of* Freedom's Journal, *Freedom's Journey.* Lothrop, 1970. The subject is interesting both as a little-known figure in antebellum black history in the United States and as an important one in the turbulent early days of Liberian history. 12-15

☆ SACAJAWEA (1786–1884)
Farnsworth, Frances Joyce. *Winged Moccasins; The Story of Sacajawea,* ill. by Lorence Bjorklund. Messner, 1954. An interesting and authentic account of the life of Lewis and Clark's Indian guide. 12-15

SAMPSON, DEBORAH. See GANNETT, DEBORAH (SAMPSON).

SCHLIEMANN, HEINRICH (1822–1890)
Braymer, Marjorie. *The Walls of Windy Troy.* Harcourt, 1960. Distinguished biography of Heinrich Schliemann, who achieved his dream of archeological research on the site of ancient Troy. 12-16

SCHUMANN, CLARA (1819–1896)
SCHUMANN, ROBERT (1810–1856)
Kyle, Elisabeth. *Duet: The Story of Clara and Robert Schumann.* Holt, 1968. 11-14

● SINGER, ISAAC BASHEVIS (1904–)
Singer, Isaac Bashevis. *A Day of Pleasure; Stories of a Boy Growing Up in Warsaw,* ill. with photos by Roman Vishniac. Farrar, 1969. National Book Award. 11 up

☆ SITTING BULL, SIOUX CHIEF (1831–1890)
Garst, Shannon. *Sitting Bull, Champion of His People,* ill. by Elton C. Fax. Messner, 1946. 11 up

§ SMALLS, ROBERT (1839–1915)
Meriwether, Louise. *The Freedom Ship of Robert Smalls,* ill. by Lee Jack Morton. Prentice, 1971. Sim-

ply told, the story of the captain of *The Planter.* 8-10
Sterling, Dorothy. *Captain of the Planter; The Story of Robert Smalls,* ill. by Ernest Crichlow. Doubleday, 1958. 12-15

§ SMITH, BESSIE (1894–1937)
Moore, Carman. *Somebody's Angel Child; The Story of Bessie Smith.* T. Crowell, 1970. The dramatic and sad story of the greatest blues singer of them all. 11-14

☆ SQUANTO, PAWTUXET INDIAN (d. 1622)
Bulla, Clyde. *Squanto; Friend of the Pilgrims,* ill. by Peter Burchard. T. Crowell, 1954. 7-9

STANTON, ELIZABETH CADY (1815–1902)
Faber, Doris. *Oh, Lizzie; The Life of Elizabeth Cady Stanton.* Lothrop, 1972. 12-16

● STEIN, GERTRUDE (1874–1946)
Greenfeld, Howard. *Gertrude Stein; A Biography.* Crown, 1973. 12 up

STEINMETZ, CHARLES (1865–1923)
Lavine, Sigmund. *Steinmetz; Maker of Lightning,* ill. with photos. Dodd, 1955. This biography of the crippled German immigrant is a fine combination of good characterization and scientific information. 13 up

§ STEVENS, THADDEUS (1792–1868)
Meltzer, Milton. *Thaddeus Stevens and the Fight for Negro Rights.* T. Crowell, 1967. 13 up

STEVENSON, ROBERT LOUIS (1850–1894)
Proudfit, Isabel. *The Treasure Hunter, the Story of Robert Louis Stevenson,* ill. by Hardie Gramatky. Messner, 1939. A full-length biography of a favorite children's author. 10-14
Wood, James Playsted. *The Lantern Bearer; A Life of Robert Louis Stevenson,* ill. by Saul Lambert. Pantheon, 1965. 12 up

§ STILL, PETER (1800–?)
Mann, Peggy. *The Man Who Bought Himself.* Macmillan, 1975. 12-15

SUN YAT-SEN (1866–1925)
Spencer, Cornelia. *Sun Yat-sen; Founder of the Chinese Republic.* Day, 1967. 12-15

☆ TALLCHIEF, MARIA (1925–)
Tobias, Tobi. *Maria Tallchief,* ill. by Michael Hampshire. T. Crowell, 1970. 7-9

TERESHKOVA, VALENTINA VLADIMIROVA (1937–)
Sharpe, Mitchell R. *"It Is I, Sea Gull," Valentina Tereshkova, First Woman in Space,* ill. with photos. T. Crowell, 1975. Excellent view of the woman who made space-flight history. 11-15

TERRY, ELLEN ALICIA (1848–1928)
Fecher, Constance. *Bright Star; A Portrait of Ellen Terry.* Farrar, 1970. The author makes her subject move with reality and warmth. Excellent both as a personal portrait and as a large plummy slice of theatrical history. Enticing photographs. 12 up

§ TOUSSAINT L'OUVERTURE, PIERRE DOMINIQUE (1746?–1803)
Syme, Ronald, *Toussaint; The Black Liberator,* ill. by William Stobbs. Morrow, 1971. 10-13

§ TUBMAN, HARRIET (1820–1913)
Lawrence, Jacob. *Harriet and the Promised Land,* ill. by author. Windmill, 1968. In this story of Harriet Tubman, the writing is simple, rhythmic, and effective and the pictures are dramatic and vigorous. 7-9
Petry, Ann. *Harriet Tubman; Conductor on the Underground Railroad.* T. Crowell, 1955. A well-documented, thrilling story. 12-16
Sterling, Dorothy. *Freedom Train; The Story of Harriet Tubman,* ill. by Ernest Crichlow. Doubleday, 1954. 10-12
Swift, Hildegarde. *Railroad to Freedom; A Story of the Civil War,* ill. by James Daugherty. Harcourt, 1932. 12-14

TYLER, JOHN (1790–1862)
Hoyt, Edwin P. *John Tyler.* Abelard, 1970. A clear demonstration of how the times and the person are mutual influences. 11-15

VAN GOGH, VINCENT. See GOGH, VINCENT VAN.

VERRAZANO, GIOVANNI DA (c. 1480–1527?)
Syme, Ronald. *Verrazano; Explorer of the Atlantic Coast,* ill. by William Stobbs. Morrow, 1973. Direct, brisk account of the explorer, written with Syme's usual concern for accuracy. 9-11

VESPUCCI, AMERIGO (1451–1512)
Baker, Nina Brown. *Amerigo Vespucci,* ill. by Paul Valentino. Knopf, 1956. 9-12

§ WASHINGTON, BOOKER TALIAFERRO (1859?–1915)
Graham, Shirley. *Booker T. Washington; Educator of Hand, Head and Heart.* Messner, 1955. 10-12
Washington, Booker T. *Up from Slavery.* Houghton, 1917. 12 up
Wise, William. *Booker T. Washington,* ill. by Paul Frame. Putnam, 1968. 7-9

WASHINGTON, GEORGE (1732–1799)
Bulla, Clyde. *Washington's Birthday,* ill. by Don Bolognese. T. Crowell, 1967. 6-8
d'Aulaire, Ingri and Edgar Parin. *George Washington,* ill. by authors. Doubleday, 1936. 7-9
Eaton, Jeanette. *Leader by Destiny,* ill. by Jack Manley Rosé. Harcourt, 1938. 12-15
Foster, Genevieve. *George Washington.* Scribner's, 1949. 9-11
Judson, Clara Ingram. *George Washington, Leader of the People,* ill. by Robert Frankenberg. Follett, 1951. 11-15
McNeer, May. *The Story of George Washington,* ill. by Lynd Ward. Abingdon, 1973. Handsome pictures and simple text. 7-9

WASHINGTON, MARTHA (1731–1802)
Vance, Marguerite. *Martha, Daughter of Virginia; The Story of Martha Washington,* ill. by Nedda Walker. Dutton, 1947. 9-11

WAYNE, KYRA PETROVSKAYA
Wayne, Kyra Petrovskaya. *Shurik; A Story of the Siege of Leningrad,* ill. Grosset, 1970. A dramatic, true story of World War II. A nurse in a hospital during the siege of Leningrad adopts Shurik, a homeless orphan. Chilling descriptions of the besieged city and impressive pictures of compassion and courage. 12-15

● WEST, BENJAMIN (1738–1820)
Henry, Marguerite, and Wesley Dennis. *Benjamin West and His Cat Grimalkin,* ill. by Wesley Dennis. Bobbs, 1947. An enchanting biography of one of America's first artists. 9-12

§ WHEATLEY, PHILLIS (1753?–1784)
Graham, Shirley. *The Story of Phillis Wheatley,* ill. by Robert Burns. Messner, 1949. 12-14

WHITMAN, NARCISSA (PRENTISS) (1808–1847)
Eaton, Jeanette. *Narcissa Whitman; Pioneer of Oregon,* ill. by Woodi Ishmael. Harcourt, 1941. This inspiring life of a great pioneer woman is based on early letters and memoirs. 12-16

WHITMAN, WALT (1819–1892)
Deutsch, Babette. *Walt Whitman; Builder for America,* ill. by Rafaello Busoni. Messner, 1941. A sensitive study of the man, illustrated with copious selections from his poems. 14-16

WILDER, LAURA INGALLS (1867–1957)
Wilder, Laura Ingalls. *West from Home; Letters of Laura Ingalls Wilder, San Francisco, 1915,* ed. by Roger Lea MacBride; historical setting by Margot Patterson Doss. Harper, 1974. For all those who have loved the Wilder "Little House" books.

WILLIAMS, ROGER (1603?–1683)
Eaton, Jeanette. *Lone Journey; The Life of Roger Williams,* ill. by Woodi Ishmael. Harcourt, 1944. Story of the courageous Puritan who left the Massachusetts colony and helped establish Rhode Island. 12-16

Jacobs, William Jay. *Roger Williams,* ill. with authentic prints and documents. Watts, 1975. Authoritative introduction to a genuine free spirit. 10-12

WILSON, WOODROW (1856–1924)
Peare, Catherine Owens. *The Woodrow Wilson Story; An Idealist in Politics.* T. Crowell, 1963. 12-15

WOODHULL, VICTORIA (1838–1927)
Meade, Marian. *Free Woman; The Life and Times of Victoria Woodhull.* Knopf, 1976. Stockbroker, journalist, actress, this colorful woman was the first woman to run for President of the United States. 12–15

ZAPATA, EMILIANO (1869?–1919)
Syme, Ronald. *Zapata, Mexican Rebel,* ill. by William Stobbs. Morrow, 1971. 9-11

ZENGER, PETER (1697–1746)
Galt, Tom. *Peter Zenger; Fighter for Freedom,* ill. by Ralph Ray. T. Crowell, 1951. Biography of a famous pre-Revolutionary War printer, who faced trial and prison rather than yield the right of freedom of the press. 12-15

Informational Books Chapter 13

If there is one trait that is common to children of all ages, of all backgrounds, of all ethnic groups, it is curiosity. Children read informational books to satisfy that curiosity, whether their books have been chosen to answer questions on a particular subject or to fulfill a desire for broader knowledge. While the criteria (discussed on the following pages) by which all informational books can be judged should serve as a basis for evaluating the thousands of factual children's books in print, additional qualities invest some of them with such distinction that they can be called fine literature; originality of presentation or concept can contribute to this distinction, but it rests primarily with that least tangible of literary virtues, distinguished style. It is apparent in the clarity and vigor of Isaac Asimov's writing, in the scholarship and wit of Alfred Duggan, in the lyric simplicity of Jean George's *Spring Comes to the Ocean*. Each author uses prose in a way that is individual, each uses phrase and cadence appropriate to the subject, and each achieves distinctive style without sacrificing the basic qualifications for good informational writing.

Evaluating Informational Books

The variety of informational books is vast, ranging from the simplest concept books (which, along with alphabet and counting books, are discussed in Chapter 4, Books for Early Childhood) to books for older readers on a variety of complex subjects. The best informational books are written by authors who know their subjects well, and who write about them imaginatively, with an understanding of the needs and limitations of their audience. An expert on a subject may tend toward verbosity or a heavy use of jargon or unnecessarily technical terminology. A practiced writer, on the other hand, may lack the subject knowledge to write with depth. Each book must be judged on its own merits, and those who evaluate books should consider the author's purpose in writing a book and judge not only whether the book meets all criteria for factual writing but also whether the author has written the book so as to fulfill its purpose.

Accuracy

What are the basic criteria by which nonfiction may be judged? Probably the first tenet that would occur to anyone is accuracy. While, clearly, we seek only correct information about a subject, all we can ask of authors is that they be accurate within the boundaries of knowledge at the time a book is written. There is no reason for a book about prehistory to be inaccurate, unless startling new facts have come to light since the book's publication; on the other hand, the author of a survey of the American political system as it functions today must be very guarded about statements on congressional control of election procedures, for example, since this is a fluid situation. To avoid inaccuracy, an author must specify that an event, or a piece of legislation, or a procedure was functioning in a certain way at a certain time.

In writing for young children, who are limited in experience, vocabulary, and knowledge of concepts, authors often find it necessary to omit material; in such cases, their obligation is to omit nothing that is of major importance; that is, the book need not be comprehensive but it must cover major points or it will have the same effect as inaccuracy. We should not substitute simplified terminology if the correct word is not too difficult for young children; that, too, is a form of inaccuracy. A first book on human anatomy need not, for example, use "clavicle" rather than the more familiar "collarbone," but there is no reason not to use "lymph" even if it is an unfamiliar word, since there is no acceptable substitute.

If we supply children with factual information which is out of date or superficial, we only add to their confusion. Suppose, for instance, we give children purportedly modern books about the Holland of picturesque costumes and quaint, old-fashioned customs or about the old China of rickshaws and queues or about the South America of primitive Indian villages only. Meanwhile, newspapers, magazines, and television newscasts show them pictures of progressive Holland today, China's program of industrialization, and large South American cities. Discerning children can only conclude that books are less reliable references than other sources.

Obviously, accuracy is one of the most important criteria for judging any informational book. There has never been a greater need for accurate information than there is today to help counteract the widely disseminated misinformation to which children are subjected. Adults should encourage them to check so-called facts in reliable sources. This is one way of arming children against credulity and teaching them to weigh arguments, question sources, and search for facts.

Viewpoints

I like books of knowledge; not those that want to encroach upon recreation, upon leisure, pretending to be able to teach anything without drudgery. There is no truth in that. There are things which cannot be learned without great pains; we must be resigned to it. I like books of knowledge when they are not just grammar or geometry poorly disguised; when they have tact and moderation; when, instead of pouring out so much material on a child's soul that it is crushed, they plant in it a seed that will develop from the inside. I like them when they do not deceive themselves about the quality of knowledge, and do not claim that knowledge can take the place of everything else. I like them especially when they distill from all the different kinds of knowledge the most difficult and the most necessary—that of the human heart.—Paul Hazard. *Books, Children and Men* translated by Marguerite Mitchell, The Horn Book, Inc., 1944, p. 43.

Currency

Currency is closely related to accuracy. In many informational books, the date of copyright is especially important. For some subjects, this is of minor importance—Scheele's books on prehistoric life, for example, have been for many years, and are likely to be for many more, some of the best of their type—but even in history or archeology there are new discoveries or new theories. Informational books should represent not only the heritage and the knowledge of the past, but the latest research and contemporary experience as well.

Currency is usually a preeminent factor in choosing the best science books. In many science experiment books, great changes have taken place, and any evaluation of these books would need to consider their currency. Formerly, directions might be given something like this: "Take a teaspoon of this, a teaspoon of that, mix, and . . . will happen." This kind of instruction reflected traditional teaching methods: the teacher demonstrated an experiment, the students tried to duplicate it, and results were expected to be identical. With the discovery method, which emphasizes why things happen, new books give children options as they experiment, and stress observation of scientific method, keeping records, and drawing inferences from conclusions. Conversion to the metric system obviously affects our choices of science experiment books. Changes in educational practices in any area, then, should be reflected in changes in the literature; methods as well as content should be up-to-date.

Organization and Scope

In considering the accuracy and currency and therefore the effectiveness of any informational book, we must decide how successfully the author has simplified material and limited the scope of the subject for the intended audience. One reason the Crowell science books for beginning readers have been successful is that the authors and editors, in limiting the scope of their material, have been careful to select the important facts about a subject and to present them in logical sequence. Too much information, or information that is supplementary, may confuse and mislead a child even though there are no inaccurate statements in the text.

The presentation of material in logical sequence is particularly important. Only in very short books is a continuous text appropriate; in books of substantial length, the text should be broken up with heads and subheads that clarify the relations of the separate parts. A table of contents can also help make clear the organization of the text and the contents of each chapter. Though few books for very young children have an index, even here such aids are found more frequently than before. For most informational books for children in the middle grades and up, an index is a necessity, and the best indexes have cross-references.

The text material should move from the familiar to the unfamiliar, or progress from the simple to the complex, or be in chronological order; arrangement will vary with the nature of the subject. Historical material lends itself to chronological treatment, project books to a simple-to-complex arrangement, and an explanation of an aspect of human physiology, for example, to the familiar-to-unfamiliar sequence.

The Author's Responsibility

Any book that teaches a child how to make something, as in experiment books, should include safety rules and should present lists of materials needed and sources for acquiring them if they are not available in the home. Science experiment books and cookbooks should also make clear when adult supervision or adult participation in a stage of the procedure is needed. Activities suggested should conform with scientific method.

It is also the author's responsibility to ensure the absence of stereotyping by sex, race, age, or religion either in the text or in the illustrations. There are women chemists and business executives; a black doctor may have a white nurse; children of all ethnic backgrounds may be interested in a physics experiment and should be so represented in illustrations.

The writing should reflect a scientific attitude, not only in *what* is said, but in *how* it is said: no "Mother Nature" in books about plants and animals, no anthropomorphism in animal characters, although for the very young child some personification of animals is permissible. The facts must not only be current and accurate, but they should be presented so that they build toward concepts and principles. And it is incumbent on the author to keep the intended audience in mind so that the vocabulary, scope, and concepts are close to the child's ability to comprehend.

Authors should carefully distinguish between fact and theory or opinion. To signal an opinion or a theory, they should use such phrases as "In my opinion," "It may be that," or "One group of scientists believes." They should avoid the unsupported generalization and the untenable, all-inclusive generalization, which lets readers assume that the part they have been reading about is the whole. It just isn't true that if you've seen one, you've seen them all, and to imply this is particularly reprehensible in a book about people. Professional men and women often have a bias about theories in their field, and the dependable author informs the reader that he or she holds one idea, but that there are others, or that the text covers only some aspects of a subject. Some of these facts can be learned from the author's background; both the limitation of coverage and the adherence to a theory should be clear.

The Author's Competence

One of the clues to the author's competence is the material considered, that is, the material he or she chooses to include and to omit. John Navarra, for example, includes a chapter on pollution and politics in *The World You Inherit* presumably because, as an expert in the field, he is aware of the urgency of getting enabling legislation for corrective measures.

Authors who have scientific backgrounds should be aware of, and should make explicit, the social implications of their subjects, the effects on people and institutions. An author who is an authority on a subject can write with more originality than the writer who can only reassemble facts provided by others. A true scientist, for example, is not hesitant about showing that—at certain stages—answers must be inconclusive.

Evaluation of the writer's competence is made easier if his or her credentials are given. The book's accuracy may be further confirmed by a list of readers whose specialties qualify them to vouch for the book's information. A list of sources, a bibliography, a glossary, or a chronology add to the value of a book and usually attest to the authoritative knowledge or research involved.

Format

Format should be examined in evaluating an informational book. The child in fifth grade will scorn the book that, because of its size or shape or style of illustration, looks like second-grade fare. The type size and page layout are of more importance in informational books than in other types of books, since confusion may lead to misinterpretation. The reader can be confused by paragraphs irregularly arranged on a page with not enough blank space to make sequence apparent. The chapter heads and subheads should be explicit indicators of content. A photograph or map can lose its value if it is located too far from the discussion to which it pertains. The illustration should always be accurate and should complement and clarify the printed text; it can give too little information or too much. Inadequate labels or captions can lessen or obviate the value of maps, pictures, and diagrams. Photographs that are posed or that are decorative rather than informative can be an irritant. There are some books for which photographs are the best illustrative medium, as they are in *A Life of Their Own* by Aylette Jenness and Lisa Kroeber, and here even the posed pictures of a Guatemalan family *are* informative. The best illustrations reflect some quality of the text, as Leonard Everett Fisher's black-and-white scratchboard drawings reflect the sturdy individuality of the colonial craftsmen in books like *The Tanners*, or as Edwin Tunis's meticulous drawings enhance the reference use of *Frontier Living*.

Viewpoints

In all media, the reviewer of nonfiction most of the time limits himself to asking how much information the book contains. And how accurate or up-to-date it is. Infrequently a reviewer will compare the book with others on the same subject, but only as to factual content. Rarely will he ask what more there is to the book than the mere facts. I would want to ask how well it is organized. What principle of selection animated the writer; what is the writer's point of view; does the writer acknowledge other opinions of value? And then, beyond all this, what literary distinction, if any, does the book have? And here I do not mean the striking choice of word or image but the personal style revealed. I ask whether the writer's personal voice is heard in the book. In the writer who cares, there is a pressure of feeling which emerges in the rhythm of the sentences, in the choice of details, in the color of the language. Style in this sense is not a trick of rhetoric or a decorative daub; it is a quality of vision. It cannot be separated from the author's character because the tone of voice in which the book is written expresses how a human being thinks and feels. If the writer is indifferent, bored, stupid, or mechanical, it will show in the work. The kind of man or woman the writer is—this is what counts. Style in any art is both form and content; they are woven together.
—Milton Meltzer. "Where Do All the Prizes Go? The Case For Nonfiction," *The Horn Book Magazine,* February 1976.

Style

Finally, informational books must be clearly and interestingly written. Nonfiction can be abysmally dull. The wrong way to combat dullness is to dress it up. Information can and should be written in a straightforward fashion; young readers need no palliative with books on science or geography or nature study. No "Mother Nature knew it was springtime" is admissible in children's nonfiction books, nor does a squirrel need to be referred to as "Little Nutsy." Children don't like to be talked down to. They can take information straight, although they can be bored stiff if the writing is too dry or too heavy. A book may be useful—and there are many that are mediocre in style but useful—but a child will not cherish it unless it is also interesting.

The vocabulary should be geared to the reading ability of the child. Books that are used by young children for identification, or concept books (discussed in Chapter 4), should present ideas simply but with the grouping or repetition that will encourage observation, classification, and deduction. A controlled vocabulary may be helpful for the beginning reader, but most children enjoy writing that has some unfamiliar words. Older children appreciate the challenge of some new terms that expand their vocabulary and widen their horizons.

With the increasing use of trade books to supplement texts and other curricular materials, the criteria for evaluation seem even more important today than in the past. Even in those books for young children in which a fictional framework is used, the purpose of an informational book is to inform. The best of such books expose a child to differences and lead to questioning and comparing books, to evaluating conflicting theories. The best nonfiction goes beyond the presentation of facts to presentation of principles, concepts, theories, interpretation, and evaluation.

Accuracy, currency, careful organization and presentation, a scientific attitude, responsibility in dealing with fact and opinion, format, and interesting style are some of the criteria by which informational books can be judged. In the rest of this chapter, these criteria will be further examined as they pertain to particular books. The first section presents in alphabetical order twenty-eight outstanding authors of informational books for children and some of the books they have written. The second section discusses briefly a number of other important authors and significant books organized by subject matter (the biological sciences, the physical sciences, the social sciences, religion and the arts, activities and experiments, and reference books). This discussion gives a glimpse of the variety and the riches available in today's informational books.

Irving Adler

The Wonders of Physics

Irving Adler, who has been a teacher of mathematics at the high-school and college levels, is the author of more than fifty books on scientific subjects. His work is notable for the skill and lucidity with which he makes complicated material comprehensible. In *The Wonders of Physics* (1966), for example, written for older children, the clarity of his prose is such that the book can be given even to a seven-year-old child to explain the difference between the Centigrade and Fahrenheit temperature scales.

The Wonders of Physics bears out Jerome Bruner's assertion that ". . . the foundations of any subject may be taught to anybody at any age in some form."[1] Adler defines the four states of matter (solid, liquid, gaseous, and plasma) succinctly, then discusses them, using subheadings and drawings to make the material easier to understand. In discussing temperature scales, the author carefully identifies each type, along with the scientist after whom it was named, and provides complete descriptions and diagrams. In discussing heat engines, Adler skillfully explains the three laws of thermodynamics. The index includes "see also" references. Page numbers in boldface type refer to a page where there is an illustration of the subject. Throughout the text, cross-references are excellent.

Tools in Your Life (1956) is an account of the development of tools from the primitive

[1]Jerome S. Bruner, *The Process of Education* (Harvard Univ. Press, 1966), p. 12.

ax to atomic energy, tracing the sociological effects of the adoption of new tools or of the clinging to old ones. *Magic House of Numbers* (1957; 1974) describes number systems built on bases other than ten, and includes many intriguing puzzles. These books are illustrated by Ruth Adler, who was also coauthor and illustrator of more than thirty titles in "The Reason Why" series. These are short, useful books with descriptive tables of contents but no indexes. Three books for children in the middle grades are *Evolution* (1965), *Sets* (1967), and *Petroleum* (1975), which is written by Irving Adler alone, and for those even younger, *Sets and Numbers for the Very Young* (1969).

Isaac Asimov

Words from History

Biochemist Isaac Asimov has written his own reference book, *Asimov's Biographical Encyclopedia of Science and Technology*, and his writing covers a wide range of subjects, from authoritative discussions of astronomy (*Jupiter; The Largest Planet*, 1973; 1976) and distinctive science fiction to a story for the preschool child, *The Best New Thing* (1971).

Words from History (1968) is a good example of Asimov's work in a field outside his own. Like all of his other books, it is distinguished for a witty, informal style that smoothly carries authoritative information. Using one page of text for each word, he gives its etymology and sets it in historical perspective. The following quotation shows how clearly Asimov writes and how much to the point his explanations are:

> *Along the Roman roads, the legions tramped, guarding the frontiers and suppressing revolts (and sometimes marching on Rome itself to snatch at the Imperial crown). Distance was important and was measured off by the tireless pacing of the legionaries in convenient units of a thousand paces. In Latin, a thousand paces is "milia Passuum," and this was gradually shortened to the first word alone, in English mile. Our present "mile" is a little longer than the Roman, however, and comes to about 1050 paces or 1760 yards. (p. 141)*

Among his other "Word" books are *Words on the Map* (1962) and *Words of Science; and the History Behind Them* (1959). Each of these books follows the same format as *Words from History*, that is, one word and its explanation on one page. *Words from the Exodus* (1963) and *Words in Genesis* (1962) show how much of our everyday speech comes from the Bible.

The Shaping of North America (1973) and its sequel, *The Birth of the United States 1763–1816* (1974), are two of several Asimov books about the formative years of a country; his fresh viewpoint and easy, informal style make history interesting even when he covers familiar information. In *The Shaping of France* (1972) and *The Shaping of England* (1969), his tendency to crowd the pages with names and dates may be some obstacle to readers in the United States, while Canadian readers, better acquainted with British and French history, will have an advantage. All of Asimov's history books, despite such crowding, have a breadth and sweep that give readers perspective on events, personalities, and factions.

Building Blocks of the Universe (1957) is an excellent book on chemistry and contains little sidelights which make the scientific words come alive for young people. *Realm of Numbers* (1959) is a popularizing of arithmetic for those who don't have a knowledge of algebra, geometry, and calculus. One of the most successful of Asimov's many books about space is *ABC's of Space* (1969), which is illustrated with photographs and drawings from the space program, with short paragraphs for each item. This may be used with very young children, despite the fact that the terminology is sometimes complex.

Jeanne Bendick

Names, Sets and Numbers

An author or illustrator of more than 100 books for children, Jeanne Bendick is probably best known for her lively, humorous illustrations. Her easily recognizable style, which she describes as "relaxed representational" is echoed in the brisk and vigorous writing that skillfully clarifies difficult concepts. Her interest in science developed after she had illustrated a number of science books and had done a lot of reading in order to draw her pictures accurately. She found that she had the ability to present a complex subject in simple terms and in a light, often breezy manner.

Names, Sets and Numbers (1971) is typical of her direct, crisp approach. Although it is recommended by the publisher for grades four to six, the content and style are suitable for younger children:

First, we give names to things.
People have names, like Mike and Karen.
Planets have names, like Earth and Mars.
Every plant we know has a name.
"Buttercup" is a name. So is "pine."
Every animal we know has a name.
"Earthworm" is a name. So is "lion." (p. 8)

Beginning with names of things as a reference point, the author then moves into sets in a smooth transition. Making small things out of big ones gets across the concept of subsets and classification, another subject to which very young children are being exposed.

Jeanne Bendick has written a number of books, all with the same straightforward tone, in the Watts "First Book" series. *A First Book of Space Travel* (1969, revised several times) is a comprehensive yet simplified look at the subject, from "What Space Is" to "What Space Science Has Done for Earth." *The First Book of Time* (1963) begins with a question: what do we know about time? It discusses measurement of time, calendars, and clocks, including plant and animal clocks. *A Place to Live* (1970) is for the read-aloud audience and deals with the interdependence of human, plant, and animal life. Some of Bendick's books deal with weather phenomena. *The Wind* (1964) gives scientific information about how winds are caused and how they travel, preceded by a discussion of myths and superstitions the world over. Some of her books deal with aspects of the physical sciences; *Solids, Liquids and Gases* (1974) uses the process approach to explain the differences between the three states of matter, suggesting basic criteria for comparison and testing, and exemplifying the scientific method. *What Made You You?* (1971) asks

Did you come like a chicken out of an egg? Like a flower out of a bud? Like a rainbow out of raindrops? Like music out of a horn? No, but just as wonderful. YOU were born! (pp. 38, 39)

Blithe as it is, the text gives accurate and explicit information about reproduction and heredity.

Electronics for Young People (1960) and *How Much and How Many* (1960) are for older children and contain more text than pictures. *Television Works Like This* (1965) and *The Consumer's Catalog of Economy and Ecology* (1974) were written in collaboration with the author's husband, Robert.

Sonia Bleeker

The Ibo of Biafra

Sonia Bleeker said, in *The Ibo of Biafra* (1969), "A man must dance the dance of the times, is an Ibo proverb. To the Ibo, it means that they are ready to accept change." And change is what the Biafrans have had, and more than their share, since October of 1960, when Nigeria obtained independence from Britain.

Sonia Bleeker was an anthropologist whose books are distinguished for their simplicity of style and for the objective assessment of cultural patterns. There is never any insinuation in her writing that a food is exotic or a rite strange; from her viewpoint as a scientist, all customs of all peoples have an equal validity, and this admirable attitude is communicated to her readers. All of her books give both historical background and a description of the tribe's way of life today, but the major portion of each is devoted to an examination of cultural patterns. In *The Ibo of Biafra,* for example, early chapters of the book deal with the people, their mores, home and marketplace, clothing, and economy. "Growing Up" is a detailed description of the way a child is born, is raised, and matures. Many pages are given over to the courtship and marriage ceremonies. "The Marketplace" discusses the slave trade, which was not abolished until early in the nineteenth century, and actually continued on a small scale until the beginning of the twentieth century.

Illustration by Edith G. Singer for The Ibo of Biafra *by Sonia Bleeker. Copyright 1969. Reproduced by permission of William Morrow & Company, Inc.*

Sonia Bleeker went to Africa four times to do research, and each of her books is made vivid by the small details that can come only from personal observation. In *The Pygmies; Africans of the Congo Forest* (1968) she describes a ceremony of the Mbuti, one of the four major Pygmy groups. The Molimo is a beautiful and moving rite, a memorial honoring the Pygmy dead, usually a beloved old person, in which the participants give thanks to the forest for its abundance.

In addition to her more recent books on Africa, Bleeker wrote seventeen books about Indians of the Americas, among which are *The Sea Hunters; Indians of the Northwest Coast* (1951), which describes the history and living patterns of Indians on the Alaskan and Canadian coasts, and *The Maya; Indians of Central America* (1961), which includes some discussion of archeological exploration in the area. In *The Eskimo; Arctic Hunters and Trappers* (1959), Bleeker presents a mass of factual material in a writing style that is simple but always vivid.

Franklyn M. Branley

The Milky Way; Galaxy Number One

Franklyn Branley was, before retirement, an astronomer on the staff of the American Museum-Hayden Planetarium, and Director of Educational Services. Both his professional knowledge and his familiarity with presenting facts to the lay person are reflected in his many books on astronomy and other scientific subjects. He collaborated with Eleanor K. Vaughan in two interesting books for the very young, *Mickey's Magnet* (1956) and *Timmy and the Tin-Can Telephone* (1959), which present scientific facts in attractive format.

The Milky Way (1969) is one of his books for older readers, using scientific terminology and a scholarly approach. It begins with a history of astronomy, describing early telescopes, the beliefs of early scientists and the ordinary people, and the conflict between Ptolemaic and Copernican theories.

Chapter 4 describes a development of the 1940s, exploring by radio astronomy. With this new device the shape of the Milky Way became more discernible. The last chapter describes the way in which the galaxy may have evolved, and makes conjectures about where it may go from here. The book includes an appendix for finding stellar magnitudes and distances, intended for those who understand logarithms, and a bibliography for further reading. Other books for older readers are *Mars; Planet Number Four* (1966), a revision that includes the findings of Mariner IV, and *The Sun; Star Number One* (1964).

Branley has also written many books for younger children. *The Sun; Our Nearest Star* (1961) is a simple explanation in picture-book format, and *A Book of Mars for You* (1968) speculates about an unmanned landing. *The Moon Seems to Change* (1960), handsomely illustrated with woodcuts by Helen Borten, is a clear explanation for the changes in the moon's appearance. These books are in the Crowell "Let's-Read-and-Find-Out Science Books" series. Branley is particularly skilled at selecting salient facts and omitting minor ones, so that his books for readers in lower and middle grades are succinct as well as accurate. In *Eclipse* (1973) he defines terminology in order to explain clearly the phenomenon of total solar eclipse, and in *Pieces of Another World* (1972) he discusses the collection and analysis of moon rocks, carefully distinguishing between fact and theory, and making clear the interdisciplinary effort of scientists in the investigation.

None of Franklyn Branley's books has been more popular than *The Christmas Sky* (1966), which is based on the Christmas lecture at the Hayden Planetarium. It discusses the Biblical, historical, and astronomical clues to the true date of the birth of Jesus, and deftly combines scientific facts and a reverent approach.

Leonard Everett Fisher

The Tanners

The Glassmakers (1964) was the first of a series of books by Leonard Everett Fisher on "Colonial Americans and Colonial American Craftsmen." The books are well designed, with a full-page picture on the right facing three-quarters of a page of text on the left, with an occasional double-spread picture. The scratchboard illustrations, drawn with vigor, depict costume details and customs, and there are many small, accurate drawings of the tools of each trade, carefully labeled and described. The first third of *The Tanners* (1966) is devoted to history, the last two-thirds to technique, an arrangement used for all books in the series. The author includes a glossary of terms and an index, but provides no bibliography or acknowledgments of any kind. The text is replete, however, with references which are evidence of research. Fisher explains how the tanner played an important part in the economy of the American colonies. The tanner prepared the skins for the parchment-maker, who in turn made vellum, a superior writing surface—on which were written both the Declaration of Independence and the Constitution of the United States.

Illustration by Leonard Everett Fisher from The Architects. *Copyright © 1970 by Franklin Watts, Inc. Reprinted by permission.*

Among his books on Colonial Americans are *The Schoolmasters* (1967), *The Architects* (1970), and *The Homemakers* (1973). In the series on Colonial American craftsmen are *The Cabinetmakers* (1966), *The Blacksmiths* (1976), and others. For younger children he wrote a book about fire engines entitled *Pumpers, Boilers, Hooks and Ladders* (1961). *Two If by Sea* (1970) is a dramatic description of the actions of Paul Revere and three others during two hours of an eventful evening: April 18, 1775.

Genevieve Foster

George Washington's World

Because the subject of history confused her as a schoolgirl, Genevieve Foster, when she decided to write history books for children, thought in terms of what events were going on at the same time all over the world, and what people lived at the same time. By using primary sources from which she quotes, she imparts a sense of nearness to the happenings of long ago.

George Washington's World (1941) is divided into six parts beginning when Washington was a boy and ending with his presidency. The book does an admirable job of presenting a horizontal look at history, a slice of life crosswise instead of strung out chronologically. When George Washington was a farmer, for instance, James Watt invented the steam engine, James Cook discovered Australia on the other side of the world, and Pompeii was uncovered. California was settled, Japan was a feudal state closed to the world, Marie Antoinette was married in France. All of these events and more were taking place during the period when Boston had a tea party and Paul Revere took his ride.

This book, like its counterparts in the series, is a large volume with interesting illustrations, full index, and separate indexes of places, nations, and events. Although these books are rather formidable, and graded for eleven-to-fourteen-year-olds, the style is so lively and understandable that they are excellent sources for teachers and parents to read to younger children.

The World of Columbus and Sons (1965) and *The World of William Penn* (1973), two other books in the series, are richly documented and have the same original approach to history; the former seems more difficult than *George Washington's World,* and is not so fully illustrated. The Penn book gives a broad view of world events in the years in which Penn was most active as a Quaker and was establishing the Pennsylvania settlements.

The Year of the Pilgrims—1620 (1969), for a younger audience, is more simply written and introduces color in a small volume of 62 pages. In this and in *The Year of the Horseless Carriage—1801* (1975), also for younger children, the text extends beyond the date given in the title.

Jean Craighead George

All Upon a Stone

All of Jean George's books are distinguished for her authoritative treatment of biological subjects and minute knowledge of the habits and the habitat of wild creatures. *All Upon a Stone* (1971) has been singled out not because it is more profound or perceptive than the others, but because of the unusual and explicit way in which it presents ecology to young children.

The book is notable for the harmony between the graceful writing and the handsome pictures by Don Bolognese, who painted a three-foot by four-foot canvas in acrylics first, then used details of the larger work to fill each

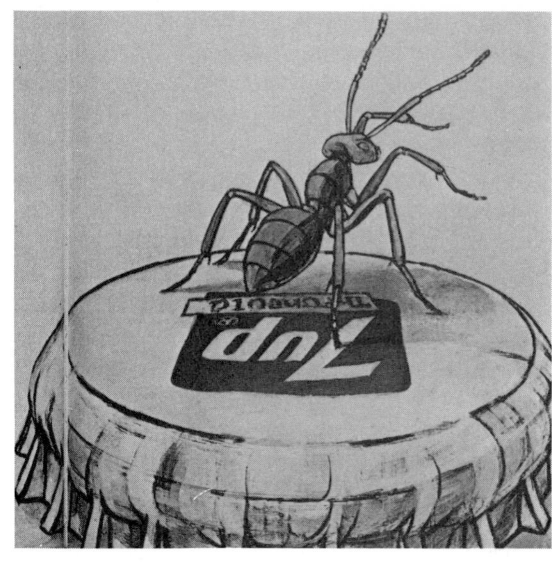

From All Upon a Sidewalk *by Jean Craighead George, illustrated by Don Bolognese. Copyright © 1974 by Jean Craighead George and Don Bolognese. Reprinted by permission of the publishers, E. P. Dutton & Co., Inc., and Curtis Brown, Ltd. (Original in color)*

of the pages of the book. Bolognese chose this technique to reflect the unity of the microcosm of the life on the stone. The whole picture is shown at the end of the book. The opening paragraph draws the analogy:

> *A stone by a stream in the woods is like a tiny country. It has its own forests, valleys, and pools. It has its own creatures that live out their lives, hunting, sleeping, and working all upon a stone.* (p. 1)

As a mole cricket tunnels under the ground and makes his way upon the stone, he meets all of the animal and plant life in this environment, including algae, rotifers, fresh-water jellyfish, and sponges in the water of the rock pool.

In *All Upon a Sidewalk* (1974) it is a yellow ant that explores her small world. George brings into the text, simply written as it is, such aspects as chemical messages and mutually profitable relationships between species. Again in this book the whole world of the sidewalk is pictured only at the end of the book.

The Hole in the Tree (1957), profusely illustrated by Jean George, can be enjoyed by very young children. It is the story of various occupants: a bark beetle, a carpenter bee, a black-capped chickadee family, and so on to the family of raccoons that is born there. *The Moon of the Bears* (1967) is one of a series of nature books, "The Thirteen Moons." These books have grown out of Jean George's interest in ecology, especially in the study of the relationship between climate and periodic biological events. As part of her research for *The Moon of the Wild Pigs* (1968), she visited the Arizona-Sonora Desert Museum, where she talked with scientists and observed the peccaries in their natural habitat.

Most of George's books for older readers are fictional, but all of them are concerned with some facet of the natural sciences: wolf behavior in *Julie of the Wolves* (1972), the effects of pollution on wild creatures in *Who Really Killed Cock Robin?* (1971), and the protection of wild animals in *Going to the Sun* (1976). None of her fiction for older readers, however, surpasses in writing style *Spring Comes to the Ocean* (1965), in which each chapter describes one form of marine life, beginning with the stirring of the reproductive instinct in the spring. Authoritative, accurate, logically organized, the book is imbued with a sense of wonder and pleasure in the marvelous intricacies of ocean life.

Sonia and Tim Gidal

My Village in Ghana

Sonia and Tim Gidal traveled abroad to acquire facts and photographs for their "My Village" books, and the wealth of detail in that series is evidence of their careful observation. Limiting their subject to one child's friends and family, they give a detailed account of the activities which take place in home, school, and recreation areas during the span of one day, although there may be references to past events.

My Village in Ghana (1969) has a full-color photograph of young James Kodjo Badu on its cover and it is through his first-person, present-tense account that we learn about life in Makranso, which is the center of Ghana. Through Kodjo we learn about the customs, schooling, food, folklore, dress, arts and crafts, and economy of the village as well as the interpersonal relations within his extended family. Kodjo's day begins in his Aunt Lucretia's household as he helps with the chores, then joins a group of younger children to hear a story about Ananse the spider and why the snake has no legs, told by Nana, the chief. As the day progresses we look into almost every side of village life.

The book has more than eighty black-and-white photographs of many aspects of life in the village. While some are obviously posed, others are candid. In addition, there is a well-drawn map at the end of the book, as well as a sketch of the village in a two-page spread at the beginning. A glossary of foreign words appears (although they are explained the first time they are used in the text). There is also a one-page history of Ghana.

The "My Village" series has had many imitators, but few authors have achieved the natural quality of the Gidals' books, which include *My Village in Germany* (1964), *My Village in Italy* (1962), *My Village in Denmark* (1963), and others, numbering over twenty volumes in the series. Two volumes have been written by Sonia Gidal alone: *My Village in Portugal* (1972) and *My Village in Hungary* (1974).

Shirley Glubok

The Art of Ancient Greece

Shirley Glubok majored in art and archeology, received her master's degree in early childhood education, and lectures to children's groups at the Metropolitan Museum of Art. She is well prepared, then, to explain and introduce the arts and crafts of ancient cultures, and her books are impressive because of the combination of authoritative knowledge, simple presentation, dignified format, and a recurrent emphasis on the relationships between an art form and the culture in which it was created.

The Art of Ancient Greece (1963) has clear photographs of sculpture, architecture, pottery, and reliefs in a survey of Greek art. Presented for the middle grades, it is a guided tour in print of art objects gathered from museums all over the world. The book begins with a paragraph describing Greece, and then discusses ancient Greek vases, their beauty, and their various uses. Greek sculpture is discussed, with reproductions of Aphrodite and Apollo and of the Parthenon and its sculpture. Enlarged photographs of the heads are shown so that readers can see the details in the carving. The pages on armor are particularly well designed, with the figures facing each other from opposite pages, both backed by squares of brilliant pink to set off the black-and-white photographs. Glubok has expanded this theme into an entire book, *Knights in Armor* (1969), which is based mostly on the collection of armor in the Metropolitan Museum of Art.

In all of Shirley Glubok's books the page layout and the quality of the reproductions are good; the correlation between the text and the pictures has been careful, and locations in museums are given for all objects pictured.

The Art of Ancient Mexico (1968) is simply written and includes some materials children would be interested in for their familiarity: a pottery figure which appears to be a child in a swing, a man playing a drum and one blowing on a conch shell, and a series of pieces on an ancient ball game, including a player wearing helmet, knee guards, and ankle guards for protection. *The Art of the Etruscans* (1967) gives a good look at the Etruscan civilization through its art, much of it bronze statues and terra-cotta figures of athletes, gods, and warriors.

While most of the books in the series are about ancient cultures, Glubok has also written many books about art in the United States, including *The Art of Colonial America* (1970), *The Art of the Old West* (1971), *The Art of the Plains Indians* (1976), and *The Art of America in the Gilded Age* (1974), all of which have supplementary curricular use. This series is unique in its field. It does not give a comprehensive art history of a culture, but it is unexcelled as an introduction for the beginner.

James Haskins

The Consumer Movement

As a teacher at every level from elementary school to university, James Haskins has become familiar with the interests of young readers as well as with their problems, some of which he describes in *Diary of a Harlem Schoolteacher*. He has written many biographies about black men and women as well as nonfiction in the social sciences; his writing is notable for its forthright tone, its casual but dignified style, its objectivity, and the research that is evident in the glossaries, bibliographies, and carefully compiled and cross-referenced indexes.

The Consumer Movement (1975) is, like most of Haskins's books, written for older readers but has minor reference use for children in the middle grades. It is organized by such topics as "The Consumer Movement and the Drug Industry" and "The Consumer Movement and the Toy Industry." Within each section, there is some background material, followed by a history of problems, dangers, consumer action, and legislation; each chapter concludes with a summary statement on ways the consumer may encourage solutions to problems. The subject chapters are preceded by discussions on the consumer movement and consumer needs, and the final chapter emphasizes consumer awareness and the importance of joining the consumer movement.

Street Gangs, Yesterday and Today (1974) is a serious investigation based on newspaper accounts, sociological studies, and interviews. It covers the subject from colonial times to the present, pointing out the fact that there have always been ties of political and criminal elements, and that there are no easy solutions for a social phenomenon that has as some of its causes poverty, loneliness, low status, and class distinctions. In *Your Rights Past and Present* (1975) Haskins does not attempt coverage of all issues but concentrates on the historical development and present status of the rights of youth in five areas: labor, school, justice, in the home, and in choosing a home. Candid and impartial, the book is based on research and the author is careful to point out that some issues are in a state of flux, thereby ensuring the fact that his readers will not assume what was current at the time of writing necessarily remains true. He has also written on such diverse topics as *Religions* (1973), a survey of five major faiths,

Witchcraft, Mysticism and Magic in the Black World (1974), *Jobs in Business and Office* (1974), and *The Creoles of Color of New Orleans* (1975).

Holling Clancy Holling

Paddle-to-the-Sea

In a book as imaginative as its title, Holling C. Holling sets down the travels of a little wooden Indian sitting in a canoe carved of wood. Launched in the water in Nipigon country in Canada, the carving floats down through all of the Great Lakes, and finally reaches the sea. During this odyssey of *Paddle-to-the-Sea* (1941), he becomes frozen into the lake water, caught in a forest fire, and picked up by strangers, but always they heed the carving on the bottom of the canoe: "Please put me back in the water. I am Paddle-to-the-Sea," and he is put back in the water to continue his journey.

Fictionalized, this is also a geographical tour de force and a description of the ecology of the land through which Paddle floats. While *Paddle-to-the-Sea* is in truth a demonstration that water from north of Lake Superior makes its way to the Atlantic Ocean, it is much more. It is an imaginative dream of the real-life Indian boy who made the carving, and who later heard that it had gone far across the ocean to France; it is a picture of the wildlife that surrounds Lake Superior; it is all these things, but because it is the sum rather than the parts, it is a unique work of art. *Paddle-to-the-Sea* was a Caldecott Honor Book in 1942.

Each chapter consists of one page of print alternating with full-page illustrations in full color, so that the story unfolds quickly as Paddle makes his way from the north, through the locks at Sault Ste. Marie, and on down to the ocean. The author shapes each chapter or page around a momentous happening, such as the breaking up of the ice on the river, or going over Niagara Falls. His easy, descriptive style, interspersed with lively conversation, makes the book attractive to children. Just as attractive are the pencil drawings which decorate the margins of the text, intricate accurate diagrams of the locks at the Soo, of a sawmill, or a lake freighter. Labeled well, they describe material which is not covered in the text. Coupled with the full-color paintings, these drawings both complement and enlarge the text, and they show as well as the text does the extensive historical research that Holling did for his books.

Illustration from Paddle-to-the-Sea *by Holling Clancy Holling. Copyright 1941 & 1969 by Holling Clancy Holling. Reprinted by permission of Houghton Mifflin Company. (Original in color)*

Although *Minn of the Mississippi* (1963) is almost identical in format and approach with *Paddle-to-the-Sea*, it is usually classified as a book about a reptile rather than fiction. Minn is a three-legged turtle who travels down the Mississippi from Lake Itasca, Minnesota, to the Gulf of Mexico, which enables Holling to describe the history, geography, climate, and geology of the river's regions.

Holling is also the author of *Pagoo* (1957), which describes in detail the life of a hermit crab, and *Tree in the Trail* (1942), the story of a tree's life over two centuries.

Aylette Jenness

Along the Niger River; An African Way of Life

Living in different parts of the world while on anthropological projects, Aylette Jenness has become interested in the lives of the people she met, and she has recorded them in several excellent photodocumentary volumes. She does not write as an uninvolved observer, but as a sympathetic visitor who hopes to be accepted by those she visits. She writes of peoples who lead lives that are, in varying degrees, primitive, but she does not write with an attitude of superiority nor does she assume that customs, foods, or clothing are odd or quaint—a weakness in many books about people of other countries.

Along the Niger River (1974) is based on observations made during the three years that Jenness lived in Nigeria. The photographs are excellent, some informative and others merely decorative. The text discusses tribes of the savanna lands that border the Niger in northern Nigeria, and it gives historical background that is a firm base for understanding how modern technology is impinging on traditional living patterns. The material is divided by such locations and occupations as "The Farmers," "The Fishing People," and "People of the Town." Comments on customs, mores, and cultural integration are perceptive, and the writing has both objectivity and the warmth that comes only from personal observations and relationships.

Jenness writes, in fact, only about things she has observed. While her first book, *Gussuk Boy* (1967), is fiction, it is based on a year of life in a village on the Bering seacoast. It incorporated many details of Alaskan Eskimo life, but there is far more of interest in *Dwellers of the Tundra* (1970), which gives a vivid picture of the same community, Makumiut, and of the impact of white culture on the residents, particularly on the restless adolescents of the village. The writing style is casual and conversational but the tone is serious; Jenness writes with candor and sympathy. The same qualities are in *A Life of Their Own; An Indian Family in Latin America* (1975), written with Lisa Kroeber. The authors spent much time with one family, but also explored the school, the health clinic, the market, and the government of a Guatemalan town, so that the text and photographs together give a well-rounded picture of a community.

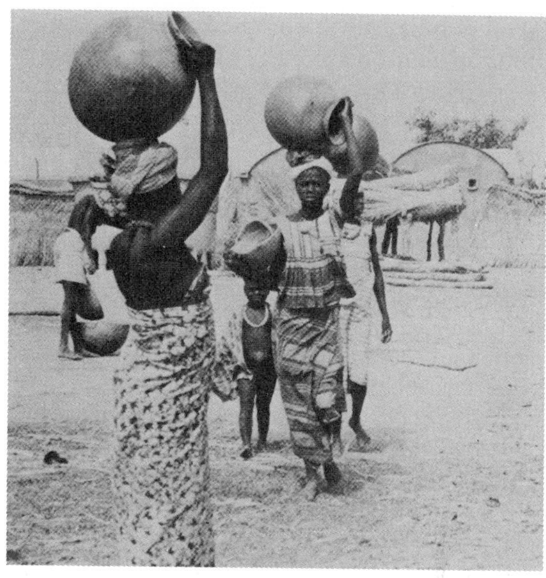

Copyright © 1974 by Aylette Jenness. Photograph from Along the Niger River *by Aylette Jenness, reprinted by permission of Thomas Y. Crowell Company, Inc., publisher.*

Patricia Lauber

Who Discovered America?

In a sharp departure from her earlier works, Patricia Lauber, in *Who Discovered America?* (1970), has written a speculative view of early explorers of America beginning with the people who may have crossed the land bridge between Siberia and Alaska; the Paleo-Indians, who may have inhabited the state of California 17,000 years ago; people who may have come from Southeast Asia to Middle America; the ones who named Vinland; and on through the voyages of Columbus. Lauber has done an excellent job of gathering and synthesizing the often controversial material about this important subject.

Two chapters are particularly interesting: "Visitors from Distant Lands" and "Vinland the Good." In the first, the author presents photographs and documentation of inventions, designs, and motifs that are common to Asia as well as Latin America and asks the question, "Borrowed from the old world or invented in the new?"

This story is not easy to believe. It seems almost impossible that the fishermen could have drifted 8,000 miles and landed in Ecuador, where they taught the Indians to make pottery. Yet archeologists cannot find another way to explain the sudden appearance of this particular pottery in a region where there are no traces of earlier pottery.

About 2,000 years ago, Ecuador seems to have had another visit by voyagers from Asia. The evidence is a collection of pottery objects that were common in Asia but have not been found anywhere else in the New World. They were discovered by archeologists digging near the north coast of Valdivia . . .

These pottery objects found together in one part of Ecuador are nearly impossible to explain, unless they were introduced by people from Asia. They appear suddenly in Ecuador. They seem unrelated to New World pottery objects, but they are like objects that were widely used in the Old World. (p. 64)

In the chapter on Vinland she presents the evidence for the discovery of Vinland as it is outlined in *The Saga of Eric the Red* and *The Greenlander's Saga* and tends to agree with scholars who think that the basic events of these sagas are true. The format of the book is attractive, and the reproductions of photographs, prints, and maps are excellent. The book's nine chapters are well organized and well indexed.

Lauber has written widely in the fields of the sciences and social studies. *All About the Planets* (1960), which includes an introductory chapter on the formation of the solar system, a chapter on the moon, and information on the planets, is a competent work. *All About the Ice Age* (1959) is illustrated with drawings, maps, and twelve pages of photographs of glaciers and the scientists exploring them. Three easy-to-read volumes are: *Your Body and How it Works* (1962), *The Story of Numbers* (1961), and *The Friendly Dolphins* (1963). Her interest in ecology and conservation is evident in *Everglades Country; A Question of Life or Death* (1973) and *Too Much Garbage* (1974). A quality that makes Lauber's books stimulating is their sense of lively curiosity, a provocative relish that can be shared by the reader and may send one seeking more information.

Robert M. McClung

Thor; Last of the Sperm Whales

In a book with overtones of *Moby Dick*, Robert McClung begins with the story of a sperm whale which destroyed the ships of whalers hunting him 150 years ago. *Thor* (1971) goes on to describe a sperm whale of today that bears the same marking as his ghostly forebear, ramming into the stern of a modern-day catcher boat carrying harpooners. In between there is a detailed description of the birth, feeding, growth, mating, and death of the great sperm whale as it travels the oceans, a great monster of the deep, fifty feet in length and "forty tons of bone and muscle, overlaid by an insulating blanket of blubber nearly a foot thick on his breast." While this is a scientific description of the life of the sperm whale, it is also a story of the slaughter of whales in our century, destruction so great that three species, the great blue whales, the finbacks, and the sei whales, are in danger of extinction. McClung graphically describes modern hunting techniques and their relentless efficiency.

McClung, a prolific author in his field, has written sympathetically but without sentimentality of all kinds of wildlife. He manages to be thorough, but not dry, and weaves a story without anthropomorphism into his factual approach. Threaded through all of his work is the persistent theme of good conservation practices, and his very early work *Spike; The Story of a Whitetail Deer* (1952) is a fine illustration of this. In it, the reader is exposed to the illegal practice of hunters shining a flashlight at night to attract deer. His books for younger children have large type, and clear, simple writing that never descends to oversimplification. In *Shag, Last of the Plains Buffalo* (1960), the author documents the savage slaughter of the buffalo as the white men drove westward with their guns and railroad tracks. *Honker; The Story of a Wild Goose* (1965) and *Black Jack; Last of the Big Alliga-*

tors (1967), which contains an afterword about the alligator being an endangered species of American wildlife, continue the conservation story.

While McClung's illustrations are not always labeled, they are always accurate and well placed in relation to textual references. His ability to write for different age levels is evident in comparing *Sea Star* (1975), which is written in concise prose, and *Gypsy Moth* (1974), which is detailed enough for adult readers; at both levels the writing is lucid and the information accurate. An excellent book on animal camouflage, *How Animals Hide* (1973) uses color photographs, showing examples of protective adaptation far better than any drawing could.

Milton Meltzer

In Their Own Words

The first of the three-volume survey of black history in America, *In Their Own Words*, contains material not previously known to many readers, drawn from letters, diaries, journals, autobiographies, speeches, resolutions, newspapers, and pamphlets of black people in slavery. It traces life on the plantation and conditions in the North in letters from escaped slaves in the free states, and tells of the day of Emancipation. In these excerpts, one can see Milton Meltzer's selectivity in showing the wide range of activity and writings of slaves and freed slaves. The three books are an excellent source of information on what living conditions have been for black people through American history. Volume One is illustrated with black-and-white paintings, drawings, engravings, and photographs, and includes reproductions of a list of slaves belonging to Thomas Jefferson and of posters announcing the sale of slaves. Each excerpt is short, some only two pages; occasionally a document is quoted in full. Each has an introduction by Meltzer and the source is identified at the close. The volumes cover three periods: 1619–1865, 1865–1916, and 1916–1966.

Meltzer's books show his interest in social reform and its effects on the American people. *Time of Trial, Time of Hope* (1966), written with August Meier, describes the many problems and few victories of black people in the United States between the First and Second World Wars. The authors write with authority and from a broad viewpoint that includes political, economic, educational, and cultural problems as well as the role of labor.

Meltzer's book on the labor movement in the United States, *Bread and Roses* (1967), gives a vivid history of the struggles of the laboring class up to 1915. Using comments from contemporary sources, Meltzer documents the grim story of child labor, sweat shops, and defeated attempts to organize. As is true in all his books, the sources cited in *Bound for the Rio Grande; the Mexican Struggle, 1845–1850* (1974) give evidence of the author's meticulous research. Several of Meltzer's books are concerned with the Jewish people: *Never to Forget; The Jews of the Holocaust* (1976) discusses the treatment of Jews in Nazi Germany; Jewish life in Eastern Europe is described in *World of Our Fathers* (1974); and in *Remember the Days* (1974) Meltzer writes a brief history of American Jewry. The last two books were finalists for the National Book Award.

Anthony Ravielli

Wonders of the Human Body

Wonders of the Human Body (1954) has never been surpassed in showing children the intricate marvels of the human form. Written by a man with a passion for communicating by word and illustration, the book has on every page a dramatic and illuminating picture that reveals the inner workings of the body. Anthony Ravielli is fascinated by what holds us together and makes us function, and he makes the subject equally intriguing for his readers. The book describes the skeleton, the muscles, the digestive system, and the brain and nervous system. One double-page spread shows the spine as a long string of spools. Then Ravielli uses two pages for a labeled, anatomically correct drawing of the spine, and the text describes what the spine is and does. In like fashion, another two-page picture shows wire

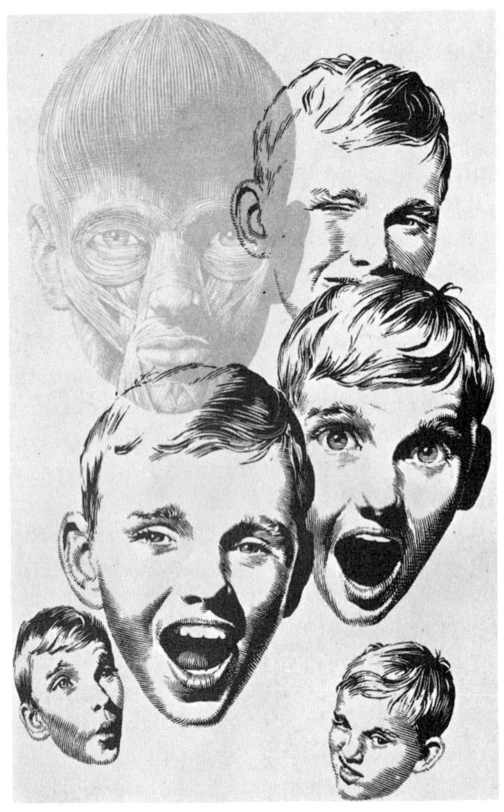

Illustration by Anthony Ravielli from Wonders of the Human Body *by Anthony Ravielli. Copyright 1954 by Anthony Ravielli. Reprinted by permission of The Viking Press, Inc. (Original with color)*

attached to the spools: "These are your ribs." The next page likens the thorax, or rib cage, to a bird cage. And there it is—a black-and-white bird cage, complete with bird, slipped down over the realistic drawing of the actual rib cage. The economy of Ravielli's prose and the grace of his style are evident. He limits his description always to one or two pages, and always the illustrations are coordinated. There is a very full table of contents.

Ravielli has written *An Adventure in Geometry* (1957), a book bursting with action drawings which relate forms in nature with geometric forms. *The World is Round* (1963) deals with the earth as a large spinning sphere, and likens human life on the earth to that of a fly on a giant ball the size of a house. Ravielli gives a history of people's beliefs about the shape of the earth, and concludes with a prophetic statement about humans landing on the moon. In *From Fins to Hands; An Adventure in Evolution* (1968), the author-illustrator has produced another handsome book, printed in two colors, on the importance of the development of the hand from prehistoric times to the present day of automation. Ravielli says of hands that "The human brain made man a civilized being, but it was his hands that recorded his progress and made human culture possible." In *What Is Bowling?* (1975) and *What Is Golf?* (1976), he gives histories of both sports, explains how they are played, and gives succinct advice on play, with excellent stop-action drawings.

Katharine Savage

The Story of World Religions

A historical as well as descriptive approach, Katharine Savage's *The Story of World Religions* (1967) is a comprehensive, well-written book, useful at both the junior-high and elementary levels, which gives a dispassionate, objective view of religions of the world. The book covers the world's major religions, but it does not include the area south of the Sahara in Africa, or reflect the many changes in the rituals and dress in the Roman Catholic religion, nor does it encompass the unrest in the priesthood of the Roman Catholic Church. It is organized into fourteen chapters which are roughly chronological, and each treats one religion, sometimes several, of a given area. Well researched, the book has an extensive bibliography, and in her acknowledgments the author cites numerous sources of information as well as sources for the photographs.

Savage's style is dignified but not dry, sympathetic but not sentimental, and her distinction as a writer of informational books is based on comprehensive treatment, reliable research, logical organization of material, and a sense of perspective which sees and emphasizes those aspects of a subject that have real importance. Her other works include *The Story of the United Nations* (1962), in which the first third of the book describes the inception and formation of the U.N., and the last third chronicles crises such as the birth of Israel, the Berlin airlift, and attempts to bring peace to the Congo; and *The Story of Africa;*

South of the Sahara (1961), which gives a history of the exploration and exploitation period in Africa and a look at some of the countries—Ghana, Nigeria, Rhodesia, and Kenya, among others.

Millicent E. Selsam

Benny's Animals

Millicent Selsam, one of the most dependably competent authors of science books, writes for all age levels, but she is undoubtedly best known for her books for young readers. Her style is simple and clear, with no extraneous material and no trace of popularization. She defines good science books as "those that show the methods of science at work, that elucidate basic principles of science and are not a mere assembly of facts, that convey something of the beauty and excitement of science, and that interest young people in thinking up good questions for new young scientists to test by experiment."[2]

Benny's Animals (1966) is a particularly good example of the inclusion of methodology and basic principles in a science book for the beginning reader. It is a clear lesson in how animals are classified, with a fictional framework that facilitates the explanation. Benny was a child with a passion for neatness and order, who wanted to organize his collection of material from the seashore, and this led to questions about the differences between animals. Finally Benny went to the museum to talk with Professor Wood, who suggested that he put the specimens in two piles according to whether or not they had a backbone; then his next step was to divide the animals with backbones into fish, amphibians, reptiles, birds, and mammals. Benny wanted to take classification a step further, but Professor Wood dissuaded him, saying that it would be a lifelong job. The book ends on just the right note, having explained the basic steps in classification and having made the point that there is a rational way of dividing living things. The format is excellent, with continuous text, large print, and plenty of space between the lines. Arnold Lobel's illustrations are appropriate in their earth colors, casually realistic when he portrays the boys and the family, and close enough to reality to be recognizable when he draws the animals, often giving them a little personality. *Greg's Microscope* (1963) and *Let's Get Turtles* (1965) are other titles in this "Science I Can Read" series.

How Kittens Grow (1975) is a succinct book for preschool children, illustrated with sharp photographs.

The Carrot and Other Root Vegetables (1971) and *Bulbs, Corms, and Such* (1974) are for independent readers in lower and middle grades, illustrated with large handsome photographs, some in color, by Jerome Wexler. A group of books which are illustrated by several different artists are *See Through the Jungle* (1957); *See Through the Sea* (1955), a story of

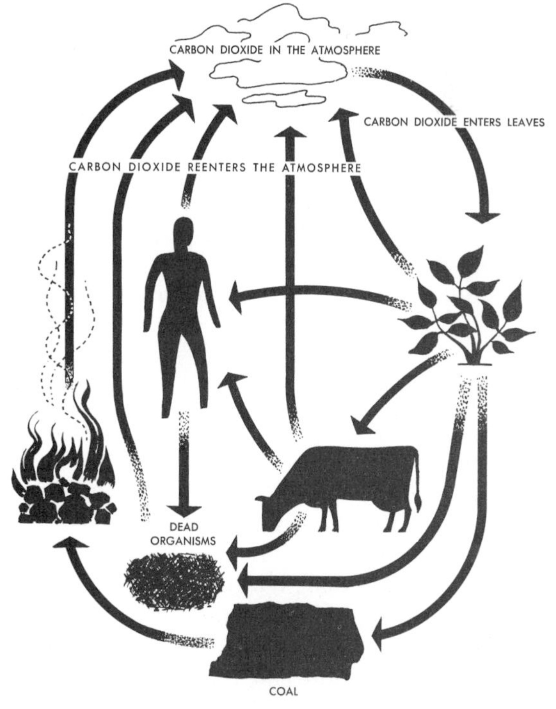

Illustration by Weimer Pursell from Biography of an Atom *by J. Bronowski and Millicent E. Selsam. Copyright © 1963 by J. Bronowski; renewed 1965 by J. Bronowski and Millicent E. Selsam. Reprinted by permission of Harper & Row, Publishers, Inc.*

[2]"Writing About Science for Children," by Millicent E. Selsam. From *A Critical Approach to Children's Literature*, edited by Sara Innis Fenwick. © 1967 by the University of Chicago. Reprinted by permission.

underwater life; and *See Along the Shore* (1961), a colorful volume which deals with tides and animals and plants of the seashore.

For still older children are *Animals as Parents* (1965) and *The Language of Animals* (1962), the latter a fascinating story of communication between animals including sounds, smells, facial expressions, and tail positions. In *Plants That Move* (1962), Selsam tells about the sundew plant, which catches insects, as well as the better-known venus flytrap; and in *Plants That Heal* (1959), she writes an intriguing chapter on plant medicines that are in use today. One of Selsam's most interesting books for older readers was written with Jacob Bronowski—*Biography of an Atom* (1963), which traces the history of one carbon atom from its birth in a young star, through the millennia, to a conjectural fate today.

Katherine B. Shippen

Men, Microscopes, and Living Things

Katherine Shippen's books reflect a wide-ranging interest: science, biography, history, music, industry, and other fields. *Men, Microscopes, and Living Things* (1955) exemplifies her careful research and the vitality and grace of a writing style that give her work authority and elegance. In this survey of the work of great biologists, she uses quotations from their writings to enliven the book. Each chapter deals with some aspect of experimental science, concluding with Thomas Hunt Morgan's work in this century, using the fruit fly in studies of heredity. Anthony Ravielli's spidery, delicate line drawings, quite unlike his other work in children's books, give added appeal. It is indexed in full; for example, there are eighteen entries under "Darwin, Charles."

Quotations are used also, as chapter introductions rather than within the text, in *The Great Heritage* (1947), which is timely because of the wide interest in conservation. *Miracle in Motion; The Story of American Industry* (1955) concisely gives a history of three centuries of industry, from the "Buy American" slogan after the American Revolution to Henry Ford's "Five Dollars a Day." In another book for older readers, Shippen collaborated with Anca Seidlova in writing *The Heritage of Music* (1963), a comprehensive and scholarly history of music from its beginning to Edgar Varèse's electronic music. *This Union Cause* (1958) is a history of organized labor in the United States and *The Pool of Knowledge; How the United Nations Share Their Skills* (rev. ed., 1965) is an informative contribution to young people's understanding of many of the peoples of this world as well as some of the work of the U.N.

Paul and Kay Showers

Before You Were a Baby

Before You Were a Baby (1968), the only book by Paul Showers for which he has a coauthor, is an excellently paced book for readers in the second and third grades, and it is clear enough to be read aloud to younger children. There are repetition and rhythm in sentences like "This new cell grew and grew and grew. And at last it became you." Particularly dramatic are the pictures which show, in color, the increasing size of the baby inside the uterus. On these pages the text is almost nonexistent, and the reader's eye is carried forward by the power of the graphic drawings as they progress from the hunchback figure at six weeks to the completely formed baby of eight months. Using all of the correct terms, such as *testes, sperm,* and *penis,* the book gives an accurate explanation of conception without being either coy or evasive. The book's tone is captured in its opening and closing paragraphs:

> *Once you were a baby. You were very small. A*
> *little boy could lift you easily and carry you.*
> *Before you were a baby, you were much smaller.*
> *No one could even see you.*

then,

> *Now the baby is born.*
> *This baby,*
> *and you,*
> *and every baby in the world—*
> *came from two tiny cells that nobody could see—*
> *an ovum*
> *and a sperm.*

The simple style and use of large print, with a minimum of labeled diagrams, is typical of the Crowell series which includes *Before You Were a Baby*. Showers gives accurate information in the very simplest language, chooses important facts, and tells them in logical sequence, so that the child can read the books alone or the adult can use them as a springboard for discussion.

Showers's other books include *Your Skin and Mine* (1965) and *Look at Your Eyes* (1962). The first gives some of the basic facts about skin: sensation, temperature adjustment, hair follicles, and color differences, explaining the latter so that the message about skin color is casual, while the illustrations show children of various colors in connection with the text rather than as an ethnic spectrum for its own sake. For example, a black child's daily activities are used to show how eyes adjust to light, that eyes are different colors, how the parts of the eye work.

Use Your Brain (1971), *Where Does the Garbage Go?* (1974), and *Sleep Is for Everyone* (1974) are other concise, informative science books by Paul Showers, and he has also written *Indian Festivals* (1969) and *Columbus Day* (1965) in the same direct and pithy style.

Viewpoints

If his knowledge is to grow through the books a child reads because of his desire to know, it must be the kind of knowledge that grows with his growth. Even a simple, elementary presentation of a subject that has interest for quite young children can awaken curiosity and suggest extensions of knowledge through books beyond the one a child is immediately reading. His interest in the subject may thus become a reading interest developed through childhood into maturity. The satisfactions of such continuous reading interests in the field of knowledge have permanent and rewarding values for children. Their reading of these books is complementary to their pleasure in creative literature, and both are necessary to the mental and imaginative growth of children.—Lillian H. Smith, *The Unreluctant Years,* American Library Association, Chicago, 1953, pp. 180–181.

Alvin and Virginia Silverstein

Hamsters; All About Them

Alvin Silverstein is a biology professor and Virginia Silverstein a translator of Russian scientific literature; they have collaborated on over thirty books for young people, from books that deal with a narrow area, such as *Apples; All About Them* (1976) to books on such complex topics as *Sleep and Dreams* (1974). Their work is carefully organized and written in a clear, direct style, and is dependably accurate. The more complicated subjects are not always covered in depth, but they are given balanced treatment, and the Silversteins' writing usually shows their attention to current research and always maintains a scientific attitude.

Hamsters (1974) is one of a series of books for the middle elementary school grades, all subtitled "All About Them." It is illustrated with photographs that are well placed in relation to textual references, although not all the pictures are informative. Following a brief discussion of the way in which hamsters were introduced into the United States as research animals and became popular as pets, the text gives detailed advice on the care of hamsters, including information on housing and breeding. A concluding chapter describes the importance of the hamster in laboratory studies. Pervading the book is an attitude of respect for the rights and well-being of pets, and there is no trace of fictionalization or anthropomorphism.

The Silversteins have written many books in a series called "Systems of the Body," with books like *The Skeletal System* (1972) and *The Skin* (1972) that have accurate texts, include facts on recent research, and give lucid explanations of intricate physiological functions. In *Exploring the Brain* (1973) the authors give a good overview of what is known on the subject, discussing both the functioning of the brain and the nervous system, and citing laboratory experiments on the effects of drugs and of illness on the human brain. They also discuss memory, intelligence, dreams, and extrasensory powers. Their emphasis on current research is evident in this book as in others; it is stressed particularly in *The Code of Life* (1972), which explores genetic engineering as well as genetic inheritance and how it functions, and in *The Chemicals We Eat and Drink* (1973), which discusses the benefits or dangers of chemicals in foods, with findings based on testing programs and research studies. The book also considers, as do other Silverstein books, effects on the society, and suggests citizen support of pollution control and of supervisory legislation.

Hilda Simon

Living Lanterns; Luminescence in Animals

As a student of art and biology, Hilda Simon is well qualified both as author and artist for the books she has written and illustrated in the field of biology. Her drawings are beautifully detailed and accurate, and the same accuracy is evident in her writing, which is informal and lucid. While there are scientific terms used, the writing is not laden with jargon but can be understood by readers with little background. However, since Simon uses neither anthropomorphism nor condescension and since she treats her subjects in some depth, her books are also appropriate for readers who do have background in biology.

In *Living Lanterns* (1971) Simon begins with a brief survey of what has been known about the phenomenon of luminescence in the past, then describes luminescent creatures according to their habitats (land, air, or sea), and concludes with a discussion of the anatomy of luminescence. Observations are validated by citing research, and the text is explicit in stating the fact that not all the questions about bioluminescence have been answered. Simon's books exemplify the best kind of science writing, authoritative and accurate, illustrated with pictures that are carefully placed and informative, and supplied with indexes, bibliographies, and—in some books—maps that show the ranges of species.

Most of her books are for older readers, but Simon's *The Amazing Book of Birds* (1958) is for the middle grades. Written in a light, informal style, it gives many facts about birds, but the random arrangement makes it less cohesive and therefore less useful than her later work. A study of imitative patterns or adaptations in the insect world, *Insect Masquerades* (1968), is a more typical example of Simon's writing: logically organized, and leading from the discussions of individual creatures to conclusions about the survival potential of insects which have such advantages. The full-color drawings in *Snakes; The Facts and the Folklore* (1973) and *Frogs and Toads of the World* (1975) have crisp, useful captions and can be used for identification. *Snakes* includes a chapter on keeping a snake as a pet, and both books describe the habits and habitats of species in great detail.

A. Harris Stone

The Chemistry of a Lemon

In a disarmingly simple volume of experiments, *The Chemistry of a Lemon* (1966), A. Harris Stone has presented a series of approaches to some aspects of chemical phenomena. The approaches are brief, open-ended, and thought-provoking, and teach much about scientific method. The child is

From the book The Chemistry of a Lemon *by A. Harris Stone, illustrated by Peter P. Plasencia. © 1966 by A. Harris Stone. Published by Prentice-Hall, Inc., Englewood Cliffs, New Jersey. (Original with color)*

encouraged to think beyond the pages of the book.

"Cleaning with lemon juice," for example, begins with two questions: "What does lemon juice do to a dirty copper penny?" and "Are there other liquids that will clean pennies?" A discussion of the process of oxidation is followed by a brief explanation of why the lemon juice acts as it does. Then the section ends, as it began, with a series of six questions leading to six experiments. This is far different from most other chemistry books in print, many of which set up experiments with only one conclusion, and guide the child each step of the way.

After twenty-five of these brief experiments, the author leaves the child with still more motivating ideas in a section called "A Last Word."

If you've experimented right to this page, you are now an experienced chemist. If you have kept notes on your work, you will be able to check each idea that you worked on. You can design and write about your own experiments, too. Look around! Have you overlooked other elements you can combine with a lemon or some part of a lemon to get a new chemical reaction? Keep trying and see what you can discover. (p. 58)

A glossary of twenty-one terms is furnished, and a paragraph for each explanation. No index is given, none is needed.

The humorous black-and-white line drawings by Peter Plasencia complement the casual, off-hand style the author establishes throughout. Stone uses short sentences, short paragraphs, and uncomplicated vocabulary, but never writes down to his readers. Thus, while the book might conceivably be used by junior-high students where experiments are regularly in the science curriculum, the appeal is wide enough so that elementary students can use the book, both at home and in the elementary-science programs.

Stone's other books include *Puttering with Paper* (1968), coauthored with Bertram Siegel; *Experiments in Ecology* (1973), which was written with Stephen Collins; and *Biology Project Puzzlers* (1973), for which the coauthor is Robert Stein, and in which the text frequently suggests adult supervision. *Puttering with Paper*, which is based on discoveries of important scientists from Leonardo da Vinci to Sir Robert Hooke, is certainly more than "puttering." Children are likely to be intrigued by the title, however, and if they heed the advice in the introduction, they will "be willing to experiment without much knowledge about the problem and to experiment in ways not described in this book." Experiments range from testing the tension and absorption rate of paper to making folded paper airplanes. As in other Stone books, the drawings demonstrate procedures in step-by-step fashion.

Stone was one of the first authors to use the process approach that is now a part of the science curriculum; and his writing is so imbued with an enjoyment of investigation that it stimulates the child's need to know.

Alvin Tresselt

The Beaver Pond

Alvin Tresselt and his illustrator, Roger Duvoisin, have produced in *The Beaver Pond* (1970) a beautiful picture book which vividly describes the chain of ecological events that result from the damming of a stream. We see beavers gnawing down aspen trees for food and material for their beaver dam. As the dam grows in the small stream, ducklings and fish join the pond family, and green reeds grow along the shore. As the years pass, the stream brings fine silt into the pond, and the beavers finally move on to newer, deeper water. Without the industrious beavers to dam up the pond, the swiftly running water eats away at the remains of the dam and beaver houses, sweeping all of them away; and the stream reverts to its former leisurely pattern. The calm picture of winter quiet that the artist has painted is echoed in this prose:

The frost bit deeper and deeper into the ground as a sheet of ice spread over the top of the pond.
And the frogs slept deep in the mud at the bottom.
The winter snows swept down, filling the hollows
and covering the secret runways of field mice.

The frozen earth slept under the snow.
The pond slept under the ice,
and the beavers were safe from the wolf,
the prowling lynx, and the wolverine,
under the icy roof of the pond and the frozen domes
of their houses.

The Beaver Pond is both an explanation of ecological balance and a story of an animal's life cycle, and its text demonstrates the reason for Tresselt's durability as a writer for small children. His prose is direct and unornamented, yet it has a poetic quality, and he sees in natural beauty, in wild life, and in the variations of weather those aspects that are exciting or curious to a child.

His earlier books of nature are still favorites with children. *Sun Up* (1949) describes a day on a farm, from the time the rooster crows until nightfall. *Rain Drop Splash* (1946) is the story, in very large print and large pictures, of rain and its travels through a pond, a brook, a lake, and a river down to the sea. This book is illustrated by Leonard Weisgard, but most of Tresselt's work is illustrated by Roger Duvoisin, and the two have made an important team over the years. *White Snow Bright Snow* (1947; Caldecott Award) is the delightful story of a big snowstorm and the troubles of all the people who have to brave the elements, compared with the delight of the children in being snowed in. These early books have always stressed ecology and the interdependence of life and its surroundings. *Hide and Seek Fog* (1965), a poetic description of a weather phenomenon, was a Caldecott Honor Book. *It's Time Now!* (1969) portrays in light and easy tone the drama of the changing seasons as they affect activities in the city. It is an evocative book that should help small children associate the cycle of weather and the passage of time.

Illustration by Roger Duvoisin for The Beaver Pond *by Alvin Tresselt. Copyright 1970. Reproduced by permission of Lothrop, Lee & Shepard Co. (Original in color)*

In *The Dead Tree* (1972) the text follows a tree's life from maturity to its return to the rich humus of the forest floor from which it first sprang. This book is perhaps the best of Tresselt's work in showing the intricacy and balance in an ecological biome.

Edwin Tunis

Frontier Living

The immense amount of detail produced in *Frontier Living* (1961) reflects painstaking research; the text contains little conjecture, but only fact upon fact about all aspects of frontier living. Organized generally in an east-to-west pattern, the book, by the author's admission, concentrates mostly east of the Mississippi because, as he said, "Nearly every phase of the far West has been dealt with . . . while the forest frontier, with a few notable exceptions, has been bypassed since James Fenimore Cooper stopped romancing about it." And so the book progresses from sections dealing with the Piedmont, in which Indians, forts, and medicine and witchcraft are described, on through the old Northwest Territory, passing then out to Kansas, Colorado, and California. "The Old Northwest" has much excellent material on day-to-day living, and the section on housekeeping is an example of both the author's style and the meticulousness of his research.

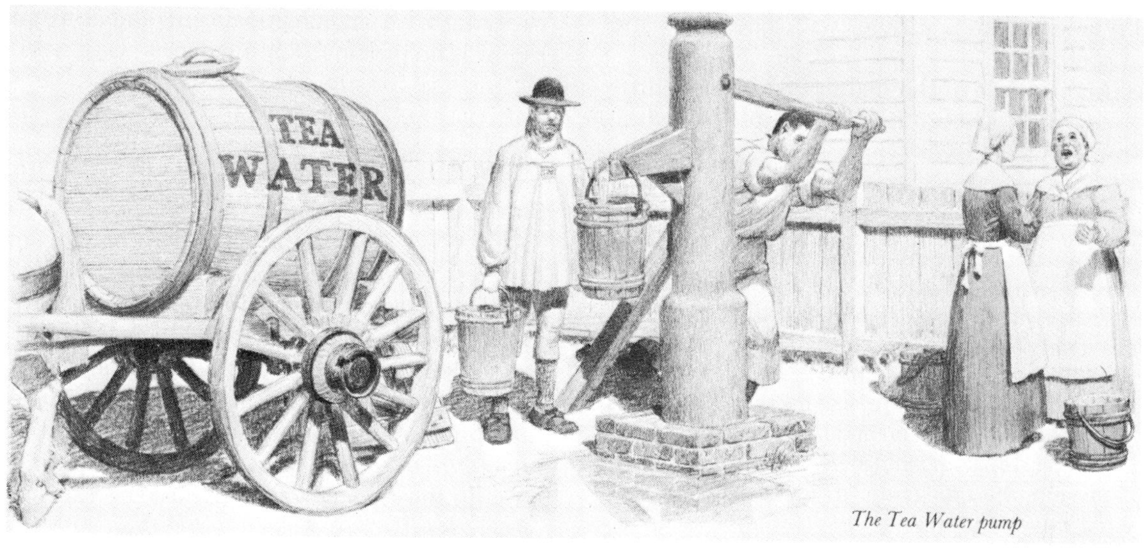

Copyright © 1969 by Edwin Tunis. Illustration from The Young United States—1783–1830 *by Edwin Tunis. Reprinted by permission of Thomas Y. Crowell Company, Inc., publisher, and Curtis Brown Ltd.*

The black-and-white line drawings are of uniform excellence and accuracy, whether of a panoramic view of moving half of a canal boat over a mountain, or detailing the intricate works of a small arsenal of early western arms. The author's captions are revealing, too, and often humorous. Of the illustrations of the Bowie knife, he wrote: "The mild and quiet Colonel Bowie didn't design this toadsticker; he gave it his name by way of the mayhem he did with it."

Frontier Living was a Newbery Honor Book, and *Colonial Living* (1957), with a similar format, won the Thomas Alva Edison Foundation's Children's Book Award for special excellence in portraying America's past. *Wheels; A Pictorial History* (1955) and *Indians* (1959) are so comprehensive and profusely illustrated with authoritatively detailed drawings that they have reference use. *Shaw's Fortune* (1966), the picture story of a plantation, differs from earlier books in being chronological, following the growth of the plantation from a cabin in the wilderness clearing to a self-sufficient community in 1752. *The Young United States—1783 to 1830* (1969) is topically organized, covering both daily life and historical events. In *The Tavern at the Ferry* (1973), Tunis follows the changes that occur in the life of a Quaker family and in the building they own; through this, he gives an immediacy to the colonial way of life and to events of the Revolutionary War. Tunis's wit had been evident in his other books, but with the publication of *Chipmunks on the Doorstep* (1971), his first book in the field of natural science, he added a wry humor to the appeals of perceptive observation and beautiful pictures.

Harvey Weiss

Pencil, Pen and Brush; Drawing for Beginners

A major criterion for an activity book is that the instructions tell the reader exactly how to perform the activity. Harvey Weiss's arts and crafts books are clear in explaining procedures, and they encourage readers to use their own initiative.

Pencil, Pen and Brush (1961) has a sophisticated approach for a how-to-do-it book. Using the work of major artists, from Leonardo da Vinci to Maurice Sendak, as well as photographs for models, Weiss presents his instructions in easy steps, never talking down to his readers. Practical advice is given for each step, and readers are given suggestions for striking out on their own; the discussion ends on an encouraging note, with questions and suggestions.

An example of the matter-of-fact procedure used throughout the book is this selection from "Tones":

A tone is a shade of black or a shade of color. When you use a tone combined with simple line, your drawing will look more solid and more interesting. Here is a way to make a figure drawing using tones. Get a small sponge, or a piece of sponge. (If you can't find a sponge a crumpled-up facial tissue will do.) Pour two or three drops of ink onto a plate and add about two tablespoons of water. Mix the ink and water. Dip your sponge lightly into the mixture then press the sponge down lightly on a piece of scrap paper and quickly lift it straight up again. You'll see that the sponge leaves a large and pleasantly textured tone of gray.

Use the sponge to put the main masses of the figure on paper—a few big dabs for the body, some slimmer dabs (with the narrow part of the sponge) for the arms and legs. Then take your pencil, or pen and ink, and draw in the figure with lines. Try using colored ink, instead of black ink, for your tones. Or use water color, which is a transparent paint. (p. 24)

At the end of the book the artist has included a section "About the illustrations" identifying each artist included in the book by the title of his work, and giving the museum in which the original art is located.

Other books deal with three-dimensional materials: *Clay, Wood and Wire* (1956), *Ceramics from Clay to Kiln* (1965), and *Carving* (1976). Again, the artist uses pieces of sculpture, artifacts, woven fabrics, a Buckminster Fuller geodesic dome, masks, and Egyptian pottery as his models. *Paper, Ink and Roller* (1958) is on printmaking for beginners. Although Weiss has reproduced some artists' prints for this book, he uses many examples of his own prints.

Weiss is always clear and explicit, moving from simple projects to more complicated ones; in *Model Cars and Trucks and How to Build Them* (1974), for example, the first model is a solid, one-piece racing car, and the last a large, intricate car that can be ridden.

Weiss has also written *Sailing Small Boats* (1967) and *Motors and Engines and How They Work* (1969), an accurate and useful book for the child with a mechanical bent, and one that requires no previous knowledge.

Herbert Zim

Dinosaurs

Among the many books that Herbert Zim has written in various scientific fields, *Dinosaurs* (1954) is a good example of the logical organization, simple and succinct writing, and provision of background information that make his approach admirably suitable for presenting complex information to a reader unfamiliar with the subject. Zim explains the ways in which fossils are formed and the ways in which scientists are able to determine what dinosaurs looked like, and what they ate, by comparing their skeletal structure with those of known creatures. He describes the evolution of dinosaurs, gives details on how the species differed, and provides brief descriptions of some of the better-known kinds. The meticulously drawn black-and-white illustrations parallel the text and are always adequately captioned. The book concludes with a discussion of the ways in which dinosaurs changed during the Age of Reptiles and offers possible reasons for their extinction.

Herbert Zim has taught for over thirty years in the fields of science and science education. With his first wife, Sonia Bleeker, he wrote *Life and Death* (1970), which stands alone in the field of children's literature; no one else has attempted a work quite like it for children of elementary school age. The book discusses life expectancy, aging, the clinical definition of death, and the rituals and legal procedures that are followed after death occurs. It concludes with a brief description of death rituals as they are practiced throughout the world.

Zim's lifelong interest in collecting nature specimens is reflected in *Golden Hamsters* (1951) and *Frogs and Toads* (1950), two of a series of small volumes with large print that have proved most attractive to young children. In them, as in *Crabs* (1974) and *Snails* (1975), both written with Lucretia Kranz, the continuous texts are comprehensive, giving classification, varieties, and facts about habits, habitat, and structure. His books on the human body, *Our Senses and How They Work* (1956) and *Your Heart and How It Works* (1959), are for the slightly older child. A professor of science education, Zim exemplifies the objectivity of the scientist's attitude. In *Medicine* (1974), which is a survey of products, not of the profession, he includes information based on research. He has also contributed to the field of informational books as editor and coauthor of a series of Golden Nature Guides, pocket-sized volumes in full color. They are widely circulated in outlets other than libraries and are probably the one most handy tool for quick identification of trees, fish, seashells, fossils, and flowers.

It is obviously impossible to include, in the discussion and the bibliography that follow, all the good informational books or indeed books on every subject. The chapter and the reading lists are meant to give the reader a broad picture of the kinds of material that are available to provide children with pleasure and to satisfy their need for information.

Whenever books are classified as in the following discussion, problems arise, because some of them simply refuse to fit neatly into preordained slots. For example, the early concept books (discussed in Chapter 4) for very young children could be in a separate group here, also: books that present ideas of big and small, books that simply introduce familiar objects, books that familiarize a child with colors. There are books that bridge the physical and biological sciences, books that are about religious holidays but are also activity books, books that describe musical instruments and also tell the reader how to make simple instruments. Books on pollution, for instance, involve weather, natural resources, and chemical change; they involve living things; and they illustrate the problems created by our careless destruction of our environment, problems that have sociological repercussions. Since pollution is a tragedy created by humanity, such books have been placed in the social science list.

The books have been arranged in five broad categories: physical sciences, biological sciences, social sciences, religion and the arts, and activities and experiments. The bibliography for this chapter follows the same pattern.

The Biological Sciences

Partly because of the nationwide concern for more science in the schools, the list of science books grows phenomenally each year as publishers rush more of them to press. The list has also grown in breadth of subject. No longer are books in the biological sciences confined to those about familiar plants and animals—today they cover almost every topic from a hen's egg to cryogenics and space medicine. Children's books have abandoned, for the most part, the pseudo-scientific stories and watered-down information of the past and have adopted instead a seriousness and a straightforward approach that children and adults alike can appreciate.

Reports from teachers and librarians show that science rates high in both the types of questions children ask and in the types of books they request. Properly presented, almost any area of scientific knowledge can be made both fascinating and comprehensible to children.

The criteria for informational books discussed earlier in this chapter (see pp. 444–448) of course are applicable in evaluating science books. It is important that the author keeps in mind the child's point of view.

Authors should begin within the framework of the child's limited world. They must expand that world *step by step* at a pace which the child can follow—if they leap, they may leave the child behind. Leading, though, is not enough, for the child will choose to stay behind if the journey becomes uninteresting. What, therefore, is necessary to maintain interest?

Naturally clarity and good organization are of primary importance. Yet no matter how carefully and logically an author develops material, if it sounds like an article for an encyclopedia, the child will often lose interest. Unfortunately many adults look upon science as a cold collection of facts. To them it is devoid of emotion, entirely unrelated to imaginative writing. To the child, however, finding out about science is full of excitement, fascination, joy, and reassurance. What are some more of the books that not only present information clearly and understandably but maintain the reader's interest?

Illustration by Peter Parnall is reprinted by permission of Charles Scribner's Sons from Year on Muskrat Marsh *by Bernice Freschet, illustrated by Peter Parnall. Illustration copyright © 1974 Peter Parnall.*

Some books include both the biological and the physical sciences, like Bertha Parker's *Golden Book of Science* (1956), which is designed to introduce the child to a many-faceted field and to encourage pursuing the facets in detail.

Books like Sarah Riedman's *Naming Living Things* (1963) discuss seriously the classification of plants and animals. There is a wide spread between the sophistication of this book and the simple approach of *Benny's Animals* by Millicent Selsam, described earlier, but in terms of accuracy each fulfills its purpose.

With the current stress on ecological balance, many books explore both the plants and the animals of a living community. *The Living Community* (1966) by Carl Hirsch is an introduction to interrelationships among plants and animals; and Berniece Freschet's *Year on Muskrat Marsh* (1974) gives a similar picture of an ecosystem for younger children.

In Margaret Waring Buck's *In Yards and Gardens* (1952) the relationships among living things in an easily accessible environment are made as interesting as are those of the more exotic flora and fauna in *Tropical Rain Forests* (1957) by Delia Goetz.

Lucy Kavaler's *The Wonders of Algae* (1961) is an engrossing report on the versatility of one of the simplest of plant forms and of the experiments that have proved its usefulness to people: as a food, as a life-sustaining system for space ships, or as fuel. Kavaler's *Wonders of Fungi* (1964) discusses the myriad uses of some of the 100,000 known species of fungi that are disease producers or that are used as food or medicine. Among the most beautifully illustrated books about plants are Anne Dowden's *Wild Green Things in the City* (1972) and *The Blossom on the Bough* (1975), both of which can be used for identifying plants. The latter can be used as an introduction to botany; it also stresses the importance of plants in the ecology. For younger readers, a good book about the plant kingdom is *Green Is for Growing* (1964) by Winifred and Cecil Lubell. The illustrations are accurate and beautiful; the rhythmic, flowing text describes the characteristics of each group of plants, and it is pervaded with an awareness of the importance of ecological balance.

Both plants and animals are discussed in Glenn Blough's *Soon After September* (1959), the story of what happens in winter to plants, hibernating animals, and migrating birds. *After the Sun Goes Down* (1956) is a story of animals at night, and *Who Lives in This House* (1957) is about animal families. All of these books are illustrated by Jeanne Bendick and are appealing to younger children; the typeface is large and clear, and the language is simple.

The accurate details of Olive Earle's drawings correspond to the meticulous details of her books about animals. In *Praying Mantis* (1969), for example, about half the book describes the life cycle of the female mantis, the other half being notes on the behavior of a single mantis. The tone is often poetic, but the facts are quite accurate. Earle also has written about plant life in *The Rose Family* (1970) and *State Trees* (1973).

Probably the greatest number of books about the animal kingdom are accounts of a single animal. Alice Goudey's stories are authoritative and simply written, giving the life cycle, habits, and habitat in such books as *Here Come the Lions* (1956) and *Here Come the Dolphins* (1961). Another author whose books are dependably accurate and have a direct and dignified style is Dorothy Shuttlesworth, who writes chiefly about insects, although her works include *The Story of Rodents* (1971) and *To Find a Dinosaur* (1973). The evidence here of thorough research is seen also in Shuttlesworth's similar books on ants and on spiders.

Roy Chapman Andrews's *All About Whales* (1954) has the stamp of personal observation, since Andrews worked with these great mammals. *The Whales Go By* (1959) by Fred Phleger is a simple, easy-to-read picture book about whales, and Jane Werner Watson's *Whales; Friendly Dolphins and Mighty Giants of the Sea* (1975) is a well-rounded book for the middle grades. Certainly the most beautifully written book on the subject is Victor Scheffer's *Little Calf* (1970).

Of all the books about dinosaurs, Roy Chapman Andrews's *All About Dinosaurs* (1953) adds another dimension to information, for a large part of the book is devoted to his own experiences, and he conveys with relish the excitement of locating the first dinosaur eggs found in our time. He also wrote, for younger children, *In the Days of the Dinosaurs* (1959). Basic information on the subject is given clearly and briefly in two quite similar books, *Dinosaurs* (1955) by Marie Bloch, and *Discovering Dinosaurs* (1960) by Glenn Blough.

Louis Darling's most impressive book is *The Gull's Way* (1965). Here there is excellent correlation between Darling's text and his pictures. On a remote coastal island, he observed closely the behavior of two herring gulls as they courted, mated, brooded their eggs, and departed when their offspring became independent. Darling's style changed, in this book, from his competent but conventional description of a bird in *Greenhead* (1954), the study of a mallard duck, to a philosophical, almost tender, outlook on wildlife.

The Bird Watcher's Guide (1961) by Henry Collins is a comprehensive book on all aspects of bird-watching. In addition to books for identifying birds, there are many that describe a single kind of bird. Barbara Brenner's *Baltimore Orioles* (1974) gives accurate information for beginning readers, describing the oriole's life cycle; Berniece Freschet, in *The Flight of the Snow Goose* (1970), uses the life cycle also, but includes ecological aspects. Alice Schick, in *The Peregrine Falcons* (1975), uses a life cycle but bases the description on real birds observed along the Hudson, and also discusses the efforts by scientists to breed the birds after their numbers dwindled because of ingestion of DDT.

A good book for identifying seashells is Elizabeth Clemons's *Shells Are Where You Find Them* (1960), which gives advice on collecting and on a separate page describes each shell listed. A good choice for use with very young children is Alice Goudey's *Houses from the Sea* (1959). The slow, easy pace and the delicate illustrations by Adrienne Adams make it a good choice for reading aloud; the fact that two children, wandering along the beach, find fifteen kinds of shells means that there is not too much information for small children to assimilate. The book is prefaced by a note on collecting and closes with a brief account of how shells are formed. *Houses from the Sea* was a Caldecott Honor Book.

In addition to books on animal species, there are excellent ones that explore some special aspect of animal life. Dorothy Shuttlesworth, for example, in *Animal Camouflage* (1966), explains countershading, disruptive coloration, and mimicry. Jack Scott discusses characteristics that have enabled some species to flourish in *The Survivors* (1975). J. H. Prince describes patterns of courtship and mating in *The Universal Urge* (1973), and Dorothy Patent, a zoologist, writes lucidly of chemical stimuli in *How Insects Communicate* (1975).

All kinds of vertebrate life are considered in Margaret Cosgrove's *Bone for Bone* (1968), a study of comparative anatomy by a medical artist. One of the first drawings in the book, for example, shows skeletons of the mouse and the elephant, divergent outwardly but strikingly alike in their skeletal patterns. Cosgrove discusses, in graceful prose, the relationships between parts of the body, the graduation from simple to complex vertebrates, and the adaptive process by which each animal fits into a way of life.

Cosgrove's *Eggs—and What Happens Inside Them* (1966) is for a slightly younger audience, and deals with eggs that develop in water or on land, and eggs without shells, concluding with a discussion of the parts of the egg that develop into different parts of the body. A book with remarkable photographs is

Window into an Egg; Seeing Life Begin (1969) by Geraldine Lux Flanagan. Through a glass window sealed into an eggshell, we see an embryo develop into a chick.

The miracle of reproduction is described in books for every age, from Paul and Kay Showers's *Before You Were a Baby*, discussed earlier in this chapter, and Margaret Sheffield's *Where Do Babies Come From?* (1973), both of which are clear explanations that use correct terminology yet have a reverent approach toward the miracle of birth, to Eric Johnson's *Love and Sex in Plain Language* (1974), which discusses sexual intercourse and sex mores with frankness and dignity. For the child of eight to ten, Sidonie Matsner Gruenberg's *The Wonderful Story of How You Were Born* (1970) is a direct and simple text, illustrated with tender and dignified drawings by Symeon Shimin. Photographs are used to illustrate the candid, clear text for the same age range in a book translated from the Swedish, Lennart Nilsson's *How Was I Born?* (1975). For children just a bit older, Sadie Hofstein's *The Human Story* (1967) adds to its information on reproduction such practical concerns as voice changes in boys, acne, and menstrual hygiene.

Although the subject of hereditary characteristics is touched on in many books for younger children, the complexity of genetics is fully explored only in books for older readers. Two excellent books that complement each other are Aaron Klein's *Threads of Life* (1970), which surveys the work of scientists whose findings contributed, over the centuries, to the body of knowledge that led to the discovery of DNA; and *The Language of Life* (1966) by George and Muriel Beadle, a comprehensive and authoritative book on genetics that uses only the minimum of necessary scientific terminology.

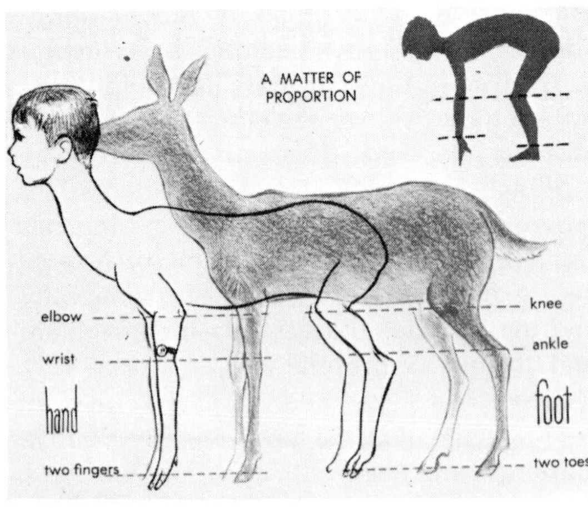

Illustration by Margaret Cosgrove. Reprinted by permission of Dodd, Mead & Company, Inc. from Bone for Bone *by Margaret Cosgrove. Copyright © 1970 by Margaret Cosgrove.*

The Physical Sciences

Many of today's children know more about science than do some adults. Parents can sympathize with the mother and father who hadn't the remotest idea of the answer when their fourth-grader asked them whether the ionosphere or the troposphere was nearer the earth. Teachers can report numerous situations similar to the one in which a fifth-grader was able to give the class an impromptu lecture in answer to another child's question on how a rocket works. Where are the children getting this information?

Some of it may come from television programs, but science books for children are certainly one of the most important sources of information. In both the extent of subjects covered and in the vocabulary used, children's science books show that there is a new respect for the reader's intelligence and interest.

Many of the concept books for young children, like Eric Carle's *My Very First Book of Shapes* (1974) can stimulate curiosity. Mae Freeman's *Gravity and the Astronauts* (1971) links an important phenomenon in physics to a subject children find alluring, and includes simple home demonstrations.

Alvin Tresselt's picture books about the weather; Isaac Asimov's story about gravity, *The Best New Thing* (1971); books like Illa Podendorf's *Things Are Alike and Different* (1970); and *How Big Is Big? From Stars to Atoms* (1950) by Herman and Nina Schneider all lead young children to curiosity about the world in which they live and about why things happen the way they do. When children begin to ask "how" and "why," then we know that they are ready to explore further in the world of science. It is the primary purpose of all of these books to encourage this desire to know more.

One of the first things a child becomes aware of is the weather. A good first book on the subject is Julian May's *Weather* (1967), which uses technical terminology rather heavily but gives broad coverage. *The First Book of Weather* (1966) by Rose Wyler is for readers in the middle grades and includes simple experiments. Benjamin Bova's *Man Changes the Weather* (1973) describes the ways in which man has affected the atmosphere, including pollution and a discussion of control agencies, and in John Navarra's *Wide World Weather* (1968), older readers can investigate the scientific, social, and governmental aspects of getting and sharing information, and of weather control and weather satellites.

Walter Buehr's *Water; Our Vital Need* (1967) and Melvin Berger's *The New Water Book* (1973) explain the water cycle and the variation in rainfall in different parts of the earth; the latter also describes the uses of water, water resources, and water pollution. A good first book about the earth is *Your Changing Earth* (1963) by Hy Ruchlis, which describes the beginnings of the earth and the solar system; the development of land, sea, and air; and the ways in which natural forces change the earth's surface. For older readers, a book that is as enjoyable for its fluency and wit as for the breadth of its treatment is George Gamow's *A Planet Called Earth* (1963), which discusses theories of planetary formation, composition of bodies in the solar system, weather, the living cell, and earth's future. One of the most provocative books about our earth is Alan Anderson's *The Drifting Continents* (1971), which describes the evidence that has led to acceptance of the theory (not new, but long disputed) of continental drift, and the possibilities of new research that may stem from this revolution in geological thinking.

Oceanography is another rapidly expanding frontier; like many other areas of science, it is a subject in which many books bridge the scientific disciplines. Although newer books report some of the more recent knowledge about the sea floor, no book on the subject is more exciting than Rachel Carson's *The Sea Around Us* (1958), which describes the formation of the oceans, tides and currents, marine flora and fauna, and the ocean floor with its volcanic activity. A book that adds immediacy to the information it gives is Peter Briggs's *Science Ship* (1969). Briggs spent three weeks aboard an oceanographic research vessel, *The Discoverer*, and his report gives facts about techniques, equipment, and findings; it also shows how today's scientific investigations demand the skills of scientists from many fields. Melvin Berger's *Oceanography Lab* (1973) is a competent survey of the work of oceanographers that makes clear the way they draw on help from other scientific disciplines.

Books about the earth and volcanic activity may stimulate a child's interest in the past ages in which the earth as we know it was shaped. *First Days of the World* (1958) by Gerald Ames and Rose Wyler explains the formation of the solar system, the beginnings of oceans, atmosphere, and living things, and goes on to describe the geological changes through the ages. *The First Book of Volcanoes and Earthquakes* (1972) by Rebecca Marcus describes both the causes of these phenomena and the work of seismologists; in Julian May's *Why the Earth Quakes* (1969) the explanations of what causes earthquakes and volcanic eruption is clarified by Leonard Everett Fisher's illustrations. For older readers, Charlton Ogburn's *The Forging of Our Continent* (1968) is a concise overview of the geology and physiography of North America, with emphasis on the area of the United States.

People have always been fascinated by stars, but never before the space age has there been such general interest and such immediate concern with the far reaches of our universe. Two of the best introductions to astronomy for children of ten to twelve are *The New Golden Book of Astronomy* by Rose Wyler and Gerald Ames (1965), which covers the atmosphere, seasons, and phases of the moon, the members of the solar system, gravity and tides, how stellar measurements are made, and plans for the continuous exploration of space; and Roy Gallant's *Exploring the Universe* (1968), which presents the theories of early astronomers in an easy, informal style.

Many of Franklyn Branley's books were discussed earlier in the chapter; no writer in the field of astronomy is more adept at writing simply for young children. For older readers, Robert Richardson's *The Stars and Serendipity* (1971) introduces astronomical discoveries made by scientists who were working on another problem and came across an exciting new find.

Another clever approach, designed for beginners, can be found in *You, Among the Stars* (1951) by Herman and Nina Schneider. As in other books by these same authors, the emphasis is on orienting the young child. Through the theme of an envelope address, the child moves from the family home outward into space step by step until the familiar street address becomes greatly elaborated.

Ask children today what area of science they want to study, and more often than not they will answer "space." In the minds of today's children, studying space often means studying rockets and satellites, not the sun and moon. Franklyn Branley's *Man in Space to the Moon* (1970), for readers in the middle grades, explains each step in the historic flight of Apollo 11. John Wilford's *We Reach the Moon* (1969) is based on the original adult book and gives the step-by-step development of the NASA program, concluding with some results of the scientific experiments carried out by the astronauts. Bernice Kohn, in *Communications Satellites* (1975), describes the principles by which satellites function, and Ben Bova's *Workshops in Space* (1974) discusses knowledge garnered from satellites.

To understand the mechanics of the space program, so much of which is based on intricate mathematics, readers must be aware of the mathematical computations on which scientists rely. Lancelot Hogben's *The Wonderful World of Mathematics* (1968) relates the growth of mathematics as a science to changing human needs. With the modern curriculum, in which children are learning new concepts at earlier stages, there have been many books published that use the process approach or deal with one aspect of mathematical concepts. Rolf Myller's *How Big Is a Foot?* (1962) is a fictionalized picture book, but it lucidly presents the reasons that standards of measurement are needed. An excellent series, the Crowell "Young Math Books," examines one aspect in each volume. Typical of the series is *Long, Short, High, Low, Thin, Wide* (1971) by James Fey, which discusses measurement and encourages the reader to observe and compare; some of the others are *Number Ideas Through Pictures* (1974) by Mannis Charosh, Robert Froman's *Less Than Nothing Is Really Something* (1973) and Jane Srivastava's *Averages* (1975). These books teach something about scientific methods as well as the immediate subject with which they are concerned. Jeanne Bendick's *Take Shapes, Lines, and Letters* (1962), written with Marcia Levin, deals with ideas and relationships rather than with numbers, and the basic principles of computer mathematics are explained in *The New World of Computers* (1965) by Alfred Lewis.

To prepare children for conversion from our traditional system of measurement to the metric system, many authors have discussed its advantages. June Behrens, in *The True Book of Metric Measurement* (1975), gives a clear explanation for readers in the primary grades. For slightly older readers, both Franklyn Branley's *Think Metric!* (1973) and Miriam Schlein's *Metric—The Modern Way to*

Viewpoints

To write about science for children an author needs to know science, to know children, and to know how to write. . . .

. . . It is not enough to say, "Here is an exciting thing. See the way a caterpillar spins a cocoon." The role of the writer is to write the book so that a child can feel he is *participating* in an observation. . . .

Good science books should communicate some of the excitement of discovery—and the triumph that goes with the solution of scientific problems. They should make a young person understand why Archimedes could jump out of his bath to rush through the streets of Syracuse shouting "Eureka" when he discovered a new physical principle.—Millicent E. Selsam, "Writing About Science for Children," *A Critical Approach to Children's Literature,* edited by Sara Innis Fenwick, The University of Chicago Press, Chicago and London, 1967, pp. 96, 98–99.

Measure (1975) discuss both the way in which the metric system works and the reasons it is preferable to the old system of measuring. More background and more details are given in books for readers in the upper elementary grades and in high school. They describe historical development and discuss opposition to the change as well as explaining the need for conversion and the functioning of the metric system.

When we come to physics and chemistry we are entering realms of science which have increasingly enabled humanity to reorder natural existence to suit particular desires or needs. While we want our children to appreciate fully these achievements of applied science, they must also be helped to recognize its limitations if they are to gain a realistic picture of the world in which they live. In this nuclear age, it is perhaps more apparent than ever before that science can bring great good or harm, depending on how we put it to use.

The science of chemistry can be traced back to early times. Roy A. Gallant's *Exploring Chemistry* (1958), for example, begins with the discovery of fire and thereafter tells the absorbing history of efforts to understand and change matter. Ira M. Freeman elaborates upon this story for older children in *All About the Wonders of Chemistry* (1954), describing at greater length such things as molecular structure, the elements, chemical change, and the many ways in which chemistry has contributed to medicine, farming, and industry, for the benefit of modern life. Older children may also enjoy *Elements of the Universe* (1958) by Glenn T. Seaborg and Evans G. Valens, which contains dramatic accounts of some of chemistry's greatest discoveries, written by men who have directly participated in the thrill of such achievements. Ira Freeman and A. Rae Patton, in *The Science of Chemistry* (1968), give basic facts about the ways in which atoms and molecules function chemically, and formulas are introduced only in relation to relevant theory. Isaac Asimov, in *Building Blocks of the Universe* (1961), makes clear, in his usual witty and informal style, the chemical elements that are the foundation of all matter. While the complexities of chemistry are seldom explored as a whole for younger children, aspects of the subject are discussed in such books as *Millions and Millions of Crystals* (1973) and *Oil; The Buried Treasure* (1975) by Roma Gans, who makes complicated topics very clear in both books by wise selection of facts.

In the purest sense, chemistry is the study of matter only—its composition, its nature, and the changes it constantly undergoes—while physics is the study of matter and energy and the relationship between them. Even at the elementary-school level, more and more books are appearing that cross boundary lines and reveal the strong interrelationship between these sciences. For example, there are now several books which borrow learnings from chemistry regarding atoms and molecular structure and then go on to apply these learnings to the recent developments in physics regarding atomic energy and its many uses.

An excellent example for younger children is John Lewellen's *The Mighty Atom* (1955), which very simply, with the aid of familiar analogies and Ida Scheib's clever illustrations, moves from a discussion of the atom with its neutrons, protons, and electrons, to molecular structure and the basic elements and finally to atomic power, the construction and operation of atomic furnaces and engines, and the uses of atomic energy in both war and peace. Margaret Hyde's *Atoms Today and Tomorrow* (4th ed., 1970), written with Bruce Hyde, describes the production and uses of atomic energy, and David Woodbury's *The New World of the Atom* (1965) stresses the uses of atomic energy in medicine, in carbon-14 testing, and in nuclear power plants for space exploration.

Mechanics, an area of great interest to children, paves the way for a study of transportation, and is one of the areas in which children can observe and experiment from the first time they are fascinated by the moving parts in their toys. An interesting book for young children is *The True Book of Toys at Work* (1953), in which John Lewellen describes the mechanical principles involved in such things as whistles, electric trains, and balloons. An excellent book for the reader in the middle grades is *The Simple Facts of Simple Machines* (1975) by Elizabeth James and Carol Barkin, a book that discusses principles of

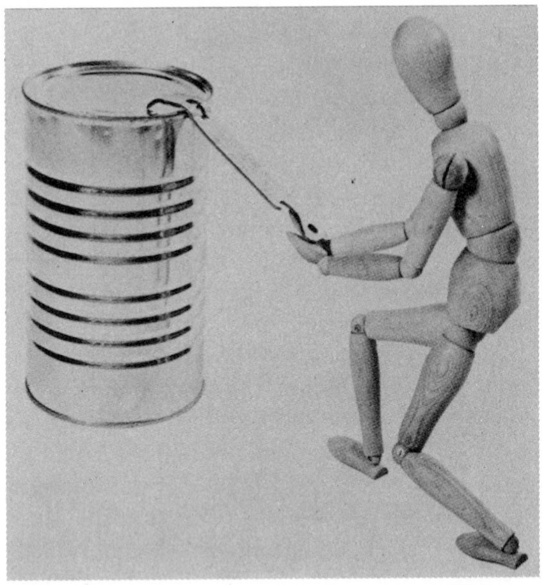

Illustration by Daniel Dorn, Jr. for The Simple Facts of Simple Machines *by Elizabeth James & Carol Barkin. Reproduced by permission of Lothrop, Lee & Shepard Company.*

physics. Hy Ruchlis's *Orbit; A Picture Story of Force and Motion* (1958) successfully explains Newton's law of universal gravitation as well as his three laws of motion in terms that can be understood by most children above the fourth grade. Action-packed photographs of such things as "flying" cars, acrobatic stunts, and daredevil sports, plus excellent diagrams by Alice Hirsch, help to illustrate these scientific laws, all of which contribute a great deal toward an adequate understanding of transportation vehicles and particularly of space flight.

Naturally the machines which people have built on the principles of mechanics would have limited use indeed without the harnessing of some type of energy other than human power to run them. One of the most comprehensive books on this subject, excitingly illustrated in color by John Teppich, is Lancelot Hogben's *Wonderful World of Energy* (1957). This book constantly reminds the child that, of all the many sources of energy, the greatest is the one which has mastered the others—humanity's own will and drive to go forward. We learn how people have gradually harnessed and put to work energy from wind, water, steam, fire, electricity, and now the atom and the sun. This last source of energy, vast and unlimited, still requires a great deal of study. Its history and future possibilities have been extensively discussed by Franklyn M. Branley in *Solar Energy* (1957). The problems of diminishing sources of energy and the social implications for the future are described in Daniel Halacy's *The Energy Trap* (1975) and Laurence Pringle's *Energy; Power for the People* (1975). Both discuss possible solutions through new developments and action by individuals and authoritative bodies.

Of all the forms of energy, however, the one with which the child has had the most direct experience is usually electricity. This is not an easy subject for children, and yet it plays such an important role in their everyday lives that we should help them gain at least an appreciation of its great value and some understanding of how it operates. One of the clearest and simplest explanations of this complex subject can be found in *The First Book of Electricity* (1953) by Sam and Beryl Epstein. Since this book is designed for the beginner with no previous knowledge of electricity, new concepts have been fully explained. In addition, there are pages of easy-to-follow instructions for experiments. For older children who already have a basic knowledge of this subject, the greater complexities of electricity are explained in Ira M. Freeman's *All About Electricity* (1957), which introduces a good deal of the history of the development of electrical power and contains whole chapters on various uses of electricity.

Actually, the science concerned with the communications devices just mentioned is electronics. John Lewellen's *Understanding Electronics* (1957) and Jeanne Bendick's *Electronics for Young People* (1960) are clear, detailed books for children of twelve and up.

Many of the topics we have mentioned are included in *Understanding Science* (1956) by William Crouse. It is a panoramic view in which no subject is treated in depth, but it gives the reader a broad picture of the worlds of pure and applied science. For such background, books like Corinne Jacker's *Window on the Unknown; A History of the Microscope* (1966) and Aaron Klein's *The Electron Microscope* (1974) are most useful.

The Social Sciences

Under the rubric of the social sciences are those subjects that have to do with people in their association with other groups of people: history, political science, anthropology, economics, geography, law, and many others, often—as is true of other sciences—overlapping each other or other disciplines. With so broad a scope, this chapter can only mention some of the good books in areas so extensive yet so finely divided.

Since an understanding of many of these areas is partially dependent on seeing a relationship between past and present, perhaps the best background book for a young child is one that clarifies time concepts. Three such are *The True Book of Time* (1956) by Feenie Ziner and Elizabeth Thompson, which teaches children that there are other ways, in addition to clocks, for measuring time; Miriam Schlein's *It's About Time* (1955), which helps clarify the puzzling relationships implied in "long time, short time"; and Melvin Berger's *Time After Time* (1975), which discusses days, seasons, time measurement, and the inner time-sense of living things in a clear, open-ended text.

Often small children are fascinated by dinosaurs before they understand the earth's time scale, and books about dinosaurs can be used to introduce the beginnings of human prehistory. Julian May's *The First Men* (1968), for the early grades, may be followed in the middle grades by *The First People in the World* (1958) by Gerald Ames and Rose Wyler. For older readers, Eleanor Clymer's *The Case of the Missing Link* (1968), which describes the search for our ancestors and the theories held about them, gives a good account of the way scientists carefully evaluate evidence.

Two reliable books about prehistoric people in North America are William Scheele's *The Earliest Americans* (1963), which investigates the puzzle of when humans first migrated to this continent, and Anne Terry White's *Prehistoric America* (1951), which describes modern discoveries that have led to a better understanding of prehistoric times. Scheele's *The Mound Builders* (1960) reconstructs what may have happened when a new burial site was created at Hopewell, Ohio.

To understand how information about prehistory and early civilizations is acquired, children may turn to a book about archeology as a science. Anne Terry White's *All About Archeology* (1959) or Leonard Cottrell's *Digs and Diggers; A Book of World Archeology* (1964) give information about the development of the science, its methodology, and some of the great discoveries of the past. Dora Hamblin's *Pots and Robbers* (1970) tells some true stories about the dramatic aspects of archeology, many incidents involving thefts and forgeries. Her *Buried Cities and Ancient Treasures* (1973) is based on her own observation of archeological sites in Turkey.

There is a wealth of material on ancient civilizations, for many facets of which the art books by Shirley Glubok are good supplementary reading. Victor von Hagen's *Maya, Land of the Turkey and the Deer* (1960) is based on scholarly documents and vividly evokes the people and the period; Ruth Karen's *Kingdom of the Sun* (1975) describes the Inca empire with the same combination of vigorous style and scholarly research. Hans Baumann's *In the Land of Ur* (1969) is written with a sense of excitement, and Joan Joseph's *Black African Empires* (1974), while it lacks such excitement, gives a broad overview of the rich

From the book Kingdom of the Sun *by Ruth Karen, published by Four Winds Press. Photograph courtesy of The American Museum of Natural History.*

and powerful African empires of the past.

Many of the Columbian biographies include conjecture about the first "discoverers" of America, with honors usually divided between Columbus and the Vikings. Ellen Pugh, in *Brave His Soul* (1970), presents convincing evidence for the theory that a Welsh prince exiled himself and came to North America in 1170. A stunning book that uses source material and binds the excerpts smoothly with the compiler's comments is *The New Land* (1967) by Phillip Viereck.

There is a gratifying abundance of books in world history. One book that exemplifies a fine series about major cultures of the world, published by World, is Thomas Chubb's *The Byzantines* (1959). The learning, the technological skills, and the pride of a prosperous civilization are made excitingly real by the vivid writing. Each volume in the series has a chronological chart that correlates other world events. Alfred Duggan, who was one of the great historical writers of our time, illumined his subject in *Growing Up in 13th Century England* (1962) with authoritative knowledge and sophisticated wit; by portraying five households at different social levels, he was able to show minute details of daily living as well as social customs, recreation, and education.

Often books that are not written as history can illuminate a period. One such book is *The Bayeux Tapestry* (1966) by Norman Denny and Josephine Filmer-Sankey, which describes the Norman Conquest as it is told in the tapestry; another is Grant Uden's *A Dictionary of Chivalry* (1968), which won the Greenaway Medal for Pauline Baynes's exquisite illustrations and was a runner-up for the Carnegie Medal, a book as useful as it is handsome.

Books which give children a factual account of the early history of America, its discovery and settlement, include Alice Dalgliesh's *America Begins* (1958) and Louise Rich's *The First Book of New World Explorers* (1960). And for a record of United States history from 1492 to the present, we have *The First Book of American History* (1957) by the noted historian Henry Steele Commager.

Enid Meadowcroft's *The Land of the Free* (1961) reflects the careful study, shown in her bibliography, which preceded the writing of the book. It is a brief history, but it weaves together the threads of events that form America's history from 1492 to the end of the Second World War. Reading like fiction, *The Land of the Free* points out America's failures as well as triumphs and so places the country's character in true perspective.

The American Revolution and the Declaration of Independence are events of special significance for children, and there are many good books about this period of revolution and confederation. *The First Book of the American Revolution* (1956) by Richard B. Morris will help younger readers understand what these events meant then and what they mean today. Jean Fritz's *Who's That Stepping on Plymouth Rock?* (1975) is as lively as her brief stories of colonial leaders. At the junior-high level *The Golden Book of the American Revolution* (1959), adapted by Fred Cook from the *American Heritage Book of the Revolution*, provides an excellent summary of events leading to the war and covers the tactics of battles on land and sea, the development of the armed forces, the contributions of allies, and the final victory. George Sanderlin's *A Hoop to the Barrel* (1974) discusses the issues and compromises that shaped the writing of the Constitution. Prominent men of the newly formed government are well drawn in *The Great Declaration* (1958) by Henry Steele Commager. The author uses excerpts from official documents, letters, and diaries in weaving together the story of the Declaration of Independence. The crucial role of women is described in Linda De Pauw's *Founding Mothers* (1975). An unusual viewpoint is given by Clorinda Clarke in *The American Revolution 1775–83; A British View* (1967), a book that has a judicious, long-range outlook and a lively style.

For the very young child interested in American pioneers, Mabel Harmer's *The True Book of Pioneers* (1957) is brief but does an admirable job of covering the subject. Ruth Franchere's *Westward by Canal* (1972) describes the impact of the building of the Erie Canal. William O. Steele's *Westward Adventure* (1962) comprises the true stories of six pioneers and is based on material in diaries and journals. One of the few humorous books about the past, Suzanne Hilton's *The Way It Was—1876* (1975) describes daily life vividly.

Charles Flato's *The Golden Book of the Civil War* (1961) is adapted from an American Heritage picture history. Profusely illustrated, it gives a broad and vivid picture of the war years. G. Allen Foster's *Sunday in Centerville* (1971) is as interesting for the discussion of the complex causes of the war, and the preparations for it, as it is for the detailed account of the first Battle of Bull Run.

Daniel J. Boorstin's *The Landmark History of the American People* (2 vols., 1968, 1970) deviates from the usual compilation of facts and dates to discuss the people who influenced patterns of change, and its emphasis is on movements and on regional and national patterns. The approach is stimulating, the style informal, and the analyses acutely perceptive, as might be expected from an eminent historian.

Of the many books on black history in the United States, some of the best are Robert Goldston's *The Negro Revolution* (1968), Dorothy Sterling's *Tear Down the Walls!* (1968) and *The Trouble They Seen; Black People Tell the Story of Reconstruction* (1976), and Johanna Johnston's *Together in America* (1965), all comprehensive and as objective as is consistent with a history of slavery and oppression. Marcella Thum, in *Exploring Black America* (1975), is not chronological but discusses a number of topics in relation to the holdings of specialized museums. Unfortunately, no comparable body of material exists for other minority groups in the United States. The Native American, for example, is represented by very few books, and most of those are concerned with a tribe, an Indian leader, or an event. Ann Nolan Clark's *Circle of Seasons* (1970) is a dignified and reverent description of the rites and observances of the Pueblo year. *Red Hawk's Account of Custer's Last Battle* (1970), like other books by Paul and Dorothy Goble, is historically accurate. The story is told dramatically from the viewpoint of a boy who realizes, after the battle at Little Big Horn, that while the Indian victory was definitive, the Indian's fight against white invasion was hopeless. Franklin Folsom's *Red Power on the Rio Grande* (1973) gives the Indian point of view on the Pueblo Revolution of 1680, and Dee Brown has ably adapted *Wounded Knee* (1974) from the moving and powerful *Bury My Heart at Wounded Knee*. There is a wealth of material in Sonia Bleeker's books on individual Indian cultures: *The Sea Hunters; Indians of the Northwest Coast* (1951), *The Sioux Indians* (1962), and others, or in a compendium of information like *Indians* (1959) by Edwin Tunis. Robert Hofsinde, adopted by the Chippewas, wrote with meticulous attention to details in books that dealt with aspects of Native American cultures. *Indian Warriors and Their Weapons* (1965) describes martial weapons and costumes of seven tribes, *Indian Sign Language* (1956) is a glossary of over 500 universal signs of North American tribes, and *Indian Music Makers* (1967) discusses musical instruments. Probably the two best books available are *The American Indian* (1960) by Oliver La Farge, which has both historical and contemporary material, and May McNeer's *The American Indian Story* (1963), which is more an introduction than a survey, but is distinguished in illustration.

In addition to Milton Melzer's history of American Jews discussed earlier, other books about minority groups include Harold Coy's *Chicano Roots Go Deep* (1975) and Alberta Eiseman's *The Spanish-Speaking in the United States* (1973), which are candid and sympathetic evaluations of discriminations suffered by Hispanic peoples in the years they have lived in the United States. Edwin Hoyt, in *Asians in the West* (1975), examines with equal candor the record of Caucasian discrimination.

Several books provide information about Canada. Regina Tor, in *Getting to Know Canada*, describes the people of the various provinces, their government, customs, and industries. Lithographs by Lynd Ward help to make May McNeer's *Canadian Story* an exciting account of the history of Canada from the time of the Vikings to the opening of the St. Lawrence Seaway.

Among the books that, in addition to those by Sonia and Tim Gidal, give information about countries in other parts of the world are *The First Book of South America* (1961) by William Carter, which gives an account of the folklore, religions, and history of the continent; John Gunther's books about Africa; the Lippincott series on "Land and People of . . ."; Armstrong Sperry's *All About the Arctic and Antarctic* (1957); and Lois Hobart's *Mexican Mural* (1963). In fact, there are so many that a representative list would be impossible in one chapter on informational books.

Because of the spread of urbanization, the interest in cities is greater today than it has ever been, both from the standpoint of allure and, alas, from the standpoint of the complex problems in urban life. Few are more urgent than pollution. In *Dangerous Air* (1967), Lucy Kavaler cites the causes of air pollution throughout the world and discusses what government, industry, and individual citizens must do to eliminate this danger. John Navarra considers the same problem in *The World You Inherit; A Story of Pollution* (1970) and adds, in a cogent chapter, the legislation and litigation that are involved; in *Our Noisy World* (1969), he discusses the problem of noise pollution. James and Lynn Hahn look to solutions in *Recycling* (1973); and in *The Population Puzzle* (1973) by A. H. Drummond, the associated problem of increasing population density and decreasing resources is examined.

No author has made cities more enticing than Miroslav Sasek. Despite the crime and grime, New York is beautiful in *This Is New York* (1960), with gay, colorful pictures and a lively, humorous text describing the grandeur of a bridge span, the bustle of the garment district, the biggest traffic jams in the world. Of his other books in the series, two of the most attractive are *This Is Edinburgh* (1961) and *This Is Greece* (1966). A sharply different picture emerges in John Holland's *The Way It Is* (1969), a series of photographs, with captions, taken by black and Puerto Rican schoolboys in their home neighborhood.

Alvin Schwartz, in *Old Cities and New Towns* (1968), shows Philadelphia as it is, and as it could be, following renovation and renewal. In a book for young children, *Let's Look Under the City* (1954), Herman and Nina Schneider show the maze of service facilities but emphasize the interdependency of people in making services universally available. Carl Hiller's *Babylon to Brasilia* (1972) describes the same problems investigated by Alvin Schwartz but adds more recent information, especially about some of the model cities established in various parts of the world.

Children are indefatigably curious about the way other people live and where they live—and why they live there if it's hot (or cold, or rainy, or mountainous . . .). They are curious about differences, open-minded rather than insular. Books can help foster their awareness of the superficiality of differences and the similarity of people everywhere. *Why We Live Where We Live* (1953) by Eva Knox Evans helps them understand the interdependence of people and the geographic limitations upon the choice of homes.

Many of the recent books for children have been written with the objective of making the story of our past and present a "real experience" rather than a superficial one. A stimulating volume to which older children can be guided is *People and Places* (1959) by Margaret Mead. The book is richly informative, springing out of Mead's expert knowledge of people and countries. She begins her first chapter, "Man's Discovery of Man," by stating that human beings are curious about each other and that even the most primitive peoples in the world today wonder about those unlike themselves, and she concludes with

Viewpoints

In the hunt for facts and the ascertaining of truth, the historian must be as conscientious as the scientist. In the presentation he must be an artist, a true one, not one of those who favor vain embellishments. . . .

The historian's means of communication with the public is writing, as color is for painters. An historian who uses so dull a style that he will not be read is as useless as a painter who should use invisible colors. He is, moreover, sure not to do justice to realities, thus swerving from truth, for realities are not dull. Those for whom they are so suffer from a dull mind and a dull heart. In them is the fault, not in the things.—From *The Writing of History* by Jean Jules Jusserand, Wilbur Cortez Abbott, Charles W. Colby, and John Spencer Bassett, Charles Scribner's Sons, New York, 1926, pp. 3–4, 5.

discussions about "Man Asks About Man," in which she talks about similarities and differences among peoples of the world. She also offers suggestions as to what steps must be taken to solve humanity's problems so that all may live in a more orderly world. All in all, Mead's book challenges its readers to a deeper understanding not only of themselves but also of other people and places.

Religion and the Arts

Books of religious instruction and prayers are used by devout families in the home, and biographies of religious leaders or stories that present religious diversity can help children understand and respect the beliefs or the nonbelief of others. Books on comparative religion, however, belong in any collection to which children turn for information.

Ruth Smith's *The Tree of Life* (1942) is an anthology consisting of selections from the world's great religions, and is an excellent companion volume to Katharine Savage's *The Story of World Religions,* discussed earlier in this chapter, or the Haskins book, also previously mentioned. *Religions Around the World* (1967) by Leonard and Carolyn Wolcott is not as detailed as the Savage book, nor is the scope as great, but it discusses people and beliefs that are not included in the other. Edward Rice's *The Five Great Religions* (1973) differs from the other books that examine major faiths by giving more background, since Rice believes that the mystical aspects of each are rooted in its beginnings.

The series of books about religious denominations by Kathleen Elgin, of which *The Unitarians* (1971) is an example, describes the history and the beliefs of the denomination, lists some of its famous members of past and present, and gives at length a biography of a leader or prominent member. In *The Vatican* (1970), the managing editor of *Commonweal,* John Deedy, describes the Vatican community's members and its art and history. Roland Gittelsohn, a rabbi, discusses the origins of Jewish tradition and observances in *The Meaning of Judaism* (1970), and describes the differences among the three groups within that faith. Elizabeth Seeger describes Buddhism, Confucianism, Hinduism, Shinto, and Taoism in *Eastern Religions* (1973).

Books that encourage the child's interest in music range from such narrow treatments as Larry Kettelkamp's *Flutes, Whistles and Reeds* (1962), which introduces woodwinds and explains how they produce sounds, to the comprehensive treatment in *The Wonderful World of Music* (1958) by Benjamin Britten and Imogen Holst, a history of music, musicians, and instruments that is mature in concept. Much of the book can be appreciated by the reader with no musical background, but the discussions of theory and harmony may present difficulties for the general reader. A similar book is *The Heritage of Music* (1963) by Katherine Shippen and Anca Seidlova, which describes musical forms and instruments, and is enlivened by anecdotes about musicians. David Ewen is one of the most prolific and authoritative authors of books about music, writing on musical forms: *Opera* (1971), *Orchestral Music* (1973), *Vocal Music* (1975), and others. Roy Hemming, in *Discovering Music* (1974), gives suggestions for the collector of tapes and records.

There is comparatively little material available about the music of other countries. Betty Warner Dietz and Michael Babatunde Olatunji have written an outstanding book about the way music is used in African cultures south of the Sahara in *Musical Instruments of Africa* (1965); and in *Folk Songs of China, Japan, and Korea* (1964) Dietz collaborated with Thomas Choonbai Park. These books have been compiled with scholarly care, and can help children understand other cultures through their music.

Langston Hughes wrote several books about music: *The First Book of Rhythms* (1954), *Famous Negro Music Makers* (1955), and *The First Book of Jazz* (1955). The latter presents a concise history of the development of jazz in the United States and of its spread to other countries. Hughes discusses the diverse elements that contributed to the complex rhythms of jazz: African, French, and Spanish elements in New Orleans; worksongs and blues; spirituals, ragtime, and minstrel music. James Collier defines jazz and analyzes its forms in *Inside Jazz* (1973). Although not written as an informational book, Nat Hentoff's *Jazz Country* (1965) conveys the essence of the jazz world. (See Chapter 10 discussion.) Another book that gives a history of a popular type of music is Arnold Shaw's *The Rock Revolution* (1969), which includes discussions of performers and comments of critics. In *Golden Guitars* (1971), Irwin Stambler and Grelun Landon tell the story of country-and-western music.

Books about opera, libretti of individual operas, many collections of songs, and books that describe the composition and arrangement of orchestras are listed in the bibliography, as are some of the many song books published for children. There is also a considerable amount of information about music and musicians in the biographies cited in Chapter 12.

A book that bridges the worlds of music and dance is *American Indians Sing* (1967) by Charles Hofmann, in which the information about music, dances, and song-poems includes melodic and dance notation. The relationship of dance to religious observance is emphasized in Lee Warren's *The Dance of Africa* (1972), which discusses also the impact of cultural changes on traditional forms. Perhaps the most comprehensive book on the dance is Arnold Haskell's *The Wonderful World of Dance* (1969). In an impressively authoritative volume, Haskell describes the evolution of the dance and dance forms, with biographical material about famous dancers and choreographers, and with many diagrams of dance notation. There is an especially good section on ritual dances of the Orient; and, throughout the book, dance forms are related to the cultural context in which they evolved. Narrower in scope, *Ballet; A Pictorial History* (1970) by Walter Terry is a good introduction for the reader who is not a balletomane, but it has enough material about outstanding dancers of each historical period to appeal to the lover of ballet. Noel Streatfeild's *A Young Person's Guide to Ballet* (1975) gives a wealth of interesting detail about techniques and ballet history.

Olga Maynard's *American Modern Dancers; The Pioneers* (1965) is an excellent survey of the evolution of modern dance through discussions of the work of great dancers, giving authoritative analyses of techniques, theories, trends, influences, and comparative schools. Maynard gives, in *The Ballet Companion* (1957), a detailed guide to four ballets, and a glossary of ballet terms and techniques.

Undoubtedly because dancing is a performing art there is comparatively little written about it. When we turn to books about art, however, there is a positive cornucopia of fine books. One of the best general surveys is Janet Moore's *The Many Ways of Seeing* (1968), which discusses the relationship between art and nature, and the relationship between the artist and the world. It analyzes the ways an artist perceives in terms of light, color, composition, and line; it also describes media, materials, and techniques, and suggests ways in which the reader can try some of the ideas discussed and learn to see the elements of an art form. A similar book, with examples ranging from ancient treasures to contemporary works, is *Looking at Sculpture* (1968) by Roberta Paine.

Marion Downer's *The Story of Design* (1964) uses a variety of art objects, shown in photographs, to illustrate the appreciation of design the world over, from primitive times to today. M. J. Gladstone's *A Carrot for a Nose* (1974) and Elinor Horwitz's *Contemporary American Folk Artists* (1975) discuss folk art. In *Looking at Art* (1966) Alice Elizabeth

Viewpoints

The difference between the good and bad historian is not so much the difference between a wide, regular, well-ordered and a narrow, irregular, and ill-ordered reading of record. It lies much more in the two qualities of proportion and imagination. Two men, for instance, may sit down to write as historians the events of an ancient battle.

. . . But the space of each is limited, and even if each had an unlimited canvas on which to paint, the truth of the result would still depend upon proportion—upon the discovery of the essential movements and the essential moments in the action; and upon imagination, the power of seeing the thing as it was; landscape, the weather, the gestures and the faces of the men; yes, and their thoughts within.—Hilaire Belloc, *One Thing and Another,* Hollis and Carter, London, 1955, pp. 24, 25.

Chase, an art historian, describes the ways in which artists have interpreted their worlds, and the author's explicit and clearly presented views on the nature of art make the book an excellent choice for the reader who is on unfamiliar terrain. Howard Greenfeld writes with authority and zeal in *The Impressionist Revolution* (1972) and *They Came to Paris* (1975).

The Pantheon Story of Art for Young People (1964; 1975) by Ariane Ruskin Batterberry is competently written but slights contemporary work; it has, however, an unusually large number of full-page, full-color illustrations. Some of the series are by Ariane Ruskin under that name, some by Michael Batterberry, some written jointly by the two, as is *Primitive Art* (1973). Ruskin's *Art of the High Renaissance* (1970) emphasizes painters and painting, but the comprehensive text covers all art forms. All of the books in this series are profusely and handsomely illustrated.

There are few art books written for adults that cannot be enjoyed by children, if the books are illustrated. The Time-Life Library of Art has magnificently illustrated volumes, each devoted to a single artist. The biographies by Elizabeth Ripley could almost as well be in this chapter as in Chapter 12. Shirley Glubok's books are discussed earlier in this chapter. Books on color for the preschool and primary-age child can encourage aesthetic appreciation as well as teach colors, and some of the first concept books, like Tana Hoban's *Shapes and Things*, can stimulate an awareness of form as well as encourage observation. In other words, information about art can come from many sources other than books about art.

Friedrich von Schlegel called architecture "frozen music," and in Mary Louise King's *A History of Western Architecture* (1967), the illustrations show the patterned precision of Greek temples and the soaring lift of Gothic cathedrals that make this phrase so apt. King emphasizes the new developments of each period, and discusses the factors that influence style. A simpler book that gives architectural history more succinctly is *Understanding Architecture* (1971) by George Sullivan, which explains styles and construction techniques from the rudimentary post-and-lintel buildings to today's skyscrapers and the plans for ecologically oriented homes of tomorrow.

Anne Rockwell's *Glass, Stones and Crown; The Abbe Suger and the Building of St. Denis* (1968) is as interesting for its historical background as it is for the story of Suger, the boyhood friend of Louis Capet, whose life as abbot was devoted to rebuilding St. Denis and incorporating those features that became popular throughout Europe: stained glass windows, flying buttresses and piers, and ribbed vaulting.

The construction of a modern building is described in Ely Jacques Kahn's *A Building Goes Up* (1969), in which the erection of an office building is detailed from planning to completion. Although David Macaulay's books are discussed in Chapter 5, they also belong here as outstanding books on architecture.

Activities and Experiments

One of the most popular kinds of activity books is the puzzle book. Martin Gardner's *Perplexing Puzzles and Tantalizing Teasers* (1969) contains riddles, scrambled words, mazes, and puzzles that require logic for solution. It has enough difficult puzzles to tempt the quick child but not so many as to discourage the one who is slow. More difficult is *Math Menagerie* (1970) by Robert Kadesch, in which the material is grouped under such headings as probability, binary numerals, and soap-film mathematics. Another kind of brain-teaser is Martin Gardner's *Codes, Ciphers, and Secret Writing* (1972), which describes codes used in history, explains how to concoct or decipher messages, and explains the difference between codes and ciphers. *Egyptian Hieroglyphs for Everyone* (1968) by Joseph and Lenore Scott gives an explanation of how the language developed and makes it easier for the reader to understand hieroglyphic writing.

At the other end of the spectrum are the books that give instruction for physical activities, usually sports. One such is S. H. Freeman's *Basic Baseball Strategy* (1965), which is packed with so much information that it can be used by players older than the middle-grades audience to whom it is addressed, or by coaches for the clear explanations of such fine arts as base stealing, the squeeze play, and when to use the hit-and-run. *Better Softball for Boys and Girls* (1975) by George Sullivan gives advice on play and explains the game clearly. *Bicycling* (1972) by Charles Coombs tells the reader how to choose, use, and take care of a bicycle. In Jim Moore's *Football Techniques Illustrated* (1962), there are discussions of offensive and defensive play, advice on running, kicking, passing, and tackling, and the rules of play. Other how-to-do-it sports books can easily be found listed under the names of the sports in such guides as *Children's Catalog*.

A useful group of activity books are those in the fields of arts and crafts: Jan Adkins, in *Toolchest* (1973), gives succinct advice to the amateur carpenter; in *Collage* (1968), Mickey Klar Marks gives instructions for seven different kinds of collage; *The Complete Crayon Book* (1969) by Chester Jay Alkema suggests a variety of projects, from simple to complex, and gives an excellent discussion of media and techniques. *Mask-Making with Pantomime and Stories from American History* (1975) by Laura Ross gives good background history as well as clear instructions. Among the many books on puppetry, two of the best are Eleanor Boylan's *How to Be a Puppeteer* (1970), which gives directions for making and

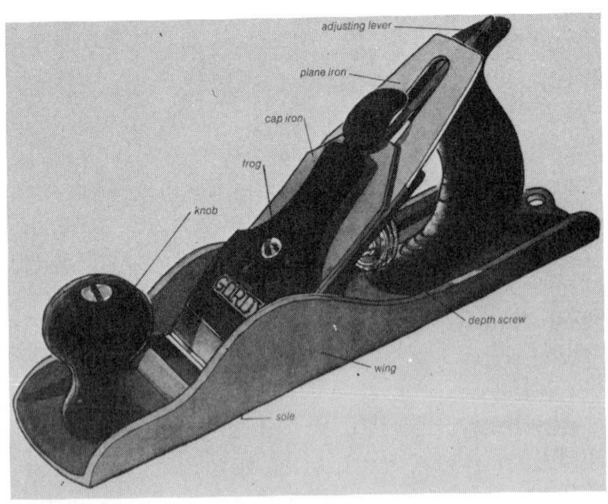

From the book Toolchest: a Primer of Woodcraft *by Jan Adkins. Published by Walker & Company, Inc. New York, N.Y. © 1973 by Jan Adkins.*

costuming puppets, manipulating them, making sets and scenery, etc., and David Currell's *The Complete Book of Puppetry* (1975), which is comprehensive enough to have reference use.

There are general craft books like Susan Purdy's *Festivals for You to Celebrate* (1969), in which the projects are grouped by seasons and suggestions are given for group activities, or Carolyn Meyer's *Christmas Crafts* (1974), which proposes a project a day through December. Camille Sokol's *The Lucky Sew-It-Yourself Book* (1966) is a hand-sewing book with very simple projects for the seven- to nine-year-old. An example of the specialized book is Jan Beaney's *The Young Embroiderer* (1967), with imaginative suggestions that can stimulate original work; another is Meyer's *Rock Tumbling* (1975). Older children can use almost any cookbook, but *Kids Cooking* (1970) by Aileen Paul and Arthur Hawkins makes cooking easy by listing ingredients and implements on one page, and giving the instructions on the facing page. *The Natural Cook's First Book* (1973) by Carole Getzoff stresses wholesome recipes.

Filmmaking has become tremendously popular, and both Joan Horvath's *Filmmaking for Beginners* (1974) and Robert Ferguson's *How to Make Movies* (1969) give detailed and practical advice on every aspect of the art. Yvonne Andersen gives both the techniques of preparation and the intricacies of filming in *Make Your Own Animated Movies* (1970).

One of the most sensible books on pets is Dorothy Broderick's *Training a Companion Dog* (1965), which is explicit and detailed and gives advice on equipment. Harriet Howard's *If You Had a Pony* (1965) uses photographs to teach the care and training of a pony and to give some information on riding. In *Look What I Found!* (1971), Marshal Case explains how to capture small wild creatures, with suggestions for duplicating the animal's natural habitat and an emphasis on showing kindness and respect for all life forms, and Roger Caras, in *A Zoo in Your Room* (1975) gives sensible advice on pet care. William Weber's *Wild Animal Babies* (1975) does the same for the care of abandoned or injured small creatures.

In addition to the books that describe specific activities and crafts, there is the comprehensive "doing" book, which presents information about a variety of scientific topics through suggested experiments and activities. And there are books in very specialized areas, like Remy Charlip's *Handtalk; An ABC of Finger Spelling and Sign Language* (1974).

The experiment book has a definite value in that it guides the child toward direct participation in the discovery of knowledge, and, since so many experiences must be gained vicariously, first-hand discovery should be encouraged whenever possible. But experiment books also have a more subtle value. We realize today that education must do more than impart knowledge—it must also teach the child how to use that knowledge in the solution of problems. Glenn Blough once stated:

> *If pupils are to grow in ability to solve problems they must grow in ability to think of appropriate things to do to discover solutions.*[3]

Teaching children how to set up sound experiments and how to interpret the results of these experiments is one way of training them to "think of appropriate things to do."

Good experiment books, for obvious reasons, will suggest only those activities which are safe and those which can be performed with readily available and inexpensive materials, and there are such books today for every age level. Whatever the interest, a child who likes to experiment can benefit from Thomas Moorman's *How to Make Your Science Project Scientific* (1974), which exemplifies the scientific attitudes and methods it describes.

Prove It! (1963) by Rose Wyler and Gerald Ames is for the beginning reader and presents simple experiments performed with ordinary objects. Harlow Rockwell's *I Did It* (1974) has varied, simple experiments and projects for beginning readers to try. Rose Wyler's *What Happens If . . . ?* (1974) has safe, easy experiments designed by a teacher of science and science education. Franklyn Branley's *Timmy and the Tin-Can Telephone* is written as a story in which two children learn about the transmission of sound by making a "telephone" out of tin cans, string, and buttons. Harry Milgrom's *Adventures with a Paper Cup* (1968) has an assortment of easy experiments in which a cone-shaped cup is used to demonstrate such phenomena as air resistance and sound amplification. This and similar books by Milgrom, or Nancy Larrick's *See for Yourself* (1952), which has simple experiments with air, water, and heat, can stir or encourage an interest in scientific exploration and discovery in young children. For the child with a short attention span, Herman Schneider's *Science Fun for You in a Minute or Two* (1975) offers experiments that are brief and require little equipment.

One of the most varied books of experiments, containing material in many of the sciences, is *700 Science Experiments for Everyone*, compiled by UNESCO in 1956. William Moore's *Your Science Fair Project* (1964) has projects grouped by levels from grades three to eight, and is particularly useful for the average student who is required to participate. Alfred Morgan's *Boys' Book of Science and Construction* (1959) has more advanced experiments, and also includes instructions for making such things as steam turbines, pinhole cameras, and weather vanes.

Elizabeth Cooper's *Science in Your Own Back Yard* (1958) suggests way of observing, collecting, and experimenting in the field of nature study, in a book that can stimulate the individual reader or be used by a group. There is an emphasis on conservation in Ted Pettit's *A Guide to Nature Projects* (1966). Each section of the book deals with a single aspect of the subject and gives background information before discussing experiments.

For the child who has a specific interest, there are such books as Harry Sootin's *Experiments with Magnetism* (1968) or his mineralogy book, *The Young Experimenter's Workbook* (1965), written in collaboration with Laura Sootin. Paul Czaja's *Writing with Light* (1973) shows how one can make pictures without a camera. Both books require only materials that are available in the home or are inexpensive, and the experiments are practical and clearly explained. Rocco Feravolo's *Easy Physics Projects; Air, Water and Heat* (1966) and A. Harris Stone's books are for

[3]Glenn O. Blough, "Quality Is What Counts!" *Instructor*, September 1958, p. 6.

children of the same age, but they are quite different in approach. Rather than using the open-ended process approach of the Stone experiment books, Feravolo answers the questions raised; little is left to the student's imagination, but the concepts are lucidly presented and the book can be useful to children hesitant about taking initiative.

Reference Books

Although encyclopedias and dictionaries, fact books and almanacs, and indexes and bibliographies are the kinds of books usually meant when reference books are referred to, it should be remembered that many other kinds of books have reference use.

Children's rooms in public libraries often have books that reflect the particular interests of their community, such as foreign language source books, reference materials that give information about local industries, or books about indigenous flora and fauna. School library collections may stress books that fit into curricular units. Both will gather as much as they can about local history, and both will include in their collections some books intended for adult reference use.

There are so many dictionaries and encyclopedias that are valuable, that guides to them are reference books in themselves. Most professional journals include reviews of reference books; *Booklist* and *Wilson Library Bulletin* have special sections devoted to them. Carolyn Sue Peterson's *Reference Books for Elementary and Junior High School Libraries* is a useful annotated bibliography that suggests in its introduction methods of evaluation, most of which require examination of the volumes being considered. Another good source is *General Encyclopedias in Print.* Almost every dictionary and encyclopedia has a coterie of devoted users who feel that their favorites are the best. Each differs, and libraries that can afford to buy all the reference books which meet critical standards usually do so.

In assembling a home reference library, parents would do well to examine carefully the different reference books they are considering. If possible, a home collection for children should include one of the major children's encyclopedias, a reliable dictionary appropriate for the ages of the children in the family, and an atlas. Parents of children with limited vision may want an atlas printed in large type, which is also useful for younger children because the maps are easy to read. In making decisions, parents will want to examine the way material is arranged and to make sure that the type is uncrowded and is large enough to read without strain; they will look for the quality and placement of illustrations and the adequacy of captions or labels, and they will consider aids to pronunciation, glossaries, indexes, and other auxiliary material provided on prefatory or appended pages, including an explanation of symbols used, or other features of the book.

Most adults feel that children should have their own dictionaries, but they are not so sure that children need their own encyclopedias. In homes where books must be carefully budgeted, many families feel that an adult encyclopedia is the better investment. When children are young, parents can help them use the books, and the older children can use them themselves. The best adult encyclopedias last for a lifetime; they may become dated in some respects, but the bulk of the material will carry a child through high school, college, and adult life. If a choice must be made, then decidedly the adult set should be purchased because of its greater richness and long-range value. But when a family can afford both, the children should have their own set. And let's face it—many families cannot afford *any* set. For them, using library copies is an answer.

Many informational series books have reference use, from such erudite books as the Time-Life Library of Art and the American Heritage historical series, to Leonard Everett Fisher's books on colonial crafts. But each book in a series must be evaluated on its own merits. As is true in library collections, a home reference collection will include such books when they are appropriate for the family's particular interests. And if a member of the family is a bird-watcher or a stamp collector, Roger Tory Peterson's *Field Guide to the Birds* or *Scott's Standard Postage Stamp Catalogue* may seem an absolute necessity.

Some families may feel that reference books that reflect their interests are a better investment than an encyclopedia, since it is possible to keep such a subject collection current with less financial outlay than the purchase of an encyclopedia would require. Library-owned encyclopedias are apt to be more current than home sets and are therefore more useful for school assignments.

The library reference collection should include the Bible and other sacred writings and books on comparative religion, whether they are discussions of denominations like Kathleen Elgin's separate treatments or a compendium like Katharine Savage's *The Story of World Religions*. Also useful for information about religion are biographies of religious leaders and such books as Susan Purdy's *Jewish Holidays; Facts, Activities and Crafts*.

Despite the abundance and variety of informational books, they are often given short shrift in discussion of literary quality. To be sure, some are distinguished more for their usefulness than for their style, but many of these books, such as *Chipmunks on the Doorstep* by Edwin Tunis, are as graceful in their prose as are some of the works of fiction that have won awards. And remember that the first Newbery Medal was given to Hendrik Willem Van Loon for *The Story of Mankind*, a history of humanity's origin and evolution that is witty and authoritative, the sort of informational book that amuses, informs, and stimulates readers to further inquiry. What more could one ask?

Adult References[4]

DEASON, HILARY J., comp. *The AAAS Science Booklist.*

FISHER, MARGERY. *Matters of Fact: Aspects of Non-Fiction for Children.*

HUUS, HELEN. *Children's Books to Enrich the Social Studies for the Elementary Grades.*

IRWIN, LEONARD B., comp. *A Guide to Historical Reading; Non-Fiction.*

LOGASA, HANNAH. *Science for Youth.*

PETERSON, CAROLYN SUE. *Reference Books for Elementary and Junior High School Libraries.*

SUTHERLAND, ZENA. *History in Children's Books; An Annotated Bibliography for Schools and Libraries.*

TITOWSKY, BERNARD. *American History.*

VANCE, LUCILLE, and ESTHER TRACEY. *Illustration Index.*

WILTZ, JOHN E. *Books in American History; A Basic List for High Schools.*

[4]Complete bibliographic data are provided in the combined Adult References in the Appendixes.

In the following bibliography these symbols have been used to identify books about a religious or a particular ethnic group:

§ Black
★ Chicano or Puerto Rican
☆ Native American
● Religious minority

The Biological Sciences

ADLER, IRVING and RUTH. *Evolution,* ill. by Ruth Adler. Day, 1965. 8-10

ALIKI. *The Long-Lost Coelacanth and Other Living Fossils,* ill. by author. T. Crowell, 1973. A clear explanation of how fossil finds enable scientists to recognize living fossils. 7-9

AMON, ALINE. *Reading, Writing, Chattering Chimps,* ill. by author. Atheneum, 1975. A report on projects in which chimpanzees learn to communicate. 10-12

ANDREWS, ROY CHAPMAN. *All About Dinosaurs,* ill. by Thomas W. Voter. Random, 1953. 9-12

_____. *All About Whales,* ill. Random, 1954. 9-11

_____. *In the Days of the Dinosaurs,* ill. by Jean Zallinger. Random, 1959. 8-11

ASIMOV, ISAAC. *ABC's of Ecology.* Walker, 1972. 8-11

BEADLE, GEORGE and MURIEL. *The Language of Life; An Introduction to the Science of Genetics.* Doubleday, 1966. 14 up

BENDICK, JEANNE. *How Heredity Works; Why Living Things Are As They Are.* Parents' Magazine, 1975. A good introduction to genetics. 7-9

_____. *A Place to Live,* ill. by author. Parents Magazine, 1970. 5-8

_____. *What Made You* You? ill. by author. McGraw, 1971. 4-7

BLOCH, MARIE H. *Dinosaurs,* ill. by George F. Mason. Coward, 1955. 8-10

BLOUGH, GLENN O. *After the Sun Goes Down,* ill. by Jeanne Bendick. McGraw, 1956. 7-9

_____. *Discovering Dinosaurs,* ill. by Gustav Schrotter. Whittlesey, 1960. 8-9

_____. *Soon After September; The Story of Living Things in Winter,* ill. by Jeanne Bendick. McGraw, 1959. 7-9

_____. *Who Lives in This House; A Story of Animal Families,* ill. by Jeanne Bendick. McGraw, 1957. 7-9

BRENNER, BARBARA. *Baltimore Orioles,* ill. by J. Winslow Higginbotham. Harper, 1974. 6-7

BUCK, MARGARET WARING. *Pets from the Pond,* ill. by author. Abingdon, 1958. Good fresh-water biology. 9-11

_____. *In Yards and Gardens,* ill. by author. Abingdon, 1952. 9-12

CLEMONS, ELIZABETH. *Shells Are Where You Find Them,* ill. by Joe Gault. Knopf, 1960. 8-10

COLLINS, HENRY HILL, JR. *The Bird Watcher's Guide,* ill. with photos; line drawings and cover by Richard Harker. Golden Pr., 1961. 10-13

COSGROVE, MARGARET. *Bone for Bone,* ill. by author. Dodd, 1968. 11-15

_____. *Eggs—And What Happens Inside Them,* ill. by author. Dodd, 1966. 8-12

DARLING, LOUIS. *Greenhead.* Morrow, 1954. 10-14

_____. *The Gull's Way,* photos and ill. by author. Morrow, 1965. 11-15

DOWDEN, ANNE OPHELIA TODD. *The Blossom on the Bough; A Book of Trees,* ill. by author. T. Crowell, 1975. 11 up

______. *Wild Green Things in the City; A Book of Weeds,* ill. by author. T. Crowell, 1972. 10-14

EARLE, OLIVE L. *Paws, Hoofs, and Flippers,* ill. by author. Morrow, 1954. Mammals are classified by their feet. 10-14

______. *Praying Mantis,* ill. by author. Morrow, 1969.

______. *The Rose Family,* ill. by author. Morrow, 1970. 8-10

______. *State Trees,* rev. ed., ill. by author. Morrow, 1973. 9-12

EARLE, OLIVE LYDIA, and MICHAEL KANTOR. *Nuts,* ill. by Olive L. Earle. Morrow, 1975. Botanical information that has minor reference use. 8-10

FEGELY, THOMAS D. *Wonders of Wild Ducks.* Dodd, 1975. Good scope in a text that stresses conservation. 10-14

FENNER, CAROL. *Gorilla Gorilla,* ill. by Symeon Shimin. Random, 1973. A narrative framework for a life-cycle book. 8-10

FLANAGAN, GERALDINE LUX. *Window into an Egg; Seeing Life Begin,* ill. with photos. Scott/Addison, 1969. 9-11

FLEMING, ALICE. *Alcohol; The Delightful Poison.* Delacorte, 1975. Historical background plus a discussion of excessive drinking. 12-16

FRESCHET, BERNIECE. *The Flight of the Snow Goose,* ill. by Jo Polseno. Crown, 1970. 7-9

______. *The Web in the Grass,* ill. by Roger Duvoisin. Scribner's, 1972. Handsome illustrations show the spider's world. 4-7

______. *Year on Muskrat Marsh,* ill. by Peter Parnall. Scribner's, 1974. 8-10

GEORGE, JEAN. *All Upon a Sidewalk,* ill. by Don Bolognese. Dutton, 1974. 7-8

______. *All Upon a Stone,* ill. by Don Bolognese. T. Crowell, 1971. 7-8

______. *The Hole in the Tree,* ill. by author. Dutton, 1957. 8-10

______. *The Moon of the Bears,* ill. by Mac Shepard. T. Crowell, 1967. One of a series. 9-11

______. *Spring Comes to the Ocean,* ill. by John Wilson. T. Crowell, 1965.

GOETZ, DELIA. *Tropical Rain Forests,* ill. by Louis Darling. Morrow, 1957. 8-11

GORDON, SOL. *Girls Are Girls and Boys Are Boys; So What's the Difference?* ill. by Frank C. Smith. Day, 1974. 8-9

GOUDEY, ALICE E. *Graywings,* ill. by Marie Nonnast. Scribner's, 1964. The life cycle of a herring gull. 6-10

______. *Here Come the Dolphins,* ill. by Garry MacKenzie. Scribner's, 1961. 7-9

______. *Here Come the Lions!* ill. by Garry MacKenzie. Scribner's, 1956. 7-9

______. *Houses from the Sea,* ill. by Adrienne Adams. Scribner's, 1959. 5-7

GROSS, RUTH BELOV. *Snakes.* Four Winds, 1975. An especially competent treatment of habits and habitat; coverage of reproduction is scanty. 8-10

GRUENBERG, SIDONIE MATSNER. *The Wonderful Story of How You Were Born,* rev. ed., ill. by Symeon Shimin. Doubleday, 1970. 8-10

GUILCHER, J. M., and R. H. NOAILLES. *A Fern Is Born.* Sterling, 1971. Clearly detailed photographs and a concise style make this and other books in the series admirable examples of nature writing. 9-12

______. *A Tree Grows Up,* Sterling, 1972. Same format as *A Fern Is Born.* 10-12

HALMI, ROBERT. *Zoos of the World.* Four Winds, 1975. Focuses on the increasing attention paid to the comfort and security of zoo animals. 10-12

HELLMAN, HAL. *Biology in the World of the Future,* ill. Evans, 1971. A knowledgeable and witty foray into the frontiers of biological research, well organized and provocative. 12 up

HIRSCH, S. CARL. *The Living Community; A Venture into Ecology,* ill. by William Steinel. Viking, 1966. 12-14

HOBAN, TANA. *Big Ones, Little Ones,* photos by author. Greenwillow, 1976. 2-5

HOFSTEIN, SADIE. *The Human Story; Facts on Birth, Growth, and Reproduction.* Lothrop, 1969. 10-12

HOLLING, HOLLING C. *Pagoo,* ill. by L. W. Holling. Houghton, 1957. 8-10

HOPF, ALICE L. *Biography of a Rhino,* ill. by Kiyo Komoda. Putnam, 1972. A narrative framework incorporates accurate information smoothly. 7-9

______. *Biography of an Ostrich,* ill. by Ben F. Stahl. Putnam, 1975. No anthropomorphism despite a fictional framework. 7-9

______. *Misplaced Animals and Other Living Creatures.* McGraw, 1976. A survey of animal life that has been accidentally introduced into new environments. 11-14

HUTCHINS, ROSS E. *The Ant Realm,* ill. with photos by author. Dodd, 1967. The author describes, with his usual zest, the fascinating behavior of various species of ants, both group and individual behavior. 10-14

______. *The Bug Clan,* photos by author. Dodd, 1973. A comprehensive and well-organized survey. 10 up

______. *The Travels of Monarch X,* ill. by Jerome P. Connolly. Rand, 1966. The description of a southward migration of a tagged Monarch butterfly from Toronto to Mexico. 8-10

JACKER, CORINNE. *The Biological Revolution; A Background Book on the Making of a New World.* Parents' Magazine, 1971. A comprehensive, exciting survey of biological frontiers. 13 up

JOHNSON, ERIC W. *Love and Sex in Plain Language,* rev. ed., ill. by Russ Hoover. Lippincott, 1974. 12-17

KAVALER, LUCY. *Life Battles Cold,* ill. by Leslie Morrill. Day, 1973. A discussion of the many ways living things adapt to extreme cold. 11-15

______. *The Wonders of Algae,* ill. with photos and with drawings by Barbara Amlick and Richard Ott. Day, 1961. 11-14

______. *The Wonders of Fungi,* ill. with photos and with drawings by Richard Ott. Day, 1964. 11-14

KLEIN, AARON E. *Threads of Life; Genetics from Aristotle to DNA,* ill. Natural History Pr., 1970. 12 up

LAUBER, PATRICIA. *Everglades Country,* photos by Patricia Caulfield. Viking, 1973. 11-14

______. *Your Body and How It Works,* ill. by Stephen Rogers Peck, photos by Florence Burns. Random, 1962. 8-10

LAVINE, SIGMUND A. *Wonders of the Eagle World.* Dodd, 1974. Describes physical characteristics, behavior, and the eagle in history and mythology. 9-11

LEVINE, EDNA S. *Lisa and Her Soundless World,* ill. by Gloria Kamen. Behavioral Publications, 1974. A discussion of the abilities and limitations of a deaf child. 8-10

LUBELL, WINIFRED and CECIL. *Green Is for Growing,* ill. by Winifred Lubell. Rand, 1964. 8-10

McCLUNG, ROBERT M. *Black Jack: Last of the Big Alli-*

gators, ill. by Lloyd Sandford. Morrow, 1967. 8-10

______. *Gypsy Moth,* ill. by author. Morrow, 1974. 10-14

______. *Honker,* ill. by Bob Hines. Morrow, 1965. 8-10

______. *How Animals Hide.* National Geographic, 1973. 7-10

______. *Mice, Moose, and Men; How Their Populations Rise and Fall.* Morrow, 1973. A description of the causes and problems of overpopulation. 9-12

______. *Sea Star,* ill. by author. Morrow, 1975. 7-9

______. *Shag, Last of the Plains Buffalo,* ill. by Louis Darling. Morrow, 1960. 8-10

______. *Spike; The Story of a Whitetail Deer,* ill. by author. Morrow, 1952. 8-9

______. *Thor; Last of the Sperm Whales,* ill. by Bob Hines. Morrow, 1971. 8-10

McCOY, J. J. *The Hunt for the Whooping Cranes; A Natural History Detective Story,* ill. by Rey Abruzzi. Lothrop, 1966. A detailed and fascinating account of the search for the nesting grounds of the whooping cranes and efforts to save this endangered species. 13 up

MARI, IELA and ENZO, ills., *The Apple and the Moth* and *The Chicken and the Egg.* Pantheon, 1970. First published in Italy, two charming books for the youngest biologists that tell their stories clearly without text. 3-5

NAPIER, JOHN. *The Origins of Man,* ill. by Maurice Wilson. McGraw, 1969. A fine introductory interpretation of evolution. The author (Director of the Primate Biology Program of the Smithsonian) adds to his professional competence a sense of drama and a simplicity of approach. 9-11

NILSSON, LENNART. *How Was I Born? A Photographic Story of Reproduction and Birth for Children.* Delacorte/Seymour Lawrence, 1975. 8-11

NOURSE, ALAN E. *The Body,* by Alan E. Nourse and the Editors of *Life.* Time-Life, 1964. Illustrated with superb photographs. 13 up

PARKER, BERTHA MORRIS. *The Golden Book of Science,* ill. by Harry McNaught. Golden Pr., 1956. 8-10

PATENT, DOROTHY HINSHAW. *Frogs, Toads, Salamanders and How They Reproduce,* ill. by Matthew Kalmenoff. Holiday, 1975. A lucid and authoritative text, broad in scope. 9-12

______. *How Insects Communicate.* Holiday, 1975. 9-12

PERRY, BILL. *Our Threatened Wildlife; An Ecological Study,* ill. Coward, 1970. An excellent survey of wildlife resources. Discusses extinct and endangered species, conservation agencies, types of refuges, and kinds of research. 12-15

PHLEGER, FRED. *The Whales Go By,* ill. by Paul Galdone. Random, 1959. 6-7

PRINCE, J. H. *The Universal Urge; Courtship and Mating Among Animals.* Nelson, 1973. 11 up

PRINGLE, LAURENCE. *This Is a River; Exploring an Ecosystem.* Macmillan, 1972. Includes a description of the water cycle and discusses pollution and damming. 9-11

RAVIELLI, ANTHONY. *From Fins to Hands; An Adventure in Evolution,* ill. by author. Viking, 1968. 9-11

______. *Wonders of the Human Body,* ill. by author. Viking, 1954. 10-12

RIEDMAN, SARAH R. *Naming Living Things; The Grouping of Plants and Animals,* ill. by Jerome P. Connolly. Rand, 1963. 10-12

RUSSELL, SOLVEIG PAULSON. *Like and Unlike; A First Look at Classification,* ill. by Lawrence Di Fiori. Walck, 1973. Authoritative introduction to classification of plants and animals. 8-10

SCHALLER, GEORGE B., and MILLICENT E. SELSAM. *The Tiger; Its Life in the Wild,* ill. with photos, drawings, and maps. Harper, 1969. The author's firsthand experiences add interest to this account of much that is known about tigers. Myths about these animals are also recounted. 10-12

SCHEELE, WILLIAM E. *Prehistoric Animals,* ill. by author. World, 1954. Describes the first five million years of earth's life forms. Cites locations of fossils in museums. 9 up

SCHEFFER, VICTOR. *Little Calf,* ill. by Leonard Everett Fisher. Scribner's, 1970. 12 up

SCHICK, ALICE. *Kongo and Kumba; Two Gorillas,* ill. by Joseph Cellini. Dial, 1974. A comparison of the lives of a gorilla in the wilds and another in a zoo. 8-10

______. *The Peregrine Falcons,* ill. by Peter Parnall. Dial, 1975. 11-15

SCOTT, JACK DENTON. *Loggerhead Turtle; Survivor from the Sea,* photos by Ozzie Sweet. Putnam, 1974. A vivid prose essay on the creature so graceful in the sea and so clumsy on land. 10 up

______. *The Survivors; Enduring Animals of North America,* ill. by Daphne Gillen. Harcourt, 1975. 10-14

______. *That Wonderful Pelican,* photos by Ozzie Sweet. Putnam, 1975. An authoritative and comprehensive text. 10 up

SELSAM, MILLICENT E. *Animals as Parents,* ill. by John Kaufmann. Morrow, 1965. 10-12

______. *The Apple and Other Fruits,* photos by Jerome Wexler. Morrow, 1973. Excellent magnified photographs accompany a lucid botanical description. 8-10

______. *Bulbs, Corms, and Such,* photos by Jerome Wexler. Morrow, 1974. 8-10

______. *Benny's Animals, and How He Put Them in Order,* ill. by Arnold Lobel. Harper, 1966. 6-8

______. *The Carrot and Other Root Vegetables,* photos by Jerome Wexler. Morrow, 1971. 7-9

______. *Greg's Microscope,* ill. by Arnold Lobel. Harper, 1963. 6-8

______. *The Harlequin Moth; Its Life Story,* photos by Jerome Wexler. Morrow, 1975. Designed to encourage observation by pointing out differences. 7-9

______. *How Kittens Grow,* photos by Esther Bubley. Four Winds, 1975. 4-7

______. *The Language of Animals,* ill. by Kathleen Elgin. Morrow, 1962. 10-14

______. *Let's Get Turtles,* ill. by Arnold Lobel. Harper, 1965. 7-8

______. *Peanut,* ill. with photos by Jerome Wexler. Morrow, 1969. 7-9

______. *Plants That Heal,* ill. by Kathleen Elgin. Morrow, 1959. 11-14

______. *Plants That Move,* ill. by Fred F. Scherer. Morrow, 1962. 8-11

______. *See Along the Shore,* ill. by Leonard Weisgard. Harper, 1961. 7-9

______. *See Through the Jungle,* ill. by Winifred Lubell. Harper, 1957. 7-9

______. *See Through the Sea,* ill. by Winifred Lubell. Harper, 1955. 7-9

SHEFFIELD, MARGARET. *Where Do Babies Come From?* ill. by Sheila Bewley. Knopf, 1973. 5-7

SHIPPEN, KATHERINE B. *Men, Microscopes and Living Things,* ill. by Anthony Ravielli. Viking, 1955. 13-15

SHOWERS, PAUL. *Look at Your Eyes,* ill. by Paul Galdone. T. Crowell, 1962. 6-7

______. *Sleep Is for Everyone,* ill. by Wendy Watson. T. Crowell, 1974. 6-8

______. *Use Your Brain,* ill. by Rosalind Fry. T. Crowell, 1971. 5-8

______. *Where Does the Garbage Go?* ill. by Loretta Lustig. T. Crowell, 1974. 7-8

§ ______. *Your Skin and Mine,* ill. by Paul Galdone. T. Crowell, 1965. 6-8

SHOWERS, PAUL and KAY. *Before You Were a Baby,* ill. by Ingrid Fetz. T. Crowell, 1968. 7-8

SHUTTLESWORTH, DOROTHY. *Animal Camouflage,* ill. by Matthew Kalmenoff. Natural History Pr., 1966. 11-14

______. *To Find a Dinosaur.* Doubleday, 1973. 9-12

______. *The Story of Rodents,* ill. by Lydia Rosier. Doubleday, 1971. 9-12

SILVERSTEIN, ALVIN and VIRGINIA B. *Apples; All About Them,* ill. by Shirley Chan. Prentice, 1976. 9-12

______. *The Code of Life,* ill. by Kenneth Gosner. Atheneum, 1972. A detailed, comprehensive study of genetic heritage. 12 up

______. *Exploring the Brain,* ill. by Patricia De Veau. Prentice, 1975. 10-13

______. *Gerbils; All About Them,* photos by Frederick Breda. Lippincott, 1976. 9-12

______. *Hamsters; All About Them,* photos by Frederick Breda. Lothrop, 1974. 9-12

______. *The Skeletal System; Framework for Life,* ill. by Lee J. Ames. Prentice, 1972. 9-11

______. *The Skin; Coverings and Linings of Living Things,* ill. by Lee J. Ames. Prentice, 1972. 9-11

______. *Sleep and Dreams.* Lippincott, 1974. 12-15

SIMON, HILDA. *The Amazing Book of Birds.* Hart, 1958. 9-11

______. *Exploring the World of Social Insects,* ill. by author. Vanguard, 1963. A study of group behavior. 9-13

______. *Frogs and Toads of the World,* ill. by author. Lippincott, 1975. 11-14

______. *Insect Masquerades.* Viking, 1968. 11-14

______. *Living Lanterns; Luminescence in Animals,* ill. by author. Viking, 1971. 11 up

______. *Snakes; The Facts and Folklore,* ill. by author. Viking, 1973. 11-15

STEVENS, CARLA. *The Birth of Sunset's Kittens,* ill. with photos by Leonard Stevens. W. R. Scott, 1969. No cute posed pictures, no saccharine comment, just the miraculous facts of kittens being born. 5-8

STONE, A. HARRIS, and STEPHEN COLLINS. *Experiments in Ecology,* ill. by Peter Plasencia. Watts, 1973. 9-12

STONE, A. HARRIS, and ROBERT J. STEIN. *Biology Project Puzzlers,* ill. by David Lindroth. Prentice, 1973. 9-12

STOUTENBURG, ADRIEN. *A Vanishing Thunder: Extinct and Threatened American Birds,* ill. by John Schoenherr. Natural History Pr., 1967. A sobering reminder of human carelessness. 10-12

TRESSELT, ALVIN. *The Beaver Pond,* ill. by Roger Duvoisin. Lothrop, 1970. 5-7

______. *The Dead Tree,* ill. by Charles Robinson. Parents' Magazine, 1972. 5-7

TUNIS, EDWIN. *Chipmunks on the Doorstep,* ill. by author. T. Crowell, 1971. 10 up

WATSON, JANE (WERNER). *Whales; Friendly Dolphins and Mighty Giants of the Sea,* ill. by Richard Amundsen. Western, 1975. 9-12

ZIM, HERBERT S. *Dinosaurs,* ill. by James G. Irving. Morrow, 1954. 9-11

______. *Frogs and Toads,* ill. by Joy Buba. Morrow, 1950. 8-10

______. *Golden Hamsters,* ill. by Herschel Wartik. Morrow, 1951. 8-10

______. *Medicine,* ill. by Judith Corwin. Morrow, 1974. 9-11

______. *Our Senses and How They Work,* ill. by Herschel Wartik. Morrow, 1956. 9-11

______. *Your Heart and How It Works,* ill. by Gustav Schrotter. Morrow, 1959. 9-11

ZIM, HERBERT S., and SONIA BLEEKER. *Life and Death,* ill. by René Martin. Morrow, 1970. 9-12

ZIM, HERBERT, and LUCRETIA KRANZ. *Crabs,* ill. by René Martin. Morrow, 1974. 8-10

______. *Snails,* ill. by René Martin. Morrow, 1975. 8-10

The Physical Sciences

ADLER, IRVING. *The Changing Tools of Science; From Yardstick to Cyclotron,* ill. by Ruth Adler. Day, 1958; 1973. 12-14

______. *The Giant Golden Book of Mathematics,* ill. by Lowell Hess. Golden Pr., 1960. An explanation of fundamental concepts. 10-14

______. *Magic House of Numbers,* ill. by Ruth Adler. Day, 1957; 1974. 10-14

______. *The New Mathematics,* ill. by Ruth Adler. Day, 1958. An explanation of advanced math, 11-14

______. *Petroleum; Gas, Oil and Asphalt,* ill. by Peggy Adler. Day, 1975. 9-11

______. *The Stars; Steppingstones into Space,* ill. by Ruth Adler. Day, 1956. This emphasizes scientific investigation of astronomy. 12-14

______. *The Sun and Its Family,* ill. by Ruth Adler. Day, 1958. 12-14

______. *Tools in Your Life,* ill. by Ruth Adler. Day, 1956. 10-14

______. *The Wonders of Physics; An Introduction to the Physical World,* ill. by Cornelius DeWitt. Golden Pr., 1966. 12 up

ADLER, IRVING and RUTH. *Sets,* ill. by Ruth Adler. Day, 1967. 9-11

______. *Sets and Numbers for the Very Young,* ill. by Peggy Adler. Day, 1969. 6-8

AMES, GERALD, and ROSE WYLER. *First Days of the World,* ill. by Leonard Weisgard. Harper, 1958. 8-10

ANDERSON, ALAN H. *The Drifting Continents.* Putnam, 1971. 12 up

ASIMOV, ISAAC. *ABC's of Space,* ill. Walker, 1969. 8-10

______. *The Best New Thing,* ill. by Symeon Shimin. World, 1971. 5-7

______. *Building Blocks of the Universe,* rev. ed. Abelard, 1961. 14-17

______. *How Did We Find Out About Comets?* ill. by David Wool. Walker, 1975. A fine example of a text incorporating scientific method in the explanation of knowledge accruing over centuries. 9-11

______. *Jupiter; The Largest Planet.* Lothrop, 1973; 1976. 12 up

______. *More Words of Science,* ill. by William Barss. Houghton, 1972. Lively prose defines and explains terminology. 12-15

______. *Realm of Measure,* ill. by R. Belmore. Houghton, 1960. A discussion of measuring systems. 12 up

______. *Realm of Numbers,* diagrams by Robert Belmore. Houghton, 1959. 12 up

______. *Words of Science; and the History Behind Them,* ill. by William Barss. Houghton, 1959. 12-17

BEHRENS, JUNE. *The True Book of Metric Measurement.* Childrens Pr., 1975. 7-9

BENDICK, JEANNE. *All Around You; A First Look at the*

World, ill. by author. Whittlesey, 1951. 6-8

______. *Electronics for Young People,* 4th ed., ill. by author. McGraw, 1960. 11-13

______. *The First Book of Space Travel,* rev. ed., ill. by author. Watts, 1969. 8-10

______. *The First Book of Time,* ill. by author. Watts, 1963. 9-11

______. *How Much and How Many; The Story of Weights and Measures,* ill. by author. McGraw, 1960. 10-12

______. *Names, Sets and Numbers,* ill. by author. Watts, 1971. 7-10

______. *The Shape of the Earth,* ill. by author. Rand, 1965. 9-11

______. *Solids, Liquids and Gases,* ill. by author. Watts, 1974. 8-10

______. *The Wind,* ill. by author. Rand, 1964. 8-10

BENDICK, JEANNE, and MARCIA LEVIN. *Take Shapes, Lines and Letters,* ill. by Jeanne Bendick. McGraw, 1962. 10-12

BENDICK, JEANNE, and ROBERT BENDICK. *Television Works Like This,* 4th ed., ill. by Jeanne Bendick. McGraw, 1965. 10-12

BERGER, MELVIN. *The New Water Book,* ill. by Leonard Kessler. T. Crowell, 1973. 9-11

______. *Oceanography Lab.* Day, 1973. 9-11

BOVA, BENJAMIN. *Man Changes the Weather.* Addison, 1973. 10-13

______. *The Weather Changes Man.* Addison, 1974. A review of man's adjustment to weather, and its influence on his life, from Ice Age to Space Age. 10-12

______. *Workshops in Space.* Dutton, 1974. 11-14

BRANLEY, FRANKLYN M. *A Book of Flying Saucers for You,* ill. by Leonard Kessler. T. Crowell, 1973. A discussion of the phenomena that have been reported as flying saucers. 8-9

______. *A Book of Mars for You,* ill. by Leonard Kessler. T. Crowell, 1968. 6-10

______. *A Book of Planet Earth for You,* ill. by Leonard Kessler. T. Crowell, 1975. A study of earth as seen from an imaginary planet. 8-10

______. *The Christmas Sky,* ill. by Blair Lent. T. Crowell, 1966. 9-11

______. *Eclipse; Darkness in Daytime,* ill. by Donald Crews. T. Crowell, 1973. 7-9

______. *The End of the World,* ill. by David Palladini. T. Crowell, 1974. A projection of the distant event is based on astronomical changes. 10-14

______. *Energy for the 21st Century,* ill. by Henry Roth. T. Crowell, 1975. An analysis of energy resources and needs includes discussion of solutions for future needs. 11-14

______. *Man in Space to the Moon,* ill. by Louis S. Glanzman. T. Crowell, 1970. 9-11

______. *Mars: Planet Number Four,* rev. ed., ill. by Helmut K. Wimmer. T. Crowell, 1966. 12-15

______. *The Milky Way: Galaxy Number One,* ill. by Helmut K. Wimmer. T. Crowell, 1969. 12 up

______. *The Moon Seems to Change,* ill. by Helen Borten. T. Crowell, 1960. 6-7

______. *Pieces of Another World; The Story of Moon Rocks,* ill. by Herbert Danska. T. Crowell, 1973. 10-13

______. *Shakes, Quakes, and Shifts; Earth Tectonics,* ill. by Daniel Maffia. T. Crowell, 1974. An explanation of the shifting continents distinguishes between known facts and theories. 10-15

______. *Solar Energy,* ill. by John Teppich. T. Crowell, 1957. 11-14

______. *The Sun; Our Nearest Star,* ill. by Helen Borten. T. Crowell, 1961. 5-8

______. *The Sun; Star Number One,* ill. by Helmut K. Wimmer. T. Crowell, 1964. 11-14

______. *Think Metric!* ill. by Graham Booth. T. Crowell, 1973. 9-11

BRANLEY, FRANKLYN M., and ELEANOR K. VAUGHAN. *Mickey's Magnet,* ill. by Crockett Johnson. T. Crowell, 1956. 5-7

BRIGGS, PETER. *Science Ship; A Voyage Aboard the Discoverer.* Simon, 1969. 11-15

BRONOWSKI, JACOB, and MILLICENT E. SELSAM. *Biography of an Atom,* ill. by Weimar Pursell and with photos. Harper, 1965. 10-14

BUEHR, WALTER. *Water; Our Vital Need,* ill. by author. Norton/Grosset, 1967. 9-11

CARLE, ERIC. *My Very First Book of Shapes.* T. Crowell, 1974. 2-4

CARSON, RACHEL. *The Sea Around Us,* ad. by Anne Terry White, ill. with photos, maps, and drawings. Golden Pr., 1958. 11-14

CHAROSH, MANNIS. *Number Ideas Through Pictures,* ill. by Giulio Maestro. T. Crowell, 1974. 7-9

______. *Straight Lines, Parallel Lines, Perpendicular Lines,* ill. by Enrico Arno. T. Crowell, 1970. One of a series of mathematics books for the young, each volume examining basic ideas and demonstrating patterns and relationships. Brisk, straightforward text; large, clear illustrations. 8-9

COOMBS, CHARLES. *Lift-Off; The Story of Rocket Power,* ill. by R. H. Foor. Morrow, 1963. A clear explanation of rocket engines and guidance systems. 9-11

CROUSE, WILLIAM H. *Understanding Science,* rev. ed., ill. by Jeanne Bendick and D. Mahanes. McGraw, 1956. 10-14

DEMING, RICHARD. *Metric Power; Why and How We Are Going Metric.* Nelson, 1974. 11-15

EPSTEIN, SAM and BERYL. *The First Book of Electricity,* ill. by Robin King. Watts, 1953. 9-12

§ FEELINGS, MURIEL. *Moja Means One,* ill. by Tom Feelings. Dial, 1971. Soft illustrations add appeal to a counting book that gives numbers 1-10 in Swahili. 5-8

FEY, JAMES T. *Long, Short, High, Low, Thin, Wide,* ill. by Janie Russell. T. Crowell, 1971. 7-9

FREEMAN, IRA M. *All About Electricity,* ill. by Evelyn Urbanowich. Random, 1957. 10-13

______. *All About the Wonders of Chemistry,* ill. by George Wilde. Random, 1954. 10-13

FREEMAN, IRA M., and A. RAE PATTON. *The Science of Chemistry,* ill. by Zenowij Onyshkewych. Random, 1968. 10-12

FREEMAN, MAE (BLACKER). *Finding Out About Shapes,* ill. by Bill Morrison. McGraw, 1969. A good introduction to spatial conceptualization, with simple definitions. 5-8

______. *Gravity and the Astronauts,* ill. by Beatrice Darwin. Crown, 1971. 10-12

FROMAN, ROBERT. *Less Than Nothing Is Really Something,* ill. by Don Madden. T. Crowell, 1973. 7-9

GALLANT, ROY A. *Exploring Chemistry,* ill. by Lee Ames. Garden City, 1958. 9-13

______. *Exploring the Universe,* ill. by Lowell Hess. Garden City, 1956; rev. ed., 1968. 9-13

GAMOW, GEORGE. *A Planet Called Earth.* Viking, 1963. 13 up

GANS, ROMA. *Millions and Millions of Crystals,* ill. by Giulio Maestro. T. Crowell, 1973. 7-8

______. *Oil; The Buried Treasure,* ill. by Giulio Maestro. T. Crowell, 1975. 7-8

GOUDEY, ALICE E. *The Day We Saw the Sun Come Up,*

ill. by Adrienne Adams. Scribner's, 1961. Two children rise before dawn, and Mother explains night and day, shadows, and the turning earth. 5-7

HALACY, DANIEL S. *The Energy Trap.* Four Winds, 1975. 12-15

HIRSCH, S. CARL. *Meter Means Measure; The Story of the Metric System.* Viking, 1973. 11-15

HOGBEN, LANCELOT. *Beginnings and Blunders; or Before Science Began.* Grosset, 1970. Primitive man moves toward the earliest civilization, from the first tools to the first cities. 11-14

______. *The Wonderful World of Energy,* ill. by Eileen Aplin and others. Garden City, 1957. 11-14

______. *The Wonderful World of Mathematics,* ill. by Andre, Charles Keeping, Kenneth Symonds. Garden City, 1955; rev. ed., 1968. 10-14

HYDE, MARGARET O., and BRUCE G. HYDE. *Atoms Today and Tomorrow,* rev. ed., ill. by Ed Malsberg. McGraw, 1970. 11-13

JACKER, CORINNE. *Window on the Unknown; A History of the Microscope,* ill. by Mary Linn and with photos. Scribner's, 1966. 13 up

JAMES, ELIZABETH, and CAROL BARKIN. *The Simple Facts of Simple Machines,* photos by Daniel Dorn, diagrams by Susan Stan. Lothrop, 1975. 9-11

KLEIN, AARON E. *The Electron Microscope; A Tool of Discovery.* McGraw, 1974. 13 up

KOHN, BERNICE. *Communications Satellites; Message Centers in Space,* ill. by Jerome Kuhl. Four Winds, 1975. 9-11

LAUBER, PATRICIA. *All About the Ice Age,* ill. Random, 1959. 10-12

______. *All About the Planets,* ill. by Arthur Renshaw. Random, 1960. 9-11

______. *The Story of Numbers,* ill. by Mircea Vasiliu. Random, 1961. 8-10

LEWELLEN, JOHN. *The Mighty Atom,* ill. by Ida Scheib. Knopf, 1955. 8-10

______. *The True Book of Toys at Work,* ill. by Karl Murray. Childrens Pr., 1953. 6-8

______. *Understanding Electronics,* ill. by Ida Scheib. T. Crowell, 1957. 12-14

LEWIS, ALFRED. *The New World of Computers,* ill. with photos. Dodd, 1965. 9-12

MARCUS, REBECCA. *The First Book of Volcanoes and Earthquakes.* Watts, 1972. 9-11

MAY, JULIAN. *Weather,* ill. by Jack White. Follett, 1967. 7-9

______. *Why the Earth Quakes,* ill. by Leonard Everett Fisher. Holiday, 1969. 9-11

MYLLER, ROLF. *How Big Is a Foot?* Atheneum, 1962. 5-7

NAVARRA, JOHN GABRIEL. *Wide World Weather.* Doubleday, 1968. 11 up

OGBURN, CHARLTON. *The Forging of Our Continent.* American Heritage, 1968. 11-13

PODENDORF, ILLA. *Things Are Alike and Different,* ill. by John Hawkinson. Childrens Pr., 1970. 7-8

PRINGLE, LAURENCE. *Energy; Power for People.* Macmillan, 1975. 11-13

RAVIELLI, ANTHONY. *An Adventure in Geometry,* ill. by author. Viking, 1957. 14-17

______. *The World Is Round,* ill. by author. Viking, 1963. 7-10

REED, W. MAXWELL. *The Stars for Sam,* rev. ed., ed. by Paul Brandwein, ill. with photos. Harcourt, 1960. Describes the solar system and the universe and exploration of outer space. Reed's books on the earth and the sea, all durable sources of information, have also been revised. 10-13

RICHARDSON, ROBERT. *The Stars and Serendipity.* Pantheon, 1971. 11-14

RUCHLIS, HY. *Orbit: A Picture Story of Force and Motion,* ill. by Alice Hirsch. Harper, 1958. 10 up

______. *Your Changing Earth,* ill. by Janet and Alex d'Amato. Harvey, 1963. 7-9

SCHLEIN, MIRIAM. *Metric—The Modern Way to Measure.* Harcourt, 1975. 8-10

SCHNEIDER, HERMAN and NINA. *How Big Is Big? From Stars to Atoms,* ill. by Symeon Shimin. W. R. Scott, 1950. 8-11

______. *You, Among the Stars,* ill. by Symeon Shimin. W. R. Scott, 1951. 8-10

SEABORG, GLENN T., and EVANS G. VALENS. *Elements of the Universe,* ill. with photos, charts, and diagrams. Dutton, 1958. 12 up

SELSAM, MILLICENT E. *Birth of an Island,* ill. by Winifred Lubell. Harper, 1959. The evolution of a volcanic island. 8-10

SHANNON, TERRY, and CHARLES PAYZANT. *Windows in the Sea; New Vehicles That Scan the Ocean Depths.* Childrens Pr., 1973. A description of panoramic-view submersibles and the way they are used in marine exploration. 10-13

SILVERBERG, ROBERT. *Wonders of Ancient Chinese Science,* ill. by Marvin Besunder. Hawthorn, 1969. Following a brief background history of China from 1994 B.C., this most informative book surveys the achievements of Chinese scientists, some familiar but many neglected for centuries. 12 up

SILVERSTEIN, ALVIN and VIRGINIA. *The Chemicals We Eat and Drink.* Follett, 1973. 10-13

SRIVASTAVA, JANE JONAS. *Averages,* ill. by Aliki. T. Crowell, 1975. 7-9

______. *Statistics,* ill. by John J. Reiss. T. Crowell, 1973. An excellent introduction explains both the ways statistics are compiled and the ways compilation can affect results. 7-8

TRESSELT, ALVIN R. *Hide and Seek Fog,* ill. by Roger Duvoisin. Lothrop, 1965. 5-8

______. *It's Time Now,* ill. by Roger Duvoisin. Lothrop, 1969. 5-8

______. *Rain Drop Splash,* ill. by Leonard Weisgard. Lothrop, 1946. 4-8

______. *Sun Up,* ill. by Roger Duvoisin. Lothrop, 1949. 5-8

______. *White Snow, Bright Snow,* ill. by Roger Duvoisin. Lothrop, 1947. Caldecott Medal. 5-7

TRIVETT, JOHN V. *Building Tables on Tables,* ill. by Giulio Maestro. T. Crowell, 1975. A lucid presentation of the concepts that are basic to multiplication. 7-9

TUNIS, EDWIN. *Wheels; A Pictorial History,* ill. by author. World, 1955. 11 up

WEISS, HARVEY. *Motors and Engines and How They Work,* ill. by author. T. Crowell, 1969. 10-12

WILFORD, JOHN NOBLE. *We Reach the Moon,* based upon the original book published by *The New York Times* and Bantam Books. Norton/Grosset, 1969. 10-12

WOODBURY, DAVID O. *The New World of the Atom.* Dodd, 1965. 9-11

WYLER, ROSE. *The First Book of Weather,* ill. by Bernice Myers. Watts, 1966. 9-11

WYLER, ROSE, and GERALD AMES. *The New Golden Book of Astronomy,* rev. ed., ill. by John Polgreen. Golden Pr., 1965. 10-12

The Social Sciences

ABELES, ELVIN. *The Student and the University; A Background Book on the Campus Revolt.* Parents' Magazine, 1969. The "background" of the subtitle is the prime emphasis of the book, which traces European and American developments from feudal times to today. The final sections which discuss the changing university and the contemporary student movement are measured and objective. 13 up

ADAMSON, WENDY WRISTON. *Saving Lake Superior; A Story of Environmental Action.* Dillon, 1974. A citizens' group fights pollution. 11-14

§ ADOFF, ARNOLD, ed. *Black on Black; Commentaries by Negro Americans.* Macmillan, 1968. A collection of material spanning the thinking of black Americans from Frederick Douglass to Dick Gregory. Their viewpoints may differ but they unite in speaking of the problems of a fragmented society. 13 up

AMES, GERALD, and ROSE WYLER. *The First People in the World,* ill. by Leonard Weisgard. Harper, 1958. 8-10

ARCHER, JULES. *The Extremists; Gadflies of American Society.* Hawthorn, 1969. Illustrated with old prints and cartoons, a detailed and objective history of extremists in this country. Useful as a source book and eminently readable. 13 up

ASHE, GEOFFREY. *King Arthur in Fact and Legend.* Nelson, 1971. A scholarly, lively investigation of the fictional Arthur and the Arthur of historical and archeological fact. 12 up

ASIMOV, ISAAC. *The Birth of the United States 1763–1816.* Houghton, 1974. A sequel to *The Shaping of North America.* 11-15

______. *The Dark Ages,* ill. Houghton, 1968. From the year 1000 to the advent of chivalry. 12-17

______. *Our Federal Union.* Houghton, 1975. Third in the series on the United States. 13 up

______. *The Shaping of England.* Houghton, 1969. 13 up

______. *The Shaping of France.* Houghton, 1972. 13 up

______. *The Shaping of North America; from Earliest Times to 1763.* Houghton, 1973. 13 up

______. *Words from History,* ill. by William Barss. Houghton, 1968. 11 up

______. *Words from the Exodus,* ill. by William Barss. Houghton, 1963. 11 up

______. *Words in Genesis,* ill. by William Barss. Houghton, 1962. 11 up

______. *Words on the Map,* ill. by William Barss. Houghton, 1962. 12 up

BALES, CAROL ANN. *Chinatown Sunday; The Story of Lilliann Der.* Reilly and Lee, 1973. A photodocumentary examines the life of a Chinese-American family in Chicago. 8-10

☆ ______. *Kevin Cloud; Chippewa Boy in the City.* Reilly, 1972. A photodocumentary that is both candid and dignified. 8-10

BAUMANN, HANS. *In the Land of Ur; The Discovery of Ancient Mesopotamia,* tr. by Stella Humphries, ill. Pantheon, 1969. 13 up

______. *Lion Gate and Labyrinth,* tr. by Stella Humphries, ill. Pantheon, 1967. The archeological discoveries of Troy, Crete, and Mycenae are described along with some of the history, myths, and legends of those civilizations. Includes color plates of archeological sites and finds. 12-15

☆ BAYLOR, BYRD. *Before You Came This Way,* ill. by Tom Bahti. Dutton, 1969. Walking in the quiet of a canyon in the southwest, you wonder if you are the first to pass this way and then you see the wall paintings of the past. A handsome, thought-provoking book. 7-9

BENDICK, JEANNE, and ROBERT BENDICK. *The Consumer's Catalog of Economy & Ecology,* ill. by Karen Watson. McGraw, 1974. 12 up

BERGER, MELVIN. *Time After Time,* ill. by Richard Cuffari. Coward, 1975. 7-9

§ BERNHEIM, MARC and EVELYNE. *African Success Story; The Ivory Coast,* ill. Harcourt, 1970. A lucid and authoritative description of the growth and prosperity of the Ivory Coast since it gained independence. 11-14

§ ______. *In Africa.* Atheneum, 1973. A survey of life styles in a coastal village, a city, a savannah, a forest, and a nomad community. 5-8

BERTON, PIERRE. *The Golden Trail: The Story of the Klondike Rush,* ill. by Alan Daniel. Toronto: Macmillan, 1954. A vivid account by a major Canadian author. 11 up

BIRMINGHAM, JOHN, ed. *Our Time Is Now: Notes from the High School Underground.* Praeger, 1970. Excerpts from high-school papers show the intense concern of young people. 13 up

BLEEKER, SONIA. *The Eskimo: Arctic Hunters and Trappers,* ill. by Patricia Boodell. Morrow, 1959. 9-12

§ ______. *The Ibo of Biafra,* ill. by Edith G. Singer. Morrow, 1969. 10-12

☆ ______. *The Maya, Indians of Central America,* ill. by Kisa N. Sasaki. Morrow, 1961. 9-12

§ ______. *The Pygmies: Africans of the Congo Forest,* ill. by Edith G. Singer. Morrow, 1968. 9-12

☆ ______. *The Sea Hunters: Indians of the Northwest Coast,* ill. by Althea Karr. Morrow, 1951. 9-12

☆ ______. *The Sioux Indians; Hunters and Warriors of the Plains,* ill. by Kisa N. Sasaki. Morrow, 1962. 9-11

§ BONTEMPS, ARNA. *Story of the Negro,* 3rd. ed., ill. by Raymond Lufkin. Knopf, 1958. An authoritative and perceptive black history. 11-14

BOORSTIN, DANIEL J. *The Landmark History of the American People,* 2 vols., ill. Random, 1968 and 1970. 10-14

BRANLEY, FRANKLYN M. *The Mystery of Stonehenge,* ill. by Victor G. Ambrus. T. Crowell, 1969. An exploration of theories about the erection of Stonehenge. 9-11

☆ BROWN, DEE. *Wounded Knee.* Holt, 1974. Adapted by Amy Ehrlich from the adult title, *Bury My Heart at Wounded Knee.* 11-14

CARLSON, DALE BICK. *Girls Are Equal Too; The Women's Movement for Teenagers,* ill. by Carol Nicklaus. Atheneum, 1973. A discussion of the causes and solutions in contemporary sexism. 11-14

CARTER, WILLIAM E. *The First Book of South America.* Watts, 1961. 9-12

CHASE, STUART. *Danger—Men Talking! A Background Book on Semantics and Communication.* Parents' Magazine, 1969. The author writes with profound perspective about the tyranny of words, discussing human speech and semantics, techniques of improving communications in human dialogue, and many ancillary topics. 12-17

CHUBB, THOMAS CALDECOT. *The Byzantines,* ill. by Richard M. Powers. World, 1959. One of a fine series of books about major cultures of the world (Arabs, Aztecs, Slavic peoples, etc.). 11 up

CLARK, ANN NOLAN. *Circle of Seasons,* ill. by W. T. Mars. Farrar, 1970. 10-14

CLARKE, CLORINDA. *The American Revolution 1775–83; A British View,* ill. McGraw, 1967. 10-14

CLYMER, ELEANOR. *The Case of the Missing Link,* rev. ed. Basic, 1968. 15 up

☆§ COHEN, ROBERT. *The Color of Man,* ill. with photos by Ken Heyman. Random, 1968. A fine book on the physical differences among people, and on the nature and dangers of prejudice. 10-13

COMMAGER, HENRY STEELE. *The First Book of American History,* ill. by Leonard E. Fisher. Watts, 1957. 10-12

______. *The Great Declaration; A Book for Young Americans,* ill. by Donald Bolognese. Bobbs, 1958. 12-14

COOK, FRED, ad. *The Golden Book of the American Revolution,* adapted from *The American Heritage Book of the Revolution,* ill. Golden Pr., 1959. 12-14

COOLIDGE, OLIVIA. *Tales of the Crusades,* ill. adapted from prints by Gustave Doré. Houghton, 1970. Each of the stories that chronicle some facet of the long years of the Crusades is a splendid entity, wonderfully evocative, and vividly written. The book is not a cohesive picture but is impressive both as a literary and a historical work. 13 up

COOMBS, CHARLES. *Cleared for Takeoff; Behind the Scenes at an Airport.* Morrow, 1969. An interesting backstage view. 11-15

______. *Spacetrack; Watchdog of the Skies,* ill. with photos and diagrams. Morrow, 1969. Describes the work of the North American Air Defense Command. 10-12

COTTRELL, LEONARD. *Digs and Diggers; A Book of World Archaeology,* ill. with photos. World, 1964. 13 up

★ COY, HAROLD. *Chicano Roots Go Deep.* Dodd, 1975. 11 up

DALGLIESH, ALICE. *America Begins; The Story of the Finding of the New World,* rev. ed., ill. by Lois Maloy. Scribner's, 1958. 8-11

DENNY, NORMAN, and JOSEPHINE FILMER-SANKEY. *The Bayeux Tapestry; The Story of the Norman Conquest: 1066,* ill. Atheneum, 1966. 11-15

DE PAUW, LINDA. *Founding Mothers; Women of America in the Revolutionary Era.* Houghton, 1975. 12 up

★ DOBRIN, ARNOLD. *The New Life—La Vida Nueva; The Mexican-Americans Today.* Dodd, 1971. A survey of attitudes, problems, and factors that influence the Chicano, using interviews. 10-12

DRUMMOND, A. H. *The Population Puzzle; Overcrowding and Stress Among Animals and Men.* Addison, 1973. 12-15

DUGGAN, ALFRED. *Growing Up in 13th Century England,* ill. by C. Walter Hodges. Pantheon, 1962. 11-14

§ DURHAM, PHILIP, and EVERETT L. JONES. *The Negro Cowboys,* ill. with photos. Dodd, 1965. A great deal of information about the blacks who participated in the westward expansion. 13 up

★ EISEMAN, ALBERTA. *Mañana Is Now; The Spanish-Speaking in the United States.* Atheneum, 1973. 12 up

ELLIOT, SARAH. *Our Dirty Air,* ill. with photos. Messner, 1971. Suggests ways that children can help. 8-10

EPSTEIN, BERYL and SAMUEL. *Who Says You Can't?* Coward, 1969. Instances of causes that seemed lost and the determined people who campaigned for those diverse causes are described in a lively and provocative book. 12 up

EVANS, EVA KNOX. *Why We Live Where We Live,* ill. by Ursula Koering. Little, 1953. 9-12

FISHER, LEONARD EVERETT. *The Architects,* ill. by author. Watts, 1971. 10-12

______. *The Blacksmiths,* ill. by author. Watts, 1976. 10-12

______. *The Cabinetmakers,* ill. by author. Watts, 1966. 10-12

______. *The Glassmakers,* ill. by author. Watts, 1964. 10-12

______. *The Homemakers,* ill. by author. Watts, 1973. 9-11

______. *The Peddlers,* ill. by author. Watts, 1968. 10-12

______. *Pumpers, Boilers, Hooks and Ladders,* ill. by author. Dial, 1961. 5-8

______. *The Schoolmasters,* ill. by author. Watts, 1967. 10-12

______. *The Silversmiths,* ill. by author. Watts, 1964. 10-12

______. *The Tanners,* ill. by author. Watts, 1966. 10-12

______. *Two If by Sea,* ill. by author. Random, 1970. 10-11

§ FLATO, CHARLES. *The Golden Book of the Civil War,* ad. from *The American Heritage Picture History of the Civil War.* Golden Pr., 1961. 10-12

FLEMING, ALICE. *Trials That Made Headlines.* St. Martin's, 1975. A description of ten United States trials that affected judicial development. 12-15

☆ FOLSOM, FRANKLIN. *Red Power on the Rio Grande; The Native American Revolution of 1680,* ill. by J. D. Roybal. Follett, 1973. 12-15

FOSTER, G. ALLEN. *Sunday in Centerville; The Battle of Bull Run, 1861,* ill. by Harold Berson. White, 1971. 12 up

FOSTER, GENEVIEVE. *George Washington's World,* ill. by author. Scribner's, 1941. 11-14

______. *The World of Columbus and Sons,* ill. by author. Scribner's, 1965. 11-14

______. *The World of William Penn,* ill. by author. Scribner's, 1973. 9-12

______. *The Year of the Horseless Carriage—1801,* ill. by author. Scribner's, 1975. 10-11

______. *The Year of the Pilgrims—1620,* ill. by author. Scribner's, 1969. 8-10

FRANCHERE, RUTH. *Westward by Canal.* Macmillan, 1972. 10-13

FRIEDLANDER, JOANNE K., and JEAN NEAL. *Stock Market ABC,* ill. by Tom Dunnington. Follett, 1969. A lucid description in a light tone of the intricacies of the stock market. 12 up

FRITZ, JEAN. *Who's That Stepping on Plymouth Rock?* ill. by J. B. Handelsman. Coward, 1975. 8-10

GIDAL, SONIA. *My Village in Hungary.* Pantheon, 1974. 9-11

______. *My Village in Portugal.* Pantheon, 1972. 9-11

§ GIDAL, SONIA and TIM. *My Village in Ghana.* Pantheon, 1970. And other titles in the series. 9-12

☆ GOBLE, PAUL, and DOROTHY GOBLE. *Brave Eagle's Account of the Fetterman Fight; 21 December 1866,* ill. by Paul Goble. Pantheon, 1972. An Oglala Sioux chief describes Indian resistance to white encroachment. 10-12

☆ ______. *Red Hawk's Account of Custer's Last Battle,* ill. by authors. Pantheon. 1970. 10-12

§ GOLDSTON, ROBERT C. *The Negro Revolution,* ill. Macmillan, 1968. 13 up

GORODETZKY, CHARLES W., and SAMUEL T. CHRISTIAN. *What You Should Know About Drugs.* Harcourt, 1970. The dispassionate tone and straightforward style add to the usefulness of this source of information for the young reader. 10 up

GREENFELD, HOWARD. *The Waters of November,* ill. Follett, 1969. A dramatic, detailed account of the Florentine flood of 1966. Included is a description of the sophisticated techniques of restoration of the art treasures. 13 up

GURNEY, GENE, and CLARE GURNEY. *The Launching of Sputnik, October 4, 1957; The Space Age Begins.* Watts, 1975. 10-13

HABENSTREIT, BARBARA. *Men Against War.* Doubleday, 1973. A survey of pacific protest from colonial times to today. 12-15

HAHN, JAMES, and LYNN HAHN. *Recycling; Re-Using Our World's Solid Wastes.* Watts, 1973. 9-12

HALL, ELIZABETH. *Why We Do What We Do; A Look at Psychology.* Houghton, 1973. An authoritative discussion of behavior is based on experimental research. 11-14

HAMBLIN, DORA JANE. *Buried Cities and Ancient Treasures.* Simon, 1973. 12 up

______. *Pots and Robbers.* Simon, 1970. 12 up

HANFF, HELENE. *The Movers and Shakers; The Young Activists of the Sixties.* Phillips, 1970. Often passionate, always candid, carefully researched, and only occasionally given to generalized statements, this is exciting to read and furthermore is a valuable document about the youth movement of the 60's. 13 up

HARMER, MABEL. *The True Book of Pioneers,* ill. by Loran Wilford. Childrens Pr., 1957. 7-9

HASKINS, JAMES S. *The Consumer Movement.* Watts, 1975. 12 up

§ ______. *The Creoles of Color of New Orleans,* ill. by Don Miller. T. Crowell, 1975. 11-14

______. *Jobs in Business and Office.* Lothrop, 1974.10-12

______. *Street Gangs, Yesterday and Today.* Hastings, 1974. 13 up

§ ______. *Witchcraft, Mysticism and Magic in the Black World.* Doubleday, 1974. 11-14

______. *Your Rights Past and Present; A Guide for Young People.* Hawthorn, 1975. 12-17

HILLER, CARL E. *Babylon to Brasilia; The Challenge of City Planning.* Little, 1972. 10-13

HILTON, SUZANNE. *The Way It Was—1876.* Westminster, 1975. 11 up

HIRSCH, CARL. *The Globe for the Space Age,* ill. by Burt Silverman. Viking, 1963. A book that traces the development of globes and stresses their advantage over maps in studying the sphere on which we live. 11-14

HOBART, LOIS. *Mexican Mural: The Story of Mexico, Past and Present.* Harcourt, 1963. 15 up

HODGES, C. WALTER. *Magna Carta,* ill. by author. Coward, 1966. An excellent survey of the conditions leading to the signing of the Magna Carta. 10-14

______. *The Norman Conquest,* ill. by author. Coward, 1966. A companion volume to the above title. The text is crisply informational; the illustrations unusually beautiful and informative. 10-14

______. *Shakespeare's Theatre,* ill. by author. Coward, 1964. The beautiful pictures are filled with informative detail and the text is written with simplicity and authority. The book is a delight. 11 up

HOFFMAN, EDWIN D. *Pathways to Freedom; Nine Dramatic Episodes in the Evolution of the American Democratic Tradition,* ill. Houghton, 1964. Nine episodes in the history of this country, each episode illustrating some facet of the democratic tradition. Well-written and well-researched. 13 up

☆ HOFSINDE, ROBERT (GRAY-WOLF). *Indian Sign Language,* ill. by author. Morrow, 1956. 9-13

☆ ______. *Indian Warriors and Their Weapons,* ill. by author. Morrow, 1965. 8-13

☆ ______. *Indians at Home,* ill. by author. Morrow, 1964. A discussion of six major types of Indian homes. One of the best of the author's books on the cultures of North American Indians. 9-12

§ HOLLAND, JOHN, ed. *The Way It Is,* ill. with photos. Harcourt, 1969. 8-10

HOLLING, HOLLING C. *The Book of Cowboys,* rev. ed., ill. by author and Lucille Holling. Platt, 1968. 12 up

☆ ______. *The Book of Indians,* rev. ed., ill. by author and Lucille Holling. Platt, 1962. 12 up

______. *Minn of the Mississippi,* ill. by author. Houghton, 1951. 10-12

______. *Paddle-to-the-Sea,* ill. by author. Houghton, 1941. 9-11

______. *Tree in the Trail,* ill. by author. Houghton, 1942. 9-12

HOYT, EDWIN P. *Asians in the West.* Nelson, 1975. 12 up

______. *Whirlybirds: The Story of Helicopters,* ill. by George J. Zaffo. Doubleday, 1961. Attractive color illustrations. 10-13

§ HUGHES, LANGSTON. *The First Book of Africa,* rev. and rewritten, ill. with photos. Watts, 1964. Explorers, missionaries, the history of ancient Africa, and an evaluation of Africa today are included in this fine introductory book. 10-12

§ ______. *The First Book of Negroes,* ill. by Ursula Koering. Watts, 1952. Not comprehensive, but a competent introduction to black history. 9-11

JANEWAY, ELIZABETH. *The Vikings,* ill. by Henry C. Pitz. Random, 1951. Includes a chapter on Vineland. 9-11

§ JENNESS, AYLETTE. *Along the Niger River; An African Way of Life,* photos by author. T. Crowell, 1974. 10 up

______. *Dwellers of the Tundra: Life in an Alaskan Eskimo Village,* photos by Jonathan Jenness. Crowell-Collier, 1970. 11-14

JENNESS, AYLETTE, and LISA W. KROEBER. *A Life of Their Own; An Indian Family in Latin America,* photos by authors, drawings by Susan Votaw. T. Crowell, 1975. 10-13

JOHNSON, GERALD W. *America Grows Up: A History for Peter,* ill. by Leonard E. Fisher. Morrow, 1960. One of a series of lively and lucid books on the history and government of the United States. 10-13

______. *America Is Born: A History for Peter,* ill. by Leonard E. Fisher. Morrow, 1959. 10-13

______. *America Moves Forward: A History for Peter,* ill. by Leonard E. Fisher. Morrow, 1960. 10-13

______. *The Congress,* ill. by Leonard E. Fisher. Morrow, 1963. 9-12

______. *The Presidency,* ill. by Leonard E. Fisher. Morrow, 1962. 9-12

______. *The Supreme Court,* ill. by Leonard E. Fisher. Morrow, 1962. 9-12

§ JOHNSTON, JOHANNA. *Together in America; The Story of Two Races and One Nation,* ill. by Mort Künstler. Dodd, 1965. 11-14

§ JOSEPH, JOAN. *Black African Empires.* Watts, 1974. 10-12

☆ KAREN, RUTH. *Kingdom of the Sun; The Inca, Empire Builders of the Americas,* ill. with photos. Four Winds, 1975. 12 up

☆ ______. *Song of the Quail; The Wondrous World of the Maya.* Four Winds, 1973. A vivid account of the impressive achievements of the Mayan civilization. 11 up

KAVALER, LUCY. *Dangerous Air,* ill. by Carl Smith. Day, 1967. 12 up

☆ KIRK, RUTH. *David, Young Chief of the Quileutes: An American Indian Today,* ill. with photos by author. Harcourt, 1967. The true story of a Pacific coast tribe that has moved gracefully into modern life while keeping its respect for Quileute tradition. 9-11

______. *The Oldest Man in America: An Adventure in Archeology,* ill. with photos by Ruth and Louis Kirk. Harcourt, 1970. The story of a search for records of prehistoric man is made more dramatic by the fact that a new dam threatened the project. 10-14

KURELEK, WILLIAM. *Lumberjack,* paintings by author. Houghton, 1974. A depiction of life in a Canadian lumber camp. 10 up

______. *A Prairie Boy's Summer,* ill. by author. Houghton, 1975. This (and the title below) recreates in text and pictures the quality of life on a Manitoba farm. 8-10

______. *A Prairie Boy's Winter,* ill. by author. Houghton, 1973. 8-10

★ KURTIS, ARLENE HARRIS. *Puerto Ricans; From Island to Mainland.* Watts, 1965. A simply written survey, with historical background provided. 9-12

☆ LA FARGE, OLIVER. *The American Indian.* Golden Pr., 1960. 10-12

LANGONE, JOHN. *Death Is a Noun; A View of the End of Life.* Little, 1972. Objective, thorough in coverage, and candid, this explores euthanasia, fear, funeral customs, death by crime, and other aspects of the subject. 12-16

LAUBER, PATRICIA. *Too Much Garbage.* Garrard, 1974. 7-9

______. *Who Discovered America? Settlers and Explorers of the New World Before the Time of Columbus.* Random, 1970. 9-11

§ LESTER, JULIUS. *To Be a Slave,* ill. by Tom Feelings. Dial, 1968. Excerpts from source material, chronologically arranged, give a moving and explicit picture of slavery. 11-14

LIFTON, BETTY JEAN. *Return to Hiroshima,* ill. with photos by Eikoh Hosoe. Atheneum, 1970. A matter-of-fact, serious, objective assessment of the enduring ramifications of the bombing of Hiroshima. Excellent photos. 10-17

LIPSYTE, ROBERT. *Assignment: Sports.* Harper, 1970. A compilation of articles covering many sports and sports figures. The author, sports columnist for *The New York Times,* writes with authority and a facility for quick and vivid character portrayals. 11-15

LISTON, ROBERT A. *Who Really Runs America?* Doubleday, 1974. An analysis of the power structure in the United States. 12-15

§ LOBSENZ, NORMAN M. *The First Book of Ghana,* ill. with photos. Watts, 1960. A competent historical and cultural overview. 9-11

LONGSTRETH, T. MORRIS. *The Scarlet Force: The Making of the Mounted Police,* ill. by Alan Daniel. Toronto: Macmillan, 1953. First in the "Great Stories of Canada" series. 11 up

McHUGH, MARY. *Law and the New Woman.* Watts, 1975. A discussion of the variety of specializations within the legal profession. 12 up

☆ McNEER, MAY. *The American Indian Story,* ill. by Lynd Ward. Farrar, 1963. 9-11

MAY, JULIAN. *The First Men,* ill. by Lorence F. Bjorklund. Holiday, 1968. 7-9

MEAD, MARGARET. *Anthropologists and What They Do.* Watts, 1965. The interview technique is used to introduce some of the specialized fields and diversified techniques of anthropology. A lively, varied, and informative career guidance book. 12 up

______. *People and Places,* ill. by W. T. Mars and Jan Fairservis and with photos. World, 1959. 12-14

MEADOWCROFT, ENID LA MONTE. *The Land of the Free,* ill. by Lee J. Ames. T. Crowell, 1961. 8-10

★ MELTZER, MILTON. *Bound for the Rio Grande; The Mexican Struggle 1845–1850,* ill. with prints and photos. Knopf, 1974. 12 up

______. *Bread and Roses: The Struggle of American Labor, 1865–1915,* ill. Knopf, 1967. 12-15

● ______. *Never to Forget: The Jews of the Holocaust.* Harper, 1976. 12 up

● ______. *Remember the Days; A Short History of the Jewish American,* ill. by Harvey Dinnerstein. Doubleday, 1974. 12 up

______. *The Right to Remain Silent.* Harcourt, 1972. A comprehensive survey of man's right to refrain from giving self-incriminating testimony. 12 up

● ______. *World of Our Fathers; The Jews of Eastern Europe.* Farrar, 1974. 12 up

§ ______, ed. *In Their Own Words: A History of the American Negro;* Vol. 1, 1619–1865. T. Crowell, 1964.

§ ______, ed. *In Their Own Words: A History of the American Negro;* Vol. 2, 1865–1916. T. Crowell, 1965.

§ ______, ed. *In Their Own Words: A History of the American Negro;* Vol. 3, 1916–1966. T. Crowell, 1967. 12-15

§ MELTZER, MILTON, and AUGUST MEIER. *Time of Trial, Time of Hope: The Negro in America, 1919–1941,* ill. by Moneta Barnett. Doubleday, 1966. 11-14

MORGAN, EDMUND S. *So What About History?* Atheneum, 1969. In this stimulating and unorthodox approach to history (this is not a history book), the author stresses the significance of historical interpretation of material objects, from discarded junk to imposing government buildings, as evidence of living patterns. 9-11

MORRIS, RICHARD B. *The First Book of the American Revolution,* ill. by Leonard E. Fisher. Watts, 1956. 9-13

NAVARRA, JOHN. *Our Noisy World: The Problem of Noise Pollution.* Doubleday, 1969. 11-14

______. *Supertrains.* Doubleday, 1975. Pollution, energy resources, and traffic problems are factors in planning new transportation systems. 9-12

______. *The World You Inherit: A Story of Pollution.* Natural History Pr., 1970. 12-14

● NAYLOR, PHYLLIS REYNOLDS. *An Amish Family,* ill. by George Armstrong. O'Hara, 1975. A competent survey of Amish society is based on a study of a three-generation family. 11 up

§ NICKEL, HELMUT. *Arms and Armor in Africa,* ill. Atheneum, 1971. The Curator of Arms and Armor for the Metropolitan Museum of Art describes both contemporary and ancient weapons and armor and relates this information to facts about the cultures of the peoples discussed. 9-14

§ NOLEN, BARBARA, ed. *Africa Is People; Firsthand Accounts from Contemporary Africa,* ill. with photos. Dutton, 1967. An interesting anthology, each selection preceded by a brief note on the context of the excerpt and on the author. Varied backgrounds and varied topics. 13 up

OGLE, LUCILLE, and TINA THOBURN. *I Spy; A Picture Book of Objects in a Child's Home Environment,* ill. by Joe Kaufman. American Heritage, 1970. Two labeled pictures on each page afford small children the pleasure of recognizing familiar objects or learning new ones. Useful for extending vocabulary, for classifying objects, and for environmental concepts. 2-5

PACE, MILDRED (MASTIN). *Wrapped for Eternity; The Story of the Egyptian Mummy,* ill. by Tom Huffman. McGraw, 1974. A description of Egyptian death practices includes many facts about the culture of ancient Egypt. 10-14

PARNALL, PETER. *The Mountain,* ill. by author. Doubleday, 1971. Pollution ruins the peace and beauty of a mountainside. 5-7

§ PERKINS, CAROL MORSE, and MARLIN PERKINS. *"I Saw You from Afar"; A Visit to the Bushmen of the Kalahari Desert,* ill. with photos. Atheneum, 1965. The daily life of the bushmen in photographs and simple text. The treatment is sympathetic and dignified. 9-11

PERL, LILA. *America Goes to the Fair; All About State and County Fairs in the USA,* ill. with photos. Morrow, 1974. A description of fairs past and present. 10-13

PRICE, CHRISTINE. *Made in Ancient Egypt,* ill. Dutton, 1970. Written in a direct and dignified style, this is a fascinating study of the ancient Egyptians through their tombs, temples, and the many artifacts recovered from burial chambers. A dynastic table and map precede the text, which is profusely illustrated. 11 up

PUGH, ELLEN, with the assistance of DAVID B. PUGH. *Brave His Soul,* ill. Dodd, 1970. 12-15

RAU, MARGARET. *The People's Republic of China.* Messner, 1974. Gives both historical background and a full discussion of China today. 10-12

RICH, LOUISE DICKINSON. *The First Book of New World Explorers,* ill. by Cary Dickinson. Watts, 1960. 9-11

SANDERLIN, GEORGE. *A Hoop to the Barrel.* Coward, 1974. 11-15

SASEK, MIROSLAV. *This Is Edinburgh,* ill. by author. Macmillan, 1961.

______. *This Is Greece,* ill. by author. Macmillan, 1966.

______. *This Is Historic Britain,* ill. by author. Macmillan, 1974. 8-11

______. *This Is New York,* ill. by author. Macmillan, 1960. 8-11

§ SAVAGE, KATHARINE. *The Story of Africa; South of the Sahara,* ill. with photos and maps. Walck, 1961. 12 up

______. *The Story of the United Nations,* maps by Richard Natkiel. Walck, 1962, rev. ed., 1970. 13 up

SCHECHTER, BETTY. *The Peaceable Revolution,* ill. with photos. Houghton, 1963. The nonviolent way of solving human problems is traced through the perspective of history: Thoreau, Gandhi, and into today's civil rights movement. 13 up

☆ SCHEELE, WILLIAM E. *The Earliest Americans,* ill. by author. World, 1963. 10-14

☆ ______. *The Mound Builders,* ill. by author. World, 1960. 10-14

SCHLEIN, MIRIAM. *It's About Time,* ill. by Leonard Kessler. W. R. Scott, 1955. 6-8

SCHNEIDER, HERMAN and NINA. *Let's Look Under the City,* rev. ed., ill. by Bill Ballantine. Scott/Addison, 1954. 8-10

SCHWARTZ, ALVIN. *The City and Its People: The Story of One City's Government,* ill. with photos by Sy Katzoff. Dutton, 1967. An excellent description of a city of 300,000 people, its administrative structure, problems, and planning. 9-12

______. *The Night Workers,* photos by Ullie Steltzer. Dutton, 1966. Interesting chronological treatment. 7-10

______. *Old Cities and New Towns,* ill. with photos. Dutton, 1968. 11-14

______. *University: The Students, Faculty, and Campus Life at One University.* Viking, 1969. An overview of student activity and the roles of faculty and administration. 12-15

SEED, SUZANNE. *Saturday's Child; 36 Women Talk About Their Jobs,* photos by author. O'Hara, 1973. Interviews with women who describe their jobs and how they prepared for them. 12-17

SHIPPEN, KATHERINE B. *The Great Heritage,* ill. by C. B. Falls. Viking, 1947; rev. ed., 1962. 12-16

______. *Miracle in Motion: The Story of America's Industry.* Harper, 1955. 12-17

______. *The Pool of Knowledge: How the United Nations Share Their Skills,* rev. ed., ill. with photos. Harper, 1965. 11 up

______. *This Union Cause: The Growth of Organized Labor in America,* ill. with photos and drawings. Harper, 1958. 14-17

SHOWERS, PAUL. *Columbus Day,* ill. by Ed Emberley. T. Crowell, 1965. 5-8

☆ ______. *Indian Festivals,* ill. by Lorence Bjorklund. T. Crowell, 1969. 5-8

SPERRY, ARMSTRONG. *All About the Arctic and Antarctic,* ill. by author. Random, 1957. 9-11

SPIER, PETER. *Of Dikes and Windmills,* ill. by author. Doubleday, 1969. A remarkably interesting book about the long struggle of the Netherlands to claim and hold land from the sea. Written with articulate ease, the book contains a large amount of historical information. 11 up

STEELE, WILLIAM O. *Westward Adventure; The True Stories of Six Pioneers.* Harcourt, 1962. 9-11

§ STERLING, DOROTHY. *Tear Down the Walls! A History of the American Civil Rights Movement,* ill. Doubleday, 1968. 12 up

§ ______, ed. *The Trouble They Seen: Black People Tell the Story of Reconstruction.* Doubleday, 1976. 12 up

STEVENS, LEONARD A. *The Town That Launders Its Water,* ill. with photos. Coward, 1971. A California town has eight man-made lakes for recreation, the water reclaimed from sewage. 11 up

§ STEVENSON, JANET. *The School Segregation Cases; (Brown v. Board of Education of Topeka and others); The United States Supreme Court Rules on Racially Separate Public Education.* Watts, 1973. A comprehensive examination of protest, dissent, and legislation about school integration. 10-14

STOUTENBURG, ADRIEN. *People in Twilight: Vanishing and Changing Cultures,* ill. with photos. Doubleday, 1971. A moving description of the struggle to maintain cultural identity. 11-14

§ THUM, MARCELLA. *Exploring Black America; A History and Guide.* Atheneum, 1975. 11 up

TOYE, WILLIAM. *Cartier Discovers the St. Lawrence,* ill. by Laszlo Gal. Toronto: Oxford, 1959. An authoritative account of Cartier's three exploratory voyages. 10-12

TREASE, GEOFFREY. *This Is Your Century,* ill. Harcourt, 1966. An impressive twentieth-century history—chiefly of the western world—written in an easy but dignified style, with good organization and reasonable objectivity. 13 up

TRIPP, ELEANOR B. *To America,* ill. Harcourt, 1969. The author, in an unusual approach, has chosen nine highly localized sources of American newcomers, each demonstrating a different reason for coming to a new land. A vivid picture of the diversity of our forebears. 11-14

TUNIS, EDWIN. *Colonial Craftsmen and the Beginnings of American Industry,* ill. by author. World, 1965. Well-organized and superbly illustrated, the text is comprehensive, lucid, and detailed. 11-14

______. *Colonial Living,* ill. by author. World, 1957. 10-12

______. *Frontier Living,* ill. by author. World, 1961. 10 up

☆ ______. *Indians,* ill. by author. World, 1959. 11 up

______. *Shaw's Fortune; The Picture Story of a Colonial*

Plantation, ill. by author. World, 1966. 9-12

● TUNIS, EDWIN. *The Tavern at the Ferry,* ill. by author. T. Crowell, 1973. 9-12

———. *The Young United States—1783–1830,* ill. by author. World, 1969. 10-14

§ TURNBULL, COLIN M. *Tradition and Change in African Tribal Life,* ill. World, 1966. An anthropologist looks at the institutions of tribal life in an effort to see how they meet the needs of people. 13 up

UDEN, GRANT. *A Dictionary of Chivalry,* ill. by Pauline Baynes. T. Crowell, 1968. 11 up

UNSTEAD, R. J. *Living in a Medieval Village,* ill. by Ron Stenberg. Addison, 1973. One of a series of informative books about medieval times stresses the occupations of villagers. 9-11

VAN LOON, HENDRIK WILLEM. *The Story of Mankind,* ill. by author. Liveright, 1921, rev. ed., 1951. Newbery Medal. 12-14

VIERECK, PHILLIP, comp. *The New Land; Discovery, Exploration, and Early Settlement of Northeastern United States, from Earliest Voyages to 1621, Told in the Words of the Explorers Themselves,* ill. by Ellen Viereck. Day, 1967. 14 up

☆ VON HAGEN, VICTOR W. *Maya, Land of the Turkey and the Deer,* ill. by Alberto Beltrán. World, 1960. 11-14

WALTON, RICHARD J. *America and the Cold War.* Seabury, 1969. An important book, this is a detailed and passionate history of the tangled international situation that followed World War II. The author offers neither verdict nor solution and is careful to so state when comments are conjectural. 12 up

———. *Beyond Diplomacy; A Background Book on American Military Intervention.* Parents' Magazine, 1970. A fine history of aspects of American foreign policy, objective in appraising the discrepancies between fact and popular belief. 12-17

WARREN, RUTH. *Pictorial History of Women in America.* Crown, 1975. A survey of women's contributions from colonial times on. 12 up

WESTMAN, WESLEY C. *The Drug Epidemic: What It Means and How to Combat It.* Dial, 1970. A thoughtful and objective book, written for the mature reader, by a clinical psychologist working in the field of drug abuses. He discusses the medical, psychological, and sociological aspects of the problem. 12 up

WHITE, ANNE TERRY. *All About Archaeology,* ill. by Tom O'Sullivan and with photos. Random, 1959. 10-13

———. *Prehistoric America,* ill. by Aldren Watson. Random, 1951. 9-11

WHITNEY, DAVID. *The First Book of Facts and How to Find Them,* ill. by Edward Mackenzie. Watts, 1966. Author discusses the sorts of questions that can be answered by reference books and describes the major types of reference sources. Not comprehensive, but clear; valuable for the discussion of opinions vs. facts and of discrepancies. 9-11

WINN, MARIE. *The Fisherman Who Needed a Knife; A Story About Why People Use Money,* ill. by John E. Johnson. Simon, 1970. A companion book to the following title, this introduces the concept of money as a common medium of exchange. 4-7

———. *The Man Who Made Fine Tops; A Story About Why People Do Different Kinds of Work,* ill. by John E. Johnson. Simon, 1970. A light fictional framework describing the father who made his son a top is used to explain the division of labor. The ideas are perfectly clear and the author wisely stopped when her point was made. 5-7

☆ WOLF, BERNARD. *Tinker and the Medicine Man; The Story of a Navajo Boy of Monument Valley,* photos by author. Random, 1973. A small boy learns the arts practiced by his father, a medicine man. 9-11

ZINER, FEENIE, and ELIZABETH THOMPSON. *The True Book of Time,* ill. by Katherine Evans. Childrens Pr., 1956. 6-8

Religion and the Arts

BATTERBERRY, ARIANE (RUSKIN). *The Pantheon Story of Art for Young People,* rev. ed. Pantheon, 1975. 10 up

BATTERBERRY, MICHAEL. *Art of the Middle Ages.* McGraw, 1972. Well organized and cohesive, a beautifully illustrated book. 12 up

BATTERBERRY, MICHAEL, and ARIANE RUSKIN, ads. *Primitive Art.* McGraw, 1973. 12 up

☆ BIERHORST, JOHN, ad. *Songs of the Chippewa;* ad. from the collections of Frances Densmore and Henry Rowe Schoolcraft, and arranged for piano and guitar by John Bierhorst; ill. by Joe Servello. Farrar, 1974. Simple musical notation is provided; lyrics are in English. 9 up

BONI, MARGARET BRADFORD, ed. *The Fireside Book of Favorite American Songs,* arr. for piano by Norman Lloyd, ill. by Aurelius Battaglia. Simon, 1952. From songs of the Pilgrims to ballads of the Nineties. 8 up

BORTEN, HELEN. *A Picture Has a Special Look.* Abelard, 1961. Describes and illustrates some of the media used by artists. 9-11

BRITTEN, BENJAMIN, and IMOGEN HOLST. *The Wonderful World of Music,* rev. ed. Doubleday, 1968. 8-12

§ BRYAN, ASHLEY. *Walk Together Children; Black American Spirituals,* selected and ill. by Ashley Bryan. Atheneum, 1974. Only the melodic line is provided, so no musical training is necessary to pick out the notes. 8-10

BULLA, CLYDE ROBERT. *Stories of Favorite Operas,* ill. by Robert Galster. T. Crowell, 1959. Twenty-three libretti of popular operas. 10-14

CHASE, ALICE ELIZABETH. *Famous Artists of the Past,* ill. with reproductions. Platt, 1964. A very good sampling of the works of some two dozen great artists. There is discussion of the artists and some analysis of most of the pictures in the book. 11-15

———. *Looking at Art,* ill. T. Crowell, 1966. 12 up

COLLIER, JAMES LINCOLN. *Inside Jazz.* Four Winds, 1973. 12-15

COMINS, JEREMY. *Art from Found Objects.* Lothrop, 1974. Directions for using scrap to make objects by collage, assemblage, vacuum forming, and other techniques. 10-12

DEEDY, JOHN. *The Vatican,* ill. with photos. Watts, 1970. 10-12

DE MILLE, AGNES. *The Book of the Dance,* ill. by N. M. Bodecker. Golden Pr., 1963. Social, ritual, and theatrical dance history in full, with many color photographs. 11 up

§ DIETZ, BETTY WARNER, and MICHAEL BABATUNDE OLATUNJI. *Musical Instruments of Africa,* ill. by Richard M. Powers and with photos. Day, 1965. 11-12

DIETZ, BETTY WARNER, and THOMAS CHOONBAI PARK. *Folk Songs of China, Japan, and Korea,* ill. by Mamoru Funai. Day, 1964. 9 up

DOWNER, MARION. *Discovering Design.* Lothrop, 1947. An analysis of the elements of design in nature. 11 up

______. *The Story of Design,* ill. with photos. Lothrop, 1964. 11 up

______. *Roofs Over America,* ill. with photos. Lothrop, 1967. Two or three paragraphs on each page, accompanied by full-page photographs introduce 32 roofs in this unified treatment of American architecture from the Plymouth Colony to the present. 11-15

ELGIN, KATHLEEN. *The Unitarians,* ill. by author. McKay, 1971. And others in the series. 9-11

EWEN, DAVID. *Opera; Its Story Told Through the Lives and Works of Its Foremost Composers.* Watts, 1972. 12 up

______. *Orchestral Music; Its Story Told Through the Lives and Works of Its Foremost Composers.* Watts, 1973. 12 up

______. *Solo Instrumental and Chamber Music; Its Story Told Through the Lives and Works of Its Foremost Composers.* Watts, 1974. Discusses instruments, composers, and musical forms. 13 up

______. *Vocal Music; Its Story Told Through the Lives and Works of Its Foremost Composers.* Watts, 1975. 12 up

FREEDGOOD, LILLIAN. *An Enduring Image; American Painting from 1665,* ill. T. Crowell, 1970. A good survey of American painting, the emphasis on individual artists, with background discussion of trends here and influences from abroad and with a lucid discussion of contemporary art. All illustrations are in black and white. 12 up

● GITTELSOHN, ROLAND. *The Meaning of Judaism.* World, 1970. 13 up

GLADSTONE, M. J. *A Carrot for a Nose; The Form of Folk Sculpture on America's City Streets and Country Roads.* Scribner's, 1974. 10-13

GLAZER, TOM. *Eye Winker, Tom Tinker, Chin Chopper; Fifty Musical Fingerplays,* ill. by Ron Himler. Doubleday, 1973. Fifty songs are included, as are directions for hand movements. 5-11

GLUBOK, SHIRLEY. *The Art of America in the Early Twentieth Century,* ill. with photos. Macmillan, 1974. Reflects, more than do most of Glubok's books, the breadth and variety of art forms within a given period. 10-13

______. *The Art of America in the Gilded Age,* ill with photos. Macmillan, 1974. 9-12

______. *The Art of Ancient Greece,* ill. with photos. Atheneum, 1963. And other books in this series. 10-13

______. *The Art of China,* ill. with photos. Macmillan, 1973. Not comprehensive, but a fine introduction to an art heritage that spans four millennia. 9-11

______. *The Art of Colonial America,* ill. with photos. Macmillan, 1970. 9-12

______. *The Art of the Old West,* ill. with photos. Macmillan, 1971. 9-12

☆ ______. *The Art of the Plains Indians,* ill. with photos. Macmillan, 1975. 9-12

★ ______. *The Art of the Spanish in the United States and Puerto Rico,* ill. with photos. Macmillan, 1972. Includes architecture, room interiors, crafts, and religious art objects. 8-10

______. *Dolls, Dolls, Dolls,* ill. with photos. Follett, 1975. 8-11

______. *Knights in Armor,* ill. with photos. Harper, 1969. Clear descriptions and photos give minor reference use to a handsome book. 9-14

GREENFELD, HOWARD. *The Impressionist Revolution.* Doubleday, 1972. 12 up

______. *They Came to Paris.* Crown, 1975. 13 up

GRIGSON, GEOFFREY. *Shapes and Stories: A Book About Pictures.* Vanguard, 1965. Perceptive comments about a selected group of pictures. 10-12

HASKELL, ARNOLD LIONEL. *The Wonderful World of Dance.* Doubleday, 1969. 11-14

HASKINS, JAMES. *Religions.* Lippincott, 1973. 11-14

HEMMING, ROY. *Discovering Music; Where to Start on Records and Tapes, the Great Composers and Their Works, Today's Major Recording Artists.* Four Winds, 1974. 12 up

HIRSCH, S. CARL. *Printing from a Stone: The Story of Lithography,* ill. Viking, 1967. A most interesting book that describes the history of lithography. The writing style is straightforward, lucid, and a bit dry. 12 up

HOAG, EDWIN. *American Houses; Colonial, Classic, and Contemporary,* ill. Lippincott, 1964. Writing in a straightforward style, the author relates developments always to influences of heritage, materials and climate, function, or period-fashion. 12-15

HOBAN, TANA. *Look Again!* ill. Macmillan, 1971. A book of photographs that can pique the young child's curiosity. Blank pages with a square cut out of them expose a portion of a picture behind. 2-4

______. *Shapes and Things,* ill. Macmillan, 1970. This wordless book is illustrated with white-on-black silhouettes. 2-5

HODGES, CYRIL WALTER. *Playhouse Tales,* ill. by author. Coward, 1975. Six tales of the Elizabethan theater are more interesting as information than as fictionalized history. 12-15

☆ HOFMANN, CHARLES. *American Indians Sing,* ill. by Nicholas Amorosi. Day, 1967. 10-13

☆ HOFSINDE, ROBERT (GRAY-WOLF). *Indian Arts,* ill. by author. Morrow, 1971. An intriguing and decorative book on aspects of North American Indian cultures. 8-11

☆ ______. *Indian Music Makers,* ill. by author. Morrow, 1967. 9-12

HORWITZ, ELINOR. *Contemporary American Folk Artists.* Lippincott, 1975. 11 up

§ HUGHES, LANGSTON. *Famous Negro Music Makers.* Dodd, 1955. 11-14

§ ______. *The First Book of Jazz,* ill. by Cliff Roberts, music selected by David Martin. Watts, 1955. 11 up

______. *The First Book of Rhythms,* ill. by Robin King. Watts, 1954. 11-14

§ JOHNSON, JAMES WELDON, and J. ROSAMOND JOHNSON. *Lift Every Voice and Sing: Words and Music.* Hawthorn, 1970. Simply arranged for piano and guitar chords, a song that has endured as a hymn of black hope since it was written in 1900. 9-11

KAHN, ELY JACQUES. *A Building Goes Up,* ill. by Cal Sacks. Simon, 1969. 10-14

KETTELKAMP, LARRY. *Flutes, Whistles, and Reeds,* ill. by author. Morrow, 1962. 9-11

KING, MARY LOUISE. *A History of Western Architecture,* ill. with photos and diagrams. Walck, 1967. 12-16

☆§ LANGSTAFF, JOHN M., comp. *The Season for Singing; American Christmas Songs and Carols,* musical settings by Seymour Barab. Doubleday, 1974. Some songs are of European origin; Native American and black music are included. all ages

LARRICK, NANCY, comp. *The Wheels of the Bus Go Round and Round; School Bus Songs and Chants,* ill. by Gene Holtan. Golden Gate, 1972. Songs—many of which are old favorites—for singing while riding. 8-10

MACAULAY, DAVID. *Cathedral; The Story of Its Con-*

struction. Houghton, 1973. All three of Macaulay's books give almost as much information about the culture as they do about the architectural details of the construction of great edifices. The illustrations are profuse and meticulously detailed.

_____. *City; A Story of Roman Planning and Construction.* Houghton, 1974.

_____. *Pyramid.* Houghton, 1975. 10 up

MANCHEL, FRANK. *When Movies Began to Speak,* ill. with photos and line drawings by James Caraway. Prentice, 1969. A history of the industry from the time of *The Jazz Singer* to the advent of the large screen, the impact of television, and the competition of foreign films. 12-15

_____. *When Pictures Began to Move,* ill. by James Caraway. Prentice, 1969. One of the best histories of the motion picture industry for young people, ending with the death of the silent film. Good bibliography. 11-14

MAYNARD, OLGA. *American Modern Dancers: The Pioneers.* Atlantic/Little, 1965. 11 up

_____. *The Ballet Companion.* Macrae, 1957. 11-15

MILLS, JOHN FITZ MAURICE. *Treasure Keepers.* Doubleday, 1974. A description of problems faced by museum curators in dealing with art forgeries, analysis and display of objects, and restoration. 12 up

MOORE, JANET GAYLORD. *The Many Ways of Seeing; An Introduction to the Pleasures of Art,* ill. World, 1968. 13 up

MYLLER, ROLF. *From Idea into House,* ill. by Henry K. Szwarce. Atheneum, 1974. A detailed explanation of the planning and building of a house. 10-14

§ NAYLOR, PENELOPE. *Black Images; The Art of West Africa,* photos by Lisa Little. Doubleday, 1973. Relates art objects to the cultural beliefs and traditions they reflect. 12 up

PAINE, ROBERTA M. *Looking at Sculpture,* ill. Lothrop, 1968. 9 up

POSTON, ELIZABETH, comp. *The Baby's Song Book,* ill. by William Stobbs. T. Crowell, 1972. Includes songs from other languages as well as English in a collection for young children. 2-5

PRATSON, FREDERICK J. *The Special World of the Artisan.* Houghton, 1974. Stresses the creativity of the artisan in pottery, woodcarving, glassblowing, weaving, and making musical instruments. 11-13

§ PRICE, CHRISTINE. *Made in West Africa,* ill. with photos. Dutton, 1975. Descriptions of art objects are arranged by techniques and media. 11 up

§ _____. *Talking Drums of Africa.* Scribner's, 1973. Discusses the drums, the drumming, and the songs and dances of the Ashanti and Yaruba peoples. 8-10

● PURDY, SUSAN GOLD. *Jewish Holidays; Facts, Activities, and Crafts,* ill. Lippincott, 1969. Each holiday is described and each is followed by directions for some project associated with it. Useful for religious education or for craft groups. 10-12

● RADFORD, RUBY L. *Many Paths to God.* Theosophical, 1970. The basic ideas of twelve living religions and many of their parallel teachings. Each chapter has a list of suggested readings. 10-14

REISS, JOHN. *Colors,* ill. by author. Bradbury, 1969. Not only useful for color identification, but for awakening aesthetic appreciation. 2-5

● RICE, EDWARD. *The Five Great Religions,* photos by author. Four Winds, 1973. 12-15

ROCKWELL, ANNE. *Glass, Stones, and Crown: The Abbe Suger and the Building of St. Denis.* Atheneum, 1968. 11-13

ROGERS, W. G. *A Picture Is a Picture: A Look at Modern Painting.* Harcourt, 1964. An informed survey of the development of modern painting, including schools, techniques, and theories. 13 up

_____. *What's Up in Architecture; A Look at Modern Building.* Harcourt, 1965. Trends, styles, and architects are discussed in informal, lively writing. 11 up

RUSKIN, ARIANE. *Art of the High Renaissance,* ill. McGraw, 1970. 12 up

_____. *History in Art.* Watts, 1974. Not history as represented in art, but a history of art, authoritative and comprehensive. 12-15

_____. *Nineteenth Century Art.* McGraw, 1968. 13 up

_____. *The Pantheon Story of Art for Young People,* ill. Pantheon, 1964. 11-14

_____. *17th and 18th Century Art,* ill. McGraw, 1969. Lucid and informative, a book that serves as an excellent introduction to the art history of two centuries, but is comprehensive and authoritative enough for the knowledgeable reader. 12 up

SAMACHSON, DOROTHY and JOSEPH. *The First Artists,* ill. Doubleday, 1970. A competent survey, with good photographs of cave paintings and engravings, more extensive than the usual treatment of the subject. 10-14

● SAVAGE, KATHARINE. *The Story of World Religions,* ill. with photos and maps. Walck, 1967. 13 up

● SEEGER, ELIZABETH. *Eastern Religions.* T. Crowell, 1973. 12-15

SHAW, ARNOLD. *The Rock Revolution,* ill. Crowell-Collier, 1969. 12 up

SHIPPEN, KATHERINE BINNEY, and ANCA SEIDLOVA. *The Heritage of Music,* ill. by Otto van Eersel. Viking, 1963. 12-16

●☆ SMITH, RUTH, ed. *The Tree of Life,* ill. by Boris Artzybasheff. Macmillan, 1942, 1946. 13 up

SPIER, PETER, ill. *The Star-Spangled Banner.* Doubleday, 1973. Pictures are filled with historic details; text includes a discussion of the War of 1812 and a chart of official flags. 8-11

STAMBLER, IRWIN, and GRELUN LANDON. *Golden Guitars, the Story of Country Music,* ill. with photos. Four Winds, 1971. 12-16

STREATFEILD, NOEL. *A Young Person's Guide to Ballet,* ill. by Georgette Bordier. Warne, 1975. 9-12

SULLIVAN, GEORGE. *Understanding Architecture.* Warne, 1971. 10-14

TERRY, WALTER. *Ballet: A Pictorial History,* ill. Van Nostrand, 1970. 10-12

VAN DER HORST, BRIAN. *Rock Music.* Watts, 1973. A survey of types of rock music and of forms that preceded and contributed to it. Much of the book is devoted to individual performers and groups. 12-17

§ WARREN, FRED and LEE. *The Music of Africa; An Introduction,* ill. with photos and line drawings by Penelope Naylor. Prentice, 1970. Includes lists of books and recordings. 11-14

§ WARREN, LEE. *The Dance of Africa; An Introduction,* ill. by Haris Petie, photos by Vyvian D'Estienne and others. Prentice, 1972. 11 up

§ _____. *The Theater of Africa; An Introduction.* Prentice, 1976. Varied and comprehensive. 11 up

WATSON, ALDREN AULD. *Country Furniture,* ill. by author. T. Crowell, 1974. A detailed and comprehensive discussion of the craft as practiced in the past. 11 up

WILDER, ALEC, music by. *Lullabies and Night Songs,* ed. by William Engvick, ill. by Maurice Sendak. Harper, 1965. The choice of songs is very good, the arrangements are simple, the lyrics smooth; the illustrations are delectable. all ages

WINN, MARIE, ed. *The Fireside Book of Fun and Game Songs,* musical arrangements by Allan Miller, ill. by Whitney Darrow. Simon, 1974. Amusing pictures, a wide variety of songs. all ages

● WOLCOTT, LEONARD and CAROLYN. *Religions Around the World,* ill. by Gordon Laite. Abingdon, 1967. 11 up

WOODS, GERALD, PHILIP THOMPSON, and JOHN WILLIAMS, eds. *Art Without Boundaries.* Praeger, 1974. A description of the work of artists from many countries, and of the blurring of traditional boundaries between disciplines and media in the visual arts. 13 up

Activities and Experiments

ADKINS, JAN. *The Craft of Sail,* designed and ill. by author. Walker, 1973. The text moves from physical principles and facts about sailboats to techniques of sailing. 11 up

______. *Toolchest,* ill. by author. Walker, 1973. 10 up

ALKEMA, CHESTER JAY. *The Complete Crayon Book.* Sterling, 1969. 10 up

ANDERSEN, YVONNE. *Make Your Own Animated Movies; Yellow Ball Workshop Film Techniques.* Little, 1970. 10-13

§ ARCHER, ELSIE. *Let's Face It: The Guide to Good Grooming for Girls of Color,* rev. ed. Lippincott, 1968. Hair, complexion, makeup, clothes, speech, manners are all covered in this guide. 11-14

BEANEY, JAN. *The Young Embroiderer.* Warne, 1967. 10-13

BOYLAN, ELEANOR. *How to Be a Puppeteer,* ill. by Tomie de Paola. McCall, 1970. Gives directions for making and costuming puppets, manipulating them, making sets and scenery, etc. Plays for a single puppeteer and a group are included. 8-10

BRANLEY, FRANKLYN M., and ELEANOR K. VAUGHAN. *Timmy and the Tin-Can Telephone,* ill. by Paul Galdone. T. Crowell, 1959. 5-7

BRODERICK, DOROTHY. *Training a Companion Dog,* ill. by Harris Petie. Prentice, 1965. 9-12

BUSCH, PHYLLIS. *A Walk in the Snow,* ill. with photos by Mary M. Thacher. Lippincott, 1971. An unusually good correlation of pictures and text make clear the methods of observing and enjoying some of the natural phenomena in snow time. 7-9

CARAS, ROGER. *A Zoo in Your Room,* ill. by Pamela Johnson. Harcourt, 1975. 10-13

CASE, MARSHAL T. *Look What I Found! The Young Conservationist's Guide to the Care and Feeding of Small Wildlife,* ill. with photos by author. Chatham/Viking, 1971. 9-11

CHARLIP, REMY, MARY BETH and GEORGE ANCONA. *Handtalk; An ABC of Finger Spelling & Sign Language.* Parents' Magazine, 1974. 8 up

CHEKI HANEY, ERENE and RUTH RICHARDS. *Yoga for Children,* ill. by Betty Schilling. Bobbs, 1973. Simple instructions and adequate warnings about not overdoing. 8-10

COCHRANE, LOUISE. *Tabletop Theatres,* ill. by Kate Simunek. Plays, 1974. Directions for making stages, puppets, and costumes plus scripts for plays. 10-13

COLMAN, HILA. *Making Movies; Student Films to Features,* ill. by George Guzzi. World, 1969. Explicit and very comprehensive, written in a direct style. The advice is pertinent to career guidance. 12-15

COOMBS, CHARLES IRA. *Bicycling,* ill. with photos and diagrams. Morrow, 1972. 10-13

COOPER, ELIZABETH K. *Science in Your Own Back Yard,* ill. by author. Harcourt, 1958. 10-13

CURRELL, DAVID. *The Complete Book of Puppetry.* Plays, 1975. 11 up

CZAJA, PAUL CLEMENT. *Writing with Light; A Simple Workshop in Basic Photography.* Chatham/Viking, 1973. 11 up

FENTEN, D. X. *Indoor Gardening,* ill. by Howard Berelson. Watts, 1974. Brisk, sensible advice about caring for a wide variety of plants. 9-12

______. *Plants for Pots: Projects for Indoor Gardeners,* ill. by Penelope Naylor. Lippincott, 1969. Informal style and precise drawings give information on the propagation, potting, and care and feeding of house plants. 10-14

FERAVALO, ROCCO V. *Easy Physics Projects: Air, Water and Heat,* ill. by Lewis Zacks. Prentice, 1966. 8-10

FERGUSON, ROBERT. *How to Make Movies: A Practical Guide to Group Filming.* Viking, 1969. 13 up

FREEMAN, S. H. *Basic Baseball Strategy,* ill. by Leonard Kessler. Doubleday, 1965. 10-14

GARDNER, MARTIN. *Codes, Ciphers and Secret Writing.* Simon, 1972. 11 up

GARDNER, MARTIN. *Perplexing Puzzles and Tantalizing Teasers,* ill. by Laszlo Kubinyi. Simon, 1969. 8-11

GETZOFF, CAROLE. *The Natural Cook's First Book; A Natural Foods Cookbook for Beginners,* ill. by Jill Pinkwater. Dodd, 1973. 9-11

HAWKINSON, JOHN. *Pastels Are Great.* Whitman, 1968. The author explains the basic skills of the technique with enticing examples and explicit instructions. 8-10

HELFMAN, HARRY. *Making Your Own Movies.* Morrow, 1970. Lucid instructions on preparation, equipment, and filming. 10-14

HOLZ, LORETTA. *Mobiles You Can Make,* ill. by author, photos by George and Loretta Holz. Lothrop, 1975. Clear, step-by-step instructions for making three kinds of mobiles. 10-14

HORVATH, JOAN. *Filmmaking for Beginners.* Nelson, 1974. 11-15

HOWARD, HARRIET SHRIVER. *If You Had a Pony,* ill. with photos by Susan Rosenthal. Harper, 1965. 9-11

HUDLOW, JEAN. *Eric Plants a Garden,* ill. by author. Whitman, 1971. Clear photographs show a beaming young gardener planning, planting, tending, and harvesting his crop. 7-9

HUSSEY, LOIS J. and CATHERINE PESSINO. *Collecting for the City Naturalist,* ill. by Barbara Neill. T. Crowell, 1975. 9-11

KADESCH, ROBERT R. *Math Menagerie,* ill. by Mark A. Binn. Harper, 1970. 11-14

KIDDER, HARVEY. *Illustrated Chess for Children,* ill. by author. Doubleday, 1970. A really fine book for the beginning chess player. The clear diagrams are very helpful as is the proceeding from basic moves to increasingly complicated ones. 10-13

KUJOTH, JEAN. *The Boys' and Girls' Book of Clubs and Organizations.* Prentice, 1975. Gives sources of information for activities and projects described in the text. 9-12

LAFFIN, JOHN. *Codes and Ciphers; Secret Writing Through the Ages,* ill. by C. de la Nougerede. Abelard, 1964. An excellent book on cryptography, written with style and clarity and well organized. Cryptograms and solutions for the reader are appended. 12 up

LARRICK, NANCY. *See for Yourself,* ill. by Frank Jupo. American Bk., 1952. 6-8

LASSON, ROBERT. *If I Had a Hammer; Woodworking with Seven Basic Tools,* photos by Jeff Murphy. Dutton, 1974. Shows incorrect as well as correct procedures in completing simple projects. 10-13

LOPSHIRE, ROBERT. *A Beginner's Guide to Building and Flying Model Airplanes.* Harper, 1967. Step-by-step instructions for assembling planes, and many small tips to ensure good workmanship. 10-12

______. *It's Magic?* ill. by author. Macmillan, 1969. Simple tricks are described within the framework of a humorous story. 7-9

LYTTLE, RICHARD. *The Complete Beginner's Guide to Backpacking.* Doubleday, 1975. Straightforward, sensible advice on equipment, safety rules, and hiking. 11 up

MARA, THALIA, and LEE WYNDHAM. *First Steps in Ballet: Basic Exercises for Home Practice,* ill. by George Bobrizky. Garden City, 1955. Twelve basic barre exercises meant to be used in conjunction with formal training. 8-14

MARKS, MICKEY KLAR. *Collage,* ill. by Edith Alberts and with photos by David Rosenfeld. Dial, 1968. 8 up

______. *Painting Free: Lines, Colors and Shapes,* ill. by Edith Alberts and with photos by David Rosenfeld. Dial, 1965. Step-by-step instructions for the beginner interested in abstract painting. 11 up

MEILACH, DONA Z. *Creating with Plaster.* Reilly, 1966. A straightforward text with tips on techniques that give a professional touch. 12 up

MEYER, CAROLYN. *Christmas Crafts; Things to Make the 24 Days Before Christmas,* ill. by Anita Lobel. Harper, 1974. 10 up

______. *Saw, Hammer and Paint; Woodworking and Finishing for Beginners,* ill. by Tony Martignoni. Morrow, 1973. Materials and techniques are described; projects range from simple to difficult. 11 up

MEYER, CAROLYN, and JEROME WEXLER. *Rock Tumbling,* photos by Jerome Wexler. Morrow, 1975. 10-14

MILGROM, HARRY. *Adventures with a Paper Cup,* ill. by Leonard Kessler. Dutton, 1968.

______. *Adventures with a Straw,* ill. by Leonard Kessler. Dutton, 1967. 4-7

______. *First Experiments with Gravity,* ill. by Lewis Zacks. Dutton, 1966. A series of home demonstrations, each prefaced by an explanation of the principle involved. 8-10

MOORE, EVA. *The Seabury Cook Book for Boys and Girls,* ill. by Talivaldis Stubis. Seabury, 1971. A very good first cook book containing nine easy recipes. 7-9

MOORE, JIM. *Football Techniques Illustrated,* rev. ed., ill. by Tyler Micoleau. Ronald, 1962. 10-14

MOORE, WILLIAM. *Your Science Fair Project.* Putnam, 1964. 8-13

MOORMAN, THOMAS. *How to Make Your Science Project Scientific.* Atheneum, 1974. 10-14

MORGAN, ALFRED POWELL. *Boys' Book of Science and Construction,* rev. ed., ill. with plates and diagrams. Lothrop, 1959. 11-14

MOTT, CAROLYN, and LEO B. BAISDEN. *The Children's Book on How to Use Books and Libraries,* ill. Scribner's, 1961. Meets a wide variety of elementary grade needs ranging from writing a book review to using reference books and the library catalog. 9-11

NEUMANN, BILL. *Model Car Building,* ill. with photos. Putnam, 1971. Full instructions on building, painting, tools, materials, and adhesives. Big, clear photographs of equipment and procedures. 10-14

PAUL, AILEEN, and ARTHUR HAWKINS. *Kids Cooking.* Doubleday, 1970. 8-11

PETERSON, JOHN. *How to Write Codes and Secret Messages,* ill. by Bernice Myers. Four Winds, 1966. Lucid explanations of an alluring subject. 9-11

PETTIT, FLORENCE H. *How to Make Whirligigs and Whimmy Diddles; and Other American Folkcraft Objects,* ill. by Laura Louise Foster. T. Crowell, 1972. Instructions are lucid; projects are varied; a lively writing style makes the book particularly enjoyable. 12 up

PETTIT, TED S. *A Guide to Nature Projects,* ill. by Walt Wenzel. Norton/Grosset, 1966. 9-12

PURDY, SUSAN. *Festivals for You to Celebrate: Facts, Activities, and Crafts.* Lippincott, 1969. 9-12

RAVIELLI, ANTHONY. *What Is Bowling?* ill. by author. Atheneum/SMI, 1975. 9-11

ROCKWELL, HARLOW. *I Did It.* Macmillan, 1974. 6-7

ROSS, LAURA. *Hand Puppets: How to Make and Use Them,* ill. by author. Lothrop, 1969. Includes suggestions for a puppet play. 9-12

______. *Mask-Making with Pantomime and Stories from American History,* ill. by Frank Ross. Lothrop, 1975. 9-11

______. *Puppet Shows Using Poems and Stories,* ill. by Frank Ross, Jr. Lothrop, 1970. Each poem, story, or excerpt from a book is provided with production notes. Simple enough for children to use alone, yet good source material for adults. 9-11

ROTH, ARNOLD. *Pick a Peck of Puzzles,* ill. by author. Norton, 1966. Varied selections; riddles, rebuses, tongue-twisters, pictures with hidden clues, etc. 8-10

SARNOFF, JANE, and REYNOLD RUFFINS. *The Code and Cipher Book.* Scribner's, 1975. Includes such variant puzzlers as pig Latin and cockney slang as well as the usual kinds of codes and ciphers. 9-12

SCHNEIDER, HERMAN, and NINA SCHNEIDER. *Science Fun for You in a Minute or Two; Quick Science Experiments You Can Do,* ill. by Leonard Kessler. McGraw, 1975. 7-10

SCOTT, JOSEPH, and LENORE SCOTT. *Egyptian Hieroglyphs for Everyone: An Introduction to the Writing of Ancient Egypt.* Funk, 1968. 11 up

SIMON, SEYMOUR. *The Rock-Hound's Book,* ill. by Tony Chen. Viking, 1973. Describes varieties of rocks, with an identification table, and gives advice on collecting. 9-11

SOKOL, CAMILLE. *The Lucky Sew-It-Yourself Book,* ill. by Bill Sokol. Four Winds, 1966. 7-9

SOOTIN, HARRY. *Experiments with Magnetism,* ill. by Julio Granda. Norton/Grosset, 1968. 9-12

SOOTIN, HARRY, and LAURA SOOTIN. *The Young Experimenter's Workbook: Treasures of the Earth,* ill. by Frank Aloise. Norton/Grosset, 1965. 8-11

STONE, A. HARRIS. *The Chemistry of a Lemon,* ill. by Peter P. Plasencia. Prentice, 1966. 8-11

STONE, A. HARRIS, and BERTRAM M. SIEGEL. *Puttering with Paper,* ill. by Peter P. Plasencia. Prentice, 1968. 9-12

______. *Turned On: A Look at Electricity,* ill. by Peter P. Plasencia. Prentice, 1970. 10-12

SULLIVAN, GEORGE. *Better Softball for Boys and Girls.* Dodd, 1975. 9-14

SWENINGSON, SALLY. *Indoor Gardening.* Lerner, 1975. Simple, explicit, and adequately illustrated. 8-10

TISON, ANNETTE, and TALUS TAYLOR. *The Adventures of the Three Colors.* World, 1971. Shows color mix by use of transparencies. 5-8

UNESCO. *UNESCO Source Book for Science Teaching: 700 Science Experiments for Everyone,* 2nd ed. UNESCO, 1962. 10-14

UNKELBACH, KURT. *You're a Good Dog, Joe: Knowing and Training Your Puppy,* ill. by Paul Frame. Prentice, 1971. Includes warnings on safety of the puppy and very sensible training procedures. 7-9

WEBER, WILLIAM. *Wild Orphan Babies; Mammals and Birds.* Holt, 1975. 10 up

WEISS, HARVEY. *Carving; How to Carve Wood and Stone.* Addison, 1976. 11-14

______. *Ceramics from Clay to Kiln.* W. R. Scott, 1964. 10-14

______. *Clay, Wood and Wire; A How-To-Do-It Book of Sculpture.* W. R. Scott, 1956. 8-17

______. *Collage and Construction,* ill. W. R. Scott, 1970. A good do-it-yourself book in art, simple enough for the younger reader, dignified enough for the older. Discusses not only the materials (easy-to-get) and techniques, but artistic conception. 9-12

______. *How to Make Your Own Books,* ill. with photos. T. Crowell, 1974. Instructions for making different kinds of books follow explanations of procedures like folding, binding, and making covers. 10-14

______. *Model Cars and Trucks and How to Build them,* ill. with photos, plans, and drawings. T. Crowell, 1974. 9-12

______. *Paper, Ink and Roller; Print-Making for Beginners.* W. R. Scott, 1958. 9 up

______. *Pencil, Pen and Brush; Drawings for Beginners.* W. R. Scott, 1961. 11 up

______. *Sailing Small Boats,* ill. by Peter Barlow. Scott/Addison, 1967. 10 up

WYLER, ROSE. *What Happens If . . . ? Science Experiments You Can Do by Yourself,* ill. by Daniel Nevins. Walker, 1974. 7-9

WYLER, ROSE, and GERALD AMES. *Prove It!* ill. by Talivaldis Stubis. Harper, 1963. 5-8

YOUNG, RAY. *Bridge for People Who Don't Know One Card from Another,* ill. by Tom Dunnington. Follett, 1964. There's no assumption of previous knowledge, yet the author never talks down. A lucid book for beginners. 11 up

Part 4
Bringing Children and Books Together

14. Patterns of Response to Literature
15. Encouraging Response to Literature
16. Introducing Literature to Children

Patterns of Response to Literature

Chapter 14

From the earliest times, people have waited with anticipation for the wandering storyteller, bard, or minstrel. The old tales such as "The Bremen Town-Musicians" must have brought laughter and a muttered agreement that the poor old animals did, indeed, deserve the comforts they won by their own wits. Other tales, such as "Rumpelstiltskin" or "Tom Tit Tot," may have brought a sense of relief that the imp who would strike such a hard bargain was outwitted at the end of the story. "Cinderella" was a wonderful fantasy for poor people as they entered into the role of the poor cinder girl, seeing the ball through her eyes and experiencing her rise from rags to riches.

A good storyteller saw, in the faces of listeners, response to the story, and shared the audience's reactions to the plight of the characters, feeling their suspenseful interaction with a good plot. Sometimes there was response to the style of the telling. People listening to "The Three Billy-Goats Gruff" came to expect and to repeat, with the storyteller, "Who's that walking over my bridge?" and the favorite ending, "Snip, snap, snout. This tale's told out." This variety of response still is heard and seen when children hear a story well told.

The old tales inspire not only the obvious reactions of laughter or tears, but also the deeper sense of a story linking us to human lives over the ages, a story that has been told time and again in many parts of the world. As Paul Hazard wrote, "Once upon a time, . . . at a period so far removed from us that we are unable to visualize it to ourselves, there was the very same story."[1]

New tales may bring the same quality of response from readers and listeners. A nine-year-old tells of reading and rereading Laura Ingalls Wilder's *The Long Winter* because the descriptions of the blizzards sent chills up her spine and made her wish that she could be with Laura and Mary beside a roaring fire. A five-year-old nods wisely as Peter, in Ezra Jack Keats's *The Snowy Day,* discovers that the snowball he put in his pocket yesterday has melted.

This chapter and the two chapters that follow are concerned with children's response to literature—the different forms it can take and some ways of encouraging it. We start with the assumption that responding to literature is a positive, enriching experience, one we would like to share with children. But activities to encourage response should never be simply busy work. They should be rooted in the material and should serve the needs and interests of the children. This point bears repeating: Activities to encourage response to literature must grow naturally out of the reading, and different responses—both in variety and quality—must be respected and nurtured.

A giggle over some amusing passage and a

[1]Paul Hazard. *Books, Children and Men* translated by Marguerite Mitchell, The Horn Book, Inc., 1944, p. 158.

tear shed in sympathy for a story character's misfortunes are signs that the reader is interacting with the story. Such interaction is the substance of response. Response to literature need not be overt, as with giggles or tears, but we hope it occurs whenever children become involved with books which have stimulating content and are well written. Reading becomes enjoyable when children experience adventure right along with a story character, find answers to their questions in a book of nonfiction, or remember and repeat favorite poems. Literature becomes enlightening when children begin to interpret incidents and conversations which take place in a story, when they begin to tie fictional events to circumstances in their own lives. Books become intriguing as children gain the sophistication needed to understand the themes that run through them, become aware of the techniques an author has used to develop interesting characters, or begin to appreciate a certain style of writing. Literature can be challenging if children are encouraged to evaluate content in terms of general quality, interesting ideas, or accuracy of information. All of these experiences involve the response of a reader to a book.

Forms of Response

Response can take many forms. It can be overt and immediate. Then again, it may not be distinguishable at once and, perhaps, not ever. Many responses to literature do not surface until long after the book has been put down. Even then, the response may be a composite of responses to many literary works which have influenced the reader. A composite literary response can emerge, for instance, when we try to deal with a minor misfortune by stating our belief in humanity's ability to succeed through perseverance, an idea we may have encountered in many works of literature, popular as well as classic. A response may surface in an unexpected way, as when children respond to a cartoon character with giggles because the character reminds them of Henry Huggins. More clearly defined is the response of children saying, simply, that the story character has the same problems that they themselves have.

Viewpoints

Literature teachers often discuss but seldom define response to literature. They know it is important in the literature classroom and is an assumption in every literature curriculum. Aware that it is not quite the same as what psychologists call response to a stimulus, teachers realize that response to literature is mental, emotional, intellectual, sensory, physical. It encompasses the cognitive, affective, perceptual, and psychomotor activities that the reader of a poem, a story, or a novel performs as he reads or after he has read.—Alan C. Purves with Victoria Rippere. "Elements of Writing About a Literary Work: A Study of Response to Literature," NCTE Research Report No. 9, National Council of Teachers of English, 1968, p. xiii.

Many responses of children and adolescents involve an emotional interaction with the story or with a story character. Other responses are more complex, sometimes involving the emotional response along with an awareness of the meaning of the story or an evaluation of its quality. Occasionally, a response shows the child's ability to note the author's style or means of developing plot or characterization. It is not likely or even desirable that all of these kinds of responses appear at the same time. If we set a priority, very likely the most important form of response is involvement with a story. Without emotional interaction, young people are not likely to go on to develop a broad range of responses.

Literary response can stem from the experience of an individual child with an individual book; from group experience with literature through storytelling, choral speaking, story theater, or some other dramatic activity; or from literature presented and accompanied by discussion.[2] A response need not be active. It does not increase in value because it is overt. It is enough that a child has read or heard a literary selection that inspired interaction with the characters or ideas in the work.

We should not insist or even hope that all response to literature be observable. Never-

[2]D. W. Hardy, "Response to Literature; The Report of the Study Group," in *Response to Literature*, ed. J. Squire (Nat. Council of Teachers of English, 1968).

Viewpoints

Prolonged contact with literature may result in increased social sensitivity. Through poems and stories and plays, the child becomes aware of the personalities of different kinds of people. He learns to imaginatively "put himself into the place of the other fellow." He becomes better able to foresee the possible repercussions of his own actions in the life of others.—Louise M. Rosenblatt, *Literature as Exploration,* Revised Edition. Noble and Noble, New York, 1968, p. 184.

theless, response frequently can be seen and it can also be encouraged. As teachers or librarians, we can become aware of the occasions which draw a response, the selections that inspire interaction of readers with books, and the signs of response in faces of readers, listeners, or players. Increasing our awareness, we are better able to nurture response and to make it an important part of a child's reading experience. The key is to watch for and acknowledge response without interfering with it. A response is a very personal thing for a child, and if it is made public by an unthinking adult, the youngster's attitude toward reading may be severely affected. It goes without saying that any response should be treated with the utmost respect and that it should be recognized by adults as a sign that the experience with a story or poem has been strong enough to evoke a reaction.

As you note responses children make to literature, you may also absorb information about the kinds of literary selections particular children enjoy. They may be especially alert to aspects of characterization, plot, or an author's way of creating humor or suspense, or empathic with the predicaments of a story character. Use your observations as a guide to book recommendations for the child or ideas for offering active involvement with other books.

This emphasis on literary response is not new. Writing in 1938, Louise Rosenblatt suggested that the point at which a student meets and interacts with a piece of literature is crucial to response.[3] Her interest was in the way that response may bring a recognition of a value structure in the literature. Response may include an awareness of a universal truth that is passed on from one generation to the next through the literary tradition. Such awareness may help a young reader to cope more easily with life's problems.

More recently, the 1966 Dartmouth Conference papers showed a clear focus on the importance of response to the literary experience. Scholars from Great Britain and the United States met to consider the relationship of response to literary experiences at all age levels. Strong recommendations were made for an elementary English curriculum which allows students to respond to aspects of literature which affect them personally—to make an emotional response as well as a response to literary form and style.

A number of researchers in recent years have investigated the nature and form of literary response. Two of them, James Squire and Alan Purves, have made important contributions to our knowledge about responses of older students, and the information has triggered interest in the responses of younger students, as well. The work of those two men will be used here to provide a framework for the discussion of literary response.

The Emotional Reaction

When we become engaged with a story we are reading so that we interact with it, one of the consequences is an emotional response to the work. Test this out by thinking of a piece of fiction you have read and become involved with. Emotional response is shown when a child comments that she could almost feel the cold on the frozen tundra as she read about Julie's experiences with survival (Jean George's *Julie of the Wolves*). When children remark that the bully, Martin, in Mary Stolz's *The Bully of Barkham Street* is like a school bully who terrifies many of them, they are making personal responses to the story. Similarly, children who remark that the house in Elizabeth Hill's *Evan's Corner* looks much like their own are reacting in a personal way. You can also observe nonverbal emotional responses. Emotional reaction can show in children's body movements and in facial

[3]Louise Rosenblatt, *Literature as Exploration* (Appleton. 1968; 1938).

expressions when they read or listen to stories. Nonverbal response is evident, too, in dramatization and in pantomime.

Far from being a low-level response to literature, as some English specialists in the past suggested, the emotional response is probably the most important base upon which to build other responses, those involving evaluations of the literary qualities of a work or interpretation of the selection. In fact, Squire, studying the responses of ninth- and tenth-grade students to short stories, found that students who were personally involved with the stories also responded by evaluating the literary qualities of those works.[4] We do not know just how the two forms of response complement each other, but the evidence does at least show the importance of involvement.

In a study of the elements of response present when students write about a work of literature, Alan Purves and Victoria Rippere identified a number of responses termed "engagement-involvement."[5] They range from personal reaction to the work or the author to involvement with characters and relating incidents in the story to the reader's own life. As you begin to bring children actively together with books you will find that many such responses result, though they are more likely physical or oral, than written. The child who expresses pleasure on hearing another story by Robert McCloskey is showing engagement with the work of a particular author. Another youngster who laughs at old Sneep in McCloskey's *Lentil* and comments that he'd like to see the school principal in the same position is making an emotional response to the work. A student responding to Farley Mowat's *Owls in the Family* by describing his own hilarity when his dog chased its tail so hard it tripped and rolled over and over, is showing emotional reaction to the story.

Children who can respond through pantomime may show emotional involvement in their evident relish of a character part or a particularly interesting scene. One child was so engrossed in her characterization of Goldilocks that she forgot to be frightened when Little Bear woke her up. Instead, she greeted him joyfully and took him on home with her to meet her parents! Dramatization opens many doors to active involvement with a story, as does oral interpretation of literature. Emotional response is present, too, when children read or speak character parts with evident enjoyment and good interpretation. Such emotional responses should be valued and encouraged.

The Interpretive Reaction

Teachers and librarians responsible for recommending books to children hope that their recommendations will be books that readers can relate to and interpret. Teachers of reading are (or should be) very concerned about developing interpretation skills. Therefore, it is important to look for and recognize interpretive responses that children are capable of making and to provide opportunities for them to gain experience in interpreting literature.

Several types of interpretive response have been identified.[6] Responses made by relatively unsophisticated readers generally have to do with interpretation of stylistic devices such as metaphor, allusion, irony, and symbols; inferences about happenings prior to and following the action of the story, based on information given in the text; and inferences about the nature of a character, about the setting, or about the author's motive.

A child makes an inference or an interpretation when she decides that Russell Hoban's *A Bargain for Frances* was probably written because the writer wanted to show that it is not good to trick your friends. Another inferential response is saying that Sara, in Betsy Byars's *Summer of the Swans*, was really a great person but she was kind of hard to get along with because she didn't have much self-confidence. A student may be so inspired by the clear descriptions in Sheila Burnford's *The Incredible Journey* that he asks to illustrate several of the most memorable scenes. His explanation, that he wants to re-create an atmosphere that goes beyond the bare descrip-

[4]James R. Squire, *The Responses of Adolescents While Reading Four Short Stories* (Nat. Council of Teachers of English, 1964).
[5]Alan C. Purves with Victoria Rippere, *Elements of Writing About a Literary Work; A Study of Response to Literature* (Nat. Council of Teachers of English, 1968).

[6]Ibid., pp. 30–41.

tion, suggests that he is making inferences about the setting and is reconstructing scenes from the story.

We cannot emphasize strongly enough that much of what seems essentially interpretation of a story has with it a solid element of personal involvement. If the personal reaction triggers enough interest in a character, setting, bit of action, or underlying idea, the reader will be willing to enter into the spirit of the work and try to interpret it. The obvious need is for us as adults to provide material for response that intrigues, excites, or simply compels the reader to become immersed in the story.

The Critical Reaction

James Squire, in his study of adolescents' responses, defines a category of responses in which the reader judges the general literary quality of the story or reacts specifically to language, style, or characterization. In the Purves classification scheme, some responses to literary elements are included which can be seen in reactions of even young children. They are those responses that show attention to the language and the content of a work. Responses dealing with language include comments a reader makes about writing style, use of rhetorical devices such as personification, use of metaphor and simile, and of imagery. The reaction to language also includes response to the author's use of dialogue and description. The response to content includes reactions to the subject matter or topic, to action in the work, to character description, character relationships, and setting. Other responses identified by Purves as literary perception responses and of interest here are reactions to plot, mood, point of view assumed by the author, and attempts to define the genre of the work.

An example of a child's reaction to literary qualities is a statement that a book was boring because there was not enough action. A child who smiles over a poem because it is a limerick is responding to a literary element. So is a child who expresses pleasure over the perfect little people Mary Norton creates in *The Borrowers*. A reader may laugh at Astrid Lindgren's *Pippi Longstocking* because the author always lets Pippi get the better of adults who try to take advantage of her. Recognizing the author's way of developing humor is a response to a literary element.

Children's responses to literary characteristics may be as specific as: "I didn't get interested in any of the characters because there wasn't enough information about how they looked and felt." Literary judgment may also reflect the specific interest in language, as when a child repeats over and over the line, "I think mice are nice," and pronounces it a favorite line because of the good sound of *mice* and *nice*. On a more general level, children have been known to respond to a book by wondering, aloud, why the author bothered to write it or by excitedly asking whether there are any other books in the library that are like that one.

Responses that reflect some degree of literary judgment often reflect a strong emotional response as well, as is shown by the above examples. We may encourage the literary dimension of a response, if it seems appropriate, by taking a few minutes to talk with the child about the way an author is developing humor, or what an author might do to make a story character really interesting by use of dialogue as well as description.

The Evaluative Reaction

Although Squire includes judgments about the story in the same category as comments about the literary qualities of the work, he defines another kind of judgment which he calls a "prescriptive judgment." Responses in this category are those in which a reader tells what he or she thinks a character ought to do, based on some absolute standard. Such responses occurred infrequently in the patterns of ninth- and tenth-graders he studied and may not be very common among responses made by young children, either.

Purves, in his scheme for classifying responses, identifies a whole group of responses he terms "elements of evaluation." Among them are responses in which the reader evaluates the emotional appeal of the story. In addition, there are responses which evaluate an author's method: for instance, whether a work is a good or bad example of its genre (as a good or bad poem), or whether the author has used a fresh and interesting approach. Another kind of evaluative response deals with the moral significance of the work and the moral acceptability of lessons taught through the work.

Children are likely to make some kinds of evaluative responses more frequently than others. You should be alert to them so that they can be acknowledged and perhaps discussed further. The prescriptive judgment is easily recognized and can be expanded through discussion. For example, if a reader says emphatically that Harriet, in Louise Fitzhugh's *Harriet the Spy*, ought to throw away her notebook, it would be interesting to ask the child why Harriet might need to keep her notebook about people. What good is it doing her? By helping a reader to explore a response, some reaction to the literary characteristics may also emerge. At the elementary level, however, we are not as interested in instruction as we are in releasing response in children.

We hear fairly often evaluative responses which represent some of the types included in the Purves scheme. Children who say a book is one of the funniest they have ever read are responding with an affective evaluation. A reader who likes this mystery because the plot is different from most is evaluating the author's method of writing as well as evaluating the selection as a good example of its genre. The following response to Robert Lipsyte's *The Contender* shows an evaluation of the moral significance of the book: "It's worth reading because it shows that if you work hard you can get ahead."

Levels of Response

The preceding discussion of responses purposely did not give a value judgment on which kind of response—emotional, interpretive, critical (literary judgment), or evaluative—is most important or sophisticated. All are important and frequently occur in combination with each other. If we were to judge which response mode is most important for elementary school children, the answer would undoubtedly be the emotional involvement response.

There is a growth factor observable in response, as shown by a study of responses of children in grades three through twelve.[7] The pattern in that study showed that the youngest subjects, the third-graders, made a large number of responses that were literal retellings of the story, as well as some that were evaluative. Fourth-grade students were beginning to add personal involvement responses to the narration and, by fifth grade, children were making fuller retellings of the stories along with evaluations and personal reactions. At the sixth-grade level, interpretive responses began to emerge. The proportion of interpretive responses continued to increase at succeeding grade levels. The interpretive response, then, can be seen as a sign of greater maturity.

Retelling the Story

When we are asked to discuss or react to books we have not really understood, our response is likely to be a retelling of the material we have read. Our response may not include any emotional reaction and we usually do not attempt to interpret the work. Essentially, our response is literal. It might be considered a less mature or lower-level response than one which involves interpretation or evaluation of the story.

When you discuss books with children, you may find how often your question of "Why did the story end this way?" is met with an answer that is nothing more than a narration of the entire story, without any attempt to interpret events to determine why the author gave it such an ending. It may, at first, seem that the child is avoiding your question. More likely, the child has not reached a level of maturity or experience to be able to respond on a higher level, or perhaps the story was too complex or difficult for the reader. We should recognize if either case is true and offer children opportunities to develop the ability to interpret and evaluate literature and, certainly, to interact with that literature on an emotional level.

[7]Alan C. Purves, "Research in the Teaching of Literature," *Elementary English*, April 1975, pp. 463–466.

The Bettmann Archive

Christa Armstrong/Rapho/Photo Researchers

In contrast to the formality of early libraries, modern facilities are designed so that children find it easy to share reactions to new books. Over the years, rules for library conduct have changed and those changes have led to library programs that encourage reader response. The effect of a book on a reader is as highly valued as the book itself.

The Bettmann Archive

Ken Heyman

The discomforts of hard benches and formal recitations in early schools cannot have inspired much love for books. In contemporary classrooms, an important goal is to provide enjoyable experiences with books. Informality allows children to play active roles as listeners and readers.

Making Literary Judgments

A response that suggests literary judgment of a book or literary judgment of some aspect of the writing may range from the relatively unsophisticated to the very mature. Children frequently make a summary judgment about a book by pronouncing it "Great!" or "a real drag." If the reader volunteers more information (or responds to follow-up questions) to indicate that the book is great because the characters are so realistic and interesting or it is boring because the author has included a lot of information that is not necessary for the plot, a higher-level, more mature response is evident. Similarly, a judgment backed by the comment, "I didn't like this as well as the author's other books because I didn't feel as sympathetic to the characters," indicates that the reader has reacted emotionally to the story and is also probably making a judgment based on the character descriptions in the book. A mature reader would be able to discuss, in some detail, differences between two books in terms of logical plot development or author's style. Such responses are rare from elementary age children and are not a goal of an elementary literature program. Nevertheless, if we are aware of the many forms a judgmental response can take, we can distinguish the earliest attempts and encourage them to grow to responses of a more mature and thoughtful type.

Involvement Leading to Interpretation

Children who express involvement with a story or a character and who make some inferences based on information presented are responding to key story elements. At the elementary school level, the emotional and interpretive responses are probably the most important responses because they allow readers to enter completely into a story and to relate it to their own experiences.

At this level, watch for responses that indicate feeling about the treatment of a story character or the outcome of a plot. After reading *The Incredible Journey*, a boy remarked with emotion that he suffered along with the old dog but admired him for his persistence and thought it showed that animals, as well as people, will often suffer great hardships if they think the cause is worth it. Another reader commented at the end of a mystery story that it was exciting and the plot ended as she thought it would because one of the clues in the first chapter helped her figure out the solution. A young child responds to Pat Hutchins's *Rosie's Walk* first with squeals of delight at the plight of the fox and then a pronouncement that she guessed the fox deserved it since he was trying to hurt Rosie and he didn't really watch where he was going.

Through questions, discussion, and activities, you can encourage children to interact with books. Techniques to encourage response are discussed in the following chapter. This interaction may move children to interpret the events in books in ways that will add greater depth to what they know about life in general and their own lives in particular. Such is the force of literature and one of the major reasons that books and poems are written and read.

Response and Reading Comprehension

The relationship of literary response to reading comprehension is an important idea for teachers and librarians who work with children of elementary school age, for a good literary experience can help to develop the higher-level comprehension skills necessary for effective reading. On the other hand, a good reading program which aims to develop a child's ability to make inferences about, evaluate, and appreciate literature can also enhance children's response to literature.

Writing about the development of reading comprehension abilities, Robert Ruddell describes comprehension as occurring on three levels—*factual, interpretive,* and *applicative.*[8] He notes that the *factual* level involves mostly the information and ideas the reader finds. A child comprehending at the *interpretive* level, however, analyzes the information and infers such relationships as cause and effect, infers main ideas, and predicts the outcome of an event in the story. Also at this lev-

[8]Robert B. Ruddell, *Reading-Language Instruction; Innovative Practices* (Prentice, 1974).

el, readers begin to deal with their own values by inferring or interpreting character traits or identifying the author's motive. They bring personal judgment and their own experiences to bear on their interpretations.

At another comprehension level, which Ruddell terms *applicative,* readers apply the knowledge from the story to new situations, make and substantiate value judgments, and engage in problem solving. The comprehension skills at the interpretive and applicative levels can be related to the literary response abilities we have been discussing. At the interpretive level, the ability to infer is closely related to the interpretive response to literature. A child who identifies traits of a key story character by inferring from that character's actions, speech, and unspoken thoughts, is engaging in character trait analysis and also noting, though perhaps not intentionally, the techniques an author uses to develop a character. Thus, a child may describe the protagonist in Beverly Cleary's *Henry Huggins* as a boy who is not especially brave or confident and may judge Henry's actions as inappropriate by suggesting a better way to deal with a problem. In response to the follow-up question, "Why doesn't Henry seem to have much self-confidence?" a child may reply that Henry was not sure he could convince his mother to let him keep the stray dog. The reader may also note that Henry sounds fearful when he calls his mother and that his lack of confidence is also clear when he tries to get on the bus with his dog. Such responses do indicate that the reader is aware of some ways an author can give depth to characterization. Many children would make an emotional as well as a literary response to a question about Henry Huggins. Some would admit that they sometimes act the way Henry does or that they would be embarrassed—or would laugh—if they had the same predicament on the bus as Henry had when the dog got loose. Children may also suggest that Henry did not use good sense in handling the problem but should have tried some other scheme or given up entirely on the new dog. Value judgments call for a knowledge about the character and the situation. They also require the reader to infer and predict on the basis of what is known. Furthermore, an emotional response gives reason to believe that the child is responding to the story as a piece of literature and that the author has succeeded in drawing captivating

Viewpoints

Last fall, soon after finishing *Where the Wild Things Are,* I sat on the front porch of my parents' house in Brooklyn and witnessed a scene that could have been a page from one of these early notebooks. I might have titled it "Arnold the Monster."

Arnold was a tubby, pleasant-faced little boy who could instantly turn himself into a howling, groaning, hunched horror—a composite of Frankenstein's monster, the Werewolf, and Godzilla. His willing victims were four giggling little girls, whom he chased frantically around parked automobiles and up and down front steps. The girls would flee, hiccuping and shrieking, "Oh, help! Save me! The monster will eat me!" And Arnold would lumber after them, rolling his eyes and bellowing. The noise was ear-splitting, the proceedings were fascinating.

At one point Arnold, carried away by his frenzy, broke an unwritten rule of such games. He actually caught one of his victims. She was furious. "You're not supposed to catch me, dope," she said, and smacked Arnold. He meekly apologized, and a moment later this same little girl dashed away screaming the game song: "Oh, help! Save me!" etc. The children became hot and mussed-looking. They had the glittery look of primitive creatures going through a ritual dance.

The game ended in a collapse of exhaustion. Arnold dragged himself away, and the girls went off with a look of sweet peace on their faces. A mysterious inner battle had been played out, and their minds and bodies were at rest, for the moment.

I have watched children play many variations of this game. They are the necessary games children must conjure up to combat an awful fact of childhood: the fact of their vulnerability to fear, anger, hate, frustration—all the emotions that are an ordinary part of their lives and that they can perceive only as ungovernable and dangerous forces. To master these forces, children turn to fantasy: that imagined world where disturbing emotional situations are solved to their satisfaction.—Maurice Sendak. "Caldecott Award Acceptance," *The Horn Book Magazine,* August 1964.

characters and situations. The evidence of literary response is even more clear at the applicative level where readers are expected to make value judgments and also to substantiate those judgments by referring to the story.

Mature readers understand the material and are able to relate it to their own experiences or to other information that they have. Reading comprehension, then, is the key to literacy. Although literary responses and reading comprehension skills are not specifically the same abilities, there are relationships which can be identified and used so that development of reading skills grows naturally into a mature response to literature.

The relationship of reading comprehension to literary response is evident from the Barrett Taxonomy of Reading Comprehension:[9]

Figure 1

1.0 *Literal Recognition or Recall*
 Recall of details, main ideas explicitly stated in the selection, sequence, comparisons (among characters, or historical times or places), cause and effect relationships, and character traits

2.0 *Inference*
 Inferring supporting details, main idea, sequence, comparisons (likenesses and differences in characters, time, or places), cause and effect relationships, and character traits
 Predicting outcomes
 Inferring literal meanings from figurative language

3.0 *Evaluation*
 Judgments of reality or fantasy; fact or opinion; adequacy/validity (of author's treatment of the subject); appropriateness (in terms of relevancy of selections or parts of selections to a particular topic); and worth, desirability, or acceptability (of a character's action)

4.0 *Appreciation*
 Emotional response to content, plot, or theme
 Reactions to author's use of language, including connotations of words and effect of figures of speech
 Reaction to author's use of imagery

The Barrett Taxonomy includes affective as well as cognitive reading skills. The addition of affective responses to reading, shown in the category termed "Appreciation," draws the classification toward the concerns we have about response to literature—emotional involvement with the story or poem *plus* an attempt to interpret it, evaluate it, and, perhaps, discuss aspects of its literary structure.

When we look at the reading comprehension and response to literature schemes together, the interrelationships are clear.

Figure 2

Reading Comprehension
Literal Recall[10]*—Recall of details, main idea, sequence, comparisons, cause and effect, character traits*

Literary Response
Narration[11]*—Squire's term for a factual retelling of the story*

A response to a story or poem which is simply a retelling appears to be similar to and rest upon the comprehension skills identified as literal recall. This retelling relies mainly on the ability to recall details in sequence.

The details might be important if the reader uses them to infer cause and effect, to figure out the solution to a mystery, to interpret the behavior of a story character, or to form a response to the beautiful setting described by an author. Unless the information that is recalled is extended to other modes of response, the factual retelling is of no great importance when we talk of literary response. Recalling information about character traits can be useful if a child goes on to see how an author develops characterization. Similarly, recall of sequence may be important when a child points out similar plots in two stories. Recognizing character traits and plot structure in these two instances constitutes a response to literary qualities. A number of inferential comprehension skills are important when children respond to literature by trying to interpret it.

Children who have developed skills de-

[9]Adapted from Barrett, Thomas C., "A Taxonomy of Reading Comprehension," *Reading 360 Monograph (1972)*. Lexington, Massachusetts, Ginn and Company (Xerox Corporation). Reprinted by permission.

[10]Ibid., pp. 53–54.

[11]See James Squire, *The Responses of Adolescents While Reading Four Short Stories* (Nat. Council of Teachers of English, 1964).

fined in *Figure 3* have background for comparing the clothing of Laura and Mary (the *Little House* books) with current clothing styles (inferring comparisons), talking about why an author included certain characters in the story (inferring cause and effect), or suggesting events that could occur after the story has ended (inferring sequence).

Figure 3

Reading Comprehension

Inference[12]—Inferring supporting details, main idea, sequence, comparisons, cause and effect, and character traits; predicting outcomes; inferring literal meanings from figurative language

Literary Response

Interpretation—Making sense of the story; relating the work to what the reader knows about life

A child who says of *Owls in the Family,* "Wol's bad experience when he first flew came because he didn't have a mother owl to teach him how to fly," shows comprehension of cause and effect. If you look at the statement in terms of literary response, it shows an *interpretation* of a story character's problem.

The difficulties of Ramona (*Ramona the Pest* by Beverly Cleary) were explained by one child as caused by the fact that Ramona wants to do the right thing but usually doesn't succeed. That child cited several instances when Ramona's obedience actually got her into trouble (as when she sat in her seat all morning "for the present"). The character interpretation is built on character trait inference. By asking open-ended questions ("why" rather than "what, who, and where"), you give children experience with inference. Those "why" questions can enrich reading instruction as well as discussion of literature. When you are aware of the important ties between reading instruction and a literature program, you can strengthen them by building experience with literature into the reading program. You can also extend reading experiences by encouraging children's response to books during library and free reading periods.

Evaluative reading is an important skill which is related directly to evaluation of literature, as the following comparison shows.

Figure 4

Reading Comprehension

Evaluation[13]—Judgments of reality/fantasy; fact/opinion; adequacy/appropriateness; worth, desirability, or acceptability

Literary Response

Evaluation; Literary Judgment—Judgments of the worth of a story or of the quality of writing, depth of characterization, or effectiveness of plot; comments about the appropriateness of a character's behavior

A classification of reading skills which includes affective as well as cognitive abilities shows the close relationship between reading comprehension and emotional involvement with literature.

Figure 5

Reading Comprehension

Appreciation[14]—Emotional response to content, plot, or theme; reaction to author's use of language

Literary Response

Emotional Involvement with Literature—Comments showing interaction with a story or poem which may reflect joy, excitement, dislike, or a range of other emotions

Children who are encouraged to respond to characters, content, plot, and theme and to react to the author's use of language are being given experiences that can open the door to a satisfying emotional response to literature. Children who have begun to show involvement with literature may respond with comments like these: "I just hated Martin (*The Bully of Barkham Street*) until he stopped beating up on little kids," "That description of the doughnuts (*Homer Price* by Robert McCloskey) falling all over the floor was really funny," or "If I had been Ramona, I would have pulled that girl's curls, too."

[12]Smith and Barrett, pp. 54–56.

[13]Ibid., pp. 55, 56.
[14]Ibid., pp. 56–57.

It is interesting to note that the Barrett organization of comprehension abilities is described as a taxonomy rather than a hierarchy; that is, no order of importance is imposed on the levels of comprehension. However, the appreciation skills are based on inference and evaluation. The appreciation level represents ability to react emotionally in addition to grasping the meaning of the story. And it is that emotional reaction that you can consciously foster through the reading program. If emotional response is considered a base for other responses which occur at the same time or even at later stages of development, the emotional response must be encouraged and emphasized whenever possible.

Interpretation of Pictures

Young children are often taught, as a part of the beginning reading program, to get information from pictures and to interpret them. When they are asked for factual information, they are then often asked to use that information to predict what will happen to characters in the pictures or to interpret what is taking place in the scene.

Picture reading is very likely an important readiness activity for literary response as well as for reading comprehension. A child who is asked to "tell the story" in a book that is completely or almost entirely without text is being asked to respond to the illustrations. John Goodall's *The Ballooning Adventures of Paddy Pork* and Mercer Mayer's *The Great Cat Chase* are examples of wordless books that give children a chance to infer a story from illustrations. Young children of kindergarten age and below may, as often as not, respond with a factual account of what they see in the pictures. Older or more mature "picture readers" are more likely to respond by combining factual observations with their own inferences about what goes on in the story.[15] The younger children are giving a narrational response, the older or more mature ones a response that usually combines emotional involvement with inferences about the pictorial information. Such a story "told" by more mature children may include a considerable number of inferences about the characters and about the plot, including predictions of what may occur as the story progresses. The response, therefore, is a literary response at the same time that it is an exercise in picture comprehension. By providing good experiences with picture books and asking appropriate questions, we can help young children to develop inference skills.

The need for a strong library reading program to complement the skill instruction that goes on in reading class should be evident. Through planned library activities, children can be brought into contact with—and, we hope, interaction with—fine and interesting books. They can have time and opportunity to respond emotionally to the books, to whet their curiosity through reading experiences, and to begin to reorganize some perceptions of the world they live in. They can use vicarious literary experiences as guides to the interpretation of some of life's events.

Developing Values Through Literary Response

In Chapter 1, "Children and Their Books," we observed that children are constantly struggling to keep a balance between their personal happiness and social approval and that sensitively written books help children to understand themselves and others. The struggle to satisfy basic needs is one which all people engage in. The basic needs identified in Chapter 1 are a need for physical well-being, the need to love and be loved, the need to belong, the need to achieve, the need for change, the need to know, and the need for beauty and order. Striving to attain those universal needs can bring children into situations that test their value structures. Observing story characters dealing with those same needs can provide some reassurance to young readers.

Responding to Universal Needs

Exposure to worthwhile literature can help give children a sense of physical well-being

[15]Mary Jett Simpson, *Children's Inferential Responses to a Wordless Picture Book; Development and Use of a Classification System for Verbalized Inference* (Unpublished doctoral dissertation. University of Washington, 1976).

because they are engaged in a relaxed and pleasant activity. They can also experience a sense of physical well-being through the feelings and actions of story characters if they are able to enter emotionally into a story. With Laura and Mary (the *Little House* books), they learn to be grateful for their sense of sight and to realize some of the difficulties blind people face. They identify with Colin and Dickon in Frances Hodgson Burnett's *The Secret Garden* and realize the joy of moving freely and painlessly.

Children take satisfaction in reading about children who are loved, and about story characters that they can love and respond to emotionally. One of the satisfying qualities of the *Little House* books is the great sense of love that dominates all the relationships within the Ingalls family. Some children may experience that love vicariously. They often mention not the adventure or the historical interest but the nice deeds the Ingallses did for one another. Some readers respond to Karana, in Scott O'Dell's *The Island of the Blue Dolphins,* by pointing out the great love she must have had for her brother to swim back to the island in search of him. The aura of love in a sensitive story like Madeleine L'Engle's *A Wrinkle in Time* sometimes brings a response from readers that shows how completely they have been wrapped up in the warmth of this family group.

The need to belong and the need for security concern all people. A child who is a stranger in a new neighborhood may take refuge in reading about a familiar story character or find a story that shows such strong friendships among story characters that some of their security extends to the reader. Reading Irene Hunt's *Up a Road Slowly* sometimes causes children to comment on the problems the protagonist had and how hard it was for her to live with relatives. In Louisa Shotwell's *Roosevelt Grady* children may respond to Roosevelt's constant moving and lack of opportunity to stay in one place long enough to belong. Such responses can bring a growth in empathy as well as vicarious satisfaction of needs.

Children can learn to value growth and achievement as they experience those needs in such books as Rebecca Caudill's *Did You Carry the Flag Today, Charley?* and Joseph Krumgold's *. . . and now Miguel.* Charley's need to achieve the expected behavior of a kindergartner is shown through his failures, struggles, and eventual success. The book often elicits an emotional response from children who realize that they are a little bit like Charley. The need to achieve the status of manhood drives Miguel into a risky situation before he reaches his goal. Response to Miguel's struggle may show that the reader is also challenged to prove that he or she has achieved adulthood. As readers participate vicariously with story characters like Miguel, they can begin to work out some of their own concerns.

The need for change is met through books in which a story character has an experience quite different from the life of the reader. *My Side of the Mountain* by Jean George offers experience in outdoor living that appeals to many children. They respond so fully that they enter into the story with Sam, living a wilderness retreat life right along with him. *Hills End* by Ivan Southall brings much the same sense of immediacy to readers as they relive the experience of isolation by a flash

Viewpoints

To teach children's literature from the point of view of the reader would seem to be the only defensible way to approach the task whether you are teaching literature to children or to adults. If the purpose for teaching is to introduce readers to books to which they can respond and to encourage self-directed reading, then the responsibility for considering the reader's point of view is clearly evident.

Children's literature is taught to children and to adults; it is taught to adults so that they can be more effective when teaching children. The methods used should reflect the teacher's recognition of the interrelatedness of the two groups of students. College students studying children's literature will try to predict the responses of the child who will read or hear the story or poem, i.e., try to see it from the point of view of the reader.—Norine Odland, "Teaching Children's Literature: From the Point of View of the Reader," in *Elementary English,* November 1972, p. 993.

flood and of desperate struggle for survival. Readers who are encouraged to respond openly to such stories can also benefit from observing and sometimes playing out the way in which a character in the book deals with a problem.

The quest for knowledge sends students of all ages to informational books. Here, too, a well-written book can involve children so completely that they begin to integrate the material with previous knowledge and to evaluate the book. A book like Jean George's *All Upon a Sidewalk* presents information about the yellow ant in such a way as to engage the reader's curiosity and to cause some readers to continue their own research in other books to add information or double-check what is presented. An informational book such as Patricia Lauber's *The Friendly Dolphins* stimulates curiosity about dolphins and the ways they communicate. Children may even begin to compare dolphin behavior with human behavior.

A beautifully illustrated book surely helps to satisfy the need for beauty and order. A child reads a poem and comments that she likes it because everything rhymes as it should. That evaluation may not single out a quality of poetry that sophisticated adults desire, yet the poem has obviously satisfied the child and fit her sense of order. Similarly, a story in which all elements of plot are resolved by the ending can provide a sense of satisfaction that all is in order. Children exposed to so much that is trite and unfinished in television need the security and satisfaction of a well-ordered story.

The basic needs, then, represent the sorts of experiences a developing personality seeks. Children sense the deeper questions they need to be concerned with. They are aware, however vaguely, of the decisions they must make and some of the possible consequences of those decisions. As young readers respond to the basic needs presented in literature, they begin to get a sense of the story characters' values and how they were formed. Readers may perceive that they face many of the same problems faced by their favorite characters in literature and that they must make thoughtful decisions about their own problems just as the people in the stories do.

Interacting with Problems of Story Characters

When children interact emotionally with stories, they frequently become involved with characters with whom they can identify. Sometimes readers also meet characters whose lives are very different from their own. The child who reads William Armstrong's *Sounder* and learns from it what it is to be poor and discriminated against may be seeing the problems of ill-treated people for the first time. A youngster, listening to the story of the life of a barrio child, wonders at the problems of daily existence many children face. Discussion and role-playing of story characters' problems can bring children into closer relationship with the characters and help them to begin to develop a sense of empathy.

A scale of empathic behavior has been developed on the basis of elementary school children's responses to filmed literature. While these findings are based on response to film, they have a clear application to children's response to literature as well.

Figure 6

A Hierarchy of Empathy[16]

I. Identification. *A sensory-motor response shown as imitation of self or another. It is carried out purely for its own sake and is seen in facial* expressions, *body posture, movement, or sounds of a person or animate being that is observed.*

II. Differentiation. *An affective response characterized by conscious awareness of feeling for or against another,* Differentiation *occurs in dramatized or verbalized expression of difference between self and other. At this level, empathy can take the form of* Resistance, *shown through exaggerated imitation in body or speech and physical or verbal withdrawing from a person. It can also emerge as* Re-identification, *shown through behavior such as friendly imitation in body, sound or speech, friendly overtures, gentle teasing, joining another person's plans.*

III. Empathy. *This primarily cognitive response also includes sensory-motor and affective response. It is characterized by active considera-*

[16]Dorothy Jean Woodbury. "A Hierarchy of Empathy" from *Toward a Theory of Empathy: A Developmental Hierarchy Applied to Response to Filmed Literature*, an unpublished doctoral dissertation, University of Washington, 1975, pp. 57-60.

tion of and placement of value on both self and other to generate goodwill. The highest stage constitutes altruistic goodwill or empathy.

The ascending order of behavior begins with simple imitation of behavior and moves to a conscious feeling for or against another person. The level of conscious feeling is superseded by conscious placement of value on both oneself and another which is known as goodwill. At the highest level of response, the person realizes that understanding of self and others is important because each profits from the welfare of the other.

A student responding at the first level on the empathic hierarchy to Jean Little's *From Anna* might simply imitate Anna as a caricature of someone who doesn't see well and bumps into things. At a higher level, the child might observe that Anna was different because she did not have good vision but that she had the same feelings about wanting to do well in school that other people have. At the highest level, a reader might note that a sighted child who got to know Anna and help her could learn about the problems of being partially sighted and could help other people. Role-playing a situation can lead students to identify with and eventually begin to understand the fears and difficulties of others. Such responses can best be described as emotional. At the same time, however, they may also be interpretive since the reader is trying to interpret the motives and behavior of story characters.

You can provide a basis for development of empathy by giving young children time and opportunity to interact with literature. Well-chosen stories can influence the way children view themselves in relation to others. A sensitively written story such as Anne Holm's *North to Freedom* is best read independently so that children can think about the subtle implications for understanding people who are different from them. Other stories, excerpts, or poems may be more effective if interaction is developed through dramatic activities such as role-playing or through discussion. When you read literature that seems to have special significance for value formation, keep in mind discovering the best way to encourage interaction with it.

Observing Value Formation by Literary Characters

Value clarification programs are one way to help children formulate a personal value structure. Typically, those programs use the technique of placing children in situations that require decision making and analysis of the consequences of decisions. Experiences with literature can usually give children this background for valuing without the use of contrived situations. Furthermore, literature not only can provide well-developed situations but also can show desirable and undesirable consequences of a course of action. Role-playing or follow-up discussion can help children to consider the options open to them when they face problems and to think, also, about the consequences of a particular way of behaving. Books with well-developed plot and characterization can provide children with fine insights into ethical ways of dealing with problems. Therefore, experiences with good literature selections should help children to think about the values held by story characters and relate those values to situations in their own lives.

A number of value hierarchies have been developed, among them a classification of types by Lawrence Kohlberg.

Figure 7[17]

Stage 0: Amoral. *Response to specific situations without understanding the ethical question.*

Stage 1: Fearful-Dependent. *Concern with punishment that may follow an action. Issues are considered only from child's point of view but power and prestige may influence actions.*

Stage 2: Opportunistic. *Based on the idea that the best action is that which benefits the person who acts. No response to moral principles.*

Stage 3: Conformist: Person Oriented. *Main concern is with pleasing others. This can lead to conforming to stereotypes held by the majority.*

Stage 4: Conformist: Rule Oriented. *Authority, often legalistic, replaces the "other people" who influence behavior at Stage 3.*

Stages 5 and 6: Principled Autonomy. *At Stage 5 there is recognition of social utility in behavior; at Stage 6, values of justice, mutual respect, and trust dominate the decisions.*

[17]See Richard L. Gorsuch, "Moral Education from a Psychological View of Man as an Ethical Being," *The Educational Forum*, January 1973, p. 173.

In a sense, this hierarchy resembles Woodbury's empathy hierarchy, with the shift from a self-centered response to one which recognizes mutual respect and universality of application.

The study of value formation can help in our work with children and books. Essentially, all good literature deals with values. Children who read widely and hear stories read and told cannot help but interact with story characters involved in decision making, in formulating personal values, in learning to empathize with the difficulties of people the world over. We can help children to select books that will give them some experience with the valuing process. Even beyond that, we can take note of their responses and can encourage young readers to observe the actions of story characters and to think through the motivations for, and consequences of, their actions. Going from there, children can talk about similar situations in their own lives and determine whether the outcome was good or whether they would behave differently if given another chance.

A valuing response to literature can come from reading a book like *The Bully of Barkham Street.* Children are able to identify Martin's recurring problem—the teasing he gets from classmates because he is fat. When they look at his actions in the first part of the story, as he tries to deal with his problem, they see that he strikes out at children younger than himself whom he can easily out-fight. He also eats more because he dislikes himself for his actions. The consequences are that he sinks deeper into his original problems. Not until his teacher helps him to understand himself is Martin able to change his behavior and to see changes in the consequences of his actions. He becomes, in the end, slimmer and happier. There are many situations in the book which can be used for role-playing or discussion. Our main concern is to be sure children see how clearly a good writer can show a character's thoughts and actions so that we can examine the valuing process that is taking place.

Children can experience and respond to characters like Queenie in Robert Burch's *Queenie Peavy.* At the beginning of the story, she acts at the amoral level, doing what she pleases even though she knows she will be punished. As she matures, she progresses at least to the rule-oriented conformist level. Another story character, Kate, in *The Good Master* by Kate Seredy is purely opportunistic at the start but, by the end of the sequel, *The Singing Tree,* she has moved up to a level of valuing which shows some ability to deal on an ethical level. Many stories show a child character who at first cares only about pleasing peers, but who learns to forego peer pressure and to abide by rules which are, presumably, for the good of all.

We approach value exploration through literature from an emotional response coupled with character interpretation. We can recognize and encourage reader interaction with the values of story characters. Using techniques for discussion, role-playing, and puppetry, it is possible to enhance the process of personal value formation.

Evaluating Response

Evaluation of children's learning about literature is seldom done formally. Nevertheless, there are literary behaviors which can be identified and observed throughout a school year. Formal and informal observation can also help you to look at the success of your literature program. Evaluation, carried out throughout the course of a program, can give information about these behaviors:

1. knowledge about literature;
2. ability to apply that knowledge in comparing stories or poems or tracing their cultural roots;
3. expressed response—either through oral, dramatic, or artistic form; or through talking or writing about response; and
4. willingness to participate in literary experiences or to respond to literature.[18]

Behaviors (3) and (4) above are closely related to experiences described in the two chapters that follow. You might, for example, evaluate whether oral reading and discussion develops more positive attitudes in your students than

[18]Alan C. Purves, "Evaluation of Learning in Literature," in *Handbook of Formative and Summative Evaluation of Student Learning,* Benjamin S. Bloom, J. Thomas Hastings, and George Madaus, eds. (McGraw, 1971), pp. 703–710.

role-playing, as shown by children's comments that indicate greater emotional involvement with a story or poem. The best means of assessing response to literature at the elementary level seems to be through adult observation of children's behavior and reactions to literature heard and read. Written responses and objective tests are more useful for evaluating responses of older students.

Willingness to participate in literary experiences and to respond to literature can be assessed by observing children's reading habits, either informally or with a questionnaire, and by noting reactions to literature presented in class. A questionnaire asking children to rank reading according to its importance in their lives might include such other choices as television viewing, participating in sports, or spending time with hobbies. By using such a questionnaire at the beginning and end of a year, it is possible to get some idea of the success of a literature program. Informally noting whether individuals or a group can better interpret literature at the end of the year can add to this evaluation. So, too, can the use of tests of knowledge about literature.

Judgment of the success of an entire program serves its purpose when we make plans for future programs. Evaluation carried out during a program can help us to make changes while the program is still in use. If creative dramatics is not an effective way of involving a certain group of children with literature, frequent observations should make that clear. Another approach, such as discussion, can be substituted and a check made of changes in attitude and/or knowledge as a result of the new strategy. The evaluations need not be more formal than observations of children's reading behavior. However, conscious evaluation can help to keep a literature program interesting and develop mature responses.

As adults who are involved in bringing children and books together, we would like to make that experience a rewarding one. In this chapter we have discussed a wide range of current theory and research on children's response to literature. Our purpose in this discussion has been to provide a basis for thinking about children's experiences with literature and for organizing activities—the subject of the two chapters that follow.

Recommended Activities

1. Make it a practice, over the period of a week or so, to ask children who have finished a book what they thought of it. Make a simple tabulation of how many responses fit each of the categories: emotional involvement, interpretation, literary judgment, evaluation.
2. Read a story aloud to one or more children. At the close of the reading, pause for spontaneous comments or ask some open-ended questions to help children respond. Notice the types of responses made, in terms of the categories described in this chapter.
3. Read several books for any age level you choose. As you read, try to notice types of responses that you are making to the story. An alternate plan would be to work with a partner, both reading the same book. Interview each other at intervals during your reading to see what types of responses you make.
4. Begin to develop a list of books you think give especially good opportunity for each kind of response development.
5. Read a story from the bibliography at the end of Chapter 10, "Modern Fiction." Determine what level of empathy or what stage of valuing the characters exhibit. How could you help a young reader to discover his or her own value structure through response to the book?

Adult References

Gorsuch, Richard L. "Moral Education from a Psychological View of Man as an Ethical Being." *The Educational Forum,* January 1973, p. 173.

Hazard, Paul. *Books, Children, and Men.* Horn Book, 1960.

Purves, Alan C. "Research in the Teaching of Literature." *Elementary English,* April 1975, pp. 463–466.

Purves, Alan C., ed. *How Porcupines Make Love; Notes on a Response-Centered Curriculum.* Xerox College Publications, 1972.

Purves, Alan C., with Victoria Rippere. *Elements of Writing About a Literary Work; A Study of Response to Literature.* Research Monograph No. 9, Nat. Council of Teachers of English, 1968.

Rosenblatt, Louise M. *Literature as Exploration.* Appleton, 1938, 1968.

Ruddell, Robert B. *Reading Language Instruction; Innovative Practices.* Prentice, 1974.

Squire, James, ed. *Response to Literature.* Dartmouth Seminar Paper No. 6, Nat. Council of Teachers of English, 1968.

______. *The Responses of Adolescents While Reading Four Short Stories.* Nat. Council of Teachers of English, 1964.

Encouraging Response to Literature

Chapter 15

To become mature readers children need opportunities to respond to a variety of reading material. Some children will respond easily to selections that interest them, showing response in their comments as well as in their facial expressions as they read, hear, or recall a story or poem. Other children will need more encouragement and may respond more freely if they are allowed to use physical as well as verbal response, as in a puppet production of a story. Your role is to encourage but never force response, to offer activities that will allow children to actively respond to a selection, to observe and help to extend responses to literature so that they include interpretation and evaluation. At the same time, you should realize that some of the most deeply reflective responses are not observable and that those responses must be honored and not destroyed by too much emphasis on activity. Remind yourself that your goal is not a polished dramatic production but a group of children enjoying an experience with a fine story.

Response-centered activities discussed in this chapter begin with those designed for listening enjoyment—reading aloud to children and storytelling. A third activity, discussion, adds active verbal interchange to listening, and leads to interpretation and evaluation of a selection. The chapter then moves to dramatic activities—role-playing, creative dramatics, story theater, oral interpretation, and puppetry—activities which encourage physical/motor response as an aid to involvement with a story. Writing activities are described last. The act of writing about a literary work requires a certain amount of skill in written expression. Children who have only minimal writing skill will be inhibited in developing response to literature if made to write about what they have read. For that reason, written responses may be fine for some children and some situations but should be used selectively.

Reading Aloud to Children

Parents, teachers, librarians, baby-sitters, all of us who work with children, can enrich our lives as well as those of children when we provide and encourage delight in hearing a good story read aloud well. Pleasurable experiences in listening can create interest in books that carries on through years of adolescence and adulthood. Listening can also provide natural opportunities for development of a listening vocabulary and acquaintance with English syntax. When you read to children, you give them a chance to hear an author's style, to identify with well-developed characters, and sometimes to try to predict the direction the plot will take in tomorrow's installment. Most important of all, you help them to know good books and poems in a relaxed, warm atmosphere.

Oral reading will be most successful when

you give the listeners time to get ready to hear a story. For most groups, that readiness involves a few minutes of quiet and a chance to get as comfortable as possible. If the illustrations are important to the story, it also means settling the children close enough to you so that all can see. When you read from a picture book, it is important that you either hold the book so that they can see as you read or pause at the end of a page and take time to show the illustrations.

Selecting Material to Read Aloud

For many people and certainly for inexperienced readers, the two basic guidelines for selecting materials to read aloud are (1) that you like the selection and (2) that it is well written. As to the first guideline, you are more likely to draw an emotional reaction from listeners if you are involved with the story yourself. You will probably also do a better job of interpreting the characters and developing a sense of mood. However, unless you have chosen a well-written story, you may fail on both counts even though you like the book. A poorly written selection can cause you to feel awkward, to stumble over words, and to fail to make sense of the syntax because the writing lacks grace and polish.

Vivid characterization and a fairly fast-paced story line (a compact, factual account that concentrates more on action and less on description) are also important factors to keep in mind when you select a book to read aloud. Choose characters who will interest listeners and whose dialogue will be interesting and comfortable for you to read. Choose a plot or an organizational scheme that moves at a pace fast enough to keep reader attention, exercising your judgment about what may appeal to the group and keeping in mind age, past experiences, and interests.

The amount of time you can devote to an oral reading session will also influence the way you select material. Never try to read a long selection when you know the attention span of the children is likely to be no more than twenty minutes. You can usually find good stopping points if you have skimmed the material in advance. Sometimes an intriguing question can give the children a chance to wonder about what will happen next. If the story must be continued for several days, let the children, rather than you, review the story before continuing on with the next reading. Longer selections require special treatment but they are often very appealing to children because they allow fuller appreciation of a good plot and a chance to get well acquainted with the characters. Reading full-length books also gives some children a chance to know certain books they would never read on their own. If you cannot continue a story with the same group of children, consider the many fine poems that they may like. Think, too, of books like Beverly Cleary's *Henry Huggins* and Robert McCloskey's *Homer Price* which have episodic plots, each chapter usually a self-contained experience.

Reading aloud should not be limited to young children. Older children also enjoy being read to and often will read books they have heard previously. Additionally, the oral

Viewpoints

Reading aloud by the teacher to the students is a delightful way to open the world of literature to children. Oral reading is important not just to primary grade students but to upper grade boys and girls as well. To interact with the hero of *Call It Courage, Island of the Blue Dolphins, The Biggest Bear, Charlotte's Web,* or *Tom Sawyer,* to name just a few, by listening to the teacher read is a surefire way to create excitement about books and to entice children into reading them. Reading a chapter a day, after lunch, for instance, can certainly whet the reading appetite by giving children new insights into good literature.

We, as teachers, have the important and responsible privilege of giving children the gift of reading. A large part of this gift must be accepted in the form of skills and controls that are taught in a developmental, sequential manner. However, as teachers, we are responsible also to see that this gift of reading is used. It takes time, perhaps, to evaluate our reading programs and find just what opportunities we are opening up so that our students can become readers of books, not people who just know how to read.—Dewey W. Chambers, *Children's Literature in the Curriculum,* Chicago: Rand McNally & Company, 1971, pp. 31–32.

reading provides a group experience with literature in contrast to the more frequent silent reading activities that older children engage in.

Oral Reading Techniques

When you have chosen a story that is right for you and your children, you are ready to begin preparing to read aloud. Even experienced readers often use some pre-presentation techniques to make a reading more effective. They focus on the literary aspects of a story, qualities such as characterization and author's style, which must be conveyed when you read aloud. That can be done only if you have read, or at least skimmed, the selection to note high points in the plot. The same is true for noting crucial points to be emphasized when you are reading biography or informational material.

Previewing, or studying a selection in advance, will call your attention to the general tone the author uses. Is it serious, cynical, humorous, matter-of-fact? How should the narrator's parts be handled to provide contrast with character parts? Previewing should also show you the personality traits of the story characters so that you can use that information in your interpretation of dialogue. Skimming combined with a more complete reading of some sections of a story can give you an idea of the author's style. Are there long descriptive phrases? Does the author use short, action-packed sentences to instill excitement? Does the writer use unusual words? Are there words or word clusters that must be emphasized as you read? Skimming can help you to prepare quickly to make the most of a character part, a well-written line, or a build-up of conflict within the plot.

If you are a beginner at oral reading, you may want to practice a story aloud several times before reading it to the group. If you are reading from your own copy of a book, you may even want to mark it, underlining words needing emphasis and key punctuation marks so that you will make the most of a phrase or a sentence. If you have trouble keeping a wide enough eye-voice span to read ahead a sentence at a time, try at least to read for phrases so that your oral reading is smooth. The smoothness is the mechanical part of the reading. Beyond that, you must try to give listeners the mood of a selection. Creating mood requires you to bring together all of your knowledge about a work—understanding of theme, plot structure, characterization, and style. Using your voice, you can create a mood that helps listeners into their own interpretation of a story and brings them far enough into a work so that they are able to react intellectually as well as emotionally. Your level of pitch, tone of voice, and the pace of your reading all contribute to mood—a quiet, hushed reading for parts of Robert McCloskey's *Time of Wonder* and a brisk, rapid one for his *Homer Price*.

When you work on characterization, you should consider what you know about the character's personality. How would the person talk? Should you interpret the character as good-natured? domineering and aggressive? frightened or unsure? angry? Would the character generally speak slowly? fast? softly? Would the rate and loudness of speech vary, depending on what was being said? You may find it easier and more rewarding to try to think as the story character thinks and to really put yourself into the role, reading each bit of dialogue as though you were in the shoes of that character. Regardless of the technique you use, you should achieve enough of the spirit of the story so that characters are distinguishable from one another and so that they evoke some emotional response from children who are listening to the story.

Oral reading of fiction requires you to interpret mood and character. Oral reading of informational books calls for attention to key facts and emphasis on those facts as you read. Since the information is much more compressed in nonfiction, you would be wise to pause slightly at the end of a major section to allow listeners to absorb and reflect on some of the ideas before you go on to the next part. Although informational books are not read aloud as frequently as fiction or poetry, they are interesting to many children and are useful in a library or classroom program. The section of this chapter dealing with discussions will be helpful in guiding your use of informational material with elementary-grade children.

Poetry is one of the literary forms most often read aloud. It surely deserves to be. Poetry must be read to children who are not fluent enough readers to appreciate their own poetry reading. Poetry presents a visual barrier to many children reading it—a barrier that doesn't exist when the poetry is heard read aloud.

The question is often asked, "How can a person with little knowledge of poetry and less knowledge of oral interpretation learn to read poetry acceptably?" The answer is to read a poem aloud repeatedly until its tune and its meaning grow. Fortunately, the nonsense ditties of *Mother Goose*, Edward Lear, and Laura Richards, with their crisp or explosive consonants and brisk rhythms, practically force the reader into vigorous, precise speech and give one a sense of tempo and variety. A. A. Milne, too, writes his lines so that they compel a correct interpretation. The subtle lyrics of William Blake, Christina Rossetti, and Walter de la Mare, and the thought-provoking poetry of Robert Frost, however, require something more than vigor and swing. The works of these poets demand delicate, precise interpretation, and such interpretation must be grown into. So read a poem aloud to yourself first to get the general mood or feeling. Obviously, Blake's "Laughing Song" carries a gentle gaiety with it; listen to your own reading and see if you hear the suggestion (and only a suggestion) of laughter growing and finally coming to a climax in the last line. "Some One" by Walter de la Mare is mysterious and hushed—you can almost hear the speaker listening and whispering his speculations about the unseen knocker-at-the-door.

You make many discoveries when you read poetry aloud, because skilled poets write for the ear, and they employ melody and movement consciously for specific ends: (1) sometimes melody and movement are used to suggest the action described in the poem; (2) sometimes they help to establish the mood of the poem; or (3) they may furnish clues to its meaning. When you read a poem aloud, therefore, you catch elements you miss when you read it silently. The second time you try it orally you will interpret it even better because you understand it better.

Observing Response

Responses to the oral reading of a story or poem are usually spontaneous. Watch for the grin as you show an illustration that captures the humor of a *Homer Price* episode or the sober expressions as listeners enter into the boy's problems in Louisa Shotwell's *Roosevelt Grady*. Many of the responses are likely to reflect emotional involvement with the selection as it is being read. Frequently, however, at the end of a reading, children will spontaneously offer an evaluation, saying, "Oh, that was really good! Can we hear it again?" or "I can't wait until tomorrow to find out how that ends." Unfavorable evaluations occur just as often while a story is being read; watch for yawns or shuffling of papers or eyes too easily distracted by something else going on in the room. A request (or demand) at the end of the session that you read some other book tomorrow should be a clear message that a book is boring. You can follow with a question as to why the child disliked the book, in order to encourage a greater depth of response and to determine whether the evaluation was based entirely on an emotional response or whether it took into account a literary judgment. Occasionally a child will venture to compare a story just heard with another, as the girl who remarked that "Inviting Jason" from *Altogether One at a Time* sounded like something out of *About the B'nai Bagels*. She was interested when the librarian told her that they were both by the same author, Elaine Konigsburg.

A pause at the end of a story or poem can give children time to wonder about the selection and try to make some interpretations. Comments like "If Jim were nicer, he would probably get into the club" or "I think they'll find the little boy pretty soon because there have been some clues to where he is" indicate an attempt to interpret a story. A child who comments that he knows how the boy in the story feels because he lost his bike once, too, is making a sort of interpretation by showing empathy for a story character. He is also responding emotionally to the story. Another child may remark that she doesn't like a story character because he often hurts other children and makes them afraid to play outside. She further reflects that this would be a terrible place to live if there were many bullies like that. Value judgment shows up in her response. At the same time, the judgment might reflect interpretation of the theme of a story and an evaluation of a story character's behavior.

Reading aloud may generate many kinds of responses. They should be accepted and encouraged, extended by questions when the occasion is right. Above all, remember that a good book, well read, brings responses from children who could not enjoy and respond to the book on their own because their reading ability would not permit it.

Storytelling

The storyteller's concerns are much like those of the oral reader, with the most apparent difference being that the storyteller does not use a book in presenting material to children. If you want to be a storyteller who re-creates a story so that it captivates your listeners, you might keep these three ideas in mind:

1. Choose a story that you *like*. If you enjoy the story, you will be able to infuse it with your special insight.
2. Know the story well enough to be comfortable with it and to avoid worry about a lapse of memory.
3. When you tell a story, it is important to establish a relationship with the audience so that they will share the mood of the story with you.

A person with a head full of stories to tell never needs to carry books. When a class goes on a field trip, the bus is often late. A good storyteller can gather the class around and make the time pass quickly. Many a situation which can alarm children unnecessarily or require a restless waiting has been soothed with a story.

The successful storyteller learns how to capture the attention of the audience and hold it. You learn to observe those subtle signs of interest: staring eyes, still hands. You also learn the signs of flagging interest: wiggling, head-turning. By interpreting these signs correctly, the storyteller uses the tricks of the trade to revive interest, to retrieve the child who is on the verge of distraction. With the knowledge of your audience, you emphasize those elements of a story that you know will be relished.

Selecting a Story to Tell

The easiest stories to begin with are folk tales. They are easy because they were created orally by storytellers and have perfect form for narration. The form is invariable: a clear, brief introduction that launches the conflict or problem; the development or body of the story with a rising action, increasing suspense, and an exciting climax that marks the turning point in the story and the fortunes of the hero; and, finally, a satisfying conclusion that winds up everything—problems, conflicts, and villains all suitably disposed of. From the simplest cumulative "Pancake" type of story, through "Snow White" and "The Bremen Town-Musicians," to the more subtle "Clever Manka" for the oldest children, these folk tales tell themselves with ease and will help you fall into the storytelling habit and develop your own unique style.

Another good source of stories to tell are the myths. Many of the myths are long and may take two or three story periods to tell; for example, the stories of Perseus and of Theseus. Fortunately, these two tales have been well told by Ian Serraillier in *The Gorgon's Head* and *The Way of Danger*. Reading these books will show you why even the simplest myths demand more imagination in the telling and a more choice vocabulary than the folk tales.

Most stories written these days are for reading, not for telling, but here and there you will find little stories that are as perfect for telling as any folk tale. "Paddy's Three Pets" by Mary Phillips is a good example, also *Torten's Christmas Secret* by Maurice Dolbier, "Peter the Goldfish" by Julian Street, and *The Bears on Hemlock Mountain* by Alice Dalgliesh.

If you begin with your favorite folk tales and tell enough of them to get the feel and fun of storytelling in your very bones, then you will be better able to spot a likely candidate for your repertoire, whether it is old or new.

Learning and Telling a Story

Probably no two people learn and re-create stories in quite the same way, but visualizing characters and scenes often helps. In "The Pancake," you might see a snug kitchen with a mother standing close to the stove, her seven hungry children crowding much too near her to watch that fat, sizzling pancake. An old grandfather is sitting over in the corner smoking his pipe. Through the open door—it must be open because the pancake rolls through it—you might see a road winding over the hills and across the country and clear out of sight. You must see the characters, too, some in more detail than others, depending upon how dramatic their words or their roles are in the tale. Visualizing them undoubtedly helps in characterizing them; so if you see the sneering faces of Cinderella's sisters, undoubtedly something of the sneer gets into your interpretation of their words and behavior. Not that you do actually sneer, of course—that is stage business, not storytelling—but still a sneerful suggestion undoubtedly creeps in. And if you are telling a hero tale, something noble and serious comes into your voice, face, and manner.

Storytelling is an art that requires disciplines of many kinds, and one of these is the choice of words. As a storyteller, you cannot go far with a meager vocabulary; moreover, you must develop a sensitivity to language, so that you cannot possibly tell an Irish tale with the same vocabulary and cadence you use for a Norwegian story. Read the story aloud first until you get the feel and flavor of its special vocabulary and word patterns. While exact memorizing is usually the wrong approach to the folk tale, the other extreme is much worse—a slipshod telling, a careless use of words.

Such modern colloquialisms as "Boots got real mad," or "The princess looked really great," or "'OK,' said the lad," can ruin the mood and magic of a tale. Words must be chosen with a sensitive perception of the individual style of each tale. The dreamlike romance of "Sadko" calls for a very different choice of words from the rural dialogue of the old man and his good wife in "Gudbrand on the Hillside." Voice, diction, and vocabulary demand the training of your ear. Listen to yourself—to your voice, your speech, and above all, to the words appropriate for your story.

Obviously, if you are going to tell a story you must know it thoroughly. This involves overlearning to such a degree that you cannot possibly forget the tale, but can stand aside and play with the interpretation of the story because you have no worries about the mechanics of recall. Some people feel that memorizing is the only solution. Others consider memorizing the wrong approach to the folk tale for two reasons: First, these naive tales do not have the formal perfection of the literary story; they were always kept fluid and personal by the old tellers. If they are memorized, they are likely to sound stilted and impersonal. Ruth Sawyer, in *The Way of the Storyteller*, pays a tribute to the storytelling of her Irish nurse, who was proud of her art and used it with great dignity. She would close a story with the saying, "Take it, and may the next one who tells it, better it." This is exactly what happens.

A second reason that exact memorizing is

Viewpoints

Our aim, then, should be to refine and develop responses the children are already making—to fairy stories, folk songs, pop songs, television serials, their own game-rhymes, and so on. Development can best be described as an increasing sense of form. In literature, I have suggested this means principally a sense of the pattern of events, and this, however rudimentarily, children certainly feel in the stories that satisfy them. . . . Progress lies in perceiving gradually more complex patterns of events, in picking up clues more widely separated and more diverse in character, and in finding satisfaction in patterns of events less directly related to their expectations and, more particularly, their desires; . . .

But the forms of language itself—its words with their meanings and associations, its syntax, its sounds and rhythms, its images—these contribute to the total form, not as fringe benefits but as inseparable elements of a single effect.—James Britton. "Response to Literature" in *Response to Literature* edited by James R. Squire, National Council of Teachers of English, 1968, pp. 4–5.

not recommended is that forgetting a single phrase or a connecting sentence may throw you completely off, so that you have to stop or start over or pause awkwardly while you rack your brain for the lost word. This, of course, spoils a story. On the other hand, if the story is thoroughly learned but not memorized it will remain in your memory for years.

The beginnings and endings of your stories, particularly, should be polished until they are smooth and sure. The beginning requires special care because it establishes the mood of your tale. You may announce your story informally in any of a dozen ways: "Today we are going to hear about our old friends, 'The Three Billy-Goats Gruff.' " Or, "I've a new story for you today, and it's called 'The Fox and His Travels.' " Or, "You have all heard stories about 'Jack the Giant Killer,' but do you know there was a woman who got the best of a powerful giant? Our story is about her, and her name is 'Molly Whuppie.' "

Then, having announced your story, pause a moment—not too long, not long enough to let the children start squirming again, just long enough for a deep, quiet breath—and then begin.

Observing Response

A storyteller who has established rapport with the group and is able to maintain eye contact with the audience is in a unique position to notice the children's response to the story. The response in a listener's eyes or facial expression that indicates interest, enjoyment, or sadness is the kind of emotional response that is basic to other responses that may follow. That signal, subtle though it may be, indicates a grasp of the story and an ability to interact with characters, with the story line, or with a particular word choice which the listener finds appealing. In a sense, then, a good storyteller monitors the listener's reactions to a story by noticing physical responses and, primarily, facial expressions. You might ask yourself these questions when you have finished telling a story to a group of children:

1. Which children showed response during the story period?
2. What parts of the story evoked the most response?
3. How did the children show their reactions?
4. Did any child comment about the story at some time after the story hour? If so, did the comment indicate emotional response? interpretation of the story? attention to literary characteristics such as style?
5. Do the reactions give you ideas for future story choices for this group?

Book Discussions

Book discussions can range from a highly structured classroom situation to a simple exchange of opinions between a librarian and a child after a storytelling session has broken up. Discussions can serve many purposes. They give children opportunity to vent their feelings about a story or poem. The give-and-take of discussion may help children interpret the meaning of a selection. Under adult guidance, book discussions can give children insight into an author's purpose and a character's motives and can help them to make reasoned evaluations of the general quality of a book. Discussions can also open children's minds to the many life experiences they meet vicariously through books—the problems of the aged, poor, orphaned, or handicapped, or the way a story character forms values and changes behavior accordingly. Talking about incidents from a story can help children to develop empathy for people they might never know personally. Discussions can also point out ways that books help us to know ourselves better.

Book discussions can help you to gain insight into children's values and can permit you to observe children's responses. Sometimes putting problems in terms of book characters makes them easier for children to discuss.

Selecting Material for Discussion

Book discussions may be based on selections children have read or on stories they have listened to. A natural opportunity for discussion is following a storytelling or reading aloud session. Stories that are worthy of discussion have clearly developed themes of enough depth to raise questions that will encourage children to draw on their own experiences, interests, and concerns. Select material that allows children to discuss the humorous as well as the serious incidents in literature. Through the humor of Rosemary Wells's *Noisy Nora*, children see a view of life that makes it easier to accept misfortunes and disappointments. Humorous incidents as well as serious ones can lead children to examine their own values.

Fiction, poetry, nonfiction, picture books—all can be effective for stimulating discussion. Children's interests and reading and listening abilities should, of course, be taken into account when selecting material for discussion. The length of time available for the session, too, will influence your decision of how many aspects of a selection, or how complex a work, you will be able to explore. A third guideline should be your own knowledge of the literature you plan to use. In order to conduct a good discussion, you should have a thorough grasp of the themes and literary structure of the work, including an understanding of each character and of the techniques the author has used for character development. Your pre-assessment of a selection influences the depth and quality of a guided discussion because you draw on that assessment as you plan your sequence of questions.

Discussion of wordless picture books is a fine vehicle for encouraging young children to respond to illustrations and to develop a sense of plot structure at the same time. The best wordless picture books interest children enough to evoke emotional involvement with the story told through the pictures. They also have enough plot so that the action carries a child along from one page to the next. Perhaps most important, however, the pictures supply some details necessary to create a good story but they leave enough to the child's imagination to encourage inference about details of characterization and plot. Those inferences are the heart of response to wordless picture books. They can be encouraged by repeated experiences in telling the story from the pictures, especially in a one-to-one situation between an adult and a child. An adult guiding the retelling of a wordless picture book story can encourage inferences by asking questions such as: What do you think will happen next? Why is she doing that? Where do you think he is going? and others specific to the story.

Formulating Questions

As you prepare for a book discussion, you will need to keep in mind both the qualities of the selection and the abilities of the children. In order to make a pre-assessment of the material, you might ask yourself these questions:

1. What are the important ideas to be gained from the selection?
2. What aspects of the story will require exploration if children are to understand and interpret them?
3. Which story characters are children most likely to identify with?
4. Will they need help in understanding a character's motives?
5. Are there aspects of style or figurative language that should be discussed in order to aid in interpretation?
6. How can this selection be related to children's experiences, interests, and concerns?

Using these questions as stepping-stones, you can formulate specific questions that will guide children to interpret and evaluate literature, to note devices an author or poet has used, and, above all, to interact emotionally with the story.

Studies of teachers' questions during reading instruction have indicated that teachers rely too much on factual questions which have only one right answer. Such questions do not lead to a discussion of a work, they simply result in a sort of tennis game between adult and children. (What was the name of the dog? Where did the pirate bury the treasure? etc.) Aside from a few factual questions which may be necessary in order to produce information to serve as a basis for later discussion, most of your questions should ask children to infer, to interpret, to evaluate, and to identify with characters. Their answers of course may vary because each child comes to a literary experience with a different background.

Examples of some open-ended questions based on Maurice Sendak's *Where the Wild Things Are* follow, with types of possible responses shown in parentheses:

What did you like best about the wild things? (involvement, evaluation)
Why do you think Max went to the land where the wild things were? (interpretation, comprehension skill of cause and effect)
If you had been Max, what would you have done when the wild things crowned you king? (involvement, interpretation)
Were you satisfied with the story ending, or how would you have wanted it to end? (evaluation, recognizing plot structure)
Have you ever felt, as Max did, that you wanted to be where someone loved you best of all? When? (involvement, understanding a character, empathy)
How do the pictures show us Max's moods? (interpreting illustrations)

A discussion based on one chapter of Farley Mowat's *Owls in the Family* might be guided by questions such as:

In what ways are the owls, Wol and Weeps, different? (comparing characters and identifying characterization)
Why do you think the author made the two owls so different? (literary judgment, interpretation)
What questions would you like to ask Billy about his owls? (involvement, interpretation)
What was the funniest part of the story? (involvement, evaluation)
What is so funny about the scene where two owls try to learn to fly? (literary judgment, involvement)
How did Wol feel when he fell to the ground the first time he flew? Have you ever felt that way? How did *you* behave? (involvement, empathy)
Were the owls tame or wild? What information did you get from the story to back your answer? (interpretation, literary judgment regarding character traits)

Many other questions could, of course, also be used. A discussion should be fluid and kept personal in terms of the story and the group, following up on answers so that students can pursue a question to greater depth. As a follow-up to the last question above, you might want to ask: What can happen to a wild animal after it has been tamed? What is the author telling you in this story that might apply to any wild animal?

In general, then, discussion questions focus on characters, on favorite parts of the plot, on the relationship between episodes, on the author's message, and on evaluation of a selection. Some basic question types which can be adapted to many books are:

Which story character did you like best? Why? (evaluation, involvement)
If you had been a character in this story, how would you have acted if ____? (involvement, empathy, interpretation)
Do you think ____ did the right thing when he/she ____? (evaluation, valuing)
How else could ____ have handled the problem about the ____? What would you have done? (involvement, evaluation, valuing, interpretation)
What do you think this author is trying to tell us about the way people learn to have respect for themselves? (interpretation, literary understanding of theme)
What important idea (or theme) did you find throughout this story? (interpretation of main idea, literary understanding of theme)
What was the most interesting or exciting part of the story? (evaluation, involvement)
Did you learn anything from the story that will help you get along better with people and perhaps to understand yourself better? (valuing, empathy)
How is this story like ____ (another story they know)? (literary judgment, interpretation)
How did the author manage to make this so funny that you laughed out loud? What techniques did he/she use? (literary judgment of style, involvement)
What does ____ (figure of speech) mean in this poem? (literary knowledge, interpretation)

In general, the questions beginning with *why*, *what*, and *which* lead to a more open discussion than the sorts of questions beginning with *when* and *where*.

A questioning technique which can be very effective in helping children to become involved with a story character or situation requires that you preface a question by asking the child to take the point of view of a story character. As an example, you could say to a child: "You are Max. What were your thoughts when your mother sent you to bed without your dinner?" or "What did you think when you saw the land of the wild things?" By asking children to look at a story from the point of view of a story character, you can help them to interact with the story and so enhance involvement. This technique works not only to create involvement with human characters, but also with animal characters in some stories. In *Owls in the Family,* for instance, some children become so involved with the owls that they are easily able to respond to a question like: "You are Mutt [the family dog]. Why do you defend Weeps from other dogs even though you don't seem to like owls yourself?" Answers may show that children recognize that quality in a family dog that feels responsible to protect all who live under that roof and perhaps senses that the weaknesses of some family members require greater care. Using the character-point-of-view question as a beginning, you can help children to sense the author's point of view by asking questions such as: "How would the story be told if the author were telling it through Wol's eyes?" "Who is the author using as the storyteller here?" "Is it one of the story characters or is the author reporting everything that all characters experience and think?"

Pacing a Discussion

An adult guiding a book discussion has the responsibility of keeping it going by interjecting appropriate questions. The ability to know *when* to ask another question or to probe an answer more deeply is one of the keys to an effective discussion. Linked to that ability is the sense of how long and when to pause so that students can reflect on the question and synthesize their thoughts to formulate a good answer.

Some work has been reported in science education which relates to pace of questioning.[1] Essentially, the work has involved monitoring the amount of time between questions to see whether the length of time allowed influences the kinds of responses given. Findings suggest that a greater amount of "wait-time" leads to responses showing higher levels of thinking about the problem (above factual reporting, for example). These findings in turn have led to some work in training teachers to increase the amount of time they allow students before going on to another question or giving the answer themselves.

The increase in interpretation and other higher-level responses in science activities may be a guideline to adults who lead book discussions. A factual question, as "Who were the characters in this story?" may not require a very long wait for answers. It simply requires recalling information. A question that requires interpretation or evaluation, however, requires children to relate their own experiences to the story and, in the case of evaluation, to make judgments based on that synthesis. If you ask, "Do you think that Max acted wisely in the way he treated the wild things? Why or why not?" children will need a longer time. Questions of this sort require an interaction with the story to formulate an answer and will usually require some reflection. The same is true when you ask them to answer a question such as: "Why do you think the author let you know that the cat Wol killed had been a menace to the neighborhood?" Or, "Have you ever had wild animals in your neighborhood? How were they like Wol and Weeps?" When you ask questions such as these, you might try to pause at least three full seconds before probing with other questions to help children get at the important ideas. The combination of open-ended questions and enough time for reflective answers should encourage literary responses that show involvement with a story but also some attempt to interpret the story or to make judgments about it.

Organizing for Discussion

Many book discussions are adult-led because they follow the reading or telling of a story to

[1]Mary Budd Rowe, "Reflections on Wait-time; Some Methodological Questions," *Journal of Research in Science Teaching* 11 (1974): 263–279.

a group. The adult may be a parent, librarian, or a teacher. A large-group discussion requires a leader who is able to maintain a good pace, to encourage many children to participate, and to keep the discussion on the track. Obviously, the open-ended question, especially one which asks for a personal involvement with some aspect of the story or an interpretation based on personal experiences, can permit almost every child to respond if there is time. A leader must be able to accept all responses but to keep children focused on the question. Furthermore, the leader should try to maintain a neutral attitude in conducting discussions and not interject his or her own opinions. If children know that you censure the behavior of a certain story character, they are less likely to give you open, candid answers. On the other hand, you can build on their naive responses in some cases to lead them to a better understanding of a character's behavior and why certain kinds of behavior are not highly valued in our society.

An adult-led small-group discussion is often more enjoyable for children than a large-group discussion. They need to be at ease with the other participants and to feel free to ask as well as answer questions. Small-group discussions can follow oral reading or storytelling by an adult. They can also work well when the children have all read the same story on their own. In working with gifted children, a seminar version of the small-group discussion is effective. In this arrangement, each student either reads the same book or reads a book that represents a particular genre. For example, all may choose one book of modern fantasy. Your questions in the discussion guide the students to see how all of their books are similar in terms of fantasy. Have characters been manipulated so that they are talking animals, small people, superhuman beings? Is the setting on another planet, inside our earth, or in a mythical country? Has the time been manipulated so that the story takes place far in the future? Such a discussion can help children to note literary devices used by an author. It can also lead to evaluation of the books and to interpretation of events in the stories.

Another kind of small-group discussion is that in which one child acts as leader. Though a child must be relatively mature to keep a discussion going, the group's responses can be much freer than when an adult is in the group.

One method of establishing peer-led discussions is to have children sign up under one of several headings (humorous story, animal story, mystery, nonfiction, etc.), indicating the title of a book they are completing. A date is set for the discussion and a child is appointed leader for each group. Sometimes it is wise to give the child-leader some guidelines or suggested questions to use. Generally, though, the discussions center on how the books read were alike and how they were different, even though they belong to the same genre. Questions can point out the clues an author gives to the solution of a mystery, call attention to the use of pictorial material to support nonfiction, or draw out the relationship of the nonfiction information to the lives of children in the group. Questions can also call attention to information given about animals in books read by group members and ways in which an animal's behavior is like or different from other accounts they have read. Because student-leaders will not be adept at keeping a discussion going at a good pace, the amount of time alloted should be fairly short, probably not more than fifteen minutes.

Book discussions can occur in many situations, among them a one-to-one discussion of child-adult or child-child. In these informal discussions, the child can use an adult as a sounding board as was the case when a child asked, "Were you disappointed when Sam [Jean George's *My Side of the Mountain*] had people as visitors?" Children need time to sit quietly and chat with one another about books, too. When you overhear some of those conversations, notice the kinds of information discussed. (Needless to say, you do not intrude.) Some of the most persuasive "bookselling" goes on in those meetings and some good ideas about favorite passages are also exchanged. To facilitate discussions, you can set up a classroom or library corner where children and adults feel free to talk about books in their spare time. By providing the right atmosphere, you can inspire a natural response to literature and a love for many kinds of books.

Dramatic Activities

Dramatic activities provide marvelous opportunities for children to interact with literature. They are especially good for young children who are able to respond physically even though they may not be able to respond verbally with much ease. The activities we will discuss which work well as vehicles for literary response are role-playing, creative dramatics, story theater, oral interpretation (including Readers Theatre), and puppetry.

Role-playing

Role-playing is an educational strategy. It sets up a problem situation for children to come to grips with and allows them to "play through" the problem in order to discover alternate solutions and the results of those solutions. The emphases are on decision-making and its consequences, and the goal is to promote social values. In the process, personal values may be influenced rather significantly.

Experiences with literature can be enhanced by role-playing. When children are involved with a character and are confronted with that character's problem as they are in role-playing, the way is open to a satisfying literary response. By sharing the challenges and frustrations of a literary character, children may develop personal and social values and at the same time learn to appreciate an author's way of handling plot and characterization.

The material best suited to role-playing is the problem story, so-called because it develops a problem which students can become involved with and try to deal with. Some stories written especially for the role-playing situation are included in *Role-Playing for Social Values* by Fannie and George Shaftel. A well-written piece of realistic fiction can also provide thought-provoking problem situations. In choosing episodes from literature, be certain that the characters are well developed and the problem situation is clearly defined. Beyond these points, the plot should have a logical stopping place so that students can play out their endings. Books with episodic plot structure, with each chapter an almost self-contained story, work well because the length of the selection is easier to handle than a full-length book.

Viewpoints

Yet the primacy of pleasures as an end in reading is now quite widely accepted, and we have indeed gone further and asked some searching questions about the nature and sources of that pleasure. And because those sources properly lie in only two places—the written work before the reader and the mind of the reader himself—we have been led to concentrate upon that unique, immediate encounter between book and reader, largely and quite deliberately, neglecting such peripheral matters as the biography of the author, the circumstances under which the book was composed, its reputation, or—as I've already suggested—its "lesson." And in consequence we find ourselves driven to think, not primarily about authors and subject matters and "reading" generally, but about specific books and their readers—what goes on in books, what goes on in the people, young and old, who read them.—Edward W. Rosenheim, Jr. "Children's Reading and Adults' Values" in *Only Connect* edited by Sheila Egoff, G. T. Stubbs and L. F. Ashley. Oxford University Press (Canadian Branch), 1969, p. 18.

What kinds of problems provide good material for role-playing? First of all, they should be problems that students can identify with. That means well-stated universal fears, concerns, or temptations—difficulties common to people in all kinds of environments. If the setting and story characters are familiar to your students, the problem situation may also be easier for them to deal with. A second basis for judging material is whether the problem it raises will help students to develop a personal value system.

The problem stories included by the Shaftels involve situations dealing with integrity, responsibility for others, being fair, accepting others, and wishing you were bigger or better. Some books with sections that develop these problems are:

Responsibility for Others—*Don't Take Teddy* by Babbis Friis-Baastad

Being Fair—*A Bargain for Frances* by Russell Hoban

Accepting Others—*After the Goat Man* by

Betsy Byars, *Take Wing* and *From Anna* by Jean Little, "Inviting Jason" from *Altogether, One at a Time* by Elaine Konigsburg

Accepting Others, Surmounting Prejudice—*The Other Side of the Fence* by Molly Cone, *Berries Goodman* by Emily Neville, and *The Borrowed House* by Hilda van Stockum.

Wishing You Were Bigger or Better—*Wait for William* by Marjorie Flack, *The Ears of Louis* by Constance Greene.

The general procedure for conducting a role-playing session includes these nine steps recommended by the Shaftels:[2]

1. Warm-up (teacher introduction and reading of the problem story)
2. Selecting role players
3. Preparing the audience to observe
4. Setting the stage
5. The enactment
6. Discussion and evaluation
7. Further enactments
8. Further discussion
9. Generalizing

In Step 1, the adult encourages children to think about how the story might end. This alerts them and helps them to identify with literary characters. A typical question would be, "What do you think will happen now?" In Step 2, the adult can ask students to describe characters and then ask a student who seems to identify with a character to play that role. Step 3 requires that the audience members be prepared for their part. They may be asked to watch carefully to decide whether the solution is a realistic one. In Step 4 (setting the stage), the players decide what they are going to do but do not practice dialogue. The adult can help them get into the roles by encouraging them to describe the staging they are using. Step 5 focuses on the role-playing itself with each actor playing the part of the character he or she represents. Acting ability should not be criticized, since the focus is on the problem solution. Step 6 includes the follow-up discussion and evaluation. During that period the observers discuss their opinions of the character portrayals and of the consequences of their actions. Adults should encourage children to think in terms of consequences and alternative behaviors. In Steps 7, 8, and 9, the role-players try new interpretations based on ideas that came from the discussion in Step 6. The final step is important because it encourages students to make some assessment of the outcomes of each portrayal and to determine what they think is the best way to deal with the problem.

Although the approach to role-playing, as developed by Fannie Shaftel, uses an unfinished problem story which children must work with, this procedure can be adapted so that after reading an entire book, as a sort of post-reading or listening experience, children are asked to respond to a problem situation set up by the adult by playing the roles of story characters as they might deal with that problem. For example, this situation might be set up for Vera and Bill Cleaver's book *Where the Lilies Bloom:* You are Mary Call Luther and her family. You have been offered a lot of money to let a motion picture company film your home and tell the story of your lives. How are you going to handle this? What will you decide? In this technique, as with point-of-view questioning, broach the first question as "You are ______" to help children get into their roles and see the problem through their characters' eyes.

During steps 5–9 of the Shaftel strategy for conducting role-playing, children's responses should be obvious to the adult observer. Questions such as the following will help you to evaluate the kinds and degrees of responses made:

1. Do students seem able to interpret a character's feelings about the problem?
2. Do students show emotional involvement with characters and with the problems posed? Are they able to put themselves into a character role?
3. In discussion and enactment, do students show empathy for characters?
4. Does the question of values enter into the discussion, either explicitly or implicitly?

In role-playing, response is, of course, the key to success. And as in other activities, some

[2]From *Role-Playing for Social Values* by Fannie R. Shaftel. ©1967 by Prentice-Hall, Inc. Reprinted by permission.

responses show greater depth of interpretation than others. Certainly, a child who is able to speak convincingly in the role of a story character is making an attempt to interpret that character's approach to the problem. If a child is also able to assume some of the emotions of a character, so much the better. In many children, a strong interaction with a character shows in the content of what is spoken, in the tone of voice used, and in nonverbal signals such as facial expression and body movements.

As important as response to characters is, however, the crucial reaction in role-playing is a reasoned response to the problem situation. Children's responses often show them grappling with their own values in order to seek out a solution to the problem. Sometimes a response is complete enough to include reasons for the solution or to show the mental steps the child went through before arriving at the solution. Children who are able to carry out dialogue effectively while staying within the roles of their story characters can arrive at a problem solution through the conversation. This shows a high level of response in terms of interpretation, emotional involvement, and evaluation of a situation. Whether their problem solution achieves a high moral value should be looked at separately.

Creative Dramatics

While role-playing develops responses that show interpretation of a story problem and involvement with characters, creative dramatics develops responses that indicate a child's involvement with characterization and plot structure. In role-playing, you ask children to deal with a "what if" proposition, to extend a plot in order to create their own conclusions. In creative dramatics, you ask children to interpret a story which is structurally complete, using suitable voice and actions. The dramatization centers on interpreting character and plot to draw out the major themes. Dialogue is improvised but is true to the sense of characters and theme.

Children who participate in creative dramatics need certain technical skills, to be sure. They must be able to recall the sequence of episodes in the plot, to interpret an author's characterization so as to create real characters, to use vocal ability and body gestures to produce a dramatization that is believable. With guidance, children grow in ability to handle these literary and dramatic interpretation skills. They become skilled in interpreting a story, learning to infer missing details they need for their re-creation of a character, dialogue, or plot. Children also gain personally from experiences with creative dramatics. In addition to the value of the experience itself, they learn to work together and to express themselves unaffectedly and fluently as the dramatization provides an avenue for release of tension and for enjoyment of a story. Development of personal values and appreciation for good literature can also grow from participation in creative dramatization.

A well-written story, one interesting to the children, with some kind of conflict and a fair amount of action, provides good material for dramatization. Characters should be well enough developed so that children can distinguish different character types in the story. Good dialogue is important for children who are not very adept at improvising dialogue.

Some stories successful with primary-age children are: single chapters from Beverly Cleary's *Ramona the Pest, Ramona the Brave,* or *Henry Huggins;* Marjorie Flack's *Ask Mr. Bear;* Pat Hutchins's *Rosie's Walk* and *The Surprise Party;* and folk tales such as "The Three Billy-Goats Gruff," "The Three Little Pigs," or "The Pancake." The repetitious plot structure of folk tales makes them easy for young children to handle and the characters, though not highly developed, contrast well enough so that children can portray them effectively.

Material for older students might include: "The Bremen Town-Musicians" and other more complex folk tales like "Urashima Taro and the Princess of the Sea" and "The Tiger, the Brahman and the Jackal"; Dr. Seuss's *The King's Stilts;* episodes from Mark Twain's *Tom Sawyer* or Kenneth Grahame's *The Wind in the Willows,* or scenes from contemporary stories such as Jean George's *Julie of the Wolves* or Elaine Konigsburg's *From the Mixed-Up Files of Mrs. Basil E. Frankweiler.*

Some poetry is well suited to dramatization and can be especially good for use with young children who are not able to handle a more involved story. Poems must have action, of course, to work as creative dramatics material. Conflict is useful, too, but not essential. The poems should provide experiences children are familiar with and can participate in with understanding. Many poems create a mood that children are able to convey in the dramatizations, whether it be joy, fear, curiosity, or pensiveness.

A few poems that have worked well for creative dramatization are "Galoshes" by Rhoda Bacmeister and *Mother Goose* rhymes such as "Jack Be Nimble" or "The Grand Old Duke of York." Edward Lear's "The Owl and the Pussy-Cat" works well, as does his "You Are Old, Father William." In quite a different vein, a serious poem like "Swift Things Are Beautiful" by Elizabeth Coatsworth makes a challenging but effective dramatization. Add to the collection poems like "Trains" by James S. Tippett, "Fog" by Carl Sandburg, "Mud" by Polly Chase Boyden, and "Doorbells" by Rachel Field. Read these poems to see how their qualities are suited to dramatization. Then, as you find other appropriate poems, add them to your collection.

The adult who guides a creative dramatization has many things to keep in mind. The adult leader has the responsibility to set the mood for a dramatization and to plan warm-up activities that will prepare children to move freely and speak easily. A simple warm-up activity is pantomiming favorite animals while classmates try to guess what they are. A similar activity for older students involves pantomiming an awkward or embarrassing experience so that other members of the group can tell what it is. Once a mood for drama has been set, it is time to tell or read (preferably tell) the story or poem you have chosen. This presentation should be made vivid by your use of description and emphasis on important parts of the plot. Above all, the story line must be clear so that the plot is easy for children to grasp.

Following the telling of the story, help children to identify the scenes they will need to dramatize and write them on the board. This requires you to think through the story in advance in order to give help in working through the scenes. Taking one scene at a time, help the children break it down into a sequence of smaller actions, thinking of characters who will be needed and the action that is involved. At this point you may analyze each of the major scenes until all have been discussed, or you may begin by having students dramatize just the first scene before they analyze the others.

The first step of dramatization should include discussion of characters—how they look, how they act, even what they think. You may want to let all the students pantomime the characters before proceeding to the dramatization of the scene. At that point, children should be given a chance to volunteer for the parts they wish to play. Remember that in creative dramatics the cast and the audience both have a part to play. To prepare the cast, after characters have been discussed and progression of the plot has been reviewed, give them some time in a private place to rehearse and work out their dramatization. Encourage them to create dialogue they think is natural for those characters. Prepare the audience members so that they are ready to look for good things in the performance and also for some things that they think could be changed in order to create a better production.

The first playing of a scene should be carefully set up so that the area where the production will be given is cleared except for any necessary furniture. (Most costumes and props can be left to the viewer's imagination.) A signal should be given by the adult leader to show the students when to begin and bring to a close their dramatization, since it is sometimes necessary to limit the amount of time allowed or to stop so that some action can be discussed. You may simply hold up your hand, or you may prefer to dim the lights or use a soft bell so that you can be heard even though the players are not looking at you.

When children have played a scene (or sequence of scenes), engage the audience in discussion of the performance to help them evaluate the effectiveness of characterization and dialogue. Try to get them also to judge the faithfulness to the plot structure of the original story. Following the discussion, the scene may be replayed by the same group of children or by another group selected from the audience. This procedure of playing, discussing, and replaying continues until the entire

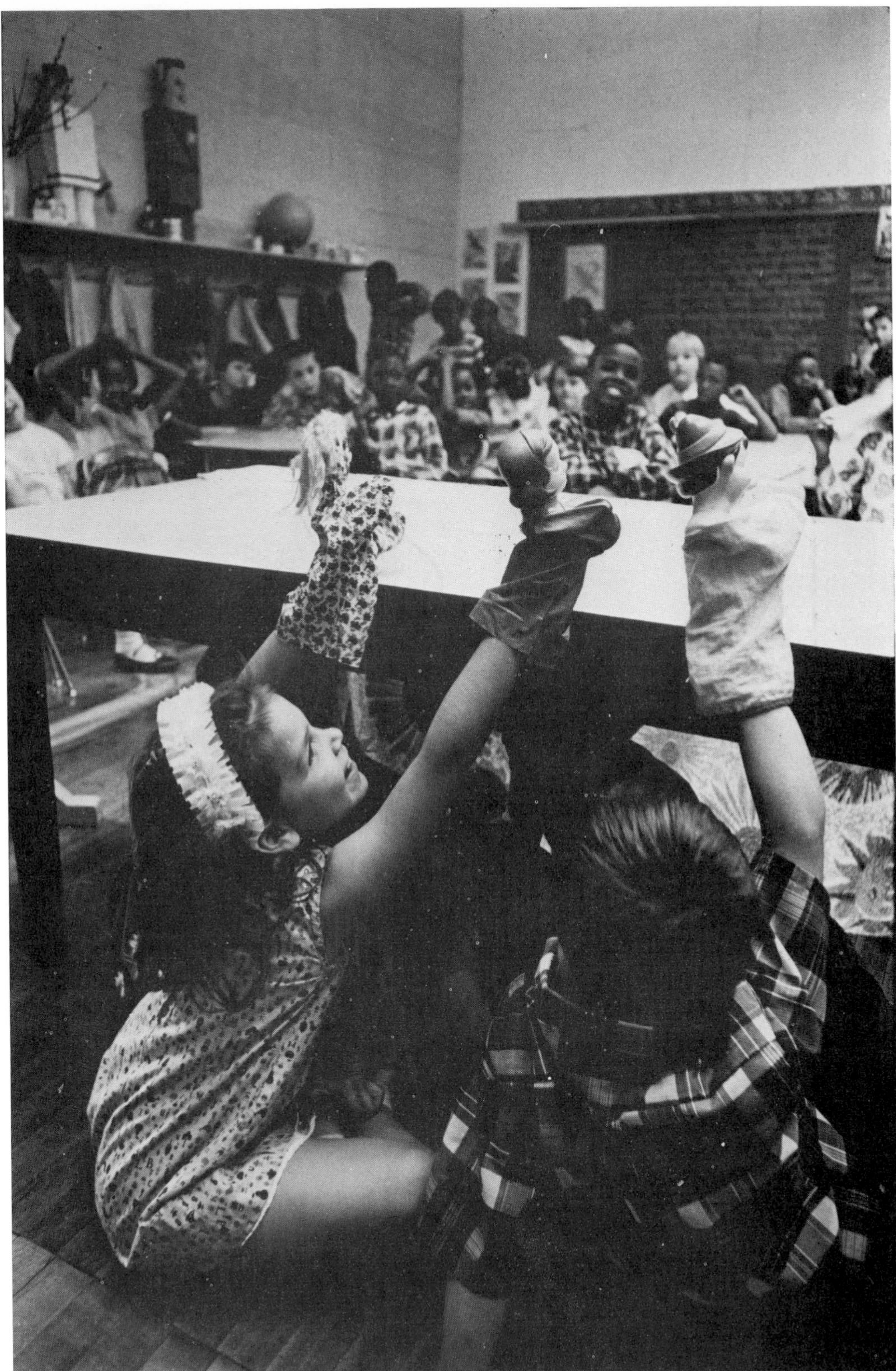

Hand puppets and a table used as a stage free children to use voices and gestures to interpret a story. Bruce Roberts/Rapho/Photo Researchers.

With ample space for moving and some adult guidance, these young children took the part of mice in a story theater dramatization. Photo by Steven Tryber.

This Readers Theatre production, staged at one end of a classroom, required only an open space and a few props. Stock, Boston/Donald C. Dietz.

The effectiveness of an informal atmosphere and good oral reading shows in the faces of these listeners. Paul Fusco/Magnum.

A story told with imagination and skill can create an image as vivid as an illustration. Paul Fusco/Magnum.

The comradery of reading and talking together about a good story is one of the rewards of a response-centered program. Photo by Suzanne Szasz.

story has been enacted. If students have done one scene at a time, they then put together the entire sequence in one performance with the audience watching to see how smoothly they can connect the scenes.

In summary, the steps in guiding a creative dramatics production are:

1. Choose a good story or poem.
2. Tell or read it to the children.
3. Involve them in identifying the characters and the scenes needed for the dramatization.
4. Carry out in-depth discussion of character traits and allow time for pantomiming of characters.
5. Let children decide who will play each character part.
6. Give the players a short time to analyze the first scene and to plan and practice their performances, creating their own dialogue.
7. Prepare the audience to critique the performance.
8. Have the scene played before the audience.
9. Guide audience discussion of the scene.
10. Allow for a replaying of the scene, either with the same cast or with a new group.
11. Work on each scene in the same way, then play through the entire story.
12. Guide audience discussion of the complete enactment.
13. Replay, if there is time.

Creative dramatics allows for many forms of response to a selection. Children are challenged to identify and interpret an author's development of characterization and plot. During the dramatization itself and also during the discussion that follows, notice responses related to recognition of literary characteristics of the story and interpretation of the work. Some children are able to talk of plot structure, for example, as the child who said it was important for the big billy goat to walk over the bridge, too, before he butted the troll to pieces because the story should show the same thing happening to all three of the goats. That recognition of plot structure is a literary response, as is the comment by an older child that Georgie's accident, in Robert Lawson's *Rabbit Hill*, is an important part of the plot because it adds to other parts of the story that show the ways people and animals affect each other. Children respond to characterization by pointing out words an author uses to describe a character, by conveying through facial expression something of the character's personality, or by using dialogue which shows a character's feelings. Such responses show a grasp of the literary qualities of a piece. Response to characterization can also emerge as an emotional response when a student shows vividly, through actions, an involvement with a character.

Interpretation of literary qualities adds greatly to effective dramatization. A child who realizes that the boy in Rebecca Caudill's *A Pocketful of Cricket* loves his cricket because he is a farm child and it is his special security in the strange school environment may slip in some dialogue expressing that idea. Another child who recognizes, in a story problem, something he or she has also struggled with may express the similarity of experiences through dialogue. Interpretation is shown by facial expression and bodily gesture as well, though these are more limited to interpretation of a character's feelings.

A spirited dramatization is usually evidence of emotional response to the story. So is a thoughtful discussion after the playing, a discussion that reveals interest of the audience in the story as well as in the quality of the dramatization. When the emotional response is added to an intelligent interpretation of the ideas in the story, a very good dramatization usually is given.

Story Theater

Story theater is a kind of dramatization in which a narrator reads or tells the story while the actors pantomime the action. In story theater, inanimate objects—a rock, for example—are represented by the player along with the animal or human characters who carry the story along.

Directing story theater is not difficult. The emphasis on pantomime rather than more formal acting with dialogue removes some of the demands and complexity of creative dramatics. The important steps in directing are these:

1. Read aloud or tell the story to be dramatized.
2. Help children to identify characters (animate and inanimate).
3. Guide the group pantomiming of each character part and make sure some child will be responsible for that part in the dramatization.
4. Review the story plot with the group so that children will be ready to participate.
5. Allow time for individuals to practice the actions they plan to use for their pantomimes.
6. Arrange the area where the dramatization will take place. As with creative dramatics, no props are needed. Instead, in story theater, children can portray inanimate objects referred to in the story.
7. Read or tell the story as the actors pantomime it. (Note: a child may also serve as a narrator, especially if the story is read.)

A description of the preparation for a story theater production of *Anansi the Spider,* illustrated by Gerald McDermott, will illustrate the steps outlined above. With the children sitting comfortably around her, the leader read the story of Anansi, showing McDermott's brilliantly colored illustrations as she went along. At the close of the reading, she asked students to think back through the story to identify the characters they would need if they were to dramatize it. She wrote the names of characters on the board as they were mentioned and again showed the illustration of the globe of light to remind the children that they might also need to include it as well as the forest in which it was seen. The character list complete, the leader called attention to one character at a time, asking children how they would pantomime that character and giving them a few minutes to try out the characterization. When all the characters had been discussed and dramatized, the leader asked for volunteers to take the character parts in the story theater production. She then reviewed the plot briefly with the group. They arranged themselves in the proper locations for the beginning of the story (some outside of the "stage" area, waiting for entrance) and the leader began reading the story, pacing it so that children had time to carry out their actions and to make entrances. When the story was over, several children expressed a desire to try it again because they weren't quite satisfied with their performances. After a short discussion of the problems they encountered, they practiced for a few minutes and the leader again read the entire story. What evaluation there is must be done by the actors, since everyone is a participant. (If you have a large group, expand the numbers and kinds of inanimate objects portrayed such as trees, doors, flowers, etc.) However, the focus is not on evaluation so much as on freedom to participate and a genuine enjoyment of the experience. That freedom is enhanced because there is no audience. The experience is really one of group cooperation toward a common goal.

When you select material for story theater, bear in mind that the best material for work with children is a folk tale or a myth with distinctive characters and a relatively uncomplicated plot. Since children will interpret the characters through pantomime only, the best selections will provide clear distinctions among characters that can be shown easily through large body movements. In *Anansi the Spider,* for example, the six sons have such names as Roadbuilder, River Drinker, Stone Thrower, Game Skinner, See Trouble, and Cushion. Children find it easy to devise movements that will indicate who the character is.

The cumulative plot commonly found in folk tales works well for story theater, especially with young children who need a fairly simple plot structure. Stories such as "The Three Billy-Goats Gruff" or "The Three Little Pigs" are fun for preschool and primary age children. In "The Three Little Pigs" the cast of characters can be augmented by allowing some children to play the roles of the pig's houses. A more elaborate folk-tale plot, such as "The Bremen Town-Musicians," is great fun for older children. In addition to the four animals, you can have as large a band of robbers as the staging area can accommodate.

As you read folk literature, try to pick out tales and myths that would lend themselves well to pantomime. Keep your own file of good story theater selections. Remember that children (even intermediate-grade children) enjoy playing animal roles as much as they do human roles. Don't overlook tales such as "Gudbrand on the Hill-side" where the husband sets off to sell his cow but trades it stupidly for a whole succession of animals and comes home with only a shilling. That story has enough animal roles and interesting human characters to make it a good choice. *Why Mosquitoes Buzz in People's Ears,* told by Verna Aardema and illustrated by Leo and Diane Dillon, is a fine choice for younger children.

Story theater material need not be limited to folk literature. Picture books such as *Drummer Hoff* by Ed and Barbara Emberley, *Rosie's Walk* by Pat Hutchins, or *Mr. Gumpy's Outing* by John Burningham are good sources for dramatization. So are poems like "Days That The Wind Takes Over" from Karla Kuskin's *Near the Window Tree,* "The Monkeys and the Crocodile" from Laura Richards's *Tirra Lirra,* and any number of *Mother Goose* rhymes like "Hey! diddle, diddle."

Material for use with older students should include some of the more complex folk tales and myths. Many of Aesop's fables are effective in story theater, among them "The Lion and the Mouse" or "Belling the Cat." Good folk tales are "Momotaro; Boy-of-the-Peach," "The Tiger, the Brahman and the Jackal," or "Anansi's Hat-shaking Dance." Myths and epics that make effective productions are "Atalanta's Race," "Cupid and Psyche," and "The Curse of Polyphemus." Selected episodes from *Robin Hood* also provide good material for pantomime as do episodes from *Pippi Longstocking, Homer Price* (especially the doughnut machine scene with students representing the machine), *The Pushcart War,* and other contemporary books. Once you begin to work with story theater, you will find many poems, tales, and episodes from full-length books which work well.

Response to literature is seen in story theater in creative character portrayal which shows appreciation for the story character in relation to the complete story. Response is also revealed through the smoothness with which a child fits a character interpretation into the ongoing dramatization. When this happens, a child has grasped the plot structure and, in some cases, shows an appreciation for the style of the story by attempting to suit the style and pace of the action to the style of the selection. A young child responding to the rhythm of "Ride a cock horse" by playing the character role in perfect rhythm with the *Mother Goose* rhyme, is acknowledging the style of a piece. As you observe children engaged in story theater, you will notice many other examples of emotional response, interpretation, and response to the literary qualities of a piece.

Oral Interpretation

Another response activity for children to try is to orally interpret a story. By oral interpretation we mean a degree of dramatization with the voice to re-create a story vividly for listeners and to give a sense of the kinds of people the story characters might be. Notice that we said "dramatization with the voice." Oral interpretation does not include physical acting out except for an occasional gesture. Oral interpretation techniques are, of course, necessary for any successful oral reading, and are frequently used by adults who read to children and by children who read aloud, either voluntarily or as part of a classroom assignment. People who read aloud effectively, whether adults or children, have mastered the art of using the voice expressively. Because children need guidance and practice in that skill, oral interpretation work should be part of every classroom literature and reading program.

Oral interpretation enriches the literary experience for reader and listener. At its best it grows out of interaction with a story and its characters. It is a re-creation of the original story, not a transformation of it as in creative drama, but a reading in which the reader interprets underlying themes, characters, and plot, and projects the combined image for listeners. The child who reads obviously must understand and appreciate the story. It is also important that the story characters take shape and become almost real for the reader. As to plot, the reader must recognize major scenes and transition passages so that the reading carries on at a pace that highlights important events and contrasts one character with another. Because oral interpretation does not demand the more physical interpretation involved in role-playing, creative drama, and story theater, children who are hesitant about performing may find it a more rewarding and less threatening response activity.

As with all the activities we have been discussing, the first and most important consideration in selecting material is that it should be interesting to the children who will read it. In many cases, that means it should be about experiences they have shared. A fast-paced mystery or action story is another good choice to interest readers and listeners.

In choosing stories for oral interpretation, look for selections that have a number of characters, preferably characters that differ in ages and/or personality so that the reader, or readers, will be challenged to use their voices expressively to differentiate one character from another. The quality of the dialogue is, therefore, of prime importance.

Material for use with younger readers might include Else Minarik's *A Kiss for Little Bear* or any of the other *Little Bear* books. They are easy reading books, yet are well written with dialogue that makes sense and is not stilted. The cumulative folk tales like "Henny Penny" or "The Gingerbread Boy" provide enough dialogue and repetition to keep young readers interested. Pat Hutchins's *The Surprise Party* works well, too. Another book which does not have dialogue but can work for oral interpretation is *Drummer Hoff* by Barbara and Ed Emberley. Stories that are superior in characterization and style of writing and that give children a chance to use their voices to interpret joy, anger, fear, a range of emotions, can be used for a good oral interpretation experience. A book that is weak in style or characterization will not work. You can easily get a sense of an author's style by reading aloud a page or two. A book written by a good stylist practically reads itself and you find yourself making the most of every nuance. Identify and keep a file of books you feel have these qualities.

It is easier to find oral interpretation material for children above third grade. Some authors seem to write dialogue more naturally than others. E. L. Konigsburg, Madeleine L'Engle, and Beverly Cleary are three authors who write character parts that children enjoy interpreting and dialogue that seems natural. *The Wind in the Willows* and *The Hobbit* have chapters which make excellent material for oral interpretation, too. As you find other authors you enjoy reading aloud, add their books to your list of recommended materials. Remember, though, that a book should be scanned for those passages which may be too difficult or less interesting for young readers.

Poetry is a rich source of material for practice of oral interpretation skills. The second stanza of "The Pied Piper of Hamelin" by Robert Browning is a good one to use; so are Carl Sandburg's "Buffalo Dusk" (*Smoke and Steel*), "Seal" by William Jay Smith (*Boy Blue's Book of Beasts*), and "Sliding" by Myra Cohn Livingston (*Whispers and Other Poems*).

We can slide
down
the
hill
or
down
the
stair
or
down
the
street
or anywhere.

Or down the roof
where the shingles broke,
Or down the trunk
of the back-yard oak.

Down
the
slide
or the ice
or the slippery street,

We can slide
on our sled
or our skates
or our feet.

Oh, it's lots of fun to go outside
And slide
and slide
and slide
and slide.[3]

[3]"Sliding" from *Whispers and Other Poems*. Copyright © 1958 by Myra Cohn Livingston. Reprinted by permission of McIntosh and Otis, Inc.

This poem, like some others that are good for oral interpretation, is written in a form that immediately gives a young reader some clues about how it should be read. The phrase "down the" is repeated several times and it suggests a feeling which can be conveyed by the voice, a long slur that moves across several pitches.

Another poem that is great fun to read aloud is David McCord's "The Pickety Fence." The form of this poem urges the reader to establish the rhythm of a fence by emphasizing each word that rhymes with "pickety."

The pickety fence
The pickety fence
Give it a lick it's
The pickety fence
Give it a lick it's
A clickety fence
Give it a lick it's
A lickety fence
Give it a lick
Give it a lick
Give it a lick
With a rickety stick
Pickety
Pickety
Pickety
Pick[4]

These poems not only read aloud exceptionally well, but they sharpen children's sensitivity to the use of language and the creation of mood.

When you guide students in preparation for the oral interpretation of a story or poem, you first need to encourage them to read the passage through carefully in order to note (1) the characters—who they are, what kinds of people they are, and how each might talk, (2) the plot—how it develops, what the climax is, and where it occurs, (3) high points of the plot which should be emphasized in the reading, and (4) specific words or phrases which should be emphasized. In reading poetry, this last point is the crucial one. Obviously such close analysis will require several close readings of the selection. You may want to encourage students to underline (mentally or with a soft pencil) the crucial words, to show where the voice would be raised or lowered, or to mark critical punctuation marks so that important pauses will be observed.

Once this kind of analysis has been completed, children should turn to the vocal interpretation of what is on the page. And this involves an interpretation of character roles which draws on the reader's ability to interact with the feelings and ideas of those characters. Vocal interpretation also involves manipulation of the voice to produce tone, inflection, and pauses that will create the desired effect and convey the emotional tone of the passage.

Two techniques are helpful as children move into the vocal interpretation. One is a short warm-up period to give a chance to try the limits of loud, soft, high, and low tones available vocally. A music session when children sing familiar songs works well when it creates a mood of relaxation and enjoyment. That, after all, is what you are after in your oral interpretation activity. The choral reading of a poem that allows for good vocal range also works well. You might try the pattern in which you read a story or poem and pause for the group to fill in special words or sounds. The words in this case should be written on the board or on cards so that you can simply point to the appropriate word. Furthermore, it is a good idea to let children practice each word first before the story is read. Several stories which are usable for young children are Roger Duvoisin's *Petunia* and Verna Aardema's *Why Mosquitoes Buzz in People's Ears*. For older students, you can use a choral reading of any poem.

A second technique which can aid in interpretation practice is taping several readings of the selection, playing back each reading so children can listen for weak spots and can try to improve those places on the next attempt. For children who need a great deal of help, have them use pencil to underline key words and punctuation marks and even to indicate vocal highs and lows. As they listen to the tape, the marked version can guide their analysis of the reading.

If the oral interpretation involves poetry, children should practice the oral reading until

[4]"The Pickety Fence" from *Every Time I Climb a Tree* by David McCord. Copyright 1925, 1929, 1949, 1950, 1952 by David McCord. Reprinted by permission of Little, Brown and Co., and Curtis Brown, Ltd.

the flow of words is appropriate to the rhythm pattern of the poem. When children work with free verse, they may need even more guidance in suiting the pace of reading to the mood of the poem. When they have had time to perfect the reading of poem or story, the finished performance should be taped or presented to an audience.

Readers Theatre. In addition to oral interpretation in which a single reader reads to a group, the form known as Readers Theatre has become popular as a means of staging oral interpretation presentations. Readers Theatre requires not one reader, but a narrator and as many readers as are needed to cover all the character parts. This more formal technique is especially effective for children who are secure enough readers that they can direct their attention to the interpretation of character parts, following the written story only as a sort of script.

When you look for Readers Theatre material, look for good characterization and a style that reads aloud comfortably. You can judge the effectiveness of the style by reading a section aloud and listening for a natural flow of language. Selections for Readers Theatre should have enough characters to make the reading interesting but probably not more than five or six for a smooth production. The narrator provides the description that cannot be handled through dialogue and serves as a bridge between dialogue sections so that the plot moves along clearly. If the narrator's part includes lengthy discussions or descriptions and if the selection is otherwise effective, you might want to consider cutting the length of such passages. Some books that provide good excerpts for Readers Theatre are Robert O'Brien's *Mrs. Frisby and the Rats of NIMH*, Elaine Konigsburg's *From the Mixed-Up Files of Mrs. Basil E. Frankweiler* and *About the B'nai Bagels*, and Else Minarik's *A Kiss for Little Bear*. Although this last book may be read completely, short sections of the other books may be selected on the basis of the criteria we have been discussing.

Guiding Readers Theatre requires a somewhat more elaborate sequence of steps than other forms of interpretation. First, the children who are going to interpret the story must choose the character parts they will play. Generally, the narrator should be a strong reader. In fact, when Readers Theatre is adapted for use with young children, an adult can read the narrator's part, cuing the children if they have trouble following the format.

When character parts have been decided on, Readers Theatre practice proceeds in much the same way as oral interpretation. The readers should be encouraged to become familiar with the whole selection so that they identify the themes to be emphasized and are aware of unique qualities of the author's style. Each reader turns next to an in-depth analysis of his/her part, getting to know the character (in the case of the narrator, getting acquainted with all characters) and trying to decide how that character looks, acts, and talks. Allow time for the children to practice their parts, providing a tape recorder for them to use, if possible. And remind them not to read the "he said's" and "she said's." The production will sound smoother without them.

When individual parts have been rehearsed, it is time to put the production together. This involves, at first, rather informal practice sessions with the readers standing or sitting facing the narrator. Enough time

Viewpoints

There are those who regard children only as potential adult readers and think it does not matter greatly what they read as children. We do indeed hope that children will continue to read after they become adults, yet would anyone doubt that a child who, for instance, has read *Treasure Island,* has had an immediate experience which lights a child's world where he is? The impact of even one good book on a child's mind is surely an end in itself, a valid experience which helps him to form standards of judgment and taste at the time when his mind is most sensitive to impressions of every kind. The reading in childhood of *Treasure Island,* or any good book, may well be a prelude to further reading carried into adult life. The strong and lasting impression of such a prelude will bring to adult reading some recognition of vitality and permanence. – Lillian H. Smith, *The Unreluctant Years,* The American Library Association, Chicago, 1953, pp. 16–17.

should be allowed for these rehearsals so that students are able to read expressively and coordinate the reading with other parts. The help of an adult at this point can be valuable. If you notice that a reader is having trouble coming in at the right time, help the child to circle the key words that the previous reader will say and to listen for cues.

The final step is to stage the production. Because no props or costumes are used, this is really quite simple. You should try to find enough folders alike so that the readers can use them to hold their copies of the story. If high stools are available, they can be used also. If not, readers may sit on low chairs and rise to read or they can remain standing throughout the reading. Whichever arrangement is used, it is effective to have the readers of character roles facing the narrator and placed in a semi-circle so that they can see one another. In that way, both audience and readers have a feeling of interaction among the characters and a recognition that the narrator is keeping the thread of the plot running smoothly.

The Readers Theatre production is now ready for an audience. Younger children often enjoy watching and listening to this kind of presentation. If the readers have done a good job preparing, they can serve as good models to the younger children, too. An alternative to presentation before an audience is to prepare a videotape or a regular tape recording. If this is done, you can add background music or other sound effects which enhance the performance. A videotape is especially interesting to children later on, as they can notice how well they complemented the vocal interpretation with facial gestures and other bodily motions, limited though they are by staying in one place and holding a script.

The readers' responses to the story are most evident in tone of voice and facial expressions used to convey character interpretation. A lively interpretation or one which is especially moving indicates a high degree of emotional response by the reader. A reader who is able to show a character's feelings clearly has also been successful in interpreting the motives of the character and has probably recognized some fine points of the author's talent for characterization. The reader may also have sensed the author's purpose in including that character in the story. A narrator who successfully keeps the production moving shows awareness of the progression of incidents in the plot, of the importance of each incident, and, often, recognition of the relationships among story characters. Though Readers Theatre is not a discussion technique or a form that utilizes dramatization, it does, nevertheless, give opportunity for in-depth response to literature.

As sometimes happens, a reader may fail to interpret a role effectively or a narrator may show, by halting voice and stilted presentation, that he or she does not sense where the plot is going. You can seize those opportunities to engage the readers in interpretation of the story by such questions as: How does Jamie feel toward Claudia? How would he show it? What will happen as a result of the conversation? Working from questions that guide the readers in understanding the story more clearly, you can move to questions that require them to re-think their interpretations of character and narrator parts, questions such as: What tone of voice would Jamie use to show that he is a little afraid of Claudia even though he does admire her? How can the narrator effectively lead up to the next happening in the story by changing his or her reading? How can you show, by your voice and face, what Claudia is thinking? By working from story interpretation to character interpretation, you may help the readers to an increased emotional response to the characters and to the story itself.

Choral speaking. If your class is responsive to poetry, you may want to introduce them to choral speaking to give an added dimension to their enjoyment. Choral speaking is another oral interpretation activity which gives children opportunity to enjoy and experiment with the sound of literature. Although some prose, especially folk literature, adapts well to choral speaking, poetry is the easiest form to use and usually the most effective, since a poet is generally concerned with the effects of sound. The rhyme and meter of poetry appeal to children, and rhymes that are pleasant to hear can also be fun to say. The pleasure of interpreting a favorite poem orally is one of the rewards of choral speaking. Another is the sense of group participation toward an artistic effect. When children are accustomed to hearing poetry, when they have discovered how much like music it is in its variety of rhythms, moods, and melodies, and when they like it well enough to explore further, you may tell them something about choral speaking or speaking choirs.

Effective choral speaking requires the same attention to key words and pauses as effective oral interpretation of any kind. Children should probably hear a poem several times in order to sense the mood they will want to convey, whether rollicking, funny, sad, mysterious, or wondering. The next step is to help them identify key words in a line that should be emphasized. That helps to develop a natural flow to the speaking, one that clarifies the sense, and can help to eliminate some of the sing-song quality that often goes with poetry reading. In that regard, you may want to call attention to the punctuation marks which are signals to pause—periods, commas, and dashes. Attention to them can help to keep a group together as well as to increase the effectiveness of the presentation.

Mood is important in choral speaking and can be enhanced by building contrast between parts of the selection. Grouping voices for effect is a good technique. A mysterious or scary part can be taken by a group of children with lower voices. By contrast, children with high voices can be grouped to speak lines that have a lilt and a happy swing. Another way of achieving contrast in sound is to have the whole group speak most of the lines and assign lines requiring special effects to a single voice.

Choral speaking is much like singing. Careful breath control and attention to rhythm are important. Sometimes, with formal verse choirs, one person acts as a director, using hand movements similar to those used with a singing chorus, but this is rare. For most informal situations, you need not direct the children but just get them started together, letting the rhythm of the piece carry them through.

Familiar lines and phrases in poetry and prose can be a good introduction to choral speaking. If you are reading aloud a folk tale such as "The Three Billy-Goats Gruff," encourage children to join you in "Trip, trap! Trip, trap! Trip, trap! went the bridge," increasing in volume when the middle-sized goat crosses and becoming very loud for the big billy goat's crossing.

For older children, "Overheard on a Saltmarsh" by Harold Monro is a good introduction to choral speaking through unison speaking of lines. This poem is essentially a dialogue between a goblin and a nymph. After several unison readings, you might want to read the goblin part (marked with a *G*) and let the whole group of children read the nymph part (*N*). Later, you can divide the children into two groups so that one group takes each part. This same procedure can be useful in introducing other poems, too.

Overheard on a Saltmarsh[5]

(G) *Nymph, nymph, what are your beads?*
(N) *Green glass, goblin. Why do you stare at them?*
(G) *Give them me.*
(N) *No.*
(G) *Give them me. Give them me.*
(N) *No.*
(G) *Then I will howl all night in the reeds,*
Lie in the mud and howl for them.
(N) *Goblin, why do you love them so?*
(G) *They are better than stars or water,*
Better than voices of winds that sing,
Better than any man's fair daughter,
Your green glass beads on a silver ring.
(N) *Hush, I stole them out of the moon.*
(G) *Give me your beads, I desire them.*
(N) *No.*
(G) *I will howl in a deep lagoon*
For your green glass beads, I love them so.
Give them me. Give them.
(N) *No.*

A good file of choral speaking poetry and prose is useful. Anthologies of children's literature such as *The Arbuthnot Anthology*[6] contain many poems and folk tales suitable for choral speaking. Try to find at least ten poems you would like to use plus several folk tales or other short prose pieces. Keep them in a loose-leaf notebook or in a card file so that you can add new selections as you find them.

[5]"Overheard on a Saltmarsh" by Harold Monro from *Children of Love* (London: The Poetry Bookshop, 1913). Reprinted by permission of Lynn McGregor.
[6]See *The Arbuthnot Anthology*, Parts One and Two.

Puppetry

Puppetry allows children to plan a dramatization, create dialogue, and work for effective use of the voice. In those respects it is similar to creative dramatics. However, since the puppeteer is not in view of the audience, the voice becomes extremely important as the means of creating a story interpretation. Like Readers Theatre, puppetry can be a more easily accepted activity for children who do not feel comfortable physically performing before an audience. Creating a puppet that will suit the character part unites puppetry with art in much the same way that drama relies on the artistic sense of set and costume designers. In puppetry, as in other forms of drama, the goal is to produce a unified visual and auditory effect that will effectively show the plot and the characters but, above all, will capture the spirit of the story. If the mood of the story is humorous, the puppet production should reflect that accurately. That is why so much literary response is involved in the planning of any successful dramatic presentation.

Action is an important ingredient in a good story for puppetry. Conflict is also a desired, though not necessary, attribute. The number of characters is limited by the size of a puppet stage (not more than five or six characters, as a rule) and those characters should contrast enough to make the production interesting. Subtle character differences will be lost. The popular Punch and Judy shows are good examples of the effectiveness of action, conflict, and strong characterization.

In creative dramatics and other theater productions, the actors are able to create three-dimensional characters with a range of emotions. The use of puppets tends to make the characters flat, often limiting them to such strong emotions as anger, fear, or joy but rarely showing much depth of feeling. Again, subtle emotions will be lost. For that reason, folk tales with their relatively flat characters are a good choice for puppet presentation.

Although puppet shows can involve a fairly elaborate plot, including several acts and scenes, beginners should choose stories with simple plots. The repetitive plot structure of many folk tales is another good reason for selecting them. If you produce "The Three Billy-Goats Gruff," for example, you have action consisting of three similar conflicts between the goats and the troll. The progression is easy to follow because of the order in which the goats enter the story—small to large—and the ending is easy to remember. The plot structure and the small number of characters make it a good choice.

Bear in mind the kind of setting you might need for a story and think about ways that the characters could be made into puppets. In "The Three Billy-Goats Gruff" the only necessary additions to a bare puppet stage would be the bridge and a hill with green grass. The characters can easily be constructed as paper bag puppets, or hand puppets with papier-mâché heads. They can be made distinctive because of the contrasting sizes of the three goats and because the troll is evil and menacing in contrast to the goats. Remember that the puppet production will highlight the plot and the contrast between characters.

"Gudbrand on the Hill-side" is suitable for puppetry because it has a repetitive plot and the cast of characters can be whittled down to eleven by having only the animals and their owners appear on stage. "The Pancake" works well because of its repetitive language and cast of nine characters. Children's voices offstage can be used for several parts. "The Bremen Town-Musicians" can be easily adapted for puppetry by using an open box at one end of the stage for the robber's house. Some other tales which can be adapted for puppetry are "Tom Tit Tot," "Snow White," "Henny Penny," "The Three Little Pigs," and "The Three Bears."

A puppet production can take several forms, depending upon the kind of puppets used and whether a script is read or the dialogue is created by the puppeteers. Those decisions are made on the basis of the story you choose and the age level of children who will participate. Marionettes (puppets moved by strings from overhead) require a good deal of skill to handle but finger puppets, hand puppets, stick puppets, paper bag puppets, balloon puppets, and adaptations of these are easy for preschool and elementary school children to make and handle. With these options in mind, you can easily help children find or create puppets to go with a story.

When you have chosen a story for the production—and you may wish to do this on your own or with the help of the children—read it to the group, asking them to listen first for the characters they will need to represent by puppets. At the close of the reading, involve the children in a discussion so that they identify the characters and talk about the personality of each, whether that character's actions are predictably good or bad, whether the character is happy, sad, angry, funny, and so forth.

When the characters have been listed and discussed, children are ready to begin planning the puppets they will want to use. At this point, you may want to have several different types of puppets to show if you want the children to help with the decision of what kind to make. In preparation, you should think through the story to determine the most suitable kind of puppet for the characters, also keeping in mind the amount of time available to produce the puppets and the abilities of the children.

Although we will not give specific instructions here for making puppets, a description of some means for preparing them may be helpful. Hand puppets may be purchased. They may be made from old stockings with eyes, ears, noses, and mouths made of felt or some other material. Papier-mâché heads can also be fitted with mittens or stockings for use as hand puppets. Finger puppets can be made from toilet-paper rolls or from mittens, in which case each finger can represent a different character. Stick puppets usually have heads made of papier-mâché set onto a dowel rod. A dress or clothing of some sort can be attached to the head, covering the stick and allowing the puppeteer to simulate arm movements of the puppet. Paper bag puppets, among the simplest to make, require only decoration with eyes, ears, hair, etc. The balloon puppets are decorated with cut paper features and arms and limbs. They can be manipulated by a length of small dowel rod attached to the balloon opening.

When children design the facial features of the puppets, they should keep in mind the most important personality traits of the characters. If a puppet must appear happy as well as sad in the show, what kind of features will be best? The change of mood can be made by manipulating the face of a stocking puppet. Can it also be shown by the way the puppet moves on the stage? How should the villain of a play look? the hero? How can a puppet's looks show kindness or helplessness? Such problems must be dealt with by puppeteers, and children will learn about character traits as they work with puppets. Encourage them to refer to the story from time to time to refresh memories about the characters.

When the puppets have been produced, guide the children in a review of the story in preparation for the show. The review should focus on identification of key episodes (later translated to scenes) which can be portrayed by the puppets and sections of the story which can be told by the narrator. You might want to help children make a simple chart showing a breakdown of the story line as this example for "The Three Billy-Goats Gruff" shows:

Narrator
Scene 1: Smallest goat walks over bridge
Narrator
Scene 2: Middle-sized goat walks over bridge
Narrator
Scene 3: Biggest goat walks over bridge and fights with troll
Narrator

When the simple outline has been made, the puppeteers may rehearse their dialogue for each of the scenes. When dialogue is created by the children, only one child is needed to operate the puppet and supply the voice. If you have students read dialogue from a story, they will probably have to work in pairs, one child reading and the other operating the puppet.

The puppet show should be rehearsed so that children learn to use a puppet stage to the best effect, especially to show the conflicts between characters clearly. If a puppet stage is not available, a table may be used as a stage by turning it on its side or by leaving it upright and covering it with a sheet, the children crouching out of sight behind it. Children should have opportunities to present their puppet shows to audiences so that they see the effect the characters and voices have on spectators. A videotape of the performance can also let them see the results of their work.

Response to the puppet show should reveal enjoyment as well as some understanding of the literary components of the story. Children who are eager to give their show to another class or to watch a show again reveal emotional involvement. A young child who comments that he likes the witch because she looks as scary as she sounds is responding to the quality of the characterization. Children often respond to plot by working hard to get just the right build-up of suspense or by highlighting an ending.

Written Response

If writing about literature is to be truly response, the students should be good enough writers that the act of writing does not interfere with expression of their feelings and ideas about a selection. The writing assignment should be structured for less mature writers so that they are not required to produce lengthy reports or essays about books. Whatever the format used, you should keep in mind the purpose of written response—to encourage children to think about the meaning of a story or poem and to react to its value.

Writing activities can develop awareness of the literary characteristics of prose and poetry. Sometimes a written response will carry a child beyond a response to that single book and inspire a creative effort to write an original story or poem. Through written response, children can experiment with form and style, trying to develop their own stories or poems based on plot structure or poetic form they have enjoyed. They may respond to point of view and characterization by trying to rewrite a story or episode as it might have been seen through the eyes of one of the characters. They can become more aware of the interaction of characters by trying to write a script for a favorite story.

For some children, the written response may be the fullest expression of their responses to literature. These may be children who are somewhat shy about entering into a discussion or into dramatic activities. They most certainly are children who have well-developed writing skills. They may also be children who delight in mulling over a selection, thinking it through and pondering its meaning. That takes time and, for some children, it also takes solitude.

Keeping a diary record of books read, including a reaction to each book, is one kind of written assignment that older children can handle. The writing need not be lengthy, but children should be encouraged to record every book they begin even though the reaction may be, "I didn't finish it because it wasn't interesting." You may also want to encourage them to comment about ideas they gained from the book. Children may evaluate the books according to whether they are good enough to recommend to other students. If you sit down with a child after the diary has been kept for a period of time you both will find it interesting to identify favorite types of books and to look at the kinds of reactions to each book. If a diary has been kept for an entire year, children will find changes in their reading interests over that period of time, moving perhaps from an exclusive interest in animal stories to some interest in fantasy, and you will often find an increase in ability to show several different kinds of responses, including interpretation, evaluation, or literary judgment as well as emotional involvement.

Keeping a diary may lead students to illustrate a story in order to express their response to it. Children who are not adept at writing can illustrate key episodes and write a caption of one or two sentences for each. To do this the reader must determine which episodes are important and which can also be illustrated. The written caption should describe what is happening in the picture and should tell how it relates to the rest of the story. The exercise calls for close attention to character description and ability to interpret the descriptions artistically. The illustrations may be kept by a child as a sort of diary of books read or they may be used as part of a bulletin board display about books.

The traditional written book report is generally not the best way to encourage response to a story. It usually becomes an exercise to be read only by the teacher, especially when the writing process is a burden to the child who is required to write the report. A slight change in approach can make these reports useful to other students and give some purpose to the project. A card file of book reviews written by the children can be set up and can become an important part of the reference section of a classroom or library. A recommended format for the cards includes title and author, a short plot summary, and some comments indicating what the student felt was good or not good about the book. This written work should encourage an evaluation response and often some reaction to literary qualities as well.

Another variation on the traditional book review is the point-of-view book report. To introduce this format, you might ask a child who has just finished a book to name his or her favorite character from the story. Follow by saying, "You are _____ *(name of story character)*. Tell the story the way you saw it." Once children become accustomed to the idea, you can simply instruct them to choose one story character and retell the story as they think that character would tell it. This approach leads to many opportunities for identifying with story characters, to emotional involvement with the story, and to interpretation of events.

Reports are not the only kinds of useful written responses to books. Creating a script from a favorite book can allow children a good deal of creative interpretation. The script can be designed for a puppet show or for a dramatization of the story. This activity requires that the child select an episode and decide which ideas can be conveyed by means of the dialogue already in the story and what information will have to be supplied by a narrator. Some of the narration can be drawn from the story, but the child will have to write an introduction to the episode, to be read by the narrator. The finished script can be played through before an audience. Seeing his or her script produced, however simply, should encourage the writer.

Creative writing often is inspired by books and poems children read. They may experiment with the plot structures and poetic forms they have enjoyed in their recreational reading. Many stories for young children—Pat Hutchins's *Rosie's Walk* and John Burningham's *Mr. Gumpy's Outing*, for example—follow a simple plot in which the principal character sets out on a journey and returns home at the end of the story. Stories with that structure can be shown on a flannelboard or chalkboard as circle stories, with the beginning and ending scenes at the top of the circle and the others proceeding around clockwise. After reading or hearing several such stories, children can make their own circle stories, drawing the illustrations, placing them on a large piece of chart paper, and writing a caption or short sentence under each picture so that the story can be told by words or by pictures.

A more complex writing activity but a very enjoyable one for many children is the photo essay. As a follow-up to reading an informational book about animals, for example, a child may decide to make a photo essay about how wild animals in the neighborhood spend the winter. If a camera is available, the child might take pictures of the wildlife, developing them and selecting certain ones to use for the essay. If photography is impossible, pictures from magazines and newspapers can be used. The pictures are arranged in the order needed to tell the story and an account is written, telling about the struggles of the animals and birds. The final step is to arrange the pictures and the text artistically on each page so that they complement one another. This may be done on large sheets of construction paper or on half sheets.

When children enjoy reading so much that they want to write their own stories or poems, they are showing a special kind of response. Creative writing is often a much greater effort than children think it will be, but the reward of having someone else read their stories is usually worth the work involved. Children usually need some guidance in thinking through these questions:

1. Who will your characters be and how will you describe each one?
2. Where and when will the story take place?
3. What kind of conflict (or problem) do you plan for the characters?
4. How will the plot lead up to the climax?
5. How will the conflict be solved and the story end?

You might want to ask the children to think

about how these questions were treated in a book they recently read. Encourage them to proceed from there to devise their own characterizations and plot. The finished draft may be read by younger children or placed on a "writing corner" table to be read by others in the classroom or library.

The activities described in this chapter are suggested as ways of providing active participation in literature for those children who respond well to an activity-centered literature program. The ideas should also provide means of tempting and drawing out the child who is less enthusiastic about books and reading. Regardless of the approach you use, be ever alert to the hint of a response, whether it is a look of pleasure or concern over a book, poem, or passage; awareness of literary structure, style, or characterization; or interpretation of some aspect of a selection or judgment of the merit of a piece. By fostering that early response, you may lead a child to a depth of response that can produce an avid and sensitive reader.

Recommended Activities

1. Select a story or poem that you enjoy. Practice reading it aloud, taping your reading, if possible. Play the tape back to see how well you have done with the use of pauses and vocal flexibility to make the reading interesting. You may want to practice and retape it before reading it to a group of children.

2. Write the titles of two or three of the best children's books you know. Think carefully about each book and decide which strategy or strategies discussed in this chapter you might use to encourage response to them.

3. Using suggestions from this chapter, find a book that would be suitable for dramatization. Read the book carefully and identify an episode that children could dramatize. Outline the scenes that might be practiced and list character parts that would be needed. If possible, plan a creative dramatics session based on the outline given in this chapter and try it with a group of children.

4. Read a number of collections of poetry recommended in Chapter 9, and select a poem that you would like to read and discuss with the children. Using oral interpretation techniques to guide you as you practice, read the poem aloud. Reread the section on discussion in this chapter and plan a good sequence of questions to guide the discussion. Try to plan so that you give children a chance to respond emotionally and to show ability to deal with interpretation, evaluation, or the literary characteristics of the poem.

5. As you read books suggested in Chapter 10, "Modern Fiction," try to identify episodes which could be adapted for Readers Theatre presentation. Keep a file of those selections, indicating the pages you would use and the names of characters that would be needed.

6. From the folk-tale collections mentioned in Chapter 6, select several tales that would be good for story theater dramatizations. Read each one carefully to list all characters that would be necessary. Plan a brief warm-up and outline the scheme you would use to assign character parts and provide practice in pantomiming the parts. Try to use your plan with a group of children.

7. Read one of the articles or books in the bibliography for this chapter. Using an idea from that reading, plan a lesson to involve children with literature.

Adult References

ARTLEY, A. STERL. "Oral Reading as a Communication Process." *The Reading Teacher,* 26 (October 1972), pp. 46–51. Identifies classroom situations for oral interpretation and includes a description of teacher-guided interpretation.

BAMMAN, HENRY A., MILDRED A. DAWSON, and ROBERT J. WHITEHEAD. *Oral Interpretation of Children's Literature,* 2nd ed. Brown, 1971. Includes recommended selections as well as guidelines for improving oral reading and oral interpretation.

BRIDGE, ETHEL B. "Hickory Dickory Dock; Prelude to Choral Speaking." *Elementary English,* 49 (December 1972), pp. 1169–70. Develops ideas for choral reading sessions.

CARLTON, LESLIE, and ROBERT H. MOORE. *Reading, Self-Directive Dramatization and Self-Concept.* Merrill, 1968. Reports research results of studies dealing with self-directive dramatization. Chapters on selection of materials are also included.

CHAMBERS, DEWEY W. *Literature for Children; Storytelling and Creative Drama.* Brown, 1970. Recommendations for organizing storytelling and creative drama sessions are accompanied by discussion of educational implications for those activities.

COGER, LESLIE IRENE, and MELVIN R. WHITE. *Readers Theatre Handbook; A Dramatic Approach to Literature,* 2nd ed. Scott, Foresman, 1973. Provides sample scripts and suggestions for casting and rehearsing Readers Theatre productions.

CURRELL, DAVID. *The Complete Book of Puppetry.* Plays, 1975. A comprehensive book on making and using every kind of puppet.

DURLAND, FRANCES. *Creative Dramatics for Children.* Kent State Univ. Pr., 1952, 1975. Covers sources and techniques.

FORDYCE, RACHEL. *Children's Theatre and Creative Dramatics: An Annotated Bibliography of Critical Works.* Hall, 1975. A most useful compilation of pertinent articles and books.

HOETKER, JAMES. *Dramatics and the Teaching of Literature.* Nat. Council of Teachers of English, 1969. Considers the evidence of drama's effectiveness and mentions the most promising means of uniting drama and literature.

McCASLIN, NELLIE, ed. *Children and Drama.* McKay, 1975. Essays by fourteen leaders in the field.

MOORE, VARDINE. *The Pre-School Story Hour,* 2nd ed. Scarecrow, 1972. Lists useful stories and includes ideas for setting story-hour situations.

PIERINI, MARY FRANCIS. *Creative Dramatics; A Guide for Educators.* Seabury, 1971. A useful guide for developing creative dramatics from simple pantomimes to story dramatization.

POST, ROBERT M. "An Oral Interpreter's Approach to the Teaching of Elementary School Literature." *The Speech Teacher,* 20 (September 1971), pp. 167–173. Materials and techniques for introducing elementary grade children to oral interpretation.

ROSS, EULALIE STEINMETZ, ed. *The Lost Half-Hour; A Collection of Stories.* Harcourt, 1963. Recommendations for planning effective storytelling sessions.

ROWE, MARY BUDD. "Reflections on Wait-time; Some Methodological Questions." *Journal of Research in Science Teaching,* 1974, pp. 263–279.

SEBESTA, SAM LEATON. "The Neglected Art; Thought Questions." *Elementary English,* December 1967, pp. 888–95. Describes the use of the point-of-view question and other questioning techniques.

SHAFTEL, FANNIE R., and GEORGE SHAFTEL. *Role-Playing for Social Values; Decision-Making in the Social Studies.* Prentice, 1967. Describes procedures for guiding role-playing experiences and includes stories developed for role-playing.

SHEDLOCK, MARIE L. *The Art of the Storyteller,* 3rd ed. Dover, 1951. A treatment of storytelling that grows from a richness of literature.

SIKS, GERALDINE B. *Creative Dramatics; An Art for Children.* Harper, 1952. Comprehensive guide to developing creative dramatics with children.

STEWIG, JOHN WARREN. *Read to Write.* Hawthorn, 1975. Suggestions for writing activities based on children's literature.

TOOZE, RUTH. *Storytelling.* Prentice, 1959. Recommendations for selecting and telling stories.

WAGNER, JOSEPH A. *Children's Literature Through Storytelling.* Brown, 1970. Includes suggestions for preparing and using visual aids and puppets as well as guidelines for telling stories.

WARD, WINIFRED. *Playmaking with Children from Kindergarten Through Junior High School,* 2nd ed. Prentice, 1957. Procedures and suggested materials for developing extemporaneous drama.

WHITEHEAD, ROBERT. *Children's Literature; Strategies of Teaching.* Prentice, 1968. Suggestions for oral reading practices and recommended books.

Introducing Literature to Children

Chapter 16

In the earlier chapters of this book (Chapters 4 through 13) we discussed the various types of writing for children—poetry, fantasy, and biography, for example. Suggestions for introducing children to these specific kinds of books are developed in this chapter. In a sense, this material represents a synthesis and application of ideas discussed in the preceding two chapters, where we considered the patterns of response to literature and methods of encouraging that response. The suggested activities here were planned on the basis of this question: How can I best present this book to encourage children's responses? These responses may show involvement, interpretation, awareness of literary qualities, and/or evaluation of the story.

The goal of a literature program is to develop reading habits that will stay with children through adulthood. As children grow older, more and more of their reading should be independent reading from books of their own selection. Activities such as those discussed here may be used with less frequency as children become more involved in their private reading. The activities are designed to open doors to literature and to encourage reaction to books.

Formal study of literature is not usually a part of the elementary school curriculum. Experiences with literature most often come through the library program, the reading program, or the language arts program. A review of Chapter 15 will show the close ties of many of the activities there with what is typically included in language arts. A review of Chapter 14 will suggest relationships between what is considered literary response and the comprehension skill development included in a good reading program. Librarians will recognize that ideas from both chapters are related to sound objectives of a library program. A strong literature program can contribute substantially to the general educational experience.

Underlying any recommendations for literature-related activities are certain questions: What abilities can children develop at this level? What materials and activities are appropriate for developing those abilities? The answers are closely tied to developmental characteristics of children. Communication skills continue to grow from infancy but require guidance and practice for fullest development. Listening skills are developed through storytelling and oral reading to children. They are also fostered through planned book discussions, where children must respond to one another's ideas about a story. Speaking skills come into play in discussion, in role-playing, and in activities related to creative dramatics, puppetry, and oral interpretation. Writing skills are practiced when children respond to a literary selection with a writing activity. Ability to relate to others, to empathize, to appreciate problems common to people everywhere, is encouraged through book discussions and role-playing of problem situations.

Materials for developing these abilities must be selected carefully so that they are appropriate to their uses. Making the story or poem serve the activity by changing or manipulating a character or plot is generally not a good idea, as it shows a certain lack of respect for literature and for an author's purposes. Sensitive selection of material, on the other hand, can enhance the appeal of literature by showing how it helps us to understand and deal with our uncertainties and fears, how it provides release from tension through laughter, and how it gives us appreciation for the beauty of the language.

Careful matching of activities with books is critical if those activities are to enhance rather than detract from the literary work. The activity should focus on a significant quality of the literature and not distort a poem or story simply for the sake of providing some activity for children. For instance, some stories should not be used for puppetry because the literary qualities of plot, characterization, or style may be trivialized by such an adaptation. The same caution holds true for other activities such as creative dramatics, story theater, role-playing, and oral interpretation. When activities are carefully selected and developed around appropriate material to generate responses, the combination can take a child into a book so that a memorable experience results. That is the goal of the abbreviated plans in this chapter.

The chart on pp. 558–559 suggests how a teacher or librarian could expose children to a wide variety of books and encourage various kinds of responses. The chart lists recommended book activities discussed later in the chapter. Included are books for young children (preschool to age six), for primary-age children (ages six to eight or nine), and for children in the intermediate grades (ages nine to twelve). Books for the first group are coded with a *(1)*, for the second group with a *(2)*, and for the third group with a *(3)*. A number of the books are usable with a broad range of ages, indicated by more than one number. Not all blocks on the chart are filled in. Some are blank because activities do not seem appropriate for certain types of literature as, for example, storytelling with informational books. Others are open so that you can use ideas from previous chapters in combination with books you select to create your own additions to the chart.

You will discover that many books can be used appropriately with more than one activity. In the discussion that follows, a number of possible activities are sometimes suggested for a book. For the sake of example, one activity is developed in some detail. Starred books on the chart are those for which activity plans are included in this chapter.

You should not, by any means, look upon the books and activities described here as guidelines to be followed to the letter. They are simply included as models with the hope that you will try them and then use the ideas to create your own activities for books and poems you choose. If you follow through with the presentation of stories and poetry suggested here (or alternate selections of your own choice), a fairly well-balanced, response-centered literature program can result. The program would not be complete, of course, unless children also were involved in a great deal of independent reading of library materials.

Picture Books

Since picture books appeal to primary-age children as well as preschoolers, some of the activities have been developed for primary-grade and could even be used with intermediate-grade children. This is especially true of the story theater presentation. Some of the activities require little time to carry out. Others would best be done over a period of several days.

Story Theater (Choral Speaking, Storytelling, Reading Aloud)[1]

Why Mosquitoes Buzz in People's Ears by Verna Aardema, illustrated by Leo and Diane Dillon.

Picture books that have illustrations with a strong sense of rhythm and movement are good sources of material for story theater productions. Story theater is closely related to

[1]Activities in parentheses would also be suitable.

Genres	Suggested Activities			
	Reading Aloud	**Storytelling**	**Discussion**	**Role-Playing**
Picture Books and Wordless Picture Books	**May I Bring a Friend?* (1) **One Frog Too Many* (1)	*The Tale of Peter Rabbit* (1)	*Nothing Ever Happens on My Block* (1, 2)	*Where Is It?* (1)
Folk Literature	**Tikki Tikki Tembo* (1)	*"The Fisherman and His Wife" (2, 3)	**Tom Tit Tot* (2) *"Rumpelstiltskin" (2)	*Once a Mouse* (2)
Poetry	*Far and Few* (2, 3)		*"Low Tide" (3) *"Mummy Slept Late and Daddy Fixed Breakfast" (2)	
Fantasy	*Mr. Rabbit and the Lovely Present* (1) *The Wizard in the Tree* (3)	"The Emperor's New Clothes" (2)	**The Borrowers* (2)	*The Pushcart War* (3)
Animal Stories	*Nobody's Cat* (1, 2) *The Incredible Journey* (3)		**Owls in the Family* (2, 3)	**The Biggest Bear* (2) *A Bargain for Frances* (1, 2)
Realistic Fiction	**A Pocketful of Cricket* (1)		*The Hundred Penny Box* (3) *Do You Have the Time, Lydia?* (2)	**The Bully of Barkham Street* (2, 3) *Julie of the Wolves* (3)
Historical Fiction/ Biography	**And Then What Happened, Paul Revere?* (2)	**The Story of Johnny Appleseed* (1)	*The King's Fifth* (3)	*Cesar Chavez* (2, 3)
Informational Books	**Jambo Means Hello* (2, 3)		**All Upon a Sidewalk* (2, 3)	**Handtalk* (2, 3)

(1) Preschool (2) Primary (3) Intermediate *Book is discussed in Chapter 16.

Suggested Activities

Creative Dramatics	Story Theater	Oral Interpretation	Puppetry	Writing Activities
**Where the Wild Things Are* (1, 2)	**Why Mosquitoes Buzz in People's Ears* (2, 3) *Drummer Hoff* (1, 2)	*A Kiss for Little Bear* (1, 2)	"The Three Billy-Goats Gruff" (1)	**Time of Wonder* (2, 3)
"The Four Musicians" (2)	"The Hare and the Tortoise" (1) "The King's Drum" (2)		*"The Pancake" (1, 2)	
Wide Awake and Other Poems (1, 2)	*"Little Miss Muffet" (1)	"Mice" (2)	*"The Monkeys and the Crocodile" (2)	*Hailstones and Halibut Bones* (2, 3)
Caps for Sale (1, 2)	**In the Forest* (1) *The King's Stilts* (3)	**Mrs. Frisby and the Rats of NIMH* (3)		*Paul Bunyan* (2, 3)
Rabbit Hill (2, 3)	*The Story of Ferdinand* (1, 2)			**The Bat-Poet* (3)
The Adventures of Tom Sawyer (3)	*The Time-Ago Tales of Jahdu* (2, 3)	*From the Mixed-Up Files of Mrs. Basil E. Frankweiler* (3) **Ramona the Pest* (2, 3)		*My Side of the Mountain* (3)
The Witch of Blackbird Pond (3)		The *Little House* Books (2, 3)		**North to Freedom* (3)
Push-Pull, Empty-Full (1)			*How to Be a Puppeteer* (2) *Puppet Shows Using Poems and Stories* (3)	*Codes, Ciphers and Secret Writing* (3)

dance. Like dance, it requires an interaction with mood and a depiction of that mood through movement. In a fine picture book, the mood is conveyed directly through the illustrations and also, usually, through the words of the story.

In *Anansi the Spider,* Gerald McDermott's graphics are beautifully designed. The book is a fine vehicle for story theater because the actions of story theater do not have to "use" the book, they develop spontaneously from interaction with it. The same thing is true of *Why Mosquitoes Buzz in People's Ears,* in which the Dillons' illustrations show strong, flowing movement. Indeed, every curve of an animal functions as part of the overall design. The rhythm of the prose and stylistic touches of onomatopoeia elaborate the movements made by the animals. Going through the book, reading the text and looking at the illustrations, you are struck with the strong sense of physical movement. Children who have listened to the story and studied the pictures may interact with them to give a meaningful interpretation. Responses which may be encouraged through the story theater experience are an emotional response to the characters and their common problem; literary response, showing appreciation for style of illustrations and style of writing, especially the onomatopoeia; and interpretation of the theme, telling how the tribal people arrived at the mythical explanation of the mosquito as a nuisance.

The story should be read with much attention to the oral interpretation of character parts and of onomatopoetic words. Pictures should be displayed so that all children can see them. When the reading is completed, you might want to let children review the story, identifying the key characters in the order of their appearance.

At the close of the reading, children will want to talk about the sequence of events that lead up to the mosquito's banishment from the council of the animals. You might explain that this is a folk tale and ask them how such a story might have started. In the discussion, you may want to introduce the myth as one way early people tried to explain happenings they could not really understand, such as earthquakes and volcanic eruptions.

Since the pictures tell the story so beautifully, you would be wise to go through the book once again, just showing the pictures and encouraging children to look at them carefully to notice how the animals look and how they seem to move.

If the story is to be used for story theater dramatization, you probably should plan that activity for a second day, beginning that day with a second reading of the story. Ask children to listen for sounds used to describe each animal and for the sequence of events in the story. When the reading is completed, ask children to repeat the onomatopoetic sounds ("mek, mek," etc.) used in the story to describe each animal. Give them a few minutes to develop their own interpretations of the animal, basing them on illustrations and on the verbal descriptions. They might enjoy trying to show how an iguana might move so as to make a sound like "mek, mek, mek, mek." At this time, children might also want to decide who will play the part of each animal during the story theater production. When they have had time to practice and have decided how to use available space for a stage, you are ready for the reading. Read with the best oral interpretation techniques, pacing the story so that children have time to pantomime the character parts and emphasizing the onomatopoetic words so that your reading inspires the actors.

For follow-up discussion to the story theater production, you might focus on such questions as:

What strange events in nature are being explained in this story?

How did the storyteller and the illustrators let us know what the characters were like?

Which illustration(s) do you like best? Why?

The format of this plan can be adapted for use with other folk tales, including many of the Anansi stories.

Reading Aloud (Choral Speaking, Role-Playing)

May I Bring a Friend? by Beatrice Schenk de Regniers, illustrated by Beni Montresor.

This is a fine book to read aloud to preschoolers who are delighted by the imaginative quality of the colorful illustrations. The "reading" of the pictures shares importance with listening to the lively text, so children should be seated where they can see the illustrations as the story is read.

Responses which can be developed are emotional response to the fun of the story and literary response to the amusing illustrations, to the rhythm and rhyme of the verse, and to a recognition of the problems and solutions that make up each episode of the plot.

You can use the cover illustration effectively to introduce the story by asking children whom they see on the cover and who the little boy's friend is. Encourage them to listen and watch the illustrations to see what happens in this story about a queen, a king, and a little boy. As you read, be sure to emphasize the rhythm and rhyme of the lines, as young children generally respond well to those effects.

To encourage greater interaction with the events of the plot, you might want to pause after reading "So I brought my friend . . . ," inviting children to guess at who the friend might be or whom they would take if they were having tea at the palace. The words spoken by the king and queen provide opportunity for use of good oral interpretation techniques and you will probably find children joining you on "Hello" each time the king greets a new guest. Children may also enjoy guessing at the problems that may arise when the latest guest (for example, the hippopotamus) sits down to tea. They might like to try to decide where the elephant can sit and will be amused at the solution.

Throughout the reading, show the illustrations carefully. You might want to take time following the story to show all of them again, inviting children to look for surprising things in the pictures, such as the king and queen hanging their feet over the dock while they fish and the dismayed look on the king's face when the hippopotamus tries to sit next to him. Children will want to hear the story many times. Encourage them to join you on familiar verses so that they learn to use their voices to interpret rhythm and rhyme.

Reading Aloud (Discussion)

One Frog Too Many by Mercer and Marianna Mayer.

Even though this is a wordless picture book, it can be read aloud, in a fashion. As young children become used to the idea that a sequence of pictures tells a story, they will be more able to give their own verbal descriptions of what they see, eventually producing a sort of story line.

Responses that may be developed are, first and foremost, emotional involvement with the story told through pictures. Enjoyment is the key response. Some children will understand the story in terms of their own experiences with jealousy toward a new brother or sister. Frog's wicked delight in the mishaps he creates for the young frog is a familiar experience for many children. With a little help, they may begin to interpret the story, making some inferences about the need for Frog's change of heart and acceptance of the newcomer when he hops in through the window. Emotional involvement comes, of course, through the pictures and is a direct result of appreciation of them. Children may show some form of empathy for the characters. They may also begin to develop readiness for literary response to a plot structure based on conflict and resolution from experiences in "reading" a wordless picture book like this one. Picture interpretation and inference about the happenings provide important prereading experiences.

Because the pictures are small and have many details that children will enjoy, they should be used with a single child or, at most, two or three. A good way to get a child involved with the story is to read the title and ask the child to look at the cover picture to find out what seems to be the trouble between the two frogs. With that preview, you might just let the child move from page to page. Some children will tell the story out loud as it unfolds on the page. Others will simply make comments about details in the pictures. If the child is unfamiliar with picture reading, you may want to "read" a book first, then let the child "read" another one to you. To encourage children to make more inferences about the picture on page one, you might ask what could possibly be in the box and why the box has holes in it. To start children thinking about the problem situation in the plot, ask them to notice the expression on Frog's face in pictures two and three. Why does he look so unhappy? As the plot develops and Frog's treatment of the newcomer becomes more unkind, you can ask children what causes Frog to behave as he does. Ask, too, whether they have ever felt the way Frog feels. Some children will spontaneously respond to the ending by expressing relief that the small frog finds his way back and that Frog accepts him this time. You may want to ask whether the ending is a good one. How else could the story end? What ending would they prefer?

Creative Dramatics (Reading Aloud, Story Theater)

Where the Wild Things Are by Maurice Sendak.

This picture book is well known to many children. They are attracted to the vivid illustrations and enter gladly into the wild rumpus, enjoying the humor of the situation and reveling in the rhythm of the ungainly dance. And, at the close of the festivities, they understand Max's desire to go home to where "someone loved him best of all," which expresses the need most humans have for a close relationship with others rather than the adulation of a large number of strangers.

Responses which can be encouraged by means of dramatization include emotional response through enjoyment of story and pictures and empathy for Max's situation. Some children will also recognize and interpret the theme that being with people who love you is the most important thing. Children may also respond to the literary style and artistic qualities of the book. The plot structure really reveals a story within a story and this can be clearly shown through the dramatization. The characterization of Max and the marvelous illustrations add to enjoyment. Children will note Max's changes of mood, shown by his posture and facial expressions, and use that information to develop their own pantomimes.

Introduce this splendid picture book so that all the children in the group can enjoy the pictures. You might introduce it by showing the cover picture as you read the title, then asking the children whether they would like to go to a land inhabited by creatures resembling the one in this illustration. What kinds of adventures might they have? Turn, next, to the first-page illustration of Max in his wolf suit and tell children to listen and watch the pictures to find out what happens to Max in the story. Each picture has a wealth of detail that children will enjoy, so pace your reading to allow time for them to examine each picture before you move on to the next page. Allow time, too, for the spontaneous expressions of delight that are likely to come from the listeners. When the story has been read completely, you can decide whether to continue with the dramatization or to save it for a second session. A good picture book is enjoyed even more at a second reading so it may be better, especially with children below first-grade level, to read the story at two sessions.

Whenever possible, give children a chance to enjoy the pictures on their own between the two readings. Prior to the second reading, you may want to show the pictures to the group and give them time to tell what they especially enjoy in each. You can call attention to changes in Max's facial expression as the story progresses, asking children to try their own expressions of wickedness, shrewdness, delight, and sadness. This is a good activity to prepare for a dramatization of the story. In fact, with young children, a "dramatization" may be no more than your rereading of the story while all children mime the part of Max, or participate in the wild rumpus scene.

During the second reading, older children should listen carefully to notice the order in which the events take place. Ask them also to listen for the sayings that are repeated several times during the story. When you have finished reading, you might ask the children where the story begins and ends (in Max's house) and where the rest of it takes place (the ocean and the kingdom of the wild things). To further establish the setting for older children, you might help them identify scenes of the story: Max's house, Max's room, the ocean, the land of the wild things, the ocean, and Max's room, in that order.

With those scenes in mind, ask children to decide what characters they will need for dramatizing each scene. They may include Max's dog and inanimate objects, such as the vines and the boat, which are important for the action of the story. There can be any number of wild things, so that all children in the group will be involved in the dramatization.

The next steps are to let children decide

who will play each part and to give them time to practice pantomiming their roles and to improvise dialogue where it is needed. At this point, be sure those who want to are able to look at the illustrations again to notice the movement in each picture.

Prior to the dramatization, the staging should be planned so that children know what areas of the room will be used as Max's room, as the ocean, and as the land of the wild things. You will want to remind the children to listen well so that they come in at the right time. If the children are very inexperienced, you might want to provide the narration by reading from the text and pausing at the speaking parts to let children supply the dialogue. A word of caution: Since Max has a very active part, it might be wise to choose a child who is quite independent and able to remember the story line to play that part.

As a follow-up to the dramatization, you can talk with the children about their performance. What did they especially enjoy about the story? Why did Max go on his journey and why did he return home? Was his behavior similar to anything they have done? If you want to emphasize the literary structure, you might reread the first and last sections which take place in Max's room and ask children whether that part could be a story by itself. Then read the "journey" section, beginning and ending with the boat trips so that children can see the story within a story.

This book has many possibilities for extending enjoyment of literature and, indeed, the arts. If an appropriate record is available, you might want to use that during the wild rumpus scene to help children get into the spirit of the sort of dance that is shown in the illustrations.

Writing Activity (Discussion, Oral Interpretation)

Time of Wonder by Robert McCloskey

The illustrations in this fine picture book are matched by equally sensitive prose. The story is a challenge to the oral interpretation skills of an adult reader. Such descriptions as "the sound of growing ferns . . . slowly unfurling, slowly stretching" encourage children to hear and visualize the picture. To get the full effect, children deserve to hear as well as look at this book. They may well respond with their own creative use of words and pictures.

Many kinds of responses may be opened up through *Time of Wonder*. Certainly a good reading of it will stir some children to ask for a repeat because "the words are so nice." After a second reading, you can ask which were their favorite descriptions. Some children will respond emotionally because they, too, have had an experience at the seashore or at a lake in the wilderness. With a few thought-provoking questions from an adult, some children may be able to deal with an underlying theme which emerges in the last paragraph with the question, "Where do hummingbirds go in a hurricane?" With encouragement, children will appreciate the dramatic changes in weather shown in the illustrations. They will notice the contrast between scenes with a great turbulence and those of great serenity, the contrasts in people's moods as well as the contrasts in nature.

When the story has been read once with a sensitive interpretation and plenty of time for children to enjoy the illustrations, you might want to substitute a showing of the Weston Woods film for a second reading. Whichever plan you choose should help children to focus on the effective use of illustrations to re-create the many moods of weather and the out-of-doors.

Find time for some discussion of favorite scenes from the story and encourage children to think of the way they felt as they looked at the pictures and listened to the words this author used to describe the coming storm and the clearing afterward.

If children have shown interest in the story, you might suggest that they make their own picture essays, selecting some aspect of nature that they see every day. They should decide for themselves what to describe, draw the illustrations or take photographs, and write the creative descriptions that will go alongside each picture and create a story. You might remind them of the care with which McCloskey chose words to make the verbal description as vivid as the pictures. When the illustrations and creative writing have been completed, children should have a chance to plan the layout of the work, using a photo-album format made from sheets of construction paper.

Folk Literature

Reading Aloud (Storytelling, Story Theater)

Tikki Tikki Tembo, retold by Arlene Mosel, illustrated by Blair Lent.

This retelling of a Chinese folk tale has enough suspense to involve children with the problems and misfortunes of Chang and his brother, Tikki Tikki Tembo. The illustrations capture the rather easygoing mood of the village but they also describe quite explicitly the dangerous position of being in the bottom of a well!

Responses which may be generated through a reading of the story are emotional involvement with the story as children feel concern for the safety of first one boy and then the other. Children may also respond to literary qualities of the story, particularly the cumulative plot structure and the use of rhythm and rhyme in the long name. And children will love to repeat that with you: "Tikki, tikki, tembo-no sa rembo-chari bari ruchi-pip peri pembo."

You might preface the story by asking children to think of the longest name they have ever heard. Then read the title of the story and tell them that this is just part of the name of one of the boys they will hear about. His whole name was so long that it got him into lots of trouble. They are to listen to see how he got into and out of that trouble.

As you read, use your voice and hand gestures to emphasize the development of plot and the movement of the action from one place to another (from the well to the stream to the old man and again to the well) and try to pause during the second episode, when Tikki Tikki Tembo falls into the well, so that children have a chance to think ahead and try to decide what will happen next, based on their knowledge of Chang's escapade. Let children join you each time Chang struggles to pronounce Tikki Tikki Tembo's long name. They will want to hear the story again and again and will enjoy retelling it themselves. In fact, you can show the illustration at the end of the story and let children use it to prompt their retelling of the tale.

Storytelling (Story Theater, Puppetry)

"The Fisherman and His Wife" from *Grimm's Household Tales*, translated by Margaret Hunt.

Folk tales are part of the oral tradition and are the single richest source for storytelling. "The Fisherman and His Wife" is a story with a moral children cannot miss. It is a good choice for storytelling because the incidents are repetitious, yet they build in such a way that it is quite easy to keep the plot sequence in mind. The rhyme that is repeated each time the fisherman goes to seek the flounder also provides a kind of structure for the story and children will enjoy repeating it with you as they become familiar with it.

Responses that develop rather naturally to this story are emotional involvement with the woman's greed and her undoing as well as interpretation of the theme of the story and literary response through appreciation for the repeated rhyme. Responses may also show that children are examining their own values.

The story is not difficult. A fisherman catches a flounder that is really an enchanted prince. The fisherman gladly releases the fish when he finds it can talk. But his wife, when she learns of it, is furious that he has not asked the flounder to grant a wish. The upshot of it is that the poor fisherman returns to the sea, calls back the flounder, tells his wife's wish, and the flounder grants it. This process is repeated six times until finally the flounder has had enough and sends the couple back to their original living quarters, a hovel. The secret in memorizing the story is to think of the sequence of the wishes: (1) to live in a cottage, (2) to live in a castle, (3) that the wife should be King, (4) that she should be Emperor, (5) that she should be Pope, and (6) that she should be like God. The last is too much for the flounder and he returns the couple to their condition at the start of the story.

There is certainly a lesson in the story, and when you pause at the end you can give children time to reflect on the outcome of the wife's greedy ways. If children respond spontaneously or with a little encouragement to "think about what that story tells us," the way is open to a discussion in which they may share their own experiences that bear on the same lesson. If children do not share their ideas quite spontaneously, do not force a discussion. That would put the focus on the "lesson" and perhaps on self-righteous moralizing and not on enjoyment of the story itself.

Children may notice that the same episode is repeated over and over with just a little change each time. If they do, you might encourage them to think about other stories like "The Three Billy-Goats Gruff" that have similar repetitive story patterns.

Discussion (Storytelling, Role-Playing, Puppetry).

Tom Tit Tot, illustrated by Evaline Ness.

The story can be read aloud with time allowed afterward for a discussion, or it may be paired with "Rumpelstiltskin" to show children how very similar stories can appear in different countries in somewhat different forms.

Responses to *Tom Tit Tot* may include emotional reaction to the girl's predicament and elation when she finds out the strange creature's name. Children may also recognize the language of the tale as unique to another time in history and therefore an important quality of the folk tale. They may respond also to the literary characteristics of the plot, recognizing that the creature appears three times to the girl – the magic number three that they have seen in such other tales as "The Three Billy-Goats Gruff" and "The Three Little Pigs." Literary response may also be encouraged when children have heard and compared "Rumpelstiltskin" and *Tom Tit Tot.* Children will recognize similarities and differences in the characters and plot as well as differences in the language of the two versions.

When you have read *Tom Tit Tot,* you might pause to see what kinds of spontaneous responses children make. You may work from these responses to develop a discussion of aspects of the story that mark it as a folk tale. You might ask children to recall some of the words used to describe the girl. What did her mother call her? What could the word "gatless" mean? Ask them to think of other words used that sound old-fashioned. They should recognize "upped and oped it" and "Noo, t'ain't" as well as others. You might also ask what they especially enjoyed about the story to allow them to express emotional reaction to plot and characters. To develop response to literary characteristics, you can ask how many times the creature returns for the girl to guess its name, encouraging children to recall other tales they know that are built on a repetition of three similar episodes. If the children know "Rumpelstiltskin," questions can help them to note the main character in each and to compare them, to identify the problem and its solution in each story, and to compare the language in the British version with the translation of "Rumpelstiltskin" from the German.

Creative Dramatics (Story Theater, Storytelling)

"The Four Musicians" from *The Oak Tree Fairy Book,* ed. by Clifton Johnson.

This tale has enough action and enough surprises to provide good material for creative dramatics. Children will respond with empathy to the plight of the animals and express pleasure at the good turn their lives take. Emotional response may also be evident in laughter as children realize that the robber has misunderstood the rooster's crowing for the cries of a man on the roof shouting, "Chuck him up to me." Children are sure to enjoy the dramatic experience. In addition, they may react to literary structure by recognizing the common folk-tale theme of the poor but good person overcoming the villain.

When the tale has been told or read, ask the children to think about the story characters. Who were the musicians, and what talents did they use to make their journey a success? Before proceeding further with the plot review, you might want to let the whole class pantomime each character, adding sound effects if your walls are thick enough! Be certain to remind them that these are old, unwanted animals, poor in spirit at the beginning, but gaining courage when they are together. They may also want to pantomime the robbers as they are surprised at their meal. With that background, ask children to recall the sequence of events they will need for producing a dramatization. Essentially, there are three major scenes: the first when the four animals meet along the road; the second when they come upon the house, see the robbers inside, frighten them away, and finish the feast; and the third when the robbers return and are frightened away again by the animals. Once characters have been chosen, the scenes can be practiced one at a time, first pantomimed and then with dialogue created by the children. Finally, all three scenes are played in a continuous dramatization.

Puppetry (Storytelling, Choral Speaking)

"The Pancake" from *Tales from the Fjeld* by Peter Asbjörnsen and Jörgen Moe, translated by Sir George Webbe Dasent.

"The Pancake" is one of several versions of this tale. Another well-known one is *Journey Cake, Ho!* by Ruth Sawyer. "The Pancake" can be adapted quite easily for puppetry, using paper bag puppets, finger puppets, or balloon puppets. A balloon puppet attached to a stick is especially effective in creating a sense of movement, for the pancake is, of course, always moving. This idea is adapted from a production of "Henny Penny" by Aurora Valentinetti.[2]

Responses will include emotional reaction as children enjoy the escapades of the pancake and foresee its demise. In terms of literary response, children may notice the use of rhyming names and repeat them along with the storyteller. They will notice the cumulative plot structure, with the pancake repeating the names of all the animals it has outwitted each time a new character appears. You may want to give a chance for evaluation of the story by reading *Journey Cake, Ho!* after children have completed the puppet production of "The Pancake." Ask them to decide which version they most enjoyed.

A number of words and sayings are repeated throughout the story, so the telling of the story should be true to the original to keep the flavor of the language. Unless you can memorize it, a reading will probably be more effective than a telling. When the story has been presented and perhaps repeated, with the children joining in on the familiar parts, they will be ready to assemble the cast of characters needed for a puppet show. If balloon puppets are used, the features of each animal (and of the people) can be made from colored paper cut and fastened onto the balloon with tape. During the show, one child is responsible for each character. Using a table turned on its side as a stage, the action takes place with the pancake crossing in front of the stage over and over, each time meeting one of the hungry creatures, beginning with Manny Panny and ending with Piggy Wiggy. As Piggy Wiggy swallows the pancake, the puppeteer behind the table can pop the balloon, creating an ending that will satisfy young audiences. In order to keep the story line going well, the adult reader should pay careful attention to pacing.

[2]Alvina Burrows, et al., *New Horizons in the Language Arts* (Harper & Row, 1972), p. 163.

Poetry

Discussion (Oral Interpretation)

"Low Tide" from *The Malibu and Other Poems* by Myra Cohn Livingston.

Found. One red starfish
at low tide. One
plump, prickly starfish wrested by arm,
by leg, squirming among
purple, bubbling sea urchins.

Plop him in a pail? Scoop up the
salt water? His color will fade.
He will miss his bubbling urchins.

Grab him by the arm. Return him
to his rock, his pink anemone.
One red starfish. Lost.[3]

If a poem is to be discussed, it should have form and content that will inspire discussion. That is essential because a forced discussion will become simply a question-answer period and will very likely lead to a dislike for poetry. "Low Tide" is a poet's description of an experience many children have had. They may never have seen a live starfish or an anemone, but they have probably captured tadpoles or even small water bugs in puddles.

Response may be an emotional reaction, centering on the joy of finding something as fascinating as a starfish. Children may relate to the speaker in the poem, explaining what they would have done if they had found the starfish, perhaps thinking of their values concerning ecology. There may also be a reaction

[3]From *The Malibu and Other Poems* (A Margaret K. McElderry Book). Copyright © 1972 by Myra Cohn Livingston. Used by permission of Atheneum Publishers and McIntosh and Otis, Inc.

to the literary qualities of the poem, responses that show a listener's attention to description or to form.

The title is a good introduction to the poem. Read it and ask children what they would expect to see on a beach at low tide. If your children are not acquainted with ocean and tidal changes, it may be necessary to explain briefly the way a beach looks when the water sweeps out to sea, leaving hundreds of yards of exposed sand. Read the poem once, not too quickly, emphasizing the first and last words so that children get a sense of the form of this free verse. Let them discuss it informally if they offer comments. Then read it again.

After the second reading, you may want to open up a discussion by asking children whether they have ever had an experience like this poet is describing. Why did the speaker in the poem decide not to keep the starfish? Is the last part of the poem as fast-moving and happy as the first? Why not? How does the pace of the poem reflect the speaker's mood?

To help children think about the use of descriptive words and phrases, ask if they could draw a picture of what they heard. If necessary, reread, asking them to listen for all the ways this poet paints a word picture for us. How is the starfish described? The sea urchins? Children may also become aware of form if you show the poem so that they can see the one-word beginning and ending. Ask children how "Found" and "Lost" shape the poem, even though it does not have a regular rhyme scheme.

Story Theater (Reading Aloud, Puppetry)

"Little Miss Muffet" from *Mother Goose.*

This favorite *Mother Goose* rhyme has enough of a story line so that it is fun for young children to pantomime. They can respond emotionally to the threat of the spider and the relief that Miss Muffet did, indeed, escape from the creature. Dramatizing the scene gives vent to the emotions and makes the experience more vivid.

The two characters, Miss Muffet and the spider, can be created easily through pantomime. Children should have a chance to create the movements of a spider and to decide whether their spiders will be threatening or just innocent intruders. They can work out the character of Miss Muffet, showing the motions of eating curds and whey, and can make her reaction to the spider quite dramatic. When the entire group has participated in these warm-ups, you might want to let pairs of children pantomime the poem as it is read aloud or told by other children.

Discussion (Oral Interpretation, Writing Activities)

"Mummy Slept Late and Daddy Fixed Breakfast" from *You Read to Me, I'll Read to You* by John Ciardi.

Daddy fixed the breakfast.
He made us each a waffle.
It looked like gravel pudding.
It tasted something awful.

"Ha, ha," he said, "I'll try again.
This time I'll get it right."
But what I got was in between
Bituminous and anthracite.

"A little too well done? Oh well,
I'll have to start all over."
That time what landed on my plate
Looked like a manhole cover.

I tried to cut it with a fork:
The fork gave off a spark.
I tried a knife and twisted it
Into a question mark.

I tried it with a hack-saw.
I tried it with a torch.
It didn't even make a dent.
It didn't even scorch.

The next time Dad gets breakfast
When Mommy's sleeping late,
I think I'll skip the waffles.
I'd sooner eat the plate![4]

Ciardi's poem is sure to bring giggles from listeners. They will have personal stories to relate about the times someone in their family who doesn't usually cook has tried it. The emotional reaction to the humor of the poem is a good way to lead children to look at *how* the poet produced the humor, leading to a lit-

[4]From *You Read to Me, I'll Read to You* by John Ciardi. Copyright © 1962 by John Ciardi. Reprinted by permission of J. B. Lippincott Company.

erary response. Children may note figurative language they find interesting. They may also recognize the poet's use of exaggeration to evoke humor.

After the first reading, give children time to share their emotional reactions to the poem. Prepare them for the second reading by asking that they listen for all the ways the poet makes them laugh. Why are the descriptions funny? Which are the most impossible exaggerations? Why are they so funny? A discussion of these questions can help children to see that great exaggeration, or an impossible situation, is often the source of humor in a story or a poem.

Puppetry (Choral Speaking, Story Theater)

"The Monkeys and the Crocodile" from *Tirra Lirra* by Laura Richards.

Five little monkeys
Swinging from a tree;
Teasing Uncle Crocodile,
Merry as can be.
Swinging high, swinging low,
Swinging left and right:
"Dear Uncle Crocodile,
Come and take a bite!"

Five little monkeys
Swinging in the air;
Heads up, tails up,
Little do they care.
Swinging up, swinging down,
Swinging far and near:
"Poor Uncle Crocodile,
Aren't you hungry, dear?"

Four little monkeys
Sitting in the tree;
Heads down, tails down,
Dreary as can be.
Weeping loud, weeping low,
Crying to each other:
"Wicked Uncle Crocodile,
To gobble up our brother!"[5]

This is an example of poetry that can be adapted for use with puppets without ruining the effect of the poem. Indeed, the brief but neatly developed plot presents a strong visual effect. Children will enjoy showing the transition from verse 2 to verse 3 (five teasing monkeys to four sad monkeys) with puppets.

The activity described here can involve children in several different kinds of responses. The foremost response should be enjoyment of the poem, shown through spontaneous reaction to the poem's words and rhythm. Response may also involve interpretation as children realize that too much teasing can indeed lead to sad consequences for children as well as monkeys. They may also grow in literary awareness as they develop a sense of the plot structure. This should, however, be developed informally, not through direct instruction.

Actual work with puppets should be preceded by several readings of the poem. On the second or third reading, encourage children to join you on the conversational lines at the end of each stanza. In that way, the whole group can eventually be involved and can experience the rhythm of the poem.

The puppets can be simple finger puppets. In order to create a production that enhances the poetic qualities, the children must hear the poem many times. Emphasize the rhythm of lines like "Swinging high, swinging low" and "Weeping loud, weeping low," encouraging children to repeat them with you. You might also suggest that children move their hands or their bodies in rhythm as the monkeys might move, trying to convey the feeling of happiness or sadness. The final reading, done with puppets, can combine your reading of the poem with children joining in on the last lines of each verse.

Fantasy

Discussion (Oral Interpretation, Writing Activities)

The Borrowers by Mary Norton.

This book can give children some ideas about the characteristics of fantasy. Most important, it can generate strong emotional response. Children are intrigued with the lives of the tiny people; they share the Borrowers' fear of discovery and they enjoy the clever uses the Borrowers have for items we "lose." The stories are so intriguing that more

[5]From *Tirra Lirra* by Laura E. Richards. (Boston: Little, Brown and Company), 1955.

than one child has remarked that it almost seems possible there could be little people behind the walls. Children can also respond to literary aspects of the story. They begin to appreciate the use of point of view to create an effect and it is rather a surprise when they realize that the "human beans" described by the tiny Borrowers in this story are very much like themselves. With some guidance, children can also see that the author has used manipulation of characters in a clever way to create this fantasy. For in this story it is the characters who make it a fantasy. They are not talking animals as in Russell Hoban's *A Bargain for Frances,* nor are they people from another planet. They are tiny people who look and talk and feel just like us. The setting is realistic; only the characters have been manipulated to produce the fantasy.

There is enough suspense in these episodes to hold attention as you read them aloud. Take advantage of the places where good oral interpretation skills will pay off. At the end of the first chapter, pause and give children a few minutes to react spontaneously to the story if they wish. Some children will enter into the spirit of the story if you ask them what they have lost lately and how the Borrowers might be able to use it. Give them a chance to think about how the Borrowers must feel when they hear the heavy tramp of footsteps entering a room near them. You might try some point-of-view questions such as: You are Pod. Where were you when you first realized the boy had seen you? What were your first thoughts? That information is quite clearly given in the book. To switch point of view, you might then say: You are the boy. What did you think when you saw the tiny creature halfway up the curtain in the nursery?

When the book has been completed, you should give children a chance to think back over the story. Did it seem real to them? What could have happened? What could not be possible? How did the author change the characters so that she made the story a fantasy rather than a realistic story? Interpretation may come into play, too, when children discuss the reasons that some things terrified the Borrowers but seem completely harmless to us.

Story Theater (Reading Aloud)

In the Forest by Marie Hall Ets.

This enjoyable story is simple enough so that young children can dramatize it. There are twelve animal characters in addition to a boy and his father, so it is possible to involve quite a large group. Response to the story will surely be at the emotional level as children interact with the joyousness of the walk. Some children will show involvement with the characters through good pantomime.

Because the pictures are not large, you may want to gather children closely around you for the reading. Following that, let them think over the characters to decide which they enjoyed most. A second look at the pictures may aid them in remembering the cast of characters. As a story character is identified, you might want to let children imitate the character, encouraging them to use bodily motion and good facial expressions to develop the pantomime. When all characters have been identified and mimed, let children choose their parts and find places in the room. Read the story, pausing so children can play out the character roles, adding appropriate noises when they can. You will need these characters: boy, his father, big wild lion, old gray stork, two elephant babies, two little monkeys, two big brown bears, rabbit, and mother and father kangaroo and their baby.

Oral Interpretation (Discussion, Writing Activities)

Mrs. Frisby and the Rats of NIMH by Robert O'Brien.

This story offers children a marvelous opportunity for adventure. Many children also develop a feeling of empathy for the rats as well as for Mrs. Frisby and her family. Underlying it all is the question: Where can the mass of new scientific information take us? This fantasy, through humor and pathos, gives readers a chance to consider that important question. Responses may take the form of emotional reaction to the problems of the story characters and should also include inferences about the events that lead to interpretation of the author's purpose.

Children find it easy to identify with the rats and to interpret their behavior. Readers

Theatre is a good way to build on the interpretation. It is particularly effective for this story because there are a number of sections with extended dialogue involving several characters. In order to prepare children for the oral interpretation, agree upon the cast of characters in the section. For example, the episode from page 115 (mid-page) to 119 would need: narrator, Nicodemus, Justin, Dr. Schultz, Julie, and George. Ask the children to think about the personalities of those characters, so far as they know them. What are their motives in this scene? What tone of voice would they assume in speaking to one another? What does each character have to gain from what happens? You might also ask them how this scene relates to the outcome of the story. What significance does it have? The last question is based on the assumption that, in order to do a good Readers Theatre presentation, children have read the entire story so that they understand the interrelationships among characters and events.

When children have some ideas about the role each character plays in the scene, let them choose parts and practice their reading independently. You might want to read the narrational parts or work with the narrator so that the child makes that part a good structure for the dialogue.

If children enjoy this section of the story, they may want to search for other short passages they can adapt for Readers Theatre. One other good section is from page 200 (last paragraph) to page 202 (next to last paragraph).

Animal Stories

Discussion (Oral Interpretation, Writing Activities)

Owls in the Family by Farley Mowat.

Farley Mowat, a Canadian naturalist, wrote this highly entertaining story about a boy and his two pet owls. Oral reading of part or all of the story followed by discussion gives children a chance to share their enjoyment and to appreciate what the author is telling them about wild creatures. Emotional response should emerge in the form of laughter at amusing incidents and descriptions and, for some children, in an understanding of Billy's friendship with his owls. Feelings of empathy for one or another of the characters may also be expressed. Through discussion, children may become aware of a literary quality of the story as they see how frequently the author injects humor involving a story character's mishaps. Evaluation can be a part of the response pattern if children are asked how the author has succeeded in giving the owls qualities that are both human and animallike.

The entire book is suitable for reading aloud and is written with an episodic plot structure so that each chapter stands alone. Too much discussion of any book can interfere with enjoyment of the story. Nevertheless, there are times when discussion is important so that children can share their thoughts about a story and, with your guidance, begin to understand why they appreciate the writing. Discussion can be reserved for the end of the story or, as we suggest here, initiated at the end of a chapter or of several chapters.

To set a situation for discussion of the Mowat book, you might want to read the first five chapters aloud, pausing after Chapter 5 to give the children a chance to react. You can begin the discussion by noting parts of the story that brought laughter from the group as you read. Ask why they laughed. What had the author done to create a funny scene? Why did they laugh when Wol falls with a thud as he is learning to fly? Why did they laugh when Weeps refuses to even try to open his wings and falls like a rock instead? Perhaps they will recognize the ridiculousness of each situation and also the fact that we often laugh at another person's misfortune. (They may recall laughing when a friend got his trousers caught in a bicycle wheel and tumbled off.) Why does that makes us feel good?

Children may be interested in talking about the relationship Bill has with his owls. Why does he seem to know what they are thinking? Some children may be able to compare their relationships with pets to the example in the story. A natural extension of this questioning tack leads to student evaluation of the way these animals are presented. You can pursue this by asking children in what ways the owls in the story appear human and in what ways they appear like wild animals. If students are able to make these comparisons, you might ask whether they think the author should have included the wild animal episodes (such as the killing of the cat) as well as the accounts of the owls' almost human behavior. What is he telling us?

Role-Playing (Discussion, Reading Aloud)

The Biggest Bear by Lynd Ward.

The fact that this animal story is based on an underlying set of values makes it possible for readers to relate to the situations Johnny finds himself in. Children should be encouraged to respond emotionally to the story—to enjoy the pictures as well as the story line and to identify with Johnny's feelings about his bear. They may also evaluate the story ending by role-playing and then discussing the author's solution to Johnny's problem.

Successful role-playing depends on the degree to which children can interact with a problem and work out their own solutions. The story must set up a problem children understand and care about. *The Biggest Bear* can draw a strong emotional response from children and can also encourage interpretation of the story and sometimes evaluation of the story ending. Responses may also indicate that the story involves children in value formation.

To involve children to the fullest, it is a good idea to read the story aloud to the group, showing the pictures so that all the children can enjoy them. There are several good places to stop for role-playing of a story problem situation. The first is on page 47 when Johnny is told that the bear must go. When the children have looked at that picture, you might pose this point-of-view situation: You are Johnny. Talk the situation over with your father. What will you do? Ask two children to volunteer to play the roles of Johnny and his father and let them carry on a conversation to help Johnny decide what to do about the bear. Several other pairs of children may also want to participate when the first group is finished.

Continue reading the story. You may want to stop again on pages 52, 56, and 60 so that Johnny and his father can try to solve the problem of the bear each time he returns. Or you may prefer an uninterrupted reading of the story, stopping at page 76 where the bear is captured for a zoo. Children will enjoy giving opinions of that problem solution. You may want to invite them to be Johnny and his friends. Ask: Was this a good solution to the problem for Johnny *and* for the bear? What other ending can you think of? Which do you prefer?

Writing Activity (Reading Aloud, Discussion, Oral Interpretation)

The Bat-Poet by Randall Jarrell.

This story, with prose interwoven with poetry, is unusual and beautifully written. Because of its quality, it deserves to be read aloud by an experienced reader. The approach suggested here is a combination of oral reading, discussion, and follow-up writing activities.

Responses to be encouraged are an emotional response to the bat's need to share his experiences with others. Many children will empathize with the bat's frustration at not being able to interest the other bats in the wonderful things he sees during his daytime excursions. Children will respond, also, to the content of the poems as well as to such literary characteristics as the author's choice of words. Certainly they should hear the poems several times so that they are aware of the musical quality combined with superb description.

You might present the book to children by asking whether they have ever thought what the world might look like to an animal, such as a squirrel or a bird. What would they notice? What could be important to such creatures? In this book, they will view life through the eyes of a bat. The story is too long to be read at one sitting, so you may read only certain parts or find good stopping points. It would be a good idea to stop occasionally to let children repeat and enjoy some of the poetry and other especially fine descriptive passages. In order to prepare for later writing activities, you may want to begin a chart titled "Good Descriptions," writing a few phrases from the opening of the story and encouraging children to help you decide what to add to the chart as you go along. Some ideas for the beginning are: "the color of coffee with cream in it," "a fur wave went over them," and "squirrels chattered . . . like two rocks being knocked together."

The follow-up writing activity can be based

on children's appreciation of descriptions used in the story. You might simply ask them to choose some animal (or bird) that they are quite familiar with and perhaps can observe frequently. Several options are available for a writing activity based on this story. Some children may want to write a prose and poetry description of the creature, as was done in *The Bat-Poet*. Others may prefer to describe the world as it might be seen by the creature, getting experience in writing from a different point of view. In either case, emphasis should be on producing fresh, descriptive phrases, emphasizing some of the techniques used by the writer of this fine book.

Realistic Fiction

Reading Aloud (Discussion, Role-Playing)

A Pocketful of Cricket by Rebecca Caudill.

Young children look forward to that magic time when they will go to school. They can also be somewhat fearful about that important event, especially if they have listened to stories told by older children. Caudill's story about the first day at school for a country boy is told with sensitivity, and when it is read aloud well, it can draw young children to the boy so that they, too, experience some of his sadness at trading his free farm existence for a life of school buses and classrooms. Although the story is rather slight, it is a moving description of a teacher's sympathy for a small boy who finds a sort of security in his cricket. The most important responses will be those which show emotional involvement and empathy with the boy and his problem. Children may also interpret the situation as similar to times when they may have wanted a familiar object (such as a doll or a teddy bear) near them in a strange place.

Role-Playing (Discussion, Writing Activity)

The Bully of Barkham Street by Mary Stolz.

By sharing Martin's crises with him, children can be encouraged to take a look at some of their own difficulties, at some of the circumstances that motivate them, and at the results of unpleasant behavior.

There are plenty of opportunities for emotional responses to this story, responses that may include some laughter but will lead most children to develop empathy with one or more of the story characters as they notice similarities to situations they, too, have met from time to time. The responses of interpreting the selection and analyzing the literary elements are close to the emotional response here. Children will begin to appreciate the complexities of Martin's character and to see how the author has used young Edward, other children in Martin's class, and his teacher, Mr. Foran, as mirrors of his behavior and to show how one problem led Martin to another so that his overeating became both cause and symptom of his troubles.

Many scenes provide good role-playing situations. The beginning of Chapter 2, where Martin beats up Edward because he calls him "Fatso," works well. End your oral reading at the point where Edward has finally said "Uncle" and is starting away from Martin. Let children think about how both boys must feel at the moment and then tell them that a neighbor has been watching. Now the neighbor talks to Martin. Ask for a volunteer to play the role of Martin and another to be the elderly man (Mr. Eckmann) who was watching. Let them play out the conversation as they think it might have occurred. Then read the lines from the story.

Another good section is the beginning of Chapter 5. Read up to the part where Martin leaves the table, sending his chair to the floor, and storms up to his room. Tell the children to think for a moment how his words and behavior might have affected the family and ask for volunteers to role-play a conversation that might take place among Mr. and Mrs. Hastings and Marietta. These and other episodes in the story can give children a chance to be involved in Martin's struggle to be a better person. They can be used to good effect, especially when discussion follows the role-playing.

Oral Interpretation (Discussion, Creative Dramatics)

Ramona the Pest by Beverly Cleary.

This is a delightful book to read aloud. Listeners are amused at Ramona's antics, but they also realize that she is a little person with fears and needs quite like their own. They can respond emotionally by laughing at her but also by feeling compassion and empathy for her. Building on the emotional response, children can begin to interpret the story by inferring that Ramona seems to be a little girl who doesn't mean to be naughty but who sometimes gets into trouble because she thinks she has been badly treated by someone. They may also infer that the author is trying to show us the things that can happen to make kindergarten (or any school experience) difficult for children.

Oral reading of the story should take advantage of the many dialogue parts that help to build Ramona as a character. Numerous sections of the story are appropriate for Readers Theatre work. It is preferable, of course, that children read or hear the entire story before singling out one section for oral interpretation. An effective section is near the beginning, where Ramona goes to school for the first time (pp. 10–17, ending with the amusing "present" misunderstanding). Parts needed are: narrator (preferably an adult or superior reader), Ramona, Mrs. Quimby, Mary Jane, Beezus, Mrs. Kemp, Howie, a group of first-grade boys, and Miss Binney. Another good section is the scene where Ramona is stuck in the mud and must be pulled out by Henry Huggins (pp. 114–125). Characters are: narrator, Ramona, Henry, Miss Binney, a group of kindergarten children, a man in his car, and some older boys calling through an open window. A third choice is the "dawnzer" episode (pp. 171–173). The characters needed are: narrator, Beezus, Ramona, Mr. Quimby, and Mrs. Quimby. Third- and fourth-graders are far enough advanced to read these sections and they are also enough older than Ramona that they can feel a sort of security in having passed through the difficult kindergarten period.

Historical Fiction and Biography

Reading Aloud (Discussion, Creative Dramatics)

And Then What Happened, Paul Revere? by Jean Fritz.

A cleverly illustrated description of old Boston opens this account of some of Paul Revere's adventures. Emotionally, children will respond to the humorous descriptions such as Paul's advertisement for his art in making false teeth, and they will enter into the excitement of his life as a secret agent and an express rider between Boston and Philadelphia. They may make some evaluation of the story if they are able to compare it with other sources.

There are many human touches in this telling of Paul Revere's life as a patriot. Your reading can add greatly to children's interest in the man as a person as well as a patriot. You can pause in strategic places to give children a chance to think about the situation and consider what Paul might do next. A good example of that is the picture of Paul and his friends on the dock when he realizes he has no spurs, with a caption reading, "What could be done?" Children may come up with the same idea as Paul—to send the dog home with a note so that his wife could attach the spurs to the dog's collar and send them back.

An important part of this book is the inclusion of notes from the author. Children should be made aware of them and you may want to read some or all aloud as part of the story.

Storytelling (Reading Aloud, Discussion)

The Story of Johnny Appleseed by Aliki.

Young children are interested in living things. They enjoy planting seeds and watching them sprout. Though they may not be able to imagine a country without carefully tended orchards and fields, they will be interested in this story about a man who cared enough about trees and about people to spend part of his life planting seeds that could eventually produce fine orchards. Children respond emotionally to the character of Johnny Appleseed, especially when the story is told convincingly. The picture book by Aliki provides a basic story line which storytellers can use or adapt. You may want to show the illustrations from the book as you tell the story of Johnny Appleseed's life.

Writing Activity (Reading Aloud, Discussion, Role-Playing)

North to Freedom by Anne Holm.

This touching story tells about a boy's discovery of the outside world after spending his early years in a concentration camp. Children generally can respond emotionally to the boy David. Often their comments show empathy for him and sensitivity to the problems he struggles with. A discussion of the story can also show that children are able to evaluate the plot structure, especially the story ending.

David's story is told in such a way that children become closely involved with him. When they relate so well to a character, they often find it easy to assume his or her point of view. That ability to assume a character's point of view can be used to extend the reading experience to a writing activity, at the same time giving children a chance to make inferences about a story character's behavior. Some situations from the story that can stimulate good writing responses are these:

You are David. Describe your feelings as you were running from the barbed wire fence of the camp to take cover in the thicket.

You are David. Suppose that you had not overheard the conversation between Carlo and Andrea's parents and run away. Describe what your life might have been like in their home.

You are David. Write a letter to a friend, describing your first experience with a friendly dog.

How else might the story have ended? Write your own ending from the time David arrived in Copenhagen.

Informational Books

Reading Aloud (Discussion, Role-Playing)

Jambo Means Hello by Tom and Muriel Feelings.

This beautifully illustrated picture book is an alphabet book that will interest older children as well as those in the primary grades. Information in the book ranges from an introduction with a map showing countries where Swahili is spoken to definition and pronunciation of twenty-four Swahili words, one for each letter of the Swahili alphabet. Word concepts are elaborated in the double-page illustrations.

Do not neglect the introduction when you read the book aloud, for it presents important information about the people who speak Swahili. You can also use it to acquaint children with the fact that an introduction is an important part of many nonfiction books. As you read the book, show the pictures so that children can see how the pictures help to develop word concepts. You may want to let children speak some of the words together, pantomiming the concepts as they say the new words. That is an effective procedure for words like *heshima* (respect), *jambo* (hello), *rafiki* (friend), and *Karibu* (welcome).

Responses to be sought and encouraged are, of course, enjoyment of the language and curiosity about word meanings, responses which touch on emotional reaction, interpretation, and attention to literary qualities. Children may show interest in similarities between Swahili and English, evident in words for father, mother, and school. Discussion may lead children to seek other information about how words enter a language.

Discussion (Reading Aloud, Writing Activities)

All Upon a Sidewalk by Jean George.

The illustrations are an important part of this informational book. For that reason, children should have an opportunity to view them as the book is being read and to study them independently later.

Responses that indicate curiosity about and interest in the yellow ant, expressions of emotional response to the material, should be encouraged. Children may also comment on the form of the illustrations, in particular the technique of extracting small segments from a large picture to illustrate each page. Since a yellow ant's territory is limited, it was possible for the illustrator to draw three scenes which account for all the story action. Each page of the book is illustrated with a segment of the scene, greatly magnified, that is the setting for that part of the story. Some children will comment on a literary element—the writing style used to describe the ant's surroundings and the effectiveness with which the author shows us the microcosmic world of the ant.

When the book has been read and the pictures studied, you might allow children time to informally share information they gained from the story. Let them discuss their ideas about the most interesting things they learned. Next, you might call attention to the full-sized illustration on the last page and follow that with a look at the illustration on the first page. Ask whether they can locate that microscopic view in the large picture. Why did the illustrator choose to blow up the pictures that way? What is he trying to make us think about? Encourage them to discuss the illustrator's purpose in trying to have us see the world from an ant's viewpoint. To establish that comparison with our own way of observing, you might again show the picture on the last page and ask what the cat must look like to an ant.

To help children identify important information from the book, ask them to recall the things that seem most important to Lasius. How does the yellow ant go about satisfying her needs and wants? What dangers does she meet? How did the author tell us that even raindrops can be dangerous to an ant? As a follow-up, some children may want to investigate the movements of an insect they observe after school and write an illustrated account of what they saw.

Role-Playing (Discussion)

Handtalk by Remy Charlip, Mary Beth and George Ancona.

Handtalk is a book which builds children's curiosity about ways of communicating without speech. If you introduce the book by describing the world of a deaf person who must rely on eyes alone for communication, you can create sensitivity to the handicap of deafness. Experience with the book should help children to develop empathy with deaf people and admiration for the way they are able to communicate. The illustrations in the book include signing as well as finger spelling. As one example, the letter *L* is introduced with *LOVE*. A large colored picture shows Mary Beth signing *love* by crossing her hands over her chest. At the bottom of the page, small photos show the correct finger spelling for each letter of the word. The inside book cover shows a large number of other words or ideas which can be signed.

You may want to introduce this informational book by letting children look at each of the pictures, practicing several of the signs. When children have had a chance to study the book, they will be ready for a role-playing situation in which you ask a question and ask them to answer it by signing, as though that were their only means of communication. Examples of questions are:

What is your favorite food?
How do you like to spend your spare time?
How do you feel about animals?

A follow-up discussion might give children a chance to compare the advantages of signing and finger spelling to decide which is the more effective and which might communicate more easily.

Summary

In all the books recommended and activities suggested in this chapter and in all the books and activities you find work well in your own experiences, the key to your success will be building on children's enjoyment. Response to literature can take place only when children have enjoyed a story or poem. This idea may seem obvious on the surface, and yet it can be lost sight of so easily when choosing books and activities for a particular group of children with particular needs and tastes. If you take pleasure or enjoyment as the starting point and as the goal of a literature program, you are likely to have most success measured in terms of enthusiastic readers. Through the enjoyment, a sense of literary structure may develop and children may be encouraged to try to interpret aspects of the work. Occasionally, they will look at the story or poem critically, evaluating it in some fashion. Most important, however, we hope children will enjoy these experiences with literature so much that they will want to read and reread books independently, to take time alone with favorite picture books, and to investigate the books of other authors.

A second hope is that you, the adult, will seek out other books and poems that you would enjoy sharing with children, adapting some of the activities in this chapter to your own material. A further hope is that you can provide plenty of books and a pleasant reading environment. An activity-centered program in combination with a strong program of independent library reading can provide the basis for ever increasing enjoyment of and reliance on reading as a leisure-time pursuit.

Children's Books Discussed in This Chapter

AARDEMA, VERNA. *Why Mosquitoes Buzz in People's Ears,* ill. by Leo and Diane Dillon. Dial, 1975.

ALEXANDER, LLOYD. *The Wizard in the Tree,* ill. by Laszlo Kubinyi. Dutton, 1975.

ALIKI. *The Story of Johnny Appleseed,* ill. by author. Prentice, 1963.

ARBUTHNOT, MAY HILL, and ZENA SUTHERLAND. *The Arbuthnot Anthology of Children's Literature,* 4th ed. Scott, Foresman, 1976. (See for "The Fisherman and His Wife," "The Bremen Town-Musicians," "The Hare and the Tortoise," "The Pancake," and "Rumpelstiltskin.")

BOYLAN, ELEANOR. *How to Be a Puppeteer.* McCall, 1970.

BROWN, MARCIA. *Once a Mouse,* ill. by author. Scribner's, 1961.

______, ill. *The Three Billy-Goats Gruff.* Harcourt, 1957.

BURNFORD, SHEILA. *The Incredible Journey,* ill. by Carl Burger. Little, 1961.

ANDERSEN, HANS CHRISTIAN. *The Emperor's New Clothes,* ill. by Virginia Lee Burton. Houghton, 1962.

CAUDILL, REBECCA. *A Pocketful of Cricket,* ill. by Evaline Ness. Holt, 1964.

CHARLIP, REMY, MARY BETH and GEORGE ANCONA. *Handtalk,* ill. with photos. Parents, 1974.

CIARDI, JOHN. *You Read to Me, I'll Read to You,* ill. by Edward Gorey. Lippincott, 1962.

CLEARY, BEVERLY. *Ramona the Pest,* ill. by Louis Darling. Morrow, 1968.

COURLANDER, HAROLD. *The King's Drum,* ill. by Enrico Arno. Harcourt, 1962.

DE REGNIERS, BEATRICE SCHENK. *May I Bring a Friend?* ill. by Beni Montresor. Atheneum, 1964.

EMBERLEY, BARBARA. *Drummer Hoff,* ill. by Ed Emberley. Prentice, 1967.

ETS, MARIE HALL. *In the Forest,* ill. by author. Viking, 1944.

FEELINGS, MURIEL. *Jambo Means Hello,* ill. by Tom Feelings. Dial, 1974.

FRANCHERE, RUTH. *Cesar Chavez,* ill. by Earl Thollander. T. Crowell, 1970.

FRITZ, JEAN. *And Then What Happened, Paul Revere?* ill. by Margot Tomes. Coward, 1973.

FYLEMAN, ROSE. *Fifty-One Nursery Rhymes.* Doubleday, 1931, 1932.

GARDNER, MARTIN. *Codes, Ciphers and Secret Writing.* Simon, 1972.

GEISEL, THEODOR SEUSS. *The King's Stilts,* ill. by author. Random, 1939.

GEORGE, JEAN CRAIGHEAD. *All Upon a Sidewalk,* ill. by Don Bolognese. Dutton, 1974.

______. *Julie of the Wolves,* ill. by John Schoenherr, Harper, 1973.

______. *My Side of the Mountain,* ill. by author. Dutton, 1959.

HAMILTON, VIRGINIA. *The Time-Ago Tales of Jahdu,* ill. by Nonny Hogrogian. Macmillan, 1969.

HOBAN, RUSSELL. *A Bargain for Frances,* ill. by Lillian Hoban. Harper, 1970.

HOBAN, TANA. *Push-Pull, Empty-Full.* Macmillan, 1972.

______. *Where Is It?* Macmillan, 1974.

JARRELL, RANDALL. *The Bat-Poet,* ill. by Maurice Sendak. Macmillan, 1967.

KONIGSBURG, E. L. *From the Mixed-Up Files of Mrs. Basil E. Frankweiler,* ill. by author. Atheneum, 1968.

LAWSON, ROBERT. *Rabbit Hill,* ill. by author. Viking, 1944.

LEAF, MUNRO. *The Story of Ferdinand,* ill. by Robert Lawson. Viking, 1936.

LIVINGSTON, MYRA COHN. *The Malibu and Other Poems,* ill. by James Spanfeller. Atheneum, 1972.

______. *Wide Awake and Other Poems,* ill. by Jacqueline Chwast. Harcourt, 1959.

MATHIS, SHARON BELL. *The Hundred Penny Box,* ill. by Leo and Diane Dillon. Viking, 1975.

MAYER, MERCER and MARIANNA. *One Frog Too Many,* ill. by Mercer Mayer. Dial, 1975.

McCLOSKEY, ROBERT. *Time of Wonder,* ill. by author. Viking, 1957.

McCORD, DAVID. *Far and Few,* ill. by Henry B. Kane. Little, 1952.

MERRILL, JEAN. *The Pushcart War,* ill. by Ronni Solbert. Scott/Addison, 1964.

MILES, MISKA. *Nobody's Cat,* ill. by John Schoenherr. Little, 1969.

MINARIK, ELSE. *A Kiss for Little Bear,* ill. by Maurice Sendak. Harper, 1968.

MOSEL, ARLENE. *Tikki Tikki Tembo,* ill. by Blair Lent. Holt, 1968.

MOWAT, FARLEY. *Owls in the Family,* ill. by Robert Frankenberg. Little, 1962.

NESS, EVALINE. *Do You Have the Time, Lydia?* ill. by author. Dutton, 1971.

______, ill. *Tom Tit Tot.* Scribner's, 1965.

NORTON, MARY. *The Borrowers,* ill. by Beth and Joe Krush. Harcourt, 1953.

O'BRIEN, ROBERT C. *Mrs. Frisby and the Rats of NIMH,* ill. by Zena Bernstein. Atheneum, 1971.

O'DELL, SCOTT. *The King's Fifth.* Houghton, 1966.

O'NEILL, MARY. *Hailstones and Halibut Bones,* ill. by Leonard Weisgard. Doubleday, 1961.

POTTER, BEATRIX. *The Tale of Peter Rabbit,* ill. by author. Warne, 1903.

RASKIN, ELLEN. *Nothing Ever Happens on My Block,* ill. by author. Atheneum, 1966.

RICHARDS, LAURA E. *Tirra Lirra,* ill. by Marguerite Davis. Little, 1955.

SAWYER, RUTH. *Journey Cake, Ho!* ill. by Robert McCloskey. Viking, 1953.

SENDAK, MAURICE. *Where the Wild Things Are,* ill. by author. Harper, 1963.

SHEPHARD, ESTHER. *Paul Bunyan,* ill. by Rockwell Kent. Harcourt, 1941.

SLOBODKINA, ESPHYR. *Caps for Sale,* ill. by author. W. R. Scott, 1947.

SPEARE, ELIZABETH GEORGE. *The Witch of Blackbird Pond.* Houghton, 1958.

STOLZ, MARY. *The Bully of Barkham Street,* ill. by Leonard Shortall. Harper, 1963.

WARD, LYND. *The Biggest Bear,* ill. by author. Houghton, 1952.

WILDER, LAURA INGALLS. *The Little House in the Big Woods,* ill. by Garth Williams. Harper, 1953. (See others in the series also.)

ZOLOTOW, CHARLOTTE. *Mr. Rabbit and the Lovely Present,* ill. by Maurice Sendak. Harper, 1962.

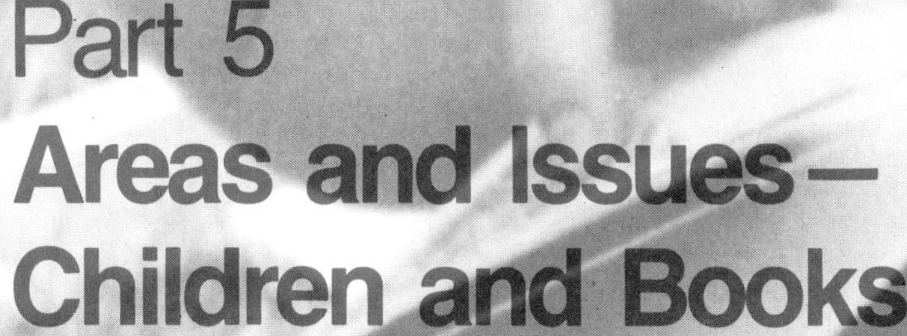

Part 5
Areas and Issues—Children and Books

Research in Children's Literature

Censorship: Perpetual Threat to Librarians and Teachers

Television: Its Impact and Influence

Sexism in Children's Books

Pressure for Pluralism

Internationalism in Children's Literature

Popular Literature

Children's Access to Materials

Areas and Issues

Introduction

As the title suggests, Part 5, "Areas and Issues—Children and Books," is not strictly about children and books in that even when the discussion is directed at print materials, it is not always concerned with adult-approved reading materials. An assumption that runs through all the following discussions is that media, in whatever form, do more than provide information: they do have an impact and influence upon behavior and attitude formation, even though it is still impossible to isolate in research the precise nature of such influence.

The areas and issues presented here are crucial ones for students, teachers, librarians, and all adults interested in children's reading and in child development. Since most of the topics have had books written about them and others have been the subjects of major research studies, the purpose of the discussions here is to provide introductions to the topics, supply bibliographies, and suggest questions for further study and research ranging from term papers to doctoral dissertations. The bibliographies reflect as wide a range of opinion as possible. In Donelson's article, for example, the bibliography provides access to books and articles that support censorship as well as to those that oppose it and to those that take a middle ground.

Obviously, these eight topics represent only a small proportion of possible areas of concern available for research studies. As Lukenbill observes in "Research in Children's Literature," the entire field of children's literature is open for study. Among the numerous topics that are not covered here, but might have been, are: (1) the extent and nature of specialized children's book collections; (2) the various book award organizations and the criteria established for the awards; (3) the quantity and quality of newspapers and magazines for children; (4) the quantity and quality of criticism and evaluation of children's books and related media as exemplified by various review media; (5) the issues raised by the current controversy over the structure and role of the public-school system; and (6) special facets of the censorship question, such as the inclusion of sex education books in schools and libraries.

Solid research in a field does more than establish the respectability of that field. It aids the practitioners in identifying what is known as well as what remains to be discovered. It also aids in the development of new research techniques as older, established methodologies prove inadequate to the needs of the field under study. In the area of children's literature in relationship to its impact upon children's reading and attitudes, it may be that new techniques will have to be developed before the critical questions can be answered.—*Dorothy M. Broderick, Editor, Part 5, Areas and Issues—Children and Books.*

Research in Children's Literature

*W. Bernard Lukenbill**

A General Premise

To reiterate a statement made in the 1972 edition of this article, social science research seeks to establish normative principles rather than to search for laws. Therefore, accepting the study of children's literature as a part of the social sciences entails developing research studies which are capable of adding to broad and correct generalizations and principles concerning children and their relationships to books, literature, and reading. Researchers might view their work as contributing to an eventual understanding of youth literature and its possible environmental and behavioral influences.

Often assertions are made by teachers, librarians, and parents concerning the positive effects of good books and literature on the behavioral patterns of youth. Yet very few of these traditional assumptions have been consistently determined through research evidence. Helen Huus wrote in 1964 that researchers had not been able to ascertain the effects of various social variables on children and their reading, and subsequently on their behavioral patterns; nor had they formulated research techniques and designs capable of answering some of the basic problems posed in their studies. The same generalization can be drawn today as well.

In attempting to verify certain claims, the researcher in children's literature must become allied with research methodologies originated in other disciplines, yet applicable to children's literature study. The investigator will find several methods and techniques available; but whichever methods are selected, the researcher should always operate on the assumption that the work will add something to the general understanding of children's literature as an influence on children's behavior.

*W. Bernard Lukenbill is Assistant Professor in the Graduate School of Library Science at the University of Texas, Austin.

Research Trends

Today, most research in children's literature is conducted either as masters' theses or as doctoral dissertations. Although some research is conducted by practitioners or academicians acting as independent investigators, most researchers seldom have adequate time or finances required to carry out a well-designed and executed research project. Interestingly enough, psychologists and behavioral scientists have intermediately conducted studies in the area of reading's influence on behavioral changes, but only rarely have these studies involved children's literature. Nevertheless, such studies do exist, and they offer examples of techniques and procedures to be studied and perhaps emulated. Such studies also help in the establishment of generalizations concerning reading as a behavior-influencing factor. More often the research conducted by sociologists and psychologists has been concerned with the effects of nonbook media on children's behavior patterns. Research relating to television's effects on behavior has been especially plentiful in recent years.

Research scholars in the humanities also have begun to show more interest in children's literature as a serious and respected topic for research. This seems evident by the increasing number of studies appearing in leading humanities-oriented journals as well as the increased activities related to research in children's literature under the auspices of organizations such as the Children's Literature Association, the Seminar on Children's Literature of the Modern Language Association, and the International Research Society for Children's Literature.

Historically, probably the most popular areas of investigation in children's literature have been reading-interest studies. Generalizations based on these reading-interest studies usually can be accepted, but even here one will find contradictions and changes, depending upon the samples and time periods.

How best to teach young people to enjoy literature and how to use children's literature in the instructional curriculum are popular topics of investigation. But these studies often suffer from inadequate statistical and sampling techniques. Another common deficiency of these studies is their evaluation instruments. Two opposing questions can be raised about these instruments: (1) are they sensitive enough to measure the extent of learning taking place in the children involved in the experiment; and (2) do they over-measure the degree of learning taking place? Again, generalizations about the effectiveness of such teaching methods should not be accepted without question.

Specialized historical studies have also been popular as research topics. Literary developments in the colonial period, the Civil War period, the post–Civil War period, etc., have proven popular with investigators. Many studies both here and abroad have also been devoted to the history of foreign children's literature; and a number of translations of works concerned with children's literature in other countries are available, especially works from Germany, Spain, and France. England has also published some notable historical studies. The study of the historical development of juvenile periodicals is becoming increasingly popular with researchers. Periodical development in the late nineteenth century has proven itself especially popular as a topic of investigation. Nevertheless, much work still remains to be done in this area. More critical interpretative historical studies are certainly needed.

Literary studies in children's literature based on the general historical method of inquiry have produced studies dealing with various genres, including biography, drama, fantasy, historical fiction, humor, and poetry. This method has also lent itself to author studies and literary criticism.

In recent years, many studies have been devoted to the sociological aspects of children's literature. Researchers have shown special interest in analyzing the content of books for children depicting blacks, Native Americans, Mexican Americans, Puerto Ricans, Asian Americans, and other minority groups. An interest in analyzing books and other media for sexist biases has also become popular. Unfortunately, a great deal of the research devoted to these topics which has appeared in the less research-oriented professional press has been too emotionally and politically based to stand as examples of model research studies, although findings from such studies have often been confirmed by the findings of more objectively researched studies. Some studies have also attempted to determine how exposure to youth literature might affect attitude change toward minority groups and women. Although most of these studies have shown some sort of attitude change, additional study is required before sound generalizations can be drawn regarding this question. Social values and attitude concepts appearing in youth literature have also been popular areas of investigation. Examples of such social values and attitude concepts include death and its relationship to children, mental retardation, the aged, sexual identification and the acquiring of an appropriate expression of sexuality, pro social role behavior, and variations in familial life patterns.

Research Methods

Most research methodologies used in social sciences are applicable to research in children's literature. These methods include (1) the historical; (2) the descriptive—including its many techniques (survey, questionnaire, interview, group behavior analysis, content analysis, observational studies, and appraisal techniques); (3) the experimental; (4) the case study; and (5) the genetic or developmental study. The researcher should have some familiarity with all these techniques. Three excellent sources for background reading in research methodologies are Good's *Essentials of Educational Research* (1966), Kerlinger's *Foundations of Behavioral Research; Educational and Psychological Inquiry* (1964), and Selltiz and Jahoda's *Research Methods in Social Relations* (1959). Excellent articles on research also appear in Lindzey and Aronson's *Handbook of Social Psychology* (1968–1969) and Sills's *International Encyclopedia of the Social Sciences* (1968).

Of the methods cited above, the historical and the descriptive methodologies have been most widely used in research in children's literature. Further study requiring the experimental method seems also warranted in order to increase our understanding of the effects of books, reading, and literature on the learning and on the behavioral and attitudinal changes and patterns of children. But it should be remembered that in the experimental method, environmental and social variables are extremely difficult to control.

The case study method has not been widely used in children's literature research, although it is applicable. Prominent educators such as Frances Henne and the late Alice Brooks McGuire have suggested that this method be used more extensively in studying characteristics, interests, and responses of readers. The genetic or developmental study method seems to be seldom used in children's literature study. Its purpose is to study the developmental pattern of an individual or group over an extended period of time; consequently, it is often too involved and expensive for most researchers to undertake, even though it would be beneficial to children's literature.

Research Procedures and Sources

Before a research idea can be formed into a research design and executed, the researcher must obtain a sound knowledge of the general area to be investigated. This knowledge can be acquired through experience and association, and/or through reading. It is advisable to first formulate a general theory or concept about the area to be studied. This theory should normally include some broad generalizations which have not yet been tested. From this generalized theory, a hypothesis should be formulated. The hypothesis is a simple statement asserting that some element contained in the general theory is true under certain conditions and can be tested through research. Once the hypothesis has been stated, the research design, including appropriate research methodologies and techniques, can be developed.

Students and teachers who are interested in finding research topics need to keep abreast of professional developments and to read extensively in professional journals and monographs. A review of the bibliography for this article will identify periodicals which present current problems involving children's literature. Actual research studies are often found in these periodicals, offering examples for the researcher. Research journals such as *Review of Educational Research* also occasionally carry research studies devoted to children's literature, and in the last few years two periodicals especially devoted to research in children's literature have made their appearance. These are *Phaedrus; a Newsletter of Children's Literature Research*, and *Children's Literature: The Great Excluded*. Another indication of the widening appeal of children's literature as an area of research interest was the founding of the International Research Society for Children's Literature in May of 1970. This association seeks to encourage and coordinate the exchange of information concerning both theoretical questions of interest to researchers in the field as well as to disseminate information about on-going projects. Biennial professional meetings for interested researchers are part of the association's activities.[1] One who is interested in conducting research should also be aware of social issues and cognizant that social developments influence children's literature, thus providing fruitful areas for research.

Several bibliographic sources which list research studies in children's literature are included in the following bibliography. These sources should be consulted before any serious research planning is done. The researcher should also read as many actual research studies, including dissertations, as possible. In this way, the novice will develop an understanding and feel for methodology and research procedures and will learn to identify the strengths and weaknesses of various research techniques.

Primary sources for the study of children's literature are extremely important to the researcher, especially if biographical, literary, or historical studies are contemplated. Although the *National Union Catalog of Manuscript Collections* is available and should be consulted, its holdings now are generally sparse and incomplete in the area of children's literature. Carolyn Field's *Subject Collections in Children's Literature* (1969) is an excellent source for locating both collections of children's books and manuscripts relating to children's literature and is now being updated and expanded.

[1]Inquiries may be addressed to the International Research Society for Children's Literature, Tjärhovsgatan 36, S-11621, Stockholm, Sweden.

Suggested Research Needs

The entire area of children's literature is available for research. The following general topics seem to be particularly in need of study:

1. The effects of reading on behavior and learning patterns (bibliotherapy, retarded readers, etc.).
2. The sociology of children's literature (both past and present).
3. The publishing industry both in the United States and abroad (including regional presses).
4. The history of children's literature (including regional developments).
5. The teaching of children's literature (including college instruction, use of innovation, mediated approaches, group and simulation techniques).
6. The review media (including regional coverage, characteristics of reviewers, etc.).
7. Linguistic features of children's literature (including reading levels, etc.).
8. Art and media format studies (illustrations, paperbacks, typography).
9. Prognostic studies (prediction of future developments in book or media forms, reader-use characteristics, etc.).
10. Books and nonbook media as behavior modeling devices for children, especially children from minority and lower socio-economic backgrounds.
11. Information needs and information-seeking behavior of children and how books and nonbook items serve those needs and affect those behavior patterns.
12. Studies using children's literature in creative dramatics for children (focus of such studies might include the study of recently published books for children considering their adaptability to children's creative dramatics experiences).
13. Children's literature in the open school and classroom (a study of the teacher and pupil behavior in relationship to functions, roles, and literature availability).

Bibliography

Research Reviews

BEKKEDAL, TAKLA K. "Content Analysis of Children's Books." *Library Trends* 22 (1973): 109–126. Beginning with a discussion of content analysis as a research tool, this article comments upon major content analysis studies conducted in the area of children's literature. Included are studies pertaining to culture and social values, as well as racism and ethnic group content. Suggestions for additional research are also included.

BROWN, GEORGE I. "Literature in the Elementary School." *Review of Educational Research* 34 (1964): 187–194. Although becoming dated, an excellent review of research studies pertaining to reading interests; the elementary-school library and its relationship to literature programs; evaluation and analysis of children's literature; individualized reading and literature; and psychological processes and literature. Calls for more significant research work in the areas mentioned.

BUSBY, LINDA J. "Sex-role Research on the Mass Media." *Journal of Communication* 25 (1975): 107–131. Summarizes and categorizes the most significant recent research on sex roles as depicted in mass media, with an emphasis on content and effects studies. Mass media areas analyzed include television, children's TV programming, magazines, newspapers, children's literature, and textbooks. Extensive bibliography included.

BURTON, DWIGHT L. "Research in the Teaching of Literature." *Review of Educational Research* 19 (1949): 125–134. Cites research studies in the area of teaching techniques, evaluation, social and personal adjustment, and reading interests. National and state surveys are also discussed. Bibliography of research studies included.

CHAMBERS, DEWEY W. "The Didactic Theory," in *Children's Literature in the Curriculum,* pp. 137–162. Rand, 1971. Discusses several major research studies dealing with the ability of literature to influence behavior.

HUUS, HELEN. "Interpreting Research in Children's Literature." In *Children, Books, and Reading,* pp. 123–145, edited by Mildred Dawson, Perspectives in Reading, no. 3. Newark, Del.: International Reading Association, 1964. Major discussion on research in children's literature. Outlines five areas of popularity: (1) reading preferences, (2) poetry, (3) mass media, (4) reading materials, and (5) effects of reading. Lists areas of needed research. Bibliography of studies included.

KINNEL, ERIC. "Can Children's Books Change Children's Values?" *Educational Leadership* 28 (1970): 209–214. Discusses selected studies dealing with both the effects of reading on children and the social content of books that might influence behavior. An excellent selected bibliography included.

LOWRY, HEATH W. "A Review of Five Recent Content Analyses of Related Sociological Factors in Children's Literature." *Elementary English* 46 (1969): 736–740. Reviews studies by Chambers, Homze, Lowry, Shepherd, and Walker. Concludes that these studies have contributed to an understanding of social values appearing in children's materials. Suggests areas for additional research.

PURVES, ALAN C., and RICHARD BEACH. *Literature and the Reader: Research in Response to Literature, Reading Interests and the Teaching of Literature.* Nat. Council of Teachers of English, 1972. Presents a critical and important analysis of numerous research studies of significance which were conducted through 1969 in the areas of reader response to literature, reading interest, and the teaching of literature. Well-selected bibliographies of major research studies are included. An excellent summary chapter presents conclusions drawn from the review and discusses implications for further research.

ROBINSON, HELEN M., and SAMUEL WEINTRAUB. "Research Related to Children's Interests and to Developmental Values of Reading." *Library Trends* 22 (1973): 81–108. Presents a readable review of significant studies on: (1) the reading interests of children including preschool and primary children, middle-grade children as well as secondary-school children, and (2) a discussion of the developmental values of reading, including the effects of reading in changing children's value and behavior systems. An excellent bibliography is included.

SHAFER, ROBERT I. "The Reading of Literature." *Journal of Reading* 8 (1965): 345–349. Brief review of several major studies in reading and literature. Calls for additional research to develop an understanding of the impact of literature on human behavior.

SQUIRE, JAMES R. "English Literature." In *Encyclopedia of Educational Research.* 4th ed., pp. 461–473. Macmillan, 1969. Gives an extensive review of research studies relating to the teaching of literature. Both elementary and secondary level approaches are given with emphasis on the secondary-school aspect. Comprehensive bibliography included.

TEMP, GEORGE. "Literature in the Secondary School." *Review of Educational Research* 34 (1964): 195–202. Surveys of the more important studies conducted in the area and comments on the problems of research in literature. Studies discussed are noted in the bibliography.

Source Guides

"Children's Literature Collections and Research Libraries." *Wilson Library Bulletin* 50 (1975): 128–169. Entire issue devoted to discussing developments in child culture and children's literature. Topics include the need for material planning for research collection development; Yiddish juvenilia; the juvenile book collection of the Essex Institute in Salem, Mass.; U.C.L.A.'s collection of rare children's books; and the Morgan Library's children's book collection. Also included are discussions on the cataloging and organization of material in the Information Center on Children's Culture in New York; and a brief review of the printed catalogs of the Osborne Collection of children's books.

Dissertation Abstracts and *Dissertation Abstracts International.* 1952–(monthly). Includes abstracts of dissertations accepted by participating colleges and universities. Comprehensive subject and author indexes are available.

FIELD, CAROLYN W., ed. *Subject Collections in Children's Literature.* New York: Bowker, 1969. Describes the holdings of collections useful in children's literature research. Books, manuscripts, and other items included. Currently being updated and expanded.

HAVILAND, VIRGINIA, et al. *Children's Literature: A Guide to Reference Sources.* Library of Congress, 1966.

______. *Children's Literature: A Guide to Reference Sources.* First Supplement. Library of Congress, 1972. Extensive guides to various sources of materials relating to children's literature. Subject approach provided.

Children's Literature Abstracts, May 1973– (quarterly). International Federation of Library Associations. This service abstracts material appearing in educational and library science journals from around the world. English, American, and continental sources predominate. Access to material is provided through a broad subject arrangement.

Library Literature, 1933/35– (quarterly). Contains lists of masters' and doctoral theses on children's literature under the heading "Library Schools—Theses."

LITTLE, LAWRENCE, comp. *Researches in Personality, Character and Religious Education; A Bibliography of American Doctoral Dissertations, 1885–1959.* Pittsburgh: Univ. of Pittsburgh Pr., 1962. Provides a specialized approach to research in children's literature. Annotations are not given for entries.

LUKENBILL, W. BERNARD. *A Working Bibliography of American Doctoral Dissertations in Children's and Adolescents' Literature, 1930–1971.* Occasional Paper, no. 103. Urbana-Champaign: University of Illinois, Graduate School of Library Science, 1972. Identifies and describes over 100 doctoral dissertations accepted by American colleges and universities. Extensive bibliography included.

McNAMEE, LAWRENCE F. *Dissertations in English and American Literature; Theses Accepted by American, British and German Universities, 1865–1964.* Bowker, 1968.

______. *Dissertations in English and American Literature. Supplement One; Theses Accepted by American, British and German Universities, 1964–1968.* Bowker, 1969.

______. *Dissertations in English and American Literature. Supplement Two; Theses Accepted by American, British and German Universities, 1969–1973.* Bowker, 1974.
Although limited, these works offer access to some foreign dissertations dealing with children's literature.

Modern Language Association, Seminar on Children's Literature. *Children's Literature: The Great Excluded,* 1972– (annual). Published by the English Department at the University of Connecticut, this periodical presents essays on all aspects of children's literature and interest. Topical coverage includes all ages from preschool through high school. Most essays are developed from a viewpoint of research in the humanities.

Phaedrus; a Newsletter of Children's Literature Research. Fall 1973– (biannual). Attractively printed newsletter, edited by James Fraser, which disseminates information about research in children's and adolescents' literature. The newsletter covers periodicals, textbooks, comics, song books, boxed games, films, television, and the oral literature of children. Excellent bibliographic features are included which cite material drawn from diverse scholarly fields and languages.

Research Studies in Education; A Subject and Author Index of Doctoral Dissertations, Reports and Field Studies, and a Research Methods Bibliography. 1941/51– (annual). Excellent source both for dissertations completed during the preceding year and for proposals accepted. Children's literature topics generally appear under the subject heading "Methods of Teaching; Teaching Aids; Libraries."

U.S. Educational Research Information Center. *Resources in Education.* 1966– (monthly). Commonly known as ERIC, this is a comprehensive source for all types of material dealing with education, including children's literature. Entries include dissertations, reports, conference proceedings, books, unpublished material, etc.

U.S. Library of Congress. *National Union Catalog of Manuscript Collections.* 1959– (annual). Describes the manuscript holdings of participating libraries in the United States. Subject-index approach offers access to a limited amount of material relating to children's literature.

Research Guides

BARZUN, JACQUES, and HENRY GRAFF. *The Modern Researcher.* Rev. ed. Harcourt, 1970. Suggests ways to do research. Especially strong in library and document analysis.

GOOD, CARTER V. *Essentials of Educational Research; Methodology and Design.* Appleton, 1966. An update and adaptation of Good's earlier work, *Introduction to Educational Research,* this edition discusses and outlines basic research method concepts applicable to most areas of the behavioral sciences, including education. Quantitative details of testing and measurement statistics and data processing are not included.

KENT, SHERMAN. *Writing History.* 2d ed. Appleton, 1967. Classical work which describes the historical research method. Gives details on topic selection, writing styles, and language usage suggestions.

KERLINGER, FRED N. *Foundations of Behavioral Research; Educational and Psychological Inquiry.* Holt, 1964. Considers technical and methodological problems in research at length. This is an excellent guide to a fundamental understanding of scientific research methodology applied to human behavior.

LINDZEY, GARDNER, and ELLIOT ARONSON, eds. *The Handbook of Social Psychology.* 2d ed., 5 vols. Addison, 1968–1969. Excellent background guide for those interested in research in socio-psychological relationships. Especially worth noting are excellent articles on interviewing and content analysis techniques as well as detailed discussions on the effects of the mass media, socialization, and attitudes and attitude change.

RILEY, MATILDA WHITE, and CLARICE S. STOLL. "Content Analysis." In *International Encyclopedia of the Social Sciences,* vol. 3, pp. 371–377. Macmillan, 1968. Explanation of the content analysis technique as used in social science research. Includes excellent bibliography.

SELLTIZ, CLAIRE, et al. *Research Methods in Social Relations.* Rev., one-vol. ed. Holt, 1959. Outlines basic approaches to the practical application of research. Standard research techniques are explained.

Representative Studies

APSELOFF, MARILYN. "Death in Current Children's Fiction: Sociology or Literature." Paper presented at the Forum on the Criticism of Children's Literature of the Midwest Modern Language Association, St. Louis, Mo., November 1974. ERIC document no. ED 101 371. An interesting examination of four children's books for their sociological and psychological attitudes toward death. Literary values in terms of style, plot, and characterization were also examined.

DARLING, RICHARD L. *The Rise of Children's Book Reviewing in America, 1865–1881.* Bowker, 1968. Traces the growth of children's literature in the post–Civil War period through a study of the contemporary review media.

DEANE, PAUL C. "The Persistence of Uncle Tom: An Examination of the Image of the Negro in Children's Fiction Series." *Journal of Negro Education* 37 (1968): 140–145. Interesting analysis of stereotypical and demeaning racial characteristics often applied to blacks as characters in popular mass-produced, series-fiction books published throughout the early and mid-twentieth century in the United States.

FALKENHAGEN, MARIA, et al. "Treatment of Native Americans in Recent Children's Literature." *Integration Education* 11 (July 1973): 58–59. Using a modified version of the David Gast analysis instrument, presents data on a content analysis of twenty-two children's books containing Native American characteristics, concepts, and stereotypes.

JENNINGS, S. A. "Effects of Sex Typing in Children's Stories on Preferences and Recall." *Child Development* 46 (1975): 220–223. Study describes how a group of preschool children reacted to sex roles as portrayed in story books. Calls for more books which offer boys wider model choices as well as presenting girls with more active and competent role models.

KARLINS, MARVIN, and HERBERT IL ABELSON. *Persuasion; How Opinions and Attitudes Are Changed.* 2d rev. ed. Springer, 1970. Gives summaries with discussion of research. Discusses many forms of change instruments, including reading.

KIEFER, MONICA MARY. *American Children Through Their Books, 1700–1835.* Univ. of Pa., 1970. Study of the adult concept of childhood as pictured in contemporary books written for children.

KUJOTH, JEAN SPEALMAN, comp. *Reading Interests of Children and Young Adults.* Scarecrow, 1970. A collection of actual research studies on reading interests. An excellent source book.

WEITZMAN, L. J., et al. "Sex-role Socialization in Picture Books for Pre-School Children." *American Journal of Sociology* 77 (1972): 1125–1150. Excellent and detailed presentation of data systematically gathered concerning sexual role behavior as presented in modern children's picture books.

Child Behavior Theory

BALDWIN, A. L. *Behavior and Development in Childhood.* Dryden, 1955. Ground-breaking textbook which has played a significant role in helping psychologists redefine and reconceptualize their understanding of the mental and behavior processes of children.

BANDURA, ALBERT. *Aggression: A Social Learning Analysis.* Prentice, 1973.

———. *Principles of Behavior Modification.* Holt, 1969. These two significant studies, conducted within the context of behavioral theory, demonstrate that children can and do acquire new response patterns through observation and imitation, without the need for external reinforcement, or even extensive rehearsal or practice. These studies reinforce the implication for modeling behavior gained through media as well as face-to-face encounter.

Literary Theory

ALBRECHT, MILTON C. "The Relationship of Literature and Society." *American Journal of Sociology* 59 (1964): 425–436. Theoretical discussion of the interplay of social organization and literature.

WELLEK, RENÉ, and AUSTIN WARREN. "Literature and Psychology." In *Theory of Literature*. 3d ed. pp. 81–93. Harcourt, 1956, discusses theoretical aspects in the study of psychology of the writer, the creative process, and psychological types and laws within literature. "Literature and Society," (pp. 94–109) discusses literature as a social institution, cautioning researchers not to use literature uncritically as social documents.

Censorship: Perpetual Threat to Librarians and Teachers

*Ken Donelson**

Censorship is hardly new. Throughout history, some people have worried that the rest of humanity could not safely discern the true from the false, the orthodox from the heretical, the beautiful from the ugly, and have gladly tried to forbid dissemination of what they regarded as objectionable material. Plato recommended censorship in his perfect society for religious and moral reasons. Hobbes advocated it as a politically practical way to control the state. Thomas Bowdler rewrote Shakespeare's plays to eliminate "those words and expressions which cannot with propriety be read aloud in the family." Anthony Comstock, our premier national censor, worried incessantly about the potentially corruptive power of the printed word, especially on young people, and in forty years worried several publishers, writers, and booksellers into jail. Censors' concern with *their* truth, the *only* truth fit to print or speak or teach, is illustrated in a manifesto of the Texans for America: "The stressing of both sides of a controversy only confuses the young and encourages them to make snap judgments based on insufficient evidence. Until they are old enough to understand both sides of a question, they should be taught only the American side." Censorship may not be new, but it is always contemporary.

*Ken Donelson is Professor of English at Arizona State University, Tempe.

Intellectual Freedom and Extralegal Censorship

Intellectual freedom, the freedom to read and write and speak and think and pursue any vision of the truth wherever that takes one, is presumably basic to the lives and work of librarians and teachers. But they will find others who do not accept the tenets of intellectual freedom, some antagonistically and openly, some quietly and insidiously. Public libraries have customarily been less vulnerable to attack, though a rapid skimming of the *Newsletter on Intellectual Freedom* (a basic reference for anyone concerned about the current state of intellectual freedom and *must* reading for librarians and teachers) will prove that public libraries are attacked. More likely to suffer are school librarians and teachers because they work with young people, and some parents would deny their children (and sometimes others' children) any rights of intellectual freedom.

Our nation has witnessed many attacks on schools and intellectual freedom during the past few years. Most attacks have been extralegal; that is, outside the courts or legal niceties, and teachers and librarians soon learn that extralegal censorship is common. When a teacher in Drake, North Dakota, taught Vonnegut's *Slaughterhouse-Five*, the school board objected to the book's alleged obscenity and ordered the book burned, and the teacher was fired. Though the teacher was ultimately vindicated in the courts and school officials were ordered to allow Vonnegut's novel back into the school, the teacher was not rehired and the likelihood of Drake teachers, or other teachers nearby, using this book or any other widely censored work is remote, the court order notwithstanding. A debate about drug and sex education in Ridgefield, Connecticut, touched off a two-year battle about teaching approaches and materials which more and more focused on books by and about blacks, notably Cleaver's *Soul on Ice*. The best publicized and certainly most volatile censorship incident occurred in Kanawha County, West Virginia. A controversy in early 1974 over textbooks some parents claimed were "anti-Christian, ungrammatical, and immoral" opened a running battle between school people and protestors. The conflict may have stemmed from the different values and value systems of the two groups, but the conflict soon centered around the freedom of teachers and librarians to select materials they believed effective and worthwhile. Teachers were called atheists, communists, perverts, filth-mongers, and corrupters. Beatings, shootings, and bombings threatened the lives of everyone involved, and intellectual freedom was jeopardized.

Local censorship cases rarely go to the courts. Commonly, unofficial charges against a book and a teacher or librarian begin as rumors and end in telephone calls to administrators. Starting because someone thought the work obscene (or suggestive, pornographic, filthy, un-American, anti-Christian, etc.) for some reason, the censorship incident is likely to be tried in the court of public opinion where pressure and power and rumors count more than the value of the book or education. The interpretations or definitions of obscenity (or un-American, anti-Christian, etc.) used in this extralegal court may have no legal or logical bases, but they are operationally effective in assuring a speedy verdict. These extralegal proceedings tend not to be concerned with accuracy or fairness or reasoning or justice.

The Supreme Court and Obscenity Decisions

On those rare occasions when a case involving censorship of a work used in schools goes before a legally constituted court, teachers or librarians may find that the court's definition or interpretation of obscenity is only slightly better than that of the extralegal proceedings. Though the First Amendment of the Constitution provides that "Congress shall make no law . . . abridging the freedom of speech, or of the press," the United States Supreme Court over the years has determined that certain freedoms may be abridged for the common good. Specifically, the Court has determined that obscenity is not protected by the First Amendment, but in so determining, the Court has never arrived at any precise definition of obscenity. As William Lockhart and Robert McClure wrote in the March 1954 *Minnesota Law Review*, "No one seems to know what obscenity is. Many writers have discussed the obscene, but few can agree upon even its essential nature . . . most writers have found the term hopelessly subjective and lacking in any definite or acceptable meaning."

The modern era of Court definitions of obscenity began with *Roth* v. *United States* (354 U.S. 467) in 1957. The *Roth* test was "whether to the average person, applying contemporary community standards, the dominant theme of the material taken as a whole appeals to prurient interest." In 1964, *Jacobellis* v. *Ohio* (378 U.S. 184) clarified the meaning of "contemporary community standards" when Justice Brennan, speaking for the majority, said that ". . . the constitutional status of an allegedly obscene work must be determined on the basis of a national standard. It is, after all, a national Constitution we are expounding." It is worth noting that Chief Justice Warren disagreed with Justice Brennan and argued for a local meaning of the word "community." Such was the law of the land until 1973. In two decisions, *Miller* v. *California* (93 S.Ct. 2607) and *Paris Adult Theatre I et al.* v. *Slaton* (93 S.Ct. 2628), Chief Justice Burger, delivering the majority opinion, repudiated the use of national community standards and stated that the community standard should be local. A certain confusion in whether the Court was really ready to accept *local* rather than *national* community standards crept into the 1974 decision in *Jenkins* v. *Georgia* (94 S.Ct. 2750). Justice Rehnquist attempted without much clarity to explain why *local* community standards were to be used, but not in all cases at all times. While the concept of *local* community standards seems likely to persist for many years, given the present group of Supreme Court Justices, the interpretation of the concept may alter slightly as new cases come before the Court.

Some Assumptions About Censorship

Because censorship is ubiquitous, because extralegal proceedings are common, and because the courts may offer little help or solace, teachers and librarians must face the likelihood of censorship in their schools and libraries. The following assumptions should be kept in mind.

(1) Any work of literature at any level is potentially censorable by someone, some-

where, sometime, for some reason. One mother argued that *Silas Marner* was bad because "You can't prove what that dirty old man is doing with that child between chapters." Another parent objected to *Treasure Island* because "You know what men are like and what they do when they've been away from women that long." A teacher objected to the last line in May Swenson's poem, "Southbound on the Freeway," because she thought the word *guts* was inappropriate for children.

(2) If any work can come under attack, the most likely to be attacked are *new* books or films. New works are more likely to be popular with young people, and they are more likely to be about the reality of the world today. Reality disturbs many people who would prefer their children had little contact with it in school and out.

(3) Censorship more often than not comes unexpectedly, often to teachers and librarians convinced that they are somehow immune from censorship, that censorship strikes only other people. Because they regard themselves as immune, they do not prepare to face the censor and they are easy prey.

(4) Censorship is capricious and arbitrary, books under attack in one school being safely used in another school nearby. Several surveys of censorship reveal that School I may come under attack for one book while School II, in the same district and only a mile away, may use the same book without incident. Even more absurd, but true, surveys reveal that Teacher A may come under attack while Teacher B, in the same school, uses the same book with impunity.

(5) Censorship often causes ripples in nearby schools. A censorship battle is almost certain to produce news, and teachers, librarians, and school administrators in other schools may grow nervous or fearful and avoid using the works under attack, at least until the furor dies down. Rumors fly, none faster than during censorship confrontations, and too many people prefer to be cautious, even at the expense of students. Fear leads easily to cowardice in book selection. Often, teachers or schools under attack remain justifiably fearful for years thereafter.

(6) Censorship most often begins with parental pressures, but other censors include board members, administrators, librarians, and teachers. Some in-house censorship by teachers and librarians may arise from fear of repercussions from using works recently censored in a nearby school or town. Other censorship may come from a belief that the old and classic is always superior to the new and relatively untried and potentially troublesome. Teachers and librarians may be guided by prior censorship because they fear any kind of trouble from any book anyone might have any remote objections to. One teacher was quoted as saying, "I would never use any book anyone might have any objection to." Given the many quite different books under attacks for many reasons, such a statement could lead to teaching no works at all since nothing is totally safe from attack. Other teachers and librarians may feel (or know) that they will receive no support from their school officials should attacks come. They might take refuge in statements like these: "We have no censorship problems. No, nobody here would support us. When they hire English teachers in my town, they make sure that English teachers are either cowards or pliable. Those that are cowards present no threat to anything (especially good literature for kids). Those that are pliable are brainwashed. Nobody here ever taught anything remotely worth censoring." "We could have had many complaints, but most of our teachers, myself included, steered clear of books that might offend." "After an investigation of both sides of a censorship problem, the principal might agree with the parents since we have been warned by the School Board that as far as book selection is concerned, we are on shaky ground. In other words, we cannot force the issue because we will not get *any* support."

Materials Likely to Be Attacked

While some books under attack are difficult to categorize, eight categories of objections cover most books likely to be censored.

(1) Sex ("suggestive situations," "immoral," "obscene"). This includes books as different as Huxley's *Brave New World*, Klein's *Mom, the Wolf Man and Me*, Keyes's *Flowers for Algernon*, Renvoize's *A Wild Thing*,

Brown's *Manchild in the Promised Land*, and Zindel's *The Pigman*.

(2) Politics or an attack on the American Dream ("liberal," "Communist-inspired," "un-American"). Orwell's *Animal Farm*, Steinbeck's *The Grapes of Wrath*, Hentoff's *I'm Really Dragged But Nothing Gets Me Down*, Steig's *Sylvester and the Magic Pebble*, Baum's *The Wizard of Oz*, and Plato's *Republic*.

(3) War and peace ("un-American," "peaceniks," "the author ought to go back where he came from"). Frank's *Alas Babylon*, Trumbo's *Johnny Got His Gun*, Heller's *Catch-22*, Remarque's *All Quiet on the Western Front*, Hersey's *Hiroshima*, and Cobb's *Paths of Glory*.

(4) Religion ("anti-God," "violates separation of church and state," "sacrilegious"). Levin's *Rosemary's Baby*, Vonnegut's *Slaughterhouse-Five*, Waugh's *The Loved One*, Hesse's *Siddhartha*, Parks's *The Learning Tree*, and *The Bible*.

(5) Sociology, race, and ethnic literature ("do-gooders," "pro-black," "anti-black," "biased on the race question," "do kids really have to read all that ugly stuff?"). Deloria's *Custer Died for Your Sins*, Cleaver's *Soul on Ice*, Neufeld's *Edgar Allan*, Armstrong's *Sounder*, Fox's *The Slave Dancer*, Merriam's *The Inner City Mother Goose*, Taylor's *The Cay*, Bannerman's *Little Black Sambo*, Lofting's *Dr. Doolittle*, Lipsyte's *The Contender*, Ellison's *Invisible Man*, Lee's *To Kill a Mockingbird*, and Westheimer's *My Sweet Charlie*.

(6) Language ("dirty words," "profane," "unfit for human ears"). Wojciechowska's *Don't Play Dead Before You Have To*, Miller's *The Cool World*, Salinger's *The Catcher in the Rye*, Chaucer's *The Canterbury Tales*, Joseph's *The Me Nobody Knows*, Fitzhugh's *Harriet the Spy*, and Neufeld's *Freddy's Book*.

(7) Drugs ("my kid doesn't need to know this stuff," "depressing," "don't contaminate kids with dirty stuff like this"). *Go Ask Alice*, Wojciechowska's *Tuned Out*, Kerr's *Dinky Hocker Shoots Smack*, Hinton's *That Was Then, This Is Now*, and Kingman's *The Peter Pan Bag*.

(8) Inappropriate adolescent behavior ("poor models for our children," "kids don't really act that way," "kids ought to know better than to act that way"). Zindel's *My Darling, My Hamburger*, Frank's *The Diary of a Young Girl*, Swarthout's *Bless the Beasts and Children*, McCullers's *Member of the Wedding*, and Donovan's *I'll Get There. It Better Be Worth the Trip*.

Obviously, some books under attack for one reason might as easily be attacked for another reason or a series of reasons. Orwell's *1984* has been censored because it is "obscene" and contains "filthy sex," but equally likely are attacks because the book is "un-American," "anti-God," "profane," "full of drug scenes," and "kids will be harmed by this book. They might like that life." Indeed, *1984* has been censored for all these reasons and others too numerous to mention.

Today ethnic literature is probably the most vulnerable to the censor. Censors may openly question its worth; sometimes their public statements mask their real objections. For example, many works by black authors were attacked in Kanawha County because they were "ungrammatical" or "used bad English" or "lacked merit as literature," though few teachers had any doubt about the real underlying reasons. Much racist hatred lies only slightly below the surface in too many censorship incidents.

Speaking at the 1975 meeting of the National Council of Teachers of English, Robert C. Small, Jr., pointed up the absurdity of much censorship when he described what would happen to a library if every group were allowed to eliminate any book objected to for any reason. Small noted that some people would object to any book in any way dealing with sex, another group would object to anything remotely religious, another group would oppose anything they construed as un-American, yet another group would do away with the occult or supernatural, still another group might object to anything they thought depressing, and other groups might come along objecting to feminist literature, antifeminist literature, ungrammatical literature, and on and on until there would be no books left for anyone. Once the librarian or teacher knuckles under and gets rid of *any* book, *nothing* is safe.

Why do censors fear ideas and books? Some censors want to protect young people against reality, and they feel that if certain ideas and facts can be withheld, young people will be safe from contamination. Ignorance does not lead to happiness, nor can any idea be fought effectively with ignorance, a thesis Milton advanced in his *Areopagitica* more than 300 years ago. Some censors have no faith in education and would prefer indoctrination. Education may open eyes and minds; indoctrination is intended to close eyes and minds to all but one mode of thought or one point of view. People fearful of the implications of education, that is the free inquiry into ideas and their consequences, naturally fear books which freely explore ideas, and this fear manifests itself as censorship.

What Teachers and Librarians Can Do About Censorship

Nothing anyone can do will necessarily stave off the possibility of censorship, but acting upon the following five suggestions might minimize the number or intensity of attacks.

First, teachers and librarians need to develop policy statements explaining clearly and succinctly the rationales they have for teaching or stocking literature. The statements should be honest and direct and understandable to the layperson. Statements about selection procedures would naturally follow. Both statements should be easily accessible to the public, for the public has the right to know not merely *what* books are used, but more importantly, *why* they are used and *how* they are used. Somewhere in the selection statement should occur some distinction between censorship and selection since the two terms are frequently confused or misused. The classic distinction comes from Lester Asheim's "Not Censorship But Selection" in the September 1953 *Wilson Library Bulletin*.

> *Selection, then, begins with a presumption in favor of liberty of thought; censorship with a presumption in favor of thought control. Selection's approach to the book is positive, seeking its values in the book as a book, and in the book as a whole. Censorship's approach is negative, seeking for vulnerable characteristics wherever they can be found anywhere in the book, or even outside it. Selection seeks to protect the right of the reader to read; censorship seeks to protect—not the right—but the reader himself from the fancied effects of his reading. The selector has faith in the intelligence of the reader; the censor has faith only in his own.*
>
> *In other words, selection is democratic while censorship is authoritarian, and in our democracy we have traditionally tended to put our trust in the selector rather than in the censor.*

The selection statement should clearly differentiate the problems involved in selecting books for different groups and individuals. Because they rarely have any understanding of the selection process, parents lack insight into the difficulties teachers and librarians face in selecting materials. Nor do they understand that a teacher must establish different criteria in selecting a book for an entire class, for small groups, or for individuals. Teachers and librarians are often asked to recommend a book to someone seeking leisure reading, and still different criteria operate then. Educating parents and other laypeople to problems like these is part of the responsibility of teachers and librarians.

One aspect of the selection process presents a real problem to librarians. Reevaluation, or the selective weeding of book collections, should not always be misinterpreted as censorship, but in fact, the first can easily become an excuse or justification for the latter. The *Interracial Books for Children Bulletin* has rightly called for care in selecting books honest to cultures and beliefs and peoples, but taken only slightly further, their recommendations can all too easily become censorship. Two excellent articles presenting divergent viewpoints appeared in the *School Library Journal*, Dorothy Broderick's "Censorship—Reevaluated" in November 1971 and James Harvey's "Acting for Children?" in February 1973. Librarians attempting to justify reevaluation might ponder what they would do if parents came to the library insisting that they wanted the same rights to weed out of the library whatever they thought bad or outdated or devoid of literary merit or prejudicial to one group. *The Charleston Gazette*, on November 14, 1974, carried an ad by the Business and Professional People's Alliance for Better Textbooks. The bulk of the huge ad featured quotations from textbooks the Kanawha County parents wanted removed from the schools, but a portion of the statement that followed contained words that looked suspiciously like library reevaluation.

> *We understand why certain groups object to* Little Black Sambo, *and we honor their objection. All we ask is that our group be given the same consideration. We do not insist that they agree with our position, but we do expect them to honor it.*
>
> *It is possible that if all minority objections were honored the schools might be reduced to teaching the basics, but would that be so bad?*

Second, teachers and librarians should become aware of the basic arguments for censorship (Plato and Hobbes) and against censorship (Milton's *Areopagitica* and Mill's *On Liberty*). They should recognize the current ploys of censors and their current targets. Reading *School Library Journal*, *English Journal*, *Language Arts*, *Wilson Library Bulletin*, and the *Newsletter on Intellectual Freedom* is essential in keeping up to date with the state of intellectual freedom.

Third, they should establish and implement a formal policy to handle objections to any materials. The National Council of Teachers of English pamphlet *The Students' Right to Read* (1962, revised 1972) suggests a procedure for handling censorship. The American Library Association's "Library Bill of Rights" (1961 and 1967) along with several interpretations and readings of the document is available in the *Intellectual Freedom Manual* (1974). Also included in the book are other statements librarians and teachers should know and use: the "Freedom to Read Statement" (1953, 1972), the "School Library Bill of Rights" (1955, 1969), and "How Libraries Can Resist Censorship" (1962, 1972). A form requesting specific reasons for any objections should be duplicated and distributed to any complainant, and all objections should be required in writing before any further action is taken. Complainants should be treated equally and politely. The school board should be consulted frequently as the policy is developed, and in some cases, teachers and librarians will need to convince board members of the necessity of yet another policy and the dangers inherent in any school operating without means to protect themselves if they are attacked. *Without school board support and formal approval and without administrator follow-up, any policy to handle censorship is merely an exercise in frustration and futility.*

Some cautions need to be sounded. Parents *do* have the moral right to deny their children access to ideas or books, *their* children, not other children. Parents might sometimes be right in objecting to a teacher's use of a book, not necessarily for attacking the book but in questioning the wisdom of assigning it. In working with parents at any time, but especially in dealing with objections, teachers and librarians must be models of fairness and tact.

Fourth, they should devote some time to public relations about their libraries and classes. Friends of books abound in every community, but their attention is seldom sought until censorship strikes. Groups like the ACLU, AAUP, NEA, AFT, former teachers and librarians, and readers who favor freedom of choice are not unaware of the dangers of censorship, but they rarely know that teachers and librarians need their support, both before and during censorship battles. While the final determination of selection and retention *must* stay with teachers and librarians, lay people could be invited to help with the selection process. The invitation might be a pleasant surprise to some parents who are unaware that anyone would be interested in what they think, and the education that could follow might be mutually beneficial, teachers and librarians learning about what parents believe and parents learning about the troublesome problems of book selection.

Finally, teachers and librarians need to accept their ultimate responsibility to select and use and recommend books. The process of selecting and using books is not easy, but that is presumably the reason they were hired. But are they qualified? Leo N. Flanagan notes in the October 15, 1975, *Library Journal:*

> *Unfortunately, many librarians doubt their ability to make decided judgments regarding materials and patrons. Again and again I hear the question, from librarians, at library conferences, "Who are we to judge?" A better question might be, "Who else is to judge?" Doctors judge illness and the means of curing it, and they strongly recommend but do not force the cure. Lawyers judge the nature*

of individual human conflict and recommend courses of action to conclude it to the satisfaction of their clients. Generals judge the conflicts of nations and recommend campaigns to end them. And we trust them because they have greater expertise in their areas of specialty than we do as laymen. Do we trust librarians? Do librarians trust themselves?

In that the answer to the latter question appears to be "no" lies the single greatest tragedy of librarianship. Most librarians hide behind a definition of intellectual freedom which demands no responsibility, which simply commands them to do nothing. And I would suggest that is because they are fearful of making decisions about materials and people with the low level of substantive knowledge that they possess.

And what is the lesson to be learned from Flanagan's words? Read widely, study, wonder, ponder, and learn. Then accept responsibility as teacher or librarian. Responsibility is not given to a professional; it is *demanded* of a professional.

Suggested Research Needs

1. Rather than approach this question in lofty, philosophical terms, it is suggested that teachers and school librarians, jointly, develop questionnaires that will help them discover what level of commitment to intellectual freedom exists among the various groups concerned with education. The questionnaire could be administered to students, teachers, administrators, and PTA members. The value of this approach would be to see how much agreement and how much disagreement existed among the groups.

2. School personnel should also consider in-depth discussion on how much the "right-wrong" answer approach to education contributes to people's inability to see issues in terms other than one side is totally right and the other side totally wrong and there are no ambiguities in between.

3. School personnel might also consider whether censorship of school newspapers produced by students contributes to a belief that censorship is an acceptable activity.

Bibliography

Bibliographies

GREGORY, RUTH W. "Readings on Book Selection and Intellectual Freedom; a Selected List, 1962–1967." *ALA Bulletin* 62 (January 1968): 64–69. An annotated bibliography of important books and articles that can serve as resources for the librarian.

HARVEY, J. A., comp. *Librarians, Censorship and Intellectual Freedom; An Annual Annotated Comprehensive Bibliography, 1968–1969.* ALA, 1970. Principles, practices, and various activities related to intellectual freedom are included in this list of annotated articles. Especially useful is the section on case histories of libraries and librarians involved in censorship issues.

Books and Pamphlets

American Civil Liberties Union. *Combatting Undemocratic Pressures on Schools and Libraries; A Guide for Local Communities.* American Civil Liberties Union, 1964. The primary aim of this pamphlet is to prepare citizens to cope with community pressures that infringe on intellectual freedom.

American Library Association, Office for Intellectual Freedom. *Intellectual Freedom Manual.* ALA, 1974. Reprints all of the ALA's major documents, gives a historical overview, and contains a bibliography.

BERNINGHAUSEN, DAVID K. *The Flight from Reason; Essays on Intellectual Freedom in the Academy, the Press, and the Library.* ALA, 1975. A solid presentation of the threats to freedom as seen by one of the ALA's most respected experts on intellectual freedom.

BLANSHARD, PAUL. *The Right to Read; The Battle Against Censorship.* Beacon, 1955. A history of censorship, changing standards, and legal interpretations.

BOYER, PAUL S. *Purity in Print: Book Censorship in America.* Scribner's, 1968. Historian Boyer traces the rise of anti-vice societies in the nineteenth century through the heyday of censorship cases in the 1920s to the leveling off in the 1930s. By relating censorship activities to the social and political climate rather than viewing them in isolation. Boyer makes such activities meaningful and shows them to be far more complex than many writers on the subject would lead the reader to believe.

CHANDOS, JOHN, ed. *'To Deprave and Corrupt . . .': Original Studies in the Nature and Definition of 'Obscenity.'* Association Pr., 1962. A British look at the problem of censorship and obscenity that is urbane, scholarly, witty, thought-provoking, and creative.

DANIELS, WALTER MACHRAY, ed. *The Censorship of Books.* (Reference Shelf, v. 26, no. 5.) Wilson, 1959. Basic material on the pros and cons of censorship, including reprints of important documents.

DOWNS, ROBERT B. *The First Freedom.* ALA, 1960. An anthology of notable English and American writings on literary censorship. Especially important is Chapter VIII, "The Librarians Take a Stand."

FISKE, MARJORIE. *Book Selection and Censorship: A Study of School and Public Libraries in California.*

Univ. of Calif. Pr., 1959. The effects of self-censorship on book selection in school and public libraries are revealed in this famous study.

GARDINER, HAROLD C., S.J. *Catholic Viewpoint on Censorship.* Hanover House, 1958. The aims and methods of the National Legion of Decency and the National Office for Decent Literature are studied as well as the charges made against them by the American Civil Liberties Union and the American Book Publishers Council.

HANEY, ROBERT W. *Comstockery in America: Patterns of Censorship and Control.* Beacon, 1960. A member of the Unitarian ministry shows the complexities of censorship in a free, pluralistic society and discusses the question of who really does the censoring.

Issues in Children's Book Selection. Bowker, 1973. Part II is devoted to "Intellectual Freedom or Censorship?" and contains five articles on varying aspects of this complicated subject.

KRONHAUSEN, EBERHARD, and PHYLLIS KRONHAUSEN. *Pornography and the Law.* Rev. ed. Ballantine, 1964. One of the most important books on the subject, in which the Kronhausens make clear the differences between erotic realism and hard-core pornography. For readers who have never encountered hard-core pornography, the section detailing the plot structure of the more famous titles will be of major importance.

KUH, RICHARD H. *Foolish Figleaves? Pornography in-and-out-of-Court.* Macmillan, 1967. Writing from his experiences as an assistant district attorney, Kuh outlines the problem of defining obscenity and pornography, traces the legal history in this country, and discusses memorable cases, including Lenny Bruce's. His detailed recommendations for legislative action that would bar the sale of pornography to young people are reflected in the New York State law that was upheld by the Supreme Court in the *Sam Ginsberg* v. *New York* ruling.

McCLELLAN, GRANT S., ed. *Censorship in the United States.* Wilson, 1967. Reprints of articles and excerpts from books, this compilation is designed to show how our freedoms are currently affected by censorship activities.

McKEON, RICHARD, ROBERT K. MERTON, and WALTER GELLHORN. *The Freedom to Read; Perspective and Program.* Bowker, 1957. An examination of the philosophical, political, and moral arguments for and against censorship.

MERRITT, LE ROY CHARLES. *Book Selection and Intellectual Freedom.* Wilson, 1970. Following a chapter on book selection in public libraries are directions for writing a book selection policy, sample policies, and methods of evaluation. The basic documents concerning intellectual freedom are also included.

MOON, ERIC, ed. *Book Selection and Censorship in the Sixties.* Bowker, 1969. Primarily an anthology of articles written for *Library Journal,* these essays contribute to a full understanding of the development of intellectual freedom during the 1960s.

National Council of Teachers of English. *Meeting Censorship in the School: A Series of Case Studies.* Nat. Council of Teachers of English, 1967. Each report describes the community, school, complaint, the objector, and the reaction to the complaint. Cases include the ones the censor won as well as those lost.

New Jersey Committee for the Right to Read. *A Survey of New Jersey Psychiatrists Pertaining to the Proscription by Legislation of Sexually Oriented Publications for Persons Under 18 Years.* Final Report. New Jersey Committee for the Right to Read, 1967. The results of a questionnaire concerning the effects on a young person of reading sexually oriented material are tabulated and summarized.

The Report of the Commission on Obscenity and Pornography. Bantam, 1970. The report pleased no one. The President, who commissioned it, refused to accept it; those who see a need for curtailing pornography found it too liberal; those who advocate no restrictions found it too confining. Nevertheless, it is essential reading.

Articles

ASHEIM, LESTER E. "Not Censorship But Selection." *Wilson Library Bulletin* 28 (September 1953): 63–67. Probably the most quoted article in library literature in which the selector's approach is differentiated from the censor's.

ASHER, THOMAS R. "A Lawyer Looks at Libraries and Censorship." *Library Journal* 95 (October 1, 1970): 3247–3249. A workable balance between the risks of absolute censorship and the objectives of intellectual freedom is suggested by a lawyer who is active in the American Civil Liberties Union.

BERNINGHAUSEN, DAVID K. "The Librarian's Commitment to the Library Bill of Rights." *Library Trends* 19 (July 1970): 19–38. The Director of a library school and deeply involved in the ALA Intellectual Freedom Committee, Berninghausen traces the historical development of library dedication to intellectual freedom.

BOOTH, WAYNE. "Censorship and the Values of Fiction." *English Journal,* March 1964.

BRODERICK, DOROTHY M. "Censorship—Reevaluated." *School Library Journal,* November 1971.

"Censorship: Librarians, Administrators and Boards." *Library Journal* 95 (December 15, 1970): 4309. Censorship activities throughout the country are reported. They vary from the removal of forty pages on human sexuality from a high-school textbook to restrictions on underground newspapers.

DONELSON, KEN. "Censorship in the 1970's: Some Ways to Handle It When It Comes (And It Will)." *English Journal* 63 (February 1974): 47–51. Summary of books that have been objected to and an analysis of issues lying beneath the surface.

ESCOTT, RICHARD H. "Reality and Reason: Intellectual Freedom and Youth." *Top of the News* 31 (April 1975): 296–301. A superintendent of schools discusses the pressures educators face in light of the 1973 Supreme Court ruling in selecting books for English classes.

FARLEY, JOHN J. "The Reading of Young People." *Library Trends* 19 (July 1970): 81–88. The dean of a school of library science explains why the question of intellectual freedom becomes most perplexing when a high-school youngster is involved.

FLANAGAN, LEO N. "Defending the Indefensible: The Limits of Intellectual Freedom." *Library Journal* 100 (October 15, 1975): 1887–1891. Attack on the "Introduction" to ALA's *Intellectual Freedom Manual,* which is described as timid, simplistic, naive, and anti-intellectual—among other things.

GARD, ROBERT R. "Censorship and Public Understanding." *English Journal* 60 (February 1971):

255–259. The necessity for building public trust and some recommended procedures for the educator.

GAYLIN, WILLARD M. "The Prickly Problems of Pornography." *Yale Law Journal* 77 (1968): 579–597. In the course of reviewing Kuh's *Foolish Figleaves?* psychiatrist Gaylin analyzes the problem of pornography from a mental health viewpoint. He makes the point, among others, that a child reading pornography with the knowledge that it is disapproved of will not likely be harmed, but a child reading pornography without such knowledge may be harmed.

GOTHBERG, HELEN. "YA Censorship: Adult or Adolescent Problems?" *Top of the News* 22 (April 1966): 275–278. A high-school librarian describes her methods of preventing censorship. Important factors are anticipating needs, recognizing the latent censor in the student, and teaching the young person how to handle reactions to certain types of materials.

GREEN, BERNARD. "Obscenity, Censorship, and Juvenile Delinquency." *University of Toronto Law Journal* 14, no. 2 (1962): 229–252. After reviewing what we know and don't know about the relationship between reading and juvenile delinquency, a Canadian lawyer makes suggestions for legal controls that will protect the young but leave adults free.

HARVEY, JAMES. "Acting for Children?" *School Library Journal,* February 1973.

Interracial Books for Children Bulletin, 6, nos. 3 and 4 (1975). This double issue was prepared specially for the 1975 annual conference of the ALA and focuses on the dilemma librarians face in trying to eliminate racism without becoming censors. Important.

KILLIFER, CONSTANCE. "Double Standards: Intellectual Freedom and the Post-Modern Generation." *Top of the News* 25 (June 1969): 392–399. A high-school librarian sees the need for new standards and believes that the questioning attitude of the "post-modern" generation is a step toward their attainment. The article also appeared in the October 1968 *Bay State Librarian.*

KLEIN, NORMA. "More Realism for Children." *Top of the News* 31 (April 1975): 307–312. The author of *Mom, the Wolf Man, and Me* discusses the two major restrictions authors face in trying to write for children: language and subject matter.

KOSINSKI, JERZY. "Against Book Censorship." *Media & Methods* 12 (January 1976): 22–24. The noted novelist makes the point that, if not encouraged to respond to all literature imaginatively, students may not be able to handle real and potentially damaging events. Short but powerful article.

KRISTOL, IRVING. "Pornography, Obscenity and the Case for Censorship." *The New York Times Magazine,* March 28, 1971, pp. 24 +. A strongly reasoned statement, stressing the dehumanizing effects of pornography. Kristol describes the difference between repressive laws and laws that regulate and concludes that "liberal censorship" is both possible and desirable.

LADOF, NINA SYDNEY. "Censorship—The Tip of the Iceberg." *American Libraries* 2 (March 1971): 309–310. An experienced librarian suggests that there may be more to the problem of censorship than what we see or hear. The harassment of bookstores by police is one form of extralegal pressure.

MAZER, NORMA FOX. "Comics, Cokes, and Censorship." *Top of the News* 32 (January 1976): 167–170. An author and mother relates very personal experiences and asks, but does not answer, the question of whether there is material inappropriate for the young.

NEILL, S. D. "Censorship and the Uncertain Librarian." *Canadian Library Journal* 32 (October 1975): 345–348. Analyzes the discrepancy between official library association policies and behavior of librarians as individuals and concludes that no association policy should supersede individual conscience.

PAGE, ROBERT L. "Holden Caulfield Is Alive and Well and Still Causing Trouble." *English Journal* 64 (May 1975): 27–31. Written in a parody of Holden's style, this is a madman rap about obscenity and censorship and the insanity surrounding the issues as experienced by a teacher.

RAFFERTY, MAX. "The Other Side: Hardest of All to Come By." *Wilson Library Bulletin* 42 (October 1967): 181–186. The text of an address given by the ex-Superintendent of Public Instruction in California to the Library Trustees' meeting at the annual ALA Convention in San Francisco, 1967. Among Rafferty's points concerning the relationship of schools and libraries to youth is a strong plea for censoring what youth reads.

REISCHE, DIANA. "Censorship and Obscenity: What's Happened to Taste?" *Senior Scholastic* 89 (October 14, 1966): 12–15. Changing tastes and public morals are part of the reason why censorship questions are so difficult. The problems and judicial attempts to clarify and solve them are explained.

SABADOSH, AUDREY. "Teenagers View Censorship." *Top of the News* 22 (April 1966): 278–280. Thought-provoking responses to a questionnaire on reading that was distributed to high-school English students. Thirty-six percent indicated a definite belief in censorship.

SEREBNICK, JUDITH. "The 1973 Court Rulings on Obscenity: Have They Made a Difference?" *Wilson Library Bulletin* 50 (December 1975): 304–310. Report of a survey of ten medium-sized cities to determine how school and public librarians were responding to the "community standards" ruling by the Supreme Court. Still unanswered is the question: do librarians impose restrictions upon themselves or are the restrictions imposed upon them?

SHUMAN, R. BAIRD. "Making the World Safe for What?" *Education Digest* 34 (December 1968): 36–38. (Condensed from *Illinois Schools Journal,* Fall 1968.) As a professor of education, Shuman speaks out against pressure groups that would decree curricular matters and notes the folly of those who think censorship is necessary to protect youth.

SIEBERT, SARA, and LINDA LAPIDES. "Shuddered to Think . . ." *Top of the News* 22 (April 1966): 259–268. Two young adult librarians describe a complaint concerning a book in Baltimore's Enoch Pratt Free Library and explain precisely how the complaint was handled.

STEINER, GEORGE. "Night Words." *Encounter* 25 (October 1965): 14–19. The point is made that mass-produced pornography is not only monotonous, but it does our imagining for us, invades our privacy, and markets our dreams wholesale. A plea for reticence.

WHITE, LUCIEN W. "The Censorship Dilemma." *Illinois Libraries* 49 (September 1967): 612–621. A brief chronology of major landmarks in censorship legislation and suggestions for implementing intellectual freedom at the practicing level.

Periodicals

American Libraries. The official journal of the ALA carries a regular column "Intellectual Freedom" written by the Director of the Office for Intellectual Freedom in which are reported major concerns affecting libraries and how they are handled.

Newsletter on Intellectual Freedom. Published bimonthly by the ALA Intellectual Freedom Committee. Available from: American Library Association, 50 East Huron Street, Chicago, Illinois 60611. The *Newsletter* is one of the most valuable resources for locating information concerning censorship activities across the nation. It brings together items that are, of necessity, scattered throughout magazines and newspapers.

Other Resources

American Library Association, Intellectual Freedom Committee, 50 East Huron Street, Chicago, Illinois 60611. The Office for Intellectual Freedom will provide, upon request, a packet of material, containing, among other items, the Library Bill of Rights and the statement on Freedom to Read.

California Library Association, Intellectual Freedom Committee. *Intellectual Freedom Kit.* Sacramento, 1964. This is an example of the type of kit provided by some professional associations to help the local librarian resist censorship. Basic documents are included as well as bibliographies of pertinent readings and reprints of articles.

National Council of Teachers of English. Champaign, Illinois. The NCTE has endorsed a document entitled "The Student's Right to Read," which is available from that organization, as well as other documents concerned with the problems of teaching in a free atmosphere.

Television: Its Impact and Influence

*Deirdre Breslin and Eileen Marino**

The impact and influence of television on the lives of today's children is clearly presumed by Buckminster Fuller in his statement that "television may be regarded as the American child's third parent."

One measure of the truth of Fuller's statement can be found in the amount of time children spend watching TV. In 1948 fewer than one percent of all American homes had television sets. In 1976, ninety-eight percent of all homes contained at least one set, more homes by far than have adequate heat and plumbing. Twenty-five percent of all American homes now contain two or more television sets. By the time of high-school entrance, the average North American child will have spent some 22,000 hours watching TV. Viewing begins early, as shown by Dr. Spock's estimation that preschoolers watch TV about fifty hours per week, more time than is given to any other activity except sleep. Gerbner and Gross found that nearly half the 12-year-olds in their sample average six or more hours of television every day. Regardless of which study one consults, the evidence is clear that children spend a large amount of time watching television.

It is because children spend so much time before TV sets that researchers concern themselves with what is being seen and what influence the content has upon behavior. It is important for adults to understand the messages being transmitted by television if they are to help children know how to make the best use of it.

Content Analysis

Perhaps the most obvious and therefore most discussed aspect of television content is violence. Many parents who carefully monitor what their children may view during evening hours blithely assume that the Saturday morning children's shows are free of violence. An analysis of Saturday morning shows by F. Earle Barcus revealed that "about three out of ten dramatic segments were saturated with violence and 71 percent had at least one instance of human violence with or without the use of weapons." A similar analysis of evening shows by Gerbner and Gross revealed that "More than half of all characters on prime-time TV are involved in some violence, about one-tenth in killing."

Robert Liebert, a psychology professor, has stated that children are using violence on TV as a partial guide for their own actions. In 1972, a University of Arizona study indicated that by the age of 14, an American child has seen 18,000 human beings killed on TV. Dr.

*Eileen Marino is completing her Ph.D. degree at New York University in the field of Media Ecology and is a teacher in the Syosset School District. Deirdre Breslin is the Early Childhood Coordinator for the Office of Urban School Services of the New York State Education Department.

Bertram S. Brown, director of the National Institute of Mental Health, states that repeated exposure to violent programming can produce insensitivity to cruelty and violence because it gradually extinguishes the viewers' emotional responses and builds the feeling that violent behavior is appropriate. Not only does TV violence influence people to think of violence as appropriate behavior, it also "leads viewers to perceive the real world as more dangerous than it really is, which must also influence the way people behave," as Gerbner and Gross concluded.

Television is also a transmitter of cognitive skills and the best-known effort is *Sesame Street* and its spin-off, *Electric Company*. Research done by the Educational Testing Service has demonstrated that *Sesame Street* is an effective teacher for both middle-class and disadvantaged children. Letter and number recognition plus assorted other concepts are presented to youngsters in a snappy entertainment format with a magazine arrangement. *Electric Company* introduces reading, vocabulary, and decoding skills via the same format.

Social skills are highlighted in such TV shows as *Vegetable Soup*, *Villa Allegre*, and *Big Blue Marble* which aim to present to the audience various forms of positive social behavior. Each show attempts to deal with a situation revolving around social interaction and interpersonal relationships. Positive solutions to everyday life situations are presented.

More than any other medium, television furnishes a common body of information for the early socialization of children. The Jacques Costeau specials present the wonders of the sea in a graphic way. *Welcome Back, Kotter* exposes children to an off-beat but empathic teacher and humanizes the members of the "special" class found in most schools. Mister Rogers of *Mister Rogers Neighborhood*, with his message of "I like you just as you are," has undertaken to help his viewers acquire understanding of and sensitivity for children with handicaps. Each week one of the programs introduces viewers to children with physical handicaps.

While television offers viewers an occasional insight into genuine human beings functioning in the real world, the bulk of its content is stereotyped. The following are samples of the stereotyped messages being transmitted to all television viewers, not just children.

1. The world in which we live is, in the main, white, middle-class, and suburban. Saturday morning programs include minority representation in only four out of 39 shows. On major network programs, 80 percent of all characters are white—this despite the fact that the majority of the world's population is nonwhite.

2. Minority group members believe in and support the conventional rules of society. Police shows, such as *The Rookies* and *Hawaii Five-O*, are consistent in presenting minority people as staunch supporters of the status quo. Other popular programs, such as *Ironside* and *Kojak*, go further in suggesting that power and ideas always emanate from the white man.

3. Racial and ethnic slurs are funny. *All in the Family* has legitimatized and given respectability to racial and ethnic slurs. The audience laughter elicited by such shows conveys to viewers the idea that such slurs are not vicious or symbolic of an oppressive system but are primarily funny. They are the modern day equivalent of the black-face minstrel show. Surveys show that most viewers are not laughing *at* Archie Bunker but *with* him.

4. Women are extraneous and/or unimportant. Between 75 and 80 percent of all leads are male—the precise percentage varies slightly depending on when a survey is made, but has yet to fall below 75 percent. Even when women are the lead characters, the plot solution almost always involves being rescued by a male co-worker. The message that high-status women must look to lower-status males for rescuing is particularly true of police dramas. Thus, TV has failed to recognize the contributions of women to the workings of society by lessening their roles and lowering their visibility to the child viewer.

5. Women can only be employed in certain jobs, and shown in specific, limiting roles. They are usually mothers, sweethearts, or wives. If employed, they are nurses and secretaries. When depicted outside these socially approved roles, such as doctors, they are then more neurotic than their male counterparts.

6. The other side of this restrictive depiction of women is what it does to the men. Since women must be "kept," it then follows that men must do the "keeping." In many crime shows the motivation given for male criminal activity is the need to support the woman in the style to which she has become accustomed. Perceptive TV viewers might reasonably conclude that criminal activity would be eliminated if it were not for men trying to satisfy grasping women.

7. Possessions bring you success and happiness. The right brand of sneakers will make you an Olympic gold medal winner; the right soft drink will assure your popularity; another product puts you on the moon with the astronauts.

8. Beauty, particularly female beauty, comes from external products. The right face cream, soap, bath oil, and deodorant will get you what you want from life—a man. Only in public service announcements are women allowed to worry about anything other than physical appearance.

9. Important as beauty is, it cannot compare with being young. The ideal age in TV land is between nineteen and twenty-five. The cult of youth predominates and downgrades the validity of other ages, leaving both childhood and old age in limbo.

10. Old age, when depicted at all, is usually shown in destructive stereotypes. With the demise of the extended family, many children only see their grandparents once or twice a year, if that often. The image TV gives them of old people as objects of ridicule, or pathetic, meddling nonentities, hardly helps them look forward to encounters with their grandparents or other older members of the family.

Rather than ignore television, teachers could do a great deal of good by assigning television viewing to students and then analyzing the hidden—and not so hidden—messages being transmitted. Only by learning to apply rigorous analysis to television can the young avoid automatically internalizing the messages.

Techniques for Using TV with Children

Following are some ideas for helping children view television critically. Since the study of television really begins when the watcher is made aware of the unique combination of sights and sounds that make up the medium, we begin with ideas for making clear the importance of the visual and the audio and their relationship to each other.

If your local television station has a library of videotapes, see if you can borrow one that will be of interest to your students. First show the videotape with the sound off and ask the students to write down what they think the show was about. If the students are too young to write complicated analyses, tape record their reactions. Then run the video with the sound and no picture. Ask the students to talk about which process is more compelling/distracting. Do we have to pay more attention when we can see but not hear? Why?

Teachers working with upper elementary or junior high school students can assign them to monitor shows in terms of camera techniques. How long does the camera remain in one position? What kind of programs have short takes? long takes? What do these camera techniques suggest about the programs?

Commercials contain both overt and hidden messages. Teachers wishing to help students deal with the hidden messages of television may have to first learn how to detect them for themselves. School systems should offer in-service training programs for teachers in this highly specialized field of content research. Some school systems, such as the North York Board of Education (Ontario, Canada), have hired highly trained television producers to teach consumer education in terms of television commercials. Lacking that quality of teacher, school systems can assure a basic knowledge for all teachers by hiring consultants for in-service programs.

Even without specialized training, all of us can help young children analyze the impact of commercials on overt behavior. Do children nag their parents to buy products advertised on TV? Do they ever want a product just to get the "gift" which is inside the package? Does the gift live up to its promises?

Most important of all, teachers can ask students whether they believe certain products will make them popular, happy, or smart. In schools where "value education" is a part of the curriculum, watching television commercials can provide the basis for discussing whether it is the externals or internals that make a person what he or she really is.

We are past the point in history where we ask *if* television has influence. Advertisers would not spend their money if they did not believe television influenced people. Now we must ask what television is doing to people and whether we want the kind of world television is selling.

Suggested Research Needs

Here are some proposals and recommendations for needed research.

1. What is the best length of a TV program for children of different ages?
2. Does active involvement in a TV show which demands use of sensory-motor skills improve retention?
3. Can TV viewing by preschool children become habit forming?
4. Should there be a mandatory code concerning permissible levels of violence for all TV programs?
5. What are the critical age levels for promoting children's understanding of pro-social behavior?
6. Would a series of TV programs utilizing children of various cultural and racial groups reading easy and familiar stories to the TV audience interest the young viewer in learning to read those same books?
7. Do children remember the content of a TV book dramatization any better than an in-person reading of the same story?
8. Can an interest in poetry be fostered and maintained as a result of TV exposure to poetry?
9. Can more age specific TV programs be created?

Bibliography

Books and Pamphlets

Association for Childhood Education International. *Children and TV: Television's Impact on the Child.* Assoc. for Childhood Education International, 1967. A collection of articles examining television and its relationship to children's viewing habits.

BELSON, W. A. *The Impact of Television: Methods and Findings in Program Research.* Archon, 1967. A presentation of research techniques used in England to analyze television's influence.

BENTON, CHARLES W., et al. *Television in Urban Education: Its Application to Major Educational Problems in Sixteen Cities.* Praeger, 1969. A wealth of information, often graphic, about TV and its relationship to urban educational problems.

BLUEM, A. WILLIAM, and ROGER MANVELL. *Television: The Creative Experience.* Hastings, 1967. A collection of articles dealing with educational TV and its impact on the public.

BRONFENBRENNER, URIE. *The Two Worlds of Childhood; U.S. and U.S.S.R.* Russell Sage Foundation, 1970. Chapter 4 of this book gives a cogent analysis of TV and its impact on American children.

BROWN, LES. *Television: The Business Behind the Box.* Harcourt, 1971. A discussion of the politics involved in the TV industry.

Carnegie Commission on Educational TV. *Public Television: A Program for Action.* Harper, 1967. This report discusses the need for a broader method of supporting important programming which does "not at the moment seem appropriate or available for support by advertising."

CARTER, DOUGLAS, and STEPHEN STRICKLAND. *TV Violence and the Child.* Russell Sage Foundation, 1975. The book deals successively with television as an object of concern, research findings, response of critics, and TV industry response.

FEINSTEIN, PHYLLIS. *All About Sesame Street.* Tower, 1971. A critical evaluation of "Sesame Street" since its inception.

FESHBACK, SEYMOUR. *Television and Aggression: An Experimental Field Study.* Jossey-Bass, 1971. The report of a research project conducted with children who watched violent television while in a residential setting.

FRANK, JOSETTE. *Television: How to Use It Wisely with Children.* Child Study Assn. of Am., 1969. A discussion of how much time a child should spend before TV and what content should be selected.

GATTEGNO, CALEB. *Toward a Visual Culture.* Outerbridge and Diestenfrey, 1969. A discussion of the impact and influence of TV and suggestions for dealing with TV.

GERZON, MARK. *A Childhood for Every Child.* Outerbridge and Lazard, 1973. A discussion dealing with TV and its relationship to early development.

HALLORAN, J. D., and P. R. ELLIOT. *Television for Children and Young People.* International Publications Service, 1971. A study dealing with English television for children.

HALLORAN, JAMES D., ed. *The Effects of Television.* Panther Books, 1970. The chapter called "Television and Education" is an excellent resource on the topic.

HALLORAN, JAMES, R. L. BROWN, and D. C. CHANEY. *Television and Delinquency.* Leicester University Press, 1970. A comprehensive review of English information about TV and its relationship to delinquency.

HIMMELWEIT, HILDE, A. N. OPPENHEIM, and PAMELA VINCE. *Television and the Child.* Oxford, 1959. A survey of English children's viewing habits. Diaries, questionnaires were used to analyze the television viewing habits of ten- to fourteen-year-olds. This study was of major importance in evaluating the role of television in all areas of the subjects' lives.

JOHNSON, NICHOLAS. *How to Talk Back to Your Television Set.* Little, 1970. The author tells the various important aspects of television, especially the educational value of television, and describes how the public can reform television.

KAYE, EVELYN. *The Family Guide to Children's Television.* Panther, 1974. A book for parents on what to watch, what to miss, what to change, and how to do it.

KLAPPER, JOSEPH. *The Effects of Mass Communication.* Free Pr., 1960. This author attempts to integrate research findings and expert conjecture into some tentative generalizations about mass media influences on attitudes and behavior.

LESSER, GERARD. *Children and Television: Lessons from "Sesame Street."* Random, 1974. The history and background of the program. The book discusses the research done about the show, written by the show's research director.

LIEBERT, ROBERT, JOHN NEAL, and EMILY DAVIDSON. *The Early Windows: Effects of Television on Children and Youth.* Pergamon, 1973. The history of television and its role in today's world. A good review of research done on this topic and a look at some new research to come. Good resource book.

McLUHAN, MARSHALL, and QUENTIN FIORE. *The Medium Is the Message.* Bantam, 1967. An in-depth discussion of media and their effects on society. Gives the reader a background in understanding the medium.

MAYER, MARTIN. *About Television.* Harper, 1972. This book presents television as a most persuasive form of communication.

MELODY, WILLIAM. *Children's Television: The Economics of Exploitation.* Yale University Press, 1973. A study of the economic characteristics of commercial children's television. Focuses on TV's economic forces and trends and evaluates the public's attitude toward commercial children's TV.

MORRIS, NORMAN. *Television's Child.* Little, 1971. A book which gives the reader a wide range of opinions from various interested experts. This is a book to use as a basic background for dealing with television.

PEARCE, ALAN. *The Economics of Children's Television Programing.* Federal Communications Commission, 1972. An examination of the financial aspects of the television industry.

PENNYBACKER, JOHN, and WALDO BRADEN. *Broadcasting and the Public Interest.* 1969. A series of articles by experts in the television field. Particularly good analysis chapters.

PROWITT, MARSHA O'BANNAN. *Guide to Citizen Action in Radio and TV.* Office of Communication, United Church of Christ, N.Y., 1971. Presents the various aspects of television and radio and the ways a citizen can deal with aspects they dislike.

QUINLAN, STERLING. *The Hundred Million Dollar Lunch: The Broadcasting Industry's Own Watergate.* O'Hara, 1974. Presents the case of the deviant side of the broadcasting industry.

RUTSTEIN, NAT. *"Go Watch TV!" What and How Much Should Children Really Watch?* Sheed, 1974. A major contribution to the question of the analysis of television.

SARSON, EVELYN, ed. *Action for Children's Television.* Avon, 1971. A compilation of the speeches presented at the First National Symposium on the Effect of Television Programming and Advertising on Children.

SCHWARTZ, TONY. *The Responsive Chord.* Anchor Press/Doubleday, 1972. An in-depth discussion on communication theory and practice. The author makes the valid point that this medium has not been extended to its fullest potential.

SHAYON, ROBERT LEWIS. *The Crowd-Catchers: Introducing Television.* Sat. Review, 1973. An interesting and important discussion of the principles involved in dealing with television.

STEINER, GARY. *The People Look at Television: A Study of Audience Attitudes.* Knopf, 1963. A scientific investigation of television. It merits reading.

Television and Social Behavior. A Technical Report of the Surgeon General's Advisory Committee on Television and Social Behavior. U.S. Government Printing Office, 1972. vol. 1: *Media Content and Control,* Papers and Reports, G. A. Comstock and E. A. Rubinstein, eds. vol. 2: *Television and Social Learning,* Papers and Reports, G. A. Comstock and E. A. Rubinstein, eds. vol. 3: *Television and Adolescent Aggressiveness,* Papers and Reports, E. A. Rubinstein, G. A. Comstock, and J. P. Murray, eds. vol. 4: *Television in Day-to-Day Life, Patterns of Use,* Papers and Reports, E. A. Rubinstein, G. A. Comstock, and J. P. Murray, eds. vol. 5: *Television's Effects: Further Explorations,* Papers and Reports, G. A. Comstock, E. A. Rubinstein, and J. P. Murray, eds. A description of all the research done for the Surgeon General. The original research designs are included and discussed. These five volumes of research represent an outstanding effort to discover the effect TV has on today's children.

WARD, SCOTT. *Effects of Advertising on Children and Adolescents.* Marketing Science Institute, Mass., 1971. An important study in the way advertising controls children.

WITTY, PAUL. *Studies of Mass Media, 1949-1965.* Television Information Service, 1966. A summary of the results of Witty's annual survey of children's viewing habits. It was the first research of any merit.

Articles

ALBERT, ROBERT, and HARRY MELINE. "The Influences of Social Status on the Uses of Television." *Public Opinion Quarterly* 22 (1958): 145-151. The study examines television-use patterns of children from higher and lower social classes. Researchers found much disagreement between children's reports and parental responses.

BAILYN, LOTTE. "Mass Media and Children: A Study of Exposure Habits and Cognitive Effects." Psychology Monograph 73V48 (1959). Analysis of the media habits of 600 fifth- and sixth-grade children, related to social psychological characteristics.

BANDURA, ALBERT. "Social Learning Through Imitation." In *Nebraska Symposium on Motivation,* pp. 211-274. University of Nebraska Press, 1962. The studies indicate that exposure to human models portraying aggression on film is the most influential method of producing and shaping some aggressive behavior.

______. "Vicarious Processes: A Case of No-Trial Learning." In *Advances in Experimental Social Psychology,* vol. 2, edited by Leonard Berkowitz, pp. 1-55. Academic Press, 1965. A review of how children learn by observation, both theory and research findings. A good reference source.

BANDURA, ALBERT, D. ROSS, and SHEILA ROSS. "Imitation of Film-Mediated Aggressive Models." *Journal of Abnormal and Social Psychology* 66 (1963): 3-11. A study of young children's imitation of aggressive behavior when exposed to film aggression.

BARCUS, F. EARLE. "Network Programming and Advertising in the Saturday's Children's Hours; A June-November Comparison." Prepared for Action for Children's Television, Mass., 1972, pp. 1-95. The update of programs shown on Saturday mornings in the Boston area. A good review of the quality and social aspects of these shows.

______. "Parental Influence on Children's Television Viewing." *Television Quarterly* 88 (1969): 63-73. Research shows parents, though expected to exercise control over TV, do not. Parents are more interested in quantity than quality of TV.

BOGART, LEO. "Violence in the Mass Media." *Television Quarterly* 8 (1969): 36-47. The author feels that the greatest impact of the media may derive from the diffuse increase of general public anxiety rather than from individual acts in response to specific media images.

CARPENTER, C. R. "Approaches to Promising Areas of Research in the Field of Instructional Television." In *New Teaching Aids for the American Classroom.* Stanford: Institute for Communication Research, 1960. Useful gathering of summaries of research from studies of teaching film through 1949. Many of these results are applicable to instructional television.

"Children's TV Commercials: Policy and Research." *Journal of Communication* 4 (Autumn 1974): 113-144. An interesting view of how TV commercials are bought by programs and the research aspect of their use with the viewers.

COHEN, DOROTHY. "Is TV a Pied Piper?" *Young Children,* November 1974, pp. 4-14. Is the promise of television living up to its expectations or are we dealing with a very different kind of learning? The article deals with this important question.

CULHANE, JOHN. "Report Card on Sesame Street." *New York Times Magazine,* May 24, 1970, pp. 34-35. The article points out that Sesame Street gets high marks in cognitive-skills development, but fails when social science is involved.

FEELEY, JOAN T. "Television and Reading in the Seventies." *Language Arts* 52 (September 1975): 797-801+. A review of the research done to determine what type of show a child will choose.

GERBNER, GEORGE, and LARRY GROSS. "The Scary World of TV's Heavy Viewer." *Psychology Today* 9 (April 1976): 41-45 +. Adults who watch television four or more hours per day have a warped view of the dangers of the real world based on the violence they see on the screen. This fear is preparing people to play the role of victim and may be contributing to the flight from the cities, and "television may have become our chief instrument of social control."

GRAY, MARYJANE. "The Effect of Home Televiewing on School Children." *Elementary English,* March 1969, pp. 303-310. The report of a study which reflects that children do choose TV over another form of pleasure.

HESS, ROBERT D., and HARRIET GOLDMAN. "Parents' Views of the Effects of Television on Their Children." *Child Development* 33 (1962): 411-426. Questionnaires in this research found that mothers are somewhat ambivalent toward TV and that parents do not use control over the set.

LARRICK, NANCY. "Children of Television." *Teacher,* September 1975, pp. 75-76. An article which gives emphasis to the role of parents and teachers in dealing with the television child.

LEIFER, AIMEE, NEAL GORDON, and SHERRYL GRAVES. "Children's Television More Than Mere Entertainment." *Harvard Educational Review* 44 (May 1974): 213-219. The authors state that while TV is entertaining to children, it also socializes them. The authors deal with the question of economic factors being more important than children's learning, involving commercial TV.

NIVIN, HAROLD. "Who in the Family Selects the TV Program?" *Journalism Quarterly* 37 (1963): 110-111. Beginning research about which family member selects programs. It seems evident that at this time only one TV set per family was involved.

ROBINSON, JOHN P. "Television and Leisure Time: Yesterday, Today, and (Maybe) Tomorrow." *Public Opinion Quarterly* 33 (1969): 210-223. A substantial amount of time that was previously devoted to other mass media and leisure activities is now devoted to TV watching. In the investigator's view, there is a predictable, but yet unspecified, limit to the amount of time people in a given society will spend watching TV.

"TV's Effects on Children and Adolescents: A Symposium of Eleven Studies." *Journal of Communication* 25 (Autumn 1975). A wealth of information covering all major concerns.

Periodicals

Better Radio and Television. National Association for Better Broadcasting, 373 N.W. Avenue, Los Angeles, Cal. 90004. One issue each year includes the annual guide to "Television for the Family: A Comprehensive Guide to Family Viewing."

Journal of Advertising Research. Advertising Research Foundation, 3 E. 54th St., New York, N.Y. 10022. Articles about television advertising and other advertising research.

Journal of Broadcasting. Broadcast Education Association, Temple University, Philadelphia, Pa. 19122. This magazine is dedicated to all aspects of the broadcasting industry.

Journal of Communication. Anneberg School of Communications in cooperation with the International Communication Association, P.O. Box 11358, Philadelphia, Pa. 19101. All aspects of communication are reviewed in this magazine.

TV Guide. Box 4000, Radnor, Pa. 19088. Popular and informative; articles involved with television. Lists shows for the week.

Television Quarterly. National Academy of Television Arts and Sciences, 291 South La Cienega Blvd., Beverly Hills, Cal. 90211. Many subjects covered in this magazine including news, art design, TV, radio, and news.

Other Resources

Action for Children's Television. 33 Hancock Avenue, Newton Centre, Mass. 02159.
National Association for Better Broadcasting. 373 N. Western Ave., Los Angeles, Cal. 90004.
National Association of Broadcasters. 1771 N. Street, N.W., Washington, D.C. 20036.
National Association of Educational Broadcasters. 1346 Connecticut Avenue, N.W., Washington, D.C. 20036.
Television Information Office. 745 Fifth Avenue, New York, N.Y. 10022.

Sexism in Children's Books

*Diane Gersoni**

The problem of sexism in juvenile books is a threefold problem for adults: (1) how to assess it; (2) how to keep new books free of it; and (3) how to deal with it in old books. Sexism is defined as the *unwarranted* omission or stereotyping of female characters. (The word "unwarranted" is important because there are situations in life when it is reasonable that females will not be present.) Some people would extend this definition to include the unwarranted omission or stereotyping of male characters as well as female. Feminist criticism applied to juvenile books seeks to ensure that the books will provide children and teenagers with an authentic, humanistic sense of the world, other people, and their own complex personhood. Books presenting strictly one-dimensional views of females or males obviously cannot do this.

That juvenile literature in the past has not featured authentic female characters is very well known by now. We have an impressive collection of critical studies documenting sexism in textbooks and in trade books. These studies come from both sides of the Atlantic Ocean and have zeroed in on basal readers; Caldecott Medal books; folk and fairy tales; Newbery Medal books and other novels; biographies; children's encyclopedias; social studies, history, and literature textbooks; women's studies books; and even supposedly neutral books such as math and science texts.

The findings of the many studies have been clear-cut and statistically significant. In both textbooks and trade books male characters clearly outnumbered female characters; dress was stereotyped; males were depicted in a broader range of geographic locations; males were more often shown outdoors; females were usually passive, docile, fearful, and dependent while males were curious, aggressive, independent, and striving. The pattern held for both adult and child characters, and mother/father roles in particular were stereotyped. Adult women seldom worked outside the home and then only in stereotyped capacities. Linguistically, the pronoun "he" was used indiscriminately in referring to both females and males.

These studies have sparked some initial change. In picture books, considered important early socializing agents, females have become more visible. Instead of showing four boys playing together in a schoolyard, a picture book may now show two boys and two girls playing together. With greater visibility have come role changes for females. Instead of showing the boys roughhousing and the girls playing with dolls, picture books may now show the boys and girls interacting. While too many illustrations still feature girls in stereotyped passive positions, these small improvements are progressive steps and will undoubtedly lead to further improvement.

Females have been making inroads in books for older children as well. More biographies are being written about women, including famous Native American women, fliers, dancers, abolitionists, writers, and blacks. General nonfiction topics previously perceived as male concerns (e.g., books about the armed forces or careers) now acknowledge the potential for women. As for fiction, it is highly unlikely that any novelist in the future will be pressured to change the sex of his or her protagonist from female to male as authors have stated happened to them in the past.

Other changes have occurred in children's trade fiction as a result of the new awareness engendered by feminist criticism. An unraised consciousness is no longer a valid excuse for authors who, for example, unreflectingly and

*Diane Gersoni, editor of *Sexism and Youth* (Bowker, 1974), was formerly Associate Editor of *School Library Journal* Book Review and is now a writer/editor at Scholastic Magazines, Inc.

automatically make a weak man a sympathetic character, and the man's strong, dissatisfied wife a domineering, unlikable character. If authors make excuses for male characters, if they attempt to present the full humanity, good and bad, of male characters, then feminist critics expect them to do the same for female characters. Authors can no longer expect to be applauded for including an admirable female character if they present her as some kind of oddity. Feminist reviewers no longer accept books in which women are represented only as homemakers and all girls as aspiring homemakers. In children's books, as in the real world, women are holding jobs outside the home and are finding psychic as well as financial satisfactions in working.

The changes taking place in children's books occur in greater or lesser degree from author to author, book to book, and publisher to publisher. They are valid changes, but they do not, by themselves, ensure ultimately valid characterizations or a full recognition of human complexity and diversity. Depicting a fictional mother as a professional woman, for example, is not enough for the character to emerge as a powerful literary portrait. For that to happen the author must faithfully evoke the conflicts such a woman may experience today as she tries to be wife, mother, homemaker, and career woman. Does the author capture the character's possible guilt and frustration about neglecting "her" family while balancing those emotions by showing the self-respect she experiences as a competent member of the work force? Does the author make clear that her family experiences the similar conflict of feeling pride in her achievements while feeling annoyed that she no longer has the time to give to their needs? Giving attention to one thing automatically means that we have less time to give to something else, and whether we like it or not, in the everyday world children often resent it if their busy parents—male or female—seem to have little time for them.

We have to ask whether the authors believably depict the compromises—and the pressures stemming from them—that may have to be made within the home regarding the allotment of domestic chores. Do authors demonstrate sensitive understanding of pressures on and the problems of mothers raising families alone? Do authors help young readers understand that social conditioning often makes men feel inadequate if their wives *must* work to meet the financial needs of the family? Since many women want both personal and professional fulfillment—the ultimate desirable option—authors must find themselves capable of portraying the committed, dedicated, loving, working mother who increasingly exists in real life. And they must equally show young readers the ways men interact with, are influenced by, and learn from these women.

If, in the past, mothers have been stereotyped, single women have been maligned. They have been portrayed as unhappy spinsters, weird eccentrics, gruff but good-natured pals, or ambitious castrators. We know that single women have personal interests, strong friendships, romances, and family relationships and that these facets of the "single-woman personality" should be present in books. Such women should be portrayed as taking pride in their survival skills and having a sense of competence often lacking in other women. But single women should not be presented as having no problems. Like single men, single women are often lonelier than married ones—especially those women who do not have a powerful career drive.

Women who do not work outside the home are entitled to genuine respect for what they do as full-time homemakers. They are not vapid creatures who sit around all day in aprons doing nothing. Though the physical labor required of women in the home today is less than it used to be, studies show that in terms of sheer physical output homemakers still work harder than most other groups of workers. Women who do not work outside the home should not be eliminated from juvenile books or presented in innocuous or derogatory ways. Full-time mothers must be shown as individuals, with their own believable aspirations, frustrations, satisfactions, and disappointments.

If an author shows a female character at a crisis point in her life (and many authors do focus on crisis points because they make for more dramatic reading than do simple evocations of daily routine), then the author is justified in presenting the character as being totally disgusted with her life. She might be a disgruntled, single career woman afraid of growing old, or a bored homemaker who feels stymied and unappreciated. But the author shouldn't imply to readers that it's inherently bad to be a career woman, or inherently bad to be a homemaker. The individual character may just be unhappy with the limitations of a particular role at that particular point in her life. And always, an author must reflect the fact that a character's internal reality is more important than her external situation.

The studies, books, and articles listed in the bibliography will raise many more points about the wide range of female images that should be present somewhere in children's books. What is most important for us to keep in mind is that substituting new kinds of formula fiction—for example, idealized egalitarian family life—for old-style family life with traditional sex roles is no answer. We must remember that just as problems will always exist in life, so traditional clichés, movement clichés, sublimely happy characters, and happily-ever-after endings will always be invalid in realistic fiction.

Also, we must take care not to overreact in judging fiction. It is wrong to attack a good novel just because it has no female characters. It is wrong to reject a good novel for presenting a basically unpleasant female character, because if it is a good novel, the character will be a believable one with a background and motivations we can understand. It is right, however, to raise objections to an otherwise well-written novel if it presents stereotyped or inauthentic female characters. There is no way a serious novel can stereotype characters and still be first-rate. In this, social criticism and aesthetics go hand in hand.

What should librarians, teachers, and parents do when new books fail to live up to expectations regarding sexism? For example, what if otherwise solid nonfiction titles stint in their coverage of women? Do we buy them? Perhaps if they are good in all other respects we would be foolish not to purchase them. But we would be at fault if we did not point out their limitations in reviews, to the books' publishers, to each other, and perhaps even to children. However, if otherwise solid nonfiction titles actually give misinformation about or stereotype women's problems and contributions, they may be rejected with a clear conscience. Books with omissions can be supplemented, especially for older children; books featuring misinformation or misrepresentations can be permanently damaging.

Most difficult of all is the question of how to handle sexist books already in homes and libraries. No matter how we might object to the stereotyping of females in folk and fairy tales, for example, we cannot deny that these stories offer rich, wonderful fantasy, action, and adventure which rightfully delight children.

Few people would seriously suggest rewriting the classics or historical fiction, or discarding them altogether. Teachers, librarians, and parents can, however, make available to young people materials which explain the limitations of books with stereotyped depictions, why they were written, and how and why society used to be different. They can speak to students about perceived differences between cultural conditioning and genetic inheritance. They can use blatantly sexist books—even the classics—to start a discussion of the unfairness of sexist depictions. Children have a strong sense of fair play and they respond well to such discussions. Finally, librarians might consider building strong collections on women to counter older sexist titles and to accommodate the ever growing number of girls seeking materials about women.

Since it is obviously easier to eliminate sexism from books yet unpublished than it is to deal with it in books already at hand, librarians, teachers, and parents should be sure to let publishers know what they think juvenile books should fairly include regarding male and female characters, behavior patterns, dress, occupations, life goals, and so on. Such letters should be written and received as valuable input, not dictatorial mandates.

Suggested Research Needs

1. Should sexism be a criterion for weeding library collections? When, if ever, might such weeding be considered censorship?

2. What criteria qualify a book as nonsexist?

3. Androgynous characters, that is, people exhibiting both masculine and feminine traits, are very much in vogue now and are said by some to represent the ultimate in mental health for human beings. Does psychological research confirm or deny this view?

4. Should there be different standards for books assigned for classroom reading and discussion and those available for free reading on library shelves?

5. Can the new trend in books in discussing menstruation, masturbation, and development of secondary sex characteristics of females be considered feminist? Or, is this an entirely different category of fiction?

Bibliography

Books and Pamphlets

GERSONI, DIANE, ed. *Sexism and Youth.* Bowker, 1974. Essential anthology containing almost fifty of the most significant articles on sexism in children's literature, schools, socialization games, toys, and films.

HEILBRUN, CAROLYN. *Toward a Recognition of Androgyny.* Harper, 1974. Explores the concept of androgyny in life and in literature.

KEY, MARY R. *Male/Female Language with a Comprehensive Bibliography.* Scarecrow, 1975. Examines mechanisms of language change, androgynous language, etc.

LAKOFF, ROBIN. *Language and Woman's Place.* Harper, 1975. Analyzes how the mechanics of language reflect and create societal mores and power structure.

MASON, BOBBIE ANN. *The Girl Sleuth: A Feminist Guide.* Feminist Pr., 1975. This analysis of series heroines, e.g., Nancy Drew, considers how emancipated and/or clichéd they are.

Women on Words and Images. *Channeling Children: Sex Stereotyping on Prime Time TV.* Princeton, N.J.: Women on Words and Images, 1975. The group that gave us *Dick and Jane as Victims* turns its attention to television and analyzes commercials as well as the top shows. Not a definitive work, but food for thought.

Articles

The Gersoni title cited above contains the important articles published through early 1973. The following articles represent the more significant ones to appear since then.

BEEBE, SANDRA. "Women in American Literature." *English Journal* 64 (September 1975): 32-35. Describes setting up a high-school elective course on the topic, and includes lists of books and characters studied, suggestions for activities, films, etc.

CLARK, LINDA. "Jack and Jill Fight Back." *Media and Methods* 12 (October 1975): 23-27. Tells how to use polls, records, role-playing, etc., in activities to inspire students to discuss sexism and their own attitudes toward it.

KELTY, JEAN McCLURE. "The Cult of Kill in Adolescent Fiction." *English Journal* 64 (February 1975): 56-61. The author feels that even more detrimental than the stereotyping of girls in teenage fiction is the stereotyping of boys to regard killing as a step necessary to manhood.

KRAMER, CHERIS. "Folk Linguistics: Wishy-Washy Mommy Talk." *Psychology Today* 8 (June 1974): 82-85. Gives procedures for ascertaining how students sex-type real versus stereotyped language in TV shows, cartoons, etc.

LUKENBILL, W. BERNARD. "Fathers in Adolescent Novels." *School Library Journal* 20 (February 1974): 26-30. Seeks to extend sexism studies to cast new light on social structures by studying the depiction of fathers in youth literature.

NELSON, GAYLE. "The Double Standard in Adolescent Novels." *English Journal* 64 (February 1975): 53-55. Nelson examines five novels that equate sex with pregnancy and concludes that teen literature is not offering adequate models for females.

NEUMANN, BARBARA A. "Sex Stereotyping in Elementary Textbooks." *Vassar Quarterly* (August 1975). Describes previous research on the subject and cites the author's own findings in a study of fifteen elementary social studies texts and twelve elementary science texts. Contains bibliography.

RUSS, JOANNA. "The Image of Women in Science Fiction." *Vertex* 1 (February 1974): 53-57. While often set in the future, science fiction is a stronghold of present-day values and standards when treating women characters.

Newsletters and Periodicals

Acorn Groweth. $1 per yr. From: Rita Kort, 48 Sunset Ave., Venice, Cal. 90291. This began as an ALA/CSD publication but has gone independent while remaining library oriented.

Booklegger. 555 29th St., San Francisco, Cal. 94131. Contains regular column on books for children and teenagers, plus many other features.

Emergency Librarian. C/O Barbara Clubb, 697 Wellington Crescent, Winnipeg, Manitoba, Canada R3M OA7. Emphasis is on Canadian-produced materials.

Good Newsletter. Clearinghouse for feminist media, P.O. Box 207, Ancaster, Ontario, Canada.

Interracial Books for Children Bulletin. Council on Interracial Books for Children, Inc., 1841 Broadway, New York, N.Y. 10023. Has expanded its coverage from its original emphasis to give good coverage to feminist materials in both reviews and articles.

Young Adult Alternative Newsletter. 37167 Mission Blvd., Fremont, Cal. 94536. While the focus of this newsletter is the exchange of information between librarians working with teenagers, it is sensitive to the needs of adolescent women.

Every major periodical is now devoting entire issues to feminist concerns. A glance through *Education Index* and the index, *Library Literature,* as well as *Reader's Guide to Periodical Literature* will unearth a wealth of information.

Other Resources

AHLUM, CAROL, and JACQUELINE M. FRALLEY, eds. *Feminist Resources for Schools and Colleges: A Guide to Curricular Materials.* Feminist Pr., 1973. Includes bibliographies, multimedia resources, games, kits, posters.

______. *High School Feminist Studies.* Feminist Pr., 1976. Descriptions of pioneer high-school and junior high school feminist studies courses from across the country. Includes a collection of high-school syllabi.

ARLOW, PHYLLIS, and MERLE FROSCHL. *Women in the High School Curriculum: A Review of U.S. History and English Literature Texts.* Feminist Pr., 1975. Illustrated analysis with source bibliography.

Feminist Resources for Equal Education. Catalog may be obtained from: P.O. Box 3185, Saxonville Station, Framingham, Mass. 01701.

A Filmography of New Female-Male Images for Young People. Annotated list of more than 100 films for ages 5-17. Available for self-addressed stamped envelope and request for information from: New Images, 1305 Oxford St., Berkeley, Cal. 94709.

FRIEDLAND, SANDRA S. *Consciousness Raising in the Classroom or Activities for/to Free Children.* Available from: Greater Champaign Area Chapter, NOW, 809 South Fifth St., Champaign, Ill. 61820.

FROSCHL, MERLE, et al., eds. *Women's Studies for Teachers and Administrators: A Packet of Inservice Education Materials.* Feminist Pr., 1975. Shows how to start inservice courses on sexism in education, and includes resource group lists, sample curriculum materials, model course syllabi, etc.

HALLER, ELIZABETH S., comp. *Images of Women: A Bibliography of Feminist Resources for Pennsylvania Schools.* Available from: Pennsylvania Department of Education, Box 911, Harrisburg, Pa. 17126.

HART, L. B. *A Feminist Looks at Educational Software Materials.* Available for $1.25 from: Everywoman's Center, Munson Hall, Univ. of Massachusetts, Amherst, Mass. 01002.

Audiovisual, Graphic, and Multimedia Materials

And That's What Little Girls Are Made Of. Send $10.00 tape fee to: San Francisco Women's Media Workshop, 905 Diamond St., San Francisco, Cal. 94114.

Community Helpers. A collection of eight photographs depicting women in a variety of non-stereotyped roles, e.g., mechanic. Send $2.75 to; Feminist Resources for Equal Education, P.O. Box 3185, Saxonville Station, Framingham, Mass. 01701.

Mothers Do Many Kinds of Work. Free from: Scott, Foresman, Educational Division, 1900 East Lake Avenue, Glenview, Ill. 60025.

SCHIMMEL, NANCY. *The Handsome Prince.* This film (rental $10) comes with an instruction booklet. Available from: Franciscan Films, Inc., P.O. Box 6116, San Francisco, Cal. 94101.

Sugar and Spice. Women's Action Alliance, producers. Thirty-two-minute film on nonsexist education. Distributed by: Odeon Films, Inc., 1619 Broadway, New York, N.Y. 10019.

This Book Is Rated "S." A slide show (rental $15) available from: Berry Bock, 2617 Hartwook Drive, Fort Worth, Tex. 76109.

Women at Work. A collection of fifteen photographs showing women in nontraditional jobs. Write to: Change for Children, 2588 Mission St., #226, San Francisco, Cal. 94110.

Women in Sports. A collection of six photographs including suggestions for use. Write to: Cathy Cade, 2103 Emerson St., Berkeley, Cal. 94705.

Women's Graphics Collection. A catalog of posters and other graphics. Write to: Chicago Women's Liberation Union, 852 W. Belmont, Chicago, Ill. 60657.

Pressure for Pluralism

The Editors

Two very divergent themes have run through American history: (1) the idea that America's doors were open to all, but (2) once having arrived, the immigrants were expected to willingly take their place within "the melting pot." The doors have been closed for some time to all but a select group of potential immigrants, and in recent years the melting-pot psychology has been challenged seriously by a wide variety of groups.

The most active groups demanding change in American attitudes are (1) the blacks, (2) the Chicanos (Mexican-Americans), (3) the Native Americans (Indians), and (4) women. Puerto Ricans and Asian Americans are also asking for an acknowledgment of their heritage and an acceptance of them as individuals.

Until very recently, despite high visibility in one sense, these groups also shared a type of invisibility. Women were simply adjuncts to men, while the other groups were barred from access to the mainstream of American society for a multiplicity of reasons.

The first three groups also share a common characteristic, although it may not be quite so obvious: they are all Americans because the status was forced upon them. The blacks were brought in chains; the Mexican-Americans became Americans when Mexico lost its territories; and the Native Americans were physically defeated by the United States.

In place of the melting pot has come pressure for pluralism. Each group is demanding the right to live its own life in its own style, with control over its own destiny. While much of this rejection of white middle-class values can be traced to the black power revolution, some of it owes a debt to the millions of white young people who, during the 1960s and early 1970s, were rejecting society in one way or another. As white youth spoke sharply against the school system in underground newspapers, in demonstrations, and on occasion, in riots, it became clear that they felt participation in the mainstream might not be worth their effort.

All of this is placing great pressure on the school system and creating something akin to chaos in many areas of the country. Educators are beset with problems arising out of the need to rethink the traditional role of public education. They must also consider whether it is possible to achieve cultural equality without simultaneously working for economic equality. When public schools were begun, the need was to take many diverse groups of immigrants and show them how to become Americans. The schools did the job well but at a price that we are only beginning to recognize. Reflecting the domination of our society by white males, they imposed roles upon members of minority groups rather than seeing them as individuals. Native Americans and Spanish-speaking peoples were made to feel ashamed of their native languages; women were thought odd if they wanted to be something other than mothers and housewives; blacks were taught that they must learn to think in white terms. Teachers, librarians, and parents who have been educated in a unicultural perspective must develop insights into other cultures and value systems.

For schools and libraries the challenge is twofold. In those areas where one of the minority groups predominates, the need is to understand the value system of the group, accept it, and work within its parameters. In order to accomplish this, teachers and librarians must immerse themselves in the history and culture of the group. They cannot be content to read children's books and expect to learn what they need to know. No one who has not read *The Autobiography of Malcolm X*, for example, is in a position to evaluate black materials for children.

A second area of concern is the need to develop programs in pluralistic culture for students in all-white schools. Their need to understand that there are as many ways of life as there are different peoples is vital for reaching some national understanding of our problems and possibilities.

Neither the problems nor the possibilities are the sole province of those concerned with children's literature, but they do have the opportunity, through the conscious dissemination of children's literature that is neither sexist nor racist, to help reshape our society.

Books that denigrate third world cultures or portray only conventional sex roles can be harmful. Books in which characters have stereotypical jobs (the Chinese laundry man) or in which they have stereotypical appearance (the barefoot Chicano) as described in the text or shown in the illustrations, can be harmful. It is not that there are no Chinese laundry workers or barefoot Mexicans or mothers in aprons or Japanese gardeners, but that such portrayals reinforce existing stereotypes, and that they militate against minority group members and women being regarded as individuals, and especially as individuals who may (as they do in real life) vary drastically in appearance and appear in any role in our society.

For many years the third world characters in children's books turned to white characters for help in solving problems; men and boys assumed an active role while girls and women were passive; acceptance of minority members meant acceptance by whites. It is not that cultural differences should not be portrayed but that they should be portrayed without stereotyping. The historical group experience should be treated honestly. All children should have books that give positive reinforcement to their self-image. They have a right to books that bolster their sense of worth and their pride in their cultural heritage.

Suggested Research Needs

1. Is there a difference in the image of Native Americans in books found under the library subject-headings "Indians of North America—Fiction," and in books carrying the heading "Frontier and Pioneer Life—Fiction"?

2. Compare the images of minority groups found in the English Carnegie-Medal books

and the American Newbery-Medal books for the same selective time period.

3. What differences in images of the black experience, if any, can be found in books written by blacks and those written by whites?

4. A CBS survey of children's reactions to television programs showed that they identify with the personal characteristics of the performers and not with their racial origin. Do white children relate to minority characters in books as individuals or as representatives of a racial/ethnic group? Do minority group children relate differently?

5. What image of minority groups is found in general nonfiction books such as those dealing with sex education, books about camping, or illustrated cookbooks?

6. What image of minority groups is found in children's dictionaries?

Bibliography

On July 23, 1976, the Council of the American Library Association passed a resolution entitled "Racism and Sexism Awareness." One portion of that resolution directs the Committee on Accreditation to collect data showing that library schools are educating students to an awareness of racism and sexism. Unlike other bibliographies in this section of the book, which present a wide range of opinions, this bibliography consists of materials that will aid students in schools of education and library schools to systematically raise their consciousnesses about the nature of institutionalized racism and sexism. Because most of us have grown up in a racist society, it is not enough merely to present students with information about the history and culture of minorities; first we must realize how our perceptions of minorities have been distorted by the pervasiveness of racism. The materials can be used by individuals or as formal course readings in awareness training programs. This bibliography was prepared by the Council on Interracial Books for Children (1841 Broadway, New York, N.Y. 10023).

Multi-Racial Materials

Books

BANKS, JAMES, ed. *Teaching Ethnic Studies.* Nat. Council for the Social Studies, 1973. One of the best resources for teachers. Part I deals with racism and cultural pluralism; Part II, Teaching the Ethnic Minority Cultures, includes articles by an Asian American, a Chicano, a Puerto Rican, a Native American, and an article of great value, "Teaching Black Studies for Social Change." Part III deals with teaching about white ethnic groups and women's rights and is the weakest section.

CARLSON, ROBERT A. *The Quest for Conformity: Americanization Through Education.* Wiley, 1975. To practice cultural pluralism in education, the opposite phenomenon—Americanization through education—needs to be understood. This study explains how Americanization indoctrination created a hostility toward nonconformity, and traces its history from the seventeenth century to the 1970s. A necessary book because its historical perspective and detail reveal the dimensions of American conformity and the need to counteract it.

CARLSON, RUTH KEARNEY. *Emerging Humanity; Multi-Ethnic Literature for Children and Adolescents.* Brown, 1972. Describes values and criteria for multiethnic literature, suggests ways to use it. Separate chapters discuss black, American Indian, and Mexican-American books.

CIBC Racism and Sexism Resource Center for Educators. *Human and Anti-Human Values in Children's Books: Guidelines for the Future.* New York, 1976. This volume analyzes over 200 books and identifies what values they transmit to young readers. The books are examined for sexism, racism, materialism, elitism, individualism, conformism, escapism, and ageism—as well as for their cultural authenticity and their effect on the self-image of female and/or minority children. The reviews explore the "hidden messages" which every author, intentionally or unintentionally, transmits to young people.

FORBES, JACK D. *The Education of the Culturally Different: A Multi-Cultural Approach.* Berkeley, Cal.: Far West Laboratory for Educational Research and Development, 1969. An authoritative, well-documented account of how the mono-cultural orientation of schools has created educational disadvantages for *all* pupils. Forbes provides in detail a cross-cultural strategy for combating this problem. An essential book for everyone concerned with children.

HOTCHKISS, JEANETTE, comp. *African-Asian Reading Guide for Children and Young Adults.* Scarecrow, 1976. Divided by countries and by genre.

KEATING, CHARLOTTE MATTHEWS, comp. *Building Bridges of Understanding.* Palo Verde, 1967. An annotated bibliography of books about blacks, Indians, Spanish-speaking ethnic groups, Chinese-Americans, Japanese-Americans, Jews, and other minority groups.

______. *Building Bridges of Understanding Between Cultures.* Palo Verde, 1971. A companion volume to the title above, the annotations arranged by age level within each minority group.

KELLY, ERNECE B. *Searching for America.* Nat. Council of Teachers of English, 1972. In addition to the critiques of twelve English textbooks at the college level, this book includes four background essays which provide insights for those working with literature at any level (even elementary and junior high). These essays are by black, Chinese American, Chicano, and Native American scholars, and they offer a clear picture of the kind of exclusions and distortions found in works of literature as well as suggestions for change. The book includes NCTE's "Criteria for Teaching Materials in Reading and Literature" by the NCTE Task Force on Racism and Bias in the Teaching of English.

KNOWLES, LOUIS, and KENNETH PREWITT. *Institutional Racism in America.* Prentice, 1969. A classic in racism literature, this book gives an explanation of the ideological roots of racism in America. It also dramatically illustrates the institutional racism perpetuated by political, economic, legal, health and welfare, religious and educational institutions.

RYAN, WILLIAM, *Blaming the Victim.* Pantheon, 1971. A "must" book for all interested in understanding the way in which white society defines people of color as both the cause and effect of their circumstances. Written in easy-to-understand language, the author brilliantly exposes some of the myths of racism and social science.

STEINFIELD, MELVIN. *Cracks in the Melting Pot: Racism and Discrimination in American History.* Glencoe, 1970. A collection of readings designed to provide an overview of racism in accurate perspective, to provide insights into racist practices directed toward ethnic minorities. Shows how racism has influenced territorial acquisition, presidential thought, immigration laws, etc.

STENT, MADELON D., WILLIAM R. HAZARD, and HARRY N. RIVLIN. *Cultural Pluralism in Education: A Mandate for Change.* Appleton, 1973. Excellent collection of papers originally given at the Conference on Education and Teacher Education for Cultural Pluralism in Chicago in 1971. They are by prominent educators and leaders from different cultural groups.

TERRY, ROBERT W. *For Whites Only.* Eerdmans, 1970. Terry's book largely concerns white racism in industry. However, few books are so clear as this in analyzing the processes of racism—the liberal who will not see blacks as individuals, the conservative who will not see blacks as a group. There is an outline of basic strategies for bringing change in the society, including educational institutions. It is one of the few "how to" books for those determined to follow a new white consciousness.

Articles

BANKS, JAMES A. "Teaching Ethnic Studies: Key Issues and Concepts." *Social Studies* 66 (May/June 1975): 107-113. Shows that the total curriculum must change to reflect the role of ethnicity in American life and history. Cites research indicating that students must study more than one sample in order to develop valid generalizations. An excellent guide to curriculum planning, with concepts drawn from different disciplines (anthropology, history, geography, etc.) which contribute to ethnic literacy.

Educational Leadership 32 (December 1974) and 33 (December 1975). Twelve articles in the December 1974 issue are grouped under the heading "Toward Cultural Pluralism," offering many points of view. Eight articles in the December 1975 issue deal with the general theme, "Multicultural Curriculum: Issues, Designs, Strategies." Highly useful for the theoretical as well as practical discussions by leading educators.

TATE, BINNIE. "The Role of the Children's Librarian in Serving the Disadvantaged." *Library Trends* 20 (October 1971): 392-404. A plea for library involvement in community life, which in turn would lead to materials which reflect community needs. Provides an explanation of why libraries are currently offering "not the best for the most, but the most to the best," and suggests ways to correct this injustice.

THOMAS, NIDA. "Out of the Melting Pot." *Library Journal* 97 (October 15, 1972): 3421-3423. Explains why the first priority for educators and librarians should be to sensitize people to cultural differences in ethnic groups. "A sense of identity and self-realization . . . must be based on accurate information, freedom from ignorance, prejudice, and stereotypes, and a positive view of self."

Pamphlets

CITRON, ABRAHAM F. *"The Rightness of Whiteness": The World of the White Child in a Segregated Society.* Michigan-Ohio Regional Educational Laboratory, 1969. Distributed by P.A.C.T., 163 Madison, Detroit, Mich. 48226. A nonprofit organization, supported in part by U.S. Office of Education funds, has gathered evidence to show how preschool white children have a distorted, racist view of nonwhite people. White stereotypes about blacks are also documented. Focuses on those factors generating white superiority: i.e., textbooks, role models, perpetuation of black stereotypes.

DOWNS, ANTHONY. *Racism in America and How to Combat It.* U.S. Commission on Civil Rights; Clearinghouse Publication, Urban Series No. 1. U.S. Government Printing Office, Washington, D.C. 20402, 1970. This publication is the place to start a study of racism. It has a good development of a definition of racism and a unique six pages on "How Racism Provides Benefits to Whites." It also features strategies for combating racism; while not mentioning education specifically, the strategies can be applied to educational institutions.

Black Americans

Bibliographies

DODDS, BARBARA, comp. *Negro Literature for High School Students.* Nat. Council of Teachers of English, 1968. A valuable reference guide offering a historical survey of black writers, an annotated list of works about blacks, annotated lists of novels for boys and girls, and biographies, both historical and modern, as well as suggested classroom uses of black literature. Extensive bibliography.

IRWIN, LEONARD, comp. *Black Studies: A Bibliography.* McKinley, 1973. For young people and adults, annotations grouped under such headings as biographical material, African background, essays and anthologies, etc.

LATIMER, BETTYE I., et al., eds. *Starting Out Right: Choosing Books About Black People for Young Children, Pre-School Through Third Grade,* 1972. Distributed by Division for Administrative Services, Wisconsin Hall, 126 Langdon St., Madison, Wis. 53702. The introduction to this bibliography contains an outstanding chapter on criteria for selecting children's books on black themes. There is also a chapter that demonstrates in detail how the criteria can be applied to a particular book. Thumbnail reviews of 300 books include reasons why some of the books were not recommended. Unfortunately, the introductory criteria were not applied to all the books listed.

MILLS, JOYCE WHITE, comp. *The Black World in Literature for Children; A Bibliography of Print and Non-Print Materials.* Atlanta Univ., 1975. Divided by broad age groups and subject areas, this is for children ages 3–13.

ROLLINS, CHARLEMAE, ed. *We Build Together; A Reader's Guide to Negro Life and Literature for Elementary and High School Use.* 3rd ed. Nat. Council of Teachers of English. 1967. A selected, annotated bibliography of picture books, fiction, history, biography, poetry, folklore, music, science, and sports, with an introduction dealing with the criteria by which the books were selected.

ROLLOCK, BARBARA, comp. *The Black Experience in Children's Books,* rev. ed. New York Public Library, 1974. An annotated bibliography, classified by age and subject matter about black life in America, in the Islands, in Africa, and in England.

Books

BRODERICK, DOROTHY M. *The Image of the Black in Children's Fiction.* Bowker, 1973. An excellent analysis of the different forms of racism in books recommended by established library periodicals and reference sources from 1827 to 1967.

LERNER, GERDA, ed. *Black Women in White America.* Random, 1972. Lerner notes the double invisibility of the black woman in this fine documentary history. The book includes speeches, letters, essays covering education, slavery, racism, sexism, work, achievements, etc.

McCANN, DONNARAE, and GLORIA WOODARD, eds. *The Black American in Books for Children: Readings in Racism.* Scarecrow, 1972. A compilation of twenty-five articles which pinpoint racist attitudes in books from the past and the present. Urges the active involvement of black Americans at every juncture in book publishing, criticism, and distribution.

Articles

BARONBERG, JOAN. "Black Representation in Children's Books." ERIC/IRCD Urban Disadvantaged Series, 1971. ERIC Document Reproduction Service, Leasco Information Products, Inc. P.O. Drawer O, Bethesda, Maryland 20014. A summary of the effects of racist books on children in general, plus brief commentaries on books containing black characters for the early elementary school level. Provides a statistical review of the availability of books at this level.

BAXTER, KATHERINE B. "Combating the Influence of Black Stereotypes." *The Reading Teacher* 27 (March 1974): 540-544. Describes how one elementary school tries to teach children to read critically by means of discussions and questions about racism which have been pasted inside such books as *Sounder* and *Charlie and the Chocolate Factory.*

BRODERICK, DOROTHY M. "Lessons in Leadership: Caricatures of Black People in Recommended Juvenile Fiction Books." *Library Journal* 96 (February 15, 1971): 699-701. Contends librarians must evaluate books by relating them to contemporary issues. Failure to do this in children's books has led to the degradation of blacks and other minority groups in children's literature.

COHEN, SOL. "Minority Stereotypes in Children's Literature: The Bobbsey Twins, 1904-1968." *Educational Forum* 34 (November 1969): 119-134. Analyzes the stereotyped blacks found in the popular children's series.

CORNELIUS, PAUL. "Interracial Children's Books: Problems and Progress." *The Library Quarterly* 41 (April 1971): 106-127. Describes the representation of blacks in children's books since 1890; discusses the forces which impede the publication of interracial books; and traces the Black Power Movement in children's literature.

DYBEK, CAREN. "Black Literature for Adolescents." *English Journal* 63 (January 1974): 64-67. A short bibliography of novels, short-story collections, and nonfiction by black writers. The author introduces this list by commenting upon genres and the use of black English.

GRANSTROM, JANE, and ANITA SILVEY. "A Call for Help: Exploring the Black Experience in Children's Books." *The Horn Book Magazine*, August 1972, pp. 395-404. A summary of a meeting in New England which provided a candid interchange between several librarians and a panel of experts on interracial books. The need for black writers and illustrators was emphasized by some and challenged by others.

JOHNSON, EDWINA. "Black History: The Early Childhood Vacuum." *Library Journal* 94 (May 15, 1969): 2057-2058. An excellent article contending that "simply blackening the characters' faces" is not enough. Children's books should present: (1) black history—the record of what black people have created, nurtured, and produced in the past, and (2) black culture—the totality of black people's modes of living.

McCANN, DONNARAE. "Sambo and Sylvester." *Wilson Library Bulletin* 45 (May 1971): 880-881. The author argues that attempts to draw a parallel between the racism in *Little Black Sambo* and the picture of pigs as policemen in *Sylvester and the Magic Pebble* are wrong. While Sambo is racist, Sylvester is by no stretch of the imagination anti-law enforcement.

MATHIS, SHARON BELL. "Parent's Guide to Racism in Children's Books." *Reflect* 1 (1971): 16. Includes an 18-point checklist to apply in judging the many books about blacks by white writers and illustrators. For example, "Does the black child lack a name, home life, friends, toys, hobbies, etc., while the white child is fully described? Is black pride, in the story, dependent upon white acceptance?" and so on.

SCHMIDT, NANCY J. "Books by African Authors for Non-African Children." *Africana Library Journal* II (Winter 1971): 11-13. Describes twenty-two children's books and tells how they reflect, or fail to reflect, the African origin of the authors. The books mentioned include folk tales, autobiographies, picture books, and history and fact books about African society. The American or British publishers and the dates of publication are given.

TATE, BINNIE. "In House and Out House: Authenticity and the Black Experience in Children's Books." *School Library Journal,* October 1970. Examines books on the black experience written by white authors and shows in a fascinating way how even the most careful authors are unable completely to shed their biases.

———. "Integrating Culture." *Library Journal* 94 (May 15, 1969): 2053-2056. After three centuries of distortion of and indifference to black Americans and their African heritage, Tate feels that children's books must play a major role in exploding the myths and racist caricatures of blacks.

WERNER, JUDY. "Black Pearls and Ebony." *Library Journal* 93 (May 15, 1968): 2091. Argues that while honest character representation of the black is important, some stories or books still injure the black child's self-concept through racist symbolism in which white symbolizes good and black, bad.

WILKERSON, DOXEY A. "Understanding the Black Child." *Childhood Education* 46 (April 1970): 351-354. A brief summary of myths pertaining to the learning potential of black children in the urban environment, and a refutation of these myths. The author cites some of the research studies which offer the supporting data for each refutation.

YUILL, PHYLLIS J. *Little Black Sambo: A Closer Look.* Council on Interracial Books for Children, 1976. An in-depth study of Helen Bannerman's controversial children's book. Chapters include "Origins," "Popularity," "Protest and Controversy," and "Sambo Today."

Periodicals

Africana Library Journal: A Quarterly Bibliography and Resource Guide. 101 Fifth Ave., New York City, N.Y. 10003. Includes articles with detailed evaluations of books on Africa published throughout the world, plus comprehensive current bibliographies, and information on African writers and scholars. Includes children's books and AV materials, as well as adult books. Articles about children's books make a point of cautioning the reader about Eurocentric bias in books and an inadequate non-European viewpoint whenever this imbalance occurs. Also valuable as a guide to British books which can be easily acquired by writing London book dealers.

The Black Scholar. P.O. Box 908, Sausalito, Cal. 94965. This is a highly influential black-oriented monthly publication, and features a valuable book review section.

Black World. Johnson Publications, 820 S. Michigan Ave., Chicago, Ill. 60605. Unfortunately, this excellent monthly ceased with the April 1976 issue. From the time of its change from the *Negro Digest, Black World* was the major communication vehicle for black writers and remains an invaluable tool for librarians.

Chicanos

Bibliographies

QUINTANA, HELENA. *A Current Bibliography on Chicanos, 1960-1973.* The Cultural Awareness Center, College of Education, University of New Mexico, 1974. Both fiction and nonfiction are included in this annotated bibliography. Material is coded to indicate recommended scholastic levels. A list of Chicano periodicals and publishers is also included.

TREJO, ARNULFO D. *Bibliografia Chicana: A Guide to Information Sources.* Gale, 1975. A thoughtfully annotated guide which will serve teachers and librarians in the sections dealing with education, librarianship, history, biography, folklore, and the fine arts.

Books

ACUÑA, RUDOLFO. *Occupied America: The Chicanos Struggle Toward Liberation.* Harper, 1972. A Chicano view of American history missing from textbooks. Professor Acuña started one of the first university courses on the history of Chicanos (Mount St. Mary's College, Los Angeles, 1966). In this excellent book, he combines a definitely Chicano perspective with an academic-activist approach to history.

MARTINEZ, ELIZABETH S., and ENRIQUETA L. VÁSQUEZ. *Viva La Raza!* Doubleday, 1974. Two Chicanas, long active in many efforts to advance the Chicano cause, have written a forceful and fervent account of some of the most significant events and personalities in recent years of the Chicano movement. An important aspect of many of these events which no writers have yet captured is the role of Chicanas, *las mujeres.* The authors' special contribution is that they place the focus of Chicano nationalism on the *Familia de la Raza.*

Mexican American Education Study. U.S. Commission on Civil Rights, Washington, D.C., 7 volumes, 1971–1974. A thoroughly documented and fascinating study of the miseducation and destruction of Chicano children in modern America.

POBLANO, RALPH (RAFA). *Ghosts in the Barrio: Issues in Bilingual-Bicultural Education.* San Rafael, Cal.: Leswing Press, 1973. Essays by Chicano educators dealing with personal experiences as well as research. Educational objectives are discussed and practical solutions suggested in the areas of curriculum and administration.

ROMANO-V, OCTAVIO IGNACIO. *Voices: Readings from "El Grito," a Journal of Contemporary Mexican-American Thought,* 1967-1971. Quinto Sol Publications, Inc. (P.O. Box 9275, Berkeley, Cal. 94709), 1971. Offers much substantial and authentic background information for teachers and librarians. Particularly apropos for educators are the four articles under the heading "Stereotypes and the Distortion of History," and three articles in the section on "Education and the Chicano."

SOTOMAYOR, MARTA, and PHILIP D. ORTEGO. *Chicanos and Concepts of Culture.* Prepared by Marfel Associates for The Western Interstate Commission on Higher Education, 1974. (P.O. Drawer P, Boulder, Colorado, 80302.) Shows how several traditional concepts of culture have lead to a misinterpretation of Chicano culture, and explains each false conclusion in terms of Chicano perspective. This is a brief essay, but will provide significant help to teachers and librarians in their effort to detect the stereotypes attached to any group.

Articles

GEREZ, TONI DE. "Books for Miguel." *Library Journal* 92 (December 15, 1967): 4587-4589. Describes the lack of books and bibliographic tools in the area of

Spanish-language children's books, but shows how to minimize this problem to a degree. A sampling of books is listed for the elementary-school Spanish language collections, including dictionaries, picture books, folk tales, classics, and so on.

GURULE, KAY. "Truthful Textbooks and Mexican Americans." *Integrated Education: A Report on Race and Schools* XI (March/April 1973): 35-42. Describes the deficiencies in teaching materials in California and makes many recommendations in the areas of teaching strategies, and materials and resources. The author was chairperson of the Textbook Task Force for the Mexican American Education Commission in Los Angeles, and she summarizes the events leading to a class action suit against the California State Board of Education for adopting racist textbooks.

HARO, ROBERT P. "Bicultural and Bilingual Americans: A Need for Understanding." *Library Trends* 20 (October, 1971): 256-270. A brief survey of the sociocultural differences between Mexican American and Anglo children, followed by a description of three democratic, innovative library programs in Mexican American communities. This article is recommended less for its section on cultural differences than for its revelation of how real local control can be achieved even in a tradition-bound institution.

Interracial Books for Children Bulletin 5 (Fall, 1974). This special issue analyzes 200 children's books on Chicano themes and provides a comprehensive checklist for evaluating materials about Chicanos.

ORTEGO, PHILIP D. "Schools for Mexican-Americans: Between Two Cultures." *Saturday Review* 54 (April 19, 1971): 62+. A superb overview of the problems facing Mexican Americans in Anglo schools. A strong plea for bilingual education plus recognition of the historical and cultural heritage of the Chicanos.

TAYLOR, JOSÉ. "The Chicano in Children's Literature." *The California Librarian* 34 (January 1973): 38-39. A general statement about the need for books which reveal insights into Mexican American history, for books by Mexican American authors, and for the elimination of negative images and stereotypes.

TREJO, ARNULFO D. "Library Needs for the Spanish Speaking." *ALA Bulletin* 63 (September 1969): 1077-1081. Outlines the problems of Mexican Americans in the schools—notably a language barrier and the task of acculturation. Schools and libraries can help by providing materials in Spanish and by recognizing the viability of bilingual culture.

Wilson Library Bulletin 44 (March 1970). Except for "Regular Features," the entire issue is devoted to the theme "Libraries and the Spanish-Speaking."

Periodicals

Aztlán: Chicano Journal of the Social Sciences. 405 Hilgard Ave., Los Angeles, Cal. 90033. Published by Chicano students at the University of Southern California, Los Angeles. The journal carries in-depth academic articles.

El Grito: A Journal of Contemporary Mexican American Thought. P.O. Box 9275, Berkeley, Cal. 94719. This journal was created as an intellectual forum for Mexican Americans to articulate their own sense of identity. It serves also to counteract the plethora of writings (many in the field of education) which include and promote racial clichés.

La Raza. P.O. Box 310004, Los Angeles, Cal. 90031. This is the longest lived of the approximately 200 Chicano periodicals in existence today. It is published by La Raza Unida Party.

Other Resources

The Chicano Chronicle. Chicano Studies Center at Claremont College, 919 No. Columbia, Claremont, Cal. 91711. This presents Chicano history in an exciting newspaper format and is currently in preparation. It is an innovative way to present history to young people.

Puerto Ricans

Books

FIGUERA, LOIDA. *History of Puerto Rico.* Las Americas Publishing Company (40-22 23rd Street, Long Island City, N.Y. 11101), 1975. The best history of Puerto Rico available in English.

MALDONADO, DENIS. *Puerto Rico: A Socio-Historic Interpretation.* Vintage, 1972. An eye-opening account of the imperialist oppression of Puerto Ricans under both Spain and the U.S.

WAGENHEIM, KAL. *Puerto Rico: A Profile.* Praeger, 1970. Suggested less for perspective than for valuable background, facts, and dates.

YURCHENCO, HENRIETTA. *Hablamos! Puerto Ricans Speak.* Praeger, 1971. An unusually good documentary about Puerto Ricans. Recorded interviews by an author who consciously tries to write from a perspective that is not ethnocentric.

Articles

Interracial Books for Children Bulletin. Special Issue. New York, 1972. The following articles in this issue are useful to librarians and teachers: "100 Children's Books about Puerto Ricans—a Study in Racism, Sexism and Colonialism"; "The Colonialist Mentality: Distortions and Omissions in Children's History Books"; "Relevant Literature for Classroom Use"; "Children's Books from Puerto Rico: An Annotated Listing"; "Feminists Look at the 100 Books"; "U.S. Distributors and Suppliers of Puerto Rican Materials"; and "Book Publishers in Puerto Rico: A Survey."

Periodicals

Puerto Rico Libre! Bulletin of the Puerto Rican Solidarity Committee, P.O. Box 319, Cooper Station, New York, N.Y. 10003. Covers news in Puerto Rico and the U.S. from an *independentista* perspective.

The Rican Journal, 2409 Geneva Terrace, Chicago, Ill. 60614. This quarterly, begun in 1971, is a "voice for second generation Puerto Ricans." Somewhat academically oriented, it has excellent coverage of the Puerto Rican experience in the U.S.

Native Americans

Bibliographies

ABLER, THOMAS S., and SALLY M. WEAVER. *A Canadian Indian Bibliography, 1960-70.* University of Toronto Press, 1974. The well-annotated education section will lead teachers and librarians to research studies which involve Native American children and which suggest beneficial changes in the educational system.

BYLER, MARY GLOYNE. *American Indian Authors for Young Readers.* New York: Association on American Indian Affairs, 1974. This bibliography has an outstanding introductory essay that takes non-Native American authors to task for failing to depict Native Americans in roles that are not stereotypic. She calls on publishing houses to offset the damage by projecting realistic images of Native Americans.

HIRSCHFELDER, ARLENE B. *American Indian and Eskimo Authors; A Comprehensive Bibliography.* New York: Association on American Indian Affairs, 1973. This book will direct teachers and librarians to authentic works in the fields of poetry, art, folklore, autobiography, and so on. Sources are noted where these materials can be obtained.

HOYT, ANNE K. *Bibliography of the Cherokees.* Little Rock, Arkansas: South Central Regional Education Laboratory, 1968. Lists books, government documents, and periodical articles about Cherokee life. Also has an extensive section devoted to Cherokee life as depicted in children's books.

STENSLAND, A. L. *Literature By and About the American Indian for Junior and Senior High Schools.* Nat. Council of Teachers of English, 1973. The useful portions of this book are those leading the reader to authentic materials and to Native American sources for additional materials (e.g., there is a section on Indian authors plus autobiographies, myths, poetry). In other sections the author often indicates that the work is "from the white man's point of view," but in many cases the books are stereotyped and demeaning, and this is not indicated in the annotation.

ULLOM, JUDITH C., ed. *Folklore of North American Indians; An Annotated Bibliography.* Library of Congress, 1969. Lists historical source material and anthologies of Native American folk tales for adults and children. Divided by geographical areas: Woodland, Eskimo, MacKensie, etc. Children's editions are noted.

Books

Akwesasne Notes. *BIA: I'm Not Your Indian Anymore.* Mohawk Nation via Rooseveltown, N.Y. 13683. The story of the Trail of Broken Treaties group which occupied the Bureau of Indian Affairs headquarters in Washington, D.C., in 1972. Also contains the Twenty Points position paper presented to the White House which would revolutionize Indian/U.S. relationships.

Akwesasne Notes. *Voices From Wounded Knee 1973.* Mohawk Nation via Rooseveltown, N.Y. 13683. A first-hand account of the occupation of Wounded Knee in the words of the participants, culled from 100 hours of tape recorded while the occupation was in progress. It is accompanied by 200 dramatic photographs. It is "must" reading for teachers and librarians who need to understand this episode of the struggle for human dignity and freedom in the U.S.

CAHN, EDGAR S. *Our Brother's Keeper: The Indian in White America.* Community Press, 1969. (Distributed by World Publishing.) A searing indictment of white America's treatment of Native Americans—especially the chapter, "Education as War."

Council on Interracial Books for Children. *Chronicles of American Indian Protest.* Fawcett, 1972. A documentary history of the oppression of Native Americans by the white conquerors.

HENRY, JEANNETTE. *Textbooks and the American Indian.* American Indian Historical Society, 1970. (Order from *The Indian Historian,* 1451 Masonic Avenue, San Francisco, Cal. 94117.) While concerned with textbooks, the volume has implications for trade books as well. The first chapters are especially important, and Chapter 3, "The General Criteria," can be applied to all media.

Articles

BAYNE, STEPHEN L. "Cultural Materials in Schools' Programs for Indian Students." *Journal of American Indian Education* 9 (October 1969): 1-6. Explains how Native American cultural material (myths, arts, language) will not, per se, perpetuate the holistic values of Indian cultures, but outlines the valuable role of these materials in the curriculum: (1) they show the official sanction of Indian culture which in turn helps the child's self-image; (2) they constitute in-service training for the teachers on Indian culture; (3) they help bring the child's home and school together.

BYLER, MARY GLOYNE. "The Image of American Indians Projected by Non-Indian Writers." *School Library Journal,* February 1974, pp. 36-39. This is a reprint of the author's outstanding critical essay published in the bibliography cited above, *American Indian Authors for Young People.* The article was later attacked by editor and children's book writer Ferdinand N. Monjo in the May 1974 issue of *School Library Journal.* In an article titled, "Monjo's Manifest Destiny: Authors Can Claim Any Territory in Literature," he accuses Byler of censorship and tampering with his romanticized (and highly stereotypic) image of Native Americans.

FALKENHAGEN, MARIA, CAROLE JOHNSON, and MICHAEL A. BALASA. "The Treatment of Native Americans in Recent Children's Literature." *Integrated Education: Minority Children in Schools* XI (July-October 1973): 58-59. A useful content analysis of twenty-two books published since 1965. Thirty-eight Native American characters were studied in these books, and the conclusion was reached that they all contain subtle stereotypes and should be used only in conjunction with discussion of Native American history and culture.

HENNINGER, DANIEL, and NANCY ESPOSITO. "Indian Schools." *The New Republic* 160 (February 15, 1969): 18-21. Exposes the inhumane conditions in many schools operated by the Bureau of Indian Affairs. Also gives a brief description of the experimental school in Rough Rock, Arizona, which illustrates the improvements possible when a school is staffed largely by Native Americans.

HERBT, LAURA. "That's One Good Indian; Unacceptable Images in Children's Novels." *Top of the News* 31 (January 1975): 192-198. Describes many racist books, noting the specific scenes and incidents which portray the Native American as inferior, savage, or superficially quaint.

MALLAM, R. CLARK. "Academic Treatment of the Indian in Public School Texts and Literature." *Journal of American Indian Education* 13 (October 1973): 14-19. An anthropologist describes the inadequacy and counter-productive nature of the curriculum and the teaching materials in a Midwestern elementary school. He discusses the materials about Native Americans which are "ethnocentric, inaccurate, distorted."

SMITH, WILLIAM F., JR. "American Indian Literature." *English Journal* 63 (January 1974): 68-72. A professor of American Indian Civilization recommends and describes books in four categories: anthologies, autobiographies, poetry, and traditional narratives (myths, tales, legends). They include only the literature created by Native Americans, although some are edited by those from other cultural groups. Teachers at any grade level can select the materials appropriate for their classes, especially among the books of poetry and traditional narratives.

Social Education 36 (May 1972). This issue deals primarily with the education of the Native American and contains essays and bibliographies which promote intensive and authentic curricula.

"Textbook Bias Toward Alaskan Natives." Documentary Report by Dept. of Education, University of Alaska College, March 14, 1969. *Integrated Education: Race and Schools* 60 (March-April 1971): 44-49. This report constitutes part of the hearings of the Subcommittee on Indian Education in the Senate Committee on Labor and Public Welfare in 1969. It discusses the bias against Eskimos (the preferred term for Eskimos is Innuit) and illustrates each example with excerpts from ten elementary-school textbooks and seven high-school textbooks. Each error of fact in the example is explained.

Periodicals

Akwesasne Notes. Rooseveltown, N.Y. 13683. Newspaper of the Mohawk Nation. A "must" for every high-school library. Accounts of current and past events from the Native American viewpoint.

The Indian Historian. American Indian Historical Society, 1451 Masonic Ave., San Francisco, Cal. 94117. This quarterly is published by Native Americans and deals with issues of concern to Native Americans. It is more traditional in scope than *Akwesasne Notes.*

Journal of American Indian Education. Tempe, Arizona: Arizona State University, 1961. Covers all levels of education, all types of schools, and all regions in the U.S. Content includes general articles, research studies, new items, book reviews, and poetry.

Asian Americans

Bibliographies

Books for the Chinese-American Child; A Selected List, comp. by Cecilia Mei-Chi Chen. Cooperative Children's Book Center, 1969. A carefully selected list of books, included for their honesty and literary quality.

Interracial Books for Children Bulletin. Vol. 7, nos. 2 and 3, 1976. Special issue on the "Image of Asian Americans in Children's Books." The special issue evaluates the sixty-six children's books—currently in print or widely available in schools and public libraries—in which one or more central characters are Chinese American, Japanese American, Filipine American, or Korean American. All the books are critically reviewed. The reviews' conclusion: the books, with perhaps one or two exceptions, are blatantly racist, sexist—and elitist.

Books

Asian Women's Journal. "Asian Women." University of California at Berkeley, 1971. Thought-provoking collection of historical, analytical, and personal articles, artwork, photos, poetry, and short stories expressing the opinions and consciousness of Asian women. Interviews and poetry are especially interesting, as is the undercurrent of compassion/contrast with the white feminist movement.

Bulletin of Concerned Asian Scholars. "A Special Issue on Asian Americans." 4 (Fall 1972). Rm. 1001, 604 Mission St., San Francisco, Cal. The BCAS was established by students and scholars of Asia who felt that an alternative was needed to counter traditional Asian studies scholarship with anti-imperialist research. Born in opposition to U.S. intervention in Vietnam, it continues to publish interesting and well-researched articles on Asia and Asian America.

CHIN, FRANK, JEFFERY PAUL CHAN, LAWSON FUSAO INADA, and SHAWN HSU WONG. *Aiiieeeee! An Anthology of Asian-American Writers.* Howard University Press, 1974. Representative selections from works of the most important Asian American writers—including novelists, poets, short-story writers, and playwrights. The fifty pages of introduction are valuable and provide important insights into the Asian American experience.

NEE, VICTOR G., and BRETT DE BARY. *Longtime Californ': A Documentary Study of an American Chinatown.* Pantheon, 1972. Based on hundreds of interviews with San Francisco Chinatown's people, this is the best single volume on the subject. Transcribed sections of the interviews are preceded by narrative introductions—all divided into five major sections including "The Bachelor Society," "Refugees," and "Radicals and the New Vision."

TACHIKI, AMY, EDDIE WONG, FRANKLIN ODO, and BUCK WONG. *Roots: An Asian American Reader.*

Asian American Studies Center, University of California at Los Angeles, 1971. A reader divided into three sections: history, community, and identity. It contains a variety of materials written from a multitude of perspectives and provides a good introduction to Asian Americans.

THOMAS, DOROTHY, and RICHARD MISHIMOTO. *The Spoilage.* Berkeley: University of California Press, 1946. An account—based on the records of social scientists and of relocation camp inmates—of the erosion of Japanese American civil and human rights as U.S. citizens during the World War II period. Among the issues discussed are the repressive measures of government agencies, including martial law, incarceration, and internment, and Japanese American protests against these repressions.

Article

SCOTT, DOROTHEA. "Chinese Stories: A Plea for Authenticity." *School Library Journal,* April 1974, pp. 21-25. A critical analysis of the strengths and weaknesses in books about China or Chinese Americans.

Periodicals

Amerasia Journal (irregular), Asian American Studies Center, 3232 Campbell Hall, UCLA, Los Angeles, Cal. 90024.

Asian American Review (irregular), Asian American Studies, 3407 Dwinelle Hall, Berkeley, Cal. 94720.

Chinese Affirmative Action Newsletter (monthly), in English and Chinese, 699 Clay St., San Francisco, Cal. 94111.

Other Resources

Additional information may be obtained from these organizations:

Visual Communications, Asian American Studies Central, Inc. 1601 Griffith Park Blvd., Los Angeles, Cal. 90026.

UCLA Asian American Studies Center, 3232 Campbell Hall, Los Angeles, Cal. 90026.

Japanese American Curriculum Project, P.O. Box 367, San Mateo, Cal. 94401.

Chinese Media Committee of the Chinese for Affirmative Action, 699 Clay St., San Francisco, Cal. 94111.

Internationalism in Children's Literature

*Anne Pellowski**

Internationalism in children's literature has at least three important aspects. One has to do with the development of printed and visual materials for children in areas of the world which have until recently had no such materials and the development as well of opportunities for children to experience these materials, as in libraries and cultural centers. A second involves the exchange of children's books from one country to another, either in original form or in translation. A third, and the one which is perhaps most important for the teacher or librarian working with children, is concerned with the way different cultures are depicted and represented in the children's books of any given country.

The international organizations which have been most active and influential in the field of children's books and libraries are the International Bureau of Education (Geneva), the United Nations Educational, Scientific and Cultural Organization (UNESCO, Paris), the United Nations Children's Fund (UNICEF, New York), the International Board on Books for Young People (IBBY, Zurich), and the International Federation of Library Associations (IFLA, The Hague). The World Confederation of Organizations of the Teaching Profession (WCOTP) is currently attempting to organize support for children's materials in school libraries at the international level. They have set up a special sub-organization, the International Association of School Librarianship, for the purpose of expanding support for school library services, especially in developing countries. In addition to this, there are numerous national organizations, such as Franklin Book Programs (New York) of the United States and the International Youth Library (Munich) of the Federal Republic of Germany, which have done very much to promote internationalism and children's books.

A few national groups and organizations are

*Anne Pellowski is Director-Librarian, Information Center on Children's Cultures, UNICEF.

carrying out projects that have promoted internationalism and children's books. For example, since 1968 the Children's Services Division of the American Library Association has given the Batchelder Award annually for a children's book considered to be the most outstanding of those books originally published in a foreign country and subsequently translated and published in the United States. The Loughborough Seminar on Children's Literature, originally begun by the Loughborough University Department of Library Studies (England) in 1968, has moved each summer to a new country, and each year gives some 100 children's librarians the opportunity to meet and discuss aspects of children's literature, national and international.

There is still an enormous amount of research to be undertaken before we can come to more firm conclusions about the different methods of exposing children to literature; the relative merits of oral, visual, and print exposure; and the differences in response that depend on cultural and social values of the child reader/listener/viewer, rather than on the intrinsic qualities of the literature itself. Such research is hampered by the fact that ninety percent of current print and audiovisual literature for children is produced in a handful of countries, and represents less than one-tenth of the world's population of children.

The exchange of children's books can thus hardly be called international, except in a limited sense. The number of translations grows each year, but this is limited to translations to and from the Western European languages, with only a few exceptions. African and Asian countries use a sizable number of materials from England, the United States, and France, because in many of these countries children are growing up with English or French as their school language. A tiny bit of comparison can be found in the current use of East African Swahili and Spanish materials now being used in a few American schools.

By far the most common aspect of internationalism, then, is the introduction to other cultures, through children's literature. Now culture is not something that can be separated easily into categories like "adult" and "children's." Anyone preparing to expose children in a meaningful way to another culture must first have some understanding of it or be as open and receptive as the young child is.

The evaluation and selection of the materials that are to introduce children to another culture is most difficult. Our standard selection lists do not include enough items related to each area, and those which are included tend to stress the past more than the present. Specialized lists are more helpful, but very few have been compiled with stated criteria of selection. One must be prepared to use a wide variety of sources in tracking down sufficient materials.

In establishing the validity of *fictional and folkloric materials,* the following represent some of the questions we must ask:

1. Was the material created by a participant of the culture or by an observer of it?
2. Has it been edited to remove all elements which are morally or socially not accepted in our culture or have some of these intrinsic values of the society concerned been allowed to remain intact, e.g., polygamy, matter-of-fact acceptance of body functions, early marriage or love relationships?
3. If it is historical, is this clearly indicated?

In regard to *illustrations, photographs, or films,* the following questions can be asked:

1. Is there obvious stereotyping, such as *always* depicting Chinese children with pigtails, African children without clothes, Mexican children as barefoot boys with burros, etc.?
2. Are the facial characteristics of any race *always* the same, without regard for the fact that there are infinite varieties within all races?
3. Is the comparative wealth or poverty of a nation or people illustrated with honesty or is it exaggerated?
4. Is there overemphasis of rural or village life with no proportionate attention to urban life?
5. Are the unusually different customs depicted more for their shock value than as illuminations of parts of the total structure of the culture?

For *factual materials* we can ask:

1. What is the copyright date? Does this limit the usability of the work?
2. If the copyright date is recent, do geo-

graphical and political facts truly reflect the latest changes?

3. Whose point of view is represented – the insider or the outsider or both?

4. What kind of sources are given?

To answer some of these questions demands a firsthand knowledge, which many of us do not have and which is not acquired merely through the reading of a few books and the viewing of fewer films. One can partly test validity without actually knowing all the answers. A condescending tone or an oversimplified explanation of a complex question can warn of bias, even though one might not be able to pinpoint errors.

The popular adage "Every little bit helps" simply cannot apply when one is concerned about introducing children to other cultures. If the material is derogatory instead of objective, or vivid but totally inaccurate, chances are it will hinder rather than help. It would be better not to attempt an introduction to another people if it cannot be done with sensitivity and care.

Finally, there is the question of technique or method to employ in actually bringing these good materials to the attention of children.

In preschool years and the early grades, children still have few definitely formed concepts of nationality. They are, however, conscious of racial, religious, social, and cultural differences, especially if these differences are visible. Most research indicates that in these early years children need to see and experience the difference as well as the sameness of things, since this helps to build up the self-image.

At this level it is best to use good pictures or photographs showing children from many parts of the world; picture stories can be read aloud. Children at this age are very conscious of names of persons, places, and things, so time should be spent on the origin of names and describing customs in terms young children can recognize.

Picture books in other languages can be shown, especially if one is working with children who know another language. In this way, children often learn to take pride in background rather than secretly feeling ashamed of it because it is so different from that of the peer group.

Older children need materials of much more substance, materials which recognize the concepts of nationality and country, region, and continent, as well as social and cultural values.

Suggested Research Needs

1. Content analysis studies should be made of popular and recommended books from foreign countries that are translated into English and of the books published in the United States that are selected to be translated into other languages.

2. Cross-national comparisons should be attempted by persons who have had the opportunity to observe children in two or more countries, as they react to the same particular children's books, in their own language, or in the original.

3. Longitudinal experiments should be undertaken with similar groups of children, between the ages of four and ten, testing whether those intensively exposed to a wide range of literature from other cultures feel and respond differently from those children with only the usual small amount of such exposure encountered in average public schools and libraries.

4. Comparative studies should be undertaken to determine whether fictional stories, or nonfictional books, set in other countries or cultures, appear to be more successful in getting children to understand basic social studies concepts (such as family patterns, food, shelter, etc.) in the elementary grades.

5. The United States is often credited with having developed the best public library service to children in the world. Yet adult reading polls show that adults in the United States read less than adults in any of the western European countries. What factors related to children's books and reading can account for this disparity?

6. Surveys and bibliographies of foreign language children's books published in the U.S.A. (e.g., Spanish, Polish, Yiddish, etc.) should be undertaken from the historical as well as present-day point of view.

7. Different professional groups in different countries have been responsible for the promotion and study of children's books as literature. Comparative research needs to be undertaken to discover how children's literature is affected when it is promoted and studied chiefly by teachers (see, for example, the Louise Lemieux study for French Canada), or by children's librarians (the U.S. until the last decade), or by publishers and authors (as in Japan until recently).

Bibliography

Bibliographies

Asia Society. *Asia: A Guide to Books for Children.* New York: Asia Society, 112 East 64th Street, New York, N.Y. 10021. Describes 338 children's books on Asia in general and in specific Asian countries.

SCHERF, WALTER, ed. *Best of the Best: Picture, Children's and Youth Books from 57 Countries or Languages.* Bowker, 1971. Lists both classics and modern works up to 1970. Arranged within each country by age group, but books are not annotated.

SCHMIDT, NANCY J. *Children's Books on Africa and Their Authors; An Annotated Bibliography.* New York: Africana Publishing Co., 1975. Although there are many omissions in this bibliography and the annotations regarding "African" qualities of the books are sometimes unclear, this is nevertheless a helpful tool for use in locating English language children's books (regardless of country of origin) that have Africa as their setting or subject.

U.S. Committee for UNICEF. *Africa: An Annotated List of Printed Materials Suitable for Children.* New York: UNICEF, 331 East 38th Street, New York, New York 10016. A selective guide to more than 300 English language items published in nine countries. Arranged by country and general regions of the continent.

______. *Latin America: An Annotated List of Printed Materials Suitable for Children.* New York: UNICEF, 331 East 38th Street, New York, New York 10016. Similar to the African list, this bibliography contains over 500 items, including some in Spanish.

______. *The Near East: An Annotated List of Materials for Children.* New York: UNICEF, 331 East 38th Street, New York, N.Y. 10016. This list contains over 500 items covering the Near East, North Africa, Afghanistan, Iran, Greece, and Turkey. Includes a section on the Bible.

All three of the above are updated by individual country and subject lists published in mimeographed form by the Information Center on Children's Cultures, U.S. Committee for UNICEF.

Books

ANDREAE, GESIENA. *The Dawn of Juvenile Literature in England.* Amsterdam: H. J. Paris, 1925. (Available as a reprint from Singing Tree Press, 1968.) The evolution of the child's book through the centuries and the effect this development had on the whole concept of childhood in the eighteenth century. An excellent book with which to begin a detailed study of English children's literature.

BRAVO VILLASANTE, CARMEN. *Historia y Antologia de la Literatura Infantil Iberoaméricano. (History and Anthology of Hispanic-American Children's Literature.)* 2 vols. Madrid: Doncel, 1966. This is an invaluable aid to the study of Latin-American children's literature.

BROOKS, PETER. *The Child's Part.* Beacon, 1969. Historical aspects of children's literature (mainly English and French) but from quite different points of view than those found in the usual histories of children's books.

FRASER, JAMES HOWARD. *Foreign Language Children's Literature in the U.S.: An Inquiry into the Collecting Patterns of Research Institutions Together with a Proposal for a National Acquisitions Plan for Foreign Language Juvenilia.* Ph.D. dissertation, Columbia University, 1972. Ann Arbor, Michigan: University Microfilms (#75-9330), 1975.

HAVILAND, VIRGINIA, ed. "The International Scene." In *Children and Literature: Views and Reviews,* pp. 326-390. Scott, Foresman, 1972. Articles by eight international specialists are included in this chapter.

HAWKES, LOUISE R. *Before and After Pinocchio; A Study of Italian Children's Books.* Paris: The Puppet Press, 1933. (Available as a reprint from Singing Tree Press, 1968.) A history and criticism of Italian children's literature from classical Roman civilization to 1930. Books are treated as genuine literature, not a sub-genre.

HÜRLIMANN, BETTINA. *Die Welt im Bilderbuch.* Zurich: Atlantis Verlag, 1966. (Published as *Picture-Book World* by World Publishing, 1969.) After discussing picture books from twenty-four countries, the text is divided into topics for a comparison of how various illustrators treat such subjects as animals, ships, rain, and snow.

______. *Europaische Kinderbucher in Drei Jahrhunderten.* 2d ed. Zurich: Atlantis Verlag, 1963. (Published as *Three Centuries of Children's Books in Europe* by World Publishing, 1968.) A lively, personal history of European highlights of children's literature. A good background book.

JAN, ISABELLE. *Sur la Littérature Enfantine.* Paris: Les Éditions Ouvrières, 1969. (Published as *On Children's Literature* by Schocken Books, 1974.) An intriguing and quite different approach to children's literature as a part of world literature.

LEMIEUX, LOUISE. *Pleins Feux sur la Littérature de Jeunesse au Canada Français.* Montreal: Lemeac, 1972. A survey that covers the evolution of French-language children's literature in Canada. Especially interesting in the sections that cover the publishers' points of view. Short biographical data on some of the leading authors and illustrators.

LEPMAN, JELLA. *Die Kinderbuchbrücke.* Frankfurt-Main: S. Fischer Verlag, 1964. (Published as *A Bridge of Children's Books* by the ALA, 1969.) A moving, personal account of the author's attempts to build a "bridge of understanding through children's books" in the International Youth Library at Munich and later through the founding of the International Board on Books for Young People.

ØRVIG, MARY. *Children's Books in Sweden, 1945-1970: A Survey.* Stockholm: Swedish Institute for Children's Books, 1973. A succint summary in English of this important period in the development of Swedish children's literature, including sections on recent trends and studies.

PELLOWSKI, ANNE. *The World of Children's Literature.* Bowker, 1968. A monumental work, listing over 4400 items concerned with children's books throughout the world.

WEAVER, WARREN. *Alice in Many Tongues.* Univ. of Wisconsin Pr., 1964. A very lucid discussion of the problem of translation, and the checklist of editions and translations (in forty-seven languages) point out that, in fact, *Alice* is many books by many authors.

WOLGAST, HEINRICH. *Das Elend Unserer Jugendliteratur. (The Misery of Our Children's Literature.)* 7th ed. Worms: Ernst Wunderlich, 1950. This is the most important and influential book on the theory of children's literature written in the German language.

ZWEIGBERGK, EVA VON. *Barnboken i Sverige 1750-1950. (Children's Books in Sweden 1750-1950.)* Stockholm: Rabén & Sjögren, 1965. A clearly written, well-organized, and illustrated history of children's literature in Sweden.

Articles

For an abundance of articles, see Pellowski (listed above) and the subject heading "Children's Literature" with various countries as subheadings in the index called *Library Literature.*

Periodicals

Bookbird. International Institute for Children's Juvenile and Popular Literature. Fuhrmannsgasse 18a, Vienna, Austria. Quarterly (Irregular). 1957– Covers the international children's book scene; reviews recent materials about children's literature; lists recommended books for translation; and, on occasion, publishes in-depth articles.

Information Bulletin on Reading Materials. UNESCO Regional Centre for Reading Materials in South Asia, 26/A, P.E.C.H.H.S., Karachi 29, Pakistan. Quarterly, 1959– Although this publication is concerned with all of the problems of general book writing, publishing, and distribution, a major emphasis is on materials for children and new literates. An invaluable aid to the person interested in a study of the newly developing children's literature in South Asian countries.

Popular Literature

*Larry N. Landrum and Michael T. Marsden**

Throughout the history of children's literature there has always existed another reading matter, sometimes more widely enjoyed and almost always more widely available than even the best-selling juvenile classics. While it is seldom discussed as literature, it pervades the world of children in the form of comics, Big Little Books, pop-up books, fan and specialized one-issue celebrity magazines, as well as career novels and the formulaic series novels. The scope of reading matter parallels that of adults on many levels, and, of course, the low level of literacy required for many adult magazines opens them to the interest of juvenile readers.

While some of this literature has great appeal to a specialized audience, much of it is truly popular in the sense of being broadly appealing. More than any other form, it is selected by the children themselves, chosen from racks in drugstores, supermarkets, and newsstands, and traded with other children. Moreover parents and teachers usually do not share the reading experience as they may with more socially acceptable literature. This is a world of literature which grew up in the semi-private imagination of children for well over a century. It is a literature full of paradoxes: it is a reasonably accurate index of the prejudices and parochialism of society while it often affects a stilted style and unimpeachable standards of morals and etiquette; it is often at the same time realistic and fantastic; containing large amounts of mystery, gothic, and conspiratorial elements, the fiction rarely leaves unresolved problems. It creates a world steeped in misinformation, half-truths, and improbable standards of behavior, yet it usually remains faithful to the prevailing cultural ideology. In the last third of the nineteenth century, boys' series novels, for example, generally reflected the success ethic, the concern at the turn of the century for regulating competition, and the technical optimism preceding the First World War. The series novels separated into various formulas such as westerns, detective stories, mysteries, science fiction, and, more recently, career adventures. A typical series might span a number of action-adventure or ratiocinative formulas. In comics, we have seen Superman, whose only weakness was Kryptonite, replaced by Spiderman, the Fantastic Four, and others of the Marvel Group, who are plagued by critical identity problems. These major forms, the series nov-

*Larry N. Landrum is an Assistant Professor of English at Michigan State University and Michael T. Marsden is an Assistant Professor of Popular Culture and Acting Chairman of the Department of Popular Culture at Bowling Green State University.

els and the comic books, form the two central streams of popular children's literature.

Many of the factors that combined to produce what is often loosely called a mass society were significant in the production of popular children's literature. The invention of stereotype plates and then high capacity presses made it possible by the middle of the nineteenth century to produce large quantities of relatively inexpensive books. Expansion of the railroad system and more and better roads, together with rapid urbanization and the growth of a broad middle class made possible wide distribution and consumption. A more widespread literacy among the young, coupled with a thirst for adventure, resulted in an audience ripe for literary hacks as well as for craftsmen.

By the middle of the nineteenth century there were a number of minor forms of popular literature available to children. The "story papers" and "yellow-covered romances" in America and the "penny dreadfuls" in England supplemented the serialized novels in newspapers and popular adult magazines. Through the 1840s and 1850s Maturin Ballou published *The Weekly Novelette* series, each of which contained one-fifth of a novel and sold for four cents a copy. The House of Beadle and Adams began in 1860 to publish the famous dime novels, printing them in lots of sixty or seventy thousand until the 1890s, when they began to succumb to the depression and to competition from pulp magazines. The total sales of Beadle and Adams and their four major competitors ran into the tens of millions. Though the readership for dime novels was initially adults, these novels became more and more a juvenile form.

Popular children's literature has endured numerous critics. Though Dr. Bowdler did not begin expurgating texts until 1818, the practice began about forty years earlier and was common by the 1850s. Critics of popular reading matter have included persons and organizations such as Anthony Comstock, the Watch and Ward Society of Boston, and, more recently, the National Office of Decent Literature (NODL).

Competing with the dime novels on a purely juvenile level and at a much lower level of violence and sensationalism were the Oliver Optic novels of William Taylor Adams. Adams combined the didacticism of the primers and Sunday School readers with the adventure of the dime novels and produced what were to be the general guidelines of the boys' and girls' series novels up to the present. Though the stories usually involved incredible plots, the adventure was subservient to the concern with social and moral platitudes. It was Adams who discovered Horatio Alger, Jr. It might be significant that Adams was a school teacher and Alger a failed clergyman, but it was Alger who added the prevailing economic and social ideology to the popular juvenile novel. This ideology became the trademark of Alger: be honest, thrifty, and conscientious, and be alert to the opportunity for great wealth that will some day come your way. Alger fostered the ideals of the Gilded Age perhaps better than any other author of children's books, but by the end of the nineteenth century many of these ideals were highly suspect. The choice among free enterprise, socialism, and corporate capitalism passed by the writers as it did most other adults and the popular juveniles congealed into characteristic patterns. Significant adults fell into the background; a freedom of movement associated with the West became integrated with urban and suburban settings; economic success began to be replaced by an understood status; and career preparation became more significant than will-o-the-wisp luck.

Gilbert Patten and Edward Stratemeyer, who, respectively, created the Merriwells and Rover Boys, dominated the early twentieth century. Stratemeyer quickly formed a syndicate which capitalized on outline plots, characterization, humor, and adventure. The plots were generally presented to salaried or commissioned writers who then filled in background, characterization, and added fifty jokes. Many of the pseudonyms became household names through the years: Laura Lee Hope, Carolyn Keene, Clarence Young, Arthur Winfield, and Frank V. Webster are still recognized by many of the young and the old alike. The Motor Boys, Rover Boys, and Tom Swift series alone had accumulated sales of over sixteen and a half million copies by 1920.

This period also saw the growth of the pulps, fiction magazines printed on inexpensive newsprint, which contributed to both adult and juvenile markets and competed with such magazines as *St. Nicholas*. The pulps, dime novels, and adventure series provided a stimulus to the traditional children's literature by providing an alternative to the generally dull and didactic fare that was often written *at* children rather than *for* them. Even today the challenge of series novels exists in a muted, but ever present form. Happy Hollisters and the Nancy Drew mysteries still sell very well through children's book clubs and over the counter.

The other major form of children's popular literature, the comics, is available in several types in every corner of society. There is perhaps no more pervasive popular art form in America than comics. In his impressive study of the popular arts, *The Unembarrassed Muse*, Russel Nye writes:

No popular art, whatever medium, is so pervasive and persistent in American society as the comics. Studies have continuously shown that they reach about half the total population more or less regularly. The comic strip since its beginnings has produced from eight to twelve million drawings, by far the largest body of materials of any popular art.

The appearance of the "Yellow Kid" on February 16, 1896, in Joseph Pulitzer's *New York World* marked the beginning of the comic strip, one of the staples of an American's reading diet. Most Americans, after quickly scanning the headlines, head straight for the comics page in the daily newspaper. From the Katzenjammer Kids, through Little Nemo, Krazy Kat, Gasoline Alley, Little Orphan Annie, Winnie Winkle, Tillie the Toiler, Barney Google, Blondie, Terry and the Pirates, up to Doonesbury, we have a dramatic spectrum of the changing reading tastes of the American public, young and old.

In 1950 a funny looking boy and his friends made their first appearance in America's newspapers, and they soon helped their creator to enjoy an unimagined popularity that resulted in the sale of thirty-six million copies of eighteen different Peanuts books between 1963 and 1969. The move from comic strip to book (and to animated cartoons) was easily made for popular characters like Donald Duck and sincere Charlie Brown.

A distinction needs to be made between the comic strip, as found commonly in newspapers, and the comic book, which was the logical extension of the failing pulp magazine industry. Comic books, appearing in 1938 with the first issue of *Action* comics, were inspired by the success of the pulps and were in part the outgrowth of comic strips which had earlier been collected into paper-covered books. But the comic book was not confined to the traditional four-frame panel nor so closely tied to the scrutiny of editors, and thus allowed the artists considerably more freedom.

Heroes like Superman, Batman, G.I. Joe, and the Lone Ranger were seen in brightly colored narratives. Comic books extended the more mature narratives of the pulps into visual adventure fantasies which, by the late 1940s, developed the capacity to explore numerous genres. Comics put out by E. C. Publications, Inc., combined superior art work with pithy stories of war, horror, science fiction, and social realism to pace the industry with comic books which demanded a greater degree of artistic appreciation and thought. Dr. Wertham's famous attack on these comics, *Seduction of the Innocent*, helped result in the Comics Code in 1954. E.C. retaliated with *Mad*, one of the most iconoclastic comics ever produced.

The 1960s saw the rise of the more "mature" comics, led by the Marvel Group. A 1971 survey of college America's favorite reading found Marvel's Spiderman and Fantastic Four heading the list. The success of these more sophisticated publications, the restrictions of the code, and the expression of revolutionary lifestyles among youth gave rise to the "underground comic" of the sixties and seventies. Underground comics have been oriented to a generation of comic readers maturing in what is often seen as a vast, impersonal social system. Though the impact of these publications is difficult to measure, they are now distributed through conventional means, seem to enjoy immense popularity, are read by all age groups, and have significant influence on younger people.

What the future will hold for the comic book industry remains to be seen. But the "funnies" are no longer innocuous pastimes. They are a serious part of our culture, and if presented properly, could lead younger students to a more careful and considered awareness of the world around them.

For the concerned educators, juvenile series novels, comic books, and many other forms of popular children's literature present a serious challenge. More children will read *Mad Magazine* in a year than will read the Newbery Medal books in a generation. To ignore these popular forms of literature is to run the risk of leaving unopened a wide door into the minds of the adolescent of contemporary society. To begin to learn how to use these materials is to work from what the students are most familiar with, and to build from there is to proceed in useful directions.

Suggested Research Needs

1. What are the ideals of femininity and masculinity as presented in juvenile series books? Compare and contrast two heroines or two heroes from different series.

2. What kinds of cultural stereotypes run through either a particular girls' series or a particular boys' series? For example, what are the attitudes toward immigrant national groups, racial minorities, and occupational stereotypes?

3. The argument has been raised many times that comics lead to deviant behavior in adolescents and children. Is there any solid research evidence to support this view?

4. Taking a particular comic strip that is widely syndicated, analyze it for its cultural stereotypes.

5. Does comic book reading help or hinder the reading ability of children and adolescents?

6. How many adults read comic books? Why do they read comic books and how much else do they read?

7. What impact have the "underground" comics had on young people? Have they, in many ways, replaced older forms of risque literature?

8. What is it about the medium of the comic strip, such as Doonesbury, that allows it a freedom of expression not possible in more conventional forms of popular literature?

9. How much current social and political knowledge must a reader have to fully enjoy *Mad Magazine, The National Lampoon*, or any of the other comics that are basically satiric?

10. What new forms of popular children's literature seem to be appearing on the literary horizons?

Bibliography

Bibliographies

COHEN, HAL L. *Official Guide to Comic Books and Big Little Books . . . : The Price to Buy and Sell.* Florence, Alabama: House of Collectibles, 1974.

KEMPKES, WOLFGANG. *International Bibliography of Comics Literature.* 2d rev. ed. Bowker, 1974.

WHITE, DAVID MANNING. *The Comic Strip in America: A Bibliography.* Boston Univ. School of Public Relations and Communication, 1961. A good checklist of criticism through about 1959. The 450 items include a short list of theses and dissertations on the subject.

Books

BECKER, STEPHEN. *Comic Art in America: A Social History of the Funnies, the Political Cartoons, Magazine Humor, Sporting Cartoons, and Animated Cartoons.* Simon, 1959.

BERGER, ARTHUR A. *The Comic Stripped American: What Dick Tracy, Blondie, Daddy Warbucks, and Charlie Brown Tell Us About Ourselves.* Walker, 1973.

———. *Li'l Abner: A Study in American Satire.* Twayne Publishers, 1970. A perceptive study of Al Capp and his comic art.

CAWELTI, JOHN. *Adventure, Mystery, and Romance.* Univ. of Chicago Pr., 1976. An analysis of formulaic literature.

COUPERIE, PIERRE, MAURICE HORN, et al. *A History of the Comic Strip.* Crown, 1968. Probably the best analytical study of the comics available in print. Written with wit and sympathy as well as insight, this history illustrates the key developments in the genre.

CRAVEN, THOMAS, ed., assisted by Florence and Sydney Weiss. *Cartoon Cavalcade.* Simon, 1943. An early, though valuable, study of the comics.

DILLE, ROBERT C., ed. *The Collected Works of Buck Rogers in the 25th Century.* Chelsea, 1969. Color and black-and-white reproductions of much of the famous strip which began in 1928. Ray Bradbury contributes a brief introduction to this invaluable collection.

FEIFFER, JULES. *The Great Comic Book Heroes.* Dial, 1965. A nostalgic but important celebration of the origins of the superheroes. Feiffer is able to contribute greatly to the understanding of youthful fascination with comics.

GALEWITZ, HERB. *Great Comics Syndicated by the Daily News and Chicago Tribune.* Crown, 1972. Syndicated strips reproduced in black and white with an eight-page introduction.

GOODSTONE, TONY. *The Pulps: Fifty Years of American Pop Culture.* Chelsea, 1970. Selections and illustrations, together with brief introductory comments to thematically arranged sections.

GRAY, HAROLD. *Arf! The Life and Hard Times of Little Orphan Annie, 1935-1945.* Arlington House, 1970. Introduction by Al Capp. Black-and-white reproductions of ten years of the famous weekly strip which began in 1924 and has continued until today.

GRUBER, FRANK. *Horatio Alger, Jr.: A Biography and Bibliography.* Printed by Grover Jones Pr., 1961. Contains a useful bibliography and a brief biographical sketch which corrects some of the errors of earlier biographies.

______. *The Pulp Jungle.* Sherbourne Pr., 1967. The autobiography of one of the more prolific of the pulp writers. The book gives something of the flavor of the pulp world of the thirties.

HART, J. D. *The Popular Book: A History of America's Literary Taste.* Oxford, 1950. Useful background book on the popular novel, though little on juvenile fiction as such.

HIRSCH, MICHAEL. *The Great Canadian Comic Books.* Toronto: Peter Martin Associates, 1971.

HUDSON, HARRY K. *A Bibliography of Hard-Cover Boys' Books.* Clearwater, Florida: Privately Printed, c1965. Lists the series of forty-five publishers from the period 1900-1950. A valuable source of information.

KUNZLE, DAVID. *The Early Comic Strip: Narrative Strips and Picture Stories in the European Broadsheet from c1450 to 1825.* Berkeley: University of California Press, 1973.

LEE, STAN. *Origins of Marvel Comics.* Simon, 1974.

LUPOFF, DICK, and DON THOMPSON, eds. *All in Color for a Dime.* Arlington House, 1970. Useful for its illustrations, but lacks new information on the artists in the industry.

MOTT, FRANK LUTHER. *Golden Multitudes: The Story of Best Sellers in the United States.* Macmillan, 1947. Covers the same area as Hart, but with a slightly different perspective.

MURRELL, WILLIAM. *A History of American Graphic Humor, 1865-1938.* Whitney Museum of American Art, 1938. A study of humorous art, especially political and satirical cartoons. Well illustrated in black and white.

NYE, RUSSEL B. *The Unembarrassed Muse: The Popular Arts in America.* Dial, 1970. Essential reading for any student or teacher who wishes to understand America's popular arts. A historical approach, includes sections on most popular art forms, placing them in their social and cultural contexts.

O'CONNOR, GERARD. "The Hardy Boys Revisited: A Study in Prejudice." In *Challenges in American Culture,* Browne, Landrum, and Bottorff, eds. The Popular Pr., 1970. Discusses the prejudicial stereotypes in the first edition and the generally futile attempts at later revision.

O'SULLIVAN, JUDITH. *The Art of the Comic Strip.* University of Maryland Department of Art, 1971.

PERRY, GEORGE, and ALAN ALDRIDGE. *The Penguin Book of Comics.* Penguin Books, 1967. A standard social history of the comics in England and America. Contains information not found elsewhere, but lacks the technical demonstration of the Couperie history.

PRAGER, ARTHUR. *Rascal at Large; or The Clue in the Old Nostalgia.* Doubleday, 1971. A lively discussion of popular series books.

REITBERGER, REINHOLD, and WOLFGANG J. FUCHS. *Comics: Anatomy of a Mass Medium.* Little, 1972.

ROBINSON, JERRY. *The Comics: An Illustrated History of Seventy-Five Years of Comic Strip Art.* Putnam, 1974.

ROSENBERG, BERNARD, and DAVID MANNING WHITE, eds. *Mass Culture: The Popular Arts in America.* Glencoe, 1957. Now somewhat dated, this anthology contains useful insights by a variety of writers on the comics and popular literature. The introduction contains a debate between the editors over the value of the popular arts.

SHERIDAN, MARTIN. *Comics and Their Creators; Life Stories of American Cartoonists.* Hale, Cushman, and Flint, 1942. Presents eighty comic strips, arranged by categories. Includes a brief biographical sketch of the artist, as well as an analysis of each strip. Illustrated with examples.

SMITH, HENRY NASH. *Virgin Land.* Harvard Univ. Pr., 1950. Contains a chapter on the contribution of the dime novel to popular myth of the West.

STEDMAN, RAYMOND WILLIAM. *The Serials: Suspense and Drama by Installment.* Univ. of Oklahoma Pr., 1971. A thorough study of the serials as found in comics, movies, radio, and television. Important for its discussion of the comic strips' influence on the evolution of subsequent serial forms.

STEELE, ELIZABETH. "Mrs. Johnston's *Little Colonel,*" in Browne, Landrum, and Bottorff, eds. *Challenges in American Culture.* The Popular Pr., 1970. A perceptive essay about the cultural values embodied in a very popular book.

THOMPSON, DON, and DICK LUPOFF, eds. *The Comic-Book Book.* Arlington House, 1973.

WAUGH, COULTON. *The Comics.* Macmillan, 1947. An illustrated history of cartoons from the 1890s to the 1940s, including both comic strips and comic books.

WHITE, DAVID MANNING, and ROBERT H. ABEL, eds. *The Funnies: An American Idiom.* Macmillan, 1963. A useful collection of essays by those who write the comics as well as those who read them. Essays by Al Capp, Allen Saunders, and Walt Kelley are included.

Articles

BECKMAN, MARGARET. "Why Not the Bobbsey Twins?" *Library Journal* 89 (November 15, 1964): 4612-4613+. Presents the reasons frequently given for excluding series fiction, such as Nancy Drew and the Hardy Boys, from school and public library collections for children.

BERGER, ARTHUR A. "Comics and Culture." *Journal of Popular Culture* 5 (Summer 1971): 164-178. An informal and informative analysis of the important role the comics play in our culture.

______. "Peanuts: An American Pastoral." *Journal of Popular Culture* 3 (Summer 1969): 1-8. An informal biographical sketch of Charles Schulz and his characters, with useful insights into their popularity and effectiveness.

BLACKBEARD, BILL. "From a Corner Table at Rough House's." *Riverside Quarterly* 6 (August 1973): 46-59. Fine impressionistic study of the Mickey Mouse adventure strips.

BRAUN, SAUL. "Shazam! Here Comes Captain Relevant." *The New York Times Magazine,* May 2, 1971, 32+. Discusses the growing social and environmental concern in the comic strips and especially the comic books, and the state of the industry.

CAWELTI, JOHN G. "The Concept of Formula in the Study of Popular Literature." *Journal of Popular Culture* 3 (Winter 1969): 381-390. A major contribution to the analysis of popular literature which should be valuable to the study of children's literature.

DORFMAN, ARIEL, and ARMAND MATTELART. "How to Read Donald Duck." *Liberation* 19 (March/April 1975): 33-40.

FAUST, WOLFGANG MAX (with technical assistance from R. Baird Shuman). "Comics and How to Read Them." *Journal of Popular Culture* 5 (Summer 1971): 195-202. Discusses the problems of seriously analyzing comics and suggests methods.

"For It Was Indeed He." *Fortune Magazine* 9 (April 1934): 86+. Remains one of the primary sources for information about the Stratemeyer syndicate and its competitors.

HEMENWAY, ALICE. "Cartoon Stereotypes: Do You Believe What You See?" *New Yorker* 32 (April 1974): 9-15.

LATIMER, D. A. "If Harvey Kurtzman Had Written 'Snow White,' the Dwarfs Would Have Gotten Her." *The Paperback Magazine,* No. 3: 135-151. Brief biographical sketch of one of the most influential cartoonists and editors in the genre. Shows Kurtzman's struggle for expression of his ideas in a milieu of vague standards.

MIRA, EDUARD J. "Notes on a Comparative Analysis of American and Spanish Comic Books." *Journal of Popular Culture* 5 (Summer 1971): 203-220. An interesting comparison of American comic book heroes in Spain.

MULHAUSER, FREDERICK V. "A Juvenile View of the Empire: G. M. Fenn." *Journal of Popular Culture,* 2 (Winter 1969): 410-424. A study of the imperialist ideology of a popular British writer of juveniles during the latter third of the nineteenth century.

PEKAR, HARVEY. "Rapping About Cartoonists, Particularly Robert Crumb." *Journal of Popular Culture* 3 (Spring 1970): 677-688. A valuable article for its information about the most influential of underground comic artists.

PRAGER, ARTHUR. "The Secret of Nancy Drew." *Saturday Review* 52 (January 25, 1969): 18-19 +. How Nancy Drew retains popularity after forty years.

RACKIN, DONALD. "Corrective Laughter: Carroll's *Alice* and Popular Children's Literature." *Journal of Popular Culture* 1 (Winter 1967): 243-255. Concerns the development of a popular nondidactic, but socially satirical, children's literature which culminated in Carroll's *Alice.*

SADLER, A. W. "The Love Comics and American Popular Culture." *American Quarterly* 16 (Fall 1964): 486-490. Notes persistence of "Puritan" or Algerine moralism in girls' "romance" magazines, specifically in their "integration of virtue with economic reward."

SAGARIN, EDWARD. "The Deviant in the Comic Strip: The Case of Barney Google." *Journal of Popular Culture* 5 (Summer 1971): 179-194. Presents the case of the deviant side of one of America's best-loved cartoon characters.

SONENSCHEIN, DAVID. "Love and Sex in Romance Magazines." *Journal of Popular Culture* 4 (Fall 1970): 398-409. Points up the themes of pulp romances and suggests the extent of their juvenile readership.

YOUNG, WILLIAM H., JR. "The Serious Funnies: Adventure Comics During the Depression, 1929-1938." *Journal of Popular Culture* 3 (Winter 1969): 404-427. An important study of the way in which the comic strips avoided the important social and economic issues during the depression while supporting threatened family structures.

Children's Access to Materials

*Theodore C. Hines**

Most of what is published about restrictions on access to materials for children and young people has to do with censorship—that is, the deliberate denial of access to particular materials because of their political, sexual, religious, moral, ethical, or racial content.

This is, of course, a very serious problem area—one in which it would even be possible to argue that despite the Freedom to Read statement, the Library Bill of Rights, and the School Library Bill of Rights, we have witnessed in recent years more of a shift in what is considered censorable in some areas than an overall improvement.

Despite the very great importance of the continuing struggle against censorship, the problem of seeking freedom to read (or view or listen) for children and young people is at least fairly well documented. Awareness of it exists and the professional organizations have taken a reasonably firm, if largely unenforced, stand.

There is, however, another aspect to the problem of obtaining access to materials to which much less attention is paid but which may be as corroding to the developing mind as censorship itself. This is the problem children and young people may face in obtaining materials appropriate to their needs which may happen to be in the adult section of the library the child is using, in children's or adult departments of another library in the same school or public library system, or in another

*Theodore C. Hines is Chairman of the Library Science/Educational Technology Division, School of Education at the University of North Carolina, Greensboro.

system or type of library entirely. Put in the larger context, and stated succinctly, such networking as does exist exists for the grown-ups.

Some of the barriers to access which exist are censorship-related, of course. But others seem to arise either from a failure to perceive properly how children's intellectual development does require access to a very wide range of titles, or from a setting of priorities which places children and young people very low indeed on the totem pole—simply an impatience with or fear of the idea of having to deal with children or adolescents.

Item: The parents of a ten-year-old child with a chronic illness and an estimated I.Q. of 160, in a town with a very weak public library, but willing to drive 30 miles to take him to a state university library, requested permission for him to use the library. Permission denied.

Item: A nine-year-old child had, quite literally, read out the children's room of the local public library. The father was tired of having to go to the library every time the child wanted to go and requested that the child be issued an adult card. Permission denied. The father then asked if he could give the library a letter granting the child permission to use the father's card. Permission denied.

In both of the examples the children were highly articulate and educated, and they had the active support of a parent on the scene. Visualize, if you will, how well the less articulate and less advantaged individual without active parental support would fare.

The barriers to access to materials by children and young people may be considered in three stages: (1) barriers within a given library, (2) barriers within a given school or public library system, and (3) barriers across systems and types of libraries.

In the school library, barriers to access to materials within the local school may be many, varied, and ingenious; for example:

(1) constant use of the library by scheduled classes to the point where it is nearly impossible for individually motivated students to use the library on their own;

(2) restricted hours of access with no provision for before or after school use;

(3) a pass system (like the passes slaves had to carry to show the patrollers) for permission to go to the library;

(4) teacher or librarian inspection of student-chosen materials to be sure the child has chosen "suitable" books, and "reading proficiency" checks to be sure the child can understand the title he or she has picked;

(5) limits on the number of titles which can be checked out;

(6) fines to make up for the fact that the librarian has not arranged for a petty cash fund;

(7) limitations on library access to "offenders" who have kept materials overdue or lost them;

(8) failure to acquire titles until they have aged a year or so and possibly lost a portion of their appeal or usefulness; and

(9) the requirement that a book taken out to read must be a book reported on.

The list could be made very nearly endless.

Problems of access within a single library building are just as common in public libraries, which manage to achieve most of the restrictions mentioned for school media centers plus others. The public library is even more likely to have fines, or issue cards only on parental signature.

In many instances, children are issued distinctive cards which may be used only for materials in the children's room. Also they are often more limited in the number of titles they can borrow at one time than are adults. An unpublished survey made some years ago in the Northeast indicated that restriction of children to materials in the children's room together with a later date set for achieving adult borrowing status was more likely to occur in large city systems than in suburban libraries. Similarly, studies from the not-too-distant past indicated that the central libraries of large city systems were more likely to restrict teenage children to young people's or young adult collections than were suburban libraries or even branches within the same system.

The latter situation occurs more often by policy than by specific rule: teenagers are simply discouraged from using the full range of adult facilities, apparently reflecting distaste for having them underfoot or insecurity about "discipline" as much as fear that they may obtain "unsuitable" materials.

So far as younger children are concerned, many of the libraries which issue the same card to all borrowers regardless of age still restrict the number of titles a juvenile may borrow from the children's section of the library (children's room has become an old-fashioned term) and, as a matter of policy, may still discourage or forbid altogether children from taking books from the adult departments.

When it comes to interlibrary or interbranch loan within a system, children are still very rarely allowed this service. Indeed, often no rule against it exists; it is simply assumed to be unnecessary, undesirable, or both. The logical extension of this is that interlibrary loan on behalf of children, among or across types of libraries, is practically unknown.

It should be unnecessary, of course, to remind librarians that children are people and that like other people they have an astonishingly broad range of needs, interests, and abilities. They also constitute, incidentally, a major proportion of the clientele which actually uses public libraries, though their use level drops off sharply just as they begin to become somewhat older children and need a wider diversity of titles than most children's services provide in their own collections. They make up almost the entire clientele of school media centers, which seldom even pretend to lend titles among even the libraries within the school system, much less call upon the resources of nearby public, special, or college and university libraries.

However, the discrimination is not just against children as borrowers, but against the materials themselves. Adults wishing to do research in children's literature often find that their public or university library will not attempt to interloan needed titles for them. The policy against interloaning of children's materials retards scholarship. At the other end of the scale, adult services librarians working with adults whose reading levels are low can also find themselves unable to obtain the information that might be most appropriate for an adult patron.

It is interesting that in an era of individualization in education, there appears to be little realization of the vast diversity of intellectual provender such individualization requires, and that the growing literature of the library networking concept ignores the needs of both children and adults.

Censorship of children's reading is most likely to involve fiction; denial of access probably involves largely nonfiction. In an era in which we are increasingly concerned with discrimination against women and with problems of sex-role stereotyping, it is perhaps worth noting that nonfiction collections for juveniles (or even juvenile collections as a whole) often appear weakest in areas stereotyped as "masculine" interests: engineering, technology, and science (with the exception of nature study). We may certainly draw inferences about this when we see that boys are far more likely to stop using libraries than girls as they become interested in such topics—but what about the influence on concepts of sex roles for the girls who continue to read from collections comparatively lacking in materials on "masculine" interests?

For some reason it seems often forgotten that for many topics (mathematics, computing, mechanics, electronics, minerology, to name a few) people—adults or children—with no previous background in the field start out even in knowledge. Publishers naturally publish books for such people as general titles, not as juveniles—hence, they tend not to get added to collections for juveniles. A somewhat sad commentary on selection policies.

But this is not the whole story. With the best will in the world and with excellent financial support, it would still not be feasible from an economic or space requirement viewpoint even to attempt to acquire the diversity of materials really required to meet the diversity of interests today's children may have for a single school media center collection or a public library children's collection.

Children's interests may be sparked by the radio, television, records, their own acquisition of a trail bike, family acquisition of a CB radio—any of an astonishing variety of inputs. And, like the rest of us, many will go (or want to go) on binges of reading on one particular topic: origami, electronic music, photography, rock groups, gem polishing, radio-controlled models, macrame, cooking, bonsai—you name it, and the odds are that you can find a child with an interest in it.

Failure to provide for ranging interests by exploiting library resources—in fiction or nonfiction—through networking may actually be bringing about far more effective censorship than the misguided efforts to shield children from sexual or other facts of life, or books which represent ideas or viewpoints we don't like.

Ironically, all of this shakes down more to a lack of professionalism and enterprise on the part of librarians—adult, children's, young people's, school—than it does to the lack of funding on which we can blame so many shortcomings. If, in providing services for adults, we talk about networking even if we do very little of it, in providing services for juveniles we don't even talk about it.

Asked if she ever got books from the public library for her students, one excellent school librarian admitted going to the public library and taking them out on her own card. "But," she said, "I don't *tell* anybody that I'm doing it."

Isn't it about time we told somebody, everybody? The function of a children's or of a school librarian is to use the collection to encourage wider interests, not to limit children to that collection. Materials set aside for young adults should be titles they may be particularly interested in, not a way to ban them from adult departments, and the way to deal with "disciplinary" problems is not to punish those who themselves do not cause problems—namely, the vast majority. Interloan agreements should be worked out, publicized, and *used*. Children needing browsing or searching access to adult collections, including the sacrosanct university libraries, should be able to have it.

When did you last hear a librarian say to a child, "We haven't got it but we'll get it"? One measure of a librarian's effectiveness might well be the number of items secured from other libraries for his or her users.

The right of access to materials is not an adult right. It is a right inherent in being a person, not in being a grown-up, and the librarian has even less justification in considering a child's interests frivolous or unimportant than in making the same kind of judgment about an adult. Damn little, in either case.

In addition to striking down the obvious barriers to access, we must have more analysis of user interests and user needs. We should have more outreach in the sense of demonstrating interest in children, in getting across the idea that the library or media center can and *will* get what you want, that we are with it, not against it.

Isn't it about time for us to review and discard many of the practices and policies in regard to access, since they seem so clearly in contradiction with professed goals, duties, and precepts? Let us be facilitators, not monitors.

Editor's Note

This article has no accompanying bibliography because it is a seminal work. No one has previously stated the essence of Professor Hines's viewpoint in print with this particular emphasis. It is our hope that this article will stimulate further thought on an important subject.

DMB

Appendix A
Book Selection Aids[1]

The AAAS Science Booklist, comp. by Hilary J. Deason, 3rd ed. Selected and Annotated List of Science and Mathematics Books for Secondary School Students, College Undergraduates and Nonspecialists. American Assoc. for the Advancement of Science, 1970.

About 100 Books; A Gateway to Better Intergroup Understanding, comp. by Ann G. Wolfe. American Jewish Committee, 1969. A sixth edition, largely comprising books published in 1967, 1968, and 1969, reflecting the trends and unsolved problems in intergroup relations during that period. Arranged by age.

Adventuring with Books; A Book List for Elementary Schools, ed. by Shelton Root and the Committee on the Elementary School Book List of the National Council of Teachers of English, 2nd ed., Nat. Council of Teachers of English, 1973. Annotated listings within subject categories and interest level groupings. May be used by children since it is carefully annotated for child appeal.

Africa; An Annotated List of Printed Materials Suitable for Children. ALA, Children's Services Division and the African-American Institute. Information Center on Children's Cultures, United States Committee for UNICEF, 1968. An evaluation of all in-print English language materials on Africa for children, arranged by countries.

African-Asian Reading Guide for Children and Young Adults, comp. by Jeanette Hotchkiss. Scarecrow, 1976. Divided by countries and by genre.

Aids to Choosing Books for Children, prepared by Ingeborg Boudreau. Children's Book Council, 1969. A selected, annotated bibliography of book lists and review media, designed to aid librarians, teachers, students of children's literature, and parents in book selection. Both general and specialized book lists are included as well as a list of general sources of information.

American Historical Fiction and Biography for Children and Young People, comp. by Jeanette Hotchkiss. Scarecrow, 1973. Annotations are arranged chronologically and by subject. Symbols are used for reading and interest levels.

American History, comp. by Bernard Titowsky. McKinley, 1964. Annotated selective listings.

Appraisal: Children's Science Books. Harvard Graduate School of Education, Cambridge, Mass. Published three times each year. Around 50 books reviewed in each issue, all rated on a five-point scale by both a librarian and a science specialist.

Asia: A Guide to Books for Children. The Asia Society, 1966. Asia is defined as all the countries from Afghanistan eastward to Japan. The guide is arranged by country and approximate grade levels are suggested in the annotated listings.

A Basic Book Collection for Elementary Grades. ALA, 1960. Suggested as a minimum collection, this is a helpful annotated guide to books in subject fields as well as to fiction and picture books.

A Basic Book Collection for High Schools, 7th ed. ALA, 1963. Includes paperbacks, magazines, and audiovisual aids.

[1]See also the bibliographies accompanying the eight articles in Part 5.

A Basic Book Collection for Junior High Schools. ALA, 1960. Similar in pattern to the book for elementary grades.

Basic Books in the Mass Media, comp. by Eleanor Blum, rev. ed. Univ. of Ill. Pr., 1972. An annotated, selective book list covering book publishing, broadcasting, films, newspapers, magazines, and advertising. The bibliography is intended to provide sources for facts and figures, names, addresses, and other biographical information, and to suggest starting points for research.

Behavior Patterns in Children's Books; A Bibliography, comp. by Clara J. Kircher. Catholic Univ. of America Pr., 1966. The purpose of this book is the development of wholesome principles of conduct and the prevention of delinquency through the therapeutic use of books in which good character traits are embodied. The list is arranged by such categories as making friends, spiritual values, or boy-girl relationships rather than age, and is followed by a list of selected readings and a behavior index.

Best Books for Children. Bowker, 1959 to date. An annual catalog of 4000 titles annotated and arranged under preschool to grade 3; grades 4–6; grades 7 up; adult books for younger readers; and special subjects.

The Best in Children's Books; The University of Chicago Guide to Children's Literature, 1966–1972, comp. by Zena Sutherland. Univ. of Chicago Pr., 1973. Reviews chosen from the *Bulletin of the Center for Children's Books* are indexed by developmental values, types of literature, reading level, and curricular use as well as conventional indexes.

Bibliography of Books for Children, comp. by Sylvia Sunderlin, rev. ed. Assoc. for Childhood Education International, 1971. Annotated list of books for children from preschool through elementary grades, grouped by subject or form in useful categories.

The Black Experience and the School Curriculum; Teaching Materials for Grades K–12; An Annotated Bibliography, comp. by Katherine Baxter. Wellsprings Ecumenical Center, 1968. Annotated lists of books grouped by subject matter, about black history, social studies, biography, fiction, and poetry, with additional material on teachers' guides and audiovisual aids.

The Black Experience in Children's Books, prepared by Barbara Rollock, rev. ed. New York Public Library, 1974. An annotated bibliography, classified by age and subject matter about black life in America, in the Islands, in Africa, and in England.

Black Studies: A Bibliography, comp. by Leonard Irwin. McKinley, 1973. For young people and adults, annotations grouped under such headings as biographical material, African background, essays and anthologies, etc.

The Black World in Literature for Children; A Bibliography of Print and Non-Print Materials, comp. by Joyce White Mills. Atlanta Univ., 1975. Divided by broad age groups and subject areas, this is for children ages 3–13.

Book Bait; Detailed Notes on Adult Books Popular with Young People, ed. by Elinor Walker, 2nd ed. ALA, 1969. One hundred carefully selected books that young people enjoy. Each title is followed by a summary of the contents, a paragraph indicating the particular audience to which the book appeals, ideas for book talks, and follow-up titles.

Books for Beginning Readers, prepared by Elizabeth Guilefoile, ill. by Norma Phillips. Nat. Council of Teachers of English, 1962. A useful bibliography of over 300 easy-reading books for beginners. The majority have been published to meet the need for entertainment and information.

Books for Children 1960–1965, as selected and reviewed by *The Booklist* and *Subscription Books Bulletin.* ALA, 1966. A compilation of reviews of recommended books, expressly for teachers and librarians. Reviews are grouped by subject matter and genre. The first of an annual compilation, now issued under the title *Books for Children, Preschool Through Junior High School,* with inclusive dates for each compilation.

Books for Friendship; A List of Books Recommended for Children, 4th ed. of *Books Are Bridges.* American Friends Service Committee and Anti-Defamation League of B'nai B'rith, 1968. Books of high literary quality selected to help boys and girls widen their friendships and follow the path of peace and brotherhood.

Books for the Chinese-American Child; A Selected List, comp. by Cecilia Mei-Chi Chen. Cooperative Children's Book Center, 1969. A carefully selected list of books, included for their honesty and literary quality.

Books for You; A Reading List for Senior High School Students, comp. by Nat. Council of Teachers of English, rev. ed. Washington Square Pr., 1971. An annotated bibliography divided by subject.

Books in American History: A Basic List for High Schools, comp. by John E. Wiltz. Indiana Univ. Pr., 1964. Chronological, annotated bibliography.

Building Bridges of Understanding, prepared by Charlotte Matthews Keating. Palo Verde, 1967. An annotated bibliography of books about blacks, Indians, Spanish-speaking ethnic groups, Chinese-Americans, Japanese-Americans, Jews, and other minority groups.

Building Bridges of Understanding Between Cultures, prepared by Charlotte Matthews Keating. Palo Verde, 1971. A companion volume to the title above, the annotations arranged by age level within each minority group.

Bulletin of the Center for Children's Books. The Univ. of Chicago, Graduate Library School, Univ. of Chicago Pr. Published monthly except August. Ongoing review of new titles for children and young people, annotated according to whether the book is recommended, acceptable, marginal, not recommended, or for special collections or unusual readers only. The reviews are detailed, and grade levels and prices are given.

Canadian Books for Children: Livres Canadiens pour Enfants, comp. by Irma McDonough. Univ. of Toronto Pr., 1976. Both the French and English lists are divided by subject areas and are annotated.

Canadian Children's Literature; A Journal of Criticism and Review. Canadian Children's Press/Canadian Children's Literature Association. Includes articles, reviews, and bibliographies.

Children and Poetry; A Selective Annotated Bibliography, comp. by Virginia Haviland and William Jay Smith. Library of Congress, 1969. With a preface by Virginia Haviland and an introduction by William Jay Smith, this book presents a choice selection of poetry divided into: Rhymes, Poetry of the Past, 20th Century Poetry, Anthologies, and World Poetry.

Children's Book Review Index, ed. by Gary Tarbert. Gale, 1976. Triannual publication indexing sources of reviews in over 200 periodicals.

Children's Books, comp. by Children's Book Section, U.S. Library of Congress. An annual bibliography, selective and annotated.

Children's Books; Awards and Prizes, comp. and ed. by the Children's Book Council, 1975. A compilation of honors awarded in the children's book field by organizations, schools, publishers, and newspapers. A brief description of each award is followed by a list of all the winners since it was first given.

Children's Books for $1.50 or Less. See *Good and Inexpensive Books for Children.*

Children's Books in Print. Bowker, annual. An index to 35,000 books in print at time of publication, including such books as have become children's classics based on inclusion in publishers' catalogs. There are separate author, title, illustrator, and publisher indexes. Prices are given for trade and library bindings, and for paperback editions.

Children's Books on Africa and Their Authors: An Annotated Bibliography, comp. by Nancy Schmidt. African Bibliography Series, Vol. 3. Africana Pub. Co., 1975. Full annotations, no age or reading level assigned.

Children's Books to Enrich the Social Studies for the Elementary Grades, comp. by Helen Huus. Nat. Council for the Social Studies, 1966. Excellent annotated bibliographies, topically arranged, cover world history and geography from ancient times to today.

The Children's Bookshelf; A Guide to Books for and About Children, rev. ed. prepared by the Child Study Assoc. of America. Bantam, 1974. Short articles on books and reading; annotated bibliography for different age groups and books for parents about children and family life.

Children's Books Too Good to Miss, comp. by May Hill Arbuthnot, Margaret Mary Clark, Harriet Geneva Long, and Ruth M. Hadlow, 6th ed. The Press of Case Western Reserve Univ., 1971. A select list of books suggested as the irreducible minimum, which every child should be exposed to. The books are grouped by ages.

Children's Catalog. Wilson, 1971. Annual supp. A selected, classified catalog of children's books, arranged with nonfiction first, classified by Dewey Decimal Classification, followed by fiction, short stories, and the easy books. Five-year cumulations and yearly supplements.

Children's Interracial Fiction; An Unselective Bibliography, comp. by Barbara Jean Glancy. American Federation of Teachers, 1969. Comprehensive annotated bibliography, accompanied by articles dealing with the black perspective and a survey-review of children's literature about black people.

The Dobler World Directory of Youth Periodicals, comp. by Lavinia G. Dobler and Muriel Fuller. Schulte, 1966. A revised and expanded listing, a successor to the *Dobler International List of Periodicals for Boys and Girls.*

Doors to More Mature Reading, prepared by Elinor Walker, Donald W. Allyn, Alice E. Johnson, and Helen Lutton. ALA, 1964. Detailed notes on adult books for use with young people.

The Elementary School Library Collection; Phases 1-2-3, ed. by Mary V. Gaver. Bro-Dart, 1965. Annual supplements. Contains discussion of selection policy and classification principles and policy. Books, shown on reproductions of catalog cards, are classified according to Dewey Decimal System of Classification in the first section. Section 2 contains author-title and subject indexes.

European Historical Fiction and Biography, comp. by Jeanette Hotchkiss, 2nd ed. Scarecrow, 1972. Divided by country and, within that, by period, with brief annotations.

Fables from Incunabula to Modern Picture Books: A Selective Bibliography, comp. by Barbara Quinnan. The Library of Congress General Reference and Bibliography Division, Reference Department, 1966.

Fare for the Reluctant Reader, comp. by Anita E. Dunn, Mabel E. Jackman, and Bernice C. Bush, rev. ed. State Univ. of N.Y., 1952. Annotated bibliography to help teachers and librarians select books for reluctant readers from grades 7 through 12. Books are grouped by age and subject. There are chapters on developmental and remedial reading.

Folklore: An Annotated Bibliography and Index to Single Editions, comp. by Elsie Ziegler. Faxon, 1973. Particularly useful because it gives access to single editions.

Folklore for Children and Young People: A Critical and Descriptive Bibliography for Use in the Elementary and Intermediate School, comp. by Eloise Ramsey. Reprint of 1952 ed., Krause Reprints. Originally published by the American Folklore Society. A section on literary uses accompanies the bibliography.

Folklore of the American Indians; An Annotated Bibliography, comp. by Judith C. Ullom, ill. Library of Congress, 1969. Carefully selected items arranged by culture areas.

For Storytellers and Storytelling: Bibliographies, Materials and Resource Aids. ALA, 1968. Recommended materials on storytelling, including books, pamphlets, and multi-media aids.

4000 Books for Secondary School Libraries; A Basic List, comp. by the Library Committee of the Nat. Assoc. of Independent Schools. Bowker, 1968. Arranged by Dewey Decimal Classification; periodicals and recordings are also listed.

Gateways to Readable Books, comp. by Dorothy Withrow, Helen Carey, and Bertha Hirzel. Wilson, 1975. An annotated list of titles chosen for the reluctant adolescent reader.

Good and Inexpensive Books for Children, Assoc. for Childhood Education International, rev. ed., 1972. Annotated lists, primarily paperbacks, grouped by genre.

Good Books for Children; A Selection of Outstanding Children's Books Published 1950–65, ed. by Mary K. Eakin, 3rd ed. Univ. of Chicago Pr., 1966. The bibliography consists of graded reviews chosen from the *Bulletin of the Center for Children's Books.*

Good Reading for Poor Readers, comp. by George Spache, rev. ed. Garrard, 1974. Consists primarily of bibliographies; four chapters discuss children's interests and motives in reading, choosing and using books for children, and estimating readability.

Growing Point, published by Margery Fisher. Belmont, 1962 to date. Nine issues yearly, published in England, reviews books for parents, teachers, and librarians in the English-speaking world.

Guide to Children's Magazines, Newspapers, Reference Books, prepared by Judy Matthews and Lillian Drag. Assoc. for Childhood Education International, 1974. Revised guide to provide a quick index of available materials.

A Guide to Historical Fiction, comp. by Leonard B. Irwin. 10th ed. rev. McKinley, 1971. Annotated entries are chronologically arranged within geographical regions.

A Guide to Historical Reading; Non-Fiction, comp. by Leonard B. Irwin. 9th ed. McKinley, 1970. Annotated listing in the McKinley series.

A Guide to Non-Sexist Children's Books, comp. by Judith Adell and Hilary Klein. Academy Pr., 1976. An annotated bibliography is divided by grade groups: preschool to 3, 3–7, 7–12, and one for all ages.

History in Children's Books: An Annotated Bibliography for Schools and Libraries, comp. by Zena Sutherland. McKinley, 1967. The fifth in a series of bibliographies for schools, libraries, and teachers.

The Horn Book Magazine. Horn Book. Published six times a year. A magazine about children's books, authors, illustrators, with a section for reviews.

How to Find Out About Children's Literature, comp. by Alec Ellis, 3rd ed., Pergamon, 1973. Bibliography of bibliographies as well as other useful listings of organizations and collections, both national and international.

I Can Read It Myself; Some Books for Independent Reading in the Primary Grades, prepared by Frieda M. Heller. Ohio State Univ., 1965. Annotated lists divided into three levels of competence.

Independent Reading Grades One Through Three: An Annotated Bibliography with Reading Levels. Bro-Dart, 1975. Has cross-referenced subject headings and a reading level index.

Index to Short Biographies: For Elementary and Junior High Grades, comp. by Ellen Stanius. Scarecrow, 1971. Listed by subject and by author, with pages given. Collective biographies only.

An Index to Young Readers' Collective Biographies, comp. by Judith Silverman, rev. ed. Bowker, 1975. The contents of 471 collective biographies for elementary and junior high school readers. The alphabetical arrangement by biographee includes birth dates, nationality, and profession. Section 2 is a subject listing, with cross references and divided by country. Title and subject heading indexes are appended.

In Review; Canadian Books for Children. Provincial Library Service, Ontario. Articles by and about authors are included in a journal devoted primarily to reviews of books written in French or English.

Introducing Books; A Guide for the Middle Grades, comp. by John Gillespie and Diane Lembo. Bowker, 1970. Titles for reading guidance and book talks are grouped according to the developmental goals of childhood, and a subject index groups these same titles under their conventional headings.

Junior High School Library Catalog, ed. by Estelle A. Fidell and Gary L. Bogart, 3rd ed. Wilson, 1975. Annual supp. Part 1, the Classified Catalog, is arranged with nonfiction books first, classified according to Dewey Decimal Classification system. Fiction books follow and short stories are next. Part 2 is an author, title, subject, analytical index. Cumulated every five years, with yearly supplements.

Juniorplots; A Book Talk Manual for Teachers and Librarians, comp. by John Gillespie and Diane Lembo. Bowker, 1967. Thematic discussions of specific books grouped under eight categories of basic goals of adolescence.

The Kirkus Service. A bimonthly publication; reviews are done from galleys and appear early, but information on illustrations is not always available.

Language Arts. Nat. Council of Teachers of English. Issued monthly, September through May. Besides regular book reviews, this journal has articles on children's reading and related subjects.

Latin America; An Annotated List of Materials for Children, ed. by Anne Pellowski, selected by a committee of librarians, teachers, and Latin-American specialists in cooperation with the Center for Inter-American Relations. Information Center on Children's Cultures, United States Committee for UNICEF, 1969. Materials are arranged by country and age-graded.

A Layman's Guide to Negro History, ed. and comp. by Erwin A. Salk. McGraw, 1967. Comprehensive compilation of books and teaching aids, conveniently categorized, and listings of important dates and people in black history.

Let's Read Together, Books for Family Enjoyment, 3rd ed. Children's Services Division, ALA, and National Congress of Parents and Teachers. ALA, 1969. Arranged by age levels and annotated.

Literature by and About the American Indian; An Annotated Bibliography, for Junior and Senior High School Students, comp. by Anna Lee Stensland. Nat. Council of Teachers of English, 1973. A divided bibliography with study guides and biographies of American Indian authors.

Magazines for School Libraries: A Brief Survey by Laura K. Martin. Univ. of Ky., 1967. This is a discussion, rather than a listing, of magazines useful to teachers and librarians, as well as students, covering such areas as selection of materials, general comment, family life, fine arts, etc.

Magazines Recommended for Use with Children, Grades K–12; A Comparative Survey of Six Basic Lists Compiled by Librarians and Educators, ed. by Sylvia Hart Wright, 2nd ed. Franklin Square-Mayfair Subscription Agency, 1969.

Negro Literature for High School Students, prepared by Barbara Dodds. Nat. Council of Teachers of English, 1968. A valuable reference guide offering a historical survey of black writers, an annotated list of works about blacks, annotated lists of novels for boys and girls, and biographies, both historical and modern, as well as suggested classroom uses of black literature. Extensive bibliography.

Notable Children's Books, 1940–1959. ALA, 1966. Reappraisals of books on the annotated annual lists of the *ALA Bulletin* after a five-year interval to achieve a list of "Books Worth Their Keep."

Patterns in Reading, prepared by Jean Carolyn Roos, 2nd ed. ALA, 1961. A useful selection of books for older children, youth, and young adults. The books are grouped around more than a hundred major reading interests and are well annotated and indexed. A valuable reference.

Periodicals for School Libraries; A Guide to Magazines, Newspapers, Periodical Indexes, comp. and ed. by Marian H. Scott, rev. ed. ALA, 1973. A buying guide to periodicals and newspapers for school library purchases. Entries are alphabetical, and each is accompanied by appropriate grade level, name and address of publisher, frequency of publication, and price. Annotations describe the nature and scope of the publication and possible curricular use.

Previews; Non-Print Software & Hardware News & Reviews. Bowker. Monthly, September through May. Reviews divided (filmstrips, slides, kits, etc.) and articles included. Hardware reviews thorough.

Reading Ladders for Human Relations, ed. by Virginia Reid, rev. ed. Am. Council on Education, 1972. This enlarged and revised edition contains an introduction and bibliographies on the role of reading in developing children's self-knowledge and social awareness.

Red, White and Black: (and Brown and Yellow): Minorities in America, Harold H. Laskey, director. Combined Paperback Exhibit, 1970. Catalog of paperbacks on minority groups, with an order form for purchasing books or previewing films.

Reference Books for Elementary and Junior High School Libraries, comp. by Carolyn Sue Peterson. Scarecrow, 1970. A very useful annotated bibliography divided into general reference books (dictionaries, atlases, fact books, etc.) and those for subject areas.

School Library Journal. Bowker. A journal for librarians especially, it is published monthly, September through May. Approximately 1500 titles are reviewed, sometimes with dissenting opinions. There are also many articles on library services, books, and reading for children and young people.

Science Books: A Quarterly Review. Am. Assoc. for the Advancement of Science. Reviews around 100 science and mathematics books, elementary through college and beyond. Reviews are by specialists in the field.

Science for Youth, comp. by Hannah Logasa. McKinley, 1967. Annotated bibliography in the McKinley series.

Standard Catalog for High School Libraries. Annual supplements. Wilson. Part 1, the Classified Catalog, is arranged with nonfiction first, classified by Dewey Decimal System; fiction next; and then short stories. Each book is listed under one main entry where full information is given. Part 2 contains an author, title, subject, and analytical index of all the books in the catalog.

Starting Out Right; Choosing Books About Black People for Young Children, ed. by Bettye Lattimer. Wis. Dept. of Public Instruction, 1972. A bibliography preceded by a discussion of the extent of integration in books for children.

Stories to Tell to Children, ed. by Sara C. Bryant. Carnegie Library of Pittsburgh, frequently revised. One of the outstanding bibliographies of folk and fairy literature available for the storyteller.

Subject and Title Index to Short Stories for Children. Subcommittee of the ALA Editorial Committee, 1955. Designed to assist librarians and teachers in locating stories on specific subjects. Approximate grades given.

Subject Guide to Children's Books in Print. Bowker, annual. A subject index to children's books in 7000 categories.

Subject Index to Books for Intermediate Grades, comp. by Mary K. Eakin. 3rd ed. ALA, 1963. An index of 1800 titles with emphasis on trade books.

Subject Index to Books for Primary Grades, comp. by Mary K. Eakin and Eleanor Merritt. 3rd ed. ALA, 1967. Approximately 1000 textbooks and trade books for primary grades are indexed under detailed subject headings useful for the classroom teacher and librarian.

Subject Index to Poetry for Children and Young People. ALA, 1957. Indicates grade level.

Translated Children's Books; Offered by Publishers in

the U.S.A. Storybooks International, 1968. Annotated list of books, arranged alphabetically according to language of origin, with an author index and a title index.

Treasure for the Taking, prepared by Anne Thaxter Eaton. Viking, 1957. First published in 1946, this revised, annotated bibliography is arranged according to many types of children's books.

We Build Together; A Reader's Guide to Negro Life and Literature for Elementary and High School Use, ed. by Charlemae Rollins, 3rd ed. Nat. Council of Teachers of English. 1967. A selected, annotated bibliography of picture books, fiction, history, biography, poetry, folklore, music, science, and sports, with an introduction dealing with the criteria by which the books were selected.

World Culture, comp. by Hannah Logasa. McKinley, 1963. Arranged in subject categories.

World Historical Fiction Guide, comp. by Daniel McGarry and Sarah White, 2nd ed. Scarecrow, 1973. A selective, annotated list for junior and senior high school.

The World of Children's Literature, comp. by Anne Pellowski. Bowker, 1968. An annotated bibliography giving a picture of the development of children's literature in every country where it exists.

Your Reading; A Book List for Junior High Schools, ed. by Charles B. Willard and the Committee on the Junior High School Book List of the Nat. Council of Teachers of English, 5th ed. Walker, 1975. Annotated guide to almost 1300 books.

Appendix B
Adult References[2]

ABRAHAMS, ROGER, and GEORGE FOSS. *Anglo-American Folksong Style.* Prentice, 1968. Although many songs are included as examples, this is primarily an evaluation of the style, content, and form of folksong, and of the types of ballads and the changes in ballad style.

AFANASIEV, ALEXANDER N. *Russian Fairy Tales,* tr. by Norbert Guterman, ill. by A. Alexeieff. Pantheon, 1945. See the valuable "Folkloristic Commentary" by Roman Jakobson.

ALDERSON, BRIAN. *Looking at Picture Books 1973.* National Book League, Children's Book Council, 1974. Perceptive and knowledgeable comments on children's book illustration.

ALDISS, BRIAN. *The True History of Science Fiction.* Doubleday, 1973. On the origins of science fiction and its emergence as a genre in the 20th century.

ALMY, MILLIE. *Ways of Studying Children.* Bureau of Publications, Teachers College, Columbia University, 1969. Chapter 5 relates to the use of literature in studying children.

ALMY, MILLIE, E. CHITTENDEN, and PAULA MILLER. *Young Children's Thinking; Studies of Some Aspects of Piaget's Theory.* Teachers College Pr., 1966.

ALTICK, RICHARD D. *Lives and Letters: A History of Literary Biography in England and America.* Knopf, 1965. With liberal bibliographical notes for each chapter, the author discusses the achievement and influence of literary biographers from the seventeenth century to today. A thoroughly researched and comprehensive study.

AMERICAN COUNCIL ON EDUCATION. *Helping Teachers Understand Children.* Am. Council on Education, 1945. Report of a project designed to deepen understanding of children's growth and development by analyzing and identifying causes that underlie children's behavior.

ANDERSON, HAROLD, ed. *Creativity and Its Cultivation.* Harper, 1959. A compilation of outstanding research papers in the field of creativity. Carl Rogers's paper entitled "Toward a Theory of Creativity" presents his findings on psychological safety, which he considers essential to creative thinking.

ANDERSON, ROBERT, and HAROLD SHANE, eds. *As the Twig Is Bent; Readings in Early Childhood Education.* Houghton, 1971. A collection of articles, the majority devoted to the development of the preschool child.

ANDERSON, VERNA. *Reading and Young Children.* Macmillan, 1968. A survey of the approaches to the teaching of reading, the problems and the techniques of meeting them, and the use of materials with children.

The Annotated Mother Goose, with introduction and notes by William Baring-Gould and Ceil Baring-Gould; the complete text and illustrations in a fully annotated edition, ill. by Caldecott, Crane, Greenaway, Rackham, Parrish, and historical woodcuts. With chapter decorations by E. M. Simon. Potter, 1962. Mother Goose and other rhymes, ditties, and jingles of the nursery run side by side with columns of absorbing historical notes. This impressively large, beautiful book contains over 200 illustrations with a first-line index.

ARBUTHNOT, MAY HILL. *Children's Reading in the Home,* ill. Scott, Foresman, 1969. A description of a good home environment for reading followed by a discussion of books according to age range and type.

ARBUTHNOT, MAY HILL, and ZENA SUTHERLAND. *The Arbuthnot Anthology,* 4th ed. Scott, Foresman, 1976. A source book for children's literature classes as well as a book to be used with children, containing poetry, fantasy, and realism. Special sections are "Milestones in Children's Literature," "Illustrations in Children's Books," and "Guiding Literary Experience."

ARNSTEIN, FLORA. *Children Write Poetry: A Creative Approach,* 2nd ed. Stanford Univ. Pr., 1967. A teacher's careful record of her step-by-step procedures in conducting an experiment in creative writing with a group of elementary-school children, with discussions of qualities that mark authentic poetry.

The Art of Beatrix Potter, with an appreciation by Anne Carroll Moore. Warne, 1956. In a truly beautiful book, landscapes, still life, experimental drawings, and the tiny pictures for her children's classics are reproduced, giving new insight into the versatility of Beatrix Potter.

ASBJÖRNSEN, PETER C., and JÖRGEN MOE. *Norwegian Folk Tales,* tr. by Pat Shaw Iversen and Carl Norman, ill. by Erik Werenskiold and Theodor Kittelson. Viking, 1961. Thirty-six folk tales in an excellent translation which reintroduces the original Asbjörnsen illustrators.

______. *Popular Tales from the Norse,* tr. by Sir George Webbe Dasent. Putnam, 1908. A long and rich introduction by the translator is particularly good on changes from myth to fairy tale.

ASHTON, JOHN. *Chap-Books of the Eighteenth Century.* London: Chatto, 1882. (Facsimile of the original: Singing Tree, 1968.) The author reproduces the stories and some of the pages and illustrations from the old chapbooks.

ASIMOV, ISAAC. *Words from the Myths.* Houghton, 1961. From the Greek myths come many word roots used in science and daily language. Asimov tells the legends briefly and explains origins of current usage.

AUSLANDER, JOSEPH, and FRANK ERNEST HILL. *The Winged Horse; The Story of Poets and Their Poetry.* Doubleday, 1927. Written for older children and young people, this is a thoroughly interesting book for teachers and parents as well. Fine references on ballads and epics.

BADER, BARBARA. *American Picturebooks from Noah's Ark to The Beast Within.* Macmillan, 1976. A critical and historical study.

BAIRD, BIL. *The Art of the Puppet,* ill. Macmillan, 1965. A fascinating and handsomely illustrated book "designed to tell people about puppets and how they dif-

[2]This list provides data and annotations for the Adult References in Chapters 1–13. Consult Appendix A for any reference not found here. For additional useful reading suggestions see the bibliographies accompanying the eight articles in Part 5.

fer from each other and how they are alike" by a man with "forty years of practice in a profession that has given me the greatest satisfaction."

BALDWIN, RUTH, comp. *One Hundred Nineteenth-Century Rhyming Alphabets in English.* Southern Ill. Univ. Pr., 1972. Reproductions, some in full color, of alphabets that vary in theme, tone, and degrees of difficulty or didacticism.

BAMMAN, HENRY, MILDRED DAWSON, and ROBERT WHITEHEAD. *Oral Interpretation of Children's Literature,* 2nd ed. Brown, 1972. Suggestions for techniques and materials to use in working with children.

BARCHILON, JACQUES, and HENRY PETTIT. *The Authentic Mother Goose Fairy Tales and Nursery Rhymes.* Swallow Pr., 1960. Following a scholarly introduction to the history of Mother Goose and the Perrault fairy tales, there are facsimiles of the complete *Mother Goose's Melody,* and of the 1729 English translation of Perrault's *Tales.*

BARRY, FLORENCE V. *A Century of Children's Books.* Doran, 1923; reissued, Singing Tree, 1969. A readable account of early English books for children, with unusually good evaluations.

BAUGHMAN, ERNEST. *A Type and Motif Index of the Folktales of England and North America.* Indiana Univ. Folklore Series, No. 20, 1966. Gives extensive bibliographic references to the well-known folk-tale types.

BEADLE, MURIEL. *A Child's Mind; How Children Learn During the Critical Years from Birth to Age Five,* ill. Doubleday, 1970. A review, prepared for the lay person, of what had been learned in the preceding twenty-five years about the child's mind and development.

BECHTEL, LOUISE SEAMAN, ed. *Books in Search of Children.* Macmillan, 1969. Speeches and essays by a pioneering editor and critic.

BEHN, HARRY. *Chrysalis; Concerning Children and Poetry.* Harcourt, 1968. A children's poet reminisces and writes about children and poetry.

BERRY, THOMAS ELLIOTT, ed. *The Biographer's Craft.* Odyssey, 1967. A textbook with examples of the work of seventeen biographers from Plutarch to contemporary writers, with one-page analyses of the biographers' genres and output. Introductory essay and short additional-reading list.

BETT, HENRY. *The Games of Children; Their Origin and History.* Singing Tree, 1968. Intended for both the student of folklore and the general reader, this book explores the primitive, often religious origin of many of the games still played by children.

BETTELHEIM, BRUNO. *The Uses of Enchantment: Meaning and Importance of Fairy Tales.* Knopf, 1976. A defense of the genre and an analysis of some popular fairy tales.

The Bewick Collector. A descriptive catalog of the works of Thomas and John Bewick. . . . The whole described from the originals by Thomas Hugo. M.A., F.R.S.I., etc. London: Lovell Reeve, Vol. I. 1866. Supp., 1868; reissued, Singing Tree, 1968.

BLACKBURN, HENRY. *Randolph Caldecott: A Personal Memoir of His Early Art Career,* ill. with reproductions and photographs. London: Sampson Low, 1886.

BLOUNT, MARGARET. *Animal Land: The Creatures of Children's Fiction.* Morrow, 1975. Discusses and analyzes types of animal stories.

BOLTON, HENRY CARRINGTON. *The Counting-Out Rhymes of Children; Their Antiquity, Origin, and Wide Distribution: A Study in Folk-Lore.* Singing Tree, 1969. Almost 900 rhymes in 18 languages, including Japanese, Hawaiian, Turkish, and the Penobscot dialect, as well as the more common European languages.

BOVA, BENJAMIN. *Through Eyes of Wonder; Science Fiction and Science.* Addison, 1975. An assessment of the contribution of science fiction to scientific knowledge, with some history of the development of the genre.

BOWEN, CATHERINE DRINKER. *Biography: The Craft and the Calling.* Little, 1968. Dealing with the planning, research, and techniques involved, the book analyzes four major biographies, with side excursions for further examples, and provides a good tool for writers in the field.

BRAND, OSCAR. *The Ballad Mongers; Rise of the Modern Folk Song.* Funk, 1962. An excellent survey of the interest in, and development of, the folk music of America.

BREDSDORFF, ELIAS. *Hans Christian Andersen; The Story of His Life and Work.* Scribner's, 1975. Incorporates Andersen's autobiographical writing and analyzes his stories.

BREWTON, JOHN E. and SARA W., comps. *Index to Children's Poetry.* Wilson, 1942. First supp., 1954; second supp., 1965; third supp., 1972. Helpful in finding poem sources. Indexed by author, title, subject, and first line. Thorough analysis of book contents, number of poems in a book, and grade placement.

BRIGGS, KATHARINE M. *A Dictionary of British Folk-Tales in the English Language.* Indiana Univ. Pr., 1970. Part A, Folk Narratives, Vols. 1 and 2. Part B. Folk Legends, Vols. 1 and 2. Contains complete texts and summaries of all British tales in English with extensive comparative notes.

BRODERICK, DOROTHY M. *Image of the Black in Children's Fiction.* Bowker, 1973. Limited only by the fact that later titles were chosen from headings assigned by *Children's Catalog,* thus excluding some books with major black characters, this is an incisive and perceptive analysis of issues and attitudes.

BROWN, JAMES W. *AV Instruction: Materials and Methods.* McGraw, 1959. A textbook for teacher training sources in audiovisual instruction, with emphasis on interrelatedness of all teaching aids and the role of the instructor in the presentation of such material.

BRUNER, JEROME S. *Toward a Theory of Instruction.* Belknap Pr. of Harvard Univ., 1966. A collection of essays concerned with the relation between the growth and development of the child and the art of teaching.

BRUNVAND, JAN H. *The Study of American Folklore, an Introduction.* Norton, 1968. The best introductory textbook presently available, with excellent bibliographic references for each chapter.

BULFINCH, THOMAS. *Age of Fable; or, Stories of Gods and Heroes,* introduction by Dudley Fitts, ill. by Joe Mugnaini. Heritage, 1958. This handsome edition of Bulfinch is almost completely devoted to the Greek and Roman myths, though it does include brief materials from the Norse, Celtic, and Hindu lore.

CADOGAN, MARY, and PATRICIA CRAIG. *You're a Brick, Angela; A New Look at Girls' Fiction from 1839–1975.* London: Gollancz, 1976. Stories for girls are examined as reflections of social history as well as for their place in literary history.

CAMERON, ELEANOR. *The Green and Burning Tree; On the Writing and Enjoyment of Children's Books.* Little, 1969. Critical essays by a writer for children, with a special emphasis on fantasy.

CARLSEN, G. ROBERT. *Books and the Teen-Age Reader; A Guide for Teachers, Librarians, and Parents,* rev. ed. Harper, 1971. A practical book for adults who want to help adolescents read with pleasure for growth and personal fulfillment.

CARLSON, RUTH KEARNEY. *Emerging Humanity; Multi-Ethnic Literature for Children and Adolescents.* Brown, 1972. Describes values of and criteria for multi-ethnic literature, suggests ways to use it. Separate chapters discuss black, American Indian, and Mexican-American books.

______. *Enrichment Ideas; Sparkling Fireflies.* Brown, 1970. For the elementary school classroom teacher, suggestions for dramatization, art projects, language games, and ways of using literature to enrich the curriculum. The suggestions for activities are accompanied by selected references for children and selected references for adults.

CARROLL, LEWIS (pseud.). *The Annotated Alice; Alice's Adventures in Wonderland & Through the Looking Glass,* ill. by John Tenniel. With introduction and notes by Martin Gardner. Potter, 1960. Significant quotations from Carroll biographies and other sources are placed parallel to the story text. An enriching background source for students.

CATALDO, JOHN W. *Words and Calligraphy for Children.* Van Nostrand, 1969. Reproductions of paintings, drawings, and designs by children in an art workshop intended to give, through free expression, a familiarity with language symbols. Arranged by age groups.

CATTERSON, JANE H., ed. *Children and Literature.* International Reading Assoc., 1969. A selection of papers from the Association's annual convention that should help teachers, both elementary and high school, bring literature into the curriculum and provide positive literary experience.

CHALL, JEANNE. *Learning to Read; The Great Debate.* McGraw, 1967. The findings of a three-year study on teaching beginning reading with a sober discussion of conclusions and recommendations.

CHAMBERS, AIDAN. *Introducing Books to Children.* Horn Book, 1975. A presentation of the importance of children's literature and of how to introduce it to children.

______. *The Reluctant Reader.* Pergamon, 1969. A lively account by a Britisher of why young people are reluctant to read creative fiction, with suggestions for authors, teachers, publishers, and librarians. Bibliographies for reluctant readers in appendixes.

CHAMBERS, DEWEY W. *Children's Literature in the Curriculum.* Rand, 1971. A "plea" to make children's literature "an integral part of the elementary school's curriculum" and "an important factor in the lives of children." The three sections are "The Role of Literature in the Elementary Curriculum," "How Books Can Affect Children," and "Thoughts on Some Controversial Issues in Children's Literature."

CHAMBERS, ROBERT. *Popular Rhymes of Scotland.* Singing Tree, 1969. First published in 1826, this work has been revised and expanded several times. The 1870 edition is reproduced in this volume.

CHILD, FRANCIS JAMES, ed. *English and Scottish Popular Ballads,* 5 vols. Houghton, 1882–1898. This is our most authoritative source for all English and Scottish traditional ballads. Many variants are given for each ballad, together with copious notes.

Chosen for Children; an Account of the Books Which Have Been Awarded the Library Association Carnegie Medal, 1936–1965, rev. ed. London: The Library Assoc., 1967. A discussion of the prize-winning books for children by British authors, with excerpts, illustrations, biographical material, comments by and pictures of the authors.

CHUKOVSKY, KORNEI. *From Two to Five,* tr. and ed. by Miriam Morton. Univ. of Calif. Pr., 1965. A book on the language and comprehension of the very young child written by the dean of Russian children's writers, rich in its insights and observations.

CIANCIOLO, PATRICIA. *Illustrations in Children's Books,* 2nd ed. Brown, 1976. The book deals with art and design as areas of study in the elementary school: styles, techniques, appraisal of illustrations and their use in class. Up-to-date references by chapters, and with bibliography and index.

CIANCIOLO, PATRICIA, and the NATIONAL COUNCIL OF TEACHERS OF ENGLISH, PICTURE BOOK COMMITTEE, eds. *Picture Books for Children.* ALA, 1973. An annotated bibliography for children of all ages, this focuses on illustration rather than text.

CIARDI, JOHN, and MILLER WILLIAMS. *How Does a Poem Mean?* 2nd ed. Houghton, 1975. A college text for the study of poetry in general with an analysis of specific poems.

CLARK, ANN NOLAN. *Journey to the People,* with introduction by Annis Duff, ill. Viking, 1969. Essays about a lifelong experience with teaching Indian children: Zuni, Navajo, Pueblo, and other tribes of the Southwest, as well as the Dakota Sioux and the Indians of Guatemala and Peru.

CLEARY, FLORENCE. *Blueprints for Better Reading: School Programs for Promoting Skill and Interest in Reading.* Wilson, 1970. Offers both inspiration and ideas to teachers and librarians.

CLIFFORD, JAMES L. *From Puzzles to Portraits: Problems of a Literary Biographer.* Univ. of N. Car. Pr., 1970. An approach to biography writing that deals in anecdotal style with such problems as testing authenticity, the fictional method, the pursuit of vague footnotes, and the ethics of the biographer's selectivity.

______, ed. *Biography as an Art.* Oxford, 1962. A most useful collection of forty-seven essays of selected literary criticism by biographers, ranging from writers of the 16th to the mid-20th century, with an additional bibliography of about 150 modern books and articles.

COFFIN, TRISTRAM P. *The British Traditional Ballad in North America.* The American Folklore Society, Bibliographic and Special Series II (1950, 1963). Contains bibliographic listings for all the versions of the traditional (Child) ballads collected in North America.

COHEN, MONROE, ed. *Literature with Children.* Assoc. for Childhood Education International, 1972. A collection of articles.

COLBY, JEAN POINDEXTER. *Writing, Illustrating and Editing Children's Books,* ill. Hastings, 1967. A rewritten and enlarged edition of *The Children's Book Field,* this covers all phases of juvenile publishing and provides a wealth of practical data for authors and illustrators.

COLES, ROBERT. *Children of Crisis.* Atlantic, 1964. Based on the author's interviews with black and white people in the South, a long-term study of children, analyzing their drawings as well as their conversation.

COLES, ROBERT, and MARIA PIERS. *Wages of Neglect.* Quadrangle, 1969. An examination of the behavior of young children of the poor, their special hardships, and social and personal anxieties that determine their behavior.

COLLINGWOOD, STUART DODGSON. *The Life and Letters of Lewis Carroll (Rev. C. L. Dodgson).* Gale Library of Lives and Letters: British Writers Series. Singing Tree, 1967. The biography of Lewis Carroll, written by his nephew shortly after his death, is a primary source book of information about the public and private life of this children's writer.

COLUM, PADRAIC, ed. *A Treasury of Irish Folklore.* Crown, 1954. This book gives insight into Irish history and heroism as well as folklore.

COMENIUS, JOHN AMOS. *The Orbis Pictus of John Amos Comenius.* Singing Tree, 1968. The first children's picture book and the most widely known textbook of the 17th and 18th centuries, reproduced from an 1887 photographic copy of a 1728 London edition, this volume is of interest to educators and historians alike.

COMMIRE, ANNE. *Something About the Author: Facts and Pictures About Contemporary Authors and Illustrators of Books for Young People.* Vol. I. Gale, 1971. The inclusion of biographical information and lists of writings makes this reference series useful to adults.

CONRAD, EDNA, and MARY VAN DYKE. *History on the Stage; Children Make Plays from Historical Novels,* ill. with photos. Van Nostrand, 1971. Approaches the making of plays as a teaching technique, from choosing and reading a book and improvising to developing a script, to performance. Can be used by children 11 to 14 as well as by adults.

COODY, BETTY. *Using Literature with Young Children.* Brown, 1973. A practical literature program for young children at home and in school.

COOK, ELIZABETH. *The Ordinary and the Fabulous; An Introduction to Myths, Legends, and Fairy Tales for Teachers and Storytellers.* Cambridge Univ. Pr., 1969. The author undertakes to show that an adult understanding of life is incomplete without an understanding of myths, legends, and fairy tales and that there are many ways of presenting them.

CRAVEN, PAUL R. *Biography.* Dickenson Pub. Co., 1968. An introductory textbook, organized under autobiography, journals, obituaries, personality sketches, and extracts from books such as Samuel L. Clemens's *Life on the Mississippi.*

CREIGHTON, HELEN, comp. *Songs and Ballads from Nova Scotia.* Dover, 1966. Includes Scottish and English ballads and folk songs of English and Scottish origin as well as songs native to North America.

CREWS, FREDERICK C. *The Pooh Perplex; A Freshman Casebook,* ill. by E. H. Shepard. Dutton, 1963. Brilliant parodies using Milne's stories and verses to satirize various methods of literary criticism.

CROSBY, MURIEL. *An Adventure in Human Relations.* Follett, 1965. Report of a three-year experimental project in schools in changing neighborhoods, with two main goals: improving the schools through developing appropriate curriculum and in-service teacher training, and upgrading family and community life through the development of indigenous leadership.

CROUCH, MARCUS. *The Nesbit Tradition; The Children's Novel 1945–1970.* Rowman and Littlefield, 1973. A major English critic of children's literature examines, by theme, genre, or setting, the work of contemporary writers of fiction, chiefly British and American.

———. *Treasure Seekers and Borrowers: Children's Books in Britain, 1900–1960.* London: The Library Assoc., 1962. Excellent brief appraisals of authors and books, chiefly British, published during the first sixty years of the twentieth century.

CULLINAN, BERNICE E. *Literature for Children: Its Discipline and Content.* Brown, 1971. For elementary classroom teachers, this book is intended to build effective courses in literature. Well constructed and researched with numerous references for each chapter.

A Curriculum for English. The Nebraska Curriculum Development Center. Univ. of Nebraska Pr., 1966. This excellently worked-out curriculum covers the years of kindergarten through high school and also makes suggestions for the first year of college.

DARLING, RICHARD L. *The Rise of Children's Book Reviewing in America, 1865–1881.* Bowker, 1968. A scholarly and thorough examination of the publishing and reviewing of children's books, set in the historical context. Thirty-six periodicals are examined, including the most important literary periodicals of the time.

DARTON, F. J. H. *Children's Books in England: Five Centuries of Social Life,* 2nd ed. Cambridge Univ. Pr., 1958. A scholarly study of children's books, from the fables to Robert Louis Stevenson. Chapter VII is about John Newbery and the first English books for children.

DAVIS, MARY GOULD. *Randolph Caldecott 1846–1886: An Appreciation.* Lippincott, 1946. An evaluation of the great English artist's contribution to children's literature.

DeANGELI, MARGUERITE. *Butter at the Old Price.* Doubleday, 1971. A grande dame of the children's book world describes, in her autobiography, her long career as an author.

DeAUGULO, JAIME. *Indian Tales,* ill. by author, foreword by Carl Carmer. Hill, 1953. The author lived 40 years among the Pit River Indians and thinks as they think and writes in English as they speak in their language. The time of these stories is the historic dawn, "when men and animals were not so distinguishable as they are today." Chiefly an adult source book.

DeMONTREVILLE, DORIS, and DONNA HILL, eds. *Third Book of Junior Authors.* Wilson, 1972. A companion volume to the Kunitz and Fuller titles cited below.

DENNISON, GEORGE. *The Lives of Children: The Story of the First Street School.* Random, 1969. A fascinating account of a free school working with twenty-three students, white, black, and Puerto Rican, all from low-income homes, half of them rejects from the public schools, with severe learning and behavior problems.

DEUTSCH, MARTIN, and others. *The Disadvantaged Child.* Basic, 1967. Selected papers on the social environment for learning, and on such factors as race, social class, and language in the education of the disadvantaged child.

DeVRIES, LEONARD. *Little Wide-Awake: An Anthology from Victorian Children's Books and Periodicals in the Collection of Anne and Fernand G. Renier,* ill. World, 1967. Interesting examples of what was read by children during the 60 years of Victoria's reign.

DeWITT, MARGUERITE E., and others. *Practical Methods in Choral Speaking.* Expression, 1936. A compilation of papers by American teachers covering methods from the primary grades through the university, with many practical suggestions.

DOMAN, GLENN. *How to Teach Your Baby to Read; The Gentle Revolution.* Random, 1964. Work with brain-injured children has led to more complete understanding of how all children learn and the development of a startling reading program.

DORSON, RICHARD M. *American Folklore.* Univ. of Chicago Pr., 1959. A very readable general survey of prose forms of oral folklore in the United States. Devotes little attention to folksong.

______. *Buying the Wind, Regional Folklore in the United States.* Univ. of Chicago Pr., 1964. A good selection of authentic folklore texts with useful notes and introduction.

______. ed. *Folktales of the World.* Univ. of Chicago Pr. This most impressive series for the student of folklore has been published under the general editorship of Richard Dorson, a professor of history and director of the Folklore Institute at Indiana University. In each volume, his foreword is learned, informative, and beautifully written. The editor for each volume is a distinguished folklorist in his or her own right. The full notes, index of motifs, glossary, bibliography, and general index in each volume add to their usefulness for the scholar. Each book contains from fifty to one hundred tales; several titles are discussed in Chapter 6.

______. ed. *Folktales Told Around the World.* Univ. of Chicago Pr., 1975. Sources are cited for each tale; included are indexes by motif and type, notes on contributors, and a general index.

DOUGLAS, NORMAN. *London Street Games.* Singing Tree, 1968. Greatly expanded from an article published in *English Review* in 1913, this running account of English street life in the early part of the century captures the vocabulary and tone of the children Douglas collected from.

DOYLE, BRIAN, comp. and ed. *The Who's Who of Children's Literature,* ill. Schocken, 1969. Full and lively biographical sketches of authors and illustrators.

DREW, ELIZABETH, and GEORGE CONNOR. *Discovering Modern Poetry.* Holt, 1961. "There is no single 'meaning' to much poetry. Different interpretations are always possible. . . . Analysis is not destructive, it is creative." These are clues to the authors' approach to the interpretation of modern poetry. Modern authors are examined with an appreciation that should help the most skeptical to a better understanding of modern poetry.

DUFF, ANNIS. *"Bequest of Wings"; A Family's Pleasures with Books.* Viking, 1944. A pleasant account of one family's use of books, pictures, and music.

______. *"Longer Flight"; A Family Grows Up with Books.* Viking, 1955. Another pleasant, anecdotal account of a family and its reading, and some apt generalizations about what books mean to children and adolescents.

DUNNING, STEPHEN, and ALAN B. HOWES. *Literature for Adolescents; Teaching Poems, Stories, Novels, and Plays.* Scott, Foresman, 1975. Suggestions for ways to stimulate students' enjoyment of literature and to insure their growth as readers.

DURKIN, DOLORES. *Teaching Young Children to Read,* 2nd ed. Allyn, 1976. Techniques for teaching language skills and reading to children from preschool through third grade. Includes a discussion of reading readiness.

EASTMAN, MARY HUSE. *Index to Fairy Tales, Myths and Legends.* Faxon, 1926. First supp., 1937; second supp., 1952. Useful for locating various sources in which individual tales may be found. There are geographical and racial groupings and lists for storytellers. See entry for Ireland, Norma.

EASTMAN, MAX. *The Enjoyment of Poetry.* Scribner's, 1921, 1951. This book is an excellent introduction to the pleasures of poetry. Chapter I, "Poetic People," in which he gives his reasons for listing the child as one of the "poetic people," and Chapter V, "Practical Values of Poetry," should be noted.

ECKENSTEIN, LINA. *Comparative Studies in Nursery Rhymes.* London: Duckworth, 1906; reissued, Singing Tree, 1968. A study of the ancient folk origins of the Mother Goose verses and their European counterparts.

EDEN, HORATIA K. F. *Juliana Horatia Ewing and Her Books.* Gale Library of Lives and Letters: British Writers Series. Singing Tree, 1969. The biography of Juliana Horatia Ewing (1841–1885), her letters, and a bibliography, compiled by the younger sister of this esteemed writer for children.

EDWARDS, MARGARET A. *The Fair Garden and the Swarm of Beasts; The Library and the Young Adult,* rev. ed. Hawthorn, 1974. The writer's own experience in developing a young adult library department, recounted in a lively, provocative manner.

EGOFF, SHEILA. *The Republic of Childhood; A Critical Guide to Canadian Children's Literature in English.* Oxford, 1967. Creative writing for children by Canadian authors between the years of 1950 and 1965.

EGOFF, SHEILA, G. T. STUBBS, and L. F. ASHLEY, eds. *Only Connect: Readings on Children's Literature,* ill. Oxford, 1969. A compilation of essays by well-known, competent writers and critics covering literary criticism and history, standards, changing tastes, children's responses, writers and their writing, and illustration.

ELLIS, ALEC. *A History of Children's Reading and Literature.* Pergamon, 1968. History of schools, educational practice, and library development in England.

ELLIS, ANNE W. *The Family Story in the 1960's.* Archon Books & Clive Bingley, 1970. A survey, with comments on trends, on family stories, almost all of British origin, published during the decade. Good commentary and checklist.

ENGEN, RODNEY. *Kate Greenaway.* Harmony Books, Crown, 1976. A brief discussion of Greenaway's work is followed by pages of reproductions from original editions of her best-known books.

ERIKSON, ERIK H. *Childhood and Society,* 2nd ed., rev. and enl. Norton, 1964. The noted psychoanalyst's summary of his studies of childhood, emphasizing the importance of early experiences in the development of adult attitudes and actions.

ERNEST, EDWARD, comp., assisted by PATRICIA TRACY LOWE. *The Kate Greenaway Treasury,* ill. World, 1967. A biography of Kate Greenaway, an evaluation of her art, a fine essay about her work by the late Anne Carroll Moore, and an introduction by Ruth Hill Viguers, make this rich collection the definitive study of a beloved children's book illustrator.

ESBENSEN, BARBARA JUSTER. *A Celebration of Bees; Helping Children Write Poetry.* Winston Press, 1975. An informally written guide by an experienced teacher.

EVERTTS, ELDONNA, ed. *Explorations in Children's Writing.* Nat. Council of Teachers of English, 1970. Papers growing out of a conference on teaching elementary English, in which teachers discuss experiences with children's writing.

EYRE, FRANK. *British Children's Books in the Twentieth Century.* Dutton, 1973. A revised edition of the 1952 title, *20th Century Children's Books,* this historical survey discusses trends and includes an extensive divided bibliography.

FADER, DANIEL N., and ELTON B. McNEIL. *Hooked on Books; Program and Proof.* Putnam, 1968. A detailed description of a program to get bored and apathetic students to read, accompanied by a description of a research project evaluating the program.

FEATHERSTONE, JOSEPH. *Schools Where Children Learn.* Liveright, 1971. These are pieces on schools, learning, and teaching that have appeared in *The New Republic.* Part One is about the Primary School Revolution in Britain; Part Two, about The State of the Profession with varieties of good practice and bad.

FELDMAN, EDMUND BURKE. *Becoming Human Through Art: Aesthetic Experience in the School,* ill. Prentice, 1970. An interdisciplinary approach to visual education, primarily for teachers and teachers of teachers.

FENNER, PHYLLIS. *The Proof of the Pudding.* Day, 1957. An entertaining discussion of many books children enjoy.

———. ed. *Something Shared: Children and Books.* Day, 1959. A spirited compilation from many authors interested in children and books offers genuine entertainment as well as inspiration.

FENWICK, SARA INNIS, ed. *A Critical Approach to Children's Literature.* Univ. of Chicago Pr., 1967. Collected papers from a conference on children's literature, representing a variety of aspects.

FIELD, CAROLYN W., ed., with VIRGINIA HAVILAND and ELIZABETH NESBITT, consultants. *Subject Collections in Children's Literature.* Bowker, 1969. Identifies and publicizes special collections of children's literature, especially for those interested in research.

FIELD, ELINOR WHITNEY, comp. *Horn Book Reflections: On Children's Books and Reading.* Selected from eighteen years of *The Horn Book Magazine*—1949–1966. Horn Book, 1969. Contributors are writers, illustrators, teachers, librarians, and parents.

FIELD, LOUISE F. *The Child and His Book: Some Account of the History and Progress of Children's Literature in England.* Singing Tree, 1968. An important scholarly work tracing the history of English books for children from before the Conquest to the 19th century, this book is also a social history of England.

FISHER, MARGERY. *Intent Upon Reading.* Watts, 1962. A refreshing and critical approach to children's books, both recent and standard selections. Though many of the titles are English publications, a great number are familiar to American readers.

———. *Matters of Fact: Aspects of Non-Fiction for Children.* T. Crowell, 1972. An excellent guide to evaluative criteria.

FOLMSBEE, BEULAH. *A Little History of the Horn Book.* Horn Book, 1942. A tiny book, beautifully printed, with a history of hornbooks, in all their variations, both in England and New England.

FORD, PAUL LEICESTER, ed. *The New England Primer.* Dodd, 1897, 1962. The subtitle explains the content: "A history of its origin with a reprint of the unique copy of the earliest known first edition."

FORD, ROBERT. *Children's Rhymes, Children's Games, Children's Songs, Children's Stories: A Book for Bairns and Big Folk.* Singing Tree, 1968. The collection is a pioneer effort of the late 19th century to record the natural literature of the children of Scotland; it includes nursery and counting-out rhymes, rhyme games, songs and ballads, anecdotes, and stories.

FOSTER, FLORENCE P., comp. *Literature and the Young Child.* N.J. Dept. of Education, 1967. Criteria for selecting books for young children, techniques for reading aloud and storytelling, and suggestions for ways of stimulating continuing interest.

FRANK, JOSETTE. *Your Child's Reading Today,* rev. and updated. Doubleday, 1969. Sensible advice from a pioneer in the child study movement concerning a child's reading, given from the standpoint of the child's social-emotional development. Don't deprecate children's tastes, she advises, but capitalize on reading enjoyment.

FRANKENBERG, LLOYD. *Pleasure Dome: On Reading Modern Poetry.* Houghton, 1949, 1968. In his Foreword the author says, "I hope to provide a bridge to modern poetry for readers like myself, brought up on prose."

FRAZER, SIR JAMES GEORGE. *The Golden Bough; A Study in Magic and Religion,* 1 vol. abr. ed. Macmillan, 1922. First published in 1890, this is a monumental study (originally 13 volumes) in comparative folklore, magic, and religion.

FREEMAN, LA VERNE, and RUTH SUNDERLIN FREEMAN. *The Child and His Picture Book,* ill. Century House, 1967. A reissue of a pioneer study, updated with particular attention to methods for using picture books to help underprivileged preschoolers and kindergartners get a head start toward successful school adjustment.

FRIEDMAN, ALBERT B. *The Viking Book of Folk Ballads of the English Speaking World.* Viking, 1956. Contains many ballads, with useful notes.

FRYATT, NORMA R., ed. *A Horn Book Sampler.* Horn Book, 1959. Selected articles on authors, artists, and books that appeared in *The Horn Book Magazine* between 1924 and 1948 provide illuminating background to some of the most significant years in children's book publication.

FRYE, BURTON C., ed. *A St. Nicholas Anthology; The Early Years,* ill. Meredith. 1969. A selection from the years 1870 to 1905 of stories, articles, and poems, as well as illustrations which appeared in this most beloved of all children's magazines.

FULLER, MURIEL, ed. *More Junior Authors.* Wilson, 1963. Companion volume to *The Junior Book of Authors,* 1951, rev. ed. Contains biographical material on current juvenile authors and illustrators not included in that work. See Kunitz and Haycraft.

Funk and Wagnalls Standard Dictionary of Folklore, Mythology and Legend, ed. by Maria Leach and Jerome Fried, 2 vols. Funk, 1949. Working with a staff of internationally known folklorists and anthropologists, the editors have compiled an invaluable source on national folklores, characters, and symbols in folklore and mythology.

GERSONI-STAVN, DIANE, ed. *Sexism and Youth.* Bowker, 1974. An anthology of fifty previously published articles.

GESELL, ARNOLD, and FRANCES ILG. *Child Development; An Introduction to the Study of Human Growth.* Harper, 1949. This research study considers child growth in its broadest sense—intellectual, emotional, and social—from infancy through adolescence. Lucid style and revealing case histories make this a readable and essential book for parents and teachers.

GESELL, ARNOLD, and others. *The First Five Years of Life; A Guide to the Study of the Preschool Child.* Harper, 1940. Discusses the nature of mental growth, developmental changes, and such facets of growth as language development and personal-social behavior.

GILLESPIE, MARGARET C. *Literature for Children: History and Trends.* Brown, 1970. Covering time from the 15th century to the present, the book has chapters on fantasy, poetry, realism (catechisms, religion, manners, primers, etc.), and landmarks of publishing, with selected references and index. For elementary teachers.

GLASSER, WILLIAM. *Schools Without Failure.* Harper, 1969. This book presents suggestions for making "involvement, relevance, and thinking realities in our schools . . . combined into a total program they can provide a foundation upon which to build the schools our children need."

GODDEN, RUMER. *Hans Christian Andersen: A Great Life in Brief.* Knopf, 1955. "Life itself is the most wonderful fairy tale." So wrote Andersen, and no one could have told his fairy tale more poignantly than Rumer Godden, the English novelist.

GOODRIDGE, JANET. *Creative Drama and Improvised Movement for Children.* Plays, 1971. Practical techniques, tested in schools and studios, for teaching creative drama and correlating it with other school subjects, such as English, physical education, music, and art.

GOTTLIEB, GERALD. *Early Children's Books and Their Illustration.* Godine, 1975. Witty and erudite commentary accompanies beautiful reproductions of books in the collection of the Pierpont Morgan Library.

GREEN, PERCY B. *A History of Nursery Rhymes.* Singing Tree, 1968. Detailed explanations of children's games, potentially useful to kindergarten and nursery school teachers as well as parents.

GREEN, PETER. *Kenneth Grahame,* ill. with photos. World, 1959. This very welcome biography is authoritatively and perceptively written.

GREEN, ROGER LANCELYN. *Tellers of Tales,* enl. ed. E. Ward, 1953; reissued, Watts, 1965. This is a delightfully written discussion of English authors of children's books. Only twenty pages are devoted to modern writers.

GRIMM, JACOB and WILHELM. *Grimm's Fairy Tales,* tr. by Margaret Hunt, rev. by James Stern, ill. by Josef Scharl. Pantheon, 1944. The "Introduction" by Padraic Colum and "Folkloristic Commentary" by Joseph Campbell are important contributions.

GUERBER, HELENE A. *Myths of Greece and Rome.* American Bk., 1893; reissued, British Book Center, 1963. A standard reference, retelling and reinterpreting the myths.

GULLAN, MARJORIE. *The Speech Choir.* Harper, 1937. This is one of the most useful of all Gullan's books because it is both an anthology and a methods text. It contains American poetry as well as English ballads, with a detailed description of the presentation and development of each poem. Most of the poems are for upper-grade children and the high schools.

HALES, JOHN W., and FREDERICK J. FURNIVALL, assisted by FRANCIS J. CHILD. *Bishop Percy's Folio Manuscript.* London: Trübner, 1967. Here are the ballads that Bishop Percy found, together with the reproduction of an actual page of the manuscript with Percy's notes scribbled in the margin.

HALLIWELL-PHILLIPPS, JAMES O. *Popular Rhymes and Nursery Tales: A Sequel to the Nursery Rhymes of England.* Singing Tree, 1968. This mid-nineteenth-century book is a collection of material of interest to folklorists as well as teachers and librarians.

HALSEY, ROSALIE V. *Forgotten Books of the American Nursery; A History of the Development of the American Story-Book.* Singing Tree, 1969. A reissue of a book first published at the turn of the century, this volume traces the history of children's books in America from colonial days to the early part of the nineteenth century, with emphasis on the light children's books shed on the social history of the country.

HASKINS, JAMES. *Diary of a Harlem Schoolteacher.* Grove, 1969. A year's notes kept by a black teacher and author show starkly the educational deficiencies and social problems that affect Harlem children's learning.

HAVILAND, VIRGINIA. *Children's Literature: A Guide to Reference Sources,* ill. Library of Congress, 1966. The only reference tool of its kind in scope and coverage, this book offers bibliographic guidance to books available today and to the history of children's literature. First supplement, 1972.

HAVILAND, VIRGINIA, and MARGARET COUGHLAN, comps. *Yankee Doodle's Literary Sampler of Prose, Poetry, & Pictures.* T. Crowell, 1974. A sampling of writing and illustration drawn from the collection of the Library of Congress.

HAZARD, PAUL. *Books, Children and Men,* tr. by Marguerite Mitchell, 4th ed. Horn Book, 1960. A member of the French Academy and professor of comparative literature both in France and in the United States has written engagingly of the great children's books of many countries.

HELMS, RANDALL. *Tolkien's World.* Houghton, 1974. A discussion of the relevance of Tolkien's writings as mythic literature.

HENTOFF, NAT. *Our Children Are Dying,* and JOHN McPHEE. *The Headmaster.* Four Winds, 1967. Two accounts of the problems and challenges of educators, one set in a public school in Harlem, the other in a private boys' boarding school.

HERNDON, JAMES. *The Way It Spozed to Be; A Report on the Crisis in Our Schools.* Bantam, 1969. An innovative teacher in a slum school reports on war in the classroom. Penetrating and wryly humorous.

HEWINS, CAROLINE M. *A Mid-Century Child and Her Books.* Singing Tree, 1969. The autobiography of a pioneer children's librarian who was also the author of many books on children's literature, this book provides a detailed picture of what life was like for a book-loving child in New England in the mid-nineteenth century.

HIGGINS, JAMES E. *Beyond Words; Mystical Fancy in Children's Literature.* Teachers College Pr., 1970. The author discusses the importance of mystical fantasy in the development of the child and its significance as a literary form, with special detailed analysis of the work of such great authors as George Macdonald, W. H. Hudson, Saint-Exupéry, Tolkien, and C. S. Lewis.

HILDICK, WALLACE. *Children and Fiction.* World, 1971.

A critical study of the artistic and psychological factors involved in writing fiction for and about children, suggesting the application of high standards in examining children's literature both from the literary and the sociological point of view.

HILLYER, ROBERT. *In Pursuit of Poetry.* McGraw, 1960. A distinguished poet and winner of the Pulitzer Prize, Hillyer has written an entrancing introduction to the appreciation of poetry, old and modern, with unforgettable examples from some of the finest English poetry.

HODGART, M. J. C. *The Ballads.* Hutchinson's Universal Library, 1950. Useful general discussion of the traditional ballads, stressing the literary approach.

HOFFMAN, MIRIAM, and EVA SAMUELS, eds. *Authors and Illustrators of Children's Books; Writings on Their Lives and Works.* Bowker, 1972. A compilation of articles from magazines gives more depth than many of the briefer entries in other sources, although the coverage is not as broad.

HOLT, JOHN. *How Children Fail.* Pitman, 1964. An important book, based on records of classroom experience, dealing with the ways children meet or dodge the demands adults make on them, the interaction between fear and failure, the difference between what children are expected to know and what they really know, and finally how the schools fail to meet the real needs of children.

———. *How Children Learn.* Pitman, 1967. This book, written in journal form about the reactions of various children in games, experiments, reading, talking, and being involved in arts and math, throws light on using their minds effectively and on the relationship between encouragement and progress in learning.

———. *What Do I Do Monday?* Dutton, 1970. A school teacher's innovative observations on modern education and theories of the learning process, supported by ideas, exercises, and examples in several subjects.

HOMER. *The Odyssey,* tr. by George H. Palmer, ill. by N. C. Wyeth. Houghton, 1929. This cadenced prose will sing in your memory like poetry. For children who are superior readers, this edition illustrated by Wyeth is a superb source for these tales.

HOPKINS, LEE BENNETT. *Books Are by People,* ill. Citation, 1969. Human interest interviews with 104 writers and illustrators for children, to be used with children to make their authors "come alive."

———. *Let Them Be Themselves.* Citation, 1969. Recommendations for enriching the language arts curriculum for all children, but especially the disadvantaged.

———. *More Books by More People.* Citation, 1974. Interviews with 65 children's authors give information about the author's work and his or her personal life.

HUBER, MIRIAM BLANTON. *Story and Verse for Children,* ill. Macmillan, 1965. With introductory chapters on the selection and history of children's books, followed by an anthology of poetry and prose, this book is intended primarily for teachers, librarians, and parents.

HUCK, CHARLOTTE S. *Children's Literature in the Elementary School,* 3rd ed., ill. Holt, 1976. A reorganized and updated revision of a well-known textbook.

HUDSON, DEREK. *Arthur Rackham; His Life and Work.* London: Heinemann, 1960, 1974. A biography that includes perceptive analysis of Rackham's art, with a fully annotated bibliography.

HUGHES, TED. *Poetry Is.* Doubleday, 1970. Based on a series of BBC talks, a discussion of poetry intended for young writers, but interesting for poetry readers as well.

HURLIMANN, BETTINA. *Picture-Book World,* ed. and tr. by Brian Alderson, ill. World, 1969. Modern picture books for children from 24 countries, with introductory chapters on particular countries and with a bio-bibliographical supplement.

———. *Three Centuries of Children's Books in Europe,* ed. and tr. by Brian Alderson, ill. World, 1968. A comparative study as well as a history which includes a survey of contemporary books for children in all of the countries of Europe.

HUTT, S. J., and CORINNE HUTT, eds. *Early Human Development.* Oxford, 1973. A collection of studies on various aspects of early human behavior.

HYMES, JAMES LEE. *Understanding Your Child.* Prentice, 1952. This is a practical and entertaining discussion of child behavior and parent-child conflicts. It is built around these four major considerations: children grow, there is a plan to their growth, they want things out of life, and there is a reason for their behavior.

ILG, FRANCES L., and LOUISE BATES AMES. *Child Behavior.* Harper, 1955. Frances Ilg, M.D., and Louise Ames, Ph.D., give direct advice, based on their research at the Gesell Institute, to parents concerning problems of child behavior.

Insights: A Selection of Creative Literature About Childhood. Child Study Assoc. of America. Aronson, 1974. Excerpts and short stories about aspects of childhood.

IRELAND, NORMA. *Index to Fairy Tales, 1949–1972: Including Folklore, Legends and Myths in Collections.* Faxon, 1973. A supplement to the Eastman indexes, which indexed fairy tales through 1948. A useful addition, this indexes material in collections, not single tales.

ISAACS, J. *The Background of Modern Poetry.* Dutton, 1952. Scholarly first aid to adults who find modern poetry hard to take.

Issues in Children's Books Selection; An Anthology of Articles from School Library Journal/Library Journal. Bowker, 1973. A broad array of provocative writings on many aspects of book selection.

JACOBS, JOSEPH. See listings of his collections of English, Celtic, and Indian folk tales in the Chapter 6 bibliography. They contain significant introductions, and the notes in each appendix are treasures of folklore information.

JACOBS, LELAND B., ed. *Using Literature with Young Children.* Teachers College Pr., 1965. A collection of papers on providing good literature for young children, storytelling, reading aloud, poetry, choral speaking, dramatization, and relating literature to other school experiences.

JENKINS, GLADYS GARDNER. *Helping Children Reach Their Potential.* Scott, Foresman, 1961. Describes how teachers have handled the particular emotional needs and problems of their pupils.

JENKINS, GLADYS GARDNER, HELEN S. SHACTER, and WILLIAM W. BAUER. *These Are Your Children,* 4th ed. Scott, Foresman, 1975. A series of case studies with charts of normal child development and the special needs of children at various ages, enlivened by photographs of children in problem situations or normal activities.

JOHNSON, EDNA, EVELYN SICKELS, and FRANCES

CLARKE SAYERS. *Anthology of Children's Literature,* 4th ed. Houghton, 1970. The editors in this latest edition have attempted to hold to the long view, choosing from the present that which gives promise of lasting value and fitting it into the interstices of the proven past.

JORDAN, ALICE M. *From Rollo to Tom Sawyer.* Horn Book, 1948. Here in beautiful format with decorations by Nora Unwin are 12 little essays on some of the most important nineteenth-century writers for children.

JOSEPH, STEPHEN M., ed. *The Me Nobody Knows; Children's Voices from the Ghetto.* Avon, 1969. Moving and revealing writing by children, mostly black and Puerto Rican, in the most impoverished city neighborhoods.

KAMM, ANTONY, and BOSWELL TAYLOR. *Books and the Teacher.* Univ. of London Pr., 1966. A handbook on the choice, requisition, and use of books. References are to British authors and publishers, and organizations listed are also exclusively British.

KARL, JEAN. *From Childhood to Childhood: Children's Books and Their Creators.* Day, 1970. An editor's views on children's books.

KELLOGG, RHODA, and SCOTT O'DELL. *The Psychology of Children's Art,* ill. Random, 1967. Selected examples from a collection of over a million pieces of children's art, accompanied by text explaining the developmental phases common to all children.

KIEFER, MONICA. *American Children Through Their Books, 1700–1835.* Univ of Pa. Pr., 1948, 1970. The American child at the beginning of the 18th century was too insignificant for physicians to waste time on, the author tells us. She traces the child's developing place in the world through an examination of children's books.

KINGMAN, LEE, ed. *Newbery and Caldecott Medal Books: 1956–1965.* Horn Book, 1965. A biographical sketch of each author or illustrator, along with his or her acceptance paper and related material from *The Horn Book.*

______, ed. *Newbery and Caldecott Medal Books 1966–1975.* Horn Book, 1975. A companion volume to others in the series of acceptance speeches and articles taken from the magazine.

KINGMAN, LEE, JOANNA FOSTER, and RUTH GILES LONTOFT, comps. *Illustrators of Children's Books, 1957–1966,* ill. Horn Book, 1968. This volume, a supplement to *Illustrators of Children's Books, 1744–1945,* and *Illustrators of Children's Books, 1946–1956,* reviews the decade, offers biographies of active illustrators and a bibliography of their works.

KINGSTON, CAROLYN. *The Tragic Mode in Children's Literature.* Teachers College Pr., 1974. Discusses tragedy in realistic fiction for ages 8–12, using books published before 1970.

KIRK, GEOFFREY S. *Myth.* Univ. of Calif. Pr., 1970. Discusses the function of myth in various cultures.

KITTREDGE, GEORGE LYMAN, ed. *English and Scottish Popular Ballads: Student's Cambridge Edition,* ed. by Helen Child Sargeant. Houghton, 1904. This is the invaluable one-volume edition of the Child collection. It contains the 305 ballads, a few variants of each, brief notes, and the excellent glossary giving the definitions and pronunciations of the difficult ballad words.

KLEMIN, DIANA. *The Art of Art for Children's Books,* ill. Potter, 1966. Examples and commentary on the work of 64 illustrators of children's books.

______. *The Illustrated Book: Its Art and Craft,* ill. Potter, 1970. A contemporary survey with examples and commentary on the work of 74 artists. A chapter on drawing for reproduction is included, which clarifies the process involved in printing.

KOCH, KENNETH. *Wishes, Lies, and Dreams; Teaching Children to Write Poetry,* ill. with photos. Random, 1971. Working with the children of P.S. 61 in New York City, the author, himself an outstanding poet, has developed ways of getting children to release their ideas and feelings into writing. The book is a collection of their poetry preceded and accompanied by his description of his teaching methods.

KOHL, HERBERT R. *The Open Classroom: A Practical Guide to a New Way of Teaching.* New York Review, 1969. Primarily addressed to public school teachers, this book is a "handbook for teachers who want to work in an open environment. . . . [and] is based upon the experience of teachers: their problems, failures, and frustrations, as well as their successes."

______. *Teaching the Unteachable; The Story of an Experiment in Children's Writing.* New York Review, 1967. An innovative approach to teaching in East Harlem, illustrated by examples of the children's writing.

______. *36 Children,* ill. by Robert George Jackson. New Am. Lib., 1967. The author's experiences in a sixth-grade Harlem classroom demonstrate the progress that children can make when a good teacher meets their needs.

KOZOL, JONATHAN. *Death at an Early Age; The Destruction of the Hearts and Minds of Negro Children in the Boston Public Schools.* Houghton, 1967. Serving as a substitute in a ghetto school, the author found the segregated schools rife with prejudice, with black children condemned by brutality, hostility, neglect, and wholly inadequate provisions for physical needs. A bitter indictment.

KRAPPE, ALEXANDER HAGGERTY. *The Science of Folk-Lore.* Dial, 1930. This book covers various types of folk literature, evaluates theories of origin and content, and analyzes motives. Chapter IX, "The Popular Ballad," discusses the ballad as part of the great stream of folklore, related to the epic, the carol, and the folk tale, migrating even as they have.

KREIDER, BARBARA. *Children's Plays in Collections.* Scarecrow, 1972. An interalphabetized author, title, and subject listing. Plays are also listed by cast size; no listings are annotated.

KUJOTH, JEAN SPEALMAN. *Reading Interests of Children and Young Adults.* Scarecrow, 1970. A collection of research findings and observations by teachers, authors, and librarians on reading interests and how they are influenced. Divided by age groups.

KUNITZ, STANLEY J., and HOWARD HAYCRAFT, eds. *The Junior Book of Authors,* 2nd ed. Wilson, 1951. Biographical sketches of outstanding authors and illustrators of books for children.

LANDECK, BEATRICE. *Learn to Read; Read to Learn; Poetry and Prose from Afro-Rooted Sources.* McKay, 1975. Suggestions for broadening and enriching the approach to teaching reading, writing, and speech in the elementary school.

LANE, MARGARET. *The Tale of Beatrix Potter; A Biography,* ill. Warne, 1968. Revised and updated, with new material from the secret code journals of Beatrix Potter.

LANES, SELMA G. *Down the Rabbit Hole; Adventures*

and Misadventures in the Realm of Children's Literature, ill. Atheneum, 1971. A series of essays, by an editor of children's books, exploring the literary and artistic merits of a particular selection of books. A small bibliography of choice books is appended.

LANG, ANDREW, ed. *Perrault's Popular Tales.* London: Clarendon, 1888. A careful study of Perrault and the tales he edited.

LARRICK, NANCY. *A Parent's Guide to Children's Reading,* rev. and enl. 4th ed., ill. Doubleday, 1975. Sponsored by the National Book Committee, this is a comprehensive handbook for parents' use in developing reading interests from infancy on.

______. *A Teacher's Guide to Children's Books,* ill. Merrill, 1960. How to stimulate and develop reading interests in the elementary grades, accompanied by extensive bibliographies for the child and the teacher.

______, ed. *Somebody Turned on a Tap in These Kids.* Delacorte, 1971. A lively collection of articles on changing the attitudes and expectations of young people toward poetry, with liberal examples of what they like and what they write themselves.

LEACH, MacEDWARD. *Folk Ballads and Songs of the Lower Labrador Coast.* Ottawa: Queen's Printer and Controller of Stationery, 1965.

______, ed. *The Ballad Book.* Harper, 1955. Gives about 250 ballads, many in several variants. The major section is "Ballads of England and Scotland with American and Danish Variants." "American Ballads by Origin and Adoption" contains 45 ballads. The headnotes to each ballad are useful and a general introduction gives a brief survey of ballad scholarship.

LENNON, FLORENCE BECKER. *Victoria Through the Looking-Glass.* Simon, 1945; reissued as *The Life of Lewis Carroll,* Collier Books, 1962, paperback. A fine biography of Lewis Carroll.

LENSKI, LOIS. *Adventure in Understanding; Talks to Parents, Teachers and Librarians by Lois Lenski, 1944–1966,* with decorations by the author. Tallahassee, 1968. The author's ideas concerning books and literature in general, young people, the state of the world, and particularly her own ideas on writing books for children.

LEPMAN, JELLA. *A Bridge of Children's Books,* tr. by Edith McCormick. ALA, 1969. Fascinating autobiographical account of bringing books of all nations to the children of postwar Germany to replace their Nazi-oriented literature.

LEWIS, C. S. *Of Other Worlds: Essays and Stories,* ed. by Walter Hooper. Harcourt, 1966. A posthumous collection which includes essays on fantasy and science fiction, three unpublished short stories, and the first chapters of a novel.

LIEBERT, ROBERT, JOHN NEALE, and EMILY DAVIDSON. *The Early Window; Effects of Television on Children and Youth.* Pergamon, 1973. A survey of studies done on content of programs and their effects on children.

LINDSTROM, MIRIAM. *Children's Art; A Study of Normal Development in Children's Modes of Visualization,* ill. Univ. of Calif. Pr., 1970. Illustrated study of stages of development in expression of visual imagery.

LINES, KATHLEEN, ed. *Walck Monographs.* Walck. Personal anecdotes and a pleasing style make these brief biographies and critical evaluations of internationally known authors invaluable to the teacher or student of children's literature. The series includes:

Louisa M. Alcott, Cornelia Meigs
J. M. Barrie, Roger Lancelyn Green
Lucy Boston, Jasper Rose
Lewis Carroll, Roger Lancelyn Green
Walter de la Mare, Leonard Clark
Eleanor Farjeon, Eileen H. Colwell
Kenneth Grahame, Eleanor Graham
Rudyard Kipling, Rosemary Sutcliff
Andrew Lang, Roger Lancelyn Green
C. S. Lewis, Roger Lancelyn Green
John Masefield, Margery Fisher
Mrs. Molesworth, Roger Lancelyn Green
Beatrix Potter, Marcus Crouch
Howard Pyle, Elizabeth Nesbitt
Arthur Ransome, Hugh Shelley
Ruth Sawyer, Virginia Haviland
Noel Streatfeild, Barbara Ker Wilson
Rosemary Sutcliff, Margaret Meek
Geoffrey Trease, Margaret Meek

LIVINGSTON, MYRA COHN. *When You Are Alone/It Keeps You Capone; An Approach to Creative Writing with Children.* Atheneum, 1973. An insightful discussion by a well-known children's poet.

LOMAX, JOHN A., ed. *Songs of the Cattle Trail and Cow Camp.* Duell, 1950.

LOMAX, JOHN A., and ALAN LOMAX, comps. *American Ballads and Folk Songs.* Macmillan, 1946.

______, eds. *Cowboy Songs and Other Frontier Ballads,* rev. and enl. Macmillan, 1948. The Lomax collections of our native ballads are of major importance as sources, not only because they were the first ones made, but also because they were gathered first-hand and the tunes were recorded on wax cylinders, on the spot, unedited.

LOWNDES, BETTY. *Movement and Creative Drama for Children.* Plays, 1971. A description of the movement and drama work carried on in an infants' school in North London with an emphasis on how both can be used to get children to communicate and to learn with enjoyment.

LUKENS, REBECCA. *A Critical Handbook of Children's Literature.* Scott, Foresman, 1976. A discussion of the criteria for, and elements of, imaginative literature for children.

LURIE, ALISON, and JUSTIN SCHILLER, eds. "Classics of Children's Literature 1621–1932," Garland. A series of photo-facsimile editions of hard-to-find books. The 117 titles include books by Bunyan, Edgeworth, Grahame, Goodrich, Lang, Molesworth, and others.

MacCANN, DONNARAE, and OLGA RICHARD. *The Child's First Books.* Wilson, 1973. A discussion of the role of picture books in the history of children's literature.

MacCANN, DONNARAE, and GLORIA WOODWARD, eds. *The Black American in Books for Children: Readings in Racism.* Scarecrow, 1972. A broad selection of brief essays, with notes on contributors.

McGUFFEY, WILLIAM HOLMES. *Old Favorites from the McGuffey Readers,* ed. by Harvey C. Minnich. Singing Tree, 1969. Selections from all six of the readers are of special interest to students of educational and social history.

MacLEOD, ANNE SCOTT. *A Moral Tale; Children's Fiction and American Culture 1820–1860.* Archon, 1975. Explores the concepts and the concerns of a period of rapid change as reflected in the stories for children, especially what adults expected of children and what they wanted for them.

MAHONY, BERTHA E., and ELINOR WHITNEY FIELD. eds. *Newbery Medal Books, 1922–1955.* Horn Book, 1955. Here in one handsome volume are brief biographies of Newbery authors along with their acceptance speeches. See also supplementary volumes by Kingman.

MAHONY, BERTHA E., LOUISE P. LATIMER and BEULAH FOLMSBEE, comps. *Illustrators of Children's Books, 1744–1945.* Horn Book, 1947. A superb history of illustration in children's books considered as a part of the whole stream of art. Many pictures are reproduced from early books as well as from more recent ones. A major reference. See also supplementary volumes by Viguers and others and by Kingman and others.

MAIER, HENRY W. *Three Theories of Child Development: The Contributions of Erik H. Erikson, Jean Piaget and Robert R. Sears, and Their Applications,* rev. ed. Harper, 1969. The expanded psychoanalytic theory of Erikson, Piaget's theory of Erikson, Piaget's theories on the development of behavior, and those of Robert Sears are explicated and compared, and the last two chapters deal with how they can be used in working with children. A useful bibliography is appended.

MATHEWS, MITFORD M. *Teaching to Read; Historically Considered.* Univ. of Chicago Pr., 1966. Survey of methods of teaching reading and the theories behind them.

MAYERSON, CHARLOTTE LEON, ed. *Two Blocks Apart; Juan Gonzales and Peter Quinn,* ill. with photos by the Still Photography Workshop Harlem Youth Unlimited. Holt, 1965. Biographies, from tapes, of two boys in New York, living in the same neighborhood, going to the same school, sharing the same religion, one white middle class, the other Puerto Rican, members of two cultures separated by social and economic conditions.

MEEKER, ALICE M. *Enjoying Literature with Children.* Odyssey, 1969. A book for parents and teachers, with annotated bibliographies for the preschool years, for the culturally deprived, storytelling, poetry, choral speaking, holidays, and teachers' browsing. Though short, the book is full of practical suggestions for helping children enjoy books.

MEIGS, CORNELIA, ANNE EATON, ELIZABETH NESBITT, and RUTH HILL VIGUERS. *A Critical History of Children's Literature,* rev. ed. Macmillan, 1969. Three librarians and an author of children's books have surveyed the field from ancient to recent times. The evaluations of books, authors, illustrators, and trends make this a valuable reference.

MILLAR, SUSANNA. *The Psychology of Play.* Penguin, 1968. Chapter V, "Phantasy, Feeling, and Make-Believe Play."

MILLER, BERTHA MAHONY, and ELINOR WHITNEY FIELD, eds. *Caldecott Medal Books: 1938–1957.* Horn Book, 1957. Stories of artists who have won awards for the most distinguished picture book of each year, together with their acceptance speeches. An invaluable source for schools and libraries. See also supplementary volume by Kingman.

MOE, CHRISTIAN, and DARWIN REID PAYNE, eds. *Six New Plays for Children.* Southern Ill. Pr., 1971. This is an interesting collection of new plays for child audiences.

MONTGOMERIE, NORAH. *To Read and to Tell,* ill. by Margery Gill. Arco Pub. Co., 1964. Fairy stories, folk tales, fables, and legends from many lands.

MOORE, ANNE CARROLL. *A Century of Kate Greenaway.* Warne, 1946. An appreciation of the artist and her distinctive contribution.

______. *My Roads to Childhood.* Doubleday, 1939. A distinguished librarian and critic of children's books comments on outstanding books up to the year 1938.

MOORE, VARDINE. *Pre-School Story Hour,* 2nd ed. Scarecrow, 1972. A discussion of the techniques, programming, and physical arrangements for the story hour, and a chapter on the needs and characteristics of the preschool child is followed by a subject-oriented bibliography and a chapter on games and rhythmic play.

MORRIS, RONALD. *Success and Failure in Learning to Read,* rev. ed. Penguin, 1973. Various aspects of the reading process are examined. Introduction and appendixes are valuable commentaries in themselves.

MUIR, PERCY. *English Children's Books, 1600 to 1900.* Praeger, 1954, 1969. Muir acknowledges his indebtedness to the books of Darton and the Opies, but his work adds to both. There are excellent indexes and lavish illustrations from the books discussed.

MUNCH, PETER A. *Norse Mythology, Legends of Gods and Heroes,* rev. by Magnus Olsen, tr. by Sigurd B. Hustvedt. American-Scandinavian Foundation, 1926; reissued, Singing Tree, 1968. Authoritative and complete interpretation of sources.

MYRUS, DONALD. *Ballads, Blues, and the Big Beat.* Macmillan, 1966. A survey of the singers and the songs of today, with separate chapters on musical genres.

NICHOLSEN, MARGARET. *People in Books: A Selective Guide to Biographical Literature Arranged by Vocations and Other Fields of Reader Interest.* Wilson, 1969. Appended: an index by century and by country; an index to autobiographical books; and an index of persons about whom a book or part of a collective biography is included in the main section.

Once upon a Time . . ., rev. ed. New York Library Assoc., 1964. Help for librarians with preschool hours, picture-book hours, and story hours. Suggested programs and bibliographies are included.

OPIE, IONA and PETER. *Children's Games in Street and Playground.* Oxford, 1969. This record of the games children play draws its authority from more than 10,000 children in England, Scotland, and Wales.

______. *The Lore and Language of Schoolchildren.* Oxford, 1959; Oxford paperbacks, 1967. "The curious lore passing between children about 6–14, which today holds in its spell some 7 million inhabitants" of Great Britain includes rhymes, riddles, childhood customs, and beliefs. Some can be traced back for generations and others are current. "The present study is based on the contributions of some 5000 children attending 70 schools."

______, comps. *A Family Book of Nursery Rhymes,* ill. by Pauline Baynes. Oxford, 1964. In addition to the rhymes, this contains excellent notes on origins.

______, eds. *The Oxford Dictionary of Nursery Rhymes.* Oxford, 1951. This is the most exhaustive and scholarly study yet made of the origins of the nursery rhymes, their earliest recordings, and variations through the years. Copious illustrations from old plates add to its real interest.

The Original Mother Goose's Melody, As First Issued by John Newbery, of London, about A.D. 1760. Reproduced in Facsimile from the Edition as Reprinted by Isaiah Thomas of Worcester, Mass., about A.D. 1785, with Introductory Notes by William H. Whitmore. Singing Tree, 1969. Whitmore's introductory notes discuss the origin, development, and popularity of the Mother Goose rhymes in this reprint.

OVID. *The Metamorphoses,* tr. by Henry T. Riley. McKay, 1899. A literal prose translation of the Latin versions of the Greek myths and hero tales, with copious notes explaining their fable or allegorical significance.

PERRAULT, CHARLES. *Perrault's Complete Fairy Tales,* tr. by A. E. Johnson and others, ill. by W. Heath Robinson. Dodd, 1961. The unabridged fairy tales of Perrault, together with tales by Mme. de Beaumont and Mme. d'Aulnoy.

PIAGET, JEAN, and BARBEL INHELDER. *The Psychology of the Child,* tr. from the French by Helen Weaver. Basic, 1969. A comprehensive summary of Piaget's child psychology, tracing the stages of cognitive development over the entire period of childhood, from infancy to adolescence.

PILGRIM, GENEVA HANNA, and MARIANNA McALLISTER. *Books, Young People, and Reading Guidance.* Harper, 1968. For use by teachers, librarians, and parents, and also as a college text. Emphasis is chiefly on contemporary books.

PINES, MAYA. *Revolution in Learning: The Years from Birth to Six.* Harper, 1967. A report on the growing number of research projects on increasing intellectual growth in childhood.

PITZ, HENRY C. *Illustrating Children's Books: History, Technique, Production.* Watson-Guptill, 1963. Detailed and authoritative, profusely illustrated, a book that is particularly useful for its lucid explanations of techniques of art reproduction and how the artist prepares his work.

______. *The Practice of American Book Illustration.* Watson-Guptill, 1947.

______, ed. *A Treasury of American Book Illustration.* Watson-Guptill, 1947. A distinguished artist discusses illustration as one of the seven lively arts. With many pictures from modern sources he proves his point. The second volume contains a good chapter on "Pictures for Childhood."

Plays, the Drama Magazine for Young People. Plays, Inc. 8 Arlington Street, Boston, Mass. 02116. This useful magazine is published monthly, October through May. Each issue, in addition to providing plays for lower grades, middle grades, and junior and senior high, always has a special feature—a dramatized classic, a radio play, or material for an assembly.

POUND, LOUISE, ed. *American Ballads and Songs.* Scribner's, 1922, 1969. A good collection of United States remnants of old ballads along with our native compositions. No music. Excellent introduction.

______. *Poetic Origins and the Ballad.* Macmillan, 1921; Russell and Russell, 1961. The author furnishes lively evidence against the communal origin of the ballad, besides adding ballad history.

POWER, EFFIE. *Bag O'Tales; A Source Book for Story-Tellers,* ill. by Corydon Bell. Dutton, 1969. Stories for little children, folk tales, myths, and tales of heroes and chivalry, with good lists of source material for the storyteller at the end of each section.

PURVES, ALAN C., and RICHARD BEACH. *Literature and the Reader: Research in Response to Literature, Reading Interests, and the Teaching of Literature.* Nat. Council of Teachers of English, 1972. Each of the three areas is treated separately, with a discussion of the factors, instruments, and quality of studies that have been made, followed by a very extensive bibliography. The citations for Reading Interests run 34 pages, for example. A most useful survey.

QUAYLE, ERIC. *The Collector's Book of Children's Books,* photos by Gabriel Monro. Potter, 1971. Profusely illustrated with pictures of old books, a history of British and American children's books that is erudite and enthusiastic, emphasizing early books.

QUIMBY, HARRIET, CLARA JACKSON, and ROSEMARY WEBER. *Building a Children's Literature Collection.* Choice, 1975. *Choice* Bibliographic Essay Series, No. 3. This useful paperback consists of two parts: a suggested reference collection for academic libraries, consisting of guides and background reading for a children's literature collection, and a suggested basic collection of children's books.

RANK, OTTO. *The Myth of the Birth of the Hero: A Psychological Interpretation of Mythology,* tr. by F. Robbins and Smith Ely Jellife. Brunner/Mazel, 1952. A classic exposition of the connection between the form of myths and the unconscious emotions of the child. Studies the myths of the birth of the hero from Moses to Lohengrin, interpreting each myth in terms of the Oedipus complex.

READ, HERBERT. *This Way, Delight.* Pantheon, 1956. An excellent anthology, mentioned here because of its unusual introduction in which the author defines poetry and gives practical suggestions for writing it.

RIBNER, IRVING, and HARRY MORRIS. *Poetry: A Critical and Historical Introduction.* Scott, Foresman, 1962. Designed to help the beginning poetry reader read with greater understanding and appreciation.

RICHARD, OLGA. "The Visual Language of the Picture Book." *Wilson Library Bulletin,* December 1969. A discussion of criteria by which to evaluate picture book art.

RICHARDSON, ELWYN. *In The Early World.* Pantheon, 1969. Written by a New Zealand teacher, this is an exploration of the stimulation of activity and creativity, particularly with reference to appreciation of nature and particularly expressed in the children's writing. Good book on teaching; good book on children's expression of appreciation of the world around them.

ROBINSON, EVELYN ROSE. *Readings About Children's Literature.* McKay, 1966. Excerpts from books, magazines, journals, and newspapers providing an understanding of the child as a reader, criteria for book selection, and appropriate materials. Contributors are well-known writers, librarians, and teachers of children's literature.

ROSELLE, DANIEL. *Samuel Griswold Goodrich, Creator of Peter Parley; A Study of His Life and Work,* ill. State Univ. of N.Y., 1968. The Peter Parley books, now largely forgotten, entertained children in the first half of the 19th century with cautionary tales, instructive fables, and reports of strange lands.

ROSENBACH, ABRAHAM S. W. *Early American Children's Books with Bibliographical Descriptions of the Books in His Private Collection,* foreword by A. Edward Newton. Southworth Pr., Portland, Me., 1933; Dover (paperback), 1971. Facsimile pages and illustrations (many in color) of American children's books published between 1732 and 1836. Probably the greatest and most comprehensive book on juvenile Americana.

ROSENBLATT, LOUISE M. *Literature as Exploration,* rev. ed. Noble, 1969. A probing evaluation of the nature of the literary experience.

ST. JOHN, JUDITH. *The Osborne Collection of Early Children's Books 1566–1910; A Catalogue,* introduction by Edgar Osborne. Toronto Public Library, 1958; vol. 2, 1976. Descriptive notes on this world-famous collection, illustrated with many facsimiles. Fascinating background material for scholars and students of children's literature.

SALWAY, LANCE, ed. *A Peculiar Gift.* Penguin, 1976. (Kestrel Books) An anthology of essays on children's literature written by or about authors of the 19th century.

SANDBURG, CARL, ed. *The American Songbag.* Harcourt, 1927. While this collection borrows from others, Sandburg's illuminating notes make it a particularly useful and enjoyable volume.

SANDERS, THOMAS E. *The Discovery of Poetry.* Scott, Foresman, 1967. An introduction to the aesthetics of poetry, this book discusses how poetry is written and how it can be read in the same creative way.

SAWYER, RUTH. *My Spain; A Storyteller's Year of Collecting.* Viking, 1967. Pleasant account of a journey through Spain in search of folk tales.

______. *The Way of the Storyteller.* Viking, 1942, 1962. Informally written in Ruth Sawyer's fine style, this is a contribution both to the art of storytelling and to the history of the old tales.

SAYERS, FRANCES CLARKE. *Summoned by Books; Essays and Speeches by Frances Clarke Sayers,* comp. by Marjeanne Jenson Blinn. Viking, 1965. Essays by an outstanding and influential children's librarian.

SCHWAB, GUSTAV. *Gods and Heroes,* tr. by Olga Marx and Ernst Morwitz, ill. with designs from Greek vases. Pantheon, 1946. This large, handsome book is not comprehensive, and the English translation from a German adaptation is not always satisfactory, but it is an excellent source nevertheless.

SCOTT, JOHN ANTHONY. *The Ballad of America: The History of the United States in Song and Story.* Grosset, 1966. Chronologically arranged, with musical notation and with substantial comment on the background for each selection.

SHARP, CECIL J., comp. *English Folk-Songs from the Southern Appalachians,* ed. by Maud Karpeles, rev. and enl., 2 vols. Oxford, 1953. A major contribution by an English collector and musician.

______. *Nursery Songs from the Appalachian Mountains,* 2 vols. London: Novello, 1921–1923. A collection that should be better known in our schools. Many selections for the youngest children.

SHAW, JOHN MacKAY. *Childhood in Poetry: A Catalogue,* with Biographical and Critical Annotations, of the Books of English and American Poets Comprising the Shaw Childhood in Poetry Collection in the Library of the Florida State University, with Lists of the Poems that Relate to Childhood, 5 vols. Gale 1967. Although the price ($135) of this work makes it inaccessible to many individuals and small libraries, it is a comprehensive bibliographic guide to English-language children's poetry.

SHEDLOCK, MARIE. *Art of the Story-Teller,* 3rd ed., bibl. by Eulalie Steinmetz. Dover, 1951. Guidance in selection of material, techniques of storytelling, and useful bibliographies are included.

SIKS, GERALDINE BRAIN. *Creative Dramatics.* Harper, 1958. Various suggestions for encouraging children to use their imaginations in dramatization.

SILBERMAN, CHARLES E. *Crisis in the Classroom; The Remaking of American Education.* Random, 1970. Addressed to laymen and professionals alike, its four parts include: The Educating Society, What's Wrong with the Schools, How the Schools Should Be Changed, and The Education of Educators. A fascinating account based on a three-and-a-half-year study commissioned by the Carnegie Corporation of New York.

SMITH, DORA V. *Fifty Years of Children's Books,* with an introduction by Muriel Crosby, ill. Nat. Council of Teachers of English, 1963. From Dora Smith's years of experience with children and books, she has selected and discussed significant titles which appeared between 1910 and 1959. Numerous illustrations are reproduced from the original books.

SMITH, IRENE. *A History of the Newbery and Caldecott Medals.* Viking, 1957. Excellent historical background material on two major annual awards for distinguished children's books in the United States.

SMITH, JAMES STEEL. *A Critical Approach to Children's Literature.* McGraw, 1967. A serious, careful analysis of children's books as creative literary works.

SMITH, LILLIAN. *The Unreluctant Years.* ALA, 1953; reissued, Viking, 1967. A Canadian librarian writes discerningly of children's literature from the standpoint of literary quality only.

SMITH, RUTH, ed. *The Tree of Life,* ill. by Boris Artzybasheff. Viking, 1942. A distinguished text for a comparative study of religious ideas. It is a compilation of the "testaments of beauty and faith from many lands." Excerpts from the expressions of religious ideals of the Navaho Indians, the Norse, Hindu, Buddhist, Confucian, and other religions (including the Hebrew and Christian) make up the content of the book, which is for adolescents or for adults to use with older children.

Some British Ballads, ill. by Arthur Rackham. Dodd, 1920. This is a superb edition for home and school.

SPACHE, GEORGE, D. *Parents and the Reading Program.* Garrard, 1965. Suggestions for a program to inform parents on what is involved in teaching pupils to read; a question-and-answer format is used.

STEWART, CHRISTINA. *The Taylors of Ongar: An Analytical Bio-Bibliography.* 2 vols. Garland, 1975. A superb source of information about the works of the prolific family that included Isaac, Jane, and Ann.

STEWIG, JOHN WARREN. *Read to Write: Using Children's Literature as a Springboard to Writing.* Hawthorn, 1975. A description of a writing program designed to help children improve their ability by becoming conscious of the nature of the writing process.

STIRLING, MONICA. *The Wild Swan; The Life and Times of Hans Christian Andersen.* Harcourt, 1965. Thoroughly documented, a serious and mature study of Andersen's life and work.

STIRLING, NORA. *Who Wrote the Classics?* 2 vols., ill. Day, 1965, 1968. Short biographies of nineteen English and American writers.

STRICKLAND, RUTH G. *The Language Arts in the Elementary School,* 3rd ed., ill. Heath, 1969. Comprehensive treatment of all aspects of language development with three chapters on reading.

TARG, WILLIAM, ed. *Bibliophile in the Nursery.* World, 1969. Articles by scholars, collectors, and authors have been combined into a delightful whole, highlighting developments in children's literature and the joys of collecting. Lavishly illustrated.

TATLOCK, JESSIE M. *Greek and Roman Mythology.*

Appleton, 1917. Although intended for high-school study, this is a useful book for teachers. Tatlock retells the myths, gives excerpts from the "Homeric Hymn" and modern poetry, and presents some fine photographs of Greek sculpture.

Teaching Literature in Wisconsin. Wisconsin English Language Arts Curriculum Project. State of Wisconsin Department of Public Instruction, 1965. (Madison) A carefully developed approach to a literature curriculum for kindergarten through grade twelve.

Teaching Reading Through Children's Literature: Proceedings of the 1971 First Annual Reading Conference, June 21–22. Curriculum Research and Developmental Center, School of Education, Indiana State University, Terre Haute. Articles include "Role Playing in Children's Literature and Its Effect Upon the Affective Domain of Children's Thinking," "Teaching Reading Through the Use of Films and Children's Literature," and "Reading the Pictures in Children's Books."

TERRY, ANN. *Children's Poetry Preferences: A National Survey of Upper Elementary Grades.* Nat. Council of Teachers of English, 1974. Results of a survey in which students in over 500 classes participated.

THOMAS, KATHERINE ELWES. *The Real Personages of Mother Goose.* Lothrop, 1930. Scholarly research into the historical origins of the Mother Goose rhymes as political diatribes, religious philippics, and popular street songs.

THOMAS, R. MURRAY, and SHERWIN G. SWARTOUT. *Integrated Teaching Materials,* rev. ed. McKay, 1963. Designed to help teachers improve their skills in choosing, creating, and using audiovisual teaching materials, including reading sources, this book also presents specific classroom illustrations—both verbal and photographic—which add to its practicality.

THOMISON, DENNIS. *Readings About Adolescent Literature.* Scarecrow, 1970. A collection of 25 articles from professional journals.

THOMPSON, STITH. *The Folktale.* Dryden, 1946. A standard work in the field discusses the nature and forms of folk tales, traces their spread, analyzes types, describes the North American Indian folk tale in detail, and examines studies of folk tales.

______, comp. *One Hundred Favorite Folktales.* Indiana Univ. Pr., 1968. Tales chosen by a famous folklorist "as the result of more than a half century of almost daily familiarity with these tales." (p. xi)

THWAITE, MARY. *From Primer to Pleasure in Reading,* 2nd ed. London: The Library Assoc., 1972. A history of English children's books from the invention of printing to 1914, with some material on developments in other countries.

TOOZE, RUTH. *Storytelling.* Prentice, 1959. Extensive bibliographies add to the value of this helpful guide for storytellers.

TOWNSEND, JOHN ROWE. *A Sense of Story.* Longmans, 1971. An analysis of the work of 19 writers of children's books, American, British, and Australian, with some notes by the authors on their own writing, and short biographical notes.

______. *Written for Children: An Outline of English Children's Literature,* rev. ed., ill. Lothrop, 1974. A short, selective survey of prose for British children from its beginnings to today.

TRAVERS, PAMELA L. *About the Sleeping Beauty.* McGraw, 1975. Six versions of the story are accompanied by an essay in which it is analyzed as a part of a discussion of fairy tales.

TREASE, GEOFFREY. *Tales Out of School: A Survey of Children's Fiction,* 2nd ed. Dufour, 1964. A highly personal, entertaining, critical survey of juvenile fiction.

TUER, ANDREW W. *Pages and Pictures from Forgotten Children's Books; Brought Together and Introduced to the Reader,* ill. Singing Tree, 1969. The introduction offers a description of the various methods used to illustrate children's books published in England in the 18th and 19th centuries: wood blocks, copper plates, and stone lithographs.

______. *Stories from Old-Fashioned Children's Books; Brought Together and Introduced to the Reader.* Singing Tree, 1968. A collection of old children's stories, by a nineteenth-century publisher.

VANCE, LUCILLE, and ESTHER TRACEY. *Illustration Index,* 2nd ed. Scarecrow, 1966. A topical index to illustrations in periodicals such as *Life, National Geographic,* and *American Heritage,* ranging from abacus to Zurich.

VIGUERS, RUTH HILL. *Margin for Surprise; About Books, Children, and Librarians.* Little, 1964. Essays by a dedicated and enthusiastic children's librarian.

VIGUERS, RUTH HILL, MARCIA DALPHIN, and BERTHA MAHONY MILLER, comps. *Illustrators of Children's Books, 1946–1956.* Horn Book, 1958. An outstanding supplement to *Illustrators of Children's Books, 1744–1945.* Includes art trends, artists' biographies, and a wealth of illustrations from modern children's books.

Volsunga Saga: The Story of the Volsungs and Niblungs, with Certain Songs from the Elder Edda, tr. by Eirikr Magnusson and William Morris. London: Walter Scott, n.d. This prose translation of the difficult verse form of the *Elder Edda* is easy to read and is the basis for Morris's beautiful verse version of the saga. (In 1962, Collier Bks. published a paperback version using the Morris translation.)

WALSH, FRANCES, ed. *That Eager Zest; First Discoveries in the Magic World of Books.* Lippincott, 1961. Almost 50 delightful verses and sketches about their own childhood reading experiences by such well-known writers as Carl Sandburg, James Thurber, Sherwood Anderson, and Lewis Mumford.

The Wandsworth Collection of Early Children's Books. London: Wandsworth Public Library, 1972. A descriptive bibliography.

WARD, MARTHA E., and DOROTHY A. MARQUARDT. *Authors of Books for Young People,* 2nd ed. Scarecrow, 1971. Biographical sketches of authors.

______. *Illustrators of Books for Young People.* Scarecrow, 1970. Biographical information about 370 illustrators of books for children.

WEISS, HARRY B. *A Book About Chapbooks; The People's Literature of Bygone Times,* ill. Singing Tree. 1969. A history of chapbooks, their printers, authors, and salesmen, with reproductions of woodcuts and title pages.

WELSH, CHARLES. *A Bookseller of the Last Century, Being some Account of the Life of John Newbery, and of the Books he published with a Notice of the later Newberys.* London: Griffith, Farran, 1885; reissued, Singing Tree, 1969. A readable history of Newbery, his famous bookshop, and his varied activities.

______, ed. *The Renowned History of Little Goody Two Shoes, Otherwise Called Mrs. Margery Two Shoes,* attributed to Oliver Goldsmith. Heath, 1930.

WHALLEY, JOYCE IRENE. *Cobwebs to Catch Flies: Illustrated Books for the Nursery and Schoolroom,*

1700–1900. Univ. of Calif. Pr., 1975. Profusely illustrated, a text that focuses on instructional works.

WHITE, DOROTHY MARY NEAL. *About Books for Children.* Oxford, 1947. Although the author selects predominantly British children's books, she also discusses many American publications.

______. *Books Before Five,* ill. by Joan Smith. Oxford, 1954. A New Zealand children's librarian's study of her two-year-old daughter's progression in the experience of books over three years, ranging over more than 100 books, from Adams's *First Things* to Tolkien's *The Hobbit.*

WHITEHEAD, ROBERT. *Children's Literature; Strategies of Teaching.* Prentice, 1968. Specific practices which help the teacher present an attractive and effective program in literature.

WILLIAMS, SIDNEY H., and FALCONER MADAN. *The Lewis Carroll Handbook,* rev. and enl. by Roger Lancelyn Green. Oxford, 1962. A valuable and comprehensive bibliography of Lewis Carroll's own writings and what others have written about his life and works. Descriptive notes are comprehensive and scholarly.

WILSON, BARBARA KER. *Writing for Children; An English Editor and Author's Point of View.* Watts, 1960. Sound comment on writing fiction, nonfiction, and picture books for children.

WILSON, ROY R. *Teaching Children Language Arts.* Parker Pub. Co., 1970. Wilson says that the purpose of his book is to provide practical, imaginative ideas—specifics to try as well as ideas to stir the reader's thinking about "what needs to be done in the language arts classroom."

WITUCKE, VIRGINIA. *Poetry in the Elementary School.* Brown, 1970. An illuminating treatment of strategies for generating interest in poetry, with generous references and unhackneyed selections of examples, including audiovisual materials.

WOLSCH, ROBERT A. *Poetic Composition Through the Grades; A Language Sensitivity Program. Practical Suggestions for Teaching,* ed. by Alice Miel. Teachers College Pr., 1970. A teacher's handbook for teaching poetry writing in the elementary school.

WYNDHAM, LEE. *Writing for Children and Teen-Agers.* Writer's Digest, 1968. Practical, detailed advice presented in a lively style and covering all phases of writing children's books, marketing them, and seeing them through publication, by a woman who is herself a prolific writer for children.

Yale French Studies: The Child's Part. Yale Univ. Pr., 1969. A collection of essays exploring children's literature as a vast subspecies, attention to which can illuminate culture, society, literature itself.

YARDLEY, ALICE. *Young Children Thinking.* Citation, 1973. A British educator discusses the mental development of young children, giving suggestions for adding intellectual dimensions to the child's education.

YOLEN, JANE. *Writing Books for Children.* The Writer, Inc., 1973. Discusses genres and the children's book market as well as the literary, financial, and legal aspects of writing books.

Appendix C Publishers and Their Addresses[3]

ABELARD. Abelard-Schuman, 666 Fifth Ave., New York, N.Y. 10019
ABINGDON. Abingdon Pr., 201 Eighth Ave. S., Nashville, Tenn. 37202
ABRAMS. Harry N. Abrams, Inc., 110 E. 59th St., New York, N.Y. 10022
ACADEMIC. Academic Press, Inc., 111 Fifth Ave., New York, N.Y. 10003
ADDISON. Addison-Wesley Pub. Co., Inc., Jacob Way, Reading, Mass. 01867
ALA. American Library Assoc., Pub. Dept., 50 E. Huron St., Chicago, Ill. 60611
ALLYN. Allyn & Bacon, Inc. 470 Atlantic Ave., Boston, Mass. 02210
AM. ASSOC. FOR THE ADVANCEMENT OF SCIENCE. 1776 Massachusetts Ave., N. W., Washington, D.C. 20036
AMERICAN BK. American Book Co., 450 W. 33rd St., New York, N.Y. 10001
AM. COUNCIL ON EDUCATION. 1 Dupont Circle, N. W., Washington, D.C. 20036
AMERICAN HERITAGE. American Heritage Pub. Co., Inc., 1221 Ave. of the Americas, New York, N.Y. 10020
APPLETON. Appleton-Century-Crofts, 440 Park Ave. S., New York, N.Y. 10016
ARCHON. See Shoe String
ARIEL. Ariel Books. See Farrar
ARLINGTON. Arlington House Pubs., 165 Huguenot St., New Rochelle, N.Y. 10801
ARONSON. Jason Aronson, Inc., 59 Fourth Ave., New York, N.Y. 10003
ASSOC. FOR CHILDHOOD EDUCATION INTERNATIONAL. 3615 Wisconsin Ave. N. W., Washington, D.C. 20016
ASSOCIATION PR., Association Press, 291 Broadway, New York, N.Y. 10007
ASTOR. Astor-Honor, Inc., 48 E. 43rd St., New York, N.Y. 10017
ATHENEUM. Atheneum Pubs., 122 E. 42nd St., New York, N.Y. 10017
ATHERTON. Lieber-Atherton, Inc., 1841 Broadway, New York, N.Y. 10023
ATLANTIC. Atlantic Monthly Pr., 8 Arlington St., Boston, Mass. 02116
ATLANTIC/LITTLE. Atlantic Monthly Pr. in association with Little, Brown & Co.
AVON. Avon Books, 959 Eighth Ave., New York, N.Y. 10019
BALLANTINE. Ballantine Books, Inc., 201 E. 50th St., New York, N.Y. 10022
BANTAM. Bantam Books, Inc., 666 Fifth Ave., New York, N.Y. 10019
BARNES. Barnes & Noble Books, 5th Ave. and 18th St., New York, N.Y. 10003
BASIC. Basic Books, Inc., 10 E. 53rd St., New York, N.Y. 10022
BEACON. Beacon Pr., 25 Beacon St., Boston, Mass. 02108

[3]For the address of any publisher not listed here consult the latest *Literary Market Place* or Bowker's *Books in Print*.

BEECHURST. Beechurst Pr. See A. S. Barnes
BEHRMAN. Behrman House, Inc., 1261 Broadway, New York, N.Y. 10001
BOBBS. Bobbs-Merrill Co., Inc., 4300 W. 62nd St., Indianapolis, Ind. 46206
BOWKER. R. R. Bowker and Co., 1180 Ave. of the Americas, New York, N.Y. 10036
BRADBURY. Bradbury Pr., Inc., 2 Overhill Rd., Scarsdale, N.Y. 10583
BRO-DART. Bro-Dart Pub. Co., 1609 Memorial Ave., Williamsport, Pa. 17701
BROWN. William C. Brown Co., Publishers, 2460 Kerper Blvd., Dubuque, Iowa 52001
CAMBRIDGE UNIV. PR. 32 E. 57th St., New York, N.Y. 10022
CANADIAN WOMEN'S EDUCATIONAL PRESS. Canadian Women's Educational Press, 280 Bloor St. West, Suite 305, Toronto, Ontario, Canada
CAXTON. The Caxton Printers, Ltd., Caldwell, Idaho 83605
CHATHAM/VIKING. 15 Wilmot Lane, Riverside, Conn. 06878. Distributed by Viking
CHELSEA. Chelsea House Publishers, 70 W. 40th St., New York, N.Y. 10018
CHILD STUDY ASSOC. OF AM. Child Study Association of America/Wel Met Inc., 50 Madison Ave., New York, N.Y. 10010
CHILD STUDY PR. The Child Study Press, 50 Madison Ave., New York, N.Y. 10010
CHILDREN'S BOOK COUNCIL. Children's Book Council, Inc., 67 Irving Place, New York, N.Y. 10003
CHILDRENS PR. Childrens Press, Inc., 1224 W. Van Buren, Chicago, Ill. 60607
CHILTON. Chilton Book Co., Chilton Way, Radnor, Pa. 19089
CITATION. Citation Press. Imprint of Scholastic Book Services, Div. of Scholastic Magazines, 906 Sylvan Ave., Englewood Cliffs, N. J. 07632
COPP CLARK. The Copp Clark Pub. Co., 517 Wellington St. W., Toronto 135, Ont., Canada
COUNCIL ON INTERRACIAL BOOKS FOR CHILDREN, 1841 Broadway, New York, N.Y. 10023
COWARD. Coward, McCann & Geoghegan, Inc., 200 Madison Ave., New York, N.Y. 10016
COWLES. Henry Regnery Co., 180 N. Michigan Ave., Chicago, Ill. 60601
CRITERION. Criterion Books, Inc., 666 Fifth Ave., New York, N.Y. 10019
CROWELL-COLLIER. Crowell Collier and Macmillan, Inc., 866 Third Ave., New York, N.Y. 10022
T. CROWELL. Thomas Y. Crowell Co., 666 Fifth Ave., New York, N.Y. 10019
DAY. Thomas Y. Crowell Co., 666 Fifth Ave., New York, N.Y. 10019
DELACORTE. Delacorte Pr. See Dell
DELL. Dell Pub. Co., Inc., 1 Dag Hammarskjold Plaza, 245 E. 47th St., New York, N.Y. 10017
DEVIN. Devin-Adair Co., 143 Sound Beach Ave., Old Greenwich, Conn. 06870

DIAL. The Dial Pr., Inc. See Dell
DODD. Dodd, Mead & Co., 79 Madison Ave., New York, N.Y. 10016
DOUBLEDAY. Doubleday & Co., Inc., 245 Park Ave., New York, N.Y. 10017
DOVER. Dover Pubns., Inc., 180 Varick St., New York, N.Y. 10014
DRYDEN. Dryden Pr., 901 N. Elm, Hinsdale, Ill. 60521
DUELL. Duell, Sloan & Pearce. See Hawthorn
DUFOUR. Dufour Editions, Inc., Chester Springs, Pa. 19425
DUTTON. E. P. Dutton & Co., Inc., 201 Park Ave. S., New York, N.Y. 10003
EERDMANS. William B. Eerdmans Pub. Co., 255 Jefferson Ave., S. E., Grand Rapids, Mich. 49502
ERIKSSON. Paul S. Eriksson, Inc., Pub., 119 W. 57th St., New York, N.Y. 10019
EVANS. M. Evans & Co., Inc., 216 E. 49th St., New York, N.Y. 10017
EXPRESSION. Expression Co., 155 Columbus Ave., Boston, Mass. 02116
FARRAR. Farrar, Straus & Giroux, Inc., 10 Union Sq., W., New York, N.Y. 10003
FAWCETT. Fawcett World Library, 1515 Broadway, New York, N.Y. 10036
FAXON. F. W. Faxon Co., Inc., 15 Southwest Park, Westwood, Mass. 02090
FEMINIST PR., Feminist Pr., SUNY/College at Old Westbury, Box 334, Old Westbury, N.Y. 11568
FERNHILL. Humanities Pr., Inc., Atlantic Highlands, N.J. 07716
FLEET. Fleet Pr. Corp., 160 Fifth Ave., New York, N.Y. 10010
FOLLETT. Follett Pub. Co., 1010 W. Washington Blvd., Chicago, Ill. 60606
FOUR WINDS. Four Winds Pr. See Scholastic
FREE PR. The Free Press, 866 Third Ave., New York, N.Y. 10022
FUNK. Funk & Wagnalls, Inc., 53 E. 77th St., New York, N.Y. 10021
GALE. Gale Research Co., Book Tower, Detroit, Mich. 48226
GARDEN CITY. See Doubleday
GARLAND. Garland Publishing, Inc., 10 E. 44th St., New York, N.Y. 10017
GARRARD. Garrard Pub. Co., Champaign, Ill. 61820
GLENCOE. Glencoe, Inc., 8701 Wilshire Blvd., Beverly Hills, Calif. 90211
GODINE. Godine Press, Inc., 306 Dartmouth St., Boston, Mass. 02116
GOLDEN GATE. Golden Gate Junior Books, 1247½ North Vista St., Hollywood, Calif. 90046
GOLDEN PR. Golden Press, Inc., 850 Third Ave., New York, N.Y. 10022
GREENWILLOW. Greenwillow Books, 105 Madison Ave., New York, N.Y. 10016
GROSSET. Grosset & Dunlap, Inc., 51 Madison Ave., New York, N.Y. 10010
GROVE. Grove Press, Inc., 53 E. 11th St., New York, N.Y. 10003
HALE. E. M. Hale & Co., Inc., 20 Waterside Plaza, New York, N.Y. 10010
HANOVER HOUSE. See Doubleday
HARCOURT. Harcourt Brace Jovanovich, Inc., 757 Third Ave., New York, N.Y. 10017
HARPER. Harper & Row, Pubs., 10 E. 53rd St., New York, N.Y. 10022
HARVEY. Harvey House, Inc., 20 Waterside Plaza, New York, N.Y. 10010
HASTINGS. Hastings House Pubs., 10 E. 40th St., New York, N.Y. 10016
HAWTHORN. Hawthorn Books, Inc., 70 Fifth Ave., New York, N.Y. 10011
HILL. Hill & Wang, Inc., 19 Union Sq. W., New York, N.Y. 10003
HOLIDAY. Holiday House, Inc., 18 E. 53rd St., New York, N.Y. 10022
HOLT. Holt, Rinehart & Winston, Inc., 383 Madison Ave., New York, N.Y. 10017
HORN BOOK. Horn Book, Inc., 585 Boylston St., Boston, Mass. 02116
HOUGHTON. Houghton Mifflin Co., 2 Park St., Boston, Mass. 02107
HUBBARD. Hubbard Pr. See Rand
INDIANA UNIV. PR. Tenth and Morton Sts., Bloomington, Ind. 47401
INTERNATIONAL PUBLICATIONS SERVICE, 114 E. 32nd St., New York, N.Y. 10016
JOSSEY-BASS. Jossey-Bass, Inc., Pubs., 615 Montgomery St., San Francisco, Calif. 54111
KNOPF. Alfred A. Knopf, Inc., 201 E. 50th St., New York, N.Y. 10022
KNOW. KNOW, Inc., P.O. Box 86031, Pittsburgh, Pa. 15221
LERNER. Lerner Pubns. Co., 241 First Ave. N., Minneapolis, Minn. 55401
LIBRARY OF CONGRESS. Supt. of Documents, U.S. Govt. Printing Office, Washington, D.C. 20402
LIPPINCOTT. J. B. Lippincott Co., E. Washington Sq., Philadelphia, Pa. 19105
LITTLE. Little, Brown & Co., 34 Beacon St., Boston, Mass. 02106
LONGMANS. Longmans, Green & Co. See McKay
LOTHROP. Lothrop, Lee & Shepard Co., Inc., 105 Madison Ave., New York, N.Y. 10016
LUCE. Robert B. Luce, Inc., 2000 N. St., N. W., Washington, D.C. 20036
MCCALL. McCall Books, 230 Park Ave., New York, N.Y. 10017
MCGRAW. McGraw-Hill Book & Educational Services Group, 1221 Avenue of the Americas, New York, N.Y. 10020
MCKAY. David McKay Co., Inc., 750 Third Ave., New York, N.Y. 10017
MCKINLEY. 112 S. New Broadway, Brooklawn, N.J. 08030
MACMILLAN. Macmillan Co., 866 Third Ave., New York, N.Y. 10022
MACRAE. Macrae Smith Co., 225 S. 15th St., Philadelphia, Pa. 19102
MEREDITH. Meredith Pr. See Hawthorn
MERRILL. Charles E. Merrill Pub. Co., 1300 Alum Creek Dr., Columbus, Ohio 43216
MESSNER. Julian Messner, Inc. See Simon & Schuster
METHUEN. Methuen Pubns., 2330 Midland Ave., Agincourt, Ont. MIS 1P7, Canada
MORROW. William Morrow & Co., Inc., 105 Madison Ave., New York, N.Y. 10016
NAT. COUNCIL FOR THE SOCIAL STUDIES. National Education Assoc., 1515 Wilson Blvd., Arlington, Va. 22209
NAT. COUNCIL OF TEACHERS OF ENGLISH. 1111 Kenyon Rd., Urbana, Ill. 61820
NATURAL HISTORY PR., 501 Franklin Blvd., Garden City, N.Y. 11530
NELSON. Thomas Nelson, Inc., 30 E. 42nd St., New York, N.Y. 10017
NEW AM. LIB. New American Library, 1301 Avenue of the Americas, New York, N.Y. 10019

NEW YORK LIBRARY ASSOC. P.O. Box 521, Woodside, N.Y. 11377
NEW YORK PUBLIC LIBRARY. Room 50A, Fifth Ave. and 42nd St., New York, N.Y. 10018
NOBLE. Noble & Noble Pubs., Inc., 1 Dag Hammarskjold Plaza, New York, N.Y. 10017
NORTON. W. W. Norton & Co., 500 Fifth Avenue, New York, N.Y. 10036
NORTON/GROSSET. W. W. Norton in association with Grosset & Dunlap
OBOLENSKY. See Astor-Honor
ODYSSEY. See Bobbs-Merrill
O'HARA. J. Philip O'Hara Inc., Pubs., 20 E. Huron St., Chicago, Ill. 60611
OUTERBRIDGE. Outerbridge & Lazard, 200 W. 82nd St., New York, N.Y. 10023
OXFORD. Oxford Univ. Pr., 200 Madison Ave., New York, N.Y. 10016
PANTHEON. Pantheon Books, 201 E. 50th St., New York, N.Y. 10022
PANTHER. Panther House, Ltd., P.O. Box 3552, New York, N.Y. 10017
PARENTS' MAGAZINE. Parents' Magazine Pr., 52 Vanderbilt Ave., New York, N.Y. 10017
PARNASSUS. Parnassus Pr., 4080 Halleck St., Emeryville, Calif. 94608
PENGUIN. Penguin Books, Inc., 625 Madison Ave., New York, N.Y. 10022
PERGAMON. Pergamon Pr., Inc., Maxwell House, Fairview Park, Elmsford, N.Y. 10523
PHILLIPS. S. G. Phillips, Inc., 305 W. 86th St., New York, N.Y. 10024
PHOENIX HOUSE. See Univ. of Chicago Pr.
PITMAN. Pitman Pub. Corp., 6 E. 43rd St., New York, N.Y. 10017
PLATT. Platt & Munk, Inc., 1055 Bronx River Ave., Bronx, N.Y. 10472
PLAYS. Plays, Inc., 8 Arlington St., Boston, Mass. 02116
POCKET BOOKS. See Simon & Schuster
POPULAR PR. Popular Library, 600 Third Ave., New York, N.Y. 10016
POTTER. Clarkson N. Potter, Inc., 419 Park Ave. S., New York, N.Y. 10016
PRAEGER. Praeger Pubs., Inc., 111 Fourth Ave., New York, N.Y. 10003
PRENTICE. Prentice-Hall, Inc., Englewood Cliffs, N.J. 07632
PRESS OF CASE WESTERN RESERVE UNIVERSITY. Quail Bldg., Cleveland, Ohio 44106
PUTNAM. G. P. Putnam's Sons, 200 Madison Ave., New York, N.Y. 10016
QUADRANGLE. Quandrangle/The New York Times Book Co., 10 E. 53rd St., New York, N.Y. 10022
RAND. Rand McNally & Co., P.O. Box 7600, Chicago, Ill. 60680
RANDOM. Random House, Inc., 201 E. 50th St., New York, N.Y. 10022
REILLY. Reilly & Lee Books, 114 W. Illinois St., Chicago, Ill. 60610
RITCHIE. The Ward Ritchie Pr., 474 S. Arroyo Pkwy., Pasadena, Calif. 91105
RONALD. The Ronald Press Co., 79 Madison Ave., New York, N.Y. 10016
ROY. Roy Pubs., Inc., 30 E. 74th St., New York, N.Y. 10021
ST. MARTIN'S. St. Martin's Pr., Inc., 175 Fifth Ave., New York, N.Y. 10010
SAT. REVIEW. Saturday Review Pr., 201 Park Ave. S., New York, N.Y. 10003
SCARECROW. The Scarecrow Pr., 52 Liberty St., Metuchen, N.J. 08840
SCHOCKEN. Schocken Books, Inc., 200 Madison Ave., New York, N.Y. 10016
SCHOLASTIC. Scholastic Book Services, 50 W. 44th St., New York, N.Y. 10036
W. R. SCOTT. See Addison-Wesley
SCOTT/ADDISON. See Addison-Wesley
SCOTT, FORESMAN. Scott, Foresman and Co., 1900 E. Lake Ave., Glenview, Ill. 60025
SCRIBNER'S. Charles Scribner's Sons. 597 Fifth Ave., New York, N.Y. 10017
SEABURY. Seabury Pr., 815 Second Ave., New York, N.Y. 10017
SHEED. Sheed & Ward, Inc., 6700 Squibb Rd., Mission, Kan. 66202
SHERBOURNE PR. Sherbourne Pr., 1640 La Cienega Blvd., Los Angeles, Calif. 90035
SIGNET. See New American Library
SIMON. Simon & Schuster, Inc., 630 Fifth Ave., New York, N.Y. 10020
SINGING TREE. See Gale
SPRINGER. Springer Publishing Co., Inc., 200 Park Ave. S., New York, N.Y. 10003
STANFORD UNIV. PR. Stanford, Calif. 94305
STEIN & DAY. 7 E. 48th St., New York, N.Y. 10017
STERLING. Sterling Pub. Co., 419 Park Ave. S., New York, N.Y. 10016
STOKES. Frederick A. Stokes Co. See Lippincott
SWALLOW. The Swallow Press, Inc., 1139 S. Wabash Ave., Chicago, Ill. 60605
TAPLINGER. Taplinger Pub. Co., 200 Park Ave. S., New York, N.Y. 10003
TEACHERS COLLEGE PR. Teachers College, Columbia Univ., 1234 Amsterdam Ave., New York, N.Y. 10027
TIME-LIFE. Time-Life Books. Time-Life Bldg., Rockefeller Center, New York, N.Y. 10020
TOWER. Tower Pubns., Inc., c/o Belmont-Tower Books, Inc., 185 Madison Ave., New York, N.Y. 10016
TROUTMAN. Troutman Pr., Sharon, Conn. 06069
TUNDRA. Tundra Books of Northern New York, 18 Cornelia St., Box 1030, Plattsburgh, N.Y. 12901
TUTTLE. Charles E. Tuttle Co., Inc., 28 S. Main St., Rutland, Vt. 05701
TWAYNE. Twayne Pubs., 70 Lincoln St., Boston, Mass. 02111
UNIV. OF CALIF. PR. 2223 Fulton St., Berkeley, Calif. 94720
UNIV. OF CHICAGO PR. 5801 Ellis Ave., Chicago, Ill. 60637
UNIV. OF PA. PR. 3933 Walnut St., Philadelphia, Pa. 19104
VANGUARD. Vanguard Pr., Inc., 424 Madison Ave., New York, N.Y. 10017
VAN NOSTRAND. Van Nostrand Reinhold Co., 450 W. 33rd St., New York, N.Y. 10001
VIKING. Viking Pr., Inc., 625 Madison Ave., New York, N.Y. 10022
VINTAGE. See Random House
WALCK. Henry Z. Walck, Inc., 750 Third Ave., New York, N.Y. 10017
WALKER. Walker & Co., 720 Fifth Ave., New York, N.Y. 10019
WARNE. Frederick Warne & Co., Inc., 101 Fifth Ave., New York, N.Y. 10003
WASHBURN. Ives Washburn, Inc. See McKay
WATSON-GUPTILL. Watson-Guptill Pubns. Div. of Billboard Pubns., Inc. 1 Astor Plaza, New York, N.Y. 10036
WATTS. Franklin Watts, Inc., 730 Fifth Ave., New York, N.Y. 10019
WESTMINSTER. The Westminster Pr., 902 Witherspoon

Bldg., Philadelphia, Pa. 19107

WESTERN. Western Pub. Co., 1220 Mound Ave. Racine, Wis. 53404

WEYBRIGHT. Weybright and Talley, Inc. See McKay

WHITE. David White Co., 60 E. 55th St., New York, N.Y. 10022

WHITMAN. Albert Whitman & Co., 560 W. Lake St., Chicago, Ill. 60606

WHITTLESEY. Whittlesey House. See McGraw-Hill

WILEY. John Wiley & Sons, Inc., 605 Third Ave., New York, N.Y. 10016

WILSON. H. W. Wilson Co., 950 University Ave., Bronx, N.Y. 10452

WINDMILL. Windmill Books, Inc., 201 Park Ave. S., New York, N.Y. 10010

WORLD. William Collins & World Publishing Co., 2080 W. 117th St., Cleveland, Ohio 44111

YOUNG SCOTT. Young Scott Books. See Addison-Wesley

Appendix D
Children's Book Awards

The awards and prizes given in the children's book field by organizations, schools, publishers, and newspapers, in the United States and other countries, have grown to a sizable number.[4] The Newbery and Caldecott Medals and National Book Award for Children's Literature, all given annually, are the best-known United States awards, and the Hans Christian Andersen Medal, given biennially, the best-known international award. The Carnegie and Kate Greenaway Medals are major British awards for children's books, and the Canadian Library Awards are the most significant given in Canada. In most cases, the awards are given for books published during the preceding year.

Following are brief histories of these awards and listings of the winners and runners-up.

The Newbery Medal

Frederic G. Melcher, editor of *Publisher's Weekly Magazine,* donated and named this award as a tribute to John Newbery (1713–1767), the first English publisher of books for children. Beginning in 1922 and every year since, the Newbery Medal has been given by an awards committee of the Children's Services Division of the American Library Association to the author of the most distinguished contribution to literature for children published in the United States during the preceding year. The author must be a citizen or resident of the United States.

1922 *The Story of Mankind* by Hendrik Willem van Loon, Liveright

Honor Books: *The Great Quest* by Charles Hawes, Little; *Cedric the Forester* by Bernard Marshall, Appleton; *The Old Tobacco Shop* by William Bowen, Macmillan; *The Golden Fleece and the Heroes Who Lived Before Achilles* by Padraic Colum, Macmillan; *Windy Hill* by Cornelia Meigs, Macmillan

1923 *The Voyages of Doctor Dolittle* by Hugh Lofting, Lippincott

Honor Books: No record

1924 *The Dark Frigate* by Charles Hawes, Atlantic/Little

Honor Books: No record

1925 *Tales from Silver Lands* by Charles Finger, Doubleday

Honor Books: *Nicholas* by Anne Carroll Moore, Putnam; *Dream Coach* by Anne Parrish, Macmillan

1926 *Shen of the Sea* by Arthur Bowie Chrisman, Dutton

Honor Book: *Voyagers* by Padraic Colum, Macmillan

1927 *Smoky, the Cowhorse* by Will James, Scribner's

Honor Books: No record

1928 *Gayneck, The Story of a Pigeon* by Dhan Gopal Mukerji, Dutton

Honor Books: *The Wonder Smith and His Son* by Ella Young, Longmans; *Downright Dencey* by Caroline Snedeker, Doubleday

[4]Children's Books: Awards and Prizes (comp. and ed. by the Children's Book Council, 1975) is a complete compilation of honors awarded in the children's book field.

1929 *The Trumpeter of Krakow* by Eric P. Kelly, Macmillan

Honor Books: *Pigtail of Ah Lee Ben Loo* by John Bennett, Longmans; *Millions of Cats* by Wanda Gág, Coward; *The Boy Who Was* by Grace Hallock, Dutton; *Clearing Weather* by Cornelia Meigs, Little; *Runaway Papoose* by Grace Moon, Doubleday; *Tod of the Fens* by Elinor Whitney, Macmillan

1930 *Hitty, Her First Hundred Years* by Rachel Field, Macmillan

Honor Books: *Daughter of the Seine* by Jeanette Eaton, Harper; *Pran of Albania* by Elizabeth Miller, Doubleday; *Jumping-Off Place* by Marian Hurd McNeely, Longmans; *Tangle-Coated Horse and Other Tales* by Ella Young, Longmans; *Vaino* by Julia Davis Adams, Dutton; *Little Blacknose* by Hildegarde Swift, Harcourt

1931 *The Cat Who Went to Heaven* by Elizabeth Coatsworth, Macmillan

Honor Books: *Floating Island* by Anne Parrish, Harper; *The Dark Star of Itza* by Alida Malkus, Harcourt; *Queer Person* by Ralph Hubbard, Doubleday; *Mountains Are Free* by Julia Davis Adams, Dutton; *Spice and the Devil's Cave* by Agnes Hewes, Knopf; *Meggy Macintosh* by Elizabeth Janet Gray, Doubleday; *Garram the Hunter* by Herbert Best, Doubleday; *Ood-Le-Uk the Wanderer* by Alice Lide and Margaret Johansen, Little

1932 *Waterless Mountain* by Laura Adams Armer, Longmans

Honor Books: *The Fairy Circus* by Dorothy P. Lathrop, Macmillan; *Calico Bush* by Rachel Field, Macmillan; *Boy of the South Seas* by Eunice Tietjens, Coward; *Out of the Flame* by Eloise Lownsbery, Longmans; *Jane's Island* by Marjorie Allee, Houghton; *Truce of the Wolf and Other Tales of Old Italy* by Mary Gould Davis, Harcourt

1933 *Young Fu of the Upper Yangtze* by Elizabeth Foreman Lewis, Winston

Honor Books: *Swift Rivers* by Cornelia Meigs, Little; *The Railroad to Freedom* by Hildegarde Swift, Harcourt; *Children of the Soil* by Nora Burglon, Doubleday

1934 *Invincible Louisa* by Cornelia Meigs, Little

Honor Books: *The Forgotten Daughter* by Caroline Snedeker, Doubleday; *Swords of Steel* by Elsie Singmaster, Houghton; *ABC Bunny* by Wanda Gág, Coward; *Winged Girl of Knossos* by Erik Berry, Appleton; *New Land* by Sarah Schmidt, McBride; *Big Tree of Bunlahy* by Padraic Colum, Macmillan; *Glory of the Seas* by Agnes Hewes, Knopf; *Apprentice of Florence* by Anne Kyle, Houghton

1935 *Dobry* by Monica Shannon, Viking

Honor Books: *Pageant of Chinese History* by Elizabeth Seeger, Longmans; *Davy Crockett* by Constance Rourke, Harcourt; *Day on Skates* by Hilda Van Stockum, Harper

1936 *Caddie Woodlawn* by Carol Brink, Macmillan

Honor Books: *Honk, the Moose* by Phil Stong, Dodd; *The Good Master* by Kate Seredy, Viking; *Young Walter Scott* by Elizabeth Janet Gray, Viking; *All Sail Set* by Armstrong Sperry, Winston

1937 *Roller Skates* by Ruth Sawyer, Viking

Honor Books: *Phebe Fairchild: Her Book* by Lois Lenski, Stokes; *Whistler's Van* by Idwal Jones, Viking; *Golden Basket* by Ludwig Bemelmans, Viking; *Winterbound* by

Margery Bianco, Viking; *Audubon* by Constance Rourke, Harcourt; *The Codfish Musket* by Agnes Hewes, Doubleday

1938 *The White Stag* by Kate Seredy, Viking
Honor Books: *Pecos Bill* by James Cloyd Bowman, Little; *Bright Island* by Mabel Robinson, Random; *On the Banks of Plum Creek* by Laura Ingalls Wilder, Harper

1939 *Thimble Summer* by Elizabeth Enright, Rinehart
Honor Books: *Nino* by Valenti Angelo, Viking; *Mr. Popper's Penguins* by Richard and Florence Atwater, Little; *"Hello the Boat!"* by Phyllis Crawford, Holt; *Leader by Destiny: George Washington, Man and Patriot* by Jeanette Eaton, Harcourt; *Penn* by Elizabeth Janet Gray, Viking

1940 *Daniel Boone* by James Daugherty, Viking
Honor Books: *The Singing Tree* by Kate Seredy, Viking; *Runner of the Mountain Tops* by Mabel Robinson, Random; *By the Shores of Silver Lake* by Laura Ingalls Wilder, Harper; *Boy with a Pack* by Stephen W. Meader, Harcourt

1941 *Call It Courage* by Armstrong Sperry, Macmillan
Honor Books: *Blue Willow* by Doris Gates, Viking; *Young Mac of Fort Vancouver* by Mary Jane Carr, T. Crowell; *The Long Winter* by Laura Ingalls Wilder, Harper; *Nansen* by Anna Gertrude Hall, Viking

1942 *The Matchlock Gun* by Walter D. Edmonds, Dodd
Honor Books: *Little Town on the Prairie* by Laura Ingalls Wilder, Harper; *George Washington's World* by Genevieve Foster, Scribner's; *Indian Captive: The Story of Mary Jemison* by Lois Lenski, Lippincott; *Down Ryton Water* by Eva Roe Gaggin, Viking

1943 *Adam of the Road* by Elizabeth Janet Gray, Viking
Honor Books: *The Middle Moffat* by Eleanor Estes, Har-Court: *Have You Seen Tom Thumb?* by Mabel Leigh Hunt, Lippincott

1944 *Johnny Tremain* by Esther Forbes, Houghton
Honor Books: *These Happy Golden Years* by Laura Ingalls Wilder, Harper; *Fog Magic* by Julia Sauer, Viking; *Rufus M.* by Eleanor Estes, Harcourt; *Mountain Born* by Elizabeth Yates, Coward

1945 *Rabbit Hill* by Robert Lawson, Viking
Honor Books: *The Hundred Dresses* by Eleanor Estes, Harcourt; *The Silver Pencil* by Alice Dalgliesh, Scribner's; *Abraham Lincoln's World* by Genevieve Foster, Scribner's; *Lone Journey: The Life of Roger Williams* by Jeanette Eaton, Harcourt

1946 *Strawberry Girl* by Lois Lenski, Lippincott
Honor Books: *Justin Morgan Had a Horse* by Marguerite Henry, Rand; *The Moved-Outers* by Florence Crannell Means, Houghton; *Bhimsa, the Dancing Bear* by Christine Weston, Scribner's; *New Found World* by Katherine Shippen, Viking

1947 *Miss Hickory* by Carolyn Sherwin Bailey, Viking
Honor Books: *Wonderful Year* by Nancy Barnes, Messner; *Big Tree* by Mary and Conrad Buff, Viking; *The Heavenly Tenants* by William Maxwell, Harper; *The Avion My Uncle Flew* by Cyrus Fisher, Appleton; *The Hidden Treasure of Glaston* by Eleanore Jewett, Viking

1948 *The Twenty-one Balloons* by William Pène du Bois, Viking
Honor Books: *Pancakes-Paris* by Claire Huchet Bishop, Viking; *Li Lun, Lad of Courage* by Carolyn Treffinger, Abingdon; *The Quaint and Curious Quest of Johnny Longfoot* by Catherine Besterman, Bobbs; *The Cow-Tail Switch, and Other West African Stories* by Harold Courlander, Holt; *Misty of Chincoteague* by Marguerite Henry, Rand

1949 *King of the Wind* by Marguerite Henry, Rand
Honor Books: *Seabird* by Holling C. Holling, Houghton; *Daughter of the Mountains* by Louise Rankin, Viking; *My Father's Dragon* by Ruth S. Gannett, Random; *Story of the Negro* by Arna Bontemps, Knopf

1950 *The Door in the Wall* by Marguerite de Angeli, Doubleday
Honor Books: *Tree of Freedom* by Rebecca Caudill, Viking; *The Blue Cat of Castle Town* by Catherine Coblentz, Longmans; *Kildee House* by Rutherford Montgomery, Doubleday; *George Washington* by Genevieve Foster, Scribner's; *Song of the Pines* by Walter and Marion Havighurst, Winston

1951 *Amos Fortune, Free Man* by Elizabeth Yates, Aladdin
Honor Books: *Better Known as Johnny Appleseed* by Mabel Leigh Hunt, Lippincott; *Gandhi, Fighter Without a Sword* by Jeanette Eaton, Morrow; *Abraham Lincoln, Friend of the People* by Clara Ingram Judson, Follett; *The Story of Appleby Capple* by Anne Parrish, Harper

1952 *Ginger Pye* by Eleanor Estes, Harcourt
Honor Books: *Americans Before Columbus* by Elizabeth Baity, Viking; *Minn of the Mississippi* by Holling C. Holling, Houghton; *The Defender* by Nicholas Kalashnikoff, Scribner's; *The Light at Tern Rock* by Julia Sauer, Viking; *The Apple and the Arrow* by Mary and Conrad Buff, Houghton

1953 *Secret of the Andes* by Ann Nolan Clark, Viking
Honor Books: *Charlotte's Web* by E. B. White, Harper; *Moccasin Trail* by Eloise McGraw, Coward; *Red Sails to Capri* by Ann Weil, Viking; *The Bears on Hemlock Mountain* by Alice Dalgliesh, Scribner's; *Birthdays of Freedom,* Vol. 1 by Genevieve Foster, Scribner's

1954 *. . . and now Miguel* by Joseph Krumgold, T. Crowell
Honor Books: *All Alone* by Claire Huchet Bishop, Viking; *Shadrach* by Meindert DeJong, Harper; *Hurry Home Candy* by Meindert DeJong, Harper; *Theodore Roosevelt, Fighting Patriot* by Clara Ingram Judson, Follett; *Magic Maize* by Mary and Conrad Buff, Houghton

1955 *The Wheel on the School* by Meindert DeJong, Harper
Honor Books: *The Courage of Sarah Noble* by Alice Dalgliesh, Scribner's; *Banner in the Sky* by James Ullman, Lippincott

1956 *Carry on, Mr. Bowditch* by Jean Lee Latham, Houghton
Honor Books: *The Secret River* by Marjorie Kinnan Rawlings, Scribner's; *The Golden Name Day* by Jennie Lindquist, Harper; *Men, Microscopes, and Living Things* by Katherine Shippen, Viking

1957 *Miracles on Maple Hill* by Virginia Sorensen, Harcourt
Honor Books: *Old Yeller* by Fred Gipson, Harper; *The House of Sixty Fathers* by Meindert DeJong, Harper; *Mr. Justice Holmes* by Clara Ingram Judson, Follett; *The Corn Grows Ripe* by Dorothy Rhoads, Viking; *Black Fox of Lorne* by Marguerite de Angeli, Doubleday

1958 *Rifles for Watie* by Harold Keith, T. Crowell
Honor Books: *The Horsecatcher* by Mari Sandoz, Westminster; *Gone-Away Lake* by Elizabeth Enright, Harcourt; *The Great Wheel* by Robert Lawson, Viking; *Tom Paine, Freedom's Apostle* by Leo Gurko, T. Crowell

1959 *The Witch of Blackbird Pond* by Elizabeth George Speare, Houghton
Honor Books: *The Family Under the Bridge* by Natalie S. Carlson, Harper; *Along Came a Dog* by Meindert DeJong, Harper; *Chucaro: Wild Pony of the Pampa* by Francis Kalnay, Harcourt; *The Perilous Road* by William O. Steele, Harcourt

1960 *Onion John* by Joseph Krumgold, T. Crowell

Honor Books: *My Side of the Mountain* by Jean George, Dutton; *America Is Born* by Gerald W. Johnson, Morrow; *The Gammage Cup* by Carol Kendall, Harcourt

1961 *Island of the Blue Dolphins* by Scott O'Dell, Houghton

Honor Books: *America Moves Forward* by Gerald W. Johnson, Morrow; *Old Ramon* by Jack Schaefer, Houghton; *The Cricket in Times Square* by George Selden, Farrar

1962 *The Bronze Bow* by Elizabeth George Speare, Houghton

Honor Books: *Frontier Living* by Edwin Tunis, World; *The Golden Goblet* by Eloise McGraw, Coward; *Belling the Tiger* by Mary Stolz, Harper

1963 *A Wrinkle in Time* by Madeleine L'Engle, Farrar

Honor Books: *Thistle and Thyme* by Sorche Nic Leodhas, Holt; *Men of Athens* by Olivia Coolidge, Houghton

1964 *It's Like This, Cat* by Emily Cheney Neville, Harper

Honor Books: *Rascal* by Sterling North, Dutton; *The Loner* by Ester Wier, McKay

1965 *Shadow of a Bull* by Maia Wojciechowska, Atheneum

Honor Book: *Across Five Aprils* by Irene Hunt, Follett

1966 *I, Juan de Pareja* by Elizabeth Borten de Trevino, Farrar

Honor Books: *The Black Cauldron* by Lloyd Alexander, Holt; *The Animal Family* by Randall Jarrell, Pantheon; *The Noonday Friends* by Mary Stolz, Harper

1967 *Up a Road Slowly* by Irene Hunt, Follett

Honor Books: *The King's Fifth* by Scott O'Dell, Houghton; *Zlateh the Goat and Other Stories* by Isaac Bashevis Singer, Harper; *The Jazz Man* by Mary H. Weik. Atheneum

1968 *From the Mixed-Up Files of Mrs. Basil E. Frankweiler* by E. L. Konigsburg, Atheneum

Honor Books: *Jennifer, Hecate, Macbeth, William McKinley, and Me, Elizabeth* by E. L. Konigsburg, Atheneum; *The Black Pearl* by Scott O'Dell, Houghton; *The Fearsome Inn* by Isaac Bashevis Singer, Scribner's; *The Egypt Game* by Zilpha Keatley Snyder, Atheneum

1969 *The High King* by Lloyd Alexander, Holt

Honor Books: *To Be a Slave* by Julius Lester, Dial; *When Shlemiel Went to Warsaw and Other Stories* by Isaac Bashevis Singer, Farrar

1970 *Sounder* by William H. Armstrong, Harper

Honor Books: *Our Eddie* by Sulamith Ish-Kishor, Pantheon; *The Many Ways of Seeing: An Introduction to the Pleasures of Art* by Janet Gaylord Moore, World; *Journey Outside* by Mary Q. Steele, Viking

1971 *Summer of the Swans* by Betsy Byars, Viking

Honor Books: *Kneeknock Rise* by Natalie Babbitt, Farrar; *Enchantress from the Stars* by Sylvia Louise Engdahl, Atheneum; *Sing Down the Moon* by Scott O'Dell, Houghton

1972 *Mrs. Frisby and the Rats of NIMH* by Robert C. O'Brien, Atheneum

Honor Books: *Incident at Hawk's Hill* by Allan W. Eckert, Little; *The Planet of Junior Brown* by Virginia Hamilton, Macmillan; *The Tombs of Atuan* by Ursula K. Le Guin, Atheneum; *Annie and the Old One* by Miska Miles, Atlantic/Little; *The Headless Cupid* by Zilpha Keatley Snyder, Atheneum

1973 *Julie of the Wolves* by Jean George, Harper

Honor Books: *Frog and Toad Together* by Arnold Lobel, Harper; *The Upstairs Room* by Johanna Reiss, Crowell; *The Witches of Worm* by Zilpha Keatley Snyder, Atheneum

1974 *The Slave Dancer* by Paula Fox, Bradbury

Honor Book: *The Dark Is Rising* by Susan Cooper, Atheneum/McElderry

1975 *M. C. Higgins, the Great* by Virginia Hamilton, Macmillan

Honor Books: *Figgs & Phantoms* by Ellen Raskin, Dutton; *My Brother Sam Is Dead* by James Lincoln Collier & Christopher Collier, Four Winds; *The Perilous Gard* by Elizabeth Marie Pope, Houghton; *Philip Hall Likes Me. I Reckon Maybe* by Bette Greene, Dial

1976 *The Grey King* by Susan Cooper, Atheneum/McElderry

Honor Books: *The Hundred Penny Box* by Sharon Bell Mathis, Viking; *Dragonwings* by Lawrence Yep, Harper

The Caldecott Medal

This award is named in honor of Randolph Caldecott (1846–1886), the English illustrator whose pictures still delight children. In 1937, Frederic G. Melcher, the American editor and publisher who had conceived the idea of the Newbery Medal some years earlier, proposed the establishment of a similar award for picture books, and since 1938 the Caldecott Medal has been awarded annually by an awards committee of the American Library Association's Children's Services Division to the illustrator of the most distinguished picture book for children published in the United States during the preceding year. The award is limited to residents or citizens of the United States.

In cases where only one name is given, the book was written and illustrated by the same person.

1938 *Animals of the Bible* by Helen Dean Fish, ill. by Dorothy P. Lathrop, Lippincott

Honor Books: *Seven Simeons* by Boris Artzybasheff, Viking; *Four and Twenty Blackbirds* by Helen Dean Fish, ill. by Robert Lawson, Stokes

1939 *Mei Li* by Thomas Handforth, Doubleday

Honor Books: *The Forest Pool* by Laura Adams Armer, Longmans; *Wee Gillis* by Munro Leaf, ill. by Robert Lawson, Viking; *Snow White and the Seven Dwarfs* by Wanda Gág, Coward; *Barkis* by Clare Newberry, Harper; *Andy and the Lion* by James Daugherty, Viking

1940 *Abraham Lincoln* by Ingri and Edgar Parin d'Aulaire, Doubleday

Honor Books: *Cock-A-Doodle Doo . . .* by Berta and Elmer Hader, Macmillan; *Madeline* by Ludwig Bemelmans, Viking; *The Ageless Story,* ill. by Lauren Ford, Dodd.

1941 *They Were Strong and Good* by Robert Lawson, Viking

Honor Book: *April's Kittens* by Clare Newberry, Harper

1942 *Make Way for Ducklings* by Robert McCloskey, Viking

Honor Books: *An American ABC* by Maud and Miska Petersham, Macmillan; *In My Mother's House* by Ann Nolan Clark, ill. by Velino Herrera, Viking; *Paddle-to-the-Sea* by Holling C. Holling, Houghton; *Nothing at All* by Wanda Gág, Coward

1943 *The Little House* by Virginia Lee Burton, Houghton

Honor Books: *Dash and Dart* by Mary and Conrad Buff, Viking; *Marshmallow* by Clare Newberry, Harper

1944 *Many Moons* by James Thurber, ill. by Louis Slobodkin, Harcourt

Honor Books: *Small Rain: Verses from the Bible* selected by Jessie Orton Jones, ill. by Elizabeth Orton Jones. Viking; *Pierre Pigeon* by Lee Kingman, ill. by Arnold E. Bare, Houghton; *The Mighty Hunter* by Berta and Elmer Hader, Macmillan; *A Child's Good Night Book* by Margaret Wise Brown, ill. by Jean Charlot, W. R. Scott; *Good Luck Horse* by Chih-Yi Chan, ill. by Plao Chan, Whittlesey

1945 *Prayer for a Child* by Rachel Field, ill. by Elizabeth Orton Jones, Macmillan

Honor Books: *Mother Goose* ill. by Tasha Tudor, Walck; *In the Forest* by Marie Hall Ets, Viking; *Yonie Wondernose* by Marguerite de Angeli, Doubleday; *The Christmas Anna Angel* by Ruth Sawyer, ill. by Kate Seredy, Viking

1946 *The Rooster Crows . . .* (traditional Mother Goose) ill. by Maud and Miska Petersham, Macmillan

Honor Books: *Little Lost Lamb* by Golden MacDonald, ill. by Leonard Weisgard, Doubleday; *Sing Mother Goose* by Opal Wheeler, ill. by Marjorie Torrey, Dutton; *My Mother Is the Most Beautiful Woman in the World* by Becky Reyher, ill. by Ruth Gannett, Lothrop; *You Can Write Chinese* by Kurt Wiese, Viking

1947 *The Little Island* by Golden MacDonald, ill. by Leonard Weisgard, Doubleday

Honor Books: *Rain Drop Splash* by Alvin Tresselt, ill. by Leonard Weisgard, Lothrop; *Boats on the River* by Marjorie Flack, ill. by Jay Hyde Barnum, Viking; *Timothy Turtle* by Al Graham, ill. by Tony Palazzo, Viking; *Pedro, the Angel of Olvera Street* by Leo Politi, Scribner's; *Sing in Praise: A Collection of the Best Loved Hymns* by Opal Wheeler, ill. by Marjorie Torrey, Dutton.

1948 *White Snow, Bright Snow* by Alvin Tresselt, ill. by Roger Duvoisin, Lothrop

Honor Books: *Stone Soup* by Marcia Brown, Scribner's; *McElligot's Pool* by Dr. Seuss, Random; *Bambino the Clown* by George Schreiber, Viking; *Roger and the Fox* by Lavinia Davis, ill. by Hildegard Woodward, Doubleday; *Song of Robin Hood* ed. by Anne Malcolmson, ill. by Virginia Lee Burton, Houghton

1949 *The Big Snow* by Berta and Elmer Hader, Macmillan

Honor Books: *Blueberries for Sal* by Robert McCloskey, Viking; *All Around the Town* by Phyllis McGinley, ill. by Helen Stone, Lippincott; *Juanita* by Leo Politi, Scribner's; *Fish in the Air* by Kurt Wiese, Viking

1950 *Song of the Swallows* by Leo Politi, Scribner's

Honor Books: *America's Ethan Allen* by Stewart Holbrook, ill. by Lynd Ward, Houghton; *The Wild Birthday Cake* by Lavinia Davis, ill. by Hildegard Woodward, Doubleday; *The Happy Day* by Ruth Krauss, ill. by Marc Simont, Harper; *Bartholomew and the Oobleck* by Dr. Seuss, Random; *Henry Fisherman* by Marcia Brown, Scribner's

1951 *The Egg Tree* by Katherine Milhous, Scribner's

Honor Books: *Dick Whittington and His Cat* by Marcia Brown, Scribner's; *The Two Reds* by Will, ill. by Nicolas Harcourt; *If I Ran the Zoo* by Dr. Seuss, Random; *The Most Wonderful Doll in the World* by Phyllis McGinley, ill. by Helen Stone, Lippincott; *T-Bone, the Baby Sitter* by Clare Newberry, Harper

1952 *Finders Keepers* by Will, ill. by Nicolas, Harcourt

Honor Books: *Mr. T. W. Anthony Woo* by Marie Hall Ets, Viking; *Skipper John's Cook* by Marcia Brown, Scribner's; *All Falling Down* by Gene Zion, ill. by Margaret Bloy Graham, Harper; *Bear Party* by William Pène du Bois, Viking; *Feather Mountain* by Elizabeth Olds, Houghton

1953 *The Biggest Bear* by Lynd Ward, Houghton

Honor Books: *Puss in Boots* by Charles Perrault, ill. and tr. by Marcia Brown, Scribner's; *One Morning in Maine* by Robert McCloskey, Viking; *Ape in a Cape* by Fritz Eichenberg, Harcourt; *The Storm Book* by Charlotte Zolotow, ill. by Margaret Bloy Graham, Harper; *Five Little Monkeys* by Juliet Kepes, Houghton

1954 *Madeline's Rescue* by Ludwig Bemelmans, Viking

Honor Books: *Journey Cake, Ho!* by Ruth Sawyer, ill. by Robert McCloskey, Viking; *When Will the World Be Mine?* by Miriam Schlein, ill. by Jean Charlot, W. R. Scott; *The Steadfast Tin Soldier* by Hans Christian Andersen, ill. by Marcia Brown, Scribner's; *A Very Special House* by Ruth Krauss, ill. by Maurice Sendak, Harper; *Green Eyes* by A. Birnbaum, Capitol

1955 *Cinderella, or the Little Glass Slipper* by Charles Perrault, tr. and ill. by Marcia Brown, Scribner's

Honor Books: *Book of Nursery and Mother Goose Rhymes,* ill. by Marguerite de Angeli, Doubleday; *Wheel on the Chimney* by Margaret Wise Brown, ill, by Tibor Gergely, Lippincott; *The Thanksgiving Story* by Alice Dalgliesh, ill. by Helen Sewell, Scribner's

1956 *Frog Went A-Courtin'* ed. by John Langstaff, ill. by Feodor Rojankovsky, Harcourt

Honor Books: *Play with Me* by Marie Hall Ets, Viking; *Crow Boy* by Taro Yashima, Viking

1957 *A Tree Is Nice* by Janice May Udry, ill. by Marc Simont, Harper

Honor Books: *Mr. Penny's Race Horse* by Marie Hall Ets, Viking; *1 Is One* by Tasha Tudor, Walck; *Anatole* by Eve Titus, ill. by Paul Galdone, McGraw; *Gillespie and the Guards* by Benjamin Elkin, ill. by James Daugherty, Viking; *Lion* by William Pène du Bois, Viking

1958 *Time of Wonder* by Robert McCloskey, Viking

Honor Books: *Fly High, Fly Low* by Don Freeman, Viking; *Anatole and the Cat* by Eve Titus, ill. by Paul Galdone, McGraw

1959 *Chanticleer and the Fox* adapted from Chaucer and ill. by Barbara Cooney, T. Crowell

Honor Books: *The House That Jack Built* by Antonio Frasconi, Harcourt; *What Do You Say, Dear?* by Sesyle Joslin, ill. by Maurice Sendak, W. R. Scott; *Umbrella* by Taro Yashima, Viking

1960 *Nine Days to Christmas* by Marie Hall Ets and Aurora Labastida, ill. by Marie Hall Ets, Viking

Honor Books: *Houses from the Sea* by Alice E. Goudey, ill. by Adrienne Adams, Scribner's; *The Moon Jumpers* by Janice May Udry, ill. by Maurice Sendak, Harper

1961 *Baboushka and the Three Kings* by Ruth Robbins, ill. by Nicolas Sidjakov, Parnassus

Honor Book: *Inch by Inch* by Leo Lionni, Obolensky

1962 *Once a Mouse . . .* by Marcia Brown, Scribner's

Honor Books: *The Fox Went Out on a Chilly Night* by Peter Spier, Doubleday; *Little Bear's Visit* by Else Holmelund Minarik, ill. by Maurice Sendak, Harper; *The Day We Saw the Sun Come Up* by Alice E. Goudey, ill. by Adrienne Adams, Scribner's

1963 *The Snowy Day* by Ezra Jack Keats, Viking

Honor Books: *The Sun Is a Golden Earring* by Natalia M. Belting, ill. by Bernarda Bryson, Holt; *Mr. Rabbit and the Lovely Present* by Charlotte Zolotow, ill. by Maurice Sendak, Harper

1964 *Where the Wild Things Are* by Maurice Sendak, Harper

Honor Books: *Swimmy* by Leo Lionni, Pantheon; *All in the Morning Early* by Sorche Nic Leodhas. ill. by Evaline Ness, Holt; *Mother Goose and Nursery Rhymes* ill. by Philip Reed, Atheneum

1965 *May I Bring a Friend?* by Beatrice Schenk de Regniers, ill. by Beni Montresor, Atheneum
Honor Books: *Rain Makes Applesauce* by Julian Scheer, ill. by Marvin Bileck, Holiday; *The Wave* by Margaret Hodges, ill. by Blair Lent, Houghton; *A Pocketful of Cricket* by Rebecca Caudill, ill. by Evaline Ness, Holt
1966 *Always Room for One More* by Sorche Nic Leodhas, ill. by Nonny Hogrogian, Holt
Honor Books: *Hide and Seek Fog* by Alvin Tresselt, ill. by Roger Duvoisin, Lothrop; *Just Me* by Marie Hall Ets, Viking; *Tom Tit Tot* by Evaline Ness, Scribner's
1967 *Sam, Bangs & Moonshine* by Evaline Ness, Holt
Honor Book: *One Wide River to Cross* by Barbara Emberley, ill. by Ed Emberley, Prentice
1968 *Drummer Hoff* by Barbara Emberley, ill. by Ed Emberley, Prentice
Honor Books: *Frederick* by Leo Lionni, Pantheon; *Seashore Story* by Taro Yashima, Viking; *The Emperor and the Kite* by Jane Yolen, ill. by Ed Young, World
1969 *The Fool of the World and the Flying Ship* by Arthur Ransome, ill. by Uri Shulevitz, Farrar
Honor Book: *Why the Sun and the Moon Live in the Sky* by Elphinstone Dayrell, ill. by Blair Lent, Houghton
1970 *Sylvester and the Magic Pebble* by William Steig, Windmill
Honor Books: *Goggles!* by Ezra Jack Keats, Macmillan; *Alexander and the Wind-Up Mouse* by Leo Lionni, Pantheon; *Pop Corn & Ma Goodness* by Edna Mitchell Preston, ill. by Robert Andrew Parker, Viking; *Thy Friend, Obadiah* by Brinton Turkle, Viking; *The Judge* by Harve Zemach, ill. by Margot Zemach, Farrar
1971 *A Story—A Story* by Gail E. Haley, Atheneum
Honor Books: *The Angry Moon* by William Sleator, ill. by Blair Lent, Atlantic/Little; *Frog and Toad Are Friends* by Arnold Lobel, Harper; *In the Night Kitchen* by Maurice Sendak, Harper
1972 *One Fine Day* by Nonny Hogrogian, Macmillan
Honor Books: *If All the Seas Were One Sea,* by Janina Domanska, Macmillan; *Moja Means One: Swahili Counting Book* by Muriel Feelings, ill. by Tom Feelings, Dial; *Hildilid's Night* by Cheli Duran Ryan, ill. by Arnold Lobel, Macmillan
1973 *The Funny Little Woman* retold by Arlene Mosel, ill. by Blair Lent, Dutton
Honor Books: *Anansi the Spider* adapted and ill. by Gerald McDermott, Holt; *Hosie's Alphabet* by Hosea, Tobias and Lisa Baskin, ill. by Leonard Baskin, Viking; *Snow-White and the Seven Dwarfs* translated by Randall Jarrell, ill. by Nancy Ekholm Burkert, Farrar; *When Clay Sings* by Byrd Baylor, ill. by Tom Bahti, Scribner's
1974 *Duffy and the Devil* by Harve Zemach, ill. by Margot Zemach, Farrar
Honor Books: *Three Jovial Huntsmen* by Susan Jeffers, Bradbury; *Cathedral: The Story of Its Construction* by David Macaulay, Houghton
1975 *Arrow to the Sun* adapted and ill. by Gerald McDermott, Viking
Honor Book: *Jambo Means Hello* by Muriel Feelings, ill. by Tom Feelings, Dial
1976 *Why Mosquitoes Buzz in People's Ears* retold by Verna Aardema, ill. by Leo and Diane Dillon, Dial
Honor Books: *The Desert Is Theirs* by Byrd Baylor, ill. by Peter Parnall, Scribner's; *Strega Nona* retold and ill. by Tomie de Paola, Prentice

The Laura Ingalls Wilder Award

This prize, administered by the American Library Association Children's Services Division, was first awarded in 1954. Since 1960 it has been given every five years to an author or illustrator whose books, published in the United States, have made a substantial and lasting contribution to children's literature.
1954 Laura Ingalls Wilder
1960 Clara Ingram Judson
1965 Ruth Sawyer
1970 E. B. White
1975 Beverly Cleary

The National Book Award

In March 1969, the National Book Awards included for the first time in its twenty-year history a prize for Children's Literature. The $1000 prize, contributed by the Children's Book Council and administered by the National Book Committee, is presented annually to a juvenile title that a panel of judges considers the most distinguished written by an American citizen and published in the United States in the preceding year.
1969 *Journey from Peppermint Street* by Meindert DeJong, Harper
Leading Contenders: *Constance* by Patricia Clapp, Lothrop; *The Endless Steppe* by Esther Hautzig, T. Crowell; *The High King* by Lloyd Alexander, Holt; *Langston Hughes* by Milton Meltzer, T. Crowell
1970 *A Day of Pleasure: Stories of a Boy Growing Up in Warsaw* by Isaac Bashevis Singer, Farrar
Leading Contenders: *Pop Corn & Ma Goodness* by Edna Mitchell Preston, Viking; *Sylvester and the Magic Pebble* by William Steig, Windmill; *Where the Lilies Bloom* by Vera and Bill Cleaver, Lippincott; *The Young United States* by Edwin Tunis, World
1971 *The Marvelous Misadventures of Sebastian* by Lloyd Alexander, Dutton
Leading Contenders: *Blowfish Live in the Sea* by Paula Fox, Bradbury; *Frog and Toad Are Friends* by Arnold Lobel, Harper; *Grover* by Vera and Bill Cleaver, Lippincott; *Trumpet of the Swan* by E. B. White, Harper
1972 *The Slightly Irregular Fire Engine* by Donald Barthelme, Farrar
Leading Contenders: *Amos & Boris* by William Steig, Farrar; *The Art and Industry of Sandcastles* by Jan Adkins, Walker; *The Bears' House* by Marilyn Sachs, Doubleday; *Father Fox's Pennyrhymes* by Clyde Watson, T. Crowell; *Hildilid's Night* by Cheli Duran Ryan, Macmillan; *His Own Where* by June Jordan, T. Crowell; *Mrs. Frisby and the Rats of NIMH* by Robert C. O'Brien, Atheneum; *The Tombs of Atuan* by Ursula K. Le Guin, Atheneum; *Wild in the World* by John Donovan, Harper
1973 *The Farthest Shore* by Ursula K. Le Guin, Atheneum
Leading Contenders: *Children of Vietnam* by Betty Jean Lifton and Thomas C. Fox, Atheneum; *Dominic* by William Steig, Farrar; *The House of Wings* by Betsy Byars, Viking; *The Impossible People* by Georgess McHargue, Holt; *Julie of the Wolves* by Jean Craighead George, Harper; *Long Journey Home* by Julius Lester, Dial; *Trolls* by Ingri and Edgar Parin d'Aulaire, Doubleday; *The Witches of Worm* by Zilpha Keatley Snyder, Atheneum
1974 *The Court of the Stone Children* by Eleanor Cameron, Dutton

Leading Contenders: *Duffy and the Devil* by Harve Zemach, Farrar; *A Figure of Speech* by Norma Mazer, Delacorte; *Guests in the Promised Land* by Kristin Hunter, Scribner; *A Hero Ain't Nothin' But a Sandwich* by Alice Childress, Coward; *Poor Richard in France* by F. N. Monjo, Holt; *A Proud Taste for Scarlet and Miniver* by E. L. Konigsburg, Atheneum; *Summer of My German Soldier* by Bette Greene, Dial; *The Treasure Is the Rose* by Julia Cunningham, Pantheon; *The Whys and Wherefores of Littabelle Lee* by Vera and Bill Cleaver, Atheneum

1975 *M. C. Higgins, the Great* by Virginia Hamilton, Macmillan

Leading Contenders: *The Devil's Storybook* by Natalie Babbitt, Farrar; *Doctor in the Zoo* by Bruce Buchenholz, Studio/Viking; *The Edge of Next Year* by Mary Stolz, Harper; *The Girl Who Cried Flowers* by Jane Yolen, T. Crowell; *I Tell a Lie Every So Often* by Bruce Clements, Farrar; *Jo! Bangla!* by Jason Laure with Ettagale Laure, Farrar; *My Brother Sam Is Dead* by James Lincoln Collier and Christopher Collier, Four Winds; *Remember the Days* by Milton Meltzer, Zenith/Doubleday; *Wings* by Adrienne Richard, Atlantic/Little; *World of Our Fathers* by Milton Meltzer, Farrar

1976 *Bert Breen's Barn* by Walter D. Edmonds, Little

Leading Contenders: *As I Was Crossing Boston Common* by Norma Farber, Dutton; *To the Green Mountains* by Eleanor Cameron, Dutton; *Of Love and Death and Other Journeys* by Isabelle Holland, Lippincott; *The Star in the Pail* by David McCord, Little; *El Bronx Remembered; A Novella and Stories* by Nicholasa Mohr, Harper; *Ludell* by Brenda Wilkinson, Harper

The Carnegie Medal

The Carnegie Medal, established in 1937, is awarded annually by the British Library Association to an outstanding children's book written in English and first published in the United Kingdom.

1936 *Pigeon Post* by Arthur Ransome, Cape
1937 *The Family from One End Street* by Eve Garnett, Muller
1938 *The Circus Is Coming* by Noel Streatfeild, Dent
1939 *Radium Woman* by Eleanor Doorly, Heinemann
1940 *Visitors from London* by Kitty Barne, Dent
1941 *We Couldn't Leave Dinah* by Mary Treadgold, Penguin
1942 *The Little Grey Men,* by B. B., Eyre & Spottiswoode
1943 No Award
1944 *The Wind on the Moon* by Eric Linklater, Macmillan
1945 No Award
1946 *The Little White Horse* by Elizabeth Goudge, Brockhampton Press
1947 *Collected Stories for Children* by Walter de la Mare, Faber
1948 *Sea Change* by Richard Armstrong, Dent
1949 *The Story of Your Home* by Agnes Allen, Transatlantic
1950 *The Lark on the Wing* by Elfrida Vipont Foulds, Oxford
1951 *The Wool-Pack* by Cynthia Harnett, Methuen
1952 *The Borrowers* by Mary Norton, Dent
1953 *A Valley Grows Up* by Edward Osmond, Oxford
1954 *Knight Crusader* by Ronald Welch, Oxford
1955 *The Little Bookroom* by Eleanor Farjeon, Oxford
1956 *The Last Battle* by C. S. Lewis, Bodley Head
1957 *A Grass Rope* by William Mayne, Oxford
1958 *Tom's Midnight Garden* by Philippa Pearce, Oxford
1959 *The Lantern Bearers* by Rosemary Sutcliff, Oxford
1960 *The Making of Man* by I. W. Cornwall, Phoenix
1961 *A Stranger at Green Knowe* by Lucy Boston, Faber
1962 *The Twelve and the Genii* by Pauline Clarke, Faber
1963 *Time of Trial* by Hester Burton, Oxford
1964 *Nordy Banks* by Sheena Porter, Oxford
1965 *The Grange at High Force* by Philip Turner, Oxford
1966 No Award
1967 *The Owl Service* by Alan Garner, Collins
1968 *The Moon in the Cloud* by Rosemary Harris, Faber
1969 *The Edge of the Cloud* by K. M. Peyton, Oxford
1970 *The God Beneath the Sea* by Leon Garfield and Edward Blishen, Kestrel
1971 *Josh* by Ivan Southall, Angus & Robertson
1972 *Watership Down* by Richard Adams, Rex Collings
1973 *The Ghost of Thomas Kempe* by Penelope Lively, Heinemann
1974 *The Stronghold* by Mollie Hunter, Hamilton
1975 *The Machine-Gunners* by Robert Westall, Macmillan

The Kate Greenaway Medal

This medal is awarded each year by the British Library Association for the most distinguished work in illustration of a children's book first published in the United Kingdom during the preceding year.

In cases where only one name is given, the book was written and illustrated by the same person.

1956 *Tim All Alone* by Edward Ardizzone, Oxford
1957 *Mrs. Easter and the Storks* by V. H. Drummond, Faber
1958 No award
1959 *Kashtanka and a Bundle of Ballads* by William Stobbs, Oxford
1960 *Old Winkle and the Seagulls* by Elizabeth Rose, ill. by Gerald Rose, Faber
1961 *Mrs. Cockle's Cat* by Philippa Pearce, ill. by Antony Maitland, Kestrel
1962 *Brian Wildsmith's ABC* by Brian Wildsmith, Oxford
1963 *Borka* by John Burningham, Cape
1964 *Shakespeare's Theatre* by C. W. Hodges, Oxford
1965 *Three Poor Tailors* by Victor Ambrus, Hamilton
1966 *Mother Goose Treasury* by Raymond Briggs, Hamilton
1967 *Charlie, Charlotte & the Golden Canary* by Charles Keeping, Oxford
1968 *Dictionary of Chivalry* by Grant Uden, ill. by Pauline Baynes, Kestrel
1969 *The Quangle-Wangle's Hat* by Edward Lear, ill. by Helen Oxenbury, Heinemann; *Dragon of an Ordinary Family* by Margaret May Mahy, ill. by Helen Oxenbury, Heinemann
1970 *Mr. Gumpy's Outing* by John Burningham, Cape
1971 *The Kingdom Under the Sea* by Jan Pienkowski, Cape
1972 *The Woodcutter's Duck* by Krystyna Turska, Hamilton
1973 *Father Christmas* by Raymond Briggs, Hamilton
1974 *The Wind Blew* by Pat Hutchins, Bodley Head
1975 *Horses in Battle* by Victor Ambrus, Oxford; *Mishka* by Victor Ambrus, Oxford

The Canadian Library Awards

This award, first presented in June 1947, was established by the Canadian Library Association. It is given annually to a children's book of outstanding literary merit, written by a Canadian citizen. Since 1954 a similar medal has also been awarded yearly to an outstanding children's book published in French.

1947 *Starbuck Valley Winter* by Roderick Haig-Brown, Collins
1948 *Kristli's Trees* by Mabel Dunham, Hale
1949 No Award
1950 *Franklin of the Arctic* by Richard S. Lambert, McClelland & Stewart
1951 No Award
1952 *The Sun Horse* by Catherine Anthony Clark, Macmillan of Canada
1953 No Award
1954 No English Award
Mgr. de Laval by Emile S. J. Gervais, Comité des Fondateurs de l'Eglise Canadienne
1955 No Awards
1956 *Train for Tiger Lily* by Louise Riley, Macmillan of Canada
No French Award
1957 *Glooskap's Country* by Cyrus Macmillan, Oxford
No French Award
1958 *Lost in the Barrens* by Farley Mowat, Little
Le Chevalier du Roi by Béatrice Clément, Les Editions de l'Atelier
1959 *The Dangerous Cove* by John F. Hayes, Copp Clark
Un Drôle de Petit Cheval by Hélène Flamme, Editions Lémèac
1960 *The Golden Phoenix* by Marius Barbeau and Michael Hornyansky, Walck
L'Eté Enchanté by Paule Daveluy, Les Editions de l'Atelier
1961 *The St. Lawrence* by William Toye, Oxford
Plantes Vagabondes by Marcelle Gauvreau, Centre de Psychologie et de Pédagogie
1962 No English Award
Les Iles du Roi Maha Maha II by Claude Aubry, Les Editions du Pélican
1963 *The Incredible Journey* by Sheila Burnford, Little
Drôle d'Automne by Paule Daveluy, Les Editions du Pélican
1964 *The Whale People* by Roderick Haig-Brown, William Collins of Canada
Feerie by Cécile Chabot, Librairie Beauchemin Ltée.
1965 *Tales of Nanabozho* by Dorothy Reid, Oxford
Le Loup de Noël by Claude Aubry, Centre de Psychologie de Montréal
1966 *Tikta'Liktak* by James Houston, Kestrel
Le Chêne des Tempêtes by Andrée Maillet-Hobden, Fides
The Double Knights by James McNeal, Walck
Le Wapiti by Monique Corriveau, Jeunesse
1967 *Raven's Cry* by Christie Harris, McClelland & Stewart
No French Award
1968 *The White Archer* by James Houston, Kestrel
Légendes Indiennes du Canada by Claude Mélancon, Editions du Jour
1969 *And Tomorrow the Stars* by Kay Hill, Dodd
No French Award
1970 *Sally Go Round the Sun* by Edith Fowke, McClelland & Stewart
Le Merveilleuse Histoire de la Naissance by Lionel Gendron, Les Editions de l'Homme
1971 *Cartier Discovers the St. Lawrence* by William Toye, Oxford University
La Surprise de Dame Chenille by Henriette Major, Centre de Psychologie de Montréal
1972 *Mary of Mile 18* by Ann Blades, Tundra
No French Award
1973 *The Marrow of the World* by Ruth Nichols, Macmillan of Canada
Le Petit Sapin Qui A Poussé Sur Une Étoile by Simone Bussières, Presses Laurentiennes
1974 *The Miraculous Hind* by Elizabeth Cleaver, Holt of Canada
No French Award
1975 *Alligator Pie* by Dennis Lee, Macmillan of Canada
No French Award
1976 *Jacob Two-Two Meets the Hooded Fang* by Mordecai Richler, Knopf
No French Award

The Canadian Library Association has awarded the Amelia Frances Howard-Gibbon Medal annually since 1971 for outstanding illustrations in a children's book published in Canada. The illustrator must be a native or resident of Canada.

1971 *The Wind Has Wings,* ed. by Mary Alice Downie and Barbara Robertson, ill. by Elizabeth Cleaver, Oxford
1972 *A Child in Prison Camp* by Shizuye Takashima, Tundra
1973 *Au Dela du Soleil/Beyond the Sun* by Jacques de Roussan, Tundra
1974 *A Prairie Boy's Winter* by William Kurelek, Tundra
1975 *The Sleighs of My Childhood/Les Traineaux de Mon Enfance* by Carlos Italiano, Tundra
1976 *A Prairie Boy's Summer* by William Kurelek, Tundra

The Hans Christian Andersen Award

This award was established in 1956 by the International Board on Books for Young People and is given every two years to one living author who, by his or her complete work, has made an important international contribution to children's literature. Since 1966 an artist's medal has also been given. Each national section of the International Board proposes one author and one illustrator as nominees and the final choice is made by a committee of five, each from a different country.

1956 Eleanor Farjeon (Great Britain)
1958 Astrid Lindgren (Sweden)
1960 Erich Kästner (Germany)
1962 Meindert DeJong (U.S.A.)
1964 René Guillot (France)
1966 Author: Tove Jansson (Finland)
Illustrator: Alois Carigiet (Switzerland)
1968 Authors: James Krüss (Germany)
Jose Maria Sanchez-Silva (Spain)
Illustrator: Jiri Trnka (Czechoslovakia)
1970 Author: Gianni Rodari (Italy)
Illustrator: Maurice Sendak (U.S.A.)
1972 Author: Scott O'Dell (U.S.A.)
Illustrator: Ib Spang Olsen (Denmark)
1974 Author: Maria Gripe (Sweden)
Illustrator: Farshid Mesghali (Iran)
1976 Author: Cecil Bødker (Denmark)
Illustrator: Tatjana Mawrina (U.S.S.R.)

Appendix E
Pronunciation Guide

Symbols used in the pronunciation are as follows: a as in *hat;* ā as in *age;* ã as in *care;* ä as in *father;* e as in *let;* ē as in *see;* ėr as in *term;* i as in *pin;* ī as in *five;* o as in *hot;* ō as in *go;* ô as in *order, all;* oi as in *oil;* ou as in *house;* th as in *thin;* ŧh as in *then;* u as in *cup;* u̇ as in *full;* ü as in *rule;* ū as in *use;* zh as in *measure;* ə as in the unaccented syllables of *about, taken, pencil, lemon, circus;* H as in the German *ach;* N as in the French *bon* (not pronounced, but shows that the vowel before it is nasal); œ as in the French *peu* and the German *könig* (pronounced by speaking ā with the lips rounded as for ō); Y as in the French *du* (pronounced by speaking ē with the lips rounded as for ü). All other symbols represent the consonant sounds that they commonly stand for in English spelling.

Aardema är′de mä
Abrashkin a brash′kin
Adoff ā′dof
Afanasiev ä fä nä′syif
Agle ā′gu̇l
Agra ä′grə
Aiken-drum ā kən drum
Alcock, Gudrun al′kok, gü′drun
Aldis ôl′dis
Aliki ä lē′kī
Allingham al′ing əm
Almedingen al′mə ding′ən
Ambrus ôm′bru̇sh
Analdas ə näl′dəs
Ananse ə nan′si
Anckarsvärd äng′kȧs verd
Ankhsenpaaten anH′sen pät′en
Arawn ä ron′
Ardizzone är di zō′ni
Arora ə ro′rə
Arrietty ãr i e′tē
Artzybasheff är tsi ba′shif
Asbjörnsen äs′byėrn sen
Asimov as′im ov
Aucassin ō ka saN′
Averill ā′və ril
Ayars ãrz
Ayme e mā′
Baba Yaga bä′bə yä′gä
Babar bä′bär
Bacmeister bok′mī ster
Bandai ban dī′
Banneker ban′nə kėr
Barbauld bär′bōld
Barchilon, Jacques bär shē yoN′, zhäk
Bartusis bär tü′sis
Basho bä shō
Baudouy, Michel-Aimé bô dü ē′, mē shel-e mā′
Baumann bou′män
Behn bān
Beim bīm
Benary-Isbert, Margot ben ãr′ē-is′bėrt, mär′gō
Benedetti, Mario bā′nā dāt′ tē
Benét be nā′
Benezet ben′ ə zet′
Beowulf bā′ə wu̇lf
Berquin, Armand bėr kaN′, ar mäN′
Bertol bãr′tôl
Beskow bes′kō
Bethune, Mary McLeod bə thūn′, mak loud′
Bevis bē′vis
Bewick bū′ik
Bidpai bid′pī
Binnorie bin′ə rē/bin′ô rē
Bishop, Claire Huchet œ shā′
Blegvad bleg′vad
Blough blou
Bogosian bô gōz′yun
Bolognese bō lō nā′zē
Bontemps, Arna bôN tôN′, är′nə
Brinsmead, Hesba Fay hez′bə
Bryson brī′sən
Bubo bū′bō
Budulinek bu dū′lin ek
Bulla bu̇l′ə
Burchard bœr′chärd
Cabeza de Vaca kä bā′thä dā vä′-kä
Carigiet, Alois cä rē zhē ā′, al wä′
Caudill kô′dl
Cavanna kə van′ə
Cayuse kī ūs′
Chaga chä′gä
Chakoh chä′kō
Chincoteague ching′kə tēg
Christiansen, Reider kris′tyän-sən, rēd ər
Chukovsky, Kornei chu kôf′-skē, kôr nā′
Chute, Marchette chüt, mär shet′
Chwast kwäst
Ciardi chär′dē
Cinderlad, Per, Paal, Espen sin′-dər läd, pãr, pôl, es′pən
Coblentz kō′blents
Collodi kōl lô′dē
Colman, Hila hī′lä
Coombs kümz
Colum, Padraic kol′um, pä′drig
Comenius kə mē′ni us
Contes de Ma Mère l'Oye kôNt də mä mãr lwä
Cowper kü′pėr
Credle crā′dəl
Cruikshank kru̇k′shangk
Cuchulain kü kü′lin
Dahl, Roald däl, rō′äl
Dalgliesh däl glēsh
D'Amelio da mēl′ē yō
D'Armancour där môN kür′
Dasent dā′sənt
d'Aulaire dō lãr′
d'Aulnoy dōl nwä′
De Angeli də an′jel ē
De Beaumont, Madame Leprince də bō môN′, ma dam′ lə-praNs′
De Brunhoff, Jean də brün′ôf, zhôN
De Gasztold, Carmen Bernos də gaz′tōl, bėr′nōs
De Genlis, Madame də zhôN lē′, ma dam′
DeJong, Meindert də yung′, mīn′dėrt
De la Mare də la mãr′
De Luca dā lü′kä
Demetrius of Phalerum də mē′-tri us, fu lēr′əm
De Pareja dā pə rā′hä
De Regniers də rān′yā
Derleth dėr′leth
De Trevino dā trə vē′nyō
Deucher dü shā′
Deutsch, Babette doich, bab et′
Ditlabeng dit′lə beng
Dobry dō′brē
Dodge,Mary Mapes māps
Domanska, Janina dô män′skä, yä nē′nä
Doob düb
Douty dü′tē
Du Bois, William Pène dY bwä, pen
Duvoisin dY vwä zaN′
Eckenstein, Lina ek′en stīn, lē′nä
Edda ed′ə
Eichenberg ī′ken bėrg
Engdahl əng′dôl
Epaminondas i pam i non′dəs
Evers, Alf ev′ėrs, älf
Farjeon fär′jun
Farquharson fär′kwėr sən
Feagles fē′gləs
Fenians fē ni ənz
Fflewddur Fflam flü′dœr flam
Figgis fig′is
Fiorello fē ō rel′ō
Fjeld fē el/fyel
Forberg, Ati ä′tē
Forten fôr′tən
Franchere frän′shãr
Frascino frə shē′nō

Frasconi, Antonio frans kō′nē, än tō′nyō
Frolov, Vadim frō′lof, vä dim
Fyleman fīl′man
Gaer gār
Gaetano gä′ā tä nō
Gág gäg
Galdone gal dōn′
Galland, Antoine gə läɴ′, äɴ-twōn′
Gaudenzia gou den′tsya
Gautama Buddha gô′tə mə bu̇′də
Geisel gī′z′l
Gengi gən′jē
Gerda ger tə
Gidal gi dal′
Gilgamesh gil′gə mesh
Giuliano jü lyä′nō
Glubok glü′bok
Gobhai gō bī
Goff gof
Gottschalk, Fruma gät′shəlk, frü′-mə
Goudey gou′dē
Gramatky gra mat′kē
Gripe grēpu
Gudbrand gu̇d′bränd
Guillot, René gē yō, ru̇ nā′
Guion gī′ôn
Guiterman git′ėr mən
Gurgi gœr′jē
Gwydion gwi′dē on
Gylfi gʏl′fə
Haar, Jaap Ter här, yop tėr
Haas häs
Haber hä′bėr
Hader hā′dėr
Haida hī′du
Hakon hô′kən
Hallard hal′lärd
Hanff hänf
Haugaard hou′gärd
Hautzig hout′zig
Hazard a zär′
Hazeltine hāz′əl tīn′
Heinlein hīn′līn
Hepzibah hep′zi bah
Hesiod hē′si od
Heumann hoi′män
Heyerdahl, Thor hā′ėr däl, tu̇r
Heyward, Du Bose du̇ bōz′
Hidalgo y Costilla ēd häl′-go ē kōs te′yä
Hieatt hi′at
Hitopadesa hi tō pa dā′sha
Hoban hō′ban
Hofsinde hof′sin də
Hogrogian, Nonny hō grō′-gē an, no′nē
Hokusai hō ku̇ sī
Homily hom′i lē
Hosford hôs′fərd
Hyndman hīnd′man
Ignatow ig nä′tō
Ishi ē shē
Ish-Kishor, Sulamith, ish′ki shor′, su lam′ith
Issa is′ə
Jahdu jä′dū
Jancsi yan′sē
Jansson, Tove yän′sən, tō′vā
Janosh yä′nōsh
Jarrell jar′rel
Jataka jä′tä kə
Jean-Claude zhôn klōd
Jeanne-Marie zhan′mä rē′
Jenness jen es′
Josian jō sī′ən
Kaa kä
Kahl käl
Karana kä rä′nä
Kästner, Erich kest′nər, ā′rik
Katia kä′tyə
Kaula kô lu
Kavaler ka′vu̇l ėr
Kävik kä′vik
Kenofer ken′o fėr
Kim Van Kieu kēm vən kyū
Kinder und Hausmärchen kin′-dėr u̇nd hous′mār′ʜən
Kjelgaard kel′gärd
Konigsburg kō′nigs bėrg
Krakatoa krak ə tō′ə
Kroeber krō′bər
Krush krush
Krylov kril ôf′
Kumin kew′min
Kuskin kus′kin
La Fontaine, Jean de lä fon ten′, zhôɴ də
La Gallienne lə gal′yən
Lakshmi lok′shmē
Lalu la lü
Latham lā′thum
Lathrop lā′thrəp
Ledoux lə dʏ′
Le Guin le gwin′
Le Hibou et la Poussiquette lē-bü′ ā lä pü si ket′
Lexau lex ô
Liam lē′am
Liddell lid′əl
Liers lirs
Lindgren, Astrid lind grən, äs′-trid
Lionni lē ō′nē
Lipkind lip′kind
Lippiza lip′it za
Llyn-Y-Fan ʜlin′ə van′
Lobel lō bel′
Lorenzini lô ren tsē′nē
Lueders lwē′dėrs
Lurs lürz
McKuen mak kū′ən
Mafatu ma fa tu
Mahabharata mə hä′bä′rə tə
Mali mä′lē
Manolo män′ō lō
Mara mä rə
Mari, Iela and Enzo mä′rē, ī′-la, en zō
Mārchen mār′ʜən
Mary-Rousselière, Guy mä rē′-rü se li ā′, gē
Massee ma′sē
Massignon mas ē nyōɴ′
Matthiesen math′i sən
Maurois, André mô′rwā, än drā′
Mayne mān
Megrimum me′grə məm
Mei Li mā lē
Melendy mə lən′dē
Miers mirz
Miklagard mik′la gärd
Milne miln
Minarik min′ə rik
Mirsky, Reba Paeff mėr′skē, rē′-bā paf
Mizamura, Kazue mi′zä mü rä, kä zü′ā
Moe, Jörgen mō ə, yėr′gən
Momolu mo′mō lü
Monjo mon′jō
Montresor, Beni mōn′trə sôr, bā′nē
Monvel, Boutet de môɴ vel′, bü tā′də
Moonta mün′tə
Mordvinoff mord′vin of
Mosel mō zəl′
Moskof mos′kof
Mowgli mou′glē
Mulready mu̇l′red ē
Munari, Bruno mü nä′rē, brü′nō
Navarra na va′ra
Nefertiti ne fėr tē′ti
Nibelungs/Niblungs nē′bə lu̇ngz/nē′blu̇ngz
Nic Leodhas, Sorche nic ly ōs′, sôr′ä
Nicolette nē kô let′
Noguchi, Hideyo no gu′che, hē de yo
Nootka nu̇t′kə
Okada Rokuo ō ka da, rō ku̇ ō
Olatunji, Michael Babatunde o lä tu̇n ′jē, bä bä tu̇n′dē
Orgel or′gel
Orisha ôr ē′sha
Ormondroyd ôr mond roid
Orphelines ôr fel ēnz′
Padre Porko pä′t͟hre pôrk′ō
Palazzo pa lat′zō
Panchatantra pän chə tän′trə
Pandu pän′dü
Pantaloni pan tə lō′nē
Papashvily pa pash vē lē
Paracelsus par ə sel′səs
Pecos pā kəs
Pegeen pe gēn′
Pelle pel′lə
Perrault pe rō′
Petrides, Heidrun pə trē′dēz, hīd′drun
Petry pē′tri
Pettit pe tē′
Piatti, Celestino pyät′-tē, chā lās tē′nō
Pibroch of Donnel Dhu pē′-broʜ, don′nel dū
Picard, Barbara Leonie pi′-kärd, lā′ō nē
Pincus pin′kəs
Planudes plə nū′dēz
Plasencia plä sen′thyä
Plouhinec plü′i nek
Podkayne pod kān

Politi pō lē'tē
Prelutsky pre lut'skē
Prishvin, Mikhail prēsh'-vin, mē hä ēl'
Procyon prō'si on
Prydain pri dān'
Pulga pủl'gȧ
Pwyll and Pryderi pü'il, pru dā'rē
Quarles kwôrlz
Rabe rāb
Raman rä'mən
Ramayana rä mä'yə nə
Ranke räng'ke
Rasmussen, Knud räs'-mus ən, nủd
Ravielli rav ē el'li
Repplier rep'lēr
Rey rā
Ripopet-Barabas rē'pō pā-bä'-rä bä
Rocca, Guido rôk'kō, gwē dō
Roethke ret'kē
Rojankovsky rō jan kôf'skē
Rossetti rō set'ē
Rugh rü
Rukeyser rü'kī zėr
Rus, Vladimir rüs, vlad'i mir
Saba sä'bä
Sadko säd'kô
Saemund sā'mủnd
Saint Exupéry, Antoine de san tāg zy pā rē, än twän'də
Sasek, Miroslav sä'sek, mī'-rō släv
Savigny säv'in yē
Scheele shē'lē
Schoenherr shủn'hār
Schweitzer shvī'tsər
Seignobosc, Françoise sāngn'-yō bosk, fräɴ swäz'
Sellew se'lü
Selsam sel'səm
Sendak sen'dak
Seredy shār'ə dē
Serraillier sə räl'yā
Seuss süs
Shawneen shä nēn'
Shecter shek'tėr
Sheftu shef'tü
Shimin, Symeon shi'min, sim'-ē un
Shogomoc shō gō môk
Showalter shō'wäl tėr
Shulevitz, Uri shü'lə vitz, ü'rē
Sidjakov sij'ə kof
Sigurdson si'gûth son
Singer, Isaac Bashevis bə shā'vis
Sita sē'tä
Slobodkin slō bod'kin
Slote slōt
Smolicheck smol'i chek
Snegourka snye gür'kä
Sojo, Toba sō jō, to bä
Sokol sō'kol
Sonneborn son'ne born
Soupault sü pō'
Southall south'ôl
Spier spēr
Stahl stäl
Steegmuller steg mul'ər
Steig stīg
Stolz stōlts
Strachey strā'chi
Streatfeild, Noel stret'feld, nō'əl
Sture-Vasa stủr-vä sä
Spyri, Johanna shpē'rē, yō hän'ä
Sturluson, Snorri stür'-le sôn, snôr'ā
Suba sü'bə
Sundiata sün dē ä'tä
Syme sīm
Tagore, Rabindranath tä'-gōr, rā bēn'drā nät'
Taliesin tal ē ā'zin
Taran ta'ran
Tashjian täs jun
Tatsinda tat sin'dä
Tenniel ten'yel
Terzian ter'zian
Thorne-Thomsen, Gudrun thôrn tom'sen, gü'drun
Thorvall, Kerstin tủr'vāl, char'-stin
Tistou tē stü'
Tituba ti'tū bä
Tlingit tling'git
Tolkien tôl'ken
Treece trēs
Tresselt tre'selt
Truro trủr'ō
Tunis tū'nis
Turska, Krystyna turs'kä, kris tē'-na
Tutankhaten tüt änʜ ä'tən
Uchida, Yoshiko ü chē dä, yō shē kō
Udry ū'dri
Ullman ủl'män
Undset, Sigrid ūn'set, si'grid
Ungerer, Tomi un'gœ rœr
Unnerstad un'nėr stadt
Ushinsky ủ shin'skē
Van Iterson, Siny vän ē'ter sôn, sē nē
Vasilisa va syē'le sa
Vedge vej
Viehmann vē'män
Viollet vē ō let'
Vivier viv ē ā'
Volsung vol'sủng
Vulpes vul'pēz
Watie wā'tē
Wayah wā ä
Weisgard wīs'gärd
Weiss wīs
Whippety Stourie wip'ə tē stür'-ē/stủr'ē
Whuppie wủp'ē
Wibberley wi'bėr lē
Wier wēr
Wiese vē'zə
Wild, Dortchen vilt, dôrt'shən
Wodehouse wủd'hous
Wojciechowska, Maia woi je-hov'-ska, mä'ē ä
Wuorio, Eva-Lis wür yō, ā vä-lēs
Yashima, Taro yä'shi ma, tä'rō
Yonge yung
Yonie Wondernose yō nē wun'-dər nōz
Yorubaland yôr u'ba land
Yulya yü lyä
Zamani zä mä nē
Zemach zē'mak
Zhenya zhā'nyə
Zolotow zol'ə tou

Subject Index

Author, Illustrator, Title Index*

Major discussions of authors and illustrators are indicated in the following index by boldface type.

*The color section appears between pp. 132 and 133. See also Appendixes A and B for additional authors not included here.